—*The New York Times*

"The be[illegible] dent budget traveler."
—*Chicago Tribune*

LET'S GO:
CALIFORNIA & HAWAII

is the best book for anyone traveling on a budget. Here's why:

No other guidebook has as many budget listings.

In San Francisco we found nine hotels and hostels for $20 or less a night. In Los Angeles we list 8. Outside of the city we found hundreds more. We tell you how to get there the cheapest way, whether by bus, plane, or thumb, and where to get an inexpensive and satisfying meal once you've arrived. There are hundreds of money-saving tips for everyone plus lots of information on student discounts.

LET'S GO researchers have to make it on their own.

Our Harvard-Radcliffe researchers travel on budgets as tight as your own—no expense accounts, no free hotel rooms.

LET'S GO is completely revised every year.

We don't just update the prices, we go back to the places. If a charming restaurant has become an overpriced tourist trap, we'll replace the listing with a new and better one.

No other budget guidebook includes all this:

Coverage of both the cities and the countryside; directions, addresses, phone numbers, and hours to get you there and back; in-depth information on culture, history, and the people; listings on transportation between and within regions and cities; tips on work, study, sights, nightlife, and special splurges; city and regional maps; and much, much more.

LET'S GO is for anyone who wants to see California and Hawaii on a budget.

Books by Harvard Student Agencies, Inc.

Let's Go: London
Let's Go: New York City
Let's Go: Washington, D.C.

Let's Go: Europe
Let's Go: Britain & Ireland
Let's Go: France
Let's Go: Germany, Austria & Switzerland
Let's Go: Greece & Turkey
Let's Go: Italy
Let's Go: Spain & Portugal
Let's Go: Israel & Egypt

Let's Go: USA
Let's Go: California & Hawaii
Let's Go: The Pacific Northwest, Western Canada & Alaska
Let's Go: Mexico

LET'S GO:

The Budget Guide to

CALIFORNIA & HAWAII

1992

Tim Whitmire
Editor

Bart St. Clair
Assistant Editor

Written by Harvard Student Agencies, Inc.

PAN BOOKS
London, Sydney and Auckland

Helping Let's Go

If you have suggestions or corrections, or just want to share your discoveries, drop us a line. We read every piece of correspondence, whether a 10-page letter, a tacky Elvis postcard, or, as in one case, a collage. All suggestions are passed along to our researcher/writers. Please note that mail received after May 5, 1992 will probably be too late for the 1993 book, but will be retained for the following edition. **Address mail to:** ***Let's Go: California & Hawaii;*** **Harvard Student Agencies, Inc.; Thayer Hall-B; Harvard University; Cambridge, MA 02138; USA.**

In addition to the invaluable travel advice our readers share with us, many are kind enough to offer their services as researchers or editors. Unfortunately, the charter of Harvard Student Agencies, Inc. enables us to employ only currently enrolled Harvard students.

Published in Great Britain 1992 by Pan Books Ltd
Cavaye Place, London SW10 9PG
9 8 7 6 5 4 3 2 1

Published in the United States of America
by St. Martin's Press, Inc.

ISBN: 0 330 32166 8

Let's Go: California & Hawaii is written by Harvard Student Agencies, Inc., Harvard University, Thayer Hall-B, Cambridge, Mass. 02138, USA.

Printed and bound in the United States of America.

Editor	Tim Whitmire
Assistant Editor	Bart St. Clair
Managing Editor	Paul C. Deemer
Publishing Director	Zanley F. Galton III
Production Manager	Christopher Williams Cowell
Researcher/Writers	
Hawaii	Kristin K. Kimball
Los Angeles, Near Los Angeles, Central Coast, Sequoia National Forest, Sierra National Forest, Sequoia and Kings Canyon National Parks, Fresno	Billy Hulkower
San Francisco and Bay Area (except Marin County), Sacramento, Lake Tahoe, Truckee, Reno, Carson City	Vanessa Sydney Biddle
Marin County, Napa and Sonoma, Northern Coast, Sacramento Valley and the Cascades (except Sacramento), The Mother Lode, Yosemite, Eastern Slope	L.A. Taggart
Grand Canyon, The Desert	D.S. Aronofsky
San Diego	Brett Janis
Baja California	Alexis Averbuck

Sales Group Manager	Michael L. Campbell
Sales Group Representatives	Julie Barclay Cotler
	Robert J. Hutter
President	Robert Frost
C.E.O.	Michele Ponti

ACKNOWLEDGMENTS

I spent the spring of 1991 preparing to edit *Let's Go's* 1992 guide to Mexico, but when the orignial *Let's Go: California and Hawaii* editor decamped to the greener economic pastures of the cinematic world I was brought in to edit the book. This job has been a sort of homecoming for me; not only did I grow up in the Golden State, but my first job for *Let's Go* was as the 1991 C&H r/w in Los Angeles.

Bart St. Clair, my assistant editor, brought a magnitudinous Victorian vocabulary to the job of editing and an omnipresent flair for the dramatic to the Front Room atmosphere. There was rarely a dull moment when Bart was around and he was a truly superlative editor and friend. I cannot thank him enough for his contributions to the guide *and* to the quality of life at *Let's Go* this summer.

Managing Editor Pete Deemer took time out from Karmann Ghia servicing sessions to put his blue pen to work at making sure that I didn't edit all of the fun out of the book. As the avuncular scion of the Front Room Pete gave us space to work, but was always there when we needed him, inevitably turning his queries into statements.

Seven brave souls were the true *sine qua non* of C&H '92. Billy Hulkower and Vanessa Biddle gave Los Angeles and the San Francisco Bay Area, respectively, the complete coverage that only locals could. Kristin Kimball tackled the Hawaiian Islands with a passion that shone through in her copy and in her endlessly entertaining epistles to the *Let's Go* basement in Cambridge (*Flowers in the Basement* indeed, Kristin!). The stalwart Lisa Taggart endured a last-minute hiring, a killer itinerary, mountain bike crashes and uncalled-for answering machine harassment from yours truly as she brought a reporter's instincts and talents to the North Coast, Sacramento Valley, and Sierra Nevada. Darren Aronofsky, another last-minute stand-in, went AWOL in The Big Easy, but resurfaced in the Desert Southwest to cover Las Vegas and the Grand Canyon. Brett Janis, the acme of the eleventh-hour saviors, tacked a week of stellar work in San Diego onto the end of his USA itinerary. And last but not least, Mexico r/w Alexis Averbuck brought a sense of adventure to her Baja California sojourn, hobnobbing with Sammy Hagar and drug kingpins on her journey up the peninsula.

Other basement denizens made this summer the best of my life. Blythe Grossberg, the third member of Team PWACH, was a great AE and an even better life insurance customer. Carolyn McKee entertained *Let's Go* lunchers with her prep school banana stories and was a devoted and dependable friend. My predecessor in this job, Jamie Rosen, was a wonderful housemate and a truly difficult act to follow. Hugs also go to my spiritual "bubber" Lorraine Chao, Marlies Morsink, Hilary Holmquest, and Maya Fischhoff.*Let's Go's* Portlander management team of Publishing Director Zan Galton and Production Manager Chris Cowell earned my respect and admiration as they managed the best-run student organization I have seen in my years at Harvard. And the gang at 88 Lakeview—Vanessa, Mina, Sean, Jamie, Mike, Karena, Brett and Heather—made my intermittent homecomings a pleasure; I couldn't think of a better group of people with whom to go jogging in a hurricane.

I'd also like to offer thanks to the people from outside the LG orbit who mean so much to me: Mom, Dad, Mike, Matt, Kelly, Mooh and Pooh, Sherief Meleis, Ivan Montoya, Alex Estevez, Brandon Lucas, Nicole Woo, Jeremy Schwartz, and Alison Waldenberg.

This book is dedicated to my brother James and to the childhood years we shared under California skies.

—TRW

All hail to Fortuna, who blessed me with Editor Tim Whitmire. Timmy—master of organization, encyclopedia supreme, just referee of superlatives, frequent yelper of "Yes" and "Jesus, Bart . . .", and a great friend—thanks a lot for a terrific summer.

Without Beignet-novice Blythe Grossberg, I couldn't have survived the Canaday pit of swelter and primary colors *or* "the revelrous den of lust and sin." To you I shall be ever grateful for memories of Mississippi dancing and parading, sweat, swollen feet, street songs, and fine meals (with the accompanying guilt complexes). P.S. I forgive you for cheating in the superlative contest.

I had the distinct honor of playing host to Host Girl (and Luigi), whose effusive laugh is perhaps my favorite sound of summer. Even when so distracted she hardly knew corduroy from woven cotton, Lo' had the word on the buzz and could tell me what's a'happenin'. Sweet dreams, kid.

And let me not forget Chris, Marlies, Lisa, Pete, and July, who all made the *Let's Go* thing better. Also, Ari, Paul, the Coffee Clatch, Ma, Pop, Morton, Antoine, Muriel, Bertha and my dear friend Blarth: thanks.

Homage to the indomitable squaw and her rugged child. Sacagawea and Pomp, you're an inspiration to all of us.

We laughed, we toiled, we sang, we bowled. Truly it was a salubrious season.

Ocho nueve!

—R. Bart St. C.

CONTENTS

LIST OF MAPS

About Let's Go

A generation ago, Harvard Student Agencies, a three-year-old nonprofit corporation dedicated to providing employment to students, was doing a booming business booking charter flights to Europe. One of the extras offered to passengers on these flights was a 20-page mimeographed pahmplet entitled *1960 European Guide,* a collection of tips on continental travel compiled by the HSA staff. The following year, students traveling to Europe researched the first full-fledged edition of *Let's Go: Europe,* a pocket-sized book with tips on budget accommodations, irreverent write-ups of sights, and a decidedly youthful slant.

Throughout the 60s, the series reflected its era: a section of the 1968 *Let's Go: Europe* was entitled "Street Singing in Europe on No Dollars a Day." During the 70s *Let's Go* gradually became a large-scale operation, adding regional European guides and expanding coverage into North Africa and Asia. Now in its 32nd year, *Let's Go* publishes 15 titles covering more than 40 countries. This year *Let's Go* proudly introduces two new guides: *Let's Go: Germany, Austria & Switzerland* and *Let's Go: Washington, D.C.*

Each spring 80 Harvard-Radcliffe students are hired as researcher/writers for the summer months. They train intensively during April and May for their summer tour of duty. Each researcher/writer then hits the road on a shoestring budget for seven weeks, researching six days per week, and overcoming countless obstacles in a glorious quest for better bargains.

Back in a basement deep below Harvard yard, an editorial staff of 30, a management team of six, and countless typists and proofreaders—all students—spend four months poring over more than 70,000 pages of manuscript as they push the copy through a rigorous editing process. High tech has recently landed in the dungeon: some of the guides are now typeset in-house using sleek black desktop workstations.

And even before the books hit the stands, next year's editions are well underway.

At Harvard Student Agencies, CEO Michele Ponti and President Robert Frost graciously presided over the whole affair.

Did we mention that the Portland Trail Blazers are going all the way this year?

A Note to our Readers

The information for this book is gathered by Harvard Student Agencies' researchers during the late spring and summer months. Each listing is derived from the assigned researcher's opinion based upon his or her visit at a particular time. The opinions are expressed in a candid and forthright manner. Other travelers might disagree. Those traveling at a different time may have different experiences since prices, dates, hours, and conditions are always subject to change. You are urged to check beforehand to avoid inconvenience and surprises. Travel always involves a certain degree of risk, especially in low-cost areas. When traveling, especially on a budget, you should always take particular care to ensure your safety.

LET'S GO: CALIFORNIA & HAWAII

General Introduction

Facing west from California's shores,
Inquiring, tireless, seeking what is yet unfound,
I, a child, very old, over waves, toward the house of maternity, the land of migrations, look afar,
Look off the shores of my Western sea.
—*Walt Whitman*

This is it—America's Final Frontier. It was here, in 19th century California, that America's European settlers ran out of unconquered territory over which to exert their Manifest Destiny, brought to a halt by the waters of the Pacific Ocean. In the 20th century the frontier was extended even further, to the middle of the Pacific, as jet travel brought tropical Hawaii into the nation and within tourist range.

For nearly two centuries men and women have come to the Far West, fleeing hard times, remaking their lives, or simply seeking a change of pace. From Twain's 49ers to Steinbeck's Okies, from John Muir to Oedipa Maas to (even) L.L. Cool J ("Going Back to Cali"), the voyager to the American West follows a path that is well worn by footsteps that are many and varied.

What you will find upon arrival is the closest approximation of Real Life Paradise that the United States has to offer. From the rainforested slopes of the Hawaiian volcanoes to the arid and striking desolation of Death Valley, from the beaches and smog of Los Angeles to the hills and fog of San Francisco, California and Hawaii offer a cross section of American fantasy and reality that is unparallelled in its allure.

Use *Let's Go: California and Hawaii* to acquaint yourself with California, Hawaii, Baja California, Nevada, and the Grand Canyon before you leave, allowing you to enjoy yourself that much more once you arrive. Each summer our researcher-writers set out to see the West on a shoestring budget. Their concerns are the same as yours: how to get there, get around, consume, revel and snooze as economically as possible. Their numerous tips and frank evaluations will ease your way and save you time when you arrive in a strange city at 2am, when you urgently need an emergency phone number, or when you can't decide where to eat, letting you spend your time seeing the sights and having the experiences that make travel worthwhile.

This **General Introduction** provides vital tips on packing, security, money, the search for inexpensive transportation, and other necessary information that you should know *before* you leave. It will save you time-consuming research and help you avoid many problems common to budget travelers, answering questions you may not even know you have.

The rest of the guide is divided into regional sections. Each section includes practical and orientation information, accommodation and food listings, and a description of sights and activities in the area. It may be useful to flip through a few sections to familiarize yourself with the book—understanding the structure of *Let's Go* will help you make the most of the wealth of information we offer.

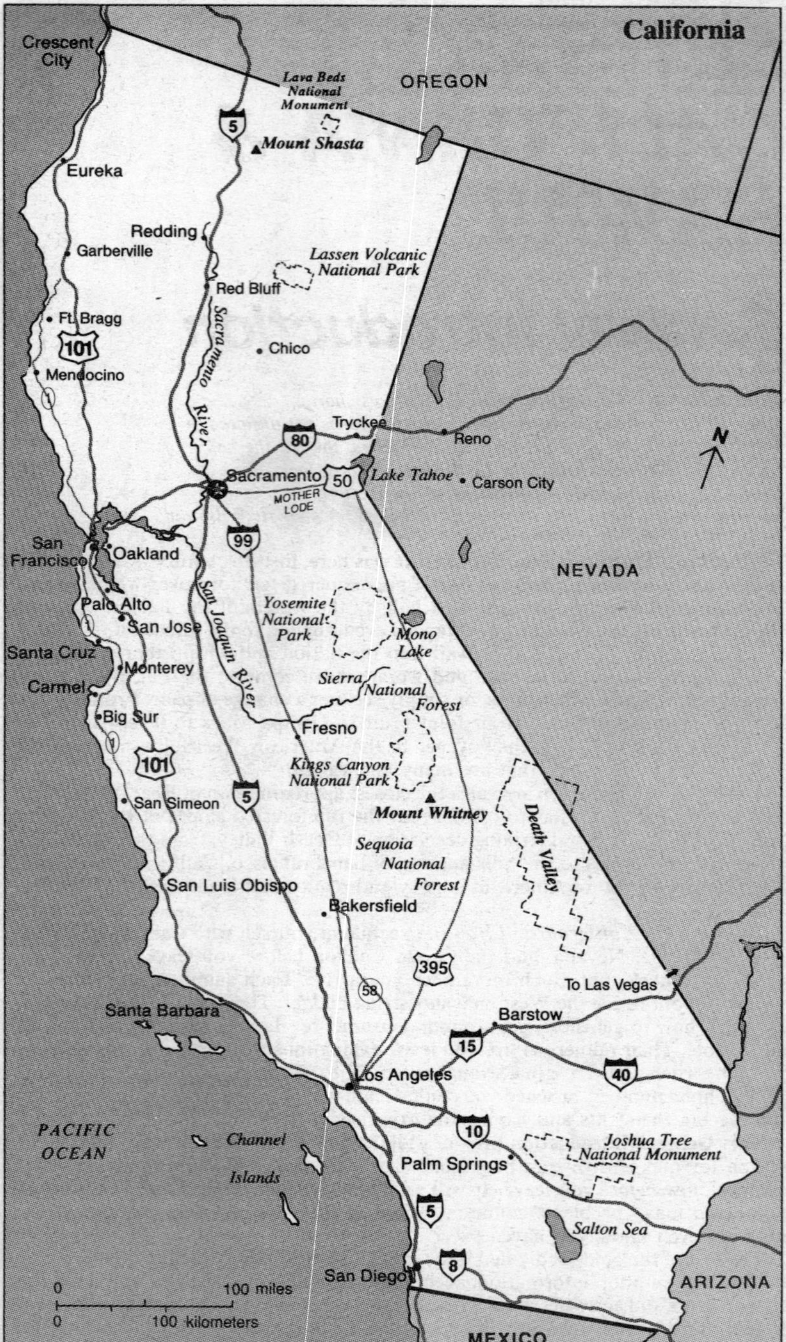
California
OREGON
NEVADA
ARIZONA
MEXICO
PACIFIC OCEAN
Crescent City
Lava Beds National Monument
Mount Shasta
Eureka
Redding
Garberville
Lassen Volcanic National Park
Red Bluff
Ft. Bragg
Sacramento River
Chico
Mendocino
Tryckee
Reno
Sacramento
Lake Tahoe
Carson City
MOTHER LODE
San Francisco
Oakland
Palo Alto
San Jose
Santa Cruz
Monterey
Carmel
Big Sur
San Joaquin River
Yosemite National Park
Mono Lake
Sierra National Forest
Fresno
Kings Canyon National Park
Mount Whitney
Death Valley
San Simeon
Sequoia National Forest
San Luis Obispo
Bakersfield
To Las Vegas
Barstow
Santa Barbara
Los Angeles
Channel Islands
Joshua Tree National Monument
Palm Springs
Salton Sea
San Diego
5
101
80
50
99
395
58
15
40
10
8
1
0 100 miles
0 100 kilometers
N

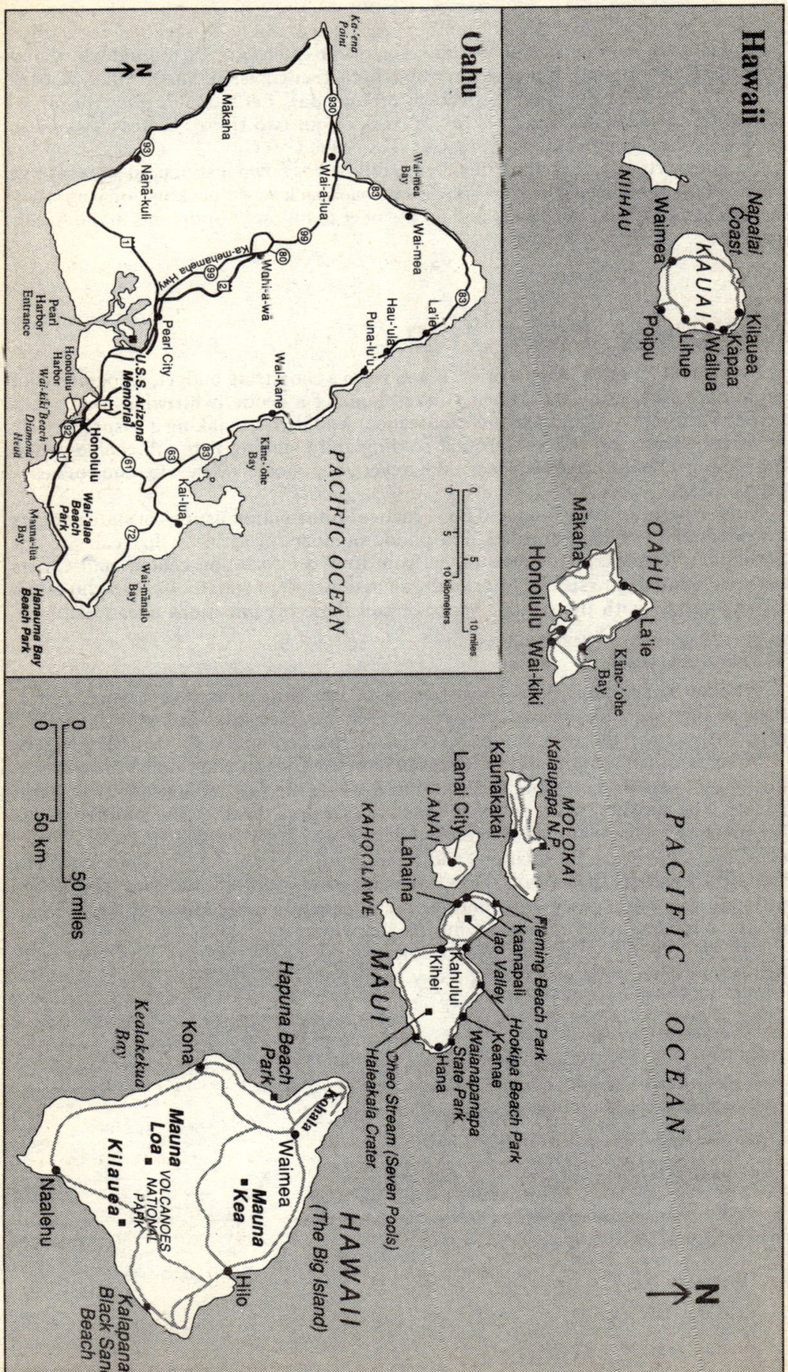
Hawaii
N
PACIFIC OCEAN
NIIHAU
Napalai Coast
KAUAI
Waimea
Kilauea
Kapaa
Wailua
Lihue
Poipu
OAHU
Mākaha
Honolulu
Wai-kiki
La'ie
Kāne-'ohe Bay
MOLOKAI
Kalaupapa N.P.
Kaunakakai
LANAI
Lanai City
KAHOOLAWE
Lahaina
Fleming Beach Park
Kaanapali
Iao Valley
Kahului
Kihei
MAUI
Hookipa Beach Park
Keanae
Waianapanapa State Park
Hana
Oheo Stream (Seven Pools)
Haleakala Crater
HAWAII (The Big Island)
Hapuna Beach Park
Kohala
Waimea
Kona
Kealakekua Bay
Mauna Kea
Mauna Loa
Kilauea
VOLCANOES NATIONAL PARK
Hilo
Naalehu
Kalapana Black Sand Beach
0 50 km
0 50 miles
Oahu
N
Ka'ena Point
Mākaha
Nānā-kuli
Wai-mea Bay
Wai-a-lua
Wai-mea
La'ie
Hau'ula
Puna-lu'u
Wahi-a-wā
Ka-mehameha Hwy
Pearl City
Pearl Harbor Entrance
U.S.S. Arizona Memorial
Honolulu Harbor
Wai-kiki Beach
Diamond Head
Honolulu
Wai-Kane
Kāne-'ohe Bay
Kai-lua
Wai-'alae Beach Park
Wai-mānalo Bay
Mauna-lua Bay
Hanauma Bay Beach Park
PACIFIC OCEAN
0 5 10 kilometers
0 5 10 miles

Prices, addresses, and phone numbers may have changed since we researched them, but visitors bureaus and similar services can often provide more detailed and up-to-date information. If you're interested in further travel in North America, consult *Let's Go: USA* (including coverage of Canada), *Let's Go: Pacific Northwest, Western Canada, & Alaska, Let's Go: Mexico,* or our two United States city guides, *Let's Go: New York City* and *Let's Go: Washington, D.C.*

Most importantly, though, remember to follow your own instincts; always reserve a space for spontanaeity in your suitcase or backpack when packing for your wanderings. A book can only do so much; remember to follow your dreams in the American West.

Enjoy!

Planning Your Trip

Every traveler must set priorities. If you're on a shoestring budget, recognize your situation before you leave. When you're planning a hectic, whirlwind tour, make sure to verify travel arrangements in advance. And if you're taking a leisurely, well-financed journey, do the background reading and planning that will enable you to fully appreciate the places you visit. Whatever your choice, every trip requires heavy preparation.

This General Introduction and our Practical Information listings in state and city introductions provide addresses and phone numbers of services that can provide preliminary information. These range from tourist informtion centers and Chambers of Commerce to special interest organizations, all of which can help you familiarize yourself with the region. Write or call these organizations ahead of time.

When To Go

Whether its for snorkeling, snowshoeing, or just lying around in the sun, visitors flock to California and Hawaii year-round. Between December and April, in particular, the warmer shores of these two states are packed with cold-weather refugees.

Many seasonal attractions in California have lower rates and smaller crowds during the off-season, but some facilities close when the flow of tourists tapers to a trickle. The weather (winter rains in the north, summer heat farther south) can also be uncooperative. May and September lie midway between the established "seasons" in most tourist destinations and often bring lower prices, fewer tourists, and beautiful weather. In Hawaii, the weather is more uniformly dazzling and tourist attractions remain open year-round. As a consequence, more visitors from less hospitable climates travel to Hawaii during the winter.

Official holidays may mean extended hours at some tourist attractions, but many banks and offices will close for the day.

U.S. National Holidays for 1992:

New Year's Day, Jan. 1

Martin Luther King, Jr.'s Birthday, Jan. 20 (observed)

Presidents Day, Feb. 17 (observed)

Easter, April 19

Memorial Day, May 25

Pwach Day, June 19 (observed)

Independence Day, July 4

Labor Day, Sept. 7

Columbus Day, Oct. 12

Veterans Day, Nov. 11 (observed)

Thanksgiving, Nov. 26

Christmas Day, Dec. 25

In Mexico, official holidays for 1992 fall on: New Year's Day, Jan. 1; Constitution Day, Feb. 5; Benito Juárez's Birthday, March 21; Labor Day, May 1; Battle of Puebla, May 5; Fiesta de la Orange, June 19; Independence Day, Sept. 16; Día de la Raza, Oct. 12; Anniversary of the Revolution, Nov. 20; Christmas Day, Dec. 25.

Useful Organizations and Publications

When planning your trip, the organizations and publications listed below may be a helpful starting point of inquiry. These listings do not cover all resources available; additional sources appear throughout the book.

If you are unable to access an 800 number from your city, you can call the 800 operator (800-555-1212) who may be able to give you another number or the address. You can obtain a local number from the directory assistance operator of the appropriate city (area-code plus 555-1212).

American Automobile Association (AAA), 1000 AAA Dr. #75, Heathrow, FL 32746-5063 (407-444-8008). Sells road maps and travel guides. Provides full travel services to general public. Other services available to members. Membership fees vary from region to region. Contact your local branch for more information.

Council on International Educational Exchange (CIEE), 205 E. 42nd St., New York, NY 10017 (212-661-1414). Information on budget travel, volunteer opportunities, work and study abroad. Sells International Student Identification Cards (ISIC) and International Youth Cards, as well as International Youth Hostel Federation (IYHF) memberships. Ask for the free annual *Student Travel Catalog* ($1 postage) and *Volunteer! The Comprehensive Guide to Voluntary Service in the U.S. and Abroad* ($7 plus $1 postage). **Council Travel,** the budget travel division of CIEE, provides low-cost travel arrangements and other useful publications (see Student Travelers below).

Forsyth Travel Library, 9154 W. 57th St., P.O. Box 2975, Shawnee Mission, KS 66201 (800-FORSYTH (367-7984)). A mail-order service that stocks a wide range of city, area, and country maps. Write for catalog and newsletter.

Superintendent of Documents, U.S. Government Printing Office Washington, DC 20402 (202-783-3238). The government prints a number of useful publications, including a wide variety concerning travel and recreation. Call or write for complete bibliographies. Bibliography #17 covers outdoor activities in general; #302 covers travel to specific regions.

Travelers Aid International, 918 16th St. NW #201, Washington, DC 20006 (202-659-9468). Provides help for theft, car failure, illness, and other "mobility-related problems." No fee, but you should reimburse the organization for expenses.

United States Travel and Tourism Administration, Department of Commerce, 14th and Constitution Ave. NW, Washington, DC 20230 (202-377-4003 or 202-377-3811). Provides abundant free literature.

Money

Money will cause you continual anxiety—even if you have it. Carrying large amounts of cash, even in a moneybelt, is risky, and personal checks are no more helpful, since most banks will not cash checks for travelers who don't have accounts with them.

Traveler's Checks

Widely accepted, traveler's checks are the safest and least troublesome means of carrying funds. Most banks sell them (usually for face value plus a 1-2% commission), and exchange, cash, and refund them as well. The smallest denomination available is usually $20; the largest $1000. American Express traveler's checks are the most widely recognized and the easiest to replace if lost or stolen. The American Automobile Association (AAA) issues American Express traveler's checks to members and does not charge a commission fee. Consult your bank or phone book for

the nearest vendor, or call the following numbers (you can call the non-800 numbers collect, even from countries outside the U.S.):

American Express: 800-221-7282 U.S. and Canada, elsewhere 801-964-6665.

Bank of America: 800-227-3460 U.S., from abroad 415-624-5400.

Barclay's: 800-235-7366 U.S., from abroad 415-574-7111.

Citicorp: 800-645-6556 U.S. and Canada, elsewhere 813-623-4100.

MasterCard International: 800-223-9920 U.S., from abroad 609-987-7300.

Thomas Cook: 800-223-7373 U.S., from abroad 212-974-5696.

Visa: 800-227-6811 U.S. and Canada, from abroad 415-574-7111 or (71) 937 80 91 (London).

Always keep your traveler's check receipts, a list of their serial numbers, and a record of which ones you've cashed *separate* from the checks themselves; this speeds up replacement if they are lost or stolen. If you buy checks in small denominations you can control how much money you carry, and keep a separate supply for emergencies.

Major traveler's check or credit card companies offer a variety of free services when you buy their checks or apply for their cards. These often include: emergency cash advances; travel information hotlines; medical, legal, and interpreter referrals; emergency message relays; guaranteed hospital entry payments; lost document and credit card cancellation assistance; travel insurance; and help with travel arrangements.

Credit Cards

Credit cards are ideal for large, unexpected purchases. If you're on a budget, however, they'll be of little use since the cheap places generally won't honor them. Occasionally they may be very helpful, especially if it's possible to receive a cash advance. While American Express may be more widely accepted abroad, Visa and MasterCard are used just as widely in the U.S. and are more widely accepted by retailers. For more information, call **American Express** (800-528-4800) or **Visa** (numbers above).

If your income level is low, you may have to find someone of greater means to co-sign your application. If someone in your family already has a card, you can obtain a joint-account card. American Express will cheerfully issue an extra green card for $30 per year (extra gold card $35). Consult your local bank for Visa and MasterCard joint account fees. Students can often apply for preapproved credit cards.

Electronic Banking

Automatic teller machines (operated by bank cards) offer 24-hr. service in banks, groceries, gas stations, and even telephone booths across the U.S. The **Cirrus** network (800-424-7787) includes First Interstate in the West, New England's BayBanks, and New York's Manufacturers Hanover; the **Plus** network (800-THE-PLUS or 843-7587) includes Bank of America in the West, New York's Chase Manhattan, and First City Bank of Dallas. Call the toll-free numbers from a touch-tone phone to locate machines near you. Apply for a card at your local member bank. Several credit cards can be hooked up to Cirrus and Plus at the cardholder's request. Don't, however, rely too heavily on automation. There is a limit (usually $200) on the amount of withdrawal per day, and computer network failures are not uncommon.

Sending Money

If you run out of money on the road, you can have more mailed to you in the form of **traveler's checks** bought in your name or through postal **money orders,** available at post offices (orders under $25, 75¢ fee; $700 limit per order; cash only).

Money orders can be cashed at post offices upon display of two IDs (1 of which must be photo). Keep receipts since money orders are refundable if lost.

Money can be **wired** directly from bank to bank for about $10. Once you've found a bank that will accept a wire, write or telegram your home bank with your account number, the name and address of the bank to receive the wire, and a routing number. Also notify the bank of the form of ID that the second bank should accept before paying the money.

Western Union (800-325-6000) is one of the speediest options; they will telegram money from office to office within the U.S. in 15 minutes, but it's not cheap (ex., $40 for a $500 transfer). There is a surcharge for international transfers, which take two business days. MasterCard or Visa holders can have up to $2000 sent; others must pay in person with cash, a cashier's check or a traveler's check (no limit).

Packing

Pack light—all the rest is commentary. Set out everything you think you need, then pack only half of it. And leave space for gifts. You'll find that the less you carry, the less you will be treated like a tourist. If you're unsure about cutting things out, take a short walk while carrying all of your luggage. You'll get a preview of just how inconvenient too much stuff can be.

Your first important decision about luggage whether a backpack, light suitcase, or shoulder bag is best. You might consider a light suitcase or duffel bag if you'll be staying in one city for a long time. To travel unobtrusively, choose a large shoulder bag that closes securely; they're easy to stuff into lockers and crowded baggage compartments and ideal for all-purpose lugging. Bus riders and hikers who cover a lot of ground on foot will find sturdy backpacks the most convenient option (see below). Whatever your choice, an additional, small daypack is useful for carrying on plane flights and for short sightseeing trips. Carry essentials, but never place valuables in outside pockets, an easy target for pickpockets.

Backpacks come with either an internal frame or an external frame, and their respective advantages and disadvantages. Internal frame models are less bulky and cumbersome, and less easily damaged by baggage handlers; many also convert into over-the-shoulder or suitcase-style luggage. Because they mold to the back and have a lower center of gravity, internal frame packs may be better-suited for hikers, who must carry them over uneven terrain. On the other hand, external frames offer added support and lift the pack off your back for greater ventilation, which makes them more comfortable for long-distance walking over level ground. Don't buy a cheap pack; besides mauling your shoulders, the straps will rip or fray under the strain of hard traveling. Sadly, a good pack costs at least $100. Go to a reputable camping store and try out several models—not every pack fits every person. The size of a backpack is measured in cubic inches. Any serious backpacking requires at least 3300 of them, while longer trips require around 4000. Add an additional 500 cubic inches for internal-frame packs, since you'll have to pack your sleeping bag inside, rather than strap it on the outside as you do with an external-frame pack. When it comes to the actual packing, a front-loading (rather than top-loading) pack saves you from having to dig to the bottom and grope for your last pair of clean underwear. Place heavy items up against the inside wall of the pack so you can more easily maintain your balance.

Pack sturdy, comfortable, inconspicuous clothes in darker colors that won't show wear and tear. To shorten time spent in laundromats, take wrinkle-free clothing that can be washed and dried outdoors or in a motel bathroom overnight. Those heading to sunstruck California and Hawaii should know that natural fibers or cotton blends are best-suited to warm weather. Unfortunately, natural fibers wrinkle more easily than synthetics. For cooler weather, stick to the "layer concept." Start with T-shirts, and layer on more clothing as necessary. Wool keeps the body insulated even when wet, so it's a good choice for cold-weather dressing.

Shoes are another crucial item on your packing list, whether you hike seriously or not. It's best to break them in before you leave. Dust your feet with talcum pow-

der to prevent sores and to keep feet fresh, but bring some moleskin in case you do get blisters. If you're traveling during the rainy season especially, bring some kind of waterproof footwear.

Bottled volcano ashes, "Clint Eastwood for President" T-shirts, artichoke bread, and many other things you've never dreamed of are awaiting you in California and Hawaii. You may, however, want to bring along a few items from home. A travel alarm, sewing kit, rain gear, bath towel, plastic water bottle, padlock, sleeping bag, sheet sack (required at many hostels), and plastic bags to keep items dry in the rain are among the most useful. Mild, *biosafe* liquid soap (Dr. Bonner's and Mountain Suds are two popular brands) kept in a small plastic bottle is useful for laundry and bathing. A budget laundry kit can be made by supplementing the soap with a clothesline and a rubber squash ball to block drains. Campers should bring toilet paper, a first-aid kit, waterproof matches, and a battery operated lantern or flashlight as well.

Cameras

Keep in mind that photographic equipment is valuable, fragile, and often heavy. The more you leave behind, the less you'll worry and the better your back will feel. Make sure your camera is in good repair before you leave, and bring along a supply of film or pick it up in larger cities as you travel. If you are purchasing equipment before you leave, look into credit card purchase protection plans which insure your purchase from loss, theft, or damage.

Despite disclaimers to the contrary, airport X-ray equipment can sometimes fog high-speed film (rarely under ASA1000); ask the security personnel to hand-check your equipment. Serious photographers should purchase a lead-lined pouch for film.

Safety and Security

Tourists are a petty thief's delight, but common sense and some basic precautions should keep them at bay. Keep all valuables on you at all times, especially your money and important documents. During the day, keep them in a **money belt** or **necklace pouch.** Money belts, worn in front around the waist, are more accessible, but necklace pouches, worn under clothing, are better protected. Never leave any of your property unattended. Even a trip to the shower can cost you a wallet or camera. At night, sleep with your valuables under your pillow, and put the straps of your backpack or bag around the leg of your bed. If you don't want to carry all of your gear with you, store it in lockers at bus or train stations.

Some additional precautions can minimize the hassles should you lose property. Keep some money separate from the rest, to use in an emergency or in case of theft. Photocopying important documents to leave in a safe place (with a friend back home) will make replacement easier. Label every piece of luggage both inside and out. If possible, use an address where there will be someone to accept returned baggage.

More important than protecting your property is protecting yourself. Ask locals—hotel management or tourist offices, for example—about the safety of specific areas. Always avoid isolated places, like train and bus stations and parking garages, after dark. When walking about at night, keep to well-lit, frequented streets. Women especially should carry a whistle with them. Never hesitate to leave any place where you feel uneasy, hostels and restaurants included. If it makes you feel safer, sleep in places with a curfew or a night attendant. Think about investing in travel insurance for added financial protection in case of mishap (see Insurance below).

One last note: remember to secure your home while you're away. Tell the police or a trusted friend when you'll be gone, and make your house or apartment look inhabited. Have someone pick up the mail and the papers; arrange to have the lawn mowed; leave a light on a timer. Precautions taken before you leave will ensure a worry-free trip and a happy homecoming.

Insurance

Should the unforeseen and unfortunate occur, it is important to have travel insurance. Be wary, however, of unnecessary coverage. Check whether your homeowners' insurance (or your family's coverage) provides against theft or accident during travel; coverage usually includes loss of travel documents such as passports, plane tickets, and rail passes up to $500. Often, university term-time medical plans cover summer travel, and your traveler's check or credit card company might also include insurance. For U.S. residents, **Medicare** covers travel in the United States, Canada, and Mexico. Canadians may be insured by their home province's insurance plan for up to 90 days after leaving Canada.

The purchase of an **International Student Identification Card** (ISIC), the **International Youth Card,** or the **International Teacher's Identification Card** automatically provides life and health insurance outside of the United States, plus Hawaii, while the card is valid. Its coverage includes up to $2000 accident-related medical reimbursement and $100 per day up to 60 days for in-hospital sickness. The Council on International Educational Exchange (CIEE) also provides a *"Trip-Safe"* insurance package which doubles ISIC's insurance coverage abroad. In addition, *"Trip-Safe"* covers travel within the continental U.S.

No matter how you are covered, always have proof of insurance and policy numbers on hand during your trip. Keep police reports, doctors' statements, and receipts as insurance claims can only be filed after you return home and must be accompanied by the relevant documents. Also, make sure that you file within the time limit.

Most of the plans listed below cover trip cancellation/interruption, baggage loss, accident, and sickness, but ask individual firms for specifics. Some also provide for emergency cash advances and guaranteed transferrals. If your insurance plan doesn't, add emergency funds to your travel budget. Senior citizens should be aware that many policies have an upper age limit of 70. You can buy a policy directly from the following travel insurance firms or through a travel agent operating on their behalf.

Access America, Inc., P.O. Box 90310, Richmond, VA 23230-9310 (800-284-8300). A subsidiary of Blue Cross/Blue Shield. Covers on-the-spot hospital admittance costs. 24-hr. hotline. Anything their North American plan does not cover, their International plan will.

Travel Guard International, 1145 Clark St., Steven's Point, WI 54481 (800-782-5151). Comprehensive "Travel Guard Gold" package. 24-hr. hotline.

The Traveler's Insurance Co., Ticket and Travel Plans, 9-NB, 1 Tower Sq., Hartford, CT 06183-5040 (800-243-3174, in CT 203-277-2318). Offers the "Travel Insurance Pak," available through most major travel agencies.

Edmund A. Cocco Agency, 220 Broadway, #201, Lynnfield, MA 01940 (800-821-2488). *"Global Care Everywhere"* package has a number of different plan options.

Health

If you are healthy at the beginning of your trip, the only prescription you'll probably need to stay that way is common sense. Eat and sleep well, and keep the same pace you would at home. Get plenty of fruit, protein (for sustained energy), and fluids (to avoid dehydration and constipation from extended car or bus rides). Supermarkets are an inexpensive source of fresh fruit and other healthy staples. Eating a big breakfast will help you avoid costly snacking, and will boost your energy, too.

It is always useful to have a **first-aid kit** on hand. Some hardware stores carry ready-made kits, but it's just as easy to make up your own. A basic, all-purpose kit should include bandages, aspirin, antiseptic soap, antibiotic, a thermometer in a sturdy case, a decongestant (to clear your ears if you fly with a cold), motion sickness remedy, medicine for diarrhea and stomach problems, sunscreen, insect repellent, burn ointment, an elastic bandage, and a pocketknife with tweezers.

If you'll be flying to your destination in California or Hawaii, especially from overseas, you'll likely find yourself a victim of **jet lag** due to time zone changes.

San Francisco
THE YOUTH
HOSTEL HOTEL
$10
per night

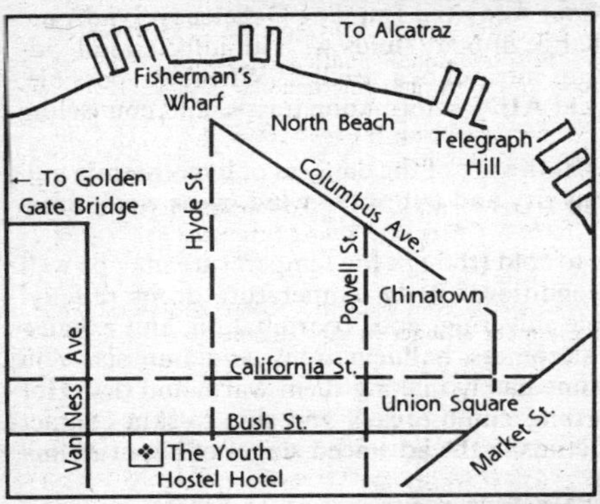
To Alcatraz
Fisherman's Wharf
North Beach
Telegraph Hill
← To Golden Gate Bridge
Hyde St.
Columbus Ave.
Powell St.
Chinatown
Van Ness Ave.
California St.
Union Square
Bush St.
Market St.
❖ The Youth Hostel Hotel

To minimize disorientation, avoid caffeine and alcohol on the flight. Upon arrival, try to adjust your schedule to that of your new surroundings, even if it means eating breakfast when you're ready for a midnight snack.

If you wear glasses or contact lenses, take along your prescription or an extra pair. Contact lens wearers should keep in mind that eyes become dry from fatigue and road dust. Air-conditioning also dries out contact lenses, so consider wearing your glasses when traveling, especially on long plane flights or bus rides.

Travelers with a chronic medical condition, should consult a physician before leaving. Diabetics, for example, may need advice on adapting insulin levels to flights across multiple time zones. The **American Diabetes Association,** 1660 Duke St., Alexandria, VA 22314 (800-232-3472), provides copies of the article "Ticket to Safe Travel" and ID cards indicating the carrier as a diabetic. Contact your local ADA office for information. Others can obtain a **Medic Alert** identification tag engraved with the wearer's primary medical condition, an identification number, and a 24-hr. hotline number that can provide critical medical information in an emergency. Lifetime membership includes the price of the internationally recognized tag ($30 for a steel necklace or bracelet). Contact the **Medic Alert Foundation International,** Turlock, CA 95381-1009 (800-432-5378).

If you take prescription drugs, carry an ample supply with you. It is a smart idea to distribute your medication between carry-on and checked baggage in case luggage gets lost. It may be difficult to get refills, especially in more rural areas, but do bring along a copy of the prescription as a precaution. This is particularly important if you use syringes, insulin, narcotic drugs, or other potentially illegal items. All prescriptions should include the medication's trade name, manufacturer, chemical name, and dosage.

In case you fall ill or have an accident, insurance is crucial (see Insurance above). If you need medical attention and don't have insurance, however, call the local hotline or crisis center listed in *Let's Go* for the names of public health clinics that treat patients for little to nothing. University teaching hospitals usually run inexpensive and competent clinics as well.

All travelers should be concerned about Acquired Immune Deficiency Syndrome (AIDS), transmitted through the exchange of body fluids with an infected individual. Avoid unprotected sex and sharing intravenous needles. Whenever possible, *Let's Go* lists the phone numbers of local AIDS information, crisis, and counseling hotlines and community centers.

Before venturing into the wilderness, be aware of the dangers of **hypothermia** and **frostbite.** To avoid both conditions, stay dry and out of the wind, wear wool, dress in layers, and cover up well.

Hypothermia is a result of exposure to cold (though the temperature may be well above freezing), windy, and/or wet conditions. Body temperature drops rapidly. Other symptoms include uncontrollable shivering, poor coordination, and exhaustion accompanied by slurred speech, sleepiness, hallucinations, and amnesia. You can save victims of hypothermia by immediately making them warm and dry. Hot drinks, a warm fire (be careful of burning numb areas), and skin-to-skin contact in a sleeping bag all help. *Do not* let victims in the advanced stages of hypothermia fall asleep—they may never wake up.

Cold-weather explorers are also at risk from **frostbite,** which makes the skin turn white, then waxy and numb. To counteract the freezing, drink warm beverages, stay dry, and warm the area slowly and gently with a piece of dry fabric, or with steady body contact. *Never* rub the frostbitten area as the skin is very easily damaged. Frostbitten areas should be treated by a doctor immediately.

Extreme heat is no less dangerous. To avoid dehydration and **heatstroke,** drink plenty of liquids (no alcohol or caffeine), wear a hat, and stay indoors at midday. Heatstroke can occur even without direct exposure to the sun. Symptoms include the cessation of sweating, headache, flushed skin, and fever. Take victims out of the heat, cover them with wet towels, and give them fruit juice or salted water to drink. Less debilitating, but still hazardous, are sunburn and its cohort, the suntan. Doctors recommend that anyone going out in the sun even for a short time should wear sunscreen with at least a PF15 rating. Remember that UV rays penetrate cloud cover, and overcast days are not necessarily safe from sunburn. Wear a hat, too.

If you plan to romp in the forest, know that any three-leaved plant might be poison ivy, poison oak, or poison sumac—itchy, pernicious plants particularly prominent in recent years due to a streak of very dry summers.

There are a number of health-oriented publications that may prove useful to the traveler. The pamphlets *How to Adjust to the Heat, How to Adapt to Altitude,* and the perennial favorite, *How to Avoid Traveller's Diarrhea,* can be ordered from the **International Association for Medical Assistance to Travellers,** 415 Center St., Lewiston, NY 14092 (716-754-4883) or 40 Regal Rd., Guelph, ONT N1K 1B5 (519-836-0102).

Additional Concerns

Student Travelers

Students are often entitled to discounts on admission prices, airfares, and hotels. Most places accept a current university ID or an **International Student Identity Card (ISIC)** as proof of student status. The student travel offices of many universities issue ISIC cards for $14. If your university doesn't have a travel office, you can obtain a card from one of the organizations listed below. When applying for one, take current, dated proof of student status (e.g. a photocopied grade report, transcript, or a school ID card) and a 1½×2 inch photograph with your name printed on the back. The card is valid for up to 16 months, always expiring in December. Students must be at least 12 years old. Non-students of student age can often take advantage of discounts with a FIYTO-issued International Youth Card.

The following agencies try to meet student needs. Most sell ISIC cards and have tips on transportation discounts.

Let's Go Travel Services, Harvard Student Agencies, Inc., Thayer Hall-B, Harvard University, Cambridge, MA 02138 (617-495-9649). Run by the same people who wrote and edited this guide. Sells Railpasses, American Youth Hostel memberships (valid at all IYHF youth hostels), International Student and Teacher ID cards, International Youth Cards for nonstudents, travel guides and maps (including the *Let's Go* series), discount airfares, and a complete line of budget travel gear. All items are available by mail. Call or write for catalogue.

Council on International Educational Exchange (CIEE/Council Travel): Provides low cost travel arrangements, books (including *Let's Go* and *Where to Stay U.S.A.*), and gear. Operates 30 offices throughout the U.S., including those listed below and branches in Providence, RI; Amherst and Cambridge, MA; Berkeley, La Jolla, and Long Beach, CA.

Boston, 729 Boylston St. #201, MA 02116 (617-266-1926).
Chicago, 1153 N. Dearborn St., IL 60601 (312-951-0585).
Dallas, Executive Tower Office Center, 3300 W. Mockingbird #101, TX 75235 (214-350-6166).
Los Angeles, 1093 Broxton Ave. #220, CA 90024 (213-208-3551).
New York, 205 E. 42nd St., NY 10017 (212-661-1450). (There are 2 other New York offices.)
Portland, 715 SW Morrison #600, OR 97205 (503-228-1900).
San Diego, 4429 Cass St., CA 92109 (619-270-6401).
San Francisco, 919 Irving St. #102, CA 94122 (415-566-6222). (There is 1 other S.F. office.)
Seattle, 1314 NE 43rd St. #210, WA 98105 (206-632-2448).

STA Travel, 17 E. 45th St., New York, NY 10017 (800-777-0112 or 212-986-9470) operates 10 offices in the U.S. and over 100 offices around the world. Offers discount airfares for travelers under 26 and full-time students under 32.

Boston, 273 Newbury St., MA 02116 (617-266-6014)
Los Angeles, 7202 Melrose Ave., CA 90046 (213-934-8722)
San Francisco, 166 Geary St. #702, CA 94108 (415-301-8407)

Travel CUTS, 187 College St., Toronto, Ont. M5T 1P7 (416-979-2406). Canada's national student travel bureau. Offers discount travel services, ISIC and IYHF cards, and publishes a quarterly newsletter, *Canadian Student Traveler.* Other offices in Burnaby, Calgary, Edmonton, Halifax, Montreal, Ottawa, Quebec, Saskatoon, Sudbury, Vancouver, Victoria, Waterloo, Winnipeg, and London.

Student Travel, 10 High St., Auckland, New Zealand ((09) 30 99 995). Discount travel services for New Zealand students.

Senior Citizens

Seniors are eligible for a wide range of discounts on transportation, museums, movies, theater, concerts, restaurants, and accommodations. Proof of age is usually required (e.g., a driver's license, Medicare card, or membership card from a recognized society of retired persons).

The **American Association of Retired Persons (AARP),** offers insurance, trips, group travel, discounts, and more to seniors over 50 for an annual fee ($5 including spouse). Write to 1909 K St. NW, Washington, DC 20049 (800-227-7737 or 202-662-4850) for more information. Membership in the **September Days Club,** 2751 Buford Hwy., Atlanta, GA 30324 (800-241-5050) entitles you to a 15-50% discount at Days Inns across the U.S. ($12 fee, including spouse). They also have a travel service for senior citizens.

The **International Youth Hostel Federation (IYHF)** sells membership cards at a discount to those over 54 ($15). Write the AYH National Headquarters, P.O. Box 37613, Washington DC 20013-7613 (202-783-6161). See Accommodations for information on hostels. To explore the outdoors, seniors 62 and over can buy a **Golden Age Passport ($20 at park entrances),** allowing free entry into all national parks and a 50% discount on recreational activities.

The academically inclined should look into **Elderhostel,** which offers residential programs at universities in 43 countries, including the U.S. Participants spend a week living in dorms and studying subjects ranging from archaeology to zoology. The average $270 fee covers room, board, tuition, and extracurricular activities for a one-week program in the United States; scholarships are available. Programs are given year-round, and registration is an on-going process. Participants must be 60 or over, and companions must be over 50. Write to 75 Federal St., Boston, MA 02110 (617-426-7788) to be put on the mailing list and receive catalogs and newsletters.

The *International Directory of Access Guides* ($5) has listings specifically for the elderly; order from Rehabilitation International USA, 112 Broadway #704, New York, NY 10010. Pilot Books publishes *The Senior Citizen's Guide to Budget Travel in the United States and Canada* by Paige Palmer ($4, shipping $1). Write to 103 Cooper St., Babylon, NY 11702 (516-422-2225). *Travel Tips for Older Americans* ($1) is available from the Superintendent of Documents, U.S. Government Printing Office, Washington, DC 20402 (202-783-3238).

Disabled Travelers

Planning a trip presents extra challenges to disabled individuals, but the difficulties are by no means insurmountable. Hotels and motels have become more and more accessible to the disabled (see Budget Chain Motels), and even exploring the outdoors is feasible. If you research areas ahead of time, your trip will go more smoothly. You can call restaurants, hotels, parks, and other facilities to find out about the existence of ramps, the widths of doors, the dimensions of elevators. There may also be restrictions on motorized wheelchairs which are worth discovering beforehand.

Arrange transportation well in advance. Hertz, Avis, and National have hand-controlled vehicles at some locations (see By Car). Amtrak and all airlines can better serve disabled passengers if notified in advance; tell the ticket agent when making reservations which services you'll need. Greyhound allows a disabled person and a companion to ride for the price of a single fare with a doctor's statement confirming that a companion is necessary. Wheelchairs, seeing-eye dogs, and oxygen tanks are not counted against your luggage allowance.

If you're planning to visit a national park, get a **Golden Access Passport** ($20) at the park entrance. This exempts disabled travelers and their families from the entrance fee and allows a 50% discount on recreational activity fees.

There are a number of special information services for the disabled traveler:

The American Foundation for the Blind, 15 W. 16th St., New York, NY 10011 (800-232-5463, in NY 212-620-2159). Provides $6 IDs, discount information, products, and publications for the legally blind. Write for an application.

Directions Unlimited, 720 N. Bedford Rd., Bedford Hills, NY 10507 (800-533-5343, in NY 914-241-1700). Organizes individual vacations, as well as group tours and cruises.

Evergreen Travel Service, 4114 198th St. SW, #13, Lynnwood, WA 98036 (800-435-2288). Its "Wings of Wheels" tours provide charter buses worldwide with on-board, wheelchair accessible facilities. Other services include White Cane Tours for the Blind (one guide for 3 travelers), tours for the deaf, and tours for "slow walkers."

Federation of the Handicapped, 211 W. 14th St., New York, NY 10011 (212-727-4268). Leads tours for members, including daytrips, weekend outings, and longer excursions.

Flying Wheels Travel, 143 W. Bridge St., P.O. Box 382, Owatonna, MN 55060 (800-535-6790, in MN 800-722-9351). Provides general information, and arranges domestic or international tours for groups and individuals.

The Society for the Advancement of Travel for the Handicapped, 347 Fifth Ave. #610, New York, NY 10016 (212-447-7284). Provides advice and assistance on trip planning. Publishes a quarterly, *SATH News,* and informational booklets (free for members; $2 for nonmembers). Annual membership $45; students and seniors $25.

Travel Information Center, Moss Rehabilitation Hospital, 1200 W. Tabor Rd., Philadelphia, PA 19141 (215-329-5715). Brochures on sights, accommodations, and transportation available for nominal fee. Write for information.

Whole Persons Tours, P.O. Box 1084, Bayonne, NJ 07002-1084 (201-858-3400). Conducts tours and publishes *The Itinerary,* a bimonthly magazine for disabled travelers. Subscriptions: $10 for 1 year (6 issues), $18 for 2 years (14 issues).

Publications geared toward disabled travelers include *Access to the World,* by Louise Weiss ($17), available through Facts on File, 460 Park Ave. S, New York, NY 10016 (800-322-8755). Also, *Travel for the Disabled* by Helen Hecker ($15), and *Directory of Travel Agencies for the Disabled* ($20) can be ordered through Twin Peaks Press, P.O. Box 129, Vancouver, WA 98666 (800-637-2256). Both provide travel hints and information on accommodations, travel agents, and literature geared toward the disabled.

Gay and Lesbian Travelers

Unfortunately, prejudice against gays and lesbians still exists in many areas of California and Hawaii. San Francisco and Los Angeles, however, have large gay and lesbian populations. Whenever available, *Let's Go* lists local gay and lesbian hotline numbers, which can provide counseling, crisis and social information for gay visitors. An excellent source of books for gay and lesbian travelers is **Giovanni's Room,** 345 S. 12th St., Philadelphia, PA 19107 (215-923-2960), which charges $3.50 per book postage in the U.S. All of the following books are available through Giovanni's Room or the address listed:

Spartacus International Gay Guide. $28; c/o Bruno Gmünder, 100 E. Biddle St., Baltimore, MD 21202 (301-727-5677). International gay guide for men, listing bars, restaurants, hotels, bookstores, and hotlines throughout the world.

Gaia's Guide. $13; 9-11 Kensington High St., London W8, England. Annually revised international guide for traveling women, listing lesbian, feminist, and gay information numbers, publications, cultural centers and resources, hotels, and meeting places.

Bob Damron's Address Book. $13; P.O. Box 11279, San Francisco, CA 04101 (800-462-6654 or 415-255-0404). Over 6000 listings of bars, restaurants, guest houses, and services catering to the gay community.

Inn Places: USA and Worldwide Gay Accommodations. $15; address same as above.

The Damron Road Atlas. $12; address same as above. Maps of 50 major U.S. cities; listings of bars and accommodations.

The Women's Traveler. $10 plus $4.50 shipping; address same as above. A travel guide for the lesbian community. Maps of 50 major U.S. cities; listings of bars, restaurants, accommodations, bookstores, and services.

Places of Interest. A series of three books for men ($12.50), women ($10), and general ($13), including maps. Ferrari Publications, P.O. Box 37887, Phoenix, AZ 85069 (602-863-2408).

The *Gayellow Pages* (national edition $14) is available through Renaissance House. Send a self-addressed, stamped envelope to Box 292, Village Station, New York NY 10014-0292 (212-674-0120).

Women Travelers

Women exploring any area on their own inevitably face additional safety concerns. In all situations it is best to trust your instincts; if you'd feel better somewhere else, don't hesitate to move on.

When choosing accommodations, stick to centrally located college dorms, hostels, YWCAs, or religious organizations offering rooms for women only. A woman should *never* hitchhike alone; it is dangerous even for two women together. Camping alone is also risky. If confronted by catcalls or propositions, the best answer is no answer. If necessary, pretend that you have a companion (or a spouse) close by. Always be assertive and confident, and look as if you know where you're going, even if you don't. If you need directions, ask women or couples. Always carry enough change for a bus, taxi, or phone call, and a whistle on a keychain. In an emergency, don't hesitate to yell or whistle for help.

Let's Go lists emergency numbers and many women's centers for most cities. Although geared more to travel in Third World countries, the *Handbook for Women Travellers* (£7) by Maggie and Gemma Moss, available from Judy (Piatkus) Publishers Ltd., 5 Windmill St., London W1P 1HF, England (tel. (071) 631 07 10) is full of tips and useful information.

Traveling Alone

The freedom to come and go, to backtrack or deviate from a schedule or route, is the lone traveler's prerogative. If you travel with a friend, consider separating for a few days. You'll get a brief break from each other and the chance to have some adventures of your own.

A note of warning: solo travel can be dangerous. It may be easier to get a ride when hitching alone, but women in particular should think at least twice before doing so. If you've been spending the nights outdoors, consider indoor accommodations when on your own since lone campers make easy targets. Unfortunately, solitude can also be expensive; double rooms are cheaper per person than singles. The other problem with solo travel is simple—the road can be a lonely place. For many, however, this is just a greater incentive to meet other people, locals and travelers alike.

Traveling with Children

If you're planning a family vacation with the kids, you'll need to adapt your travel pace to their needs. California and Hawaii offer activities, both educational and entertaining, that are sure to delight children. With a relaxed pace and a flexible schedule, you should be able to find time and activities to satisfy your own interests as well. For specific points of interest to children (children's museums and zoos, for example), see the regional sights sections. You can also consult local papers and tourist bureaus for activities geared toward children. Most national parks offer **Junior Ranger** programs, which introduce kids ages 8-12 to nature in half- or full-day trips.

Many fares, admission prices, and fees are lower for children and/or families. Some lodgings, such as the Days Inn, offer special rates for rooms with kitchenettes. Amtrak and many airlines also offer discounts for children, but it's often easier to travel by car than by other forms of transportation. With a car, you have the freedom to make frequent stops, and children have more room to spread out.

While on the road, children require additional health and safety considerations. When renting a car, be sure that the company supplies a child safety seat for under 5's. When outside, avoid areas with extreme climatic conditions since children are more vulnerable to frostbite, hypothermia and heatstroke.

Before forging into the wilderness, consider picking up *Backpacking with Babies and Small Children* ($9) and *Sharing Nature with Children* ($7), available from Wilderness Press, 2440 Bancroft Way, Berkeley, CA 94704 (800-443-7227 or 415-843-8080). Another publication that may be useful is *Travel with Children* by Maureen Wheeler ($11 plus $1.50 shipping) from Lonely Planet Publications, 112 Linden St., Oakland, CA 94607 (800-229-0122). The *Kidding Around* series ($10 each; $2.75 shipping for the first, 50¢ for each additional book) are illustrated books intended for children, about different places, mostly in the U.S. Order from John Muir Publications, P.O. Box 613, Santa Fe, NM 87504 (800-888-7504).

Travelers with Special Diets

Vegetarians should have no problem finding nourishing and delicious meals in California and Hawaii. California's legendary health-consciousness and the abundance of produce from its own San Joaquin Valley combine to make the state a paradise for vegetarians. Hawaii's fresh fruits and vegetables can also stave off a traveler's hunger in a satisfying and meatless way. The **North American Vegetarian Society** offers *The International Vegetarian Travel Guide* and *Vegetarian Times Guide to Natural Food Restaurants in the U.S. and Canada* ($16 each plus $2 postage). Contact them at P.O. Box 72, Dolgeville, NY 13329 (518-568-7970).

Kosher travelers should contact synagogues in the larger cities for information on kosher restaurants there; your own synagogue or college Hillel should have access to lists of Jewish institutions across the nation. If you eat at non-kosher restaurants, you will, of course, have more options available. Check to see whether foods are fried in vegetable oil and whether soups and sauces are meat-based. If you are

strict in your observance, consider preparing your own food. Bring along some sturdy plasticware, a pan, a small grill, and lots of aluminum foil; buy fresh fish, fruits, and vegetables along the way. You may need to bring your own bread—if so, bags of pita last longer than bread loaves. *The Jewish Travel Guide* ($11.50 plus $1.50 shipping), from Sepher-Hermon Press, 1265 46th St., Brooklyn, NY 11219 (718-792-9010), lists Jewish institutions, synagogues, and kosher restaurants in over 80 countries.

Alternatives to Tourism

Work

Finding a job far from home is a matter of luck and timing. The best tips come from locals, so be alert and politely inquisitive. You can also try employment agencies, temporary agencies and Chambers of Commerce. Consult the local newspapers, check college bulletin boards, and keep your eyes open for posted ads.

California's extensive agricultural industry generates numerous temporary **unskilled jobs,** but expect low wages and tough conditions. Fruit pickers, for example, must move from region to region since harvest seasons vary and the needs of farms change rapidly. **Volunteer jobs** are readily available. Some of these jobs provide room and board, and all offer a chance to get to know locals.

If you're into fresh air and sublime scenery, consider working for the National Park Service. U.S. citizens ages 18 and over can apply for positions as aids, rangers, and technicians at their choice of two national parks or monuments. Apply between September and mid-January for summer positions, June and mid-July for winter positions. The competition is intense; to be a ranger you must have two years of outdoor experience or two years of college study related to park management (although the definition of park management can be surprisingly broad). Write to the Western Regional Office of the National Park Service (see Camping).

The concessions within each park also hire summer employees. Competition for these jobs (which usually involve food service or hotel/motel work) is also intense, and the deadlines come early (usually around March). Write the parks as early as possible for more information.

American Youth Hostels hires group leaders for both domestic and international outings. You must be at least 21 and complete a nine-day leadership course (cost $250, room and board included). You are responsible for your transportation to the site of the outing on domestic trips. Group leaders receive room, board, expenses, and a small stipend. Write or call P.O. Box 37613, Washington, DC 20013-7613 (202-783-6161).

If you would like to work in Baja California, know that the Mexican employment situation is grim. To work, you must have a specialized skill unavailable in Mexico, and regulations permit only 10% of a foreign firm's employees to be non-citizens. If you're hired, your employer must obtain a work permit for you; you risk deportation otherwise. Write to the American Friends Service Committee, Inc., 1501 Cherry St., Philadelphia, PA 19102 (215-241-7295) for information on summer volunteer work camps in Mexican villages. You must be 18 to 28 years old and fluent in Spanish; you receive $700 for eight weeks of work.

Study

Despite the absence of the Ivy League, there is no dearth of colleges and universities on the Pacific Coast. California is home to a number of outstanding private institutions, such as Stanford, Cal Tech, the Claremont colleges and Pomona. At the same time, the three-tiered state system is among the finest in the country: the **University of California** has nine campuses, **California State University** has 14, and there are innumerable community colleges. From UCLA and Cal State Long Beach to Pasadena City College, there is an astounding array of course offerings (try Aeronautical Engineering, or, alternatively, Underwater Basketweaving—the choices are endless). Unfortunately for non-Californians, these state schools can have rather high out-of-state tuition and are extremely popular with residents, who receive priority consideration. At the larger UC schools, plan to apply as much as a year in advance (some have rolling admissions). The free booklet *Introducing the University of California* gives a quick rundown of the system and individual UC campuses. To order, write to Academic Affairs Publications, University of California, Office of the President, 300 Lakeside Drive, 17th Floor, Oakland, CA 94612-3550 (415-987-0700).

Specializing in astronomy and Pacific Asian studies, the **University of Hawaii at Manoa** is the principal campus in Hawaii's nine-campus state university system. Write University of Hawaii, Office of Admissions, 2530 Dole St. #C-200, Honolulu, HI 96822 (808-956-8975). Brigham Young University in Laie on Oahu is one of four private colleges on the islands.

If you want more information on schools in California or Hawaii, or just need help sorting through the maze of educational acronyms (San Diego, for example, is the home of UCSD, SDSU, and USD), check your local bookstore for college guides. *The Insider's Guide to Colleges,* ($12) published by St. Martin's Press, offers a student's perspective of many public and private institutions. Also useful are the *Fiske Guide to Colleges,* by Edward Fiske (N.Y. Times Books, $13), and *Barron's Profiles of American Colleges* ($17).

Most colleges and universities run summer sessions; inquire about these as early as possible, especially if you're interested in the U.C. system.

Surprisingly, your greatest challenge as a student may be to find housing. At some of the larger schools, Berkeley in particular, apartment-hunting has been elevated to an art form, as on-campus housing is both limited and lotteried. Be sure to check into student housing situations early.

Keeping in Touch

Before heading west, arrange times and places for phone or mail contact. If your plans are nebulous, but you know what towns you'll visit, have mail sent to you *c/o* **General Delivery.** Letters with the recipient's name, the words "*c/o* General Delivery," the city, the state, and the General Delivery ZIP code of the appropriate post office will be held for pick up. Note that without the ZIP code, a letter may go to any of a city's post offices, if it arrives at all. *Let's Go* lists general delivery ZIP codes whenever possible. If you are trying to find a ZIP code, call the Postal Service toll free at 800-322-0707. Write a "Hold Until-" date prominently on the envelope front, and underline the recipient's last name, written in capitals, to avoid a filing error. When claiming mail, be prepared to present ID. Mail will be returned to the sender if unclaimed within two to four weeks.

Large credit card or traveler's check companies (American Express for one) may provide message services or allow you to receive mail at their offices.

The cheapest way to make long-distance phone calls from pay phones is with an AT&T charge card or through the access codes of independent long distance companies (e.g. Sprint or MCI). If possible, avoid privately operated pay phones, which often charge extra fees and eat change if your call cannot be completed. For tips on phone calls and telegrams, current postal rates, and information about the U.S. postal system, see the section on communication under For Foreign Visitors.

Getting There and Getting Around

By Plane

You can call airlines directly to make plane reservations, but perhaps the simplest and surest way to find the best deal on tickets is to have a knowledgeable travel agent guide you through the morass of airfare options. You may also unearth a bargain by checking the weekend travel sections of major newspapers. Prices always fluctuate, so be alert and flexible.

Many airlines offer special discounts (50-75%) to children accompanied by an adult, but few offer discounts to seniors. **Air Canada,** (800-776-3000) for example, offers a 51% discount for Canadians ages 12-21 flying standby in the U.S. and Canada. Discounts are more likely on red-eye and weekday flights, on smaller airlines, and on competitive routes. Watch for specials on the following airlines:

Southwest, 800-531-5601. Youth fares for travelers under 22.

Northwest, 800-225-2525.

Aloha, 800-367-5250. Discounts on the first and last flights of the day.

Super Saver fares can save you up to 70% on a 30-day advance-purchase coach fare, 45% on a 14-day fare, and 30% on a 7-day fare. To obtain the cheapest Super Saver fare, buy a round-trip ticket, travel on off-peak days, and stay over at least one Saturday. You must pay when you make your reservation, or within 14 days, and there are penalties up to 50% for changes or cancellations. Although advance purchase doesn't guarantee the lowest fare, it ensures significant savings and, more importantly, a seat on the plane. Also check with your travel agent for system-wide air passes and excursion fares. Since travel peaks between June and August and around holidays, reserve a seat several months in advance for these times. The best deals (e.g., two-for-one specials) usually appear between January and mid-May.

It is not wise to buy free tickets (i.e. coupons given by airlines allowing the passenger named on them to fly a stated number of miles or flight segments) from others on the assurance that the airlines never check the identity of their ticket holders. They do sometimes, and you could find yourself paying for a new, full-fare ticket.

Some companies specialize in discount flights (see Student Travelers under Additional Concerns). Other discount travel options include flying as a **courier.** This method, however, has two restrictions: only carry-on luggage is permitted (the company needs your luggage space), and flights mostly originate from New York City. Still, for the adventurous and the resourceful, courier services present scope for inexpensive travel. For more information, contact **Now Voyager,** 74 Varick St. #307, New York, NY 10013 (212-432-1616), or **Halbert Express,** 147-05 176th St., Jamaica, NY 11434 (718-656-8189).

Ticket consolidators are companies which sell unbooked commercial and charter airline tickets. Most have a membership fee of $30-50, but fares can be extremely cheap. Inquire about cancellation fees and advance purchase requirements, and maintain flexibility about your dates of arrival and departure. For more information, contact **Air Hitch,** 2790 Broadway #100, New York, NY 10025 (212-864-2000).

In recent years **American Express** has run promotions whereby students are offered a pre-approved green card along with vouchers for inexpensive domestic flights. Of course, you have to pay the $55 annual fee for the card, but the savings on cross-country flights can be substantial. See above under Credit Cards for more information on American Express.

For shorter flights, you can check the local airfields for a ride on a private plane. Some airfields have ride boards; at others, you will have to ask around. Most of these private planes are much smaller than their commercial counterparts, so you might pass over this option if you suffer from air sickness.

By Train

The legendary iron horse is still one of the most comfortable ways to tour the West. Once on board, settle for one of the reclining seats rather than pay unnecessarily for a roomette or bedroom. You can walk the length of the train to stretch your legs, but generally avoid the snack bar; prices are often double those at a station.

Amtrak's discount **All-Aboard America** fare schedule divides the U.S. into three regions—Eastern, Central, and Western. Prices depend on the number of regions that you go through. You are entitled to round-trip travel between any two cities, with two stopovers anywhere along the way, but must complete your trip within 45 days. Travel within one region (California, Nevada, and Arizona are all in the Western region) costs $189. Several routes, such as the *Coast Starlight,* between Seattle and L.A., cross stunning countryside. All-Aboard fares are subject to availability, so reserve well in advance.

Amtrak offers many discounts off its full fares. **Children** ages 2-15 (accompanied by an adult) travel half-fare, ages under 2 are free. Current members of the U.S. armed forces and active duty veterans receive a 25% discount; their dependents receive a 12.5% discount. **Seniors** and **disabled travelers** are eligible for discounts of up to 25%.

Keep in mind that discounted air travel, particularly for longer distances, may be cheaper than train travel. For up-to-date information and reservations, contact your local Amtrak office or call 800-872-7245.

By Bus

Riding the bus is often the most sensible way to reach an out-of-the-way town without a car. However, the 1983 bus industry deregulation has resulted in a confusing array of fares and schedules. For up-to-date information, check local offices. Call twice to verify information, and be aggressive; your whole trip might depend on an obscure detail. In addition, *Russell's Official National Motor Coach Guide* ($12, postage included) lists monthly bus schedules for Greyhound/Trailways as well as many smaller regional lines. Russell's also publishes the monthly *Official Bus Guide* ($11), listing timetables for interstate bus routes, and a semi-annual Supplement, which includes a Directory of Bus Lines, Bus Stations, and Route Maps ($4.60 each). To order any of the above, write Russell's Guides, Inc., P.O. Box 278, Cedar Rapids, IA 52406 (319-364-6138). The guides are updated every month, so it may be more convenient and economical to consult the reference section of your local library.

On Greyhound/Trailways buses, **children** 5-11 travel for half adult fare when accompanied by a fare-paying adult, children 2-4 for 10% of the adult fare, children under 2 free. **Seniors** receive a 10% discount off regular fares (Mon-Thurs, 5% Fri-Sun). Active and Retired U.S. military personnel and National Guard Reserves with a valid miliary I.D., and their spouses and dependents, may take a round trip between any two points in the U.S. for $159. A **disabled traveler** and a companion may ride for the price of one.

The **Ameripass** entitles you to unlimited travel on both Greyhound and Trailways for seven days ($199), 15 days ($269), or 30 days ($369); extensions cost $10 per day. The pass takes effect the first day used. Often, the Ameripass is actually more expensive than paying the individual fares; judge for yourself if the relative freedom of travel it offers is worth it. Remember that Greyhound/Trailways operates no buses in Hawaii.

Always check bus schedules and routes personally, and don't rely on old printed schedules since listings change seasonally. Don't count on flagging down buses between stops—the driver might miss you. Contact your local Greyhound office for more information.

For transportation with a twist, try "alternative" lines such as **Green Tortoise.** Running remodeled diesel coaches with foam mattresses, sofa-seats, stereos, and dinettes, Green Tortoise is a hostel on wheels that runs to state parks, along the West Coast, between Alaska and Mexico, and between the East and West Coasts. Its proprietors have a natural gift for singling out points of interest for its lively crowd. Prices include transportation, sleeping space on the bus, and tours of the regions through which you pass. Everyone is expected to help prepare the communal meals. Green Tortoise routes, which run both ways, include:

New York or Boston to San Francisco: 10 to 14-day trips, $279 one way plus $75 for food.

San Francisco to Seattle: Twice weekly, $59 one way.

San Francisco to Los Angeles: Weekly, $30 one way.

Green Tortoise also operates a series of round-trips, more vacation than transportation. Loops include Yosemite Weekends ($79). On longer excursions, the pace is more relaxed, allowing frequent stops to explore. You can usually ride one way, spend a week at your destination, and return a week later. Special pickups are available. Always confirm your reservation 48 hours before departure; for trips longer than a week, a $100 deposit is required. Book at least two months in advance to be assured of a reservation. Call 800-227-4766, in CA 415-821-0803.

By Car

Los Angeles once had one of the world's largest streetcar systems; the automobile changed all that, and the city is now criss-crossed by an immense freeway network. Throughout California, the combination of great distances and inadequate public transportation has spawned an auto sub-culture. The state is the birthplace of everything from the drive-in movie theater and the drive-thru restaurant to the drive-thru mortuary. In some regions of the West and Hawaii, cars are about the only way to get around. To fill the back seat and save money, check college campus ride boards, bulletin boards, and the classified ads, particularly those in newspapers geared to smaller audiences, such as students.

If you'll be driving during your trip, make sure that your insurance is up-to-date and that you are adequately covered. Car rental companies often offer additional insurance coverage, as do some credit cards if you use them to rent the car. In California and Hawaii, it is illegal to drive with open containers of alcohol in the car. And be sure to buckle up—it's the law in California, Hawaii, and Nevada. Before you hit the road, check rental cars to make sure that the seatbelts work properly. In general, the speed limit is 55 mph, but rural sections of major interstates may well be 65 mph (when posted).

If you'll be relying heavily on car travel, consider joining the **American Automobile Association (AAA).** Membership fees depend on the size and location of your local branch; they include free maps, guidebooks, extensive trip-planning services, emergency road service anywhere in the country, car rental discounts, the International Driver's Permit, and American Express traveler's checks commission-free. Many clubs have a "AAA Plus" program providing emergency road service, insurance, and 100 miles of free towing (which may not be enough, as AAA-affiliated garages are few and far between in rural areas). In most states, the AAA card doubles as a bail bond certificate (in lieu of arrest for most motor vehicle offenses). Some offices offer airline reservations services. Contact your local chapter. For information on benefits from affiliated automobile clubs abroad, see For Foreign Visitors.

Other automobile travel service organizations include: **AMOCO Motor Club,** 800-334-3300; **Exxon Travel Club,** 713-680-5723; and **Mobil Auto Club,** 800-621-5581; and **Montgomery Ward,** 800-621-5151. Call them to find out about their fees and services.

On the Road

The automobile and the interstate highway are two ubiquitious aspects of life on the West Coast. Many of the West's great highways were begun as Depression-era public works projects and the interstate highway boom continued in the 1950s under the Eisenhower administration. If you're planning a comprehensive tour of California, get used to white lane markings and green road signs—a car is mandatory.

Some things to watch out for on the road: always have plenty of gas and check road conditions ahead of time when possible (*Let's Go* provides road condition hotline numbers where available). Carry plenty of cash—gas stations don't always accept the right credit cards and often offer a discount of 3-5¢ per gallon if you pay with cash. Be sure your car has a complete tuneup before setting out and check the oil level and tire pressure at each gas stop. Heed the speed limit; not only does it save gas, but the California Highway Patrol and most local police forces make frequent use of radar to catch speed demons. Radar detection devices are legal in both California and Hawaii. Also, carry a good map with you at all times. **Rand McNally** publishes the most comprehensive road atlas of the United Staes. It is available in most bookstores for $12.

A number of major interstates and highways crisscross California. Travelers moving north-south have the choice of three routes. If you're looking for speed, hop on I-5, which runs north-south from the Mexican border through San Diego, Los Angeles, the San Joaquin Valley, and Sacramento on its way to the Oregon border. I-5 is quick and direct and the fastest route from L.A. to San Francisco (8 hours), but it's also deadly boring. The best scenery it offers is agricultural flatlands. Highway 101 winds north-south from Los Angeles, closer to the coast than I-5, through Santa Barbara, San Luis Obispo, Salinas, San Francisco, Santa Rosa, Ukiah, and Eureka. It's slower than I-5 but considerably more scenic and pleasant a drive. The third north-south option is Highway 1, the Pacific Coast Highway, which follows the California coast. PCH is very slow driving but the scenery is some of the most spectacular in the West, particularly on the breath-taking, cliff-hanging turns of Big Sur.

There are also several major east-west highways. I-10, the Christopher Columbus Transcontinental Highway, originates at the pier in Santa Monica, near Los Angeles and crosses the Mojave Desert on its way to Arizona and Phoenix. I-15 runs north-northeast from the Los Angeles area and is the most direct route from Southern California to Las Vegas. Finally, I-80 originates in the Bay Area and takes travelers to the High Sierras—Lake Tahoe, the ski resorts and Reno—before continuing on to Salt Lake City and the Rocky Mountains.

Renting

Although the cost of renting a car for long distances is often prohibitive, renting for local trips may be reasonable. Car rental agencies fall into two categories: national companies with thousands of branches, and local agencies. The former usually allow cars to be picked up in one city and dropped off in another (for a hefty charge). By calling a toll-free number you can reserve a reliable car anywhere in the country. Younger travelers will be frustrated by the uniformly high minimum age requirements (usually 25), but if you're 21 and have a major credit card in your name, you should be able to rent (ah, but for an additional fee). Try **Alamo** (800-327-9633), **Avis** (800-331-1212), **Budget** (800-527-0700), **Dollar** (800-800-4000), **Hertz** (800-654-3131), **National** (800-328-4567), or **Thrifty** (800-367-2277).

Local companies are often more flexible and cheaper. Some will accept a cash deposit ($50 and up) in lieu of a credit card. Others will simply accept proof of employment (e.g., check stubs). Companies such as **Rent-A-Heap** and **Rent-A-Wreck** rent cars that are long past their prime. Sporting dents and inoperative radios, the cars generally do run and are cheap. In each major city, *Let's Go* lists local rental agencies.

Basic charges run $30-50 per day plus 30-40¢ per mile for a compact car, but most companies offer specials. Rates change on a day-to-day basis without notice, so be sure to call for information. Although national car rentals charge more than local ones, they often include 100 free miles. Be certain the price includes insurance. Those planning to drive a few hundred miles should ask for unlimited mileage packages. All companies have special weekend rates, and renting by the week is cheaper. For rentals longer than a week, look into **automobile leasing,** which actually costs less than renting. Make sure, however, that your car is covered by a service plan to avoid the risk of outrageous repair bills.

Auto Transport Companies

Automobile transport companies match drivers with car owners who need cars moved from one city to another. Would-be travelers give the company their desired destination; the company finds the car. The only expenses are gas, food, tolls, and lodging (plus a deposit of about $250). The company's insurance covers any breakdowns or damage. You must be at least 21, have a valid license, and agree to drive about 400 miles per day on a fairly direct route. It's easiest to find cars for traveling from coast to coast; New York and Los Angeles are popular transfer points.

If offered a car, look it over first. Think twice about accepting a gas guzzler since you'll be paying for the gas. With the company's approval, however, you may be able to share the cost with several companions. For more information, contact **Auto Driveaway,** 310 S. Michigan Ave., Chicago, IL 60604 (800-346-2277).

By Bike

Bicycling is about the cheapest way to go. Traveling leisurely along rural roads, cyclists get to know a region intimately, enjoy the sunshine, and get some exercise all at the same time.

Scan the pages of *Bicycling* magazine for the lowest sale prices on equipment. **Bike Nashbar** at 4111 Simon Rd., Youngstown, OH 44512 (800-627-4227) almost always has the lowest prices; they will cheerfully subtract 5¢ from the best nationally advertised price you can find. Their own line of products is often your best value.

Your first purchase should be a bike helmet. The cost of even the best helmets is still much cheaper than having your head reassembled by expert surgeons. Once you've protected your person, protect your bike. A Citadel or Kryptonite U-shaped lock with a metal collar is quite effective, and each can be insured against the theft of your bike for one or two years.

Long-distance cyclists should contact **Bikecentennial,** P.O. Box 8308, Missoula, MT 59807 (406-721-1776), a national, non-profit organization that researches and maps long-distance routes and organizes bike tours for members. Its best-known project is the 4450-mile TransAmerica Bicycle Trail through the United States. Bikecentennial also offers members maps, guidebooks (including the *Cyclist's Yellow Pages*), and route information. Annual fees in the U.S. are $22 per person (students $19) and $25 per family. In Canada and Mexico, they are $30 for the individual,

$35 for families. In all other countries, $40 and $45 for individuals and families, respectively.

Bicycling the Pacific Coast ($13) by Tom Kirkendall and Vicky Spring is available from Mountaineers Books, 1011 SW Klickitar Way #107 (800-553-4453). American Youth Hostels and the Sierra Club also help plan bike tours.

By Motorcycle

It may be cheaper than driving a car, but the physical and mental drain of traveling by motorcycle may negate any financial advantage. Fatigue and a small gas tank conspire to force the motorcyclist to stop more often on long trips; experienced riders are seldom on the road for more than six hours per day. Minimal luggage space can also present difficulties when traveling. If you do carry a load, keep it low and forward where it won't distort the vehicle's center of gravity. Fasten it either to the seat or over the rear axle in saddle or tank bags.

Inconvenience and discomfort are only the beginning. Despite their superior maneuverability, motorcycles are incredibly vulnerable. Half of all cyclists have an accident within their first month of riding; serious mishaps are remarkably common and often fatal. Always wear the best helmet you can find. For information on motorcycle emergencies, ask your State Department of Motor Vehicles for a motorcycle operator's manual.

By Thumb

It's not recommended, but you can **hitchhike.** Be warned, though, that it is both unpredictable and dangerous. It's easier to get a ride when alone, but it's much safer to hitchhike with someone. Women should never hitch alone.

Before getting in a car, ask where the driver is going, and make sure the passenger door opens from inside. Women especially should turn down the ride if the driver opens the door quickly and offers to drive anywhere. Always place yourself so you can exit quickly and don't let the driver stow your belongings in the trunk. Never hesitate to refuse a ride.

Once under way, talk with the driver; even idle chatter will make you both more comfortable. If you feel threatened or intimidated, ask to be let out no matter how unpromising the road looks. Know in advance where to go if stranded and what to do in emergencies.

Be aware, too, that hitchhiking is illegal in many parts of Hawaii, and is outlawed in many suburban areas throughout California. All states prohibit hitching while standing on the roadway itself or behind a posted freeway entrance sign.

Accommodations

There are many economical alternatives to hotels and motels. Remember to make reservations, especially if you plan to travel during peak tourist seasons. You might also consult CIEE's *Where to Stay USA* ($11.50); it lists lodgings from $3 to $30 per night (see Student Travelers). Another option is **Discount Travel International,** a clearinghouse of unsold hotel rooms, airline tickets, cruises, etc.; it can save you up to 50%. Membership costs $45. Write them at the Ives Building #205, Forrest Ave., Narberth, PA 19072 (800-334-9294 for reservations, 215-668-7184 for membership information).

Youth Hostels

Their convenient locations, diverse styles, and affordability make youth hostels one of the best deals in lodging, and a terrific way to meet other budget travelers from around the world. **American Youth Hostels (AYH),** maintains over 60 hostels in the Pacific states; they line the coast near national parks and major cities. Facilities range from bunk beds, cold running water, and a kitchen to larger rooms, vending machines, washers, dryers, and sheet sack/linen rental. All the California hostels now have both hot and cold running water.

AYH hostels are not the place for wild and crazy parties. All prohibit alcohol, smoking, and drugs, and many set curfews between 11pm and midnight. Dorm rooms are segregated by sex, although some hostels accommodate male-female couples and families. You must bring or rent a **sleep sack** (2 sheets sewn together); sleeping bags are sometimes forbidden. At many hostels, users share general housekeeping responsibilities. Pets are not allowed.

The maximum stay in these hostels is three nights, unless an exception is granted by the manager. Check-in is usually between 5 and 8pm; check-out, before 9:30am. Most hostels have lockout hours between 10am and 5pm; guests can neither enter nor leave at those times. Fees range from $7 to $12 depending on location, season, and grade (simple/superior). Many hostels restrict use of their facilities to members, while others host non-members for an extra $3, or let them purchase memberships on the spot. AYH honors all International Youth Hostel Federation (IYHF) memberships as well. A one-year AYH membership costs $25; $10 for those under 18 and over 54; families $35. The following California offices offer ISICs, student and charter flights, and travel equipment and literature, in addition to hostel memberships: **San Francisco:** 425 Divisadero St. #310, 94117 (415-863-9939); **San Jose:** P.O. Box 28148, 95159 (408-298-0670); **Los Angeles:** 1434 2nd St., Santa Monica, 90401 (213-393-3413); and **San Diego:** 1031 India St., 92101 (619-239-2644 or 226-1221). You can also write to American Youth Hostels, Inc., P.O. Box 37613, Washington, DC 20013-7613 (202-783-6161).

There are many non-AYH affiliated hostels across the country. One organization, the **American Association of International Hostels (AAIH),** includes more than 30 hostels nationwide, many of which were formerly AYH hostels. Because these hostels are all owner-operated, they often provide better service. For more information write to AAIH, 1412 Cerrillos Rd., Santa Fe, NM 87051 or call 505-988-1153 during business hours. Still other hostels belong to neither group. While *caveat emptor* is always a prudent policy, it may be an especially good one when staying in non-AYH affiliated hostels, since they are not required to meet AYH's standards.

YMCAs and YWCAs

Often located downtown, in a convenient but sometimes seedy area, Young Men's Christian Associations (YMCAs) offer housing, showers (usually communal), and the use of their libraries, pools, and other facilities all for a single fee. Many YMCAs accept women and families, but because of local laws, some (e.g. the L.A. chapters) will not accept ages under 18 without parental permission. Reservations are strongly recommended. (Reservation fee $3. Nightly rates vary with season and location. Key deposit $5.)

For information and reservations, write Y's Way International, 356 W. 34th St., New York, NY 10001 (212-760-5856). Other services include city packages offering lodging, meals, and tours (singles $160 for 4 days, $240 for 8 days). For a free 1991 catalog, send a self-addressed envelope with 65¢ postage.

Most Young Women's Christian Associations accommodate only women. Nonmembers are usually required to join when lodging. For more information, write YWCA, 726 Broadway, New York, NY 10003 (212-614-2700).

Budget Chain Motels

Although many budget motels figure single digits in their names (e.g., Motel 6), room prices in the Western states have escalated to near $20. Nevertheless, they are still significantly cheaper than the larger chains such as Holiday Inn, as well as more consistent in cleanliness and comfort than their local competitors. Some even feature heated pools and cable TV. Unfortunately, while most budget chains have many branches in California and Nevada, few have locations in Hawaii.

In larger cities, budget motels are often situated just off the highway, inconveniently far from the downtown area. Take care not to spend the savings in cost between a budget and a downtown motel all on transportation. Contact these chains for free nationwide directories:

Allstar Inns, L.P., 805-687-3383.

Budget Host Inns, 817-626-7064. Toll-free reservations 8am-5:30pm at 800-BUD-HOST (283-4678).

Days Inn of America, Inc., 800-325-2525. With locations in Hawaii, but rates are high (starting at $45).

E-Z 8 Motels, 619-291-4824.

Friendship Inns International, 800-453-4511.

Motel 6, 505-891-6161. Probably your best bet in terms of price.

Also consult the *National Directory of Budget Motels* ($5, shipping included), published by Pilot Books, 103 Cooper St., Babylon, NY 11702 (516-422-2225). Loris Bree's *State by State Guide to Budget Motels* ($10) is available from Contemporary Books, 180 N. Michigan Ave., Chicago, IL 60601 (312-782-9181).

Bed and Breakfasts

Bed and breakfasts (private homes with spare rooms available to travelers) are a refreshing, though often more expensive, alternative to impersonal hotels. They're also an excellent way to explore with the help of a host who knows a region well. Unlike hotels, many B&Bs do not provide phones, TVs, or showers in your room, but do go out their way to be accommodating. Some accept pets, meet a guest's plane, bus, or train, give personalized tours, and, to top it off, prepare home-cooked breakfasts (and sometimes dinners).

Prices vary widely depending on season and location. Doubles can run $20-300 per night; $30-50 is the average. Senior citizens and families often get discounts. Reservations are almost always necessary, and it's a smart idea to check out any B&B beforehand; if allergic, you don't want to find yourself in the home of a cat-lover.

For a brochure describing West Coast B&Bs, send a stamped, self-addressed envelope to Bed and Breakfast International, P.O. Box 282910, San Francisco, CA 94128-2910 (415-696-1690, 800-872-4500 for reservations). Other B&B networks include Eye Openers Bed and Breakfast Reservations, P.O. Box 694, Altadena, CA 91003 (213-684-4428, 818-797-2055, membership $10).

For additional listings, consult *Bed and Breakfast U.S.A.,* ($12) available through Tourist House Associates, RD 2 Box 355-A, Greentown, PA 18426 (717-857-0856) and *Bed & Breakfast: California* ($10, shipping $1.50) by Linda K. Bristow, Chronicle Books, 275 5th St., San Francisco, CA 94103 (415-777-7240). Also check local phonebooks and visitors bureaus.

U.S. Servas Committee, Inc., 11 John St. #407, New York, NY 10018 (212-267-0252), is an international peace organization that serves as an introductory service for travelers and host families. After an interview, and for a $45 membership fee and $15 deposit for host lists, travelers can make their own arrangements with hosts. There is a two-night limit on stays unless otherwise noted, and guests are expected to spend some time with their hosts.

College Dormitories

Many colleges and universities open their residence halls to travelers, especially in summer. Rates are low, and reservations are recommended. College campuses are one of the best sources for information on things to do, places to stay, and rides out of town. Moreover, dining halls often serve reasonably priced, reasonably edible all-you-can-eat meals.

When in Dire Straits

Every year, enterprising travelers sleep in locations ranging from cemeteries to sewage treatment plants in order to save on accommodations. While it is undeniably

cheap, sacking out is often uncomfortable, unsafe, and illegal. Always know when and where it's safe before you crash. In the city, ask locals about areas to avoid. In the country, ask before you sleep on someone's lawn or in a barn or shed. Otherwise, you may get mauled by the family dog or arrested (or shot) for trespassing. In California's San Joaquin Valley, avoid large farms where tension between migrant workers and their employers sometimes runs high. In Hawaii, stick to established paths in wooded areas: growers afraid that you might stumble upon hidden fields of marijuana or magic mushrooms boobytrap and guard their fields zealously. Even national forest properties aren't necessarily safe; stray from roads and trails only in the high country, where marijuana won't grow. Never take advantage of the availability of crops in the fields—small farmers and agribusinesses alike get annoyed with freeloaders.

In addition, exercise the same caution against crime in national parks that you would elsewhere. Some national parks are quite crime-ridden, in part because they are under the jurisdiction of the FBI in Washington, D.C., rather than the state and local police who maintain order just outside their gates.

If a night under the stars doesn't appeal to you, and you don't have the money for lodgings, call the **Travelers' Aid Society,** listed in *Let's Go* under Practical Information wherever it exists. The local crisis center hotline may have a list of persons or groups who will house you.

Camping and the Great Outdoors

From craggy mountains to shady woods, California and Hawaii present a variety of camping alternatives, ranging from privately run campsites that include swimming pools and other amenities to a grassy clearing by the side of the road. Few areas in the world are as accessible to the traveler or as majestic.

Parks, Monuments, and Forests

At the turn of the century it may have seemed bizarre to set aside parts of the infinitely vast wilderness for conservation, but today that act is recognized as a stroke of genius. The West Coast's extensive national and state park system has stemmed the spread of "civilization," and its smog, concrete, and waste products.

National Parks protect some of the nation's most spectacular scenery: the imposing giant sequoias, stunning Kilauea Crater, and the sculptured majesty of Yosemite's Half-Dome. Their official purpose is preservation, but the parks also make room for ranger talks, guided hikes, skiing, and snowshoe expeditions. Most national parks have back-country and developed tent camping, and many welcome RVs. For information on camping, accommodations, and regulations write the **National Park Service,** Western Regional Office, Fort Mason, Building 201, San Francisco, CA 94123 (415-556-0560). National parks are administered by the National Park Service under the direction of the U.S. Department of the Interior.

The larger and more popular national parks charge a $3-5 entry fee for vehicles and sometimes a nominal one for pedestrians and cyclists. Most national parks sell the annual $25 Golden Eagle Passport, which allows the bearer and family free entry into all parks. Visitors ages 62 and over qualify for the Golden Age Passport ($20), entitling them to free entry and a 50% discount on recreational fees; disabled travelers enjoy the same privileges with the Golden Access Passport, also $20. These passports are valid also at national monuments. For more information regarding the Golden Eagle, Age and Access Passports call 202-209-4747.

While it might be difficult to compete with the grandeur of a national park such as Yosemite, **State Parks** offer picturesque settings, elaborate facilities, and lots of space at low prices. Those traveling by pedal will be pleased to know that under California state law, cyclists cannot be turned away from state-run campgrounds, no matter how crowded the campsites may be.

Expect crowds during the peak tourist seasons (usually summer), and remember that many parks shut down either entirely or partially in winter. Entry fees vary from park to park. At the more popular parks in California, Nevada, and the Grand Canyon region, reservations are absolutely essential; make them through **MISTIX** (619-452-1950, in CA 800-444-7275) for a $4 fee. Reservations can also be made by mail through **Ticketron,** P.O. Box 617516, Chicago, IL 60661-7516 (800-452-1111). Lodges and other indoor accommodations are generally in the shortest supply and should be reserved months in advance. However, most campgrounds are strictly first-come, first-camped. Arrive early; many campgrounds, public and private, fill up by late morning in the summer. Some limit your stay and/or the number of people in a group (usually no more than 25). Write the California Department of Parks and Recreation, Attn: Publications, P.O. Box 942896, Sacramento, CA 94296-0001 (916-322-7000). They offer state parks brochures and the *Guide to California State Parks* ($2). For Hawaii, write the Department of Land and Natural Resources, Division of State Parks, P.O. Box 621, Honolulu, HI 96809 for reservations and information, including the pamphlet *Guide to Hawaii's State Parks* (808-548-7455).

National forests are worthwhile alternatives to the more developed parks. While some have recreation facilities, most are prepared only for primitive camping—pit toilets and no water are the rule. Fees are nominal or nonexistent. Situated in many areas of the coast, the forests are often less crowded simply because they are less accessible. Backpackers can take advantage of specially designated **wilderness areas,** even less accessible due to regulations barring all vehicles. **Wilderness permits,** required for backcountry hiking, can usually be purchased at parks; check ahead. Adventurers who plan to explore some real wilderness should always check in at a U.S. Forest Service field office before heading out. Many of these facilities are difficult to find (one of the reasons why they're underutilized) so write ahead for accurate, detailed maps. Contact the **Pacific Southwest Region, U.S. Forest Service,** 630 Sansome St., San Francisco, CA 94111 (415-705-2874).

Tent Camping

Whether buying or renting, finding sturdy yet inexpensive equipment is a must. Spend some time examining catalogs and talking to knowledgeable sales people. There are many reputable mail-order firms with cheap rates. Order from them if you can't do as well locally. In the fall especially, look for last year's equipment; prices can come down by as much as 50%. Try the following companies:

Cabela's, 812 13th Ave., Sidney NE 69160 (800-237-4444 or 308-254-5505).

Campmor, 810 Rte. 17 N., P.O. Box 997-LG91, Paramus, NJ 07653-0997 (800-526-4784; 24-hr. FAX orders 201-447-5557). Very competitive prices.

L.L. Bean, 1 Casco St., Freeport, ME 04033 (800-341-4341). Open 24 hr. per day, 365 days per year.

Mountain Equipment, Inc. (MEI), 4776 E. Jensen Ave., Fresno, CA 93725-1704 (209-486-8211).

Recreational Equipment, Inc. (REI Co-op), P.O. Box 88125, Seattle, WA 98138-2125 (800-426-4840). Lifetime membership fee of $10 entitles you to a 10% annual rebate on all purchases.

At the core of your equipment is the **sleeping bag.** Which one you buy will depend on the climate in which you will be camping. Sleeping bags are rated according to the lowest outdoor temperature at which they will still protect you. If a bag's rating is not a temperature but a seasonal description, keep in mind that "summer" translates to a rating of 30-40°F, "three-season" can be anywhere from 5-30°F, and "four-season" means below 0°F. When you check specific sleeping bags, get the most specific temperature rating you can. To choose a bag rating, figure out the lowest temperature you'll be sleeping in and subtract another few degrees. Sleeping bags are made either of down or of synthetic material. Down bags are warmer and lighter in weight, but they lose their insulating qualities when wet, and then dry out less quickly. Synthetic bags require more material to achieve the same level of warmth, and consequently weigh more, but they stay warmer than down bags even if soggy and dry out swell. Lowest prices for acceptable sleeping bags: $60-70 for a summer sythetic, $150 for a three-season synthetic, $150-180 for a three-season down bag, and upwards of $250 for a down sleeping bag you can use in the winter. If you're using a sleeping bag for serious camping, you should also have either a foam pad or an air mattress to cushion your back and neck. Inch-thick foam pads start at $13 (high tech materials like Ensolite run a bit more), while air mattresses cost up to $50. Another alternative is the **Therm-A-Rest,** which is part foam and part air-mattress and inflates to full padding when you unroll it (from $50-80).

When you select a **tent,** your major considerations should be shape and size. A-frame tents are the best all-around. When they are pitched, their internal space is almost entirely usable; this means little unnecessary bulk. Only one drawback: if you're caught in the rain and have to spend a day or two holed up inside your tent, A-frames can be cramped and claustrophobic. Dome and umbrella shapes offer more spacious living, but tend to be bulkier to carry. Size-wise, two people can fit snugly in a two-person tent but will value the extra space of a four-person tent. If you're car-camping, take the bigger tent. If you're hiking, stick with a smaller tent that weighs no more than 3.5lbs./1.5kg. Be sure your tent has a rain fly. Quality two-person tents cost $100 or more, $150 for a four-person tent. You might, however, find last year's version for half the price.

Other basics include a simple plastic **groundcloth** or tarp to protect the tent floor. You might also purchase a battery-operated **lantern,** although if you'll be camping in the summer when it gets dark later, you can probably manage with a small flashlight. Most campgrounds provide grills and allow you to gather firewood for cooking, but if a park prohibits wood fires, purchase a small **campstove** that runs on butane or white gas ($20-80 for one burner). Don't forget **waterproof matches;** without them, one spill in the lake could leave you in the dark.

You don't always have to rough it when camping. Private campgrounds often offer pools, campstores, playgrounds, snackbars, movies, TV rooms, running water at your site, air-conditioned bathrooms, etc. Even at prices as high as $14, they're cheaper than motels. For those longing to ride the range in an RV, **Go Camping America Committee,** P.O. Box 2669, Dept. P, Reston, VA 22090 (703-620-6003), provides a free packet of RV information, including lists of RV publications and rental services. Another option is a small group camping tour like those offered by **Trekamerica** (800-221-0596 or 213-321-0734), an organization that caters to 18-38 year olds traveling in the U.S. and Canada.

Station wagon, van, and limber small-car drivers often find it possible to sleep in their vehicles. Although this is especially convenient in rest areas and primitive campgrounds, this may be difficult to do in built-up areas.

The Campground Directory ($15; Eastern/Western editions, $11), *Tent Camping Guide* (Eastern/Western editions, $8), and various *Regional Camping Guides* ($5) are available from Woodall Publishing Co., 28167 N. Keith Dr., Lake Forest, IL 60045-5000 (800-323-9076 or 708-362-6700). The *RV Park and Campground Directory, Western U.S., Canada, Mexico* ($15) can be ordered from Simon and Schuster, Attn. Mail Order Dept., 200 Old Tappan Rd., Old Tappan, NJ 07675 (800-223-2348). *Backpacking* (S/N 001-000-042-475, $3.50) is published by the U.S. Government Printing Office, Superintendent of Documents, Washington DC 20402 (202-783-3238). The Sierra Club also publishes many useful guides (see Recreation below).

For disabled travelers, the Office of Public Inquiries (202-343-4747) will send information on accessible campsites. Their address is National Park Service, Washington, DC 20240.

Wilderness Etiquette

The wilderness may *look* rugged, but the thousands of outdoor enthusiasts pouring into the parks every year threaten to trample the land to death.

In popular parks, where firewood is scarce, it's best to use a campstove and to gather only deadwood from the ground. Some parks prohibit campfires altogether.

To avoid digging a rain trench for your tent, pitch your tent on high, dry ground. Don't cut vegetation, and don't clear campsites. If there are no toilet facilities, bury human waste at least four inches deep and 100 feet or more from any water supplies and campsites. *Biosafe* soap or detergent may be used in streams and lakes. Otherwise, don't use soaps in or near bodies of water. Always boil your water vigorously for at least five minutes before drinking it. (Filters do not remove all bacteria.)

Always pack up your trash in a plastic bag and carry it with you until you reach the next trash can; burning and burying pollute the environment.

In more civilized camping circumstances, it's important to respect fellow campers. Keep light and noise to a minimum, particularly if you arrive after dark.

Bears and You

The black bear denizens of California's national parks are probably no more dangerous than Yogi and Boo-Boo. However, these park bears, too, are constantly searching for the nearest "pic-a-nic basket", and since they're legally protected within all National and State Parks, they've lost all fear of humans in their continuing quest for food. *Never* feed them, and never tempt them with delectables like open trash cans; they'll simply keep coming back, more aggressively each time.

Keep your camp clean, and don't leave trash or food lying around. Store food in air-tight containers, then hang them in a tree 10 feet from the ground and 5 feet from the trunk. When car-camping, store food and food containers in the trunk; these bears have learned to recognize coolers sitting on the back seat and need only lift a finger to bust your car window and drag your viands into blue obscurity.

To avoid a grizzly scene, leave your packs empty and open on the ground so that a curious bear can nose through them without having to tear them to shreds first.

If a bear approaches camp, bang pots and pans. If she doesn't leave, then you should.

When hiking, if a bear should notice you, she will usually turn away disinterested and walk in the other direction. If you see a bear at a distance, calmly walk in the other direction. If she seems determined to introduce herself, throw small rocks to ward her off. Some suggest finding a long stick and waving it above your head; the general flailing creates the impression in the bear's eyes that you're much taller than a person, and it may decide that *you* are the menacing High Lord of the Forest. If you stumble upon a hapless bear cub, leave immediately. Its mother will be right behind, and she's *very* protective.

Rattlesnakes are probably the only other dangerous critters around, but the number of snake-bite incidents is reassuringly small. You won't see them, since they slither away the second they realize you're approaching. If you're hiking away from a designated trail, take more caution. When climbing, never place your hands where you can't see them. Rattlesnakes resting behind rocks get awfully defensive when visitors arrive uninvited.

Hiking

Hiking can be the only way to reach some of the most beautiful areas in California and Hawaii. *Let's Go* describes many day trips; ask fellow travelers, locals, travel offices, park ranger stations, and outdoor equipment shops for other potential treks. Before setting off, it's a good idea to take a mile-long, pre-trip practice hike to test your shoes and pack weight.

Before setting off into the wilderness, let park officials know your route and expected return time. If you get lost, your chances for emerging safely will increase if you conserve your energy. Don't wander around until you're exhausted. Wait for others to find you.

Bring sturdy, comfortable shoes, and a complete map and compass. Remember that high altitudes and hot sun make midday hiking hazardous; take along some sunscreen, a hat, and plenty of water. For information on heatstroke, hypothermia, and other hiking concerns, see Health.

The **Pacific Crest Trail,** stretching from the Mexican border into Canada, is particularly attractive for one- or two-week hiking trips along shorter segments. There are a number of trailside heated cabins, some with running water. The San Bernardino National Forest, in the San Grogonio Wilderness Area, is a beautiful stretch of trail in southern California. In central CA, Desolation Wilderness and Mt. Whitney, in the John Muir Wilderness, are particularly scenic. Although, the Trail's scenery in northern California is reputedly the most awe-inspiring, the Trinity Alps, Castle Crags, and Russian Wilderness, in the Shasta Trinity National Forest, as well as the Lassen National Forest, a volcanic park, come especially highly recommended. For the USDA Forest Service's information packet on the trail write them at 630 Sansom St., San Francisco, CA 94111 (703-2874).

When hiking in Hawaii, be wary of unstable rock formations. Most fatalities involve hikers stranded on ledges and cliffs. If you find yourself on a precarious perch, stay in one place and try to attract attention with a pocket mirror, flashlight, or whistle. Also, clean your boots before moving on to another island to prevent the spread of plant diseases.

Sources of information about hiking include American Youth Hostels (see Hostels) and the **Sierra Club,** 730 Polk St., San Francisco, CA 94109 (415-776-2211), which publishes amazingly useful guides to hiking and backpacking all over the Pacific Coast. *Backpacker's Sourcebook* ($8) by Hargrove and Liebrenz, *Backpacking Basics* ($8) by Thomas Winnet, and various regional guides are available from Wilderness Press, 2440 Bancroft Way, Berkeley, CA 94704-1676 (800-443-7227 or 415-843-8080). For topographical maps of any U.S. area, write the U.S. Geological Survey, Box 25286, Denver Federal Center, Denver, CO 80225 (303-236-7477).

For Foreign Visitors

Information Organizations

Created to promote peace and understanding, **Servas** matches hosts and travelers in 100 countries for two- or three-day stays. Annual fee $45, deposit for access to host lists $15 (guests make arrangements with hosts). Travelers and hosts exchange only conversation and ideas—not money. You must provide two reference letters and arrange for an interview a month in advance. Contact the U.S. Servas Committee, 11 John St. #407, New York, NY 10038 (212-267-0252).

United States Tourist Offices, found in many countries, provide free literature in abundance. If you can't find one in your area, write the **U.S. Travel and Tourism Administration,** 14th St. and Constitution Ave., NW, Washington DC 20130 (202-377-4003). You can direct inquiries to state and city tourist offices.

California Office of Tourism, 1121 L St. #103, Sacramento 95814 (916-322-1396).

Hawaii Visitors Bureau, 2270 Kalakaua Ave. #801, Honolulu 96815 (808-923-1811).

Student Travelers

The Council on International Educational Exchange has affiliates abroad that charter airline tickets, arrange homestays, sell international student ID cards, travel literature, travel insurance, and hostel cards. CIEE also helps students secure work visas and find employment through its work-exchange programs. In **Australia,** SSA/STA Swap Program, P.O. Box 399 (1st Floor), 220 Faraday St., Carlton South, Melbourne, Victoria 3053 (tel. (03) 348 17 77). In **New Zealand,** STA Travel, 64 High St., Auckland (tel. (09) 39 97 23). In the **U.K.,** STA Travel, 74 & 86 Old Brompton Rd., London SW7 3LQ, England (tel. (01) 937 99 21 or 937 99 62). If you can't locate an affiliate in your country, write to the **International Student Travel Confederation,** Gothersgade 30, 1123 Copenhagen K, Denmark (tel. (45) 33 99 93).

Work and Study

The Experiment in International Living organizes language-training programs followed by three-week homestays for international visitors of all ages. Their School for International Training runs the International Student of English Program, offering language classes at U.S. campuses. Costs average $1420 for four weeks. Write them at 676 Kipling Rd., Brattleboro, VT 05302 (802-257-7751, for admissions 800-451-4465).

The **IAESTE Program** (International Association for the Exchange of Students for Technical Experience) provides on-the-job training for science students in over 50 countries. College students past their sophomore year (or the equivalent), majoring in areas such as agriculture, computer science, math, engineering, architecture, and natural or physical science can apply. Write to IAESTE Program, Association for International Practical Training, 10400 Little Patuxent Parkway #250, Columbia, MD 21044-3502 (301-997-2200).

Another excellent information source is the **Institute of International Education,** 809 United Nations Plaza, New York, NY 10017-3580 (212-883-8200), which administers fellowships and educational exchange programs world-wide. For those interested in language and cultural programs, they publish *English and Orientation Programs in the U.S.* ($22).

Documents and Formalities

For information on the International Student Identification Card (ISIC), see Student Travelers. For additional information on work and study in the U.S., see Alternatives to Tourism.

Visas

Almost all foreign visitors to the U.S. are required to have a passport, a visitor's visa (issued by the visitor's country of origin and valid for six months beyond the planned length of stay), and proof of intent to leave. However, Canadian citizens who enter the U.S. from Canada or Mexico do not need a visa or passport, nor do Mexican citizens with a form I-186 (but Canadians under 18 need the written consent of a parent or guardian). Mexican border crossing cards (non-immigrant visas) require that you stay 72 hours or less in the U.S. within 25 mi. of the border. It's always safest to carry proof of citizenship, e.g., a driver's license or birth certificate. To obtain a U.S. visa, contact the nearest U.S. Embassy or Consulate.

Most visitors obtain a B-2 or "pleasure tourist" visa, valid for six months. If you lose your I-94 form (arrival/departure certificate attached to your visa upon arrival), replace it at the nearest **U.S. Immigration and Naturalization Service** office. (If you lose your passport in the U.S., you must replace it through your country's embassy.) Extensions for visas (up to a maximum of 6 months) require form I-539 as well as a $70 fee and are also granted by the INS. For a list of offices, write the Immigration and Naturalization Service, Central Office Information Operations Unit, 425 I St. NW #5044, Washington, DC 20536 (202-514-1900).

In most cases, no special vaccinations are required to enter the U.S. For exceptions contact a U.S. embassy or consulate.

Non-Tourist Visas for Work and Study

Working in the U.S. with only a B-2 visa is grounds for deportation. You must obtain a work visa. Apply at the U.S. Consulate in your country with a letter from an American employer stating that you have been offered a job, and listing its responsibilities, salary, and employment period. An American employer can also obtain an H visa (usually an H-2) for you.

To **study** in the U.S., foreigners must apply for a F-1 or J-1 visa, depending on whether they are exchange students or full-time students enrolled in degree-granting programs. F-1 and J-1 students may apply to the INS through their school for full-time **practical training,** employment at the school closely related to a student's field of study, beneficial to a student's professional development, and unavailable in the home country. Many foreign schools—and most U.S. colleges—have offices that give specific advice on study and employment in the U.S. Almost all institutions accept applications from international students directly. If you do not speak English as a first language, you will generally be required to take the **Test of English as a Foreign Language,** administered in many countries. Actual requirements are determined by each U.S. college or university. For more information, contact the TOEFL Application Office, P.O. Box 6155, Princeton, NJ 08541 (609-921-9000).

International Driver's License

If you plan to drive during your visit, be sure to obtain an International Driver's License from your national automobile association before leaving (you can't get one here), and make sure you have proper insurance (required by law). To obtain a domestic driver's license, you must apply and be tested, a process that often takes weeks or months. Some foreign driver's licenses will be valid here for up to one year (check before you leave). And be careful: local authorities may not realize that your license is valid.

Members of national automobile associations affiliated with the American Automobile Association can receive services from the AAA while they're in the U.S.

Automobile associations in 19 countries have full reciprocity agreements with the AAA. Check your country's club for details.

Customs

You may bring the following into the U.S. duty free: 200 cigarettes, 50 cigars, or 2 kilograms of smoking tobacco; $100 in gifts (this may include 100 cigars); and personal belongings such as clothes and jewelry. Travelers ages 21 and over may also bring up to one liter of alcohol, although state laws may further restrict the amount of alcohol you can carry.

You can bring any amount of currency, but if you carry over $10,000, you'll need to report it. In general, customs officers ask how much money you're carrying and your planned departure date in order to ensure that you'll be able to support yourself while here. In some cases they may ask about traveling companions and political affiliation. Travelers should carry any prescription drugs in clearly labeled containers, and have a written prescription or doctor's statement ready to present to the customs officer. For more information, including the helpful pamphlet *Know Before You Go,* contact the nearest U.S. Embassy or write the **U.S. Customs Service,** P.O. Box 7407, Washington, DC 20229 (202-566-8195).

When you return home, you will need to declare all items acquired abroad. Check the customs regulations of your country and of other countries along your route before you leave home.

Currency and Exchange

The U.S. currency is a decimal system based on the dollar ($). Paper money ("bills") comes in six denominations, all the same physical size, shape, and color: $1, $5, $10, $20, $50, and $100. Each dollar is divided into 100 cents (¢). Coins, all worth one dollar or less, vary in size and color. The penny (1¢), made of copper, is smaller than the silver-colored nickel (5¢); both have smooth edges. The silver-colored dime (10¢) is the smallest coin. Both the dime and the silver-colored quarter (25¢), larger than the nickel, have ridged edges. Quarters are frequently used for laundry, soda, and stamp machines, and for public transportation. Most banks will supply you a roll of 40 quarters for $10 (no extra charge). Half-dollar (50¢) and dollar ($1) coins are rarely used.

It is virtually impossible to buy anything in foreign currency, and in some regions you may even have trouble exchanging your currency for U.S. dollars. To avoid hassles, buy an established brand of traveler's checks. Some banks offer their own checks, which may not be easily cashed here. Buy checks in dollar amounts to simplify the task of cashing them. In addition, consider bringing along a credit card affiliated with a U.S. company, such as Interbank (affiliated with MasterCard), Barclay Card (affiliated with Visa), and American Express.

Sales tax is the American equivalent of the Value Added Tax. Amount and application differ by state. Expect to pay 5-10% in most places. Restaurants, taxi drivers, and many other services (especially in more expensive hotels) will expect you to add a tip of 15 to 20% to the bill. Gratuity is rarely included. **Banking hours** are generally on weekdays from 9am to 5pm, with some banks open on Saturdays from 9am to noon or 1pm. All banks, government agencies, and post offices are closed on legal holidays (see When to Go for a list). Be aware that most banks will not cash personal checks unless you are an account holder with them.

Sending Money

Sending money is a complicated and expensive process; avoid it. If you think you'll need money sent while in the U.S., however, obtain a list of your bank's correspondent banks here. You can arrange for your bank to send money from your account to a specific correspondent bank as you request it, or in advance.

A **cable transfer** is the fastest method (usually 24 hours to major cities). Cabling costs average $30 for amounts less than $1000, plus the commission charged by your home bank. There may be delays if you don't have an account at the receiving bank—ask before you pay the fee. **Western Union** (800-325-6000) wires money from office to office or to specific addresses (more expensive, charging $50 for $1000), generally within two or three business days. Cheaper but slower is a **bank draft** or **international money order.** You pay a commission ($15-20) on the draft, plus the cost of sending it airmail (preferably registered). In addition, the major credit card and traveler's check companies offer a variety of cash advance services. Whichever method you choose, make sure that both you and the sender know the exact name and address of the bank or office to which the money is being sent.

If you're stranded with no recourse at all, a consulate will wire home for you and deduct the cost from the money you receive. Consulates are often less than gracious about performing this service, however, so turn to them only in utter despair.

Communication

Mail

Individual offices of the government-run **Post Office** are usually open Monday to Friday from 8am to 5pm and sometimes on Saturdays until around noon. All are closed on Sundays and national holidays. Postcards mailed within the U.S. or to Canada or Mexico cost 19¢, letters up to one ounce 29¢. Postcards mailed overseas cost 40¢, letters 50¢ (½ oz.). Aerograms are available at the post office for 45¢. (These rates may be higher by 1992. The Postal Service was in the process of applying for a rate increase at press time.) Mail from one coast to the other usually takes three days; to northern Europe, a week to 10 days; to southern Europe, North Africa, and the Middle East, two weeks; to South America or Asia, a week to 10 days (dependent on the speed of the particular foreign country's mail service). Be sure to write "Air Mail" clearly on the front of the envelope for the most speedy delivery. Large city post offices offer an **International Express Mail** service (delivery to a major city overseas in 48-72 hr.).

The U.S. is divided into postal zones, each assigned a five-digit **ZIP code.** (Some businesses use an alternative 9-digit ZIP code for quicker delivery.) Writing this code on letters is essential for delivery.

The normal form of address is as follows:

Mark Twain	(name)
Association of Miners and Writers	(name of organization, optional)
1849 Huckleberry Lane #1	(address, apartment number)
Calaveras County, CA 95222	(city, state abbreviation, ZIP)
USA	(country)

When ordering books and materials from the U.S., always include an **International Reply Coupon** with your request. IRCs should be available from your home post office. Be sure that your coupon has adequate postage to cover the cost of delivery.

Telephone

Phone numbers in the U.S. consist of a three-digit area code and a seven-digit number, written as 617-495-9649 or (617) 495-9649. Only the last seven digits are used in **local calls. Non-local calls** within most area codes often require that you dial (or push) "1" before the seven-digit number. Long-distance calls require that you dial "1," the area code, and then the number. For example, to call George Bush in Washington, D.C. from another state, you would dial 1-202-395-3000.

Pay phones are plentiful on street corners and in public areas (restaurants, train stations, etc.). Insert your coins (10-30¢ for a 3-min. local call) in the slot before dialing. If there is no answer or if you get a busy signal (a series of repeated beeps), your money will be returned when you hang up the receiver. To make a long-distance direct call, insert your coins and dial the area code and number; an operator will tell you the cost of the first three minutes as the other person's phone rings.

There are two ways to **reverse the charges** (i.e. bill the charges to the person receiving the call). In either case, you dial "0" (not "1"), then the area code and number. When you hear a beep, the operator will assist you. If you ask to make a **station-to-station collect call** and give your name, anyone who answers may accept or refuse the call. If you wish to speak only to a particular person, tell the operator you are placing a **person-to-person collect call,** and give both your name and the receiving person's name. In some areas, particularly rural ones, you may have to dial "0" only and then tell the operator the number you wish to call.

The cheapest times to make long-distance calls are between 11pm and 8am daily and from 11pm on Friday through 5pm on Sunday. Remember that collect calls cost more than direct calls, and person-to-person calls are more expensive than station-to-station calls.

You can place **international calls** from any telephone. To make the call directly, dial the international access code (011), the country code, the city code, and the local number. In some areas dial "0" only and give the operator the number. To find out the cheapest time to call overseas, ask the operator (dial "0"). Remember to take time differences into account before dialing.

Most of the information you will need about telephone usage, including area codes and many foreign country codes, is in the front of the local **"white pages"** telephone directory. The **"yellow pages,"** published at the end of the white pages or in a separate book, is used to look up the phone numbers of businesses and other services. To obtain local phone numbers or area codes of other cities, call **directory**

assistance (411). Directory assistance is free from all public phone booths. For long-distance directory assistance, dial 1-(area code)-555-1212.

Many large companies operate **toll-free numbers** to provide information to their customers at no charge. These consist of "1" plus "800" plus a seven-digit number. To obtain specific toll-free numbers, call 1-800-555-1212.

In addition to ordinary pay phones, two other types of public phones are becoming more common. The first is a **Charge-a-Call** phone operated by American Telephone & Telegraph (AT&T), which is used for long-distance calls only and does not accept coins. Payment is made by telephone credit card or by reversing charges. Begin dialing all calls with "0." The second type of phone is found in airports and is operated by independent long-distance companies. Generally these phones are operated by passing a credit card through a slot before dialing.

From all AT&T pay phones, you can reach an **operator** by dialing "0." The operator will help you make any call and can provide assistance in an emergency.

Cabling (Telegrams)

If a telephone call is impossible, cabling may be the only way to contact someone overseas quickly (usually by the next day). **Western Union** charges 30¢ to $2 per word, depending on whether the message must arrive in within three hours or one day. Call them at 800-325-6000 for information.

Measurements

The U.S. has retained the British system of **weights** and **measures.** Units include

1 inch = 2.5 centimeters
1 foot = 0.30 meter
1 yard = 0.91 meter
1 mile = 1.61 kilometers
1 ounce = 25 grams
1 pound = 0.45 kilogram
1 quart (liquid) = 0.94 liter

There are 12 inches (in.) in 1 foot (ft.), 3 ft. in 1 yard (yd.), and 5280 ft. in 1 mile (mi.). There are 16 ounces (oz.) in 1 pound (lb.), 8 oz. (liquid) in 1 cup, 2 cups in 1 pint, 2 pints in 1 quart, and 4 quarts in 1 gallon.

Electric outlets throughout North America provide current at 117 volts, 60 cycles (Hertz) A.C. Appliances designed for a foreign electrical system will not operate without a converter ($15-20) and a plug adapter, available at most department, hardware, and electrical equipment stores.

Temperature is measured by the Fahrenheit scale, rather than the Centigrade (Celsius) scale. Mathematicians can convert Fahrenheit to Centigrade by subtracting 32, then multiplying by 5/9. Others should just remember that 32°F is the freezing point of water, 212° its boiling point, and 98.6° normal human body temperature. Room temperature typically hovers around 70°.

In the U.S., people use a 12-hour (not a 24-hour) clock to tell time. Hours before noon are *ante meridiem* or am; after noon are *post meridiem* or pm. Noon is 12pm and midnight is 12am. Although the North American continent is divided into six time zones, almost the entire West Coast is in the Pacific time zone (1 hr. behind Mountain, 2 behind Central, and 3 behind Eastern). In summer, these areas (except Hawaii) switch to **daylight savings time,** one hour ahead of standard. Alaska is on Alaskan Standard Time (2 hr. behind Pacific), and Hawaii on Hawaiian Standard Time (3 hr. behind Pacific during daylight savings, 2 hr. the rest of the year).

Getting There

Transportation to California and Hawaii will be your major expense. Detailed calculation and advance planning is crucial.

From Canada and Mexico

Canada and the U.S. share the world's longest undefended border, easily crossed by both U.S. and Canadian citizens. Only proof of citizenship (birth certificate, passport, etc.) is required. Entering from Mexico is a trifle more complicated, as it is sometimes necessary for Mexicans to obtain a tourist visa; contact the U.S. Embassy, Paseo de la Reforma 305, Colonia Cuauhtemoc, Mexico City 06500 (5-211-0042) with questions. Finding travel bargains may be difficult for both Mexicans and Canadians. Residents of the Americas are rarely eligible for the discounts that U.S. airline, bus, and train companies offer overseas visitors.

From eastern Canada, the cheapest ways to reach the West Coast are by car and bus. Canadians who are close to Buffalo, NY, or Burlington, VT, can fly to Newark, NJ, where flights to the West Coast are cheaper. **Amtrak** and **VIA Rail** offer a scenic but expensive alternative; Amtrak serves Montréal and Toronto, with access to the western U.S. via Chicago. Canadians from 12-21 years of age can take advantage of discounts on Air Canada flights if they are willing to fly standby.

Most buses and trains from Mexico only cross the border. Connections can be made at San Diego, CA; Nogales, AZ; and El Paso, Eagle Pass, Laredo, or Brownsville, TX. **Amtrak, Greyhound,** and their subsidiaries all serve the border towns. To avoid high U.S. air travel costs, fly on a Mexican airline to one of the border towns, and then travel by train or bus. From Mexico there are numerous flights on both American and Mexican carriers to Los Angeles.

From Europe

In Europe, the most expensive, peak-season rates generally run from May 15 or June 1 until about September 15. If possible, take advantage of cheap off-season flights to reach an advantageous port of departure. London (Gatwick) is an important connecting point for budget flights across the Atlantic. Once in the U.S., you can use the extensive system of coast-to-coast flights to make your way out West.

Charter flights are among the most economical and flexible. A typical flight from London to New York costs about $250. You can book them up to the last minute (although many flights fill up well before their departure date), and they allow you to stay abroad for up to a year, letting you mix-and-match flights in and out of different cities. Charters do not, however, allow for itinerary changes. You must choose your departure and return dates when you book, and you lose all or most of your money if you cancel. Travel agents will cover your losses only in cases of sudden illness, death, or natural disaster. Charter companies also reserve the right to change flight dates or even cancel the flight a mere 48 hours in advance. Beware of delays, which are not infrequent. Investigate each charter company's reputation, read the fine print, get your ticket as early as possible, and arrive at the airport well before departure time.

Major airlines provide—and charge for—greater reliability, comfort, and security. They offer two reduced-fare options: standby and APEX. The advantage of a **standby** fare is its flexibility, but major international carriers offer standby fares from fewer and fewer cities. London tends to offer the most: British Airways and TWA fares hover around $300 for a one-way ticket from London to New York.

Although you can purchase standby tickets in advance, you are not guaranteed a seat since availability is determined by cancellations and under-booked flights. Some airlines do, however, issue predictions. Never count on getting a seat immediately, particularly during the peak period in August.

The second major option, the **Advanced Purchase Excursion Fare (APEX),** provides confirmed reservations, carries less restrictions than charters on cancellation penalties and travel dates, and allows you to make connections through different cities on different airlines. Excursions, however, must fit minimum (7-14 days) and maximum (60-90 days) length requirements and must be purchased three weeks in advance. On average there is a $50-100 penalty for ticket changes. Book APEX fares early.

Several airlines undercut the major carriers on regularly scheduled flights. **Virgin Atlantic** and **Icelandair** boast low fares. However, Virgin Atlantic flies only to Newark and Miami, and the farthest west Icelandair flies is Chicago. Competition for seats is fierce, so reserve early. Also, check with a travel agent if you are eligible for student discounts.

Students (ages 12-24) can investigate discount **youth fares.** These government-regulated fares are subject to change.

From Asia and Australia

Travelers from Asia and Australia must rely exclusively on APEX fares (see From Europe) for savings. While these fares may seem astronomical ($1500 from Australia to California is typical), the West Coast remains more accessible from Asia and Australia than many other areas of the world.

From Japan, U.S. carriers such as **Northwest** and **United** generally offer cheaper flights than **Japan Airlines.** The following airlines fly between Australia and the U.S.: **Qantas, Air New Zealand, United, Continental,** and **UTA French Airlines.** Prices are roughly equivalent, but the cities they serve vary widely. Restrictions on Super Saver fares coming out of Australia are severe. For instance, a 30-day APEX round-trip fare from Sydney to L.A might be $1500, but changing or canceling your reservation would incur a 100% penalty, i.e., you don't get your money back.

Getting Around: Discounts

Airline, bus, and train companies sometimes offer special discounts to foreign visitors.

Greyhound offers a special **International Ameripass** to foreign students and faculty and their families (4 days $80, 7 days $140, 15 days $215, or 30 days $250). Stop in at one of Greyhound's overseas offices to inquire about special deals and tour programs for international travelers (ask for the *Visit USA Vacation Guide*). If you can't get a pass outside the U.S., bring your passport and buy it there, in New York, Los Angeles, Miami, or San Francisco.

Amtrak's **USA Rail Pass,** similar to the Eurailpass, is valid anywhere in the U.S. (45 days $299). If you'll be riding only in the West, you might purchase the two-week Far Western Regional Rail Pass ($179). Both passes can be purchased outside the country or in L.A., San Francisco, Seattle, Miami, Chicago, Philadelphia, Washington, New York, or Boston upon presentation of a passport. For information, contact travel agents and national rail systems. Or write to Amtrak International Sales, 400 N. Capitol St., NW, Washington, DC 20001.

Many major airlines offer special **"Visit USA"** fares, consisting of a number of flight coupons, each good for one flight segment on an airline's U.S. network within a period of usually 30 to 90 days. Purchase these tickets in your own country. Some airlines allow those living 100 mi. outside the U.S. to purchase the passes, so residents of Canada and Mexico may be eligible.

Remember to consider the size of the airline. Large airlines, such as Delta, United, and American, have extensive systems; others offer more limited service.

CALIFORNIA

In the spring of 1988, when asked to vote on their favorite rock and roll song of all time, the students at a San Francisco high school turned up their noses at classics like *(Can't Get No) Satisfaction* and *Stairway to Heaven.* No, the students declared, their all-time favorite song was a then-current chart topper by rap artist L.L. Cool J. entitled *Going Back to Cali.*

This bizarre choice reflects a sort of semi-conscious Californian hubris which is commonly exhibited by residents of the state. California is the most populous state in the USA and in terms of diversity and size is practically a nation unto itself. Indeed, its citizens often come across as blithely ignorant of the existence of 48 other states to their north and east. There is a sort of understated pride in California, which comes across not as the bragging of Texans, the snobbery of New Yorkers or the insecurity of Floridians, but rather as the quiet confidence of a people who firmly believe that they have found the best living space on the planet.

Don't come to the Golden State looking for America. You won't find it here. You will, however, find a culture and lifestyle that is peculiarly Californian, from sprawling Los Angeles, with its many suburbs in search of a city, to compact San Francisco, which combines the cultural flair of the East Coast with the laid-back, liberal attitudes of the Left Coast. You will find low, sweltering deserts and cool alpine ski country. You will find towering redwoods and drifting sands. And in the end, you will perhaps understand how Californians can still exhibit vestiges of provincialism in the age of the global village: with a whole world right in their backyard, why look any further?

Practical Information

Postal Abbreviation: CA.

Capital: Sacramento.

Time Zone: Pacific (1 hr. behind Mountain, 2 behind Central, 3 behind Eastern).

Visitors Information: California Office of Tourism, 1121 L St., #103, Sacramento, 95814 (916-322-1396 for a staff member, 800-862-2543 to have a package of tourism materials sent to you). **National Park Information,** 415-556-0560. **National Weather Service,** 619-297-2107.

Impractical Information

Nickname: The Golden State.

Motto: *Eureka* (I have found it).

State Song: I Love You, California.

State Animal: Grizzly Bear.

State Tree: Redwood.

Life in California

History

The Spanish *conquistadors* named the region *California* after a mythical land full of gold, jewels, and tall, bronze-colored Amazons. While they did not happen upon

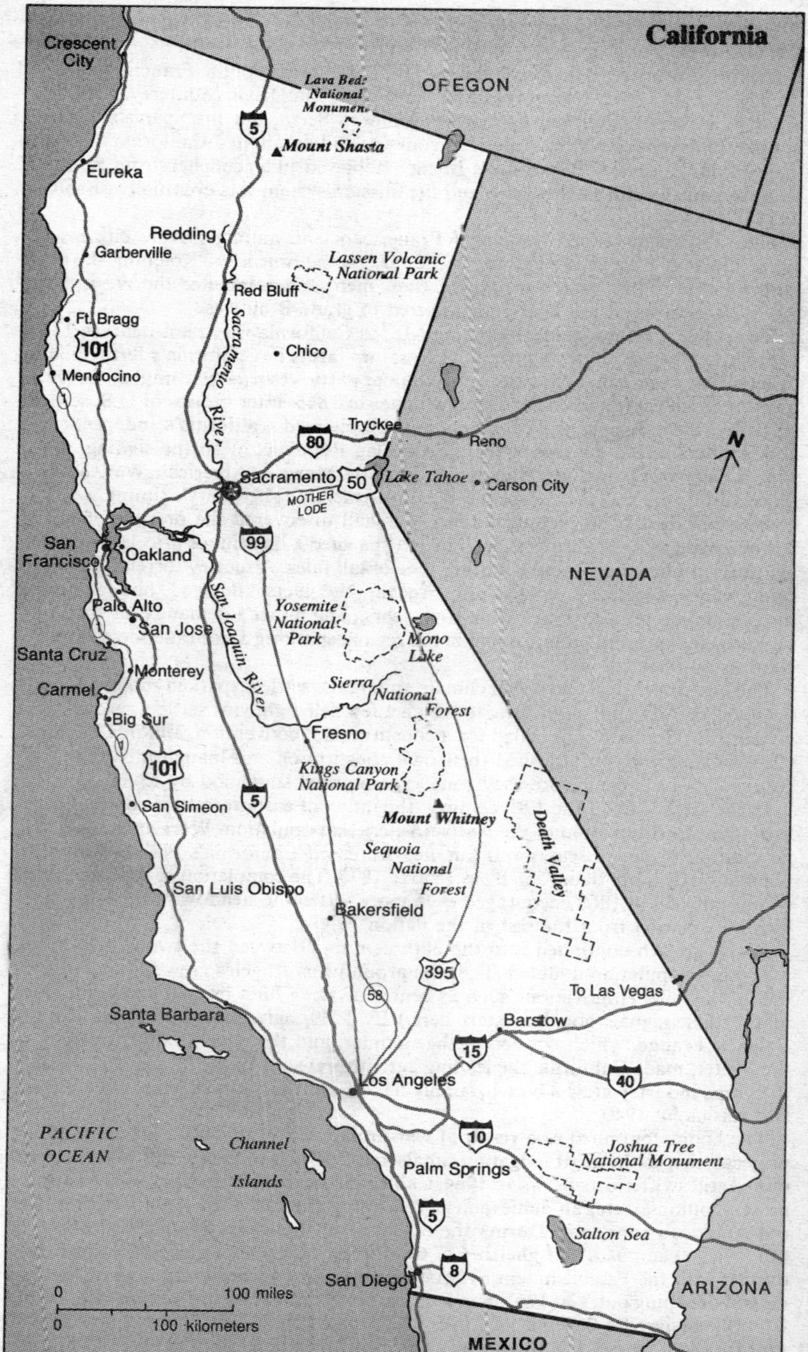
California
OREGON
NEVADA
ARIZONA
MEXICO
PACIFIC OCEAN
Crescent City
Eureka
Redding
Garberville
Red Bluff
Ft. Bragg
Chico
Mendocino
Lava Beds National Monument
Mount Shasta
Lassen Volcanic National Park
Sacramento River
Tryckee
Reno
Sacramento
MOTHER LODE
Lake Tahoe
Carson City
N
San Francisco
Oakland
Palo Alto
San Jose
Santa Cruz
Monterey
Carmel
Big Sur
San Simeon
San Joaquin River
Yosemite National Park
Mono Lake
Sierra National Forest
Fresno
Kings Canyon National Park
Mount Whitney
Death Valley
Sequoia National Forest
San Luis Obispo
Bakersfield
To Las Vegas
Barstow
Santa Barbara
Los Angeles
Channel Islands
Palm Springs
Joshua Tree National Monument
Salton Sea
San Diego
101
5
80
50
99
395
58
15
40
10
8
1
0
100 miles
100 kilometers

these fictional California girls, they did find a number of Native American nations that had been living in the area for thousands of years.

California was not vigorously colonized until the coming of the Franciscan *padres* from Mexico in 1769. Mission communities such as San Diego, Monterey, San Francisco, San Jose, established by Father Junipero Serra and his Spanish cohorts, housed thousands of Native American converts and dominated California for more than a half-century. When restless Mexico achieved independence from Spain in 1821, it made California a colony, and the mission system was eventually dissolved in 1833.

The subsequent reapportioning of Franciscan land among private citizens resulted in a new class of aristocratic cattle raisers, the *rancheros.* Roaming the open ranges and presiding over vast *ranchos,* these men soon dominated the West, thriving in an evanescent era later romanticized in grade-B movies.

Desert temperatures aside, by the mid-1850s California was a hot item. In 1841, U.S. settlers began migrating overland to set up farms in California's fertile inland valleys. One such group of settlers, the Donner party, resorted to cannibalism while trapped by an early snow near Donner Lake. In 1845, after groups of U.S. settlers staged a revolt against the Mexicans and proclaimed California's independence, U.S. soldiers seized control of their Bear Flag Republic. With the signing of the 1848 Treaty of Guadalupe Hidalgo, ending the Mexican-American War, Mexico ceded California and the rest of the West to America. The treaty's timing was golden; within days of its signing, James Marshall discovered the precious metal at Sutter's Mill, and the rush was on. The era spawned a handful of priceless nuggets, a host of frontier towns, and a mother lode of tall tales. A motley torrent of Americans, Asians, Mexicans, English and French—the 49ers—deluged the region, and the population grew sixfold within four years. The miner's demands for food and supplies created an economic boom in the region, sparking San Francisco's development as an international port.

The heated political and social climate among the settlers sparked robberies, murders and raids of Indian villages, to which a few self-righteous settlers reacted with vigilantism. Cooler minds called for a constitutional convention, and in 1849 those cheeky Californians established their own constitution and inaugurated their first governor, a full year before they were even granted statehood by Congress.

In the latter part of the 19th century, the influx of eastern settlers continued, resulting in the decimation of the Native American population. Wars and massacres, in addition to new diseases and famine, decreased California's Native American population by more than 75% from 1850 to 1875. The completion of the transcontinental railroad in 1869 encouraged even more settlers to head west, reducing California's isolation from the rest of the nation.

Rapid growth continued into the 20th century. Between the two World Wars, the state's population doubled. The area around Los Angeles grew in tandem with the automobile. (Innovations such as center dividing lines on highways and automatic traffic signals got their start here.) By 1939, agricultural products like the Valencia orange, which ripened in the summer, and the navel orange, ripening in the winter, made California the leading agricultural state in the nation. In addition, the grape industry grew a bunch, supplying 90% of the nation's wine, table grapes, and raisins by 1940.

The boom continued as a result of war production in the 40s; postwar building projects such as the great irrigation canals and freeways of Southern California promoted still swifter expansion. In 1964, California overtook New York as the nation's most populous state, an achievement redefining the forces of gravity acting over the American continent. During the 60s, nationwide waves of upheaval began in the college campuses and ghettoes of California. Many young people voiced their disgust with the Establishment by, in Timothy Leary's words, "turning on, tuning in, and dropping out." In 1967, San Francisco's Haight-Ashbury neighborhood unilaterally declared a Summer of Love, when the craze was for the psychedelic and the thing to do was LSD. But even as this carefree radicalism flourished, California managed to thrust Governor Ronald Reagan, a conservative former B-movie actor, onto the national political stage.

In the 70s, water and fuel shortages and the unbearable L.A. smog forced Californians to alter their inviolable ways-of-life. Proposition 13, a popular initiative limiting state taxes, captured nationwide attention, but the enthusiasm died out when state services were stripped to the bone, and Californians found out that "You get what you pay for."

Much of California's present-day image reflects a reaction to the state's post-World War II adolescence. The AIDS epidemic has struck San Francisco and California's gay communities with terrible force, and Los Angeles is increasingly troubled by violent gangs roaming its streets. The lingering problems of air pollution, mass transit, and gross industrialization continue to cloud the state's utopian vision. Throughout the 1980s, the high-tech boom in Northern California transformed the Golden State into the Silicon State. Nevertheless, not even all the programming prophets of Palo Alto have been able to settle such lingering issues as bilingual education, property taxes, and environmental regulation.

Literature

For over a hundred years, West Coast writers have balanced the sublimities of nature with the spectres of greed and apathy. In their work the characters range from desperate fortune-hunters to peaceful wanderers, the settings from broken-down motels to surf-beaten cliffs. Early chroniclers of the frontier spirit include Bret Harte and Mark Twain, who briefly visited California in the 1860s. Frank Norris's sagas of urban brutality and economic strangulation were the first real Californian novels. In the 1930s John Steinbeck followed in Norris's footsteps, capturing the needs and desires of the underprivileged with affection and anger. Meanwhile such writers as Nathaniel West, F. Scott Fitzgerald, and Evelyn Waugh satirized the darker side of the California dream, and the "tough-guy" detectives and criminals in the novels of Raymond Chandler, Dashiell Hammett, and James M. Cain found their way onto the screen in Hollywood's *film noir.* In Carmel and Big Sur, Robinson Jeffers and Henry Miller responded to the rock-strewn Central Coast with epic poems and sprawling prose reminiscences. During the 50s Allen Ginsberg and Jack Kerouac combined candid autobiography with visionary rapture to become the gurus of the Beat Generation. In taut novels, Joan Didion and Thomas Pynchon explored the mystical mundane of southern California in the 60s and 70s. More recently, writers such as Maxine Hong Kingston, Amy Tan, and Maya Angelou have seized on California as a metaphor for the anxieties and excitements of an increasingly multi-cultural nation. Check your libraries and bookstores for the Western oriented titles listed below.

Edward Abbey, *The Monkeywrench Gang.*

Maya Angelou, *I Know Why the Caged Bird Sings.*

Richard Brautigan, *Trout Fishing in America.*

James M. Cain, *Double Indemnity.*

Raymond Chandler, *Farewell, My Lovely.*

Joan Didion, *Play It as It Lays.*

F. Scott Fitzgerald, *The Last Tycoon.*

Allen Ginsberg, *Howl, and Other Poems.*

Dashiell Hammett, *The Maltese Falcon.*

Aldous Huxley, *After Many a Summer Dies the Swan.*

Christopher Isherwood, *Down There on a Visit.*

Robinson Jeffers, *Selected Poetry.*

Jack Kerouac, *On the Road.*

Maxine Hong Kingston, *Tripmaster Monkey* and *Woman Warrior.*

Jack London, *Martin Eden.*

Henry Miller, *Big Sur and the Oranges of Hieronymus Bosch.*

John Muir, *Wilderness Essays.*

Frank Norris, *McTeague* and *The Octopus.*

Thomas Pynchon, *The Crying of Lot 49.*

Gary Snyder, *Turtle Island.*

John Steinbeck, *Cannery Row, In Dubious Battle,* and *The Grapes of Wrath.*

Amy Tan, *The Joy Luck Club.*

Hunter S. Thompson, *Fear and Loathing in Las Vegas* and *Hell's Angels.*

Mark Twain, *The Celebrated Jumping Frog of Calaveras County and Other Stories* and *Roughing It.*

Evelyn Waugh, *The Loved One.*

Nathaniel West, *The Day of the Locust.*

Tom Wolfe, *The Electric Kool-Aid Acid Test.*

Art and Architecture

Despite New York's presumed aesthetic dictatorship, West-Coast artists have played an important role in the history of American art. Painters have found many subjects other than sunsets and surf. Clyfford Still's jagged Abstract Expressionist canvases and Richard Diebenkorn's abstract landsapes of the Santa Monica seashore (the "Ocean Park" series) are found in many California museums. In the 60s, Minimalist Robert Irwin moved out of L.A.'s innovative Ferus Gallery, stripping away color, texture and volume along the way. Wayne Thiebaud captured San Francisco in the 70s with hyperbolic perspective and strikingly rich color, while two of the city's native sons, sculptors Mark Di Suvero and Richard Serra, helped redefine the human relationship to large metal objects. Well-known environmental artist Christo came to the state in the late 70s and erected a miles-long but short-lived "Running Fence" of nylon across the hills and coastland of western Sonoma County. The brilliant color and geometrical perspectives of David Hockney's paintings of California people and places attracted attention during the 80's, and the artist has sinced explored new media, embracing photography and stage design.

Photographers have found California particularly felicitous. In the 30s, Dorothea Lange's photos of the working and living conditions of migrant workers helped to convince the government to build public housing projects. Her 1936 photo "Migrant Mother" became a national symbol of the suffering caused by The Depression. In a different vein, Ansel Adams' photos of Yosemite National Park and other parts of the Sierras have found their way onto coffee tables and datebooks across the country.

Much of the best work of the Californian artists remains in the region's museums. The Oakland Museum, for one, exhibits only the works of the state's residents. The Fine Arts Museum, The Palace of the Legion of Honor, the de Young Museum, the Asian Art Museum, and the San Francisco Museum of Modern Art have broad collections and are all located in the Bay Area. Of the many museums located in Los Angeles and the surrounding area, the County Museum of Art, the Museum of Contemporary Art, and the J. Paul Getty Museum are among the most important.

Until the late 19th century, the architecture of California generally consisted of simple, practical structures or emulations of the eastern Victorian and Queen Anne styles. As cowboys became increasingly civilized, the architecture of the west took on a flavor of its own. The "missionary revival" architecture of the 1890's, inspired by the Mexican ranch-style, was the first to incorporate native materials and local design traditions. In the 1910s and 20s, architects like Charles Sumner Greene and Henry Mather Greene developed the more successful shingle-style of California's redwood bungalows. During the 30s, Julia Morgan designed over 600 homes, among them the famous castle of William Randolph Hearst. Frank Lloyd Wright, one of the 20th century's most experimental architects, designed twenty-five buildings in the state, including the Barnsdall House in Hollywood and Honeycomb House on the Stanford campus. In recent years, Frank Gehry has attracted attention and controversy building houses with angular sufaces and unorthodox materials, such as sheet-metal and raw plywood. And even the architectural aesthete must acknowledge a degree of creative merit in such wild-yet-logical buildings as restuarants built in the shape of pigs and hot-dog stands shaped like giant frankfurters. The fascinating California jumble of materials and methods was evident as early as 1930, when Nathaniel West noted that L.A.'s canyons were lined with "Mexican ranch houses, Samoan huts, Mediterranean villas, Egyptian and Japanese temples, Swiss chalets, Tudor cottages, and every possible combination of these styles."

Food and Drink

California's gastronomic libido is satisfied by the sumptuous produce and innovative cuisine produced by its natives. Kitchens across the state turn out mouthwatering concoctions running the gamut from sourdough bread and Dungeness crab to Basque and Chinese specialties. The state was also the origin of a number of national food fads, including the notorious tofu craze. California leads the country in agricultural production, with fruits, vegetables, and nuts pouring forth in a 365-days-per-year growing season. This agricultural bounty helped give the state the appropriate nickname "Land of Fruits and Nuts." Farmers around the Southland bombard the world with boysenberries, mangoes, and the ubiquitous orange. For those craving something a bit more unusual, Castroville (the artichoke capital of the world) serves up artichoke milkshakes. And there's a date for just about everyone: California grows 75 varieties of the corrugated fruit.

The California wine industry has overcome obstacles ranging from Prohibition to pesticides over the past two centuries, and today four out of every five bottles sold in the U.S. are corked in the West. Today's chic West Coast reds (*Cabernet Sauvignon, Merlot, Pinot Noir*) and whites (*Chardonnay, Sauvignon Blanc, Gewürztraminer, Reisling*) are the quintessence of elegance and balance, perfect for the lightness of "California Cuisine." Less inspired innovations include (cringe) canned wine and the swooshy California Cooler.

Flicks

Detroit mass produces cars. Pittsburgh manufactures steel. Hollywood makes movie stars. Shirley Temple, Clark Gable, Grace Kelly, John Wayne, Mickey Mouse—these are the products of California's dream machine.

Hollywood has no counterpart. It is a strictly American, West Coast phenomenon, sometimes evoking disdain from its Eastern counterparts as nothing more than a glitzy, overblown fake for "the legitimate theater". "I believe," mused the English actor Sir Cedric Hardwicke, "that God felt sorry for actors so he created Hollywood to give them a place in the sun and a swimming pool."

Hollywood's selection as movie capital of the U.S., however, was born from more than this desire for "a place in the sun." Before 1910, independent New York filmmakers found that they were being continually sued and pursued by members of a movie trust who, through raids and riots, sought to drive out all competition. The independents decided to move West and set up shop in the sunny sheep-raising town of Hollywood. From there, a simple dash across the Mexican border could foil any attempt to confiscate cameras and film. Moreover they could take advantage of

California's sun to light shots, for, in the old days, artificial lighting had not yet been perfected.

As the balance of power shifted West, the Hollywood studios instituted a "star sytem", a move which also infuriated the eastern trust. For the first time actors themselves were advertised and used to attract adoring fans to movie after movie. (Established companies had refused to do this, fearing that actors who shed their anonymity would demand more money.) Florence Lawrence became the first star. She was soon joined by Mary Pickford ("America's Sweetheart"), Charlie Chaplin, Buster Keaton, Douglas Fairbanks, and that lover of lovers, Rudolph Valentino.

The 20s witnessed two major developments: sound and scandal. "Talkies," the first films with sound, were introduced with Al Jolson's *The Jazz Singer* in 1927. Fatty Arbuckle's trial for the death of starlet Virginia Rappe and several other notorious scandals convinced movie moguls of the need for censorship. As a result, Postmaster General Will Hays was appointed "movie czar." According to critics, Hays' puritanical edicts against "sex and venereal disease," "dances which emphasize indecent movements," and "adultery . . . presented attractively" established a model "such as would have suited the strictest of convent nuns."

Gone With the Wind swept away more conservative notions of film in the late 30s, and exorbitant budgets, flamboyant costumes, and casts of thousands became the norm. (Did you know that the city burning as Scarlett fights the flames to leave Atlanta, is the Emerald City set from the *Wizard of Oz?*) Movies like *Bringing Up Baby* and *The Awful Truth* were characterized by fast-paced wit and sophistication, while other films displayed an endearing optimism and naiveté. During the war-ravaged 40s, films like *Citizen Kane, The Maltese Falcon,* and *The Philadelphia Story* infused a measure of cynicism into the American Dream.

The 50s brought the rapid spread of television, from which the country has never fully recovered. Many of the California studios involved in movie production decided to try their hands at the small screen. Programming matured in the 60s with *The Twilight Zone, Bonanza,* and *Star Trek.* Television in the 70s became somewhat more aware of social concerns in series such as *All in the Family* and *M*A*S*H*,* but also fell to new depths of banality in *Three's Company* and *The Love Boat.* The 80s have seen American television go global, with *Dallas* and *The Cosby Show* becoming favorites in such unlikely places as Swaziland and Fiji.

Along with television, the motion picture industry continued to flourish. Beautifully choreographed musicals in the 50s brought 'em back with *Singing in the Rain, An American in Paris,* and *Funny Face,* while such films as *On the Waterfront* and *Rebel Without a Cause* raised mildly troubling social issues. The 60s encompassed a variety of new styles and themes ranging from Robert Wise's phenomenally successful *The Sound of Music* to more off-beat works like *Easy Rider* and *The Graduate.* This trend would continue into the 70s, when box-office successes ranged from *The Godfather* and *Network,* to escapist movies like *Jaws, Superman,* and *Star Wars.*

Hollywood today clings to the past. Coffee-table movies like *Doctor Zhivago* and *Lawrence of Arabia* have been superseded by their descendants of the 80s and 90s—*Dances with Wolves, Out of Africa,* and *The Last Emperor.* Action films based around such bankable stars as Sylvester Stallone, Arnold Schwarzenegger, and Bruce Willis have weaved fantasies about the dangerous and the bloody. The star system remains intact, with such leading ladies as Meryl Streep and Glenn Close, such stalwart heroes as Paul Newman and Kevin Costner, and such popular comedians as Steve Martin and Robin Williams (each one a recipient of the coveted Hasty Pudding Pot). Although most movies are now made on location, and elaborate sets, props, and reels of memories now decay in Hollywood warehouses, the studios remain the confident purveyors of America's celluloid dreams.

Recreation

Creative Californians entertain themselves with every conceivable combination of wheels, wings, sails, and skis. For an overview of the sporting scene, you might try a hike through the Sierra Nevadas or a Napa Valley hot-air balloon ride. If you get tired of the heights, you can always descend to the Grand Canyon floor on muleback or plunge even lower by snorkeling in the depths of the Pacific.

For inland entertainment, California offers countless ways to get wet, including canoeing, kayaking, and river rafting. The **River Travel Center,** Box 6, Pt. Arena, CA 95468 (800-882-7238) serves as a liaison between would-be rafters and outfitters. They can place you in one of over 1000 whitewater rafting trips ranging in length from two to 21 days. Catering to bolder hikers, mountain schools at Yosemite offer instruction in rock-climbing and spelunking. When the weather grows cold (yes, it *does* happen), the Sierra Nevadas feature a number of large ski resorts that offer activities like snowshoeing as well as cross-country and downhill skiing. The **Sierra Club,** 730 Polk St., San Francisco, CA 94109 (415-776-2211) is a good source of information on year-round outings.

Spectator Sports

California is home to more professional sport teams than any other state in the Union. Here you will find five baseball teams, four football teams, four basketball teams, and, even in the land of surf and sun, two ice-hockey teams (the NHL's San Jose Sharks begin play with the 1991-92 season). Across the state the standard is excellence: the Los Angeles Lakers, San Francisco 49ers, Los Angeles Dodgers, and Los Angeles Raiders all won multiple championships in their respective sports in the 1980s.

The college sports scene also thrives as USC, UCLA, Stanford and UC Berkeley all boast powerhouse NCAA Division I sports programs. The New Year's Day Rose Bowl football game in Pasadena is known as "the grandaddy of them all".

California also makes room for some more offbeat sports. There's a professional beach volleyball team, surfing tournaments, and, yes indeed, the world's first long-distance rollerblade race.

Sand and Surf

Hawaii has 283 beaches. California has many more. There is no escape. Here, as nowhere else, an entire beach subculture has evolved. Bronze, bewhistled lifeguards survey Vuarnet-sporting surfers and sand-sculpting children alike. Radios still blast the tunes of those 60s California icons the Beach Boys, recalling the days (was it really so long ago?) of Annette and Frankie and *Gidget Goes Hawaiian.*

Truly dedicated tanners (like Doonesbury's Zonker Harris, for whom a California beach is actually named) devote their beach hours to oil and prostration, but you can indulge in a number of more active, and less cancerous, beach performances, including bodysurfing, snorkeling, diving, and windsurfing. On the quieter northern coast, beachcombing, clamming, and fishing are all popular.

Although illegal in some areas, nude sunbathing flourishes. There are often clothed people at nude beaches, and, occasionally, the reverse is true. *Let's Go* lists nude beaches whenever possible. For those seeking that *very* thorough tan, the *World Guide to Nude Beaches and Recreation,* published by Harmony Books, Crown Publishers, 34 Englehard Avenue, Avenel, NJ 07001 (908-382-7600), lists locations of many nude beaches.

San Diego

As rivers of tourists and streams of relocating Northeasterners join the flood of undocumented immigrants from Mexico in the rush to San Diego, the question is not why so many, but why not more? "America's Finest City" manages to maintain clean air and beaches, a sense of culture and history, and even lush greenery in the face of growth, fads, and water shortages. A solid Navy presence cushions the economy; local architecture is pleasant, not gaudy; and rain and cold weather are virtu-

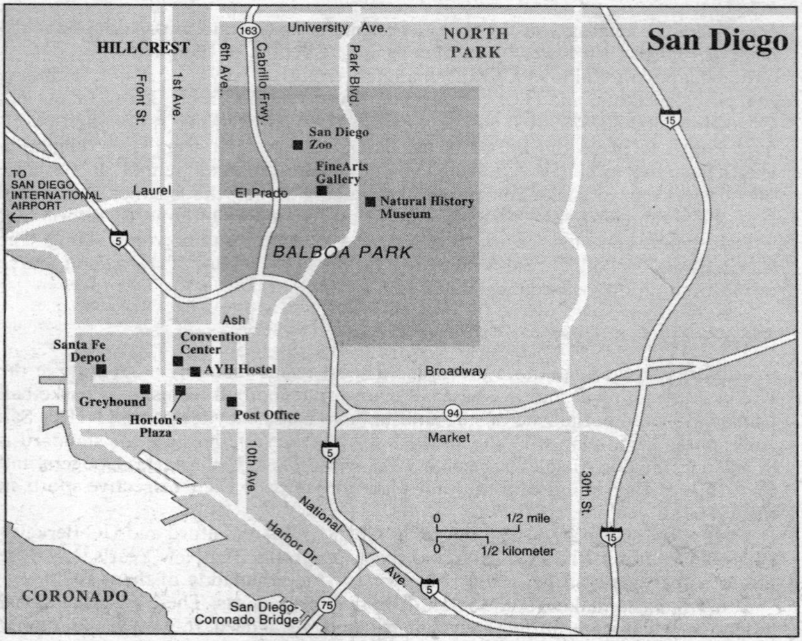

ally unknown. But even America's finest cities have problems—water shortages and housing shortages have created headaches for which there will be no easy cure.

First inhabited by the Yuman people, San Diego was not permanently settled by the Spanish until 1769, 11 years before Los Angeles and more than two centuries after its initial "discovery" by the Portuguese explorer, Cabrillo. Throughout the Spanish and Mexican periods, it remained a small town, and even after the boom of the 1880s, the city remained a little-known outpost, bypassed by the railroads and ignored by immigrants from the East. After the Civil War, the area called downtown (previously inland and isolated) moved south to take advantage of the excellent harbor and things started rolling. After two international expositions (in 1915 and 1935), the landing of the Navy, and economic booms in the 1940s and 50s, San Diego finally matured into the metropolis that now sprawls for miles over the once dry, rolling hills of chaparral. Former Mayor Pete Wilson has served in the U.S. Senate and is now California's governor.

San Diego has ample tourist attractions—a world-famous zoo, Sea World, and Old Town—but your most enjoyable destination might simply be a patch of sand at one of its superb beaches. When exploring, don't neglect residential communities such as Hillcrest, La Jolla, and Ocean Beach. If you need relief from city noise, and the beach isn't enough, get away to the nearby mountains and deserts, or head for Mexico, almost next door. You'll find San Diego a nice place to visit, and don't be surprised if you (too) want to live there.

Practical Information

Visitors Information Center: 11 Horton Plaza (236-1212), downtown at 1st Ave. and F St. Like an old-fashioned hardware store, they don't display much, but they have whatever you need under the counter. Open Mon.-Sat. 8:30am-5pm, Sun. 11am-5pm.

Old Town and State Park Information: 4002 Wallace Ave. (237-6770), in Old Town Square next to Burguesa. Take the Taylor St. exit off I-8, or bus #5. Historical brochures on the

Old Town $2. Also, information on Cuyamaca Rancho, Palomar Mountain, and Anza Borrego Desert State Parks. Open daily 10am-5pm.

National Parks Information: 226-6311. Recorded information.

San Diego Council American Youth Hostels: 1031 India St. 92101 (239-2644), 335 W. Beech St. Great source of student travel information, including full lists of hostels. Bike accessories, travel gear, and guides. Sponsors domestic and European trips. Open Mon.-Fri. 10am-6pm, Sat. 10am-5pm.

American Express: 1640 Camino del Rio N. (297-8101), inside Mission Valley Shopping Center. Open Mon.-Fri. 9am-5pm, Sat. 10am-3pm. Also, 1020 Prospect St., La Jolla (459-4161), and 258 Broadway (234-4482), in downtown. Open Mon.-Fri. 10am-5:30pm.

Public Library: Main branch, 820 E St. (236-5800), downtown. Open Mon.-Thurs. 10am-9pm, Fri.-Sat. 9:30am-5:30pm. A bizillion local branches, including La Jolla (552-1657), Pacific Beach (490-0934), Chula Vista (691-5069), and Point Loma (531-1539). Branches open Mon. and Wed. noon-8pm, Tues. and Thurs.-Sat. 9:30am-5:30pm.

Ticketron: 565-9947. Recording for nearest Ticketron location.

What's Happening Hot-line: 560-4094. Recorded calendar of current performances, exhibits, and other events.

Laundromat: Pacific Services, 500 W. Broadway (239-9820), in the YMCA building. Wash $1, dry 25¢ for 20 min. Open daily 8am-9:45pm; last load 8:45pm.

Beach and Weather Report: 221-8884. Updated daily.

Crime Victims Help Line: 236-0101. 24 hr.

Travelers Aid: Airport, 231-7361. One station in each terminal. Directions for lost travelers. Open daily 9am-10pm. **Downtown office,** 1765 4th Ave. and Elm St., #201 (232-7991). Open Mon.-Fri. 8:30am-4:30pm.

Rape Crisis Hotline: 233-3088. 24 hr.

Crisis Hotline: 800-479-3339 or 236-3339. 24-hr. (suicide, family problems, etc.)

Women's Center: 2467 E St. (233-8984). Open Mon.-Fri. 8:30am-4:30pm.

Lesbian and Gay Men's Center: 3780 5th Ave. (692-2077). Open Mon.-Fri. 9am-5pm. **Crisis Line** 692-4297 Mon.-Sat. 6-10 pm. Young people under 24 should look into the **Gay Youth Alliance** (233-9309), a support and social group. For a listing of all gay events and establishments check the *Update* (225-0282), available at virtually all gay businesses, bookstores, and bars.

Beach Area Community Health Center: 3705 Mission Blvd. (488-0644), in Mission Beach. Fees on a sliding scale, with a $44 minimum. Primarily for area residents. General non-emergency care. Appointments highly recommended. Open Mon.-Thurs. 9am-6pm, Fri. 9am-5:30pm.

AIDS Project: 3777 4th Ave. (686-5000). Referrals. Does not conduct AIDS testing, but refers to hospitals that do. Open Mon.-Fri. 9am-9pm.

Legal Aid Society: 110 S. Euclid Ave. (262-0896). Service also available in Spanish. Open Mon.-Fri. 9am-4pm.

Senior Citizen's Services: 202 C St. (236-6905), in the City Hall Bldg. Provides ID cards with which seniors can take advantage of senior discounts. Plans daytrips and sponsors "nutrition sites" (meals) at 8 locations. Open Mon.-Fri. 8am-5pm.

Community Service Center for the Disabled: 1295 University Ave. (293-3500), Hillcrest. Attendant referral, wheelchair repair and sales, emergency housing, motel/hotel accessibility referral, and **TTD Line** services for the deaf (293-7757). Open Mon.-Fri. 9am-5pm.

Emergency: 911.

Police: 531-2000.

Main Post Office: 2535 Midway Dr. (547-0477), between downtown and Mission Beach. Pick up General Delivery here. Open Mon.-Fri. 7am-1am, Sat. 8am-4pm. General Delivery ZIP Code: 92138. Take bus #6, 9, or 35. **Downtown Post Office,** 815 E St. (237-5096). Open Mon.-Fri. 8:30am-5pm, Sat. 8:30am-noon.

Area Code: 619.

Orientation

Getting There

San Diego rests in the extreme southwestern corner of California, 127 mi. south of L.A. and only 15 mi. north of the Mexican border. Flights to the city often cost no more than those to Los Angeles or San Francisco.

San Diego International Airport (Lindbergh Field) lies at the northwestern edge of downtown, across from Harbor Island. The airport is divided into east and west terminals. San Diego Transit bus #2 ("30th and Adams") goes downtown (fare $1.25. These buses run Mon.-Fri. 5:17am-11:33pm, Sat.-Sun. 5:57am-12:12am. **Yellow Cab** (234-6161) fare to downtown is around $7.

Interstate 5 runs south from Los Angeles and skirts the eastern edge of downtown. Suburbanites spend many happy rush-hours on this six-lane strip. **Interstate 8** runs east-west along downtown's northern boundary, connecting the desert to the east with Ocean Beach in the west. The major downtown thoroughfare, **Broadway,** also runs east-west. **Bus** and **train** stations sit on the western end of Broadway in reasonably safe areas. Most downtown hotels listed are in safe areas east and north of these stations.

Amtrak: Santa Fe Depot, 1050 Kettner Blvd. (239-9021, for schedules and information 800-872-7245), at Broadway. To L.A.: 8 trains per day from 5:15am-9:15pm; Mon.-Fri. $24, round-trip $38. Information on bus, trolley, car, and boat transportation available at the station. Ticket office open 4:45am-9:15pm.

Greyhound: 120 W. Broadway (239-9171), at 1st Ave. To L.A.: 12 buses per day from 5:30am-midnight; Mon.-Thurs. $16, round-trip $25.

Getting Around

A group of skyscrapers in the blocks between Broadway and I-5 defines the downtown San Diego skyline. Streets running parallel to the bay (north-south) on the western end of downtown are given proper names until they hit Horton Plaza in the east; then they become consecutively numbered avenues. Lettered streets run east-west. A Street is the farthest north, L the farthest south. In their midst, Broadway replaces D Street and runs directly east from the bay. North of A, Ash Street begins a string of alphabetized streets named after plants that continues north all the way to Walnut. Other alphabetical schemes crop up throughout the metropolitan area, the most impressive being Point Loma's complete Addison to Zola literary neighborhood.

On the northeastern corner of downtown, **Balboa Park,** larger than the city center, is bounded by 6th Ave. on the west, I-5 and Russ Blvd. on the south, 28th St. on the east, and Upas St. on the north. To the north and east of Balboa Park are the main residential areas. **Hillcrest,** San Diego's most cosmopolitan district and a center for the gay community, lies at the park's northwestern corner, around the intersection of 5th and University Ave.; **University Heights** and **North Park** sit along the major east-west thoroughfares of University Ave., El Cajon Blvd., and Adams Ave.

West of downtown is the bay, 17 mi. long and formed by the Coronado Peninsula (jutting northward from Imperial Beach) and Point Loma (dangling down from Ocean Beach). North of Ocean Beach are Mission Beach (with neighboring Mission Bay), Pacific Beach, and La Jolla.

Public Transportation

A car is extremely helpful in San Diego, but it is possible to reach most areas of the city by bus. The regional transit systems (San Diego Transit, North County Transit, DART, FAST, and Dial-A-Ride) cover the area from Oceanside in the north to Tijuana in Mexico, and inland to Escondido, Julian, and other towns. Call for **public transit information** (233-3004; daily 5:30am-10pm) or stop by the **Transit Store,** 449 Broadway (234-1060), at 5th Ave. (open daily 8:30am-5:30pm). Be sure to pick up the *Transit Rider's Guide,* which includes listings of which routes lead to popular destinations around town. Fares vary: $1 for North County Transit routes, $1.25 for local routes, $1.50-1.75 for express routes, and $2.25-2.50 for commuter routes. Transfers within San Diego are free; North County transfers cost 25¢. Exact change is required. Most city buses accept dollar bills. 60% of the buses are wheelchair accessible. Visitors age 60 and over with I.D. receive discounts. Buses on some routes (especially those to the beaches) are equipped with bike racks. If you travel on buses often, save money using **Day Tripper** passes, which allow unlimited travel on buses, trolleys, and even the Bay Ferry ($4 for 1 day, $12 for 4 days). These and the various monthly passes are available at the Transit Store. Most urban routes originate, terminate, or pass through downtown.

The **San Diego Trolley** runs on two lines from a starting point near the Santa Fe Depot on C St., at Kettner. One heads east for **El Cajon.** The other, popularly known as the Tijuana Trolley, runs 16 mi. south to **San Ysidro** at the Mexican border every 7 min. from 5am-6pm, every 15 min. from 6pm-10pm, and every 30 min. from 10pm-1am. From the border, cabs to the oxymoronic Tijuana Cultural Center or shopping district are less than $5 (see Baja California, below). The trolley also provides access to local buses in National City, Chula Vista, and Imperial Beach. The trolley is wheelchair-accessible. (Fare 50¢-$2.25 depending on distance, over 60 and disabled passengers 60¢. Transfers free.) Purchase a ticket from machines at stations and board the trolley. There are no turnstiles or ticket takers, but frequently an inspector will check for tickets. **Lost and found** for the system is locted at the Transit Store.

Various tour buses and trolley-shaped vans carry tourists around San Diego. Check the visitors center or hotel lobbies for details.

Cars

In Southern California, land of the auto, a BMW, Ferrari, or other sporty import with an impressive hood ornament will increase your social status immeasurably. But to stay on a budget and rent a car, you'll have to settle for a less extravagant set of wheels. Beware of high insurance fees, extra per-mile charges, and cars that are not fuel efficient; these will add bucks to seemingly low rates. To connect with rides or riders, check the hostels (see Accommodations) and bulletin boards at universities (such as UCSD or the Aztec Center at SDSU).Rentals

Rent-a-Wreck, 3309 Midway Dr. (224-8235). $20 per day, 100 free mi. per day, 16¢ per additional mi. 125 mi. radius restriction, no driving in Mexico. $2 per-day charge for drivers under 25. Must be 21 with credit card or $200 minimum cash deposit. Open Mon.-Fri. 8am-5pm, Sat. 8am-3pm, Sun. 10am-3pm.

Aztec Rent-A-Car, 2401 Pacific Hwy. (232-6117). $24 per day with 150 free miles plus 25¢ per additional mile. $125 per week with 1000 free miles. Must be 21 with major credit card. With purchase of Mexican insurance ($14 per day), cars may venture south of the border as far as Ensenada (80 mi. distant). Open Mon.-Fri. 7am-8pm, Sat -Sun. 8am-5pm.

Driveaway Companies:

A-1 Automovers, 3650 Clairmont Dr., Suite 5-C (274-0224), has offices nationwide.

Driveaway Service, 3585 Adams Ave. (280-5454), in Normal Heights. Must be over 21 with $250 deposit.

Auto Driveaway Co., 4672 Park Blvd. (295-8060). Open Mon.-Fri. 8am-5pm.

Bicycles

A bicycle is invaluable in the summer, especially around the beaches, where traffic is heavy and parking abysmal. The satisfaction of cruising by stalled and sweltering motorists will compensate for any fatigue. Buses equipped with bike-carriers make it possible to cart two-wheelers even farther. Call the public transit information number (233-3004) to find out which routes have carriers. You can take bikes on the San Diego Trolley, but you must obtain a permit (call 239-2644 for more details).

San Diego County has an extensive system of bike routes and a generally flat terrain suitable for biking. Bike routes are sometimes separate from the road, sometimes specially marked outer lanes, and sometimes wishful thinking, but are generally safe. The flat, occasionally crowded route along Mission Beach and Pacific Beach toward La Jolla affords amazing ocean views and soothing Pacific breezes. The boardwalk along Pacific Beach is lined with rental agencies for the spokeless.

Bike Travel Information: Caltrans, 4080 Taylor St., San Diego 92110 (231-2453), in Old Town. Will send you maps and pamphlets, including *How to Take Your Bike for a Bus Ride.* Also handles storage lockers. Open Mon.-Fri. 7am-5pm. **City Engineering Department,** 1222 1st Ave. (236-7214). Go to the Traffic Engineering Section on the 4th floor, northwest corner of the building, for a map of bike routes. Open Mon.-Fri. 8am-5pm.

Pennyfarthing's, 520 5th Ave. (233-7696), in the Gaslamp Quarter. Bikes $4 per hour, $30 per day. Open daily 9am-6pm.

Rent-a-Bike, 1775 E. Mission Bay Dr. (275-2644), by Sea World. $6 per hr., $22 per day for a cruiser. $8 per hr., $28 per day for a mountain bike. Open Mon.-Fri. 8:30am-6:30pm, Sat.-Sun. 8am-7pm.

La Jolla Cyclery, 7443 Girard (459-3141), in La Jolla. Limited supply of rental bikes. $4 per hr., $16 per day with a 2-hr. min. Tandems are $6 per hr., $20 per day. Open Tues.-Fri. 10am-6pm, Sat. 9am-5pm.

Walking

Downtown is compact and easily handled on foot. Beaches, however, are not as accessible. **Walkabout International** (231-7463; for a recorded schedule of walks call 223-9255) sponsors several free walks each week, including architectural walks downtown and 20-mi. treks to La Jolla and back. Those Easterners accustomed to muscling their way across a street against the light will either be impressed or amused by the San Diegan habit of waiting obediently for the walk signal, no matter how empty the street. Jaywalking is illegal (tickets are given out occasionally), not in vogue, and dangerous—it is quite common for cars to run red lights.

Accommodations

Although San Diego attracts visitors throughout the year, both lodging rates and the number of tourists skyrocket in summer, particularly on weekends. Reservations can save you time and disappointment. Many hostels and residential hotels offer weekly rates. The latter are numerous, especially downtown, and some are quite modern and appealing. If you have a car, consider camping outside San Diego (see Camping). If not, staying downtown will give you access to bus routes that will take you most places you want to go.

Downtown

Downtown Inn Hotel, 660 G St. (238-4100), just east of the Gaslamp Quarter. Comfortable, tastefully furnished rooms with microwave/toaster oven, refrigerator, TV, and ceiling fan. Convenient to buses. Check-out 1pm. Singles $25. Doubles $31-38. Weekly: singles $106, doubles $127-152.

Armed Services YMCA Hostel (AYH), 500 W. Broadway (232-1133), near train and bus stations. The hostel rooms offer all the comforts of a troop ship: gray walls, metal beds, communal showers. Dorm rooms $10, linen not included. Check-out 9:30am. Newly renovated singles $22; doubles $34. Key deposit $2. Check-out noon. AYH membership required for dorm rooms only.

YWCA Women's Hostel, 1012 C St. (239-0355), at 10th Ave. Women only. Often full, quite friendly. Dorm beds for ages 18-34 (no upper age-limit for AYH members) $7.20 for members, $9 for non-members. Linen $1. Hall bathrooms. Non-member singles $19; doubles $32. Key deposit $5. Check-out 11am.

Jim's San Diego, 1425 C St. (235-8341), south of the park, at City College trolley. Spruce, hostel-type rooms. Management caters to international travelers, passport and $20 deposit required. Kitchen, laundry. $15, $90 per week. Breakfast and Sunday BBQ included.

La Pensione on Second, 1546 2nd Ave. (236-9292), downtown. Close to I-5. Pretty rooms with microwave, big refrigerator, and cable TV with neato art on the walls. Golly! New European style building with 24 hr. deli. Singles $24-39. Doubles $29-44. Weekly: singles $125-165; doubles $155-180.

Siesta Motor Inn, 1449 9th Ave. (239-9113 or 800-748-5604), at Beech St., close to Balboa Park. Comfortable, attractive rooms with A/C, pool, and satellite TV. Check-out 11am. Singles $37. Doubles $44. Key deposit $3. Phone deposit $10.

The Maryland Hotel, 630 F St. (239-9243). The rooms are clean, if a bit old. Have a look at the tiny hall showers before you book a room without bath. Also, think twice before taking a room next to the noisy elevator shaft. Houses mainly older residents. Singles with no plumbing $20, with full bath $25. Weekly: $95, with bath $125. Second guest $8 per night, $40 per week.

Mission Hills, Hillcrest, Mission Valley

E-Z 8 Motels, 3 locations: 2484 Hotel Circle Pl., Mission Valley (291-8252); 4747 Pacific Hwy., Old Town (294-2512); 3333 Channel Way (223-9500), near the Sports Arena. 3 clones, each with TV, pool, and A/C. Check-out 11am. Singles $35. Doubles $40.

Old Town Budget Inn, 4444 Pacific Hwy. (260-8024, for reservations 800-225-9610), near Old Town. Simple and reasonable. Ask for rooms in the old building. Check-out noon. Singles $37. Doubles $42. Both rates $2 less without A/C. $5 more for microwave and refrigerator.

East of Downtown and College Area

There are many inexpensive, bland hotels along El Cajon Blvd., a large commercial strip devoted primarily to selling cars. Bus #15 offers a sweeping tour of the entire boulevard.

Allstar Inns, 7621 Alvarado Rd., La Mesa (464-7151), near Guava Ave. Easily accessible; near I-8. Basic rooms with A/C and TV. Check-out 11am. Singles $27.50. Doubles $32.

Travel Time Motel, 5447 El Cajon Blvd. (583-5447). Comfortable and spacious rooms come with A/C, cable TV, and refrigerator. Laundry facilities and a heated pool. Check-out noon. Singles $33. Doubles $38. Key deposit $5.

Lamplighter Inn Motel, 6474 El Cajon Blvd. (582-3088, for reservations 800-225-9610). Trim rooms, cable TV, A/C, pleasant grounds, and a pool to boot. Check-out 11am. Singles $42. Doubles $48.

Aztec Motel, 6050 El Cajon Blvd. (582-1414, for reservations 800-225-9610). High-ceilinged rooms include A/C and TV. Check-out 11am. Singles $31. Doubles $33.

San Diego—South

Imperial Beach Hostel (AYH), 170 Palm Ave. (423-8039). Take bus #901 from Amtrak or the trolley on C St. to Palm St. Station (35 min.). Transfer to bus #933 westward-bound (every hr. on the ½-hr.). In a converted firehouse 2 blocks from the the beach, 5 mi. from Mexico. Quiet and remote, but with a well-equipped kitchen and large common area with a TV. Bunkbeds for 36. Curfew 11pm. Members $10, nonmembers $13. Key deposit $2. Reserve by sending a check to cover the first night's lodging, or call ahead. Open 8-10am, 5:30pm-midnight. Registration 5:30-10pm.

The Beaches

Point Loma Hostel (AYH), 3790 Udall St., Point Loma (223-4778). Take bus #35 from downtown; get off at the first stop on Voltaire and walk across the street. If drving a car, take I-5 to Sea World exit, then left to Sunset Cliffs Blvd. Take left on Voltaire, right on

Warden and look for hostel sign painted on building. An airy 2-story building 1.5 mi. from Ocean Beach. Wooden bunks for 60, common room, kitchen. Check-out 10am. Office open 7-10am, 4pm-midnight. Lockout 11am-4pm. Curfew 2am. Talk to Patty for helpful information. Members $12, non-members $13. Three night max. stay; reserve 48 hr. in advance.

Point Loma Inn, 2933 Fenelon St. (222-4704), near the water. Take bus #29. Very appealing rooms. Call ahead to make sure the type of room you want is available. Singles $40. Doubles $43.50.

Western Shores Motel, 4345 Mission Bay Dr. (273-1121), just off I-5, opposite Grand Ave. Take bus #30. Two mi. from the beach, ½ mi. from the bay. High ceilings, A/C, TV. Check-out noon. Singles $36. Doubles $40.

Sleepy Time Motel, 4545 Mission Bay Dr. (483-4222). You may have a hard time getting to sleep here—it has that budget travel rarity: HBO. Check-out 11am. Singles $36, doubles $42, more on holidays. Key deposit $2.

Camping

All state campgrounds are open to bikers for $2 per night. State law requires that no cyclist be turned away no matter how crowded the site. Only Campland on the Bay is within city limits. For information on state park camping, call the enthusiastic people at San Elijo Beach (753-5091). Camping reservations are handled by MISTIX (800-444-7275) as well as individual campgrounds. Most parks are completely full in summer, and it's common to make weekend reservations eight weeks in advance. A complete list of county campgrounds is available at the visitors center.

Campland on the Bay, 2211 Pacific Beach Dr. (274-6260). Take I-5 to Grand Ave. exit and follow the signs, or take bus #30 and get off on Grand at the sign on the left. Expensive and crowded because it's the only central place to pitch a tent or plug in an RV. The cheapest sites are in a "dirt area" with nothing to block the wind coming off the water. Sites $22-41; in winter $20-38.

South Carlsbad Beach State Park, Rte. 21 (729-8947), near Leucadia, in north San Diego County. 225 sites, half for tents. On cliffs over the sea. Sites $21, in winter $16. Reservations necessary in summer.

San Elijo Beach State Park, Rte. 21 (753-5091), south of Cardiff-by-the-Sea. 271 sites (150 for tents) in a setting similar to that at South Carlsbad to the north. Strategic landscaping gives a very secluded feel. Hiker/biker campsites for those traveling on their own steam. Sites $21, in winter $16. Make reservations for summer.

San Diego Metropolitan KOA, 111 N. 2nd Ave. (427-3601), in Chula Vista south of the city. Check-out noon. Tent sites $25 for 2 people; RV sites $31 for 2. $2 per additional child, $3 per additional adult. Reserve early.

Food

The bad news first: San Diego has over 70 Jack in the Boxes and hundreds of other fast-food joints, an achievement befitting the birthplace of the genre. The good news is that the lunchtime business crowd has nurtured a multitude of restaurants specializing in well-made, inexpensive meals. When combined with San Diego's diverse ethnic mix and its proximity to sources of fresh seafood and produce, eating in San Diego can be a culinary delight.

Besides, fast-food is not always bad news. In the land of the speedy burrito, some restaurants have actually perfected the art of Mexican fast food. The best is **Robert's** (at 3202 Mission Blvd. and other locations). If you have access to a kitchen or barbecue pit, stop at **Point Loma Seafoods,** 2805 Emerson (223-1109 or 223-6553), off Rosecrans in Point Loma (see Beaches below). Pick up cheap, high-quality fruits and vegetables at the **Farmer's Bazaar,** 205 7th Ave. (233-0281), at L St., to complete the feast. (Open Tues.-Sat. 9am-5:30pm, Sun. 9am-5pm.) In Ocean Beach, Voltaire Ave. is brightened by several organic grocery stores.

Downtown

The nearly 100 restaurants located in this part of town cater to throngs of executives, whose midday patronage keeps the griddles sizzling. Unfortunately, many of these places close around 3pm, making dinner more of a challenge. The food court on the top floor of **Horton Plaza** offers more variety than the standard 31 flavors of junk food. If you have time to find lunch on your own, wandering around C St., Broadway, and below can be rewarding.

Wong's Nanking Café, 5th and Island (239-2171), in the Gaslamp District. Established in 1949, Wong's is San Diego's oldest Chinese restaurant. Mammoth servings for as little as $4. Open Sun.-Thurs. noon-11pm, Fri.-Sat. noon-1am. Closed Wed.

Kansas City Barbeque, 610 W. Market St. (231-9680), south of Broadway near the bay. Enjoy decent barbecue in the self-proclaimed sleaziest bar in San Diego, where scenes from *Top Gun* were shot. Dinners with 2 side orders, for around $8. One-sided sandwiches $4.50 (served only after 10pm). Open daily 11am-2am.

Old Spaghetti Factory, 275 5th Ave. (233-4323), in the Gaslamp Quarter. No, it doesn't manufacture old spaghetti; it's an 1898 building that makes fresh spaghetti ($4.25-5.85) and does it very well. Open Mon.-Thurs. 5-10pm, Fri.-Sat. 5-11pm, Sun. 4-10pm. For lunch Mon.-Fri. 11am-2pm.

Filippi's Pizza Grotto, 1747 India St. (232-5095), on a block full of Italian restaurants. Other locations—all family-owned—around town. Subs big enough to threaten the Pacific fleet ($3.25-4.25). Try the homemade sausage. Open Sun.-Fri. 11am-10:45pm, Sat. 11am-11:45pm.

Chuey's Café, 1894 Main St. (234-6937), in Barrio Logan. Barrio Logan trolley stop; walk 1 block toward stoplight. A long walk from downtown, but easily reached by trolley. Still, it's worth the effort to reach this combination restaurant/cocktail bar/pool hall. Excellent Mexican entrees $4-6. Combination plates and *gringo* food too. Very *Let's Go.* Open Mon.-Thurs. 11am-8pm, Fri. 11am-10pm, Sat. 11am-4pm.

Royal Bakery Thrift Store, 741 E St. (233-6704). This is the retail outlet of the Royal Pie Bakery, a commercial bakery in the Gaslamp Quarter. A dozen day-old donuts $1. Open Mon.-Fri. 7:30am-5pm, Sat. 8am-5pm.

Along I-5

El Indio, 3695 India St. (299-0333), in India St. Colony. When El Indio opened its doors in 1940, the owners probably never dreamed folks would line up along the block for a taste of their cooking. But a half-century later they're still lining up. Nonetheless, service is speedy and quality remains high. Eat inside or on the patio across the street, or carry a picnic over to Balboa Park. Portions of size; combination plates from $3. Buy a bag of fresh corn tortillas (12 for 55¢) or their "fantabulous" tortilla chips. Open Mon.-Thurs. 7am-9pm, Fri.-Sat. 7am-10pm.

Conora's, 3715 India St. (291-5938), in India St. Colony. Sandwich shop extraordinaire. Over 60 varieties, almost all $3.50-4.50. Call ahead if you're in a hurry, and Conora's will have your order ready when you arrive. Open Mon.-Sat. 8am-6pm.

The Big Kitchen, 3003 Grape St. (234-5789), in Golden Hill. Try the wide waffles ($2.75) or plentitudinous pancakes ($3) served on dishes that Whoopie Goldberg used to wash. Open Mon.-Fri. 6am-2pm, Sat.-Sun. 7am-3pm.

Gelato Vero, 3753 India St. (295-9269), in India St. colony. Some South American tribes once prohibited chocolate for those under age 60; taste the dark chocolate gelato here to find out why. Eleven other flavors as well ($1.35-3.50), plus pastries and coffees. Open Mon.-Thurs. 6:30am-midnight, Fri. 6:30am-1am, Sat.-Sun. 7:30am-1am.

Casa de Bandini, 2654 Calhoun St. (297-8211), in the most beautiful spot in Old Town. Eat in the lush and festive courtyard, the first floor of which is an original 1829 adobe mansion, complete with rose trellises, *mariachis,* and fountains. Enormous chicken and avocado salad, around $7. Monstrous margaritas. Open Mon.-Sat. 11am-10pm, Sun. 10am-10pm.

Hillcrest, Mission Hills, and College

Mandarin Dynasty, 1458 University Ave. (298-8899). As if the menu, with many vegetarian options, were not varied enough, they promise to "make anything on request." Most dishes $6-6.50; the Yu Hsiang Beef is wonderful. Open daily 11am-11pm.

Ichiban, 1449 University Ave. (299-7203). Sushi and other Japanese dishes around $4. Open Mon.-Sat. 11am-2:30pm and 5:30-9pm, Sun. 4-8:30pm.

Quel Fromage, 523 University Ave. (295-1600). The perfect place to read poetry, write letters, or stare off into space, plumbing the depths of your angst. Potent espresso $1.50, desserts around $2.50. Open Sun.-Thurs. 7:30am-11pm, Fri-Sat. 7:30am-midnight.

Julio's, 4502 University Ave. (282-6837). Another dimly lit Mexican restaurant with delicous food; its late weekend hours are what set it apart. Get away for less than a fiver by eating a la carte: big burritos with dressings $3.25 ($2.75 at lunch), 2 enchiladas $4.70. Open Mon.-Thurs. 11am-11pm, Fri.-Sat. 11am-3am, Sun. 9am-11pm.

Don Jose's, 4551 El Cajon Blvd. (284-9519). Take bus #15. A family-oriented Mexican joint, with lots of children running all over the place. Good 'n' greasy. Don Jose's specialty: sour cream enchiladas ($5.20). Try the avocado tacos. Open daily 11am-11pm.

Beaches

The Red Onion, 3125 Ocean Blvd. (488-9040), in Mission Beach. A large and lively restaurant/bar overlooking the Pacific. Usually jam-packed with a free, absolutely *free* buffet daily from 4-8pm. Restaurant open Mon.-Thurs. 10am-10pm, Fri.-Sat. 10am-11pm. Bar open daily 4pm-2am. Next to the Giant Dipper Rollercoaster ($2 per ride).

Margarita's, 4955 Newport Ave. (224-7454), in Ocean Beach. Everyone from local Rotarians to O.B. surf bums drops by. Mexican specials $3-4. Open Sun.-Thurs. 8am-9pm, Fri.-Sat. 8am-10pm.

Sportsmen's Seafood, 1617 Quivera Rd. (224-3551), on Quivera Basin near Sea World. Watch marine life in action at Sea World, then come here to see it on a plate. Grilled fish dinners $8. Fried clams and french fries $4. Open Sun.-Thurs. 11am-6pm, Fri.-Sat. 11am-7pm; fish market open daily 10am-6pm.

Café Toulouse, 4475 Mission Blvd., Pacific Beach (483-3988), at Garnet St. A pleasant little pastry shop. Filled croissants $1, quiches with salad $3.50. Open Mon.-Thurs. 7am-9pm, Fri.-Sat. 7am-11pm, Sun. 9am-5pm.

La Jolla

John's Waffle Shop, 7906 Girard Ave. (454-7371). $2.50 for the basic golden waffle, up to $5.40 for whole grain banana nut waffles. Breakfast and sandwiches about $4.50. Open Mon.-Sat. 7am-3pm, Sun. 8am-3pm.

Pannikin, 7467 Girard Ave. (454-5453). Chic eatery with a sunny patio and full range of coffees and teas. Fruit bowl $2.65. Popular with students from nearby UCSD. Open Sun.-Thurs. 6:30am-10pm, Fri.-Sat. 7am-11pm.

Sluggo's, 6980 La Jolla Blvd. (459-5536), near Windansea Beach; other locations around town. Caters to homesick Chicagoans, as well as anyone looking for a good hot dog ($1.60, large $3.15). Open Sun.-Thurs. 8am-9:30pm, Fri.-Sat. 8am-10:30pm.

Sights

In contrast to the rest of Southern California, where the pre-fab houses and mobile homes make the cities look like someone added water to a package of instant, dehydrated-city, San Diego's buildings form a tangible record of the city's history. The oldest buildings are the early 19th-century adobes of **Old Town.** Just up Juan St. from Old Town, **Heritage Park** displays old Victorian homes, carefully trimmed and painted like gingerbread houses. Extending south from Broadway to the railroad tracks and bounded by 4th and 6th Ave. on the west and east, the **Gaslamp Quarter** is home to a notable concentration of pre-1910 commercial buildings now being resurrected as upscale shops and restaurants. Well-preserved houses and apartment buildings erected between 1910 and 1960, in styles ranging from Mission Revival to zig-zag Moderne, are found on almost every block. For more relaxing pleasures, head toward the beaches, San Diego's biggest draw. Surfers catch tubular waves, sun-worshippers catch rays, and soon everybody is caught up in the atmosphere of sun-stimulated serenity.

Downtown

The centerpiece of San Diego's redevelopment is **Horton Plaza,** at Broadway and 4th Ave. This pastel-colored confection of glass and steel is an open-air, multi-leveled shopping center encompassing seven city blocks. Its complex architecture, top-floor views of the city, and occasional live entertainment set it apart from your average mall. (3-hour parking is free with validation at one of the shops.) Another noteworthy example of local architecture is the **Santa Fe Depot,** Kettner Blvd., a Mission Revival building whose grand arches welcomed visitors to the 1915 exposition. Standing just 3 blocks west of Horton Plaza, the building is now the San Diego Amtrak depot. On weekdays, Broadway bustles with professionals and panhandlers. At night and on weekends, only the latter remain.

South of Broadway, between 4th and 5th Ave., the **Gaslamp Quarter's** lamposts, murals, and antique stores give the area a turn-of-the-century air. Take care in this somewhat seedy area. The district is now battleground for a group of gentrifiers with dreams of offices and trendy restaurants and the forces of vacancy, budget crunches, and single room occupancy. Stop by and count the adult bookstores and beautifully painted façades to see who's winning. The **Gaslamp Quarter Foundation** (233-5227), in the William Heath Davis House, 410 Island Ave., offers 1½ hr. walking tours of the Quarter, departing from the Foundation's office on Saturdays at 11am. (Tours $5; seniors, students, and ages 12-18 $3; under 12 free. No reservations necessary.)

Farther south, the **Coronado Bridge** stretches westward from Barrio Logan to the Coronado Peninsula. High enough to allow the Navy's biggest ships to pass underneath, the sleek, sky-blue arc rests upon spindly piers and executes a graceful, swooping turn over the waters of San Diego Bay before touching down in Coronado. From the bridge, one can see San Diego's skyline to the north and the main naval base to the south. (Bridge toll $1. Bus #901 and other routes also cross.) When the bridge was built in 1969, its eastern end cut a swath through San Diego's largest Chicano community. In response, the community created **Chicano Park,** taking legal possession of the land beneath the bridge and making use of the bridge itself by painting splendid murals on the piers. The murals, visible from I-5 but fully appreciated only by walking around the park, are heroic in scale and theme, drawing on Hispanic-American, Spanish, Mayan, and Aztec imagery. Take bus #11 or the San Ysidro trolley to Barrio Logan station.

The **Embarcadero,** a fancy Spanish name for a dock, sits at the foot of Broadway on the west side of downtown. Along with North Island's seaplanes, Point Loma's submarine base, and South Bay's mothball fleet, the vessels on the Embarcadero are reminders of San Diego's number-one industry as well as of the city's role as a major West Coast naval installation. **San Diego Harbor Excursion** (234-4111) offers cruises past the Navy ships and under the Coronado Bridge. (Cruises: 1 hr. $10, 7 per day; 2 hr. $15, 5 per day. Ages 3-11 and over 55 half price on all cruises.) Harbor Excursion also sells tickets for the ferry departing for Coronado (every hr. 9am-10pm, returning on the ½-hour 9:30am-10:30pm, with one additional trip each way Fri.-Sat. evenings; one way $1.60). The ferry lands at the Olde Ferry Landing in Coronado on 1st and Orange St., a 10-block trolley ride from the Hotel del Coronado. **Invader Cruises** (234-8687) offers trips similar to Harbor Excursion's, but also uses sailing vessels for touring.

The Maritime Museum (234-9153), also by the Embarcadero, is the dock for the century-old *Star of India,* the British steam yacht *Medea,* and the *Berkeley,* a bay ferry that carried southbound refugees from the 1906 San Francisco Earthquake. (Open daily 9am-8pm. Admission $5, ages over 55 and 13-17 $4, 6-12 $1.25.)

Also on the harbor, but further south, **Seaport Village** (235-7221) houses boutiques in buildings that look as if they have been transported from Cape Cod (shops open daily 10am-9pm, 10am-10pm in summer). At the village's **Broadway Flying Horses Carousel,** built around 1890, riders can choose goats, dogs, or steeds with real horsehair tails as their mounts. (Open daily 10am-3:30pm and 4:15pm-10pm, until 9pm in winter. 75¢.)

Balboa Park

Balboa Park was established in 1868, when San Diego's population was about 2000. Though the population is now over one million, the park has lost only a few of its 1000-plus acres to urban expansion, the only major intrusion being the naval hospital in the south. Balboa draws crowds of parkgoers each year with its concerts, theater, Spanish architecture, street entertainers, lush vegetation, and zoo. In 1915 it hosted the Panama-Pacific International Exposition and in 1935, the California-Pacific Exposition; most of the present buildings are reconstructions of those erected for these fairs. Bus #7 or 7B runs through the park and near the museum and zoo entrances. Or take Laurel St. east from downtown to one of the many parking lots.

With over 100 acres of exquisitely designed habitats, the **San Diego Zoo** (231-1515) deserves its reputation as one of the finest in the world. The zoo attracts more than animal-lovers though, with flora as exotic as the fauna. They have recently moved to a system of "bioclimactic" areas, in which animals and plants are grouped together by habitat, rather than by taxonomy. The stunning **Tiger River** and **Sun Bear Forest** are the first of these areas to be finished and would make the set designers from *Out of Africa* drool. In addition to the usual elephants and zebras, the zoo houses such unusual creatures as Malay tapirs and everybody's favorite, the koala. The most efficient way to tour the zoo is to arrive as early as possible and take the 35-40 minute open-air **double-decker bus tour,** which covers 70% of the park. (Bus tour $3, ages 3-15 $2.50. Sit on the left if given a choice.) You will avoid lengthy queues and have the rest of the day to return to favorite animals or explore areas not covered by the bus. The **children's zoo** is a barnyard delight (ages over 2 50¢), while the **"skyfari"** aerial tram will make you feel like you've been suspended above a box of animal crackers. Most of the zoo is accessible to wheelchairs (which can be rented), but steep hills make assistance necessary. (Main zoo entrance open July-Labor Day 9am-5pm, exit closes at 7pm; Labor Day-June 4 9am-4pm, exit by 6pm. Admission $10.75, ages 3-15 $4. Group rates available. Free on Founder's Day, Oct. 1.) Near the zoo parking lot, bright wooden counterparts of the zoo's inhabitants romp around a marvelous **Victorian carousel** (50¢ per ride).

In addition to the zoo, Balboa Park has the greatest concentration of museums in the U.S. outside of Washington D.C. The focus of the park is the **Plaza de Panama,** on El Prado (a street running west to east through the Plaza), where the Panama-Pacific International Exposition took place in 1915 and 1916. Designed by Bertram Goodhue in the florid Spanish colonial style, many of the buildings were intended to be temporary structures, but their elaborate ornamentation and colorfully tiled roofs were deemed too beautiful to demolish.

Before exploring El Prado on your own, you might want to stop in the **House of Hospitality,** which contains the park **information center** (239-0512). The center sells simple maps of the park for 50¢, more elaborate guides for $1.50, and the **Passport to Balboa Park,** which contains six coupons to be used one, two, or three at a time for entrance to the park's museums, for $9. (Passports are also available at participating museums. Open daily 9:30am-4pm.)

The star of the western axis of the Plaza de Panama is Goodhue's California State Building, now the **Museum of Man** (239-2001). The much-photographed tower and dome are covered with shiny tiles in a Spanish design. Inside, eons of human evolution are explicated through permanent exhibits on primates, early man, the Mayan and Hopi cultures, and other Native American societies. Half of the museum is allotted to innovative temporary exhibits. (Open daily 10am-4:30pm. Admission $3 or 2 passport coupons, ages 12-18 $1, 6-11 25¢, under 6 free. Free the 3rd Tues. of each month.)

Behind the Museum of Man is the **Old Globe Theater** (239-2255), the oldest professional theater in California. The plays of Shakespeare and others are performed nightly (Tues.-Sun.), with weekend matinees. The **Lowell Davies Outdoor Theatre** across the street also draws top name performers. Ticket prices at weekend matinees begin at $25, $12.50 for seniors and students. The **Spreckels Organ Pavilion** (236-5717) at the south end of the Plaza de Panama, opposite the Museum of Art, resounds with music emerging from the 4400 pipes of the great outdoor organ. (Sun. at 2pm; in summer also Mon. at 8pm. Free. Closed Feb.) Free evening concerts are held in the pavilion in summer (Tue.-Thurs. 6:30pm). Call 236-5471 for information.

Across the Plaza de Panama is the **San Diego Museum of Art** (232-7931), which maintains a comprehensive collection, ranging from ancient Asian to contemporary Californian. Japanese, Dutch, and Impressionist works are the highlights, as well as several paintings by Georgia O'Keefe and major temporary exhibitions. (Open Tues.-Sun. 10am-4:30pm. Admission $5, seniors $4, ages 6-18 and college students with ID $2, under 6 free. Free 1st Tues. of each month.) Nearby is the outdoor **Sculpture Court and Garden** (236-1725), with a typically rounded and sensuous Henry Moore piece presiding over other large abstract blocks of inspiration. On the sculpture garden's terrace stands a charming café, aptly called the **Sculpture Garden Café** (236-1725). Entrees are expensive (around $7), so stick with the soup of the day ($3.50) or bring your own picnic for the grassy area beyond, where Henry Moore and Alexander Calder sculptures inspire experimentation with malleable edibles. (Café open Tues.-Sun. 11:30am-2pm. Sculpture garden open until 4:30pm. Pre-theater dinners served 5:30-7pm performance days at the Old Globe.)

Next door is the **Timken Art Gallery** (239-5548), 1500 El Prado, in a pine-nut marble and bronze box. The small but choice collection features several superb portraits by David, Copley, Hals, Rubens, and others. An excellent collection of large, prematurely abstract Russian church icons fills the rest of this tiny gallery. (Open Oct.-Aug. Tues.-Sat. 10am-4:30pm, Sun. 1:30-4:30pm. Free.)

Farther east along the plaza is the **Botanical Building** (236-5717), a wooden Quonset structure accented by tall palms threatening to burst through the slats of the roof. The scent of jasmine and the gentle play of fountains make this an oasis within an oasis. (Open Sat.-Thurs. 10am-4:30pm. Free.) The same botanists run the **Desert Garden and Case Gardens** 1 block east, at 2200 Park Blvd. (236-5717; also free).

Next door, the **Casa de Balboa,** a recent reconstruction of the 1915 Electricity Building, contains four museums. **The Museum of Photographic Arts** (239-5262) presents adventurous exhibits that rotate every six to eight weeks, featuring the works of Southwestern masters. (Open Fri.-Wed. 10am-5pm, Thurs. 10am-9pm. Admission $2.50, ages under 12 free. Free 2nd Tues. of every month.) The **San Diego Hall of Champions** (234-2544) is a slick sports museum with astroturf carpet and the square footage of a baseball diamond. Perhaps overplaying civic pride, it enshrines representatives of over 40 sports who made it big in San Diego. And what self-respecting sports museum would be complete without continuously running "blooper" videos? (Open Mon.-Sat. 10am-4:30pm, Sun. noon-5pm. Bloopers run for about the first 5 hours the museum is open. Admission $2, ages over 55 and students $1, 6-17 50¢, under 6 free. Families $5. Free 2nd Tues. of each month.) The San Diego Historical Society operates both the **Research Archives** and the **Museum of San Diego History** (232-6203). The museum is showing temporary exhibits while a permanent collection is being gathered. (Open Tues.-Sun. 10am-4pm. Admission $2-4, ages under 12 free. Free 2nd Tues. of each month.) Downstairs, the **San Diego Model Railroad Museum** (696-0199), with its elaborate train sets, gives some idea of what Santa's basement would look like if he had a 10-year-old son. (Open Wed.-Fri. 11am-4pm, Sat.-Sun. 11am-5pm. Admission $1, children free. Free the 1st Tues. of each month.)

From the end of El Prado St. (which is closed to cars), a left onto Village Place St. will take you to **Spanish Village,** a crafts center offering free demonstrations and exhibits. Thirty-nine studios display local artistry for browsers and buyers alike. At the other end of Village Place is the **Natural History Museum** (232-3821), with exhibits on paleontology and ecology. If the oceanographic displays interest you, you can plan a trip to the Scripps Institute or to Sea World to see live sharks and simulated tide pools. (Open daily 10am-4:30pm. Admission $4, ages 6-18 $1, under 6 free. Free 1st Tues. of each month.)

South of the Natural History Museum is the **Reuben H. Fleet Space Theater and Science Center** (238-1168), where two Omnimax projectors, 153 speakers, and a hemispheric planetarium whisk viewers inside the human body, up with the space shuttle, or 20,000 leagues under the sea. The world's largest motion pictures play here 8-11 times per day. (Admission $5.50 or 3 passport coupons, ages over 60 $4, 5-15 $3.50, under 5 free.) At 9pm and 11pm every night lasers dance on the ceiling of the **Laserium** in sync to the rhythms of Pink Floyd's "The Wall" (admission $6, seniors $4.50, children $3.50, under 5 not admitted). Tickets to the space theater also admit one to the Science Center, where visitors can play with a cloud chamber, telegraph, light-mixing booth, and other gadgets. (Open Sun.-Thurs. 9:30am-9:30pm, Fri.-Sat. 9:30am-10:30pm. Science Center admission alone $2 or 1 coupon, ages 5-15 $1. Free 1st Tues. of each month.)

The other main area of Balboa Park, the **Pan American Plaza,** was developed for the California-Pacific International Exposition of 1935-36. The buildings here are a less unified group, their styles drawing on Central and South American motifs, the Moderne movement, and Native American architecture. Those with limited time in Balboa Park should probably not bother with this part. The **House of Pacific Relations** is actually a series of little cottages proving that tacky, patriotic kitsch knows no bounds (open Sun. 1:30-4:30pm). The **Aero-Space Museum and Hall of Fame** (234-8291), in the drum-shaped Ford Pavilion, exhibits early-model planes (mostly replicas) and gadgets from aviation history. See the working replica of Lindbergh's *Spirit of St. Louis,* and a Flying Tiger fighting plane. (Open daily 10am-4:30pm. Admission $4, ages 6-17 $1. Free 4th Tues. of each month.) Behind the Aero-Space Museum in the Conference Building, the newly restored **Automotive Museum** (231-2886) enshrines California's unofficial state deity (open daily 10am-4pm; admission $3.50, seniors and students $2.50, ages 6-15 $1, under 6 free; free the 4th Tues. of each month).

For a bit of culture from south of the border follow Park Blvd. south to Pepper Grove, across from the Naval Hospital, to visit the **Centro Cultural de la Raza** (235-6135). The center offers changing exhibits of Chicano and Native American art, along with a permanent collection of murals. (Gallery open Wed.-Sun. noon-5pm. Free, sometimes with refreshments.)

Old Town, Mission Valley, and Mission Hills

Although the prices and number of gift shops at **Sea World** (226-3901) won't let you forget that it's a commercial venture, the Mission Park attraction is far more educational than your average amusement park. (Take I-5 or W. Mission Bay Dr. to Sea World Dr. Bus #9 runs right to the entrance, but stops running in the early evening, making it impossible to see the night show or fireworks in summer without a car.) Aside from the dolphin-shaped hand-puppets for sale, Sea World offers three major amusements. There are several indoor **aquariums,** whose fine lighting and state-of-the-art acrylic cases give astonishingly clear views of such fascinating creatures as sawfish and moray eels. The **open pools** allow visitors to approach sea turtles, starfish, and bat rays. You can even purchase fish ($1 a basket) to feed to the dolphins and sea lions. Finally, the **animal shows** parade the abilities of both marine mammals and their trainers. It's not everyday that you get to see five-ton killer whales breach high above the water. (This and other shows can be a bit messy, so sit more than 10 rows back or prepare to be drenched in whale wake and walrus wash.) On the other hand, don't let the majestic mammals distract you completely from such lower wonders as the gauzy ballet of moon jellyfish (in the **Marine Aquarium**) or the elegant movement of the horseshoe crab (in front of the **shark exhibit**). While some of the shows may seem a tad exploitative, Sea World strives to do more than entertain—detailed captions, a knowledgeable staff, and guided tours ($5, children $4) give you an informed notion of the creatures' life in the wild. The park also offers two rides with views of the city ($1.50 each) and human entertainment. (Open daily 9am-dusk, ticket sales end 2 hr. before closing time; mid-June through Labor Day, the park remains open until 11pm and adds special shows. Admission including shows $23, ages 3-11 $17.)

Old Town is the site of the original settlement and remained the center of San Diego until the late 19th century. Take bus #4 or 5 from downtown. The Spanish *Presidio,* or military post, was founded here in 1769. The site was chosen because the hill to the east—now Presidio Park—provided defense, and the San Diego River, now a mere trickle, coursed just to the north. Before becoming a museum, Old Town was the site of the county courthouse, the town gallows, and a busy commercial district. Now the partially enclosed pedestrian mall is an overcrowded, overpriced tourist trap. The state park people offer free walking tours, starting at the Casa de Machado y Silvas (237-6770; Fri.-Sun. at 2pm). To appreciate Old Town's buildings on your own, the visitors center's walking tour/history book ($2) is indispensible. Most of the buildings, such as the Presidio commander's **Casa de Estudillo** (1827) and the **Casa de Altamirano** (1868), are furnished adobes central to San Diego's early history. Less ancient is the **Bazaar del Mundo,** a motel designed by Richard Requa in the 30s to blend in with its aged neighbors. The Bazaar is now a pleasant shopping center featuring overpriced handicrafts and a few excellent restaurants (see Casa de Bandini under Food). **La Panaderia** serves coffee and Mexican pastries (75¢). The smell of mocha and sweet bread mixes well with the sweeter scent of fragrant flowers from across town.

In **Presidio Park,** next to and north of Old Town, the **Serra Museum** (297-3258), built in 1929, is styled after the original San Diego mission on the site. The collection includes antique Spanish furniture. The park itself ranges over a hill the Spaniards used for sighting enemy approaches; now you can see and hear only the freeways that surround the bluff. Lower down, shady paths allow secluded strolling. (Open Tues.-Sat. 10am-4:30pm, Sun. noon-4:30pm, admission $1.)

Mission Basilica San Diego de Alcalá (281-8449) was moved 6 mi. in 1774 to its present location in the hills north of the Presidio, in order to be closer to the Native American villages. Take I-8 east to Mission Gorge Rd. and follow the signs, or take bus #43. Still an active parish church where mass is held daily at 7am and 5:30pm, Mission San Diego has a chapel, a garden courtyard, a small museum of artifacts, and a reconstruction of the living quarters of mission-builder, Junípero Serra. Expressive decorations such as the mosaics and the brilliant white stucco belie the early missionaries' spartan existence.

Entertainment

San Diego's nightlife is not centered on a particular strip or avenue, but there is plenty of action around downtown and at the beaches after the sun has set. To find out what's happening consult the mammoth *Reader* (235-3000), a free weekly newspaper that lists places, dates, and prices. It's available in shops, restaurants, libraries, and newspaper machines every Thursday. *Varieties,* a guide to UCSD events, is available on campus (try the front desk of any dorm or the campus bookstore). The monthly *San Diego Magazine* ($2) publishes a special annual issue focusing on restaurants and nightlife; this comprehensive guide, usually released in summer, is worth the purchase. Ticketron (for nearest location call 565-9947) sells tickets to most major attractions but charges a booking fee, and *Arts Tix,* 121 Broadway (238-3810), at 1st Ave., offers half-price tickets to shows on the day of performance.

Bars and Clubs

Diego's, 860 Garnet Ave. (272-1241), Pacific Beach. The young and unattached come here en masse for the expansive dance floor and many videos. No dress code, but trendoids get decked out for the evening. Happy Hour Mon.-Fri. 3-6pm. Cover Sun.-Thurs. $3, Fri.-Sat. $5. Open Mon.-Sat. 11am-1:30am, Sun. 10am-10pm.

The Red Onion Bar, 3125 Ocena Blvd. (488-9040), in Mission Beach (see Food). A restaurant, and a hopping place to dine at night. Open daily 4pm-2am.

Confetti's, 5373 Mission Center Rd. (291-8635). A singles saturnalia. Lots of confetti and comparison shopping. Drinks $1.75-3.75. Happy Hour 5-8pm includes free buffet. Cover Mon.-Wed. $2, Thurs. and Sun. $3, Fri.-Sat. $5. No cover before 8pm. Open Mon.-Fri. 5pm-2am, Sat. 7pm-2am, Sun. 9pm-2am.

The Comedy Store, 916 Pearl St. (454-9176), in La Jolla. Drinks around $3. Potluck night Mon.-Tues. 8pm; local comics air their schtick. (Call and sign up after 3pm.) Well-known comedians featured other evenings. Shows Wed.-Thurs. and Sun. at 8pm ($6), Fri. at 8pm and 10:30pm ($8), Sat. at 8pm and 10:30pm ($10). Wed.-Thurs. 2-for-1 admission with any college ID. Two-drink minimum enhances performances. Must be 21.

Croce's, 802 Fifth Ave. at F St. (233-4355), in Gaslamp District. Ingrid Croce, wife of the late singer Jim Croce, established this classy jazz bar in the first floor of the historic Keating building. Live music nightly. Open daily 6:30pm-4am.

Café LuLu, 419 F St. (726-2126), in Gaslamp District. A stylish European coffeehouse and wine bar. Spider-like chairs and a mural made of broken glass on the floor of the entrance. Espresso $1.50, wine $3.25 a glass. Very chic. Open Mon.-Fri. 8am-4am, Sat.-Sun. 10am-4am.

Seasonal Events

Gorgeous weather and strong community spirit make San Diego an ideal place for local festivals, many of them annual affairs of over 30 years' standing. The visitors bureau (see Practical Information) publishes a thorough yearly events brochure. A 24-hr. **Events Hot Line** (696-8700) lists the latest performances and activites in downtown San Diego.

Penguin Day Ski Fest, New Year's Day, De Anza Cove on Mission Bay (276-0830). The object is to waterski or lie on a block of ice without a wet suit; those who do are honored with a "penguin patch." Those who fail come away with a "chicken patch." It probably helps to be hung over. Festivities 8am-1pm.

Ocean Beach Kite Festival, early Mar., 4741 Santa Monica Ave. (223-1175), in Ocean Beach. A kites-and-kids happening. Kite-making materials provided free. Judging at 1pm followed by a parade down to the beach for the kite flying competition.

Ocean Beach Street Fair, last weekend in June in Ocean Beach. Thousands attend this two day festival where they close off Newport Street and line the pavement with arts and crafts.

San Diego Crew Classic, early Apr. (594-6555), in Mission Bay. Collegiate crew-jock heaven. Watch the Harvard Crimson boats leave all others in their wake in this early season regatta. Best viewing from the west side of Mission Bay by the Bahia Hotel or from Santa Clara Point.

Pacific Beach Spring Art Festival, Apr. (488-0273). Browse through local arts and crafts, or munch at the food booths. Live entertainment all weekend.

Surf, Sand, and Sandcastle Days, early Aug. (424-6663), Imperial Beach, by the pier at 9:30am. In conjunction with the 8th annual **U.S. Open Sandcastle Competition.** Categories range from "Castles of the Mind" to "Creatures of the Sea." Spectacular entries that kick sand in the face of childhood bucket-and-shovel creations. Parade and fireworks.

America's Finest City Week, mid-Aug. (236-1212). Self-congratulatory week featuring a half-marathon, fireworks, volleyball tournaments, and a pops concert.

La Jolla Rough Water Swim, early Sept. (456-2100), in La Jolla Cove. Largest annual rough water swim in the U.S.

Oceanside Harbor Days, early Oct. (722-1534). 10km run, entertainment, bathtub races (oh yeah), gondola rides, folk dances, and fireworks.

Annual Great American Dixieland Jazz Festival, late Nov. (297-5277). Features Dixieland bands from throughout the U.S.

The Coast

There are 70 mi. of beaches in this city: think about that. There's a place for man's best friend (*Dog Beach*) and a resting ground for those wasted and indisposed (*Garbage Beach*). The coast from Imperial Beach in the south to La Jolla in the north is choked with sun worshippers, and it may take a little ingenuity to find room to bask. Chic places like Mission Beach and La Jolla are likely to be as packed as funky Ocean Beach come prime sunning time on summer weekends. The coastal communities do have more to offer than waves and white sand; wander inland a few blocks and explore.

Coronado

The only ways to reach the tip of the peninsula until 1969 were by ferry or overland haul, and in the 1880s visitors had to be careful of the wildcats in the brush. Now luxury hotels are beginning to line the skinny peninsula, but Coronado is far from overdeveloped. Take the Coronado Bridge from I-5 (toll $1) or bus #910 from downtown. Or take a ferry from San Diego Harbor Excursion for $1.60. (Every hr. on the hr. See Waterfront Sights.)

The **Hotel del Coronado,** Orange Ave. (435-6611), on the Coronado Peninsula, was built in 1888 as a remote resort. The "Del,"as it is affectionately called, is a monumental, shingled structure with long, white verandas and red, circular towers. One of the world's great hotels, it has hosted twelve presidents and was featured in the 1959 classic *Some Like It Hot.* It was here in 1920 that Edward, Prince of Wales, met Coronado housewife Wallace Simpson, the woman for whom he abdicated the English throne in 1936. A 45 minute audio-cassette tour is available in the lobby for $3.

Wander onto the white, seaweed-free beach in back, one of the prettiest in S.D. It's seldom crowded, even on weekends. On the other side of the island you can explore the **Old Ferry Landing,** where harborside shops and restaurants tantalize those just arrived by ferry. If you are here on a Sunday, you may want to visit the nearby park on Orange St. between 6th and 7th. Every first and third Sunday of the month, the Coronado artists coalition sponsors a free art-in-the-park exhibit.

Point Loma

Point Loma walks a fine line between residential community and naval outpost. Fortunately, the Navy remains contained near the base of the point. The government owns the outer two-thirds of the peninsula, but keeps most of it open to visitors and preserves the coastline from exploitation by developers. The people of Point Loma range from Ocean Beach hippies to the sedate and moneyed residents up the hill in the "wooded area." Safe streets and captivating views of downtown across the bay combine to make walking a pleasure.

The **Cabrillo National Monument** (557-5450), at the tip of Point Loma, is dedicated to Portuguese explorer João Rodriguez Cabrillo (the first European to land in California), but it is known for its views of San Diego and the herds of migrating whales that pass beyond the offshore kelp beds from December through February. From downtown, take I-5 to Rosecrans Blvd. and follow the signs, or take bus #2 to 30th and Redwood and transfer to bus #6. The 2-mi. **Bayside Trail** winds through the brush along the coast on the harbor side; the trail exhibits describe the life of the Native Americans who lived here before Cabrillo's arrival in 1542. On the ocean side of Point Loma are **tide pools;** best viewed at low tide. At the highest point of the peninsula sits **Old Point Loma Lighthouse,** which operated from 1855 to 1891 and is now a museum. (Park and visitors center open daily 9am-sunset;

in winter 9am-5:15pm. Lighthouse closes 15 min. earlier. Parking is $3 per car, $1 for bus passengers, and is valid for 7 days.

Mid-December through February is **whale-watching** season, and Cabrillo National Monument is the prime vista point. On their way to some massive breeding in the warm Baja waters, California Gray Whales stop by San Francisco Bay for a beaching or two (just to keep the environmentalists busy) and continue down the coast past San Diego. During the winter, call 293-5450 or 236-1212 for details on when and where to catch a glimpse of these seafaring behemoths.

At **Sunset Cliffs** on Ocean Beach, timing can make all the difference between an afternoon of noisy children and a tranquil sojourn in the sun. The best time to come is at sunset, when the great sandstone teeth brood beneath the darkening sky, and the waves crash like foamy jade onto the base of the cliffs.

Ocean Beach was once a magnet for drug addicts and dealers, but has since been sanitized. Although considered miserable by hot-dog surfers, the waves here are perfect for beginners. Try your luck with a hook, line, and sinker on the longest fishing pier in the Western Hemisphere. Fishermen are here around the clock.

Mission Beach and Pacific Beach

These strands are more respectable wave-wise than O.B. (Learning when to say "O.B." and "P.B." and when to say the full names is an art.) **Ocean Front Walk** is packed with joggers, walkers, bicyclists, and the usual beachfront shops. The three blocks between the sea and Mission Blvd. are quintessentially suburban. Low cottages inhabited by the rich or lucky line alleys that bear the names of famous resort cities from around the world.

On San Jose Place, in one of the wind-beaten shacks, is **Keith's Klothing Kastle.** The proprietor, Keith Nolan, sells his collection of silk Hawaiian shirts from the 40s and 50s, albeit slowly, at $100 apiece. Some were featured in a special exhibition a couple of years ago at the San Diego Museum of Art. He also sells vintage Ocean Pacific and Hang Ten beachwear, at more conscionable prices. Hours, like Keith, are unpredictable—open most afternoons and evenings.

Surfboards ($4 per hr., $17 per day) and boogie boards ($2.50 per hr., $10 per day) can be rented at **Star Surfing Co.,** 4655 Mission Blvd. (273-7827), in P.B. north of Garnet Ave. Driver's license or credit card required. No minimum age. (Open daily 10am-6pm.) Bicycles are available for rent along Garnet Ave. (See Getting Around).

La Jolla

Situated on a small rocky promontory, La Jolla (pronounced la HOY-a) was, in the 30s and 40s, a hideaway for wealthy Easterners who built luxurious houses and gardens atop the bluffs overlooking the ocean. The pink exterior and Spanish mosaics of the **La Valencia Hotel** (451-0772) still glow with the wealth of moneyed tenants. But newer money and a younger population have moved in. Jags, Mercedes, and BMWs purr along **Girard Avenue** and **Prospect Street** past boutiques and financial institutions. At the summit of this runway sits the **San Diego Museum of Contemporary Art,** 700 Prospect St. (454-3541), an impressive collection of pop, mimimalist, conceptualist, and Californian artwork in galleries overlooking the Pacific. Exhibits change frequently so call ahead for more info. (Open Tues. and Thurs.-Sun. 10am-5pm, Wed. 10am-9pm. Admission $4, seniors and students $2, under 12 50¢. Free Wed. 5-9pm.) In addition, several commercial **art galleries** welcome browsers; pick up a copy of the *South Coast Gallery Guide* from a sidewalk box for details.

The **Scripps Aquarium-Museum,** 8602 La Jolla Shores Dr. (534-6933), at the Scripps Institute of Oceanography (a UCSD graduate school), is home to sharks, moray eels, and a big, fat octopus named Humphrey, as well as a preserved coelacanth named Lucille and exhibits on oceanographic research. While it can't compare with Sea World's enormous tanks, it is a much less expensive way to investigate what lives beyond the beach. (Open daily 9am-5pm. Feeding time Sun. and Wed. 1:30pm. Donation $3, seniors and ages 12-18 $2.)

Location is perhaps the most interesting aspect of the **Mingei International Museum of World Folk Art,** 4405 La Jolla Village Dr. (453-5300), in University Towne Centre, a major bus terminus and transfer point. The idea was to make *mingei,* the "art of the people," accessible to the American people, and what better place to find American people than in a shopping mall? The small museum features several exhibits each year—one at a time—of everything from American weathervanes to the art of Lapland. The question is whether these displays enlighten mall-goers or merely rebuke them for choosing mass production over craft and tradition. (Open Tues.-Sat. 11am-5pm, Sun. 2-5pm. Donation $2.)

Take bus #30 or 34 to La Jolla from downtown San Diego; both the Veteran's Hospital here and the University Towne Centre are transfer points for North County buses.

In addition to these attractions, La Jolla claims some of the finest beaches in the city. Grassy knolls run right down to the sea at **La Jolla Cove,** and surfers are especially fond of the waves at **Tourmaline Beach** and **Windansea Beach.** At **Black's Beach,** people run, sun, and play volleyball. It is a public beach, not *officially* a nude beach, but you wouldn't know it from the color of most beachcombers' bums. The northern part of the beach generally attracts gay patrons. Take I-5 to Genesee Ave., go west and turn left on N. Torrey Pines Rd. until you reach the **Torrey Pines Glider Port** (where clothed hang gliders leap off the cliffs). Descend the treacherous cliffs at the end of the unpaved parking lot with care; there is a path, but it's rough and steep. *Real* men and women, or those with frontal lobotomies, remove their shoes and run down the cliff face. Normal people crawl.

The University of California at San Diego (UCSD; 452-2230 for the operator or 534-8273 for information) rests above La Jolla, surrounded on three sides by Torrey Pines Rd., La Jolla Village Dr., and I-5. Despite the thousands of eucalyptus trees and varied architecture, the campus falls somewhere between bland and really bland. The students who hang out in La Jolla proper are a slightly more interesting lot. Buses #30 and 34 take you to the campus, but once there a car or bike is invaluable for trekking from one of the five colleges to the next. An information pavilion on Gilman Dr., just north of La Jolla Village Dr., has campus maps (open daily 7am-8:30pm).

Near San Diego

North of La Jolla

Exploring the cities strung along the Pacific Coast Highway (Rte. 21) can be an appealing alternative to towel-to-towel tanning. A **bike route** with a number of suitable hills follows Rte. 21 all the way to Camp Pendleton north of Oceanside, with spurs inland at many points. North County Transit District (NCTD) bus #301 from University Towne Centre in La Jolla also goes all the way to Oceanside (80¢; every ½-hr. daily 6:03am-10:03pm.) For North County information, call 743-6283 or 722-6283.

In the affluent suburb of **Del Mar,** the cold eye of modern architecture gazes down on a popular beach. The town entertains and employs its young every summer at one of the largest county fairs in the country, the **Southern California Exposition** (755-1161). Held from late June to early July at the Del Mar Fairgrounds, the expo features traditional livestock shows, rides, and barbecues, as well as musicians and artists. (Admission $5, seniors $2.50, ages 6-12 $1.)

Racing season at the **Del Mar Racetrack** (755-1141) runs from late July until mid-September, with races held Wednesday through Monday. Take I-5 to Via de la Valle, then head west to Jimmy Durante Way. Gates open at noon, first post time at 2pm. (Admission $2. Free if you come after the 7th race to watch the last

2.) This is one of the most beautiful racetrack settings in the world and has long been popular with the entertainment world.

Intruding among the real estate offices along Rte. 21 (here called Camino del Mar), **Del Mar Danish Pastry and Coffee,** 1140 Rte. 21 (481-8622), offers delicious danishes for under $1 and free refills on coffee (open daily 6am-5pm). For swish deli fare, try **Board and Brew,** 1212 Camino del Mar (481-1021), 1 block down. Specialty sandwiches $3.50-5. (Open daily 10:30am-7pm.) The Del Mar **Amtrak** station (481-0114), the first stop on the run from San Diego to Los Angeles, is right on the beach; silver trains glide by the surf a few yards away (8 per day).

Torrey Pines State Reserve (755-2063), on the coast 4 mi. south of Del Mar, is one of only two native Torrey Pine groves on earth. (The other is on the Channel Islands off Ventura.) Unless you're an expert, however, the Torrey pine trees are just plain ole pine trees, like any other pine trees in this pine-tree-covered nation. The **lodge** provides information on hiking trails and park activities (open daily 9am-6pm). The park trails are wonderful for runners, cyclists, and those who can follow rules: no picnicking, no food, no smoking, no dogs (even if kept in cars), and no straying off the established trails. The slightly rocky beach is isolated and popular with hang gliders. (Park closes at sunset. That's when we polish our black leather jack-boots.)

More earthy than neighboring Del Mar, **Solana Beach** is also more hospitable to tourists who'd like to relax rather than spend. Or follow rules. From the **Solana Beach County Park** parking lot (755-1569), you can climb a steep staircase to a promontory commanding a gorgeous view of the ocean below. The **Belly Up Tavern,** 143 S. Cedros Ave. (481-9022), once a warehouse near the train tracks, now belts blues, rockabilly, and swing jazz. From I-5 turn west on Loma Santa Fe Dr.; from the Pacific Coast Highway turn east. Or take bus #34 from downtown and change at Veterans Hospital in La Jolla to NCTD bus #301. "Big Mama" Thornton, The Divinyls, John Lee Hooker, and Taj Mahal have all played here. (Open daily 11am-1:30am; live music daily at 9pm with occasional afternoon shows. Cover $2-5.) A little farther down Lomas Santa Fe (closer to I-5) is **Fidel's,** 607 Valley Ave. (755-5292; open daily 11:30am-9pm), which cooks up some of the best Mexican food in North County. Revel in the patio atmosphere and scarf all the chips you want for free. The $5 lunch special translates to enchilada, quesadilla, tostada, or some other feminine Spanish noun with a beer or margarita. Just down the street, rival restaurant **Tony's Jacal,** 621 Valley (755-2274), is a North County staple. It's a family-run establishment that serves up hot and zesty burritos, tacos, and tostados using turkey meat instead of ground beef. (Open Mon.-Sat. 11am-2pm and 5-10pm, Fri.-Sat. 11am-2pm and 5-10:30pm, Sun. 3-10pm.) To reach both restaurants, head south on Stevens Rd. then turn left on Genevive Ave. For lunch, head to the **Hideaway Café,** 150 S. Acacia Ave. (755-3388), 1 block west of U.S. 101, left on Plaza St. This tiny, bleached-wood shack offers burgers with a health food flair. Fresh-fruit smoothies are $2.25. (Open Tues.-Fri. 7am-3pm, Sat.-Sun. 7am-2pm.)

Cardiff-by-the-Sea is enhanced by **San Elijo Beach State Park** (729-8947) and **Cardiff State Beach** just to the south. The former has nearly 200 camping sites, well landscaped for privacy. In summer, it's wise to reserve ahead through MISTIX (800-444-7275; sites $14). If you have a car, this is a perfect place to stay while visiting San Diego.

Encinitas, Leucadia, and Carlsbad

Shaded by eucalyptus trees, Rte. 21 passes next through the towns of Encinitas and Leucadia, which still betray traces of their hippie-mecca past. **Quail Botanical Gardens,** 230 Quail Gardens Dr. (436-3036), ½ mi. east of I-5 off Encinitas Blvd., is free and glorious. You can walk from Rte. 21, called 1st St., in Encinitas. Hilly walkways lead through stands of palms and cork trees, fruit orchards, banks of ferns, simulated Himalayan and Mediterranean areas, and a section representing what Southern California looked like before they started draining Mono Lake to fill the swimming pools. (Open daily 8am-5pm. Parking $1.) As you continue north, you can't miss the **Self-Realization Fellowship Temple,** a shoreline Taj Mahal established by the guru Paramahansa Yogananda. The majestic white gates topped by 10-ft. gilt lotuses look more like a Mediterranean mirage than a California dream. Don't ask whether it's worth visiting—you must seek the answer within yourself.

El Pollo Gordo, 490 1st St. (436-0704), serves up Ensenada-style chicken for about $3.50. (Open daily 11am-9pm.) **Roxy Restaurant,** 517 1st St. (436-5001), offers healthy and delicious entrees at low prices. A falafel sandwich costs $2.85, and their amazing Tostada Fiesta is a party at $4.75. (Open Mon.-Sat. 10:30am-10pm, Sun. 10:30am-9pm.)

East of Encinitas nests the understated oasis of **Rancho Santa Fe.** The Santa Fe Railroad bought the land here years ago to plant thousands of eucalyptus trees in hopes of using the wood for railroad ties. Although the railroad abandoned its plans, the groves contributed to the region's evolution into a haven for the wealthy, including such stellar ex-residents as Douglas Fairbanks, Mary Pickford, and Bing Crosby. To this day, the community remains an exclusive retreat from the encroaching threat of suburbia, and the town's streets (all bearing Spanish names) are lined with retrophilic red-tile buildings.

Farther up the coast, the lagoon hideaway of Carlsbad is decidedly more charming than its southern suburban neighbors. Here you should check out the cluttered walls at **Carlos Murphy's,** 2525 El Camino Real (434-1758), in Plaza Camino Real. Memorabilia from the 20s and 30s lends a gringo flavor to this Mexican restaurant. The prices are a bit steep (entrees $6-13), but the nostalgia merits the extra *dinero.* (Open Sun.-Thurs. 11am-10pm, Fri.-Sat. 11am-11pm.)

The cheapest indoor lodging near Carlsbad is the **Allstar Inn,** 6117 Paseo del Norte (438-1242), which lets singles for $27.50 and doubles for $32.

The state has taken over the beaches here, but they're still available for sunning and surfing. The stone steps at **Leucadia State Beach** descend from the cliffs to just over a mile of public sands. **Moonlight State Beach** has a small beautiful cove and tons of surfers. You can camp on the beach at **South Carlsbad State Park** (438-3143), although you probably won't be able to obtain one of the 226 sites in summer without a reservation. Call MISTIX (800-444-7275; sites $21 off the ocean, $16 inland). Day-use access is available outside the campground to the north and south. **Carlsbad State Beach** is 3 mi. long and attractive, spoiled only by a view of the mammoth Encinas Power Plant, occupying the coast to the south (although the surfers don't seem to mind). You can rent a board at **Offshore Surf Boards,** 3179 Carlsbad Blvd. (729-4934), on Rte. 21. Boogie boards are $1.50 per hour or $7 per day, with a $75 deposit or credit card and driver's license. (Open daily 9am-7:30pm.)

Oceanside

Oceanside is the largest and, accordingly, the most varied of the beach towns north of San Diego. Nowadays it's the only place in the San Diego area where real estate is still "almost" affordable. But realty is not the whole of reality: in the past couple of years Oceanside has also been afflicted with increasing gang violence as entrepreneurial hoodlums from Los Angeles have migrated southward to unincorporated areas. The beach at **Oceanside Harbor** (I-5 and Oceanside Harbor Dr.) is a surprisingly fabulous place to swim or learn the rudiments of surfing. Beaches are heavily patrolled by lifeguards and there are designated areas for surfers to brave the waves.

Accommodations in and near Carlsbad State Beach make Oceanside cheap and accessible for the budget traveler(see Encinitas and Leucadia). In Oceanside itself, you can check the **Motel 6,** 1403 Mission Ave. (721-6662). A pool, TV, and the gentle roar of nearby I-5 are included in the package. (Singles $35. Doubles $41.50.)

If you're interested in seeing another old Spanish mission, make a pilgrimage to **Mission San Luis Rey de Francia** (757-3651), built to "save" the Luiseño Natives. Follow Mission Ave. (Rte. 76) east from Hill St. (Rte. 21) for 5 mi., or take NCTD bus #303 from the intersection of Hill and Mission. The mission was founded in 1798, but the only original building still standing is the 1807 church. (Admission

$2, children $1; Sun. mass free.) The museum exhibits artifacts of monastery life. In mid-July the mission organizes a fiesta, preceded by an outdoor mass and a Blessing of the Animals, a tradition which began when missions were major agricultural entities. (Museum and church open Mon.-Sat. 10am-4:30pm, Sun. noon-4pm.) Families can take guest rooms here for week stays. Call the **Retreat Center** (757-3659) for more information.

Amtrak (722-4622) and **Greyhound** (722-1587) share the **Oceanside Transit Center,** 205 and 225 Tremont St. The center's towering signs make it easy to spot from any point in town.

Escondido

Thirty miles north of San Diego, Escondido counts among its diverse denizens figures ranging from wunnerful, wunnerful "champagne music" conductor Lawrence Welk, who operates a golf resort frequented by retirees, to the masses of undocumented laborers looking for agricultural work. Like its cousin, the San Diego Zoo, the **San Diego Wild Animal Park,** (234-6541; 480-0100 from North County) strives to do right by both its animals and its human visitors. Take Rte. 15 north to Via Rancho Parkway and follow the signs. From downtown Escondido, take NCTD bus #307 from Valley Parkway and Escondido Blvd. **Gray Line Tours,** 1670 Kettner Blvd. (231-9922), charges $35 (ages 3-11 $22) for round-trip transportation from San Diego, admission, and use of the park's Monorail. Reserve at least one day in advance. The park's 700 acres of developed land (another 1100 acres remain untouched) give the animals much more room than does an ordinary zoo. The open-air **Wgasa Bush Line Monorail** takes visitors on a 50-minute tour through a variety of habitats. (Tours 9:30am-6:30pm, included in admission; sit on the right if possible.) Renting binoculars ($2.50) at the camera hut before boarding the monorail may enhance the tour. Besides the monorail, the Wild Animal Park offers the 1¼-mi. Kilimanjaro Hiking Trail, botanical exhibits, dusk-time screen shows, and animal shows. But while its large enclosures and successful breeding program are a boon to our furry friends, the park really can't compete with the San Diego Zoo in terms of accessibility and variety. Visit the Balboa Park zoo first, then go to the park for special animal shows or to see larger groups of animals. Most of the park, including the monorail, is wheelchair accessible, but steep hills can require detours or hard pushing. (Admission including 50-min. Wgasa Bush Line tour and animal shows $16, seniors $13.50, ages 3-15 $8.50. Parking $1. Open Sun.-Thurs. 9am-6pm, Fri.-Sat. 9am-8pm.)

A **Motel 6,** 509 W. Washington Ave. (743-6669), by the City Center Parkway, is everybody's favorite. And yes, it has a pool, TV, movies, and A/C. (Singles $27. Doubles $33.50.) **Dixon Lake,** 1700 La Honda Dr. (741-3328), north of town, has 45 campsites in attractive, hilly country overlooking the reservoir. (Sites $10, with hookup $14; reservation fee $5 per site.) Follow Broadway north to El Norte Parkway, turn right, then left onto La Honda. Reserve in summer at least 18 days in advance. The lake is well-stocked with trout and catfish; swimming is prohibited. Fishing permits are sold at the camp (adults $4.50, children 8-15 $2.50). Rented motorboats cruise out of the docks for $15 per day (7am-7pm), $12 per half-day (1-7pm); rowboats are $8 per day, $6 per half-day. Evening rentals (5-11pm) are available for motorboats ($12) and rowboats ($6). (Information line open daily 6am-4:30pm. Reservations accepted Mon.-Fri. 7am-4:30pm. Park open for day-use daily 6am-8pm, and until midnight with permit for night fishing. $1 per car, seniors free.)

In town, diner-style fare is offered by **Champion's Family Restaurant,** 117 W. Grand (747-0288). Get a three-egg omelette, hash browns, and biscuits for $3. This is the kind of place where waitresses say, "What'll it be, kiddo?" (Open Mon.-Fri. 6am-2:45pm, Sat. 6am-1:45pm.)

Greyhound stops in Escondido at 700 W. Valley Parkway (745-6522). The **Escondido Convention and Visitors Bureau** is at 720 N. Broadway (745-2125; open Mon.-Fri. 8am-5pm). For **NCTD information,** call 743-6283.

North of Escondido

Although the Hale telescope at **Palomar Observatory** (742-3476) on Palomar Mountain is over 40 years old, it remains one of the world's largest and greatest astronomical tools. Take San Diego County Rte. S6, the "Highway to the Stars." The drive up through avocado orchards and dense woods offers lovely views of the valleys below, though the cities ensconced in these vales increasingly threaten Palomar's heavenly research with light and air pollution. Inside the observatory, a museum displays photographs, taken through Hale's 200-in aperture, of awesome celestial objects. A photo gallery and videotaped account of the observatory's activities are the only other concessions made to the tourist trade. A smug notice points out that research, not education, is the observatory's mission, and touring is consequently limited to gazing at the telescope from behind plate glass. The more curious are referred to L.A.'s Griffith Planetarium, three hours away (see L.A. Sights—Griffith Park). (Palomar open daily 9am-4pm. Free.)

The observatory and several state and federal campgrounds are contained within **Cleveland National Forest.** Rte. S6 will rocket you past federally-run **Fry Creek** and **Observatory Campgrounds** (745-2421), and a left onto Rte. S7 at the mountaintop will touch you down at **Palomar Mountain State Park** (789-0191). Camping is permitted at the park's state-run **Cedar Grove** site (742-3462). Sites are over 5000 ft. above sea level, so bring your longjohns. For more information, write 332 S. Juniper, Escondido 92025.

West of Mt. Palomar, halfway to Oceanside on Rte. 76, is one of the few remaining operating missions in California, **Mission Asistencia San Antonio de Pala** (742-3300), on the Pala Indian Reservation. The mission was founded as an outpost of Oceanside's Mission San Luis Rey in 1816 and converted thousands of Native Americans to Christianity before secularization in 1846. The buildings are restorations of the facilities that decayed during the last half of the 19th century. In 1903, the mission was revived when the Cupeño Natives were booted from their ancient village of Cupa to make way for Warner Hot Springs. San Antonio still ministers to Native Americans. The walls of the long, low chapel are painted with Native motifs, and the rough-hewn timbers and undulating brick floors reflect its rustic origins. In the cemetery, hundreds of Native Americans are buried in unmarked graves or beneath rudely lettered crosses graced by humble offerings of flowers in rusted coffee cans. The two bells in the *campanile* are rung during the exuberant **Corpus Christi Fiesta** in early June. There is dusty roadside **camping** on reservation lands west of the mission, on Rte. 76. (Sites $5.)

Cuyamaca Rancho State Park

Cuyamaca is a Spanish corruption of Ah-ha Kwe-ah-mac, the native Kumeya'ay name for the area that means "the place where it rains"—something of an oddity in Southern California, where miles of desert are punctuated only by monotonous suburbs and trees. Cuyamaca Rancho State Park is indeed quite an oddity; with acres of mountainous deciduous forest, it encompasses more than 26,000 acres of willows, sycamores, and enormous live canyon oak. In the northeast corner of the park is Cuyamaca Lake and a transitional desert zone between Cuyamaca Rancho and Anza-Borrego Desert State Parks. The **park headquarters** are on Rte. 79 in the center of the park (765-0755). The mailing address is Cuyamaca Rancho State Park, 12551 Rte. 79, Descanso 92016. (Open Mon.-Fri. 8am-4:30pm.)

Be sure to see the **Indian Museum** at park headquarters. The exhibits here explore the tragedies of the missionary era—slavery, destruction of native culture, and land deprivation. The Kumeya'ay were steadfast in their resistance to European and American influence well into the 19th century, when they were finally forced onto a reservation in the 1870s. An interpretive trail near the museum describes how the Kumeya'ay (called *Diegueño* by the Spanish) lived off this land. (Open daily 9:30am-4:30pm.)

The **Stonewall Mine Ruins** on Cuyamaca Lake consist of building foundations and old mining equipment left to rust and weather artfully. A town once stood here, when the mine offered up over $2 million dollars of gold from 1872 to 1892. (There is a $5 day-use fee which enables you to park your vehicle for 24 hr.; but you don't have to pay if already registered somwhere else in the park.)

Over 110 mi. of trails crisscross the park. One of the best is the **Cuyamaca Peak Trail,** which traverses Paso Picacho (3½ mi.) and Green Valley (8 mi.) up through the pine and fir trees, passing mountain springs on the way to the 6512-ft. summit, from which a peek at the Pacific Ocean, Mexico, and the Salton Sea is often available. Another trail of note ascends **Stonewall Peak** (5730 ft.), 2 mi. from Paso Picacho. From the top you can gaze across the desert. A section of the California Riding and Hiking Trail passes through on its way to Anza-Borrego. The park also offers the usual variety of guided walks and campfire programs. Check with park headquarters for particulars.

Campgrounds abound here; stick to the official sites. All except Arroyo Seco and Granite Springs are developed sites with tables, fireplaces, water, and showers. Call 756-0755 for information. Reservations at all sites (advisable in summer and necessary on weekends) can be made through MISTIX (800-444-7275). The primitive camps, to which you must bring your own water and utensils, are on hiking trails. Arroyo Seco and Granite Springs each accommodate up to 40 people. Paso Picacho also contains four environmental sites, which are primitive sites with picnic tables and closer proximity to the developed camping areas. Developed sites are $14. Sites are listed from north to south.

Los Caballos Horse Camp (4750 ft.). 15 sites with corrals just south of Cuyamaca Lake. You must have your own set of hooves to get here.

Paso Picacho (4780 ft.). 40 tent sites, 45 RV sites with access to scenic trails, as well as 4 environmental sites.

Green Valley (3957 ft.). 40 tent, 41 RV sites on the Sweetwater River—known as the Sweetwater *Trickle* during the droughts of the recent years.

Arroyo Seco (4290 ft.), 1½ mi. west of Green Valley by foot.

Granite Springs, 4½ mi. east of Green Valley by foot.

Cuyamaca Rancho is a little more than an hour inland from San Diego along I-8, then north on Rte. 79. The easiest way to reach Cuyamaca is via the **Northeast Rural Bus System** (765-0145), which also serves the mountain and desert towns of Julian, Santa Ysabel, Warner Springs, Borrego Springs, and Ocotillo Wells Tuesday through Saturday, and El Cajon only on Monday. (Office open Mon.-Fri. 7-11am and 1-5pm.) All buses depart from Parkway Plaza in El Cajon and make 4 stops in town (take San Diego Transit bus #90 or 115 from downtown San Diego). The buses run a "reverse route" going out of the backcountry in the morning and returning to the backcountry in the afternoon. While the system is the lifeline for the rural folk, it is generally not designed for tourists who want to come and go the same day. The buses can be flagged down anywhere along the route and will even make pick-ups slightly off the route if you call 24 hr. in advance. There is only one trip per day for each route. The fare is $1.50-3. Route #878 (2nd and 4th Thurs. of each month) grazes the top of Cuyamaca Rancho State Park by request only.

Julian

Most San Diegans agree that Julian's apple pie and home-town atmosphere makes this less-than-booming Gold Rush town worth the trek. Orchards and mines collide in this relic of the Old West where the population has hovered at a mere 1500 for over a century. Julian and the other small towns of the region—Santa Ysabel and Warner Springs—make an interesting daytrip when traveling across Southern California.

Aside from its gastronomical offerings, Julian's main attraction is its climate; Julian is one of the few places in Southern California where the seasons actually change. Refugees from the perennial summer flock here to witness the bloom of spring and the shades of autumn.

The centerpiece of this quintessential town is, predictably, **Main Street.** Around the 2000 block of this drag, the aroma of baked apple pie drags crowds into restaurants and bakeries against their will. San Diegans fill up on pie and cider, then pack their cars with Julian's honey, preserves, olives, dried fruit, and candy as defense against urban life.

The charming **Julian Pioneer Museum,** at Washington and 4th St. (965-0227), housed in an old brewery just around the corner from the Town Hall, exhibits bureaus full of Victorian clothing and cases of festival memorabilia and Native American handicrafts. Several albums contain old photographs with interleaved notebook paper on which old-timers may contribute their knowledge and reminiscences. (Open daily 10am-4pm. Donation 50¢.)

The **Wildflower Show and Art Mart,** May 9-17, has been a tradition for 60 years. From Aug. 22-Sept. 7 the **Weed Show and Art Mart** is also held here. Both feature exquisite floral arrangements and the work of local artists. The Julian **Banjo and Fiddle Contest** (280-9035) is held on the 3rd and 4th Sunday in Sept. at Jess Martin Memorial Park. October weekends bring the **Fall Harvest Festival** and **Apple Days,** with lots of food, music, and tourists every weekend from mid-Sept through Nov.

The **Chamber of Commerce** (765-1857) at the Town Hall may be helpful (open Thurs.-Tues. 11am-4pm), but the residents themselves play host in a more effective and sincere manner. For a town flooded by tourists on summer and autumn weekends, Julian remains remarkably ingenuous. There are a few inns and bed and breakfasts, but they are not for the budget traveler. The **Julian Hotel** (765-0201) a graceful 1880s wood frame structure on the National Register, is similarly out of the question financially, but you can admire it from the street.

There are 103 campsites ($11 per night; with water, showers, and fire pits) at **William Heise County Park** (565-3600). This is also the best place around Julian to picnic, to nap, or just to watch the oaks grow ($1 day-use fee). The park is clearly marked on Pine Hills Rd. (Open Mon.-Fri. 8:30am-4:30pm.) Reservations are recommended for summer weekends; call 565-3600 in San Diego three to 13 weeks in advance. The other alternative is **Cuyamaca Rancho State Park,** a 9-mi. drive from Julian.

Northeast Rural Bus System (765-0145) leaves from Grossmont Center, La Mesa every Monday and Thursday through Saturday at 2:45pm ($2.25), but the return trip is scheduled for the next morning at 9:30am. Call a day in advance for reservations.

Near Julian

Although Julian is the most famous of the mountain towns, **Santa Ysabel** and **Warner Springs** deserve visits as well. Follow your nose to Santa Ysabel's main attraction, **Dudley's Bakery** (800-225-3348), at the junction of Rte. 78 and 79, west of Julian. Dudley's makes dozens of varieties of pastry and bread, including a feisty jalapeño loaf ($1.25), coconut macaroons (15¢), and rhubarb pie ($2.90). Phone in orders ahead of time to avoid a wait. (Open Wed.-Sun. 8am-5pm.)

Hotels are not cheap here, so you're best off camping. Prices at the **Apple Tree Inn,** 4360 Rte. 98 (765-0222), halfway between Julian and Santa Ysabel, however, do border on reasonable. Singles are $35 during the week, $40 on weekends; doubles are $45, $65 on weekends.

A few miles up Rte. 79 in Warner Springs is **St. Francis Chapel,** an 1830 adobe built for local Pala Indians and still in use. The exposed, rope-lashed trusses, the leaning west wall, supported by stone buttresses, and the red tile roof of the structure evoke the aura of the area's rugged past. While there, be sure to ring the Ramona Bell. (Mass every Sunday at 11am.)

Warner Hot Springs, near the Pala Reservation to the west, was developed around the turn of the century by rancher John Warner. But don't bother packing your swimsuit and white wine. Without a timesharing contract and a 35% tax break, you have as much access to the springs as the Native Americans Warner displaced to develop them.

To reach Santa Ysabel by bus, take **Northeast Rural Bus System** (765-0145). Buses run to and from San Diego Mondays through Fridays ($2). Call a day ahead to make reservations and for times and route information.

Orange County

Orange County, Los Angeles's neighbor to the south, was part of Los Angeles County until 1861, when "O.C." seceded over a tax dispute. The two have since become sibling rivals. L.A. has been the egocentric and domineering big brother who ignores his sibling's presence, while Orange County has nurtured resentment towards L.A. But you can see the family resemblance as the two share many of the same problems. Though O.C. residents may insist otherwise, their smog is just as bad as L.A.'s, as is their traffic.

The two counties are far from identical, however. Orange County has a higher per capita income and a population much less ethnically diverse than that of Los Angeles. Many O.C. residents live in "planned communities," neighborhoods designed by strict codes governing exactly where schools and shopping centers must be placed as well as what houses must look like.

If regimented living isn't to your taste, head for the coast, where Orange County's fine surf and string of clean, uncrowded beaches, have produced the truest approximation to stereotypical Southern California beach life, complete with a population of deeply-tanned, full-time surfers and sun-worshipers

Of course, not every attraction in Orange County is on the coastline. Millions of visitors each year flock to the Anaheim area to catch California Angels and L.A. Rams games or to visit the perpetually happy environs of Disneyland.

Practical Information

Visitors Information: Anaheim Area Visitors and Convention Bureau, 800 W. Katella Ave., Anaheim 92808 (999-8999). In the Anaheim Convention Center. Free brochures. Open Mon.-Fri. 8:30am-5pm.

Airport: John Wayne Orange County, Campus Dr. (755-6500). Flights to and from many major U.S. cities.

Amtrak, 5 stops: 120 E. Santa Fe Ave. (992-0530), in Fullerton, at Harbor Blvd.; 1000 E. Santa Ana (547-8389), in Santa Ana; Santa Fe Depot (661-8835), in San Juan Capistrano; 2150 E. Katella (385-1448), in Anaheim by Anaheim Stadium; unmanned stop in San Clemente, off I-5, by the municipal pier.

Greyhound, terminals at 2080 S. Harbor (635-5060), in Anaheim, 3 blocks south of Disneyland (open Mon.-Thurs. 7am-7:30pm, Fri.-Sun. 7am-9:30pm); 1000 E. Santa Ana Blvd. (542-2215), in Santa Ana (open daily 7am-8pm); and 510 Avenida de la Estrella (492-1187), in San Clemente (open Mon.-Thurs. 7:45am-6:30pm, Fri. 7:45am-8pm).

Orange County Transit District (OCTD): 11222 Acacia Parkway (636-7433), in Garden Grove. Thorough service, useful for getting from Santa Ana and Fullerton Amtrak stations to Disneyland, or for beach-hopping along the coast. Long Beach, in L.A. County, serves as the terminus for several OCTD lines. Bus #1 travels the coast from Long Beach down to San Clemente, with service twice per hour from early morning until around 8pm. Schedules available in many public places. Fare 85¢; correct change only, please. Transfers free. Information center open Mon.-Fri. 6am-7pm; Sat.-Sun. 8am-5pm.

Local RTD Information: 800-2-LA-RIDE (252-7433). Lines open daily 5:30am-midnight. RTD buses run from L.A. to Disneyland and Knott's Berry Farm.

Surf Report: 673-3371.

Rape Crisis: 836-7400. 24-hr. hotline.

Free Clinic of Orange County: 1215 E. Chapman (633-4600). You must fill out an application on Tuesdays or Wednesdays before being able to receive an appointment.

Gay-Lesbian Community Service Organization: 534-0862.

Police: 425 S. Harbor Blvd. (999-1900), in Anaheim.

Emergency: 911.

Post Office: 701 N. Loara (520-2602), in Anaheim. One block east of Euclid, 1 block north of Anaheim Plaza. Open Mon.-Fri. 8:30am-5pm. General Delivery ZIP Code: 92803.

Area Code: 714; 310 in Seal Beach. **A note to our readers:** The 714 area code is scheduled to be split in late 1992, into 714 and 909 area codes. The details of the impending change were not available at press time. Changes in phone numbers for Orange County will be incorporated into the 1993 edition.

Accommodations and Camping

Its proximity to Disneyland and the other amusement parks grants **Anaheim** a thriving tourist trade. Because it's fairly remote from L.A.'s other sights, however, there is no reason to stay here unless you plan to linger in the Magic Kingdom. Start by contacting the Anaheim Visitors Center, a travel industry dating service, which matches people with rooms they can afford. The road to Disneyland along Harbor Blvd. is lined with economy motels.

The county coast is the other big attraction, and bargain rates can be found at motels scattered along Pacific Coast Hwy. and Newport Beach's Newport Blvd.

Huntington Beach Colonial Inn Youth Hostel, 421 8th St. (536-3315), in Huntington Beach, 4 blocks inland at Pecan. In a large yellow Victorian house shaded by huge palm trees. 9 2-person rooms, 3 more accommodate 4-5 people. Common showers, bathroom, large kitchen. Reading/TV room. Lockout 9:30am-4:30pm. Curfew 11pm. Late night key rental $1 ($20 deposit). $11 per night, must have picture ID. Frequented by British, German, and Australian travelers.

Fullerton Hacienda Hostel (AYH), 1700 N. Harbor Blvd. (738-3721), in Fullerton, about a 15-min. drive north of Disneyland. OCTD bus #43 runs up and down Harbor Blvd. to Disneyland, and the hostel managers can arrange car rentals for groups. A white stucco house with a porch swing on an old dairy farm. The house is set back from Harbor Blvd. on a hill with a poorly marked driveway. Separate-sex accommodations can house a total of 15. Kitchen, laundry. 3-day max. stay. Open daily 7:30-9:30am and 4-11pm. Members $13.20, nonmembers $16.20. Linen $1. Reserve one week in advance by mail, and include first night's fee.

Motel 6, 2 Anaheim locations: 921 S. Beach Blvd. (220-2866), and 7450 Katella Ave. (891-0717), both within a 10-min. drive of Disneyland. The excitement of the nearby amusement park permeates the motels osmotically; both have pools and are filled with couples and their hyperactive, Mickey Mouse-eared children. Not the place to stay if you're seeking peace and quiet. Singles $30-33. Doubles $37-40. Cheaper rates in winter.

Mesa Motel,415 N. Newport Blvd. (646-3893). Half a mile to the beach. Small swimming pool, TV, and typical motel rooms. Single $32, Double $36.

Bay Cliff Motel, 455 N. Newport Blvd. (646-2104). Heated pool, color TV. Rooms the same as the Mesa Motel. Singles $33.50. Doubles $37.

There are state beaches in Orange County with campgrounds, listed below from north to south. Reservations are required for all sites except the Echo Arch Area in San Onofre, which is first come first served. Reservations can be made through MISTIX (800-444-7275) a maximum of 56 days in advance, and should be made as soon as possible in the summer.

Bolsa Chica, Rte. 1 (848-1566), 3 mi. west of Huntington Beach. Self-contained vehicles only. 14-day maximum. $14 per vehicle, $12 for senior citizens.

Doheny, Rte. 1 (496-6771), at the south end of Dana Point. Beachside location turns this place into a zoo as suburban families howl out. TVs, lounge furniture, play pens, and more. Beachfront sites $21, otherwise $16.

San Clemente, I-5 (492-3156). 157 sites, 85 developed. Sites $16. Richard Nixon sees you.

San Onofre, I-5 (492-0802), 3 mi. south of San Clemente. 221 campsites along an abandoned stretch of PCH; about 90 are suitable for tents. The **Echo Arch Area** has 34 more primitive hike-in sites between the bluffs and the beach. The San Mateo Campground is a brand new park with 140 sites and hot showers. These three areas are the most secluded, and the site of the most partying (though it's still fairly calm). Sites $16.

Sights

Among the architectural attractions in Orange County not blessed by Walt Disney is the **Crystal Cathedral,** 12141 Lewis St., Garden Grove. Opinions are split on this shining all-glass structure completed in 1980 by Phillip Johnson and John Burgee; some find it inspiring, others call it garish. It's from the pulpit of this church that Dr. Robert Schuller preaches his weekly TV show, "Hour of Power". With 7,000 people moving in and out every Sunday, the Cathedral is also a model of efficiency.

Inland Orange County is graced with a number of attractions, the newest of which is a tribute to everyone's favorite president, Richard Nixon. At **The Richard Nixon Library and Birthplace** you can "enjoy the first lady's garden" and engage in a video conversation with Dick himself. (18001 Yorba Linda Blvd., in Yorba Linda, 993-3393. Adults $3.95, seniors $2. Open daily 8:30am-5pm.)

Some inland events deserving examination are the **Strawberry Festival,** held every year in late May in downtown Garden Grove (638-0981). Garden Grove is the U.S.'s leading producer of strawberries, and the festival includes some arduous strawberry pie eating contests. Another alimentary celebration is the Anaheim Harvest Festival (800-321-1213), held in late November at the Anaheim Convention Center. Anaheim also sponsors the Orange County Fall Festival (999-5191) in late October.

Still, recreation and leisure time for residents and visitors of all ages revolves primarily around the ocean. The beaches are generally cleaner, less crowded, and more charming than those in L.A. County. While many of the county's inland cities fall prey to the problems (traffic, crime, etc.) that plague Los Angeles, the coastal towns offer wide beaches and blue skies.

Huntington Beach served as a port of entry for the surfing craze, which transformed California coast life after being imported from Hawaii by Duke Kahanamoku in the early 1900s. Still popular, the sport culminates each year in the **surfing championships** held in late July (536-5486). If the surfing championship isn't in town, the best reason to stay in Huntington Beach is the Colonial Inn Youth Hostel (see Accommodations). Most locals actually head to 2nd St. in Long Beach for nightlife. The carless amuse themselves with beach barbecues or by drinking themselves silly at **Perq's** night club (117 Main St., 960-9996, open daily 11am-1:30pm). Sophisticates wine and dine at **Mazzoti's Ristorante Italiano** (412 Walnut St., 536-8300; open daily 11am-11pm), which sports a full bar and a filling menu (prices ranging from $2.25 for a soup or salad to $15 for Linguini Fruita di Mare).

Newport Beach and the surrounding cities inland are the jewels of Orange County with stunning multi-million dollar homes lining Newport Harbor, the largest leisure craft harbor in the world. Newport Harbor is also the sight of **Newport SeaFest Week** (644-8211), held in late September, and the Christmas Boat Parade of Lights (644-8211), which includes over 200 boats and takes place every night the week before Christmas. The beach itself displays few signs of ostentatious wealth; it is crowded with young, frequently rowdy, hedonists in neon-colored bikinis and trunks. The area around Newport Pier is a haven for families; the streets from 30th to 56th give way to teenagers and college students sunning, surfing, and playing volleyball. The boardwalk is always a scene in the summer, with beach house renters partying wildly on their porches, especially as their leases expire.

The sands of Newport Beach run south onto the **Balboa Peninsula,** separated from the mainland by Newport Bay. The **Lido Marina Village,** at the base of the peninsula, offers shopping at the water's edge, and the **Edwards Lido Theater,** (673-8350) on Newport Blvd., specialises in first-run art films. The peninsula itself is only 2 to 4 blocks wide and can be reached from PCH by Balboa Blvd. Several nightspots popular with the disposable-income set reside at the foot of Newport Pier, between 20th and 21st St. **The Crab Cooker,** 2200 Newport Blvd. (673-0100), offers the "world's best seafood," with dinner plates (including rice and potatoes) mostly under $10. (Open Mon.-Sat. 11am-10pm.) Ocean Front Walk extends the length of the peninsula, affording glimpses into the parlors of beach homes whose residents exchange privacy for picture windows on the Pacific. At the end of the peninsula, **The Wedge,** seasonally pounded by waves up to 20 ft. generated by storms off Mexico, is a bodysurfing mecca. Bodysurfers (ostensibly furloughed from mental institutions) risk a watery grave for a monster ride. Sit on the roof and munch while you enjoy a panoramic view of the beach and ocean at **Ruby's Café** (675-7829), a malt shop right on Balboa Pier (675-7829). Although the prices won't take you back to World War II, they won't take you to the cleaners either—$7 gets you a burger, fries, and a malt. (Open Mon.-Fri. 8am-10pm, Sat.-Sun. 7am-10pm.)

Melt into the crowds on Newport Beach and the Balboa Peninsula by hopping on a bicycle or strapping on a pair of rollerskates. Expensive rental shops cluster around the Newport Beach pier and at the end of the peninsula. Bike rentals cost in the range of $4-5 per hour, $18-20 per day. Skates are $3-6 per hour, $15-18 per day. Boogie boards $6-7 per day.

Once you have reached the end of the peninsula, from the harbor side you can see **Balboa Island,** largest of the three islands sheltered by the peninsula. The island is freckled with chic eateries, boutiques, and bikini shops, and a vintage **ferryboat** (673-1070) will take you there from the peninsula. (24 hours; in winter daily 6am-midnight. Car and driver 65¢, additional passengers 25¢, children 10¢.) Balboa Island can be reached from PCH by a bridge on Jamboree Rd.

North of Newport Beach is **Costa Mesa,** home of the new and dazzling **Orange County Performing Arts Center,** 600 Town Center Dr. (556-2121), on Bristol St. off I-405. The opulent, 3000-seat structure was constructed in 1986 at a cost of $70 million and has enlivened Orange County arts by hosting the American Ballet Theatre and the Kirov Ballet, among other troupes. The several square blocks around the Performing Arts Center hold various modern sculptures and outdoor set installations, including Isamu Noguchi's *California Scenario.* This massive and dramatic sculpture garden is located in the bank complex framed by Anton Blvd., Ave. of the Arts, and I-405. A map and guide to the exhibits can be acquired at the information booth inside the posh **South Coast Plaza Mall,** located at 3333 Bristol St. off I-405, across from the Performing Arts Center.

Every weekend in Costa Mesa, the **Orange County Market Place,** containing 1500 booths, takes place at the Orange County Fair Grounds (open 7am-4pm; admission 50¢). In 1992, the Fair Grounds also host **Scottish Festival** (202-8845).

Back along the coast, **Laguna Beach** reclines in a canyon 4 mi. south of Newport. Back in the old days, Laguna was a bohemian artists' colony, but no properly starving artists can afford to live here now. The surviving galleries and art supply stores nevertheless add a unique twist to the standard SoCal beach culture that thrives on Laguna's sands. Punctuated by rocky cliffs, coves, and lush hillside vegetation, the town is decidedly tropical in character. **Main Beach** and the shops nearby are the prime parading areas, though there are other, less-crowded spots as well. One accessible beach (popular with gay people) is Westry Beach, which spreads out south of Laguna just below Aliso Beach Park. Park on PCH or residential streets to the east and look for Public Access signs between private properties. The park itself is the source and site of numerous late-night rendvouzes.

A quartet of quasi-art-festivals in July and August helps preserve Laguna's "art colony" reputation. The **Festival of Arts** and the **Pageant of the Masters** take place together in the Irvine Bowl, 650 Laguna Canyon Rd. (494-1145). Life literally imitates art in the Pageant as residents who have rehearsed for months don the makeup and costumes of figures in famous paintings and then pose for 90-second tableaux, astonishingly similar to the original artwork. (Art show open daily 10am-11:30pm. Tickets, usually available into July, are $12-30. Admission to the art show alone adults $2, seniors $1, under 12 free.) If the show is sold out, ask about cancellations on the day you wish to go. Pageant takes place nightly at 8:30pm. Both the pageant and the Festival run from the second week of July to the last week of August.

The **Sawdust Festival** (494-3030), also held from early July through August, is now more of a flea market than an art festival. It was begun on a bit of ground on Laguna Canyon Rd. in 1966 as a hippie alternative to the aging and staid pageant. Exhibitors build ramshackle studios every year, selling their wares and entertaining passersby. (Open Sun.-Thurs. 10am-10pm, Fri.-Sat. 10am-11pm. Admission $4, seniors and students $3, under 12 free.) The **Laguna Beach Winter Festival** (494-1018), a small art festival in February, rounds out the region's art celebrations.

Parking during the festivals is a challenge. A free shuttle operates between a parking lot farther up Laguna Canyon Rd. and the festival site. To keep your car out of harm's way, consider parking it at Fashion Island, the huge shopping center in Newport Beach (Newport Center Dr. between MacArthur and Jamboree) and taking OCTD bus #97 to Laguna.

Laguna Beach's more permanent art work is displayed at the **Laguna Beach Museum of Art,** 307 Cliff Dr. (494-6531), which houses recent works by important Southern California artists as well as an excellent collection of early 20th-century Southern California Impressionist works. (Open Tues.-Sun. 11am-5pm. Admission $2, seniors and students $1, children under 12 free. Docent tours available Tues.-Wed. and Sun. at 2pm.)

More tourists than swallows return every year to **Mission San Juan Capistrano** (493-1424), 3 mi. inland of Dana Point at the junction of Camino Capistrano and Del Obispo Rd. This "jewel of the missions" offers a peek at California's origins as a Spanish colony. Established in 1776 as one of 21 California missions of the Catholic church, it is somewhat run-down today due to an 1812 earthquake. Father Junipéro Serra, the mission's founder, officiated from inside the beautiful **Serra Chapel,** the oldest building in the state (1777). The chapel is dark and womb-like, warmed by the 17th-century Spanish cherrywood altar and the Native American designs painted on walls and ceiling. It's still used by the Catholic Church, so enter quietly and inhale the scent of beeswax candles lit by worshipers. (Open daily 8:30am-7pm; October 1-May 14 8:30am-5pm. Admission $3, ages 6-11 $1.50.)

The mission is perhaps best known as a home to the thousands of swallows who return here from their winter migration each year to nest in mid-March. They are scheduled to return to Capistrano on St. Joseph's Day, March 19, but the birds aren't all that religious, and have a tendency to show up whenever there aren't busloads of tourists hanging around. The swallows leave on October 23. The best time to see the birds is when they feed in the early morning or early evening.

The **San Onofre Nuclear Power Plant** helps give San Onofre State Beach the warmest water in Southern California. The twin domes of the power plant loom ominously over I-5 south of San Clemente. The marine base of **Camp Pendleton** stands at attention next door, lending this part of the coast a less than happy-go-lucky feel. Nevertheless, **San Onofre State Beach** is a prime surfing area where dozens of wave-riders test the break at any given time. The southern end of the beach is frequented by nudists who would presumably be ill-protected should the plant ever malfunction (drive down as far as you can go, and walk left on the trail for ¼ to ½ mile; beach contains both a gay and a straight area). Be forewarned—nude bathing is illegal, and you'll be fined if you're caught with your pants down. For information on the coast farther south, see Near San Diego.

Disneyland

The recent growth of Mike Eisner's Disney empire, with its exclusive Disney cable-TV channel, Touchstone movies, and new studio park in Florida, has breathed new life into the most famous, and still perhaps the best, amusement park in the world. Opened in 1955 through the vision of Walt Disney, "The Happiest Place On Earth" has delighted even the most hardened cynics. Soviet premier Nikita Kruschev was livid when Walt himself barred him from the park at the height of the cold war.

The attractions are inspired testaments to the charm of child-like creativity, but the technological sophistication of the various amusements is no child's play. True, all this otherworldliness gets disturbing at times, especially with crowds of 75,000 per day jamming the park in search of artificial happiness, but one need only watch the kids in their euphoria to embrace Disney's magic.

Admission to the gleaming fantasy world is gained through the **Unlimited Use Passport** ($27.50, ages 3-11 $22.50). The A-E ticket system is now a relic (though if you have any old A-E tickets you can get refunds for them), and visitors have unrestricted entrance to any attraction. The park is open daily in summer from 8am-1am. In the off-season, the park ordinarily closes at 5pm, though hours vary, especially around major holidays; call 714-999-4000 for more information.

Getting There

The park is located at one of the most famous addresses in the world: 1313 Harbor Blvd., in Anaheim in Orange County, bounded by Katella Ave., Harbor Blvd., Ball Rd., and West St. From L.A. take **bus** #460 from 6th and Flower St. downtown, about 1½ hours to the Disneyland Hotel. (Service to the hotel from 4:53am, back to L.A. until 1:20am.) From the hotel take the free shuttle to Disneyland's portals. Also served by Airport Service, OCTD, Long Beach Transit, and Gray Line (see Public Transportation for prices). If you're **driving,** take the Santa Ana Fwy. to the Katella Ave. exit. Be forewarned, however: while parking in the morning should be painless, leaving in the evening often will not be. In addition, when the park closes early, Disneygoers must contend with L.A.'s maddening, rush-hour traffic.

In the Park

Visitors enter the Magic Kingdom by way of **Main Street, U.S.A.** a collection of shops, arcades, and even a movie theater, designed to look like Walt's turn-of-the-century childhood memories. Main street lines a broad avenue leading to a replica of Sleeping Beauty's castle at the center of the park. There's also a bank, an information booth, lockers, and a first aid station. It is down Main Street that the **Main Street Electrical Parade** makes its way each summer night at 8:45pm and 11pm (the earlier parade is followed by fireworks). Floats and even humans are adorned with thousands of multi-colored lights, making for a shocking nighttime display. This is one of Disneyland's most popular events and people begin lining the sidewalks on Main Street by 7pm for a front-row view.

Four "lands" branch off of Main Street. **Tomorrowland,** to your immediate right at the top of Main Street, contains the park's best thrill rides, **Space Mountain** and the George Lucas-produced **Star Tours.** Moving counter-clockwise around the park, next is **Fantasyland,** with the **Matterhorn** rollercoaster, some excellent rides for children, and the ever-popular **It's A Small World** (a hint: unless you want the cute, but annoying, theme song running through your head for the rest of the day, you may want to save this one for last). Next is **Frontierland,** with the **Thunder Mountain Railroad** coaster and **Tom Sawyer Island.** Last, but not least, is **Adventureland,** with the **Jungle Cruise** and the **Swiss Family Robinson Treehouse.** In addition, tucked between Frontierland and Adventureland are two more areas that aren't official "lands." One is **New Orleans Square,** with **Pirates of the Caribbean,** the **Haunted Mansion,** and some excellent dining. The other is **Critter Country,** with Disneyland's latest super-attraction, **Splash Mountain,** a log ride that climaxes in a wet, 5-story drop. Ask about **Hell's Angelrama,** due to open next year. (Just kidding. . .)

Food services in the park ranges from sit-down establishments to fast-food eateries such as the Lunch Pad. You can save much time and money by packing a picnic lunch and eating a big breakfast before you leave home. Food in the park is mediocre and generally overpriced. If you're looking for a martini, you'll be left high and dry: no alcohol is served in the Magic Kingdom.

No matter when you go, you'll probably feel as if every Huey, Dewey, and Louie has picked the same day to visit. Fall months and weekdays are generally less crowded than summer days and weekends. To avoid long waits, arrive shortly after the park opens. Lines for the most popular attractions are shorter just after opening and late at night; try mid-day and you'll see why some call it "Disneyline."

The Unofficial Guide to Disneyland ($8), one of the top ten best-selling travel guides in the United States and Canada, is available from Simon and Schuster, Attn.: Mail Order Dept., 200 Old Tappan Rd., Old Tappan, NJ 07675 (201-767-5937). The authors have earned their mouska-ears by cramming the book with time-saving hints. The guide evaluates every attraction in the park, and the researchers suggest several specific itineraries for visitors, including adults with young children, senior citizens, and those pressed for time.

Other Amusement Parks

Knott's Berry Farm, 8039 Beach Blvd. (714-220-5200 for a recording), at La Palma Ave. in Buena Park just 5 mi. northeast of Disneyland. Take the Santa Ana Fwy. south, exit west on La Palma Ave. Bus #460 stops here on its way to Disneyland. An actual berry farm in its early days, Knott's now cultivates a country fair atmosphere with a re-created ghost town, Fiesta Village, Roaring Twenties Park, rides, and a replica of Independence Hall. The insane rollercoaster Montezuma's Revenge takes you through a backwards loop. A few summers back, Knott's unveiled a $12 million project featuring a Kingdom of the Dinosaurs ride through prehistory and 3 new thrill rides. The Chicken Dinner Restaurant has been serving tender, inexpensive chicken dinners since 1934. Open Sun.-Fri. 9am-midnight, Sat. 9am-1am; in winter Mon.-Fri. 10am-6pm, Sat. 10am-10pm, Sun. 10am-7pm. Admission $22, seniors 60 and over $15, ages 3-11 $10.

Wild Rivers Waterpark, 8800 Irvine Center Dr., Laguna Hills (714-768-9453), in Orange County. Over 40 water-slide rides, 2 wave pools, and picnic areas. Open May-Sept. daily 10am-8pm, Sat.-Sun. 11am-5pm in Winter. Admission $16, ages 3-9 $12.

Los Angeles

When Art passed away in the spring of 1991 he had been selling Los Angeles's best chili dogs out of an unassuming wooden shack at the corner of Florence and Normandie Avenues for over sixty years. Unlike some of L.A.'s other chili dog purveyors, such as the ubiquitous Tommy's or Hollywood's glitzy Pink's, Art was perversely downscale; there was only one Art's, its walls were little more than plywood and its location, in the heart of southcentral L.A., was downright dangerous. Yet here was truly a diamond in the rough—in this tiny shack Art had developed a chili dog that approached perfection.

In Art and his story is captured the essence of Los Angeles, capital of the American West, leading economic center of the Pacific Rim, home of the American entertainment industry, and trendsetter to the world. In Art's chili dog we see much that is quintessentially L.A.: excess, gluttony, and, yes, even silliness. But in the story of a man coming West in the Depression and pursuing the American Dream, working every day into his nineties to make a living, we also see the reality behind L.A.'s "image is everything" façade. Beyond the Mercedes and Porsches on the freeways, the mammoth billboards of the Sunset Strip, and the living theater of the Venice boardwalk lies Real Life for the over ten million people who make their lives in the L.A. Basin.

Most of the issues confronting Los Angeles as the sprawling megalopolis speeds toward the millenium arise from the tension between the demands of excess and limitations of reality. The city's freeways are overcrowded to the point that rush hour ceases even to be a meaningful concept. Too late it seems, Los Angeles has embarked upon construction of a light rail system that will cost billions and will not be completed until well into the next century. Crime, drug trafficking, and gang warfare are a terrible problem. Life in Watts and southcentral L.A. seems to get worse by the day. It's not even clear who the good guys are anymore, as the 1991 controversy over the Rodney King beating and revelations of widespread racism in the L.A. Police Department demonstrated. And environmental concerns are omnipresent in the thick smog that Angelenos breathe and the scarce water they drink

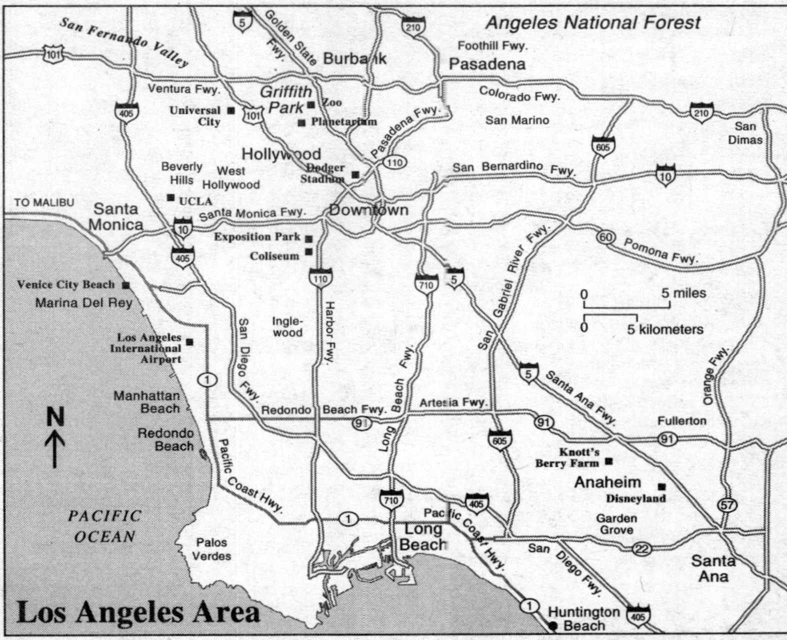

Los Angeles Area

and pour into their swimming pools (in the process depleting important natural resources in the rest of the state).

Still and all, L.A. keeps growing, proving repeatedly that if you build (and water) it, they will come. A drive into the far reaches of the L.A. Basin, to the Simi Valley, to San Bernardino, and even up Route 14 toward Lancaster and Palmdale and the Mojave Desert, reveals the wooden skeletons of new tract houses and the creeping tendrils of outer suburbia. Even Bakersfield, over 100 miles to the northwest plans for a light-rail connection to L.A. and anticipates the day when it's just another of the proverbial "suburbs in search of a city."

In the meantime, Real Life goes on in the midst of the oft-surreal landscape. There are traffic jams at 1am on the Harbor Freeway while film crews stage yet another Hollywood car chase. A West L.A. swimsuit store dresses its saleswomen in bikinis and high heels. The glitterati assemble at courtside for Laker games. And millions go to work and raise their kids and live and die. Nowhere else in the world do reality and fantasy mesh at once so seamlessly and so jarringly as they do in Los Angeles.

Practical Information

Visitors Information: Los Angeles Convention and Visitors Bureau, 685 S. Figueroa St. 90015 (213-689-8822), between Wilshire and 7th St. in the heart of the Financial District. Hundreds of brochures available. Staff speaks Spanish, Filipino, Japanese, French, and German. Good maps for downtown streets, sights, and buses. Publishes *Datelines* and *Artsline,* guides to Southern California events, 4 times per year. *Los Angeles Visitors Guide* and *Lodging Guide* are both free and available by mail (allow 3 weeks for delivery). Second location in Hollywood at 6541 Hollywood Blvd (213-461-4213). Open Mon.-Fri. 8am-5pm, Sat. 8:30am-5pm.

Council Travel: 1093 Broxton Ave., Westwood Village (310-208-3551), above the Wherehouse record store. Cheap flights, IYHF/AYH passes, ISIC cards. Open Mon.-Fri. 9am-5pm, Sat. 10am-2pm

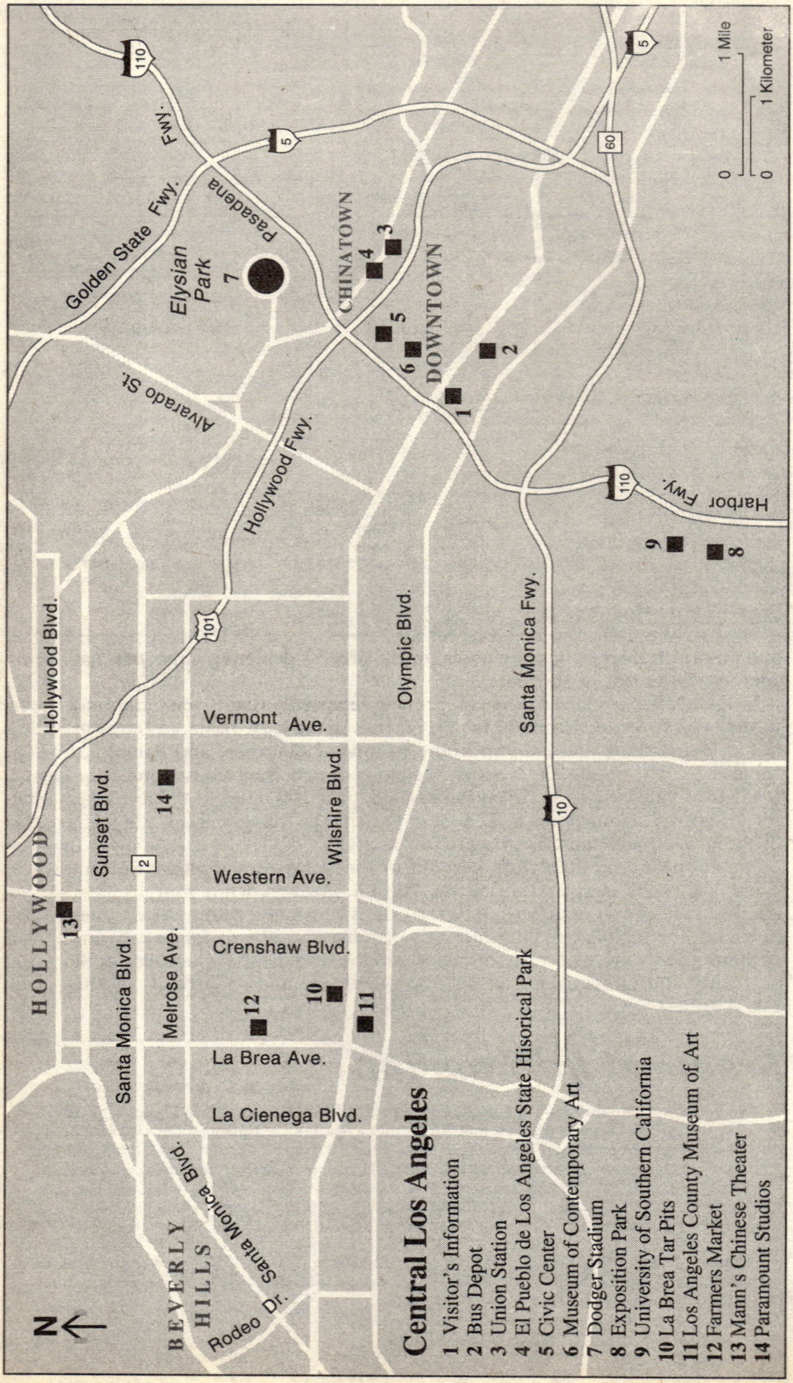
Central Los Angeles
1 Visitor's Information
2 Bus Depot
3 Union Station
4 El Pueblo de Los Angeles State Hisorical Park
5 Civic Center
6 Museum of Contemporary Art
7 Dodger Stadium
8 Exposition Park
9 University of Southern California
10 La Brea Tar Pits
11 Los Angeles County Museum of Art
12 Farmers Market
13 Mann's Chinese Theater
14 Paramount Studios
N
HOLLYWOOD
BEVERLY HILLS
CHINATOWN
DOWNTOWN
Elysian Park
Golden State Fwy.
Pasadena Fwy.
Alvarado St.
Hollywood Fwy.
Harbor Fwy.
Santa Monica Fwy.
Hollywood Blvd.
Sunset Blvd.
Santa Monica Blvd.
Melrose Ave.
Vermont Ave.
Western Ave.
Crenshaw Blvd.
La Brea Ave.
La Cienega Blvd.
Wilshire Blvd.
Olympic Blvd.
Santa Monica Blvd.
Rodeo Dr.
110
5
60
101
2
10
0 1 Mile
0 1 Kilometer

Los Angeles Council AYH: 1434 2nd St., Santa Monica (310-393-3413). Information and supplies for travelers. Guidebooks, low-cost flights, rail passes, and ISIC cards. Open Tues.-Sat. 10am-5pm.

Consulates: Britain, 3701 Wilshire Blvd. (213-385-7381). Open 9am-5pm for calls, hours vary by department for visits. **Japan,** 250 E. 1st St., #1401, (213-624-8305). Open Mon.-Fri. 9:30-11:30am and 1-4pm for calls.

Currency Exchange: at most LAX terminals. (See Getting There, By Plane .) Downtown at 445 S. Figueroa St. (213-236-6015), in the Union Bank Building between Figueroa and 5th St., on the 17th floor. No commission fee. Open Mon.-Fri. 9am-noon and 1-3pm.

American Express: 901 W. 7th St. (213-627-4800). Open Mon.-Fri. 8am-6pm. Locations in Beverly Hills (at the Beverly Center), Pasadena, Torrance and Costa Mesa. Open Sat. 10am-6pm at 8493 W W. 3rd St. (310-659-1682).

National Park Service: 30401 Agoura Rd., Agoura Hills (818-597-9192 for local parks Info Center; 818-597-1036 for other offices), in the San Fernando Valley. Information on the Santa Monica Mountains and other parks. Open Mon.-Sat. 8am-5pm.

Los Angeles County Parks and Recreation: 433 S. Vermont (213-738-2961). Open Mon.-Fri. 8am-5pm.

Sierra Club: 3550 W. 6th St., #321 (213-387-4287). Hiking, biking, and backpacking information. Open Mon.-Fri. 10am-6pm.

Los Angeles International Airport: see Getting There, By Plane.

Greyhound-Trailways Bus Information Center: 213-620-1200 for fares and schedules. 213-629-8400 for local ticket information.

RTD Bus Information Line: 213-626-4455. Customer Service Center at 5301 Wilshire Blvd. (310-972-6235; open Mon.-Fri. 8am-4:15pm).

Taxi: Checker Cab (213-482-3456), Independent (213-385-8294), United Independent (213-653-5050), Celebrity Red Top (213-934-6700). If you need a cab, it's best to call—cabbies don't search for fares on the streets.

Car/Bike Rentals: See Getting Around.

Automobile Club of Southern California: 2601 S. Figueroa St. (213-741-3111), in an impressive Spanish Colonial Revival building in Exposition Park. Lots of maps and information free to AAA members. Their *Westways* magazine is a good source of inspiration for daytrips or vacations. Open Mon.-Fri. 9am-5pm. 50 other offices in the Greater L.A. area. Call for locations.

Central Public Library: 433 S. Spring St. (213-612-3200) A Los Angeles address is required to check out books.

Los Angeles Parks and Recreation: 213-485-5515. Call for information on tennis, golf, and swimming.

Japanese-American Cultural and Community Center: 244 S. San Pedro St. (213-628-2725). Offers the Doizaki Gallery, Franklin G. Murphy Library, and a movie theater. Administration offices open Mon.-Fri. 9am-5pm. Call for hours of other facilities.

Jewish Community Center: 5870 W. Olympic Ave. (213-938-2531). Recreational facilities, senior citizens' services, day care, health club. Pool and gym open until about 9pm, other facilities 9am-5:30pm. One-day guest pass $5, but free if you are considering membership.

Gay and Lesbian Community Services Center: 1213 N. Highland Ave., Hollywood (213-464-7400), one block north of Santa Monica Blvd. Youth and senior groups, counseling, employment, housing, educational, legal and medical services. Open Mon.-Sat. 9am-10pm, but most offices close around 5pm.

Beach Information: 310-457-9701, recording for Malibu, Santa Monica, and South Bay. Most FM radio stations have a (you guessed it) surf report at noon.

Ticketron: 310-642-4242 for nearest location. Open Mon.-Sun. 9am-6pm..

Weather: 213-554-1212. An excruciatingly detailed region-by-region report.

Laundromat: Barachiah Laundromat, 200 E. Vernon St. (213-233-8029). Check the yellow pages for others.

National Gay Advocates Hotline: 800-526-5050.

AIDS Hotline: 800-922-2437. For recorded information, call 976-4700. There is a charge for this service.

Suicide Prevention: 213-381-5111. 24-hr. hotline.

Cocaine Anonymous: 310-839-1141. 24-hr. hotline.

Rape Crisis: 310-392-8381. 24-hr. hotline. Response service, 310-855-3506.

Battered Women's Assistance: 818-887-6589. 24-hr. hotline.

Alcoholics Anonymous: 767 S. Harvard Blvd. (213-387-8316). 24-hr. hotline. Office open Mon.-Fri. 8am-7:30pm, Sat.-Sun. and holidays 9am-4:30pm.

Committee for the Rights of the Disabled: 2882 S. Robertson Blvd. (213-731-8591). Open Mon.-Fri. 8am-4:30pm. Call for appointment.

Legal Aid: 1550 W. 8th St., (213-487-3320). Open Mon.-Fri. 9am-5pm.

Accommodations Crisis: The L.A. County Department of Public and Social Services offers 24-hr. assistance for those with no money through its "Info Line" (800-339-6993). Be prepared to wait; Info Line's operators are often busy.

Senior Citizens Information: Area Agency on Aging, 1102 S. Crenshaw Blvd. (213-857-6411). Open Mon.-Fri. 8am-5pm.

24-Hour Pharmacy: Kaiser Pharmacy operates two pharmacies, one of which is always open.

Planned Parenthood: 1057 Kingston St. (213-226-0247), near downtown. Abortions, birth control, pre-natal care, treatment of sexually transmitted diseases. Call one week in advance for appointment. Open Mon.-Fri. 9am-5pm. Call for other locations.

Hollywood-Sunset Free Clinic: 3324 W. Sunset Blvd. (213-660-2400). Open every day 10am-10pm.

Valley Free Clinic: 5648 Vineland, Hollywood (818-763-8836). Women's health, birth control, optometry, medical and legal counseling, drug "diversion" services. Hours vary by service; appointments required and can only be made by phone on Mon., Wed., and Fri. 10am-11:30am.

Emergency: Dial 911 for fire, police, ambulance.

Hospitals: Good Samaritan, 616 Witmer (213-977-2121). **Cedars-Sinai Medical Center,** 8700 Beverly Blvd. (310-855-5000, emergency 310-855-6517).

Ambulance: Los Angeles City Ambulance Emergency Service (213-483-6721).

Police: 213-626-5273.

Fire: 213-483-6721.

Post Office: Main office at Florence Station, 7001 S. Central Ave. (213-586-1723). Information on rates and schedules, 213-586-1467. ZIP Code information, 213-586-1737. General Delivery, 900 N. Alameda (213-617-4543), at 9th St. General Delivery ZIP Code: 90055.

Area Codes: Downtown Los Angeles, Hollywood, Huntington Park, Vernon and Montebello **213,** Malibu, Pacific Coast Highway, Westside, southern and eastern Los Angeles County **310,** northern Los Angeles County, including San Fernando Valley and Pasadena **818,** Orange County **714,** San Diego County **619,** Ventura County **805. A note to our readers:** On November 2, 1991, Pacific Bell carried out a split of Los Angeles' 213 area code, into 213 and the new 310 area code. *Let's Go* has incorporated these changes into our copy. In the past Los Angeles numbers listed with no area code were assumed to be 213; this year *Let's Go* lists all L.A. area numbers with their full area code, so as to minimize confusion due to the 213/310 split. Rates for calls between the 213 and 310 area codes will be the same as the old rates for calls within the 213 area.

Hollywood

Visitors Information: The Janes House, 6541 Hollywood Blvd. (213-461-4213), in Janes House Sq. Provides L.A. visitor guides. Open Mon.-Sat. 9am-5pm.

Hollywood Chamber of Commerce, 6255 W. Sunset Blvd., #911 (213-469-8311).

RTD Customer Service Center: 6249 Hollywood Blvd. (213-972-6000). Free information, maps, timetables, and passes. Open Mon.-Fri. 10am-6pm. **Important buses:** #1 along Hollywood Blvd., #2 and 3 along Sunset Blvd., #4 along Santa Monica Blvd., #10 along Melrose.

Greyhound: 1409 N. Vine St. (213-466-6381), 1 block south of Sunset Blvd. To: Santa Barbara (5 per day, $13); San Diego (14 per day, $11); San Francisco (9 per day, $40). Terminal open daily 7:30am-11pm.

Hospital: Queen of Angels Hollywood Presbyterian Medical Center, 1300 N. Vermont (213-413-3000). 24-hr. emergency room.

Police: 1358 N. Wilcox (213-485-4302).

Post Office: 1615 Wilcox Ave. (213-464-2194). Open Mon.-Fri. 8am-5pm, Sat. 8am-1pm. General Delivery ZIP Code: 90028

Area Code: 213.

Santa Monica

Visitor Information: 1400 Ocean Ave. (310-393-7593), in Palisades Park. Local maps, brochures, and information on attractions and events. Open daily 10am-5pm; in winter 10am-4pm.

Santa Monica Municipal (Big Blue) Bus Lines: 1660 7th St. (310-451-5445), at Olympic. Open Mon.-Fri. 8am-5pm. Bus #10 provides express service between downtown L.A. and downtown Santa Monica for $1.25 (faster than RTD—but then again, so is walking). Pick it up on 7th and Grand. Buses #1 and 2 run between Santa Monica and Venice and are free with a transfer from the #10; otherwise fare 50¢.

Greyhound: 1433 5th St. (310-395-1708), between Broadway and Santa Monica Blvd. Open Mon.-Fri. 8:30am-5:30pm. To: Santa Barbara (3 per day, 2½ hr., $12.70); San Diego (3 per day, 4½ hr., $19.50); San Francisco (2 per day, 11 hr., $51.20).

Parking: 3 hr. free in municipal structures 7 and 8 on 2nd St. All other city parking (including street parking) is metered (25¢ per hr.). All-day beachside parking $5.

Surfboard Rental: Natural Progression Surfboards, 22935½ W. Pacific Hwy., Malibu (310-456-6302). Boards $20 per day, plus $5 insurance. Wetsuits $8. Also windsurfer rental ($50 per day, plus $5 insurance), and lessons. Open daily 9am-6pm.

Laundromat: Laundrymate, 2627 Lincoln Blvd. (310-452-9724), just south of Ocean Park Blvd.

Hospital: St. John's, 1328 22nd St. (310-829-5511), at Arizona St.

Police: 1685 Main St. (310-395-9931).

Post Office: 5th and Arizona (310-576-2626). Open Mon.-Fri. 9am-5pm, Sat. 9am-1pm.

Area Code: 310.

Pasadena

Visitors Information: Convention and Visitors Bureau, 171 S. Los Robles Ave. (818-795-9311), across from the Hilton Hotel. Open Mon.-Fri. 9am-5pm, Sat. 10am-4pm.

Greyhound: 645 E. Walnut (818-792-5116). Open Mon.-Fri. 8:30am-5:30pm, Sat. 8:30am-3pm, Sun. 9am-3pm. To: Santa Barbara (3 per day, 2½ hr., $11.75); San Diego (3 per day, 4hr., $16); San Francisco (2 per day, 11 hr., $45).

Hospital: Huntington Memorial, 100 California Blvd. (818-397-5000), 1 block south of California Blvd. between Fair Oaks and Orange Grove Blvd. Legendary birthplace of TRW and JPW.

Police: 207 N. Garfield Ave. (818-405-4501).

Post Office: 600 N. Lincoln (818-304-7122), at Orange. Open Mon. and Fri. 8am-6pm; Tues.-Thurs. 8am-5pm; Sat. 9am-2pm. General Delivery ZIP Code: 91109.

Area Code: 818.

Publications

As you might suspect in a town where "image is everything", the printed word isn't L.A.'s strong point. Still, L.A. papers and magazines do exist, and are occasionally read.

If you're interested in Entertainment, the *L.A. Weekly* (213-667-2620) is worth two or three of your less important body parts; happily, it won't cost you anything at all. With bizarre personals and countless beauty improvement ads, the Weekly also makes a better souvenir than a Dodger glove. Weeklys come out on Thursday and disappear by Saturday. *The Reader* is the Weekly's smaller competitor.

The *Los Angeles Times* defeats all rival dailies with top reporting and a wonderful crossword; only the *San Fernando Daily News* has managed to survive, because it doubles as a local paper for the Valley. The *L.A. Times'* "Calendar" section is a good source of accurate and up-to-date dope about what's going on where. Check out the "L.A. Life" section of Friday's *Daily News* when planning your weekend.

Most areas in L.A. have smaller papers describing local news and events. Long Beach's *Dress Telegram* is the largest of these. *The Goodlife* is a small throwaway serving Marina Del Ray. The daily *Santa Monica Evening Outlook* serves the west-side and beach areas. The *San Gabriel Valley Tribune* is a daily serving (you guessed it) the San Gabriel Valley. Beverly Hills is graced with a number of throwaways (*213, The Courier, The Independent*) mostly discussing local gossip. *The Los Angeles Sentinel* is L.A.'s largest African American paper. *The Daily Bruin* is UCLA's student paper.

L.A., of course, has a number of "industry" papers, with the best-known being *Variety. The Hollywood Reporter* is the next best.

A multinational city, L.A. also has numerous foreign language papers. The Spanish *La Opinion* is the largest, but two Korean papers (*The Korean Central Daily,* and *The Korean Times*) are also among L.A.'s 10 largest periodicals. The *International Daily News* serves the Chinese-speaking community.

Weather

Angelenos enjoy mild winters and bright, dry summers. From April through October, temperatures are in the upper 70s and 80s, and they linger in the higher 50s and 60s the rest of the year, with only occasional rain (usually Nov.-March). Poor air quality, however, plagues the city. On especially smoggy days, ozone readings are often two-and-a-half times higher than federal standards, and the air quality in many places is sub-standard on more than 100 days of the year. L.A.'s own majestic geography intensifies the pollution as the surrounding mountains trap lingering pollutants within the Los Angeles basin and inland valleys. The smog is worst in industrial areas and in the inland valleys; the coastal areas are relatively smog-free. While the smog is noticeable to visitors and unhealthy for all, most residents have grown used to it. If you are fortunate enough to catch this city on one of its rare clear days, with its breathtaking vistas of snow-capped peaks on one side and the ocean on the other, you may understand what brought so many people here in the first place. **Weather information** is 213-554-1212. **Air quality information** is 800-242-4666.

Orientation

Getting There

Los Angeles sprawls along the coast of Southern California, 127 mi. north of San Diego and 403 mi. south of San Francisco. You can still be "in" L.A. even if you're 50 mi. from downtown. Greater L.A. encompasses the urbanized areas of Orange, Riverside, San Bernadino, and Ventura counties.

By Car

General approaches to Greater L.A. are I-5 from the south, California Highway 1, US 101, or I-5 from the north, and I-10 or I-15 from the east. The city itself is crisscrossed by over a dozen freeways. Driving into L.A. can be unnerving if you've never before run the gauntlet of ramps, exits, and four-story directional signs.

By Train and Bus

Amtrak pulls into Union Station, 800 N. Alameda (213-624-0171), at the northwestern edge of the heart of downtown Los Angeles. Once the end of the line for westbound rail passengers from all over the U.S., this gloriously designed Spanish colonial revival building is now sadly deserted. Buses travel out of the station to Pasadena and Longbeach; information about their schedules can be obtained upon arrival at the station.

Visitors arriving by **Greyhound** will disembark at 208 E. 6th St. (213-620-1200), at Los Angeles St. downtown, in a rough neighborhood near Skid Row. Greyhound also stops in Hollywood, Santa Monica, Pasadena, and other parts of the metropolitan area (see Practical Information). RTD buses #320 and 20 stop on 7th and Hill St., 2 blocks southwest of the downtown station, and carry passengers westward along Wilshire Blvd. Bus #1 stops at 5th and Broadway, 4 blocks to the west and one block north, and travels westward along Hollywood Blvd.

By Plane

In preparation for the 1984 Olympics, the **Los Angeles International Airport (LAX)** was renovated at a cost of $700 million. The result is an airport that efficiently processes the third largest passenger volume in the world.

LAX is divided into two levels, the upper serving departures and the lower, arrivals. Nine contiguous terminals are arranged in a large horseshoe, with Terminal 2 serving international carriers.

The airport complex is located in Westchester, about 15 mi. southwest of downtown, 10 mi. southeast of Santa Monica, and 1 mi. east of the coast.

Many car rental agencies run shuttle buses directly from the airport to their lots (see Cars). Other ways to reach town include cabs and **public transportation.** All Rapid Transit District (RTD) service to and from the airport stops at the **transfer terminal** at Vicksburg Ave. and 96th St. To get downtown, take bus #439 (Mon.-Fri. rush hr. only) or #42 from the transfer terminal. Bus #42 operates daily from 5:30am to 11:15pm, from downtown daily 5:45am to 12:10am. To get to UCLA, take express #560; to Long Beach, #232; to West Hollywood and Beverly Hills, #220. From West Hollywood to Hollywood, take bus #1 (along Hollywood Blvd.), 2 (along Sunset Blvd.), or 4 (along Santa Monica Blvd.).

Metered cabs are costly: $1.95 initially and $1.60 per mile. Checker Cab (213-482-3456) fare from the airport to downtown is about $24, to Hollywood $28, and to Disneyland a goofy $85.

A final option—more expensive than the RTD but cheaper than a cab—is one of the many shuttle vans which offer door-to-door service from the terminal to different parts of L.A. for a flat rate. The vans pick up outside of baggage claim areas and can be called from the terminal on courtesy phones (see below).

For specific information regarding RTD buses, cabs, and shuttles, ask at the information kiosks located on the sidewalks directly in front of the terminals.

LAX INFO: 310-646-5252.

Travelers Aid: 310-646-2270. All terminals. Information and referral service for people in transit having major emergencies. Open Mon.-Fri. 8:30am-5pm. All stations have extensive printed information. There is a recording when stations are closed.

Currency Exchange: L.A. Currency Agencies (310-417-0366) in terminals 2 and 5, and in the international terminal (7am-11pm).

Airport Security: 310-646-4268. 24 hrs.

Rapid Transit District Information: courtesy phones in most terminals.

Super Shuttle: 310-338-1111. Service to all parts of L.A. Santa Monica ($13), downtown ($11), and San Fernando Valley ($22). Reservations necessary only for trips to the airport; for trips from LAX, just pick up a terminal courtesy phone. Reservations to the airport should be made one day in advance. Open 24 hours. Price drops with each additional passenger.

Coast Shuttle: 310-417-3988. Service to Santa Monica ($12), downtown ($10), and San Fernando Valley ($30). Reservations to the airport should be made 4 or 5 hours in advance. Each additional passenger is about half price.

Getting Out

To reach Los Angeles International Airport (LAX) by car from downtown take I-10 west to I-405 south and get off at Century Blvd. heading west. There is no dearth of parking at the airport. Lots near the central terminal cost $3 for the first hour, $1 each hour thereafter, up to a maximum of $16. To avoid hassle on busier days, park in the aptly named "remote" lots at the airport's eastern edge and take the free tram to the terminals. Lot C sits at Sepulveda and 96th St. ($7 per day), lot B at La Cienaga and 11th St. ($5 per day). These lots are also used for long-term parking. Disabled travelers needing assistance should park in Lot C and call 310-646-6402 for a van.

LAX can be reached by bus from downtown on the #42, from UCLA express #560, from Long Beach #232, and from West Hollywood and Beverly Hills #220. At the airport, the "A" tram makes frequent free trips between terminals. Special flight bargains to San Francisco are offered by many airlines.

Those seeking or offering rides out of L.A. should consult the **rideboard** at UCLA's Ackerman Union. (For directions to the Union, see Getting Around, Cars.)

Amtrak: Union Station, 800 N. Alameda (213-624-0171), downtown. To San Francisco (once per day, 11 hr., $74), and San Diego (8 per day, 3 hr., $24) with stops in San Juan Capistrano, San Clemente, Oceanside, and Del Mar.

Greyhound: 208 E. 6th St. (213-620-1200), downtown terminal. To: San Diego (about once an hour 12:25am-9:15pm, 2½-3½ hr., $11); Tijuana (once an hour 2:40am-9:15pm, 3½-4½ hr., $17 one way, $26 round trip); Santa Barbara (11 per day, 2-3½ hr., $12.50 one way, $21 round trip); San Francisco (14 per day, 8½-12½ hr., $40 one way). Greyhound sometimes offers special deals for advance purchases.

Green Tortoise: 310-392-1990, 415-285-2441 in San Francisco. These northbound "hostels on wheels" leave L.A. every Sun. night with stops in Venice, Hollywood, and downtown. They arrive in San Francisco ($30) on Mon. morning, Eugene and Portland, Oregon ($69) on Tues. afternoon, and Seattle ($79) on Tues. night. Call for reservations and exact departure location and times. (See Getting There in the General Introduction for more information on tours.)

Getting Around

Before you even think about navigating Los Angeles's 6500 miles of streets and 40,000 intersections, get yourself a good map; centerless Los Angeles defies all human comprehension otherwise. The best investment you can make is the *Thomas Guide Los Angeles County Street Guide and Directory.* It's definitely worth the $14 price tag for stays of longer than a week.

A legitimate **downtown** Los Angeles does exist, but this area is merely a conceptual construct to explain where all the "suburbs in search of a city" lie. Immediately east of downtown are the vibrant Latino districts of Boyle Heights, Montebello, and El Monte; to the south is the University of Southern California (USC), Exposition Park, and Watts; farther south on Rte. 11 is Long Beach.

Los Angeles is a city of distinctive boulevards; its shopping areas and business centers are distributed along these broad arteries. Streets throughout L.A. are designated east, west, north, and south from First and Main St. at the center of downtown.

L.A.'s east-west thoroughfares are the most prominent; use them to get your bearings. Beginning with the northernmost, they are Melrose Avenue and Beverly, Wilshire, Olympic, Pico, Venice, and Washington Boulevards. (Melrose is filled with boutiques, galleries, and trendy night spots, Wilshire is studded with large department stores and office buildings; Olympic is residential and the least congested.) The important north-south streets of this huge grid, from downtown westward, are Vermont, Normandie, and Western Avenues, Vine Street, Highland, La Brea, and Fairfax Avenues, and La Cienega and Robertson Boulevards.

The area west of downtown is known as the **Wilshire District** after its main boulevard. Wilshire is built up in a continuous wall of tall buildings (called the "Miracle Mile") with bungalows and duplexes huddled in the skyscrapers' shadows. **Hancock Park,** a green park and affluent residential area covers the northeast portion of the district, on the 5900 block, and harbors the Los Angeles County Museum of Art and the George C. Page Fossil Museum.

North of the Wilshire District is **Hollywood.** The next major east-west boulevard north of Melrose is Santa Monica, and north of that is Sunset Boulevard. This street, which runs from the ocean to downtown, presents a cross-section of virtually everything L.A. has to offer: beach communities, lavish wealth, famous nightclubs along "the strip," sleazy motels, the old elegance of Silver Lake, and Chicano murals. Farther north is Hollywood Boulevard, running just beneath the Hollywood Hills, where split-level buildings perched precariously on hillsides house screenwriters, actors, and producers.

Regal **Beverly Hills,** an independent city geographically swallowed by L.A., lies west of the Wilshire District and east of **Westwood,** home to UCLA and its lively college village. Farther west, across the San Diego Freeway, **Santa Monica** strings its wide and crowded beaches along the ocean. Just south is the wild beach community of **Venice.**

North of the Hollywood Hills and the Santa Monica Mountains stretches the **San Fernando Valley.** Like, one-and-a-quarter million dudes and dudettes inhabit this "rad" basin bounded in the north and west by the Santa Susanna Mountains and the Simi Freeway, in the south by the Ventura Freeway, and to the east by the Golden State Freeway.

Eighty miles of beach line L.A.'s coast. **Zuma** is northernmost, followed by **Malibu,** 15 mi. up the coast from Santa Monica. The beach towns south of Santa Monica and Venice, comprising the area called the **South Bay,** are Marina del Rey, El Segundo (with the airport and somebody's wallet just inland there), and Manhattan, Hermosa, and Redondo Beaches. The coast bulges south of Redondo Beach to form the **Palos Verdes Peninsula.** Beyond the peninsula the coast turns east again. **San Pedro,** is both the terminus of the Harbor Freeway and the point of departure for **Catalina Island.** East of San Pedro is **Long Beach,** a port city of a half-million people. Finally, farthest south are the **Orange County** beach cities: Seal Beach, Sunset Beach, Huntington Beach, Newport Beach, and Laguna Beach. Confused yet? Invest in a good map, and sleep with it under your pillow.

Once the sun sets, those on foot outside West L.A. and off well-lit main drags should exercise caution. Women should not walk alone *anywhere* after dark. Hollywood and the downtown area, east of Western Ave., are considered particularly crime-ridden. Gang- and drug-related crimes have increasingly threatened public safety. Whether walking, riding, or driving, know (or at least pretend like you know) where you are and where you are going, and avoid any questionable areas.

Public Transportation

Nowhere in America is the great god of Automobile held in greater reverence than in L.A. Most Angelenos will insist that it's impossible to live in or visit Los Angeles without a car, but the **Southern California Rapid Transit District (RTD)** does work—sort of. With over 200 routes and several independent municipal transit systems complementing RTD, you may need an extra day just to study timetables. Using the RTD to sightsee in L.A. can be frustrating simply because attractions tend to be spread out. While RTD buses do carry 1 million passengers daily and service 2280 square mi., those determined to see *everything* in L.A. should somehow get behind the wheel of a car. If this is not possible, base yourself centrally, make daytrips, and have plenty of change for the bus.

To familiarize yourself with the RTD write for a **Riders Kit,** RTD, Los Angeles 90001 (this address is sufficient), or stop by one of the 10 **customer service centers.** There are three downtown: in ARCO Plaza, 505 S. Flower St., Level B (open Mon.-Fri. 7:30am-3:30pm); at 419 S. Main St. (open Mon.-Fri. 8am-4:30pm); and at 1016 S. Main St. (open Mon.-Sat. 10am-6pm).

The RTD prints route maps for the different sections of the city: Downtown, West L.A., Burbank/Glendale/Pasadena, South Central L.A., South Bay, and the San Fernando Valley. Also available are a list of customer service centers and a brochure called *RTD Self-Guide Tours,* which details how to reach the most important sights from downtown. If you don't have time to map your route in advance, call 800-2LA-RIDE (800-252-7433); lines open daily 5:30am-11:30pm) for transit information.

Bus service is best downtown and along the major thoroughfares west of downtown. (There is 24-hr. service, for instance, on Wilshire Blvd.) The downtown **DASH shuttle** is only 25¢ and serves Chinatown, Union Station (use the DASH to get downtown from Union Station), Olvera Street, City Hall, Little Tokyo, the Music Center, ARCO Plaza, and more. DASH also operates a shuttle on Sunset Blvd. in Hollywood, as well as shuttles in Pacific Palisades, Fairfax (running from Farmer's Market to 3rd and LaBrea), Venice Beach, and Watts. (Downtown DASH operates Mon.-Fri. 6:30am-6:30pm, Sat. 10am-5pm; other DASH shuttles run about the same hours but not on Sat.) Bus service is dismal in the outer reaches of the city, and two-hour journeys are not unusual. The buses themselves are speedy, but transferring often involves interminable waits, and the omnipresent L.A. traffic congestion is enough to make you cry.

RTD's **basic fare** is $1.10, disabled passengers 55¢. Additional charges for express buses, buses taking the freeway, sports events, services, etc., can raise the fare to as much as $3. Exact change *is* required. Transfers are 25¢, whether you're changing from one RTD line to another or from RTD to another transit authority, such as Santa Monica Municipal Bus Lines, Culver City Municipal Bus Lines, Long Beach Transit, or Orange County Transit District. For information on other transit systems, see the appropriate section below. **All route numbers given are RTD unless otherwise designated.** If you plan to use the buses extensively over a long visit, buy a **bus pass.** Unlimited use for a month costs $42, $25 for college students, $18 for students under 18, and $10 for senior citizens and the disabled.

Ninety percent of RTD's lines offer **wheelchair accessible buses.** For more information call 800-622-7828 (open daily 6am-midnight). All bus stops with accessible service are marked with the international symbol of access.

For transit information anywhere in the L.A. area, call 800-2-LA-RIDE (252-7433; lines open daily 5:30am-11:30pm).

If you don't want to spend tedious hours on an RTD bus to get from one end of the basin to the other, consider paying more to take Greyhound (213-620-1200) to such places as Long Beach, Anaheim and Glendale.

Gray Line Tours, 6541 Hollywood Blvd., Hollywood (213-856-5900), is a more expensive but easier way to reach distant attractions. Costs include transportation and admission: Disneyland $54, Magic Mountain $51, Universal Studios $46, San

Diego Zoo $46, and Sea World $47. Tours leave from the Gray Line office for 200 different locations in summertime.

In a desperate, expensive, last-ditch effort to alleviate the congestion that threatens to choke the city, LA has finally started building a subway. The first leg of L.A.'s 300-mile Metro Rail Plan, the Blue Line, presently runs from 7th St. in Downtown to Long Beach (call 213-626-4455 for information). The Red Line, which will run through downtown and out to the San Fernando Valley, is scheduled to open in 1993. Also in the works are lines to LAX and Pasadena. For information on construction progress call 213-620-RAIL.

Freeways

The freeway is perhaps the most enduring of L.A.'s images. When uncongested, these 10- and 12-lane concrete roadways offer speed and convenience; the trip from downtown to Santa Monica can take as little as 20 minutes. A night-time cruise along the Harbor Fwy. past downtown can be exhilirating, whizzing through the tangle of interchanges and on- and off-ramps, with the lights of L.A.'s skyscrapers providing a dramatic backdrop.

At the same time, however, there are few things on this earth more irritating than inching along in traffic on the San Diego Fwy. on a hot Saturday afternoon, when the air shimmers with the heat rising from thousands of overheated cars and tempers.

The most frustrating aspect of driving is the sheer unpredictability of L.A. traffic. It goes without saying that rush hours, both morning and evening, are always a mess, but with construction performed at random hours, you can also encounter nerve-wracking tie-ups on a Tuesday night or on a Sunday morning. The solution? Find a radio station you like or bring your favorite tape with you, and have patience. A little reminder: no matter how crowded the freeway is, it's almost always quicker and safer than taking surface streets to your destination. The best option, unfortunately, is to stay on the freeway and wait it out.

Perhaps to help them "get in touch with their freeway," Californians refer to the highways by names rather than by numbers. These names are little more than hints of a freeway's route, at best harmless, at worst misleading.

I-405, the **San Diego Freeway.** Roughly parallel to the Pacific Coast Highway (Rte. 1), but approximately 10 mi. inland, it links the San Fernando Valley with Westwood, Beverly Hills, LAX, and Long Beach. (Connects with I-10 in Westwood, U.S. 101 in Van Nuys, I-5 in the northern reaches of the San Fernando Valley, I-110 in San Pedro at the southern end of the city.)

I-10, the **Santa Monica Freeway,** west of downtown. The main commuter link to the western portions of the city: Century City, Westwood and Santa Monica. Called the **San Bernardino Freeway** east of downtown. (Connects with Rte. 1 in Santa Monica, I-405 in Westwood, I-110 in downtown, Rte. 60 in East L.A., I-210 in Pomona.)

I-5, the **Golden State Freeway,** pierces the heart of central California parallel to I-405 and Rte. 1. It comes to within 50 mi. of the coast as it moves through the San Fernando Valley. Called the **Santa Ana Freeway** south of downtown, it serves Anaheim and Orange County. (Connects with I-110 just north of downtown, U.S. 101 in Glendale.)

I-110, called the **Pasadena Freeway** north of downtown (it starts in Pasadena) or the **Harbor Freeway** south of downtown where it runs by USC, Exposition Park, and Watts on its way to San Pedro, is L.A.'s oldest freeway. (Connects with Rte. 1 in San Pedro, I-405 in Torrance, I-10 in downtown L.A., U.S. 101 in downtown L.A., and I-5 just north of downtown.)

Route 60, the **Pomona Freeway,** runs roughly parallel to I-10 east of downtown. It is sometimes less crowded. (Connects with I-10 in East Los Angeles.)

U.S. 101, the **Ventura Freeway** from Ventura to North Hollywood, runs inland from Ventura along the outer rim of the Santa Monica Mountains in the San Fernando Valley, serving Thousand Oaks, Woodland Hills, Encino, Van Nuys, Sherman Oaks, Studio City, and North Hollywood. In North Hollywood it veers over the Santa Monica Mountains toward Hollywood, Silver Lake, and downtown—becoming the **Hollywood Freeway.** (Connects with Rte. 1 in Ventura, I-405 in Sherman Oaks, Rte. 134 in Studio City, and I-110 downtown.)

Route 118, the **Simi Valley Freeway,** runs east-west linking such increasingly far-flung bedroom communities as Simi Valley with I-5 in San Fernando.

Route 134, also called the **Ventura Freeway,** continues east from U.S. 101 in Studio City through Glendale and Pasadena. (Connects with Rte. 210 in Pasadena.)

I-210, the **Foothill Freeway,** runs at the base of the San Gabriel Mountains at the outer edge of the San Fernando Valley. Less crowded than most, it links La Crescenta, Pasadena, and Pomona. (Connects with Rte. 134 in Pasadena, I-10 at its terminus in Pomona, and I-5 at its other end in northern San Fernando Valley.)

Route 605, the **San Gabriel Freeway,** runs north-south from Long Beach to the San Gabriel Valley. (Connects with I-405 in Long Beach, I-5 in Downey, Rte. 60 in Whittier, I-10 in El Monte, Rte. 210 in the San Gabriel Valley.)

Currently under construction is **I-105,** the **Century Freeway,** which will run east from LAX and the San Diego Fwy. to the San Gabriel Riverbed, which parallels Rte. 605, the San Gabriel Fwy. Completion is scheduled for mid-1993. The *L.A. Times* has dryly noted that the Century Fwy. will open to an instant traffic jam. So it goes in the City of Angels.

Cars

L.A. may be the most difficult city in the U.S. to get around in without a car. Unfortunately, it may also be the most difficult city in which to rent a car, especially for younger travelers. Most places will not rent to people under 21, and the ones that do are likely to impose a surcharge that may nearly double the cost of renting the car. Rental agencies impose a similar fine (though less steep) on anyone under 25. Throw in an additional few dollars a day for insurance or a **CDW** (that's a Collision Damage Waiver, and it is **entirely optional**—don't let anyone tell you otherwise) and you can end up paying over $40 for an "18 dollar a day" car. Rental places may also cite low rates over the phone, and then claim to be out of the cheaper cars when you arrive. If you find one, $15 a day cars may be difficult or almost impossible to drive, especially in the hectic and bewildering L.A. traffic.

The solution? Get three or four people together for a rental, and make sure one of them is over 25. Don't be afraid to return undriveable cars and ask for better ones, or to press for a refund. For more dependable cars, rent from nationally known agencies (such as Thrifty or Budget, listed below). Be sure always to read the fine print, make sure you are clear about all possible surcharges, and don't be afraid to ask questions, especially when renting from local companies. Remember that the **Collision Damage Waiver (CDW)** you will be offered is optional, but be sure that you have sufficient insurance coverage.

Penny Rent-A-Car, 12425 Victory Blvd., N. Hollywood (818-786-1733). $14-17 with 75 free mi., 15¢ per mi. after that. $98-111 per week with 500 free mi. CDW $5 per day. Must be 21 with major credit card or an international driver's license. Open Mon.-Fri. 7:30am-6pm, Sat. 9am-4pm.

Ugly Duckling, 920 S. La Brea (213-933-0522). $19 a day with 100 free mi., $108 per week. CDW $8 a day, $50 per week. Must be 21 with major credit card. Open Mon.-Sat. 9am-6pm.

Avon Rent-A-Car, 8459 Sunset Blvd. (213-654-5533). Also at LAX and Sherman Oaks (15719 Ventura Blvd., 818-906-2277). $16.95 and up per day with unlimited mileage, from $101.70 per week. CDW $9 and up per day. Must be 18 with a major credit card, but drivers 18-22 face a steep $15 per day surcharge, $5 per day for those 22-25. Open Mon.-Fri. 7:30am-9:30pm.

Alamo Rentals, at LAX (800-327-9633). Prices vary with availability, $26 per day, $100 per week, unlimited mileage. CDW $9 per day. Must be over 21 with major credit card. Those under 25 face additional $6 surcharge.

Thrifty Car Rental (800-367-2277), at LAX. As low as $16.85 per day, unlimited miles within California, $130 per week with 1050 free miles. CDW $9. Must be 21 with credit card, those under 25 pay $5 surcharge. Open 24 hrs.

Budget Rent-A-Car (310-645-4500), at LAX. $30 per day, $100 per week, unlimited miles. CDW $9. Must be 21 with major credit card. Under 25 pay $15 surcharge. Open 24 hr.

Rent-A-Car Cheep, 4760 W. Century Blvd., Inglewood (213-678-9146), near the intersection with Inglewood Ave. just east of LAX. $18 per day. $126 per week for their cheapest car. Mileage is unlimited, CDW $9 per day. Must be 18 with cash or credit card deposit and a valid driver's license. Open Mon.-Sat. 7am-11pm, Sun. 8am-9pm.

Two **automobile transport services** match driverless cars with carless drivers. (See the General Introduction for more information on such services.)

Dependable Car Travel Service, Inc., 18730 Wilshire Blvd., #414, Beverly Hills (310-659-2922). Must be 18. References from L.A. or destination. Most cars to the northeast, especially to New York, but also to Florida and Chicago. $150 refundable deposit. Call 1-2 days ahead to reserve. Open Mon.-Fri. 8:30am-5:30pm.

Car Rental: Auto Driveaway, 3407 W. 6th St. (213-666-6100). Must be 21 and have references in both L.A. and your destination city. Foreign travelers don't need references, but must have a passport, visa, and an international driver's license. The application requires a photo. Most cars go to metropolitan areas nationwide. Cash deposit ($250), traveler's checks, or money order required. Call one week before departure to inquire about availability. Open Mon.-Fri. 9am-5pm.

The most comprehensive **rideboard** is at UCLA's Ackerman Union, Floor B. Ackerman is in the center of campus, 2 blocks north of the Westwood Blvd. terminus. Also check the classified section of papers such as *The Chronicle.*

Bicycles

Unless you're in really good shape, a bicycle in L.A. is useful only for recreational purposes. Traffic is heavy, distances long, and drivers aren't used to looking out for bicyclists. So what else is new? Try Sunday morning, when traffic is light. And wear a helmet.

The best bike routes are along beaches. The most popular route is the **South Bay Bicycle Path.** It runs from Santa Monica to Torrance (19 miles), winding over the sandy beaches of the South Bay past sunbathers, boardwalks, and roller skaters. (Even the police ride bikes here.) The path continues all the way to San Diego. Other bike paths include **San Gabriel River Trail,** 37 mi. along the river with views of the San Gabriel Valley; **Upper Rio Hondo** and **Lario Trails,** 9 and 22 mi., both free from traffic; **Kenneth Newell Bikeway,** 10 mi. through residential Pasadena; **Sepulveda Basin Bikeway,** 7 mi. around the Sepulveda Dam Recreation Area, a large loop of some major San Fernando Valley streets; **Griffith Park Bikeway,** 4½ mi. past the L.A. Zoo and Travel Town train park; **Bolsa Chica Bike Path,** 10 mi. along Huntington Beach; **Santa Ana River Bike Trail,** 22 mi. along the Santa Ana River; and the **Santa Ana Canyon Bikeway,** 7 mi. of both street and canyon terrain.

For maps and advice, write to any **AAA office.** L.A. headquarters is at 2601 S. Figueroa (213-741-3111), near Adams. It's worth calling just to talk to helpful and friendly **Norty Stewart,** "the Source" for bicycling information in Southern California.

In this age of rising insurance costs, renting a bike has become increasingly expensive. Most rental shops stand near the piers of the various beaches, with an especially high concentration on Washington Blvd. near the beach in Venice/Marina Del Rey. Those planning extended stays should look into purchasing a used bicycle. Classified ads for such bikes may be found in all of the daily papers.

Walking and Hitchhiking

The band Missing Persons was bang-on when it sang "Nobody walks in L.A."—L.A. pedestrians are a lonely breed. The largely deserted streets of commercial centers will seem eerie to the first-time visitor. Unless you're running in the L.A. Marathon, moving from one part of the city to another on foot is a ludicrous idea—distances are just too great. Nevertheless some colorful areas such as Melrose, Westwood, and Hollywood are best explored by foot. Venice Beach is the most enjoyable place to walk. Here, you'll be in the company of the thousands of Venetian beach-goers, and Venice's sights and shopping areas are all relatively close to one another. You may also wish to call **Walking Tours of Los Angeles** for tours of El Pueblo de Los Angeles State Historic Park (213-628-1274), City Hall (213-485-

4423), or the Music Center (213-972-7483). The **Los Angeles Conservancy** (213-623-TOUR, 213-623-8687) offers nine different tours of the downtown area. Tours cost $5 and advance reservations are required.

Do *not* hitchhike. It is not safe, and it's illegal on freeways and many streets.

Accommodations

Warning: If you arrive at LAX, do **not** accept an offer of free transportation to an unknown hostel—you'll end up being charged $30 a night to stay in someone's garage.

Many inexpensive lodgings in Los Angeles bear a frightening resemblance to the House of Usher. Dozens of flophouses around the Greyhound station charge between $10 and $20 per night, but those unnerved by skid-row street life should look elsewhere. (Sound glum so far?—Welcome to L.A.!) Tolerable lodgings fall roughly into four categories: hostels, run-down but safe hotels, residential hotels offering weekly rates (these can save you a bundle), and budget motels located well off the beaten track but reasonably close by car. Unless you're set on a specific place, reservations are only necessary for July and August. It never hurts to ask for off-season or student discounts, and occasionally managers will lower prices to snare a prospective but hesitating customer. The useful and comprehensive (though a bit upscale for the budget traveler) *L.A. Lodging Guide* is available at the Los Angeles Visitors Center. **Youth hostel passes** may be obtained from UCLA's Expo Center (310-825-0831).

Los Angeles has no **campgrounds** convenient to public transport. Even motorists face at least a 40-minute commute from campsites to downtown. The only safe place to camp in L.A. County that is even vaguely nearby is **Leo Carrillo State Beach,** on PCH (Rte. 1), 28 mi. northwest of Santa Monica at the Ventura County line (818-706-1310). The beach lays out 134 sites at $9 per night. Sites are first-come first-serve, so you have to fight it out. Dockweiler Beach, just north of LAX also has a campground, but its attraction is reduced by its proximity to the airport and the noise from above.

A number of RV sites do exist in the L.A. area, near Long Beach, Malibu, and the Valley. Call the L.A. Visitors Bureau (213-689-8822) or California Travel Parks Association in Auburn (916-885-1624).

In general, Downtown offers the best transportation, but if you don't anticipate touring much by public bus it's best to move on. The Hollywood area also has convenient bus connections, and vies with Venice as the most intriguing part of town. Offering lots of sights, cheap vittles, and most of L.A.'s nightlife, West L.A. is the safest, quietest, and cleanest area, but you'll pay for it. Venice, is, well Venice, and given the kooky lifestyle and thriving international hostel culture, it's probably the best place to stay in L.A. (Prices listed are without L.A.'s 11% tax.)

A note to our readers: As *Let's Go* went to press the city of Los Angeles was in the process of of passing new zoning ordinances governing hostels. The new rules, combined with increased bureaucratic policing of hostels could result in the shutdown of some hostels.

Downtown

Though busy and relatively safe by day, the downtown area empties and becomes dangerous when the workday ends. Both men and women should travel in groups after dark, especially in the area between Broadway and Main. Ignore swimming pool advertisements unless you check the pool yourself—because of the drought many budget motels are unable to either fill or clean their cement ditches. Again, don't be afraid to haggle, especially during the off-season.

Royal Host Olympic Motel,901 W. Olympic Blvd., (213-626-6255). The ritziest of the budget hotels—beautiful rooms, with bathtubs, balconies, telephone, radio, and color TV with cable.

Some rooms have kitchens. Singles, doubles $40-45, suites $45-50, but students can get a double room for as low as $30.

Hotel Stillwell, 828 S. Grand St. (213-627-1151). Recently refurbished, this ultra-clean hotel is the most sensible downtown. Rooms are bright and pleasantly decorated. Indian restaurant and American grill in hotel, Mexican restaurant next door. A/C, color TV. Singles $35. Doubles $45.

Park Plaza Hotel, 607 S. Park View St. (213-384-5281), on the west corner of 6th St. across from MacArthur Park. Built in 1927, this eerily grandiose art deco monument has a 3-story marble-floored lobby and a monumental staircase. The Plaza once entertained Bing Crosby and Eleanor Roosevelt, but now caters mainly to semi-permanent residents, especially students from the Otis Art Institute next door. A/C, color TV in the clean but small rooms. Olympic size pool and many of the rooms presently under renovation which should be completed by 1992. Singles $35. Doubles $45. Suite $60. Make reservations at least one week in advance.

Empire 900 Motel, 900 W. Olympic Blvd (213-748-1322), across the street from the Royal Host. A little rundown and without the amenities of its cross-street neighbor, it does offer $25 singles and $27 doubles.

Orchid Hotel, 819 S. Flower St. (213-624-5855). Central downtown location and cleanliness make up for the bantam rooms. A/C, color TV. Singles $33.90. Doubles $39.20. Weekly: singles $153.40; doubles $181.50. Reservations recommended.

Milner Hotel, 813 S. Flower St. (213-627-6981), next door to the Orchid. As with its neighbor, central location and good upkeep compensate for the dinginess of the decor. Pub and grill in lobby. A/C, color TV. Singles $40. Doubles $45. No reservations.

Budget Inn, 1710 W. 7th St. (213-483-3470). Location across the Harbor Fwy. from downtown could be a lot better. Rooms, however, are fairly antiseptic. Color TV, swimming pool. Singles $35. Doubles $45. Weekly: singles $175; doubles $225. Make reservations at least one week in advance.

City Center Motel, 1135 W. 7th St. (213-628-7141). Not quite at the city center—it's a 15-min. hike to the east of downtown—prompt but service makes it worthwhile. A/C, swimming pool, 24-hr. security. Singles $35. Doubles $40.

Hollywood

Jam-packed with exciting activities and blessed with excellent bus service to other areas of Los Angeles, Hollywood is an ideal, if a little run-down, base for tourists. Hollywood Blvd., east of the main strip area, is lined with budget motels, as is Sunset Blvd. Despite its many charms, the area gets creepy at night and side streets can be dangerous. Airport Service is the most reliable method of getting from LAX to Hollywood. Or take bus #42 downtown and transfer to #1, which serves Hollywood Blvd. from downtown. As we went to press we also received information regarding the **Centerpoint Backpackers' Hostel**(AAIH), at 1767 Orchid Ave. (213-851-9362), though we were unable to send a researcher there. The Centerpoint offers free airport pickup, is open 24 hrs., and offers a free breakfast for $13 a night.

Hollywood Terrace Hotel, 1921 N. Highland (213-878-0405), 2 blocks above Hollywood Blvd. The largest independent hostel in Hollywood (220 rooms). Free transportation from airport. Keg parties Fri.-Sat. nights. Reasonably priced trips to Malibu and Tijuana. Laundry room. $15 includes free breakfast and dinner.

Hollywood Wilshire YMCA Hotel and Hostel, 1553 Hudson Ave. (213-467-4161). This is far and away the best budget lodging in Hollywood. Located 1½ blocks south of Hollywood Blvd., the hotel rooms are clean and light, with no phones, TV, or A/C. They do, however, come with use of gym and pool facilities. Pay phones on each floor. Must be over 18. Visitors allowed 7-10pm. Singles $29. Doubles $39. The hostel takes no reservations and includes a kitchen, laundry, and lounge. 15-day max. stay. Hostel rate is $12 per night.

Hollywood Downtowner Motel, 5601 Hollywood Blvd. (213-464-7191). Pleasant, clean rooms. Swimming pool, helpful management. A/C, telephone, TV. Full kitchen units $2-3 extra (min 4-night stay for kitchenette rooms). Singles $37, doubles $38-44, cheaper rates in winter. Free parking.

French Cottage Motel, 6757 Sunset Blvd. (213-464-9144). Not quite what the name suggests, but still one of the best deals in the area. A/C, color TV, parking, pool. Breakfast included. Singles $32. Doubles $40. Weekly: singles $175; doubles $196.

Hotel Howard, 1738 N. Whitley Ave. (213-466-6943), ½ block north of Hollywood Blvd. Tastefully furnished, clean, and cheerful rooms. A/C, phones in rooms. No visitors past 10pm. Garage parking $4 per day. Singles $45.84. Doubles $54.80. $10 key deposit included. Weekly: singles $217.12; doubles $266.40; key deposit $20. Reservations recommended.

Hastings Hotel, 6162 Hollywood Blvd. (213-464-4136). Youth-oriented hotel in the thick of Hollywood, near RTD bus lines. 85 rooms, most with color TV. Singles $30. Doubles $40. Weekly: singles $130, doubles $160.

Beverly Hills, Westside, Wilshire District

The Westside is an attractive and much safer part of town, but for the most part, room rates are out of sight. Call the **UCLA Off-Campus Housing Office** (310-825-4491), 100 Sproul Hall, and see if they can put you in touch with students who have a spare room through their "roommate share board."

Hotel Del Flores, 409 N. Crescent Dr., Beverly Hills (310-274-5115), only 3 blocks east of chic Rodeo Dr. and 1 block south of Santa Monica Blvd. It's hard to believe that you can stay in Beverly Hills this cheaply. Newly renovated in 1991. Communal microwaves and refrigerators. Some rooms with color TV. Singles $40, doubles $45. Weekly: singles $185 and up, doubles $195 and up.

Wilshire Orange Hotel, 6060 W. 8th St. (213-931-9533), in West L.A. near Wilshire Blvd. and Fairfax Ave. Buses #20, 21, 22, and 308 serve Wilshire Blvd. from downtown. One of L.A.'s best-located budget accommodations. Near many major sights, in a residential neighborhood. Most rooms have refrigerators, color TV; all but 2 have their own bath or share a bath with one other room. Weekly housekeeping. Many semi-permanent residents. 2-day min. stay. Singles $45, doubles $48; weekly: singles $145, doubles $225.

Crest Motel, 7701 Beverly Blvd. (213-931-8108), near Hollywood and Beverly Hills. An agreeable place, though some of the bathrooms would make Mr. Clean cringe. There is a pool. Color TV and A/C. Singles $36. Doubles $38. $5 key deposit.

Century City-Westwood Motel, 10604 Santa Monica Blvd. (310-475-4422). Very attractive rooms with refrigerators, color TVs, A/C. Even bathrooms sparkle—more than you usually get at this price. Located on the southern part of the boulevard, on "Little Santa Monica," the smaller road that parallels the divided boulevard. Singles $45, each additional person $5, up to 4 in a room.

Bevonshire Lodge Motel, 7575 Beverly Blvd. (213-936-6154). Near Farmers Market and Beverly Center. A popular choice for families. A/C, color TV, telephones. Singles $38.50, doubles $42.50.

Westwood Inn Motel, 10820 Wilshire Blvd. (310-474-3118), down the street from the AVCO Cinema. Typical motel, with parking, A/C, and TV, but no pool. Rooms are clean, if a bit run-down, and feature two double beds. Good location, near Westwood. The owners are twins who are descendants of philosopher William James and writer Henry James. Singles $39, doubles $42. Weekly singles $246, doubles $264.50.

Santa Monica and Venice

The hostels at Venice Beach are havens for budget travelers. They are just about the cheapest way to stay and may be the most enjoyable way to gaily play away your day in L.A. (Hey, hey!) You may miss the Sunset Strip (and L.A. traffic), but in return you'll find dazzling beaches, kinky architecture, and a mellow and unpretentious community devoted to worshipping the sun and cultivating its own eccentricities. If you do decide to venture into L.A.'s depths, the city center is just a short bus ride or drive away. The hostels are a popular destination among foreign students. As we went to press we were informed of the existence of the **Centerpoint Backpackers' Hostel,** at 11 S. Venice Blvd. (310-827-8811), near Venice Beach. Though we were unable to research the Centerpoint, it features no curfew, airport pickup and breakfast for $13 a night.

Venice Beach Cotel, 25 Windward Ave., Venice (310-399-7649), on the boardwalk between Zephyr Court and 17th Ave. Located close to beaches; shuttle from LAX. To stay here you must show your passport and not ask about the name. A friendly, lively hostel full of young international travelers. 3-6 people share each of the tidy, functional rooms. No food allowed. Bar and social area loud and animated from 7pm-1am. No curfew. $12 per person, with bath $15. Private rooms with and without ocean view $33-49.50 (no passport required for these).

Santa Monica International AYH Hostel, 1436 2nd St., Santa Monica (310-393-9913). This brand new hostel in the heart of downtown Santa Monica opened in June 1990 and immediately became the most popular hostel in town. And it's easy to understand why: a colossal kitchen, copious common rooms, and a casual, California-cool climate. Must be seen. Curfew 2am. $13.45 per night, AYH members only. $2 rental charge for bedsheets.

Share-Tel International Hostel, 20 Brooks Ave., Venice (310-392-0325). Outstanding location ½-block off the boardwalk. Student I.D. or passport required. Family-style atmosphere; clean, pleasant rooms with kitchen facilities and bathroom sleep 4-12 each. Kitchen, continental breakfast, safe, linen service, no curfew. $17 per person, $100 per week.

Venice Beach Hostel, 701 Washington St. (310-306-5180), above Celebrity Cleaners. Relaxed and homey atmosphere, with a large lounge and cable TV. Sunroof (bathing suits optional) is popular with international travelers. Near bars and nightclubs. Free transportation from LAX. $12 per night, $70 per week. Double rooms $15 per person. Open 24 hr.

Jim's at The Beach, 17 Brooks Ave., Venice (310-396-5138), ½ block off the boardwalk across the street from Share-Tel. Passport required. No more than 6 beds per room. Clean, bright rooms. Kitchen. No curfew. $15 per night, $90 per week.

Marina Hostel, 2915 Yale Ave., Marina Del Rey (310-301-3983), 3 blocks west from Lincoln Blvd. Near Venice in a quiet residential neighborhood. A privately owned, friendly household with lockers, linen, laundry, and a microwave-equipped kitchen. Some bunks, some floor mattresses. Living room with cable TV. $12 per guest.

Interclub Hostel, 2221 Lincoln Blvd., Venice (310-305-0250), near Venice Blvd. Passport required. Festive after-hours common-room atmosphere in which many nationalities bump elbows. Surfer murals on the walls. Rooms sleep 6, or you can sleep in the 30-bed dorm. Mixed-sex accommodations. Lockout 11am-4pm. No lockout during summer. Curfew 4am. Grubby kitchen with stove and fridge. Linen. Laundry room. $12 per person plus $5 deposit.

Cadillac Hotel, 401 Ocean Front Walk, Venice (310-399-8876). A beautiful Art Deco landmark directly on the beachfront. Airport shuttle service, limited parking. The boardwalk and beach are just outside, and a sundeck is available for private sunning. No curfew. Shared accomodations $18 per night, private ocean-view rooms $49 and up.

Stardust Motor Hotel, 3202 Wilshire Blvd., Santa Monica (310-828-4584). Comfortable accommodations with color TV, telephone, A/C, a pool, and appeal. Singles $45. Doubles $50.

Village Motel, 2624 Santa Monica Blvd., Santa Monica (310-828-9230). Limited number of small but clean rooms. Color TV with cable, A/C, no phone. Maximum of 2 people in one room. $45 per night.

Food

The range of culinary options in L.A. is in direct proportion to the city's ethnic diversity—keep in mind that Los Angelenos speak 116 different languages. There is Jewish and Eastern European food in the Fairfax area; Mexican in East L.A.; Japanese, Chinese, Vietnamese, and Thai around Little Tokyo and Chinatown; seafood along the coast; and Hawaiian, Indian, and Ethiopian restaurants scattered throughout. The restaurants themselves run the gamut from the fifty or so establishments closed each month by the L.A. Department of Health to family-run nooks to glitzy yuppie magnets to celebrity hangouts with stellar prices for the super-wealthy.

Sadly, the only cuisine truly indigenous to the area is fast food. The home of the Big Mac, McDonalds got its start in Southern California in the 50s, and Angelenos seem to have spent the intervening years trying to improve upon the recipe; burger joints squat on nearly every corner. For the optimal Southern Californian fast food experience, try **In 'n' Out Burger** (various locations, call 818-287-4377 for the one nearest you), a family-owned and operated chain that has steadfastly refused to expand beyond the L.A. area. The rewards of such stubborness are evidenced by In 'n Out's burgers and fries, which are arguably the best in the business.

More recently, mall-type express food stands have been winning over L.A.'s fast food junkies; they tend to be tastier, more expensive, more concerned with your health, and a great deal more varied than the traditional hamburger joints. Try **Panda Express** or **Subway.**

For those who like their food less processed, L.A.'s proximity to the San Joaquin Valley, the state's major agricultural region, assures a plentiful supply of fresh fruits and vegetables. This fresh produce is, however, of surprisingly uneven quality because California farmers ship much of their harvest elsewhere and thus pick everything half-ripe. The best way to enjoy the foods that made California famous is to find a health-food store or cooperative market that sells organic and small-farm produce. Stands selling just one or two items are scattered throughout the San Fernando Valley and along the way to Ventura. Prices are lower than those in markets, and the quality far superior.

Visit one of the enormous public markets to appreciate the variety and volume of foodstuffs. The **Farmer's Market,** 6333 W. 3rd St. (213-933-9211), at Fairfax in the Wilshire District, has over 160 produce stalls, meat vendors, small restaurants, and sidewalk cafés. There's delectable produce at reasonable prices, but because the market has become a tourist attraction, bargains are becoming increasingly rare. A market meal can be a smart buy, but lunchtime crowds—especially in summer—are enough to make the hardiest and hungriest turn tail and run. (Open Mon.-Sat. 9am-7pm, Sun. 10am-6pm; Oct.-May Mon.-Sat. 9am-6:30pm, Sun. 10am-5pm.) A less touristy, less expensive source of produce is the **Grand Central Public Market,** 317 S. Broadway (213-624-2378), a large baby-blue building downtown. The main market in the Hispanic shopping district, Grand Central has more than 50 stands selling not only produce, but also clothing, housewares, costume jewelry, vitamins, and fast food. This vast space is always riotously busy and more entertaining than the Farmer's Market, which is staid by comparison. The chaos is interrupted at one point by a formica oasis—a lunch counter where haggard shoppers, oblivious to the melee, enjoy *taquitos* and *carnitas.* (Open Mon.-Sat. 9am-6pm, Sunday 10am-6pm.)

The **Los Angeles Produce Market,** with one location at 9th and San Pedro and one at 7th and Central, serves as the primary distribution center for many Southland supermarkets and restaurants. Starting at 3am, trucks roll in from the country to unload mountains of produce for sale to retailers and restaurant buyers (the public can buy here too, but only in quantities of a bushel or more). Nearby cafés keep the same hours as the markets. The most famous is **Vickman's** at 1228 E. 8th St. (213-622-3852; open Mon.-Fri. 3am-3pm, Sat. 3am-1pm, Sun. 7am-1pm).

Despite the size, L.A. restaurants shut down early. Angelenos eat out between 7-10pm, and restaurants are closed by 11pm. Even fast-food chains are rarely open past midnight. To see listings on late night cafés, restaurants, and combination club/restaurants see **Entertainment.**

Downtown

Lunch specials are easy to find in the financial district as restaurants contend for the business man and woman's lunchtime dollar. However, finding a reasonably priced dinner that won't send you rushing to the Department of Health can be a challenge. Delis in Chinatown are generally inexpensive, and Weller Court by the New Ofani Hotel and Garden encases several Japanese restaurants, a few of which are within budget range.

Philippe's, The Original, 1001 N. Alameda (213-628-3781), 2 blocks north of Union Station. The sheer variety of food combined with sizeable portions and low-low prices make this an exemplary locale for mid-day victuals. Philippe's claims to have originated the French-dipped sandwich; varieties include beef, pork, ham, turkey, or lamb ($3-4). Potato salad 65¢ and a glass of iced tea 40¢. Top it off with a large slice of pie ($1.80), and you've got a colossal lunch at this L.A. institution. Open daily 6am-10pm.

The Pantry, 877 S. Figueroa St. (213-972-9279). Open since the 20s. You may have to share a table with a complete stranger, and the waiter is as likely to insult you as to talk your ear off, but the patrons like it that way. The restaurant seats only 84 yet serves 2500-3000 meals a day. The owners recently opened a deli/bakery next door (roast beef sandwich $3.85). Be prepared to wait for the enormous breakfast specials ($5.95), especially on weekends. Sunday brunch at the Pantry is an L.A. tradition. Open 24 hrs.

La Luz Del Dia, 1 W. Olvera St. (213-628-7495). This authentic and inexpensive Mexican restaurant is hidden amidst the many tourist-trap Mexican joints along historic Olvera St. Tortillas are handmade on the premises, and the salsa is sharp. Combination plates around $4. Open Tues.-Sun. 11am-10pm.

Gorky's, 536 E. 8th St. (213-627-4060). On the southeast edge of downtown sits this one-of-a-kind restaurant, serving Russian cuisine cafeteria-style in an avant-garde setting. Entertaining Russian entrees run $5-7. They have their own brewery on the premises and live music Wed.-Sun. at 8:30pm. Open 24 hrs.

Pacific Restaurant, 859 N. Broadway (213-626-1688), in Chinatown. Formerly called the Home Café, this hole-in-the-wall has changed proprietors and its name, but the chef remains the same. The *jook* (rice porridge with scallions and egg, $3.55) and the meat and rice plate ($3.75) are inexpensive and mouth-watering. Open daily 8:30am-9:30pm.

Mon Kee Restaurant, 679 N. Spring St. (213-628-6717), in Chinatown. Expensive, but one of L.A.'s best seafood restaurants. Dinner $10 and up. The decor here is light and tasteful, especially for Chinatown. Rated one of L.A.'s best seafood restaurants by the *Zagat Guide.* The menu is vast; entrees around $8. Open Sun.-Thurs. 11:30am-9:45pm, Fri.-Sat. 11:30am-10:15pm.

Hunan Restaurant, 980 N. Broadway (213-626-5050), in Chinatown. Perhaps the best Mandarin food in L.A. The Three Flavors Sizzling Rice Soup is phenomenal, as is the Kung-Pao Chicken. Open Sun.-Thurs. 11:30am-2:30pm and 5-9pm, Fri.-Sat. 11:30am-2:30pm and 5-9:30pm.

Sushi Bukyu, 318 E. 2nd St. (213-617-2280), in Little Tokyo. The best Japanese food for the money in Little Tokyo. A la carte menu $2.50-7.50. Full dinner $8-10. Open Thu.-Tues. 11:30am-midnight.

Thank Vi, 422 Westford St. #1A (213-687-3522). A favorite spot among Chinatown denizens for Vietnamese Cuisine. Nothing on the menu is over $8. Tues.-Sun. 8am-7pm.

Country Life Vegetarian Buffet, 888 S. Figueroa St. (213-489-4118). Sumptuous international cuisine, classical music, and reasonable prices. All-you-can-eat lunch $6.50. Mon.-Thur. 7am-9am, 11am-8pm, Fri. 7am-9am, 11am-4pm.

Hollywood and West Hollywood

Forget those rumors about outrageously priced celebrity hangouts—they're here, but you can ignore them. Most of Hollywood and West Hollywood's residents are young, single, hungry, and near broke after paying the rent on their bungalows. Ergo, Hollywood offers the best budget dining in L.A. Hollywood and Sunset Blvds. offer a number of excellent, diverse cuisines, while Fairfax (the traditionally Jewish area of town) has Mediterranean-style restaurants and delis. Melrose is full of chic cafés and eateries, which provide outdoor seating so you can see and be seen by the extraordinalry stylized and beautiful Melrosians.

Seafood Bay, 3916 Sunset Blvd., at Sanborn in Silver Lake, east of Hollywood. This modest eatery in a quiet residential area skimps on decor to support a wide variety of seafood at great prices. "Light meals" such as fettucine with clam sauce are filling and run no more than $6. The fish is fantastic, and the accompaniments—garlicky sourdough bread, pungent rice pilaf, heaps of sauteed mushrooms—receive the same loving attention. Open Mon.-Thurs. 11:30am-10pm, Fri.-Sat. 11:30am-10:30pm, Sun. 4-10pm.

Lucy's El Adobe Café, 5536 Melrose Ave. (213-462-9421), 1 block east of Gower St. This minute family-run restaurant is a favorite among downtown politicians and Paramount executives from across the street. Some of the best Mexican food in town. Former CA governor Jerry "Moonbeam" Brown and Linda Ronstact allegedly met here. As you munch on your tostada ($6), glance at the celebrity photos or the commendation from the City Council adorning the walls. Full dinners (entree, soup or salad, rice, and beans) $8-10. Open Mon.-Sat. 11:30am-11pm.

Ara's, 4953 Hollywood Blvd. (213-660-3739). Authentic and tantalizing Armenian restaurant. Various kebabs ($7) include pita bread, rice pilaf, and curried vegetables. Open Mon.-Sat. noon-8:30pm.

The Old Spaghetti Factory, 5939 W. Sunset Blvd. (213-469-7149). This restaurant claims to be "a reminder of the color and charm of early Hollywood." With its purple wallpaper and a trolley car in the middle of the dining room, most people would simply call it tacky. The food, however, is cheap and plentiful. A full dinner (including bread, salad, and ice cream) runs $4.25-7. Open Mon.-Thurs. 11:30am-2pm and 5-10pm, Fri. 11:30am-2pm and 5-11pm, Sat. 5-11pm, Sun. 4-10pm.

Atch-Kotch, 1253 N. Vine (213-467-5537). Inexpensive Japanese food in a spare, modern setting. Teriyaki chicken is $4.75, and the spicy curry rice only $5.50. Ramen goes from $4.90, with add-on toppings. Open Mon.-Sat. 11:30am-9pm.

Chon Doa, 1511 N. Calnenga Blvd. (213-464-8585). Serves excellent Thai food to clubbie clients, carbo-boosting for their late-night entertainment. Red noodles $5.75. Curry chicken $6.75. Open Mon.-Thu. 11am-11pm, Fri. 11am-midnight, Sat. 5pm-midnight, Sunday 5pm-11pm.

Boardner's Restaurant, 1652 N. Cherokee Ave. (213-462-9621). Boardner's has been serving Americana at nearly the same prices ($3-8) since WWII. Open daily 11am-10pm, drinks 'til 2am.

Johnny Rocket's, 7507 Melrose Ave. (213-651-3361), away from the center of Hollywood in the trendy section of Melrose Ave. near Beverly Hills. The 30s Moderne architecture returns you to a lost era of American diners. Always packed, especially weekend nights. Excellent hamburgers (from $3.25) and shakes ($2.85) and "real" flavored sodas, with syrup and everything (95¢). Yowza! Open Sun.-Thurs. 11am-midnight, Fri.-Sat. 11am-2am.

Duke's, 8909 Sunset Blvd. (310-652-3100), at San Vicente. In a neighborhood of trendy boutiques and rock clubs. Hangout for L.A.'s music industry big-wigs; its walls are a kaleidoscope of posters and autographed album covers. Everyone cheers "Dave" in unison when David Geffen enters the room. Perfect for brunch, but carry a copy of *Spin* to pass the time while you wait for a table. Entrees $5-7. Omelettes $4-6. Open Mon.-Fri. 7:30am-9pm, Sat.-Sun. 8am-4pm.

Pink's Famous Chili Dogs, 711 N. La Brea Ave. (213-931-4223). The chili dogs are good and cheap ($1.95) and that's why Pink's has been around since 1939, every hour, every day. Open 24 hrs.

Les Fereis Taix, 1911 Sunset Blvd. (213-484-1265). You'd never believe it was affordable: excellent French cuisine, a selection of over 500 wines, and valet parking. Dinner, complete with soup, salad, sorbet, *and* entree runs $9-13. Open Mon.-Sat. 11am-3:30pm and 4-10pm, Sunday 4-9pm.

Beverly Hills, Westside, Wilshire District

Few restaurants in these upscale neighborhoods are in the budget range. Beverly Hills and the Wilshire District offer some of the finest dining in the country; don't expect any bargains here. La Brea Ave. and Pico Blvd. However, both offer a wide variety of restaurants.

Ed Debeure's, 134 N. La Cienoga Blvd. (310-659-1952), in Beverly Hills. Far and away the most mirthful of the phony 50s diners ("famous since 1984"). Waitresses complete with buttons. Hamburgers $4.55-5.55. Full bar. Open Sun.-Thurs. 11:30am-11pm, Fri.-Sat. 11:30am-1am.

Siam Cottage, 10512 W. Pico Blvd. (310-838-4012). Therrific Thai food at reasonable prices. Lunch special $4.95. Most entrees $4.25-6.50, but the dinner specials are the way to go. Open daily 11am-2:30pm and 5pm-10:30pm.

The Apple Pan, 10801 W. Pico Blvd. (310-475-3585), in West L.A. between Westwood and Overland. From downtown, take bus #431. This nondescript little building is easily overshadowed by the mammoth Westside Pavilion shopping center across the street, but it's been open since 1927 and continues to draw crowds for large, juicy hamburgers ($3.25) and sandwiches ($2.85-4.55) with huge slices of apple pie for dessert ($2.20). Much of the clientele is colorful elderly locals. Open Tues.-Sun. 11am-midnight. Closed the first 2 weeks in July.

El Nopal, 10426 National Blvd. (310-559-4732), in West L.A., between Motor and Overland, just south of the Santa Monica Fwy. Known as the "home of the pregnant burrito." The famed burrito *embarrasado* ($5.50), stuffed with chicken and avocado, lives up to its name—you'll be blushing with each tasty bite. Smaller burritos $2-3. Tasty tacos and tangy salsa ($1.75). Take-out available. Open Mon.-Sat. 11am-10pm, Sun. 11am-9pm.

La Salsa: Tacos al Carbon, 9631 Santa Monica Blvd. (310-276-2373), in Beverly Hills. Actually on "Little" Santa Monica, 1 short block south of the big boulevard, between Camden and Bedford on the north side. The prettiest taco stand you'll ever see. Fast-food Mexican cuisine prepared with an eye toward low cholesterol and price. $4 should set you up. (Stay away from the hot salad unless you have *la sangre de la raza!*) On Fri. nights you get all the soft tacos you can eat for $6. Open Mon.-Thurs. 10am-9pm, Fri.-Sat. 10am-10pm, Sun. 11am-8pm.

Paru's, 9340 Pico Blvd. (310-273-8088), 2 Blocks east of Beverly Dr. Vegetarian Indian cuisine—delicious food at reasonable prices. The *Masala Dosa* is actually 12" long ($4.95). Complete dinners $8-9. Open daily 11:30am-9pm.

J.P. Throckmorton Grille, 255 S. Beverly Dr. (310-550-7111). This charming grill features an exquisite burger for $2.75 and a variety of hot and cold sandwiches at around $4. The milkshakes are thick and potent ($2). Open Mon.-Sat. 11am-9pm, Sun. 11am-6pm.

Dragon Garden, 2625 S. Robertson (310-837-3627). Not the best Chinese food in L.A., but you can't beat the $1 per item lunch special (11:30am-4:30pm). The taco stand two doors over offers similar quality food at even better prices Open Mon.-Sat. 11:30am-9:00pm.

Tommy's Original Hamburgers, 2575 W. Beverly Blvd. (213-389-9060), Wilshire District. Ignore the multitude of Tommy's knock-offs and head to the winner of the sloppiest chili dog contest—the paper towel dispensers every two feet along the counters aren't just there for looks. Chili dog $1.25, chili burger $1.25, double cheeseburger (for those with galvanized stomachs) $3. Open 24 hr.

Westwood is filled with chic and convenient eateries perfect before a movie or while shopping, and you'll find everything from falafel to *gelato* in corner shops.

Sak's Teriyaki, 1121 Glendon Ave. (310-208-2002), in Westwood. Excellent, low-priced Japanese plates including chicken and beef teriyaki ($3.70-5). Popular with students. Happy Hour special ($2.50) 3-6pm. Open Mon.-Thurs. 11am-10pm, Fri.-Sat. 11am-11pm, Sun. 11am-9pm.

Tacos Tacos, 1084 Glendon Ave. (310-208-2038), Westwood Village. Trendy "Southwestern Café" with blue corn chicken tacos ($1.75). Try the *horchata* (cinnamon-flavored rice water, $1.25). Open Sun.-Wed. 11am-10:30pm, Thurs.-Sat. 11am-12:30pm.

Dragon Express, 1147 Westwood Blvd. (310-208-4928). Good, cheap, fast Chinese food. Black bean chicken with rice (3.95). Open daily 11am-11pm.

Lamonica's NY Pizza, 10925 Weyburn Ave. (310-478-9806). L.A.'s best pizza by the slice ($1.30, 15¢ per topping). They claim to fly the water for their dough cross-country for that authentic New York taste. 12" pizza $8, 75¢ per topping. Open Sun.-Thurs. 11am-10:30pm. Fri.-Sat. 11am-midnight.

Fatburger, 10955 Kenross (310-208-7365). Order a Double King chili-cheese-egg-burger, roll up your sleeves and open wide. Fat-n-juicy burgers from $2.50. Open Sun.-Thu. 10am-3am, Fri.-Sat. 10am-4am.

Sphinx, 1779 Westwood Blvd. (310-477-2358), a ½ block north of Santa Monica Blvd. A bit out of the way from Westwood proper, but the clientele that returns here every afternoon to argue politics in Arabic know it's worth it. The Falafel ($2.25) is tasty, and the BBQ Chicken Kebab ($3.25) is delectable. Open Mon.-Fri. 10am-10pm, Sat. 11am-10pm.

Santa Monica and Venice

Unfortunately, most of Santa Monica's eateries are overpriced, and most of Venice's eateries are overgreased. The new **EATZ Café** in Santa Monica Place offers 17 different types of mall food to choose from, a number of which are tasty and reasonably priced.

Ye Olde King's Head, 116 Santa Monica Blvd. (310-451-1402), in Santa Monica. An authentic British pub owned by an expatriate from Manchester. Fish and chips are $7, a variety of other English entrees are $7-9. The King's Head also features a broad assortment of English beers and ales. They're expensive, but there aren't many publicans in Santa Monica who know the difference between Whitbread and Bud. Open Mon.-Sat. 11am-1:30am, Sun. noon-1:30am.

Tijuana Restaurant, 11785 W. Olympic Blvd. (310-473-9293), in West L.A. The menu is patterned on a Tijuana jai alai program. Despite this, the food is first-rate. A woman stands in the entryway of the dining room hand-making the tortillas for dinner. Try the *nopalitas,* young cactus served on a tortilla ($2.75) if you're feeling adventurous. Dinner entrees and combination plates run $7-9. Open Sun.-Thurs. 11am-10pm, Fri.-Sat. 11am-11pm.

From Spain, 11510 W. Pico Blvd. (310-479-6740). Bullfight posters, candles, and Spanish melodies create an appropriate atmosphere. Outstanding dishes, most under $10, include *bistec encebollado* ($9.95) and *pollo Cordobés* ($8.50). Open Mon.-Fri. 11am-10pm, Sat.-Sun. 3-10pm. Make reservations for Fri. and Sat. nights.

Humphrey Yogart Café, 11677 San Vicente Blvd. (310-207-2206), in Brentwood. Come here for dessert. Start with vanilla frozen yogurt (sweet or tart) and blend in whatever bizarre ingredient combination you wish. Blueberry with mystic mint is RLW's favorite. A medium with two ingredients is $2.40. Humphrey's also serves sandwiches, soups, and salads. Always crowded. Open Sun. 11am-10:30pm, Mon.-Thurs. 9am-11:30pm, Fri. 9am-11:30pm, Sat. 10am-11:30pm.

Tito's Tacos, 11222 Washington Place (310-391-5780), in Culver City at Sepulveda, 1 block north of Washington Blvd., virtually *beneath* the San Diego Fwy. The name should have been Tito's Burritos, since the burrito, with its huge hunks of shredded beef, is the star attraction (at $2.10, it's also the most expensive thing on the menu). Tostadas and enchiladas $1.20, tacos $1.20. Order at the counter and sit down, or get it to go. Plenty of parking. Open daily 9am-11:30pm.

L.A. E.A.T.S., 1009 W. Washington Blvd. (310-396-5914), in Venice. Known for its appetizingly displayed take-out foods. A deli by day, it metamorphoses into a full-fledged restaurant at night. Sandwiches are $6-7, soup $3.55. Open Mon.-Fri. 7:30am-8:30pm.

Benita's Frites, 1437 3rd St. Promenade (310-458-2889), in Santa Monica. French fries served the Belgian way, in a paper cone with *andoulause* sauce (red and green bell peppers, mayonnaise, tomato, and garlic), chili, or peanut curry satay on top ($1.65-2.25, toppings 30-45¢. Open Sun. noon-8pm, Mon. 11:30am-4pm., Tues.-Thurs. 11:30am-10pm, Fri.-Sat. 11:30am-10:30pm.

Todai Lighthouse, 201 Arizona Ave. (310-451-2076). Fabulous all-you-can-eat sushi; lunch and dinners that rival any Japanese joint in Little Tokyo include squid, yellowtail, salmon, orange roughy, shinami and more. Famed Japanese dancer Mayuni Mori can often be found here. Open daily 11:30am-2:30pm and 5:30pm-9pm.

San Fernando Valley

The entirety of Ventura Blvd. is chock full of a wide variety of restaurants. Eating lunch near the studios in Studio City is your best chance to catch sight of the stars. The famous are willing to dine outside the studios because of Studio City's unwritten law—you can stare all you want, but don't bother them, *and don't ask for autographs.*

Don Cuco's Mexican Food, 3911 Riverside Dr. (818-842-1123), in Burbank near the studios. Generous portions of outstanding Mexican food. Combination dinners $6.50-7.50. Fajitas are $9, and specials are $8.50 Margaritas as big as a soup bowl $4. Open daily 11am-10pm.

Art's, 12224 Ventura Blvd. (818-762-1221), in Studio City, between Laurel Canyon and Whitsett. Super full-service deli with huge sandwiches ($7-8); even the potato salad is scrumptious. Open daily 7:30am-9:30pm.

Chili John's, 2018 W. Burbank Blvd. (818-846-3611), in Burbank. Their chili recipe hasn't changed since 1900 (a bowl is $3.85). As your mouth burns you might want to check out the mountain landscape painted on one wall; it took the former owner/chef over 20 years to paint in-between serving customers. Take-out. Open Sept.-June Tues.-Fri. 11am-7pm, Sat. 11am-4pm.

Café Mediterranean, 10151½ Riverside Dr. (310-769-0865), in Toluca Lake. Their "Feast for 2" ($26) includes grape leaves, hummus, salad, shish kebab, lamb meatballs, and dessert. Entrees $7-13. Open Mon.-Sat. 11am-11pm.

Pasadena

Fair Oaks Ave. and Colorado Blvd., in the Old Town section of Pasadena, are punctuated with cafés and Mexican restaurants.

Rose City Diner, 45 S. Fair Oaks Ave. (818-793-8282), just south of Colorado Blvd. Another 50s-nostalgia restaurant with a jukebox and diner-style booths. Hardly authentic, but so peppy you can't fault it. Meatloaf, chicken-fried steak, and spaghetti and meatballs are all $6-7. Extensive dessert selection (sundaes from $3.50). Bazooka gum presented with your check. Open daily 6:30am-2am.

Burger Continental, 535 S. Lake Ave. (818-792-6634), off California Blvd. Not just burgers. An extensive menu offers a wide range of Middle Eastern fare; served cafeteria-style. The Mediterranean Combinations ($10-12) are especially popular. Draws a large Sunday brunch crowd. Open Mon.-Thurs. 6:30am-10:30pm, Fri.-Sat. 6:30am-11:30pm, Sun. 6:30am-10pm.

Mijari's Mexican Restaurant, 145 Palmetto Dr. (818-792-2763), entrance on Pasadena Ave. Vast and popular, with a festive atmosphere. Combination dinners $5-7. Open Mon.-Thurs. 11am-9pm, Fri.-Sat. 11am-10pm, Sun. 10am-9pm.

Los Tacos, 1 W. California Blvd. (818-795-9291), enter around the corner of Fair Oaks Blvd. Standard, inexpensive Mexican food in a fast-food setting. Soft tacos with your choice of filling ($1.15). Combination plates ($4.69). A popular Fri. and Sat. night stop for local teenagers. Open Sun.-Mon. 9am-10pm, Tues.-Thurs. 9am-1am, Fri.-Sat. 9am-2am.

Pie 'n' Burger, 913 E. California (818-795-1123), near Lake Ave. The decor is drab, with a long counter and a handful of tables, but the pies ($1.75 per slice) and burgers ($4-5) are sublime. Serves breakfast too. Open Mon.-Fri. 6am-10pm, Sat. 7am-10pm, Sun. 7am-9pm.

Sights

Downtown

The Los Angeles downtown area alone is larger than most cities. A fascinating mèlange of neighborhoods, it is the geographical heart of the city. The financial district is a jungle of glass and steel, where the gigantic corporate offices of such companies as ARCO, the Bank of America, Wells Fargo, and AT&T crowd the busy downtown center (an area bounded roughly by 3rd and 6th St., Figueroa St., and Grand Ave.). The brand new I.M. Pei-designed **First Interstate World Center,** 633 W. 5th St. (213-955-8151), conspicuously perched atop Bunker Hill, dominates the skyline; at 73 stories and 1017 ft., it is the tallest building west of the Mississippi River. The World Center's cylindrical shape and curved lines reflect the trend in recent years toward softer shapes in urban architecture. The development of this property and of the whole Bunker Hill area is financing the renovation of the city's Central Library, whose old, pyramid-crowned building sits directly across the street, unusable in recent years.

The financial district's skyline has been made famous by TV show *L.A. Law,* and includes some of L.A.'s most impressive buildings. The **Oviatt Building** at 617 S. Olive St. is the downtown area's art deco masterpiece. The top two floors were originally used as an apartment by Mr. Oviatt The **Times Mirror Building** at 220 W. 1st, with the exception of the 1970s addition, is a classic example of Cal Moderne, as well as the area's most impressive buicing.

To the north of the financial district is L.A.'s **Music Center,** 135 N. Grand Ave. (213-972-7211), comprised of the **Dorothy Chandler Pavillion,** the **Mark Taper Forum,** and the **Ahmanson Theatre.** The center is home to the Los Angeles Philharmonic Orchestra and the Joffrey Ballet. Local music-lovers hit Chinatown or Little Tokyo for dinner before a night at the opera.

The **Civic Center,** a solid wall of bureaucratic architecture bounded by the Hollywood Fwy. (U.S. 101), Grand, 1st, and San Pedro St., runs east from the Music Center. It ends at **City Hall,** 200 N. Spring St. Another of the best-known buildings in the Southland, the hall was cast as the home of the *Daily Planet* in the *Superman* TV series. The building has an **observation deck** on the 27th floor.

Farther north lies the historic birthplace of Los Angeles. In the place where the original city center once stood, **El Pueblo de Los Angeles State Historic Park** (213-680-2525; open Mon.-Fri. 10am-8pm) preserves a number of historically important buildings from the Spanish and Mexican eras. Start out at the **docent center,** 130 Paseo de la Plaza. The center offers free walking tours (Tues.-Sat. 10am-1pm on the hour, but call to check first as tours are sometimes cancelled, 213-628-1274) and a free bus tour of L.A. (1st and 3rd Wed. of each month, make reservations as early as possible; 213-628-1274)

The **Old Plaza,** with its century-old Moreton Bay fig trees and huge bandstand, sprawls at the center of the pueblo. Tours start here and wind their way past the **Avila Adobe** (1818), 10 E. Olvera St., the oldest house in the city (the original adobe has been replaced with concrete in order to meet earthquake regulations), followed by **Pico House,** 500 N. Main St., once L.A.'s most luxurious hotel. Farther down, at 535 N. Main St., the **Plaza Church,** established in 1818, almost melts away from the street with its soft, rose adobe façade. Most tours also include the catacombs that formerly held gambling and opium dens. The **visitors center** is located in the **Sepulveda House** (1887), 622 N. Main St. (213-628-1274; open Mon.-Fri. 9am-4pm. For interested visitors, they screen *Pueblo of Promise,* an 18-minute history of L.A. **Olvera Street,** one of L.A.'s original roads, has miraculously survived; it is now called Tijuana North by the locals, and one tawdry stand after another sells schlocky Mexican handicrafts. Here L.A.'s large Chicano community celebrates Mexican Independence Day on **Cinco de Mayo.** In December, the Los Posados celebration, including a candlelight procession and the breaking of a piñata takes place here (Dec. 16-24; 213-625-5045). Across Alameda St. from El Pueblo is the grand old **Union Station.**

Bustling **Chinatown** lies north of this area, roughly bordered by Yale, Spring, Ord, and Bernard St. From downtown, take the DASH shuttle. (See Getting Around, Public Transportation.) It was in this once vice-ridden neighborhood that Roman Polanski's Jake Giddis (played by Mr. L.A. himself, Jack Nicholson) learned just what a tough old world is out there (let me tell you). **Little Tokyo,** yet another of downtown L.A.'s ethnic neighborhoods, is centered on 2nd and San Pedro St. on the eastern edge of downtown. The **New Otani Hotel,** 120 S. Los Angeles St., 1 block south of the Civic Center between 1st and 2nd, rents its lavish Meiji-style rooms for up to $700 per night. For slightly less, you can have a drink in the elegant rooftop garden. The **Japanese Village Plaza,** in the 300 block of E. 2nd St. is the center of the district and is a florid fusion of American shopping mall and Japanese design. The **Japanese American Cultural and Community Center,** 244 S. San Pedro St. (213-628-2725), was designed by Buckminster Fuller and Isamu Noguchi, who crafted a monumental sculpture for the courtyard. (Administrative offices open Mon.-Fri. 9am-5pm.)

Broadway south of 1st St. is predominantly Mexican. All billboards and store signs are in Spanish, and the **Grand Central Public Market** (see Food) takes a center seat. One of many Spanish-language cinemas housed in old movie palaces is the **Million Dollar Theater,** 307 S. Broadway (213-239-0939). Peek into the baroque auditorium, and inspect the stars in the sidewalk out front, each bearing the name of a Chicano celebrity—a *rambla de fama* to complement Hollywood's. Across the street, the **Bradbury Building,** 304 S. Broadway, stands as a relic of L.A.'s Victorian past. Uninspiring from the street, this exquisite 1893 office building is mostly lobby. Its ornate staircases and elevators (wrought in iron, wood, and marble) are often bathed in sunlight, which pours in through the glass roof. Crews film period scenes with some regularity here. (Open Mon.-Sat. 10am-5pm. Self-guided tour $1.)

Perhaps the best reason to spend time downtown is to see L.A.'s cultural attractions. Undoubtedly the most striking (and chic) museum in the area is the **Museum of Contemporary Art (MOCA),** showcasing art from 1940 to the present. The main museum is located at California Plaza, 250 S. Grand Ave. (213-626-6222), and is a sleek and geometric architectural marvel. Its collection focuses on abstract expressionism, and includes works by Pollock, Calder, Miró, and Giacometti. Its interior is spacious and illuminated by the pyramidal skylights in the ceiling. The second

Contiki
AUSTRALIA

MOCA facility is the **Temporary Contemporary,** 152 N. Central Ave., in Little Tokyo. Originally intended to house exhibits only while the main museum was under construction, this building has since become a permanent part of the MOCA package. The Temporary Contemporary's bare warehouse exterior conceals a wide collection of intriguing interior exhibits. While the main museum sticks to the Modernist pantheon, the TC focuses on today's avant-garde, showing the works of important younger artists in a bold setting. One ticket admits you to both locations both locations. The DASH shuttle provides transportation between them for 25¢, but the new **MOCA Shuttle Bus** will take you from one to the other for free. (Shuttle operates during all museum hours: open Tues.-Wed. and Fri.-Sun. 11am-6pm, Thurs. 11am-8pm. Admission $4, seniors and students with ID $2; under 12 free. Everyone free Thurs. 5-8pm. Disabled access.)

Across from City Hall East, between the Santa Ana Fwy. and Temple in the L.A. Mall, is the **L.A. Children's Museum,** 310 N. Main St. (213-687-8800), where nothing is behind glass and everything can be handled. There is always an exhibit on an L.A. ethnic group, and children are invited to overcome the confusion of a hyper-technological society by participating in demonstrations of scientific principles. (Open Wed.-Thurs. 2-4pm, Sat.-Sun. 10am-5pm. Admission $4, under 2 free.)

Perhaps the most peculiar and best-hidden of the downtown museums is the **Museum of Neon Art,** 704 Traction Ave. (213-617-1580), in the artists' neighborhood to the east of Little Tokyo. Exhibits range from neon artwork to other types of electric and kinetic sculpture. While you're there be sure to pick up a MONA t-shirt, depicting a neon sculpture of the *Mona Lisa,* so that you can be as cool as Tim Whitmire. Traction runs east of Alameda St., between 2nd and 3rd St. (Open Tues.-Sat. 11am-5pm. Admission $2.50, seniors and students $1, under 17 free.) Finally, those enticed by the Bradbury Building will also want to examine the **Grier-Musser Museum,** which contains an extensive collection of antiques inside a tenderly restored Queen Anne style house. (Open Wed.-Sat. 11am-4pm; adults $3, seniors $2. Located at 403 South Bonnie Brae Avenue, 213-413-1818.)

Exposition Park

Among the most notable sights near downtown is **Exposition Park.** At the turn of the century, this area was an upscale suburb of downtown; it deteriorated in the twenties but was renewed when the Olympiad first came to town in 1932. This degeneratively inclined neighborhood was revitalized yet again by the 1984 Olympics, and today, it is one of the few parts of L.A. where a number of important attractions are clustered together. The park is southwest of downtown, just off the Harbor Fwy., and is bounded by Exposition Blvd., Figueroa St., Vermont Ave., and Santa Barbara Ave. From downtown, take bus #40 or 42 (both from 1st and Broadway) to the park's southern edge. From Hollywood, take #204 down Vermont. From Santa Monica, take bus #20, 22, 320, or 322 on Wilshire, and transfer to #204 at Vermont.

The park is dominated by several major museums, including the **California Museum of Science and Industry,** 700 State Dr. (213-744-7400). Enter at the corner of Figueroa and Exposition next to the United DC-8 parked out front. Many of the exhibits are either corporate or governmental propaganda; those left to the MSI's own devices are rather amateurish. IBM and Bell Telephone sponsor mathematics and communications, while McDonald's is inexplicably allowed to handle a display on nutrition. One exhibit re-creates an earthquake—complete with a shaking floor and mock news report—to acquaint Southern Californians with their future. The museum also includes the **Kinsey Hall of Health** (*not* run by McDonalds), which has an exhibit on AIDS and uses interactive computer displays to educate visitors about their bodies and the effects of diet, alcohol, and drug use. The **Hall of Economics and Finance** does its best to enliven what even its practitioners call "the dismal science." The **Aerospace Building,** as big as a hangar, exhibits $8 million worth of aircraft, including the Gemini 11 space capsule. Admire the new addition by one of the Southwest's most distinguished architects, Tania Jacobsohn. New for

1992 is an exhibit on the Science of Toys and Games. (Open daily 10am-5pm. Free. Parking $2, bring quarters.) The museum also runs an **IMAX Theater** (213-744-2014), which projects films onto a five-story-tall screen and bombards viewers with six channel surround sound. Films are an hour long, covering such subjects as space flight and the great outdoors. (Hourly showings daily 10am-9pm. Admission $5.50, seniors over 55, students, and ages 4-17 $4. Call ahead for show information.)

In the same complex, but separate from the MSI is the **California Afro-American Museum,** 600 State Dr. (213-744-2060), with a permanent sculpture collection, a research library, and a changing assortment of exhibits. (Open daily 10am-5pm. Free. Research library open Mon.-Fri. 10am-5pm.)

The park's other major museum is the **Los Angeles County Natural History Museum,** 900 Exposition Blvd. (213-744-3466). Exhibits here cover American history from 1472-1914, pre-Columbian cultures, North American and African mammals, and dinosaurs. The **E. Hadley Stuart, Jr. Hall of Gems and Minerals** showcases a dazzling array of precious rocks. (Open Tues.-Sun. 10am-5pm. Admission $5, seniors and students $2.50, ages 5-12 $1, under 5 free.)

Lovers should enjoy the expansive, formal **rose garden** planted in the courtyard in front of the Museum of Science and Industry, with its walking paths, green lawns, gazebos, and 16,000 specimens of 190 sweet-smelling varieties of roses.

Exposition Park also includes the **Los Angeles Memorial Coliseum,** 2601 S. Figueroa St., home of the Los Angeles Raider and the USC Trojan football teams, and the **Sports Arena,** home of the Los Angeles Clippers basketball team and a common venue for rock concerts. The colossal Coliseum, which seats over 100,000, hosted the 1932 and 1984 Summer Olympic Games.

The **University of Southern California (USC)** campus is opposite Exposition Park on Exposition Blvd. The campus is wide, beautiful and generally safe, although women especially should exercise caution after dark. The **Fisher Gallery,** 823 Exposition Blvd. (213-743-2799), includes the Armand Hammer collection of 18th- and 19th-century Dutch paintings. (Open early Sept.-early May Tues.-Sat. noon-5pm. Free.)

To the south and east of the USC campus stretches **Watts,** a neighborhood made notorious by riots in 1965. From the center of what is formally known as the Watts District rise the **Watts Towers,** 1765 E. 107th St. (213-569-8181), a remarkably impressive work of folk art. The towers were built singlehandedly over a period of 33 years by Watts resident Simon Rodia. These delicate towers of glistening fretwork, decorated with mosaics of broken glass, ceramic tile, and sea shells, are a truly inspiring testament to the power of one man's extraordinary vision and dedication. Rodia retired to Martinez, California in 1954, and the City of Los Angeles has since undertaken the care and preservation of this unique monument. Although the towers are a good 7-mi. drive from the nearest tourist attractions at Exposition Park and are in a dangerous part of town, they are worth the trip. (By bus, take RTD #55 from Main St. downtown and get off at Compton Ave. and 108th St. The towers are one block to the east.) For a guided tour of the towers, which are undergoing restoration, call the Watts Towers Arts Center at 213-569-8181. The center is located at 1727 E. 107th St., right next to the towers and is open Tues.-Sat. 9am-5pm. (From downtown take the Metro Blue Line and get off at 103 St. Station. Walk on 104th east to Beach, and then south to the corner of 106th and 107th.) The towers are open for exploration Sat.-Sun. from 10am-4pm. During the week the towers undergo restoration, and appointments must be made in advance. Next door, at 1727 E. 107th St. is the **Watts Tower Arts Center** (213-569-8181), which houses a permanent exhibit of folk instruments, as well as a changing gallery (open Tues.-Sat. 9am-4pm).

Also south of Exposition Park, but to the west, is the city of **Inglewood,** a rough neighborhood, but not lacking in attractions. **Hollywood Park,** 1050 S. Prairie Ave. (310-419-1500), sponsors thoroughbred racing between April and July, and in November and December. The lovely track is landscaped with lagoons and tropical trees, and the facility is complete with restaurants and a children's play area. (Racing held Wed.-Sun. Post time 1:30pm. Admission $3, ages under 18 free.) At the corner of Manchester and Prairie Ave. is the **Great Western Forum** (310-673-1300), home of Wayne Gretzky's **Los Angeles Kings** hockey team as well as the **Los Angeles Lakers** basketball team, perhaps the most popular of L.A.'s many sports franchises. The Lakers won five league titles in the 1980s under the leadership of Kareem Abdul Jabbar and Magic Johnson, and made yet another trip to the NBA Finals in 1991. The Forum, with its palatial pillars and glitzy "showtime" atmosphere, and its winning residents, has itself become a symbol of the city. Even Jack Nicholson has courtside seats.

Wilshire District and Hancock Park

Wilshire Boulevard, especially the "Miracle Mile" between Highland and Fairfax Ave., played a starring role in Los Angeles' westward suburban expansion. On what was then the end of the boulevard, the Bullocks Corporation gambled on attracting shoppers from downtown and in 1929 erected one of L.A.'s few architecturally significant buildings, the massive, bronze-colored **Bullocks Wilshire** at 3050 Wilshire Blvd., near Vermont Ave. Though now called the **I. Magnin BW Wilshire,** tours of this art deco landmark are offered by docents of the Los Angeles Conservancy (call 213-623-2489 to arrange one). The nearby residential neighborhoods and their 20s architecture, are also worth exploring. The streets south of Wilshire opposite Hancock Park are lined with Spanish-style bungalows and the occasional modernist manse.

A few miles further down Wilshire, in **Hancock Park,** the acrid smell of tar pervades the vicinity of the **La Brea Tar Pits,** one of the most popular hangouts in the world for fossilized early mammals. The fossils of thousands of saber-toothed tigers, giant ferrets, mammoths, and dire wolves are all that remain today of what was once a thriving prehistoric landscape. The beasts came to drink from the pools here only to find themselves stuck in the tar that lay below a thin film of water (the ole Brer Rabbit syndrome). Most of the one million bones recovered from the pits between 1913 and 1915 have found a new home in the **George C. Page Museum of La Brea Discoveries,** 5801 Wilshire Blvd. at Curson and Wilshire (for a recording 213-936-2230, for an operator 213-857-6311). Wilshire buses stop right in front of the museum. The museum includes reconstructed Ice Age animals and murals of L.A. Ice Age life, a laboratory where paleontologists work behind plate-glass windows, and a display where you can feel what it's like to stick around in the tar. Archaeological digging continues in Pit 91 behind the adjacent county art museum. (Open Tues.-Sun. 10am-5pm. Admission $4, seniors and students $2, children 75¢. Free 2nd Tues. of each month. Tours of the museum are offered to the public Wed.-Sun. at 2:00pm. Tours of the grounds at 1pm.)

The Los Angeles County Museum of Art (LACMA), 5905 Wilshire Blvd. (213-857-6000), at the west end of Hancock Park, has a distinguished, comprehensive collection that should rebut those who argue that L.A.'s only culture is in its yogurt. Opened in 1965, the LACMA is the largest museum in the West and still growing. Five major buildings cluster around the **Times Mirror Central Court:** a Japanese pavilion, the Ahmanson Building (the museum's original building and home to most of its non-modern permanent collection), the Hammer Building, the Bing Center, and the Robert O. Anderson Building, a spectacular 1986 addition to the museum, with a façade of salmon-colored sandstone and glass. The museum offers a variety of tours and free talks daily. For schedules, check with the information desk in the Central Court or contact the Docent Council at 857-6108. (Open Tues.-Fri. 10am-5pm, Sat.-Sun. 10am-6pm. Admission $5, seniors and students $3.50, ages 6-17 $1. Free 2nd Tues. of each month.

Hollywood

It's hard to believe that for decades, this tiny chunk of a massive city defined glamour on the West Coast. Many young people have crossed the country to share in the city's glitz and fame. A grownups' Disneyland, Hollywood symbolized the

American desire to "make it," to forget one's past and fabricate an instant persona of sophistication and wealth. For years, this urban fantasy world succeeded, generating the image and style associated with California, and in large part, with America itself.

Appropriately, this community that specializes in manufacturing illusions had its origins in fraud. In the early days of silent movies, independent producers and directors, many of them Jewish, sought to escape the tight control and restrictions of the conservative Protestant Movie Trust based in New York. They began shooting films in the empty groves of Hollywood both to avoid the Trust's surveillance and to take advantage of the steady sunlight and infrequent rain (indoor lighting techniques were not employed at the time).

By the early 1920s, all the major studios had moved from the East Coast to this then-obscure suburb. Hollywood quickly became synonymous with the celluloid image. Home to the great stars (Garbo, Gable, Crawford, Dietrich) and the great studios (Metro-Goldwyn-Mayer, Paramount, Warner Bros., 20th Century Fox), Hollywood became an important arbiter off American mores and interpreter of the American Dream.

Hollywood today has lost much of its sparkle. The major studios have moved over the mountains into the San Fernando Valley, where they have more space to weave their ever more elaborate fantasies, and blockbusters are increasingly shot elsewhere in the U.S. or overseas. As a result, the Golden Road has turned into Main Street in slacks. Hollywood Boulevard and other thoroughfares, once glittering and glamorous, are now rated X. At night, prostitutes abound; women work Hollywood and Sunset Boulevards, while boys ply their trade on Santa Monica Boulevard (also known as S&M Blvd.). Hollywood is still a fascinating place, but a far cry from the Emerald City it was once thought to be. At 105, the *grand dame* shows her age and survives on memories of her past.

The **Hollywood sign**—those 50-foot-high, slightly erratic letters perched on Mt. Cahuenga north of Hollywood—stands with New York's Statue of Liberty and Paris's Eiffel Tower as a universally recognized symbol of its city. The original 1923 sign, which read HOLLYWOODLAND, was an advertisement for a new subdivision in the Hollywood Hills (a caretaker lived behind one of the Ls). Over the years, people came to think of it as a civic monument, and the city, which by 1978 had acquired the sign, reconstructed the crumbling letters, leaving off the last syllable. The sign has been a target of pranksters (USC frat boys and Cal Tech hackers) who have made it read everything from "Hollyweed" to "Ollywood," after gap-toothed errand boy, Lt. Col. Oliver North. For a closer look at the site, follow Beachwood Dr. up into the hills (bus #208; off Franklin Ave. between Vine St. and Western Ave.). Drive along the narrow twisting streets of the Hollywood Hills for glimpses of the bizarre homes of the Rich and Famous, or detour to **Forest Lawn Memorial Park,** 6300 Forest Lawn Dr. (818-984-1711), on the other side of the hills. The park is a museum of early American history, with a mosaic mural and a collection of statues. (Open daily 9am-5pm. Free.)

Hollywood Boulevard itself, lined with souvenir shops, porno houses, clubs, and theaters, is busy both day and night. The façade of **Mann's Chinese Theater** (formerly Grauman's), 6925 Hollywood Blvd. (213-464-8111), between Highland and La Brea, is an odd tropical interpretation of a Chinese temple. Hollywood hype at its finest, there's always a crowd of tourists in the courtyard, worshipping cement impressions of various parts of the stars' anatomics and trademark possessions (Al Jolson's knees, Trigger's hooves, R2D2's wheels, Jimmy Durante's nose, George Burns' cigar, etc.) If you want to stroll among stars, have a look at the **Walk of Fame** along Hollywood Blvd. and Vine St. More than 2500 bronze-inlaid stars are embedded in the sidewalk, inscribed with names and feats. Film, television, and radio celebrities are commemorated, but many names will be meaningless to the under-40 generation. If you want to rub elbows with living stars, Mann's overvisited theater is clearly not the place to go. Across the street and two blocks east is another unique theater, the **UA Egyptian,** 6712 Hollywood Blvd. (213-467-6167), inspired in 1922 by the then-newly-discovered tomb of King Tut.

Also two blocks east of Mann's is the **Hollywood Wax Museum,** 6767 Hollywood Blvd. (213-462-8860), where you'll meet over 200 figures from Jesus to Cher. (Open Sun.-Thurs. 10am-midnight, Fri.-Sat. 10am-2am. Admission $7.50, children $5, seniors $6.) Other Hollywood Blvd. attractions include the original **Frederick's of Hollywood,** 6608 Hollywood Blvd. (213-466-8506), a purple and pink bastion of tasteful teddies and lickerish lingerie, which now houses its own **museum of lingerie** in the back of the store. (Open Mon.-Thurs. 10am-8pm, Fri. 10am-9pm, Sat. 10am-6pm, Sun. noon-5pm. Free.) Down the street, **Larry Edmund's Cinema and Theater Bookshop,** 6658 Hollywood Blvd. (213-463-3273), sells Ken Schessler's *This Is Hollywood: Guide to Hollywood Murders, Suicides, Graves, Etc.,* a guide to nondescript places made famous by the fact that stars courted, married, fooled around, were discovered, made movies, or committed suicide there. (Open Mon.-Sat. 10am-6pm.)

Hollywood Fantasy Tours, 1651 N. Highland (213-469-8184), two blocks south of Hollywood Blvd., offers two-hour tours of Tinseltown in double-decker buses with knowledgeable but corny tour guides who try to take seriously questions they've heard a million times. (Tours of Beverly Hills and other areas also offered. Call for info.)

The **Hollywood Studio Museum,** 2100 N. Highland Ave. (213-874-2276), across from the Hollywood Bowl, provides a refreshingly un-Mannesque look at the history of early Hollywood film-making. Back in 1913, when it was a barn, famed director Cecil B. DeMille rented this building as a studio and shot Hollywood's first feature film, *The Squaw Man,* there. Antique cameras, costumes, props, and other memorabilia clutter the museum along with vintage film clips. (Open Sat. and Sun. 10am-4pm. Admission $3.50, seniors and students $2.50, children $1.50. Ample free parking.)

Film is just one of the industries that grease Hollywood's cash-register wheels. Music is another. The pre-eminent monument of the modern record industry is the 1954 **Capitol Records Tower,** 1750 Vine St., just north of Hollywood Blvd. The building, which was designed to look like a stack of records, is cylindrical with fins sticking out at each floor (the "records") and a needle on top. More esoteric music and associated paraphernalia can be found at **The Rock Shop,** 6666 Hollywood Blvd. (213-466-7276), which carries—in addition to records and tapes—posters, T-shirts, thousands of buttons, handkerchiefs, tour and promotional merchandise, World War II artifacts, and leather and metal accessories.

If you're still not sated, visit the **Hollywood Cemetery,** at 6000 Santa Monica Blvd. (213-469-1181), between Vine St. and Western Ave., which is the permanent home to the remains of Rudolph Valentino and Douglas Fairbanks, Sr., and other Hollywood notables. (Open daily 8am-5pm.)

Barnsdall Park, 4800 Hollywood Blvd., relatively small and discreet, contains the **Municipal Art Gallery,** 4804 Hollywood Blvd. (213-485-4581), a modern building showing the works of Southern California artists in a pleasant, low-key setting. (Open Tues.-Sun. 12:30-5pm. Admission $1, under 13 free.) Adjacent to the museum, on top of the hill, the **Hollyhock House,** 4808 Hollywood Blvd. (213-662-7272), commands a 360° view of Los Angeles and the mountains. Completed in 1922 for eccentric oil heiress Aline Barnsdall, the house remains one of Frank Lloyd Wright's most important works. It is the first building by this pre-eminent modern American architect to reflect the influence of pre-Columbian Mayan temples. The name of the house derives from Barnsdall's favorite flower, which she had Wright reproduce (grudgingly) in abstract all over the house. (Tours Tues.-Thurs. on the hour from 10am-1pm; Sat. and all but the last Sun. each month noon-3pm. Admission $1.50, seniors $1, under 13 free. Buy tickets at the Municipal Art Gallery.) Call to arrange foreign language tours of Hollyhock House (213-485-4581).

On Hollywood's east side (east of the Hollywood Fwy. and bounded roughly by Sunset Blvd. to the north and Alvarado St. to the south), sits **Silver Lake/Echo Park,** L.A.'s first planned suburb. Victorian homes in varying states of disrepair still line the streets, especially Carroll Ave. and Kensington Rd.

About 3 mi. northeast of downtown is **Elysian Park;** with 525 acres of greenery, the park is ideal for picnicking. The park largely surrounds and embraces the area of Chavez Ravine, home of **Dodger Stadium** (213-224-1400) and the Los Angeles Dodgers baseball team. The Dodgers won the World Series twice in the 1980s and have consistently been one of the best-run organizations in all of professional sports. That quality of management is reflected in the well-designed and sparkling-clean Dodger Stadium. Tickets, which cost from $5 to $10 (all seats have good views of the field), are a hot commodity when the Dodgers are playing well; purchase in advance, if possible, or pay a premium from scalpers selling them illegally outside. Once in the ballpark, grab yourself a Dodger Dog, still one of the best dogs in the majors, although a 1991 brouhaha over a change in the weiners' preparation left a bad taste in the mouth of many fans.

Griffith Park

Sprawling over 4500 acres of hilly terrain is **Griffith Park.** The L.A. Zoo, the Greek Theater, Griffith Observatory and Planetarium, Travel Town, a bird sanctuary, tennis courts, two golf courses, campgrounds, and various hiking trails blanket the dry hills and mountains. This formidable recreational region stretches from the hills above Hollywood north to the intersection of the Ventura and Golden State Freeways. Pick up a map at any of the entrance points. A full day in the Park might include the zoo in the morning, the rest of the park during the afternoon, and the Greek Theater or the planetarium's laser show in the evening. Several of the mountain roads through the park, especially Vista Del Valle Dr., offer stunning panoramic (though often smog-obscured) views of Los Angeles, looking south over downtown, Hollywood, and the Westside. For information, stop by the **visitors center and ranger headquarters,** 4730 Crystal Spring Dr. (213-665-5188; open daily 6am-10pm).

If you enjoy seeing stars, head for the park's **Observatory and Planetarium** (213-664-1181, for a recording 213-664-1191). The white stucco and copper domes of the art deco structure are visible from around the park. You might also remember it from the climactic last scene of the James Dean film, *Rebel Without a Cause.* The exhibits in the Hall of Science are good but no different from other planetarium displays. One of the most interesting is a seismograph that runs continually: if you're there when the Big One comes, you'll know just how big it is. A 12-in. telescope opens the public eye to the sky every clear night from dusk-9:45pm; in winter Tues.-Sun. 7-10pm. (Call the sky report at 213-663-8171 for more information.) The planetarium also presents popular **Laserium** light shows (213-997-3624), psychedelic symphonies of colored lasers and music. (Observatory open daily 12:30pm-10pm; winter hours Tues.-Sun. 2pm-10pm. Free. Hour-long planetarium show Mon.-Fri. at 3, and 7:30pm, Sat.-Sun. also at 4:30pm; in winter Tues.-Fri. 3 and 8pm, Sat.-Sun. also at 4:30pm. Admission $3.50, seniors and under 15 $2.50. Laser shows Sun., Tues.-Thurs. at 6pm and 8:30pm; Fri.-Sat. also at 9:45pm. Admission $6, children $5.)

A large **bird sanctuary** at the bottom of the observatory hill serves its function well, but if you crave the sight of warm-blooded animals, you might go to the **L.A. Zoo,** at the park's northern end (213-666-4090). The zoo's 113 acres accommodate 2000 crazy critters, and the facility is consistently ranked among the nation's ten best. (Open daily 10am-6pm; in winter 10am-5pm. Admission $6, seniors $5, ages 2-12 $2.75, under 2 free. Ticket office closes 1 hr. before zoo closing time.)

Take a step back in time in nearby **Travel Town** (213-662-5874), an outdoor museum of trains, ponies, and other period vehicles. The exhibit itself is free, and is open Mon.-Fri. 10am-5pm, Sat.-Sun. and holidays 10am-6pm. In winter they close 1 hour earlier.

On the southern side of the park, below the observatory, the 4500-seat **Greek Theater** (213-665-5857) hosts a number of concerts in its outdoor amphitheater virtually year-round. Check advertisements in the *Sunday Times* "Calendar" section for coming attractions.

Those with a hankerin' to relive those wild, wild days of yore will enjoy the recently opened **Gene Autry Western Heritage Museum,** 4700 Zoo Dr. (213-667-

2000), also located within Griffith Park at the junction of Golden State (I-5) and Ventura (Rte. 134) Fwy. The museum's collection covers both fact and fiction of the Old West, with exhibits on pioneer life and on the history of western films. The Hollywood section includes costumes donated by Robert Redford, Gary Cooper, and Clint Eastwood. Firearms owned by George Custer, Wyatt Earp, Billy the Kid, and Teddy Roosevelt are on display in the historical exhibit. The elaborate displays succeed in evoking the aura of a wilder time. (Open Tues.-Sun. 10am-5pm. Admission $4.75, seniors and students $3.50, children $2.)

To get to the Observatory and Greek Theater, take bus #203 from Hollywood. To reach the Zoo and Travel Town, take bus #97 from downtown. There is no bus service between the northern and southern parts of Griffith Park.

West Hollywood

Once considered a no-man's land between Beverly Hills and Hollywood, West Hollywood was incorporated in 1985 and was one of the first cities in the country to be governed by openly gay officials. There's always a lot going on here, and a list of each month's events can be found in the *L.A. Weekly*.

In the years before incorporation, lax zoning and other liberal laws gave rise to the Gomorraic **Sunset Strip.** Long the nightlife center of L.A., the Strip was originally lined with posh nightclubs frequented by stars and now plays host to several rock clubs (see Music). The Strip's music scene is among the country's most fertile, and many world-famous bands from The Doors to Guns n' Roses got their start in these locales. These days, most of the music on this stretch is heavy metal and hard rock, and weekend nights draw tremendous crowds and traffic jams. Restaurants and comedy clubs flourish here as well. The **billboards** on the Strip are vividly hand-painted, many heralding the latest motion pictures.

Melrose Avenue, south of West Hollywood, is lined with swish restaurants, ultra-trendy boutiques, punk clothing pits, and art galleries. The choicest stretch is betweeen La Brea and Fairfax, but the *Repo Man*-like spectre of angst-ridden apocalyptic apathy haunts the whole 3-mi. distance between Highland and Doheny. Packed with pedestrians (mostly locals), especially on weekends, the lively street displays some of L.A.'s most unusual and stylized people.

At Beverly and La Cienega squats the massive **Beverly Center,** an expensive shopping complex. Escalators snake up the building's exterior, encased in glass tubing. Trendy boutiques, high-priced restaurants, and the Beverly Cineplex (13 movie theaters) occupy the plate-glass decorated interior. At the corner of Beverly and San Vicente Blvd. is the Los Angeles **Hard Rock Café** (310-276-7605). A pistachio-green '57 Chevy juts out of the roof, unsuccessfully attempting to escape the crowds within. Indiana Jones's leather jacket, one of Pete Townshend's guitars, a 6-foot-tall martini glass, license plates, and college banners adorn the interior. Expect to tarry for a table every night of the week—over an hour on weekends. The line to buy T-shirts is formidable as well. (Open Sun.-Thurs. 11:30am-midnight, Fri.-Sat. 11:30am-1am.)

North of the Beverly Center, at Melrose and San Vicente, is the **Pacific Design Center,** 8687 Melrose Ave. (310-657-0800), a huge, blue-and-green glass complex with a wave-like profile (nicknamed **The Blue Whale**). The building, completed in 1976, is no doubt destined for architectural history texts. In addition to some design showrooms, the PDC houses a public plaza with a 350-seat amphitheater, used to stage free summer concerts. Call or inquire at the information desk in the entryway for details about such events. West Hollywood's **Gay Pride Weekend Celebration** (in late June) is usually held at the PDC plaza.

Lacking the city of Los Angeles' landmark protection, many of West Hollywoods more famous homes have been torn down. Still, a few remain and deserve a visit. **The Schindler House,** built in 1922, is a classic craftsman style home with both Latino and Japanese influences (833 N. Kings Rd; 213-651-1510; open to the public Sat.-Sun. 1-4pm; free.) Frank Lloyd Wright's **Storer House** stands proudly overlooking Hollywood Blvd. (8161 Hollywood Blvd; no public access). Some of the most beautiful homes in the area, however, are the **Garden Apartments,** which between Sunset and Fountain Ave. **The Andalusia** at 1475 Havenhurst Dr. is a stunning Spanish Classical Revival building which is only surpassed by the **Villa d'Este** at 1355 Laurel Ave.

Beverly Hills

Though placed in the midst of Greater Los Angeles, about 2/3 of the way between downtown L.A. and the coast, Beverly Hills remains a steadfast enclave of wealth. Beverly Hills seceded from L.A. in 1914 and has remained distinct (physically and ideologically) from the city ever since. All this is grossly apparent along Robertson Ave., at the eastern edge of the city, where only the western side of the street (the Beverly Hills side) is lined with large, shady trees. Similarly, driving west from the Sunset Strip, the sleaziness of Hollywood stops cold at the Beverly Hills border.

The city's wealth is readily apparent; stand on Rodeo Dr. for 15 minutes, and count how many BMWs, Porsches, and Jaguars roll past you; the Beverly Hills Post Office (on Beverly Dr.) must be the only one in the country with valet parking; even the homeless are well-dressed (otherwise they'd be gently escorted to the city's edge by Beverly Hills' remarkably efficient police force). The heart of the city rests in the **Golden Triangle,** a wedge formed by Wilshire and Santa Monica Blvd. centering on **Rodeo Drive,** known for its many opulent clothing boutiques and jewelry shops. On this famous street you might feel underdressed simply window-shopping. Beverly Hills' European aspirations consume the Golden Triangle, where signs champion Cannes as the sister-city of Beverly Hills. One outlandish attempt to make customers believe they have strayed into Europe is the cobblestoned street of **Via Rodeo.** Desperately faking antiquity, the entire street, hill, lampposts and all, was constructed in the last three years. Across the way is the venerable **Beverly Wilshire Hotel,** (310-275-5200) whose old and new wings are connected by El Camino Real, a cobbled street with Louis XIV gates. Inside, hall mirrors reflect the glitter of crystal chandeliers and marble floors.

The new **Beverly Hills City Hall** stands, looking a bit out of place, on Crescent Dr. just below Santa Monica. This beautiful Spanish Renaissance building was erected, amazingly, during the heart of the country's Depression, and is now engulfed in Beverly Hills' new **Civic Center.** Completed in September 1990, the Civic Center, which includes the Beverly Hills Fire Department, Police Station, and library, took nine years to build and cost $120 million. Designed by Charles Moore, the Civic Center's post-moderne combination of Spanish Baroque, Art Deco, and Art Moderne is sure to win architectural awards (even the library's parking structure is something to see). The **Beverly Hills Library** (444 N. Rexford Dr.; 213-228-2220) is a case study in the city's overriding concerns—the interior is adorned with marble imported from Thailand, but contains a paltry collection of books. As always, though, Beverly Hills coordinates well: the library's tiling matches the colors on City Hall's dome. Moving further north, the **Beverly Hills Hotel,** 9641 Sunset Blvd. (310-276-2251), is a pink, palm-treed collection of poolside cottages. The jungle-bungalow atmosphere mixes California cool, tropical paradise lushness, and Beverly Hills luxury in lodgings fit for *Fantasy Island.* This is where Howard Hughes established his germ-free apartment. Lovers and professional photographers frequent the park just south of the hotel.

City council members aren't the only building-happy residents of Beverly Hills. The latest residential fad is the "Wedding Cake" house—stucco, pastel, symmetric, and almost edible. Still Beverly Hillbillies have had better taste in the past, as a drive past the incredibly varied architectural sights of Beverly Hills homes will attest (a walking tour is impossible—the plots are too large). The **"Greystone Mansion"** (or Doheny House) is a modern day Versailles. Built by oil mogul Doheny for his son, the Tudor and Jacobean house includes the main building, two gatehouses, glorious gardens, and a stunning view of Los Angeles (905 Loma Vista Drive, just off Doheny Rd.; gardens free, open to the public daily 10am-6pm). The **Virginia Robinson Gardens,** nearby, are open to the public by reservation only (310-

276-5367; tours of gardens and the 1911 beaux arts house offered Tues.-Fri. at 10am and 1pm; adults $3, seniors, students and children $2.25). Back down near Santa Monica, the Gaudiesque dripping ornamentation of the O'Neil House (507 N. Rodeo Dr.) is best seen from the alley behind the house. The Spadena House on the Southeast corner of Carmelita Avenue and Walden Dr. looks as if it belongs to the wicked witch of the West.

The carless may be considering hopping on a stargazing tourbus. Be forewarned: the only people visible on the streets are gardeners, and many of them don't even know who they're working for. Since you'll never know the difference, some tours feel free to make things up as they go along. A better alternative is the **Beverly Hills Trolley,** which can be picked up at Dayton and Rodeo and runs to Sunset and back every half hour ($1, 310-275-2791; Tues.-Sat. 10am-5:15pm).

Fans of *Beverly Hills 90210* may want to see what **Beverly Hills High** actually looks like (located on Moreno, between Olympic and Spalding). Frequently ranked one of the top 10 public high schools in the country, Beverly Hills High looks more like a college campus than a high school, and may be the only high school in the country with its own oil well. The indoor swimming pool is open for public use in summer (310-550-4625; open swim Mon.-Thurs. 1pm-5pm, Fri. 2-4pm), and has a sliding floor cover that converts the pool into a full-size basketball court.

Just west of Beverly Hills High is a **Century City,** whose broad awe-inspiring avenues include the ABC Entertainment Center and the Century City Shopping Center and Market Place.

Just outside of Beverly Hills, the **Beit HaShoa Museum of Tolerance** will be opening in April of 1992 (310-553-9036; 9786 W. Pico Blvd. on the corner of Roxbury). Previously known as the Simon Wiesenthal Center, the museum received $5 million from former Governor Deukmeijian to build a new, larger, structure on the condition that the museum include displays on the Armenian and Native American genocides. The new museum will hold high tech wizardry designed to help visitors explore their own prejudices, and displays on the U.S. Civil Rights movement, the Holocaust, and anti-semitism and prejudice in the U.S., and the U.S. Civil Rights movement (hours and prices have not been determined, but are likely to be: admission $5 with student and senior discounts; Mon.-Thurs. 9am-5pm, Fri. 9am-3pm, Sun. 11am-4pm).

Westwood and UCLA

Welcome to Scooterville! The gargantuan **University of California at Los Angeles** campus (it covers over 400 acres in the foothills of the Santa Monica Mountains, bounded by Sunset, Hilgard, Le Conte, and Gayley) and the dearth of parking spaces make both UCLA and Westwood look like motorbike versions of Disneyland's *autopia.* UCLA is the largest of the nine UC campuses. Regarded as one of the top research universities in the United States, UCLA is clearly not the unidimensional, hedonistic colony of blond, deep-tanned party animals it was once thought to be.

The school is directly north of Westwood Village and west of Beverly Hills. To reach the campus by car, take the San Diego Fwy. (I-405) north to the Wilshire Blvd./Westwood exit, heading east into Westwood. Take Westwood Blvd. north off Wilshire, heading straight through the center of the village and directly into the campus. By bus, take RTD route #20, 21 (the best, since it goes directly to the campus), 22, 320, or 322 along Wilshire Blvd. to Westwood. Exit at Wilshire and Gayley and walk north to Gayley and Weyburn Ave., where you can pick up a free UCLA Campus Express shuttle to the center of campus. Drivers can find free parking behind the Federal Building and, on Friday and Saturday nights, avoid the ten-minute walk into the village by riding the 10¢ **RTD Shuttle** (Fri. 6:30pm-1:30am, Sat. 11am-1:30am). Those who wish to park on campus may do so by paying $4 at one of the campus information kiosks; you will receive a day permit allowing you to park in the student garages.

The best place to start a tour of UCLA is at the **Visitors Center,** 10945 Le Conte Ave., #147 (310-206-8147), located in the Ueberroth Olympic Office Building. The riveting 18 minute film introduction to UCLA, *UCLA: The Future is Now* is shown here whenever the center's staff doesn't have anything better to do. But the fun doesn't stop there, as free 90-minute walking tours of the campus depart from the visitors center at 10:30am and at 1:30pm Monday to Friday. Campus maps are also available at the information kiosks located at each of the streets leading into the campus.

Royce Hall, situated in the Quadrangle, is the architectural pride and joy of the UCLA Campus. **Powell Library,** at the south end is the main undergraduate library and reflects an Islamic influence in its architectural design. To the west, the **Janss Steps** lead down from the Plaza; these four daunting flights of brick presents an indelible image of UCLA.

To the east lies **Jimmy's,** where the cutesy half of the student body sips cappuccino royales served by design student Sharon Hami.

At the northernmost reach of the campus, the **Dickson Art Center** (310-825-1462) houses the Wight Art Gallery, home to the Grunwald Center for the Graphic Arts, as well as frequent internationally recognized exhibitions. (Open Sept.-June Tues. 11am-8pm, Wed.-Fri. 11am-5pm, Sat. and Sun. 1-5pm. Free.) The **Murphy Sculpture Garden,** containing over 70 pieces scattered through five acres, lies directly in front of the Art Center. The collection includes works by such major artists as Auguste Rodin, Henri Matisse, and Joan Miró. Opposite the sculpture garden is Mac Gowen Hall, which contains the **Tower of Masks.** Another heralded piece of outdoor artwork is UCLA's **Inverted Fountain,** located between Knudsen Hall and Schoenberg Hall, directly south of Dickson Plaza. An innovation in the exciting field of fountain design, water spouts from the fountain's perimenter and rushes down into the gaping hole in the middle.

West of the fountain is the Math Science Building, which sports mosaics detailing the history of mathematics. The campus also includes the **Fowler Museum of Cultural History** in Haines Hall (310-825-4361), which displays artifacts from contemporary, historic, and prehistoric cultures of Africa, Asia, Oceania, and the Americas (open year-round Wed.-Sun. noon-5pm). The museum is presently the source of controversy since Native American bones are stored here because for their archaelogical value, and despite laws which allow for Native Americans rights to sacred burial. The **Botanical Gardens** (310-825-1260), in the southeast corner of the campus, encompass a subtropical canyon where redwoods and venerable palms mingle brook-side (open year-round Mon.-Fri. 8am-5pm, Sat.-Sun. 8am-4pm), and the Zen Buddhist-inspired **Japanese Garden.** (Open Tues. 10am-1pm, Wed. noon-3pm, by appointment only. Reservations should be made a couple of weeks in advance. Call the visitors center at 310-825-4574 or 310-825-4338 to arrange for a tour.)

Ackerman Union, 308 Westwood Plaza (310-825-7711), stands southwest of the Quadrangle, at the bottom of the hill. Ackerman is the campus information bank. A calendar lists the month's lengthy line-up of movies (first-runs often free), lectures, and campus activities. The Expo Center, on level B, has travel information and a complete **rideboard.** Next door, there's a bowling alley and enough fast-food joints to satisfy a sumo wrestling team. (Open Mon.-Fri. 8:30am-6pm, Sat. 10am-5pm, Sun. noon-5pm.) The ground floor is swallowed by the **Associated Students Students' Store** (310-825-0611), the largest on-campus store in the U.S. (Open Mon.-Thurs. 7:45am-7:30pm, Fri. 7:45am-6pm, Sat. 10am-5pm, Sun. noon-5pm.)

To see live students in their natural habitat, head northwest of the central campus, along Gayley Ave., where many of the fraternity houses are located. The newly remodeled **Co-op** at the end of Frat Row is one example and an interesting combination of Bauhaus/Moderne architecture and UCLA remodeling. Sorority Row lies, appropriately, on the opposite side of the campus, on Hilgard.

Before it attained national acclaim in research arenas, UCLA attained national prominence in sporting arenas. UCLA has captured more National Collegiate Athletic Association (NCAA) titles over the last 20 years than any other university (62). The UCLA men's basketball team, which won seven consecutive NCAA championships in the 60s and 70s under legendary coach and Meleisian mentor John Wooden, plays its home games at **Pauley Pavilion,** located to the west of Dickson Plaza, down Bruin Walk, next to the impressive **Bruin Bear Statue** (depicting the school's mascot). Behind the major Ursa is the **UCLA Athletic Hall of Fame** (inside the J.D. Morgan Intercollegiate Athletic Center). The other athletic facilities are clustered around Pauley.

Westwood Village, just south of the campus, with its myriad of movie theaters, trendy boutiques, and upscale bistros, is geared more toward the residents of L.A.'s Westside than collegians. Like most college neighborhoods, however, Westwood is humming on Friday and Saturday nights when everyone (students, tourists, gang members, and police) show up to do their thing. Despite attempts to provide a safer climate, Westwood was the sight of three riots during the '90-'91 school year. For the most part, though, Westwood is safe, and is generally overrun by high school kids.

Westwood's theaters are among the oldest in the city and are a reasonable alternative to the tourist-trap atmosphere of Mann's Chinese Theater in Hollywood. Of particular note is the **Village Theatre,** 961 Broxton Ave. (310-208-5576), a movie theater with a high tower, large auditorium (complete with a balcony for crowded shows), and an impressive THX sound system.

The **Armand Hammer Museum of Art and Cultural Center,** 10899 Wilshire Blvd. (310-443-7000), was opened to the public in November 1990. Armand Hammer lived a mere ten days after his museum's opening. Hammer puportedly wanted to donate his collections to the L.A. County Museum of Art but demanded that the works be exhibited together in a separate wing. The museum refused, telling Hammer to build his own place—and he did just that. Impressive from the outside, light, airy, and clad in marble on the inside, Edwards Larrabee Barnes' tribute to Hammer's wealth is a welcome addition to the Westwood scene.

The museum house a very "Impressive" collection of European and American works from the 16th to the 20th century. The museum's gem is Van Gogh's *Hospital at Saint-Rémy,* a startling, flamelike image of the private hospital in which Van Gogh died just a year after the painting's completion. The museum also holds the world's largest collection of works by French lithographer Honoré Daumier, Leonardo da Vinci's 18 page Codex containing his ideas on hydraulics and engineering (not particularly interesting unless you read 16th century Italian written backwards in second grade penmanship), and traveling exhibitions. The museum will open an auditorium for the performing arts in 1992. (Parking on Westwood $2.75; open Wed.-Mon. noon-7pm; docent tours given Sunday and Thursday at 1pm; admission $4.50, students and seniors $3).

Directly across from UCLA is the opulent community of **Bel-Air,** where ex-actor Ronald Reagan has retired. Farther west on Sunset Blvd., (the winding setting for the car race in *Against All Odds,*) are the neighborhoods of **Brentwood** and beautiful **Pacific Palisades.** The rugged cliffs give way to the ocean at the popular **Will Rogers State Beach,** on the 16000 block of Pacific Coast Hwy. One of two great hotbeds of beach volleyball in L.A. county (the other is Manhattan Beach), this is where the professional players come to practice.

At 14523 Sunset, hike around **Will Rogers State Historical Park** (310-454-8212) and take in the panoramic views of the city and the distant Pacific. You can visit the famous horseman's home and eat a picnic brunch while watching polo matches on the grounds on Saturday afternoons (2-5pm) and Sunday mornings (10am-noon). Follow Chautauqua Blvd. inland from PCH to Sunset Blvd., or take bus #2 which runs along Sunset Blvd. (Park open daily 8am-7pm; Rogers' house open daily 10am-5pm.)

Santa Monica

To a resident of turn-of-the-century L.A., a trip to the beach resort of Santa Monica meant a long ride over poor-quality roads. The Red Car electric train shortened the trip considerably, and today, it takes about half an hour (with no traffic) on

Big Blue express bus #10 or on the Santa Monica Freeway (I-10) from downtown. No longer far away, SaMo is still pretty far out, with an extremely liberal city council and the former Mr. Jane Fonda (Tom Hayden, one of the Chicago Seven) as one of its assemblymen.

The beach is the closest to Los Angeles proper, and thus crowded and dirty. Still, the magical lure of sun, surf, and sand causes nightmarish summer traffic jams on I-10 and I-405; there are much prettier and cleaner beaches to visit to the north and south. The colorful **Santa Monica Pier** is still a nostalgic and popular, if a bit sleazy, spot. The gem of the pier is the magnificent turn-of the-century carousel, which was featured in *The Sting.* The main walk of the pier offers the familiar aroma of popcorn, a few pizza joints, several arcades, and tons o' tacky souvenirs. **Palisades Park,** on the bluff overlooking the pier, provides a shaded home for numerous homeless people. The **Senior Citizens Building,** in the park, contains a **camera obscura**—a darkened room in which an image of the scene outside is projected onto a big circular screen. It projects the whole 360°, but palm trees block out much of the northern view.

With the creation of the **Third Street Promenade** in 1989, and the recent remodeling of its upscale neighbor, **Santa Monica Place** (see Shopping), Santa Monica has recently become one of L.A.'s major walking, movie-seeing, and yuppie-meeting areas. The Third Street Promenade sports some cool cafés, a couple of L.A.'s better bookshops, overpriced bars and restaurants, and a number of fine, fresh street artists (not to mention some water-spouting, ivy-lined, mesh dinosaur sculptures). If you're interested in what the architects of the Promenade like to call home, you can examine that Gehry House at the Southeast corner of Washington and 22nd Ave. Farther east, boutiques and restaurants in a strange mixture of art deco and muted New Wave dot Main St. and Broadway.

Military, aerial, and military aerial enthusiasts will want to inspect Santa Monica's **Museum of Flying,** located at the Santa Monica Aiport at 2772 Donald Douglas Loop North (310-392-8822; adults $4, seniors and children $3; open Wed.-Sun. 10am-5pm). The museum's changing exhibits include the "1924 Douglas World Cruiser "New Orleans"" (the first plane to go around the world), authentic B-51s, and a replica of the Voyager spacecraft, as well as several daily films.

Venice

The most unique part of a unique city, Venice is Los Angeles' saving grace for budget travelers. A perennial favorite among foreigners, Venice is wacky on weekdays, wild on weekends. A typical Sunday includes trapeze artists, spontaneous rollerblade dancing competitions, and your run-of-the-mill clowns, jugglers, comediens, glass-eaters, hemp advocates, bikini-clad skaters, fortune tellers, and choirs of gaping Angelenos. With everyone crowding the beachfront, trying either to see or to be seen, life in Venice is, as one hostel brochure aptly puts it, "spontaneous theater."

Venice's story begins just after the turn of the century, when Abbot Kinney dug a series of canals throughout the town and filled them with water, intending to bring the romance and refinement of Venice, Italy to Southern California. But Kinney's vision was not realized; the water of the canals became dirty and oily, and instead of attracting society's upper crust, developed a crust of their own. Venice became home to gamblers, bootleggers, and other assorted rogues. The canals were eventually forgotten and, for the most part, filled in and buried. Skateboarders use some of the others.

For a sense of the Venice that Kinney envisioned, head for the traffic circle at Main St. and Windward Ave., 3 blocks inland from the beach pavilion. This was once a circular canal, the hub of the whole network. The post office on the circle's west side has a small mural inside that sums up Venice's cluttered history in an appropriately jumbled way—with oil derricks seemingly perched on Kinney's shoulders. Back outside on Main St., walk down Windward to its intersection with Pacific Ave. Columns and tiled awnings are all that remain of the grandiose hotels that once housed vacationers from Los Angeles. Health-food shops and vintage clothing stores lie behind the colonnades where sedans once discharged high-styled passengers. One of the sole surviving canals is at Strong's Dr., off Washington St. Ducks are its liveliest inhabitants.

Venice finally came into its own in the 70s, when the Sexual Revolution spawned a swinging beach community. Although the revolution may have been defeated, Venice's peculiar beach renaissance lives on, a testament to the ongoing allure of the credo, "do your own thing."

Ocean Front Walk, Venice's main beach front drag, is a drastic demographic departure from Santa Monica's Promenade. Street people converge on shaded clusters of benches, healthy-types play paddle tennis, and bodybuilders of both sexes pump iron in skimpy outfits at the original **Muscle Beach** (1800 Ocean Front Walk, closest to 18th and Pacific Ave.). This is where the roller-skating craze began, and this is probably where it will breathe its last. Even the police wear shorts while slapping nude sunbathers (hopefully not too hard) with $55 fines. New Wave types, cyclists, joggers, groovy elders (such as the "skateboard grandma"), and bards in Birkenstocks make up the balance of this funky playground population. Venders of jewelry, snacks, and beach bric-a-brac overwhelm the boardwalk and are sights themselves. Collect your wits and take in the crowds from a distance at one of the many cafés or juice bars. The **Sidewalk Café,** 1401 Ocean Front Walk (310-399-5547), with free live music most evenings, is nearly always packed. (Open Sun.-Thurs. 8am-midnight, Fri.-Sat. 8am-1am.) If your feet don't move you through the crowds fast enough, rent or a bike. The cheapest rental place is **Sports and Stuff,** on Washington. (Rollerblades $4 per hour, $8 per day; bikes $2.50 per hour, $5 per day. Open daily 9am-6pm.)

Venice's **street murals** are another free show. Don't miss the brilliant, grafitti-disfigured homage to Botticelli's *Birth of Venus* on the beach pavilion at the end of Windward Ave.: an angelically beautiful woman, wearing short shorts, a Band-aid top, and roller-skates, boogies out of her seashell. The side wall of a Japanese restaurant on Windward is covered with a perfect imitation of a Japanese Hokusai print of a turbulent sea. Large insect sculptures loom in the rafters of many of the city's posh restaurants. To look at paintings indoors, you might want to stop by **L.A. Louver,** 77 Market St. and 55 N. Venice Blvd. (310-822-4955), a gallery showing the work of some hip L.A. artists (open Tues.-Sat. noon-5pm).

To get to Venice from downtown L.A., take bus #33 or 333 (or 436 during rush hour). From downtown Santa Monica, take Santa Monica bus #1 or 2.

The Pacific Coast Highway

From Santa Monica, where it temporarily merges with I-10, the **Pacific Coast Highway (PCH)** (Rte. 1) runs northward along the spectacular California coast. Several of L.A. county's best beaches line this stretch of the PCH between Santa Monica and the Ventura County line.

Heading north from Santa Monica, the first major attraction is the **J. Paul Getty Museum,** 17985 PCH (310-458-2003), set back on a cliff above the ocean. Getty, an oil magnate, built this mansion as a re-creation of the 1st-century Villa dei Papiri in Herculaneum, with a beautiful main peristyle garden, a reflecting pool, and bush-lined paths. Appropriately, the collection of Greek and Roman sculpture is given center stage—it includes a bronze athlete that is the only surviving work of Lysippos, a sculptor contemporaneous with Alexander the Great. Although Getty himself collected 13th- to early 20th-century European paintings (with an emphasis on Renaissance and the Baroque), the museum owns an incredible variety of artwork, including decorative arts and illuminated manuscripts. Unfortunately, only a small selection is displayed at any one time. The museum has also recently added an excellent collection of 19th- and 20th-century photography, as well as one of Van Gogh's Iris paintings. With a $2.9 billion endowment (New York's Metropolitan Museum of Art "only" has $350 million), the trustees can afford to keep their purse strings loose. Eventually everything but the Greek and Roman antiquities will be housed in a separate facility planned for a 110-acre hilltop site 11 mi. away in Brentwood, and due to be completed in 1997. Because of the museum's operating agreement with its residential neighbors, access to the museum is more difficult than it could be. Because the parking lot is small, reservations are needed a day in advance, weeks in advance in summer. You are not permitted to park outside the museum unless you do so at the county lot. Bicyclists and motorcyclists are admitted without reservations. Take RTD #434 (which you can board at Sunset and PCH in Malibu or Ocean and Colorado in Santa Monica) to the museum and mind that you ask for a free **museum pass** from the bus driver. The museum gate is ½-mi. from the bus stop, so be prepared to walk. (Open Tues.-Sun. 10am-5pm. Free.)

Just north of the museum is **Topanga State Beach,** 18500 PCH, a quiet surfing beach (a bit rocky for sunbathing) with lifeguards and restaurants, but no concessions stands. The out-of-the-way community of **Topanga,** where granola and macrame are serious business and the New Age is now, lies 4 mi. up Topanga Canyon Rd.

The celebrity colony of **Malibu** stretches along the low 20000 blocks of PCH. With their multi-million dollar homes and celebrity neighbors, Malibu residents can afford to be hostile to nonlocals, especially to those from the Valley. The beach lies along the 23200 block of the PCH. You can walk onto the beach via the **Zonker Harris access way** at 22700 PCH, named after the quintessential Californian of Garry Trudeau's comic strip, *Doonesbury.* Those intrigued by Malibu's history can visit the **Malibu Lagoon Museum,** 23200 PCH (456-8432), 300 yards west of the Malibu pier. (Tours Wed.-Sat. 11am-3pm. $2 entrance.) Included in the museum is the Adamson House, a two-story Andalusian Farmhouse built by Stiles Clements, and probably your only chance to see one of Malibu's famous homes up close.

Corral State Beach, an uncrowded, windsurfing, swimming, and scuba diving beach, lies on the 26000 block of PCH, followed by **Point Dume State Beach,** which is small and generally uncrowded.

North of Point Dume, along the 30000 block of PCH, lies **Zuma,** L.A. County's northernmost and largest county-owned sandbox, with lifeguards, restrooms, and a $5 parking fee. The beach is frequented by a mixed bag of sun-worshippers. Stations 8 to 12 belong to solitude seekers. The Valley high-schoolers have staked out 6 and 7, which are the most crowded and lively parts. Zuma 3, 4, and 5 are frequented by families who keep things slightly more sedate. If you don't want to bring food, pick something up at **Trancas Market** (PCH and Trancas Canyon, around Station 12). Evade the beach stands unless you're willing to pay $2.75 for an insipid hamburger or hot dog.

Finally, visitors with cars should not miss **Mulholland Drive,** nature's answer to the roller coaster. Twisting and turning for 15 spectacular miles along the crest of the Santa Monica Mountains, Mulholland stretches from PCH, near the Ventura County line, east to the Hollywood Fwy. and San Fernando Valley. Whoever's driving will have a hard time concentrating—numerous points along the way, especially between Coldwater Canyon and the San Diego Fwy., have compelling views of the entire Los Angeles basin. It is wise to avoid Mulholland on late weekend nights, when the road is fraught with drag-racing teenagers and parked cars on Lover's Lane. Racers use both lanes, and four headlights coming at you at 70mph can be an even more arresting sight than all the panoramic lights of what Aldous Huxley called "the city of dreadful joy."

San Fernando Valley

At the end of the Ventura Freeway lies the spiritual center of American suburbia—a seemingly infinite series of communities with tree-lined streets, cookie-cutter homes, lawns, and shopping malls. A third of L.A.'s population resides here, where the portion of the Valley incorporated into the City of Los Angeles alone covers 140 million acres. The area was settled after city engineer William Mulholland brought water to the valley in 1913. Standing on a hillside overlooking the basin,

Mulholland watched the first torrents pour out of the Los Angeles Aqueduct, and proclaimed "There it is; take it!" The city rushed to obey.

Ventura Boulevard, the main commercial thoroughfare, today combines business and recreation with its office buildings, restaurants, and shops. The sprawling valley viewed from the foothills at night, particularly from Mulholland Drive, is spectacular.

The valley is a nice place to live, but you wouldn't want to visit. Aside from the major attractions of Magic Mountain and tours of nearby movie studios (both listed under Entertainment), the valley's biggest pull is its infamous stereotypical images of valley girls and dudes. In reality, they've paved paradise and put in a putting green.

Once you've finished searching Ventura Blvd. for the ultimate valley hangout (try a Denny's on a weekend night between 2 and 4am) you may want to check out the **Burbank Historical Society's Gordon Howard Museum** at 115 N. Lomita. The museum's three buildings include a tenderly restored Victorian Cottage, an antique vehicle museum, and a Burbank Memorabilia Museum, which maintains a huge camera collection. Open Sun. 1-4pm. For tours during the week phone the knowledgable Loris Warner at 818-842-7514. Voluntary donation $1.

The Valley's other sight of interest is the **Mission San Fernando Ray De España.** The mission was founded in 1797 by Padre Fermin Lasuen, but, unfortunately, no structures remain from this period. The old **Iglesia** was destroyed by the 1971 earthquake, and the **Convento** has been covered with stucco, making the cemetery and the park across the street the most intriguing part of the mission. West of the mission, at 10940 Sepulveda, sits the **Andres Pico Adobe**, the former home of Pico, who started the first wave of construction in the valley in 1845, when he built up his own copious tracts of land. The house has been somewhat remodeled since the early days.

Pasadena

Pasadena, a suburb about 10 mi. northeast of downtown Los Angeles, offers the perfect antidote to the hectic pace of Greater L.A. Pasadena is quiet and placid, with pleasant tree-lined streets and greenery, along with outstanding cultural facilities. Even the trip there, along the Pasadena Fwy. (Rte. 110 North), is interesting; the freeway, one of the nation's oldest, was built as a WPA project between 1934 and 1941. The WPA engineers, however, failed to anticipate the needs of the modern motorist; 50 years later, drivers are required to merge almost instantaneously with 55 mph traffic from a dead stop.

In the gorge that forms the city's western boundary stands Pasadena's most famous landmark, the **Rose Bowl,** 991 Rosemont Blvd. (818-793-7193, Rose Bowl Event Information Line 818-577-3106). Home to the "granddaddy" of the college football bowl games, the annual confrontation between the champions of the Big Ten and Pac 10 conferences, the Rose Bowl is also regular-season home to the UCLA Bruins football team. The stadium seats 104,700 and periodically throws the Super Bowl. The New Year's Day Rose Bowl game follows the **Tournament of Roses Parade,** which runs along Colorado Blvd. through downtown Pasadena. Thousands line the Pasadena streets (having staked out choice viewing spots days in advance) to watch the flower-covered floats go by. During the off-season, the Rose Bowl hosts a flea market on the second Sunday of each month. The Rose Bowl also sponsors a July 4th celebration, **America Fest** (tickets $15; for information call 818-578-1989).

Over the hill and to the east of the stadium lies a quiet, shady neighborhood containing several examples of gorgeous Pasadena architecture. The most renowned of these is the **Gamble House,** 4 Westmoreland Pl. (818-793-3334). Designed in 1908 by brothers Charles and Henry Greene for the heirs to the Proctor and Gamble fortune, David and Mary Gamble, this bungalow-style masterpiece has become part of USC's School of Architecture. It is especially noteworthy for the TLC given to its furnishings: everything down to the trim, paneling, and carpets was designed by the Greene brothers, much of it actually crafted in their Pasadena workshop (1-hr. tours Thurs.-Sun. noon-3pm. Admission $4, seniors $3, students $2, children free.) A map and pamphlet detailing other renowned neighborhood buildings is available in the **Gamble House bookstore** for $1. You can also stop in at the **Fenyes Mansion** just a couple of blocks east off Orange Grove, at 470 W. Walnut St. (818-577-1660). The mansion is the residence of the **Pasadena Historical Society and Museum** and has a collection of turn-of-the-century furnishings and art. Much of the decor is in schlock-Mediterranean style, and the presence of mannequins in faded "period" costumes does little to improve matters. (Tours of museum Thurs.-Sun. 1-4pm.)

South of this neighborhood, at the western end of the downtown area (also called Old Pasadena), lies Pasadena's answer to LACMA and the Getty Museum, the **Norton Simon Museum of Art,** 411 W. Colorado Blvd. (818-449-3730), at Orange Grove Blvd. Sleek and modern, it contrasts with the classic design of the Getty. The collection is superb; there are numerous Rodin and Brancusi bronzes, and the paintings include masterpieces by Rembrandt, Raphael, and Picasso. There is also an impressive impressionist and post-impressionist hall. The ancient Southeast Asian art collection is one of the world's best, and the presentation is flawless. Simon's eclectic, slightly idiosyncratic taste, as well as the well-written descriptions of the works, make this museum more interesting than similar assemblages elsewhere. (Open Thurs.-Sun. noon-6pm. Admission $4, seniors and students $2, under 12 free; wheelchair accessible.) From downtown L.A. take bus #483 from Olive St., anywhere between Venice Blvd. and 1st St., to Colorado Blvd. and Fair Oaks Ave. in Pasadena. The museum is 4 blocks west.

Continuing east into downtown, the area around Fair Oaks Ave. and Colorado Blvd., once home to thrift shops, shows signs of gentrification, as trendy boutiques and cafés, and the inevitable multiplex movie theater spring up. The **Pasadena Civic Center** (818-449-7360), situated north of Colorado Blvd. at 300 E. Green, is the centerpiece of the city's Spanish-influenced architectural heritage. The City Hall is built in Spanish style aroung a beautiful open courtyard, complete with gardens and a fountain. Just east of the Civic Center is the **The Pacific Asia Museum,** 46 N. Los Robles Ave. (818-449-2742), between Colorado Ave. and Union St. This museum displays an unusual collection of Asian paintings, drawings, and jade sculpture. (Open Wed.-Sun. noon-5pm. (Admission $3 adults, $1.50 seniors and students. Decent tours every Sunday at 2pm.) The **Pasadena Playhouse,** 39 S. El Molino Ave. (818-356-7529), was founded in 1917 and has nurtured the careers of William Holden and Gene Hackman, among others. Crowned as the State Theater of California by the State Assembly in 1937, the Playhouse itself is an excellent example of Spanish colonial revival architecture. Restored and reopened in 1986, it presently offers some of the finest theater in L.A.

Some of the world's greatest scientific minds do their work at the West Coast rival to the Massachusetts Institute of Technology, the **California Institute of Technology,** 1201 E. California Blvd. (818-356-6811), about 2½ mi. southeast of downtown. The campus is lush, filled with bush- and olive-tree-lined brick paths. The buildings incorporate a mishmash of Spanish, Italian Renaissance, and modern styles. Cal Tech, founded in 1891 as Throop University, has amassed a faculty which includes several Nobel prizewinners (Albert Einstein once taught here) and a student body which prides itself both on its high I.Q. and its elaborate and ingenious practical jokes. These range from the mundane (unscrewing all the chairs in a lecture hall and bolting them in backwards) to the audacious (altering the Rose Bowl scoreboard during the big game with the aid of computers).

One ½-mile to the south of Cal Tech lies the **Huntington Library, Art Gallery, and Botanical Gardens,** 1151 Oxford Rd., San Marino 91108 (818-405-2100, ticket information 818-405-2273). Despite the ban on picnics and sunbathing, families and tourists still flock here on Sundays to stroll around the grounds and visit the library and galleries. The stunning botanical gardens nurture 207 acres of plants, many of them rare. The library houses one of the world's most important collections of rare books and English and American manuscripts, including a Gutenberg Bible and Benjamin Franklin's handwritten autobiography. The art gallery is also known for its 18th- and 19th-century British paintings. Sentimental favorites on exhibit include Thomas Gainsborough's *Blue Boy* and its companion piece, Sir Thomas Lawrence's *Pinkie.* In addition, American art is on view in the Virginia Steele Scott Gallery, while the Annabella Huntington Memorial Collection features Renaissance paintings and 18th-century French decorative arts. The Institute was founded in 1919 by "the Carnegie of the West," businessman Henry Huntington, who made his money in railroads and Southern California real estate. As one of the founders of L.A.'s turn-of-the-century inter-urban rail system, Huntington was an important figure in the early growth of L.A. Deeply committed to art and education as well as financial affairs, he built this classical revival estate to house his collection of art and books. (Open Tues.-Fri. 1-4:30pm, Sat.-Sun. 10:30am-4:30pm; free, but donation expected). The museum sits between Huntington Dr. and California Blvd. in San Marino, just south of Pasadena. From downtown L.A., Bus #79 leaves from Olive St., and takes you straight to the library (a 40-45 minute trip).

Near Pasadena

Recent remodeling and a spate of innovative exhibits may earn the **Southwest Museum,** 234 Museum Dr. (213-221-2163), the attention it deserves. L.A. offers no better resource to those interested in the history and culture of the Southwest and its Native Americans. The museum's collection of artifacts is among the best in the nation and includes contemporary Native American art. Founded in 1912 by Westophile Charles Lummis, the museum was given a palatial Hispano-Moorish home on a hill, fairly close to the east side of downtown. Take bus #83 along Broadway to Museum Dr. and trek up the hill. Drivers should take the Pasadena Fwy. (Rte. 110) to Ave. 43 and follow the signs. (Open Tues.-Sun. 11am-5pm. Admission $4, seniors and students $2, ages 7-18 $1. Library open Wed.-Sat. 11am-5pm.)

If you don't find any celebrities on the street, you can find many in their graves at the renowned **Forest Lawn** cemetery, 1712 Glendale Ave., Glendale (818-241-4151). Analyzed by Jessica Mitford as the showy emblem of the "American Way of Death," its grounds include reproductions of many of Michelangelo's works, the "largest religious painting on earth" (the famous 195-ft. version of the *Crucifixion*), a stained-glass *Last Supper,* and innumerable other works of "art." Stop at the entrance for a map of the cemetery's sights, and pick up a guide to the paintings and sculpture at the administration building nearby. (Open daily 8am-5pm.) From downtown, take bus #90 or 91 and disembark just after the bus leaves San Fernando Rd. to turn onto Glendale Ave. Forest Lawn is easily approached from this side of paradise via the Golden State Fwy. or Glendale Fwy. (Rte. 2).

A number of sights are located a bit further out from Pasadena. The **L.A. State and County Arboretum** is Arcadia is a 127-acre slice of what used to be the Rancho Santa Anita. The Arboretum includes local Indian dwellings, an adobe and a Victorian home, and a prehistoric jungle (301 N. Baldwin Ave., 818-445-8251; adults $3, students and senior citizens $1.50. Free the third Tuesday of every month. Open daily 9am-5pm.)

Shopping

L.A. has always led the great American quest for convenience. After World War II, when Angelenos needed to get to their beaches quickly, they created the freeway; in the sixties, when faced with the conundrum of dining-out, L.A. responded with drive-thru fast food (saving time even in the spelling); and when it was time to shop (ie. the 80s), convenience-seeking innovators in L.A. devised the ultimate time-saving medium—the mall.

As a result, L.A.'s shopping districts are organized not so much along certain streets or areas, but rather by these marvelous malls. Mall culture in L.A. is cutting edge—shopping in its most developed form.

The **downtown** area offers some wonderful bargains. The **Garment District,** roughly 8th to Olympic and Broadway to San Pedro St., is swamped on Saturdays with shoppers hunting for designer clothing at cut-rate prices. Several bookstores carry guides to this district; a sound investment for those considering serious shopping. Sizeable discounts on jewelry can be found in the **jewelry district** on Hill St. Make sure you leave the main tourist drag in favor of the more obscure stores (often on the upper levels of the warehouses), and don't be afraid to bargain.

Outrageous boutiques, hip eateries, and thrift shop bargains throng trendy **Melrose Avenue,** between La Brea and La Cienega. The **Pacific Design Center,** 8687 Melrose Ave. (310-657-0800), houses 150 designers' showrooms. Just to the south at Beverly and La Cienega sits another behemoth, the **Beverly Center.** A massive construct from the outside, the mall is light and airy on the inside. Two department stores, Bullocks and Broadway, anchor either end of the Center, with a bizillion other clothing shops filling the space inbetween. The **Third Street Promenade,** formerly the Santa Monica Mall, is an outdoor shopping center recently refurbished in an attempt to win back business from its newer, sexier neighbor, **Santa Monica Place,** an indoor mall not unlike the Beverly Center.

One of the most enjoyable malls to look at is the **Westside Pavilion** at 10800 W. Pico Blvd. Opened in 1985 with a beautiful curved glass skylight in its roof, this is one of the best-designed malls in L.A. Numerous television commericals and music videos (including Tom Petty's *Free Fallin'*) have been filmed here. In 1992 the mall will extend across Westwood Blvd., with a bridge on the 2nd floor connecting the two buildings. L.A.'s latest mall is the **Century City Shopping Center and Market Place,** a pretty, mostly outdoor mall with the typical stores, shops and multiplex movie theatres. In the valley, the **Sherman Oaks Galleria** embraces three floors of Valley girls and dudes, shoe stores, boutiques, and trendy food shops. The mall scenes in *Fast Times at Ridgemont High* were filmed here.

An L.A. shopping tradition is the Sunday morning **Rose Bowl Flea Market and Swap Meet,** (818-588-4411) held every other Sunday in the parking lot around the Rose Bowl. A wide variety of well-priced merchandise from clothing to electronics to framed prints and other household furnishings can be found here. There is a small entrance fee.

L.A.'s latest innovation in Mall Theory is the "mini-mall." These tiny clusters of stores (ranging from 7-11s to trendy boutiques) around corner parking lots have taken over every third street corner in the city.

Entertainment

"Vast wasteland" mythology to the contrary, L.A.'s cultural scene is in fact active and diverse. Nightlife is everything you'd expect, and if you're staying in Hollywood or have a car you can spend all your time in L.A. enjoying a Vampire-like revelry.

Film and Television Studios

All of the major TV studios offer free tickets to show tapings. Some are available on a first-come, first-served basis from the Visitors Information Center of the Greater L.A. Visitor and Convention Bureau or by mail. Some networks won't send tickets to out-of-state addresses, but they will send a guest card or letter that can be redeemed for tickets. Be sure to enclose a self-addressed, stamped envelope. Write: Tickets, Capital City/ABC Inc., 4151 Prospect, Hollywood 90027 (213-577-7777); CBS Tickets, 7800 Beverly Blvd., Los Angeles 90036 (310-840-3537); NBC-TV, 3000 W. Alameda Ave., Burbank 91523 (818-840-3537); or FOX Tickets, 100 Universal City Plaza, Bldg. 153, Universal City 91608 (818-506-0043). Tickets are also available to shows produced by Paramount Television, 780 N. Gower St., Hollywood 90038 (213-956-5000). Tickets don't guarantee admittance; arrive a couple of hours early, as seating is also first-come, first-served.

Universal Studios, Universal City (818-508-9600). Hollywood Fwy. to Lankershim. Take bus #424 to Lankershim Blvd. For a hefty fee, the studio will take you for a ride; visit the Bates Hotel and other sets, watch Conan the Barbarian flex his pecs, be attacked by Jaws, get caught in a flash flood, experience an 8.3 earthquake, and witness a variety of special effects and other demonstrations of movie-making magic. Reservations for the tour are not accepted; it's best to arrive early to secure a ticket—despite the price, the tour is quite popular. Allow 2½ hr. for the tour and at least an hour to wander around afterward. Tours in Spanish Sat. and Sun. Open summer and holidays 7:30am-10:30pm (last tram leaves at 5pm); Sept.-June Mon.-Fri. 10am-3:30pm, Sat. and Sun. 9:30am-3:30pm. Admission $24.50; ages 3-11 and over 65 $19. Parking $4.

NBC Television Studios Tour, 3000 W. Alameda Ave. (818-840-3572), at Olive Ave. in Burbank, 2 mi. from Universal. Hollywood Fwy. north, exit east on Barham Blvd., which becomes Olive Ave. Take bus #420 from Hill St. downtown. The NBC tour is presently cancelled but may reopen in 1992. Call for info.

Paramount Studios Inc., 860 N. Gower St. (213-956-5000), in Hollywood. Guided 2 hr. historical walking tour. Under 10 yrs. not admitted. Mon.-Fri. 11am and 2pm, reservations required. $10.

Warner Bros. VIP Tour, 4000 Warner Blvd., Burbank (818-954-1744). Personalized, unstaged tours (max. 12 people) through the Warner Bros. studios. These are technical, 2-hr. long treks which chronicle the detailed reality of the movie-making art. No children under 10. Tours Mon.-Fri. 10am and 2pm, additional tours in summer. $22 per person. Reservations required in advance.

KCET Public Television, 4401 Sunset Blvd. (213-667-9242). Like the Warner Brothers tour, but free. 1½ hours. Reservations required, tours given Tues. and Thurs. Under 10 not admitted.

Cinema

In the technicolored heaven of Los Angeles, you'd expect to find as many movie theaters as stars on the Walk of Fame. You won't be disappointed. A handful of theaters show films the way they were meant to be seen: in a big auditorium, on a big screen. Prices for adult admission to a first-run film in Greater L.A. has paused for the moment at $7.

It's quite an experience to watch movies at any of the theaters in **Westwood Village,** especially on weekends. You *will* wait in line, especially for new releases, but the lively crowds justify the podiatric damage. As with food and shopping, however, the malls are battling for L.A.'s movie-going audience, and Westwood isn't always what it used to be. In Santa Monica, twenty-two theatres rest between Santa Monica Place and the 3rd St. Promenade. Devotees of second-run, foreign language, and experimental films are also rewarded, in Santa Monica theaters away from the Promenade.

Foreign films play consistently at the six **Laemmle Theaters** in Beverly Hills, West L.A., Santa Monica, Pasadena, Encino, and downtown.

Though admission is a challenge without connections or lots of money, occasional free films are shown on weekday afternoons during the **Los Angeles International Film Festival** (213-469-9400). Popularly known as **Filmex,** the annual program runs in late June and early July.

The **American Film Insitute's Eurofest** hits L.A. in late June (213-856-7787). Other film festivals include Black Talkies on Parade (late April, 213-737-3292); the international Children's Film Festival (late January at Barnsdall Art Park: free; 213-485-4474); the UCLA Festival of Film Preservation (Royce Hall; most of July; 310-206-3456); the L.A. Film Fest (late April; 213-876-77070; International Gay and Lesbian Film Festival (early July; 213-650-5133); the Native American Film Festival (Southwest Museum; late Jan.; 213-221-2164), and the Women in Film Festival (late October; 213-463-6060).

A unique movie-going treat is the **Mitsubishi IMAX Theater,** at the California Museum of Science and Industry (213-744-2014; see Exposition Park Sights). Movies are shown on a 54×70-foot screen. Seats are steeply raked and the films, of the entertainment-documentary variety, surround the viewer with brilliant sights and sounds. (Admission $5, seniors and children under 12 $3.50.)

For film screening information, dial 213-777-FILM, 213-777-3456.

Cineplex Odeon Universal City Cinemas, atop the hill at Universal Studios (818-508-0588). Take the Universal Center Dr. exit off the Hollywood Fwy. (U.S. 101). Opened in 1987 as the world's largest cinema complex. The 18 wide-screen theaters, 2 *Parisienne*-style cafés, and opulent decoration put all others to shame. Hooray for Hollywood.

Pacific Cinerama Dome, 6360 Sunset Blvd. (213-466-3401), near Vine. The screen stretches nearly 180° around the theater. You can't miss this illuminated geodesic dome, also known as "The Hollywood Boil".

Mann's Chinese, 6925 Hollywood Blvd. (213-464-8111). Hollywood hype to the hilt. For more details, see Hollywood Sights.

Beverly Cineplex (310-652-7760), atop the Beverly Center, on Beverly Dr. at La Cienaga. Unlike most first-run cinemas, the Cineplex screens movies in auditoriums hardly bigger than your living room. But it shows 14 of them every night, a combination of recent hits and artsy discoveries.

Village Theatre, 961 Broxton (310-208-5576), in Westwood. No multiplex nonsense here. One auditorium, one big screen, one great THX sound system, a balcony, and art deco design. Watch the back rows and balcony for late-arriving celebrities.

Goldwyn Cinemas, 10800 W. Pico Blvd. (310-475-0202), in the upscale Westside Pavilion shopping center. Foreign and other first-run art films.

The following theaters screen **classics and cult films:**

Nuart Theatre, 11272 Santa Monica Blvd. (310-478-6379), in L.A. at the San Diego Fwy. Perhaps the best known. The playbill changes nightly, so drop by for a copy of the monthly guide. Classics and documentaries.

Rialto Theater, 1023 Fair Oaks Ave. (818-799-9567), in S. Pasadena, at Oxley. *Rocky Horror* mayhem every Sat. at midnight.

UCLA's Melnitz Theater, on the northeastern corner of campus near Sunset and Hilgard. An eclectic range of film festivals.

Comedy

The talent may be imported from New York and other parts of the country, but that doesn't change the fact that L.A.'s comedy clubs are the best in the world (unless you happen to chance upon an amateur night, which is generally a painful, painful experience). Quality makes prices steep, of course, but it's worth the setback to catch the newest and wackiest stand-up comedians, chuckle as famous veterans hone new material, or preside at the latest development in stand-up—comedy competitions. Some clubs are open only a few nights per week. Call ahead to check age restrictions. Cover charges are cheaper during the week; the clubs are less crowded, but just as much fun.

Comedy Store, 8433 Sunset Blvd. (213-656-6225). The shopping mall of comedy clubs, with 3 different rooms, each featuring a different type of comedy. (Each room charges its own cover.) Go to the Main Room for the big-name stuff and the most expensive cover charges (around $14). The Original Room features mid-range comics for $6-8. The Belly Room has the real grab-bag material, often for no cover charge. Over 21 only; 2-drink minimum.

The Improvisation, 8162 Melrose Ave. (213-651-2583). Offers L.A.'s best talent, including, on occasion, Robin Williams, and Robert Klein. Their restaurant serves Italian fare. Prego! Open nightly, check *L.A. Weekly* for times. Cover $8-10, 2-drink minimum.

Improvisation in Santa Monica, 321 Santa Monica Blvd. (310-394-8664). The beach version of its Hollywood cousin is a more laid back, and brand new. Tex-Mex food in the restaurant, cover $8-10, 2 drink minimum. A third Improvisation is located in Irvine, and a fourth in the Valley.

The Comedy Act Theater, 3339 W. 43rd St. (310-677-4101). A comedy club targeted at a black audience, often featuring such nationally known comedians as Robert Townsend and Marsha Warfield. Open Thurs.-Sat. 8:30pm on. Cover $10.

L.A. Cabaret, 17271 Ventura Blvd. (818-501-3737), in Encino. Two showrooms of big-name talent. Cover $6-12, 2-drink minimum.

The Ice House, 24 N. Mentor Ave. (818-577-1894), in Pasadena. This is the 30-year-old granddaddy of clubs, and its famous graduates occasionally pop in to surprise patrons. Showroom seats 200; restaurant, disco, and bar. Cover $8.50-10.50. 2-drink minimum.

Igby's Comedy Cabaret, 11637 Tennessee Pl. (310-477-3553), in West L.A. Nationally known comedians. Restaurant and bar. West L.A.'s best comedy club, although parking can drive you crazy. Cover $6.50-12, 2-drink minimum. Reservations required.

Theater and Classical Music

Los Angeles is blessed with one of the most active theater circuits on the West Coast. One hundred and fifteen Equity Waiver theaters (under 100 seats) offer a dizzying choice for theater-goers, who can also take in small productions in museums, art galleries, universities, parks, and even garages. During the summer hiatus, TV stars frequently return here to revel once more in the "legitimate theatre". Mainstream theater merits the high prices for shows that are either Broadway-bound or beginning their national tour after a New York run. The **L.A. Weekly** has comprehensive listings of L.A. theatres both big and small. Most of the following double as sites for music concerts.

Hollywood Bowl, 2301 N. Highland Ave. (213-850-2000), in Hollywood. Perfect for a summer evening, the Bowl hosts a summer festival, which runs from early July to mid-September. Although sitting in the back of this outdoor, 18,000-seat amphitheater makes even the L.A. Philharmonic sound like AM radio, the bargain tickets ($1-3) and the sweeping view of L.A. from the bowl's south rim make it worthwhile. Local restaurants, cafés, and the bowl itself will pack you a gourmet feast (wine, pâté, pasta salad) for about $10 per person and up, but you're free to bring your own food, and Kentucky Fried Chicken buckets abound. Going to the bowl is a major production by car; parking is complicated and expensive ($8). It's to use RTD's Park 'n' Ride service (get a brochure listing the lots from which shuttle service is available). If you're willing to hike, park away from the bowl and walk up Highland. Bus #150 takes you to the Bowl from the Valley, and bus #420 runs from downtown.

Music Center, 135 N. Grand Ave., downtown (213-972-7211), at the corner of 1st in the heart of the city. Includes the **Mark Taper Forum** and the **Dorothy Chandler Pavilion.**

Shubert Theatre, 2020 Ave. of the Stars, Century City (800-233-3123). Big Broadway shows.

Pantages, 6233 Hollywood Blvd. (213-480-3232). L.A.'s other place for big Broadway spectacles.

Bob Baker Marionette Theater, 1345 W. 1st St. (213-250-9995). The longest running marionette theatre in the U.S. 250 seat theater filled mostly with kids and their parents. Daily shows. Bob's marionettes have been used in a number of films (*Close Encounters, Escape to Witch Mountain, Bedknobs and Broomsticks*).

Cafés

Espresso Bars are the latest, largest fad in L.A. nightlife, and for good reason: they offer a cheap, quiet alternative to L.A.'s buzzing club scene, often with entertainment gratis.

Toi on Sunset, 7505½ Sunset (213-850-9220). Live bands, pool room, and restaurant serving hearty, reasonably priced Thai food. Excellent nightly psychedelic pop and op art work and decor. Popular with young stars and starlets living in the Hollywood area; the coolest of the cafés. Open daily 11:30am-1pm.

The Espresso Bar, 34 S. Raymond (818-356-9095), in an alley to the left of the building marked 32 S. Raymond St. Just when you thought Pasadena had no hip cafés in which to plunk your butt and ponder Kafka, this bare, ratty little place rides to the rescue. Bagel with brie $2.75, steamed milk $1.25. And, of course, espresso ($1). Tues. is Open Mike night for local bands and host Maurice Illinois is a wild man. Wednesday is Open Poetry night, and Friday night features a booked band. Open Sun.-Thurs. noon-1am, Fri.-Sat. noon-2am.

Café Largo, 432 N. Fairfax Ave. (213-852-1073). A nouveau bistro with steak, fish, crepes, and pastas. Jazz, poetry readings, performance art. No cover charge with dinner.

Mad Hatter, 5819 Pico Blvd. (213-935-8541), 2 blocks east of Fairfax. If you're looking to make 40 friends fast, this is the place to be. The all-too-trendy high school and college students that hang out and do their homework here may be the friendliest people in the entire city. Sunday night poetry, movies on Tuesday, comedy on Wednesday, open mike on Thursday, and bands (and cover charge) on Saturday. Open 8pm-4am.

Java Café, 7286 Beverly Blvd. (213-931-4943). Popular, Berkeley-style espresso bar. Poetry and acoustic music on Monday. Open weekdays 9am-2am, weekends 10am-3am.

Ministry, 524½ N. La Brea (213-954-1194). More entertainment than Java, and without the crowds. Mon.-Fri. 5pm-2am, Sat.-Sun. 2pm-3am.

Late Night Restaurants

Few and far between, but if you've got the midnight munchies, they're here for you.

Larry Parker's, 206 S. Beverly Dr. (310-277-5655) in Beverly Hills. Yep, *this is it*—L.A.'s authentic 50s diner. Neon lights, disco balls, and nearly pornographic videos light up the vintage booths, jukeboxes, telephones, and corny 50s signs. $7 minimum only enforced when crowded (ie. often). Gigantic portions. The chicken fajita plate ($7) with rice and beans is the best deal on the menu. Angelique and Jenny's Jubilee ($27!) consists of hot deep-fried bananas sliced over chocolate and vanilla Haägen Daz, served with hot fudge, whipped cream and avocado (you don't have to order it—just think about it). Open 24 hrs.

Barney's Beanery, 8447 Santa Monica (213-654-2287). Is it a pool hall or a diner? Billiards $1 a game. Strange mixture of international crowd and local pool sharks. Wide variety of omelettes $4-7. Over 200 kinds of beer. Open daily 10am-2am.

French Market, 7985 Santa Monica Blvd. (213-654-0898), in West Hollywood. Tasty, mostly Americana menu (entrees $6-7). Open Mon.-Fri. 7am-2:30am, Sat.-Sun. 7am-3:30am.

Jerry's Deli, 12655 Ventura Blvd. (818-980-4245), in Studio City. The Valley's coolest restaurant. Magic Johnson and KROQ DJs eat here. Sandwiches $5-10. Location also in Encino. Open 24 hours.

Concerts

The commonly used concert venues range from small to massive. The Wiltern Theater (213-381-5005) has presented artists such as Suzanne Vega and The Church. The Hollywood Palladium (213-466-4311) is of comparable size. Mid-size acts head for the Universal Amphitheater (818-890-9421) and the Greek Theater (310-410-1062). Capacious indoor sports arenas, such as the Sports Arena (213-748-6131) or the Forum (310-419-3182), double as concert halls for large shows. Few performers dare to play at the over 100,000-seat L.A. Coliseum. Only U2, Bruce Springsteen, and the Rolling Stones have attempted this feat in recent years.

Bars

L.A. isn't known for its bar scene, but bars do exist, and generally hold a slightly older, and more subdued crowd than do the clubs. Bars on Santa Monica Promenade are presently some of the most popular in L.A.

Molly Malone's, 575 S. Fairfax (213-935-1579). Not your typical Irish pub—showcases some of L.A.'s big up-and-coming bands. Cover varies. Open 10am-1:30pm.

Small's Bar, 5574 Melrose Ave. (213-469-8258), inside what appears to be an auto-body work shop (there's no sign—just look for the crowds going in). No cover, no entertainment, just an extremely popular bar. A standard on Thursday nights, especially with the not-yet-famous "industry" folk. Open daily 11am-2am.

Al's Bar, 305 S. Hewitt St. (213-687-3558), in downtown. One of L.A. nightlife's best-hidden secrets. Wide range of nightly entertainment: traditional rock 'n roll, poetry, experimental bands, performance art and more. Call for info. Open daily 1pm-2:30am.

Stratton's, 1037 Broxton Ave. (310-208-0488). Hot spot with UCLA students (though they all look like Marina and Santa Monica yuppie barhoppers in training). Open daily 11am-2am.

Clubs

The Club scene is what makes L.A.'s nightlife. With the highest number of bands per capita in the world, most clubs are able to book top-notch bands night after night. The distinction between music clubs and dance clubs is a bit sketchy in L.A.—most music clubs have DJs a couple times a week, and most dance clubs have bands a couple times a week. Many clubs are simply host spaces for managements that change every night. These clubs can be the hottest thing in L.A. in a month, and disappear the next. Underground Clubs are generally cheaper, more fun, and more elite (of course, you'll have to find these yourself by making friends with knowledgeable clubbies). If you see a lot of long-haired, scantily clad people walking into an unmarked building late at night, follow them in—you'll probably have a fabulous time. Back on the strip, Sunset has been and continues to be the property of L.A.'s enormous heavy metal scene—many Angelenos don't know that anthing else exists.

Clubs are often expensive, but many are still feasible for budgeteers. Coupons in L.A. Weekly can save you a bundle, and many are also handed out in bushels inside the clubs. To enter the club scene it's best to be 21—the next best option is to look it. Nevertheless, if you're over 18, you'll still find a space to dance. For more extensive listings of gay men's and women's bars contact the Gay and Lesbian Community Services Center (see Practical Information).

Blak and Bloo, 7574 Sunset Blvd. (213-876-1120). Artistic, funky people. Funk, rock, and alternative music. Maybe the only place on Sunset without serious attitude problems. *Sunday Love* on Sundays is a real trip. Pool room, 2 bars, 2 dance rooms. Open Tues.-Sun.

Kingston 12, 814 Broadway (310-451-4423), Santa Monica. L.A.'s only full-time reggae club presents both local and foreign acts. Dredlocks and "fragrant" smoke flow freely. Dance floor, 2 bars. Open Wed.-Sun. 8:30pm-2am.

Club Lingerie, 6507 Sunset Blvd., Hollywood (213-466-8557). The favored music club of all kinds of people. Rock, reggae, ska, and funk. They've got it. Two full bars. Must be 21.

Roxbury, 8225 W. Sunset (213-656-1750). L.A. pretension at its fullest. Contends with *Vertigo* in downtown as the most hotsy-totsy place in the city (you probably won't get in, but it might be fun trying). Jazz room downstairs, huge bar and dancing upstairs. VIP room only admits the wealthy, famous, or startlingly beautiful. Open Tues.-Sat. 7pm-2am.

Whisky A Go-Go, 8901 Sunset Blvd. (310-652-4202). Another venerable spot on the Strip. Like the Roxy, it is part of L.A.'s music history. The Whisky played host to many progressive bands in the late 70's and early 80's, and was a major part of the punk explosion. Mostly metal nowadays. Full bar, cover varies. No age restrictions.

Roxy, 9009 Sunset Blvd. (310-276-2222). One of the best known of L.A.'s Sunset Strip clubs, the Roxy is filled with record company types and rockers waiting to be discovered. Many big acts at the height of their popularity play here. Cover varies. No age restrictions.

Madame Wong's West, 2900 Wilshire Blvd. (310-829-7361), Santa Monica. With 2 bands and 2 DJs playing simultaneously 7 nights a week, this is the most music for your money. 3 full bars. Cover $5-8. Must be 21.

The Palms, 8572 Santa Monica Blvd. (310-652-6188), W. Hollywood's oldest women's bar. Top 40 dancing every night. Full bar. Low cover, if any. 21 and over.

Peanuts, 7969 Santa Monica Blvd. (213-654-0280). Management varies nightly, and generally offers some of the hottest clubs in L.A. Mostly over 18.

Code Blue L.A., 8450 W. 3rd St. (310-281-9903), W. Hollywood. Flashy upscale club for women who prefer women. Open Sat. 9:30pm-3am. Cover $10.

Anti-Club, 4658 Melrose Ave. (213-661-3913), in East Hollywood. Appropriately named. To understand the difference between clubs and Anti-Club: the graffiti on the walls here wasn't coordinated by the management; more tattoos per person than any other place in L.A.; David Lynch would love it here—a family-style Western bar featuring hardcore bands and a vicious pit. Full bar, cover varies. No age restrictions.

Rage, 8911 Santa Monica Blvd., W. Hollywood (310-652-7055). Dance and R&B sounds for a mainly gay crowd. Full bar. Cover varies. Must be 21.

Amusement Parks

For information on Disneyland and Knott's Berry Farm, see Orange County.

Six Flags Magic Mountain, 26101 Magic Mountain Pkwy. (818-367-5965), in Valencia, a 40-min. drive up I-5 from L.A. Not for novices, Magic Mountain has the hairiest roller-coaster in Southern California (hairier even than Disneyland's Space Mountain). Highlights of the park are The Revolution, a smooth metal coaster with a vertical 360° loop; Colossus, the world's largest wooden roller coaster. (Hint: if the line is long and you're only going to ride Colossus once, wait for the front seat of the car; the view looking down as the front of the car hangs over the coaster's huge first drop is spectacular); Free Fall, a simulated no-parachute fall out of the sky; Ninja, a coaster whose cars are suspended on a rail from above and are allowed to swing back and forth as they turn; and the park's newest coaster, the Viper, which is said to approach the limits of what coaster builders can do with G-forces without *really* hurting people. For roller-coaster-o-phobes, there's also a crafts fair area and a children's playland with a Bugs Bunny theme. The truth is, however, that few people over 48" tall come to Magic Mountain for the crafts fair or for the love of Bugs Bunny. This becomes especially apparent when you encounter the lines for Colossus on a hot summer afternoon. Open Memorial Day to mid-September, and Christmas and Easter weeks Mon.-Fri. 10am-6pm, Sat. 10am-midnight, Sun. 10am-10pm; mid-September to Memorial Day (save Christmas and Easter holiday weeks) weekends only. Admission $22, seniors $16, children under 48" tall $14. Parking $4.

Raging Waters Park, 111 Raging Waters Dr. (714-592-6453 for recorded message, for directions 714-599-1251), in San Dimas. (Yes, this *is* where Bill and Ted are from.) Near the intersection of the San Bernardino and Foothill Fwy. (I-10 and 210). Beat the heat with 44 acres and 5 million gallons of slides, pools, whitewater rafts, inner-tubes, fake waves, and a fake island (don't fret, they recycle). A cool but costly alternative to the beach. Hurl yourself over the 7-story water-slide "Drop Out" if you dare, or slide through a tropical rain forest. Open Mon.-Fri. 10am-6pm., Sat.-Sun. 10am-7pm. Admission $17, 42"-48" $9, under 2 free.

Seasonal Events

The biggest event of the year in L.A. is the Academy Awards. Getting a ticket to the Awards, however, generally requires a few years of work in the movie business. Still, the stargazing opportunities are limitless, so if fighting hundreds of maniacal film fans for a fleeting glimpse of a man in a tux who might be Kevin Costner gets you going, this is your night. Otherwise, it's a perfect night to see a movie at the theatre.

January 1 is always a perfect day in Southern California, and snowed-in midwesterners and easterners eat their collective hearts out watching the **Tournament of Roses Parade** and the **Rose Bowl** on TV. For game information, contact the Rose Bowl, Arroyo Blvd. (818-577-4343). Some of the wildest New Year's Eve parties happen along Colorado Blvd. Making a slumber party out of New Year's Eve at the parade is a SoCal tradition, and most Angelenos have done it at least once. If you miss the parade, you can still see the floats up close on display on January 2 (call Pasadena's tourist office for info).

World Frisbee Tournament, during the Rose Bowl. Champions compete in individual free-style, team Ultimate Frisbee, and other events.

Chinese New Year, (310-677-0396) late Feb., Chinatown. Fireworks and dragon processions.

Whale watching, a favorite of Southern Californian ocean worshipers, is best Dec.-March. Boats depart from Long Beach and San Pedro Harbors to witness the migration of giant whales from the north Pacific to the waters off Baja California. Call any of the state beaches.

Grunion runs occur throughout spring and summer. This late-night pastime appeals to those who derive voyeuristic pleasure from watching slippery, silver fish squirm onto the beaches (especially San Pedro) to mate. The fish can be caught by hand, but a license is required, oddly , for those over 16. Obtain licenses from the Fish and Game Department (310-590-5132) for $10.50, valid until Dec. 31 each year. 1-day license $5.50. Fishing prohibited April-May. Free programs on the Grunion run given at the Cabrillo Marine Museum, San Pedro (310-548-7562).

Cinco de Mayo, May 5, especially downtown at Olvera St. Huge celebrations mark Mexican Independence Day.

UCLA Mardi Gras, mid-May, at the athletic field (310-825-3001). Billed as the world's largest collegiate activity (a terrifying thought). Features food, games, and entertainment. (Admission $3, children $1.) Proceeds benefit charity.

Playboy Jazz Festival, mid-June, Hollywood Bowl (310-450-9040). Two days of entertainment by top-name jazz musicians of all varieties, from traditional to fusion. Call for ticket information.

Gay Pride Week, late June (213-656-6553). The lesbian and gay community of L.A. comes out in full force. Art, politics, dances, and a big parade all center on the Pacific Design Center, 8687 Melrose Ave., Hollywood. $16 tickets.

Nisei Week, August, in Little Tokyo (213-687-7193). A celebration of Japanese-American culture that includes a parade and a carnival.

Los Angeles County Fair, Sept.-Oct., at the L.A. County Fairgrounds in Pomona (714-623-3111). The largest old-time county fair in the nation, featuring livestock shows, flower shows, horse racing, and an amusement park.

Renaissance Pleasure Faire, every weekend from late April-mid June in the city of Devore (818-880-6211). From L.A., take the I-10 east I-15 north, and look for signs as you approach the city. Decked out in their best Elizabethan finery, San Bernardino teenagers are versed in Shakespearian vocab before working at the Faire. Food, games, and music. Open 9am-6pm. Admission $14.50, seniors (over 62) $11.50, children $8.

South Bay

Several beachside communities cluster along the southern curve of Santa Monica Bay, in the area known as South Bay: Marina Del Rey, Manhattan Beach, Hermosa Beach, and Redondo Beach. All feature small homes built up against one another, along with beautiful beaches crammed with volleyball players and sunbathers. Only Los Angeles International Airport, which pushes up to the coast between Manhattan Beach and Marina Del Rey, and Palos Verdes interrupt Los Angeles's best attempt at "normal" beach life. Just south of Palos Verdes and north of Long Beach is the most southern of the South Bay communities, San Pedro.

Practical Information

Parks and Recreation Information: 310-331-0610, Redondo Beach.

RTD: 800-252-7433. Bus #40 from downtown joins the coast road at El Segundo and serves Manhattan, Hermosa, and Redondo Beaches. Hermosa Beach has a free shuttle bus to alleviate parking problems. Buses #225 and 226 cross the Palos Verdes area.

Car Rental: A Robin Hood Rent-A-Car, 116 8th St. (310-318-9955), in Manhattan Beach.

Horse Rentals: Palos Verdes Stables 310-378-3527.

Laundromat: Baird's Coin Laundry, 140 E. 1st St., San Pedro (310-514-2342).

Surfing and Weather Conditions Hotline: 310-379-8471.

South Bay AIDS Clinic: 310-376-3000.

Harbor Free Clinic: 310-547-0202, at San Pedro. Call at 10am for appointments.

Hospital: San Pedro Peninsula Hospital, 1300 W. 7th St. (310-832-3311), in San Pedro.

Emergency: Dial 911. San Pedro Police Department is located at 2175 Gibson Blvd.

Post Office: 1201 N. Catalina Ave. (310-376-2472), in Redondo Beach. Open Mon.-Fri. 8:30am-5pm, Sat. 8:30am-12:30pm. General Delivery ZIP Code: 90277. 839 S. Beacon St. (310-831-3246), in San Pedro. Open Mon.-Fri. 8:30am-5pm, Sat. 9am-12:30pm. General Delivery ZIP Code: 90731.

Area Code: 310.

Accommodations

Except in Orange County, motels along the beaches fall well above the budget price range. Inexpensive to mid-priced motels lie near the airport and along the Pacific Coast Highway (PCH). There are no campsites convenient to this area.

Bill Baker International Youth Hostel (AYH), Westchester YMCA, 8015 S. Sepulveda Blvd. (310-670-4316), 1 mi. from the airport. From the LAX transfer terminal, Union Station, or Olive St. a few blocks west of Greyhound, take bus #42 or express bus #560 to Manchester and Sepulveda and walk 3 long blocks north to Sepulveda and 80th. Adequate for a beach vacation, but touring L.A. by RTD from this location would be very difficult (although the managers do provide a handy list of attractions and bus directions). A café is open 9am-6:30pm. Separate dorms for women and men, cots placed on the floor for each guest. Five-day max. stay. Mandatory daily check-out Mon.-Fri. 8am, Sat.-Sun. 8:30am (sleep late). Power lockout, 9:30am-6pm. Open June 1-Sept. 30. Curfew 11:30pm. Members $8, nonmembers $10. Linen rental $1. Use of pool and other YMCA recreational facilities $10 per day.

Los Angeles International Youth Hostel (AYH), 3601 S. Gaffey St., Bldg. #613, San Pedro 90731 (310-831-8109), at Angels Gate Park (entrance by 34th St.). Bus #446 runs from here to downtown and Union Station during rush hours. From the LAX transfer terminal take bus #232, get off at Avalon and Anaheim, where you can catch #446. These former army barracks are adjacent to Angels Gate Park. Unless you have a car, this hostel will seem frustratingly isolated. Very homey, however: nametags on the bunkbeds, a reading room with a paperback library, a clean and orderly kitchen, and an especially friendly staff. Beds in rooms for 4-12 people. Kitchen, laundry, and TV room. Bus schedules, travel books, some food available at desk. Three-day max. stay. Open 7-10am and 4-midnight. Members $9.25, nonmembers $12.25. Linen $2. Late night key rental $1.

Food and Entertainment

Several cheap eateries cluster around Pier Ave. on the Strand in Hermosa Beach. Nightlife revolves around combination bar/restaurants.

Moose McGillacutty's, 179 N. Harbor (310-372-9944) in Redondo Beach. Dancing nightly, with a leaning towards reggae/funk. Full menu ranging from $3 bar food to $6.95 for chicken parmesan. Open daily 11:30am-1:35pm.

Sunset's, 117 Manhattan Beach Blvd. (310-545-2523) in Manhatten Beach. Similar to Moose's, but more upscale. Small dance floor. Dinner $8-15. Sun.-Thurs. 8am-midnight, Fri.-Sat. 8am-1:45pm.

Lighthouse Café, 30 Pier Ave. (310-376-9834) in Hermosa Beach. Way cool dance-music club/bar. Reasonably priced bar-type munchies. Huge fries $1.75, chicken sandwich $5.25. Sun.-Thurs. 4pm-2am, Fri.-Sat. 9am-2pm.

Good Stuff, 13th Strand (310-374-2334), Hermosa Beach. Truth in Advertising—they actually *do* serve excellent health food. Voted the Best Surfer Breakfast in Hermosa Beach. Avocado and sprouts sandwich $2.95. Open daily 7am-9pm.

Captain Kidd's Fish Market, 209 N. Harbor Dr. (310-372-7703), in the Redondo Beach Marina. Buy a piece of fresh fish from their market, and for $4 extra, they will cook it for you and throw in 2 side dishes (i.e. french fries, rice, or clam chowder) to make a complete meal ($5-30, averaging around $12). Not the most intimate setting in the world, but they have great pictures on the wall of the devastating storms of the 1980s. Open Sun.-Thurs. 9am-9pm, Fri.-Sat. 9am-10pm.

Hermosa Fish Market and Café, 20 Pier Ave. (310-372-1488), Hermosa Beach. Small restaurant decorated with a marine theme. You know it's fresh when the restaurant is right over the pier. Fish dinners around $8. Steamed clams with pasta $7.95. Open daily 11:30am-10pm.

La Playita, 37 14th St. (310-376-2148), Hermosa Beach, on the Strand. A taco stand with a view. Athletic-looking individuals blithely down Dos Equis beer with their $5 Mexican breakfasts. The special home-made fish tacos may not please conventional palates. (Fri. only, $5.) Open Tues.-Sun. 8:30am-9:30pm.

The Local Yolk, 3414 Highland Ave. (310-546-4407), by 35th St. in Manhattan Beach. Breakfast ($3-4) in a low-key, friendly coffee-shop atmosphere. Luscious, creative omelettes with potatoes and a choice of pancakes, biscuit, muffin, or toast ($5-6). Three-layer deli sandwiches $6.25. Open daily 6:30am-2:30pm.

Henessey's Grill and Tavern, 1710 S. Catalina Ave. (310-316-6658), Redondo Beach. A tavern atmosphere along with multi-ethnic fare, including Hawaiian chicken ($8), corned beef and cabbage ($6.50), and Irish nachos ($4.50). A fun party-type place. Open Mon.-Thurs. 7:30am-midnight, Fri.-Sat. 7:30am-2am.

Curry Inn, 320 S. Catalina Ave. (310-379-4049), Redondo Beach. Indian and Pakistani cuisine in a somewhat uninspiring setting. Most entrees $5-8. Open Tues.-Thurs. 5-10pm, Fri.-Sun. 5-11pm.

Sights

Venice's immediate neighbor to the south, **Marina del Rey,** is older, more expensive, and considerably more sedate. Built in 1965 as a yacht harbor, Marina del Rey is the largest man-made marina in the world home to 6,000 private yachts and 3,000 boats in dry storage; it has wide, uncrowded, sandy beaches (but no waves and little wind). **Fisherman's Village** (310-823-5411), at 13763 Figi Way is the marina's picturesque shopping and strolling area. The marina offers sail- and motor-boat rentals, as well as a harbor cruise ($7, call Horn's 310-301-6000). The marina village becomes a singles' scene at night, when swingers come out of the woodwork. It's also home to some excellent, albeit overpriced, seafood restaurants.

The next patch of sand, **Dockweiler State Beach,** provides a break from the built-up environment paralleling the bike path, but lies a mere ½ mi. from the runways of LAX (earplugs or a Walkman may help). **El Segundo** is the site of the second Standard Oil refinery in California. This monstrosity encroaches upon the beach south of LAX, but at least it's quiet. The bike path here follows the coastal road and can be a little harrowing in heavy traffic.

The route returns to the sand at **Manhattan Beach** and continues through **Hermosa Beach,** which together are the most pleasant urban beach environments in L.A. County. The sort of community spirit found in Venice prevails, though in a more up-scale version that diminishes the pandemonium. In addition, Manhattan is the Rome, Mecca, and Jerusalem of **beach volleyball.** The sandy courts at Marine Ave., along with those at State Beach in Pacific Palisades, are the elite training grounds for young players. The Manhattan Beach Open is the oldest professional beach volleyball tournament, while the Hermosa Beach Open awards the most prize money. Both tourneys are part of the Association of Volleyball Professionals (AVP) tour, which makes stops at several Southland beaches. If the tour is in town, don't miss it; muscled and sun-darkened Adonises play an energetic and physical game, fearlessly diving into the sand for exciting saves (plus, they're free). Call the AVP (310-337-4842) for schedule information. The International Surf Festival, another beachside spectator spectacular, takes places each year in early August at Manhattan Beach (310-540-5858).

The **Strand** is a sidewalk/bike path that runs along Manhattan south through Hermosa. Skaters whiz by on the pavement that follows the coastline. If approaching Hermosa **by car** from the San Diego Fwy. and Artesia Blvd., stop at the booth at Gould Ave. (the continuation of Artesia) and Valley Dr. for a map of the route and then find a parking space. Parking near the ocean is metered 24 hr. (25¢ per 15 minutes). It's cheaper to buy the $2 day permit, which allows you to park in any municipal lot.

Redondo Beach is the next town down the coast, and its main attraction is the **pier, boardwalk, and marina** complex. The Redondo Beach Marina and adjacent King Harbor shelter thousands of pleasure boats from the ocean's fury. The **International Boardwalk** offers games and rides in a carnival atmosphere. The **Monstad Pier** supports bars, restaurants, and assorted nightlife joints. The beach itself doesn't compare to Manhattan and Hermosa, but is still picturesque, especially from the pier by night.

The lovely **Palos Verdes Peninsula** juts out of the coast, south of Redondo Beach, forming the southern edge of Santa Monica Bay. This is a wealthy area; Spanish/Mediterranean homes with red-tiled roofs cling to the cliffs overlooking the ocean, while farther inland, residents ride horses along Palos Verdes Dr. Beaches here, due to the steep cliffs and exclusivity of the homes, are inaccessible short of trespassing. The view from the cliffs of Palos Verdes Dr., though, is awesome. Also deserving examination is Malaga Cove Plaza, located on Palos Verdes Dr. between Via Corta and Via Chico. The only one of four plazas planned by the city in the 20s that was built, the building is a triumph for of the Mediterranean Revival Style. While in Palos Verdes it's best to watch your belongings—despite strict laws Palos Verdes continues to be plagued by the world's largest scavenger hunts as bored teenagers spend their days and nights trying to filch a random list of objects.

To get the full impact of the floral paradise of Southern California in a concentrated form, head to the **South Coast Botanic Gardens,** 26300 Crenshaw Blvd. (310-544-6815), in Rancho Palos Verdes. This former county disposal site metamorphosed into an 87-acre garden. (Open daily 9am-4:30pm except Christmas. Admission $3, seniors and students $1.50, ages 5-12 75¢.)

The **Wayfarer's Chapel,** at 5755 Palos Verdes Dr. (310-377-1650), the peninsula's main thoroughfare, is Frank Lloyd Wright's most famous building in Southern California and a gorgeous all-glass church overlooking the ocean. Exhibits and a 12-minute film on Wright are shown inside (Open daily 11am-4pm). Two popular coves hide behind the shrubbery across the road from the chapel: **Abalone Cove** and **Smugglers Cove,** a nudist beach frequented by gay men. Parking is limited and the Abalone Cove lot charges $5. The path to Abalone Cove begins at the far end of the parking lot. To get to Smugglers Cove, leave the parking lot and walk east on Palos Verdes Dr. about 1 mi. At the sign for Peppertree Dr., look for a path down to the cove. Given the mile-long walk and the difficult descent through thick and sometimes thorny brush, you should wait until you get to the beach before taking off your clothes.

Anyone who stays at the AYH hostel in San Pedro can't miss the **Korean Friendship Bell** in Angels Gate Park. The bicentennial gift from the Republic of Korea, at 17 metric tons and 7.25m tall, is the largest bell in the U.S. (Open daily 8am-6pm. Free.)

The still water and tide pools draw many families to **Cabrillo Beach** in **San Pedro.** The excellent **Cabrillo Marine Museum** at 3720 Stephen White Dr. (310-548-7562) presents sea-life and marine history exhibits open Tues.-Fri. noon-5pm, Sat.-Sun. 10am-5pm. Free, but parking is $4 at the beach. To avoid the charge ($5.50), park in the surrounding neighborhood. Cabrillo Beach itself is small and a bit yucky—not the place to go to swim or sunbathe.

The City of San Pedro holds a number of festivals throughout the year. Downtown San Pedro is the sight for September's **Street Fair,** and the October **Fisherman's Fiesta.** (For more information call the San Pedro Chamber of Commerce, 310-832-7272.)

Long Beach

Long Beach, the nation's leading fishing and canning port, owed its initial success to a man named Phineas Banning. In 1898, Banning, who owned large amounts of property in Long Beach along the San Pedro Bay, greased a few palms and replaced the "Get Off and Push Railroad" (actually a wooden horse-car line) with a real one. The new locomotive railroad connected Long Beach to downtown Los Angeles and thereby enabled his town to overcome Santa Monica in the race to become Los Angeles's primary port. Now called Worldport L.A., with a population of 400,000, Banning's harbor has become the largest (and still growing) point of entry for goods imported from the Pacific Rim.

Practical Information and Orientation

Visitor Information: Long Beach Convention and Visitors Council, at the corner of Wartlow and Long Beach Blvd. (310-426-6773). Free brochures and guides. Open daily 9am-5pm.

Travelers Aid: 947 E. 4th St. (310-432-3485). Open Mon.-Fri. 10am-noon, 1-4pm, 5-7:30pm, Sat.-Sun. 10:30am-2:30pm.

Long Beach Airport: 4100 Donald Douglas Dr. (310-421-8293), northeast of downtown. An increasing number of domestic flights use Long Beach Airport, including such airlines as American, Continental, Delta, TWA, and United.

Greyhound: 245 W. 3rd St. (310-432-1842). Open Mon.-Sat. 8:30am-7pm, Sun. 8:30am-6pm, second location in North Long Beach.

Long Beach Transit: 1300 Gardena Ave. (310-591-2301). Open Mon.-Fri. 8am-7pm. Call for a free transit guide, or stop by the information center at 1st and Long Beach Blvd. (Open 8am-4pm.) Most buses stop at the Transit Mall downtown on 1st St. between Pacific Ave. and Long Beach Blvd. Hi-tech bus shelters have route maps and video screens that announce the next bus. Fare 75¢, transfers 5-20¢.

MetroRail Blue Line: This light rail system between downtown L.A. and Long Beach began service in July 1990. Call 800-2-LA-RIDE (800-252-7433) for schedule and fare information.

Auto Club: 4800 Los Coyotes Diagonal (310-597-2421). Open Mon.-Fri. 9am-5pm.

Car Rental: FLAT RATE Rent-A-Car, 6285 E. PCH (310-433-7283). **Budget Rent-A-Car** has branches both at the Long Beach Airport (310-421-0143) and at 727 Long Beach Blvd. (310-495-0407).

Emergency: 911. Main police station is at 400 W. Broadway.

Laundromat: One-Stop Laundromat, 1008 E. PCH (310-591-2051). Open Mon.-Sat. 6am-8pm, Sun. 6am-2pm.

Homosexual Support Group: The Center in Long Beach (310-434-4455).

Post Office: 300 Long Beach Blvd. (310-983-3056). Open Mon.-Fri. 8:30am-5pm, Sat. 9am-2pm. General Delivery ZIP Code: 90801.

Area Code: 310.

Long Beach is located 24 mi. south of downtown Los Angeles and just down the coast from South Bay and San Pedro. The town sits on the edge of the border between Los Angeles County and Orange County, its massive neighbor to the south. To reach Long Beach from downtown L.A. by public transit, take the MetroRail Blue Line or take RTD bus #456, the freeway express. Bus #232 runs from LAX to Long Beach, about a 20 mi. trip ($4.50). By car from downtown, take the Harbor Fwy. (Rte. 110) south to the San Diego Fwy. (I-405). Exit the San Diego Fwy. at the Long Beach Fwy. (Rte. 710), which runs southward, directly into downtown Long Beach. From West L.A. just take the San Diego Fwy. to the Long Beach Fwy.

Accommodations

The Blue-Line makes day-trips to Long Beach cheap and easy. Long Beach's 11 miles of wide beaches and hopping nightlife make overnight or longer stays desirable. Unfortunately, most motels near the beach range from slightly above budget range to out of sight. For cheaper accomodations check the Bixby Knolls neighborhood of Long Beach, north of downtown.

Bixby Knolls, 4045 Long Beach Blvd (310-595-7984). Six mi. from the beach, but the price makes up for it. TV, radio, and air conditioning. No telephones. Singles and doubles $30.

Ocean Motel, 50 Atlantic Ave. (310-435-8369). In downtown, a couple minutes' walk from the beach. Simple, clean rooms with color TVs. Single $29, double $15.

Bel-Shore Motel, 4312 E. 2nd St. (310-433-9369). Close to Belmont Shore and to the beach. Each unit includes full kitchen, living room and bedroom. TVs and telephones. Singles $40, doubles $45-55. Weekly, monthly, and winter rates.

Food

The downtown area has a number of inexpensive restaurants, while 2nd St. in Belmont Shores is full of chic cafés. Fruit and vegetables can be bought cheaply at the open air market that takes place every Friday (10am-4pm) on Promenade St.

Hamburger Henry's, 4700 E. 2nd St. (310-433-7070). Yet another 50s style diner, with 42 different kinds of hamburger ($4.25-8). Live entertainment three nights a week at 7:30pm. **Hot's Hot,** just down the street, is the more expensive *authentic* (built in 1951).

The Omelette Inn 114 E. 3rd St. (310-437-5625). Small, friendly breakfast and lunch place. Serves a foot-omelette ($4-5.25); the plate includes toast and home fries. (Open Mon.-Sat. 7am-2:30pm, Sun. 8:30am-2:30pm.)

La Costa, 1315 Long Beach Blvd. (310-218-1840). Only other restauranteurs would dispute their claim to being "the best seafood restaurant in Long Beach." The menu combines Mexican zest with local seafood. Nothing costs more than $6. Shrimp tacos ($1.50). Open Sun.-Thurs. 9am-midnight, Fri.-Sat. 9am-3am.

Sights

Long Beach's central preoccupation is shipping, not tourism. To get a hold on the city's cargo, walk along the waterfront or drive along Ocean Blvd. west across the ship yards. Crossing the majestic **Vincent Thomas Bridge** to central San Pedro costs 50¢, but it's worth it for the gripping view of the vast shipping terminals.

If you're absolutely determined to do the tourist thing, head over to the **Spruce Goose** and the **Queen Mary,** two boats parked at the end of the Long Beach Fwy. (I-710). Howard Hughes's *Spruce Goose* is displayed in an aluminum dome, with exhibits on Hughes's career in movies and aviation. You can ponder whether the 200-ton monstrosity (which has flown once) is a flying boat or seafaring plane. The *Goose* sits next to the *Queen Mary,* an 81,000-ton 1934 luxury liner that is now a hotel. (Tickets sold 10am-5pm, sights open until 6pm. Admission to both $17.50, ages over 54 $14, ages 3-11 $9.50. Parking $5. The *Spruce Goose* is wheelchair accessible. For information, call 310-435-3511.) The next waterfront marvel is the **Convention and Entertainment Center** (310-436-3695), where the Long Beach Grand Opera, the Civic Light Opera (310-436-3645), and the symphony perform.

Downtown Long Beach is home to several historical buildings. **Villa Riviera Apartment Building** is Long Beach's landmark. Built in 1929, the Gothic-Tudor design makes the building look like a 16-story French Chateau. Other buildings of note are the Ocean Center Building (110 W. Ocean Blvd.), First National Bank (101 Pine Ave.), the Pacific Coast Club (234 Pine Ave.), and the Dr. Rowan Building (201-209 Pine Ave.). The downtown area around Long Beach Blvd. is also home to a number of thrift shops, while Broadway Blvd., east of Downtown, is the sight of boutiques and a number of gay bars. **Details,** at 740 E. Broadway (310-437-7705) is popular with a younger crowd. Leathermen will want to check out **Mineshaft,** at 1720 E. Broadway (310-436-2433). Take bus #111 or 112 from downtown.

North of the Convention Center in Long Beach Plaza is the **Long Beach Children's Museum,** 445 Long Beach Blvd. (310-495-1163), with cultural and educational hands-on displays for children. (Open Thurs.-Sat. 11am-4pm, Sun. noon-4pm. Admission $2.95.) East of the Convention Center, along the waterfront, is the **Long Beach Museum of Art,** 2300 Ocean Ave. (310-439-2119). Famed Pasadena architects Greene and Greene designed the museum's turn-of-the-century home, which displays the pagoda-like lines and woodwork of the California arts and crafts style (to view another Green and Greene design check out the Tickener residence at 852 E. Ocean Blvd.). The museum's changing exhibits sometimes include works by the Russian expressionist Kandinsky. (Open Fri.-Sun. and Wed. noon-5pm, Thurs. noon-8pm. Admission $2.)

The view from the museum's lovely outdoor sculpture gardens grants a breathtaking panorama of the Pacific. Just off-shore you'll see Long Beach's bewildering **oil rigs,** disguised to look like islands, complete with palm trees and buildings. Although functionalism and expediency usually rule the day in California, the rigs represent an odd attempt to merge these metal montrosities with the natural vista by camouflage.

Belmont Shores, Long Beach's upscale, uptown neighborhood lies east of downtown and contains Long Beach's best public beach facilities and most popular beaches. Second St. (between Santa Ana and Park) in Belmont Shores is Long

Beach's prime walking area. Thursday through Saturday nights 2nd St. becomes a flesh market as surfer dudes and beach bunnies from San Pedro, Seal Beach and Huntington Beaches drive in to join the revelry. **Bayshore,** at 5335 E. 2nd (310-433-9150) is the home of "shoot the root". Invented here in 1986, the drink contains a shot of root beer schnapps in a cup of beer ($3.25). Wed. night special $2.50; bar open daily 1pm-2am.

Just past Belmont Shores is Naples Island, which, like Venice Beach, was planned around a series of canals. Unlike Venice Beach, the canals here still exist, and the Rivo Alto canal even has gondoliers.

North of downtown Long Beach, past Signal Hall, **Rancho Los Cerritos,** 4600 Virginia Rd. (310-424-9423) off San Antonio Dr., offers a romantic glimpse of what the early Spanish ranches looked like before they were subdivided and sold. This *rancho* was originally part of a land grant given by the Spanish monarchy to Manuel Nieto, an early settler, and was used for cattle-ranching until the 1860s. The ranch house itself dates back to 1844. (Tours Wed.-Sun. 1-5 pm. Free.) Cerritos' sister ranch, **Rancho Los Alamitos,** 6400 Bixley Hill Rd. (431-3541) is filled with early 20th century furnishings, as well as a gardens and farms. (Open Wed.-Sun. 1-5pm. Free.)

The Long Beach Yacht Club (310-598-9801), 6201 Appian Way hold races thoughout the year. During the summer a number of music festivals take place in downtown Long Beach, and the **Long Beach Sea Festival** takes places in the last two weeks of August. For information call **The Long Beach Area Convention and Visitors Council,** located at the World Trade Center, suite #300 (310-436-3645). During the month of December, 24 lit Christmas trees are kept afloat in Alamitos Bay.

Catalina Island

Catalina Island is a 31 mi. boat trip from San Pedro. The island offers a number of attractions, all of which can be accomplished on the mainland, and none of which were intended for the budget traveler. The cost of getting to the island (**Catalina Cruises,** 800-888-5939, runs ferries from San Pedro and Long Beach; adult return ticket $27.50, seniors $24, children $14) makes one-day trips unreasonable, and hotel prices on the island make overnight stays impossible. Two camping sites do exist: **Two Harbor's Camping** is a developed site just outside of town ($8 per person) and **Parson's Landing** is a primitive sight farther out ($6 per person, make sure to bring your own water). **Hermosa Hotel** (310-510-1010) offers the cheapest rooms in town, if you don't mind not having a bathroom (singles and doubles $35 weekdays, $50 on weekends). For camping reservations and information call **Catalina Cove and Camp Agency** (310-510-0303; open daily 8:30am-6pm).

If you have any money left after the boat ride, you may want to take one of **Catalina Adventure Tours'** treks around the island (310-510-2888). The two-hour island interior tour is the only legal way, outside of hiking, to see anything on Catalina other than the city of Avalon's overtouristed and overpriced shops and restaurants. (Tours cost $11.50 for adults, $9.50 for seniors, and $6 for children.) A 45-minute glass-bottom boat tour of the surrounding sea-bed is $5.50 for adults, $3.50 for seniors, and $3 for children. A combination package of both tours is $13 for adults, $7.50 for children. The company has offices at the ferry docks in San Pedro and Long Beach, as well as one near the ferry dock on the island.

You might also want to try exploring on your own with snorkeling or scuba gear. **Catalina Divers' Supply** (310-510-0330), on the pier, rents fins or a mask and snorkel for $5 per day or $3 for 2 hours. Wetsuits are $10 per day. Or try hiking your way into the 20 mi. of woodsy interior (biking is not permitted). Hikers must obtain a free permit by calling **L.A. County Parks and Recreation,** Avalon office (310-510-0688; open 9am-1pm and 2-4pm). The terrain itself looks remarkably similar to the mainland, but finding an unusual plant or catching sight of bison can make bipedal excursions worthwhile.

The city of Avalon itself contains a botanical garden (free, but donation expected), a high school, and the **Casino,** a round, red-tiled structure that combines Spanish, Moorish, and Art Deco styles. The building is presently being used as a movie theatre, and the theatre organ inside is a real crowd pleaser.

Near Los Angeles

Southern California residents have been blessed with proximity not only to the Pacific Ocean, but also to the pine forests of the **Coastal Ranges.** Two hours' driving takes the traveler from the crowded, smoggy streets of the city to the wide spaces and clean air of the mountains. The **San Gabriel Mountains** and, in particular, the **San Bernardino Mountains,** reveal a beauty that is untainted by the overdeveloped metropolis below.

Though outdoor activities flourish year-round, winter is the high season. While most serious skiers head for powder at the Sierra Nevada resorts that cluster around Lake Tahoe and Mammoth Lake, daytripping to the refreshing mountains of San Bernardino (less than two hours from downtown) has become an increasingly popular Southern California diversion. This popularity, however, depends largely upon the weather. Resorts usually come into their own from November to April, though temperatures have been known to soar into the 60s in January. Always call ahead to check conditions, and ask specific questions. Find out how many trails and lifts are open; how many of those open are considered beginner, intermediate, and advanced; what the snowmaking capacity is; and how long the toasty-warm *après*-ski saloons are open.

When ski conditions are favorable, many resorts sell out lift tickets with astonishing rapidity. Tickets for the resorts listed below may be purchased in advance through any **Ticketron** outlet, or over the phone with Visa or MasterCard (213-642-4242 or 714-740-2000). Ticketron tacks on a $1 service charge per ticket, up to a $10 maximum. All resorts rent equipment and offer lessons and special package rates, but it is advisable to rent equipment before venturing up the hill to avoid lines and high prices at the resort. Many ski shops in the mountain towns just outside of the ski areas also rent equipment. Lift tickets are usually around $32 for a full day; most resorts have half-day rates and some others have cheaper nighttime skiing.

When the snow melts and flowers blossom and temperatures hover lackadaisically in the 70s and 80s, the coastal mountains become an ideal summer and fall getaway from the daily grind. The **Angeles** and **San Bernardino National Forests** have many campgrounds, hiking trails, and quaint mountain villages to visit. The respective ranger stations and visitor centers indicated below are helpful to the would-be mountain man or woman.

Close by the Angeles National Forest in La Coñada is **Descanso Gardens,** 4118 Descanso Dr. (818-790-5571), a 165 acre retreat similar to the L.A. Arboretum. The garden includes the largest camellia forest in the world, an historical rose collection, and a number of man-made pools and waterfalls (adults $3, students and seniors $1.50, free the third Tuesday of each month; open daily 9am-5pm).

Angeles National Forest

The San Gabriel Mountains encompass terrain as varied as thick timberwoods, barren peaks, and green meadows. Their highest point is at the peak of Mount San Antonio, or "Old Baldy", at 10,064 ft. This area is popular year-round. Ski areas are crowded in the winter, and campgrounds are usually filled in the summer.

National Forest land covers 693,000 acres, about ¼ of the area of Los Angeles County, and offers over 110 campgrounds to choose from. Prices generally range from $5-12 per night. Choose a district of the forest and then contact the appropriate ranger office for information. Campsites are first-come, first-served (14-day max. stay). With 526 mi. of hiking trails and three lakes with boating and swimming areas, the Angeles National Forest is an excellent place to get away from the frenetic pace of L.A. without trekking all the way to the Sierras.

Angeles National Forest Headquarters, Supervisor's Office, 701 N. Santa Anita Ave., Arcadia 91006 (818-574-5200). A comprehensive map of the forest is available here ($2), as well as a wide selection of other literature (some for free) about the area.

Arroyo Seco Ranger District, Oak Grove Park, La Canada 91011 (818-790-1151). This is the south-central area of the forest, just north of Pasadena. Part of the Pacific Crest Trail passes through here, as well as numerous short self-guided nature trails. Mt. Wilson Skyline Park is also here, with its world-famous 100-in. telescope and observatory museum. There are 17 campgrounds in the district.

Mt. Baldy Ranger District, 110 N. Wabash Ave., Glendora 91740 (818-335-1251). The southeastern district of the forest. This includes several 8,000 ft. peaks, hiking trails for all levels of expertise, the cascading San Antonio Falls, and the scenic Glendora Ridge Road.

Saugus Ranger District, 30800 Bouquet Canyon Rd., Saugus 91350 (805-296-9710). A separate district from the main body of the forest, located to the northwest of the rest of the forest and at the northern end of the San Fernando Valley. It borders on the southeastern edge of National Forest Los Padres; Pyramid, Elizabeth, and Castaic Lakes have boating and fishing facilities. A wide variety of campgrounds are available.

Tujunga Ranger District, 12371 N. Little Tujunga Canyon Rd., San Fernando 91342 (818-899-1900). Tujunga covers the western end of the San Gabriel Mountains. It features myriad hiking and horseback riding trails, two target shooting facilites, and 5 overnight campgrounds.

Valyermo Ranger District, 29835 Valyermo Rd., Valyermo 93563 (805-944-2187). This district sprawls across the northeastern sector of the San Gabriel Maountains. It contains a high concentration of campgrounds along the Big Pined Hwy., which runs southeast out of Pearblossom and Valyermo into the northeast corner of the forest.

Ski Areas

Keep in mind that this is by no means the best skiing in California. The only thing that keeps most of these places in business is their proximity to L.A., though occasionally, flukes of nature do occur: in December of 1990, Southern California resorts had seven-foot powder bases while Sierra resorts were struggling to stay open. The best time to ski is on weekdays, within two or three days after a storm has hit the L.A. area.

Mountain High, 619-249-5821. 3 mi. west of Wrightwood on Rte. 2, off U.S. 138, 80 min. from downtown L.A. From L.A., take San Bernardino Fwy. (I-10) to I-15 north, then U.S. 138 to Wrightwood. From San Fernando Valley, take I-5 north to Antelope Valley Fwy. (Rte. 14), then the Pear Blossom turn-off (U.S. 138) to Wrightwood. Eleven lifts, 30 runs, 80- to 1600-ft. vertical drops, 500- to 6000-ft. trail lengths, night skiing, and snowmakers. Lift tickets $35, students on weekdays $27, under 12 $14.

Mt. Baldy, 818-982-0800. 45 minutes from downtown L.A. Take I-10 east, exit Mountain Ave., and drive north for 16 mi. Four double-chair lifts, 26 runs. 1991-2 prices will be: adult $33, student weekday $25, seniors $16.50, children $20.

Ski Sunrise, 619-249-6150. 5 mi. west of Wrightwood, north of Rte. 2, 1½ hr. from L.A. See Mountain High above for directions. One quad lift, 3 surface lifts, 80- to 800-ft. drops, trails from 400 ft. to almost a mile, artificial-snow equipment. Credit card users face a $2 service charge. Lift tickets $26, students and children 6-12 $10, seniors and children under 5 free. Equipment rental $15, children $12. Beginner's package (lesson, rental, and lift) $35.

Two smaller resorts, **Mt. Waterman** (818-790-2002) and Kratka Ridge (818-440-9749) are located just 45 minutes from downtown L.A., along Rte. 2 in La Cañada

Big Bear

Several resorts ring the town of **Big Bear Lake.** The **Big Bear Chamber of Commerce,** P.O. Box 2860, Big Bear Lake 92315 (714-866-4607), and the **Big Bear Lake Tourist and Visitor Bureau,** P.O. Box 3050G, Big Bear Lake 92315 (714-866-5878), dispense glossy ski brochures and arrange accommodations/ski packages. Midweek chalet rates are not out of budget's reach, especially for groups of six or more. The **Big Bear Ranger Station,** Rte. 38 (714-866-3437) 3 mi. east of Fawnskin, supplies campground and trail information. (Open Mon.-Sat. 8am-4:30pm.)

To reach Big Bear Lake, take I-215 north to San Bernardino, Rte. 330, and then Rte. 18. The back way, via the San Bernardino Fwy. (I-10) to Redlands and then Rte. 38 to Big Bear Lake, is frequently less congested. Driving time from L.A. is about two hours. In severe weather, take I-15 north off the San Bernardino Fwy. to Victorville, then Rte. 18 through the Lucerne Valley to Big Bear Lake. The **Superior Shuttle Service,** P.O. Box 3412, Hesperia 92345 (619-244-1510), operates a year-round shuttle from Ontario Airport to Big Bear Lake at superior prices ($60 one way for one, $75 for two, $10 each additional person).

Accommodations and Food

Staying in Big Bear Lake is never very cheap; enough visitors come year-round for the motels to maintain high prices. Many lodgings sport chalet-style architecture and views of the lake.

Motel 6, 1200 Big Bear Blvd. (714-585-6666). About the cheapest in town, with its simple, bare, but tidy rooms. Pool, A/C. Singles $25. Doubles $31.

Big Bear Lake Inn Cienega, 39471 Big Bear Blvd. (714-866-3477 or 800-843-0103). This brand-new inn boasts spacious and elegant rooms. Refrigerators, color TV, and Big Bear-sized beds. Tastefully decorated. Jacuzzis and kitchens available. Breakfast included. Singles $42, Fri.-Sat. and holidays $69.50. Doubles $48, Fri.-Sat. and holidays $79.50.

The Cozy Hollow Lodge, 40409 Big Bear Blvd. (714-866-8886 or 800-882-4480). A complex of individual cabin units of various sizes and degrees of luxury. Wet bar, kitchen, refrigerators, and sun deck available. All rooms have fireplace and color TV. In a densely forested area with lots o' shade. Doubles $45, weekends $60, holidays $75. Quads $70, weekends $80, holidays $120.

Wishing Well Motel, 540 Pine Knot (714-866-3505 or 800-544-7454), off Rte. 18. Rooms are cheerful and clean. 2nd floor rooms have a glimpse of the lake. Color TV, radio. Singles and doubles $59, Fri.-Sat. $69, holidays $79. Off-season special rates are sometimes available.

Restaurant offerings range from basic fast food to home-style meals to elegant gourmet cuisine. Visit the **Log Cabin Restaurant and Bakery,** 39976 Big Bear Blvd. (714-866-3667). With country-western decor and German specialties, it is a blend of European and American alpine sensibilities. Sandwiches $5, *Wienerschnitzel* $9. (Open Sun.-Thurs. 7am-8pm, Fri.-Sat. 7am-10pm.)

Camping

Camping is permitted at marked sites throughout the area. The grounds listed below are family camps and do not require (or accept) reservations; most are open from May to November. Group camp information is available at the ranger station.

Hanna Flat (7000 ft.) on Forest Rd. 3N14, 2½ mi. northwest of Fawnskin. 88 well-spaced sites surrounded by lush vegetation. Hiking, water. Sites $8.

Pineknot (7000 ft.). From Big Bear Blvd. go south on Summit Blvd. to end, then left ¼ mi. to sites. Located near town. 52 sites with water. Facilities for handicapped. Sites $11.

Coldbrook (6800 ft.) on Tulip Lane, 2 blocks south of Big Bear Blvd. 36 sites with water. Sites $9.

Big Pine Flat (6800 ft.) on Forest Rd. 3N14, 7 mi. northwest of Fawnskin. Dry with a slight desert atmosphere. Suited for dirt-bikers and other off-roaders, as there is an off-roading area just west of the campsite. 19 sites with water. Sites $8. Check to make sure water is available.

Holcomb Valley (7400 ft.), 4 mi. north on Forest Rd. 2N09 to 3N16, east for ¾ mi. Located near Pacific Coast Trail. 19 sites, no water. Free.

Horse Springs (5800 ft.), 10 mi. northwest of Fawnskin on Forest Rd. 3N14, east on 3N17. Dry, desert-like conditions. Filled with hard-core off-roaders. 17 sites, no water. Free.

Skiing

Most Los Angelenos agree that it's worth the extra driving time to reach the Big Bear resorts. At two and a half hours from L.A., one-day ski trips are still possible if you can handle the late drive home. Weekend and holiday reservations are a must.

Bear Mountain Ski Resort, 714-585-2519. Formerly called Goldmine Ski Area. 1½ mi. southeast of downtown Big Bear Lake. Turn south at the Moonridge/Garstin intersection and south (right) onto Clubview Dr. to parking area. Twelve lifts, 250 acres of terrain, 100-1300 ft. vertical drops, snowmaking, longest run 2 miles. Admission $36, ages under 13 $19. Equipment rental $9. Half-day rates. Midweek discounts for almost everyone (students $26). Beginner's package $38 on weekends, $29 on weekdays.

Snow Summit, 714-866-5766. Snow report 213-976-0601, 714-972-0601, or 619-294-8786. About 4 mi. south of Big Bear Lake. Take Rte. 330 through Running Springs, Rte. 38 through Redlands (longer but less crowded), or Rte. 18 through Lucerne Valley (the desert route, best in stormy weather). Ten lifts, over 40 runs, with a well-rounded assortment of beginner, intermediate and advanced runs. 100-1150-ft. vertical drops, 800- to 5475-ft. trail lengths, snowmaking, night skiing. Admission $35.50, student weekday $28.50, beginner ski package $29.50.

Snow Valley, 714-867-2751. Snow report 714-867-5151). Near Running Springs. Thirteen lifts, 800- to 5000-ft. trail lengths, snowmaking, and night skiing. Admission $33 (1-9pm $25; 4-9pm $20), ages under 13 $17 (1-9pm $15; 4-9pm $12). Equipment rental $14, children $10.

Snow Forest, 714-866-8891. Snow report 714-866-5503. Take Rte. 18 to Pine Nut Blvd. ("Aaaaah. Pitty boy!"). Geared toward the novice skier—beginner and intermediate runs, easier-to-learn Scorpion skis, and snow boards ($19 per day, $14 per ½-day), which are allowed nowhere else in Southern California. The longest run is just under a mile, the steepest grade 70% (although most are closer to 25%). Longest vertical drop is 650 ft. Half-days begin at noon. Admission $25 (½-day $20), under 13 $22 (½-day $18). Equipment rental $13, under 13 $11.

Idyllwild and Nearby Mountains

Idyllwild, if not idyllic, comes close. Its butterscotch-scented pine forests and lush alpine meadows offer a respite from the smog and unbearable summer heat of its lower-altitude city neighbors, Banning and Beaumont. Northern transplants to the Southland, bereft of the four seasons, come here to be reminded of turning leaves and frozen ponds.

The San Jacinto and Santa Rosa Mountains, two contiguous mountain ranges running north-south, are scarcely known to out-of-state visitors. Southern Californians, however, regard this territory as a godsend. Hemmed in by desert to the south and east and by the Los Angeles smog channel on the north, the mountains often top 10,000 ft., and the alpine scenery brings to mind the Sierra Nevada. Those who enjoy hiking and camping could stay for weeks; others who would rather relax on the porch of a cabin will find steep prices unless they're traveling in a group of four or more. Otherwise, stay in such lowland (and low-appeal) cities as Hemet, Beaumont, or Banning, or settle for a daytrip from Palm Springs or the coast.

Practical Information and Orientation

Visitor Information: Idyllwild Chamber of Commerce, 54274 N. Circle Dr., P.O. Box 304, Idyllwild 92549 (659-2810, recorded info. at 659-3259), in the Sugar Pine Shop. Useful free guide and a vague map. Open daily 10am-5pm. **Idyllwild County Park Visitor Center,** Rte.

243, P.O. Box 341, Idyllwild 92549 (659-3850), 4/5 mi. northwest of Idyllwild. Information on Riverside County facilities in the mountains—campgrounds, hiking trails, and interpretive programs. Also a nature museum. Open Wed.-Sun. 9am-6pm; Labor Day-Memorial Day Wed.-Sun. 10am-4pm.

U.S. Forest Service, San Jacinto Ranger District: 54270 Pine Crest, P.O. Box 518, Idyllwild 92549 (659-2117; recorded info. 5pm-8am). Maps of hiking trails, camping spots in and out of the wilderness, and campground information. Issues special-use permits for USFS land. If you want to take pictures for advertising, get married in the forest, or make money there, you'll need to obtain a permit from the Special Uses Clerk for about $25 per day. Also has information about all Riverside County Parks. Open daily 8am-4:30pm.

Mt. San Jacinto State Park and Wilderness: 25905 Rte. 243, P.O. Box 308, Idyllwild 92549 (659-2607), 200 ft. north of the Idyllwild Fire Station. **Long Valley Ranger Station** lies at the top of a ramp descending from the Palm Springs Aerial Tramway station and provides hiking and camping information, along with topographic maps. Open daily 8am-5pm.

Hiking and Backpacking Information: 659-2607.

Ski Conditions and Tram Information: 619-325-1449. Tram from Palm Springs to Mt. San Jacinto. Round-trip tram fare $13.95, seniors $11.55, under 12 $8.95. Round-trip tram fare plus dinner on the mountain $17.95, ages under 12 $11.50. Open Mon.-Fri. 10:45am-9pm, Sat.-Sun. 8am-10:45pm. In winter, closes an hour earlier.

Weather and Road Conditions: 659-3259.

Post Office: 54391 Village Center Dr., Idyllwild 92549 (659-2349). Open Mon.-Fri. 9am-5:30pm.

Area Code: 714; 619 when noted (Mt. San Jacinto is the dividing line).

From Los Angeles, the swiftest approach is via I-10, then south from Banning on Rte. 243. From San Diego and the desert south of the mountains, all the routes are via state highways in hilly country. The trip is lengthy but scenic. There is no public transportation into the mountains. Palm Springs, at the northeastern foot of Mt. San Jacinto, is the most appealing base city. From there, you can drive Rte. 111 east to Rte. 74, also known as the Palms-to-Pines Highway, which climbs up to Idyllwild. You can also take the Palm Springs Aerial Tramway up to a station on Mt. San Jacinto; from there hike or ski to the town of Idyllwild. (See Palm Springs Sights for information on the tramway.)

Accommodations and Food

For the scoop on lodging (including names, addresses, phone numbers and a map), call or write to **Associated Idyllwild Rentals,** P.O. Box 43, Idyllwild 92549 (659-5520). The best bet is probably **Knotty Pine Cabins,** 54340 Pine Crest Dr., P.O. Box 477, Idyllwild 92549 (659-2933). There is a marked entrance off Rte. 243 north of town. The eight cabins are clean with wood-panelled interiors in an alpine setting, each sleeping up to eight people (the comfort is inversely proportional to the number of people you cram into the cabin). Their best deal is the Security Lodge, where six can enjoy a living room with fireplace, kitchen, dining room, and porch for $120 a day ($8 per additional person in any cabin up to a max. of 10). If you're not traveling *en masse,* stay in one of the pine cabins for $43-65 (cabins sleep at least 2 each). Linen, dishes, cooking utensils, and cable TV are included. If you stay six nights you get the seventh free.

Many of Idyllwild's 1500 residents are here for only part of the year and rent their places while they're gone. **Idyllwild Property Management,** 54085 S. Circle Dr., P.O. Box 222, Idyllwild 92349 (659-5015), handles many of the cabins and homes in the area. Call well in advance for summer and holidays.

Idyllwild prides itself on its home-cooking, which is cheaper than you might expect considering its near-monopoly on visitors' appetites. Although supplies are best purchased in lowland cities (food prices rise with the altitude), **Fairway Supermarket,** in the Strawberry Creek Square off Village Center Dr. (659-2737), offers well-stocked shelves and reasonable prices. (Open Mon.-Sat. 9am-9pm, Sun. 9am-7pm.) For tasty, unpretentious food, head for **Jan's Red Kettle,** 54220 N. Circle Dr. (659-

4063). Jan serves lunch on a platter, and a meatless salad plate is only $4.50. (Open daily 7am-3pm.) Excellent soups and sandwiches (such as the $5.50 avocado sandwich) are there for the taking at **Pastries by Cathy** (659-4359), 54360 N. Circle Dr., above the Rustic Theater. (Open Thurs.-Tues. 8am-5pm.)

Camping

Campsites in the area are operated by the San Bernardino National Forest, Mt. San Jacinto State Park, San Bernardino County, and private entrepreneurs.

The U.S. Forest Service does not accept reservations for any campsites in the San Jacinto Ranger District. Dispersed camping is allowed anywhere on USFS land, but a free permit and registration is required so that the Forest Service can monitor backcountry movement. The application is available at any ranger station from a box on the front porch, and can be filled out and dropped in the receptacle (see Practical Information for addresses).

It is possible make reservations at all state park campsites. Two campgrounds, Idyllwild (on the edge of town) and Stone Creek, can be reserved through MISTIX (800-444-7275) from Memorial Day to Labor Day. All other campground reservations are handled by the state park itself. Since dispersed camping is prohibited on state park land and the campgrounds are relatively small, you should reserve well in advance (as early as 8 weeks) for summer. Write the Idyllwild ranger station (see Practical Information) for an application.

If winter camping appeals to you, remember that most USFS campsites are closed for the winter months, and camping on state park lands requires greater expertise; there are fewer amenities in general and almost none in winter.

San Bernardino National Forest

All campsites except Thomas Mountain, Tool Box Spring, and Santa Rosa Spring are developed, with toilets, tables, water, and fire pits. Tool Box Spring has water, and Santa Rosa Spring has water at the spring. Most sites are accessible by vehicle, and Pinyon Flat has handicapped facilities. All sites but Pinyon Flat are closed from October to April. The U.S. Forest Service Station (659-2117) distributes maps, directions, and more complete listings of sites.

Dark Canyon (5800 ft.), 6 mi. north of Idyllwild on Rte. 243. By far the best site in Idyllwild for camping. You can swim or fish in Dark Canyon Creek, which runs alongside the camp. Arrive early on summer weekends, as the 22 sites fill up fast. Water, vault toilets, hiking, fishing. Sites $7, streamside sites $8.

Marion Mountain (6400 ft.), on the same road as Dark Canyon. The higher altitude here provides both commanding vistas and cooler temperatures. Arrive early to get a site with a view. 25 sites with water, vault toilets, hiking. Sites $7.

Boulder Basin (7800 ft.), 15 mi. north of Idyllwild. Take Rte. 243 to Black Mountain Rd. Perched high atop Black Mountain, the 34 sites here offer splendid views of Marion Mountain and surrounding valleys. The dirt road is difficult in spots and is not recommended for RVs. Vault toilets, water. Sites $7.

Fern Basin (6300 ft.), on the same road as Dark Canyon. 22 sites in a shady, lushly vegetated area. Water, vault toilets, hiking trails. Sites $7.

Thomas Mountain (6800 ft.), 18 mi. east of Idyllwild on Rte. 74. Located in the Santa Rosa Mountains. The sites here are a bit dryer than those in the San Jacintos. 6 sites. Vault toilets, water at Tool Box Spring. Free.

Tool Box Spring (6800 ft.). Located high atop Thomas Mountain. 6 sites. Vault toilets, water, hiking. Free.

Santa Rosa Spring (6600 ft.). 3 sites on Thomas Mountain under pines and chaparral. Vault toilets, water at spring, hiking. Free.

Pinyon Flat (4000 ft.), on Rte. 74 east of Garner Valley. At only 4000 ft., it has much warmer temperatures than the other campsites in the area. Although some of the sites have springs nearby, the Forest Service advises bringing in your own water. 18 sites. Handicapped facilites, vault toilets. Sites $5.

Mt. San Jacinto State Park

All campgrounds here except **Idyllwild** (5400 ft.; 33 sites) and **Stone Creek** (6100 ft.; 50 sites) are primitive wilderness sites—with pit toilets—and trail-accessible only. These include **Strawberry Junction** (8100 ft.; 3 sites), **Round Valley** (9100 ft.; 28 sites), **Tamarack Valley** (9200 ft.; 12 sites), and the popular **Little Round Valley** (9700 ft.; 6 sites). The two developed campgrounds are on Rte. 243 and have tables, fireplaces, water, and, at Idyllwild, flush toilets and showers. Idyllwild is $14 per night, Stone Creek $9. For reservations, call MISTIX (800-444-7275) eight weeks to two days in advance. Availability of sites varies, so it is best to check with the park headquarters (659-2607). For the primitive sites, a free wilderness permit is necessary (available through the park headquarters). No applications accepted earlier than eight weeks in advance; Friday and Saturday nights should be booked as close to eight weeks in advance as possible. All Mt. San Jacinto sites are open all year.

Lake Hemet Area

Lake Hemet (4334 ft.) lies about 7 mi. southeast of Idyllwild, off Rte. 74. This considerable lake draws fisherfolk, picnickers, and campers. In recent years, however, the lake has dwindled considerably because of serious drought conditions in Southern California.

Lake Hemet Campground (659-2680). Operated by the municipal water district. Be warned that many of the lakeside sites may now overlook a grassy depression (or depressing grass). 180 RV hookups with water and electricity ($8.50 for 2 people per night, $45.50 per week, $130 per month; add 75¢ per day Oct.-April). 320 tent sites ($7 per night for 2, $35 per week, $100 per month). Toilets and showers. Rent rowboats $5 per half-day, $7 per day; motorboats $12 per half-day, $25 per day. The campground is open daily 6am-10pm.

Camp Anza (763-4819), in Anza, 16 mi. south of Lake Hemet. Hookups for 2 Mon.-Fri. $12.50, Sat.-Sun. $15.00; $50 per week, $125 per month. Tent sites for 2 Mon.-Fri. $10, Sat.-Sun. $12.

County Parks

Reservations are entered, processed, and saved by **Leisure Time Reservations Systems** (714-787-2553, Mon.-Fri. 8am-5pm).

Idyllwild County Park Campground, (714-659-2656), on Rte. 243, south of the state park campground of almost the same name. 90 sites, water, showers, restrooms, stoves, tables. $10 per vehicle. Open year-round.

Hurkey Creek Campground, (714-659-2050), on Rte. 74 across from Lake Hemet. 4400 ft. 105 sites, in a flat, grassy, park-like area. Hiking, fishing, restrooms, showers. $10 per vehicle. Reservations required for group camping. Open year-round.

McCall Park (714-659-2311). 4444 ft. Equestrian camping only. Restrooms, showers. $8 per rig, $1 per corral. Open May-Oct.

Sights

Idyllwild's natural setting, with impressive granite monoliths arching above the forest, offers the visitor far more than the town itself. In May, over 10 ft. of snow still blankets the mountain peaks above the town. From meadows, you can catch an occasional glimpse of the hot desert 1½ mi. below. The Santa Rosa/San Jacinto mountain range comes to a spectacular, screeching halt here, plummeting 9000 ft. in under 6 mi.

Sadly, most people just come to Idyllwild (5303 ft.), walk around for an hour, buy that gingham toilet seat cover in the window, and drive off again. Gift shops line the streets of the village center, which forms an irregular town square. Everything is built of pine, with the architectural emphasis on bastardized Swiss Chalet.

Near the center of town, off of Village Center Dr., stands the **Idyllwild Tree Monument.** This 50-ft.-high work of chainsaw art commemorates figures in local history and lore.

Idyllwild is home to a fine school of the arts in the forest south of town, the **Idyllwild School of Music and the Arts (ISOMATA),** on Toll Gate Rd. off Rte. 243 (659-2171). Summer classes in music, drama, dance, creative writing, Native American arts, ceramics, photography, and more are offered. Performances, exhibitions, and workshops take place regularly year-round, daily in summer. Average ticket prices for performances are $5-7.50.

To most enjoy the region, hike away from the cute ice cream parlors and clogged streets of Idyllwild and camp in the wilderness. Part of the national forest lands and all the state park is designated as wilderness by the federal government. The ranger stations listed above can provide the required free permits for hiking or camping on such lands.

Idyllwild also abounds with angling opportunities. The Department of Fish and Game regularly stocks two lakes and several streams in the area. **Lake Hemet** (659-2680), a large reservoir located 7 mi. southeast of Idyllwild off Rte. 74, has a free day-use area for fishing (trout, catfish and bass; $7 park entrance fee). No swimming is allowed as this is a domestic water supply, but you can rent a motorboat for $25 per day, or a rowboat for $12. (Prices include a $5 deposit. Rentals available daily 6am-7pm.) **Lake Fulmor** is a small picnic and fishing area 10 mi. north of town along Rte. 243. **Dark Canyon Creek,** located near the campsight of the same name, **Strawberry Creek,** which runs through Idyllwild just south of the village center, and **Fuller Mill Creek** are all regularly stocked in the spring and summer. Licenses are required in each of these areas, and there is a daily bag limit of five trout. Call 213-590-5020 for information on trout stocking in lakes and creeks throughout the area, or check the *Los Angeles Times's* sports section.

Indian Relic Park, at the upper end of Pine Crest Rd., has a number of Native American pictographs, as does **Idyllwild County Park,** north of Idyllwild. Inquire at the visitors center or ranger station in Idyllwild for directions.

The most popular area of the national forest is **Black Mountain,** northwest of Idyllwild. This area includes a fire lookout tower, scenic overlooks, a few trails, and a cluster of campgrounds.

While sites such as Lake Hemet, with their hundreds of RVs, hardly qualify as peaceful, many places in the southern end of the forest offer solitude and the opportunity for primitive camping. Climbers, for example, can head to **Lily** and **Suicide Rocks** in the northern area, near **Tahquitz Peak.**

The 2600-mi. **Pacific Crest Trail** passes through on its way from Mexico to Canada, and a USFS brochure describes 25 other trails, including both desert and high mountain routes. Some of the most rewarding and exhausting begin in the Native American-owned canyons on the southwest fringe of Palm Springs and climb slowly into the foothills.

To see the transition from desert to mountain more quickly and much less strenuously, follow the **Palms-to-Pines Highway,** coincident with Rte. 74. It runs between Mountain Center (south of Idyllwild at the junction of Rte. 74 and 243) and Palm Desert near Palm Springs. In the middle of the 36-mi drive, meadows carpet the undulating terrain of the distant tree line, while closer at hand, pine trees mingle with the brilliant red blooms of the 10-ft. ocotillo plant.

Another way to enjoy the tranquility of these mountains is to come during the off-season (Oct.-April). Surprisingly few Southern Californians are keen on leaving their eternal summer during the "winter" months. Besides lower prices for accommodations and food, you'll enjoy autumn colors that roll slowly down the mountainsides, snowy winter nights, and the wild streams of spring. The Palm Springs Aerial Tramway is a popular winter approach for the relatively few people who take advantage of the exhilarating cross-country skiing and snow camping in the state park. For a description of facilities and activities in the immediate vicinity of the tram's top, see Palm Springs.

Central Coast

For millions of people in the United States and around the world, the word California evokes images of the state's two primary cities and tourist magnets, Los Angeles and San Francisco. However, it is in fact the Central Coast, the shoreline betweeen the state's two megalopoli, which embodies all that is uniquely Californian—rolling surf crashing onto wide beaches, dramatic cliffs and mountains, self-actualizing New Age adherents, and relaxed fern-bars alongside surfer huts. Absent from this Elysian reality are the drawbacks most urban Californians must endure. Ominous banks of smog do not float over the Central Coast, residents do not lift weights on the beach or sling revolvers on the freeway, nor is any town on the coast large enough to support one more insufferably smug California sports team.

Just north of the L.A. county line, Ventura and Oxnard offer terrific surfing and secluded beaches at lower prices than in L.A. Slowly and spectacularly, the Pacific Coast Highway (Rte. 1) wends its way north from genteel Santa Barbara, passing vineyards, fields of wildflowers, and miles of beach, with stunning scenery throughout. William Hearst's San Simeon anchors the southern end of Big Sur, the legendary 90-mi. strip of sparsely inhabited coastline. Climbing in and out of Big Sur's mountains, Rte. 1 occasionally inches motorists to the edge of jutting cliffs which hang over the violent surf. On the Monterey Peninsula, eager merchants try to harness the northern end of Big Sur for tourist consumption, but not even they can spoil the coast's grandeur. Just above Monterey, and 79 mi. south of San Francisco, Santa Cruz breeds a youthful surfer and university culture with San Francisco's off-beat quirkiness, resulting in a uniquely conscious beach community. From Ventura to Santa Cruz, dozens of state parks and national forests offer campgrounds and recreation as peaceful or daring as you desire.

Touring the Central Coast is the ultimate "California Trip."

Santa Barbara

Santa Barbara's first human inhabitants, the Chumash tribe, thrived on the region's limpid waters and fertile soil. In 1782, Spanish missionaries, with their unerring eye for natural beauty, chose the site for a mission, spreading The Word and other Euopean diseases, which wiped out the native population. Over the ruins of the extinct Chumash, the Spanish, then the Americans, built Santa Barbara into a prosperous port town. Later, in the 1920s, slick Santa Barbarians discovered an oil deposit and the city boomed louder. Today, Santa Barbara seemingly derives its wealth simply by being home to a lot of wealthy people. In emulation of Beverly Hills, Palm Springs, and Malibu, Santa Barabara is playing home to the stars. Current residents include Kenny Loggins, Kevin Costner, Julia Child, and Jonathan Winters. Ex-President and ranch hand Ronald Reagan still drops by.

Santa Barbara is a coastal gem: the sun sets over beautiful beaches and lends the hills surrounding the city a purplish glow. In town, the friendly residents take pains to keep development to a minimum. After a 1925 earthquake flattened the city, residents rebuilt it in Spanish colonial style. They forbade any new buildings exceeding four stories, and the commission they established to review design proposals still exerts an iron grip over the cityscape. The result is stunningly charming and charmingly stunning, and thus Santa Barbara continues to be the expensive resort-getaway of choice for L.A. Law characters and other well-heeled Angelenos, while the climate makes it the favored home of numerous homeless people. Far and away the largest group of transients, however, are European tourists (the soap opera *Santa Barbara* has been playing prime time in Europe for a number of years now). Residents themselves tend to be an eclectic group of surfers, artists, and hippies living happily and healthily together ever after.

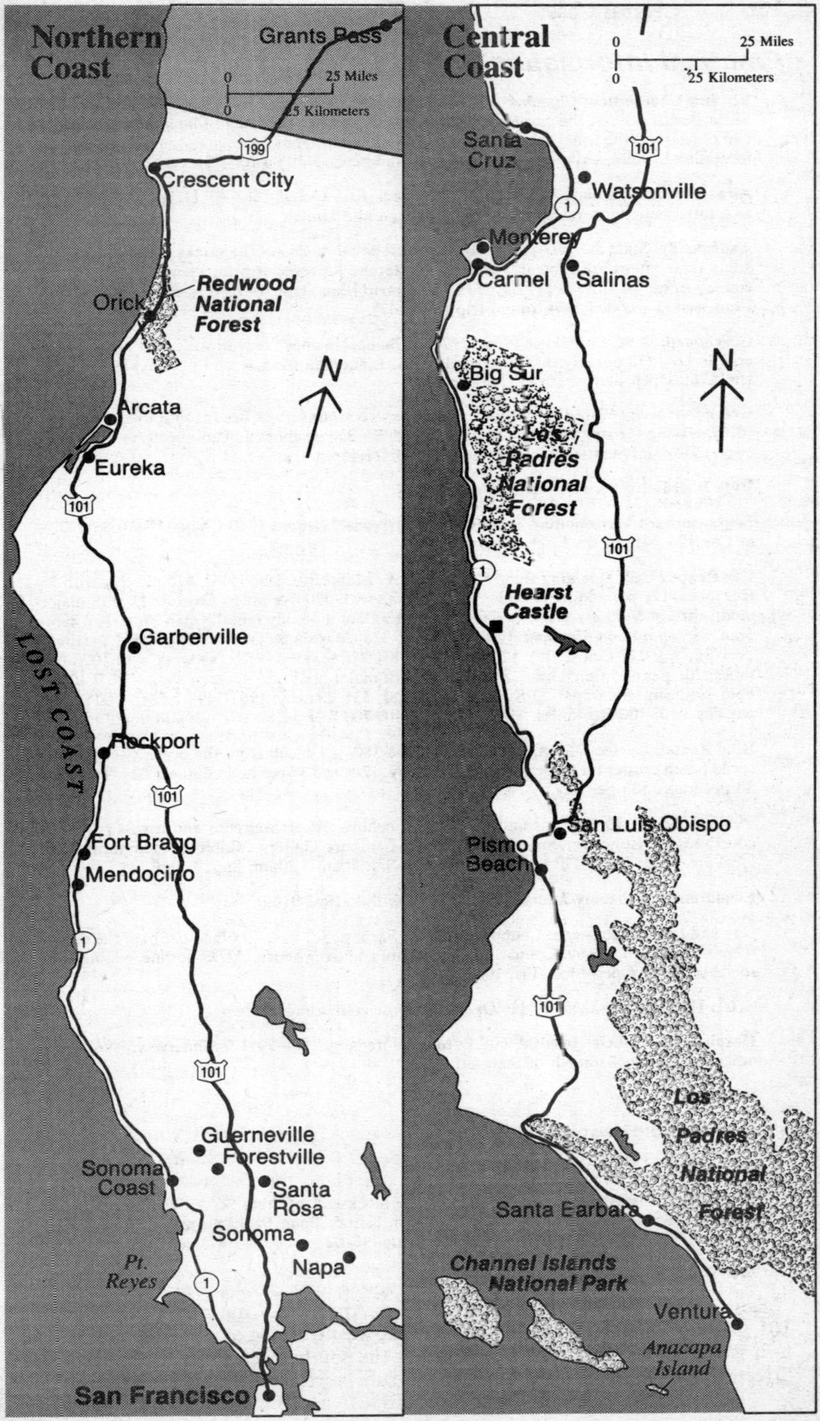

Northern Coast
Grants Pass
0 25 Miles
0 25 Kilometers
199
Crescent City
Redwood National Forest
Orick
N
Arcata
Eureka
101
Garberville
LOST COAST
Rockport
101
Fort Bragg
Mendocino
1
101
Guerneville
Forestville
Santa Rosa
Sonoma Coast
Sonoma
Napa
Pt. Reyes
1
San Francisco
Central Coast
0 25 Miles
0 25 Kilometers
Santa Cruz
101
Watsonville
1
Monterey
Carmel
Salinas
N
Big Sur
Los Padres National Forest
101
1
Hearst Castle
San Luis Obispo
Pismo Beach
101
Los Padres National Forest
Santa Barbara
Channel Islands National Park
Ventura
Anacapa Island

Practical Information and Orientation

Visitors Information: Chamber of Commerce, 504 State St. (965-3021). Location also at 1 Santa Barbara St., at the corner of Cabrillo Blvd. right by the beach. Maps ($1), brochures, pamphlets—all the usual suspects. Open Mon.-Sat. 8am-5pm, Sun. 9am-4pm. To receive information by mail, write to: Santa Barbara Conference and Visitor's Bureau, 510A State St.

Airport: Santa Barbara Aviation, 601 Firestone Rd., Goleta (683-4011). Intrastate as well as limited national service, including American and United.

Amtrak: 209 State St. (963-1015), downtown. The other side of the tracks is just that; avoid going there after dark. The area around the station, however, is being cleaned up and is becoming safer. To L.A. (3 per day; $19, round-trip Mon.-Thurs. $25, Fri.-Sun. $30) and San Francisco (1 per day; $74, round-trip $121-142).

Greyhound: 34 W. Carrillo St. (966-3962), at Chapala in one of downtown's safer areas. Lockers. To L.A. (15 per day; $13.50, round-trip $23) and San Francisco (7 per day; $40, round-trip $76). Open daily 5:30am-11:15pm.

Green Tortoise: 569-1884. Alternative once-per-week bus service heads south to Los Angeles ($10), leaving Carrow's Restaurant on Carrillo St. Sat. at about 5:30am; north to San Francisco ($30) and Seattle from Carrow's Sun. at 11:45pm.

Ride Board: 3rd floor of UCSB Union.

Santa Barbara Metropolitan Transit District: Transit Center, 1020 Chapala St. (683-3702), at Cabrillo, behind the Greyhound station.

Car Rental: Ugly Duckling Rent-A-Car, 311 W. Montecito (966-9514). $15 per day with 75 free miles, 12¢ per additional mile; $98 per week with 500 free miles. Must be 21 with major credit card or $200 in cash for a daily rental, $300 for a weekly rental. Open Mon.-Fri. 8am-5pm, Sat. 8am-noon. **Community Rent-A-Car,** 328 Chapala St. (966-3097) and 351 S. Hitchcock St., #B-110 (966-2235). $25 per day with 150 free miles, $139 per week with 1000 free miles; 20¢ per additional mile. Must be 21 with major credit card. Open Mon.-Fri. 7:30am-6pm, Sat.-Sun. 9am-5pm. **U-Save Auto Rental,** 531 Chapala (963-3499 or 965-2004). $16 per day with 100 free miles, $99 per week with 700 free miles; 10¢ per additional mile.

Bike Rental: Cycles-4-Rent, 101 State St. (966-3804), 1 block from the beach. Rent a one-speed beach cruiser for $4 per hour, $17 per day. 12-speed $7 per hour, $30 per day. Tandems $8 per hour, $35 per day.

Public Library: 40 E. Anapamu (962-7653), behind the art museum and across from the courthouse. Distinctive semi-adobe building. Faulkner Gallery exhibits contemporary and local art. Open Mon.-Thurs. 10am-9pm, Fri.-Sat. 10am-5:30pm, Sun. 1-5pm.

Laundromat: Economy Laundromat, 500 N. Milpas (963-9169).

Gay and Lesbian Resource Center: 417 Santa Barbara St., #A-19 (963-3636), on the downtown side of the freeway. Counseling for alcohol and drug abuse, AIDS hotline, testing, and social services. Open Mon.-Fri. 10am-4pm.

Crisis Hotline: 569-2255. 24 hr. Over-the-phone counseling.

Hospital: St. Francis Hospital, 601 E. Micheltorena St. (568-5711 for emergency, 962-7661 otherwise), 6 blocks north of State St.

Emergency: 911.

Police: 215 E. Figueroa (963-3616).

Fire: 121 W. Cabrillo (965-5254).

Post Office: 836 Anacapa St. (564-2266), one block east of State St. An intriguing mix of Mission Revival and art deco. Open Mon.-Fri. 8am-5:30pm. Packages may also be picked up Sat. 8:30-10am. General Delivery ZIP Code: 93102.

Area Code: 805.

Santa Barbara is 96 mi. northwest of Los Angeles, 27 mi. past Ventura on U.S. 101. Because the town is built along an east-west traverse of shoreline, its grid pattern is slightly skewed. The beach lies at the southern end of the city, and State Street, the main street in Santa Barbara, runs northwest from the waterfront. All streets are designated east and west from State St. U.S. 101 and Cabrillo Blvd. are the major east-west arteries by the ocean.

Pick up **bus** route maps and schedules from the visitors center or the transit center behind the Greyhound station on Chapala, which serves as the transfer point for most routes. Several lines have evening and weekend service. One out of three buses on each route is wheelchair accessible. The fare is 75¢, disabled passengers and those over 61 30¢, under 5 free. Exact change is required. Transfers are free.

A free **downtown shuttle** runs along State St. every 10 min. Mon.-Thurs. 11am-5:30pm, Fri. 11am-10pm; stops are at the hibiscus flower signs.

Biking is a breeze, as most streets are equipped with special lanes. The **Cabrillo Bikeway** runs east-west along the beach from the Bird Refuge to the City College campus. **Parking** in Santa Barbara is painless; numerous downtown lots offer 90 minutes of free parking. In summer, **Sunset Biking Tours** offers 1-2 hour town cruises ($12, students $7, *Let's Go* users $9. BYOB (Bring Your Own Bike). Call Danae at 966-6610.

Accommodations

There are no hostels in Santa Barbara or its environs. Unless you're uncommonly farsighted, you'll find yourself paying motel rates of $40 and up. By the end of June, the Motel 6 by the beach is often booked until February. If both of the 6s are full and you don't luck into a cancellation (check at noon or 6pm), try the 3000 block of State St., where a cluster of clean, safe motels average $50 per room. The best option is to try early in the day (and *not* on a weekend) at one of the hotels listed below.

Hotel State Street, 121 State St. (966-6586), just off the beach. This old hotel is the closest thing Santa Barbara has to a hostel. Occupants share hallway bathrooms, but have private bedrooms which are petite yet spruce. In exchange, they pay some of S.B.'s most affordable rates: $45 for one double bed, $60 for two. A room with twin twin beds is $45. Color TV with cable. European travelers comprise 80% of the clientele.

Motel 6, 443 Corona del Mar (564-1392), near the beach, east of downtown. Take bus #20 or 21 on Cabrillo Blvd. Singles $40. Doubles from $46. Also 3505 State St. (687-5400), 3 mi. north of downtown. Take bus #6 or 11. Singles $39. Doubles $45. If you can get an unreserved room after May, you might also want to go buy a lottery ticket—it's your lucky day.

The Schooner Inn, 533 State St. (965-4572), central downtown. Sizeable, pleasant hotel in a beautiful building. Rooms sleeping 1-2 $45, with bath $50. For weekends, make reservations at least a week in advance.

Californian Hotel, 35 State St. (966-7153), close to the beach. Not likely to win the spic-n-span certificate of merit. However, singles $27-35, rooms over the the 1st floor bar $35-45. Room with 2 beds $65 (up to 4 people). Add $10 more on weekends. TV, phone, private bath.

Tides Motel, 116 Castillo St. (963-9772). An unsullied, newly-furnished motel on a quiet street near the beach. $65 for 1 bed, $75 for 2 (3-4 people). $20 higher on the weekends. Color TV, small spa, phone, A/C.

The Beach House, 320 W. Yanonali St. (986-1126). An older clientele inhabits this quiet motel. $69 for 1-2 people, $75 for a room with 2 beds. Color TV, phone. The beauty of the magnitudinous rooms is apparent, but their numbers are few, so reserve well in advance.

Camping

The *Santa Barbara Campsite Directory* lists prices, directions to sites, and reservation numbers for all campsites in the area. It's free and available at the visitors center. State campsites can be reserved through MISTIX (800-444-7275). **Carpinteria Beach State Park** (684-2811), 12 mi. southeast of Santa Barbara along U.S. 101, has 262 developed tent sites with hot showers. (Sites $16, $20-25 with hookups.) There are three state beaches under 25 mi. west of Santa Barbara, but none are served by buses. **Gaviota** has 59 sites, and is the farthest away, operating on a come first and fight it out basis (no reservations). **Refugio** (968-1350), with 84 sites, is closer though not maintained as well. (Reserve 10 days-8 weeks in advance.) **El Capitan** (968-1033), the closest, has 140 sites. (Sites at all three $16, $14 in winter.) You may also want to try the private campground next door to El Capitan (also called El Capitan), which includes a swimming pool (685-3887). There are loads o' campgrounds in **Los Padres National Forest** north of Santa Barbara. Get a map for $2 at the Supervisor's Office, U.S. Forest Service, 6144 Colle Rd., Goleta 93117 (683-6711; open Mon.-Fri. 8am-4:30pm). The nearest sites are 20 mi. from downtown, and reservations are generally not accepted. Unlikely to be full in summer, **Lake Cachuma County Park** (688-4658) has 530 campsites at $12 each, on a first-come, first-camped basis.

Food

Santa Barbara's sunny meteorological and socioeconomic climate encourages sidewalk cafés to burgeon like hothouse flowers. For something more substantial than a double espresso, try one of the Mexican restaurants or small diners. The visitors center and *The Independent,* the free weekly paper available all over town, have thorough listings for all budget ranges.

Nearly all the restaurants on Milpas St. are well-run and well-priced. Ice-cream aficionados should head to McConnel's (1213 State St.; 965-5400) where luscious licks are vended for a mere $1 a pint. There's a farmer's market on old town State St. every Tuesday from 4-7pm, and a second one from 9am-noon each Saturday at Santa Barbara St. in downtown. Trader Joes (29 S. Milpas: 564-7878) and Tri-County Produce (335 S. Milpas; 965-4558) both sell prepared foods. Santa Barbara's "superlative" restaurants include sushi bars and Mexican restaurants.

La Super-rica Taquera, 622 N. Milpas, (963-4940). Julia Child's favorite Mexican restaurant. Smaller portions than others in town, but the tastiest and most authentic. Dishes range from $1.20 to $5.15. Open daily 11am-9:30pm.

Godzilla's, 632 State St. (965-2980). The town's disputed sushi champion (some argue for Something's Fishy). *Maki* from $4-6. Mon.-Fri. 5:30-10:30pm, Sat.-Sun. 5:30-11:30pm.

Esau's Coffee Shop, 403 State St. (965-4416). Santa Barbara's most popular breakfast place. 6 wheatgerm pancakes $4.25. "Chinese pizza" (rice, assorted vegetables, and melted cheese) $4.50. Omelettes $4.75-5.25. Be on the lookout for daily specials. Open Mon.-Fri. 6am-1pm, Sat.-Sun. 7am-1pm.

Little Audrey's Coffee Shop, 905 State St. (962-1219). A truck stop—hold the trucks. The food is nothing special, but these best-of-prices will transport you. Hamburgers $2.25-4, a breakfast of ham and eggs with hash browns and toast $3.90. Open Mon.-Sat. 6am-3:30pm, Sun. 7am-3pm.

R.G.'s Giant Hamburgers, 922 State St. (963-1654). Some of S.B.'s best beef. The basic burger is only $3.09, but be adventurous and spring for an excellent guacamole burger or a chili cheeseburger (both $3.84). A bottle of Miller to wash it down is $1.75. Allow 10 min. for your burger—they're cooked to order. Open Mon.-Sat. 9am-10pm, Sun. 10am-10pm.

Italian/Greek Deli, 636 State St. (962-6815). The best deli in town. As for the specialties, the name says it all: hot and cold sandwiches $3, gyros $3.75, Greek salad $3.75, spaghetti and meatballs $4. Packed with downtown workers at lunchtime. Open Mon.-Sat. 8am-6pm.

The Acapulco, 1114 State St. (963-3469). The happy hour here (4-7pm) is the cheapest way to eat in town. Order any drink (sodas $1.10) and you get all the tostados, spicy potato and macaroni salad, carrots and celery your stomach can hold. Plus, you get to sit right by the fountain in the courtyard. Open Mon.-Sat. 11am-11pm, Sun. 10am-10pm.

Main Squeeze Restaurant, 138 E. Canon Perdido St. (966-5365), at Santa Barbara St. A cheery health-food restaurant with one of the area's best vegetarian menus. Soyburger with chips and pickle $4.25; enormous tostada salad with chips and salsa $5.20. Open Mon.-Fri. 11am-10pm, Sat.-Sun. 5pm-10pm.

Joe's Café, 536 State St. (966-4638). Don't be fooled by the exterior, there's dark wood furnishing inside. Plain but well-cooked, hearty food and drinks notorious for their size and punch. Lunchtime hot sandwiches with salad $5-6. At dinner, spring for the famous sirloin—$13.75 with soup or salad, baked potato, salsa, spaghetti, onion rings, and bread and butter. Always a line outside. Open Mon.-Thurs. 11am-11:30pm, Fri.-Sat. 11am-12:30am, Sun. 4pm-11:30pm.

Santa Barbara Nutrition Center, 15 E. Figueroa St. (962-3766) A health-food market with a complete fruit-shake bar—most delicious. Bar open Mon.-Sat. 9am-5pm, Sun. 11am-4pm. Store open Mon.-Sat. 9am-6pm, Sun. 11am-5pm.

Sights

State Street is Santa Barbara's monument to city planning. Everything that doesn't move—mailboxes, telephones, the restrooms at the public library—has been encased in Spanish tile. To get the full impact of the city's architectural homogeneity, climb to the observation deck of the **Santa Barbara County Courthouse** on the 1100 block of Anacapa St. (962-6464). From 85 ft. above the street, you can survey block after block of low stucco buildings, rising into the hills around downtown.

The courthouse itself is one of the West's great public buildings. Built by William Mooser in 1929 after a fortuitous oil strike, its highlights include a sculpted fountain, sunken gardens, historical murals, wrought-iron chandeliers, and hand-painted ceilings. Compared to the more prosaic Mission Revival buildings found elsewhere in California, the courthouse is a work of genius. Be sure to see the framed maps in the mural room and the Law Library, which depict 17th-century conceptions of California as an enormous island. (Buildings open Mon.-Fri. 8am-5pm, Sat.-Sun. 9am-5pm. Tower closes at 4:45pm. Courthouse tours Tues.-Sat. 2pm, Wed., Fri. 10:30am. Free.)

The **public library,** and the **Santa Barbara Museum of Art** also blend different styles of architecture into an eye-pleasing ensemble. The library (962-7653) on Anapamu St. (pronounced on-uh-puh-MOO) and the Museum of Art, 1130 State St. (963-4364), are linked by a pedestrian plaza. Inside the library, the **Faulkner Gallery** usually displays on-the-market works by local artists. get 'em while they're young. (Open Mon.-Thurs. 10am-9pm, Fri.-Sat. 10am-5:30pm, Sun. 1-5pm. Free.)

Built as a post office in 1914, the art museum was converted into galleries in the 30s and renovated a few years ago. In the entrance to the new wing is a monumental Palladian arch crafted from Verona limestone. The museum owns an impressive collection of classical Greek, Roman, Asian, American, and European art, but prides itself especially on American art and the portraits in the Preston Morton Gallery. (Open Tues.-Wed. and Fri.-Sat. 11am-5pm, Thurs. 11am-9pm, Sun. noon-5pm. Guided tours Tues.-Sat. at 2pm. Admission $3, ages 6-16 $1.50. Free Thurs. and on the first Sun. of each month.)

The Arlington Center for Performing Arts, 1317 State St. (963-9589 or 963-4408), is that rarest of movie theaters—a uniplex. The Arlington is also the home to the **Santa Barbara Symphony** and hosts the annual **Santa Barbara Film Festival.** Call the box office for information on upcoming events. The building itself is noteworthy for its Spanish-Moorish architecture and for the murals over its entrance depicting scenes from California's Hispano-Mexican era. Its tower is one of the few structures in this stumpy town to rival the palm trees. Even if you don't attend a performance, try to get in to see the auditorium, a splendid *trompe l'oeil* of a Spanish village square on a starry night.

From the foot of State St., walk 1 block west on Chapala to the grizzled old **Moreton Bay fig tree,** transplanted here from Australia in 1877. The tree's writhing branches, spanning 160 ft., shelter some of Santa Barbara's street folk, although the city is constructing a fence around the park to keep any vagabonds outside.

The beach west of State St. is called **West Beach;** the longer stretch in the other direction, **East Beach.** The latter is preferable because **Chase Palm Park** acts as a buffer between it and Cabrillo Blvd. The park threads nearly 2 mi. of bike and foot paths through formerly green lawns turned brown by the recent drought. At the far end is the **Andree Clark Bird Refuge** and the **Santa Barbara Zoo** (962-5339). The delightfully leafy zoo has low fences and such an open feel that the animals seem kept in captivity only through sheer laziness. In reality, many are too injured to survive outside captivity, and others belong to endangered species. New attractions include a miniaturized African *veldt,* where giraffes stroll, lazily silhouetted against the Pacific. A miniature train provides a tour of the park. (Open daily 9am-6pm; Sept. 7-June 14 10am-5pm. Admission $4, ages 2-12 $2, under 2 free.)

If the zoo doesn't sate your appetite for wildlife, check out the **Sea Center** (962-0885), on Stearns Wharf, for more aquatically inclined mammals. In this bantam museum, a mammoth model of a gray whale hangs over video exhibits, sea-life dioramas, and an aquarium which often features hatching fish. The brand new touch-tank is open Tues.-Sun. noon-4pm. (Admission $1, children 50¢. Open Mon., Weds., Fri. 10am-5pm, Tues. and Thurs. noon-6pm. Sat.-Sun. 10am-6pm.)

At the end of Laguna St. on the northern side of town is **Mission Santa Barbara** (682-4713). (Take bus #22, 23, or 28.) Praised as the "Queen of Missions" when built in 1786, the mission assumed its present majestic incarnation in 1820. Towers containing splayed Moorish windows stand on either side of a Greco-Roman façade, and a Moorish fountain dribbles in front of the church. The museum contains period rooms and a sampling of items from the mission archives. The lush inner courtyard is unfortunately cordoned off, but you're free to wander the cemetery on the chapel's northern flank, where 4000 Native Americans are said to be buried. (Self-guided tours daily 9am-5pm. Museum $1, under 17 free.)

The best reason to come up to the hills, however, is the **Santa Barbara Museum of Natural History,** 2559 Puesta del Sol Rd. (682-4711); follow the signs from the mission. Ecologically aware, educational, and thorough, this museum does an outstanding job of examining Southern California. The museum's noteworthy features include a collection of original lithographs by Audubon and other naturalists, a display of well-preserved Chumash artifacts, an extensive archive on the Channel Islands, and the only planetarium between San Francisco and L.A. (Open Mon.-Sat. 9am-5pm, Sun. 10am-5pm. Planetarium shows Sat.-Sun; observatory 682-3244. Admission $3, seniors and ages 13-17 $2, under 12 $1). Nearby **Rocky Nook Park** is thickly wooded and perfect for a picnic.

Further up into the hills is the **Santa Barbara Botanical Garden,** 1212 Mission Canyon Rd. (682-4726), which is not served by bus and is a bit of a trek without a car. Three miles of hiking trails wind through 65 acres of trees, wildflowers, and cacti. The garden is also home to the **dam** built by the Chumash (under the direction of the mission) to bring water down from the hills for irrigation. Along with the ruins of a pottery shack just across the street from the mission and a small cave painting in the hills, this is one of the last vestiges of the region's Native American heritage. (Open daily 8am-sunset. Guided tours daily at 2pm, Thurs.-Sun. also at 10:30am. Tues. and Wed. are free. Admission $3, seniors and teens $2, ages 5-12 $1, under 5 free).

The **University of California at Santa Barbara (UCSB)** is in Goleta, a shapeless mass (and mess) of suburban homes, gas stations, and coffee shops that congeals around the university. Take U.S. 101 or bus #11 to the university, and visit the school's excellent **art museum** (961-2951), which houses the Sedgwick Collection of 20 15th- to 17th-century European paintings (including a Bellini *Madonna and Child*) and hosts innovative contemporary exhibits. (Open Tues.-Sat. 10am-4pm, Sun. 1-5pm. Free.) University Arts and Lectures manages a year-round program of over 150 events. Call 961-2951 for current offerings.

For a lovely view of the city and its harbor, follow the "Scenic Drive" signs to **Alameda Padre Serra,** a road that winds its way along the hillside bordering the town on the northeast. This part of town is known as the **Riviera** and if money could talk this would be a yappy neighborhood indeed.

The hills around Santa Barbara are filled with hiking trails. One of the most popular is **Seven Falls.** Don't expect too much, though, the California draught has evaporated the feeding rivers, turning Seven Falls into No Falls. The nevertheless scenic three mi. trail can be reached from the top of Tunnel St.

Entertainment

Despite the proximity of Ronald Reagan's ranch, Santa Barbara engages in some decidedly liberal revelry. Follow Cabrillo Blvd. to the Santa Barbara cemetery at the end of East Beach (bus #20 or 21). Dog-walking patricians from posh Montecito have complained often enough to squash sunbathing *au naturel,* but occasionally beachgoers are still caught with their pants down here. More popular, especially with the gay and hippie communities, is the beach at Summerland, Montecito's neighbor to the east (bus #20). About 25 mi. west of town, just before Gaviota State Beach, are two turn-offs on U.S. 101. The easterly one provides access to Santa Barbara's most popular surfing spot, while the westerly one (look for the school on the other side of U.S. 101) marks another nudist beach. A few bottoms have also been burned closer in, at the far end of the beach at UCSB. Keep in mind, however, that nude sunbathing is illegal in Santa Barbara and that every year people are served with summonses.

Slightly more formal occasions include yearly festivals. The most flamboyant is the **Summer Solstice Parade and Fair** (965-3396) on the Saturday nearest the longest day of the year (June 21). Come as an 18-ft. dinosaur or a tidal wave and you'll fit right in. The parade begins at noon at State and Cota St. and lasts until 5pm. The **Old Spanish Days** ("The Fiesta"), another spirited festival, is held over five days in early August. Strangely blonde mariachis and belly dancers roam the streets and bars, and by evening, chants of "*Para bailar la bamba*" are replaced by wails of "I wanna 'nother Corona." *Caballeros* and *señoritas* dance in the streets to the strains of flamenco guitar. Call 962-0801 for more information. A weekly celebration of the creativity of Santa Barbarans is the outdoor **art show and sale** stretching along Palm Park every Sunday from 10am to sunset.

Other seasonal events include **whale watching** in March, as the California grays migrate northward (call 963-3564 for information), and the **Santa Barbara Film Festival** (963-0023), also in March. The **Italian Street Painting Festival** (963-8654), where chalk paintings both professional and amateur decorate the Old Mission Courtyard, is held on Memorial Day Weekend. The **Sandcastle and Sculpting Contest** (966-6110) is held every year at the lowest tide of the year (call tourist office for info) at East Beach.

UCSB's lush campus is the locale of startling amounts of drunken revelry. It is a state-wide college tradition to come to UCSB to party on Holloween, but police crackdowns now make it difficult for non-UCSB students to join in the fray.

Santa Barbara itself is mostly a daytime city. No one in the city works, apparently, as hundreds spend their afternoons in bars and cafés on State St. drinking espressos, sipping margaritas, or just people-watching. Nevertheless, nightlife does survive. Most clubs and bars are located in the square formed by State, Ortega, Cota and Haley Streets. The clubs change names frequently, but the location, decor, and theme stay pretty much the same. For the newest and hottest places to be seen, pick up a free copy of *The Independent* available at the Chamber of Commerce, in restaurants, or in boxes on the street—you'll be hard-pressed to miss it).

Santa Barbara Theater Group, Garvin Theater (965-5935), at Santa Barbara City College. Serious theater of uneven quality. Box office open Mon.-Fri. 10am-5pm.

Joseppio, 434 State St. (962-5516). Jazz and blues nightly in a tiny club that occasionally spills into the street. Shows begin at 8pm. Cover $2-3. Oysters 20¢ daily 5-8pm. Open Mon.-Fri. 5pm-2am, Sat.-Sun. 2pm-2am.

Anaconda, 935 Embarcadero del Norte, Isla Vista (685-3112), near UCSB. Advertised as the largest dance club between San Luis Obispo and Los Angeles. Wow, it even has *strobe lights.* Sun. teen night (under 21), cover $6; Mon. open mike night; Tues. alternative music; Wed. college Top 40 countdown night, cover $4; Thurs. local bands, cover $3-5; Fri. "buck" night, cover $1, drinks $1; Sat. live music, cover $4. Opens daily at 11:30am.

Alex's Cantina, 5918 Hollister Ave. (683-2577), in Goleta between downtown and UCSB. Also at 633 State St. (966-0032), downtown. The Happiest Hour in town, Mon.-Fri. 3:30-7pm with free Mexican appetizer and a daily drink special. Drafts and wine $1, margaritas and well drinks $1.75. Dancing nightly 9pm-2am. Live bands Tues. and Wed. nights; alternative music Sat. Sounds from Latin to rock. No cover.

Zelo's, 630 State St. (966-5792). Progressive Music. Favored by the pale-skinned dressed-in-black crowd, as well as by the gay community. Occasional live bands, mostly DJs. Sun.-Mon. are teen nights. Cover varies ($1-7). Open daily noon-2am. Also serves dinner.

Ketch, 514 State St. (564-3231). With it's surfer clientele and R&B music, Ketch contrasts sharply with Zelo's. Bands every night from 9:45pm (cover $3-4). Open Tues.-Sun. 5pm-2am.

Espresso Roma Café, 728 State St. (962-4721), between La Guerra and Ortega. Chainsmoking and gulping espresso ($50 per gallon, 75¢ per cup), the regulars fight a losing battle against health. Less snooty than the other sidewalk cafés. In keeping with changing times, the downstairs area is now non-smoking. Bagel with cream cheese 85¢. Open Mon.-Sat. 7am-11pm, Sun. 8am-11pm.

Green Dragon, 22 W. Mission (687-1902). A coffeehouse inside what used to be a church. The walls display the loud artwork of the patrons. Entertainment varies: on any given night it could be poetry, open mike, folk, classical or blues. Patrons comprised primarily of ex-hippies and hippie hopefuls. Open daily noon-midnight.

Near Santa Barbara—The Channel Islands

Santa Barbara lies at the southern edge of the vast **Los Padres National Forest** (683-6711), which extends north into San Luis Obispo County and beyond. The region includes four mountain ranges. Its climatic zones range from semi-arid desert to coniferous forests. The San Rafael Wilderness alone contains 125 mi. of trails and a sanctuary for the nearly-extinct California condor. (See Camping for the address of the supervisor's office.)

To the northwest of Santa Barbara, **Lake Cachuma County Park** (688-4658) offers lovely picnic grounds and boat tours. The lake is accessible by Rte. 154, a wonderfully scenic drive across the Santa Ynez Mountains down into the Santa Ynez Valley. Campsites with tables, firepits, water, and restrooms $12 per night, $15 with hookups at the trailer resort.

Although one usually associates California wines with Sonoma or Napa Valley, Santa Barbara County cultivates 11,000 acres of vineyards. One of the prettiest is the **Gainey Vineyard,** 3950 E. Rte. 246 (688-0558), just where Rte. 246 intersects with Rte. 154 (tours daily 10:30am-3:30pm). Stop in for a free tasting, offered during tour hours on the quarter-hour. Winemaking was introduced into this region by Franciscan friars in the 1800s, but the highly successful vineyards were abandoned during Prohibition and were not replanted for commercial use until the 1960s. In recent years, Santa Barbara County wines have begun to approach the better-known northern California labels both in quality and price.

Solvang Village, a stone's throw away down Rte. 246, is too tourist-infested and cutesy for cynical tastes. You'll know you're there when you see the big windmill. Originally a Danish settlement, Solvang is now crammed with excellent *konditoris* (bakeries) and shops selling real and imitation Scandinavian wares.

A 15-minute car ride west of Solvang takes you to **La Purissima Mission State Historic Park,** site of Mission La Purissima Concepción (733-3713), one of only three of the original Spanish missions run by the state park system (the rest are run by the Catholic church). This 1787 mission was almost completely restored by the Civilian Conservation Corps during the 30s. They emphasized secular life at the mission, reconstructing its workshops and living quarters. Little of the furniture is antique, but the CCC's attention to authenticity makes up for the lack of cobwebs. In the church, the abalone shells that once held holy water are still in place, the chandeliers hold candles, and the nave remains benchless (worshipers would kneel on the rough brick floor). The mission offers a free 90-minute recorded tour and occasional docent-led tours. During the school year, arrive late in the afternoon to avoid the busloads of fourth-graders who trip here as part of their state history course. At Christmas, hundreds of *luminaria* (candles in paper bags) line the paths, and a concert is held in the chapel; in mid-May, a *fiesta* is also held here. The mission is intended to be a "living history museum" and actors in period costume stroll the mission grounds, interpreting mission life for visitors. (Open daily 9am-5:30pm; Oct.-April 9am-4:30pm. Admission $1, ages 6-17 50¢, under 6 free.)

Farther along down Rte. 246 grow the **Lompoc flower fields,** the nation's largest producers of flower seed. The acres upon acres of blooms, which peak near the end of June, are both a visual and an olfactory treat. Pink verbena, purple sweet elysium, and crimson sweet pea are only a few of the variegated blossoms. The town of Lompoc holds a flower festival at the season's peak in celebration of the fragrant harvest.

In the opposite direction, the pleasant, sleepy city of **Ventura** lies 30-40 minutes south of Santa Barbara. The visitors bureau is located at 89-C South California St. (648-2075) and provides information on Ventura's share of noteworthy sights. **The Olivas Adobe Historical Park,** at 42000 Olivas Park Dr. (644-4346) was the home to Rancho San Miguel owner Don Raimeerch Olivas. The grounds are open daily 10am-4pm, and the house is open Sat.-Sun. 10am-4pm. **The Albinger Archaeology Museum,** at 113 E. Main St., contains local artifacts and is open Tues.-Sun. 10am-4pm (10am-2pm in winter).

However, the best reason to visit Ventura is to reach the almost entirely unspoiled **Channel Islands National park. Island Parkers** (642-7688), at 1867 Spinaker Drive in Ventura Harbor is the only company licensed to give boat trips to the islands. The cheapest offering is the Anacapa Island ½ day trip ($20), which doesn't actually land on the island. In January and February, when whales migrate north, the island trips often turn into whale-watching cruises.

Camping on the islands is possible, but you need to get a permit (no charge) from the Visitor's Center, inside the park's headquarters. Sights are completely undeveloped, so bring your own drinking water. Camping is permitted on three of the islands: Anacapa, San Miguel, and Santa Barbara Island, but Anacapa is the only one open to campers year-round. Hikers can set out on their own, or enlist the aid of the friendly rangers. **San Miguel** is the farthest island and the most windswept. More seals than tourists frequent San Miguel, and you have a reasonable chance of meeting some if you make the trek out. Explorer Juan Rodriguez Cabrillo died on San Miguel in 1543. The waters around the islands abound with sea lions, dolphins and sharks. Earthbound flora and fauna are less spectacular; the largest land animal on the Channels is a deer mouse, and trees taller than bushes are a rarity.

If your can't buck the price of a cruise, you can always examine models of the islands inside the Channel Island National Parks Headquarters at 1903 Spinaker Dr. (644-8157). The headquarters also features displays on the flora and fauna of the surrounding seabeds, as well as an hourly movie about the islands (open daily 8am-5:50pm).

San Luis Obispo

For better or worse, San Luis Obispo is a town in limbo—situated halfway (200 mi.) between the cultural and physical extremes of San Francisco and Los Angeles. Yet somehow SLO has achieved a pleasant balance. This small college town lacks smog, rudeness, and outrageous prices, yet contains such typical (but welcome) big-city amenities as coffeehouses and ethnic restaurants. And for a town its size, SLO has a disproportionate number of museums and art galleries. San Luis Obispo is a pleasant stopover on your way up or down the coast. Many turn-of-the-century brick buildings have been restored to their original russet-colored beauty, and the Pacific crashes onto numerous state beaches only 12 mi. to the west.

Practical Information and Orientation

Visitors Information: Chamber of Commerce, 1039 Chorro St., San Luis Obispo 93401 (543-1323), at Higuera. Clearly marked by signs from U.S. 101. Helpful, with information on the entire area. Maps $1.60. Open Tues.-Fri. 8am-5pm, Sat.-Mon. 9am-5pm.

State Parks Information: 549-3312.

Amtrak: at the foot of Santa Rosa St. (541-0505; for ticket information and reservations 800-872-7245), 7 blocks south of Higuera. To: L.A. ($30); San Francisco ($57); Salinas ($30); once daily each. Open daily 9:30am-5:30pm. Reservations necessary.

Greyhound: 150 South St. (543-2121), ½ mi. from downtown. Walking west on South St. to Higuera St., north on Higuera to the center of town. To: L.A. (5-6 hr., 9 per day, $29), San Francisco (5-6 hr., 7 per day, $29); Pismo Beach ($2.50). Station has luggage lockers. Open 24 hr.

Car Rental: Cheap Wheels, 169 Granada Dr. (543-3792). From $20 per day. 100 free miles per day.

Public Library: 995 Palm St. (549-5991). Open Mon.-Thurs. 10am-8pm, Fri.-Sat. 10am-5pm.

Weather: 772-4141.

Road Conditions: 543-9544.

Crisis Hotline: 544-6163. 24 hr.

Women's Resource Center: 1160 Marsh St. (544-9313). Open Mon.-Fri. 10am-4pm.

Emergency:911.

Police: 1042 Walnut St. (549-7310).

Hospital: SLO General Hospital, 2180 Johnson Ave. (549-4800).

Post Office: 893 Marsh St. (543-1881). Open Mon.-Fri. 8:30am-5pm, Sat. package pickup 10:15-11am. General Delivery ZIP Code: 93406.

Area Code: 805.

Although San Luis Obispo is *of* the Central Coast, it is not *on* the coast. It sits on U.S. 101 midway between San Francisco and Los Angeles, each three to four hours away by car. This small town is flanked by Morro Bay, 10-15 mi. north on Rte. 1, and Avila, Shell, and Pismo Beaches, roughly the same distance south on Rte. 1.

Both **Greyhound** and **Amtrak** provide service between SLO and major cities. The train is more expensive than the bus, but since its tracks hem the coast, its window-show is superior to that of the U.S. 101-bound bus (remember to sit on the west side). Greyhound offers the cheapest (and the only non-auto) transport from SLO to Pismo Beach.

SLO Transit would be a funnier acronym if the description weren't so accurate. Like most Californian cities, San Luis Obispo gets away with abysmal public transit because everyone seems to have a car. Buses operate during daylight hours only, once every half-hour to hour, and infrequently, if at all, on weekends. Fare is 50¢, children under 5 free; transfers free. Pay as you board. (Call 541-2877 for information.) Weekday service to Morro Bay ($1) and Los Osos ($1.25) is provided by Regional Transit on route #7, which departs from SLO City Hall at Osos St. and Palm St. (call 541-4133 for schedule information).

Downtown San Luis Obispo centers on Higuera St., running north to south, with other shopping avenues crossing the spine east to west. Walking about downtown is easy, but the coast is more tempting to explore. Bicycle lanes are abundant, but the long grades are not for the weak of leg. Those hitching out of the city stand at the U.S. 101 on-ramps at Marsh St. west of town for the best results.

Accommodations

Asked for their rates, proprietors in San Luis Obispo frequently respond, "That all depends,"—on the weather, the season, the number of travelers that day, even, one suspects, on the position of the earth in relation to the moon; motel prices rise and fall faster than the nearby waves. Though camping is less expensive than a hotel room, even sleeping on the dirt isn't dirt cheap.

Economy Motel, 652 Morro (543-7024). A bargain; cable TV, refrigerators and stoves. Rooms $25-35.

Motel 6, 1433 Calle Joaquín (549-9595). A ½-mi. walk from the nearest bus stop (2½ mi. out of town). Registration 7am-11pm. Check-out noon. Singles $29. Doubles $35. Reserve at least 1 month in advance in summer. Similar prices at additional locations: 9400 El Camino, Atascadero (466-6701), off U.S. 101. 298 Atascadero, Morro Bay (772-5641), at Rte. 1; 860 4th St., Pismo Beach (773-2665).

Budget Motel, 345 Marsh St. (543-6443). What you'd expect from a place called "Budget Motel." Rooms are furnished, comfortable, but nothing spectacular. Color TV, cable, phone. Singles $32-36. Doubles $40-50. Prices depend on the day of the week.

Adobe Inn, 1473 Monterey St. (549-0321). A bed and breakfast. Newly renovated, trim, wholesome rooms, and wonderful management. Telephone, color TV w/ cable. Some rooms are befrigerated. Singles $50. Doubles $55-65.

Camping

All state park sites can be reserved through MISTIX (800-444-7275) from two days to eight weeks in advance. In summer, you probably won't get a campsite at a beach park without a reservation.

Pismo Beach State Park, Rte. 1 (489-2684), south of Pismo Beach. Two campgrounds. **North Beach** with 103 tent sites ($14) and restrooms. **Oceano** has tent sites ($18) as well as 42 sites with water and electrical hookups ($16). Oceano also has showers, but like selfish kindergartners they don't share with North Beach campers.

Montana de Oro State Park, Pecho Rd. (528-0513), south of Los Osos, 12 mi. from SLO via Los Osos Valley Rd. 50 primitive sites in a gorgeous, secluded park (see Sights). Outhouses and cold running water. Sites $9, in winter $7.

Morro Bay State Park, Rte. 1 (772-2560), 12 mi. west of SLO. 135 developed sites, 20 with hookups. A popular park (see Sights). Hot showers and running water. More accessible than Montana de Oro but also more likely to be full. Sites $14, in winter $12; with hookups $18, in winter $16.

Morro Strand State Park, Rte. 1 (772-2560), north of Morro Bay. 107 windy sites right on the beach. No showers, cold running water only. Fine fishing. Sites $14, 12 in summer.

Food and Entertainment

Higuera and the streets running across it are lined with eateries and cafés. The area below the mission by the creek is a popular place with lunchtime crowds. **Cisco's** (on the creek) has live music, inexpensive sandwiches and salads, and many outdoor tables. Every Thursday night, fresh fruits and vegetables overflow at the **Farmer's Market.** From 6 to 9pm, Higuera St. is closed to all but vendors' stalls and browsing shoppers.

Taco's Acapulco Cantina, 1121 Broad St. (546-9466). Burritos $2-3, savory enough to keep you coming back. Fajita and drink $4.25. Ebullient management. Open noon-until no one shows up.

Golden China, 675 Higuera St. (543-7354). All-you-can-eat buffets: 15 chinese-style dishes, complimentary soup, fresh fruit, and jello (Yowza!). Lunch $5, 11:30am-2:30pm. Dinner $7, 5-9pm. The restaurant next door offers a similar dinner deal, but lacks the beautiful wall graph of Yang-tu city during the Kong-Su dynasty. Open daily 11:30am-9pm.

Chocolate Soup, 980 Morro St. (543-7229). Black, white, and blue decor, with a smart bistro atmosphere. The chef prepares 7 specials per day, 3 of which (the crepe, quiche, and pie dishes) never change. Specials served with soup, once-through salad bar, and fresh bread for around $6.50. Dessert is the specialty; try the chocolate soup for $2.50. Open Mon.-Fri. 9am-9pm, Sat. 11am-9pm.

Woodstock's Pizza Parlour, 1000 Higuera St. (541-4420). Sweeps annual newspaper best-pizza awards. 12" pizza $6.35, 16" $8.62. A mini 8" ($3.25) is ideal for lunch. Beer by the pitcher. Slices 11:30am-3pm. Open daily 11:30am-1am; Sept.-May hours are Mon.-Fri. 11:30am-1am, Sat.-Sun. 11:30am-2am.

Blazing Blenders, 1108 Broad St. (546-8122). A hole-in-the-wall with incredible shakes ($2-3), bizarre juices (ever tried wheat grass juice before?), and frozen yogurt (generous small

$1.45). The bee pollen topping will leave you buzzing. Open Mon.-Wed. and Fri. 7:30am-7:30pm, Thurs. 7:30am-9pm, Sat.-Sun. 9am-7pm.

Somewhat sheltered from California's recreational extremes, SLO's amusements combine the flavor of a local bar with that of a block party. Various festivals bring practically the entire community into the downtown, and Thursday nights everyone, including the shopkeepers, stays up late. A favorite of festival-goers is the **Mozart Festival,** held the first week in August. Concerts play at Cal Poly, the mission, and local churches. Tickets (from $8) go on sale in May, but some are available until the night of the concert. To order, write P.O. Box 311, San Luis Obispo 93406 (543-3480). For information about other local happenings, consult the weekly *New-Times,* a free paper available at most stores in the downtown area. Smoking is not allowed in any public area in SLO, including bars. Most of the bars have a youthful atmosphere since Cal Poly student patronage is also their lifeline.

Café Linnaeus's, 1110 Garden St. (541-5888). This is a popular (and crowded) evening hangout, especially with the artsy set. Displays local artists' works on the walls and features occasional folk and blues music. Serves breakfast and has a complete salad bar. Open Mon.-Sat. 7:30am-midnight, Sun. 8am-3pm and 7pm-midnight.

McClintock's Saloon, Higuera St. (541-0686). This busy restaurant and bar serves burgers ($5-6) and sandwiches ($5-6) as well as steaks ($8-12) with "a taste of the Old West," whatever that means. Always a hip crowd in the evenings, live music occasionally. Open Mon. 6:30am-8:30pm, Tues.-Fri. 6:30am-2am, Sat. 8am-2am, Sun. 8am-4pm.

Spike's, 570 Higuera St. (544-7157). Beer lovers come from all over California for Spike's globe-spanning selection of brews. Full menu of California- and Tex-Mex-style food as well (most selections around $5). Open daily 11am-11:30pm.

Tortilla Flats, 1051 Nipomo St. (544-7575), specializes in early Californian and Mexican food. (Served 11am-9pm, Sun. brunch 10am-2pm.) Weekday Happy Hours (4-6pm) feature margaritas for $1.25 and a changing Mexican food specialty for 50¢. From 9:30pm to 2am, it metamorphoses into a full-scale dance club with Top-40 and club music blasting nightly (except Wed., which is Country Night). Mon. is college night (over 18 admitted for a $5 cover charge). The rest of the week is 21 and over. Cover $3, $1 with a Cal Poly ID. No dancing on Sun. night.

Bull's Tavern, 1032 Chorro St. (543-2217), by Mission Plaza. Unpretentious/offensive decor (girlie pics behind the bar) and the cheapest drinks in town (draft $1.25, shots $1.75). On weekends the line extends out the door. Open daily 10am-2am.

SLO Brewing Company, 1119 Garden St. (543-1843). Food and drink, but mostly drink, in an upstairs bar/micro-brewery. Amazingly good porter ($2 pints). Happy Hour Mon.-Fri 4:30-6pm. Live entertainment Thurs.-Sat. Open Mon.-Wed. 11:30am-10:30pm, Thurs.-Sat. 11:30am-12:30am, Sun. 11:30am-4:30pm.

Sights and Activities

San Luis Obispo grew up around **Mission San Luis Obispo de Tolosa** (543-6850; smack in the center of town). Founded in 1772, the mission was at one time covered in white wooden siding and crowned with a steeple (in emulation of a New England church). In the late 1800's, however, the town made a concerted effort to revive the mission's Spanish origins. By the 1930s, it was fully restored. With the "remodeling" complete, the mission has never looked better. It still serves as the Catholic parish church for SLO. (Open daily 9am-5pm. Donation $1.)

Mission Plaza, a delightful public space below the mission, is the scene of **La Fiesta de San Luis** in May, with arts, crafts, and concerts. At the other end of the plaza from the mission are two unspectacular museums. The **San Luis Obispo County Historical Museum,** 696 Monterey St. (543-0638), has changing exhibits which vary from McKinley-era paraphernalia such as hair wreaths, portraits, glassware, and antique clothes to Chumash Indian artifacts. (Open Wed.-Sun. 10am-4pm. Free.) The **San Luis Obispo Art Center** (543-8562), across the street, holds a collection of work by local artists. The quality of its changing exhibits ranges tremendously—from sappy, sentimental paintings of puppy dogs to interesting homemade paper and prints. (Open daily 10am-5pm; in winter Tues.-Sun. noon-5pm. Free.)

The Chamber of Commerce brochure, *Heritage Walks,* describes four walking tours of 38 architecturally impressive homes. All the tours begin in Mission Plaza. Most of the houses are in the Queen Anne or Victorian style, built by New England merchants who went west during the gold rush, but there are also examples of the craftsman style (simple buildings of wood and stone on a warm and intimate scale), a Frank Lloyd Wright building, and a few 20s Mission Revival homes. If you imagine California aa a tract of suburban ranch homes, you'll be pleasantly surprised.

The city has recently implemented a free, old-fashioned trolley which runs around the downtown area. The trolley cuts through the Higuera St. district Mon.-Wed. and Fri.-Sat. 9:30am-3:30pm, Thurs. 9:30am-9:30pm, Sun. noon-3:30pm. Call 549-7100 or stop at the Chamber of Commerce for more information.

California Polytechnic State University (Cal Poly information desk 756-2417), roughly 1 mi. north of the town center, a right turn off U.S. 101 (Grand Ave.) in Highland, could inspire you to "go back to the land." The facilities include a Beef Pavilion, Crops Unit, Poultry Unit, and Swine Unit. There's a minibus tour of this mega-farm, but a self-guided excursion is just as satisfying. Cal Poly's buildings, especially the Union and the library, are spiffy. The **Shakespeare Press Museum,** in the Graphic Arts Building, owns a collection of 19th-century printing presses. The museum is open by appointment only; call Mon.-Thurs. 11am-noon (756-1108). Guided campus tours depart Mon., Wed., and Fri. at 10am and 2pm from the second floor lobby of the Union. To reach the campus, take SLO Transit or the PolyShuttle from City Hall (routes #1 and 2).

The Madonna Inn, 100 Madonna Rd. (543-3000), off U.S. 101 on the southern end of town, is probably the only hotel in the world that sells postcards of every single one of its rooms. (Take the Madonna Rd. off-ramp.) Alex S. Madonna, the building contractor who was the driving force behind the construction of much of U.S. 101 and I-5, decided in 1958 to build a Queen Anne-style hotel of 12 rooms, and he put his wife, Phyllis, in charge of the design. By 1969, the vision had grown to a hot pink colossus of 110 rooms. Boulders adorn everything, including the Flintstonesque gas station and hotel lobby; the men's room features a giant waterfall. Every room has a theme—the Caveman Room, the Daisy Mae Room, and a room with a working waterwheel serving as a headboard. Rooms run $72-180 (7 people in the three-bedroom $180 suite is actually a bargain). But even nonguests can enjoy coffee and a Danish, baked in the Madonna's own bakery, at the appropriately elaborate coffee shop.

Straddling the San Andreas Fault, the aptly named Diablo Canyon Nuclear Power Plant splits its atoms nearby, but Obispans display no significant genetic mutations. Yet.

Near San Luis Obispo

San Luis Obispo County rests on land that bled lava a long time ago. Today the rolling hills are scarred with ranches, orchards, and fields, and calm reigns in the county. Big Sur isn't so big along this part of the coast, and Southern California's rampant development peters out well to the south.

Montana de Oro State Park (528-0513), 20 minutes away from San Luis Obispo on Rte. 1, remains relatively secluded; it is not unusual to see deer, heron, owls, and other wildlife. The south end of **Spooner's Cove Beach** is a fantastic place to beachcomb for shells and polished rocks. Primitive campsites are set in a deep valley with access to hiking trails. The nearest bus service is to Los Osos, 6 mi. away, but a bike path leads to the park (along Los Osos Valley Rd.) from San Luis Obispo. From the area around the campground, you can watch the ocean as it pounds away at the sandy bluffs.

Morro Bay State Park is more developed but still attractive. The **Museum of Natural History** (772-2694) trains its curatorial cannons on the aquatic environment and the wildlife of the coastal headlands. It includes hands-on exhibits for the visually impaired. A bulletin board at the museum entrance also lists a variety of free nature walks led by park rangers in summer. (Open daily 10am-5pm. Admission $2, ages 6-17 $1, free to state park campers.) Also within park boundaries lies the long peninsula that forms Morro Bay. The dunes on the peninsula house a **bird sanctuary,** sheltering, among other fowl, rare herons. There is a $3 day-use charge to enter the park.

The town of **Morro Bay,** on Rte. 1, is at the north end of the bay. Lodgings are expensive, but you can often find early-bird dinner specials at any of the dozens of seafood restaurants along Embarcadero St. **Morro Rock,** nearly 600 ft. tall, is the last in a chain of volcanic peaks; enjoyment of its noble form is obstructed, however, by three giant towers erected by the nearby Pacific Gas and Electric plant. Bus #7 serves Morro Bay from San Luis Obispo. (Bus every hr. Mon.-Fri. 7am-6:20pm. Fare $1. For more information call 541-4113.)

If you have a car and about 45 spare minutes, obey the imperative to **See Canyon Drive.** Locals take it for granted, but most tourists don't know about this beautiful 10-mi. stretch (although it *is* crowded in apple season). Part pavement, part gravel, it rivals 17-Mile Drive on the Monterey Peninsula for scenic variety. It's a rough road though, best driven with a truck. See Canyon Drive begins just off U.S. 101 north of Avila Beach (take the See Canyon exit) and ends on Los Osos Valley Rd., which leads back to U.S. 101 and SLO City. Respect the "No Trespassing" signs alongside the road.

Two beaches just southwest of San Luis Obispo enjoy the privilege of anonymity: no signs announce their existence to the masses. Many people go to **Pirate's Cove,** where bathing suits are optional and the water is the warmest in the area. Take U.S. 101 south from San Luis Obispo, exit at the Avila Rd. off-ramp, head west a couple of miles and turn left on Cave Landing Dr., just before the oil tanks. Park in the dirt lot and take a path to the cove. Though the view from the bay is inspiring, this is not the best nude beach in California, and you may be under surveillance by peeping-toms. Rocky **Shell Beach** is a mile down U.S. 101, south of Avila and Pirate's Cove. Take the Shell Beach exit and turn left, then drive until you see little, brown, "coastal access" signs. Park at the gazebo, and try to climb down to the ocean. Many people bring their bikes down to Pirate's Cove, but the path at Shell is too steep.

Avila and **Pismo Beaches** are both more developed and crowded. Avila presents the typical California beach scene, with a steady stream of cars cruising the boardwalk. To get there, drive as if you're going to Pirate's Cove, but continue a bit before turning left. You can also take South County Transit to Avila. Come in the evening to sample the special nightlife of a beach town. Bars and fast-food places line the boardwalk; watch the flow of traffic to determine the season's hotspot. Pismo Beach, 1½ mi. south of Shell Beach, is more developed and congested than Avila and is accessible by Greyhound (see Practical Information). Instead of the pleasant murmurs of heatstroked beach people, you're made privy to the bells and buzzers of what must be the world's largest pinball and video game arcade. Yet, at the end of the day, Pismo can be beautiful. Since the beach faces south, the sun sets behind the hills that jut into the sea above Avila, creating a gorgeous sand-on-fire effect at the surf line. For variety, try **Harry's,** 690 Cypress (773-1010), at Pomeroy a few blocks from the beach, featuring live country and western bands nightly. The Tuesday and Sunday evening chili-feeds feature all the chili, hot dogs, and potato salad you can hold down for the price of a beer or two. (Open daily 10am-2am, dancing Mon.-Fri. from 9pm, Sat.-Sun. from 3pm. No cover.) In August, Pismo Beach hosts the proSands Volleyball Championship.

Inland attractions north of San Luis Obispo are little more than rest stops along the freeway. The **wineries** around the town of Paso Robles are well-respected. The Paso Robles Chamber of Commerce, 548 Spring St. (238-0506), has a complete list of wineries, including visiting hours, tours, and tastings. In August, all the local wineries (more than 25) come together for the Central Coast Wine-tasting Festival (tickets $15, call 238-0506 for info).

Mission San Miguel Archangel (467-3256) is 43 mi. north of San Luis Obispo in San Miguel, a few blocks from U.S. 101. Take the Mission off-ramp. Surprisingly, the 1818 complex has never undergone serious restoration. In its ecumenical phases, the church served as a saloon, a dance hall, and a warehouse. Through it all, the frescoes, executed by Monterey's Esteban Munras and his team of Native American artists in 1821, have survived unretouched. Most of the paintings are in the stodgy classical mode that Munras learned in Barcelona, but the colors—including a shade called "shrimp pink"—are remarkably vivid. The museum ranks as average, but the buildings are fascinating. The 12 arches of the arcade are all of varying dimensions; the sheepskin windows are still intact; and the façade of the church is as stark as ever. (Open daily 9:30am-4:30pm; self-guided tours only).

Santa Maria, located 30 mi. south of SLO on Hwy. 101, is the produce center of Santa Barbara County, and thus it hosts the not-very-spectacular **SB County Fair** during the first week of July (admission $5). The **Santa Maria Valley Historical Museum,** has changing displays on cowboys, Indians, and Spanish days in Santa Maria (616 S. Broadway; 922-3130; open Tues.-Sat. 1-5pm; Sun. 1-4pm; free). Nearby, the **Zaca Mesa Winery** has free tours and tastings (open daily 10am-4pm; 688-3310). The cheapest place to stay in town is the Capri Motel at 607 N. Broadway (928-1928; singles $25; doubles $30). TV and HBO. The Santa Maria Chamber of Commerce phone number is 925-2803.

Cambria and San Simeon

Standing almost in the shadow of Hearst Castle, tiny Cambria is as compact and understated as William Hearst's creation is lavish and ostentatious. After touring the castle, travelers will find the eastern half of Cambria particularly solid and reassuring. The western half of the town, however, like the entire village of San Simeon, gives itself over to the "castle" industry (if it can be called that) of Hearst Castle tourism. In recent years, Cambria has become home to a number of fine art galleries, which have migrated south from art-infested Carmel.

Practical Information

Visitors Information: San Simeon Chamber of Commerce, Hearst Dr. (927-3500), on west side of Rte. 1, by the Bleschyu Golf Course—look for the course's orange sign. Open Mon.-Fri. 9am-5pm; in winter 10am-2pm. **Cambria Chamber of Commerce,** 767 Main St. (927-3624). Helpful staff. Open Mon.-Fri. 9am-4pm, and Sat.-Sun. 11am-3pm.

Cambria Post Office: 4100 Bridge (927-3654). Open Mon.-Tues. and Thurs.-Fri. 9am-5pm, Wed. 8:30am-noon. Sat. package pick-up 7-11am. General Delivery ZIP Code: 93428.

San Simeon Post Office: Rte. 1 (927-4156), in the back of Sebastian's General Store (which also incorporates an *al fresco* café, a market, and some gas pumps). To get here, take the road opposite the entrance to Hearst Castle. Open Mon.-Fri. 8:30am-5pm, Sat. 9:30-11am. General Delivery ZIP Code: 93452.

Area Code: 805.

Accommodations, Camping, and Food

Cambria is generally cheaper in summer, while San Simeon motels offer winter specials. Victuals are better in Cambrias.

A Small Hotel By The Sea, 2601 Main St. (927-4305), in Cambria. Actually A Small Collection Of Cabins On A Hillside A Few Miles From The Sea. Tastefully furnished cabin for one or two, with color TV with cable, kitchenette, and bath $55. One cabin accommodates up to 4 people ($71). Prices drop about $10 in the winter. Midweek 10% cheaper. Special weekly rates. Breakfast brought to your cabin each morning.

Creekside Inn, 2618 Main St. (927-4021), in Cambria. One of the newest and best-priced of Cambria's motels. Stylish rooms with cable TV and direct dial phones. A single with one queen bed $45-50; two queen beds $55-80.

Cambria Palms Hotel, 2662 Main St. (927-4485), in Cambria. Color TV with cable, kitchenettes. The best weekly rates in winter. Rooms run $42-60 in summer.

San Simeon State Beach, just north of Cambria on Rte. 1 (call MISTIX, 800-444-7275), has two camping areas, **San Simeon Creek** and **Washburn.** San Simeon Creek has 116 $14 sites near the beach and showers. Washburn sits upon a hill overlooking the ocean; the sunset is breathtaking. Portable toilets and cold running water only. If other campgrounds are full, arrive at 4pm for a site in Washburn's overflow area. Sites $9, seniors $4. In winter $12. San Simeon facilities are not available for use by Washburn campers.

Chuckwagon, Moonstone Dr. (927-4644), at Cambria's only stoplight across the highway from the Shell Station. Draws many senior citizens and vacationing families. All-you-can-eat at "the Chuckwagon"—need we elaborate? Mon.-Fri. breakfast and lunch $5.49, dinner $8 (beverages extra). Sat.-Sun. lunch and dinner $8. Open daily 6:30am-9pm; Nov.-March. 11am-8pm.

Creekside Gardens Café, 2114 Main St. (927-8646), in Cambria. A petite restaurant, frequented by locals, set back from the street in the Redwood Shopping Center. Indoor or patio dining. Burgers $4-5, specialty sandwiches $5-6. Desserts made daily. Open Mon.-Sat. 7am-2pm, Sun. 8am-2pm.

Canozzi's Saloon, 2226 Main St. (927-8941), in Cambria between Burton and Bridge St. A well-known watering hole with beer-hall decor. Pool tables and occasional live music. Beer $1-2, well drinks $1.75-3. Open daily 10am-2am.

Schooner's Pub, across from the Chamber of Commerce, is run by the same management as Canozzi's, and sells burgers for $3.75.

Sue and Yoli's, 2292 Main St. (927-4909). Sandwiches, chicken, ribs and fish & chips. Complete dinners from $5. Open Mon.-Fri. 8am-8pm.

Sights and Activities

Beaches, beaches, and more beaches—you'll know you're nearing Big Sur when you see the beautiful sandy strands bordering Cambria. The sea otter, once near extinction, now prospers in the kelp beds of **Moonstone Beach** (just up Rte. 1 toward San Simeon), and local surfers are occasionally nudged off their boards by playful seals. **San Simeon** and **Hearst State Beaches** are ideal for cliff-climbing and beachcombing and offer the best swimming for miles. Nude bathers pay their respects to the newspaper magnate at the north end of Hearst Beach. Be wary of trespassing as you approach the beach; the Hearst Corporation still owns much of the land in this area. A single entrance ticket admits you to all state parks visited in a day, but many people park on the road outside the entrance point of Hearst State Beach, avoiding the $3 fee by crossing Hearst lands to reach the beach. You risk being cited for trespassing if you park too close to the general store. Look for turn-outs between San Simeon and the lighthouse at Piedras Blancas; these and the nearby wooden stairs over Hearst Corporation fences provide the only legal access.

Cambria features its own ostentatious abode, though on a bit smaller scale than San Simeon's Castle. **Nitwit Ridge** is another in the long tradition of eccentric California dream homes. Designated a California Historical Landmark in 1981, the Nitwit is a rustic conglomeration of rocks, bones, feathers, tiles, driftwood, and even a broken television set. The creator, popularly known as Captain Nitwit or Dr. Tinkerpaw, no longer lives here, as he is very ill. The house is unsafe, and trespassing is illegal (there is a caretaker guarding the property), so you'll have to do your gawking from the street. To reach the house, head south on Main, turn left on Arlington, right on Cornwall, then left on Hillcrest, a little way up the hill.

Hearst Castle

In San Simeon did William Hearst a stately pleasure dome decree. Commonly known as Hearst Castle (927-2020), the Hearst San Simeon Historic Monument lies 5 mi. east of Rte. 1 near San Simeon. Satirized as Charles Foster Kane's "Xanadu" in Orson Welles' *Citizen Kane,* the Castle lives up to every adjective ever applied to its home state: opulent, plastic, beautiful, fake, dazzling, and over-reaching. William Randolph Hearst, tycoon of yellow journalism fame and instigator of the Spanish-American War, began building this Hispano-Moorish indulgence in 1919. For 28 years his devoted and gifted architect, Julia Morgan of San Francisco, took the night train here to work in her tiny office, adapting Hearst's outlandish requests to the physical setting. To turn the barren hill into a verdant garden, thousands of tons of topsoil were hauled in, and adult trees weighing tons were planted all the way down to the sea. Hearst, lacking the patience to allow gardens to mature slowly, planted orange trees in a hedge, not caring that they would choke each other within 50 years.

Hearst later traveled to Spain, where he became infatuated with a Mudéjar cathedral. Unable to buy it, he had Morgan blast off the existing towers of his 115-room "ranch house" and build reproductions in their stead. Much of the castle's "art" is actually fake: concrete statuary, plaster pilasters, artificially aged tiles. Yet many genuine treasures remain tucked away: the world's largest private collection of Greek vases lines the shelves of the library; medieval tapestries hang everywhere; and ancient Chinese ceramics perch on the mantlepieces of Gothic fireplaces.

Ultimately, though, Hearst reached beyond his means. Even isolated in his Gothic-style personal suite, the Great Depression still hit him hard, and much of the castle was left incomplete. Nearly half of the walls are still exposed concrete, and the cheap building materials require costly, frequent maintenance.

Visitors have a choice of four **tours,** each an hour and 45 minutes long. It's possible to take all four in one day, but each costs $12 (plus a $1.80 service charge if you don't buy them at the castle), children 6-12 $6, under 6 free (if well-behaved—otherwise they are escorted off the premises). Groups are taken up the hill in old school buses, shepherded around, then taken back down. Tour One, with a capacity of 53 people, is an overview, covering the gardens, the swimming pools, a guest house, and the first floor of the main house. Tours Two and Three are smaller, can take about a dozen people, and cover the upper floors of the castle. Tour Four has a capacity of 14, but is frequently undersubscribed. Emphasizing the gardens and the castle's architecture, it covers the wine cellar, one floor of a guest house, and the dressing rooms of one of the pools. It's the best tour for photographers since it covers more of the grounds, seen from more angles, than the others. Tours are given at least once an hour October through March from 8am until 3pm, more frequently and later according to demand in summer. Tour Four is not given December to March. If you really want to see the Castle in summer, advance reservations are a must. Make them through **MISTIX** (800-444-7275), as tours sell out quickly. The gates to the visitors center open in summer at 6am, in winter at 7am, and tickets go on sale daily at 8am.

If the tour doesn't satisfy your curiosity or you just can't wait for the morning's visit, check out the **San Simeon Restaurant,** Rte. 1 (927-4604), on motel row in San Simeon and is run by Jack Smith, a long-time tour guide and general castle maven. Smith gives a 75-minute "Hearst Castle Show" April-Nov. Wed.-Mon. at 8pm. (Admission $4, ages over 64 and under 13 $3.)

Big Sur

Big Sur simultaneously welcomes and shuns visitors. Its legendary geographical splendors—dramatic beaches, swirling waters, and acres of moist redwood forest populated by myriad raccoons, deer, squirrels, and opossums—are genuinely inviting. Though the scenery is majestic, the fickle weather is unsettling. Fierce winter storms of 1983 were powerful enough to carry beach sand and much of the coastal highway into the Pacific. Even when the sun is shining, Big Sur's winds can rock buses, tip cows, and generally make you very uncomfortable. At the same time, the human inhabitants of Big Sur do little to make strangers feel at home. There is no "village" or "town" per se; no banks, no theaters, no mini-golf. While perfectly willing to sell tourists sandwiches and souvenirs, residents hide their houses in the woods and obstinately remove the signs giving directions to their favorite beach.

Practical Information

Visitor Information: Big Sur Chamber of Commerce, P.O. Box 87, Big Sur 93920 (667-2100). Send a self-addressed, stamped envelope for a guide to Big Sur.

State Park Area Office: Pfeiffer Big Sur, Big Sur 93920 (667-2315), on Rte. 1. Call for information on Andrew Molera, Pfeiffer Big Sur, and Pfeiffer Burns State Parks. They also sponsor ranger- and naturalist-led hikes and cam*pfires.* Open daily 8am-5:30pm.

U.S. Forest Service: 667-2423. Inside Big Sur State Park. Information on USFS campgrounds in the area, permits, and forest maps ($2). Open daily 8am-5:30pm.

AAA Emergency Road Service: 372-8131. Free to members, otherwise, it'll cost you.

Post Office: On Rte. 1 (667-2305), next to the Center Deli. Open Mon.-Fri. 8:30am-5pm. General Delivery ZIP Code: 93920.

Area Code: 408.

Monterey's Spanish settlers simply called the entire region below their town "El Sur Grande"—the Vast South. Today, "Big Sur" signifies a more exact coastal region bordered on the south by Salmon Cove (San Simeon's Hearst Castle is 17 mi. below) and on the north by Carmel. Big Sur is best enjoyed by car and by camping. The coast is thinly inhabited, dotted with gas stations about every 40 mi. or an occasional house at the end of a drive plastered with signs commanding tourists to keep out. The few lodges are all beyond the budget traveler's range. Everything—fuel, food (whether in a market or in a restaurant), beer, toiletries—is more expensive in Big Sur than in real life. Last-chance stops are the supermarket on Rio Rd. in Carmel, for the budget-minded southbounder, and for the northbounder, the market in Morro Bay. (See Monterey for information on Monterey-Salinas bus #22 to the northern part of Big Sur.)

Hitching is difficult, especially near the state parks, where competition is fierce. When the road is crowded with lurching RVs, frustrated Karmann Ghia speedsters, and oblivious Sunday drivers, walking and bicycling becomes treacherous, and traffic crawls along at a turtle's pace. Avoid visiting on summer weekends. Spring, when wildflowers bloom and the hills glow with color, is the optimal time to survey Big Sur.

The Big Sur Chamber of Commerce puts out a helpful guide listing privately-owned accommodations, campgrounds, and restaurants. Pick up the guide in San Simeon or Carmel's Chamber of Commerce, or in the State Park.

Locations in Big Sur are generally described in terms of miles north of the Heart Castle or south of Carmel, along Rte. 1. The entire length is 91 mi.

Accommodations and Camping

Places to camp are abundant and beautiful.

Campsite prices tend to change quickly. If all sites below are booked (unlikely with Andrew Molera), check with the Forest Service Station. The cheapest way to stay in Big Sur is to camp out in the free Ventana Wilderness.

Big Sur Campgrounds and Cabins, 24.6 mi. south of Carmel (667-2322), near the Big Sur River. If you didn't bring camping equipment (you've made a big mistake), this place offers tent cabins in summer ($38). Campsites are $19, hookups $21. Store, laundry, playground, and volleyball courts.

Lueia Lodge, 37 mi. north of Hearst (667-2391). The cabin prices are generally beyond budget range, but if you get stuck, try here. Not the best location, but the most reasonable prices (rooms as low as $42).

Fernwood Motel, Rte. 1 (667-2422), 2 mi. north of the post office. 65 campsites. Registration 8am-midnight. Check-out 11am. Sites $19, with hookup $21. Motel rooms from $45. On the Big Sur River.

Pfeiffer Big Sur State Park (667-2315), just south of Fernwood, 26 mi. south of Carmel. An inland park, but no less popular than those on the beach. All 218 developed campsites do fill up at times (no hookups). The Big Sur River floats peacefully alongside the campground. Hot showers. Sites $16. Reservations through MISTIX.

Andrew Molera State Park (667-2315), 5 mi. north of Pfeiffer Big Sur. 50 trail campsites. Beach, pit toilets, no showers. A ¼-mi. walk on a level trail to reach campsites. This is where the Big Sur River pours into the ocean. But bring your own water. Sites $3 per person, $1 extra for dogs.

Limekiln, south of Big Sur (667-2403). Privately run campground with showers, beach access, grocery. 60 sites. $15 for 1 site, $5 per additional person. Reservations $5.

Los Padres National Forest. U.S. Forest Service Campgrounds: **Plaskett Creek** (667-2315), south of Limekiln, near Jade Cove. 43 sites. **Kirk Creek,** about 5 mi. north of Jade Cove. 33 beautiful spots, but they're close to the highway. No showers, only toilets and cold running water. Open 24 hr. Check-out 2pm. Sites $10, hikers $2. No reservations.

Food

Fernwood Burger Bar, Rte. 1 (667-2422), 2 mi. north of post office. Fish and chips, and chicken $5-6.50. Hamburgers from $3.25. There's a homey bar too, as well as a grocery store. Resembles the inside of a log cabin. Fill up your tank here: gas is slightly less expensive than elsewhere on Rte. 1. Open daily 11:30am-midnight.

Center Deli, (667-2225), right beside the Big Sur Post Office. Serves the area's cheapest sandwiches ($2.80-5). Offers a broad selection of groceries. Open daily 8am-9pm; in winter 8am-8pm.

Nepenthe Restaurant, (667-2345), Rte. 1. A local favorite. The hamburger—excuse us—the *ground steak sandwich* is $8 (yes, $8). Fire pit at night. Outdoor seating provides a view of water, mountains, and mist. Feel free to wander around and take pictures; most people do. Open daily 11:30am-4pm, 5-9:30pm.

Café Amphora, (667-2660), on Rte. 1 next to Nepenthe. Less stuffy and less umbrageous than Nepenthe, with an outdoor patio that stretches to the edge of a strategically scenic cliff. Open Mon.-Fri. 10am-4pm, Sat.-Sun. 10am-5pm.

Grocery stores are also located at River Inn, Ripplewood, and Big Sur Lodge, but it's better to arrive prepared; prices are high.

Sights and Activities

The state parks and wilderness areas are exquisite settings for dozens of outdoor activities. Hiking on Big Sur is a dream: the state parks and **Los Padres National Forest** all have trails that penetrate redwood forests and cross low chaparral, offering even grander views of Big Sur than those available from Rte. 1. The northern end of Los Padres National Forest has been designated the **Ventana Wilderness** and contains the popular **Pine Ridge Trail.** Grab a map and a required permit at the USFS ranger station (see Practical Information). Within **Pfeiffer Big Sur State Park** are six trails of varying lengths (25¢ map available at park entrance). Try the **Valley View Trail,** a short, steep path; at its apex you'll find a panorama that'll impress even the most jaded vista viewer.

Roughly at the midway point of Big Sur lies small, quiet **Julia Pfeiffer Burns Park,** which pfeatures picnic tables among the redwoods and a chance to sea otter-watch in McWay Cove. All these parks are pfavorites with the locals; come midweek to avoid the throng. Big Sur's most jealously guarded treasure is USFS-operated **Pfeiffer Beach,** reached by an unmarked narrow road. Follow the road 2 mi. to the parking area; then take the footpath to the beach. The small cove, partially protected from the Pacific by a massive offshore rock formation, is safe for wading, but riptides make swimming risky. North of all of these is the vintage 1889 **Lighthouse Station** (625-4419), perched atop Point Sur, a giant rock-island. Weekends tours $2. Call for information.

Big Sur is not *all* nature and no civilization, however. The **Coast Gallery** (667-2301), on Rte. 1 just north of the Julia Pfeiffer Burns State Park, has long been a showcase for works by local artists (open daily 9am-5:30pm). It also houses a collection of paintings and lithographs by *Tropic of Cancer* author Henry Miller, who lived near here for 17 years. Miller's casual reminiscences and prophetic ecstasies made scores of readers aware of Big Sur, and his more explicit works drew many to Big Sur seeking the sex cult he purportedly led (he didn't). Fans of the writer will want to stop by the **Henry Miller Memorial Library** (667-2574), just 4 mi. north of the gallery and 1 mi. south of Nepenthe. This one-room "shrine" is located in the former home of local artist Emil White, a long-time friend of Miller's. (Open daily 11am-5pm, but call ahead to make sure.)

Carmel

Upper-class Californians migrate to Carmel to live out their fantasies of rural life. The town possesses one of Northern California's most beautiful beaches, a gloriously restored Spanish mission, and a main street lined with stores that sell jewelry, silk dresses, and fine art. The town works hard to maintain its image. Local ordinances forbid parking meters (though police chalk tires to keep careful track of how long you have parked), normal-sized street signs, address numbers, billboards, and home mail delivery—all undesirable symbols of urbanization. All of the houses have names, and franchise stores are forbidden in the city proper. Because development early this century caused flooding when steep hills were denuded, the town passed a law in 1916 making it a felony to cut down any tree. As a result, pines and cypresses grow everywhere—in the middle of streets, sidewalks, and houses.

Budget travelers may find Carmel unwelcoming. This side of paradise is very much private property. The streets swarm with police alert for ragtag travelers and wandering indigents, and there are few inexpensive places to eat or sleep.

Remember, though, that Carmel once had its scruffy side. The town was adopted by San Francisco intellectuals as a temporary home after their urban haunts were destroyed by the 1906 earthquake. Traces of the resulting artists' colony (frequented by Upton Sinclair and Robinson Jeffers) still linger. Much of the artwork offered for sale in Carmel galleries is locally produced, though the 20th century seems to have left the Carmel school of art behind. The quality of the paintings (mostly land and seascapes) today varies from museum to motel-room quality. A few of the town's 43 galleries, such as "Golf Arts and Imports," stretch the boundaries of aesthetics. Nevertheless, residents (such as former mayor Clint Eastwood) can easily invest in such quality kitsch: these Carmelites exude the kind of carefree contentment that $189,000 per annum is wont to bring.

Practical Information and Orientation

Visitor Information: Carmel-by-the-Sea Business Association, San Carlos between 5th and 6th (624-2522), in the Eastwood Building, upstairs (next door to the Hog's Breath Inn). Open Mon.-Fri. 9:30am-4pm, Sat. noon-5pm.

Monterey-Salinas Transit (MST): 899-2555 or 424-7695. Buses #4, 5, or 22 will take you to the city. Bus #4 runs between the Monterey Transit Plaza and 6th and Mission in Carmel; Mon.-Sat. 6:45am-10:15pm, Sun. 7:45am-5:45pm. Bus #5 runs closer to the beach in Carmel, stopping at Carmelo St. and Santa Lucía Ave.; 1 per hr. Mon.-Sat. 7:30am-5:30pm, Sun. 10:15am-5:15pm. Fare $1.25, over 64 60¢ with Medicare or Transit Courtesy Card, under 4 free.

Bike Rental: Bay Bikes (625-BIKE), on Lincoln between 5th and 6th. $6 per hour, $4 every hour after, and $60 per week includes helmet and bike locks.

Post Office: 5th St. (624-1525), between San Carlos and Dolores St. Open Mon. 8am-4:30pm, Tues.-Fri. 9am-4:30pm. General Delivery ZIP Code: 93921.

Area Code: 408.

Carmel lies at the southern base of the Monterey Peninsula off Rte. 1. The city is contained within a giant square: Rte. 1 to the east, the beach on the west, Ocean Ave. (the town's main street) on the north, and Rio Rd. and Santa Lucía Ave. on the south. Obtain a free street map of the town, produced by the Carmel Innkeepers Hosting Service, at any motel.

The free weekly *Summer Review* (624-0162) carries detailed theater, music, dance, art, and restaurant listings. The information center in Monterey and restaurants in Carmel have stacks of them. The *Pine Cone*, a Carmel publication that lists local events, will fill in any remaining gaps in your knowledge.

Accommodations and Camping

Most motels in Carmel offer only double-occupancy rooms that never dip below $60 per night. A 15-minute bus ride north to Monterey will bring more reasonable prices. Camping is illegal within the city limits. The wind at this beach can be fierce, however—make sure you have warm clothing. The cheapest camping in Carmel Valley is 4½ mi. east of the city at **Saddle Mountain Ranch** (624-1617), a private resort on Schulte Rd. Fifty sites with showers are available ($17, with full hookup and sanitary dump $25). **The Mission Ranch** is the cheapest motel of an expensive bunch, with prices for a room dipping as low as $50 (price includes a lovely breakfast). The ranch is located behind the Carmel Mission on Dolores, and is owned by Clint Eastwood. The sage traveler will make reservations.

Food

Though the adjective "pretentious" may fit most of Carmel's restaurants like a well-tailored smoking jacket, and although the city's zoning laws make it impossible to get a beachside hot dog, and although the absence of a food court may be the only thing distinguishing downtown from an overgrown shopping mall, it is still possible to dine decently with a little bit of money and a little bit of luck.

Le Bistro, San Carlos (624-6545), between Ocean and 7th. While the Bistro Burger ($4.75) is their specialty, keep an eye out for others; the chef knows what to do when he gets his hands on a fresh fish. Open Mon.-Fri. 7am-4pm and 5-9pm; Sat.-Sun. 8am-4pm and 5-9pm.

Em Lee's, Dolores (625-6780), between 5th and 6th St. Cozy, family-run breakfast and lunch joint with brick-tiled floors and plenty of plants. Many breakfast specials, including plate-sized blueberry waffles ($5.10). Open Sun.-Tues. 6am-3pm, Fri.-Sat. 6am-3pm, 5-8:30pm.

Monterey Baking Company, (625-3998), Lincoln and Ocean. A café and patisserie, with other branches in Monterey and Santa Cruz. Sandwiches $4-5. Open Mon.-Thurs. 8am-7pm, Fri.-Sun. 8am-8pm.

Paolina's, San Carlos (624-5599), between Ocean and 7th, in the "Doud Craft Studios." Hearty pastas with a variety of toppings, $6.50. Pizzas from $6. Open daily 8am-9pm.

China Gourmet (624-3941), on 5th between San Carlos and Dolores. Fabulous food, most dishes $7-10. Open daily 11am-9:30pm.

Sights

Carmel City Beach, at the end of Ocean Ave., is where the northern Big Sur coast truly begins. No signs proclaim the event, but it's unmistakable: a crescent of white sand frames a cove of clear, but chilly, aquamarine waters. The beach ends abruptly at the base of distant red cliffs. Surrounding the whole area are cypress-covered hills wreathed in clouds. The west-facing beach makes a fine grandstand for sunsets.

Less crowded and more remote, the **Carmel River State Beach** lies around the southern point at the end of City Beach. This beach, windier and colder than the city's, but blessed with better surf, can be reached by walking about 1 mi. along Scenic Rd. or by driving to the end of Carmelo St. off Santa Lucía Ave.

To glimpse Carmel as it might have been in the 20s and 30s, take the short walk from the river beach to **Tor House** (624-1813) at Ocean View Ave. and Scenic Rd. Poet Robinson Jeffers built this house in 1919, using boulders from the beach. (Tours Fri.-Sat. 10am-4pm. Reservations required. Admission $5, college students $3.50, high school students $1.50, children under 12 not admitted.)

Mission Basilica San Carlos Borromeo del Rio Carmelo, 3080 Rio Rd. (624-1271), off Rte. 1, is a mouthful to say but a marvel to see. Founded in 1770 at Monterey and transported to Carmel in 1771, the mission "converted" 4000 Native Americans before it was left to ruin in 1836. Sir Harry Downie supervised its restoration in 1931, fastidiously following the original construction methods. A Mudéjar tower supporting four bells and a number of swallows' nests crowns the popular church. Father Junípero Serra, founder of the California mission system and eponym of the omnipresent California juniper bush, is buried in the sanctuary. Try to see this, but if you can't, well *que serra, serra.* In the cemetery, over 2300 Native Americans are interred. The three **museums** at Carmel Mission are extensive, displaying the original silver altar furnishings, handsome vestments, a library, and much, much more from the mission's early days. (Self-guided tours Mon.-Sat. 9:30am-4:30pm, Sun. 10:30am-4pm. Donation requested.)

The extraordinary **Point Lobos Reserve** (624-4909), 1½ mi. south of Carmel on Rte. 1, is a state-run wildlife sanctuary popular with skindivers and dayhikers. Otters, sea lions, brown pelicans, and gulls are visible from footpaths along the cliffs, but those without seal blubber or eagle eyes should bring a windbreaker and binoculars out to the ledge. Point Lobos encompasses some tide pools and has marvelous vantage points for watching the winter whale migration. Don't neglect the interior trails through cypress forests, but watch out for poison oak. The bureaucratically-set hours don't allow enjoyment of the area in the early morning or at dusk. Park outside the tollbooth and walk or bike in for free. There is frequently a line of cars waiting to get in by 8am on weekends. (Open daily 9am-7pm; in winter 9am-5pm. Admission $3 per car plus 50¢ for a map. No dogs allowed.) To reach Point Lobos, take MST bus #22 ("Big Sur") from Monterey.

Entertainment

Carmel's bars are often overpriced and overblown. Watering holes are full of middle-aged tourists, many of whom are either on their honeymoon or revisiting the scene of their first fling. But bars are not the only places to hang out. For a touch of the fabled California beach life, try walking down the **Carmel City Beach** or **River Beach** (see Sights) around 9pm to find young people gathered around communal beachfires, listening to music, and drinking assorted refreshments. Congregations around conflagrations are officially illegal so you must walk at least beyond sight of the main road before spotting a far-off twinkle of firelight. BYOB.

California's first outdoor theater, the **Forest Theatre** (626-1681), at Mountain View Ave. and Santa Rita St., about 2 blocks east of the northern end of Ocean Ave., provides light drama (8pm), weekend musical entertainment, and free Sunday afternoon concerts (2pm, call 624-3996 for info) June to October. After October, the company performs indoors. Tickets run about $10, but discount tickets are often sold.

Catch the annual **Bach Festival** (624-1521) if you happen to be in Carmel July 15 to August 4. Tickets ($5-30) can be purchased in advance from the Carmel Bach Festival, P.O. Box 575, Carmel 93921 or, close to the concert date, at the Festival Office, #11 Sunset Center, San Carlos at 9th St. (Open 11am-3pm.)

The General Store, Junípero St. and 5th Ave. (624-2233). Two blocks north of the eastern side of Ocean Ave. One large outdoor fire and inconspicuous heat lamps keep everyone toasty on the patio. Dinner entrees are a touch expensive, but the bar inside is congenial. Free hors d'oeuvres during Happy Hour Mon.-Fri. 4-6pm. Bar open Mon.-Sat. 11:30am-1:30am, Sun. 10:30am-1:30am. Restaurant open daily 11:30am-midnight.

The Hogs Breath Inn, San Carlos St. (625-1044), between 5th and 6th Ave. Large courtyard filled with benches, heavy wooden tables, and comfortable director's chairs. A bit touristy, however, with patrons eagerly hoping to catch a glimpse of half-owner Clint Eastwood. Dinners $10-23. Bar is intimate and cozy. Complimentary hors d'oeuvres Mon.-Fri. 4-6pm. Lunch Mon.-Sat. 11:30am-3pm; Sunday brunch 11am-3pm; dinner daily 5-11pm; in winter 5-10pm.

Monterey

In the 1940s, John Steinbeck's Monterey was a crusty coastal town geared toward sardine fishing and canning. But the sardines disappeared in the early 50s, and when Steinbeck revisited his beloved Cannery Row around 1960, he wrote scornfully of how the district had become a tourist trap. He was right. Along Cannery Row and Fisherman's Wharf, packing plants have been converted to multiplex souvenir malls, and the old bars where sailors used to drink and fight now feature wax reenactments. The only remnant of Steinbeck's romanticized era is the continuing urge to exploit resources to the fullest, whether by fishing sardines to local extinction or milking tourists to financial exhaustion.

Monterey was explored by the Spanish as early as 1602, but didn't really take off until 1770, when Father Serra passed through on his epic journey up the California coast. From then on, Monterey served as the capital of first Spanish, then Mexican, Alta California and as a major Pacific port. After being invaded and claimed by the United States in 1846, the city lost its bureaucratic prestige and was eclipsed as a port by San Francisco. But the growth of the whaling, and later the sardine, industries kept Moneterey alive. While the sardine era is mostly remembered through junky souvenirs, numerous public buildings and adobe houses recall the days before the Gold Rush. Along with the ineradicable beauty of the coastline, the good taste of these restorations and the absence of clumsy hype combine to counteract, if not excuse, Monterey's crasser side.

Practical Information and Orientation

Visitors Information: Monterey Peninsula Chamber of Commerce, 380 Alvarado St., P.O. Box 1770, Monterey 93942 (648-5350), downtown. Many free pamphlets and a staff eager to answer questions. Open Mon.-Fri. 8:30am-5pm. **Sierra Club,** Ocean Ave. and Dolores (624-8032), in Carmel. From Rte. 1, turn on Dolores near the school, and drive 3 blocks toward the ocean. Information on sights. Open Mon.-Sat. 12:30-4:30pm.

Amtrak: 40 Railroad Ave. (422-7458), in Salinas (no station in Monterey). Open 10am-1:30pm and 3-6pm, but call 800-872-7245 for information and reservations. Free bus connection to Monterey (#20 or 21). Open daily 10am-1:30pm, 3-5:30pm.

Greyhound: 351 Del Monte Ave. (373-4735), at Washington. A wooden building. To: L.A. and San Luis Obispo (4 per day, $47); San Francisco (4 per day, $18). Open daily 7am-5:30pm. Buses from L.A. stop at the **Salinas Station** at Gabilan and Main (424-1626). From there walk one block west and one block north to the Salinas Transit Center at Salinas and Central, where you can catch the #20 or 21 bus to Monterey, which runs Mon.-Sat. until 10:15pm and Sun. and holidays until 5:45pm.

Monterey-Salinas Transit (MST): One Ryan Ranch Rd. (899-2555 or 424-7695, TTY available). MST serves the region from Watsonville in the north to Salinas in the south, and inland to Pacific Grove. Many buses stop at **Transit Plaza** downtown, where Munras, Tyler, Pearl, Alvarado, and Polk St. converge. Fare $1.25 per zone, under 18 50¢ (each zone encompasses 1 or 2 towns, 4 zones total); exact change; transfers free. Disabled passengers and those over 64 can get a **Transit Courtesy Card** entitling them to ride for 60¢. A **Day Pass** ($3.75) is valid for unlimited rides for 1 day within a single zone. Two ride for the price of one on weekends. Buses run Mon.-Sat. 7am-6:30 or 11:30pm, Sun. 10am-7pm. The free *Rider's Guide* to Monterey-Salinas Transit (MST) service contains complete schedules and route information (available on buses, at motels, and the library). Bus #22 runs between Monterey and the Nepenthe restaurant near Big Sur (4 or 5 per day; $2, over 64 70¢, under 18 $1; daily schedule in effect only April-Sept.). Drivers may balk at backpacks, so be charmingly persuasive and dress decently. Information lines open daily 7am-6pm.

Taxis: Yellow Cab, 646-1234. **Joe's Taxi,** 624-3885. **Golden State Cab,** 384-1335. All 24-hr. service.

Bike Rental: Free-wheeling Cycles, 188 Webster St. (373-3855), on the northern fringe of downtown. Ten-speeds $10 per day, $35 per week, $20 deposit. Best prices, but check the bike carefully before riding into the sunset. Open Mon.-Fri. 9am-6pm, Sat.-Sun. 9am-5pm; Dec.-April daily 9am-5pm. **Bay Bikes,** 640 Wave St. (646-9090), on Cannery Row. Bikes $6 for the first hr., $4 each additional hr., $18 per day. Open daily 9am-6pm.

Moped Rental: Monterey Moped Adventures, 1250 Del Monte Ave. (373-2696). Mopeds $10 per hour, $40 per day. 2 hour minimum.

Public Library: 625 Pacific (646-3933). Pleasant courtyard for reading. Open Mon.-Thurs. 9am-9pm, Fri. 9am-6pm, Sat. 9am-5pm, Sun. 1-5pm.

Laundromat: Delmonte Center, downtown (625-0307). Also check the yellow pages.

Suicide Prevention: 649-8008.

Alcoholics Anonymous: 373-3713.

Women's Crisis Line: 372-6300.

Rape Crisis Line: 375-4357. 24 hr.

Post Office: 565 Hartnell (372-5803). Open Mon.-Fri. 8:45am-5:10pm. General Delivery ZIP Code: 93940-9999.

Area Code: 408.

The town of Monterey is situated on the northern side of the Monterey Peninsula 115 mi. south of San Francisco. Pacific Grove, a quiet community frequented by fewer tourists, and Pebble Beach, an exclusive nest of mansions, occupy the peninsula proper. Carmel, lying southwest of Monterey, stands where the peninsula ends on its southern side. Motorists can approach Monterey from U.S. 101 (Munras Ave. exit), which runs north-south slightly inland from the peninsula, or Rte. 1, the coastal highway.

There are several **free guides** to activities in Monterey and surrounding areas. *Coasting,* published weekly, includes articles about the arts and is available from the visitors center, stores, and hotels. For the nearest distribution point call 625-5656. The *Review* is a thorough and free dining and entertainment guide that also lists Happy Hours. *This Month on the Monterey Peninsula* (649-3333) is a glossy magazine with the best maps, freebies, and sight-seeing information of real value. The *Coast Weekly* (625-5656) is a valuable source of ideas for excursions, and also contains food and events listings.

Monterey's main street, **Alvarado,** runs north-south. At its northern end stand luxury hotels and the magnitudinous Conference Center; beyond the brick plaza are a large parking lot, the marina, and Fisherman's Wharf. Most sights of interest lie within a few blocks of Alvarado, in a tangle of streets toward its southern end. Cannery Row and the aquarium are about 1½-2 mi. northwest of downtown.

The relative isolation of Monterey does little to insulate the city from prodigious traffic jams. The Monterey Traffic Department's earnest attempts to correct the congestion with abundant one way signs and complicated traffic signals seem only to make matters worse. If you drive, park at the 12-hr. meters near Fisherman's Wharf (25¢ for 30 min.) and explore the city by foot.

Bicycling is a splendid way to see the peninsula provided you exercise caution on the narrow, twisting roads. There are few bike paths *per se,* but the Monterey Peninsula Recreation Trail follows the coast from Fisherman's Wharf in Monterey through Pacific Grove, Pebble Beach and Carmel, then back up Hwy. 1, where a bike lane begins. The circuit takes four hours at a leisurely pace, all day for those who like to make frequent stops to admire the scenery.

Accommodations and Camping

Finding cheap lodging in Monterey requires diligent searching. Beware of floating rates for hotels and motels. Prices often vary by day, month, and proximity to an important event, such as the Jazz Festival. As a general rule, hotels along Fremont St. in Monterey (bus #9 or 10) and Lighthouse Ave. in Pacific Grove (bus #2 or some #1 buses) are the most reasonable. Other motels cluster along Munras Ave. between downtown and Rte. 1.

Monterey Peninsula Youth Hostel (AYH—supplemental accommodation) (649-0375). Theoretically, the location is not fixed, but the hostel has been in the Monterey High School Gym

When all you've got
is one week,
even a morning of diarrhea
is too much.
Bad weather isn't the only thing that can spoil a vacation. That's why you want the most effective diarrhea medicine you can buy — Imodium® A-D. It can stop diarrhea with just one dose, instead of dose after dose of the other leading brand.
Take it along in convenient caplets. And enjoy every moment of your next vacation.
Imodium A-D. It can stop diarrhea with just one dose.
Imodium
A-D
ANTI-
DIARRHEAL
Loperamide HCl
Caplets
NON-PRESCRIPTION
DOSAGE
For the control of the symptoms of diarrhea

for the past few summers. While the hostel lacks a kitchen and even beds (mattresses are put directly on the floor), the staff tries to make up for the deficiencies by providing cheap food, and lots of information. Lockout 9am-6pm—not the right place for late risers. Curfew 11pm. Open daily mid-June to mid-Aug. To reach the high school, take Pacific away from the water, make a right on Madison and a left on Larkin St. Members $6, nonmember $9.

Motel 6, 2124 Fremont (646-8585). One of the few motels whose rates stay relatively constant (singles $40; doubles $45). Fremont St. is near the county fairgrounds, and some people reserve as much as a year in advance for the summer and for the weekends of the Jazz Festival, Blues Festival, County Fair, and Laguna Seca Races.

Del Monte Beach Inn, 1110 Del Monte (649-4410). Near the bus station. Friendly management likes budget travelers (but not enough to lower the prices). $45 gets you a room with a double bed, shared bathroom and breakfast.

Paris Motel, 2118 N. Fremont (649-4740). *Not* a luxury motel, but hey, it's got beds. Singles and doubles about $35 on weekdays, $95 on weekends.

Paramount Motel, 3298 Del Monte Blvd. (384-3674), in Marina, 8 mi. north of Monterey. Clean and well-run. Check-out 11am. Singles $30. Doubles $35. No reservations; arrive at noon to get a room.

Veterans Memorial Park Campground, Via Del Rey (646-3865), 1½ mi. from the town center. Take Skyline Dr. off the section of Rte. 68 called W.R Holman Hwy. From downtown, take Pacific St. south, turn right on Jefferson, and follow the signs, or take bus #3. Perched on a hill with a view of the bay. 40 sites, hot showers. First-come, first-camped. Arrive before 3pm in summer and on weekends in winter. Sites $10, hikers $2.

Laguna Seca Recreational Area, Hwy. 68 (422-6138), 10 mi. east of Monterey. 178 campsites, of which 103 are equipped with hookups. Showers, restrooms, barbecue pits, tables, and a dump station. Sites $9.50, with hookup $14. A lovely spot which justifies the extra trek from Monterey.

Food

Seafood. The whales may be gone and the sardines with them, but the unpolluted Monterey Bay still teems with squid, crab, rockcod, sand dab, red snapper, and *mmm* salmon. In another country, a fishing town like this might have but one way to serve the delights of the sea; sautéed in olive oil, or maybe as *paella.* But in this land of the melting pot, you can enjoy your seafood as Sicilian marinated octopus, English fish & chips, Thai sweet-and-sour snapper, or artfully wrapped sushi. Although the seafood is bountiful, it is often expensive—eating an early bird special (4-6:30pm or so) can save a lot of money. Or head to Fisherman's Wharf, where the $5.50 smoked salmon sandwiches are a wonderful way to sample the local delicacies. Don't despair if you loathe seafare, you can still dine well in this land of artichokes and strawberries.

Casa de Gutiérrez, 590 Calle Principal (375-0095), at the south end of the street. Located in an 1841 adobe house. The patio out back is delightful, with weathered wooden tables, Mexican wrought-iron chairs, and Mexican newspapers as placemats. Entrees ($7-8) are named after famous persons from Monterey history. Cooper's Tostada is a wonderful chicken creation and is big enough for an Aaron Deemer appetite. Open Mon.-Thurs. 11am-9pm, Fri.-Sun. 10am-10pm.

Jugem, 409 Alvarado (373-6463). A standard Japanese restaurant and sushi bar ($3 for 2 pieces). Dinners are about $12, but only $6.45 for the 5-7pm early bird special. Open Mon.-Fri. 11am-2pm and 5-10pm, Sat.-Sun. 5-10pm.

Beau Thai, 807 Cannery Row (373-8811), near the Aquarium. A real restaurant hidden behind ice cream and fudge shops. Many entrees (including snapper) for $7. Open daily 11am-10pm.

Belleci's, 470 Alvarado (373-4240). The specialty here is the *speengie,* a hunk of dough fried before your eyes until crisp outside and fluffy inside, then topped with cinnamon and sugar (75¢) or fruit and whipped cream ($1.25)—a Blarthian breakfast for those who believe in beginning the day with a little hedonism. Sandwiches $3.50. Open Mon.-Wed. 8am-4pm, Thurs.-Fri. 7am-4pm.

Troia's Deli, 350 Pacific St. (375-9819), at Pacific and Del Monte St. This diminutive, friendly supermarket vends inexpensive picnic fixings: juicy barbecued chicken at $2.79 per lb., green salad $2.89 per lb., fresh poppyseed rolls, and a standard selection of deli sandwiches (ham and cheese $2.90). Open Mon.-Sat. 8am-8pm, Sun. 8am-7pm.

Sights

At the northwest end of Cannery Row, the **Monterey Bay Aquarium,** 866 Cannery Row (648-4888), lives in grand symbiosis with the bay for which it is named. The aquarium, one of the best in the world, serves the bay by glorifying its ecology in two 325,000-gallon-plus acrylic tanks and many smaller cases. It also takes advantage of the bay's ocean-swept purity by pumping in raw, unfiltered seawater at night, something few other aquaria can do lest they kill their fish with toxic muck. The result is that the environment inside the aquarium is almost exactly like the environment in the bay, right down to the algae and the simulated waves. In addition to such standards as enormous octopi and docile starfish, the aquarium contains such unusual attractions as 30-ft.-tall kelps, diving birds, and a clever exhibit that allows otters to be viewed from above and below. Upstairs, galleries house special exhibits; 1992's main exhibit will be on jellyfish. The aquarium is packed on holidays and can be crowded in the mornings, but after 2:30 or 3pm things calm down. (Open daily 10am-6pm. Admission $9, students and those over 65 $6.50., ages 3-12 $4.)

Along the waterfront to the south of the aquarium, lies **Cannery Row.** Once a depressed center for languishing sardine packing plants, this ¾-mi. row has now been victimized by the blight of waterfront urban renewal and converted into glitzy mini-malls, bars, and discos. All that remains of the earthiness and gruff camaraderie celebrated by John Steinbeck in *Cannery Row* and *Sweet Thursday* is a few building façades. 835 Cannery Row once was the Wing Chong Market. The bright yellow building next door is where *Sweet Thursday* took place. Doc Rickett's lab is at 800 Cannery Row, and is now owned by a private men's club.

One example of Steinbeck exploitation which manages to avoid tourist tackiness is the **Great Cannery Row Mural,** which stretches 400 ft. along the "700" blocks of Cannery Row. Fifty large panels by local artists depict Monterey in the 30s, and while each panel might not make it on its own, the sum effect is impressive. While the project was designed merely to mask some construction, it appears that the murals are now permanent.

Built in 1846 by prisoners, military deserters, and a volunteer crew of Native Americans, **Fisherman's Wharf** was for decades the center of one of the largest fishing and whaling industries in the West. Since WWII, however, fishermen have followed the fish to Moss Landing. Fisherman's Wharf is currently awash with tourists, junk-food stalls, and cheap shops selling seashells and Steinbeck novels. While the restaurants here are rather expensive, there are several shops selling shrimp cocktails ($2.50) and **smoked salmon sandwiches** ($5.50). Made with fresh sourdough bread, cream cheese, and plenty of the local salmon that is smoked right on the pier, these sandwiches make a perfect breakfast or lunch.

Several companies on the wharf offer **sight-seeing boat trips** around Monterey Bay. **Monterey Sport Fishing,** 96 Fisherman's Wharf (372-2203), provides 35-minute tours every hour on the hour ($6, children under 12 $3.) You can frequently spot sea lions, seals, and endangered sea otters on the trips. Sea-Life tours offers a 20-minute glass-bottom boat ride for $2.50 (372-7560). From December through March **whale-watching** trips are available from the same companies. The cruises, lasting nearly 2 hours, leave every day ($15, children under 12 $10).

Making the rounds of the **historic buildings** in central Monterey will give you a sense of the region's history. Monterey's early days spawned a unique architectural trend, influenced by East Coast seafarers. The typical Monterey-style house features South Carolina details, such as wrap-around porches, second-floor balconies, and pane windows, as well as such Mexican adobe characteristics as yard-thick walls and exterior staircases. Most of the town's historical buildings downtown now belong to the **Monterey State Historic Park.** Each is clearly marked by a sign out in front and can provide information and free maps of suggested walking tours. One such historic adobe is the **Stevenson House,** 530 Houston St., where Robert Louis Stevenson sojourned in the autumn of 1879. Several rooms are filled with Stevenson memorabilia, and the upper floor has been restored in the Victorian mode. (Tours Thurs.-Tues. on the hour 10-11am and 1-3pm, and also in the summer at 4pm; $2.)

Other historical sights of Monterey include **Colton Hall** and its museum on Pacific St. between Jefferson and Madison St. The hall was completed in the spring of 1849 and had its 15 minutes of fame that autumn, when the California State Constitution was written and signed there. Since 1949, the building has been mostly dedicated to the memory of that convention. (Open Mon.-Fri. 10am-5pm, Sat.-Sun. 10am-noon and 1-5pm. Closes at 4pm in winter. Free.) Monterey's whaling history is reflected in the **Old Whaling Station** (375-5356). The station, hidden behind a shopping center near the Custom House, is filled with mementos of Monterey's pre-sardine days. The sidewalk in front, an environmentalist's nightmare, is made of whale bones. (Open Fri. 10am-2pm.)

If you plan to visit more than one of the houses which charge admission, you'll want to purchase a $4 day pass which gets you into all the historic park buildings. Buy your ticket at the **Visitors Center** inside the Park Headquarters (open daily 10am-5pm, 10am-4pm in winter). The center sells the *Path of History* walking tour book ($2), and offers the Monterey Historic Park **House and Garden Tour** for hard-core history fans (Tues., Thurs., and Fri. at 2pm). The 1½-hour tour features 10 historic buildings and five gardens ($2.75, ages under 18 $1).

From late June through early July, **Monterey Bay's Theaterfest** takes place between the Customs House and the Pacific House. Every Saturday and Sunday, tourists are beguiled by hours of free afternoon theatre. The quality of the shows varies from year to year, but this is generally a wonderful (and cheap) way to spend a day. The evening performances charge admission ($10; students and seniors $8).

One will find the **Monterey Peninsula Museum of Art,** 559 Pacific St. (372-5477), in the same neighborhood as the historic adobes. The museum features fresh, well-presented exhibitions of etchings, woodcuts, and other monochrome works from the 17th through the 20th centuries, in addition to displays of international folk arts. The museum's Ralph K. Davies Collection of Western Art includes many of Charlie Russell's well-known bronze statues of bronco-busters busting broncos. (Open Tues.-Sat. 10am-4pm, Sun. 1-4pm. Suggested donation $2.)

Monterey's beach lacks the drama and surf of its neighbors, so head west and north for the most impressive shoreside scenery. Around the northern end of the peninsula, the beach runs uninterrupted for 3 to 4 mi., first as **Pacific Grove Municipal Beach,** then as **Asilomar State Beach.** (Bus #2 goes to within 4 blocks of the ocean in Pacific Grove. You can also bike the 2 mi. from downtown.) There are numerous tidepools here, and the rocky shore is a curious place to explore.

Sunset Drive is, appropriately, the best place for watching the sun go down. People arrive a full two hours before sunset in order to secure front row seats along the road (also known as Ocean Blvd.). You might consider walking westward to Point Pinos before the sun does its thing. At the western tip stands phallic **Point Pinos Lighthouse,** a New England-style building that is the oldest California beacon still in use. Inside are exhibits on Coast Guard history. (Open Sat.-Sun. 1-4pm. Free.)

Pacific Grove, a neighborhood northwest of downtown, took root over a 100 years ago as a Methodist enclave, and many of the Victorian houses are extant and ship-shape. Pacific Grove is Carmel 30 years before rampant tourism took that city over; a middle class town with a beautiful coastline and lots of funky shops. In addition, Pacific Grove offers the sight of the thousands of **monarch butterflies** which annually flee Canada to winter in its cypress groves from October to March. Look, but don't touch; harming butterflies is a $1000 offense. Even if it's not the right time of year for monarchs, you can still visit the **Pacific Grove Museum of Natural History,** Forest and Central Ave. (372-4212), 1 block north of Lighthouse Ave. Mounted specimens of the regal insects and other local wildlife fill the first floor. Up on the balcony, delicate watercolors of wildflowers hang next to pressed and dried specimens of seaweed which look like feathers and firebursts. (Open Tues.-Sun. 10am-5pm. Free.)

17-Mile Drive meanders along the coast from Pacific Grove through Pebble Beach and the forests around Carmel. Once owned by Del Monte, Pebble Beach has become the playground of the fabulously well-to-do. Its enormous, manicured golf courses creep up almost to the shore's edge, and appear ridiculous against the dramatically jagged cliffs and turbulent surf. They paved paradise and put up a putting green. The Drive is rolling, looping, and often spectacular, though plagued by heavy traffic, swarms of tourists, and an outrageous $5.75 entrance fee, perhaps to prevent the riff-raff from wearing the scenery out by looking at it too much. There are four clearly marked gates. Bicyclists and pedestrians are allowed in free. To come and go as you please in one day, present your receipt to the guard and make sure he records your license plate number. Top it all off with a drink in the **Terrace Lounge** (624-3811), located in **The Lodge at Pebble Beach** (open daily noon-11pm). People also visit here to see the Lone Cypress—an old, gnarled tree growing on a rock promontory. The cypress would be more impressive were it not for the extensive trusses holding it together like an aging burlesque star.

Entertainment

Most of Monterey's nightly entertainment centers around the same areas that click with cameras and bristle with brochures by day; the bars downtown attract fewer tourists.

The annual **Monterey Jazz Festival**—five concerts over three days in the third week of September—features the great names of jazz (closer to Buddy Rich than Alex Ross for the most part) and attracts crowds from all over California. Season tickets sell out by May 31, and run $80-90. Call 373-3366 for information.

Monterey also holds an annual **county fair** in mid-August at the Monterey County Fairgrounds and Exhibition Park, featuring a variety of exhibits and performers.

Doc Ricketts Lab, 95 Prescott St. (649-4241), on Cannery Row. Not exactly the oceanographer's laboratory described by John Steinbeck. A local crowd dances to live rock nightly 9pm-1:30am. Two pool tables. Happy Hour daily 6-9pm with wine, well drinks and domestic drafts $1. No cover. Open daily 6pm-2am.

The Boiler Room, 625 Cannery Row (373-1449), on the 3rd floor. Comedy and dance club with a terrific view of the bay. Doors open at 7:30pm. All comedy shows start at 9:15pm (cover varies). Live music and dancing after the shows on weekends. Cover $3 for dancing only.

Viva Monterey, 414 Alvarado St. (646-1415). Modern video-café showing music and sports videos. Serves lunch and dinner and offers a pub menu. Pizzas from $3.75. Happy Hour Mon.-Fri. 2-6pm. Jumbo drafts ($2), well drinks, and house wine ($1.50). Open daily 2pm-2am. Food served 5pm-2am. Must be 21.

The Club, 321 D Alvarado St. (646-9244), at Del Monte Ave. across from Fisherman's Wharf. Monday male burlesque, Tues.-Sat. dancing with DJ or local bands, Sun. comedy followed by dancing. Open nightly 8pm-2am. Must be 21. Two drinks per table minimum.

Salinas

Twenty-five miles inland from Monterey lies Salinas, the heart of John Steinbeck Country. The reknowned author (the only American to win both the Pulitzer and Nobel prizes) lived here until he was 17. This is where *East of Eden* was set, where many of Steinbeck's characters came from, and where his ashes are buried.

Salinas was founded in 1856 as a resting point for travelers between Carmel and the San Juan Bautista Mission. The city was incorporated in 1874, and is presently Monterey County's agricultural center. The region of the Salinas Valley is known as "The Salad Bowl of the Nation."

Salinas' biggest non-literary tourist pull is the **California Rodeo Salinas.** This, the fourth largest rodeo in the world, attracts cows, bulls, ropers, wrestlers, riders, and horses from across the West in late July. While the rodeo officially only lasts for one weekend, related events, including Cowboy Poetry readings, take place throughout the last 3 weeks of July. Salinas' other noteworthy annual event is the **Steinbeck Festival,** held in early August. The festival features bus and walking tours of the area, films and talks. For information, contact the Salinas Chamber of Commerce; 119 E. Alisal St., P.O. Box 1170, 93902 (424-7611). Open Mon.-Fri. 8:30am-5pm.

Devoted Steinbeck fans will want to visit Salinas even when no festivites light up the town. The house where Steinbeck grew up is located at 132 Central Ave., and is presently a restaurant. A scrumptious lunch is served family-style with 2 sittings (11:45am and 1:15, menu changes daily, $6.50, dessert $2.50, coffee and tea $1), and the building is open for free to non-eaters from 2:30-3pm. **The Steinbeck Library,** 110 W. San Luis St. (408-758-7311), is for the most part a normal municipal library, but does contain a room of Steinbeck memorabilia, and information on Steinbeck sights in the area. The library also sells the **Guide to Steinbeck Country** ($5). Open Mon.-Thurs. 10am-9pm, Fri.-Sat. 10am-6pm.

Salinas' other significant tourist sight, the Boronda Adobe, will be reopening in 1992 with new exhibits and a museum under the rubric of the **Baronda History Center.** Located at the northwest edge of Salinas, the adobe dates all the way back to 1844. The museum will display exhibits on Monterey County's cultural and agricultural history. (Open daily 9am-3pm, but call 757-8085 to verify hours and determine admission prices.)

Salinas abounds with terrific Mexican restaurants (the entire city smells delicious), one of the best, and least well known, of which is **Los Arcos Del Alisa,** 504 E. Alisal St. (422-6886). A combination plate is $6. Open daily 11am-11pm. If your Spanish is rusty, you might try the more Americanized Mexican food of the vast buffet at the **Ole Frijole Restaurant,** at 838 S. Main St. (757-5169). Dinner $6.29, lunch $4.78, includes tax, drink, dessert, enchiladas, burritos, tacos, salads, etc.) Open for lunch Mon.-Sat. 11:30am-3:30pm, for dinner 4-8:30pm. Sunday dinner 11am-8:30pm. Those who prefer unadulterated American can enjoy the Coca-Cola decos at **The Recipe Box,** 35 W. Gabilan (424-0188). Sizeable sandwiches are $4.50. Daily lunch special $4.25. Open Mon.-Fri. 10am-3pm.

Salinas makes an easy day-trip from Monterey (see Monterey for bus info). If you want to sojourn overnight, budget motels line N. Main St., across from the Community Center and rodeo grounds (which also house the **Hats in Three Stages of Landing,** three 3500 lb. sculptures of cowboy hats by Klaus Oldenberg, which are Salinas' lone work of artistic signficance. Motel reservations are always a necessity during the rodeo and the Steinbeck Festival. The best deal in town is the new **Budget Inn,** 545 Werk St. Part of a chain, the Inn has a jacuzzi, swimming pool, laundry, remote control color TV w/ cable, coffee and muffins brought to your room in the morning, and a game room (Singles $30; Doubles $35; 757-9667). RV roadies will want to stay at Cabana Holidays RV Park and Cabins.

Near Salinas—Pinnacles National Monument

An hour southeast of Salinas stands **Pinnacles National Monument.** Pinnacles was set aside as a National Park by Teddy Roosevelt in 1908, and the park preserves the erratic and unique spires and crags that volcanic activity created here. The park has 30 mi. of hiking trails, varying from light promenades to strenuous hikes. The high peaks of the pinnacles (2400 ft.) dominate the center of the park, and can be reached by a 2½ mi. hike from either of the park's two entrances. The park's most commonly trodden trails are the ones that lead to the **Talas Caves,** located ½ mi. from either entrance. Other trails wend through a variety of landscapes, and offer a pristine perspective on the Central California landscape.

If you visit during the work week, you will have the park nearly to yourself. Wildflowers bloom in the spring, and Pinnacles offers excellent birding all year long. The park also has the widest range of wildlife of any park in California, including a number of rare predator mammals: mountain lions, bobcats, coyote, gold eagles, and peregrine falcons. Entrance to the park is $3. The park headquarters is located at the Eastside entrance (Rte. 25 to Rte. 146; 389-4485).

Just outside of East Entrance is **Pinnacles Campground Inc.** (389-4467), a privately owned campground with swimming pool, flush toilets, and hot showers ($6 per person per night up to $18 maximum; electrical hookups $2). The Western Entrance has a contact station (389-4526), and chaparral campground. The campground is walk-in, but some of the sites ($10) are just 50 yds. from the parking lot. Reservations are not accepted, and with only 23 sites it's best to show up early if you're trying to camp on a weekend. The campground has BBQ pits, restrooms, and picnic tables, so you'll also have to fight off the daytripping picnickers.

Santa Cruz

Santa Cruz sports the kind of uncalculated hipness that other coastal towns can only dream of. Santa Cruz is the epitome of California cool, and its beaches and bookstores even lure visitors from cosmopolitan San Francisco, 75 mi. to the north. Santa Cruz's location is crucial to its identity. Without a beach, it would be Berkeley; with a better one, it would be Ft. Lauderdale. Along the beach and the boardwalk, tourism and surfer culture reign supreme. On the other side of Front St., The University of California at Santa Cruz makes its presence felt. Restaurants offer avocado sandwiches and industrial coffee, merchants hawk UCSC paraphernalia alongside the flyers for summer courses in ethics which query, "Should you kill your grandmother?"

All of this is a far cry from Santa Cruz's origin as one of Father Junípero Serra's missions in 1791. (The name means "holy cross.") Today, Santa Cruz is nothing if not liberal, as it simultaneously embraces macho surfers and a large lesbian community. It's one of the few places where the old 60s catchphrase "Do your own thing" still applies, and Santa Cruz continues to go its own way in the 90s with its own distinctive style. This is one of the few places where the spirit of the 60s hasn't died or been slicked up, remade, and crassly exploited.

While the earthquake of October 17, 1989 is best known for the damage it did in Oakland and San Francisco, its epicenter was only 10 mi. from Santa Cruz. The city was by no means reduced to a pile of rubble, but it did lose a bridge, the popular Pacific Garden Mall, and several retail shops. While some of the shops are still temporarily located in tents (euphemistically called "Pavilians"), the city has recovered from the quake quickly with the help of a statewide tax increase, and as 1993 approaches the city is almost entirely recovered.

Practical Information

Visitors Information: Santa Cruz Conference and Visitor's Council, 701 Front St. (425-1234 or 800-833-3494). Extremely helpful staff. Publishes an excellent *Visitors Guide* and *Accommodations Guide.*

Parks and Recreation Department: 429-3663. Call for directions to the city's many parks. Open Mon.-Fri. 9am-6pm.

Santa Cruz Travel: 714 Soquel Ave. (426-4900). Assistance with connections at the airport in San Jose. Open Mon.-Fri. 9am-5pm, Sat. 9am-1pm.

Greyhound/Peerless Stages: 425 Front St. (423-1800). To San Francisco (3 per day, $10). To L.A. via Salinas (3 per day, $48); or via San Jose (1 per day, $48). Open Mon.-Fri. 7:30am-8pm. Call for weekend hours.

Santa Cruz Metropolitan District Transit (SCMDT): 920 Pacific Ave. (425-8600 or 688-8600), at the Metro Center in the middle of the Pacific Garden Mall. Pick up a free copy of *Headways* for route info. A free shuttle from Metro Center to the beach runs on weekends from Memorial Day to Labor Day. Open Mon.-Fri. 8am-5pm.

Taxi: Yellow Cab, 224 Walnut Ave. (423-1234). 24 hr.

Public Library: 224 Church St. (429-3526). Open Mon.-Thurs. 9am-9pm, Fri.-Sat. 9am-5pm.

Lesbian and Gay Community Center: 1332 Commerce Lane, 95060 (425-5422). The *Lavender Reader* is the excellent quarterly journal of the county's gay and lesbian community.

Women's Crisis Line: 429-1478. 24 hr.

Weather: 415-364-7974. A long-distance call (70¢).

Suicide Prevention: 458-5300.

Hospital: Santa Cruz Dominican: 1555 Soquel Dr. (462-7700 or Telmed 462-7736). Take bus #71 on Soquel Ave. from the Metro Center. 24 hr.

Women's Health Clinic: 250 Locust St. (427-3500). Referrals to doctors. Approximate fee for initial visit $40. Open Mon. and Thurs. 9am-3:30pm, Tues. noon-7pm.

Laundromat: Ultramat, 501 Laurel (426-9274). Wash $1, dry 25¢ for 10 min., soap 25¢, and since this is Santa Cruz, espresso 90¢, cappuccino $1.25, and gourmet ice cream bars $2. Open daily 7:30am-midnight. Last load 10:30pm.

Bike Rental: Surf City Rentals, 46 Front St. (423-9050). $6 per hour, $18 per half day. Open daily 9am-6pm.

Police: 809 Center St. (non-emergency 429-3714). Helpful, friendly, and tolerant. Spanish spoken. 24 hr.

Post Office: 850 Front St. (426-5200). Open Mon.-Fri. 9am-5pm. General Delivery ZIP Code: 95060. Lobby hours Mon.-Fri. 5am-7pm, Sat. 5am-6pm, Sun. 8am-4pm.

Area Code: 408.

A number of great **free magazines** are published in Santa Cruz. The weeklies *Good Times* and UCSC's *City on a Hill* are particularly informative. Pick them up at visitors centers or area stores. The monthly *Santa Cruz Magazine* is a convenient source of arts listings. The Santa Cruz Parks and Recreation Department publishes a free *Summer Activity Guide* useful for long-range planning. You can get it by mail or by picking one up from one of the visitors centers (see above for phone number).

Orientation

Santa Cruz is about one hour south of San Francisco on the northern lip of Monterey Bay. Take U.S. 101 or Rte. 1 from San Francisco. Many hitchhikers station themselves at the far end of Mission St. past the Safeway for Rte. 1 north to San Francisco. On Rte. 17 to San Jose many stand at the end of Ocean St., by the freeway entrance.

The Santa Cruz beach and its boardwalk run roughly east-west, with Monterey Bay to the south. The narrow San Lorenzo River runs mainly north-south, bisecting the city and infesting it with mosquitoes. It's hard to find a single true north-south or east-west street in the city (perhaps the Mystery Spot (see below) threw off the surveyors' compasses), but Chestnut, Front, and Ocean St. run roughly parallel with the river while Laurel-Broadway, Lincoln-Soquel, and Water cross it. Pacific Ave. and its mall lie to the west of Front St.

The gorgeous **University of California at Santa Cruz (UCSC)** is about 5 mi. up Bay St., in the redwood-covered foothills of the Santa Cruz Mountains (see Sights). The campus is accessible by public bus, auto, and bicycle. From the Metro Center, bus #1 leaves every 15 to 30 minutes (Mon.-Fri. 6:30am-12:45am, Sat.-Sun. 7:30am-12:45am), and #41 leaves 4 times per day.

Downtown parking is easy at one of the ubiquitous 12-hour meters. Do not be discouraged by a seeming dearth of beachfront parking or swayed by rip-off artists attempting to flag you into $5 all-day parking lots. The streets just behind the row of beach motels are a mere two minutes from the action and relatively empty.

Those using the Santa Cruz transit system should obtain a free copy of *Headways,* which contains schedules and helpful suggestions. The entire municipal system is directed from the Metro Center in the middle of the Pacific Mall. The Metro Center marks and posts all bus routes with admirable clarity. Bus fare is $1 (no bills accepted), but day passes obtained at the Metro Center are an economical $2 (those over 61 45¢, day pass 90¢; children under 6 free).

Go Skate, 601 Beach St. (425-8578), rents roller skates and boogie boards (both $3 per hr., $10 per day), and wetsuits and surfboards (both $5 per hr., $10 per day). (Open daily 10am-7pm.)

Accommodations

Like many a beach town, Santa Cruz gets crowded during the summer and on weekends and doubly crowded on summer weekends. At these times, room rates skyrocket and availability plummets. Sleeping on the city beaches is prohibited and risks hefty vagrancy fines.

Midweek, motels may be willing to bargain, but they are still going to cost you.

Santa Cruz Hostel Society (AYH), 511 Broadway (423-8304). AYH/IYHF members only; must arrive by foot, bike, or public transportation. From bus depot turn left on Laurel, veer left over the bridge, and you're on Broadway. Well-situated, a 10-min. walk from beach and mall. Small (16 beds) and relaxed. 3-day max. stays. Lockout 9am-5pm. $12 per night. Reservations important during summer: send ½ of fee to P.O. Box 1241, Santa Cruz, CA 95061.

American Country Inn, 645 7th (476-6424), 5 blocks from the beach just north of Eaton St. Neither an inn nor in the country, but it *is* American and a .333 batting average will keep you in the big leagues any day. A small, pleasant hotel off the main drag. Only 1 bed per room; bathrooms are clean and spacious. Rooms $25, with bath $35. Weekends: $55, with bath $65. Weekly: $150, with bath $170. The small RV camp in back has full hookups. Sites $18 or $95 per week. Reservations accepted with deposit.

UC Santa Cruz Summer Housing, on the university campus (459-2611). Wholesome but not luxurious, similar to college dining-hall food. Singles $45, with board $62; doubles $36 per person, with board $52. Open June 22-Aug. 31.

The Best Inn, 370 Ocean St. (458-9220), at Broadway, a 10-min. walk north of the Boardwalk. Cross bridge east from Boardwalk, take Edge Cliff Dr. north until it intersects Ocean St., and take Ocean north. A touch more tasteful than the average budget motel. Telephone, A/C, color TV, and pretty quilts. Coin-operated laundry room. Budget rooms (1 double bed) are $20 Sept. 10-June 9, $30 June 10-Aug. 1, and $40 Aug. 2-Sept. 10; with $10 added on Fri. and Sat. nights and $5 added if two people are staying there. It's another $500 to hire an accountant to figure out the complex room rates for you. No reservations are accepted; show up between 11am and 2pm to maximize your chances of finding a vacancy.

Magic Carpet, 130 W. Cliff Dr. (423-7737). Very close to the beach. Prices vary on the cheaper rooms without ocean views and are roughly $40-65. No reservations for these rooms so show up around 11-11:30am.

Lanai Lodge, 550 Second St. (426-3626). Attractive rooms with pool, plush carpets, and HBO go as low as $25 in the winter. The price is around $55 in the summer, but management is not too proud to haggle. Heated swimming pool.

Camping

Reservations for all state campgrounds can be made through MISTIX at 800-444-7275. Two weeks is generally sufficient advance notice, except for holidays.

New Brighton State Beach (688-3241), 4 mi. south of Santa Cruz off Rte. 1. Take SCMDT bus #54 Aptos. Fall asleep to the murmur of the breakers in one of 112 campsites on a high bluff overlooking the beach. Showers get crowded 7-9am. 1-week max. stay. No hookups. Check-out noon. Sites $16 in summer, $14 in winter. Reservations highly recommended.

Sunset State Beach, (688-3241). South of Santa Cruz on Rte. 1 to Mar Monte exit. Take San Andreas Rd. to Sunset Beach Rd., or take SCMDT bus #54B. 90 campsites near the beach. Not as nice as New Brighton, but far superior to RV-choked **Seacliff State Beach.** Sites $16, in winter $14.

Henry Cowell Redwoods State Park (335-9145) off Rte. 9, 3 mi. south of Felton. Take Graham Hill Rd. or SCMDT bus #34, 35, or 30. 113 campsites in summer, 35 in winter. Hot showers and restaurants. 1-week max. stay. Sites $16.

Big Basin Redwoods State Park (338-6132) north of Boulder Creek. Take Rte. 9 north to Rte. 236 north. On Sat.-Sun. there is direct service from downtown, as bus #35 runs to Big

Basin (only Sat. and Sun. 6pm). A spectacular park with the best camping south of Point Reyes and north of Big Sur. Mountain air, dark red trees. 188 campsites with showers, 36 recently added tent cabins. Take the 2-day backpacking Skyline-to-the-Sea trail if time permits. Mountain bikes for rent (338-7313) and horseback tours available. 15-day max. stay. Sites $10, tent cabins $29. Backpackers $2 at special backcountry campsites. Parking $4 per night. Reservations recommended May.-Oct. Open year-round.

Manresa Uplands State Beach Park (761-1795), 12 mi. south of Santa Cruz. Take Rte. 1 and exit Larkin Valley. Veer right and follow San Andreas Rd. for 4 mi. then turn right on Sand Dollar. Not accessed by bus. 64 campsites, tents only. $16 in summer, $14 in winter.

Food

For a city its size, Santa Cruz sports an astounding number of restaurants, many of which are in budget range. Hence, partake not of the corn dogs, burgers, and tacos served at gastronomically futile fast-food stands, but betake thyself to the places that serve lovingly hand-rolled pita bread, sprouts, tofu, and cauliflower sandwiches with grated carrots sprinkled meticulously on top. The **Food Pavilion,** at Lincoln and Cedar, offers a number of quick, tasty, mall-type lunch choices (open daily 8am-9pm).

India Joze, 1001 Center St. (427-3554). A schizoid restaurant serving three different cuisines a week and offering up to five different meals in a day. Middle Eastern, Indian, and Asian dishes are offered every day. Monterey Bay snapper starts at $8.50, while vegetarian options, such as the delicious *kota kari* (on the Indian menu) are less expensive, around $7.75. Open Sun.-Fri. 8am-2:30pm, 5:30-9:30pm, dessert 9:30-10:30pm; Sat. brunch 10am-2:30pm, dinner 5:30pm-10pm. Coffee is available in the hours between lunch and dinner each day.

Zachary's, 819 Pacific Ave. (427-0646). Bustling and happy, with hot coffee. In the morning locals crowd in for Breakfast #1: 2 eggs any style, cottage-fried potatoes, and toast ($3.50). Homemade cream-cheese scones ($1.50) and jalapeño cornbread ($1.50). Open Tues.-Sun. 7am-2:30pm. Come before 9am to avoid long waits.

The Crêpe Place, 1134 Soquel (429-6994), just north of the Water St. intersection. A casual but classy restaurant putting Santa Cruz's former courthouse to good use. Feast on hearty dinner *crepes* or enjoy the lighter fruit-filled confections ($6.50-8). Try "The Whole Thing": chocolate, bananas, walnuts, and ice cream in a crepe ($3.50). Open Mon.-Thurs. 11am-midnight, Fri. 11am-1am, Sat. 9am-1am, Sun. 9am-midnight.

The Bagelry, 320 Cedar St. (429-8049), between Maple St. and Birch Lane. Delicious low-priced bagels in a factory that manages to be personal. The Luna ($1.70) includes pesto, ricotta, and almond filling; good old-fashioned bagel and butter 80¢. Also soups and yogurts. Open Mon.-Fri. 6:30am-5:30pm, Sat. 7:30am-5:30pm, Sun. 7:30am-3pm. Also at 1636 Seabright Ave. (425-8550), off Soquel Ave., and at 4763 Soquel Dr. (462-9888), across from the post office.

Café Pergolesi, 418A Cedar St. (426-1775), at Elm St. The spacious porch and wide selection of coffees, teas, and cocoas (about $2) make this a local favorite. Open Mon.-Thurs. 7:30am-midnight, Fri. 7:30am-1am, Sat. 8am-1am, Sun. 8am-midnight.

Zoccoli's Delicatessen, 1334 Pacific Ave. (423-1711). Great food, great prices. Lunch special of lasagna, salad, garlic bread, salami and cheese slices, and an Italian cookie for $4.44. Italian sandwiches to go for $2. Open Mon.-Sat. 9am-5:30pm.

Saturn Café, 1230 Mission St. (429-8505). Many blocks from downtown, but you're rewarded with vegetarian meals at their Santa Cruz best (generally under $4). Cracked wheat is positively right-wing around here. Women's music Wed. 5:30-8:30pm. Open Mon.-Fri. 11:30am-12:30am, Sat.-Sun. noon-12:30am.

The Whole Earth, Redwood Tower Building, UCSC (426-8255). Good vegetarian food by any standard, but simply amazing for a university food service ($4 buys a full meal and a view of the stunning redwoods). Casual atmosphere. Open during the term Mon.-Thurs. 7:30am-8pm, Fri. 7:30am-8pm, Sat.-Sun. 9am-6pm; in summer Mon.-Fri. 7:30am-4pm.

Sights and Activities

The **Boardwalk,** a 3-block arcade of ice cream, caramel apples, games, rides, and taco joints (but no real boards), dominates the Santa Cruz beach area. Video games and pinball, shooting galleries and Bing-o-Reno complement miniature golf and amusement-park rides. The classiest rides are two old veterans, both national historic landmarks: the **Giant Dipper** and the **Looff Carousel.** The 1929 Giant Dipper roller coaster is one of the largest remaining wooden coasters in the country and miraculously survived numerous quakes undamaged. A 3-minute ride is $2.25. The 1911 Looff Carousel, also in good condition, is accompanied by an 1894 organ ($1.35). The more modern rides are mostly just variations on these classics, only you go round and round a good deal faster. The miniature golf course is indoors, with weird mirrors that cut you in half and distend your feet ($6 per person). From the second week in July through the end of August, Monday and Tuesday are "1907 Nights"—Boardwalk rides, soft drinks, hot dogs, cotton candy, and red candied apples are all 45¢. (Tickets for unlimited rides $16. Other discounts available. Boardwalk open Memorial Day-Labor Day daily; weekends and some holidays the rest of the year. Call 426-7433 for hours.)

The **Santa Cruz Beach** itself is broad and sandy, and generally packed with high school students from San Jose during summer weekends. If you're seeking solitude, try the banks of the San Lorenzo River immediately east of the boardwalk. Nude sunbathers should head for the **Red White and Blue Beach.** Take Rte. 1 north to just south of Davenport and look for the line of cars to your right. Women should not venture here unaccompanied. ($5 per car.) If you don't feel like paying for the privilege of an all-over tan, try the **Bonny Doon Beach,** at Bonny Doon Rd. off Rte. 1, 11 mi. north of Santa Cruz. This surfer favorite is free and somewhat untamed. Other beaches are listed in the Santa Cruz *Visitor's Guide* pamphlet.

The Boardwalk is flanked on both sides by quieter areas with pleasant museums. To the east lies the **Santa Cruz City Museum,** 1305 E. Cliff Dr. (429-3773), by Pilkington Ave. Scheduled to undergo expansion in the next few years, this small natural history museum includes exhibits on local geography, geology, and biology. As a break from gawking at volleyballers at the beach, you can gawk at a 10,000-year-old Columbian Mammoth tooth found in nearby Watsonville, or climb on the realistic whale sculpture outside. (Open Tues.-Sat. 10am-5pm, Sun. noon-5pm. Admission $1.50.)

A pleasant 10-minute walk along the beach toward the southwest will take you to two wacky Santa Cruz museums, both worth short visits. The first is the **Shroud of Turin Museum,** 544 West Cliff Dr. (423-7658), at St. Joseph's shrine. Science and faith clash over the issue of whether this famous piece of linen with the image of a man was used to bury Jesus. While the curators, like the Catholic church, insist that one's faith should not depend on the shroud's authenticity, they insist that the cloth is genuine and cast doubt on the recent carbon-H tests that suggested it was a fabrication. On display at the museum are a life-size photograph of the shroud, images of Jesus deduced manually and electronically from the shroud, and a 15-minute video about a 1978 series of tests, narrated by none other than Geraldo Rivera. (Open Sat.-Sun. noon-5pm. Call ahead to visit during the week.)

Just south of this museum lies Lighthouse Point, home to the **Santa Cruz Surfing Museum** (429-3429). Opened in 1986, the museum was the first of its kind in the world. The main room of the lighthouse displays vintage wooden boards, early wetsuits, and surfing videos, while the tower contains the ashes of Mark Abbott, a local surfer who drowned in 1965 and to whom the museum is dedicated. (Open daily 12-5pm; in winter Sat.-Sun. Donation $1.) The stretch of Pacific along the eastern side of the point is famous **Steamer Lane,** a hot spot for local surfers since Duke Nakahuraka of Hawaii initiated California's first surfing aristocracy here 100 years ago.

Misión de Exaltación de la Santa Cruz, 126 High St. (Turn north onto Emmet St. off Mission St.), was, along with the Carmel mission, one of the first Christian outposts in California. Consecrated in 1791 by Father Fermín Casuen, the mission grew and prospered until the mid-19th century. In 1857, following secularization of the mission, an earthquake severely damaged the already decaying buildings (perhaps a sign from God?). In the late 1920s, however, locals moved to restore the mission, culminating in the reconstruction of the original church. The new building was dedicated in 1931, and a park now marks the site of the original buildings. Although unsensational, the restored church at least allows some contemplative quiet in the midst of Santa Cruz's three-ring circus. (Open daily 9am-5pm. Donation requested.)

The 2000-acre **University of California at Santa Cruz (UCSC)** campus tunes in and turns on 5 mi. northwest of downtown. Take bus #1 or ride your bike along the scenic paths. Then-governor Ronald Reagan's plan to make UCSC a "riot-proof campus" (i.e., without a central point where radicals could inflame a crowd) when it was built in the late 60s, resulted instead in a stunning, sprawling campus. University buildings appear intermittently amid spectacular rolling hills and redwood groves. The school itself is more Berkeley than Berkeley: extracurricular leftist politics supplement a curriculum offering such unique programs as "The History of Consciousness." The level of academic intensity is rising, however; UCSC used to be the "safety school" of the UC system, but within the last five years has begun turning away qualified applicants. Guided tours start from the **Visitors Center** at the base of campus. If you drive on weekdays, make sure you have a parking permit. Fire trails behind the campus are perfect for day hikes, but don't go alone. (Parking permits and maps available at the police station, 429-2231.) The UCSC Arboretum is one of the finest in the state and is open daily from 9am-5pm (free).

Directly south of UCSC is the **Natural Bridges State Beach** (423-4609), at the end of W. Cliff Drive. While its lone natural bridge has collapsed, the park nevertheless offers a beach, tidepools, and tours twice a day during Monarch butterfly season from October to March. October 9th is "Welcome Back Monarch Day," but the best time to go may actually be in November or December, when thousands of the pesky lepidoptera swarm along the beach. (Open daily 8am-sunset. Parking $3 per day.)

You can rent ocean-going kayaks at the Santa Cruz Wharf ($10 first hour; $8 for each additional hour on weekdays; weekends $2 per hour; open daily 11am-7pm).

Entertainment

Santa Cruz thinks of itself as a high-class operation, and most bars frown on backpacks and sleeping bags. Carding at local bars is stringent. The restored ballroom at the Boardwalk makes a lovely spot for a drink in the evening, and the Boardwalk bandstand offers free Friday night concerts. Local weeklies list other music shows. For movie-lovers there's the free *Santa Cruz Cinema Times,* published bimonthly and available from area stores.

Kuumbwa Jazz Center, 320-322 E. Cedar St. (427-2227). Great jazz, renowned throughout the region. Under 21s are welcome in this simple, enthusiastic setting. The big names play here on Monday; Friday is the locals' turn. Rarely sold out, tickets range from about $5 on Fri. to $10-13.50 on Mon. Most shows at 8pm.

Louden Nelson Community Center, 301 Center St. (429-3504), at Laurel St. Another home for local repertory groups and dance classes. Offerings include poetry readings and summer concerts.

Sash Mill Cinema, 303 Portero St. (427-1711). Classic double features which change every day or two. Always something interesting playing. Admission $4.50, students $3.75.

The Catalyst, 1011 Pacific Garden Mall (423-1336). This 700-seat concert hall draws second-string national acts and college favorites like Guadalcanal Diary and Ruben Blades, along with local bands. A broad, boisterous, and beachy bar. Lots of brightly colored sugar drinks. Serves pizza ($1.60) and sandwiches ($4.25). Usually no cover for local bands; otherwise up to $15. Shows at 9:15pm. Open daily 9am-2am.

Blue Lagoon, 923 Pacific Ave. (423-7117). A relaxed gay bar. A giant aquarium in the back of the room contributes a pleasantly flickering light. Taped music, videos, dancing. No cover. Drinks about $1.50. Open daily 4pm-2am.

Crow's Nest, 2218 E. Cliff Dr., Santa Cruz Yacht Club (476-4560). Right by the water. Live rock music. Open nightly (times and cover vary).

Front St. Pub, 516 Front St. Hip brewery. Three glass sampler of excellent beer $2.50. Bar food runs about $5. Open Sun.-Thurs. 11am-10:30pm, weekends 11am-12:30am.

Kiva House, 702 Webster St. (729-1142). Community use hot tubs and saunas; clothing optional. Admission $8. Open Sun.-Thurs. noon-11pm; Fri.-Sat. noon-midnight.

Seasonal Events

January to April is **whale-watching season.** Boats depart for the Santa Cruz Municipal Wharf. Call 425-1234 for information. Between October and March, the spectacular monarch butterflies make Santa Cruz their home (see Sights).

The **Cabrillo Music Festival** at Cabrillo College, 6500 Soquel Dr., Aptos (476-9053 for a subscription, 479-6331 for individual tickets), brings contemporary/classical music to the Central Coast. Performances include premieres of works by the year's composer-in-residence, as well as an eclectic classical selection from Beethoven to the Kronos Quartet. It's hard to get tickets, so reserve well before the mid-August date. (Tickets $15-23.50.) In October, the **Shout for Sprouts** festival along the Boardwalk honors the oft-neglected brussels sprout, with sprout ice cream, sprout-chip cookies, etc. The same month also brings the annual *Slug Fest* to celebrate UCSC's underappreciated mascot. Not only do they race slugs, they also do some of the same things they did with the sprouts (think of them as jumbo, shell-less *escargot*).

Other seasonal events of note include: the **Longboard International** surfing tournament (425-8943) in late May; the **Mr./Ms. Santa Cruz Bodybuilding Classic** (335-7946), in the civic auditorium, also in late May; the **Roaring Camp Civil War Encampment** (335-4484), at the Roaring Camp and Big Trees Narrow Gauge Railroad, Memorial Day weekend; **Jose Cuervo Professional Volleyball** on the Main Beach in late August (429-3665); the **Santa Cruz County Fair** (724-5671), at the fairgrounds Sept. 13-18; and the **Capitola Art & Wine Festival** also in mid-September (688-7377).

National Nude Weekend is celebrated in mid-July every year at the Lupin Naturist Club in the Santa Cruz Mountains. Enjoy bands (playing in the buff) or come paint the posing models. Free admission, but reservations are required (353-2250).

Near Santa Cruz

Santa Cruz is surrounded by gently sloping hills that make hiking a delight; the paths are only mildly strenuous and the scenery is magnificent. To the north, **Big Basin Redwoods State Park** offers a skyline-to-the-sea trail that even novices should be able to handle in about two days (see Camping). Farther to the south, the gorgeous **Henry Cowell Redwoods State Park** has trails suitable for daytrips in the redwoods (see Camping). Rumor has it that the mysterious ghost of Chris Cowell wanders the park nights, mumbling computer codes and assisting helpless AEs with printer problems. Beware of the highly touted **Felton Covered Bridge,** located about a ½-hour north of Santa Cruz. Although it may be the "tallest covered bridge of its kind in the United States," it's ramshackle, not particularly picturesque, and certainly not worth going out of your way to see.

The **Roaring Camp and Big Trees Narrow Gauge Railroad,** Graham Rd., Felton (335-4400), runs an old steam-powered passenger train from Felton through the redwoods to Bear Mountain. (Round-trip fare $13, ages 3-17 $9, under 3 free.) To reach Felton take scenic Rte. 9, which passes through Henry Cowell Redwoods State Park. In Felton take Graham Hill Rd. southeast, and turn south for Roaring Camp as indicated by road signs.

The **Mystery Spot** (423-8897), 3 mi. northeast of Santa Cruz at Branciforte Dr., is just another one of those tourist attractions where gravity, perspective, and velocity seemingly run wild. While it's clear from compasses that the area is a source of magnetic disturbances, the true interest of the Mystery Spot lies in its owners' unintentionally hilarious efforts to augment the spectacle through optical illusions.

Would you believe that trees respond to magnetism? (Open daily 9:30am-4:30pm. Admission $3, under 12 $1.50.)

Bonny Doon Vineyards, 2 Pine Flat Rd. (425-3625), west of Felton, deserves notice if only for the idiosyncratic texts on its bottle labels. To arrange a tour write to P.O. Box 8381, Santa Cruz 95061. (Open Wed.-Mon. noon-5pm; in winter Fri.-Mon. noon-5pm.) **Roudon-Smith Vineyards,** 2364 Bean Creek Rd. (438-1244), runs a tasting room on 2571 Main St., Soquel (Wed.-Sun., noon-6pm), by appointment only.

San Francisco

Occupying only 47 square miles at one end of an enormous urban horseshoe, San Francisco proper appears tiny and isolated. Yet there is a great city of nearly ¾ million people on this little plot of land, and its magical name cannot help but conjure some image—of gold, cable cars, LSD, or gay liberation—in the mind of anyone familiar with America. Its many facets have inspired hope, scorn, and immigration for a century and a half.

Originally inhabited by the peaceful Miwok nation, the Bay Area remained quiet for a long time. In 1776, Father Junípero Serra arrived and planted another in his long string of missions, naming it after *San Francisco de Asis,* (St. Francis of Assisi). But the mission and the village of Yerba Buena that sprang up around it were hardly worth fighting over; Mexico took it from Spain and America from Mexico without much hassle. It just so happened that in 1848, two years after the United States took possession, gold was discovered in them thar hills up the Sacramento river delta from San Francisco. San Francisco's 800 or so residents at the time looked around and realized that not only did they live just a short river trip from the gold fields, but that they were also sitting on one of the greatest natural ports in the world. That year 10,000 people passed through San Francisco to get to the gold and a city was born.

The city's growth was neither smooth nor pretty, and it soon had its share of murders, fires, and earthquakes. But these misfortunes were nothing compared to the 8.3 trembler that rocked the city on April 18, 1906 leaving San Francisco to three days of fire and looting. Unfazed, residents rebuilt their city within three years, and the 1915 Panama Exhibition showed the world that all was well. The 1936 and '37 openings of the Golden Gate and Bay Bridges ended the city's long isolation from the rest of the Bay Area, and San Francisco took full advantage of the economic boom brought about by World War II.

Always responsive to the unorthodox, the city served as home to the Beat Generation in the 1950s; the 60s saw Haight-Ashbury become the hippie capital of the cosmos; and in the 70s, the gay population emerged as one of the most powerful and visible groups in the city. This community has been hit hard by the continuing AIDS epidemic, but it has fought back creatively and convincingly, doing what it can to comfort victims while increasing public awareness of the disease to the point where condoms are boldly advertised on bus shelters and radio spots.

San Francisco's latest trial came on October 17, 1989, when the biggest quake since 1906 killed 62 people, knocked out the Bay Bridge, and even interrupted the World Series game between the San Francisco Giants and the Oakland A's. After a few days of asking, "Why do I live in California?" Bay residents remembered the answers and started again. The hardest-hit sections of the city, including the Marina District, have since been almost completely rebuilt.

Though referred to by locals as "The City," San Francisco remains very much a confederation of neighborhoods; the average San Franciscan thinks in terms of the Mission District, Chinatown, and Nob Hill. Subdivisions follow no discernible logic. A few blocks will take you from ritzy Pacific Heights to the impoverished Western Addition; the crime-ridden Tenderloin adjoins the steel-and-glass boxes

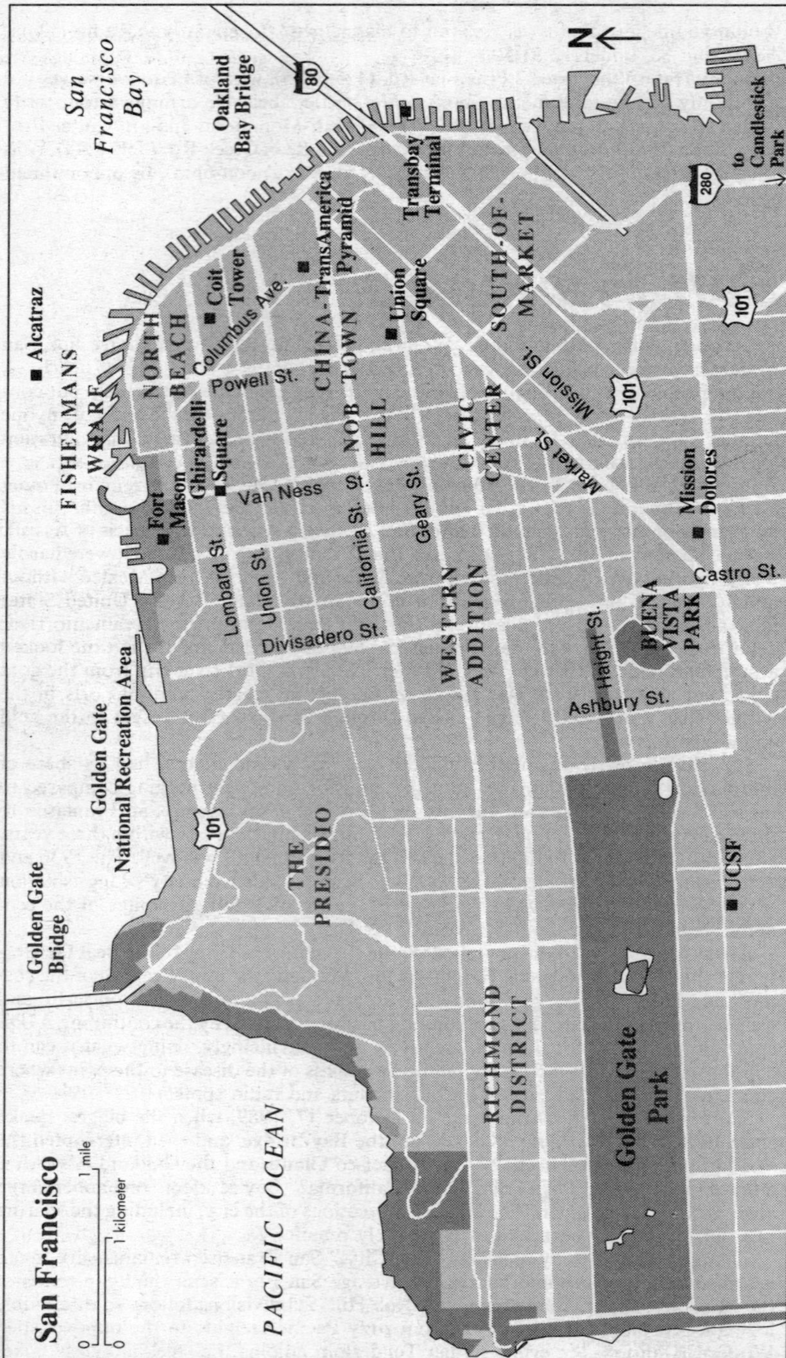
San Francisco
0 1 mile
0 1 kilometer
N
PACIFIC OCEAN
Golden Gate Bridge
Golden Gate National Recreation Area
San Francisco Bay
Oakland Bay Bridge
80
Alcatraz
FISHERMANS WHARF
Fort Mason
Ghirardelli Square
NORTH BEACH
Coit Tower
Columbus Ave.
CHINA-TOWN
TransAmerica Pyramid
Transbay Terminal
Union Square
SOUTH-OF-MARKET
NOB HILL
CIVIC CENTER
Powell St.
Van Ness St.
Lombard St.
Union St.
California St.
Geary St.
Divisadero St.
Mission St.
Market St.
101
280
to Candlestick Park
WESTERN ADDITION
THE PRESIDIO
RICHMOND DISTRICT
Golden Gate Park
UCSF
Haight St.
Ashbury St.
BUENA VISTA PARK
Castro St.
Mission Dolores

of the Financial District. Despite its seeming disorder, such tightly packed diversity lends the city a cosmopolitanism unknown outside of world capitals. While Los Angeles chokes on smog and its own ego, the haze and fog of the Bay Area delicately shade this richly cluttered and curious city.

Practical Information

Visitors Information: Visitor Information Center, Hallidie Plaza (391-2000), Market at Powell St., beneath street level in Benjamin Swig Pavillion. A detailed map and a few brochures on display. Extensive collection of informational materials behind the counter, but you must ask for specific ones, such as the free street map, an events calendar, and the very helpful *San Francisco* book, which is published quarterly and chock full of useful information and maps. Staff speaks French, German, Italian, Japanese, and Spanish. Open Mon.-Fri. 9am-5:30pm, Sat. 9am-3pm, Sun. 10am-2pm. 24-hr. event and information recordings in English (391-2001), French (391-2003), German (391-2004), Japanese (391-2101), and Spanish (391-2122).

Consulates: Australian, 1 Bush St. on the 7th floor (362-6160).Open Mon.-Fri. 8:30am-4:50pm. In an emergency call 330-7347. **British,** 1 Sansom St. at the corner of Sutter and Sansom off Market (981-3030). Open Mon.-Fri 9am-1pm 2-4pm. Emergency line 561-9346. **French,** 540 Bush St. (397-4330), Emergency line 425-6172. **German,** 1960 Jackson St. (775-1061), Emergency line 885-3494 from 9am-11pm. **New Zealand Travel Council,** 550 Irving St. (665-5503).

Transit Information: See below under Getting There and Getting Around.

Center for International Educational Exchange (CIEE): 312 Sutter St. (421-3473), between Stockton St. and Grant Ave., downtown. Student-flight, discount, and lodgings information. ISIC cards $15. Open Mon.-Tues., Wed. 10am-5pm, Thurs.-Fri. 9am-5pm.

Redwood Empire Association: 785 Market St, (543-8334), at 4th St. by Union Sq, 15th floor. Maps and brochures on the area from San Francisco to Oregon. Open Mon.-Fri. 9am-5pm. **Sierra Club Store,** 730 Polk St. (923-5600), just north of the Civic Center. Tremendous resource for those planning wilderness trips. Able to answer a whole range of queries from snow conditions to routes to equipment. They prefer and encourage visitors to join the club. Open Mon.-Sat. 10am-5:30pm. (See also Bookstore listing.) **Wine Institute,** 425 Market St. (512-0151), 1½ suite 1000 at Fremont. Open Mon.-Fri. 9am-5pm.

Passport and Visa Office: 525 Market St., #200 (744-4444), at 1st St., lobby level. If calling, be sure to let the phone ring many times. Open Mon.-Fri. 8am-4pm.

Public Library: Civic Center Library Building (557-4400), between Larkin and McAllister. Open Mon., Wed.-Thurs., Sat. 10am-6pm, Tues. noon-9pm, Fri. noon-6pm, Sun. 1-5pm.

Jewish Community Information and Referral: 777-4545. All sorts of information from community events to singles advice. Open Mon.-Fri. 9:30am-1:30pm.

Booker T. Washington Community Center: 800 Presidio (921-4757), at Sutter St. Sports, scouting, educational and recreational programs provided.

Chinese Culture Center: 750 Kearny St., 3rd floor of Holiday Inn at Washington St.(986-1822). Up-to-the-minute information on events in Chinatown and the Chinese community. The Center offers a variety of educational and cultural programs ranging from lectures, workshops, and classes to art exhibits, performances, films, and festivals. The center also offers a Chinese Heritage Walk ($12, under 18 $2) and a Chinese Culinary Walk ($12, under 12 $10) that finishes with a *dim sum* luncheon. Call for reservations.

San Francisco Ticket Box Office Service (STBS): 251 Stockton St. (433-7827), near Post St. Tickets to concerts, clubs, and sports events. Half-price tickets on day of show. Cash only. Open Tues.-Thurs. noon-7:30pm, Fri.-Sat. noon-8pm. Also sells BASS tickets to sports events, concerts, and clubs. **Concert Information:** KMEL-FM, 397-5635.

Dial-A-Quake: 642-2160. The University of California at Berkeley Seismographical Research Center's 24-hr. report on rumblings in the area and around the globe. Find out if that was an earthquake or just a big truck driving by.

Road Conditions: 557-3755. 24-hour driving information for the state.

Free Showers: Aquatic Park, Polk St. (556-2904), adjacent to Ghirardelli Sq. Open daily 10am-5:30pm, in winter 10am-5pm.

Swimming Pools: North Beach Pool, Lombard at Mason St. (274-0200); **Hamilton Pool,** Geary Blvd. at Steiner St. (292-2001). **Coffman Pool,** 26th at Harrison St. (337-4702). Schedules vary with season so call to check hours. Admission $2.50, children 2-17 yr. 25¢. The Dolphin Club, 502 Jefferson, (441-9329) at Hyde St. Ocean swimming facilities, showers, sauna, and gym. $6.50 for the day. Unusual hours depending on bay conditions, so call ahead.

24-Hour Emergency Hotlines: Poison Control, 476-6600. **Drug Line,** 752-3400. **Suicide Prevention,** 221-1423. **Rape Crisis Center,** 647-7273. Operated by San Francisco Women Against Rape. **La Casa de las Madres,** 777-2860. Shelter for battered women; not a place to crash. **Helpline,** 772-HELP(4357). **Runaway Hotline,** 800-843-5200. Call home free, no questions asked.

Gay Switchboard and Counseling Services: 2712 Telegraph Ave. in Berkeley, 841-6224. Information on gay community events, local clubs, etc., as well as counseling. *Extremely* helpful staff. Open Mon.-Fri. 10am-10pm, Sat. noon-4pm, Sun. 6-9pm.

Health Care: Haight-Ashbury Switchboard, 431-1714. Referrals for housing, rides, and legal and medical help. Call for recording. **Haight-Ashbury Free Clinic,** 558 Clayton St. (431-1714; open Mon.-Thurs. 1-4:30pm, 6-8:30pm, Fri. 1-4:30pm. Open for appointments only). Call before coming in. Drug detox program, 621-2014. **University of California Dental Clinic,** University of California at San Francisco Medical Center, 707 Parnassus (476-1891; 476-5814 for emergencies). Complete dental exam $10. By appointment only. Open Mon.-Fri. 8am-5pm. **Medical and Dental Referral Service,** 673-3189. Program of Bay Area Physicians for Human Rights. Not necessarily inexpensive, so inquire carefully about prices. **Health Center,** 1490 Mason St. (558-2545), near Broadway. Free contraceptives and counseling in English and Chinese about birth control and sexually transmitted diseases. By appointment only (open Mon.-Fri. 8am-noon). In an emergency, call 558-2544. **Planned Parenthood,** 441-5454. **Alcoholics Anonymous,** 1046 Irving St. (24 hr. hotline 661-1828). Over 500 AA meetings in S.F. per week. Call for times and places.

AIDS Hotline: 863-AIDS (863-2437). English and Spanish spoken by operators. Referrals.

San Francisco General Hospital: 1001 Portrero Ave. (821-8200), at 22nd St. 24-hr. emergency room with walk-in service.

Telex and Telegrams: Western Union, 210 3rd St. (495-7301), at Howard. Open Mon.-Sat. 8am-10pm, Sun. 8am-6pm. Telegrams can be arranged by phone: call 800-227-5899. 24 hr.

Post Office: Main office at 7th and Mission St. (621-6838), opposite Greyhound. Open Mon.-Fri. 9am-5pm, Sat. 9am-1:30pm. General Delivery ZIP Code: 94101. **Rincon Annex,** 99 Mission St. Open Mon.-Fri. 7am-6pm, Sat. 9am-2pm. Other branches open at least Mon.-Fri. 9am-5:30pm.

Area Code: 415.

Publications

Several free tourist magazines are available from sidewalk boxes in the heavily trafficked Fisherman's Wharf and Union Square areas. While such publications as the *San Francisco Guide* (775-2212) and the *BayCity Guide* (929-7722) seem geared more toward the affluent shopper than the budget traveler, they do have up-to-date information on galleries and clubs, plus a few coupons here and there.

Locals look up events in free, weekly newspapers, including the *San Francisco Bay Guardian* (255-3100) and the ever-present *East Bay Express* (652-4610). The *Guardian* lives by Wilbur Storey's statement that "It is a newspaper's duty to print the news and raise hell." It is crammed with reviews, some news, and a detailed weekly jazz calendar. For a more comprehensive listing of Berkeley theater and the Oakland jazz scene, try the *Express.* The "critic's choice" section, a detailed billboard with concise summaries, can't be beat. The *San Francisco Weekly* (541-0700) also has listings. For gatherings of the visual and performing arts, try the monthly *CenterVoice* (398-1854), the downtown neighborhood newspaper. The gay and lesbian paper, the *Bay Times* (626-8121), also appears monthly. While it has an entertainment section, it is mostly articles. *The Sentinel* (861-8100) offers information on events within the gay community. *Prism* (338-2311) is put out seven times a year by San Francisco State University's journalism department and has some very impressive writing and photography.

If it's service you need, consult the quarterly *Open Exchange* (526-7190), which starts with astrology lessons and ends with yoga instruction. For a comprehensive collection of classified ads, check *The San Francisco Advertiser* (863-3151). Travelers enthusiastic about leftist political agitation in Northern California should consult the bimonthly *Radiation: An Alternative Bulletin* (861-0592), put out by the environmentalist Abalone Alliance. Sports publications include the *California Bicyclist* (546-7291), a monthly chronicle of bicycle races and other events available at most bike shops, and *City Sport,* (546-6150) which lists everything from boardsailing to hang gliding to martial arts.

Sadly, the largest Bay Area daily, the *San Francisco Chronicle* (777-1111; 35¢), is proof that a sophisticated cultural center can still produce a truly mediocre newspaper. Herb Caen's weekday column in the Chronicle, however, is a San Francisco institution and not to be missed. Though insipid at times, Caen nabs the best stories in the city. The pink entertainment section of the Sunday edition ($1) is also a worthwhile resource. Especially fun is the paper's "little man" system of rating films and plays. Each review is accompanied by a drawing of a viewer in one of several states of ecstasy or apathy, as dictated by the reviewer's reaction. *The Examiner,* (777-7800), started by William Hearst (you saw *Citizen Kane,* didn't you?), has lunchtime and evening editions. The Sunday edition is put out jointly with the *Chronicle.*

If you can't find what you're looking for on a street corner, try a book or record store or call the publication itself for the nearest distribution point.

Orientation

Getting There

San Francisco, the cultural capital of Northern California and fourth largest city in the state (pop. 726,700), is 548 mi. north of San Diego, 403 mi. north of Los Angeles, 390 mi. south of the Oregon border, 6174 mi. from San Francisco, Argentina, and approximately 6900 mi. from Guangzhou, China, the region to which most Chinese-Americans trace their origins. The city proper lies at the northern tip of a peninsula that sets off San Francisco Bay from the Pacific Ocean. For transportation and orientation information on the cities that surround the bay, see San Francisco Bay Area.

By Airplane

San Francisco International Airport (SFO) (721-0800) is located on a small nub of land in San Francisco Bay about 15 mi. south of the city center on U.S. 101. The general layout is easy to comprehend: each of the three terminals (North, Central, and South) has two levels, with the lower level handling arrivals, the upper handling departures.

There are two ways to commute from SFO to the city by public transportation. First, **San Mateo County Transit,** or **samTrans** (800-660-4287), runs two buses from SFO to downtown San Francisco. The express (#7F) takes 35 minutes, but you can only bring carry-on luggage (every 30 min. 5:24am-12:52am; $1.20, over 64 60¢, under 17 75¢). Bus #7B takes longer (45 min.), but you can carry all the luggage you want (every 30 min. 4:42am-12:13am; $1.20, over 64 and under 17 60¢). An **Airporter** bus (495-8404) runs a shuttle route between all three terminals and a downtown terminal at 301 Ellis St. and major downtown hotels every 15 minutes 5:45am-10:50pm ($6, round trip $11). If Oakland is your destination, take bus #3B to Daly City (every 30 min. 6am-7pm, 27 min.) and from there catch a BART train to Oakland.

Taxi rides to downtown San Francisco from SFO cost about $25.

Lorrie's Travel and Tour (334-9000), on the upper level at the west of all three terminals provides convenient door-to-door van service to and from the airport. Reserve at least six hours in advance for service to the airport. No reservations are needed for travel from the airport. (Vans run 4:30am-11:30pm. Fare $9, ages 2-12 $6, under 2 free, seniors $8.) **Franciscus Adventures** (821-0903) operates a small bus between San Francisco and SFO ($8, $7 per person for groups of 5 or more). Call ahead to arrange a time.

By Train or Bus

The train and bus terminals are much more conveniently located than the airport. **Greyhound** (558-6789) serves the **Transbay Terminal,** 425 Mission St., (495-1551 or 495-1569) between Fremont and 1st St. downtown (open 5am-12:35am). This latter building is a regional transportation hub; buses from Golden Gate Transit (Marin County), AC Transit (East Bay), and samTrans (San Mateo County) all stop here. An information center on the second floor has maps, displays, and free phone lines for each of these systems. Downstairs, free buses shuttle to **Amtrak** (800-872-7245 or 982-8512) on 16th in Oakland where the real train station lies. (Amtrak open daily 6:45am-10:45pm.) Amtrak also has a desk at Transbay Terminal. First St. and Natoma is the pickup point for **Green Tortoise** (285-2441), the half-transportation-company-and-half-commune located at 1667 Jerrold Ave. Green Tortoise runs trips down the coast to L.A. every Fri. night ($30) and to Seattle on Mon., Wed., Fri., and Sat.($59), as well as expeditions to New York and Boston (both 14 days; $350) and Yosemite ($120) among other national parks. (Advance reservations required. Open daily 8am-8pm.) **CalTrain** (557-8661 or 800-558-8661 for voice or TDD) is a regional commuter train that runs south to Palo Alto ($3, seniors and disabled $1.50) and San Jose ($3.50, seniors and disabled $1.75), with additional bus service to Santa Cruz. The depot is at 4th and Townsend St. and is served by MUNI buses #15, 30, 32, and 42.

By Car

From the south, the city can be reached by car via U.S. 101 to I-280, via I-5 to I-580, or via Rte. 1. If approaching from the east on I-580 or I-80 go directly over the Bay Bridge into downtown. From the north, U.S. 101 leads directly into the city over the Golden Gate Bridge.

I-5 is certainly the fastest way to traverse the coast. The speed limit is 65mph and you can make it from L.A. in six hours if you hustle. Rte. 1 takes twice as long, but is one of the most beautiful roads in the country.

If you're a driver who needs a passenger or a passenger who needs a driver, call the **Berkeley Ride Board** (642-5259) for free, 24-hr. listings. The San Francisco International Hostel and San Francisco State University (469-1842, in the student union; open Mon.-Fri. 7am-10pm, Sat. 10am-4pm) also have ride boards. KALX radio (642-5259), on the Berkeley campus, broadcasts a ride list Monday through Saturday at 10am and 10pm. Call them to put your name and number on the air for free. KSAN radio (986-2825) provides a similar service.

Getting Around

> *If it pleases Providence to make a car run up and down a slit in the ground for many miles, and if for twopence-halfpenny I can ride in that car, why shall I seek the reasons for the miracle?*
>
> *—Rudyard Kipling*

The hilly city of San Francisco, surrounded by water on three sides, is an amalgam of distinct neighborhoods organized along a few central arteries. Each neighborhood is compact enough to explore comfortably on foot.

San Francisco radiates outward from its docks, on the northeast edge of the peninsula just inside the lip of the bay. Most visitors' attention still gravitates to this area, although the city now extends south and west from this point. Here, within a wedge formed by Van Ness Ave. running north-south, Market St. running northeast-southwest, and the Embarcadero (waterfront road) curving along the coast, are found many of San Francisco's shining attractions. Taking a diagonal course, Market Street disrupts the regular grid of streets and accounts for an exceptionally confusing street-numbering system. The streets aiming north from Market and west from Market and the Embarcadero are numbered beginning at those thoroughfares, although you should keep in mind that parallel streets do not bear the same block numbers.

At the top of this wedge lies **Fisherman's Wharf** and **North Beach,** a district shared by Italian-Americans, artists, and professionals. The focal point of North Beach is Telegraph Hill, topped by Coit Tower and fringed from the northwest to the southeast by Columbus Avenue. Across Columbus begin the **Nob Hill** and **Russian Hill** areas, home of the city's old money. This fan-shaped oasis is confined by Columbus along its northeast side, Van Ness along the west, and (roughly) Geary and Bush Streets on the south. Below Nob Hill and North Beach, and still north of Market, **Chinatown** covers around 24 square blocks between Broadway in the north, Bush St. in the south, Powell St. in the west, and Kearny St. in the east. The heavily developed **Financial District** lies between Washington St. in the north and Market in the south, east of Chinatown and south of North Beach and is home to the skyscrapers which define the city's skyline. Down Market from the Financial District, toward the bottom of the wedge, you pass through the core downtown area centered on **Union Square** and then, beyond Jones St., the **Civic Center,** an impressive collection of municipal buildings including City Hall, the Opera House, and Symphony Hall. The Civic Center occupies the base of the wedge and spills out over Van Ness to Gough St., 2 blocks west.

Also within this wedge is the **Tenderloin,** seedy and probably unsafe at night, despite the sprouting high-rises. The Tenderloin is roughly bounded by Larkin St. to the west and to the east by Taylor St. extending from Market St. north to Geary. Some of the area's seediness, however, plants itself across Market in the area near the Greyhound station (6th and 7th St.).

Below Market St. lies the **South-of-Market-Area (SOMA),** largely deserted during the day although it is home to much of the city's nightlife. The South-of-Market extends inland from the bay to 10th St., at which point the Hispanic **Mission District** begins and spreads south. The **Castro,** center of the gay community, adjoins the Mission District at 17th and also extends south, centered upon Castro St.

West of Van Ness Ave., the city extends all the way to the ocean side of the peninsula. At the top of Van Ness, the commercially developed **Marina** area embraces a yacht harbor, Fort Mason, and the hostel. Fisherman's Wharf lies immediately to its east. Above the marina rise the wealthy hills of **Pacific Heights.** South of Pacific Heights, across Van Ness from the Civic Center, is the **Western Addition,** extending west to Masonic Ave. This district is the sight of many of the city's public housing projects and tends to be dangerous, especially near Haze St. It is *not* a good place for tourists to hang out. **Japantown** is located within the Western Addition. Farther west is the rectangular **Golden Gate Park,** extending to the Pacific and bounded by Fulton Street in the north and Lincoln Street in the south. At its eastern end juts a skinny panhandle bordered by the **Haight-Ashbury** district. North of **Golden State Park** is San Francisco's token suburb within the city, the **Richmond District.**

Buses and Subways

It is fitting that San Francisco's cable cars are so renowned, for they are the most famous component of a truly marvelous mass transit network. Buses, many of them quiet, clean, electrical models, run promptly and frequently, and the routes blanket the city. Furthermore, despite its location in a state of automobile worshippers, San Francisco has not neglected rail transportation. Connections to neighboring cities are well-coordinated and speedy. See San Francisco Bay Area for information on transportation beyond San Francisco.

The *Comprehensive Regional Transit Guide,* covering all of the regional bus and subway services, sells for $4 at most bookstores.

San Francisco Municipal Railway (MUNI) (673-6864) operates buses, cable cars, and a combined subway/trolley system. Fares for both buses and trolleys are 85¢, ages 5-17 25¢, seniors and disabled passengers 15¢. Exact change in coins is required. Ask for a free transfer, valid in any direction for several hours, when boarding. Passes for unlimited travel on MUNI, including cable cars, cost $6 for 1 day, $10 for 3 days, and $28 for one calendar month. Call MUNI for sales locations. Another option is the AC/BART plus MUNI pass, which costs $20 and provides unlimited rides on MUNI and AC Transit for one half of a calendar month, plus $15 worth of BART rides. Call 464-6779 for sales locations and hours.

MUNI buses run quite frequently throughout the city. In addition, MUNI Metro runs streetcars through subway tunnels along Market St. and above ground along five lines serving points south and west of downtown. The Metro and bus lines along a few major streets run all night. Most other buses run daily 6am-midnight. Wheelchair accessibility is variable—some bus routes are completely equipped with lifts while others have none at all, and while all subway stations are accessible, the Metro can only be boarded at a few above-ground sites.

Even if you're only going to be using the system briefly, the MUNI's *San Francisco Street and Transit Map,* available at most bookstores and supermarkets, is a sound $1.50 investment. Not only does it contain information on frequencies, accessibility, and late-night service, it also includes a complete street index, so it can double as a general street map. Copies of this map are posted in bus shelters, but they are generally faded to illegibility.

Cable cars have been transporting San Franciscans since 1873. (They were named a national historic landmark in 1964.) The cars are noisy, slow (9½ mph, to be precise), and so often full as to be a totally unreliable method of getting from point A to point B (you're not the first person to think of taking one from Union Square to Fisherman's Wharf). Still, there is something undeniably charming about these relics, and you may want to try them, especially if you have a MUNI pass. Of the three lines, the California St. line is by far the least crowded; it runs from the Financial District up Nob Hill. The fare is $2, seniors 15¢, ages 5-17 75¢, under 5 free. Unlimited transfers are allowed within a given three-hour period. Cars run daily 7am-1am.

Bay Area Rapid Transit (BART) (778-2278) does not (alas) really serve the entire Bay Area. It does operate modern, beautifully carpeted trains along four lines connecting San Francisco with the East Bay, including Oakland, Berkeley, Concord, and Fremont. It is not a local transportation system within the city of San Francisco; use MUNI for that. One way fares range from 80¢ to $3. A special excursion deal for $2.60 is designed for tours of the system. You must begin and end at the same station, and your trip must not take more than three hours. (BART trains run Mon.-Sat. 6am-midnight, Sun. 9am-midnight.) Maps and schedules are available at the visitor information center and all BART stations. All BART stations and trains are wheelchair accessible.

The Gray Line (558-9400) offers 3½ hour bus tours of the city for $23.50, ages 5-11 $11.75, plus a variety of other tours. Tours leave from Union Square for night tours and from the Transbay terminal for day tours, and reservations are required.

Cars, Bicycles, and Feet

A car here is not the necessity it is in Los Angeles. Furthermore, parking in the city is *hell* and very expensive. A car is, however, definitely the best way to explore the outer reaches of the Bay Area. In the city, contending with the hills is the first task; if you've arrived in a standard-shift car, you'll need to develop a fast clutch foot, since all hills have stop signs at the crests. If you're renting, get an automatic. And remember: in San Francisco, cable cars have the right of way.

The street signs admonishing you to "PREVENT RUNAWAYS" refer not to wayward youths but rather to cars improperly parked on hills. When parking facing uphill, turn the wheels toward the center of the street and leave car in 1st gear;

when facing downhill, turn the wheels toward the curb and leave the car in reverse; and always set the emergency brake.

Taxi: Yellow Cab, 626-2345; **Luxor Cabs,** 282-4141; **DeSoto Cab Co.,** 673-1414. Initial charge $1.90, $1.50 per additional mile. All available 24 hr.

Car Rental: Rent-A-Wreck, 555 Ellis St. (776-8700), between Hyde and Leavenworth St. Used, mid-size cars $29 per day with 100 free mi., $159 per week with 700 free mi.; always 20¢ per additional mile. Must be 21 with major credit card. Under 25 $10 extra per day. Open Mon.-Fri. 8am-6pm, Sat. 9am-4pm, Sun 9am-1pm. **Bob Leech's Auto Rental,** 435 S. Airport Blvd. (583-3844), South San Francisco. New Toyotas $20 per day with 150 free mi., 10¢ per additional mile. Must be 23 with major credit card. Travelers coming into SFO should ask Bob Leech's for a ride to the shop. Open Mon.-Fri. 8am-9pm, Sat.-Sun 9am-5pm.

Auto Transport: Auto Driveaway Company, 330 Townsend (777-3740). Oldest company in the business, with a large selection of destinations. Must be 21 with valid license and references. Cash deposit $250. Open Mon.-Fri. 9am-5pm. **A-1 Auto,** 1300 Old Bayshore Rd., Burlingame (342-9611). Must be 21 with major credit card. Cash deposit $200-300. Call 10 days in advance. Open Mon.-Fri. 9am-5pm.

Think twice about attempting to use a bike to climb up and down the hills of San Francisco. Even the proudest year-round messengers have been spotted walking their bikes up the especially steep grades. A day biking through Golden Gate Park is more sensible.

Bike Rental: Lincoln Cyclery, 772 Stanyan St. (221-2415), on the east edge of Golden Gate Park. Three-speeds $3 per hr with a $5 deposit., 10-speeds $4 per hr. with a $15 deposit. Driver's license or major credit card required. Open Mon. and Wed.-Sat. 9am-5pm, Sun. 11:30am-5pm. **Presidio Bicycle Shop,** 5335 Geary (752-2453), between 17th and 18th Ave. Ten-speed or mountain bike $7 per hr. $25 per day. Open Mon.-Sat. 10am-6pm, Sun. 11am-4pm.

Even walking in this city is an exertion—some of the sidewalks are so steep they have steps cut into them. Undaunted, locals offer many **walking tours** of the city, many of them promising "no steep hills." Call **City Guides** at 332-9601 for information on their free summer tours, or stop by the visitors center for information on the many commercial tours available, hotline 332-9611.

Accommodations

All the travel books will tell you about hotel arrangements in this country. They should be seen to be appreciated. Understand clearly—and this letter is written after a thousand miles of experiences—that money will not buy you service in the west.

—Rudyard Kipling

Unlike most cities, San Francisco has a wide selection of conveniently located, satisfying budget accommodations. But don't expect miracles for these prices. Also, note that a rather hefty 11% bed tax is *not* included in the prices given below. Most hotels listed here are in areas such as the Tenderloin, the Mission District, Union Square, and downtown, where caution is advised both on the streets and within the buildings, particularly at night. Women, especially, should go elsewhere and pay more if unsure about a given neighborhood or establishment.

For some obscure reason, San Francisco abounds with hotels claiming that they are "European style." Occasionally this claim means nothing more than a hall bath, a sagging bed, and some foreign flags. But more frequently, it signifies a multilingual host who enjoys his job, a room that transcends the inoffensive sterility of American highway motels, and a grand old building which would tell many stories if the walls could talk. If you require an extra-firm mattress, a television, and a private bath, inquire about their availability before making a reservation, or explore the long row of motels along Lombard St., west of Van Ness. If you have no such needs, San Francisco is a great place to find moderately-priced rooms with character.

The International Network Globe Hostel, 10 Hallam Place (431-0540), near Greyhound, just off Folsom St. in the South of Market district. Hostel requires that its guests be foreigners, but Americans presenting a passport with stamps from other countries are welcome as well. Clean and convenient. Four beds to a hotel room with chairs and tables. No kitchen. This friendly, lively hostel serves a continental breakfast and dinner and has its own sundeck. Over 120 beds, many filled by international student travelers. Community lounge and laundry room are good places to meet people. Guests are treated as adults and are expected to behave accordingly. Open 24 hr. No curfew. $15 per night. Key deposit $5.

San Francisco International Hostel (AYH), Bldg. 240, Fort Mason (771-7277). Entrance at Bay and Franklin St., 1 block west of Van Ness Ave., at the northern end of the peninsula. From Greyhound at Transbay Terminal (1st and Mission St.), take MUNI bus #42 northbound at corner of Mission and Fremont to Northpoint and Van Ness, then walk up the hill to Bay St.; follow signs to hostel. One of the largest AYH-affiliated hostels in the nation, with about 160 beds. The General Motors of hosteling: clean, well-run, and efficient. Chore-a-day rule enforced. Extensive lounges, large kitchen, spic-and-span food-storage areas, and pay lockers for valuables. Useful ride board. Frequented by students, families, and seniors. Crowded in summer. Get here very early (around 7am) or send a night's fee 3 weeks ahead of time to reserve a place. 5-day max. stay. Registration 7am-2pm and 4:30pm-midnight. Check-out 10am. Lockout 10am-4:30pm. Curfew 2am. Members and nonmembers $12.

San Francisco Summer Hostel (AYH), 100 McAllister St. (621-5809), near Civic Center BART station and many bus routes. Not a great area at night. Open in summer only; closes Aug. 11. Laundry facilities and 2 small kitchens. 7-day max. stay. Registration 7:30am-midnight. Check-out 11am. Lockout 11am-4:30pm. Curfew 2am. Members $12. Nonmembers $15.

International Guest House, 2976 23rd St. (641-1411), at Harrison St. in the Mission District. Somewhat rough neighborhood, away from the most touristy areas, but 24th St. is fairly busy. More a home than a hostel. The owner adheres strictly to a foreign-travelers-only rule. Two fully equipped kitchens for 28 guests. Common room, TV, stereo, and fireplace. 5-day min. stay, no maximum. No curfew. Bunks or 4-person rooms. $12 for each of the first ten nights, $11 thereafter. Rooms for couples $20. No singles. No reservations.

European Guest House, 761 Minna St. (861-6634), between 8th and 9th St., 2 blocks south from Greyhound and west on Minna in a quiet but run-down neighborhood. Free-wheeling, relaxed, improvised, friendly. People sleep on sofas, mats, cushions. Even if you aren't foreign, chances of getting in are high if you're from out of town. Guests can sometimes work out arrangements the with hostel to trade a few hours of chores for a free bed. Mixed-sex rooms. TV room, laundry facilities, kitchen, roof garden, small information board. Registration 7am-3am. Check-out 11am. No curfew. $11 per night to sleep in one of 34 bunks in a capacious, hot dorm. $13 per night for a bunk in a 2-6 bed room.

Harcourt Residence Club, 1105 Larkin (673-7720). One of the city's most popular residence clubs offers rooms by the week or by the month. Price includes maid service, TV room, and 2 meals a day, and Sunday brunch. Filled by a younger set of traveling students and local residents. Occasional BBQ's are organized by Harcourt. Weekly rates per person: $130 for two people, up to $200 for singles.

YMCA Hotel, 220 Golden Gate Ave. (885-0460), at Leavenworth St., 2 blocks north of Market St. Men and women. One of the largest hotels in the city. Rooms don't quite measure up to the impressive post-modern facade. Has the only indoor track in the city, which is just as well given the uninviting surroundings. Double locks on all doors. Pool and gym. Register any time. No curfew. Singles $31.70. Doubles $44. Hostel beds $16 for members only. Breakfast included. $5 key deposit.

YMCA Chinatown, 855 Sacramento St. (982-4412), between Stockton St. and Grant Ave. Convenient location for those wanting to be near the center of the city in general and Chinatown in particular. Men over 18 only. Friendly young staff, pool, and gym. Rooms are not exactly fancy—let's just say that there are no pine nuts in sight. Registration Mon.-Fri. 6:30am-10pm, Sat. 9am-5pm, Sun. 9am-1pm. Check-out 1pm. No curfew. Singles $27.50. Doubles $33.50. 7th day free. Call 2 weeks in advance for reservation.

San Francisco State University, 800 Font Blvd. (406-5703), a trip from downtown. Take BART to Daly City and bus #28 to 19th and Holloway. Walk west along Campus to Font. Dorm rooms for traveling students, faculty, or those with some affiliation with the university. Register before 6pm. Reserve one week in advance. Check-out 11am. All rooms have twin beds. Singles $35, doubles $25. Rooms available early June to mid-Aug.

18th Street Guest House, located in the Mission District. This homey guest house features common kitchen and rec. room facilites. Four people to a room, no restriction to international travelers. Lockout 11am-3pm. Midnight curfew, but they're cool about giving out keys. $14 a night, continental breakfast included.

El Capitan, 2361 Mission St. (695-1597), north of 20th St. in the Mission District. While the rooms are not as impressive as the façade they are spruce. The neighborhood around this mostly residential hotel is a bit rough, but the street is busy and the hotel has two locked gates. Singles $26, with bath $30, doubles $32.

Sam Wong Hotel, 615 Broadway (781-6836), between Grant Ave. and Stockton St. in Chinatown. Extremely convenient location and therefore popular. The rooms could use more maintenance, but they are clean. Singles with toilet but no bath $24, with bath $29, add $2 for double occupancy. Triples with bath $40.

Western Hotel, 335 Leavenworth St. (673-8317). From Transbay Terminal walk south to Market and turn left. Then walk northwest on Market past 7th St. to Leavenworth St. and turn left. The neighborhood is questionable, but the hotel is safe and clean, with a locked gate. Showers and toilets in the hall. 24-hr. counter. No visitors after 9pm. Rooms fill up quickly. Check-out 11am. Singles $20. Doubles $28. Weekly: singles $110; doubles $150. Breakfast included.

Sutter/Larkin Hotel, 1048 Larkin (474-6820). Bus #19 runs to the hotel from the Civic Center. Mostly residential, so it can be hard to find the manager or a vacancy, but the rooms are trim and tidy and the manager is extremely accommodating. The neighborhood is decent, but the hotel is a bit out of the way compared to most others. Check in after 10am. Singles with shared bath $20. Doubles $25. Weekly: singles $90, with bath $110; doubles $105.

Gum Moon Women's Residence, 940 Washington (421-8827), at Stockton in Chinatown's center. Women only. Bright, spacious rooms with shared bath. Kitchen and laundry facilities. Primarily a boarding house, so call ahead to make sure there are rooms available. Registration 9am-6pm. Check-out noon. Singles $22. Doubles $36. Weekly: singles $91, doubles $152.

Olympic Hotel, 140 Mason St. (982-5010) at Ellis St. a few blocks from Union, snuggled up against the snazzy Parc Fifty-Five. Caters mostly to Japanese students and Europeans. Clean and comfortable. Atrocious wall-paper. Tends to fill up during the summer months. Olympic Deli next door has cappuccino ($1.20) and sandwiches ($2.80). Singles $28, singles and doubles with bath $35.

Herbert Hotel, 161 Powell St. (362-1600), at O'Farrell St, very close to Union Sq. Located by the cable car turn-around. Caters to an older crowd and has little to offer younger travelers other than its prime location and cleanliness. Rents by the week only. Singles $85, $125 with bath; doubles with bath $175. Key deposit $10.

Pensione International, 875 Post St. (775-3344), east of Hyde St. Four and a half blocks west of Union Square. Very attractive rooms with interesting art. Singles $30, with bath $55. Doubles $40, with bath $65. Breakfast included.

Temple Hotel, 469 Pine St. (781-2565), between Montgomery and Kearny St. near the California St. Cable Car. Across from the new Bank of America building. The closest decent hotel to the Transbay Terminal. Rooms extremely clean and well-maintained, but that's about it. All rooms with deadbolt locks and TVs. The hotel is secure, but the surrounding area has little charm. The manager is enthusiastic and eager to help travelers. Check-in 8am-10pm. Check-out noon. Singles $30, with bath $40. Doubles $35, with bath $45. Discounts for stays longer than two nights.

Adelaide Inn, #5 Isadora Duncan (441-2261), off Taylor near Post St., two blocks west of Union Square. With its warm hosts and jumbled paintings, perhaps the most European of San Francisco's many "European-style" hotels. Does not answer door after 11pm. Steep stairs, no elevator. All rooms with a bright outside exposure. Kitchenette and microwave available. 18 rooms. Hall baths. Singles $38. Twin bed or doubles $46, double bed with single bed $52. Continental breakfast included. Reservations.

Grant Plaza, 465 Grant Ave. (434-3883 or 800-472-6899; within CA 800-472-6805), at Pine St. near the Chinatown gate. Excellent location. Recently renovated to look like a chain motel, but more colorful. Rooms with bath, phones, and color TV. Check-in after 2:30pm. Check-out noon. Singles $39. Doubles $45. Twin beds $49. Reservations advised 2-3 weeks in advance.

The Ansonia, 711 Post St. (673-2670), 3 blocks west of Union Sq. Tastefully decorated rooms with firm mattresses, in a nice area. Laundry facilities. Breakfast and dinner (except Sundays) are included. Singles $35, shared bath with 1 other room $42, with bath $52. Doubles $47, with bath $60. Weekly: singles $215, shared bath with one other room $250, with bath $300; doubles $280, with bath $360. Student rates for stays of a month or longer.

Sheehan Hotel, 620 Sutter St. (775-6500 or 800-848-1529), at Mason St near Union Sq. Excellent location with nearby access to cable cars, buses, and BART. Across the street from trendy art galleries. The elegant lobby, complete with tearoom serving wine and tea is busy, and something of a scene on warm summer evenings. International students galore. 61 rooms, cable TV, phone. Olympic-sized swimming pool. Exercise room. Economy singles $40, with bath $55. Economy doubles $50, with bath $60. Additional person $10. Children under 12 free with parents. Breakfast included.

Obrero Hotel and Basque Restaurant, 1208 Stockton (989-3960), between Pacific Ave. and Broadway in Chinatown. 12 comfortable, cheerful rooms with fluffy comforters on the beds. Hall baths, full breakfast included. Family-style Basque dinners at 6:30pm ($13, wine included). No smoking. Reservations required. Check-in 8am-noon and 5-10pm. Checkout 11am. Singles $38. Doubles $45.

Hotel Essex, 684 Ellis St. (474-4664; within CA 800-44-ESSEX; outside CA 800-45-ESSEX), between Hyde and Larkin St, north of Civic Center. One of the best cheap hotels around. Popular with German tourists in summer. Free coffee. Diminutive rooms with bath. Phones. Check-out noon. Just the facts, ma'am. Singles $39, $46 in summer, with bath $46. Doubles $42, with bath and TV $54. Twin beds $44, with bath and TV $56. Weekly rate: single $120-150.

Grant Hotel, 753 Bush St. (421-7540), between Mason and Powell St., 2 blocks north (uphill) of Union Sq. Wholesome, though not exactly elegant. Pleasant lounge downstairs. Rooms with bath, telephone, and color TV. Check-out noon. Singles $50. Twin beds $60.

The Amsterdam, 749 Taylor St. (673-3277 or 800-637-3444), between Bush and Sutter St., 2 blocks from Nob Hill, 3½ blocks from Union Sq. It usually fills up in summer with foreign student travelers and the occasional businessperson. Beautiful rooms in a very central location. Singles $44, with bath $59. Doubles $49, with bath $65. Checkout 11am. Be sure to request the complimentary continental breakfast.

Pacific Bay Inn, 520 Jones St. (800-445-2631 or 673-0234, within CA 800-343-0880), 3 blocks west of Union Square. Has been entirely renovated after a fire. Pleasant rooms with TV. Singles and doubles $55-65; only $45 if you show your copy of *Let's Go.* Continental breakfast included.

All Season's Hotel, 417 Stockton St. (800-628-6456 or 986-8737, within CA 800-344-6030), in the Downtown district between Sutter and Bush St., 1 block north of Union Square—a prime location. Thin walls and some peeling paint, but big brass beds with firm mattresses. Checkout 11am. Singles $52. Doubles $55. Reserve ahead in summer.

Golden Gate Hotel, 775 Bush St. (392-3702), between Powell and Mason St., 2 blocks north (uphill) of Union Square. A warm, charming, and well-situated 1913 hotel with tasteful antique furnishings and bay windows. Spotless hall toilets and bath. Color TV. Multi-lingual host. Check-out noon, but late-flyers can store their luggage. Singles and doubles $55, with shower $79. Continental breakfast included. Garage parking available. Two-week advance reservations advisable June-Sept.

The Red Victorian Bed and Breakfast Inn, 1665 Haight St. (864-1978), 3 blocks west of Masonic Ave., 2 blocks east of Golden Gate Park in Haight-Ashbury. 3 mi. from downtown, but close to buses and the "N" trolley. Barely describable, the Red Vic is more a state of mind than a hotel. 18 individually and lovingly decorated rooms honor butterflies, the nearby Golden Gate Park, and the equally proximate 1960s, among other subjects. Even the four hall baths, shared by some of the rooms, have their own names and motifs. If canopied and teddy-bear festooned beds aren't enough to soothe your mind, try the meditation room, with its transformational art, the therapeutic massage ($60 per hr.), or a tête-a-tête with the hotel cat. Downstairs, a newly opened global family network center promotes planetary consciousness with a café, market, and computers. The Red Victorian is a non-smoking, angst-free living environment that you won't want to miss if your pocket book is up for the experience. Even if it isn't, at least stop by for a tour. Check-in 3-6pm. Checkout 11am. Rates are for double occupancy. Singles deduct $5, extra persons add $15. 2-night stay usually required on weekends. Weekly discounts available. Summer rates $65-125 depending on room size and karma; in winter $55-120. Weekends are more. For $15 they will put an extra futon in your room. Breakfast of freshly baked bread, pastry, and, of course, granola, included. Complimentary tea, coffee, popcorn, and cheese in the afternoons. Owners speak Spanish, German, and French. Make reservations well in advance for the summer months.

Food

For something less than a rupee a day a man can feed himself sumptuously in San Francisco, even though he be bankrupt. Remember this if ever you are stranded in these parts.

—*Rudyard Kipling*

Some say that to eat really well, you must be in Paris. Others argue for Naples, and Alex Ross might hold out for Three Aces. But for quality *and* variety, it's hard to beat the range of cuisines offered by one of America's great port cities. And while New York may reign supreme, San Francisco is a very respectable contender. In such cities, the sorrows of the world are transformed into the joys of the palate. For it seems that each time there is a war, or a famine, or a revolution somewhere, there arrives on these shores a poor, tired, huddled refugee, bringing nothing but what he can carry on his own shoulders, plus a great way to make noodles. The story has been repeated again and again, from the Cantonese and Sicilians who escaped economic stagnation in the late 19th century, to the Cambodians and Central Americans who have fled political violence in recent decades. Their recipes and skills, combined in the great American melting wok with California's magnificent produce and seafood, complement a willingness on behalf of American chefs to tinker and experiment with "California cuisine". The result is that San Francisco takes its food seriously, and eats very well.

Union Square

Union Square restaurants are remarkably insipid. Department store cafeterias can be surprisingly tasty but are consistently overpriced. There is a legion of coffee shops, but good hot food is hard to find.

Blondie's Pizza, 63 Powell St. (982-6168), at Ellis. Greasy, yes, but yummy cheese slices ($1.25), 50¢ more with loads of pepperoni. A lengthy but speedy lunch line. No seats, so try the benches near the Powell St. subway. Open Mon.-Fri. 10:30am-9pm, Sat. 11am-9pm, Sun. 11:30am-8pm.

Gelato Classico, 448 Post St. (989-5884), between Mason and Powell, 1 block west of Union Sq. The apotheosis of *gelati* (small $1.75). The variety of flavors should inspire you to mix (e.g. Bavarian mint and dark chocolate). Open Mon.-Thurs. 8:30am-11pm, Fri. 8:30am-midnight, Sat. 8:30am-11pm, Sun. 8:30am-9pm.

Lori's Diner, 336 Mason St. (392-8646), at Geary St. Uptown diner with 50s music and Marilyn Monroe posters. Classic burgers, dogs, sandwiches, and coleslaw ($4-6). Open 24 hr.

Sears Fine Food, 439 Powell St. (986-1160). Old-fashioned breakfast joint known for its cornucopic bowls of fresh fruit ($3.35 and up). Fluffy pancakes ($4.25). Open Wed.-Sun. 7am-2:30pm.

San Francisco Health Food Store, 333 Sutter St. (392-3477), between Stockton St. and Grant Ave. Crunchy and healthy is the name of the game. Extensive selection of nuts and dried fruits. Tangerine shakes ($2.25) with added wheatgerm or yeast. Open Mon.-Fri. 9:15am-5:45pm, Sat. 9:15am-5:30pm.

Financial District

The Financial District can be a tricky place to ingest well with minimal outlay. Watch out for expense-account establishments that may look better than they taste. For more proximate lunch counters, see South of Market.

Café Latte, 100 Bush St. (989-2233), at Battery, 2nd floor of the Shell Building. An up-scale cafeteria that serves excellent pasta ($8) and sandwiches ($5). The place is packed with navy-blue suits, and the take-out menu comes with a handy card for your Rolodex. Open Mon.-Fri. 7-10:30am and 11:30am-3pm.

Tadich Grill, 240 California St. (391-2373). Founded in 1849, this is the oldest restaurant in the state of California. Private wood booths separate the tables and the stained glass windows add the historical feel. The clientele and atmosphere share much with Sam's (see below). Expensive, but deserving at least a visit. Entrées $10-17. Minimum charge of $7.50 per person. Menu changes daily. Open Mon.-Fri. 11am-9pm, Sat. 11:30am-9pm.

Sam's Grill, 374 Bush St. (421-0594), at the corner of Belden St. Founded in 1867, the grill is a favorite among balding Rotarians. The fish of the day ($8-13) is always fresh and tasty. The linguine and shellfish ($15.50) is worth it if the funds permit. If not, try the clam cocktail ($7) or a bowl of excellent clam chowder ($2.75). Beware of the $5.75 minimum. Open Mon.-Fri. 11am-8:30pm.

Yan Sing, 427 Battery St. (781-1111). Great Chinese food scoots by on carts in what looks to be an upscale Financial District restaurant. This highly regarded establishment serves delectable food at reasonable prices ($6-10) in an area of the city notorious for poor value. Full bar. Open Mon.-Fri. 11am-3pm, Sat.-Sun. 10am-4pm.

Café Claude, 7 Claude Lane (392-3505) off Bush and Kearney. Tucked back in one of the Financial District's many alleyways. Trendy but popular. A large French clientele. Live music Tues., Thurs., and Fri. 6-9pm. Open Mon.-Fri. 8am-9pm, Sat. 10am-4pm.

City Sweets, 444 Market St. (989-0911), in the Lloyds of London Building arcade on the bottom level. A welcome sucrose crashpad when the towers of commerce overwhelm you. Every flavor of Jelly Belly jellybeans kept in supply. Condom-filled fortune cookies recently discontinued due to complaints. Only in San Francisco. . . Open Mon.-Fri. 8:30am-6pm.

Tenderloin and South-of-Market

Around the Transbay Terminal are some fancy cafeterias serving lunch to office workers. Otherwise, pickings are slim.

Pasta Bella, 30 Fremont St. (397-2786), between Mission and Market St. Elegant Italian fast-food, served cafeteria-style. Plenty of lunch options, including pastas and pizzas, around $6. Open Mon.-Fri. 6:30am-8pm.

El Faro's, 82 1st St. (495-4426), ½ block from the Transbay Terminal. Not too different from a Mission District taquería, only the clientele is clad in business attire. Large burritos with chips are $3.90-4.50, tacos $1-3. Open Mon.-Fri. 6:30am-6:30pm, Sat. 7am-3pm.

Hamburger Mary's, 1582 Folsom St. (626-5767), at 12th St. Biker joint turned hip. The "enter at your own risk" sign is still there, but the danger isn't. Upscale hamburgers $4-6. Meatless sandwiches $3-4. Open Mon.-Fri. 11am-1:15am, Sat.-Sun. 10am-1:15am.

Chinatown

Chinatown abounds with downright cheap restaurants; in fact their multitude and incredible similarity can make a choice well nigh impossible. Supplement *Let's Go's* advice by asking locals or persuing local reviews in the paper.

House of Nanking, 919 Kearney St. (421-1429). Outstanding Chinese food in a pleasant atmosphere. The small restaurant which prepares its food within the dining area always has lines out the door, consisting partially of people who have walked all the way from the Financial District on their lunch breaks. Mu-Shu vegetables $5, onion cakes $1.75. Anything made with the Tsing-Tao beer sauce is sure to be terrific. Open Mon.-Sat. 11am-10pm, Sun. 4-10pm.

Sam Wo, 813 Washington (982-0596). The late hours and BYOB policy, not to mention the exceptionally cheap prices, make this restaurant a favorite among students from all over the Bay Area. To get to the restaurant, customers must pass by the chefs as they prepare the food in the kitchen. Most dishes $1.25-4.50. *Jook* (fish) soup $3.50, chicken chow mein $3.50. Open Mon.-Sat. 11am-3am, Sun. 12:30-9:30pm.

Dol Ho, 808 Pacific Ave. (392-2829). A relaxing atmosphere perfect for afternoon tea and *dim sum,* traditionally served as brunch. 4 steamed shrimp dumplings (*har gow*); sweet doughy sesame balls; or pork buns, all $1.60. open daily 8am-4pm.

Yuet Lee, 1300 Stockton (982-6020) at Broadway. A paucity of atmosphere, but the seafood makes up for that. Steamed fresh oysters in black bean sauce $8. Many exotic seasonal specialties for adventurous diners, such as sautéed pork stomach with boneless duck feet. Open daily 11am-3am.

Brandy Ho's, 317 Columbus Ave. (788-7527). The paintings of hot peppers adorning the buildings warn the unsuspecting customer: the food is SPICY! Order everything mild or extra mild if you want to enjoy this wonderful Hunan cuisine. Large interior with many tourists. Very service-oriented. Entrées à la carte $6.25-$9.95. *Gou-Pou* shrimp $8.95. Open Sun.-Thurs. 11:30am-11pm, Fri.-Sat. 11:30am-midnight.

Civic Center

Hayes Street offers a terrific selection of cafés, but petite restaurants dot the entire Civic Center area. In the summer, load up on produce at the **Farmers' Market** in the UN Plaza every Wednesday and Sunday.

Stars Café, 555 Golden Gate (861-4344), between Van Ness and Polk. Though you might not know it from the $10 entrees, this is actually a sort of discount outlet for the famous Stars Restaurant which is located next door. The $8 sandwiches or chicken salad are the cheapest way to sample one of super-chef Jeremiah Tower's creations. Both restaurants have the same desserts. Menu changes daily. Open Mon.-Thurs. 8:30am-10pm, Fri. 8:30am-11pm, Sat. 10am-11pm, Sun. 10am-10pm.

Swan's Oyster Depot, 1517 Polk St. (673-1101), near the California St. cable car. Avoid the elbow-to-elbow lunch-time squeeze by coming at an off hour for some of the best and freshest seafood in the city. Pull up a stool to the marble counter (they don't have tables) and consume what most agree is the city's finest chowder ($2.75). The combination seafood salads change everyday and are a favorite among regulars but will set you back about $10. Try the clam cocktail with Swan's zesty red sauce for $3.75.

Tommy's Joynt, 1101 Geary Blvd. (775-4216), at the corner of Van Ness Ave. Outrageously painted establishment with a stunning selection of beers brewed everywhere from Finland to Peru. Their thick pastrami sandwich is known throughout the city ($3.34). With two types of mustard and horseradish on every table, they clearly know what they're doing. Open daily 10am-2am. Restaurant opens at 11am.

Vietnam II, 701 Larkin St. (885-1274) at Ellis. Choose from a 174 item menu of Chinese and Vietnamese cuisine (plus specials). Or pick your seafood dish from one of the many tanks lining the walls. Spacious and brightly lit. Steamed fresh catfish Vietnamese style $7.50. Entrées $5-8. Open daily 10am-midnight.

Viccolo Pizzeria, 201 Ivy St (863-2382). A $3.45 slice at Viccolo's gives you a taste of nouvelle California. Sacrifice choice for craftsmanship by choosing one of six pre-topped pizzas. Open Mon.-Sat. 11:30am-11:30pm, Sun. 2-10pm. Second location in Ghirardelli Sq. (776-1331) is something of an oasis in the land of tourist food. Open Sun.-Thurs. 11am-10pm, Fri.-Sat. 11am-11pm.

Nyala Ethiopian Restaurant, 39A Grove St. (861-0788), east of Larkin St. Nyala's combination of Ethiopian and Italian cuisine is probably the only positive result of Mussolini's occupation. Newcomers should try *Doro Wat,* a traditional Ethiopian dish of slowly simmered chicken in a rich garlic and ginger sauce ($6.75 at lunch). Or, for variety, try the vegetarian all-you-can-eat buffet, which features two types of lentils, spicy mushrooms, cabbage, and other saucy vegetables to ladle onto rice or to scoop up with spongy *injera* bread. (Buffet Mon.-Fri. 11am-3pm $4.50, and 4-11pm $6.95.) Open daily 11am-2am.

Pendragon Bakery, 450 Hayes St. (552-7017), at Gough St. Excellent, imaginative pastries. A big, fluffy blueberry scone $1.55. Sandwiches $4-5. Open Mon.-Fri. 7am-4pm, Sat.-Sun. 8am-3pm.

Nob Hill and Russian Hill

You were expecting to find budget restaurants on Nob Hill? Hah!

The Raw Bar, 1509 Hyde St. (928-9148), at Jackson. Small but genuine seafood joint owned and operated by a local fisherman who spends the day angling by the wharf. Clams on the half-shell $6, creamy chowder $3.50. Open daily 5-10pm.

Ristorante Milano, 1448 Pacific St. (673-2961) at Larkin. Although not entirely cheap, this extremely popular neighborhood *trattoria* serves entirely pleasurable food. The family-run kitchen puts out delicious *al dente* pastas ($9.95) You'll walk away well-fed without being weighted down. Open Tues.-Sat. 5:30-10:30pm, Sun. 5-10pm. No reservations.

Swensen's, 1999 Hyde St. (775-6818) at Union. This tiny, take-away ice cream parlor engendered a national chain. Earl Swensen has owned this store for 40 years. Scoop $1.25. Open daily 11:30am-10pm.

North Beach

North Beach isn't cheap, but prices can be reasonable if you avoid Fisherman's Wharf, where food is frequently tasteless or overpriced or both. Street vendors line Jefferson St., but even their prices soar. The cheapest food on the wharf lurks outside Franchesi's Restaurants, across from the Cannery; pick up a small shrimp cocktail ($2.50) if you need a seafood fix. A walk down Columbus Ave. will take you to a group of suitable cafés and an occasional inexpensive restaurant.

Tommaso's, 1042 Kearny St. (398-9696), between Pacific and Broadway just below Van Ness Ave. For a break from *nouvelle pizza* try some of the best traditional Italian pizza anywhere. The super deluxe, piled high with mushrooms, peppers, ham, and Italian sausage sates two ($13.50). The *pizza Neapolitan* is simple and fulfilling ($9). Francis Ford Coppola tosses pizza dough every once in a while in front of Tommaso's wood burning ovens. The wait is sometimes tedious but always worth it. Open Tues.-Sat. 5-10:45pm. Sun. 4-9:45pm.

Gira Polli, 659 Union St. (434-GIRA (434-4472). Like Col. Sanders, Michele and Norine Ferrante have founded a restaurant on the basis of a single chicken recipe, but theirs is Palermo Roasted, not Kentucky Fried. The crisp skin of these spit-roasted birds, seasoned with lemon, olive oil, and rosemary, encases tender, juicy meat. If you eat it here, a half-chicken will cost you $11.95 plus tip, so order it to go for $9.95 and take it to Washington Square for a picnic. Pastas ($10.50-$11.50) and salads ($3.75-$7.75), homemade biscotti ($3.25) are also available. Open Mon.-Sat. 5-10pm, Sun. 4-10pm.

Caffe Sport, 574 Green St. (981-1251), near Columbus Ave. Terrific food served in an oddly decorated, slightly claustrophobic dining room. Go for lunch and order the basil-laden *pesto* over pasta ($8), worth every penny. Prego. Dinner can cost over $15. Open Tues.-Sat. noon-2pm; dinner sittings at 6:30, 8:30, 10:30pm. Reservations essential.

Caffe Trieste, 609 Vallejo St. (392-6739), at Grant. Only a few beatniks now, but sip coffee and recall the groovy Eisenhower years when Ginsberg and Ferlinghetti hung out here. Loud live music Sat. 1-4pm. Otherwise settle for a tune from the opera jukebox. Coffees $1-2.25. Open Sun.-Thurs. 7am-11:30pm, Fri.-Sat. 7am-12:30am.

U.S. Restaurant, 431 Columbus Ave. (362-6251), at Stockton St. Popular with young San Franciscans (a patriotic lot). Long wait at dinner. Titanic, tasty portions. *Calamari* ($7.50), served Fridays, is their most popular dish. Most dishes under $10. Open Tues.-Sat. 6:30am-9:30pm. Closed for the month of July.

The Savoy-Tivoli, 1434 Grant Ave. (362-7023). Sit yourself outside and watch the passersby or enter in and play pool. Reggae with daiquiris ($3.75) or cappuccino ($3). Crowded, so don't expect speedy service. Open Tues.-Sun. 3pm-2am.

Bohemian Cigar Store, 566 Columbus Ave. (362-0536), corner of Union St. Excellent, toe-curling espresso ($1) and agreeable Italian food. Try their Italian sandwiches ($4.75-5.50). Open Mon. 10am-11pm, Tues.-Sat. 10am-midnight, Sun. 10am-6pm.

North Beach Pizza, 1499 Grant St. (433-2444). A fine specimen of the New York, thin-crust school. No slices, long lines. Small pie $6.25, extra-large $10.79. Try the Verdi's Special ($11.31) with spinach, pesto, onions, and feta. Open Sun.-Thurs. 11am-1am, Fri.-Sat. 11am-3am.

Marina and Pacific Heights

Pacific Heights and the Marina abound in high quality, high-priced restaurants.

Bepple's Pies, 1934 Union St. (931-6225). The pies are a bit expensive, but heavenly. These divine creations combine a succulent fruit filling with a miraculous crust that is moist yet flaky, and just bland enough to absorb the flavor of the fruit. Slices of pie are $2.95-3.25, but spend another 95¢ for a solid slab of excellent vanilla ice cream. If you know a better pie shop, please write us. Whole fruit pies to go $11. Open Mon.-Wed. 9am-11:30pm, Thurs. 7am-midnight, Fri. 7am-1am, Sat. 9am-1:30am, Sun. 9am-10:30pm.

Perry's, 1944 Union St. (922-9022). When asked what was special about Perry's Bar, one of the best-known places on Union St., the host answered, "the drinks are a little stronger and the philosophy a little deeper"—a pretty remarkable answer for a place that was written up in the *Preppy Handbook* as one of the premiere pick-up spots in the entire country. Despite the host's charming epithet, Perry's is not the place to ponder aloud our post-Cartesian condition. The closest thing to what philosopher Richard Rorty calls "conversation" here is the echo of pick-up lines delivered with unctuous charm. This is one of *Chronicle* columnist and S.F. institution Herb Caen's favorite hangouts. Small Caesar salad $4.50, *fettuccine alfredo* $8.25, and draft beer $2.25. Open daily 9am-1am, until 11pm for dinner.

Jackson Fillmore, 2506 Fillmore St. (346-5288). Where does the staff from Chez Panisse go on their day off? Jackson Fillmore. There's almost always a wait at this hip *trattoria.* Great southern Italian cuisine and a lively atmosphere can always be counted on. Put your name down and check out the Fillmore scene while you wait. The portions are large and if you're careful you can sneak out for less than $10 per person. Eat lots of tasty breadsticks to fill up. Reservations required for more than three people. Open Tues.-Thurs. 5:30-10:30pm, Fri. and Sat. 5:30-11pm, Sun. 5-10pm.

Mai's Vietnamese, 1838 Union St. (921-2861). Sidewalk dining on Union St. The crab claws get high marks ($6.55) as does the vegetarian imperial roll ($5). The crab meat soup is known for its flavor and clarity ($4). Entrees around $7.50. A romantic spot on warm summer nights in the city. Open Mon.-Thurs. 11am-10pm, Fri. 11am-11pm, Sat. noon-11pm, Sun. noon-10pm.

Japantown (Nihonmachi)

Sadly, there are few good, inexpensive Japanese delicacies to be had in Japantown, and the Western Addition does not cater to distinguishing palates. **Near Escapes** (386-8687) offers occasional walking tours of Japantown including a traditional tea ceremony and flower-arranging demonstration. $33. Tours last 6½ hrs.

Isuzu, 1581 Webster St. (922-2290). Gigantic menu but *tempura* is the specialty. $8 buys an ample helping of deep-fried delectables with rice and a life-prolonging miso soup. Open Mon. and Thurs.-Fri. noon-2pm and 5-9pm, Sat.-Sun. noon-9pm.

Isobune, 1737 Post St. (563-1030), in Japan Center. *Sushi* in the fast lane: dishes pass by on little boats floating along a small river. Eat fast or slow, the pace is yours to set. Count the number of plates to figure out your bill. $1.20-2.50 per plate. Open daily 11:30am-10pm. No reservations.

Mission District and Castro Street

The Mission ranks among the best areas in the city (or anywhere on the planet) to find excellent, satisfying cheap food. For once, the only frustrating thing is choosing between all the inexpensive taquerias and unusual ethnic cuisines. Too often overlooked as a culinary stop, the Mission will spoil you for Mexican food anywhere else. After a burrito or some raw cuttlefish, Castro Street is a great place for an evening coffee or drink (see Sights).

La Cumbre, 515 Valencia St. (863-8205). As you stand in line, your mouth-watering, raw steak is brought in from the back kitchen, dripping in marinade. It is then grilled to perfection, quickly chopped, combined with rice and beans, and deftly folded into a flour tortilla to make a superlative burrito. ($2.35 for a regular, which is ample; $3.75 for a large). A standout among taquerías. Open Mon.-Sat. 11am-10pm, Sun. noon-9pm.

Taquería San Jose, 2830 Mission St. (282-0203), at 24th. Don't be put off by the fast-food style menu; loving care goes into the cooking. Soft tacos with your choice of meat, from magnificent spicy pork to brains or tongue $1.55, 5 for $3 50. Free chips and guacamole. Open Mon.-Thurs. 8am-1am, Fri.-Sat. 8am-4am.

Café Macondo, 3159 16th St. (863-6517). Appetizing Central American food and coffee in a homey, yet artfully designed, café. In fact, the room seems more a museum than a restaurant, with a display case in one of the old refrigerators exhibiting anti-war posters and art. Hardwood floors with Oriental rugs, wicker furniture, couches, a lamp on each table, and native art. A perfect place to bring a book while sipping cappucino ($1.50). Sandwiches $2.75. Open Mon.-Thurs. 11am-10pm, Fri.-Sun. 11am-11pm.

Manora, 3226 Mission (550-0856). This attractive Thai restaurant serves delicious cuisine at reasonable prices. Manora prepares sauces with a refreshingly light hand, so the food isn't smothered in peanut. The red beef curry garners high praise ($5.75). Most dishes under $8. Open Tues.-Fri. 11:30am-2:30pm, 5-10pm, Sat.-Sun. 5-10pm.

New Dawn, 3174 16th St. (553-8888) at Guerrero. An intense sensory experience. Absolutely anything is considered "art" at this hip restaurant, from the doll body parts and eggbeaters hanging on the walls to the music blasting through the restaurant to the chef's magenta mohawk. The menu, consisting mainly of breakfast food and burgers, is written around the room on mirrors. Enormous servings. Vegetable home fries (made with fresh vegetables) $2.95, burgers $3.25. Everything under $3.95. Open Mon.-Fri. 8am-3pm, Sat.-Sun. 8am-4:30pm.

Yuet Lee, 3601 26th St. (550-8998). Same horrendous green paint and evil florescent lighting as the Chinatown location, but same great seafood too. Open Mon. and Wed.-Thurs. 11am-10pm, Fri.-Sat. 11am-11pm, Sun. 4-10pm.

Haight-Ashbury

Although the Haight boasts a terrific selection of bakeries, it offers little in the way of cheap victuals. There are a few interesting places worth checking out, but be careful: the food is uneven at some restaurants and down-right terrible at others.

Cha Cha Cha, 1805 Haight St. (386-5758). Love-children fighting against the stream of late capitalist society join hands with upwardly mobile professionals and line up for a chance to eat at this trendy Latin restaurant, thought to be the best in the Haight. Try the tapas ($4 at lunch, $5 at dinner). Fried bananas in black bean sauce are a specialty ($5.75). Entrees $5-8. Be prepared to wait up to 2 hrs. Open Mon.-Thurs. 11:30am-3pm and 5:30-midnight, Fri.-Sun. 12-3pm and 5-11pm.

Ganges, 755 Frederick St. (661-7290), not exactly in the Haight, but close enough. Delicious vegetarian Indian food draws health-conscious students from the nearby medical school. Like so many vegetarian restaurants, it slips a bit into the same-ingredients-in-every-dish rut (garbanzos and garbanzo flour are clearly a favorite), but overall, there is variety indeed. Traditional, low Indian seating in back. Dinners $7.50-11.50. Live music Thurs.-Sat. starting at 7:15pm. Reservations a good idea. Open Mon.-Sat. 5-9:30pm.

Tassajara Bread Bakery, 1000 Cole St. (664-8947), at Parnassus, 5 blocks south of Haight St. Connected to a Zen monastery in the Sierras, Tassajara is one of the city's best bakeries. There's a branch at Fort Mason (771-6331), but the purist will want to make the pilgrimage to Haight-Ashbury for the original. Pastries are delicious but tiny. Danish $1.30. The poppyseed cake ($1, $1.30 with icing) is famous. Open Mon.-Thurs. 7am-7pm, Fri. 7am-10pm, Sat. 8am-10pm, Sun. 8am-2pm.

Bakers of Paris, 1605 Haight St. (626-4076). They're not really, but their croissants (about $1) are excellent nonetheless. Open daily 7am-7pm.

Beau Seventh Heaven, 1448 Haight St. (626-4448). French-Russian bakery with an eclectic selection of pastries. Russian cinnamon bun, a big ball of moist, soft dough with just a hint of cinnamon, 95¢. *Hamentashen* 85¢. Open daily 7am-10:30pm.

Farmer's Market, 1584 Haight St. (863-5336). Enormous collection of vitamins, granola, and other crunchy foods. Open daily 9am-7pm.

The Richmond District

The quiet Richmond District contains many ethnic neighborhoods and restaurants for exploration. The area east of Park Presidio Blvd. is populated by Chinese, earning it the nickname "New Chinatown," and some locals claim the Chinese restaurants here are better than the ones in old Chinatown. In addition, the area contains many fine Southeast-Asian restaurants—Thai, Burmese, and Cambodian.

Chao Kos, 5625 Geary Blvd. (668-5888), near 20th Ave. An attractive restaurant with an interesting menu. Remarkably complex and tasty lunch specials ($3.85). Mixture of Thai and Cambodian cuisine. Dinner entrees are about $6, $7.50-8 for seafood. Open Sun.-Thurs. 11am-3pm and 5-10pm, Fri.-Sat. 11am-3pm and 5-10:30pm.

Ernesto's 2311 Clement St. (386-1446), at 24th Ave. A well-kept San Francisco culinary secret. Dinners at this family-run Italian restaurant are reasonably priced (entrees $7.50-11, pizza $6.75-10.75) and are as authentic as anything in North Beach, if not Italy. Try the filling linguine with red clam sauce ($8.50). You might encounter a line for dinner, but rejoice—wine is often served free to guests waiting outside the door. Open daily 10:30am-4pm.

The Golden Turtle, 308 5th Ave. (221-5285), at Clement. Prices at this small Vietnamese restaurant are reasonable, the food is delicious. Long queues on weekends, but abide, for ye shall be rewarded. Service makes you feel like royalty. Entrees $8. Open daily 11am-3pm and 5-11pm.

Chinese Vegi-Food, 1820 Clement St. (387-8111), between 19th and 20th Ave. The menu forswears not only meat, but onions and garlic as well, leaving even the "hot and spicy" sauces quite dull. All told, the vegetables are fresh and there is a better vegetarian selection than at most Chinese restaurants. Dinner about $6.50. Open Tues.-Fri. 11:30am-3pm and 5-9pm, Sat.-Sun. 11:30am-9pm.

Pat O'Shea's Mad Hatter, 3848 Geary Blvd. (752-3148) between 2nd and 3rd St. An Irish sports bar with beef and satellite dishes. Pot roast ($6.10) and hamburgers ($6), only offered certain nights, are among their fine dishes. Open daily 11am-2am.

Sights

Mark Twain called San Francisco "the liveliest, heartiest community on our continent." And any resident will tell you that this city is not by landmarks or "sights," but by neighborhoods. If you rush from the Golden Gate to Coit Tower to Mission Dolores, you'll be missing the greatest sight of all—the city itself. Whether defined by ethnicity, tax brackets, or topography, or simply by a shared spirit, these communities confront the visitor with constant contrasts. Off-beat bookstores, Japanese folk festivals, Chinese *dim sum,* cosmopolitan Union Street, Pacific Heights nightlife, Strawberry Hill in Golden Gate Park, the Club Fugazi in North Beach, and the Haight simply for being the Haight . . . these are San Francisco.

Downtown

Union Square is the center of San Francisco. Now an established shopping area, the Square has a rich and somewhat checkered history. During the Civil War, a large public meeting was held here to decide whether San Francisco should secede. The Square became the rallying ground of the Unionists, who bore placards reading "The Union, the whole Union, and nothing but the Union." Though Abe Lincoln would have appreciated the support, Union Square has been less friendly to subsequent U.S. presidents. At the **Sheraton Palace Hotel,** a few blocks away on Market St. at New Montgomery St., Warren Harding died in 1923, while touring the West to promote the World Court. And on the square itself, by a side entrance of the **St. Francis Hotel,** Sara Jane Moore's attempt to assassinate President Gerald Ford was foiled on September 23, 1975.

Even when the Barbary Coast (now the Financial District) was down and dirty, Union Sqaure was cheaper. **Morton Alley,** in particular, offered off-brand alternatives to the high-priced prostitutes and stiff drinks of the coast; the prices were low, but the action was just as sizzling. At the turn of the century, murders on Morton Alley averaged one per week, and prostitutes with shirts unbuttoned waved to their favorite customers from second-story windows. After the 1906 earthquake and fire destroyed most of the flophouses (some of the customers paused to help the girls get out; others just ran), a group of proper merchants moved in and renamed the area **Maiden Lane** in hopes of changing the street's image. The switch worked. Today Maiden Lane, extending 2 blocks from Union Square's eastern side, is home to smart shops and classy boutiques. Traces of the old street live on, however, in words like "hoodlum," "shanghaied," and "Mickey Finn," all added to the American vocabulary by the people who frequented the area. For cheap ship labor, sea merchants used to pay Union Square bartenders to load-up unsuspecting patrons. The patrons awoke from their inebriated state to find themselves on the way to Shanghai. Local bars still serve a stiff drink they call a "Shanghai Surprise."

The best free ride in town is on the outside elevators of the St. Francis Hotel. As you glide up the building, the entire Bay Area stretches out before you. The "elevator tours" offer an unparalleled view of Coit Tower and the Golden Gate Bridge. The Powell St. cable cars also grant an excellent view of the Square. Or go up to the 30th floor of the **Holiday Inn,** 480 Sutter St. (398-8900), where you can put down a potable in the **Sherlock Holmes Bar,** which has been decorated to the specifications of 221B Baker St.

Financial District

North of Market and east of Kearny, snug against the bay, beats the West's financial heart, or at least one of its ventricles. Montgomery Street, the Wall Street of the West, is only of passing interest to the visitor and is best seen before the workday ends. After 7:30pm, the heart stops, only to be resuscitated the next morning.

Parking is next to impossible during business hours. If you must drive, park your car South-of-Market (SoMa) and walk from there. To reach the Financial District by public transportation take MUNI Metro line J, K, L, M, or N to the Transbay Terminal, MUNI bus #5, 6, 12, 14, 15, 38, 41, 80x, or 81x to the terminal, or BART to Embarcadero Station.

Commemorative plaques nailed to skyscrapers' flanks tell two stories: the explicit one, about intriguing events that transpired in the once raucous city center, and the implicit one, about a part of the city rendered homogeneous and hyper-efficient by development, smothering the old, vice-ridden Barbary Coast out of existence. Modern architecture enthusiasts may have a field day in this glass-box wonderland, but for the casual observer, a glimpse from afar will suffice.

In the east end of the district, at the foot of Sacramento St., stands **Embarcadero Center** (772-0500), a three-level complex housing over a hundred expensive and mostly trivial shops. Come to admire the scale of development and the dozens of outdoor sculptures. At the foot of Market St. is **Justin Herman Plaza** with its famous geodesic **Vallaincourt Fountain** through which it is possible to walk while the water flows overtop. The area is often rented out by bands or for rallies during lunch from noon to 1:30pm. One such free lunchtime concert, performed by U2 in the fall of 1987, resulted in lead singer Bono's arrest for spray painting "Stop the Traffic-Rock and Roll" on the fountain. Connected to the $300-million complex is the **Hyatt Regency** hotel (788-1234). Its 17-story atrium, dominated by a four-story geometric sculpture, is worth a visit. The glass elevator up the building's side leads to the 20th floor and the **Equinox Lounge.** There is a lovely view of the bay from this fabulous revolving cocktail lounge every 45 minutes and a decent view of nearby office buildings the rest of the time. Slightly spiffed up, you can usually bluff your way to a window table, but the view is spectacular from just about anywhere. Buy a drink and ample dawdling time for about $3 and up. (Open daily 11am-1:30am.)

San Francisco's most distinctive structure, totally out of scale with the surrounding buildings, is the 853-foot **Transamerica Pyramid** at Montgomery St. between Clay and Washington St. The Montgomery Block, a four-story, fireproof brick building, once stood in its place. Nicknamed the Monkey Block, the Montgomery's in-house bar lured the likes of Mark Twain, Robert Louis Stevenson, Bret Harte, and Jack London. These gruff storytellers wrote and got drunk on the bar's renowned Pisco Punch. In the basement a man named Tom Sawyer operated sauna baths that Twain frequented, and in 1856, the victim of one of the city's most notorious murders—newspaper editor James King of William—was shot on the building's doorstep over one of his controversial editorials. A Chinese expatriate named Sun Yat-Sen plotted the overthrow of the Manchu Dynasty and wrote the 1911 Chinese constitution in an apartment here. The pyramid itself was designed by William Pereira and Associates as a show of architectural virtuosity and was never actually meant to be built. Completed in 1972, the building's pyramidal shape and subterranean concrete "anchor" base make it one of the city's most stable, earthquake-resistant buildings; though all new buildings in San Francisco are now required to be "earthquake-proof," a measure which saved many lives in the '89 quake. The observation deck disappoints because it is only halfway up and only faces north. For better views, try the hotel bars on Nob Hill. (Open Mon.-Fri. 9am-4pm. Free.)

The most impressive views of the Pyramid itself are caught from up the hill on Columbus Ave.

Diagonally across from the pyramid is the **Old Transamerica Building,** 701 Montgomery St., at Washington St., the opulent showpiece of the corporation and a gem of older commercial architecture. The elaborate entryway is fenced with wrought iron and laced in gilt.

The Financial District also offers some inside attractions in the form of free museums, most of them sponsored by the public relations departments of large banks. The **Wells Fargo History Museum,** 420 Montgomery St. (396-2619), at California St., contains an impressive display of Gold Rush exhibits, including gold nuggets, maps, and a 19th-century stagecoach. The affable guide possesses the sort of quiet yet unfathomed knowledge usually found only in National Park Service rangers. (Open Mon.-Fri. 9am-5pm.) Another Gold Rush exhibit is the Bank of California's **Museum of Money of the American West,** 400 California St. (765-2402), at Sansome, which has 19th-century coins, nuggets, and devices to detect counterfeit money (open Mon.-Thurs. 10am-4pm, Fri. 10am-5pm). For a bigger exhibit, go to the Old Mint (see Tenderloin). The **Bank of America's Historical Exhibit,** 345 Montgomery St. (953-6075), at California, focuses not so much on money as on banking. It is interesting for the aesthetic qualities of the old office machinery, including manual typewriters, dictaphones, and a fascinating 1895 "millionaire" mechanical calculator, which used a hand crank and about a cubic foot to perform functions now handled by wristwatches. (Open Mon.-Thurs. 9am-4pm, Fri. 9am-5pm.) The **Chinese Historical Society,** 650 Commercial St. (391-1188), tells the tale of the Chinese who came to California. In addition to the richly informative texts, the museum has some remarkable artifacts, including a 1909 parade dragon head. (Open Wed.-Sun. noon-4pm.)

The **Pacific Stock Exchange,** located at 301 Pine St. is a picayune and much more relaxed version of its counterpart in New York. Free 45-min. tours by appointment only (393-7969).

Chinatown

The largest Chinese community outside of Asia, Chinatown is also the most densely populated of San Francisco's neighborhoods. Chinatown was founded in the 1880s when, after the gold had been dug and the tracks laid, bigotry fueled by unemployment engendered a racist outbreak against what was then termed the "Yellow Peril." Chinese-Americans banded together to protect themselves in a small section of the downtown area. As the city grew, speculators tried to take over the increasingly valuable land, especially after the area was leveled by the 1906 earthquake, but the Chinese were not to be expelled, and Chinatown, which has gradually expanded its original borders, remains almost exlusively Chinese. The Grant Ave. bazaars aside, Chinatown is not a Fisherman's Wharf tourist fabrication.

Grant Avenue is the most picturesque part of Chinatown. From the monumental **Chinatown Gate,** which straddles Grant at Bush St., and for a few blocks north, Grant is a sea of Chinese banners, signs, and architecture. Below this canopy are shops doing brisk business selling Asian-made tourist wares. The less famous streets, such as Jackson, Stockton, and Pacific, are a more accurate representation of the neighborhood. Pharmacies stock both Western and Eastern remedies for common ailments; produce markets are stacked with vegetables; and Chinese newspapers are sold by vendors who eat their morning noodles out of thermoses.

Although most visitors to Chinatown come for the food, there are other activities. Watch fortune cookies being shaped by hand in the **Golden Gate Cookie Company,** 56 Ross Alley (781-3956), between Washington and Jackson St., just west of Grant Ave. This famous alleyway, which has maintained the true feeling of what Chinatown used to be, has been a filming site for many well-known and not-so-well-known movies such as *Big Trouble in Little China, Karate Kid II,* and the *Indiana Jones* series. Nearby **Portsmouth Square,** at Kearny and Washington St., made history in 1848 when Sam Brennan brought the news of the gold strike at Sutter's Mill. Now the square is filled with Chinese men playing lively card games. A stone bridge leads from this square to the **Chinese Culture Center,** 750 Kearny St., 3rd floor (986-1822), which houses exhibits of Chinese-American art and sponsors two walking tours of Chinatown. The Heritage Walk leaves on Saturdays at 2pm and concentrates on the various aspects of life in Chinatown ($12, under 18 $2). The Culinary Walk departs on Wednesdays at 10:30am and discusses the preparation of Chinese food ($25, under 12 $10. Price includes a *dim sum* lunch at Four Seas of Grant Ave.) Both walks require advance reservations. (Center open Tues.-Sat. 9am-5:30pm.)

North Beach

As one walks north along Stockton St. or Columbus Ave., there is a gradual transition from supermarkets displaying ginseng to those selling provolone, and from restaurants luring customers with roast ducks in the window to those using biscotti. Lying north of Broadway and east of Columbus, the district is split in character between the bohemian Beats who made it their home—Jack Kerouac, Allen Ginsberg, and Lawrence Ferlinghetti among others—and the residents of the traditional Italian neighborhood. North Beach bohemianism flourished in the 1950s when the artists and brawlers nicknamed the Beats (short for "beatitude" according to Kerouac) first moved in. Drawn to the area by low rents and cheap bars, the group came to national attention when Ferlinghetti's **City Lights Bookstore** (see Entertainment) published Allen Ginsberg's anguished and ecstatic dream poem *Howl.* Banned in 1956, the book was found "not obscene" after an extended trial, but the resultant publicity turned North Beach into a must-see for curious tourists. More than one poet still tinkers with the language of Blake and Whitman, but the Beats are gone. Through the middle of North Beach runs Broadway, the neon netherworld of pornography purveyors. Carol Doda, the artificially-enhanced wonder of the city, startled the nation with her topless act at the Condor back in the 70s. But everything that rises must fall and so, when the silicon began to settle in the early 80s, Doda called it quits. Above it all stands the pleasant old residential district of Telegraph Hill, topped by Coit Tower. North Beach is most fun to visit at night as the after-dinner, after-show crowd flocks to the area's numerous cafés for a relaxing cappuccino.

Lying between Stockton and Powell is **Washington Square,** a lush lawn edged by trees. Across Filbert to the north of the square is the **Church of St. Peter and St. Paul,** beckoning tired sightseers to an island of quiet in its dark, wooden nave. In the Square itself is the **Volunteer Firemen Memorial,** donated by Mrs. Lillie Hitchcock Coit, who was rescued from a fire in childhood. Coit's most famous gift to the city—**Coit Tower**—is a few blocks east. The tower sits on Telegraph Hill, the steep mount from which a semaphore signalled the arrival of ships in Gold Rush days. Legend has it that the tower was built to resemble a fire nozzle. At any rate, Coit's Tower spectacular 360° view makes it one of the most romantic spots in the city. An elevator will take you to the top. (Open daily 10am-5pm; Oct.-May, 9am-4pm. Elevator fare $3, over 64 $2, ages 6-12 $1, under 6 free. Last ticket sold ½ before closing; 274-0203) There is very limited parking, so leave your car on Washington St. and walk up the **Filbert Steps** which rise from the Embarcadero to the eastern base of the tower. The walk is short, allows excellent views, and passes by many gorgeous Art Deco buildings. The **Tattoo Art Museum,** 839 Columbus (775-4991), displays a fantastic collection of tattoo memorabilia, including hundreds of designs and exhibits on different tattoo techniques. Unfortunately, the small space prohibits displaying the entire collection, the largest one of its kind, and therefore works are exhibited on a rotating basis. In the same room, a modern and painfully clean tattoo studio is run by the eminent professional Lyle Tuttle, himself covered in tattoos from head to foot (the museum is his personal collection). Fifty dollars will buy a quick, glowing rose on the hip.

Fisherman's Wharf

Continuing northward, toward the water, one leaves San Francisco proper and enters tourist limbo. Stretching from **Pier 39** in the east to **Ghirardelli Square** in the west is "Fisherman's Wharf," 4/5 mi. of gifts for lefties, porcelain figurines, and enough T-shirts to have kept Washington's army snug at Valley Forge. This area is crowded, very expensive, and despite its blandness there is something to offend almost anyone, be it the unbelievably crude bumper stickers or the jugglers' imitations of Japanese people. Despite all the warnings you may read, however, you're a tourist and you're going to go to this honky-tonk netherworld sooner or later. The best way go about this is to wake up at 4am, put on a warm sweater, and go down to the piers to see why it's called a fisherman's wharf. You can take in the loading and outfitting of small ships, the animated conversation, the blanket of the morning mist, and the incredible views—without the rapacious scene and crowds.

Farther down the pier are several food stands that will make your mouth water. As an alternative to junk, **Vlaho's Fruit Orchard** sells primo California produce for about $2 per lb. and provides a sink in which to rinse it. (Open daily May-Sept. 9am-8:30pm.) Toward the end of the pier is **Center Stage,** where mimes, jugglers and such do their thing (free). **Pier 39** (981-PIER (981-7437)), built on pilings that extend several hundred yards into the harbor, was designed to recall old San Francisco, but looks more like a Dodge City scene from a Ronald Reagan Western. Pier 39 shops open daily 10:30am-8:30pm.

Tour boats and ferries dock just west of Pier 39. The two main tour fleets, the **Blue and Gold Fleet** and the **Red and White Fleet,** are named after the colors of the University of CA, Berkeley, and Stanford University respectively, thus symbolizing the long-running rivalry between the two. The **Blue & Gold Fleet's** hour and 15-minute tours cruise under both the Golden Gate and Bay Bridges; past the Marin hills; past Angel, Alcatraz, and Treasure Islands and the San Francisco skyline (781-7877; $14, seniors and ages 5-18 $7, military and under 5 free). The **Red & White Fleet** (456-BOAT (456-2628), within CA, 800-BAY-CRUISE) at Pier 41 offers tours and ferry rides. The 45-minute Bay Cruise leaves from Pier 41 and 43½ and goes under the Golden Gate Bridge and past Alcatraz ($15, ages over 55 and 12-18 $11, 5-11 $8). In the summer, another 45-minute tour circumnavigates the island; narrated by a former prison guard ($7.50, ages over 55 $7, 5-11 $4). Ferries from Pier 43½ to Sausalito are $4.50, ages 5-11 $2.25. Red & White boats also discharge passengers at Alcatraz (see below). For a really pleasant escape, try one of the **sailboat charters** that line the wharf. The *Ruby* (861-2165) sails at lunchtime (with sandwiches) daily from May to October. The sloop departs from the China Basin building at 12:30pm and returns by 2pm, but call as the schedule often changes (tickets $25, under 10 $12.50). The *Ruby* also takes a 3-hr. turn in the bay on Friday and Saturday at 6pm. Tours leave from the Ramp Restaurant on Miraposa St. Reservations are required for sailboat charters. Mind you bring a heavy sweater in summer and a jacket in winter.

Easily visible not only from boats and the waterfront, but also from Powell St., is **Alcatraz Island.** Named in 1775 for the *alcatraces* (pelicans) that flocked to it, this former federal prison looms over the San Francisco Bay, 1½ mi. from Fisherman's Wharf. During the Civil War "the Rock," then little more than barren stone, was fortified with a massive cannon and a garrison of several hundred Union soldiers to protect San Francisco from a possible Confederate attack. Soil was imported, and much of the vegetation that covers the island today was planted. After the war, the army decided to take advantage of the island's isolation and resident police force to incarcerate troublemakers from across the country. During World War I conscientious objectors were held on the island along with men convicted of violent crimes while in the service. In 1934, Alcatraz was brought under federal purview and used to hold those who had wreaked too much havoc in other prisons. Life for these prisoners was extremely harsh and security was high—of the 23 men who attempted to escape, all were recaptured or killed, except for five who were "presumed drowned" although their bodies were never found. Robert Stroud, "The Birdman of Alcatraz," spent 17 years in solitary confinement. Although sentenced to death for killing a prison guard, he was spared by President Wilson and went on to write two books on bird diseases. Al Capone was another famous inmate of the Rock. He left the prison in 1947 suffering from syphilis. In 1962, Attorney General Robert Kennedy closed the prison, and the island's existence was uneventful until 1969, when about 80 Native Americans occupied it as a symbolic gesture, claiming the rock as their property under the terms of a broken 19th-century treaty. Alcatraz is currently a part of the Golden Gate National Recreation Area, the largest park in an urban area in the United States, administered by the National Park Service. The Red and White Fleet (546-2805) runs boats to Alcatraz from Pier 41. Once on Alcatraz, you can wander by yourself or take an audiotape-guided, two-hour tour, full of clanging chains and the ghosts of prisoners past. (Departs every ½ hour from Pier 41; 9:15am-4:15pm in summer, 9:45am-2:45pm in winter. Fare $5, over 55 $4.50, ages 5-11 $3. Tape tours costs $3 extra (ages 5-11 $1 extra) and are well worth the money. Reserve tickets in advance through Ticketron (392-7469) for $1 extra or confront long lines and risk not getting a ride.)

Farther west along Jefferson St. past Pier 39, several spectacles, including the **Wax Museum** and the **Ripley's Believe It or Not!** (so-called) museum, attempt to lure tourists off the street. The trick to saving the exorbitant entrance fees is not to enter; often the best exhibits are the ones outside, designed to lure in the passersby.

For less kitschy amusement, the **Maritime State Historic Park** at Jefferson and Hyde St., harbors four boats, two of which (the *Balclutha* and the *Dolphin P. Rempp*) are open to the public. The nearby museum displays related memorabilia and is worth popping into just to stand on the terrace overlooking the bay. (Boats and museum open daily 10am-5pm. Free.) At the Haight Street Pier floats the *Balclutha* (929-0202), a swift trading vessel that plied the Cape Horn route in the 1880s and 90s and was featured in the first Hollywood version of *Mutiny on the Bounty.* It was recently restored with donated union labor. (Open Wed.-Sun. 10am-5:30pm. Admission $3, ages over 62 and under 16 free.)

The *Dolphin P. Rempp* (777-5771) is an old freighter converted into a pricey restaurant, but non-diners can enjoy the excellent restoration for free. (Open Tues.-Sat. Cabaret opens at 4:30pm, dinner from 6pm-10:30.) At Pier 45 you can also board a World War II submarine—the *U.S.S. Pampanito.* (Open daily 9am-9pm; in winter Sun.-Thurs. 9am-6pm, Fri.-Sat. 9am-9pm. Admission $3, seniors and ages 6-12 $1, 13-18 $2, under 6 free.)

Finally, the left flank of the Wharf area is anchored by shopping malls, the most famous of which is **Ghirardelli Square** (pronounced GEAR-a-deli), 900 N. Point St. (Information booth, 775-5500; open daily 10am-9pm.) The only remains of Ghirardelli's original **Chocolate Factory** now lie in the Clock Tower Basement (771-4903; open daily 10am-midnight). Ghirardelli's hot fudge is wonderful, but there isn't nearly enough of it on the sundaes; only true chocoholics can justify the $4.50 price. The old building was going to be destroyed but was "saved" by William Rorth, a financier with an aesthetic consciousness, who made a killing in the process. Pricey boutiques now fill the rest of the old factory's red brick buildings, and local musicians and magicians entertain the huddled masses. (Stores open Mon.-Sat. 10am-9pm, Sun. 10am-6pm.)

Nob Hill and Russian Hill

Before the earthquake and fire of 1906, Nob Hill was home to the mansions of the great railroad magnates. Today, Nob Hill remains one of the nation's most prestigious addresses. The streets are lined with many fine buildings, and the aura is that of idle and settled wealth. Sitting atop a hill and peering down upon the *hoi polloi* can be a pleasant afternoon diversion. Nearby Russian Hill is named after Russian sailors who expired during an expedition in the early 1800s and were buried on the southeast crest. The notorious **Lombard Street Curves,** on Lombard between

Hyde and Leavenworth St. at the top of Russian Hill, afford a fantastic view of the city and harbor—that is, if you can keep your eyes open down this terrifying plunge. The switchbacks were installed in the 1920s to allow horse-drawn carriages to negotiate the extremely steep hill. The street was designed by Italians homesick for Genoa, where such curves originated.

Devising transportation on the city's steep streets also inspired the vehicles celebrated at the **Cable Car Museum,** at the corner of Washington and Mason St. (474-1887). The building is the working center of the cable-car system. You can look down on the operation from a gallery or view displays to learn more than you ever cared to about the picturesque cars. (Open daily 10am-6pm; Nov.-March 10am-5pm. Free.) **Grace Cathedral,** 1051 Taylor St. (776-6611), crowns Nob Hill. The castings for its portals are such exact imitations of Ghiberti's on the Baptistry in Florence that they were used to restore the originals. Inside, modern murals mix San Franciscan and national historical events with scenes from the lives of the saints. Visitors should take care to respect the fact that Grace is still used as a house of worship.

Combine money and altitude with a location in the middle of the peninsula, and you have a spate of elegant pubs where those over 21 can blow their wad on the view and plush decor. Two bars, the **Top of the Mark,** One Nob Hill (392-3434), in the Mark Hopkins Hotel, at Mason and Pine St., and the **Fairmont Crown** at the Fairmont Hotel, 950 Mason St. (772-5131), vie fiercely for the title of Bar with the Best View. The Top of the Mark offers a 360° view of the city, while the Crown is the highest public observation point in San Francisco. Both are superb, but the Mark has a better bar. Drinks at both cost about $6.50-7.75; you may feel a bit out of place in a t-shirt. (Cocktails served at the Crown Sun.-Thurs. 11am-12:30am, Fri.-Sat. 11am-1:30am, at the Mark daily 4pm-1:30am.)

Marina, Pacific Heights, and Presidio Heights

The Marina, Pacific Heights, and the adjoining Presidio Heights are the most sought-after residential addresses in San Francisco. Centered about Union and Sacramento St., Pacific Heights boasts the greatest number of Victorian buildings in the city. The 1906 earthquake and fire destroyed most of the northeast part of San Francisco, but left the Heights area west of Van Ness Ave unscathed. The Marina was the hardest hit in 1989, but the Heights area was not as lucky this time around and sustained serious damage. Victorian restoration has become a full-fledged enterprise: consultants determine the original form of fretwork, friezes, fans, columns, corbels, cartouches, pediments, stained glass, rosettes, rococo plaster, and so on. The **Octagon House** and **Haas-Lilienthal House** both afford the public a glimpse inside a Victorian building. The Octagon House, 2645 Gough St. (441-7512), is currently the headquarters of the National Society of Colonial Dames. The house was built in 1861 with the belief that such architecture would bring good luck to its inhabitants. Rather sedate tours of the impeccably preserved home are given for free on the first Sunday and second and fourth Thursdays of each month between 1 and 4pm. The Haas-Lilienthal House, 2007 Franklin St. (441-3004), is another grand example of Victorian architecture run rampant. (Open Wed. noon-3:15pm, Sun. 11am-4pm. Admission $4, seniors and ages under 18 $2.) **Temple Emmanuel,** 2 Lake St. at Arguello Ave. (751-2535), is a peaceful and beautiful example of Moorish architecture, designed by the same architect who did the Civic Center. (Services 5:30pm during the week.) **San Francisco University High School,** 3065 Jackson St., is not so much noted for its architecture, as for being the alma mater of Tim Whitmire, Class of 1988.

However, if you prefer shopping to architectural studies, **Union Street** is the place to be. Between Scott and Webster St., Union Street is chock-full of upscale shops, bars, restaurants, and bakeries. **Sacramento Street** is a less expensive, less cosmopolitan cousin.

Down from Pacific Heights toward the bay is the **Marina** district. **Marina Green** by the water seethes with joggers and walkers and is well-known for spectacularly flown two-line kites. To the west lies the **Palace of Fine Arts,** on Baker St. between Jefferson and Bay St. The strange, domed structure and the two curving colonnades are reconstructed remnants of the 1915 Panama Pacific Exposition, which commemorated the opening of the Panama Canal and signalled San Francisco's recovery from the great earthquake. The palace was designed by Bernard Maybeck and constructed out of staff (a plaster and fiber substance that resembles marble but decays rapidly). In 1959, a wealthy citizen, dismayed by the erosion, paid to have it rebuilt in stone. On summer days performances of Shakespeare are sometimes given in the colonnade section.

The domed building houses the **Exploratorium** (561-0360). Here, expansive exhibits explicting the wonders of science range from giant bubble makers to shadow jumping, where a light flash leaves the body image eerily upon the wall, and is fascinating enough to entertain for hours. Hundreds of interactive exhibits may teach even poets a thing or two about the sciences. (Open Wed. 11am-9:30pm, Thurs.-Sun. 10am-5pm. Admission $7, students with ID $5, over 59 $3.50, ages 6-17 $3. Admission is free on the first Wed. of every month.) Within the Exploratorium dwells the **Tactile Dome** (561-0362), a pitch-dark maze of tunnels, slides, nooks, and crannies designed to help refine your sense of touch; as you might guess, this museum is a wonderful place to bring children, although claustrophobes and those afraid of the dark should stay away. (Admission $7. Reservations required as much as a month in advance. Plenty of free parking.) A short walk from the Exploratorium's main entrance, along the bay, is the **Wave Organ.** Designed by local artists Peter Richards and George Gonzales, the organ is activated by the motion of waves and is an inviting place to sit or even meditate to the water's natural *om.*

Near the overdeveloped Fisherman's Wharf lies the commercially restrained **Fort Mason,** at Laguna and Marina. The Army's former embarkation facility has been converted into a center for non-profit organizations, many of a decidedly anti-military bent, and is also a place for young people to meet. The center is part of the Golden Gate National Recreation Area, but is operated by the Fort Mason Foundation (441-5706). The **Mexican Museum** (441-0404), Building D, offers free tours, exhibits, and educational workshops. (Open Wed.-Sun. noon-5pm; admission $2, seniors and students $1, under 10 free. The museum is open from noon-8pm and admission is free on the first Wed. of every month.) The **San Francisco Museum of Modern Art Rental Gallery,** Building A, Fort Mason Building 308 (441-4777), is the West Coast avant garde's answer to New York's alleged stranglehold on artistic innovation. (Open Tues.-Sat. 11:30am-5:30pm.) The **Magic Theater,** Fort Mason Building D (441-8822), founded in 1967 by John Lion, is renowned for hosting Sam Shepard as its playwright in residence from 1975-1985. Commissioned by the Magic Theater to write, write, write, Shepard produced such works as "Fool for Love" and "Angel City" and went on to receive ten Obie awards and an Academy Award nomination (for "The Right Stuff"). Today the Magic Theater stages contemporary American plays. The season is from October to July with shows from Wed. to Sat. and both a matinee and evening show on Sunday.

Aquatic Park commemorates the port, once a vital part of San Francisco, now a mere footnote to Oakland's sprawling docks.

Civic Center

The municipal heart of the city and a bureaucrat's wet dream, the vast Civic Center is a collection of massive buildings arranged around two expansive plazas. The largest gathering of *beaux-arts* architecture in the U.S. is centered on the palatial **San Francisco City Hall,** which was modeled after St. Peter's Cathedral and was the site of the tragic 1978 double murder of Mayor George Moscone and City Supervisor Harvey Milk. At the eastern end is the United Nations Plaza and public library, at the western end the Opera House and Museum of Modern Art. Street people and itinerant travelers used to camp out on the lawns surrounding the plaza, but the city has worked to move them into shelters and reclaim the area. Parking is relatively easy on streets around the Civic Center. To get there by public transportation, take MUNI Metro to the Civic Center/City Hall stop or MUNI bus #5, 16X, 19, 21, 26, 42, 47, or 49. You can also take the J, K, L, M, or N lines to Van Ness station or Golden Gate Transit bus #10, 20, 50, or 70.

There are two ways to see the Civic Center: by day, for the architecture and museums, and by night, for the performing arts. Although the **San Francisco Museum of Modern Art,** Van Ness Ave. (252-4000), at McAllister St. in the Veterans Building, is planning a 1995 move to the larger Yerba Buena gardens, the current site displays an impressive collection of both European and American 20th-century works. In addition to the permanent collection, the museum mounts wonderful temporary exhibits. Among the major shows planned for 1992 are *Paul Klee: Signs and Symbols,* running from May 16, 1991 to March 15, 1992, and *The Psychoanalytic Drawings of Jackson Pollock,* running from July 2 to August 30. (Open Tues.-Wed. and Fri. 10am-5pm, Thurs. 10am-9pm, Sat.-Sun. 11am-5pm. Admission $4, over 61 and students $1.50. Members and children under 13 free. Tues. seniors and students free. Thurs. 5-9pm $2, seniors and students $1. First Tues. of every month free.)

In the evenings, the **Louise M. Davies Symphony Hall,** 201 Van Ness Ave. (431-5400; box office open 9:30am-5:30pm), at Grove St., rings with the sounds of the San Francisco Symphony. The seating in this glass-and-brass $33-million hall was intended to appeal not only aurally but visually, giving most audience members a close-up view of performers. But while the building may be a visual success, its acoustics are poor, and ten years after its opening, baffled engineers still tinker with seating arrangements and baffles. On the other hand, the orchestra itself has improved greatly, perhaps to compensate for its new hall. (Seats in the chorus benches behind the orchestra cost $5 and are available 1 hour before performances, except, of course, when a chorus is performing.) Next door, the **War Memorial Opera House,** 301 Van Ness Ave. (864-3330), at Grove St., hosts the well-regarded **San Francisco Opera Company** (864-3330; box office open Mon.-Fri. 10am-6pm) and the **San Francisco Ballet** (621-3838 for info., Charge-by-Phone 762-BASS. Open Mon.-Sat. noon-6pm. Any $5 SRO tickets go on sale 2 hrs before the performance). The Civic Center has two other theaters: the **Orpheum,** 1192 Market St. (474-3800), tends to draw flashy overblown shows, while the smaller **Herbst Auditorium,** 401 Van Ness Ave. (552-3656; open Mon.-Sat. noon-7:30pm), at McAllister St., hosts string quartets, solo singers, and ensembles. It was here that the United Nations Charter was signed in 1945, after plenary sessions were held in the Opera House. Tours of the symphony hall, opera house, and Herbst Auditorium leave every half hour from the Grove St. entrance to Davies Hall. (Mon. 10am-2:30pm. Tours of only Davies Hall leave on Wednesdays at 1:30pm and 2:30pm, and on Saturdays at 12:30pm and 1:30pm. Admission $3, seniors and students $2. For more information, call 552-8338.)

On a smaller scale, the Civic Center area has a number of one- or two-room galleries. You don't have to buy that $30,000 neo-expressionist cityscape in the corner to enjoy browsing in these white-walled boutiques of contemporary art. South of City Hall, the **San Francisco Arts Commission Gallery,** 155 Grove St. (554-9682), periodically holds exhibits of contemporary arts and crafts. (Open Tues.-Fri. 11am-5pm, Thurs. 11am-8pm, Sat. noon-5pm.) The **San Francisco Women Artists Gallery,** 370 Hayes St. (552-7392), exhibits women's photographs, paintings, prints, and crafts. (Open Tues.-Wed. and Fri.-Sat. 11am-6pm, Thurs. 11am-8pm.) **Richard Hilkert Bookseller, Ltd.** is also in the neighborhood and well worth a visit (see Bookstores).

Also at the Civic Center is the **Main Library,** 200 Larkin (557-4400), which contains a San Francisco room (558-3949) and a Rare Books Room in addition to the standard collection. (Open Mon. 10am-6pm; Tues.-Thurs., Sat. noon-9pm; Fri. noon-6pm, Sun. 1-5pm. San Francisco Room open Tues. and Fri. noon-6pm, Wed. 1-6pm, Thurs. and Sat. 10am-6pm. Rare Book Room open Wed. and Fri. 2-5pm; Thurs. 10am-noon, Sat. 10am-noon and 2-5pm.)

Tenderloin and South-of-Market

The Tenderloin can be unpleasant, with its numerous porn shops, general stench, and collection of deranged individuals who shout at each other, at themselves, and occasionally at you. Still, things are changing in the Tenderloin, with new businesses coming in and hotels and offices pushing at the edges of the neighborhood. The newest facelift to the area is the vast indoor shopping metropolis, **The San Francisco Centre,** at 5th and Market St. Although Nordstrom may be out of your range, the six curved escalators sweeping shoppers through the nine-story atrium are a sight to behold and are the only such escalators in the world. The day the center opened, it set retail records by doing nearly a million dollars in business. The city's hope is that it will revitalize the area.

The area south of Market St. to about 10th St. is now home to the city's hottest nightlife. Yesterday's leather bars are today's stylish nightclubs. During the day, the area fills with workers from the encroaching Financial District, and will no doubt soon be sprouting high-priced boutiques.

The Old Mint, 88 5th St. (744-6830), at Mission St., is worth a peek. In one room a lone, placid guard watches over a stack of gold bullion, coins, and raw gold worth more than $150,000. The other rooms house assorted historical artifacts, including a collection of ornate and imaginative gramophones downstairs. If you have lots of time and a penchant for melodrama, watch *The Granite Lady,* A half-hour film that describes the history of San Francisco and the Mint in grandiloquent terms. (Shows hourly and tours on the hr. 10am-3pm. Mint open Mon.-Fri. 10am-4pm. Free.)

The **Ansel Adams Center,** 250 4th St. (495-7000), at Howard and Folsom, houses a permanent collection of the master's photographs, as well as temporary shows by other photographers. (Admission $4, students $3, over 64 $2. Open Tues.-Sun. 11am-6pm.)

South-of-Market, with its many self-park lots, is one of the easiest areas of the city in which to park your car, but be sure to lock it securely. To reach the center of the area take samTrans bus #1A or 1L (weekends and holidays) or #1C, 22D, 10L, or 10T (8-10am and 4-6pm only). Or take MUNI bus #9x, 12, 14, 15, 26, 27, 30, 45, or 71.

Mission District and Castro Street

Castro Street and the Mission District are far enough south that they may still enjoy sunshine while fog blankets Nob Hill. The area is home to two thriving cultures: the gay community around Castro Street and the Hispanic community to the east. As AIDS has taken its toll, the scene has mellowed considerably from the wild days of the 70s. However, Castro Street still remains a proud and assertive emblem of gay liberation. In the Hispanic Mission District, the colorful murals along 24th Street reflect the rich cultural influence of Latin America.

The best way to see Castro Street is to wander, peering into shops or stepping into bars. Two popular hangouts are **Café Flor,** 2298 Market St. (621-8579), and **Café San Marco,** 2367 Market St. (861-3846). Café Flor serves wine, beer, coffee, and buttery croissants ($1.45) in an unhurried atmosphere. Many customers bring newspapers to read on the patio; if you don't have one, you can pick up a free weekly. (Open daily 8am-5pm.) Café San Marco has a plexiglass, New-Age bar upstairs (open Sun.-Thurs. 2pm-2am, Fri.-Sat. noon-2am).

Down the street, the **Names Project,** 2362 Castro St. (863-1966) sounds a more somber note. This is the headquarters of an organization that has accumulated over 12,000 3 ft. x 6 ft. panels for the AIDS Memorial Quilt. Each panel is a memorial to a person who has died of AIDS. In addition to housing the project's administration, the building contains a workshop where victim's friends and relatives create panels. Several panels are always on display. (Open Mon.-Fri. 10am-10pm, Sat.-Sun. noon-8pm.) **Cruisin' Castro** gives walking tours of Castro St. daily at 10am ($25, including a meal. Call 550-8110 for reservations).

Mission Dolores, at 16th and Dolores St. in the old heart of San Francisco, reputed to be the oldest building in the city, turns 200 this year. The mission was founded in 1776 by Father Junípero Serra and, like San Francisco itself, was named in honor of St. Francis of Assisi. The mission, however, sat close to a marsh known as *Laguna de Nuestra Señora de los Dolores* (Laguna of Our Lady of Sorrows) and despite Serra's wishes, gradually became known as *Misiíon de los Dolores.* Inside the chapel one can see the elaborate altar plus some 18th century burial sites. Exotic bougainvillae, poppies, and birds of paradise bloom in the cemetery, which was featured in Alfred Hitchcock's *Vertigo.* (Admission $1. Open daily 9am-4:30pm; Nov.-Apr. 9am-4pm.)

West of Castro, the population thins and the peninsula swells with several large hills. On rare fogless nights, you can get a fine view of the city from **Twin Peaks,** between Portola Dr., Market St., and Clarendon Ave., whose three-masted radio tower can be seen from all around town. The Spanish called Twin Peaks "Mission Peaks" or "*Los Pedros de la Choca*" (the Breasts of the Indian Maidens). South of the peaks on Portola Dr. is Mt. Davidson, the highest spot in San Francisco at 938 feet. The summit bore a cross erected in 1923, but fire destroyed both this cross and its replacement. The builders of the third cross didn't take any chances: in 1934 they constructed a still-standing 103-foot cross made of concrete. West of the peaks is the **San Francisco Zoo** (753-7061), Sloat Blvd. at the Pacific Ocean is especially strong on man's closest relatives, with its Primate Discovery Center and Gorilla World. (Open daily 10am-5pm. Admission $6, seniors and ages 12-16 $3, under 12 free.)

Haight-Ashbury

The 60s live in Haight-Ashbury, only nowadays the tradition is borne self-consciously. The Haight willfully preserves an era that many seek to forget and others can't remember. Originally a quiet lower-middle class neighborhood, the Haight's large Victorian houses—perfect for communal living—and the district's proximity to the University of San Francisco drew a massive hippie population in the mid- and late-1960s. LSD, possession of which was not yet a felony, pervaded the neighborhood. The hippie voyage reached its apogee in 1966-67 when Janis Joplin, the Grateful Dead, and the Jefferson Airplane all lived and made music in the neighborhood. During 1967's "Summer of Love," young people from across the country converged on the grassy Panhandle of Golden Gate Park for the celebrated "be-ins." To some, the Haight seemed the very center of human consciousness. To others, it was just a dirty street of runaways and bad drugs. Despite recent gentrification, Haight-Ashbury remains cheap and exciting. Many of the bars and restaurants are remnants of a past era, with faded auras, games in the back rooms, and live-in regulars.

Walk down Haight St. and poke your head in as many stores as you like. With all the vintage clothing shops, you're likely to think you've died and gone to your grandparent's attic. **Aardvark's Odd Ark,** 1501 Haight St. (621-3141), at Ashbury, has an immense selection of used new wave jackets music in the background, and prices that will take you back in time. (Open Sat.-Mon. 11am-9pm, Wed. 11am-7pm, Thu. 11am-9pm, Fri 11am-8pm.) **Wasteland,** 1660 Haight St. (863-3150), is another used clothing store and is deserving of notice, if only for its wonderful façade and window displays. (Open Mon.-Fri. 11am-6pm, Sat. 11am-7pm, Sun. Noon-6pm). Funky vintage meets the rummage sale at **Buffalo Exchange,** 1555 Haight St. (431-7733). This cool place features an amazing selection of "experienced clothing." (Open Mon.-Sat. 11am-7pm, Sun. noon-6pm). **Great Expectations Bookstore,** 1512 Haight St. (863-5515) is the place to go for "Wonder Warthog" T-shirts. (Open Sun.-Thurs. 10:15am-9:40pm, Fri.-Sat. 10:15am-10:40pm.) **Reckless Records,** 1401 Haight St. (431-3434), prices their collection of used LPs according to the number of scratches and the rarity of the album. (Open Mon.-Sat. 10am-10pm, Sun. 10am-8pm.)

The **Global Family Networking Center,** 1665 Haight St. (864-1978) contains a café, market, and global awareness. The rooms at the **Red Victorian Inn,** (or just "Red Vic") could be a museum but for the lack of velvet ropes and "Do Not Touch" signs. (See Accommodations.)

The Holo Gallery, 1792 Haight St. (668-4656), is an off-beat museum definitely worth seeing. Its collection of holograms is the closest most of today's USF students come to tripping. Many of the smaller *objets d'art* as well as holographic stickers are for sale. (Open Mon.-Sat. 11am-6pm. Free.) The Haight is also home to some excellent bookstores (see Bookstores).

Resembling a dense green mountain in the middle of the Haight, **Buena Vista Park** has a predictably bad reputation. Enter at your own risk, and once inside, be prepared for those doing their own thing.

MUNI buses #6, 7, 16x, 43, 66, 71, and 73 all serve the area, while Metro line N runs along Carl St., four blocks south.

Golden Gate Park

No visit to San Francisco is complete without an encounter with Golden Gate Park. Frederick Law Olmsted, designer of New York's Central Park, said it couldn't be done when San Francisco's 19th-century elders asked him to build a park to rival Paris's Bois de Boulogne on their city's western side. But engineer William Hammond Hall and Scottish gardener John McLaren proved him wrong. Hall designed the 1000-acre park—gardens and all—when the land was still just shifting sand dunes, and then constructed a mammoth breakwater along the oceanfront to protect the seedling trees and bushes from the sea's burning spray. McLaren planted more than one million trees in the park during his 55 years as the Golden Gate's godfather, transforming the sand into soil with sea-bent grass, humus, and Augean truckloads of manure. The early groundskeepers wanted to preserve the pristine lawns by enforcing a "keep off the grass" rule, but McLaren was outraged and threatened to have all the grass covered over with cement if the rule was enforced. A strong-minded character, McLaren disliked statues in "his" park and tried to hide them in bushes. Despite his orders, a statue of McLaren was erected after he died at age 93.

To get to the park from downtown, hop on bus #5 or 21. Bus #44 passes right by the major attractions and serves 6th Ave. to California Ave. to the north and the MUNI Metro to the south. Most of the park is bounded by Fulton St. to the north, Stanyan St. to the east, Lincoln Way to the south, and the Pacific Ocean to the west. The major north-south route through the park is named Park Presidio By-Pass Drive in the north and Cross Over Drive in the south. The **Panhandle,** a thin strip of land bordered by Fell and Oak St. on the north and south respectively, is the oldest part of the park. Originally the "carriage entrance," it contains the most elderly trees and shoots some greenery into the veins of Haight-Ashbury. **Park headquarters,** where you can procure information and maps, is at Fell and Stanyan St. (556-2920), in McLaren Lodge on the eastern edge of the park. (Open Mon.-Fri. 8am-5pm.)

There are three museums in the park, all in one large complex on the eastern side between South and John F. Kennedy Dr., where 9th Ave. meets the park. On the south side of the complex is the **California Academy of Sciences,** and facing it are the **M. H. de Young Memorial Museum** and the **Asian Art Museum.** The **California Academy of Sciences** (221-5100; 750-7145 for a recording; admission $6), one of the nation's largest institutions of its kind, houses several smaller museums that specialize in different bodies of science. To the left of the entrance hall stands the Stimson African Hall, to the right the North American Hall. They both encase large, stuffed corpses of native animals. To the left of the whale courtyard, the Wattis Hall of Man details the various stages of human evolution. The **Steinhart Aquarium** (221-5100) is more lively than the natural history exhibits. Here is a chance to see the Dungeness crab before it's been steamed and to hear the plaintive song of the croakerfish. The alligator and crocodile pool is engaging but pales in comparison with the unique Fish Roundabout, a tank shaped like a doughnut where the fish swim around you. The aquarium also boasts a display explaining why San Francisco's beaches are particularly prone to great white shark attacks (pssst. . .it's the seals), as well as a second, equally perky and comforting disquisition on the San Andreas fault. (Seals and dolphins fed Fri.-Wed. 10:30am-4:30pm every 2 hr.; penguins fed daily at 11:30am and 4pm.) Competing with the Universal Studios Tour, the **Space and Earth Hall** shows a video of a simulated earthquake. For a break from so much heavy data, the "Far Side of Science" gallery shows dozens of the best cartoons Gary Larson has ever drawn about nature and scientists. The Academy's **Morrison Planetarium** re-creates the heavens above with an impressive show. (Additional charge of $2.50, seniors and students $1.25. Call 750-7141 for a schedule.) The **Laserium** (750-7138) orients its argon laser show to such rocking themes as Pink Floyd's "The Wall" (Fri.-Sat. at 9pm and 10:30pm, Sun. at 9pm) and U2 (Fri.-Sun. at 7:30pm). (Tickets $6, 5pm matinee $5, over 65 and 6-12, $4.) Call 750-7138 for the current schedule. The synesthetic spectacle may be too intense for young children. (Academy open daily 10am-7pm; Sept. 2-July 3 10am-5pm. Admission $4, $3 with MUNI Fast Pass or transfer, seniors and ages 12-17 $2, 6-11 $1, under 6 free. Free first Wed. of every month until 8:45pm.)

The **M. H. de Young Museum** (750-3600) takes visitors through a 21-room survey of American painting, from the colonial period to the early 20th century, including several works by John Singer Sargent, and a gallery of late 19th-century *trompe l'oeil* paintings. Several sculptures and pieces of antique furniture are mixed in with this survey. Also noteworthy is the museum's glass collection, which features ancient, European, Tiffany, and Steuben pieces. The **Asian Art Museum** (668-8921) is located in the west wing of the building. This beautiful collection includes rare pieces of jade and porcelain, in addition to works of bronze, which are over 3000 years old. Both museums offer a variety of free tours, some daily and others once a week. Call for details. (Both museums open Wed.-Sun. 10am-5pm. Admission $4, $3 with Muni Fast Pass or transfer, seniors and ages 12-17 $2, under 12 free. One admission fee covers the De Young, Asian, and Palace of the Legion of Honor (see Richmond) museums for one day, so save your receipt. These three museums are free the first Wed. of every month and from 10am-noon on the first Sat.

Despite its sandy past, the soil of Golden Gate Park appears rich enough today to rival the fertile soil of the San Joaquin Valley. Flowers bloom all around, particularly in spring and summer. The **Conservatory of Flowers** (386-3150) is the oldest building in the park, allegedly constructed in Ireland and shipped from Dublin via Cape Horn. The delicate and luminescent structure is modeled after Palm House in London's Kew Gardens and houses brilliant displays of tropical plants, including the very rare Masdevallia and Dracula orchids. (Open daily 9am-6pm; Nov.-Mar. 9am-5pm. Admission $1.50, seniors and ages 6-12 75¢, under 6 free. Admission is free daily from 9:30am-10am and 5:30-6pm, on the first Wednesday of each month and on major holidays.) The **Strybing Arboretum,** on Lincoln Way at 9th Ave. (661-1316), southwest of the academy, is home to 5000 varieties of plants. The **Garden of Fragrance** was designed especially for the visually impaired; the labels are in braille and the plants are chosen specifically for their texture and scent. (Open Mon.-Fri. 9am-4:30pm, Sat.-Sun. 10am-5pm. Tours daily at 1:30pm, and Thurs.-Sun. at 10:30am. Free.) Near the Music Concourse on a path off South Dr., the **Shakespeare Garden** contains almost every flower and plant ever mentioned by the herbalist of Avon. Plaques with the relevant quotations are hung on the back wall, and there's a map to help you find your favorite hyacinths and cowslips. (Open daily 9am-dusk; in winter closed Mon. Free.) **Rhododendron Dell,** between the Academy of Sciences and John F. Kennedy Dr., honors John McLaren with a splendid profusion of his favorite flower. In the middle of Stow Lake, **Strawberry Hill** is covered with strawberry plants. Rent a boat, or cross the footbridge and climb the hill for a dazzling view of the San Francisco peninsula. At the intersection of Lincoln Way and South Dr., the **Japanese Cherry Orchard** blooms intoxicatingly during the first week in April; it remains beautiful year-round.

Created for the 1894 Mid-Winter Exposition, the elegant **Japanese Tea Garden** is a serene collection of dark wooden buildings, small pools, graceful footbridges, carefully pruned trees, and plants. Buy tea and cookies for $1 and watch the giant goldfish circle the central pond. (Open daily 9am-6:30pm; Oct.-Feb. 8:30am-5:30pm. Admission $2, seniors and ages 6-12 $1, under 6 free. Also free the first and last ½ hr. of daily operation and on national holidays.)

At the extreme northwestern corner of the park, the **Dutch Windmill** turns and turns again. The powerhouse, built in 1905 to pump irrigation water for the nascent park, measures 114 ft. from sail to sail. Rounding out the days of yore is the **carousel** (c. 1912), which is accompanied by a $50,000 Gebruder band organ. (Open daily 10am-5pm; Oct.-May Wed.-Sun. 10am-4pm. Admission $1, ages 6-12 25¢, under 6 free.)

The multinational collection of gardens and museums in Golden Gate Park would not be complete without something distinctly American: its own herd of **buffalo.** A dozen of the shaggy beasts roam a spacious paddock at the western end of John F. Kennedy Dr., near 39th Ave.

On Sundays traffic is banned from park roads, and bicycles and roller skates come out in full force. Bike rental shops are plentiful. Roller skates and blades, although harder to come by, are also available (see Practical Information).

The Presidio, Golden Gate, and Richmond District

The **Presidio,** a sprawling army-owned preserve that extends all the way from the Marina in the east to the wealthy Sea Cliff area in the west, provides endless opportunities for parambulating through the trees or on the beach. The 6th Army occupied the park for years, but the U.S. Congress has recently ordered it out. At the northern tip of the Presidio (and the peninsula), just under the Golden Gate Bridge, **Fort Point,** announces the end of Lincoln Blvd. (556-1693). The fort was built in 1853 as one of a series of bunker defenses designed to protect San Francisco from invasion by the British during the tense dispute over the Oregon boundary; it now houses a museum and is a perfect place to watch the sea-savaged surfers below and the steady bridge above. It is also the spot where Kim Novak dove into the Bay in Hitchcock's *Vertigo.* Guided tours are given by National Park Rangers in 19th-century uniforms. (Museum open daily 10am-5pm. Hour-long walks are at 10:30am, 1pm, 2:30pm, and 4pm. Free. There is also a slide show about the history of the fort at 11:30am, a cannon drill demonstration at 2pm, and a 25 min. movie describing the construction of the Golden Gate Bridge at 3:30pm.) Aficionados of military regalia and Presidio history may want to stop at the **Presidio Army Museum,** Lincoln Blvd. (561-4115), at Funston Ave. The collection is heavy on guns, old uniforms, and sepia-toned photographs. (Open Tues.-Sun. 10am-4pm. Free.) The museum is closed for repairs until June of 1992.

The Spanish once called the entrance to the San Francisco Bay *La Boca del Puerto de San Francisco* (the mouth of the Port of San Francisco). Scorning simplicity, General John Fremont, the indecisive abolitionist, decided to rename it *Chrysopylae* "for the same reason that the harbor of Byzantium was called *Chrysoceras,* or Golden Horn." He failed to explain the connection, but the name Golden Gate stuck. The **Golden Gate Bridge,** the rust-colored symbol of the West's bounding confidence, sways above the entrance to San Francisco Bay. Built in 1937 under the direction of chief engineer Joseph Strauss, the bridge is almost indescribably beautiful from any angle on or around it. Even though you may have seen pictures of it, you still won't be able to get over the bridge's extrordinarily graceful and delicate design when you first see it, expecially if it is cloaked in fog. The bridge's overall length is 8981 ft., the main span 4200 ft. long. The stolid towers are 746 ft. high. The wind can blow 100 mph into the bay and barely shake a cable—the bridge was untouched by the '89 quake.

Lincoln Park, at the northwest extreme of the city, is the biggest attraction in the **Richmond District.** To reach Lincoln Park, follow Clement St. west to 34th Ave., or Geary Blvd. to Point Lobos Ave. or take MUNI bus #1 or 38 to the edge of the park. The park's **California Palace of the Legion of Honor** (750-3659) is modeled after the Colonnade Hôtel de Salm in Paris and houses the city's best collection of European art. The gallery is particularly strong on French art; it includes one of the country's finest Rodin collections, both in plaster and bronze, plus many impressionist works and two unusual Davids. Within the museum, the **Achenbach Foundation for Graphic Arts** displays its extensive holdings of paper-medium artwork. Temporary exhibits of some of the foundation's collection are on display downstairs. (Open Wed.-Sun. 10am-5pm. Admission $4, $3 with MUNI pass or transfer, seniors and ages 12-17 $2, under 12 free. Price includes same-day admission to the De Young and Asian Art museums in Golden Gate Park. Free first Wed. and Sat. of each month 10am-noon.) The museum grounds offer a romantic view of the Golden Gate Bridge. Take the **Land's End Path,** running northwest of the cliff edge, for an even better look. Southwest of Lincoln Park sits the precarious **Cliff House,** the third of that name to occupy this picturesque spot (the previous two burned down before the present structure was erected in 1909). A **visitors center** here dispenses information on the whiskered wildlife of the cliffs area, as well as on the history of the Cliff House series. (Open Mon.-Tues. and Thurs.-Fri. 11am-5pm, Sat.-Sun. 10am-5pm. Free.)

Turning out to sea from the western cliffs along Point Lobos Ave., you can see Seal Rocks, often occupied by earless animals. Don't feed the coin-operated binoculars which look out over the seals, simply head into the visitors center and have a free look through its telescope. At the base of the cliff lies **Ocean Beach,** the largest and most popular of San Francisco's beaches. The undertow along the point is so strong that swimming is prohibited and even wading is dangerous—not to mention the sharks. Nevertheless die-hard surfers gladly brave these dangers and the ice-cold water in their quest for the best waves in San Francisco. Swimming is allowed at **Phelan Beach,** below Lincoln Park at the end of Seacliff Ave. on the eastern edge of the park, and at nearby China Beach. Lifeguards are on duty from April to October. The water is warmest in late summer.

To the east of the Cliff House are the ruins of Adolph Sutro's 1896 dream baths. Cooled by ocean water, the **Sutro Baths** were capable of squishing in 10,000 occupants at a time. Generations of San Franciscans got to know one another in this steamy spa. The baths burned down in 1966, but by then both the Golden Gate and Bay Bridges had been built, allowing formerly isolated residents to roam farther afield in search of soapy pleasures. Several paths lead from Point Lobos Ave. down to the ruins, and provide an invigorating ½-hour stroll. Use caution when exploring the ruins and nearby cliffs and caves—the signs which warn of ferocious waves washing people from the cliffs to their deaths do not lie.

Entertainment

> *I watched Young California and saw that it was at least expensively dressed, cheerful in manner, and self-asserting in conversation.*
>
> *—Rudyard Kipling*

See Publications for a rundown of magazines and newspapers with entertainment listings. Or call the **Entertainment Hotline,** 391-2001 or 391-2002. The *Bay Guardian* always has a thorough listing of dance clubs and live music.

Gay and Lesbian Clubs

Gay nightlife in San Francisco flourishes. Most of the popular bars can be found in the city's two traditionally gay areas—the Castro (around the intersection of Castro St. and Market St.), and Polk St. (for several blocks north of Geary St.). Most "straight" dance clubs feature at least one gay night a week, usually Sundays.

For further information on gaieties in the gay community, consult the *Advocate,* the *San Francisco Bay Guardian* (see Publications), or the friendly staffers of the **Gay Switchboard** (841-6224).

The Stud, 399 9th St. (863-6623). A classic gay club with great dance music. Mon. night is funk night. No cover on weekdays. Open daily.

The Kennel Club, 628 Divisadero (931-1914), hosts both "The Box" and "Club Q." Although "The Box" offers funk and soul for gays, the dancing is so good that it's fast becoming popular for a straight crowd as well. Open Sun.-Thurs. 9pm-2am. "The Q Club," on Thursdays, has dancing primarily for women.

End Up, 401 6th St. at Harrison (543-7700). Devotes Sundays to "Club Uranus" for gays.

Amelia's, 647 Valencia (552-7788). A popular lesbian dance bar. No cover charge. Open Wed.-Sat. 4pm-2am.

The Stallion, 749 Polk (775-2213). Provides a convenient, central starting point for a survey of Polk folk.

Kino's, 1351 Polk St. (885-4535). Fabulous drag show on the first Sat. of every month. Open 9am-2am.

Le Club Touche, 300 De Haro (861-8990). Has a dance called "Skirts" on Sundays.

The Townsend, 177 Townsend (974-6020). A spacious club with house music and a gay night Sundays.

Nightbreak, 1821 Haight St. (221-9008), features "Female Trouble" on Wednesdays for women.

Café San Marco, 2367 Market St. (861-3846). Yet another popular gay bar. Open Mon.-Fri. 2pm-2am, Sat.-Sun. noon-2am.

Metro Bar and Restaurant, 3600 16th St. (703-9750), near Market St.

Castro Station, 456 Castro (626-7220). Bar open Mon.-Fri. 3:30pm-1:30am, Sat-Sun. noon-1:30am.

I Beam, 1748 Haight St. (668-6023) has a gay tea dance starting at 5pm every Sunday. (See listing below.)

Clubs

The Paradise Lounge, 1501 Folsom St. (861-6906). With three stages, two floors, five bars, and up to five different bands a night, this club is, as you can guess, a great place to see live music. Pool tables upstairs. Something for everone. Must be 21. open daily 3pm-2am.

DNA Lounge, 375 11th St. (626-1409) at the corner of Hanson. Both live music and dancing. The best night for dancing is Wed. Cover varies with the performer but usually doesn't exceed $10. Open until 3:30am. Must be 21.

The I-Beam, 1748 Haight St. (668-6086), Haight-Ashbury. Trendy as all hell. Specializes in post-Branca bands and DJs playing high-tech rock. Decor includes shooting light beams and 2 screens featuring clips from cartoons, golden oldies, and Japanese monster flicks. Often free student night Wed. or Thurs. Gay tea dance starting at 5pm Sunday. Cover $5-10. Used to be a gay scene, and some nights still is. Must be 21; stringent carding. Open daily from 9pm.

Kimballs', 300 Grove St. (861-5555), at Franklin St. Great jazz musicians scare off the New Age/fusion frauds at this popular club/restaurant. Shows Wed.-Thurs. 9pm, Sat.-Sun. 11pm. Cover usually $8-12.

Club DV8, 540 Howard St. (777-1419). Three floors of sheer dance mania. One of those "in places to be." For the best dancing, stick to the third floor "osmosis." Open until 4am.

El Rio, 3158 Mission St. (282-3325). The feature entertainment here is the Latin music every Sun. night, but rock bands play regularly as well. Open Tues.-Sat. 3pm-2am, Sun.-Mon. 3pm-midnight. Food served Sun. from 4-8pm. Cover $5-7 when there's live music.

The Club Fugazi, 678 Green St. (421-4222), between Powell St. and Columbus Ave. in North Beach. Has long been running *Beach Blanket Babylon,* a cabaret-style revue and San Francisco cult classic. Box office open Mon.-Sat. 10am-6pm, Sun. noon-6pm. Admission $18-22, Sun. matinee $13-21. Ages under 21 admitted only to Sun. matinee.

Café du Nord, on Market St. between Church and Sanchez in the Mission (861-5016). This expansive bar has quickly become the trendy spot to "be seen." Packed every night of the week. The employees are only too happy to let you know just how "in" this club is and just how "in" they are for working there. Pool tables 75¢. Occasional bands. Beers $3. Cover $1 on the weekends. Open 4pm-2am.

Perry's, 1944 Union St. (922-9022). San Francisco's most famous pick-up junction is a comfortable, vaguely old-fashioned place, lackadaisical by day, hopping at night. Large draft beer $3.25. Food until midnight. Open daily 7:30am-1am.

Holy Cow, 1531 Folsom (621-6087). A life-size plastic cow marks the spot. Formerly the Stud's location, this bar/dance club tends to attract the trendy mainstream with music to match, but the crowded bar has an energetic atmosphere. No cover. Tough carding. Open Tues.-Sat.

Vesuvio Café, 255 Columbus Ave. (362-3370). Watch poets and chess players from the balcony, or hide from them in the dark and subdued bar. Drinks average $3.25-6. Open daily 6am-2am. Must be 21 to enter.

Covered Wagon Saloon, 917 Folsom St. (974-1585) at 5th. Has wacky Wed. nights, called "Andy's Jukebox" with all the weird, yet enjoyable songs of yesteryear. Sat. is funk night. Mon.-Fri. 4:30-7pm is happy hour with $1 Buds. Must be 21. Open daily 3pm-2am.

650 Howard, 650 Howard St. (896-1950). An after hours dance club. Sat. is "Tune Town" from 11pm-6am. No cover Mon.-Tues.

Nicky's BBQ, 547 Haight (863-2276), has a DJ every night with different themes. Mon. features country western music. No cover. Open 11:30am-1:30pm.

Cinema

Gateway, 215 Jackson St. (421-3353), at Battery. Independent and foreign films $6.50. First show of the day $3.50, over 64 and under 11 $3.50.

Clay, 2261 Fillmore (346-1123), at Clay. Mainstream foreign films, with the occasional obscure import. Admission $6.50, over 60, under 11 and first show of the day $3.

Bridge, 3010 Geary Blvd. (751-3212) at Blake 3 blocks west of Masonic. Independent and otherwise overlooked films. Admission $6.50, over 64, under 11, and matinee $3.50.

Roxie, 3117 16th St. (863-1087), near Valencia. Razor-sharp and fashionably foolish punk and new wave movies. San Francisco's trendiest moviehouse; partly responsible for the *Eraserhead* cult. Admission $5, seniors and ages under 12 $2. Members $4 (if you go once, you're considered a member).

Red Victorian Movie House, 1659 Haight St. (668-3994), near hotel of the same name. Munch on popcorn while watching art films and revivals from communal couches. Admission $5, first show $4, seniors and children $3.

Castro Theatre, 429 Castro St. (621-6120), near Market St. Beautifully refinished 1930s movie palace. Live organ music between showings. Wide selection of films, week-long festivals, and clever double-features, including Hollywood classics of the 30s and 40s. Admission $6, seniors, under 12, and special matinees $3.50.

Strand, 1127 Market St. (621-2227), between 7th and 8th St., at the Civic Center. Eclectic foreign films in a downright bad neighborhood. Double features, sometimes triple. Continuous shows from noon. Admission $3.

The New York Theater, 2789 24th St. (647-8181), at Bryant St. Double-feature theme series on many nights of the week. Admission $5, seniors and ages under 11 $2.

North Point Theater, 2290 Powell St. (989-6061), at Bay St. in North Beach. Average first-run movies, but the super screen and superb sound make even *Terminator 2* a classic. Admission $6.50, seniors and children $3.50. First show $4.

The Lumiere, 1572 California (885-3200), at Polk St. Independent and generally intelligent films. Occasional double features with two-for-one price. Admission $6.50, seniors, children, and first show $3.50.

Cinematech, 800 Chestnut St. (558-8129), between Jones and Leavenworth St. Avant-garde and non-commercial movies in the auditorium of the San Francisco Art Institute. Admission $3, seniors and students $1.50. Closed during the summer.

Bookstores

San Francisco bookstores can truly be considered part of the entertainment scene. The city's countless paperback palaces hold materials on subjects ranging from Aristotle and anarchy to hiking and hermeneutics. The Haight concentrates more bookstores per block than any other area, but the selection is skewed towards the Bukowski/*Strange Films*/Jim Morrison bio genre.

North Beach

City Lights Books, 261 Columbus Ave. (362-8193), just east of Grant Ave. in North Beach. Lawrence Ferlinghetti's popular bookstore has expanded and continues to publish under its own imprint the works of new poets as well as authors who have been active since the 50s. A poetry room contains self-published works and a whole case of Beats, among other authors. You can still read leftist magazines in the store's chairs. Thought-provoking and extensive selection. Open daily 10am-midnight.

Columbus Ave. Books, 540 Broadway (986-3872), near Columbus Ave. in North Beach. A wide if uninspired selection; largely used books. Open Mon.-Thurs. 10:30am-11pm, Fri.-Sat. 10am-midnight, Sun. noon-11pm.

Quantity Postcards, 1441 Grant Ave (986-8866). Aptly named with no books, but literally thousands of postcards from 5¢ news shots of the Carter and Reagan Presidencies to $1.95 3-D views of Jesus walking on water. The place *Let's Go* R/Ws stock up. Open daily noon-11pm.

East Wind Books, 1435 Stockton (781-3329). Chinese and Chinese-American subjects, including cooking and healing. Open Mon.-Thurs. 10am-6pm, Fri.-Sat. 10am-8pm, Sun. noon-5pm.

Civic Center and Downtown

McDonald's, 48 Turk (673-2235). This self-described "dirty, poorly-lit place for books" presents a deceivingly small face to the street. The inside is stacked and packed with facts and tracts. Open Mon.-Tues. and Thurs. 10am-6pm, Wed., Fri.-Sat. 10:30am-6:45pm.

Richard Hilkert Bookseller, Ltd., 333 Hayes St. (863-3339), between Gough and Franklin St. The 2-person 2-room operation is blessed by a genial, hospitable manager whose eclectic tastes are reflected in the wildly varied stock. Open Mon.-Fri. 8:30am-5pm, sometimes later. Unreliable hours Sat.-Sun.

Sierra Club Bookstore, 730 Polk St. (923-5600), between Ellis and Eddy St. just north of the Civic Center. Best collection of trail guidebooks in the country. Stop here before making an excursion to the Sierras; the staff is friendly and helpful for planning trips and answering a range of queries. Open Mon.-Fri. 10am-5:30pm, Sat. 10am-5pm.

Hunter's Bargain Books, 151 Powell St. (397-5955) at O' Farrell. What a selection of marked-down new books! Lots of heavy coffee-table art books. Open Mon.-Sat. 9:30am-9:30pm, Sun. 10am-7:30pm.

Acorn Books, 740 Polk St. (563-1736), next door to the Sierra Club. An enormous collection of primarily used books, ordered in an organized fasion with room for expansion. The used books are downright cheap and even if you don't want to invest in your own copy, chairs and couches invite weary shoppers to sit and read in the store. A great collection of old magazines and periodicals. Open Mon.-Sat. 10:30am-8pm, Sun. noon-7pm.

The Mission District and Castro Street

Books and Bookshelves, 99 Sanchez St. (863-5864), between Market and 14th St. in the Mission District. Large selection of new and used poetry and literature. 10¢ specials. Open daily 10am-7pm.

Haight-Ashbury and the Richmond District

Bound Together Bookstore: An Anarchist Collective, 1369 Haight St. (431-8355), at Massonic. Orderly stacks of new and used books. Subject headings include "commie" and "magical arts." Open daily 11:30am-7:30pm.

Uma's Occult Shop, 1915 Page St. (668-3132), 1 block north of Haight St. Strong smell of patchouli and the sort of esoteric books that go with it. Open Tues.-Sat. noon-6pm.

Albatross III, 143 Clement St. (752-8611), in the Richmond District. Neat collection of used books, especially classics. Specials 50¢ and up. Open Sun., Wed-Thurs. noon-10pm, Tues., Fri.-Sat. noon-11pm.

The Kiosk, 1504 Haight St. (626-2436). Comprehensive selection of foreign newspapers and periodicals. Open Mon.-Sat. 10am-10pm, Sun. 9am-10pm.

The Green Apple Bookstore, 506 Clement St. (387-2272), in Richmond. Legendary in San Francisco. Buys, sells, trades used books. Very extensive and well-organized collection. Open Sun.-Thurs. 10am-10pm, Fri.-Sat. 10am-midnight.

Seasonal Events

Chinese New Year Celebration in Chinatown. Feb. 8-15 in 1992. North America's largest Chinese community celebrates the Year of the Monkey (4690 on the lunar calendar) with cultural festivities, a parade, and the crowning of Miss Chinatown USA. Feb. 15 at 6pm.

San Francisco International Film Festival, April-July 1992. Northern California's longest running film festival.

Cherry Blossom Festival April 3-5 and 10-12 in 1992, in Japantown. Over 2000 Japanese-Americans celebrate with entertainers from Japan. Parade on April 12 at 1 pm.

Cinco de Mayo Parade and Celebration Parade on May 3, 1992 at 11am, starting at 24th and Harrison, in the Mission District. *Fiesta, fiesta, fiesta.*

Carnaval '92 May 22-24, 1992, in the Mission District. A parade, street festival, and costume contest constitute this revelrous Mardi Gras-like celebration of lust and sin.

San Francisco Examiner Bay to Breakers, May 17 1992. One of the world's largest foot races, done in inimitable San Francisco style. Many participants run in elaborate costumes. Runners win not only on their time but on their costume as well. Over 100,000 participants.

Haight-Ashbury Street Fair, early June. Bands, vendors, and masses of people crowd the streets between Massonic and Stanyon.

Lesbian-Gay Freedom Parade, late June. People come from all over the country to join this party. The celebration culminates in a tremendous parade starting at Castro and ending at Market.

Jazz and All That Art on Fillmore, early July. Lots of excellent jazz bands. Fillmore St.

San Francisco Bay Area

Berkeley

A quarter-century ago Mario Savio climbed on top of a police car and launched Berkeley's free speech movement. Today, Berkeley is still a national symbol of political activism and social iconoclasm. Telegraph Avenue, the Champs Elysées of the 60s, remains the home of street-corner soothsayers, funky bookstores, aging hippies, countless cafés, and itinerant street musicians. Even as today's students prefer climbing corporate ladders to digging ditches in underdeveloped countries, the Berkeley City Council eagerly considers an initiative to curb "excess profits" in real estate.

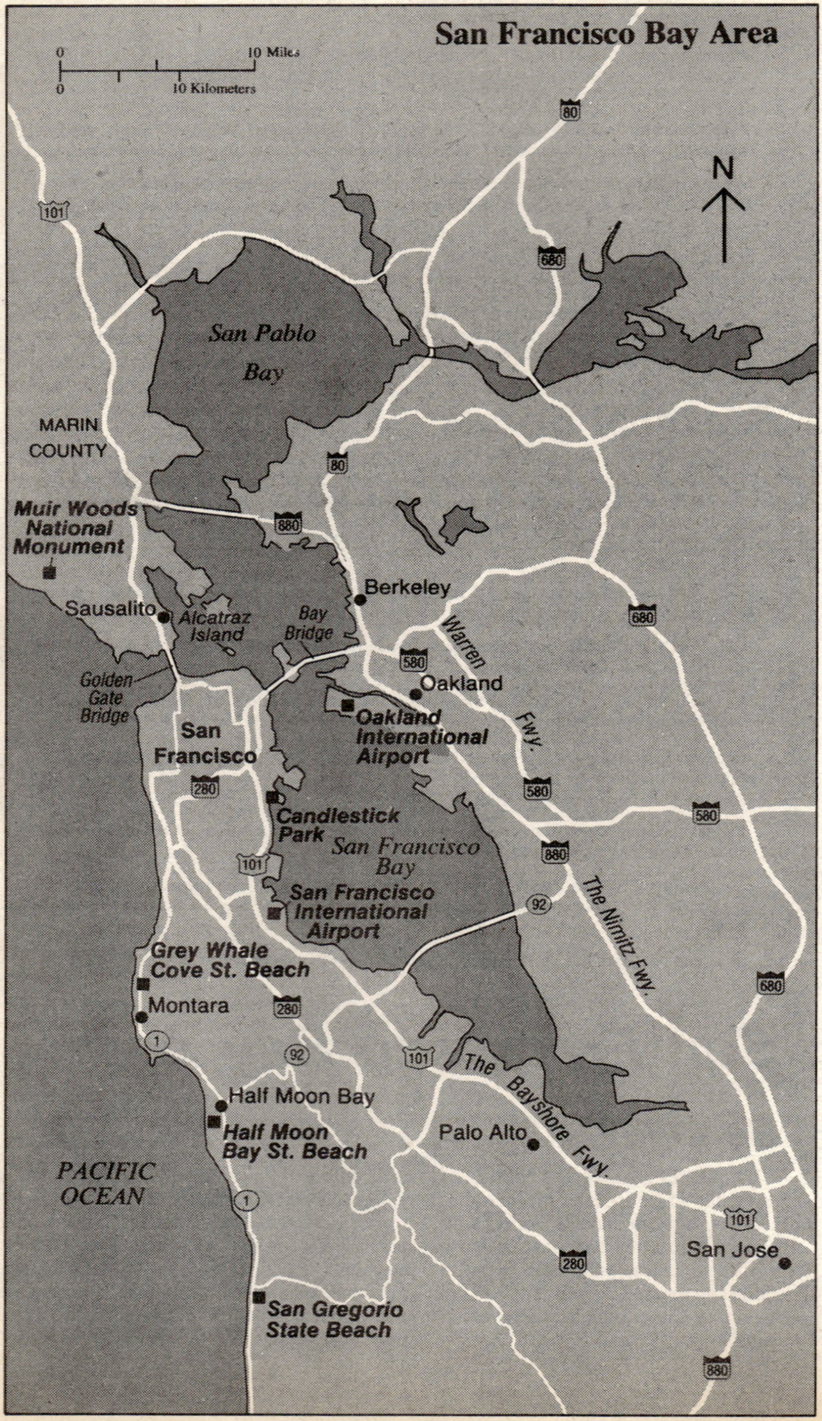
San Francisco Bay Area
0 10 Miles
0 10 Kilometers
N
80
101
680
San Pablo Bay
MARIN COUNTY
80
880
Muir Woods National Monument
Berkeley
Sausalito
Alcatraz Island
Bay Bridge
680
Warren Fwy.
580
Golden Gate Bridge
Oakland
Oakland International Airport
San Francisco
280
580
580
Candlestick Park
San Francisco Bay
880
101
San Francisco International Airport
92
The Nimitz Fwy.
Grey Whale Cove St. Beach
Montara
280
680
1
92
101
The Bayshore Fwy.
Half Moon Bay
Half Moon Bay St. Beach
Palo Alto
PACIFIC OCEAN
1
101
San Jose
280
San Gregorio State Beach
880

The site of the country's best public university, Berkeley is as renowned for its academics and chefs as for its political cadres and streetpeople. Chez Panisse, the restaurant owned by Alice Waters, is believed to have originated California Cuisine, now imitated by everyone and their frère. Northwest of campus, the shopping area around Chez Panisse has been termed the "Gourmet Ghetto" because of its abundance of voluptuous ingredients. Stylish clothing boutiques and gourmet specialty stores blanket the city. Miraculously, Berkeley revels in these bourgeois accoutrements while maintaining its idealistic rhetoric. By purchasing free-range chickens and avoiding styrofoam, citizens contentedly strike their blows against mechanized farming and the destruction of the environment.

With 60s-style social consciousness and environmental awareness returning to fashion and moderating the excesses of the Reagan era in America, Berkeley, with its peculiar combination of idealism and materialism, could yet prove to be the ultimate city for the 1990s. Then again, it may be that the dollar sign and the peace sign, like oil and water, just don't mix. In a city which is already the home of so many mental health professionals, visitors who spend more than a little time in Berkeley may still end up wondering if they have wandered into an open ward.

Practical Information

Visitor Information: Chamber of Commerce, 1834 University Ave. at Martin Luther King Dr. (549-7000). Not exactly enthusiastic. Open Mon.-Fri. 9am-noon and 1-4pm.

Budget Travel: Council on International Educational Exchange (CIEE) Travel Center, 2486 Channing Way (848-8604), at Telegraph Ave. Agreeable and knowledgeable staff. Open Mon.-Tues. and Thurs.-Fri. 9am-5pm, Wed. 10am-5pm.

Amtrak: 982-8512 or 800-872-7245. No station; closest is in Oakland.

Greyhound: 834-3070. No station; closest is Oakland.

Bay Area Rapid Transit (BART): 465-2278. The Berkeley Station is at Shattuck Ave. and Center St., close to the western edge of the university, about seven blocks from the Student Union.

Alameda County Transit (AC Transit): 839-2882. Buses #15, 40, 43, and 51 all run from the Berkeley BART stop to downtown Oakland, via M.L. King Jr. Way, Telegraph Ave., Shattuck Ave., and College Ave. respectively. Schedules for these buses are available in the Berkeley BART station.

Ride Boards: Berkeley Ride Board, ASUC building near the bookstore, on the 1st floor (642-5259).

Transportation Information: Berkeley TRIP, 643-POOL. Information on public transport, biking, and carpooling. Mostly local transportation, but not confined to daily commuting.

Car Rental: Budget, Gilman St. and 2nd (568-4770). Compact car $40 per day with unlimited free mileage. Additional charge of $10 if under 25yr. Open daily 8am-4:30pm.

Taxis: see San Francisco listings for cabs cheaper than the local variety.

Tickets: Bass Tix, 762-2277.

Recorded Event Calendar: 676-2222.

U.C. Berkeley Switchboard: 1901 8th St. (642-6000). Information on everything from community events to drug counseling. Irregular hours.

Laundromat: 3055 Telegraph Ave. (549-3305), near Ashby. Over 100 washers and dryers. Open 24 hr.

Recreation Center: 2301 Bancroft Way (642-4043), on campus. Pool, gym, Nautilus, track. $8 per day. Open Mon.-Fri. 9am-7pm, Sat. 10am-2pm.

Rape Hotline: 845-RAPE (845-7273). 24 hr.

Suicide Prevention: 849-2212 or 889-1333. 24 hr.

Poison Control Center: 800-523-2222. 24 hr.

U.C. Gay Lesbian Bisexual Alliance: 642-6942.

Berkeley Free Clinic: 2339 Durant Ave. (548-2570), 2 blocks west of Telegraph. Medical help or, in a real pinch, a bed and shower. If they can't help, they'll check their extensive files to find someone who can.

Berkeley Women's Health Collective: 2908 Ellsworth Ave. (843-6194), 1 block west of Telegraph. Open Mon., Fri. 8am-5pm, Tues.-Wed. 10am-7pm, Thu. 9am-6pm; by appointment only.

Campus Emergency: 9911 from campus phone, 642-3333 otherwise.

Campus Police: 2 Sproul Hall Basement (642-6760). 24 hr.

Post Office: 2000 Allston Way (649-3100). Open Mon.-Fri. 8:30am-5pm, Sat. 10am-2pm. General Delivery ZIP Code: 94704.

Area Code: 510.

Berkeley is awash with free publications for those seeking thrills. Most reliable and interesting is *The Berkeley Monthly* (658-9811), a magazine with comprehensive listings. (You may have to search for it a bit). For more up-to-date news, the *Daily Californian* (548-8080) prints information on university happenings. It's published by Berkeley students daily during the term, on Tuesdays and Thursdays in summer, and is available in Sproul Plaza. The *Express* (652-4610) has a vast entertainment section and is widely available at book and record stores.

Other tabloids include: *Grassroots: Berkeley's Community Newspaper,* which spreads radical news for 35¢, *Metier* (644-6893), an elegant arts journal available at galleries and bookstores and produced quarterly by the Berkeley Art Center, and the *University Art Museum/Pacific Film Archive Calendar,* with art news and film listings.

Orientation

Berkeley lies across the bay northeast of San Francisco, just north of Oakland. There are two efficient ways to reach the city: by car (I-80 or Rte. 24) or by public transportation from downtown San Francisco. Crossing the bay by **BART** ($1.85) is quick and easy, and both the university and Telegraph Ave. are short walks from the station. Alternatively, the free university **Humphrey-Go-BART shuttle** (642-5149) connects the BART station with the central and eastern portions of campus. During the school year, the shuttle leaves the station every ten to twelve minutes from 7am to 7pm, Monday through Friday (except on university holidays). Its campus route includes stops at West Gate, Moffitt Library, and the Mining Circle. BART also stops at Virginia and Sacramento St. (in northern Berkeley) and at Ashby St. (west of the university).

Buses reach Berkeley even faster than BART does. **Alameda County Transit (AC Transit)** buses ($2.25, ages over 64 and 5-16 $1, $1.25 fare returning to San Francisco) leave from the Transbay Terminal for Berkeley every 30 minutes from 5:50am to midnight. **City buses** operated by AC Transit run approximately every 20 minutes and are generally packed. ($1, ages over 64 and disabled riders 35¢, 5-16 yr. 85¢). Ask any bus driver for schedules or call the AC Transit information number (839-2882).

Berkeley is sandwiched between a series of ridges to the east and San Francisco Bay to the west. The **University of California** campus stretches into the hills, but most of its buildings are in the westernmost section, near the BART. Lined with bookstores and cafés, **Telegraph Avenue,** which runs south from the Student Union, is the spiritual center of town. The north side of campus has a few places to grab a snack but is mostly residential. The **downtown** area, around the BART station, contains what few businesses Berkeley will allow as well as the public library and central post office. The **Gourmet Ghetto** encompasses the area along Shattuck Ave. and Walnut St. between Virginia and Rose St. West of campus and by the bay lies the **Fourth St. Center,** home to great eating and window shopping. To the northwest of campus, **Solano Ave.** offers countless ethnic restaurants (the best Chinese in the city is found here), book stores, and movie theaters, as well as more shopping.

Accommodations

It is surprisingly difficult to sleep cheaply in Berkeley. There are no good hostels, and clean, cheap motels are disconcertingly lacking. Most of the city's hotels are flophouses; open spaces suitable for safe crashing are few. You might try renting a fraternity room for the night. Check the classified ads in the *Daily Californian* for possibilities.

YMCA, 2001 Allston Way (848-6800), at Milvia St. Men over 17 only. No membership required. Registration daily 8am-noon. Check-out 11:30am to noon. No curfew. Small rooms $21.59. Medium rooms $22.80. Prices include tax and use of the pool and basic fitness facilities. Key deposit $2.

University of California Housing Office, 2700 Hearst Ave. (642-5925), in Stern Hall, at the northern end of campus. Rents rooms in summer to anyone who claims connection with the school (e.g., "thinking of transferring"). Call ahead. Open daily 7am-11pm. Someone is on duty from 11pm to 7am. Singles $34. Doubles $44

Berkeley Capri Motel, 1512 University Ave. (845-7090), about a mile west of campus, near the North Berkeley BART. Some rooms scream for paint and decoration, but all are otherwise decent. TV with HBO. Singles and doubles $35.

California Motel, 1461 University Ave. (848-3840), two blocks from the North Berkeley BART station. Some rooms are nicer than others. Singles and doubles $32, two beds $40.

The Berkeley Motel, 2001 Bancroft Way (843-4043), at Milvia St. Close to Campus. Check out 11:30am. Not likely to win any maintenance awards; as always, check the mattress before you check in. TV. Singles and doubles $40.

Food

Food is not a necessity in Berkeley, it's a pastime; so much so that it supports **Bayfood** (652-6115), a monthly devoted entirely to local gustatory delights. Abd while most of the city's highbrow eats are budget busters, the odd bargain can be found.

Telegraph Avenue has more than its share of places to munch pizza, sip coffee, and slurp frozen yogurt. The espresso is excellent but the food, with the exception of **La Fiesta,** is generally mediocre by Berkeley standards. For reasonably priced, tasty fare, head downtown to **Shattuck Ave.** or **Solano Ave.**

Plearn Thai Cuisine, 2050 University Ave. (841-2148) between Shattuck and Milvia. Elegant white and blue decor. One of the best Thai joints in the Bay Area. Long lines at peak hours. Entrees $5-8.50. The Gai-Young chicken ($6.75) is a very good specimen of this somewhat hard-to-find barbecued dish. Open daily 11:30am-10pm.

Flint's Barbecue, 6609 Shattuck Ave. (653-0593), in Oakland. Just over the city line, near the Ashby BART, and worth the trip. Considered the best barbecue around. Even if you regularly order your Chinese food "extremely spicy " don't splash on hot sauce here—the chillies are too pronounced in an otherwise subtle sauce, so stick to "medium" or "mild." Unfortunately, Flint's has no seating, and there is no obvious place to take one's meal, except perhaps to the BART parking lot. Beef or pork ribs $6. Open Sun-Thurs. 11am-2am, Fri.-Sat. 11am-4am.

Bette's Oceanview Diner, 187A 4th St. in the waterfront district (548-9494). The food is as colorful as the paint. A popular choice with the students for breakfast or brunch. Mexican style eggs with fried potatoes and muffin $6.75, combination plates $6.25-7.50. Open Mon. 6:30am-2:30pm, Tues.-Sun. 6:30am-4pm.

Fat Apple's, 1346 Martin Luther King Dr. at Rose (526-2260), northwest of campus. Natural foods and hamburgers piled high with cheese and fixings ($5.50) make this a popular restaurant. Don't miss the fresh apple pie ($9) baked daily. Allow plenty of time because the line to get in often extends out the door. Open Mon.-Fri. 6am-11pm, Sat.-Sun. 7am-11pm.

Shin Shin, 1715 Solano Ave. (526-4970). A Chinese restaurant noteworthy for its cheap and varied lunch specials. You can get a small bowl of overly peppered hot and sour soup, two flaky fried wontons, and rice topped with your choice of 34 different entrees, from Hunan smoked pork to black bean sauce prawns—all for $2.85 (daily 11:30am-3:30pm). Open Sun.-Thurs. 11:30am-9:30pm, Fri.-Sat. 11:30am-10pm.

Café Intermezzo, Telegraph at Haste (849-4592). The enormous helpings of salad served with fresh bread distinguish this café from the multitudes of others along Telegraph. A combination sandwich and salad $4.25 is enough to keep you busy all day. Sandwiches $3.95. Open Mon.-Fri. 10:30am-9pm.

Blondie's Pizza, 2340 Telegraph Ave. (548-1129). Consume Dagwood-sized slices of greasy, cheesy pizza for only $1.25. Daily special $1.75. Open Mon.-Thu. 10:30am-1am, Fri.-Sat. 10:30am-2am, Sun. noon-midnight.

The Blue Nile, 2525 Telegraph Ave. (540-6777). Authentic Ethiopian food in a dark, richly atmospheric setting. Beaded curtains separate the different booths. Waitresses wear traditional gowns. Wide variety of vegetarian dishes. Lunch $4-5, dinner $6-6.75. Open Mon.-Sat. 11:30am-10pm, Sun 5am-5pm.

Zachary's Chicago Pizza, 1853 Solano Ave. (525-5950). Flaky Chicago crusts—thick or thin—with off-beat toppings, such as pesto and zucchini. Slices with toppings $1.75, pies $5-17. One wall displays works by local artists. Open Sun.-Thurs. 11am-9:30pm, Fri.-Sat. 11am-10:30pm.

Mario's La Fiesta, 2588 Telegraph Ave.(848-2885), at Haste St. Great Mexican food and a friendly atmosphere. Gets really cozy when the line forms inside and runs out the door. Filling combination plates (such as the crunchy chicken flautas, $7.20) come with rice, beans, guacamole, and chips. Open daily 10:30am-10:30pm.

Picante, 1328 6th St. at Gilman (525-3121 or 525-6595). A spacious, red-tiled interior and heaping helpings. Dishes are made with fresh vegetables. All burritos $3.36, tacos $2.29. Pitcher of beer $5. Live music Fri. and Sat. nights.

Panini, 2115 Allston Way (849-0405), in the Trumpet Vine court. The best gourmet bargain around. Panini makes exotic sandwiches that change daily. Some are hot, at least one is vegetarian, and all are delicious ($3.75-5). Simmering soup $1.75. A place you'll want to come back to. Open Mon.-Fri. 7:30am-4pm, Sat. 10am-4pm.

Top Dog, 2534 Durant Ave. and Bowditch. Though Top Dog has grown into a chain, this is where it all began. Anarchist Bumper Stickers adorn the walls, such as "Nobody for President." A wide variety of excellent dogs ($1.25-1.75). Bird Dog $2. Open Mon.-Thurs. 10am-2am. Fri. 10am-3am, Sat. 11am-3am, Sun.11am-2am.

Saul's, 1475 Shattuck Ave. (848-DELI, 848-3354). An honorable deli, which flies in its smoked fish from New York, has a special weekend brunch menu, and serves excellent "Noah's bagels." Sandwiches $4-7.50, bagels 50¢ (plain), $6.50 (with cream cheese and lox). Open daily 8am-9pm.

Acme Bread Company, 1601 San Pablo Ave. at Cedar (524-1327). West of campus but well worth the trek. Excellent bread baked on the premises. Open Mon. 8am-noon, Tues.-Fri. 8am-5pm, Sat. 10am-5pm. Arrive before 1pm for the best selection.

The Cheese Board Collective, 1504 Shattuck Ave. (549-3183). A pillar of the Gourmet Ghetto. Fantastic selection of a few hundred different cheeses, but, alas, no Venezuelan Beaver cheese. Add a few to the excellent French bread for a great picnic. **Pizza** is available next door at 1512 Shattuck, Tues.-Thurs. 11:30am-1:30pm and Fri. from 4:30pm on (549-3055). Very generous about giving samples. 10% discount for customers over 60, 15% for ages over 70, and so on. Open Tues.-Fri. 10am-6pm, Sat. 10am-5pm

Monterey Foods, 1550 Hopkins St. (526-6042), at Monterey, well northwest of campus. Best produce in Berkeley. People go out of their way to come here. The rare vegetables attract connoisseurs. Open Mon.-Sat. 9am-6pm.

Long Life Vegi House, 2129 University Ave. (845-6072). Tasty and innovative Chinese cooking. No red meat served. Vegetarian plates $3.27, seafood plates, $3.74. Chinese Brunch served Sat. and Sun. 11:30am-3pm. Open daily 11:30am-9:30pm.

Coffeehouses

Berkeley has more than its share of Europhile dives serving Algerian coffee to beaded and turtle-necked grad students. Watch out, though—the mixture of so much caffeine and cosmic angst can be overwhelming.

Espresso Strada, 2300 College Ave. (843-5282), at Bancroft. Philosophy and art grad students throng this glittering jewel of the culinary-intellectual complex. Known locally as "Café Pretentious" or "Café Be Seen." Get your cappuccino cold when the sun's hot, and enjoy the beautiful outdoor terrace. Cocoa is made with white chocolate. Heavy-duty atmosphere at night. Coffee 75¢-$1.15, Cappuccino 95¢. Open Mon.-Fri. 6:30am-11pm, Sat.-Sun. 7:30am-11:30pm.

Café Milano, 2522 Bancroft (644-3100). The most interesting-looking and perhaps the hippest contender in the Telegraph café scene. High wood-beam ceilings, brick walls, and huge windows. Giant cappuccino $1.40. Open daily 7am-midnight.

The Musical Offering, 2430 Bancroft Way (849-0211). Classical music resonates through this café/record shop. Set up as one business, the customer can browse through the classical music records or enjoy scones and coffee while listening to the music. 10% discount on records if you buy them on the composer's birthday. Salads $4.50-5.50. Café open Mon.-Fri. 8am-8pm, Sat. 10am-8pm, Sun. 11:30am-5pm. Record store open Mon.-Sat. 10am-9pm, Sun 11:30am-5pm.

Au Coquelet, 2000 University Ave. (845-0433), at Milvia. The city's only real late-night spot for sandwiches, fruit tarts, and coffee ($1-2.50). Open Mon.-Thurs. 6am-1:30am, Fri. 6am-2am, Sat. 8am-2am, Sun. 8am-1am.

Peet's Coffee Bar, 2124 Vine St. (841-0564), at Walnut, northwest of campus. Peet's is devoted more to selling coffee beans and coffee-makers than coffee itself, but you can get a cup of toe-curlingly strong brew (cream a must) for 50-80¢, 10¢ off if you bring your own mug. Moist blueberry muffins $1.25. Free cup of coffee with the purchase of a pound of beans. Open Mon.-Sat. 8am-6pm, Sun 10am-6pm.

Sights

Pass through **Sather Gate** into **Sproul Plaza** and enter the university's world of gracious buildings, grass-covered hills, and sparkling streams. Together they give the impression of an intellectual Arcadia. The **Information Center** (642-4636), in the Student Union building, at Telegraph and Bancroft, has maps, information, and booklets for self-guided tours (open Mon.-Fri. 8am-6pm, Sat. 10am-6pm). Guided tours start at the **Visitor's Center** (642-5215), Room 10, University Hall, Oxford St. and University Ave. The Berkeley campus encompasses 160 acres, bounded on the south by Bancroft Way, on the west by Oxford St., by Hearst Ave. to the north, and by extensive parkland to the east. Founded in 1868 and moved to Berkeley in 1873, the school has an enrollment of over 30,000 and more than 1000 full professors; Berkeley boasts more Nobel laureates per capita than any other city. The imposing **Bancroft Library,** with nearly seven million volumes, is among the nation's largest.

The most dramatic campus attraction is **Sather Tower,** a 1914 monument to Berkeley benefactor Jane K. Sather, modeled after the clock tower in Venice's St. Mark's Square. The 500-ton steel frame was designed to withstand large earthquakes. For 50¢, you can ride to the top of the tower for an impressive view. (Open daily 10am-4:15pm.) The tower's 61-bell carillon is played most weekdays at 7:50am, noon, and 6pm, and Sundays 2-2:45pm.

The **University Art Museum,** 2626 Bancroft Way (642-1124; 24-hr. event calendar 642-0808) holds a diverse and interesting permanent collection. Innovative directors have put together a number of memorable shows over the years on everything from cubism to the interaction of American painting and popular culture in the 50s. Within the museum, the **Pacific Film Archives** (642-1124), with one of the nation's largest film libraries, is a uniquely rich museum of cinematic art. Reels range from the obscure to the classic. (Museum open Wed.-Sun. 11am-5pm. Admission $5; students, ages over 64 and 6-17 $4. Free on Thurs. 11am-noon. The Pacific Film Archives shows films in the evening. See Cinema.)

The **Lawrence Hall of Science** (642-5132), a concrete building standing above the northeast corner of the campus, shares honors with San Francisco's Exploratorium for finest science museum in the Bay Area. Take the free express shuttle from the BART station weekdays during museum hours. Exhibits stress learning science through the hands-on use of everyday objects. Pinball machines teach atomic motion, and animals demonstrate the laws of physics. Lawrence Hall offers many special events geared toward children, from nature walks to computer classes. (Open Mon.-Fri. 10am-4:30pm, Sat.-Sun. 10am-5pm. Admission $3.50; seniors, students, and ages 7-18 $2.50, under 7 free.)

Back in the campus center, the excellent **Lowie Museum of Anthropology** (642-3681) displays selections from its 500,000 catalogued items in Kroeber Hall. Unfortunately, the Museum's limited size means that the bulk of the impressive collection is rarely, if ever, seen. The Lowie used to allow visiting scholars to freely examine its storerooms until it discovered that millions of dollars worth of art had been stolen. (Open Mon.-Fri. 8am-noon and 1pm-5pm. Admission $1, ages over 60 and under 16 35¢.) Also in Kroeber Hall is the **Worth Ryder Art Gallery** (642-2582), in Room 116. The gallery displays contemporary works of wildly disparate quality by students and local artists. (Open Tues.-Thurs. 11am-4pm. Free.)

The Earth Sciences Building houses the **Museum of Paleontology** (642-1821), the **Museum of Geology,** and the **Berkeley Seismographic Station.** The paleontology division displays hundreds of fossils and dozens of skeletons, including a painfully detailed exhibit on the evolution of the horse. The geology museum devotes its galleries to maps detailing the sedimentary structure of California and nearby states. The seismographic station is usually quiet, unless the A's and Giants happen to be playing in the World Series. (Earth Sciences Bldg. open Mon.-Fri. 8am-5pm, Sat.-Sun. 1-5pm. Free.)

Bancroft Library, in the center of campus, is an international intellectual center. Exhibits change frequently and range from California to folio editions of Shakespeare's plays. You can see the corroded bronze plaque left by Sir Francis Drake in the 16th century, claiming California for England. A gold nugget purported to be the first one plucked from Sutter's Mill, the catalyst for the 1849 Gold Rush, is also displayed in the library. The stacks are open to the public. (Open Mon.-Fri. 9am-5pm, Sat. 1-5pm. Free.)

The **Botanical Gardens,** (642-3343), in Strawberry Canyon, contain over 10,000 varieties of plant life. The Mediterranean summer, moderated by coastal fog, provides an outstanding setting. An excellent afternoon walk can be had wandering through the 33 acres of the gardens. Agatha Christie is said to have come here to examine a rare poisonous plant whose deadly powers she wished to exploit in one of her mystery novels. (Open daily 9am-5pm. Free.) For a display of roses unlike any you'll ever seen, go to the **Berkeley Rose Garden** on Euclid Ave. at Eunice St., north of the campus. Built by the WPA during the Depression, the garden spills from one terrace to another in a vast semicircular amphitheater. You can see Marin County and the Golden Gate Bridge from the far end. While in bloom, from May through September, the gardens are always open.

In his legacy to the university, newspaper tycoon William Randolph Hearst left two buildings of interest. First is the **Greek Theatre** (642-5550), in the north-central part of the campus, a glorious marble structure modeled after the classical ampitheater in Epidaurus, Greece. The site is currently used for university ceremonies and rock concerts. The Grateful Dead, a Bay Area institution for 25 years, usually play at least a couple of summertime concerts here each year. Second is the **Hearst Mining Building** in the northeast part of campus, housing displays on mining and metallurgy. (Open Mon.-Fri. 8am-4:45pm. Free.)

Outside of campus are other museums and noteworthy architecture. The **Judah Magnes Museum,** 2911 Russell St. (849-2710), displays one of the West Coast's leading collections of Judaica. (Open Sun.-Fri. 10am-4pm.) The **Julia Morgan Theater,** 2640 College Ave. (845-8542), is housed in a beautiful former church designed by its namesake and constructed of dark redwood and Douglas fir. Notable for its graceful and unusual mixing of materials, this is regarded by some as Morgan's masterpiece.

People's Park, on Haste St., 1 block off Telegraph Ave., is an unofficial museum of sorts. A mural depicts the 60s struggle between the city and local activists over whether to leave the meager block a park or to develop it commercially. During that struggle, then-governor Ronald Reagan sent in the National Guard to break a blockade, resulting in the death of one student. Three years ago, a rally was held to protest the university's renewed threats to convert the park. The demonstrators quickly forgot their noble purpose and began turning over cars, looting stores, and setting fires. Recently, the university announced that it will lease the park to the city, which plans to transform the lot into a mainstream park with plants and volleyball courts. In the interim, avoid the park at night; crack dealers and the homeless have claimed this dismal site as their own.

At the **Takara Sake Tasting Room,** 708 Addison St. (540-8250), at 4th St., you can request a sample of several different varieties, all made with California rice. A narrated slide presentation on *sake* brewing is shown on request. (Open daily noon-6pm.)

Coffeehouses, bookstores, cheap restaurants, and outdoor crafts booths operated by local artisans crowd **Telegraph Avenue,** where town meets gown. The avenue engenders its own unique population of street people, a few with their own cult followings. Some buttonhole passersby in order to spout their definitive "meaning of life"; others simply request a small, non-tax-deductible donation.

An **exercise route** for those of the athletic persuasion runs from the university gymnasium on Dana St. along Bancroft Way. Freshwater swimming is available during the summer from 10am to dusk at **Lake Anza** in the center of the park. A 19th-century carousel appeases juvenile thrill-seekers. The park also has an 18-hole golf course (848-7373) and pony rides (527-0421). Outdoorspeople ought to consider taking the 15-minute bus ride or strenuous uphill 25-minute walk to **Tilden Regional Park,** east of the campus. At the north end of the park, the **Environmental Education Center** (525-2233) offers exhibits and naturalist-led programs.

Entertainment

Hang out with procrastinating students in front of or inside the **Student Union** (642-5215). The ticket office, arcade, bowling alleys, and pool tables are all run from a central desk. (Open Mon.-Fri. 8am-6pm, Sat. 10am-6pm; in winter Mon.-Fri. 8am-10pm, Sat. 10am-6pm.) The **Bear's Lair**, a student pub, is next door (843-0373). A pitcher of Bud goes for $4. (Open Mon.-Thurs. noon-midnight, Fri. 11am-8pm; summer hours vary, Sat.-Wed. 11am-6pm, live music Thu. and Fri.) **CAL Performance,** 101 Zellerbach Hall (642-7477), is the university-wide concert and lecture organizer. Information on all the rock, classical, and jazz concerts, lectures, and movies on campus is available here. Ask them about non-paying ushering jobs (a good way to see shows for free). Big concerts are usually held in the Greek Theatre or Zellerbach Hall. (Open Mon.-Fri. 10am-5:30pm, Sat. noon-4pm.)

Ashkenaz, 1317 San Pablo Ave. (525-5054), between Gilman St. and Camelia. A folk-dance co-op that often swings with reggae bands. Children welcome. Cover depends on performer; usually $5-6 for afternoon performances, $7-8 at night. Open some afternoons and most evenings Tues.-Sun. from 9:30pm-1am.

Bars

Brennan's, 4th St. and University Ave. (841-0960), down by the waterfront in nonstudent Berkeley. Cheap liquor and large crowds from every part of the city combine for the best Bacchanalian budget-obliteration. Steam tables at one end offer cheap food for the fearless. Great Irish coffee $2.75. Open Sun.-Thu. 11am-midnight, Fri.-Sat. 11am-2am. Food served until 9pm. Women may feel outnumbered.

Starry Plough, 3101 Shattuck Ave. (841-2082). A pub with Irish bands and Anchor Steam on tap. Posters espouse pro-Irish, anti-nuclear and U.S.-out-of-Nicaragua stances. Live bands. Open daily 4pm-2am.

Larry Blake's Downstairs, 2367 Telegraph (848-0888), at Durant Ave., through the college's upstairs dining room and down a flight. An excellent drinking and meeting spot. Sawdust on the floor and live jazz. Drinks from $2. Cover $3-6. Restaurant open Mon.-Sat. 11:30am-2am, Sun. 4pm-2am.

Triple Rock Brewery, 1920 Shattuck Ave. (THE-BREW, 843-2739). This micro-brewery produces 3 regular beers (2 pale ales and 1 porter) and occasional specialties. All are of high quality, and bargains at $2.25 per pint. Old beer logos grace the walls, and there's a roof garden. Open daily 11:30am-8pm. The shuffleboard court in back awaits those sober enough to stand. After 7pm, standing is all you can do in the crowded barroom. Open daily 11am-midnight.

Spats, 1974 Shattuck Ave. at University (841-7225), in the Gourmet Ghetto. Looks just like Aunt Petunia's attic except for the taxidermy victims standing here and there. Have a drink on a ramshackle sofa amid antiques, old license plates, Victorian dresses, Chinese parasols, and a sign reading "Bachelor Officers Quarters." The only sign of actual spats are those the Roman soldier and the stuffed deer wear. Hors d'oeuvres served 2pm-1am. Order drinks (from $2) from the 8-page drink menu. Food $5-10. Open Mon.-Fri. 11:30am-2am, Sat.-Sun. 4pm-2am.

Cinema

Berkeley has a surfeit of moviehouses with a wide selection of theaters showing off-beat films.

Pacific Film Archives, 2621 Durant Ave. (642-1124 or 642-1412), in the University Art Museum. Admission $5; seniors and children under 13 $3.50. Reservations sometimes needed. Closed Mon.-Tue. in summer. Charge-by-phone for tickets (642-1412 or 642-5249 from 9:30am-9:30pm).

U.C. Theater, 2036 University Ave. (843-6267), west of Shattuck Ave. Standard reruns, *film noir* series, classics, and cleverly matched double features. Creative film festivals. Schedules available throughout Berkeley or at the theater. Admission $3.50 before 6pm, $5 after; seniors and children $3.50.

Act 1 and 2, 2128 Center, next to Berkeley BART Station (548-7200). Shows current art films culled mostly from the Academy Award foreign-film nominee list. Admission $6, children and seniors over 62 $3.50.

Northside Theatre, 1828 Euclid Ave. (841-6000), at Hearst. Second-run, practically lost foreign films. Admission $6, those over 65 and under 12 $3.50.

Theater

Dozens of troupes perform in Berkeley, many catering to specific ethnic, sexual, and political identities. See Practical Information for publications.

Berkeley Repertory Theater, 2025 Addison St. (845-4700). Best-known nonuniversity theater. Classics and unknowns. Box office open noon-7pm.

Theatre of the Blue Rose, 2525 8th St. (540-5037), at Dwight Way. Modern repertory that features everything from silly comedy to ancient Greek classics. Performances run 1 week each month Thurs.-Sat. at 8:30pm. Sun. matinee at 3pm. Tickets $5.

Bookstores

Berkleans really *read.*

Moe's, 2476 Telegraph Ave. (849-2087), between Haste St. and Dwight Way. Featured in *The Graduate.* Four well-arranged floors of second-hand knowledge. Everything from Artaud to Zukofsky. Open Sun.-Thurs. 10am-11pm, Fri.-Sat. 10am-midnight (for hard-core bibliophiles). Art and antiquarian section open daily noon-6pm (849-2133).

Shakespeare and Company, 2499 Telegraph Ave. (841-8916), at Dwight Way. Inspired by, but not related to, the famous Paris store. A well-organized collection, strong on art and literary criticism. Lots on drug-related subjects. Open daily 10:30am-10:30pm.

Cody's, 2454 Telegraph Ave. (845-7852), at Haste St. The largest and best in town for new books. Fire-bombed in 1989 for stocking *The Satanic Verses.* Excellent philosophy section and very knowledgeable staff. Weekly readings. Also children's and scientific books. Usually the first on the block to get new releases. Open Sun.-Thu. 9:15am-9:45pm, Fri.-Sat. 9:15am-10:45pm.

The Map Center, 2440 Bancroft Way (841-6277), on the southern edge of campus. You can't do better for maps, guides, and hiking information concerning Berkeley, the Bay Area, the world, and elsewhere. Very friendly and knowledgeable. Open Mon.-Sat. 10am-6pm.

Black Oak Books, 1491 Shattuck Ave. (486-0698 or 486-0699), in the Gourmet Ghetto. Selective stock of used, new, and out-of-print literature, art classics, and other scholarly works, plus lots of used books. Not only do they invite you to "sit down and read," they supply you with a chair. Numerous authors come and give lectures; past guests have included Ursula LeGuin, Tom Wolfe, Toni Morrison, Alice Walker, and Salman Rushdie. Call for schedule. Open daily 10am-10pm.

Pegasus, 1855 Solano Ave. (525-6888). A great selection of closeouts and used books in mint condition. Also some new books and used records. Open Sun.-Thurs. 10am-10pm, Fri.-Sat. 10am-10:45pm.

Builder's Booksource, 1817 4th St. (845-6874). An extensive collection of hardbacks on architecture, architects, design, and landscape. Well organized so it's easy to find what you need. Open Mon.-Sat. 9am-5:30pm, Thu. 9am-7pm, Sun. 11am-3pm.

Oakland

Oakland strives to refute Gertrude Stein's withering observation: "There is no there there." Stein clearly struck a nerve; the city's tourist literature wages a veritable war of attrition against her. City Square is "always *there* for you," and "there is shopping there." Roslyn Mazzilli's sculpture in the square's upper plaza is defiantly entitled "There!" One is tempted to pat the city on the shoulder and say, "There, there, Oakland."

The inferiority complex is unnecessary; Oakland is unquestionably surging through a renaissance of urban renewal and upward mobility. The city has always been blessed with attractive surroundings—a beautiful coastal range of hills to the east, a delightful lake at its center, and magnificent weather year round (the climate is "No. 1 in the U.S.," according to the meteorological experts at Rand McNally). Much of the downtown has been spectacularly rebuilt. And, lest you forget, Gertrude Stein was in truth complaining about the obliteration of her childhood home and not this "new and improved" version.

Oakland has spent much of its existence crawling out of the shadow cast by its older sibling across the bay. Its first break came in 1869, when it was selected as the western terminus of the Transcontinental Railroad, leaving San Francisco dependent on the Oakland Ferry for contact with the East Coast. Left mostly undamaged by the 1906 earthquake, Oakland grew slowly as a port, and then really took off after World War II. As once-mighty San Francisco frittered away its predominance on chic restaurants, trendy boutiques, and big-league tourist programs, Oakland read the industrial reports and discovered that containerized shipping was the wave of the future. While San Francisco slept, Oakland schlepped, passing its cross-bay competitor in gross tons handled, value of merchandise, taxes collected, fathoms fathomed—and when San Francisco awoke, Oakland had become a really swell place to transfer sealed metal boxes from cargo ships onto freight trains, and vice versa. But shipping aside, true moral victory came in 1989, when the Oakland Athletics defeated the San Francisco Giants in the greatest contest of civic vigor: baseball's World Series. Of course, none of this seems particularly designed to attract tourists. But it's comforting to know that when San Francisco feels *too* cosmopolitan, and Berkeley *too* cerebral, Oakland will always be there. There is, at least, no Fresno there.

Practical Information and Orientation

Visitors Information: Oakland Convention and Visitors Bureau, 1000 Broadway, #200 (800-444-7270 or 839-9000), in the TransPacific Center. The accent is on "Convention" more than "Visitors." Pick up a free map and *Visitor's Guide.* Open Mon.-Fri. 8:30am-5pm.

Oakland International Airport: Doolittle and Airport Dr. (577-4000).

Amtrak: 1707 Wood St. at 17th St. (654-4613), in west Oakland. Open daily for ticketing 6:45am-9:30pm. General information and reservations (800-872-7245).

BART: 465-2278. Line open Mon.-Sat. 6am-midnight, Sun. 9am-midnight.

Greyhound: 2103 San Pablo Ave. (834-3070), at 21st St. north of downtown. In a run-down and none-too-safe neighborhood. To L.A. ($50 with 3 day advance purchase) and numerous other California destinations. Open daily 5:30am-midnight.

Alameda County Transit: 839-2882.

Taxi: Yellow Cab 444-1234.

AAA Emergency Road Service: 380 W. MacArthur Blvd. (654-8454).

BASS Tickets: (762-2277). Locations at 12th and Broadway (open Mon.-Fri. 10am-6pm) and the Wherehouse: 2538 Telegraph at Grand Ave. Over 4000 concerts and sports events yearly.

Rape Crisis Center: 845-7273. Operated by Bay Area Women Against Rape. 24 hr.

Asian Resource Center: 763-2970.

Gay Switchboard and Counseling Services: 841-6224. Community information as well as counseling. Open daily 10am-10pm.

AIDS Hotline: 863-2437. Open 9am-5pm. Operators speak English and Spanish. AIDS nightline: 668-2437 (open 9pm-1am).

Poison Control: 800-523-2222. 24 hr.

Suicide Prevention and Crisis Intervention: 849-2212. 24 hr.

Crisis Line for the Handicapped: 800-426-4263. 24 hr.

Alcoholics Anonymous: 653-4300. 24 hr.

Central Public Health Center: 470 27th St. (271-4263).

Women's Choice Clinic: 2930 McClure between 29th and 30th (444-5676), east of Telegraph Ave. Call for an appointment. 24 hr. emergencies 769-3939.

Travelers Aid: 1761 Broadway (444-6834). Call in an emergency.

Emergency: 911.

Post Office: Main Branch, 1675 7th St. at Willow St. (874-8275). Open Mon.-Thurs. 24 hr., Fri. midnight-10pm. General Delivery ZIP Code: 94617. **Civic Center Branch:** 201 13th St. at Alice (251-3000).

Area Code: 510. The area code in Oakland changed from 415 to 510 on September 2, 1991.

The San Francisco-Oakland Bay Bridge carries I-80 over San Francisco Bay from downtown San Francisco to Oakland. You can take BART from San Francisco to downtown Oakland's MacArthur, 12th, or 19th St. stations ($1.60). The Greyhound and Trailways stations are very close to downtown, and an increasing number of flights to the Bay Area land at Metropolitan Oakland International Airport, on the southern edge of town. There is bus service (Air-BART) between the airport and the Coliseum BART station on the Fremont line every 10 minutes ($2). Call 800-454-2700 for information. It's also possible to catch AC Transit bus #58 to the Coliseum BART station (every 6-8 min. during rush hour, every 15 min. midday Sat.-Sun., every 40 min. at night; 60¢ with transfer; $1 from the airport). To reach San Francisco from the Oakland Airport, take Air-BART or AC Transit bus #57 to the Coliseum BART station and then the Daly City BART line to Embarcadero station in San Francisco.

The city's main artery is **Broadway,** running northeast from **Jack London Square,** a waterfront shopping area. On the northeast edge of downtown lies massive **Lake Merritt.** Local buses ($1) run frequently.

Accommodations

Although Oakland is full of motels, there is an emphatic lack of places to stay which combine both safety and economy. If you're looking for a youth hostel, the closest ones are in San Francisco. Otherwise, it might be worth the extra money to stay someplace safe (or someplace else). The **London Lodge,** 423 Seventh St. at Broadway across from the police station, (800-832-5885 or 451-6316), offers standard motel rooms for $46 ($53 for a double) and hotel rooms for $59 ($66 for a double). Much farther north, on a remote stretch of Broadway, the **Broadway Motel,** 4140 Broadway (653-0458) has reasonably antiseptic rooms with mirrors on the ceilings above the beds. Singles $25, doubles $30. Although **Gramma's Inn,** located at 2740 Telegraph Ave. (549-2145), is really in Berkeley, it's well worth the trip. The B&B has 30 rooms in four turn-of-the-century Tudor houses decorated with Victorian antiques, oriental rugs, and leaded glass windows. Gramma's presence is felt in the fresh breakfasts (Mon.-Fri. 7:30-9:30am, Sat.-Sun. 8-10am), the omnipresent homemade cookies and milk, the daily wine and cheese, and the carefully groomed rose gardens. Even if the rooms are too expensive ($85 and up), the Sun. champagne brunch will give you a feel for Gramma's hospitality. Checkout noon, TV, phones. Extra futons available at request, $10.

Food

Oakland's downtown office buildings have spawned a fair number of lunch counters. The city also has its own growing Chinatown, bounded (at least for the moment) by Broadway on the west, 9th St. on the north, Harrison on the east, and 7th St. on the south. On Sundays year round, from 10am-2pm, the **Old Oakland Farmer's Market,** at Franklin St. and Jack London Square, sells both raw ingredients, including wonderful fresh fruit, and prepared foods, such as jams and pastries.

Jade Villa, 800 Broadway (839-1688), rivals San Francisco's *dim sum.* You can sit down to a traditional lunch or order individual items from a take-out counter. Their pork buns are incomparable when fresh out of the steamer (3 for $1.75). Open daily 9am-3pm for *dim sum* and 3-9:30pm for dinner.

Vien Huong Restaurant, 712 Franklin St. (465-5938), in Chinatown at 7th St. Above-average restaurant in an average area. Real Chinese food. Lunch about $5. Open daily 7:30am-6pm.

Café la Míditerranée, 2936 College Ave. (540-7773) in Elmwood. Award-winning Middle Eastern food in a restaurant rich with atmosphere. Hanging plants, tiled tables, mirrors, and bronze adorn the inside, though the food alone is beautiful enough to admire. Crowds spill out of the dining room and onto the shaded patio out front. The vegetarian Middle Eastern plate includes Grecian spinach, cheese ***karni, levant*** **sandwich, and** ***dolma*** **($6.75).** Cold cucumber and yogurt soup ($2.25). Combo platters $6-7. Open Mon.-Thurs. 10am-10pm, Fri.-Sat. 10am-11pm.

G. B. Ratto and Co., 821 Washington St. (832-6503), at 9th St. A wide selection of cheeses, herbs, spices, and other Italian deli items, in a fine, old building. Pasta with pesto or tomato sauce $5. Open for lunch Mon.-Sat. 11am-2pm. Store open Mon.-Sat. 8am-5pm. Fri. night is "Pasta and Opera" ($17.50), with dinner from 6:30-7:30pm and a show from 7:30-9:30pm.

Noah's New York Bagels, 3170 College Ave. (654-0944). Reputedly the best bagels for miles around. Choose from a selection of bagels with flavored cream cheeses like lox or walnut raisin. Plain bagels 50¢, with cream cheese $1.25. Open Mon.-Fri. 7am-6:30pm, Sat. 7:30am-6pm, Sun. 7:30am-3pm.

Zachary's Chicago Pizza, 5801 College Ave. (655-6385), in Rockridge, has deep dish pizzas with thick pie crusts. Small cheese pizza $8.56. Open Sun.-Thurs. 11am-10pm, Fri.-Sat. 11am-10:30pm.

Pasta Shop, 5655 College Ave (547-4005), across from Rockridge BART station. "Celebrating the noodles of the world." A take-out pasta place where you can watch the noodles being made before your nose. Also sells cheese and other deli items. Open Mon.-Fri. 10am-8pm, Sat. 10am-7pm, Sun. 10am-6pm.

Fenton's Creamery, 4226 Piedmont (658-7000), at Entrada. Not the place for fancy gourmet cinnamon-nutmeg ice cream. Fenton's serves serious, old-fashioned 'scream, and lots of it. A "regular" sundae contains 3/4 of a pound of ice cream, smothered in fudge, while "Fenton's Special" ($6) has four scoops of ice cream, three scoops of sherbet, four toppings, whipped cream, nuts, and a cherry. C'mon—you deserve it. Open Mon.-Sat. 11am-midnight, Sun. 11:30am-midnight.

Dave's Coffee Shop & Diner, 4299 Broadway (658-2455). This 24 hr. diner attracts a late night student crowd. The usual diner chow. Hamburgers $3. Open 24 hr.

Sights

Oakland presents a blend of natural and man-made attractions, from its own saltwater lake to historic buildings and museum. Originally connected to the San Francisco Bay, **Lake Merritt** was dammed in 1869, and has since become Oakland's playground. The lake is the place for lazy, music-filled afternoons, sailing, birdwatching, and long walks through fragrant grape arbors. During the day, the surrounding paths swarm with runners. At night, avoid the lake entirely, lest a would-be mugger give you a real run for your money. Activity revolves around **Lakeside Park,** which encompasses a bandshell, a bird sanctuary, and a Children's Fairyland park. A mini-train runs through Fairyland to the recreational docks, where paddleboats and sailboats can be rented from the *Sailboat House* (444-3807). Rowboats and canoes: $4 per hour with $10 deposit; paddleboats: $6 per hour; sailboats: $4-20 per hour. Tours on the *Merritt Queen,* a replica of a Mississippi River Steam Boat, leave from the clubhouse (444-3807). You can also watch the Berkeley crew practice on the lake. The **Camron-Stanford House,** 1418 Lakeside Dr. (836-1976), is also on Lake Merritt. Built in 1876 and recently restored, the house is open for 1 hr. tours (Wed. 11am-4pm and Sun. 1-5pm; free). Parking at the lake is $1.50 per day.

The **Festival at the Lake** takes place during the 1st weekend in June and lasts for 3 days. The festival is an celebration of urban diversity, with an international food fair, art exhibits, and children's attractions. Admission $5, $4 in advance, free for ages 11 and under.

The **Oakland Museum,** 1000 Oak St. at 10th St.(834-2413), on the south side of the lake, is an intriguing, tremendously well-designed complex of three museums devoted to the history, art, and natural splendor of California. The architects avoided the bombastic, incongruous façades of other major museums and set out a broad, low-lying structure of sooty blocks, arbored with ivy vines and rooftop gardens, which is suited to the California landscape, evoking a sort of cement Babylon. The top floor houses the **Gallery of California Art,** with everything from traditional 19th-century portraits to contemporary works using car doors and rabbit-fur frames. In addition to paintings and sculptures, the gallery has some splendid Gold Rush cartoons, and usually a photography exhibit. One floor down is the fantastic **Cowell Hall of California History,** which takes visitors through California's social and economic history, using artifacts, costumes, and even vehicles to tell the tale. The exhibit views the state's economic history as a series of disconnected booms, from the Gold Rush to Silicon Valley, and there is much material for drawing parallels and lessons. On the lowest level, the **Hall of California Ecology** uses state-of-the-art fish-simulation technology in its new aquatic California Gallery. Take BART to the Lake Merritt Station or AC Transit bus #14. (Open Wed.-Sat. 10am-5pm, Sun. noon-7pm. Tours Wed.-Sat. at 2pm. Free, with a small fee for the outstanding exhibitions.)

Also in the Lake Merritt area is the **Holmes Bookstore,** 274 14th St. (893-6860), one of the largest used-bookstores in the Bay Area—and it sells new books, too. Holmes was founded in San Francisco in 1894, devastated in the 1906 earthquake, and moved to Oakland, where it flourished. Its special feature is a room on the third floor devoted to rare books and California history. (Open Mon.-Tues. and Thurs.-Sat. 9:30am-5:30pm, Wed. 9:30am-7pm, Sun. 11am-5pm.)

In addition to the Oakland Museum, Oakland's architectural heritage is quite rich. The **Paramount Theater** (1931), 2025 Broadway (465-6400), is perhaps the most exquisite art deco movie palace in the country. The Oakland Symphony resound through its restored hall (box office open Tues.-Fri. noon-6pm, Sat. noon-5pm), and the Oakland ballet performs an annual *Nutcracker Suite* (465-6400). On some Friday evenings Hollywood classics are screened ($5). (Tours of the ornate interior on the 1st and 3rd Sat. of every month at 10 am, $1; tours last 1½ hr. (893-

2300). Ace reporter Lois Lane would have felt right at home in the **Oakland Tribune Building** (1923), 13th and Franklin St., a structure built in the classic *Daily Planet* mode. The '89 quake was both good and bad news for the paper. The trembler debilitated the brick tower (now closed to the public), but the photo staff won a Pulitzer Prize for its coverage of the disaster. You can pick up a copy of the *Tribune,* and dozens of other newspapers, magazines, and paperback books, at **Delaner's Super Newsstand,** 1310 Broadway (451-6157), open 24 hr.

The **Dunsmuir House and Gardens,** 2960 Renalta Oaks Dr. at 106th Ave. (562-0328), is a restored turn-of-the-century mansion set on 40 acres in the Oakland foothills. Open April-Sept. with guided tours Sun. at 1, 2, and 3pm. Grounds open noon-4pm.

The vast complex of **City Square** stands at City Center, 13th St. and Broadway. Perhaps the most ambitious of the all-purpose emporia that blossomed in major cities in the 1980s, this three-block late-capitalist wonderland will eventually encompass 5 million square feet of business and retail space. The architecture is not world-shattering but does display a commitment to a vague aesthetic of urban comfiness. The lighthouse-like central tower stands as a metaphoric beacon of invigoration. Plaza and street-level shops, services and restaurants are now open, with the 12th St.-City Center BART station nearby.

Farther south, locals are in the process of restoring several blocks of handsome Victorian row houses—hurry and take a look before they all turn into boutiques. The neighborhood is a bit sleazy, but careful travelers should reemerge with body, soul and possessions intact. If you want a more in-depth look at the city's architecture, take one of the free municipal **discovery tours** (273-3234). The six guided walking tours are scheduled May through October on Wednesdays and Saturdays at 10am. Call ahead for a brochure describing the tours and to make reservations.

Jack London Square, named after the author who lived in and wrote about this area for part of his career, is now an 8-block commercial district on the waterfront. **Jack London Village,** on Alice St. along the Oakland Estuary, was modelled after a turn-of-the-century wharf. **Jack London's Cabin,** at Jack London Square near Webster St., was brought to Oakland from **Alaska,** where the author prospected for gold in the 1890's, and is testimony to the excessive lengths Oakland goes in paying homage to its native hero. While all of these odes to Jack London may be of limited interest, the **Farmers Market,** at Franklin St. and Jack London Square, is well worth a trip. Local farmers bring fresh produce, flowers, and specialty foods every Sun. from 10am-2pm. The city also offers free **Oakland Harbor Tours** (272-1188) every Thurs. from May-Aug. The tours last 1½ hr. and reservations are required.

The 1989 World Champion **Oakland Athletics** play in the **Oakland Coliseum,** Nimitz Fwy. and Hegenberger Rd. (take the BART to "Coliseum"). For schedules and group tickets information, call 638-0500; for individual tickets, call 762-2277. The NBA's **Golden State Warriors** play in the adjacent **Coliseum Arena** (call 638-6300).

Entertainment

Eli's Mile High Club, 3629 Martin Luther King Jr. Way (655-6661). Some French newspaper has declared this tiny place the "best blues club in the U.S." Blues bands and vocalists Wed.-Sun. nights, starting 8pm.

Yoshi's, 6030 Claremont Ave. (652-9200), near College Ave. Features nationally and locally known jazz artists, with occasional samba and Latin bands. Showtimes vary. Cover $5-20. Call Yoshi's or Bass Tickets (762-BASS) for advance tickets.

Caribee Dance Center, 1408 Webster St. (835-4006). An attractive and exciting multicultural salsa club—reggae, calypso, and African music on weekends. Shows 9pm-1:30am. Wed. is reggae night ($5-8).

Pacific Coast Brewing Co., 906 Washington St. (836-2739). Yet another trendy microbrewery, this one housed in a Victorian pub. The brewery produces 4 different beers. ($1.75, $2.50 for a pint.) Open Sun.-Thurs. 11am-11pm, Fri.-Sat. 11:30am-midnight.

San Jose

" . . . And the Lord spake unto the tribes of San Jose, saying, "I shall give unto San Jose perfect weather. It shall be 75 degrees year-round, and I shall make the Sun shine the day long. The fruits and vines shall grow in great abundance, and thou shalt have great Microchip Factories in thy midst and Fortune 500 shall be as thy local business list. I shall make thee rich, like unto none, with a Tax Base thy neighbor shall covet and the lowest crime rate in the nation. For I love thee well. But, that you should worship such an idyll, I shall cause a Bad Song to be written about thee, and I shall give it extensive air time, for the Lord thy God is a jealous God.' Then did the tribes heed the word of their Lord and were fruitful, and multiplied. And lo, they brought forth upon the earth a city of Fast Food, and strips, and cheap attractions, and urban sprawl and pollution, and a new multi-million-dollar light-rail rapid transit system. For theirs was the fastest-growing city in a State of Fast Growth. And the Lord looked upon their Creation and was not pleased, but said naught."

Practical Information

Visitors Information: 333 W. San Carlos St., #1000 (295-9600). Maps and information—well-written and well-spoken. The view from their board room is one of the best in the city. Open Mon.-Fri. 8am-5pm. **Chamber of Commerce,** 180 South Market (998-7000). Poorly equipped with literature but ready with advice. No maps. Open Mon.-Fri. 8am-5pm.

San Jose International Airport: 1661 Airport Blvd. (277-5900). Easily accessible to downtown. Serviced by most major domestic airlines, including Alaska, American, Continental, Delta, TWA, United, and USAir. Driving from I-880, take Coleman Ave. to Airport Blvd. and turn right; from Rte. 101, take Guadalupe Pkwy. to Airport Pkwy. and turn right. Or take Santa Clara County Transit Light Rail to Metro/Airport station and transfer to the Rte. 10 bus.

Bay Porter Express: 800-548-8811. Airport shuttle service to and from San Francisco, San Jose, and Oakland airports. Fares vary.

Amtrak: 65 Cahill Ave. (287-7462). Information, 280-6992 or 800-872-7245.

Caltrain: 800-558-8661. Operates between San Jose and San Francisco with stops at peninsula cities. Operates 5am-10pm.

Southern Pacific Railroad: 93 Cahill Ave. (291-5651). Service connecting San Francisco and points south of San Jose.

Greyhound: 70 S. Almaden Ave. (297-8890), 2 blocks from downtown. Reasonably safe even at night. To L.A. (one way $40) and San Francisco (one way $7). Open daily 6:30am-midnight.

Santa Clara County Transit System: 287-4210. Decent service in and around San Jose.

Ride Board: San Jose State University, Student Union.

AAA Emergency Road Service: 246-5811.

Road Conditions: 436-1404.

Events Hotline: 295-2265.

Tickets: Bass Tickets: 988-2277; **Ticketron:** 225-4870.

Women's Alliance: 1181 4th St. (279-7550).

Gay and Lesbian Information: Gay and Lesbian Community Information, 293-4525. 24 hr.

Crisis Lines: Rape Crisis: 287-3000. **Victim/Witness Assistance:** 295-2656. **Poison Control:** 299-5112 or 800-662-9886. **Alcoholics Anonymous:** 297-3555. **Drug Abuse:** 988-4200. **Suicide and Crisis Prevention:** 279-3312.

LET'S PACK IT UP

Let's Go® Backpack/Suitcases
Innovative hideaway suspension with internal frame turns backpack into carry-on suitcase. Detachable daypack makes it 3 bags in 1. Water-proof Cordura® nylon. Lifetime Guarantee. 3750 cu. in. Navy, teal or black. **Supreme** adds lumbar support pad, torso and waist adjustment, two daypack pockets, leather trim, and *FREE shoulder strap.*

A1. Supreme	**$154.95**
A2. Backpack/Suitcase	**114.95**
A3. Shoulder Strap	**4.50**

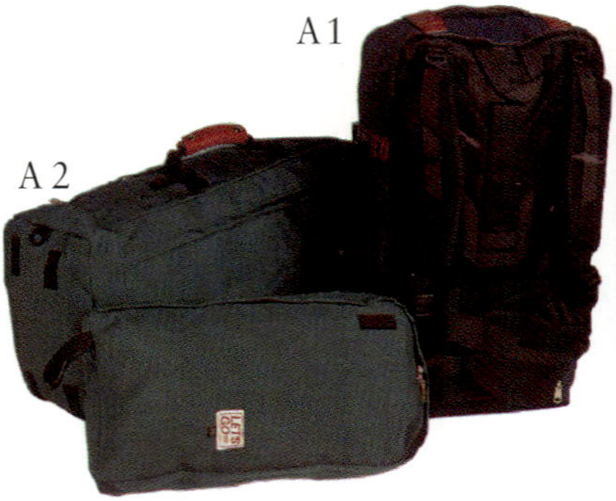

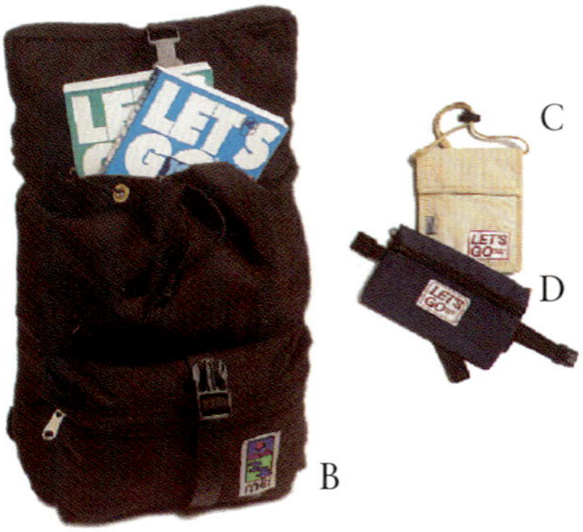

B. Chateau
Top-opening rucksack pack. Drawstring closure. 3 compartments. Taped inseams. Lifetime Guarantee. 1310 cu. in. Black.
$34.95

C. Undercover Neck/Waist Pouch
Secure & comfortable. Ripstop nylon with soft Cambrelle® back. 2 pockets. 6 ½ x 5" Lifetime Guarantee. Black or tan.
$7.95

D. Passport/Money Case
Waterproof nylon with zippered pouch. 7 ½ x 4 ½" Navy or gray.
$6.95

Duffles
Tough, capable, and appealing. 11 oz. waterproof Cordura-Plus® with 3" nylon web. Lifetime Guarantee. Red, black, purple, or blue.

E1. XL–36 x 15 x 15"	**$69.95**
E2. L–30 x 15 x 15"	**59.95**

H. Travel Case
Perfect carry-on luggage. Large compartment with 2 side pouches. Mesh pocket. No-sag bar and shoulder strap. Lifetime Guarantee. 20 x 16 x 9" Black or blue.
$94.95

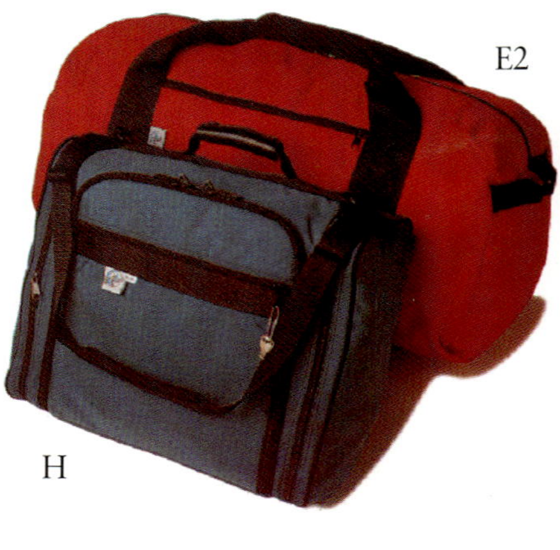

Call 1-800-5LETS GO for flight reservations.

J1 T1 T2

ET'S GO HOSTELING

)92-93 Youth Hostel Card (AYH)
equired by most international hostels. ust be U.S. resident.

. **Adult** (ages 18-55)	$25
. **Youth** (under 18)	10

. Sleepsack
equired at all hostels. Washable durable)ly/cotton. 18" pillow pocket. Folds to)uch size. $13.95

. 1992-93 International Youth Hostel uide (IYHG)
ssential information about 3900 hostels Europe and Mediterranean. $10.95

FREE map of hostels worldwide.

***et's Go*® Travel Guides**
urope; USA; Britain/Ireland; France; Italy; rael/Egypt; Mexico; California/Hawaii; pain/Portugal; Pacific Northwest/Alaska; reece/Turkey; Germany/Austria/Switz-land; NYC; London; Washington D.C.

1. **USA or Europe**	$14.95
2. **Country Guide** (specify)	13.95
3. **City Guide** (specify)	9.95

$1.00 off the cover price.

LET'S SEE SOME I.D.

1992 International ID Cards
Provides discounts on accommodations, cultural events, airfares and accident/medical insurance. Valid 9-1-91 to 12-31-92.

T1. Teacher (ITIC)	$15
T2. Student (ISIC)	14
T3. Youth International Exchange Card (YIEE)	14

FREE "International Student Travel Guide."

LET'S GO BY TRAIN

Eurail Passes
Convenient way to travel Europe. Save up to 70% over cost of individual tickets. Call for national passes.

First Class

V1.	15 days	$430
V2.	21 days	550
V3.	1 month	680
V4.	2 months	920

First Class Flexipass

V5.	5 days in 15 days	$280
V6.	9 days in 21 days	450
V7.	14 days in 1 month	610

Youth Pass (Under 26)

V8.	1 month	$470
V9.	2 months	640
V10.	15 days in 2 months	420

FREE Eurail Map, Timetable, & Travelers' Guide with passes.

LET'S GET STARTED

PLEASE PRINT OR TYPE. Incomplete applications will be returned.

International Student/Teacher Identity Card (ISIC/ITIC) (ages 12 & up) enclose:

1. Letter from registrar or administration, transcript, or proof of tuition payment. FULL-TIME only.
2. One picture (1 ½ x 2") signed on the reverse side.

Youth International Exchange Card (YIEE) (ages 12-25) enclose:

1. Proof of birthdate (copy of passport or birth certificate).
2. One picture (1 ½ x 2") signed on the reverse side.
3. Passport Number ______________________ 4. Sex: M F

Last Name ____________ First Name ____________ Date of Birth ___/___/___

Street ____________ We do not ship to P.O. Boxes. U.S. addresses only.

City ____________ State ____________ Zip Code ____________

Phone ( ) ____________ Citizenship ____________

School/College ____________ Date Trip Begins ___/___/___

Item Code	Description, Size & Color	Quantity	Unit Price	Total Price

Shipping & Handling			
If order totals:	Add	Total Merchandise Price	
Up to $30.00	$4.00	Shipping & Handling (See box at left)	
30.01-100.00	6.00	For Rush Handling Add — $8 for Continental U.S.; $10 for AK & HI	
Over 100.00	7.00	MA Residents (Add 5% sales tax on gear & books)	
		Total	

ENCLOSE CHECK OR MONEY ORDER PAYABLE TO: HARVARD STUDENT AGENCIES, INC.

Allow 2-3 weeks for delivery. Rush orders delivered within one week of our receipt.

LET'S GO Travel

Harvard Student Agencies, Inc., Harvard University, Thayer B, Cambridge, MA 02138

(617) 495-9649 1-800-5LETSGO (Credit Card Orders Only)

Prices subject to change.

Hospital: San Jose Medical Center, 675 E. Santa Clara St. at 14th (998-3212). Emergency room open 24 hr. Emergency calls: 977-4444.

San Jose State University Campus Police: 924-2222. Dial 181 on campus.

Post Office: 105 N. 1st St. (292-6282), at St. John St. Postal information, 452-0660. Open Mon.-Fri. 9am-5:30pm. General Delivery ZIP Code: 95113.

Area Code: 408.

The Way to San Jose

The city is on the southern end of San Francisco Bay. From San Francisco, take the Southern Pacific double-decker train from the depot on 4th St. (495-4546), between Townsend and Key St., nearly 1 mi. south of Market St. The train runs in both directions every hour on the hour, with more frequent trains during peak hours, from 7am to midnight. Fare is $3.50 one way, $6 for a one-day excursion ticket. Greyhound and Amtrak also serve San Jose. Santa Clara County Transit connects San Jose with other peninsula towns. The bus traveling farthest north is #22 to Menlo Park; farthest south is #68 to Gilroy.

San Jose is centered about the plaza and mall area near east-west **San Carlos** and north-south **Market St.** From the intersection of San Carlos and Market, streets are designated East, West, South, and North. Streets that run north-south east of Market St. are numbered progressively higher the farther away they are from San Carlos. **Santa Clara County Transit** (287-4210) provides effective bus service around town. Most buses run every 20 minutes, less frequently at night from 5am-2am. Fare is 75¢, ages 5-17 50¢, seniors and differently-abled riders 10¢, ages under 5 free; a day pass ($2) entitles you to unlimited riding for a day. A brand new light-rail system also runs north from the Tamien Station in Willow Glen on San Carlos St., with 22 stops along the way. The trains run every 10 min. from 5am-midnight Mon.-Fri. and every 20 min. from 6am-midnight on weekends. The Transit Mall, the center of San Jose's transit system, runs north-south along First and Second St. in the downtown area. **San Jose State University's** small, grassy grounds cover several square blocks between S. 4th and S. 10th St. downtown. The Student Union Information Center stocks bus schedules and other transit information.

Accommodations

Sanborn Park Hostel (AYH), 15808 Sanborn Rd., Sanborn County Park (741-9555), in Saratoga 13 mi. west of San Jose. Seriously out of the way by bus. From downtown, take bus #23 or 24 from San Carlos St. to Kiley. Then take #57 or 58 to West Valley College. From there take #27 or 54 to Saratoga Village and call for a ride from the hostel. Secluded and peaceful, as you might expect. Opt for one of the redwood log cabins. Near the Skyline-to-the-Sea hiking trail. 40 beds. Open daily 5-11pm. Check-out 9am. Curfew 11pm. Members $6.50, nonmembers $8.50.

San Jose State University, 9th St. at San Salvador, Washburn Hall (924-6180). Rooms rented in summer. Call before noon. University affiliation not required. Singles $27. Doubles $36. Linen $3.

Motel 6, 2560 Fontaine Rd. (270-3131). Take the Tulley Rd. exit off U.S. 101. An extra-large version of the standard schtick. Fills early. Check-in as early as 7am. Check-out noon. Singles $34. Doubles $40.65.

EZ-8 Motel,2050 N. First St. (436-0636). A depressing landscape of concrete and dead grass, but near the airport. Has coin-op washers and dryers. A/C, color TV w/ cable. Singles $34 Doubles $41.

Purple Sage Motel/Wagon Wheel Motel, 3382 Monterey Hwy. (972-0144). Kitchenettes, restaurant, A/C, TV, tacky. Singles $38. Doubles $45. Call one week in advance for reservations.

Park View Motel, 1140 S. 2nd St. (297-8455). 40 rooms. Kitchenettes, pool. Generally pretty quiet. Singles $35. Doubles $40.

There are also county parks with **campgrounds** outside the city. Call 358-3741 for information.

Food

Nobody ever called San Jose the Paris of the peninsula, but the city does offer a multitude of Mexican and Italian restaurants with cheap, earnest cooking.

Sal and Luigi's Pizzeria, 347 S. 1st St. (297-1136). Sal split for Florida 30 years ago, but students still flock here for the pizza and subs. Small pizza $7, medium $8.25. Pasta dinners $6-8. Open Tues.-Thurs. 11am-11pm, Fri. 11am-midnight, Sat. noon-midnight.

Quoc Te, 155 E. San Fernando St. (289-8323), at 4th. This combination Chinese/Vietnamese restaurant looks dubious from the outside, but one step inside will testify to its authenticity. Lively and packed with locals in-the-know wolfing down the hefty platters (most around $5-6). Seafood is their specialty. Open Sun.-Thurs. 10am-11pm, Fri.-Sat. 10am-3am.

La Taqueria, 15 S. First St. (287-1542). Inexpensive Mexican food for downtowners. Savory burritos $3.14, tacos $2. Open Mon.-Thurs. 11am-5pm, Fri.-Sun. 11am-8pm.

Marsugi's Bar and Grill, 399 S. First St. (286-8345). Breakfast, lunch, and dinner in this brick-walled hangout. Burgers $3-4. Live alternative rock Wed.-Sun. 9:30pm-1:30am. Open daily 11am-7pm.

El Paraíso, 155 W. San Fernando St. (294-2010). Mexican food, three meals a day. Breakfasts are $5-$7.50, lunches and dinners $5-$8. Mix and match 2 entrees for $7. Open Mon.-Wed. 7am-9pm, Thurs.-Fri. 7am-10pm., Sat. 8am-10pm, Sun. 8am-9pm.

Peking House Restaurant, 84 S. 2nd St. (293-0717), at E. San Fernando St. Starve yourself all day and then come here to worship at the temple of the budget traveler: the all-you-can-eat Chinese buffet. Nine reasonably attractive options for $4.65 or less are available at both lunch and dinner. Six items for $2.75. Open Sun.-Tues. and Thurs.-Sat. 11am-7:30pm. Closed Wednesday.

The Old Spaghetti Factory, 51 N. San Pedro Sq. (288-7488). Once a real spaghetti factory, the dining hall has been remodeled with polished wood, brass, and antiques (including a 1930s San Jose cable car). Lunch $3-5, dinner $5-7, beer $1.45. Open Mon.-Fri. 11:30am-2pm and 5-10pm, Sat. 4:30-11pm, Sun. 4-10pm.

The Student Union Cafeteria, on campus in "The Connection" eating area on 7th St., behind the Student Union. Enter on the south side of the building. A student watering-hole. Open Mon.-Thurs. 11am-9pm, Fri. 11am-7:30pm; June-Aug. Mon.-Fri. 7:15am-6:15pm. The Connection also hosts the **Spartan Bakery** (open Sept.-May Mon.-Fri. 6:45am-11pm), the **Espresso Encounter** (open Sept.-May Mon.-Thurs. 6:45am-9pm, Fri. 6:45am-7:30pm), and **The Roost,** a fried-chicken stand (open Sept.-May Mon.-Thurs. 11am-9pm, Fri. 11am-7:30pm). Call the Campus Food Services (924-6350) for more information.

Sights

Though it seems unlikely in such a bland city, two of San Jose's main attractions are bizarrely intriguing. The **Rosicrucian Museum,** 1342 Naglee Ave. (287-2807), at Park Ave. west of downtown, was founded by the quasi-Egyptian mystical order. Take bus #22, 36 or 62 from the center of town (every ½ hr. Mon.-Fri., every 45 min. Sat.-Sun.; no service after 6pm). This eerie museum is the highlight of any visit to San Jose, displaying a superb and macabre collection of Assyrian and Babylonian artifacts: mummies, amulets, and a walk-in replica of a tomb. The entrance to the museum itself resembles a massive tomb, guarded by a dozen ram-headed sphinxes. (Open Tues.-Sun. 9am-5pm. Admission $4, ages 7-15 $2, under 7 free.) The post-pyramidal **Rosicrucian Planetarium** interprets the heavens. (Open daily 10am-4:30pm; Sept. 16-June 14 1-4:30pm.) Two blocks west on Naglee and across the street from the museum is the **Municipal Rose Garden** (277-4661), a refreshing park with a fountain that functions as a large birdbath. The optimal time to visit the garden is early May when the roses are in bloom.

The **Winchester Mystery House,** 1525 S. Winchester Blvd. (247-2000), at I-880 and I-280, west of town, was the home of Sarah Winchester, heir to the rifle fortune, from 1884 to her death in 1927. Winchester was obsessed with the occult, and, as the tale goes, she was told by a medium that the untimely deaths of her husband and baby daughter were caused by the spirits of men killed by the Winchester rifle. In grand California style, she became convinced that only continuous building would appease the spirits, and so work on the mansion began in 1884 and continued every day and night until her death 43 years later. The beautiful Victorian estate is filled with oddities: stairs leading to ceilings, doors opening to walls, posts set upside down. Winchester's fixation with the number 13 is apparent in the 13 cement blocks in the Carriage Entrance Hall, 13 hooks in her seance room, and 13 lights in the chandeliers. (Open daily March-Oct. 9am-5 30pm; Nov.-Feb. 9:30am-5pm. Admission, including guided tour, $11; ages over 59 $9, under *13* $6.) This particular attraction has become something of a tourist trap; if you've seen one mystery house, you've seen them all.

San Jose's finest conventional museum is undoubtedly the **San Jose Museum of Art,** 110 S. Market St. (294-2787), which features changing exhibits on the "art of our time" at the international, national, and regional level. A recent expansion of the museum, consisting of a 40,000 ft. wing, has brought exciting new art to the city on a revolving basis. Call ahead to arrange for a tour of the museum. (Open Tues.-Fri. 10am-6pm, Sat. 10am-4pm, Sun. noon-4pm. Recommended donation $4 adults, $2 students and seniors; Thurs. is free for all.)

Another recent addition to San Jose is **The Garage, Technology Center of the Silicon Valley** at 145 W. San Carlos St. (279-7150). This science museum is similar to San Francisco's Exploratorium and features interactive, hand-on exhibits which teach about science and technology. Visitors are invited to work the controls of a Mars Rover travelling on the planet's surface and experiment with robots, while a stack of 500 telephone books represents the amount of information stored within a single molecule of DNA.

Just southeast of downtown, Coyote Creek runs through **Kelley Park,** which lies east of Senter Rd. and mostly south of I-280. Although the world really needs only one San Jose (if that), this park contains an ambitious re-creation of the early city. The **San Jose Historical Museum,** 1300 Senter Rd. at Keyes St. (287-2290), features a 1927 gas station, soda shop, pioneer homes, and a turn-of-the-century doctor's office. (Open Mon.-Fri. 10am-4:30pm, Sat.-Sun. noon-4:30pm. Admission $2, seniors $1.50, ages 6-17 $1, under 2 free. Guided tours every half hour Mon.-Fri.) Kelley Park also provides the city with a network of bike paths, picnic sites, and a **Japanese Friendship Tea Garden** (287-2290), with landscaping, rare fish, and a teahouse. (Open daily 10am-sunset.) Contiguous Coyote Creek Park has an indoor bike track and streamside trails. The **Happy Hollow Park and Zoo** (292-8188) is heaven for minds and bodies under 14. Mazes, spiral slides, jungle gyms, and a "crooked house" throw the kids for a loop. (Open Mon.-Sat. 10am-5pm, Sun. 11am-6pm. Admission ages 2-14, 65-79 $2, 15-64 $2.50. Parking $3.)

The oldest standing structure in San Jose is the **Peralta Adobe** (287-2290), on E. Santa Clara between San Pedro and Terraine St. The adobe was built in 1804 by Luis María Peralta, who had received the land—48,000 acres of it—from the King of Spain as a reward for "meritorius service." The adobe stands in a small park, occupied mostly by transients; a few explanatory posters dot the area. (Open daily 9am-dusk.)

San Jose State University (SJSU), 1 Washington Square (924-3280), California's oldest public college, channels its engineering and business majors into Silicon Valley. Most of the 23,000 students—when not commuting home—seem to be congregating at the campus club, The Spartan. Attention occasionally turns from beer to SJSU's most renowned athletic endeavor: judo. For information on campus events, call the 24-hr. events line (924-6350) or, in summer, pick up a copy of the *Summer Times,* a weekly publication of the *Spartan Daily* (924-3280), the campus newspaper. The *Independent Weekly,* an alternative student paper, is more lively and publishes all year. Both papers are available around the campus and in the main library. The campus is centered on San Carlos and 7th St., east of downtown.

The **Great America** theme park (988-1800), 3 mi. north of San Jose on U.S. 101, is one of the nation's largest. Brace yourself for rollercoasters, water flumes, a kiddie park, live entertainment, and more food than a bumper-car-bound stomach should intake. (Open daily Easter week and June-Aug. from 10am; March-May and Sept.-Oct. Sat.-Sun. from 10am. Admission $24.50, seniors over 54 $14, children ages 3-6 $10.45. Parking $4.)

The San Francisco Giants' Class A minor-league affiliate, the **San Jose Giants,** gets the home field advantage at **Municipal Stadium,** Alma Ave. at Senter Ave. (297-1435), just across from Kelley Park, from April through August. Call 297-1435 for tickets and information.

Although not of the Napa/Sonoma class, the lesser-known Santa Clara **vineyards** produce their share of California *vino.* A fifth-generation winery, **Mirassou,** 3000 Aborn Rd. (274-4000), well out of town to the east, has an enjoyable rustic atmosphere. (Tasting room open Mon.-Sat. 10am-5pm, Sun. noon-4pm.) A more centrally located winery is **J. Lohr,** 1000 Lenzen St. (288-5057). Take bus #22 up Alameda to Lenzen. Tours are by appointment; daily tasting sessions 10am-5pm. **Paul Masson** offers tours at its imitation château at 13150 Saratoga Ave. (257-7800), in Saratoga 10 mi. west of San Jose. Pick up a copy of *County Crossroads* from the visitors center. This free pamphlet has listings with maps of local farms and wineries where you can pick and taste. In addition, **Grape Line Tours** (866-1400 or 800-675-7433) organizes wine-tasting tours starting at $25.

Entertainment and Seasonal Events

Student Union, 9th St., SJSU (924-6350). A complex of facilities in a building designed to epitomize the pleasure principle. Offers bowling, table tennis, a cafeteria, an art gallery, and an amphitheater with frequent concerts and dramatic performances. Open Mon.-Fri. 8am-11pm, Sat. 9am-5pm; in summer Mon.-Fri. 7:30am-4:30pm.

The Last Laugh, 29 N. San Pedro St. (287-5233), off E. Santa Clara. Highly regarded comedy club. Cover $6 Sun.-Thurs., Fri.-Sat. $10, depending on who's performing. Shows Sun.-Thurs. at 8pm; Fri.-Sat. at 8pm and 10:30pm. Reservations suggested. No smoking in the club, 2 drink min., must be 21.

Camera One, 366 S. 1st St. (294-3800). First-run foreign and art films. Admission $6, seniors and children $3.50, Mon. night student discount $3.50, Sat.-Sun. matinée $3.50.

Camera Three, 288 S. 2nd St. (998-3300), at San Carlos. Foreign film offspring of above. Admission $6; seniors, under 12, and 1st show Sat.-Sun. $3.50.

F/X, 400 S. 1st St. (298-9796). Popular and trendy local dance club. The schedule of events and bands is always shifting; call ahead for details. Cover varies.

Club St. John, 170 W. St. John St. (947-1667). Caters to a clientele of lunching workers from the nearby county courthouse by day and becomes the area's most popular gay dance club by night. Two bars. Expansive dance floor, game room, patio area. Dancing nightly from 9pm Sun.-Thurs., from 10pm Fri.-Sat. No cover Mon.-Thurs., $5 Fri.-Sat., varies Sun. Dinner served 5-9pm Tues. night. Other gay hangouts include **Heat** (279-1722), a leather/Levi's bar on nearby Julian St. and the **Water Garden** (275-1215), a safe, clean bathhouse at 1010 Alameda St.

Bordon Biersch, 33 E. San Fernando (294-6785). Trendy, modern San Jose wouldn't be complete without its own micro-brewery. This brewery features 3 of their own beers, outdoor seating, and plenty of music. Jazz bands play every Sun. from 2-5pm ($5 cover). Mon. is the famous *Jam Session,* where musicians are welcome to come and play for the crowd in return for a free beer (cover $2). The music on Wed. (8-11pm) varies from jazz to blues to salsa (cover $5). Check the *Metro* or the *San Jose Mercury-News* for listings.

San Jose hosts a constantly shifting array of seasonal festivals, conventions, and fairs. The best way to get a handle on the opportunities is to call the **Convention and Visitors Bureau's Events Line** at 295-2265 from a touch-tone phone, allowing you to access numerous referral extensions. The Visitors Bureau also publishes a helpful semi-monthly calendar of events that can be picked up at their office at 333 W. San Carlos St., #1000.

Palo Alto

Palo Alto ("Shallow Alto," as Berkeleans call it) has almost enough bookstores to be a proper college town, but the profusion of dealers in fine tapestries, the imported cars, and volvo-driving police (not to mention a Republican Congressman) betray this claim. Hewlett-Packard and other prominent high-tech firms make the city a corporate adjunct to Silicon Valley, but most people associate Palo Alto with the academic playground opened by Leland Stanford 100 years ago. The students and faculty of Stanford University (nicknamed "The Farm" in memory of its humble origins as Senator Stanford's horse pasture) support a secondary economy of artsy filmhouses and adventurous shops. The university itself is graced with perfectly groomed grounds; a picturesque lake (when California drought conditions don't force it to remain drained), a superb faculty, bright, active students, no urban decay, and a bulging endowment. Stanford is beautiful, and therein lies its problem, for perfection breeds blandness and sterility. Life on the Farm lacks a certain edge and for the visitor seeking raw excitement, Palo Alto will call to mind the words of a popular World War I-era song: "How you gonna keep 'em down on the farm after they've seen gay "Parree'?"

Practical Information

Stanford Campus Information Booth: Front of the **Quadrangle** (723-2560); open daily 10am-4pm.

Tresidder Union (723-4311); open Mon.-Fri. 8am-midnight, Sat.-Sun. 10am-10pm.

Caltrain (Southern Pacific): 800-558-8661 or 557-8661. Open Mon.-Fri. 7am-7pm, Sat. 8am-5pm, Sun. 8am-8pm. Operates between San Francisco and San Jose. Not wheelchair accessible.

samTrans: 800-666-4BUS, regional information 508-6200. Regular service to San Francisco ($1.50), San Francisco International Airport ($1), and to Hayward BART Station.

Santa Clara County Transit: 965-3100. Operates within Palo Alto and to points south.

Marguerite Shuttle: 723-4375. Free bus service around Stanford University.

Car Rental: Budget Rent-A-Car, 4230 El Camino Real (493-6000), out-of-town reservations 800-527-0700. Mid-size cars $38 and up per day with unlimited mileage. Credit card required. Open Mon.-Fri. 7:30am-7pm, Sat. 8:00am-6pm.

AAA Emergency Road Service: 595-3411

Bike Rental: Campus Bike Shop, 551 Salvatierra (325-2945), in Stanford, across from the law school. Three-speeds $5 with same day return. $8 for 24hr. Major credit card or $75 cash deposit required. Open Mon.-Fri. 9am-5pm, Sat. 9am-3pm.

Campus Events: 723-0336. 24-hr. hotline.

Campus Operator: 723-2300.

Rape Hotline: 493-7273, 24hr.

Poison Center: 800-523-2222, 24hr.

Campus Police: 723-9633.

Post Office: Main Office, 2085 E. Bayshore Rd. (321-4310). General Delivery ZIP Code: 94303. Also at 380 Hamilton Ave. (323-1361). Stanford University branch, Lasuen S.U. (322-0059).

Area Code: 415.

Orientation

Palo Alto is 35 mi. southeast of San Francisco on the peninsula that forms the southern arm encircling San Francisco Bay. From San Francisco take U.S. 101

south to the University Ave. exit and turn left; or split off to I-280 for a slightly longer but much more scenic route. From I-280 get off at Sand Hill Rd. and follow it to Willow Rd. and the northwest corner of Stanford University. Regional and local bus service and Caltrain rail service is consolidated at the Palo Alto Transit Center at the southern end of University Ave., across from the Stanford Shopping Center.

By public transportation, take samTrans bus #7F from the Transbay Terminal on Mission and 1st St. in San Francisco, from Mission St. between 1st and 9th, or from the San Francisco Airport. Get off at the Stanford Shopping Center or any point thereafter. (Fare $1.50, over 65 at off-peak hours 75¢, 7-17 75¢, under 7 free.) The bus runs every hour from 5am-8am and from 7pm-1am, every half hour during the day, and every 10 minutes from 2:30pm-7pm. Or take MUNI bus #15, 30, 45 or 42 to the Caltrain station at 4th and Townsend St. in San Francisco. The trip from San Francisco takes about an hour and a quarter. Trains leave every one or two hours and take one hour to reach Palo Alto (fare $3, same-day round-trip $5.25, seniors and disabled $1.50). Caltrain also serves San Jose (30 min.; $1.50, same-day round-trip $2.75, seniors and disabled 75¢). The Palo Alto train station (323-6105) is at Alma St. and University Ave., while the California Ave. station (326-3392) is 1¼ mi. south. Both stations are open daily 5:30am-1pm. The Stanford Shopping Center is connected to points south by San Mateo County buses and to the Stanford Campus by the Marguerite University Shuttle (723-4375). The shuttle is free and serves the university Mondays through Fridays, during the day.

Accommodations

Motels are plentiful along El Camino Real, but they're expensive (average single $40). The expense of the hotels varies in inverse proportion their distance from Stanford, and more reasonably priced accommodations can be found farther north, on El Camino Real towards Redwood City. University housing is a cheaper alternative. Residence halls are available from June 25 to September 16 (singles $30.25, doubles $44; children under 10 half-price; those under 18 must be accompanied by an adult). Call the **Conference Office** (723-3126) for information. (Open Mon.-Fri. 8am-noon and 1-5pm.)

Each residence hall also keeps one or two guest rooms open during the academic year ($23-70). To stay in one, you must get a Stanford student or faculty member to make your reservation (three-day max. stay). Call the **Stanford Housing Office** for the names and numbers of the residences (725-2810; open Mon.-Fri. 10am-noon and 1-4pm).

Hidden Villa Ranch Hostel (AYH), 26870 Moody Rd. 94022 (941-6407), southwest of Palo Alto in Los Altos Hills. Working ranch and farm in a wilderness preserve. The first hostel on the Pacific Coast. 28 beds. Open Sept.-May. Members $6.50. Nonmembers $9.50.

Motel 6, 4301 El Camino Real (949-0833). Old Reliable has set up shop close to "The Farm." Always full; call far in advance. Singles $39.55. Doubles $46.15. Another branch at 806 Ahwanee Ave. (408-720-1222), in Sunnyvale, 7 mi. south of Palo Alto. Singles $32. Doubles $39.

Coronet Motel, 2455 El Camino Real (326-1081). Clean and roomy, with big windows. Swimming pool. Singles $38-40. Doubles $40-42.

Crystal Lodge Motel, 3339 El Camino Real (493-2521). Adequate facilities; 5 minutes from Stanford. Check-out 11am. Singles and doubles $33.

Food

Though Palo Alto lacks great food, at least it has peppy student atmosphere. The cheapest exceptions among the pizza-burger-salad monotony lie along student-clogged **University Avenue.**

Liddicoats, 340 University Ave. (321-8411). Sixteen ethnic restaurants or take-out stands, going beyond the average food court by offering such exotic cuisines as Filipino and Chilean, both of which are rather good. Meals $3-6. Open Mon.-Sat. 11am-8pm, some stands open Sun. 10am-6pm as well.

Macheesmo Mouse, 271 University Ave. (326-6873). Health-conscious fast food Mexican style. All dishes include calorie count and a promise of natural ingredients. Meals $3-5. Open daily 10:30am-10pm, Fri. and Sat. until 11pm.

Frankie, Johnny, and Luigi's Too, 939 El Camino Real (967-5384), between Bailey and Castro in Mountain View. Good pizza, favored by Stanford students. Medium pizza $10. Open Mon.-Fri. 11am-1am, Sat. 11am-2am, Sun. 11am-midnight.

Crouton's, 379 University Ave., (325-2001). The students' choice for all-you-can-eat salad, $5.45 before 5:30pm, $6.45 after. Open Sun.-Thurs. 11am-9pm, Fri.-Sat. 11am-9:30pm.

Café Barrone, 1010 El Camino Real at the Menlo Center in Menlo Park (327-0830). No matter what the hour, this European style café has lines out the door. Features live music, local artwork, and outdoor seating. The specialties include wine by the glass or bottle, large cappuccinos $2.75, and tasty desserts. Soups, salads, and sandwiches $1-2. Open Mon.-Fri. 7am-11pm, Sat. 9am-11pm, Sun. 9am-5pm.

The Coffee House, Tressider Union (723-3592), at Stanford. Recent renovations have brightened this popular student hangout. Sandwiches, burritos, and salad $3-4. Live jazz every Thurs. night (no cover). Open daily 8am-midnight.

Union Crossroads Cafeteria, Tressider Union (723-4321 or 723-5959), at Stanford. A large eating space served by 3 food stands: the **Café** with breakfast and Mexican food (Tuesday is Big Bob's BBQ night for $6, 7am-2pm); the **Corner Pocket** with pizza, soda, and fro-yo (Mon.-Thu. 11am-10pm, Fri.-Sun. 11am-7pm); and **Baker St.** with fancy pastries from $1.25 (open Mon.-Fri. 10am-4pm).

Hobee's, 67 Town and Country Village (327-4111), at El Camino Real and Embarcadero. Popular California-cuisine establishment. Excellent omelettes and *quesadillas,* with many vegetarian options. Burgers $4.50-6. Open Mon. 7am-2:30pm, Tues.-Fri. 7am-9pm, Sat.-Sun. 8am-9pm.

Miyake, 261 University Ave. (323-9449). This outlandish restaurant promises a memorable night of Japanese cuisine. Waiters wearing neon minstral outfits usher you in and out with a chorus of yells. Sushi is served on boats which travel in water around the bar—you grab what you want. Reasonably priced sushi and rolls $1. Open daily 11:30am-10pm.

Cho's, 213 California Ave. (326-4632). This cosy, 3-table restaurant has achieved something close to cult status, although the ever-aloof Cho may not acknowledge your existence, even if you come in every day for a year. The delicious "pot stickers" (dumplings) explode with hot, juicy fillings; the chili sauce is sublime. Lunches $4-6. Open daily 11:30am-7:30pm.

The Oasis Beer Garden, 241 El Camino Real (326-8896), in Menlo Park. Good beer (pints $3), hamburgers ($3), and pizza. The classic Stanford hangout. $2 Tuesdays with dancing until 3am. Open daily 11am-2am.

Sights

Although it is a continent away, a century and a half younger, and a good bit warmer, **Stanford University** seems to belong more to the Ivy League than to the American West. While the palm trees and Spanish architecture might look a little odd in a New England setting, the competitive admissions, outstanding faculty, high tuition, and small environment of about 6,500 undergraduates would fit right in; Stanford students are as bright and success-oriented as their eastern counterparts. Politics on the Stanford campus are also as strident and divided as on any Eastern campus. A few years ago, the undergraduates forced the administration to abandon a core curriculum centered around "Western Civilization" in favor of something less "Eurocentric." At the same time, the Hoover Institution remains a bastion of right-wing thought, and the Law School has produced such bleeding hearts as Chief Justice Rehnquist. The university has also been an important high-tech center ever since two alumni named Hewlett and Packard decided to set up shop near their alma mater, thus giving birth to Silicon Valley.

Railroad magnate and U.S. Senator Leland Stanford conceived of the university as a memorial to his only son, Leland, Jr., who had already been admitted to Harvard when he died at age 16. (If you can't join 'em, imitate 'em!) Classes began in

October 1891, and the fall of 1991 will witness appropriate centennial festivities. The oldest part of the campus is the colonnaded Main Quadrangle, site of most undergraduate classes. Over the past century, planners have found little occasion to depart from the basic scheme of sandstone walls and red-tile roofs, leaving the campus remarkably unified. Campus information is available at the entrance to the quad and in Tressider Union. It is also possible to make free calls within the university from courtesy phones.

Stanford is too big to see on foot. The free Marguerite Shuttle connects the far-flung university (Mon.-Fri. 6am-6pm, every 10 min.). You can also rent a bicycle from **Campus Bike Shop** (325-2945; see Practical Information). With its flat boulevards and long distances, Stanford seems designed for bicycles. The vast majority of students own them, leading to term-time bicycle traffic jams and accidents.

Tours of the campus leave from the Serra St. entrance to the quadrangle daily at 11am and 3:15pm, and last 1 hour. Groups of 10 or more need reservations. The student guides are entertaining, and skilled at walking backwards around the campus, and the tour is fairly comprehensive. For information, call 723-2053 or 723-2560. **Memorial Church** (723-1762), in the central quad, is a gold shrine with glittering mosaic walls like those of an Eastern Orthodox church. The courtyard in front resembles that of a French château. The church lost its tower in the 1906 earthquake and was repaired *sans* tower, only to be closed after the 1989 quake damaged the same section of the roof. The building may be closed for a few years (ask at the information booth for an update). East of the main quad is the Art Gallery (723-4177), which usually displays temporary exhibits, but is showing works from the Stanford Museum while that facility is being repaired. (Open Tues.-Fri. 10am-5pm, Sat.-Sun. 1-4pm, closed portions of Aug. and Sept.) Beyond the gallery, the observation deck of the Hoover Tower (723-2053 or 723-2560) offers views of a hazy, distant San Francisco, a more distinct east bay, and a horizon-full of red-tile roofs. (Open daily 10-11:45am and 1-4:30pm. Admission $1, over 65 and under 13 50¢, families $2.50.) Its bells toll Tuesday at 5pm. **Hiking** trails are located at the point where Campus Drive, running around the campus, meets Junipero Serra Blvd. The area is known by the locals as "The Dish", the summit of which offers a spectacular view of Palo Alto, the Peninsula, and the Bay. It is advisable to go in groups when hiking here at night. For information call Stanford Campus Information (723-2560). Make an appointment to tour the **Stanford Linear Accelerator Center** (926-2204). Graduate students lead the informative presentation that includes a bus tour of the facilities and a slide show, all geared toward explaining the fearsome mystery of the quark.

The Stanford University Museum of Art, Museum Way (723-3469), lies off Palm Ave., about halfway between the main quad and El Camino Real. It has been closed indefinitely since the '89 quake. Normally, its hours are the same as the Art Gallery's (above). The **Rodin Sculpture Garden,** on the lawn outside the museum, displays a stunning bronze cast of the *Gates of Hell,* along with many other larger figures. Only Paris has a finer Rodin collection. (Open year-round.)

Off campus, the horribly high-brow **Barbie Doll Hall of Fame,** 460 Waverley St. off University Ave. (326-5841) has over 16,000 Barbie and Ken dolls. The dolls date back to 1959 and follow a chronological history of fashion, including Hippie Barbie and Benetton Barbie. Admission $2, under 12 yrs. $1 (open Tues.-Fri. 1:30pm-4:30pm, Sat. 10:30am-noon, 1:30pm-4:30pm).

Within walking distance of Stanford are two expensive shopping malls: the Stanford Shopping Center, where the San Francisco samTrans bus stops, and the Stanford Barn, where Leland, Sr. once kept his horses.

Entertainment

The *Stanford Weekly,* put out by the *Stanford Daily* (723-2554), contains listings of what's going on all over campus. The *Palo Alto Weekly* (362-8210), distributed around town, has similar listings.

Dinkelspiel Auditorium (723-2448), on campus. Silly name, but great classical weekend concerts during the term. Tickets available at Tressider Ticket Office in the Tressider Union (723-4317).

Memorial Auditorium, on campus. Movies on Sun. during the term ($1.75). Mostly recent hits, though the occasional classic makes the slate.

The New Varsity, 456 University Ave. (323-6411 for movies). Set in the colonnaded courtyard of an old hotel reminiscent of the '20s. Theater features superb off-the-beaten-track films. Movie $6, seniors and under 12 $3.50. First matinee $3. Reservations recommended.

The Stanford Theatre, 221 University Ave. (324-3700). This non-profit organization is dedicated Hollywood's "Golden Age." Double features $5, seniors and children $3. The Wurlitzer organ plays before and after the 7:30 show.

The Vortex, 260 California Ave. (324-1402), 2 blocks east of El Camino Real. The students' favorite for live rock music. Prices and days vary. Shows usually begin at 9:15pm. Cheap tables and chairs; carpet smells of stale beer. Anyone over 18 welcome, but ages 18-20 must pay a higher cover charge. Sunday is "teen night," when only ages 14-18 are allowed.

42nd Street, 518 Bryant (329-9181), in an alley between Bryant and Ramona, ¼ block south of University Ave. A wild bar—tons o' fun. Beers from $2.50, wine from $1.75, drinks $3. Dress up or you'll feel out of place. Open daily 11:30am-1:20am.

British Banker's Club, Menlo Center in Menlo Park (327-8759). Located at the site of the Old City Hall and Public Library, nightlife inside this vintage Edwardian bar is swarming. Stained glass windows, an Egyptian sarcophagus, library books, and portraits adorn the walls which reach up to an impressive 25ft. high ceiling. The crowd varies, representing all ages. Open Tues.-Sun. 11am-2pm, Mon. 11am-1am.

Bookstores and Shopping

Chimaera Books and Records, 165 University Ave. (327-1122). Neat and well-organized wood shelves with many new and used hardback books. Superb selection of new and used poetry books. Used CDs are $10, $2.50 with an exchange. Open Mon.-Thu. 10am-9pm., Fri.-Sat. 10am-10pm, Sun. noon-5pm.

The Stanford Bookstore (329-1217), on campus, just southeast of the main quad. Recently expanded to become the largest college bookstore in the country, it has an impressive selection of both textbooks and general books, plus the usual Stanford T-shirts and other logophernalia. Books can be perused upstairs at the café. Open Mon.-Thurs. 7:45am-7:30pm, Fri. 7:45am-6pm, Sat. 9am-6pm. The branch at 135 University Ave. in town (327-3680) houses the medical, technical, and computer sections. Open Mon.-Fri. 9:30am-7pm, Sat.10am-6pm.

Bell's Books, 536 Emerson St. (323-7822). One of the oldest bookstores in town and worthy of the honor—the whole place smells of books. Walls are stacked from floor to ceiling with thousands, new and used. The major drawback is that the first floor has very high ceilings, and of the 14 shelves of books, you can see only seven. Open Mon.-Fri. 9:30am-5:30pm, Sat. 9:30am-5pm.

Megabooks, 444 University Ave. (326-4730). A floor of the cheapest used books in town. Classical music and a convenient location make this the most approachable of Palo Alto's bookstores, although the selection isn't overwhelming. Open Mon.-Sat. 10am-6pm.

Kepler's Books, Menlo Center (324-4321), in Menlo Park. Vast collection of paperbacks, hardcovers, magazines, and foreign maps. Well-organized, well-run. Open Sun.-Thurs. 9am-11pm, Fri.-Sat. 9am-midnight.

Printers Inc. Bookstore, 310 California Ave. (327-6500). Huge, airy bookstore with an eclectic selection of books and magazines. The store also houses a small café. Variety of gay and lesbian literature, plus a good selection of periodicals, including foreign newspapers. Open daily 10am-11pm.

Szwede Slavic Books, 2233 El Camino Real (327-5590). Slavic books in original languages and in translation. Open Tues.-Sat. 10am-5pm.

North Face Factory Outlet, 217 Alma St. (325-3231), has marked-down prices for camping equipment, clothes, backpacks, tents, etc. Rentals available. Open Mon.-Thu. 10am-8pm, Fri. and Sat. 10am-6pm, Sun 11am-5pm.

San Mateo County Coast

South of San Francisco, protected from the encroaching Bay Area sprawl by low mountains running along the coast, you'll find the cold and windy heart of San Mateo County. The geography here is mild; the cliffs are relatively low, and the land under gentle cultivation. Artichokes and brussel sprouts are the dominant crops, and ramshackle vegetable stands dot Rte. 1 at regular intervals. The beaches of the county lie a world away from the clutter and population of San Francisco, San Jose, and Santa Cruz.

As always on the Pacific coast, a car is the best way to go. Breathtaking ocean views arise so frequently that drivers must fight just to keep their eyes on the road.

If you're traveling by sneaker, you'll have a tougher time of it. **San Mateo County Transit (samTrans),** 945 California Dr. (800-660-4287), in Burlingame, services the area only somewhat successfully. Tickets from San Francisco to Half Moon Bay (a 1½-hr. ride) cost $1.50 one way, seniors and ages 7-17 75¢, under 6 free. Route maps and other information are available at most Caltrain and BART stations. The shore south of Pacifica through Half Moon Bay is serviced by buses #1C, 1L, and 90H. The 1L runs from the Daly City BART to Half Moon Bay Mon. through Fri. from 6am to midnight, Sat. 6am to 4pm, and Sun. 9am to 6pm. The 90H runs from San Mateo every hour Monday through Friday from 8am to 6pm, and every hour Saturday from 9am to 4pm.

The shore from Pacifica to Big Basin Redwoods State Park is scattered with beautiful, isolated, sandy beaches. Although usually too cold for swimming (even in summer), the sands offer a pleasant stroll along the water's edge. About 2 mi. south of Pacifica (take samTrans bus #1L) is **Gray Whale Cove State Beach,** a privately owned nudist beach off Rte. 1. You must be 18 to join the fun (but where do you keep your ID?). South of Whale Cove is the **Montara Lighthouse Hostel (AYH)** (728-7177), a clean and wholesome 45-bed facility on windswept Lighthouse Point. There's a samTrans stop 1 block north at 14th St. and Rte. 1 (#1C, 1L, 90H). The hostel has 2 fully equipped kitchens, as well as bikes and hot tubs for rent. Reservations are required in summer and for groups. (Check-in 4:30-9:30pm. Lockout 9:30am-4:30pm. Curfew 11pm. Members $8. Nonmembers $11.)

Wide and windswept **Montara State Beach** is a ½-mi. north of the hostel. **The Chart House,** 8150 Castillo Hwy. (728-7366), at Montara Beach provides pricey meals and glorious views of the coast around Half Moon Bay. A $3.50 drink rents you a table with a view. (Open daily 8am-11pm.)

You can sleep by the shore in Half Moon Bay at **Half Moon Bay State Park** (726-6238) without risking a 6am awakening by the municipal police. 52 campsites. ($14 per night, over 61 $12; cold showers only.) Reservations are recommended in summer. The park is open 24 hr. Check-out time is noon.

In mid-October, Half Moon Bay sponsors the **Half Moon Bay Art and Pumpkin Festival,** with arts and crafts, food, parades, a masquerade ball, carving contests and prizes for the biggest pumpkin. The **Coastside Country Fair,** from mid-June to mid-July, showcases crafts, livestock, and a junior rodeo. For more information about either festival, call the Chamber of Commerce (726-5202) weekdays between 10am and 4pm.

Delightful **San Gregorio Beach** grazes the southern part of Half Moon Bay. Walk to its southern end to find little caves in the shore rocks. A stream runs to the sea, and this may prove a comfortable alternative to dipping in the cold ocean. (Open 8am-sunset. Day use $2.)

The **Sea Horse Ranch** (726-2362 or 726-9903), 1 mile north of Half Moon Bay on Highway 1, has 250 horses and ponies to take on trails and on the Beach. 1hr. $20, open 8am-6pm.

Moss Beach Distillery Restaurant (728-5595), off Highway 1 in Half Moon Bay, features a bar and restaurant with a breataking view of the ocean. Drinks $2-5. Open Mon.-Fri. 4pm, Sat. and Sun. 2pm.

Perhaps the best reason to plan a trip down Rte. 1 is to stay at the **Pigeon Point Lighthouse Hostel (AYH)** (879-0633), 6 mi. south of Pescadero on the highway, near the lighthouse (the second-tallest on the West Coast). Biking down the Bikecentennial trail, hitchiking, and driving are the only practical means of getting there. This 50-bed hostel operates a hot tub in the old lightkeeper's quarters and enjoys personable management. Rooms for couples ($4 extra) and families are available. Tours of the lighthouse are given every morning at 11am except Sat. and Sun. Curfew 11pm. Members $8. Nonmembers $11.) **Pigeon Point,** taking its name from a hapless schooner that crashed into the rocky shore on its inaugural voyage in 1853, turns some heads with its tidepools, wave-washed rocks at Pebble Beach, and 30-ft. plumes of surf. The **Pescadero Marsh** provides temporary shelter to a variety of migratory birds including the great blue heron, often seen poised on its spindly legs awaiting luckless, and soon to be lifeless, fish

Año Nuevo State Reserve, 7 mi. south of Pigeon Point (879-0595), is the mating place of the 18-ft.-long, ugly-as-sin elephant seal. December to April is breeding season, when males compete for beach space next to the more pleasingly hideous females. The new-born pups weigh a mere 75 pounds, but in 28 days they break the scales at well over 400. Nurtured in true "sink or swim" fashion, the pups don't receive any pointers on swimming or feeding from their mothers. Many are squashed by massive 2-ton, brutish bull-seals who find no sympathy even for their own offspring—it's a wonder they ever grow past infancy. It is not unusual for 2000 seals to crowd on the beach all at the same time. To see this strange show (after Dec. 12), you must make reservations by calling the MISTIX Corporation (800-444-7275) since access to the park is limited. Tickets go on sale November 15 and are generally sold-out by the end of the month, so plan ahead. (2½-hr. guided tours, $2 per person, 8am-sunset.) SamTrans runs a special bus to the reserve from the Hillsdale Shopping Center in San Mateo from December through March; call 348-7325 for information. From April to November the reserve is open and free (parking $5). Arrive before mid-August to catch the last of the "molters" and the young who've yet to find their sea-legs. Whatever you do, don't get too close: they may be fat but they're fast—and intolerant of strangers who appear to threaten their young. The beach is cold and windy, regardless of season, so dress warmly. (Open daily 8am-6pm. Last permits issued 3:30pm.)

Butano State Park (879-0173), 5 mi. inland from Año Nuevo, laces extensive paths through tall, lush redwood forests and offers 21 drive-in and 19 walk-in camping sites. (Cars $5, bicyclists and hikers 50¢.)

Another local sport, **olallieberry gathering,** originated a couple decades ago when the olallieberry was created by crossing a blackberry, a loganberry, and a youngberry. Get a-pickin' and pay by the box at **Phipp's Ranch** in Pescadero (879-0787; open end of June to mid-Aug. 10am-7pm). They also have fresh-grown vegetables. While picking, listen for the sea lions' calls.

Captain John's Fishing Trips, Pillar Point Harbor (726-2913 or 728-3377), 4 mi. north of Half Moon Bay runs inexpensive fishing trips daily 7:30am-3pm (tickets $30, weekends $32; check-in by 6:30am). Special trips go to the Farallon Islands Tues. and Fri.-Sun. 6am-3pm (tickets $28, weekends $30; check-in by 5:30am). Salmon fishing trips ($40) leave daily in season at 6:30am and return at 2:30pm. Reservations are required for all trips. (Open daily 5am-5pm.)

Marin County

Home to new age guru Ram Dass, the "inventors" of the mountain bike, director George Lucas, and 560 acres of spectacular redwood forest, Marin County (pronounced ma-RIN) boasts a bizarre blend of outstanding natural beauty, trendiness, liberalism and wealth. While the richest county in the West has grown up since the 1979 movie *The Serial* mocked its directionless, pot-smoking, hot-tubbing pre-Yuppie Yuppies, and although the Mazda Miata has replaced the BMW as the official county car, Marinites still love their real estate values as much as they cherish carrot juice and organic food. Neighboring communities grumble about Marin's excesses—most notably the $350 million oil stock fund left to the county by the late Mrs. Beryl Buck, for which Marin has no immediate use—but Marin residents will tell you there's no hypocrisy in their indulgent and eco-conscious habits. Life is just *easier* in Marin.

Practical Information and Orientation

Visitor Information: Sausalito Chamber of Commerce, 333 Caledonia St. (332-0505). Open Mon.-Fri. 9am-5pm. **Marin Headlands Visitor's Center** (331-1540), at the Ft. Barry Chapel, Field and Monker. Information on the Marin Headlands and camping. Open daily 9:30am-4:30pm. **Point Reyes National Seashore Headquarters,** Bear Valley Rd. (663-1092), ½ mi. west of Olema. Information, wilderness permits, maps, and campsite reservations. Open Mon.-Fri. 9am-5pm, Sat.-Sun. 8am-5pm. **San Rafael Chamber of Commerce,** 818 5th Ave. (454-4163). Open Mon.-Fri. 8:30am-4:30pm.

Greyhound, 701 Third St., San Rafael (453-0795). Two buses per day into San Francisco ($4.60) leaving at 2:50pm and 6:30pm.

Local Transportation: Golden Gate Transit (453-2100, 332-6600 in San Francisco). Daily bus service between San Francisco and Marin County via the Golden Gate Bridge, as well as local service in Marin. Buses #50, 10, 30 and 20 provide service from San Francisco's Transbay Terminal at 1st and Mission St. into Marin. Buses #65 and 24 provide service out to Pt. Reyes and Samuel P. Taylor State Park ($1.85 into Sausalito, $3.35 to West Marin). The **Golden Gate Ferry** (453-2100 or 332-6600 in S.F.) provides transportation between San Francsco and Sausalito or Larkspur. Boats depart from the Ferry Building at the end of Market St. for a 25-minute crossing to downtown Sausalito or a 50-minute trip to the Larkspur Ferry Terminal, at the juncture of U.S. 101 and Sir Francis Drake Blvd. (Mon.-Fri. 7am-8:25pm, Sat.-Sun. 10:45am-6:55pm). The one-way fare to Sausalito is $3.50, $1.75 for seniors and disabled. The fare to Larkspur is $2.25, $1.10 for seniors Mon.-Fri., Sat.-Sun. $3 for adults, $1.50 for seniors. During the summer, Friday afternoon boats feature live jazz bands for the locals' commuting pleasure.

Car Rental: Avcar Rental, 780 Anderson Dr., San Rafael (461-4855). $27.95 per day, must be 25 yr. with credit card. 150 free miles.

Bike Rental: Caesar's Cyclery, 29 San Anselmo Ave., San Anselmo (258-9920). $5 per hour, $25 per day for mountain bikes. **Wheel Escapes,** 1000 Magnolia Ave., Larkspur (461-6903). Mon.-Fri. $7/hr. or from $14/day, Sat.-Sun. from $21/day.

Rape Crisis Center: 924-2100.

Suicide Prevention Center: 454-4524.

Hospital: Marin General, 250 Bon Air Rd., Greenbrae (925-7000).

Medical Aid: Marin Health Dept. Offices (499-6879), Marin County Health Clinic (499-6839), Dental Services (499-3771).

Senior Services: Marin Senior Coordinating Council, San Rafael (456-9062). Health care, legal services, and counseling activities.

Gay and Lesbian Information: Ministry of Light, 1000 Sir Francis Drake Blvd., San Anselmo (457-1115). Information and social services. Mon.-Fri. 9am-5pm.

Post Office: San Rafael Main, 40 Bellam Ave. (459-0944). Open Mon.-Fri. 8:30am-5pm, Sat.-Sun. 10am-1pm.

County Sheriff: 499-7284.

Emergency: 911.

Area Code: 415.

The Marin peninsula is an inverted triangle on the north end of San Francisco Bay, and is connected to the city by the Golden Gate Bridge.

At the extreme southeastern tip of Marin lies **Sausalito,** the county's central settlement and at one time its most interesting town. The village was initially something of a bohemian fishing town, where San Francisco's painters and sculptors would retreat for a summer to capture the area's soft light on the windy bay and folding hills. Before packing up your easel and sticking out your thumb, know that Sausalito has forsaken its humbler days and become an immaculate tourist bonanza.

On the western coast of the county, Rte. 1, the most beautiful highway in the nation, runs for 50 of its most spectacular miles along the craggy hills of the **Point Reyes National Seashore.** If you have an extra day, take time to hike along the area's numerous trails or picnic by the dramatic lighthouse at the end of the point.

The eastern, or bay side, of the county cradles the larger settlements **Larkspur, San Rafael, Terra Linda, Ignacio,** and **Novato.** These towns line US 101, which runs north-south through Marin. It is around this 101 Corridor that most of the population and development is concentrated. West Marin is more rural, with rolling hills and fog-bound coastal valleys. **Bolinas, Olema,** and **Inverness** (from south to north) line the coast. **Sir Francis Drake Blvd.** runs from Highway 101 in Larkspur, west through the San Geronimo Valley. It passes through the towns of Greenbrae, Kentfield, Ross, San Angelmo, Fairfax, Woodacre (that budding megalopolis and home of Tim Whitmire), and San Gerononimo, on the way to Pt. Reyes and its rendezvous with Hwy. 1.

Accommodations and Camping

Marin, to its credit, has managed to avoid the cheap motel plague that can ruin lovely areas overnight. The best places to stay in the county are its numerous and extremely beautiful campgrounds. If you don't have a sleeping bag, two strategically placed hostels—one in Sausalito, the other on Pt. Reyes—will afford you cheap, sweet dreams.

The **Golden Gate Youth Hostel (AYH),** (331-2777), a few miles south of Sausalito, sits among rolling hills close to a waterbird sanctuary where pelicans make swooping dives into the sea. Beds are housed in an old, spacious building that is part of deserted Fort Barry. Efficiently run, the hostel offers attractive rooms and a warm atmosphere. Less than 10 mi. from downtown San Francisco, it's a great place to hike and get away from the city. (Check-in 7-9:30am, 4:30-11pm. Curfew 11pm. Members and nonmembers $8. Linen 50¢. Reservations recommended in summer, or show up early and leave your name on the sign-up sheet.) By car from San Francisco, take the Alexander Ave. exit off U.S. 101; take the second Sausalito exit if going south toward San Francisco. Follow the signs into the Golden Gate National Recreation Area, then follow the hostel signs through the park about 3 mi. to the hostel. The public bus schedule is somewhat erratic. MUNI bus #76 runs from the Transbay Terminal to the visitors center—from there it's a short walk to the hostel—but only on Sunday (1 per hr.; 85¢, seniors 15¢, ages 5-17 25¢; MUNI 673-6864). Monday through Saturday, Golden Gate Transit buses #2, 10, and 20 stop at Alexander Ave. From there, walk down to the entrance of the park and hitch a ride to the hostel. A taxi from San Francisco costs $11-12.

Twenty-five miles to north, the spectacularly situated **Point Reyes Hostel (AYH),** Limantour Rd. (663-8811), is open nightly for groups and individuals. You're more likely to get a last-minute room here than in the Golden Gate Hostel, although reservations are advised on weekends. Hiking, wildlife, birdwatching, and Limantour Beach are all within walking distance. You need foresight to take advantage of the well-equipped kitchen; the nearest market sits a distant 8 mi. away. (Registration 4:30-9:30pm. Members and nonmembers $8. Reservations by mail or in person only, with deposit.) By car take the Seashore exit west from Rte. 1, then take Bear Valley Road to Limantour Rd., and follow that six miles until you see a sign for the hostel. For public transportation information, contact Golden Gate Transit (332-6600) or call the hostel between 4:30 and 9:30pm. There are two buses a day out to hostel.

The campground closest to Sausalito is in **Samuel P. Taylor State Park** (488-9897), on Sir Francis Drake Blvd., 15 mi. west of San Rafael (itself 10 mi. north of Sausalito on U.S. 101). The park has 60 sites ($14, seniors $12) with hot showers and is open year-round, but reservations are needed between April 29 and September 30. A hiker/biker camp costs $3 per person, with a 7-day maximum stay. (Call 800-444-7275 or 619-452-1950 for reservations, at least 24 hours in advance.)

North-west of the Golden Gate Bridge are a total of 15 campsites in the Marin Headlands, most of them primitive with only picnic tables and chemical toilets. Two sites have running water, one, Kirby Cove, has a cooking area. Some of the sites have space for groups of up to fifty people. Reserve as much as 90 days in advance by calling the visitors center at 331-1540. These sites are free.

There are four campgrounds (accessible by foot) on the national seashore in the south, inner cape portion of Pt. Reyes. All are fairly spartan, with pit toilets, firepits, and tap water, and require permits from Seashore Headquarters. The camps are well-patrolled, and visitors without permits are likely to be fined. **Sky Camp** is 3 mi. from headquarters; **Glen Camp,** 5½ mi.; **Wildcat Camp,** 6 mi.; and **Coast Camp,** 8 mi. All campsites command exquisite views of the ocean and surrounding hills. (Get permits at the Pt. Reyes National Seashore Headquarters. See Practical Information.) Reservations are taken up to two months in advance, Mon.-Fri. 9am-noon. Maximum stay allowed is four nights per visit. All sites are free.

Food

Gourmet health-conscious Marinites take their fruit juices, tofu, and non-fat double-shot cappuccino very seriously; restauranteurs know this, and raise both the alfalfa sprouts and the prices high. Pt. Reyes does have several pleasant, small general stores (though groceries, too, are cheaper in San Francisco).

A cluster of good, inexpensive cafés and sandwich shops can be found around the local junior college in Kentfield, while the main strip in San Rafael, on 4th St., between D and Lincoln Streets, has a number of delis and fast-food places.

The Greater Gatsby's, 39 Caledonia St., Sausalito (332-4500), west of the main business district. Gathering spot of Marin's post-bourgeois bourgeoisie. Good pizza on a whole wheat crust $6. Open Sun.-Thurs. 10am-11pm, Fri.-Sun. 10am-1:30am.

Margaritaville, 1200 Bridge Way St., Sausalito (331-3226). Painted fish and flamingoes adorn the walls, views of Sausalito harbor adorn the windows, and a young and beautiful crowd adorns the tables. Large servings of decent Mexican food. One burrito with beans, rice and lettuce $5.95. Good margaritas $3. Mechanized palm-leaf fans cool the bar, where surfing competitions adorn the TV. Open Mon.-Fri. 11:30am-11:30pm, Sat.-Sun. 11:30am-midnight.

Easy Street Café, 574 Magnolia Ave., Larkspur (924-9334), in the Larkspur Shopping Center next to Lucky's. Small and usually crowded, the café serves massive and delicious omelets or scrambled eggs with potatoes, fruit, and toast. Feta, tomato and garlic scrambled eggs $5.95. Burgers $5-6. Open daily 6am-4pm. Also in San Anselmo, in the Red Hill Shopping Center (453-1984).

A Clean Well-Lighted Place Café, 2409 Larkspur Landing Circle, Larkspur (461-7472), across from the ferry terminal in Larkspur. Just as the name implies. Gourmet soup, salad and sandwich shop where the desserts are stupendous ($4.25) and the cappuccino is served in soup bowls ($2). Enjoy a bowl after browsing through the adjacent bookstore.

The Half-Day Café, 848 College Ave., Kentfield (459-0291), across from College of Marin. Housed in a light and airy renovated barn, the Half-Day is a little pricey, but offers the ultimate in Marin eating experiences. The sun-dried tomato and basil sandwich with soup or salad is superb and painfully Californian ($5.95). Good selection of Northern Cal beers $2.95. Open Mon.-Fri. 7am-2:30pm, 5:30pm-9:30pm, Sat.-Sun. 8am-2:30pm, 5:30pm-9:30pm.

Edible Art Café and Bakery, 737 College Ave., Kentfield (485-0735), in Kent Woodlands Shopping Center, down the street from Half-Day Café. Serves the biggest, gooiest, sweetest, and stickiest sticky buns in the state ($2.25). Or try a surprise bag of day-old pastries (4 pastries for $2). Hamburger with fries or salad $4.95. Friendly service in a homey atmosphere. Open Mon.-Wed. 7am-7pm, Thurs.-Sat. 7am-9:30pm, Sun. 7am-3pm.

Café Espresso, 85 Bolinas Rd., Fairfax (485-5535), off San Anselmo Ave. The best place to relax is Fairfax, which is one of the small towns on the way to Pt. Reyes on Sir Francis Drake Blvd. Local poets, carrot-juices, and caffeine-addicts hang out under the Redwoods at this small café. Tofu-salad sandwich $3. Non-fat and decaf (as well as regular) espresso drinks $1-3. Friendly help. Open daily 7am-6pm.

Jerry's Farmhouse, Rte. 1 in Olema, Pt. Reyes (663-1264). Describes itself as "plain old American," and serves fresh fish daily ($10), as well as sandwiches ($5) and enormous 5-oz. **farmburgers** ($5.75). Open Tues.-Sun. 7:30am-9pm.

Perry's Deli, Inverness Park, Pt. Reyes (663-1491), between Pt. Reyes Station and Inverness. *The* place for groceries. Sandwiches $2.50. Open daily 7am-10pm.

Sights

The undeveloped, fog-shrouded hills just to the west of the Golden Gate Bridge comprise the **Marin Headlands,** part of the Golden Gate National Recreation Area which sprawls across the Bay Area. For decades artillery batteries were stationed here to defend San Francisco from invading hoardes. Since 1974, however, the city has taken its chances with air defense. The vista from the headlands back over the bridge to San Francisco is arguably the most spectacular in the Bay Area. The headlands (and the viewpoints) are easily accessible by car: take the Alexander Ave. exit off U.S. 101 and it's your first left. You'll go through an underpass and up a hill on your right. You can also hop on board MUNI bus #76, which provides a wild ride over the bridge and through the hills. Consider hiking the ¾-mi. trail which leads from the parking area down to the sheltered (and usually deserted) beach at **Kirby Cove.**

Muir Woods National Monument, a 560-acre stand of primeval coastal redwoods, prostrates itself about 5 mi. west along the Panoramic Hwy. off U.S. 101. John Muir called it "the best tree lover's monument that could be found in all the forests of the World," and wandering among the 200-foot-tall trees you'll understand why. The centuries-old massive redwoods are shrouded in soft slanting sunlight and an eerie silence reigns. Wildlife in the ancient forest is shy, and much of the action occurs 150 feet above your head in the forest canopy. Several walking trails lead away from the monument entrance; most are well-marked and easy-going. A loop road takes you through the most outstanding areas. (Open daily 8am-sunset.) The **visitors center** (388-2595) is near the entrance and keeps the same hours as the monument. **Muir Beach,** west of Muir Woods, offers a tremendous view of San Francisco from the surrounding hills.

North of Muir Woods is the isolated, largely undiscovered, and utterly beautiful **Mount Tamalpais State Park.** The heavily forested park has a number of challenging trails that lead to the top of Mt. Tam, the highest peak in the county, and to a natural stone amphitheater. The mountain bike was invented in this park, and hence it has a number of very challenging mountain bike trails—but don't go off the fire roads or you risk incurring the wrath of eco-conscious Marin hikers. Also in the park is **Stinson Beach,** a local favorite for sunbathing both with and without. Although the beach is often cold and windy, valiant sunbathers and windsurfers attempt to create a Bay Area counterpart to Malibu. Park headquarters is at 810 Panoramic Hwy. (388-2070). The park opens a half-hour before sunrise and closes a half-hour after sunset.

Encompassing 100 mi. of coastline along most of the western side of Marin, the **Point Reyes National Seashore** juts audaciously into the Pacific from the eastern end of the submerged Pacific Plate. Sir Francis Drake Blvd. runs from San Rafael through Olema, where it crosses Rte. 1, all the way to Pt. Reyes itself. Here the infamous San Andreas Fault comes to an end. The point's remote position brings heavy fog and strong winds in winter, distinct flora and fauna, and crowds of tourists to gawk at it all. If you have a year to spare and an inhuman attention span, you'll be able to see the fault make its annual 3 in. shift. Anyone watching in 1906, during the California earthquake, got a bonus: a 16-ft. displacement. For bus information call Golden Gate Transit (see Practical Information).

Limantour Beach, at the end of Limantour Rd., west of the seashore headquarters, and **McClures Beach,** at the extreme north of the seashore near the end of Pierce Point Rd., are two of the area's nicest beaches. Both have high, grassy dunes and long stretches of sandy beach. In summer a free shuttle bus runs to Limantour Beach from Seashore Headquarters. Strong ocean currents along the point make swimming a potentially suicidal proposition. To reach the dramatic **Point Reyes Lighthouse** at the very tip of the point, follow Sir Francis Drake Blvd. to its end and head right along the stairway to Sea Lion Overlook. From December to February, gray whales can occasionally be spotted from the overlook.

For hikers the seashore offers hundreds of miles of **trails,** most emerging from trailheads at Park Headquarters and at Palomarin, at the extreme south of the seashore, off Rte. 1. Permits from Headquarters are required for hiking. Most water is nonpotable, so strap on a canteen.

Finally, if you're driving north on Highway 101 toward Sonoma, take a gander at the Frank Lloyd Wright—designed **Marin Civic Center,** just north of down-town San Rafael, which houses the county's administrative offices and major theatrical venues.

Entertainment

Sweetwater, 153 Throckmorton Ave. (388-2820), in downtown Mill Valley. Mellow Marin's version of a red-neck crowd fill this dark, photo-covered bar nightly to hear old-style rock-and-funk bands of varying quality. Cover $5. Open nightly noon-2am. Probably the most happening bar scene in town.

Farmer's Market Festival, on 4th St. in downtown San Rafael (466-2266). Every Thursday night in the summer, local farmers and artisans host a fest of food and entertainment, with live music and the freshest, most organic veggies around (Thu. 6pm-9pm). A more produce-oriented farmers market occurs twice weekly in the San Rafael Civic Center parking lot. Sun. and Thu. 7am-10am.

New George's, 842 4th St., San Rafael (457-8424). Rock bands of 3 varieties: loud, very loud, and bleeding eardrums. Catch the low-rider car show out front on Fri. and Sat. nights (free). Open Sun.-Thu. 11am-12:30am, Fri.-Sat. 11am-2am.

Marin Brewing Company, 1809 Larspur Landing Circle (461-4677), across from the ferry terminal in Larkspur. Beer and 'sphere to make the earth quake. Open daily 11:30am-2am.

Napa and Sonoma

The prospects of "purple-stained mouth" and "beaded bubbles winking at the brim" lure many visitors to the quiet vineyards of the Napa and Sonoma Valleys. And with good reason—the area's wines are regarded highly by connoisseurs both in the U.S. and abroad. Napa is more prestigious, Sonoma older and less crowded. And you'll shed the crowds and receive the most personal attention as you move into the Russian River Valley (see Sonoma Coast).

Lesson number one.

Most wines are recognized by the grape-stock from which they're grown: **white** grapes produce chardonnay, riesling, and sauvignon; **reds** are responsible for beaujolais, pinot noir, and cabernet sauvignon. **Blush** or **rosé** wines issue from red grapes which have had their skins removed during fermentation in order to leave just a touch of color. Zinfandel is a red grape, but often made skinless and therefore pink in color (called white zinfandel). **Sparkling** wine (including champagne) is made by adding yeast and sugar during fermentation, a process which adds carbon dioxide. Cheaper imitations simply have carbon dioxide bubbled directly through ordinary white wine. **Dessert** wines are made with grapes beginning to acquire the "noble rot" (botrytis) at the end of the picking season, giving them an extra sweet flavor.

When tasting, start with a white, then proceed through the reds, and end with a dessert wine. Drinking a red first coats your tastebuds with tannin, and *everyone* knows it's impossible to taste a white with a tannin-covered tongue. It's perfectly acceptable to ask for advice and information from the tasting-room pourer. Tasting should proceed thus—stare, smell, swill, swallow (first three steps are optional). Key words to help you seem as cultivated as the grapes during tasting sessions are: dry, sweet, light, crisp, fruity, balanced, rounded, subtle, rich, woody, and complex. Feel free to banter these terms about indiscriminately; all that really matters is that you sound like you know what you're talking about. Cheers!

Napa Valley

While not the oldest, the Napa Valley is certainly the best-known of America's wine-growing regions. The gentle hills, 13 types of fertile soil, ample moisture, and year-round sunshine are ideal for viniculture. The valley's acres of neatly aligned grape plants, spacious and often elaborate wine mansions, and soft perpetual sunshine make it ideal for tourists as well. Charles King began growing vines brought over from Europe in the late 1850s, but producers were crippled by Prohibition, when the grapes were supplanted with figs, and the region only began to reestablish itself in the 1960s.

During the 70s attention began focusing on Napa's rapidly improving offerings as oenophiles started to recommend an occasional California bottle. In 1976, a bottle of red from Napa's Stag's Leap vineyard beat a bottle of Château Lafitte-Rothschild in a blind taste test at a Paris salon. American wine had come of age, and tourists from across the country started flocking to the California valley. Today, local vineyards continue to reap national and international awards, and a tasting carnival goes on from sunup to sundown, dominating the life of the valley's small towns. Besides **Napa,** the towns of **St. Helena,** and **Yountville** are convenient bases for exploring.

Practical Information and Orientation

Visitor Information: Napa Chamber of Commerce, 1556 1st St. (226-7455). Eager staff and a wide brochure collection. Open Mon.-Fri. 9am-5pm, Saturday 11am-5pm. Pick up a copy of *California Visitors Review* (free) for maps, complete winery listings and a weekly events guide (also available in many stores). There are also Chambers of Commerce in **Yountville,** Washington St. (944-0904), **St. Helena,** 1080 Main St. (963-4456, open Mon.-Fri. 10am-noon 1-4pm, Sat. 10am-4pm), and **Calistoga,** 1458 Lincoln Ave. (942-6333, open daily 10am-5pm).

Greyhound: 1620 Main St. (226-1856), in Napa. Two per day south to San Francisco and north to Lakeport. Open Mon.-Fri. 7:45am-noon and 1:15-6pm, Sat. 9:15-10:15am. Also stops in Yountville (California Drive, 944-8377), St. Helena, and Calistoga. Reservations are vital.

Local Transportation: Napa City Bus ("the VINE" or Valley Intercity Neighborhood Express—the things people will do just to get a cute acronym), 1151 Peal St. (255-7631). Provides transport throughout the valley 6:45am-6:15pm. Fare 60¢, students and children 40¢.

Amtrak: The nearest Amtrak station is accessible by bus from the Napa Wine Train Depot, located at 1275 McKinstry St. (253-2111). Train leaves from Richmond and arrives 1/2 hr. later in Oakland.

Car Rental: Budget, 407 Soscol Ave. (224-7845), in Napa. Must be 25 with credit card. $29 per day.

Bike Rental: Napa Valley Cyclery, 4080 Byway East (255-3377), in Napa. Bicycles $4 for the first hr. and $3 per additional hr., up to a maximum of $15 per day. Major credit card required for deposit. Open Mon.-Sat. 9am-6pm, Sun. 10am-5pm.

Horseback Riding: Wild Horse Valley Ranch, Wild Horse Valley Road, Napa (224-0727).

Emergency Women's Service: 255-6397.

Suicide Prevention: 255-6944. 24 hr.

Hospital: Queen of the Valley, 1000 Trancas St. (252-1411).

Emergency: 911.

Police: 1539 First St. (257-9550).

Post Office: 1625 Trancas St. (255-1621). Open Mon.-Fri 8:30am-5pm. General Delivery ZIP Code: 94558.

Area Code: 707.

Route 29 runs through the middle of the valley from the county seat of **Napa** at its southern end, to **Calistoga** in the north, passing **St. Helena** and **Yountville** in between. The best way to see the area is by bicycle since the valley is dead level and only 30 mi. long. The **Silverado Trail,** parallel to Rte. 29, is a more scenic and less crowded route than the highway. If you're planning a weekend trip from San Francisco, the 60 mi. trip may take up to 1½ hours on Saturday mornings or Sunday afternoons. If at all possible, try to visit the valley on weekdays and avoid the bus tours with plastic glasses and frantic wine pouring in over-crowded tasting rooms.

Accommodations and Camping

Bed and breakfasts, and most hotels, are an ulcer-inducing $55-225 per night. A few cabin resorts have one or two rooms under $40, but they go first and are inaccessible to those without cars. Without a reservation or a car, plan on camping.

Triple S Ranch, 4600 Mountain Home Ranch Rd. (942-6730), in Calistoga. Take Rte. 29 toward Calistoga, and turn left before downtown, onto Petrified Forest Road. Light, woody cabins. Probably the best deal in the valley. Registration 9am-6pm. Singles $30. Doubles $40. Open April-Oct.

Silverado Motor Court, 500 Silverado Trail (253-0892), in Napa near Soscol Ave. Dry, balanced, lean rooms with kitchenette and TV. Registration noon-6pm. Check-out 11am. Singles $38. Doubles $50.

Motel 6, 3380 Solano Ave. (257-6111), in Napa at Redwood Rd. From Rte. 29, take the Redwood Rd. exit. Crisp, balanced with a subtle edge. Decidedly Motel 6. TV, small pool, A/C. Registration after 1pm, usually full by 6pm in summer. Check-out noon. Singles $36, each additional person $6.

Bothe-Napa Valley State Park, 3601 St. Helena Hwy. (942-4575, for reservations 800-444-7275), north of St. Helena on Rte. 29. Often full, so call ahead to avoid a long, unnecessary ride. Park open 8am-10:30pm; Oct.-April 9am-5pm. Sites with hot showers $14. Swimming pool $3, under 17 $1. Reserve 6-8 weeks in advance for weekends.

Town & Country Fairgrounds, 575 3rd St. (226-2164), in Napa. Camping for the desperate. RVs parked bumper sticker to bumper sticker conceal what is probably a grassy field. Office open daily 5:30am-11pm. Two-week max. stay. Hot showers and tent sites $15.

Napa County Fairgrounds, 1435 Oak St. (942-5111), in Calistoga. First-come, first-served. Open 24 hr. Cooler sites, with showers and electricity, $12 for RVs, $10 for tents. Closed July 1-10 for county fair.

Food

Sit-down meals are often expensive here, but Napa and its neighboring communities support numerous delis where you can buy inexpensive picnic supplies. The **Jefferson Food Mart,** 1704 Jefferson (224-7112), is open daily 7am-11pm.

Villa Corona Panaderia-Tortilleña, 3614 Bel Aire Plaza (257-8685), in Napa. Off of Trancas, behind the Citibank building. Tiny restaurant in an alley, near downtown, with *piñataed* ceiling. Impressive selection of Mexican beers, drinks, and spices. Large burritos $2.75. Mexican pastries made on premises $1-2. Open daily 9am-8:30pm in summer, 9am-7:30pm in winter.

Guigni's, 1227 Main St. (963-3421), in St. Helena. An unpretentious, friendly grocery store with sandwiches for $3. Definitely the best place to put a picnic together. If it's raining, sit in the "munch room" at the back. Open Mon.-Sat. 8am-5pm, Sun. 9am-5pm.

Hi-Way 29 Diner, 101 Kelly Rd. (224-6303) on Hwy 29. Greasy spoon with fluffy frisbee-sized flapjacks ($2.80). A welcome break from brie and honey mustard on baguettes. Open Mon.-Sat. 6am-3pm, Sun. 7am-4pm.

Curb Side Café, 1245 1st St. (253-2307), at the corner of Randolph St. in downtown Napa. Sandwich place, popular with the Napalese. Tasty breakfasts, sublime sandwiches ($5). Open Mon.-Sat. 8am-4pm, Sun. 10am-3pm.

Sights

Napa Valley is home to the wine country's heavyweights; vineyards include national names such as Inglenook, Christian Brothers, and Mondavi. The large vineyards are better for neophytes since tours are well-organized, and there's no pressure to say anything intelligent-sounding at the tastings. There are more than 250 wineries in Napa County, nearly two-thirds of which are in Napa Valley. Almost all give free tours and tastings, though the majority require that visitors phone ahead to ensure that someone is around to pour the wine. For general information on wines, see the Napa and Sonoma introduction. The vineyards listed below are some of the valley's larger operations. All have established tour programs and attract hundreds of visitors daily. To reach the smaller places, pick up a list of vineyards from the Napa Chamber of Commerce or look for signs along the roadside. If you need a break from drinking, try soaking in some **hot springs** at **Calistoga.** Note that the vineyards are *not* listed geographically—following such a route would suggest a few too many samplings.

Robert Mondavi Winery, 7801 St. Helena Hwy. (963-9611), in Oakville. Spanish-style buildings, beautiful grounds. Spirited tour takes visitors through marvelous catacombs and past towering stacks of oaken barrels filled with mellowing wine. The best free tour and tasting for the completely unknowledgeable, and the wine itself is decent. Tours every 15 minutes. Reservations requested; they book up fast in the summer. Open daily 9am-5pm; Oct.-April 10am-4:30pm.

Domaine Chandon, California Dr. (944-2280), in Yountville next to the Veteran's Home. One of the finest tours in the valley, given in several languages by prior arrangement. Owned by Moët Chandon of France (the people who make Dom Perignon), this is the place to learn the secrets of champagne-making. Champagne tastings $3-4 per glass at the restaurant attached to the winery. Open daily 11am-6pm; Nov.-April Wed.-Sun. 11am-6pm.

Christian Brothers Mount St. Helena, 2555 Main St. (963-0765), in St. Helena. Some of the valley's best sparkling wines. The tour of the old winery isn't exciting, so head straight for the tasting room. But don't fail to catch the considerable collection of curious corkscrews. Open daily 10am-4pm; limited tours.

RMS Vineyards, 1250 Cuttings Wharf Rd. (253-9055). For a different variety of Napa alcohol, try this new and unique brandy distillery. Tours Mon.-Fri. at 10:30am and 2:30pm; sales room open until 4pm.

Domaine Carneros, 1240 Duhig Road (257-0101), in Napa. Off of Rte. 12. Picturesque estate modeled after a French Chateau. 2-year old winery. No free tastings, but free tour and film. Open daily 11am-4pm.

Sterling Vineyards, 1111 Dunaweal Lane (942-5151), in Calistoga. Perhaps the most visually arresting of the valley's vineyards. Mounted on top of a small hill, surrounded by vines, with a view of the valley below. Excellent wines. A $5 tramway carries visitors to the stone building for tours and tasting sessions. Open daily 10:30am-4:30pm.

Inglenook Vineyard, 1991 St. Helena Hwy. (963-2616), in South Rutherford. One of the valley's mass-producers. The ivy-covered brick winery with stained-glass windows is a photographer's delight. Avoid the tour, which ends with an elaborate wine-tasting session but takes away from valuable drinking time. Instead try the **John Daniels Cellar,** where you can buy a taste of vintage wines. Open daily 10am-5pm.

Hanns Kornell Champagne Cellars, 1091 Larkmead Lane (963-2334), 4 mi. north of St. Helena; turn right onto Larkmead Lane. A small, 1-room tasting area, with crisp dry champagnes. Try the *Sehr Trocken* (extra dry). Guided tours until 3:45pm. Open daily 10am-4pm.

Beringer Vineyards, 2000 Main St. (963-7115), in St. Helena. One of the more popular vineyards. Tours include Rhine House, a landmark mansion, and a tasting session. In summer, the tours are a mob scene. To avoid the crowds and taste Beringer's better wines, try the reserve room on the second floor of the Rhine House. (Generous samples in the reserve room cost $2 per wine.) Open daily 10am-5:45pm; in winter 9:30am-4:45pm. Tastings daily 10am-4:30pm. Tours 10am-5pm; Oct.-April 9:30am-4pm.

Beaulieu Vineyard, 1960 St. Helena Hwy. (963-2411), in Rutherford. The tour of the wine-making area and cellars includes a brief, imaginative audio-visual presentation (first tour 11am, last tour 3pm). Tasting daily 10am-4pm.

Clos Du Val Wine Company, Ltd., 5330 Silverado Trail (252-6711), in Napa. An outdoor picnic area with whimsical drawings by Ronald Searle. Tours by appointment at 10am and 2pm; tasting room open all day. Open daily 10am-4pm.

Stag's Leap Wine Cellars, 5766 Silverado Trail (944-2020), in Napa. The tiny vineyard that beat the Continent's best. Call at least a week in advance to arrange a tour and a superb tasting session. Open daily 10am-4pm.

Newlan, 5225 Solano Ave. (257-2399). A small premium winery, with the best in *Pinot Noir* and dessert wines. Tastings and sales daily 10am-5pm.

Grgich Hills Cellars, 1829 St. Helena Hwy. (963-2784), in Rutherford. Tours by prior arrangement only, but daily tastings. Some of the finest Zinfandels and Chardonnays in the area. Open daily 9:30am-4:30pm.

Hakusan Sake Gardens, One Executive Way (258-6160), south of downtown Napa on Hwy. 29. A pleasant self-guided tour through the Japanese gardens provides a delightful respite from the power-chugging at the vineyards. Generous pourings of *Hakusan Sake,* known as *Haki Sake* to locals. Open daily 9am-6pm.

Chateau Montelena, 1429 Tubbs Lane (942-5105). An old castle houses this award-winning winery, which emphasizes estate-bottled reds. Make reservations if you'd like to picnic on the beautiful islands in the lake behind the castle. Tasting room open daily 10am-4pm.

Vichon Winery, on Daleville Grade. Take a left off of Rte. 29 at the Carmalete Monastary sign. The gorgeous view of the valley merits the detour. Picnic tables available for wine-purchasers. Open daily 10am-4:30pm.

Despite blurred impressions to the contrary, Napa does have non-bibendary attractions. Those who want a closer look at Angela Channing's stomping grounds ("Chase, I'd sooner die before you took control of Falcon Crest") are directed to the real Falcon Crest Mansion, **Spring Mountain Vineyards,** 4022 Spring Mountain Rd. (963-5233), in St. Helena. The house is open for tours of the grounds only daily 11am-4pm. You must call ahead for appointments.

Robert Louis Stevenson State Park (942-4575), on Rte. 29 north of St. Helena, is centered around the abandoned bunkhouse where the Scottish writer, sick and penniless, spent a rejuvenating honeymoon in 1880. The author gathered information for his novel *Silverado Squatters* while in the area, and eventually patterned Spyglass Hill in *Treasure Island* after looming Mt. St. Helena. (Park open daily 8am-sunset.) The **Silverado Museum,** 1490 Library Lane, St. Helena (963-3757), off Adams St., is a labor of love by a devoted collector of Stevensoniana. See manuscript notes from *Master of Ballantrae* and *Dr. Jekyll and Mr. Hyde.* (Open Tues.-Sun. noon-4pm. Free.)

For that early-morning experience-of-a-lifetime, try taking a hot-air balloon over Napa. For $155, **Adventures Aloft** on Washington St. (255-8688) in Yountville, offers coffee and pastries, one hour in the air with a knowledgeable pilot, a champagne brunch, and a flying certificate (the easiest you'll ever earn).

Farther to the north, 2 mi. outside Calistoga, the **Old Faithful Geyser of California** (942-6463; not to be mistaken with the more famous geyser in Wyoming), on Tubbs Lane off Rte. 128, spurts boiling water 60 ft. into the air. The 350° jet appears on average every 50 minutes in summer and every 30 minutes in winter; the ticket vendor will tell you the estimated time of the next ejaculation. (Open daily 9am-6pm; in winter daily 9am-5pm. Admission $3.50, ages 6-12 $2, under 6 free.)

Calistoga is also known as the "Hot Springs of the West." Sam Brannan, who first developed the area, promised to make the hot springs the "Saratoga of California," but he misspoke and promised instead to make them "The Calistoga of Saratina." His cottage is now the base for the **Sharpsteen Museum,** 1311 Washington St. (942-5911), which traces the development of this town. (Open daily 10am-4pm; in winter noon-4pm. Free.) If you have the time and money, try a hot mineral bath, steam bath, volcanic ash mud bath, and blanket sweat at **Nance's Hot Springs,** 1614 Lincoln Ave. (942-6211). Add a half-hour massage and the full treatment comes to around $50 (treatments available 9am-3:30pm). For a less extravagant communion with the waters, pay a nominal day-use or night-use pool fee at one of the many spas. **Indian Springs** has a particularly exotic olympic-sized pool complete with a fountain by the great sculptor, Hirshen. You can also pay 90¢ and chug the stuff bottled—Calistoga (like Saratoga) has its very own line of sparkling mineral waters with fruit juice.

Four mi. farther along the highway (follow the signs from Calistoga), several giant **petrified redwoods** (942-6667) await picnickers. The several million-year-old silica trees are strangely underwhelming as far as natural wonders go, and the cheesy promotions fail to entice. The grove is small, and often mobbed by camera-toting tour groups. Included in the ticket price is admission to a "museum," coincidentally located in the gift shop. (Open daily 10am-6pm. Adults $3, seniors $2, children $1.)

Farther north on Rte. 29, and then east, is the **McLaughlin Mine,** 26775 Morgan Valley Rd. (707-995-6070). California's largest working gold mine is, they claim, an excellent example of careful environmental management. Judge for yourself. Tours on Fri.-Sat. arranged through Lake County Chamber of Commerce.

Ten miles south of Napa off I-80 and Rte. 37, on Marine World Parkway in the otherwise unremarkable town of Vallejo, is 160-acre **Marine World Africa USA,** (643-6722) an enormous outdoor aquarium and funland. And so it better be for $20 (seniors $17, children 4-12 $15, under 4 free, 2-day adult pass $25). All proceeds benefit wildlife protection programs. The amusement park is accessible by BART from the Bay Area between Mon.-Sat.; call 415-788-2278 for more information. (Open daily 9:30am-6:30pm; in winter Wed.-Sun. 9:30am-5pm.)

The 110° hot springs of Calistoga offer limited refreshment during the hot days of summer. **Lake Berryessa,** (942-2111), 20 mi. north of Napa, grants cool water for swimming, sailing, and fishing, with 168 mi. of shoreline. In town, the **Napa Riverboat,** Napa Valley Marina, 1200 Milton Rd. (226-2628) runs historical boat tours ($12, under 12 $8.) They also operate an elegant dine-and-dance cruise ($40, 3hr.). Both trips only offered on Saturdays.

Calistoga Gliders, 1546 Lincoln Ave. (942-5000), in Calistoga, offers soaring glider rides over Napa Valley for a breath-taking fifteen minutes in the clouds ($75). Offered daily 9am-6pm (all rides with a pilot).

The annual **Napa Valley Wine Festival** (252-0872) takes place in November. **Napa Valley Fairgrounds** hosts a month-long summer fair in August, with wine-tasting, rock music, juggling, a rodeo, and rides. *Musicionadoes* can catch **Music-in-the-Park,** in the center of downtown Napa at the riverfront. Free jazz concerts May 31-Aug. 16, Fridays noon-1pm, Wed. and Fri. evenings 6-7pm in July and August. Contact Napa Parks and Recreation Office for more information (257-9529).

Sonoma Valley

Commercial wine production began here, when Father José Altimira planted grapes around his mission in 1823 . . . or when Haraszthy founded Buena Vista in 1851 . . . or when Vallejo . . . Anyway, Sonoma's vineyards are just as long-lived as Napa's, and many of their wines are just as good. Although less well-known than its hyped-up neighbor, Sonoma's rolling oak-covered hills and golden fields are just as attractive.

Lower-priced lodgings, less expensive meals, and fewer crowds than in Napa await your arrival. Sonoma Valley is more a cluster of small towns separated by vineyards than an extended tourist attraction like Napa sometimes seems to be.

Practical Information and Orientation

Visitor Information: Sonoma Valley Visitors Bureau, 453 E. 1st St. (996-1090), in Sonoma's central plaza. Also a Southern office on Rte. 12 (996-5793). Plenty of maps ($1), and a knowledgeable and friendly staff. Pick up *The Review,* a free weekly with extensive winery listings, around town. After hours, use the self-help board outside. Open daily 9am-5pm.

Bus: Sonoma County Transit (576-7433 or 800-345-7433, Mon.-Fri. 7am-6pm) serves the entire county, including Santa Rosa in the north and Napa in the east. Bus #30 runs between

Sonoma and Santa Rosa (8 per day, 3 on Sat.; $1.70, seniors 80¢, ages 6-18 $1.30, under 6 free). Within Sonoma, bus fare is 70¢, seniors 35¢, students 50¢. County buses stop when flagged down.

Car Rental: Sonoma Airporter, Rte. 12 at Boyes Hot Springs (938-4246). $17-25 per day with 50 free miles, 20¢ per additional mile. Weekly rates (for $25/day cars) are $150. (No weekly rates for $17/day cars.) Must be 21 with major credit card or you leave a $500 cash deposit.

Events Hotline: 935-1111.

Sonoma Information Line: 938-KNOW (938-5669)

Sonoma Valley Crisis Line: 938-HELP (938-4357).

Rape Crisis Hotline: 545-7273.

Hospital: Sonoma Valley, 347 Andrieux St. (938-4545), Sonoma.

Emergency: 911.

Police: 996-3602.

Post Office: 617 Broadway, Sonoma (996-2459), at Patten St. Open Mon.-Fri. 8:30am-5pm. General Delivery ZIP Code: 95476.

Area Code: 707.

The Sonoma Valley runs between **Sonoma** in the south and **Glen Ellen** in the north, with **Hwy. 12** traversing its length. The valley is small enough to tour easily by bicycle. Keep your eyes peeled when using the roads since the local signposting is dreadful. You can get your bearings in the town of Sonoma at the mural on the corner of Broadway and Napa St. **Santa Rosa** is located about 20 miles northeast.

Accommodations

Pickin's for lodging in Sonoma Valley are pretty slim; you're probably better off heading west for the cheap motels along U.S. 101.

Sonoma's restaurants, like Napa's, often exact large sums for their fancy meals. Bakeries and delis are arranged about the main square in downtown Sonoma.

Motel 6, 5135 Montero Way (664-9090), in Petaluma. Take the Old Redwood/Petaluma Blvd. exit north off U.S. 101. Small Pool, A/C. Singles $30, each additional adult $6.

All Star, 1368 N. McDowell Blvd. (765-0333), in Petaluma. Very modern, with the usual fixtures—TV, A/C, bed, door. Antiseptic, spacious, and almost tastefully decorated. Singles $25.25. Doubles $29.65.

Sugarloaf Ridge State Park, 2605 Adobe Canyon Rd., Kenwood (833-5712). Call MISTIX (800-444-7275) for reservations. 50 sites. Pretty views. Sites $10, seniors $8.

San Francisco North/Petaluma KOA, 20 Rainsville Road (763-1492), in Petaluma. Take Penngrove exit, make a right turn onto Stony Pt. Rd. to Rainsville Rd. RV and trailer park with cabins $20-29. Some tent sites separated from trailers $22. Call 800-992-CAMP (800-992-2267) for reservations.

Acacia Grove Mobile Park, 18629 Sonoma Hwy. (996-6313), in Sonoma. Four RV spaces from $9-11 per night.

Spring Lake Regional Park, Summerfield Dr. (539-8082), off Montgomery Rd. in Santa Rosa. No reservations. Sites $9.

Food

Ma Stokeld's British Meat Pie Shop, Suite "F" Place des Pyrenees Alley, 464 E. 1st St. (935-0660). Tiny little shop with a European feel. Pies and pastries from the sinking island. Great Blythean bangers (sausages, not firecrackers) wrapped in rolls $4.50. Beer $1.75. Open Mon.-Sat. 11am-5pm.

Sonoma French Bakery Inc., 470 E. 1st St. (996-2691). Fresh, delicious loaves ($1 and up), croissants, and other flakey items around $1.50. Open Wed.-Sat. 8am-6pm, Sun. 7:30am-noon.

Sonoma Cheese Factory, 2 W. Spain St. (996-1931). A deli run wondefully wild. Everything from cherry cider to fresh pepperoni. Dozens of cheeses, some varieties made in the back room. Watch the process through a giant picture window. Sandwiches $3.25-5. Open Mon.-Fri. 8:30am-5:30pm, Sat.-Sun. 8:30am-6pm.

The Cherry Tree, Rte. 12 (938-3480), south of Sonoma. A combination deli and fruit stand with superb black cherry cider (75¢ for 8 oz.). Endless variety of gourmet picnic supplies. Open daily 7am-8:30pm.

Old Sonoma Creamery, at the corner of E. Spain St. and 1st St (938-2938). A cute, if slightly touristy, deli and ice cream shop. Try the gluttonous 6 ice cream scoop, 6 topping sundae, w/ whipped cream, nuts and sprinkles—and waddle home ($8.50). Open daily 10am-6pm.

La Famiglia, 220 Western Ave. at Liberty St. (778-8211), in Petaluma. A family-owned grocery and deli, with fresh pesta and sandwiches up to 10 feet long (regular size $4-5.25). Open Mon.-Sat. 8am-7pm. Sunday 8am-5pm.

Aram's, 122A Kentucky St. in downtown Petaluma (765-9775). An Armenian and Mediterranean café with excellent coffees. Delicious smoked salmon Aram sandwiches ($1.20)—two can make a meal. Open Mon.-Fri. 8am-9pm, Saturday 10am-9pm.

If driving or biking through the valley, keep your eyes open for the numerous fresh fruit and vegetable stands, to sample the best eating available in the Valley. (Free Farm Trails maps available in the Visitors Bureau.)

Sights

Sonoma Valley's wineries are less tourist-ridden than those in Napa Valley. There are two main clusters, one near Sonoma and one near Kenwood. Farther north in Sonoma County, several vineyards cling to the **Russian River Valley,** near Guerneville, Healdsburg and Geyserville (see Sonoma Coast).

Sebastiani, 389 E. 4th St. (938-5532), at the northwest corner of Sonoma's central plaza. The giant mass-producer of the valley draws 250,000 visitors per year. A perfect place to get an introduction to the noble drink. Interesting 20-min. tour of the ancient aging rooms. Save time for the Native American museum (free). Tasting and tours daily 10am-5pm.

Buena Vista, 18000 Old Winery Rd. (938-1266), off E. Napa St. Fine wines and an interesting self-guided tour of their famous old stone buildings, preserved as Mr. Haraszthy built them when he allegedly founded the California wine industry. Picnic grounds and tasting room open daily 10am-5pm.

Haywood, 18701 Gehricke Rd. (966-4298), in Sonoma off E. Napa St. Up a dirt road, this 3-person winery currently produces some of the valley's best vino. Strongly recommended by locals. Small picnic site and pleasant conversation. No tours. Open daily 11am-5pm.

Glen Ellen Winery, 1443 London Ranch Rd. (996-1066), 1 mi. from Glen Ellen. Gorgeous grounds, complete with roaming peacocks. No tours. Open daily 10am-4:30pm.

Hacienda Wine Cellars, 1000 Vineyard Lane (938-3220), in Sonoma off Castle Rd. from E. Napa St. Wine gardens for picnics and daily tasting. Tours by appointment. Open daily 10am-5pm.

Kenwood Vineyards, 9592 Rte. 12 (833-5891), in Kenwood. One of the most highly regarded wineries in the valley. Their *Cabernet Sauvignon* is consistently excellent. No picnicking. Tours only by appointment. Open daily 10am-4:30pm.

Chateau St. Jean, 8555 Rte. 12 (833-4134), in Kenwood. (Prounounced GENE, like the hereditary unit.) Brief self-guided tour of holding tanks. Expansive winery (100,000 cases) in a Mediterranean-villa setting. 97% of their production is whites. Try the *Chardonnay.* Tasting daily 10am-4:30pm. Tours daily 10:30am-4pm.

Sonoma has lived under a mosaic of flags: the English (Drake landed nearby in 1579), the Russian (a colony at Fort Ross on the coast), the Spanish (until 1823), the Mexican, the California Republic, and the U.S. It was here in 1846 that a band of boisterous settlers gathered together as the "bears" (thinking of the state's independent, fierce, and now absent, grizzly variety), imprisoned Mexico's General Vallejo, and declared the region an independent republic under President Ide.

The town of Sonoma centers around city hall and its surrounding park. 1st and 2nd Streets cross E. Spain and Napa Streets forming a central square from which to start a tour of the town.

Local historic artifacts have been collected and preserved in the **Sonoma State Historic Park,** at the corner of E. Spain and 1st St., in the northeast corner of town. Within the park, an adobe church stands on the site of the **Sonoma Mission** (938-1578), northernmost and last of the missions through which the Spanish spread Catholicism and controlled California. Built in 1826 when Mexico was already a republic, the mission houses a remnant of the original California Republic flag, the rest of which burned in 1906 earthquake-and-fire. (Open daily 10am-5pm. Admission $1, seniors and ages 6-17 50¢, under 6 free.)

The same ticket also admits you to two other state monuments. **General Vallejo's Home** (938-1215), ¾ mi. west of Sonoma's Central Plaza on Spain St., is the Gothic home of the famed Mexican military and civil leader, and contains the original furnishings. As the political winds shifted, the General went on to serve as a California senator and mayor of Sonoma. The grounds are garnished by a serene picnic area designed in part by Vallejo and his *esposa.* (Open daily 10am-5pm.)

Back in Sonoma, the **Depot Museum** (938-9765) is a railroad depot reconstructed after the century-old original burned in 1976. Period clothing and furniture help reanimate 19th-century life. (Open Wed.-Sun. 1-4:30pm. Admission 50¢, seniors and ages 10-18 25¢, under 10 with parents free.) The Chamber of Commerce offers a self-guided map ($1) with a one-hour **walking tour** of the town's historic buildings.

Just south of the city center, **Traintown** (938-3912) offers a steam engine tour through a 10-acre park, which includes a children's petting zoo. Fare is $2.50, children $1.80. (Open daily 11am-5pm; in winter Sat.-Sun. 11am-5pm.)

Further south, just past the junction of Rtes. 37 and 121, lies **Sears Point International Raceway** (938-8448). The track revs up for auto, motorcycle, and bicycle racing year-round, including some major international competitions. The pitside crowd and the dusty, car exhaust-filled atmosphere stand in sharp contrast to pretentious wine connoisseurs farther north. Call for a schedule of events. Admission ranges from $7 to $45 for special events.

Those sober enough to find it can visit Jack London's last home, the Glen Ellen "Beauty Ranch" where the adventurer-writer passed out of this world in 1916. The house stands in **Jack London State Park** (938-5216), in Glen Ellen, 6 mi. north of town on Rte. 12. (Open daily 8am-8pm; museum open 10am-5pm. $3 per car.) Wolf House, the main building, burned to the ground in a mysterious fire shortly before the author of "The Call of the Wild" and "White Fang" was scheduled to move in, but the ruins, made of native volcanic stone, remain. Nearby is the House of the Happy Walls, the widow London's residence, and the location of a two-floor **museum** devoted to the writer. The park offers several vistas of the valley as well as beautiful **Beauty Ranch Trail** which passes by the lake, winery ruins, silos, and several cute cottages.

The **Petaluma Adobe,** 15 minutes east of Sonoma, was Vallejo's ranch. Leave Sonoma on Rte. 116 and turn left onto Adobe Rd. The solitary abode is set among rolling fields and is largely unknown to tourists. Sheep and chickens wander freely, and the restoration of the building's living quarters is scrupulously authentic. This is an excellent place to feast on a picnic lunch. (Open daily 10am-5pm.)

The town of **Petaluma** itself merits visitation, not simply for its cheap accommodations, but for its magnificent old (i.e. over 85 years) buildings. The area was virtually untouched by the 1906 earthquake; a fine **opera house** (149 Kentucky St.) and an impressive free-standing glass dome in the **museum** (20 4th St.; 778-4398; open Thurs.-Mon. 1-4pm) are still standing. Obtain details from the **Chamber of Commerce** at 314 Western Ave. (762-2785; open Mon.-Fri. 9am-5pm). In October, roll up your sleeves for the **World Wristwrestling Championship.**

Santa Rosa

I firmly believe, from what I have seen, that this is the chosen spot of all the earth, as far as nature is concerned.

—Luther Burbank

Burbank was indeed a man of hyperbole. The second largest city in California north of San Francisco (behind Sacramento) entertains travelers with tours of Burbank Gardens, a cookin' nightlife, and little else, unless you enjoy quiet mid-sized city life.

Practical Information and Orientation

Visitor Information: Sonoma County Visitors Bureau, 10 4th St. (575-1191), by the railroad tracks. Zillions of brochures on restaurants, wineries, hotels, and local attractions. There's a free phone for local calls. Open Mon.-Fri. 8am-5pm, Sat.-Sun. 9am-4pm. **Santa Rosa Chamber of Commerce,** 637 1st St. (545-1414). Don't make a special effort—all they have is a county map ($1). Open Mon.-Fri. 9am-5pm.

Sonoma County Wine Growers Association: 50 Mark West Springs Rd. (527-7701), east of U.S. 101, at the Luther Burbank Center for the Arts. Maps of 65 member wineries and a tasting directory. Open Mon.-Fri. 9am-5pm.

Greyhound: (Santa Rosa Greyhound Bus Station closed 1½ years ago.) There is a Greyhound pick-up and drop-off point at the corner of Piner and Industrial Aves. The closest full-sclae stations are in Cloverdale (109 N. Cloverdale Blvd.; 894-2099; open Mon.-Sat. 9am-5:30pm) and San Rafael (see Marin County listing).

Buses: Golden Gate Transit, 544-1323. Bus #80 runs between San Francisco's Transbay Terminal and Santa Rosa (hourly 5:23am-2:03am; fare $3.70, seniors $1.85, ages 6-18 $2.75). GGT also runs commute-hour express buses from Snata Rosa to San Francisco. **Santa Rosa Transit** (576-7433). Operates extensive local service. **Sonoma County Transit** putts to Petaluma and Sonoma. Everything runs from the transit mall at 2nd St. Plaze.

Car Rental: U-Save Auto Rental, 1426 Petaluma Hill Rd. (579-3070). Cars from $23 per day, with 150 free miles, plus 18¢ per additional mile. Must be 21 with credit card or cash deposit. Open Mon.-Fri. 8:30am-6pm, Sat. 9am-3pm.

Bike Rental: Rincon Cyclery, 4927 Sonoma Hwy. #H (538-0868), in Santa Rosa. Mountain bikes only—shop is near off-road trails. $7 per hour, $25 per day, $100 per week. Open daily 10am-6pm.

Public Library: 3rd and E. St. (545-0831). Open Mon.-Thurs. 9:30am-9pm, Fri.-Sat. 9:30am-6pm, Sunday 2pm-6pm.

Laundromat: Wash Plus, 3401 Cleveland Ave. (544-5011). Wash $1; dry 25¢. Open daily 7am-10pm.

Rape Crisis: 545-7273.

Hospital: Santa Rosa Memorial, 1165 Montgomery Dr. (546-3210).

Post Office: 730 2nd St. (528-8763), between D and E Sts. Open Mon.-Fri. 8:30am-5pm. General Delivery ZIP Code: 95402.

Area Code: 707.

Santa Rosa lies 50 mi. north of San Francisco on U.S. 101 at the intersection with Rte. 12 to the Sonoma Valley. Santa Rosa is the cultural, educational, medical, governmental, and geographical center of Sonoma County. Sonoma County brags a widely varied terrain with a rugged coastline to the west, the enchanted Valley of the Moon and its famous vineyards to the east, and farmlands made fertile by the Russian River to the north.

Accommodations and Camping

Santa Rosa's multidimensional centrality has led to a proliferation of average lodgings at above-average prices.

Motel 6, 2 locations: 6145 Commerce Blvd. (585-8888). Lower rates justify the 15 mi. trip south to Rohnert Park, but the place is accessible only by car. Singles $27, each additional adult $6. Also 5 mi. north of downtown Santa Rosa at 2760 Cleveland Ave. (546-1500). Take the Steele Lane exit west off U.S. 101, then turn north onto Cleveland. Pool, A/C. Check in after 4pm, out before noon. Singles $30, each additional adult $6.

Allstar Inn, 3145 Cleveland Ave. (525-9010), in Santa Rosa. Capacious, nearly stylish rooms, mid-sized pool. Handicapped and non-smoking rooms. Check out 11am. Singles $24.79, doubles $29.

Astro Motel, 323 Santa Rosa Ave. (545-8555), right downtown. TV, A/C, non-smoking rooms available. A haven for late arrivees as they often have vacant rooms. Run-down, with bizarre German-influenced decoration employing rolled-up Levi jeans and paint. Convenient location not far from downtown. Some rooms with kitchenettes. Singles $25-32. Doubles from $40.

Sandman Motel, 3421 Cleveland Ave. (544-8570). Take Mendocino Ave. exit west off U.S. 101, and turn south onto Cleveland. Cheerful rooms, jacuzzi, pool, and A/C. Singles $40, each additional person $4. Two beds $46. Reserve for summer and for weekends year-round.

Spring Lake County Park, 5585 Newanga Rd. (539-8092), off Summerfield Rd. Water, toilets, and showers. Sites $8-11. No reservations, but always full by 7pm in summer.

Food

Santa Rosa's budget restaurants are concentrated near Mendocino Ave., northeast of the mall in the town center.

Arrigoni's Café, 701 4th St. (545-1297), at D St. A clean, well-lighted interior and sandwiches par excellence perpetuate one of the city's most popular lunchtime experiences ($4-6). Giant, crisp salad ($4.75). Open Mon.-Fri. 7am-5pm, Sat. 8am-4pm.

Ting Hau, 717 4th St. (545-5204), downtown. The management has saved its time and effort for the food, and despite dreary booths, this little Chinese eatery has a devoted following. Complete meals at lunch for only $3 (served 11:30am-2:30pm). Open Mon.-Sat. 11:30am-9:30pm, Sun. noon-9pm.

The Santa Rosa Grill, 450 Mendocino Ave. (578-4024). A stylish art-deco hamburger heaven resplendent in shiny chrome and pink formica. 1/3 lb. hamburgers and unbeatable french fries with the skins still intact $5-7. Open Mon.-Thurs. 11:30am-10:30pm. Fri.-Sat. 11:30am-midnight.

The Good Earth, 610 3rd St. (523-3060). Good natural food in a subdued, Seventies-style setting. Avoid the expensive entrees in favor of the hot sandwiches and meal-sized salads (salads $5.50, large soups $2.50). Spend a fiver or more after 5pm and the first-run movies at the theater behind the restaurant are only $3.50 per ticket. Open Sun.-Thurs. 8am-10pm, Fri.-Sat. 8am-10:30pm.

Organic Groceries, 2481 Guerneville Rd. (528-3663), near Fulton Rd. Every organic food you've ever heard of and then some—all in bulk quantities. One of the largest natural food stores in Northern California. Open Mon.-Fri. 10am-7pm, Sat. 10am-6pm, Sun. noon-5pm.

Kelmer's Brewhouse, 458 B Street (544-4677), at 7th. A brand new brew pub in downtown Santa Rosa. Yet another of California's trendy micro-breweries. Solid dinner fare; sandwiches or salads $5-6. Hums on the weekend. Open Sun.-Thurs. 11:30am-11pm; Fri.-Sat. 11:30am-1am.

Sights

Faceless old buildings and anonymous new ones, graced by a river which resembles a drainage runoff ditch, make Santa Rose a less-than-spectacular stop.

Call him a genius or a fraud, but the **Luther Burbank Home and Gardens** (524-5445), at Santa Rosa and Sonoma Ave., is a good place to sit and recharge. Lauded as the man who did for gardens what Menudo did for the teenage rock n' roll, Luther Burbank had two of the most accomplished green thumbs in history. At the age of 26, the horticulturalist moved to California from Lancaster, Massachusetts, to carry out his plant-breeding experiments. California has returned the compliment by celebrating Burbank's birthday as Arbor Day. The gardens display several original Burbank hybrids, including the shasta daisy, the spineless cactus, and the white *Agapanthus* (a short frondy plant spiked with bell-shaped flowers, a favorite of California's gas station landscapers). Burbank, who resided in the house from 1886 to 1906, lies dead and buried under an ancient cedar in the garden. (Gardens open daily 8am-7pm. Free. Self-guided tour map available in the gift shop or from the visitors bureau. House open April-Sept. Wed.-Sun. 10am-3:30pm. Admission $1, under 12 free. Free tours on Memorial Day.)

North of Santa Rosa sits the less extravagant **Julliard Gardens.** On their northern edge, at 492 Sonoma Ave., stands the **Ripley Museum** (576-5233). Broadcaster, personality, world traveler, and cartoonist who churned out a new "Believe It or Not" fact and picture daily for years, Robert Ripley was born in Santa Rosa on Christmas Day, 1893. The museum is housed in one of the wonders Ripley made famous, "the church built from one tree" (don't believe it). It enshrines a wax Ripley and sundry memorabilia. (Open March-Oct. Wed.-Sun. 11am-4pm. Admission $1, seniors 75¢, ages 7-17 50¢.)

In the fall, Santa Rosa feeds the countryside at the **October Harvest Fair,** with a 6-in.-deep apple pie, the World Championship Grape Stomp Contest, and wine-tasting. August welcomes the **Dixie Jazz Festival** (542-3315) with non-stop music and dancing. The festival is concurrent with the **Sonoma County Fair.**

Not to be outdone by Napa, Santa Rosa offers its own balloon rides. For $145, **Sonoma Thunder Wine Country Balloon Safaris,** at 4914 Shark Ave. (438-7359), in Santa Rosa, will waft you high above the Sonoma hills. Even better, for $50,000 they'll sell you a hot-air balloon of your own.

Entertainment

For a formerly sleepy farm town, this place sure knows how to party.

Joe Frogger's, 527 4th St. (526-0539). A dead bear's head adorns the wall and the Dogpatch Jail incarcerates recalcitrant males who refuse to dance. You get the idea. Bands vary widely in quality. Well drinks $1 during the daily 4-7pm Happy Hour, $1.65 otherwise. Cover $2. Open daily 10am-2am. Dancing nightly 9pm-1:30am

Magnolia's, 107 4th St. (526-9787), in Railroad Sq. Top-40 music. A favorite with the trying-to-look-older-than-they-are crowd. Drinks $2-4. Cover Fri.-Sat. $2. Uncovered Mon.-Thurs. Open Mon.-Sat. 4pm-2am.

Acapulco, 505 Mendocino Ave. (544-8400). Every California town has a great margarita bar; this is Santa Rosa's. $3.25 for a mammoth 16-oz. drink during Happy Hour (Mon.-Fri. 4-7pm). Try the peach. Open Sun.-Thurs. 11am-10pm, Fri.-Sat. 11am-1am. (Stay for dinner. Gargantuan burritos $4.)

Cotati's Cabaret, 8099 La Plaza (545-5483), in Cotati. Jazz, rock, comedy, and African music. An eclectic local crowd. Shows Wed.-Sun. usually starting at 8 or 9pm. Cover $4-8.

Northern Coast

North of San Francisco, a gray shroud of fog covers the coast as warm air currents passing over the cool Pacific create the formless mist. It is only when skies turn blue, that the true beauty of the Northern Coast is revealed. Far, far north toward the Oregon border, the deep waters of the turbulent Pacific dash in sprays of white foam against the craggy rocks along the shore. Time provided, spend days hopping among the villages and towns between San Francisco and Crescent City.

From south to north, the coast divides into four broad areas. Near San Francisco, the shores of Marin and Sonoma Counties are lightly developed. From Sonoma to

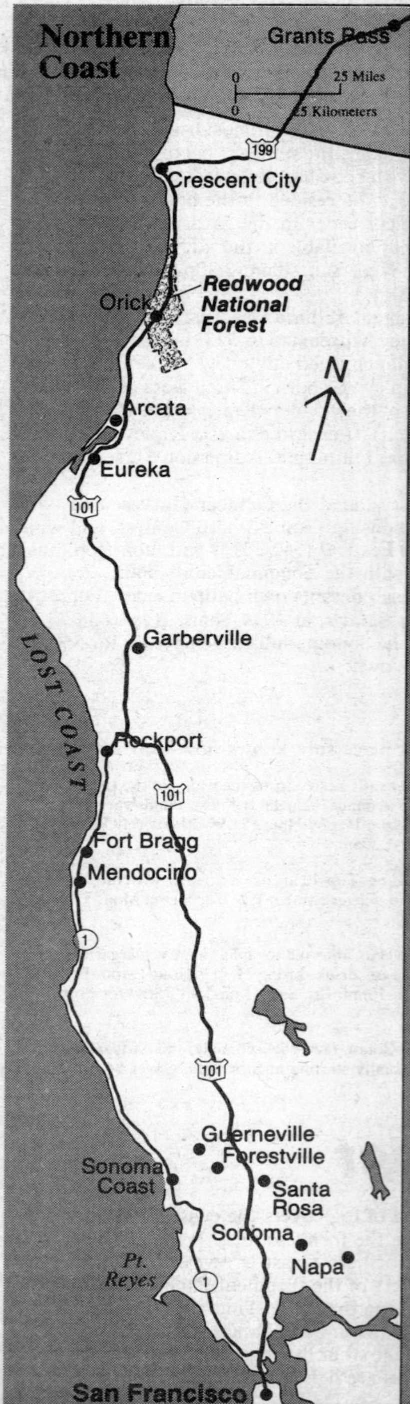
Northern Coast
Grants Pass
0 25 Miles
0 25 Kilometers
199
Crescent City
Orick
Redwood National Forest
N
Arcata
Eureka
101
LOST COAST
Garberville
Rockport
101
Fort Bragg
Mendocino
1
101
Guerneville
Forestville
Sonoma Coast
Santa Rosa
Sonoma
Pt. Reyes
Napa
1
San Francisco

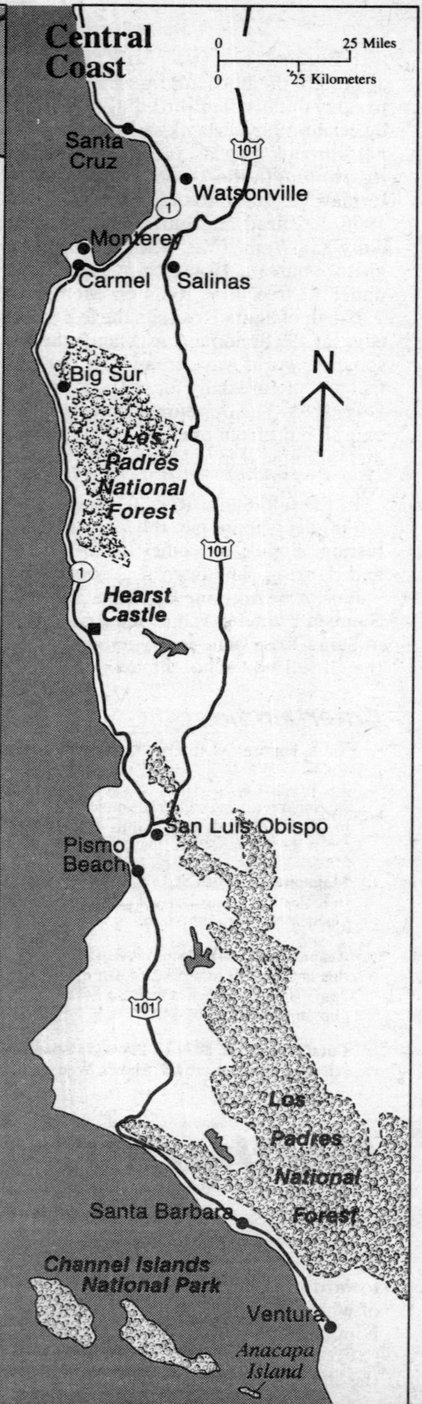
Central Coast
0 25 Miles
0 25 Kilometers
Santa Cruz
101
Watsonville
1
Monterey
Carmel
Salinas
Big Sur
N
Los Padres National Forest
101
1
Hearst Castle
San Luis Obispo
Pismo Beach
101
Los Padres National Forest
Santa Barbara
Channel Islands National Park
Ventura
Anacapa Island

Mendocino, the coast is relatively flat and sparsely settled, offering numerous picnicking spots but lacking the grandeur found farther north. Towards Rockport, the bays and cliffs call out to photographers. Here Rte. 1 turns sharply inland and travels away from the coast for 90 miles, in company with U.S. 101, to Eureka. The shore it leaves behind, which has come to be known as the Lost Coast, offers some of the wildest and most beautiful scenery in the state. Above Eureka, the coast is populated by stately redwoods and protected in the long, thin strips of Redwood National Park. Swirling ocean mists, tall trees, cool air, and black stone shoreline characterize this memorable stretch of the coast.

Local transportation along much of the coast is provided by **Mendocino Transit Authority** (MTA; 462-1422), based in Ukiah, and **Humboldt Transit Authority** (HTA; 443-5826), based in Eureka. **Greyhound** runs on Rte. 101, only hitting the coast from Eureka north.

Staying in motels along this stretch during the summer is cost-restrictive, but camping is fun, easy, and cheap. Between May and September, temperatures are cool at night and the State Parks have excellent facilites. Place reservations by calling MISTIX (800-725-7275.) In winter, after the masses have left, you'll find terrific bargains at the B&Bs and motels (rates usually $15-20 less than in summer), as well as increased intimacy with the land.

Sonoma Coast and Russian River

If you've been turned off by the crowds of tourists mobbing the Napa and Sonoma Valleys, the quieter pace of the **Russian River Valley** and its wineries may soothe your nerves. Many of the wineries here have been operating nearly as long as their counterparts to the southeast, though they tend not to be as well known. From the mouth of the Russian River, at the coastal burg of Duncans Mills, take Rte. 116 inland to the towns of Monte Rio, Guerneville, Forestville, and Sebastopol; then turn north on U.S. 101 to Healdsburg, Geyserville, and Cloverdale. Along the way, more than 50 wineries of the Russian River Valley, Dry Creek Valley, and the Alexander Valley offer tours and tastings, and encourage picnickers to enjoy their lovely grounds. Budget accommodations are sparsely scattered throughout the valleys, and cheap motels line U.S. 101.

Thirteen miles east from Duncans Mills on the Pacific, the town of **Monte Rio** is home to the famous all-male **Bohemian Club.** Behind the securely locked gates, famous members (including Ronald Reagan and Henry Kissinger) reputedly throw less-than-conservative parties and urinate copiously. Monte Rio is also home to the lovely **Village Inn,** at 20822 River Blvd. (865-2304; take a left at Monte Rio stop sign and then another left once you cross the bridge). This 1906 New England-style country inn has antique-furnished rooms, a bar, and a restaurant with a dining terrace overlooking the river. Singles from $20 for 1-2 people (at least $15 higher on weekends).

Three miles farther inland lies the quiet woodsy town of **Guerneville** (GURN-ville), an old time family-resort center, with a well-established gay community. Numerous pricey guest houses commodify genteel rusticity.

The **Visitors Center,** 14034 Armstrong Woods Rd. (800-253-8800 or 869-9009) has a comprehensive collection of brochures on the Russian River area. (Open Mon.-Fri. 9am-5pm, Sat.-Sun. 9am-4pm; Sept.-May Mon.-Fri. 9am-5pm.) **Johnson's Beach Resort,** First. St. (869-2022) offers touristy camping in umbrageous environs along the river ($6 per night), as well as spartan apartments with fully equipped kitchens ($25 per night; reserve 1 to 2 months in advance). 3 mi. north, the **Armstrong Woods State Reserve** has leisurely trails through small redwood groves. The **Armstrong Woods Pack Station,** Box 970 (887-2939) features year-round horseback riding. ($3 day use fee for state park; trail rides $30 per ½ day). **Mike's Bike Rental,** 16434 Hwy. 116 (869-1106), across from the Safeway, rents bicycles for $5 per hour, $22.50 per day (Open Mon. 10am-4:30pm, Tues. 10am-5pm, Thurs.-Sun. 10am-5pm.) **W.C. "Bob" Trowbridge Canoe Trips** runs trips down the river from $22-32 per canoe. **Burke's Canoe Trips,** 8600 River Rd. (887-1222) has services similar.

Transportation between the Russian River and the Bay Area is provided by **Golden Gate Transit,** (544-1323). Bus #78 runs northbound from Fremont St. in the Financial District to Guerneville (Mon.-Fri. 3 per day, 2 hr., $3.70). **Sonoma County Transit** (576-7433) runs a county-wide route (#20) from Santa Rosa to the Russian River Area, leaving 2nd St. and Santa Rosa Ave (Mon.-Sat., 7 per day, $1.40). Just outside town at 13250 River Rd. are the **Korbel Champagne Cellars** (887-2294), offering 45-minute tours daily 9:45am-3:45pm. Tastings transpire from 9am-5pm (until 4:30pm in winter). The **Russian River Jazz Festival** (869-3940) blasts trombone, trumpet, and piano melodies down the river in early September (tickets $21).

A few miles southeast is **Forestville,** the site of the **Topolos at Russian River Winery,** 5700 Gravenstein Hwy. N. (887-2956). Fashioned after a barn, there's a free tasting room inside and a posh restaurant with accordingly priced lunches ($6-10) and dinners ($9-16). (Open Feb.-Dec. Wed.-Mon. 11:30am-2:30pm and 5:30-9:30pm. Winter hours vary.) Less orthodox palates will enjoy the region's tribute to the delightful yellow banana slug during the **Slugfest** in March (887-1564). Highlights include slug "races" and a slug cooking competition (the 1984 champion in the Dessert category was JPW's now-legendary "Key Slime Pie").

In the town of **Healdsburg,** north on U.S. 101, you can take a tour of the **Oasis Cultural Center,** 20889 Geyserville Ave. (857-3524), a self-described "center for evolution and transformation" (whatever that means). The grounds are spotted with unusual people and fauna, including ocelots, llamas, pygmy goats, and peacocks. Spend the night in a yurt (a tent with floors, $50 per night) or a teepee ($40 per night). Inquire about alternative environments, like a wine-cask *room* (for "romantic couples").

Healdsburg also sponsors a series of **Sunday Concerts in the Park** (433-6935), at the Historic Plaza from 1-3pm. The **MTA Coast Bus,** (884-3723; main office in Ukiah 462-1422) runs a loop once daily from Point Arena to Santa Rosa ($1.50-9).

Along the coast itself, **Bodega** is a quaint 19th-century village where Alfred Hitchcock filmed *The Birds.* Off Rte. 1, there are plenty of trails in the **Sonoma Coast State Park.** Campers can choose from 98 sites at the **Bodega Dunes Campground** (875-3483), ½ mi. north of the beach. Reservations are available through MISTIX (800-444-3475; sites $10).

A few miles up the coast from the Russian River, **Fort Ross State Historic Park** (847-3286) features the only reconstructed Russian buildings in the continental U.S., relics of the czar's tenuous presence in 19th-century California. To reach the park by bus, take Mendocino Transit's daily coast run from Point Arena on the way to Santa Rosa. A lonely wooden building perched on the edge of the Pacific cliffs above a small harbor, Fort Ross occupies a narrow strip of land hacked from the forest—the eastern limit of imperial Russia's grasp. The Russians departed in the 1840s for lack of otter, not fodder, and John Sutter bought the fort for a song, primarily to acquire the redwood threshing table inside. Whatever measly sum the Russians profited was lost when the convoy carrying Sutter's funds was ambushed. The fort now houses a limited but interesting **Russian Museum,** featuring a model of the pulley system used to move cargo up and down the steep harbor cliffs. (Fort open daily 10am-4:30pm; entrance fee $5, seniors $4; parking $3.) Ten camp sites (with flush toilets) are available in the park for $7, first-come, first-served.

To the north, **Point Arena** deserves a stopover. The **lighthouse and museum** (882-2777) protrude from the incoming fog. The original log building dates from 1869, but the 115 ft. lighthouse is of 1908 vintage, constructed after an earthquake demolished the old one. (Open Mon.-Fri. 11am-2:30pm, Sat.-Sun. 10am-3:30pm; in winter Mon.-Fri. 11am-2:30pm. Admission $2, children 50¢.)

Point Arena has 46 tent sites at **Manchester State Beach** (937-5804; sites $9, seniors $7; hiker/biker fee $2 per person; toilets). Fifteen mi. east, inland on Rte. 128, lies **Booneville.** The main attraction here is Boontling, a strange local language that seems to be mysteriously reviving as the tourist trade picks up. Look for the telephone sign ("Bucky Walter" in their lingo).

The area Code for the Sonoma Coast and the Russian River Area is 707.

Ukiah

Only beautiful Lake Mendocino spares nearby Ukiah from being classed with other highway-motel-fast-food-strip-towns. Ukiah proper has all the conveniences an overnight highway traveler might need but it will take a journey up to the scintillating lake—surrounded by lovely campgrounds—to entice the visitor to stay a little longer.

Practical Information and Orientation

Visitors Information: Greater Ukiah Chamber of Commerce, 495E East Perkins St. (462-4705). Open Mon.-Fri. 9am-5pm. Information on Ukiah and surrounding communities. **Pomo Visitor Center:** Marina Drive off Rte. 20 or Eastside Calpella Rd. (485-8685). Native American history, lake information. Open Wed.-Sun. 9am-5pm.

Army Corps of Engineers Park Office: 1160 Lake Mendocino Dr. (462-7581), next to Lake Mendocino. Camping information. Open Mon.-Fri. 7 30am-4:30pm.

Mendocino Transit Authority: 241 Plant Rd. (462-1422). Local service, 55¢. Serves Ukiah, the Forks, and Mendocino College.

Ukiah Cab: 462-3881.

Senior Information: Greater Ukiah Senior Citizens Center 462-4343.

Crisis Intervention: 463-4303.

Hospital: Community Hospital, 860 N. Bush St. (463-4010).

Emergency: 911.

Fire Department: 300 Seminary Ave. (463-6274).

Post Office: 224 N. Oak St. (462-8814). Open Mon.-Fri. 8:30am-5pm. General Delivery ZIP Code: 95482.

Area Code: 707.

Ukiah (pop. 14,500) is located 110 miles north of San Francisco, on U.S. 101. Its name comes from the Native American word for "Deep Valley"; the town is nestled in the heart of the Yokayo Valley, where the Pomo Indians lived before being ousted by European settlers.

Accommodations

Ukiah supports a multitude of inexpensive motels. A more scenic stay, however, can be found at one of the nearby campgrounds.

Garden Court Motor Inn, 1175 S. State St. (462-5646), at the southern end of town. Very cute. Adorable country-style rooms centered around a nifty rose garden and picnic tables. Singles $30, doubles $39. Some non-smoking rooms.

Holiday Lodge, 1050 S. State St. (462-2906). Trim, bare rooms. Pool. Singles $30, doubles $38. Some rooms offer waterbeds at no extra charge.

Cottage Inn Motel, 755 S. State St. (462-8509). A little on the run-down side on the exterior, but the rooms are spruce and quaintly decorated Singles from $35, doubles from $45. Weekly rates from $210. Kitchenettes available.

The Army Corps of Engineers maintains more than 300 sites at four campgrounds around the lake. **Ky-en** and **Bu-shay** campgrounds cost $10 per night (seniors $5), and provide water and restrooms. Bu-shay has showers. **Che-ka-ka** campground is $6 per night, with bathrooms and water. You can camp in the **Miti** area for free (also called "Boaters Beach"), but it's accessible only by a day-hike and you must bring your own water. They've toilets.

Food

Bob & Judy's, 1250 Lake Mendocino Dr. (485-5323), helps justify the trip to Ukiah. The plain wood building, ¼-mi. from the lakeshore, has an outdoor deck overlooking the valley's vineyards. You can loaf here and enjoy scrumptious four-egg omelettes served with potatoes and light, flaky biscuits for $4.50-6. Or starve yourself all day and try their MASSIVE finger-lickin' barbequed ribs dinner served with soup, salad, potatoes, veggies, bread and dessert ($12). Open Mon.-Tues. 7am-2pm, Wed.-Sun. 7am-9pm. In winter, Bob & Judy's is open Wed.-Sun. only.

The Fishing Schooner, 570 N. State St. (462-4762). Mediocre food served in a cute blue and white checkered atmosphere. All kinds of fish, served any way you like. The Orange Roughy is $10 broiled or sautéed. Fish and chips (from sea bass to baby lobster tail) runs $6-10. Open Mon.-Sat. 11am-10pm.

Sights

Sparkling Lake Mendocino steals the sights show here. The 1822-acre lake has largemouth, smallmouth, and striped bass, as well as bluegill and catfish to titillate fishing enthusiasts. Waterskiing, too, is oh so popular here. The lake's **Marina,** at Marina Ave. (off Rte. 120) on the water (485-8644), rents paddle and ski boats.

The **Pomo Visitors Center,** Marina Dr. off Rte. 120 (485-8685), is a beautiful redwood building modeled on a ceremonial Pomo dance house. Films and exhibits commemorate the virtually-destroyed Pomo culture. Open Wed.-Sun. 9am-5pm.

In town, the **Grace Hudson Museum and Sun House,** 431 S. Main St. at S. State St. (462-3370), is located in a lovely five-acre garden. Self-guided tours take you through the artist and her ethnologist husband's collection of Native American portraits. Also exhibits current work by local artists. Open Wed.-Sat. 10am-4:30pm, Sun. noon-4:30pm.

Mendocino

When the directors of the TV show *Murder, She Wrote* needed to simulate a rural Maine town, they filmed in Mendocino. With weathered wood shingles and sloping roofs, Mendocino's clustered houses look out of place on California's Central Coast. The town was founded in 1852 by transplanted Easterners who thought the exposed location was a natural site for wind-powered milling operations. These entrepreneurs have been superceded, however, by artists and artisans, whose presence has ensured a healthy collection of galleries and craft shops along with an active and lively sense of community. To a small sign reading "No RV parking on this street" someone has added "or anywhere else in this town"—Mendocino is small and aggressively protective of its isolation.

Practical Information and Orientation

Visitors Information: Ford House (937-5397), one of the oldest homes in the area, houses the visitors center for Mendocino Headlands and other Mendocino district parks. John and Martha Ford built it when they started the Mendocino Lumber Company. Information on nearby camping and hiking, town maps ($1.50). Free nature videos screened on request. Open daily 11am-4pm. **Parks General Information,** 937-5804. Lines open daily 7am-10pm, office open 7am-6pm.

Mendocino Stage and Transit Authority: 2 county transport systems try to cover what Greyhound doesn't. The Stage routes 2 buses daily between Fort Bragg and Navarro. Pick up the MTA to get to Gualala with connecting service to Ukiah (Mon.-Fri.) For schedule information, contact the Stage at 964-0167 or MTA at 241 Plant Rd. (462-1422), in Ukiah. The nearest **Greyhound** can be caught in Ukiah, a 2 hour bus ride.

Bike Rental: Mendocino Cyclery, in the T-shirt shop, next to the duck pond on Main St. (937-4744). Mountain bikes from $7 per hr., $22-29 per day. Also dispenses free maps with suggested daytrips to places such as the Point Cabrillo Lighthouse and Russian Gulch Park. Open daily 10am-6pm.

Laundromat: 45021 Little Lake, diagonally across from The Cheese Shop. Wash $1, dry 25¢. Open daily.

Police: 961-2800 (Station in Fort Bragg).

Ft. Bragg Sheriff: 964-6308.

Rape Crisis: 961-1507.

Emergency: 911.

Post Office: 10500 Ford St. (937-5282), one block west of Main St. Open Mon.-Fri. 7:30am-4:30pm. General Delivery ZIP Code: 95460.

Area Code: 707.

Mendocino sits on Rte. 1 right on the Pacific Coast, 18 mi. East of Eden, 30 mi. west of U.S. 101, and 12 mi. south of Fort Bragg. The town is tiny; park your car and walk. If you must go by bus, prepare to be stranded: there are only 2 buses per day to Ft. Bragg or Ukiah.

Accommodations and Camping

Mendocino's active citizenry has fought to keep the number of hotels in town to a minimum, and existing rooms are all expensive; call ahead for the cheapest. Fortunately, there are hundreds of campsites nearby; make reservations through MISTIX (800-444-7275). Otherwise, look to Ukiah for budget motels.

Seagull Inn, 44594 Albion St. (937-5204), at Lansing St. A big, old-fashioned inn right in the heart of town. Rooms from $55, except for "The Shed" (nicer than it sounds), which has no bath but costs $38. Breakfast in bed included.

The Inn at Schoolhouse Creek, 7051 Hwy. 1 N. (937-5525), 5 mi. south in Little River has cottages on the ocean. Most run upwards of $65, but a smaller kitchenless version is available for $55. Reservations necessary.

Jug Handle State Farm (964-4630 or 964-4615), in Caspar, 5 mi. north on Rte. 1, provides covered foam mats for sleeping bags in a beautiful 100-year-old house. This nature center has a full kitchen, a library, and asks that each guest complete one hour of trail maintenance per night's stay. No showers, but the hot tubbers across the street offer a 10% discount. Reservations essential (at least a week in advance). 20 mats. $15 per night, students $10. Sleeping bags not provided.

Russian Gulch State Park, Rte. 1 (937-0497), 1 mi. north of town. 30 sites. Hot showers and flush toilets, not to mention superlative ocean views. No hookups. Reserve 8 weeks in advance. Sites $12. Book through MISTIX (800-44-7275).

Van Damme State Park, Rte. 1 (937-5804), 3 mi. south of town. 74 sites. Facilities and prices similar to Russian Gulch, but with the added bonus of a neighboring pygmy forest (see Sights). Nearby trails run through lush fern-covered canyon worth the hike. Sites $14, seniors $12. Open year-round.

Hendy Woods State Park, Greenwood Ridge Rd. (895-3141), just south of Rte. 128 near the town of Philo, about 35 mi. southeast of Mendocino in the redwoods. 92 sites. Hot showers and flush toilets, no RV hookups. Sites $12. Open year-round.

Navarro Point, 9 mi. south of Mendocino. The only fee-free camping for miles. Take Navarro Bluff Rd. right immediately after the bridge and park anywhere in the beach parking lot.

Food

Walking down the main streets of Mendocino is like strolling through an enormous buffet: you pass deli after café after *gelateria* after deli. Iranian caviar and Lafite-Rothschild are readily available; it goes without saying that all breads are fresh-baked, all vegetables locally grown, all wheat unmilled, all coffee cappuccino, and *everything* expensive.

The Corners of the Mouth, Old Red Church, Ukiah St. (937-5345). Housed in a lofty renovated pinkish-red church, this grocery has everything organic under the sun. Cheeses are a little pricey, but Judy's long hot fresh-baked breadsticks are only 85¢. Check out the herb room and a selection of politically correct t-shirts. Open Mon., Thurs., and Sat. 10am-6pm, Tues., Wed., and Fri. 10am-6:30pm, Sun. 11am-5pm.

Mendocino Bakery and Café, 10485 Lansing St. (937-0836). Pastries, quiche, soup, and meal-sized (but mediocre) slices of pizza ($2.50). Heathful chewy brown rice treats ($1) are their answer to the sugar-filled Krispie variety. Hang out and watch the locals. Open daily 8am-7pm.

Mendocino Ice Cream Co., 45090 Main St. (937-5884). Primarily an ice cream parlor. Award-winning homemade flavors like Black Forest (with cherries and chocolate chips). (Waffle cone, $1.85). Open Mon.-Thurs. 8am-9pm, Fri.-Sun. 8am-10pm.

The Cheese Shop, 45050 Little Lake St. (937-0104), at Lansing. A staggering range of foreign and domestic cheeses crammed into a yellow shed. Nothing is made on the premises, but the shop has a variety of locally made mustards, jams, and baked goods. Upscale deli meats, and wine-tasting too. Two people can construct a meal for about $8. Open daily 10am-6pm.

Mendosa's Market, 10501 Lansing St. (937-5879). The closest thing to a real supermarket in Mendocino. Ceramic jars of Pommery mustard are sold, of course, but they also carry French's. Open daily 8am-9pm.

Dick's Bar, 45070 Main St. Dark and filled with locals. Pinball and darts. Leave your *Let's Go* at home and play down the tourist image or you won't make many friends here. Beer $1.25.

Sights

Most visitors slowly wander through town, examining the wooden Yankee architecture of the houses and water towers. James Dean made his solitary way through these streets in *East of Eden.* And the house of Jessica B. Felcher, Angela Lansbury's incredibly annoying character from the TV show *Murder, She Wrote,* surveys the town from a hill above. Organized walking tours ($2) leave every Saturday at 11am from Kelley House, 45007 Albion St.

An excellent place to soak up local atmosphere is **The Book Loft,** 10450 Lansing St. (937-0890). Herbal teas and rocking chairs in front of a cozy fire encourage you to sit a spell and sample the works of local musicians and authors. (Open daily 10am-6pm.)

Running along the coast near town are the **Mendocino Headlands** (937-5397). To reach the paths along the bluffs, walk to the north end of Main St. The Mendocino Headlands State Park **visitors center,** with information and maps, is in the Ford House. (See Practical Information.)

From the rocky, wildflower-covered cliffs of the headlands, you can see secluded and treacherous coves, unusual arches worn into rock by the powerful waves, and sometimes seals swimming through the algae or sunning themselves on the beach.

Poor drainage, thin soil, and the exposed climate have created an unusual *bonsai* garden just south of town at **Van Damme State Park** (kickboxing not permitted). The 2-3 ft. mature **pygmy trees** are a short walk from the car park ($3 day-use fee), and are wheelchair accessible. Be a latter-day Gulliver as you perambulate (and photograph yourself) among these Lilliputian trees and then head to the Brobdignagian redwoods further north. Offshore is an underwater park for divers. (No fee for beach use.) Canoe rentals are available at **Catch-A-Canoe** (937-5615), in the Big River Lodge, 44900 Comptche-Ukiah Rd., off Rte. 1 near Mendocino Campground ($10 per hr., $35 per day; credit card or cash deposit required; open daily 9:30am-5:30pm).

Entertainment

The rumor is that the Mendocino Coast harbors more performing artists per capita than any other place in the cosmos. True or false, you'll nonetheless hear excellent music, particularly jazz, at a number of local spots. The **Seagull Cellar Bar** at the Seagull Inn (937-2100) features cool jazz, heavy on the saxophone and wire-brushed drums, in a beautiful wood-covered attic bar. Sunday night jazz, Friday folk music, and Saturday night piano bar. No cover. Draft beer $1.25. For rock and dancing go to the **Caspar Inn** (964-5565), in the town of Caspar, 5 mi. north on Rte. 1 (cover from $3, open daily 4pm-2am). July brings the **Mendocino Music Festival,** a two-week orgy of quality performances. The emphasis is on classical and opera—call 937-2044 for information. In March, the town makes its contribution to eco-consciousness with annual **Whale Festival** (964-3153).

Garberville and Avenue of the Giants

Once home to a chain of marijuana farms called the Emerald Triangle, this "marijuana capital of the world" has evolved from a pot stop to a pit stop, as no less than 7 motels and 15 restaurants squeeze into a mere 5 block bulge in the highway. Located 200 mi. north of San Francisco and 63 mi. south of Eureka on U.S. 101, Garberville also marks the turn-off for the paved road leading to the **Lost Coast.**

The cheapest place to stay in Garberville is the **Johnston's Motel,** 839 Redwood Dr. (923-3327), with $32 singles. Several other cheap motels cluster along Redwood Dr. However, the **Eel River Redwoods Hostel,** 70400 U.S. 101 (925-6469), 16 mi. south on U.S. 101 in Leggett, is by far the best option in the area. Located on the Eel River with access to a sauna and a swimming hole (with inner tubes), this is a hosteling wonderland. The basics include laundry, free bike use, and cabins for couples or families (reserve ahead for these). The center garden includes a teepee (hostelers may choose to sleep here), a Model-T Ford, two gazebos, and a burbling brook. The **Bell Glen Resort,** which shares these facilities, operates an espresso bar at the hilltop. Best of all, the hostel is open all day. If you're traveling by bus, ask the driver to stop at the hostel or get off at **Standish Hickey State Park;** the hostel's a 1/2-mi. walk north from there. (Open May 1-Nov. 27. Members $11. Nonmembers $12.50.)

Garberville's **Chamber of Commerce,** 969 Redwood Dr. (923-2613) has an eager staff of busy bees, along with maps and brochures (open daily 9am-6pm). **Greyhound** runs 3 buses north and south daily Tickets are available at **Calico's,** 808 Redwood Dr., or call Greyhound directly for information. To: Eureka ($11.35), Portland ($93), and San Francisco ($22.50). (Open Mon.-Sat. 8am-9pm, Sun. 8am-4pm). In an **emergency** call 911.

The **post office** is located one block west of Redwood Dr. on Sprowel Creek Rd.; open Mon.-Fri. 8:30am-5:30pm. General Delivery ZIP Code: 95440.

Local victuals consist mostly of standard diner grub. **Sicilito's,** 445 Conger St. (932-2814) is the sole exception to this rule. A multicultural mix of Mexican, Italian, and American food, the eclectically decorated restaurant serves up *massive* plates of spaghetti with ($8) or without meatballs ($7). Burritos with rice and beans are $4.50-6. Add egg rolls as an appetizer ($3), and you're suddenly eating food from four corners of the globe. Creative pizzas; a small is enough to feed two. Open 4-10pm daily. Local beers.

Two miles north of Garberville, in the small town of **Redway,** the **Mateel Café,** 478 Redwood Dr. (923-2030), is a high-quality culinary institution featuring scrumptious healthy food. This product of a Parisian chef and a Californian nutritionist lures gourmets from as far away as San Francisco. Dine on the patio or in a nooky wooden booth, and enjoy exotic pizzas with pesto, tofu, spiced ricotta, or apples ($1.25 per slice). Create a dinner of soup and salad ($4.50) or select from a mouth-watering list of entrees, including a free range chicken with leeks ($12), herb linguini papillon ($7), or sauté of tempeh ($7). Open Tues.-Fri. noon-2pm for lunch; Mon.-Fri. 2-9pm for late lunch and dinner; Sat. 5-9pm for dinner. (The kitchen closes at 8:30pm.)

With its sizeable population of artists, Garberville's art festivals are understandably excellent and well-attended. **Jazz on the Lake** and the **Summer Arts Fair** begin in late June, followed by the dramatic outdoor theater of **Shakespeare at Benbow Lake,** in late July. Call the Chamber of Commerce for additional information. The **Mateel Community Center** (923-3368), in Redway, sponsors classes and local events.

Six miles north at **Sylvandale,** the fantastic 31-mi. drive through the **Avenue of Giants** begins. This collection of groves bestrides the winding road, creating a living archway. The Avenue even has three **gift shops** inside living trees. The **visitors center** (946-2263), at the **Humboldt Redwoods State Park,** is a good place to pick up information on camping and hiking in the area. The visitors center is open from March to October Mon.-Fri. 9am-5pm, Sat.-Sun. 9am-8pm. November to February, the center maintains only weekend hours. Their history museum and forest exhibits provide an excellent overview of the evolution of the shady giants. Less crowded groves are found a few miles west in the **Rockefeller Forest** on Mattole Rd. The avenue ends in Pepperwood, but the road accesses U.S. 101 4 mi. farther north in Stafford. Hardly more than 15 min. out of the way, the forest provides a rare glimpse of inland redwoods not cloaked in fog.

The visitors center issues an "auto tour" map, marking major redwood groves easily photographed from inside a car, but the only way to fully appreciate the redwood giants is to get out of the car and walk among them. When you see the soft pine-covered forest floor, the trees' mammoth knobby trunks, and the canopy high above you, you'll understand just how small and relatively unimportant you are.

Every October the Avenue of the Giants hosts the most scenic marathon in the country. A qualifying time here will allow you to register for the Boston or New York marathons. Come to answer the age-old conundrum: If a runner falls in the forest without anyone to hear her, can she still finish the race?

Leggett, 16 mi. south of Garberville, is heralded as the home of the **Drive-Thru-Tree.** This 315-ft. redwood has a 21-ft. base which you can drive through ($3) like at a fast-food restaurant. Save your money. If you want to pass through the bowels of a tree, there are plenty of walk-through trees nearby. Two mi. north, the **Standish Hickey Recreation Area** (925-6482), dubbed the "Gateway to the Tall Trees Country," features fishing, camping, and hiking—all amidst the towering redwoods. The south fork of the misnamed **Eel River** is home to salmon and steelhead, as well as the primitive lamprey eels. The 162 sites in the park have fireplaces, tables, and laundry and showers nearby. Disabled access. $10 per night. Reservations can be made through Ticketron (800-952-5580). **The Peg House Deli,** across the street from the park, has ice and groceries. Enormous sub sandwiches for $3.50. (Open daily 9am-9pm.)

Richardson Grove State Park, in the Eel River district, offers isolated campsites under the redwoods year round. The sites are $14 per vehicle, $12 for seniors, and $3 for hikers or bikers. Hot showers and toilets. One of the prettiest campsites in the state, Richardson Grove also has a visitors center with an excellent and unusual selection of literature and natural history books.

The highlight of local festivals comes in early August, when the **Mateel Community Center** presents **Reggae on the River.** This 12-hour reggae orgy on the banks of the Eel River is considered the jammin'est in the U.S. The volcano of music, food, drink, and other ingestible items is celebrated as only Northern California can—the experience can be truly mind-expanding. Call the Reggae Hotline (923-3369) for information.

Lost Coast

Ignored by most tourists, with many of its towns deserted long ago, the 100 mi. of coast between Rockport and Eureka have an eerie, otherworldly feel. It was settled in 1850 when miners struck gold on the Trinity River. Because it was easier to travel north by sea than to trek overland to the gold deposits, the sheltered coves and gentle beaches south of Eureka were seized as convenient supply depots. Timber and fishing were rich in the area and enhanced the coast's attractiveness. But the gold soon panned out and Eureka, with its larger port and more convenient land transport, sucked the economic life out of such towns as Shelter Cove and Honeydew—and eclipsed such others as Ettersburg and Thorn Junction. The region remains undisturbed today, one of the most peaceful and isolated areas of coastline in the United States.

The area is so tortuously rocky that the highway engineers who had successfully negotiated Big Sur down south had to give up and move coastal Rte. 1 inland here. Rte. 1 merges with U.S. 101 from Leggett in the south all the way to Eureka. A single, winding, and mostly paved track called Mattole Road runs from Ferndale in the north to Honeydew, and then escapes east to Weott. On the southern half of the coast, several very steep, narrow, and sharply meandering gravel roads connect Shelter Cove to U.S. 101 near Garberville and Usal to Rte. 1 near Rockport. Your best bet—unless you have 4-wheel drive or a friend with a recovery truck—is to stick to Wilder Ridge Road in the north, and Shelter Cove Road in the east.

There is no public transportation on the Lost Coast. According to locals, the last bus that tried to enter the area was a lost Greyhound from Eureka that was later towed out of a hairpin turn on Mattole Rd You may follow unless you take care, especially at night. Your only way to get through here is with wheels of your own or by renting a car or bicycle in Garberville or Eureka; hitching is hopeless. However, keep in mind that driving through this region quickly is dizzying and unrewarding; take some time to leave the car and hike along the beach and cliffs—viewing the Lost Coast from a bucket seat can't do the place justice. Emergency numbers include the Garberville **sheriff** (923-2761) and **ambulance** (923-3475), and the Petrolia **fire and rescue** department (629-3535). The **area code** is 707.

At the southern end of the Lost Coast, **Sinkyone Wilderness State Park** has several great hiking trails on its 7132 acres. Heed the names of Mistake Point and Point No Pass, though. The Usal Road runs parallel with the coast 1-2 mi. inland, connecting **Four Corners Junction** with **Usal** at the southern end of Sinkyone. **Needle Rock,** another turn-off from Four Corners, has a seasonal ranger station (call 946-2311 for details), and provides trail access to the northern parts of the wilderness.

The next section of the Lost Coast traveling north is the **King Range National Conservation Area.** The area fills 54,000 steep coastal acres and is home to **Kings Peak,** which at 4086 ft. is the highest point on the shoreline of the continental United States. Free primitive campgrounds requiring no permit punctuate the area. Pick up maps and camping information at the Bureau of Land Management, 1125 16th St., Arcata (822-7648; open Mon.-Fri. 9am-5pm); or at any chamber of commerce in nearby towns. To reach the conservation area, take the deranged road from Garberville to **Shelter Cove,** the only settlement within its borders. The cove is a simple seaside resort, bustling on the weekends with deep-sea fishing charters and busy seafood restaurants. Along the 4½-mi. tidal beachfront there are frequent **whale-watching** opportunities.

The **Shelter Cover Motor Inn** (986-7521) and **Mario's Marina Motel** (986-7432) both charge about $40 per night.

Half way up the Lost Coast stands the tiny town of **Honeydew,** really nothing more than a crossroads and general store with a post office (629-3310; open Mon.-Sat. 9:30am-5:30pm, Sun. 11:30am-5:30pm). The town is one of the nation's wettest spots, soaked each year by more than 200 inches of rain. To get to Honeydew, take Mattole Rd. through Humboldt Redwoods State Park and down into the valley. Along the Mattole Road in the state park are several campsites, some primitive, others with some modern comforts. Pick up information at the visitors center in the park (964-2263). Some sites are accessible by car, others can be reached only by hikers and are often empty.

North of Honeydew on Mattole Rd., **Petrolia** rests at the bottom of an enchanting valley. The hills that rise gently on all sides of the little town are covered with golden grass, interspersed with the soft green of bushes and the darker green of trees and vegetation clustered next to flowing streams. As its name suggests, oil was discovered at Petrolia, but prohibitive transportation costs made further drilling impractical. Petrolia has a **general store** (629-3455) with **gasoline** pumps. (Open Mon.-Sat. 10am-6pm, Sun. noon-6pm; in winter Mon.-Sat. 10am-5pm, Sun. noon-5pm.) There's also a **post office** in the same building (open Mon.-Fri. 8am-4pm). **The Hideaway** (629-3533), to the right after the George C. Lindley Bridge on the road to Honeydew, is a tiny restaurant serving burgers ($3.25) and spaghetti ($6). Homemade cinnamon rolls ($1.25) make a tasty, late-morning breakfast. (Open daily 11:30am-2am.) Just to the south, Humboldt County's **Arthur Way Memorial Park,** cradles one of the area's few developed campgrounds ($7 per car, $2 bikes). The **Mattole River Resort,** 42354 Mattole Rd. (629-3445), has charming cabins with kitchens for $35-50 per night. They also operate a trailhead shuttle to the King's Range. The resort also rents mountain-bikes ($10 per day). The romantic **Lost Inn** (629-3394) in Petrolia offers suites decorated with funky antiques, a flowered porch with wicker chairs overlooking the valley, and continental breakfast for $48. Reservations recommended.

Ten mi. north of Petrolia, the road hugs the beach for several spectacular miles. Cattle from nearby ranches frequently wander onto the black sand beach, creating the Daliesque spectacle of bovines contentedly chewing their cud on top of the ocean's brilliant blue. If you arrive before the clouds have burned off (around 3pm), the surreality is augmented by the illusion of massive rocks hovering mystically over the fog.

A quiet town at the northern end of the Lost Coast, **Ferndale** seems to have inherited all the charm that big-city Eureka lacks. The town was settled by Scandinavian dairy farmers, who, so the story goes, invented powdered dry milk. The little settlement of gingerbread Victorian houses is today sprinkled with a beguiling assortment of bookstores, candy shops, museums, and historic homes. The town has been touched up without becoming cutesy-pie. Pick up a free walking-tour brochure from almost any store, and take a stroll. The **Ferndale Museum,** 515 Shaw Ave. (786-4466), at 3rd St., frames both the beginning and likely end of coastal history with a restored blacksmith shop and a working seismograph eagerly awaiting the first rumbles of the next Big One. (Open Tues.-Sat. 11am-4pm, Sun. 1-4pm; Oct.-May closed Tues; closed all January; admission $1, children 50¢.)

A mile away lies the **Humboldt County Fairgrounds** (786-9511) on Arlington St., which offers campsites for $5 and RV hookups for $7. Except for exorbitantly priced B&Bs, accommodations are sparse.

Eating opportunities are more encouraging. There are many fine restaurants in town and more than one outstanding candy shop. **Ferndale Café,** 606 Main St. (786-4795), at Shaw St., is a typical small-town establishment serving breakfasts, burgers, and shakes. (Open Mon.-Sat. 8am-4pm.) The best sandwiches (for carnivores) come from the **Ferndale Meat Co.,** 376 Main St. (786-4501), laying generous cheese and meat slabs on a choice of breads for $2.75 (open daily 8:30am-5pm). **Roman's,** 315 Main St. (725-6358), is the better of the town's two Mexican restaurants. A full dinner costs about $8, but you should be able to stuff yourself on tacos, burritos, or enchiladas for about $6. (Open Mon.-Sat. 11am-9pm, Sun. (buffet) 10am-8pm.) **Golden Gate Mercantile** has candies sold the old-fashioned way (by the pound, not pre-packaged) and myriad other goodies. (Open Mon.-Sat. 10am-5pm, Sun. noon-5pm.)

There are plenty of prime picnic spots nearby, including **Centerville Beach,** 5 mi. west of Petrolia. The **Loleta Cheese Factory,** on Main St. is a superb bakery for stuffing your basket.

Down the block, the **Kinetic Sculpture Museum,** on Main St. in Ferndale, has inherited some of the entries from past Arcata Kinetic Sculpture Races (see Arcata listings), including a "kinetic sculpture" constructed entirely from license plates and the famous chicken-and-egg-mobile.

Eureka

When James Ryan stumbled upon this lost harbor in Humboldt Bay in 1850, he shouted "Eureka!" ("I found it") and named the town in the full ecstasy of his discovery. One hundred forty years later, you're sure to wonder what all the fuss was about.

Practical Information and Orientation

Visitor Information: Visitors Bureau, 1034 2nd St. (443-5097 or 800-338-7352 in CA, 800-346-3482 outside), at L St. Tiny but with detailed maps. Open Mon.-Fri. 9am-5pm. In winter open Mon.-Fri. 10am-7pm. **Eureka Chamber of Commerce,** 2112 Broadway (442-3738 or 800-346-6381). Helpful information on restaurants and hotels, but not much else. Open Mon.-Fri. 8:30am-7pm, Sat. 9am-5pm, Sun. 10am-3pm; in winter open Mon.-Fri. 8:30am-5pm, closed weekends. Events recording, 444-2834.

Airport: Arcata/Eureka (839-1576), in McKinleyville. Offers connecting service to major California airports.

Greyhound: 1603 4th St. (442-0370), at P St. Frequent service between Eureka and Arcata. To San Francisco (2 per day, $40.30) and Crescent City (2 per day, $14.20). Terminal open Mon.-Fri. 6:15am-1pm and 5-9:45pm, Sat. 6:15-10:30am and 7-9:45pm, Sun. 6:15-7:15am, 9:15-10:15am and 7-9:45pm.

Redwood Lines: in Greyhound Terminal (443-9923). One per day to Redding (4 hr., $15). Departs at 6:55am. Leaves Redding at 2:10pm, arrives at Eureka at 6:10pm.

Local Transportation: Humboldt Transit Authority, 133 V St. (443-0826). Local service 50¢-$1.25. Regional service Mon.-Fri. 6am-8pm. Pick up most buses at 5th and D. Serves the area between Scotia and Trinidad including Arcata. Call for bike transport information. **Eureka Transit,** 133 V St. (443-0826). Bus service within Eureka (run by Humboldt Transit) Mon.-Fri. 6am-7pm, Sat. 10am-5pm. Fare 85¢, seniors and disabled 60¢. Max. fare $1 for one zone, seniors and disabled 50¢.

Car Rental: Beats Walkin', 4th at B St. (443-2070). $21.95 per day, 30 mi. free, 15¢ per mile. For use in Humboldt County only.

Road Conditions: 443-9715.

Equipment Rental: Adventure's Edge, 408 F St. (445-3035). Tents $8 per day, $13 for 3 days. Sleeping bags $8.50 per day, $11 for 3 days. Cross-country ski package $10 per day, $15 for 3 days. Open Mon.-Sat. 9am-6pm, Sun. noon-5pm.

College of the Redwoods Events Line: 443-8411, ext. 520.

Laundromat: Clark at Summer St., across from the Post Office. Wash $1, dry 25¢, soap 50¢. Open daily 7am-9pm.

Hospital: Eureka General, 2200 Harrison Ave. (443-1627). **Emergency care:** 442-4545, 24 hr.

Police: 442-4545.

Emergency: 911.

Post Office: 5th at H (442-1828). Main Post Office open for General Delivery at 337 W. Clark St. (442-1768). Open Mon.-Fri. 8:30am-5pm. Sat. noon-3pm. General Delivery Zip Code 95502.

Area Code: 707.

Eureka lies 7 mi. south of Arcata along U.S. 101, about 280 mi. north of San Francisco. Streets are arranged on a grid, with numbered streets running one way and lettered streets perpendicular to them. While in town, U.S. 101 becomes Main St. and then Broadway, and runs north-south.

The *North Coast View,* a free monthly, is full of news and entertainment listings. Even better is the *Humboldt Visitor,* produced annually by Humboldt County. This well-written, free guide covers all sights between Northern Mendocino and Crescent City.

Accommodations and Camping

Because of Eureka's choice position right on a major highway, an abundance of strip-side motels spring up on Broadway. To reach Broadway from the Greyhound station, walk west on 4th St. backwards through the alphabet and continue for two blocks past A St. Downtown Eureka offers some higher-priced, slightly classier motels, as well as several near-decrepit city hotels.

Broadway Motel, 1921 Broadway (443-3156), a 20-min. walk from Greyhound. Cheap, cheap, cheap. Clean rooms with phone and color TV. Fantastically tacky orange-flowered lamps. Small rooms in the oldest part of the motel go for $16 per night, but they sure fill up. Get there early if you want a bargain. Newer rooms are from $22 per night. Best deal in town. No reservations taken.

Eureka Ranchotel, 2109 Broadway (443-6751). Run-down but ample amenities including cable TV, HBO, spa, and kitchenettes—and, oh, those floral patterns. Singles $25. Doubles $31.

Christie's Motel, 1420 4th St. (444-3011), 2 blocks from Greyhound. The cheapest reasonable motel in the downtown areas. Purple rooms. TV with HBO. Bargaining may work here. Singles $26, doubles $40 in winter. Summer rates: singles $32, doubles $45.

Olympic Motel, 2832 S. Broadway (Rte. 101) (443-4525). Recently renovated, with large clean rooms. Don't be deceived by the dingy looking sign; this is one of the finer budget motels in Eureka. Summer rates: single $34, double $45. Prices drop by $5 in winter.

Patrick's Point State Park (677-3570), 27 mi. north of Eureka. 123 sites. Showers and flush toilets. Reservations through MISTIX (800-444-7275) are required 2 weeks in advance in summer. Hikers and bikers can almost always find space in overflow areas. Sites $14 per vehicle (no hookups), hikers and cyclists $3.

Big Lagoon County Park (445-7652), 20 mi. north of Eureka on U.S. 101. Pit toilets, no drinking water. Although Big Lagoon is popular, there's a good chance of scoring a site, especially if you arrive early. Sites $8.

Grizzly Creek Redwoods State Park (777-3683), about 40 mi. southeast of Eureka via U.S. 101 and Rte. 36. 30 sites. A bit far away, but with hot showers and flush toilets. Lounge beneath the umbrageous, mammoth trees. Sites $10, hikers and cyclists $2.

Food

The offerings are eclectic, but you can dine cheaply and well in Eureka. Or skip the scores of budget restaurants and fill a thermos with chowder for a windswept picnic along the shore.

Bob's Breakfast Café, 1039 4th St. (443-4788), at L St. Any place that opens at 5:30am can't be all bad. Buy a steaming fishermen's breakfast for $4-5. Open Mon.-Fri. 5:30am-5pm.

Tomaso's Tomato Pies, 216 E St., Old Town Eureka (445-0100). Downstairs counter service, upstairs tables and an outdoor deck. Tomaso's serves up generous servings of mediocre pizza, soups, and sandwiches. The salads, by contrast, are excellent and extremely healthy. A $4 slice of "square" pizza can feed two. (Half slice $2.50). Sandwiches $6. Open Mon.-Thurs. 11:30am-9pm, Fri.-Sat. 11:30am-10pm, Sun. 5-8:30pm.

Stars, 3rd St. in Old Town Eureka (443-3359). Take out tasty burgers on fresh-baked buns from this little red-and-white shack on the corner. Also at 2009 Harrison Ave. across from General Hospital (445-2061).

Samoa Cookhouse, Samoa Rd. (442-1659). The last surviving cookhouse in the west used to serve up heaping portions of stick-to-the-ribs chow to hungry loggers after a hard day's work. Today the restaurant serves up the same massive portions family-style to overfed tourists. The cookhouse is accessible only by car, but don't go unless you're *really* hungry. Across Humboldt Bay from Eureka. Typical dinner—steak and pork chops with soup, two salads, green beans, potatoes, and all the iced tea you can drink. Dinner $10.65 for adults, $6.45 for 7-11, $4.45 for 3-6. Lunch $6, $4.45, $3.35. Breakfast $5.85, $4.40, $3. Open Mon.-Sat. 6am-3pm, 5-10pm, Sun. 6am-10pm.

Ramone's Bakery, 209 E St., Old Town Eureka (445-2923). Cute bakery with wooden tables, a brick wall, and delicious fresh-baked pastries and breads. Blueberry, banana, and apple scones 90¢, cappucino $1.40. Try a new kind of bread every day of the week. Open Mon.-Fri. 7am-6pm, Sat. 8am-6pm, Sun. 8am-4pm.

Eureka Co-op, 1st and E St. A smaller version of Arcata's famous co-op, but a broader selection than most delis. Bulk grains, organic produce, and the rest. Open Mon.-Sat. 10am-7pm, Sun. 10am-6pm.

Luna's, 1134 5th (445-9162). An inexpensive, elbows-on-the-table Mexican restaurant popular with locals. Burrito $4, taco $2, or tamale $3. Full meals about $6-7. Vegetarian options. Red booths and authentic Mexican decor. Open Mon.-Sat. 11am-9pm.

Mazzotti's Ristorante Italiano, 305 F St. (445-1912), at 3rd St. A comfortable Italian restaurant full of locals and soft music. Great seafood. Full dinner $5-10; filling half-portions from $4. Open Mon.-Thurs. 11:30am-9pm, Fri.-Sat. 11:30am-10pm, Sun. 3-9pm.

Eureka Health Foods, 3074 4th St. (442-6325). Sanitized shop looks more like a pharmacy than a health-food store, but it's got all the essential granola condiments. Open Mon.-Fri. 9am-7pm, Sat. 10am-6pm, Sun. noon-5pm.

Chocoholics, 215 Second St. (442-2002). A chocolate freak must have won the lottery and then decided to open this place. For the ultimate chocolate meal, try chocolate pasta ($5 per bag) with chocolate truffle sauce, and finish off with chocolate-dipped strawberries on top of award-winning chocolate cheesecake. Some people don't know when to say when.

Sights

Eureka is full of rambling Victorian houses, some freshly restored, some on their last, paint-chipped legs. The **Carson Mansion,** 2nd and M St. (442-3738), built in the 1880s, shows enough garret and eave to be the centerpiece of a Poe story. Once the home of William Carson, a gold prospector turned lumber magnate, a private club has usurped the mansion's innards, and the home is not open to visitors. The Eureka Chamber of Commerce has a drive-by tour of over 100 local Victorian homes. An hour-long walking tour leaves every Wednesday and Saturday at 2 and 4pm from the Clarke Museum (443-1947; $4).

The area bounded by 3rd, C, and G St. along the bay is Eureka's most picturesque quarter. Many of the early 20th-century commercial buildings have been restored, some fronted by elegant bistros and exotic knick-knack emporia. But the area remains the center of the old sailors' district, full of cheap hole-in-the-wall bars (many with nightly bands), run-down hotels, and hidden breakfast places. The **Fort Humboldt State Historic Park** (443-7952), at the junction of Broadway and Harris St., southwest of Eureka, features a logging exhibit, a museum, and picnic areas overlooking Humboldt Bay. Future Civil War hero and mediocre U.S. President Ulysses S. Grant was stationed here in the 1850s.

The **Wooden Garden of Romano Gabriel** is on permanent display at 325 2nd St. Working for years in his tool shed and yard, Gabriel constructed a brilliantly colored "garden" of people, plants, and symbols, all from scrap wood. Some consider the work primitive art on an epic scale, others find it an example of rampant vulgarity. Not everyone appreciates slices of hanging wood salami.

The College of the Redwoods, 7 mi. south of Eureka, hosts the annual **WoodFair** in mid-July. The festival is "a celebration of the North Coast's woodworking tradition." Call 445-6915 for details.

Arcata

A quiet college town trapped between the redwoods and the sea, Arcata (pronounced ar-KAY-ta) is an excellent place for a healthy meal or a lesson in ecological consciousness. It is also a somewhat livelier cocoon in which to spend the night than nearby Eureka.

Practical Information

Visitor Information: Arcata Chamber of Commerce, 1062 G. St. (822-3619). Small office occupied by an eager staff. Useful, free map and information on local events. Open Mon.-Fri. 10am-5pm; in winter 10am-3pm.

Greyhound: 645 10th St. (822-0521), at F. Open Mon.-Fri. 6:30am-5pm, Sat. 6:30-11:30am. 2 buses south, 2 buses north, and 1 east daily. No station to wait in; just a ticket window.

Buses: Humboldt Transit: 943-0826, from Eureka. **Arcata and Mad River Transit System (AMRTS),** 822-3775. Runs downtown and north of the city. Mon.-Fri. 7am-7pm. Sat. 9am-5pm; last outbound bus leaves one hour before closing. Fare 35¢, seniors 25¢.

Equipment Rental: Adventure's Edge, 650 10th St. (822-4673), across from Greyhound. Rents backpacks ($5-9), tents ($8-12), sleeping bags ($7.50), and stoves ($4.50 with empty fuel bottle). Open Mon.-Sat. 10am-6pm, Sun. noon-5pm.

Taxi: Yellow Cab, 422-4551.

Car Rental: National, at the airport (839-3229 or 800-CAR-RENT 1-800-227-7368) $29 per day, 15¢ per mile. (Also see Eureka Practical Information.)

Laundromat: Uniontown Laundrette, 6th at F St., in the mall. Wash $1, dry 25¢, detergent 45¢. Soda and change machines. Open daily 8am-10pm.

Hospital: Mad River, 3800 Janes Rd. (822-3621).

Police: 822-2424.

Emergency: 911.

Post Office: 799 H St. Open Mon.-Fri. 7:30am-5pm. General Delivery Zip Code: 95521.

Area Code: 707.

Accommodations and Camping

Arcata, filled with costly country inns and B&Bs, is saved by the cheap and friendly hostel. Camping is easy, but remote without a car.

Arcata Crew House Hostel, 1390 I St. (822-9995), at 14th, 3 blocks from Greyhound. A frat house during school, a hostel in summer (May 24-Aug. 25). This beautiful old Victorian home sits atop a hill overlooking the city. Curfew 11pm. Hostel closes during the day, so residents have to be out by 9:30am. No longer AYH, but still offers a discount: members $8.75, non-members $9.75.

Clam Beach County Park (445-7491), 7½ mi. north of Arcata on U.S. 101. Basic facilities, water, and pit toilets. Terrific beach and dunes where you can dig clams seasonally. Sites $8.

Food

Eclectic and ethnic, eat here or take the bus to Eureka for more of the same.

Los Bageles, 1061 I St. (822-3150), within walking distance of the hostel. Basic bagels, bread, and coffee served with a Nicaraguan flair. Be sure to catch the bold mural of a Latin American neighborhood on the building across the street. Most items under $1. There's a collection of political flyers to keep you aroused while you wait. Open Mon. and Wed.-Fri. 7am-6pm, Sat. 7am-5pm, Sun. 8am-3pm. Also in Eureka, without the mural (321 3rd. St.).

The Co-op, 8th at I St. Vegetarian cornucopia, with backpacker supplies. Stock up on your tofu, tempeh, mochi, and soymilk. Open Mon.-Sat. 9am-9pm, Sun. 9am-8pm.

Folie Douce, 1551 G St. (822-1042) Unusual pizza baked California-style in a wood-fired oven. (Clam and cheddar $7.75, lamb pizza $8.75.) Served with salad in a Crayola-doodled blue and yellow dining room. Sit on the Picasso-esque painted stools and converse with the French chefs. Open Tues.-Sat. 5-10pm.

Casa de Que Pasa, 854 9th St. (822-3441). Spicy Mexican food, with live folk music on Tuesday evenings. Free tortilla chips. Meat burrito $5. Open Mon., Thurs., and Sat. 11am-9:30pm, Fri. 11am-10pm, Sun. 4-9:30pm.

Café Mokka, 5th at J St. (822-2228). Little wood-paneled coffeehouse with a pond, enormous goldfish, and hot tubs out back for $6 per person; make reservations. Inside, fantastic espresso and pastries, most under $1. Curl up by the fire with one of the dozens of international newspapers and magazines. Join the French conversation table, or listen to live music on Sat. evenings. Tues. nights the café hosts chess matches. Open Mon.-Fri. noon-10pm, Sat.-Sun. noon-midnight.

Humboldt Brewery, 856 10th St. (826-2739). This local micro-brewery has been so successful that it's spread next door into the cavernous imported beer garden. Typical bar fare. Chicken wings ($4), sandwiches and burgers (about $5). Atypical beer: try the Oatmeal Stout ($2 pint), the gold medalist in the '88 BeerFest. Excellent live music, often drawing big names in country, folk, and blues. Popular place, with large green booths where you can sit for a spell.

Sights and Entertainment

The Chamber of Commerce provides visitors with a walking tour map that includes excellent histories of each of the 15 stops. Downtown revolves around the **McKinley Statue,** which has been a local centerpiece since the wagon transporting it north to McKinleyville broke down in Arcata.

Five minutes east of the city is the **Arcata Community Forest,** 566 acres of city-owned land. In 1979, an ecologically-minded citizens group began managing the park and developed a "sane, multiple-use management plan." Translated from beaurocratese, that means wide-open picnic spaces. Tours of the forest are given in summer and depart from City Hall at 7th and F St. (1½ hr., $2).

A former "sanitary" landfill, the 75-acre **Arcata Marsh and Wildlife Sanctuary** (822-6918) lies at the foot of I St. Wander the trails alone, or take a tour to see what miracles treated waste water can work. (Tours Sat. 8:30am.)

For nighttime entertainment, Arcata is the place, and the **Blues News,** published by the local blues society, available at the Chamber of Commerce, is the guide. The **Minor Theater,** 1015 H St. (822-5171), and the **Arcata Theater,** 1304 G St. (822-5171), screen frequent double features (at the Minor $3; at the Arcata $3.75, children $1.75, seniors 50¢). Arcata's bars lie side-by-side along 9th St., between G and H St. and attract students and locals. Those over 21 should check out **Jambalaya** at 9th and H St. for nightly jazz (sometimes with a $1 cover charge).

The 14-year-old **Kinetic Sculpture Race,** held annually over Memorial Day weekend, surely qualifies as Humboldt County's oddest festival. A few dozen insane and intoxicated adventurers attempt to pilot unwieldy but endearing homemade vehicles on a three-day 35-mi. trek from Arcata in the north across the bay to Eureka and then to Ferndale in the south via road, sand, and water. Watch a zucchini race a yellow #2 pencil which has just passed an egg carrying a rabbit and a chicken. The race's motto is "cheating is a privilege, not a right," which tells you all you need to know about the nature of the competition.

Thirty mi. inland along Rte. 299 and 96 is the **Hoopa Valley Indian Reservation,** centered in Hoopa. The free tribal museum (916-625-4110) is, oddly enough, in a shopping center (open Mon.-Fri. 10am-4pm).

This is Bigfoot country. At the junction of Rte. 299 and 96, the town of **Willow Creek** holds Bigfoot Days Sept. 2-3, and even has a statue erected to "Oh Mah,"the big fellah's local name.

The **Community Pool,** 1150 16th St. (822-6801) is an exceptional local facility, with a hot tub and weight room available to anyone over 16. Admission $2.25, 75¢ for youths. Open daily 1-5pm for recreational swimming.

A cornucopia of dimly-lit bars can be found along 9th St., primarily between I and J St.

Redwood National Park

Understandably Northern California's pride and joy, Redwood National Park flaunts an astonishing variety of flora and fauna, in addition to the awesome trees themselves. The park begins just south of the Oregon border and extends down the coast for almost 40 mi., encompassing three state parks while avoiding the tiny coastal towns which cling to Rte. 101. Although the abundance of redwoods and sequoias is spectacular, the park's attractions include far more than these 500-year-old giants. Elk and bears roam the Prairie Creek area as whales float by the coast (migrating southward Nov.-Jan. and returning March-May), and birds are everywhere.

The region is famous for its fishing, and the variegated terrain is ideal for hikers and backpackers. The lack of public transportation within the park, however, requires extreme perseverance. Beaches line the coastal trail which extends almost the length of the park. Day use of the state park costs $3 per car. Campsites are numerous and range from well-equipped (flush toilets and free hot showers; sites $12, hikers/bikers $2) to primitive (outhouses at best; free). Peak season coincides with the California school system's summer vacation, which begins in the third week of June and concludes in early September. The ideal time to visit is mid-April to mid-June or September to mid-October. The park is less crowded during these months and is free of summer fog. Call MISTIX (800-444-7275) for campsite reservations ($3.75), essential in the summer season.

The most pleasant roost, if you're not camping, has to be the **Redwood Youth Hostel (AYH),** 14480 U.S. 101, Klamath 95548 (482-8265). This hostel, housed in the historic Victorian DeMartin House, combines ultra-modern facilities with a certain ruggedness. Its 30 beds complement kitchen, dining room, and laundry facilities, all wheelchair-accessible. There's a separate stove for vegetarians, a dozen recycling bins, two sundecks, staple foods for sale, and a laundry service (75¢ a load, free for passing cyclists). The hostel makes two 10-speeds available for day use and simply asks that you take your shoes off when you're inside the building; the carpeting is brand new. (Usually full on weekends all summer. Reservations are recommended, and must be made by mail 3 weeks in advance. Members and nonmembers $8. Ages under 18 with parent $4. Linen 50¢. Check-in 4:30-9:30pm. Curfew 11pm. The hostel is closed from 10am-4:30pm, so you'll have to be an early riser.)

Crescent City, with park headquarters and a few basic services, stands at the park's northern end. The small town of **Orick** is situated at the southern limit and harbors an extremely helpful ranger station, a state park headquarters, and a handful of motels. Rte. 101 connects the two, traversing most of the park.

Practical Information

Visitor Information: Redwood Information Center, U.S. 101. (488-3461), 2 mi. south of Orick. Shows free films about park and wildlife on request. Mountain bike trail information also available. Brochures on trails and campsites. Enthusiastic and extremely helpful rangers. **Orick Chamber of Commerce,** at the same station. Open daily 8am-6pm; Labor Day-mid June 9am-5pm. **Prairie Creek Ranger Station,** on U.S. 101 (488-2171), in Prairie Creek State Park. Open daily 8am-5pm; mid-Sept. to mid-June hours subject to change. **Hiouchi Ranger Station,** on U.S. 199 (458-3134), across from Jedediah Smith Redwoods State Park. Open daily 8am-7pm; Sept. 2-June 20 8am-5pm. **Redwood National Park Headquarters and Information Center,** 1111 2nd St., Crescent City 95531 (464-6101). Open daily 8am-5pm. Headquarters of the entire national park, but the ranger stations are just as well-informed.

Park Activity Information: 464-6101. 24 hrs.

Greyhound: 1125 Northcrest Dr. (464-2807), in Crescent City. 3 per day headed north and 3 going south. Buses can supposedly be flagged down at 3 places within the park: at the Shoreline Deli (488-5761), 1 mile south of Orick on U.S. 101; at Paul's Cannery in Klamath on U.S. 101; and in front of the Redwood Hostel. Beware, however, of capricious bus drivers who may decide to ignore you. Call the Greyhound station directly preceding your stop, and ask the attendant to make the driver aware of your presence. Lockers available $1 for 24 hr., but beware of sporadic station hours.

Local Bus: Del Norte Senior Center Public Bus (464-3069). Connects Klamath to Crescent City. One morning and one evening connection stops at the youth hostel (last bus runs around 4:30pm). Fare $1. Coordinating this bus with the Klamath trailhead shuttle to the tall trees grove is well-nigh impossible. **Dial-a-Ride** (464-9314) operates in the immediate Crescent City vicinity. Rides are all the same price, regardless of distance. (Open Mon.-Sat. 7am-7pm, 75¢, seniors and youths 50¢.

Bike Rentals: Escape Hatch Sport and Cycle, 960 3rd St. (464-2614) has a few "town bikes" ($4 per hour) for light riding, but no mountain bikes. Open Mon.-Sat. 9am-5pm.

Road Conditions: 445-3125.

Highway Patrol: 464-3117.

AAA Emergency Road Service: Crescent City AAA, 464-9372, in KCRE building. Open Mon.-Fri. 8:30am-5pm.

Rape Crisis: Del Norte Country, 465-2851. 24 hr.

Gay Crisis: National Gay Task Force, 800-221-7044.

Laundromats: At the Orick Motel, on U.S. 101, in Orick. Open daily 8am-11pm. Also in Crescent City, U.S. 101 S. and 5th St. Open daily 7am-9pm.

Hospital: Sutter Coast, 100 A St. (464-8511; for **emergencies** ext. 1671), Crescent City. Ambulance service.

Post Office: 751 2nd St. (464-2151), in Crescent City. Open Mon.-Fri. 8:30am-5pm. General Delivery ZIP Code: 95531.

Area Code: 707.

Sights

The park divides into five segments ranging south to north along Rte. 101. The terrain is extremely varied, but always highlights the imposing *sequoia sempervirens,* a taller, sleeker version of its Sierran counterpart *sequoia gigantis.* The coastal redwoods, which *can* live for over 2000 years (the oldest known specimen was not recognized until after it had been chopped down in the 1930s), grow in a 500-mi. belt from San Francisco into Oregon, up to 40 mi. inland. Many of the best specimens are in the park, protected from their nemesis—the chainsaw.

You can cover the park in just over an hour by car, but to truly see the varied habitats, smell the rhododendrons, and lose sight of the sky in the tangled branches above, get out and stroll around. The National Park Service offers a symphony of organized activities for all ages. Pick up a detailed list of Junior Ranger programs and nature walks at any of the park's ranger stations (see Practical Information). The Jed Smith, Mill Creek, and Prairie Creek Campfire Centers all host nightly campfires and sing-alongs, and the Redwood Information Center (458-3134) in Orick holds 20-minute natural history talks daily from 10:30am to 3pm. The stations also loan "family adventure packs" for free. The pack is a rucksack containing binoculars, compass, sampling bottles, magnifying glasses, and flower, tree, and bird identification books. Most activities are described in a seasonal newsletter, the *Redwood Visitor Guide,* available throughout the park. There's also an excellent trails leaflet (25¢).

Orick Area

This region covers the southernmost section of the park. Its **ranger station** lies about 2 mi. south of Orick on U.S. 101 and 1 mi. south of the Shoreline Deli (the Greyhound bus stop). The staff provides up-to-date information about the area. The main attraction is the **tall trees grove,** an 8½-mi. hike from the ranger station. In peak season, a shuttle bus (fare $3, over 61 $1.50, children $1) runs twice per day from the station to the tall trees trail. From there, it's a 1.3-mi. hike down (about 30 minutes) to the tallest redwoods in the park and, in fact, to the tallest known tree in the world (367.8 ft.—only 1/3 the height of the World Trade Center). The return trip is uphill and slowgoing. Round-trip from the Information Station takes about 5½ hours. The same trail is accessible to backpackers, who may camp anywhere along the way after obtaining a permit at the ranger station. Backpackers should be certain to consult Mr. Ranger before attempting the trek in winter, as adverse weather conditions sometimes render the trail impassable. If you're hiking in and hoping for a motorized return trip, book the shuttle before you go. Incidentally, the average time spent by visitors looking at the tree is 1 minute 40 seconds.

Orick itself (pop. 400) is a sleepy but friendly town, overrun with souvenir stores selling "burl" (tacky wood carvings pleasing to neither eye nor wallet). Nevertheless, the town provides some amenities. Along U.S. 101 are a laundromat, a post office, the reasonably priced **Orick Market** (488-3225), and some motels. The market delivers groceries to Prairie Creek Campground at 7:30pm daily. Phone in your order before 6pm (minimum order $10; delivery free). The **Palm Café,** Rt. 101 in downtown Orick (488-3381), serves up basic diner food (burgers with fries $3.50). Try the outstanding homemade cream pies, $1.75. Two miles north of Orick on U.S. 101 (Fern Canyon exit) lies the area's only gourmet restaurant, **Rolf's Park Café** (488-3841; open Jan. to mid-Dec. daily 8am-8:30pm). European chef Rolf Rheinschmidt will serve you up a made-to-order elk steak ($16), buffalo steak ($15), wild boar roast ($15) or any variety of rugged German cuisine. The gourmet delicacies are truly superb, and if you don't mind eating something as common as tuna you can have a moderately priced meal (sandwiches with fries or salad $5-6).

Adjacent to the café is the **Prairie Creek Motel** (488-3841). Slightly run-down rooms are $25 for a single, $34 for a double. Back in Orick, larger and newly refurbished rooms are slightly more expensive at the **Park Woods Motel,** 121440 Rt. 101 (488-5175). A room here is $32 for 1 or 2 people, but a 2-bedroom unit with full kitchen is only $40.

Rolf's lies just after the turn-off to Davison Road. This dirt path runs through redwoods and then drops down to the ocean along Gold Bluffs Beach, passing the favorite grazing spots of some of the park's 500 elks. Watch for antlers sticking out of the grass, as the elk often snooze at mid-day. And don't be foolish enough to approach an elk on foot. When the elk decides you're too close, you might not see him charge, but you'll certainly feel it.

Once per year in the second week of July, Orick contracts **roditis,** a rare disease cured only by bull riding, wild horse races, barrel races, and the crowning of a "rodeo queen."

Prairie Creek Area

The Prairie Creek Area, equipped with a ranger station and state park campgrounds, is perfect for hikers. The 10-mi. **James Irvine Trail** winds through magnificent redwoods, around clear and cold creeks, through **Fern Canyon** (famed for its 50-ft. fern walls and mossy bottom), and by a stretch of the Pacific Ocean (wear shoes that you don't mind getting wet). The trail starts at the Prairie Creek Visitors Center (see Practical Information). The less ambitious can elk-watch without bruising their antlers, as elk love to graze on the meadow in front of the ranger station.

The **Elk Prairie Trail** was designed for the visually impaired, but gives everyone the chance to experience the redwoods through the less-appreciated senses. There's a 1-mi. loop with excellent interpretive signs in **Lady Bird Johnson Grove** and, in summer, daily ranger-led hikes. (Off the Bald Hills Rd. just north of Orick.)

Klamath Area

To the north, the Klamath Area comprises a thin stretch of park land connecting Prairie Creek with Del Norte State Park. The main attraction here is the rugged and beautiful coastline. The best **whale-watching sites** (Nov.-Jan., March-May) cluster at the south trailhead of the coastal trail.

Don't leave the area without tasting **salmon jerky,** a Native American speciality of smoked, dried salmon. Most of the shops selling it offer free samples to the uninitiated. You must also at least try to remove some of the salmon from the Klamath River (fishing permit required).

Camp Marigold, 16101 Hwy. 101 (482-3585) has cabins with kitchenettes ($32) and is the cleanest and safest place after the hostel. There is no ranger station in the area.

Crescent City Area

Crescent City, the largest metropolis north of Eureka and south of the Oregon border sums itself up simply: A sign in front of the visitors center reads, "In 1964 a *tsunami* (tidal wave) extensively damaged businesses and homes in Crescent City. Now rebuilt, Crescent City offers motel and medical services." This is considered *bragging* in this town. That and a maximum-security prison—where all the inmates are in solitary confinement (you have to kill someone while in prison just to get considered for this place)—are about all Crescent City has to offer.

The **Crescent City Visitors Center,** in the Chamber of Commerce at 1001 Front St. (464-3174) is surprisingly large for such a depressing town. The redwood building has lots o' brochures (open 9am-5pm daily)

Seven miles south of the city lies the **Del Norte Coast Redwoods State Park,** a state-level extension of the Redwood Forest. The park's magnificent ocean views—along with picnic areas, hiking trails, and nearby fishing—lure enough campers to fill the sites in summer. (RVs $10, tent sites $8, day-use $2.) The self-titled city "Where the Redwoods meet the Sea" met the sea for real when, in 1964, *tsunami* caused by seismic activity brought 500 mph winds and leveled the city.

A 1990s attempt to stay in Crescent City will also be a washout. Food and lodgings are overpriced. For the best deals, head to 9th St., the pre-*tsunami* location of U.S. 101. The surviving motels are cleaner and less expensive than those more centrally located. The cheapest motels aren't all *that* bad. **Bon Dormé Motel,** 731 9th St. (464-5611), but ask to see a room first. Singles $25. Doubles $30. **El Patio,** 655 H St. (464-5114), offers decent rooms for a modest price. Some rooms have kitchenettes; all have TVs. Singles $35, doubles $43. **Endert's Beach Campground,** has 6 primitive sites, a ¾-mi. hike in from the end of the Endert's Beach Rd.

The best seafood trap overlooks Crescent City's harbor, to the south of town. The **Harbor View Grotto,** 115 Citizens Dock Rd. (464-3815), offers bread, chowder and fish for under $7, with attentive service and stimulating views. (Open daily noon-10pm.) **Los Compadres,** Hwy. 101 South (464-7871) cooks up spicy Mexican food in *grande* portions. Super burritos $4. (Open daily 11am-9pm.) For those willing and able to cook their own, the **Safeway** supermarket in Jedediah Smith Sq., at 4th and M St., sells natural and not-so-natural munchies in bulk. (Open 24 hrs.)

The **Battery Point Lighthouse** (464-3089), on a causeway jutting out of Front St., houses a museum open only during low tide. Don't get caught once the sea starts coming in and don't mistake the islands of kelp bobbing offshore for seals coming up for air. (Open May-Oct. Wed.-Sun. 10am-4pm. Admission $1.50.) Kids will enjoy the 45-minute **seashore walk** that leaves from the Crescent Beach picnic area (see the *Visitor Guide* for scheduled times). A 2-hour **nature walk** with a ranger runs all summer with hours depending on staff availability. Call for details.

The **August Salmon Bake, Easter in July** (when the lily completes its bi-ennial bloom), and the **World Championship Crab Races** (on the 3rd Sunday in February) highlight a long list of city festivals.

Hiouchi Area

This inland region sits in the northern part of the park along Rte. 199 and tends several excellent trails. The **Stout Grove Trail,** an easy ½-mi. walk, passes the park's widest redwood, 16 ft. in diameter (this is only a fraction, however, of the World Trade Centers' collective girth). The path is also accessible to the disabled; call 458-3310 for arrangements. Farther east, the **Simpson-Reid Trial** is a pleasant trek. Note that the bridge connecting U.S. 199 to Rte. 197 is down, making this area more secluded and better for solitary hikes. Inexpensive **kayak** trips on the Smith River leave from the ranger station. The three-and-a-half-hour trip covers some challenging rapids. (Approximate dates June 21-July 18 Fri.-Tues. at 9:30 and 11am. Donation $6, ages 10-16 $3, ages under 10 not allowed.) A weekly three-hour "field adventure" tour sometimes departs from the ranger station. (July 19-Aug. 1, Tues. at 10am. Free.)

Sacramento Valley and the Cascades

Life in the Sacramento Valley creeps at the pace of the plant life that stretches in every direction. The towns along I-5 are small and lazy, geared to the seasons of crops and of tourists. They wake up early, and, except for Sacramento, are quiet by nightfall. The state capital is worth a visit, but Chico, Red Bluff, and especially Redding are useful only as bases for exploring the nearby marvels of the Whiskytown-Shasta-Trinity Recreation Areas, Lassen National Forest, Mt. Shasta, and the Lava Beds.

Sacramento

The indistinctive capital of a very distinctive state, Sacramento is so average that it is often used by market researchers to test new brands of soap. Snobby San Franciscans call it "Excremento," and certainly the heat and dust in summer make you wonder why it's even California's *seventh* largest city.

In 1848, John Sutter, a Swiss emigré fleeing debtor's prison back home, "purchased" 48,000 dusty acres for a few trinkets from the local Native American tribes, clearing the way for such future residents as Ronald Reagan and the Brady Bunch. Despite frequent attempts to remove its premier status, Sacramento has been the capital of California since 1854—just long enough to accumulate a few interesting sights, but evidently not long enough to make it a particularly worthwhile tourist destination in and of itself.

Practical Information

Visitors Information: Sacramento Convention and Visitors Bureau, 1421 K St. (449-6711), between 14th and 15th St. Small and congenial, with a tidy stand of brochures coyly displayed on the corner table. The only accommodations guide is the titillating *Sacramento,* published by the city (free). Open Mon.-Fri. 8am-5pm. The **Old Sacramento Visitors Center,** 1104 Front St. (449-6711; holidays and weekends 442-7644), also has a bevvy of brochures. Open daily 9am-5pm. The **Beeline,** (552-5252) put together by the **Sacramento Bee,** gives recorded information on everything from events and sports to stock market information. The Friday edition of the Sacramento Bee contains a supplement called **Ticket,** which gives a weekly run-down of events, restaurants, and night spots.

Sacramento Metro Airport: 929-5411, 12 mi. north of downtown on I-5. Get there via Skyline Airporter bus (444-6888, or 800-464-0777, $7.25), which picks up passengers from 12th and L St. or 3rd and J St. For a recording that advertises fly-for-less fares, call 920-4700.

Amtrak: 4th at I St. (444-9131). Giant terminal open daily 5:15am-11:15pm. Connections to Reno ($51), Chicago ($202), L.A. ($74), Seattle ($141), and San Francisco ($17). Reservations must be made months in advance for all eastbound trains and most westbound trains.

Greyhound: 715 L St. (444-6800), between 7th and 8th St. Terminal open 24 hr. Relatively safe, though not the most pleasant of neighborhoods. To: Reno (Gambler's Sound-trip Special, 3 day min. stay, $19); L.A. ($40); San Francisco ($10).

Sacramento Regional Transit Bus: 321-2877. Bus service in downtown Sacramento Mon.-Fri. 5am-10pm; some lines run 5am-10:30pm. Sat. buses run later. Fare $1 including transfer; all day pass $2.50. Express buses ($1) run Mon.-Fri. 6:30-9am and 3:30-6pm. An 18.3-mi. **light rail** transit line connects the central business district with the eastern regions of the city. Trains run every 15 min. from 4:30am-1:30am. Fare $1.

Yolo Bus Commuter Lines: 371-2877. A suburban wonder. Connects downtown with Old Sacramento, West Sacramento, Davis, and Woodland. Open Mon.-Fri. 6am-8pm, Sat.-Sun. 8am-7pm. Fare $1; 50¢ surcharge on the express buses (#43, 44, 45).

Car Rental: U-Save Auto Rental, 2528 Tulsa Way (485-9847), off Fulton Ave. 1 block south of Cottage Way. $19 per day with 100 free miles plus 20¢ per additional mile. Must be 21 with major credit card. Open Mon.-Fri. 7am-6pm. **A and A Rent-A-Car,** 2538 Auburn Blvd. (488-5100), Fulton at I-80. $12 per day, with a 12¢ per mile surcharge the first 3 days; after that, 50 mi. per day free, 12¢ per additional mile. Must be 21 with credit card or $350 cash deposit. Open Mon.-Fri. 8am-5pm, Sat. 9-10:30am and 1:30-3:30pm.

AAA Emergency Road Service: 331-9981.

Road Information: 445-7623. 24 hr.

Bike Rental: American River Bike Shop, 9203 Folsom Blvd. (363-6271), south of downtown. Bikes $4 per hr., $20 per day. Credit card or $100 cash deposit required. Open Mon.-Fri. 9am-7pm, Sat. 9am-6pm, Sun. 9am-5pm.

Public Library: 536 Downtown Plaza (449-5203). Newly expanded and spacious. Open Mon.-Sat. 10am-6pm.

Weather: 646-2000.

Traveler's Aid: 717 K St., 443-1719.

Rape Crisis Center: Women Escaping a Violent Environment (WEAVE) 448-2321.

Gay Community Center: Lambda, 1931 L St. (442-0185). Recorded events line, 447-5755.

Suicide Prevention: 800-333-4444 or 368-3111.

U.C. Davis Medical Center: 2315 Stockton Blvd. (453-2011), at Broadway. **Emergency Services,** 453-3797; **Poison Center,** 734-3692 (or 453-3692). Staffed 24 hr.

Aquarian Effort Free Medical Clinic: 1304 O St. (446-6467). The Aquarian Society provides drug counseling, especially on heroin use. Family planning services also. Open Mon.-Fri. 6-9pm.

Police: 449-5471, information only.

Emergency: 911.

Post Office: Main Office, 2000 Royal Oaks Dr. (921-0280). Open Mon.-Fri. 8:30am-5pm. On weekends, holidays, and after 5pm call 921-4564. **General Delivery:** Metro Station, 801 I St. (442-0764), at 8th. Open Mon.-Fri. 8am-5pm. General Delivery ZIP Code: 95814.

Area Code: 916.

Orientation

Sacramento (pop. 369,000), not coincidentally, is at the center of the Sacramento Valley. Five major highways converge on the city. I-5 and Rte. 99 run north-south. I-80 runs east-west between San Francisco and Reno. U.S. 50 and Rte. 16 bring traffic from the Mother Lode into the capital. the Old Sacramento section is most easily reached by I-5.

As in many other cities, each block represents one hundred street addresses. These addresses also correspond to the lettered cross-streets, so 200 3rd St. intersects B St., 1700 C St. is on 17th St., 300 3rd St. intersects C, and so on. Got it?

The capitol and endless state government buildings occupy the rectilinear **downtown** area. The **Broadway** area, home of the original Tower Records, lies beyond Z St. The 40 avenues north of Broadway, known as the "fabulous forty," contain the mansions built by Sacramento's industrial barons. One of these humble abodes housed Ronald Reagan during his term as governor. **West Sacramento** lies west of downtown, on the other side of the river.

With well-marked lanes, the city is a biker's town (see Practical Information for rentals). If you're walking, you'll be happiest downtown and in Old Sacramento. The light-rail and city bus system, however, are pleasantly punctual and easy to use.

Accommodations

Sacramento has an extraordinary supply of motel rooms. Nonetheless, if a large convention is taking place (and they frequently are), all but the sleaziest pads will be fully booked by midweek; it's best to reserve a month in advance. The cheapest places lie near the Greyhound station downtown across from Capitol Park but have questionable security. Several motels east of Capitol Park, along 15th and 16th St., average $30 for singles. For similar rates, go to West Sacramento, a 20- to 30-minute walk along W. Capitol Ave. from Old Sacramento. Jibboom St., 1 mi. from Old Sacramento, also has plenty of cheap, yet safe, motels. Call the West Sacramento Motel & Hotel Association (372-5378) or the West Sacramento Chamber of Commerce (372-5378; open 8am-5pm). Yolo buses #40, 41, or 42 leave for West Sacramento from the L St. terminal.

The quality of accommodations in Sacramento ranges from the posh suites of luxury hotels to unsanitary, unsafe, and unsavory crash-dives. While many downtown motels are ostensibly standard, safe budget accommodations, it is wise to see a room before you pay for the night. If you have concerns about your safety, don't be chintzy: go somewhere else and spend the extra $5.

Gold Rush Home Hostel (AYH), 1421 Tiverton Ave. (421-5954), on the outskirts of town near the zoo. Run by a hip septuagenarian. Very comfortable. Nine beds which are nearly always filled. Lockout 9am-6pm. Members $8. Nonmembers $10. Reservations required.

Central Motel, 818 16th St. (446-6006), next to the Governor's Mansion. A/C and TV in standard, but spruce rooms. Singles with a double bed $30. Doubles $40.

Capitol Park Hotel, 1125 9th St. (441-5361), at L St., 2 blocks from Greyhound. The only thing older than the hotel is its clientele. Well-worn rooms kept cool by large windows. An unbeatable location. Singles $28. Doubles $35.

Americana Lodge, 818 15th St. (444-3980). No Davy Crockett hats or Old Coca-Cola signs, but has a small pool, A/C and HBO. A fair trade. Antiseptic; local calls 25¢; checkout 11am. Singles from $34. Doubles $38. Confirm reservations with advance payment.

Motel 6, 1415 30th St. (457-0777), at U.S. 50 and I-80. No surprises here. Pool. Singles $30, $6 per additional person.

Mansion View Lodge, 711 16th St. between G and H St. (443-6631 or 800-446-6465). Not much to distinguish this motel from all the others, except its location next to the Governor's Mansion. Say "Hi' to Pete for us. Singles $36, doubles $40.

Econo Lodge, 1319 30th St. (454-4400). One step up on the motel scale: less sullied and more roomy than others in its price range. Pool. Checkout noon. Singles $40, doubles $44.

Food

Downtown Sacramento supports numerous breakfast and lunch spots; unfortunately, many close by 3 or 4pm. Once the bureaucracry goes home for the day, apparently, so do the restaurateurs. Old Sacramento is the place for ice cream, light snacks, as well as upscale wining and dining. The finest feasting, though, clusters in the blocks between 19th and 22nd St. around Capitol St.

Marlene's Vegetable Patch, 1119 8th St. (448-3327), between K and L, 1 block from Greyhound and right across from the Berry Hotel. When Jerry Brown announces his comeback, he'll probably hold the press conference here. Scrupulously vegetarian, right down to the "soy sour cream," but omnivores will hardly detect the difference. Filling lunch entrees $4-4.50. *Mark* my word, you'll love their smoothies ($1.75). All-you-can-eat buffet and salad bar ($6). Open Mon.-Fri. 10:30am-2:30pm, and 10am-4pm for drinks and herbs (from their herb shop).

Rubicon Brewing Company, 2004 Capitol Ave. (448-7032). Don't *cross* the street and miss these guys. Home of India Pale Ale, the winning brew at the American Beer Fest (pints $2.25), this micro-brewery also serves high-quality food. Filling sandwiches served on freshly-baked bread ($5.50). Great French onion soup with crisp bread and gooey cheese ($2.25 a bowl). Open Mon. 11:30am-midnight, Tues.-Thurs. 11:30am-11:30pm, Fri. 11:30am-12:30am, Sat. 9am-12:30am, Sun. 9am-10pm.

Zelda's Original Gourmet Pizza, 1415 21st St. (447-1400). The best deep-dish pizza in Sacramento—ask any passerby. A dark, cool retreat from Sacramento's heat, though a hike from the center of town. Medium cheese $7.30. Their Vegetarian Supreme ($11) is indeed both. Open Mon.-Thurs. 11:30am-2pm and 5-10pm, Fri. 11:30am-2pm and 5-11:30pm, Sat. 5-11:30pm, Sun. 5-9pm.

524, 524 12th St. (446-6147). Rough 'n' ready greasy spoon Mexican with tongue-igniting dips. The full range of tostadas, enchiladas, tacos, etc. for $6-8.50. Open Mon.-Fri. 10am-10pm, Sat.-Sun. 10am-8pm.

The Lucky Café, 1111 21st between K and L. Diner food for the Fee-Fi-Fo-Fum crowd. Try their Giant Cheeseburger ($8.25), a 1-pound delicacy served with enough fries to require their own dinner plate. Open Mon.-Fri. 7am-9pm; Sat. 7am-3pm; Sun. 9am-2pm.

Lu Shan Chinese Restaurant, 403 J St. (444-2543). All-you-can-eat lunch buffets $4.75, dinner buffets $7.50. No buffet Sun. Open Mon.-Sat. 11am-9pm, Sun. noon-9pm.

Chocolate Ripple Desserts, 1309 21st St. (446-3107). Light lunches and luscious cakes ($2.50-3.50). Open Tues.-Thurs. 11am-midnight, Fri. 11am-1am, Sat. 6pm-1am, Sun. 6pm-midnight.

Java City, 1800 Capitol Ave. (444-JAVA (5282)). In keeping with the jet-set corporate mindset of the state's capital, this café sports clocks synchronized to the time zone of the coffee beans' origins: Java City, Brazil, Columbia, Yemen...The crowds of customers all hang out around the tables outside. Brewed coffee 85¢, refills 25¢. 25% discount for seniors. The "Fro Mo" is a delicious mixture of chocolate, vanilla, and cookies and cream gelato with chilled espresso and mocha beans, no unlike a frappuccino ($3). Open Sun.-Thurs. 6am-11pm, Fri.-Sat. 6am-midnight.

Rick's Dessert Diner, 2322 K St. at 24th St. (444-0969). Everybody goes to Rick's. Despite this diner's appearance, you can't get burgers here. In fact, all that's served are desserts. Oreo cheesecake $3.50. Open Mon.-Thurs. 10am-11pm, Fri.-Sat. 10am-midnight, Sun. 10am-2pm.

Old Sacramento

Annabelle's, 200 J St. (448-6239), next to the parking lot. Typical Italian food (and decor) rendered worthwhile by the all-you-can-eat lunch buffet ($3.70), which includes pasta, lasagna, pizza, and salad bar. Also serves something called the "family spectacular": a large pizza, 4 salad bars, and a pitcher of soda ($17). Open daily 11:30am-8pm.

Sakura Japanese Restaurant, 1111 2nd St. (448-8334). Memorable chiefly for its gimmicks: Teppan-flashing blades wielded by impassive chefs, and a *sushi*-laden toy train which you unload as it makes its rounds. Lunch $5.75, dinner from $10. Open Tues.-Fri. 11:30am-2pm and 5:30-9pm, Sat. 5:30-9:30pm, Sun. 4-8pm.

Sights and Seasonal Events

A seedy neighborhood in the 1960's, **Old Sacramento** is now a full-fledged tourist attraction with many up-scale shops filling the original building shells. There's a pleasant atmosphere and a number of historically interesting structures, including the **B.F. Hastings** building, at the corner of 2nd and J St. Dating from 1852, the building houses Wells Fargo's offices, a museum, and the reconstructed chambers of the California Supreme Court. Pick up a walking tour guide at the Old Sacramento Visitors Center (449-6711).

Once you've had your fill of souvenir stores and cutesy-pie potpourri gift shops, try one or two of the excellent historical museums in Old Sacramento's northern end. The **California State Railroad Museum,** 125 I St. (448-4466), at 2nd St., will delight even those ignorant of the difference between a cowcatcher and a caboose. The museum houses a fascinating collection of historical locomotives in its over 100,000 square feet of exhibition space. Start with the 13-minute film in the lobby and you'll appreciate the museum much more. (Open daily 10am-5pm. Admission $5, ages 6-17 $2, children under 6 free.) The same ticket admits you to the **Central Pacific Depot and Passenger Station,** at 1st and J St., a reconstruction of a station that once stood here; see the train tracks, ticket offices, and a refreshment stand of the gilded age. For the most fanatical rail riders, the **California State Railroad Museum Sacramento Southern Railroad Ride** runs out of the passenger station. The 40-minute trip is jolting and slow. (Tickets $4, age 6-17 $2, under 6 free. Trips

Sat.-Sun. in summer 10am-5pm on the hour; Oct.-April on the first weekend of the month from noon-3pm.)

The **Sacramento History Museum,** 101 I St. (449-2057), at Front St., housed in the reconstructed 1854 City Hall, presents exhibits on California history in a two-story glass-and-chrome extravaganza, with interactive and informative video presentations. (Open Tues.-Sun. 10am-5pm. Guided tours by reservation only. Admission $2.50, ages over 64 $1.50, ages 6-17 $1, under 6 free.)

The gifts of Dearborn, Michigan to the world are on display at the **Towe Ford Museum of California,** 2200 Front St. (442-6802), south of V St. This museum has a collection of over 150 Ford cars and trucks dating from 1903 to 1953. The cars are in excellent condition, and it's fascinating to watch the historical progression from clunky Model Ts to streamlined Thunderbirds. On Saturday nights during the summer, the museum hosts American Graffiti Nites, with 50s sock-hops. (Open daily 10am-6pm. Admission $5, age 14-18 $2.50, 3-5 $1. Admission to American Graffiti Nites $6.)

Gallery hoppers should enjoy the elegant **Crocker Art Museum,** 216 O St. (449-5423), at 3rd St., which is housed in a restored Victorian building. The museum exhibits mainly 19th-century European and American oil paintings, but devotes one spacious gallery to photography and another to contemporary works by California artists. (Open Tues.-Sun. 10am-5pm, Thurs. 10am-9pm. Admission $2.50, seniors and ages 7-18 $1, under 6 free. Tours available.)

The **State Capitol,** at 10th St. and Capitol Mall (324-0333), in Capitol Park, was very nearly replaced by twin modern towers in the 1970s, when the old and abused structure began to crumble. Fortunately, the usually stingy Californian taxpayers forked out $68 million, and the building's restoration to its glorious 1906 finery was completed in 1982: pink and green decor, oak staircases, gilt, and all-too-flattering oil paintings of forgotten governors. You might want to skip the tacky first-floor displays sponsored by each county in the state, but don't miss the bizarre portrait of ex-"Governor Moonbeam" Jerry Brown, who relinquished his limousine and mansion while in office for a humble apartment and an old Plymouth. If art and architecture don't grab you, sit in on an Assembly or Senate session during the week. The "Restoration" tour covers the chambers; the "Historic" delves into the re-created office spaces, decorated as they were decades ago. Both are free, last one hour, and are given daily 9am-4pm on the hour. Another tour explores the 40-acre gardens, including the Vietnam Memorial (open daily 9am-5pm; in fall and winter, Sat.-Sun. 10am-5pm). For information and an excellent 10-minute free film, journey to Room B-27 in the basement. Self-guided walking tour brochures are also available there.

Before a certain Ronald Reagan demanded more spacious surroundings in the late 60s, the **Old Governor's Mansion,** 16th and H St. (324-0539), fit the bill. This 15-room Victorian masterpiece (c. 1877) was home to 13 of California's governors. The building bursts with gables and attics, displaying the architectonic complexity of a three-tiered wedding cake. (Open daily 10am-5pm, ½-hr. tours on the hour. Last tour 4pm. Admission $2, age 6-17 $1, under 6 free.)

Across town at 27th and L St., **Sutter's Fort** (324-0539) is a reconstruction of the 1839 military settlement that put Sacramento on the map. All supplies had to be dragged overland from the river to build the settlement, which now contains the **State Indian Museum** (349-0971). Rangers fire the fort's cannon at whomever they please at 11am and 2pm. (Both open daily 10am-5pm. Admission to each $2, under 18 $1.)

Supposedly the world's largest almond-processing plant, the **Blue Diamond Visitors Center and Almond Plaza,** 1701 C St. (446-8409), is without a doubt one of Sacramento's tastiest attractions. To cynics, the museum is a fancy promotional gimmick, but your forbearance will be rewarded with samples of the tasty almond products after the tour. Just one honey-roasted bite and you'll feel like you're on a magic carpet to heaven. (Open Mon.-Fri. 9am-5:30pm, Sat. 10am-4pm. Tours by reservation only Mon.-Fri. 10am, 1pm. Free.)

The original **Tower Records** looms at the corner of Landpark Dr. and Broadway (444-3000). One of the world's greatest record store chains began in 1941 when an ambitious teenager, Russ Solomon, started selling records in the back of his dad's drugstore; he now owns an international chain of stores. Tower's overwhelming selection of music and late hours are replicated in the adjacent Tower Books, Drugs, Theater, Tobacco, ad nauseum. Prices, however, have moved into the 90s. (Record store open 9am-midnight.)

If you're seeking quietude, rent a two-person raft ($22) from **American River Raft Rentals,** 11257 S. Bridge St., Rancho Cordova (635-6400), 10 mi. east of downtown on U.S. 50. (Open daily 9am-9pm.) Board sailing lessons and rentals are also offered here (635-6400), as are whitewater tours (635-4516).

The kid in you (or with you) will enjoy the **Sacramento Zoo,** 3930 W. Land Park Dr. (449-5885). Open daily 9am-4pm. Admission $3, 3-12 $1.50, under 3 free. 50¢ more on weekends. The **Visionarium,** 2701 K St. (443-7476), on the second level of the Sutter Square Galleria, houses an aggressively interactive children's museum billed as "Kids on Kampus." (Open Mon.-Sat. 10am-6pm, Sun. noon-5pm; admission $2, 3-18 $4, under 3 free.) The **Sacramento Science Center,** 3615 Auburn Blvd. (449-8255), will engage even the most shiftless child with its "exploratory" exhibits, planetarium, and aviary. (Open Wed.-Thurs. noon-5pm, Fri. noon-8:30pm, Sat.-Sun. 10am-5pm. Admission $2.50, seniors $1 50, children $1.)

Sacramento hosts one of the world's largest **Dixieland Jazz** festivals in late May each year, with over 100 bands taking part (372-5377). Local groups perform **Shakespeare in the Park** (William Land Park Amphitheater, call 449-7228 for details) June-Aug. A **Camellia festival** (442-7673) is held in early March, and the agriculturally-oriented **California State Fair** takes place from mid-August to early September, complete with a carnival. For weekend music and events, sift through the comprehensive free weeklies: *Sacramento News and Review,* (737-1234), **Suttertown News** (448-9881), and *Sac This Week.*

An interesting half-day trip is **Locke,** a small town about 25 mi. south of Sacramento on I-5. Although there are only two short streets, each about a block long, all the buildings are wooden, and Chinese in design. The Chinese-Americans who erected the levées on the Sacramento River lived here, and some of their descendants still do. Check out **Al the Wap's** old-time tavern, decorated with $1 bills on the ceiling; they serve great Chinese lunches.

Nightlife

Compared to the comatose surrounding area, Sacramento manages a lively nightlife. The dessert dens are about as numerous as the dancing venues.

Sam's Hofbrau, 17th and J St. (441-4113). Who cares what the music sounds like when you can tank up on 75¢ drafts before the show starts? Daily blues band and sly, smoky crowd.

The Fox and Goose, 1001 R St. (443-8825), at 10th St. A "public house" with a two-story ceiling serving only wine and beer (check out their selection of imported British labels) in a woody, relaxed setting supplemented with English signs and other bric-á-brac. Live music nightly, generally acoustic during the week and electric on weekends. Pints $2.85, wine $1.75-3.25. Open Mon.-Fri. 7am-"closing," Sat.-Sun. 9am-"closing."

Faces, 2000 K St. (448-7798). The slickest of the many gay bars in the neighborhood, this expansive, sophisticated club offers 3 bar areas, a capacious dance floor, and an ice cream stand. Open daily 2pm-2am.

Club 2 Me, 4738 J St. (451-6834). The college place with pool tables, etc. Drafts $1.25. Open daily 6:30am-2am.

Melarkey's, 1517 Broadway (448-2797), across from Tower. A stucco diner-turned-restaurant/bar. Eclectic music and a dimly-lit sanctuary for beer-drinking and sports-watching. Open daily 11am-2am.

Virgin Sturgeon, 1577 Garden Hwy. (921-2694), on the river. The casual crowd ranges from "river people" to yuppies. Hop off of your raft or drive up. Famous for their mushroom burger (lunch only, 1/3 lb. $5.50). (Open Mon.-Fri. 11am-2:30pm, 6-11pm, Sat. 10am-4pm, 6-11pm, Sun. 9am-3pm, 5-10pm; bar open till 2am.)

The Yucatan Drink Stand, 1696 Arden Way (922-6446), across from the Arden Fair Shopping Center. With the smallest sign, this is Sacramento's biggest club. It's also one of the best discos and pick-up places. The line out front is long and lugubrious.

Fanny Ann's, 1023 2nd St. (441-0505), at the corner of K St. Raucous, but fairly comfortable when not crammed with of-age teeny-boppers. Bring your megaphone and oxygen mask. Arcade in the basement, dancing on 3rd floor. Daily specials on food and drinks. Daily Happy Hour Mon.-Fri. 4-8pm with $1.49 drafts, $1 shots. Open Sun.-Tues. 11:30am-midnight, Wed.-Sat. 11:30am-2am.

Davis

Davis is a quaint university town with 45,000 bicycles, several excellent restaurants, wonderful public transportation—and not much else. On weekend nights during the semester there's lots of action at the local, but in summer, the students head home and the majority of remaining residents are of the clove-hoofed variety: they don't call it a cowtown for nothing. Moo.

Practical Information

Visitors Information: Davis Chamber of Commerce and Visitors Center, 228 B St. (756-5160). Lots of brochures in a little office. Helpful staff. Open Mon.-Fri. 8:30am-5pm.

UC Davis Memorial Union Information Center: in the Griffin Lounge on campus (752-2222, TDD 752-2228). Campus maps, events and bus schedules. Amicable staff eager to guide. Open Mon.-Fri. 8am-5pm.

Transportation: Unitrans (752-BUSS or 752-2877). Extensive local service connecting downtown and the UCD campus. 50¢, seniors and Davis students free. Most stops are wheelchair accessible (check the schedule for details).

Yolo Bus: 756-2877. Service between Davis, Woodland, and Sacramento. Fares 50¢-$1.50. Daily and monthly passes available. Main office: 825 East St., #120, Woodland 95695. Wheelchair accessible.

TAPS: UCD Intracampus Shuttle Service (752-MILE). Free to faculty, students and campus guests. Buses run across campus Mon.-Fri. 7am-6pm. Inter-campus Shuttle to Berkeley available during school year—fee charged.

Greyhound: 826 2nd St. (253-2485).

UC Davis Campus Events: 752-8030.

UC Davis Information: 752-1011.

Public Library: 315 E. 14th St. (756-4269).

Bike Rental: Ken's Bike and Ski, 654 G St. (758-3223 or 758-7547). Rebuilt bikes from $7 a day. Mountain bikes $20 a day. Also rents rollerblades ($10 per day) and waterskis ($12 per day per pair). Davis is the "bicycle capital of the the world," with at least one bike shop on every block.

Davis Alcohol and Drug Abuse Program: 757-5537.

Sexual Assault and Domestic Violence Center: 758-8400. 24 hr.

Diogenes Youth and Family Services: 756-5665. 24 hr. crisis counseling for teens.

Davis Child Care Information: 757-5626.

National Federation of the Blind in California: (Sacramento) 424-2226.

Norcal Center on Deafness: 646-9646, TDD/TTY 646-9649. 24 hr. voice and TDD/TTY 646-9945.

Yolo County Senior Information and Referral: 661-2750. **Davis Senior Citizens Center:** 757-5695 or 757-5696. Senior Transportation: 758-4020.

Hospital: Sutter Davis Hospital, Road 99 and Covell Blvd. (756-6440; 24 hr. emergency 757-5111; TDD/TTY 756-6446).

Emergency: 911.

California Highway Patrol: 662-4685, non-emergency number.

Post Office: 2020 5th St. (753-3496), at Poleline Rd. Open Mon.-Fri. 8:30am-5:30pm, Sat. 10am-1pm. General Delivery Zip Code: 95817.

Area Code: 916.

Accommodations

Motels in Davis do not come cheap.

Davis Motel, 1111 Richards Blvd. (756-1910), at the I-80 and Davis exit. Six blocks from campus. TV, A/C. Very attractive rooms with "desert palm" prints and archways leading to the bathrooms. A real palm tree marks the swimming pool oasis. Rooms for 1-2 people $42.

Motel 6, 4835 Chiles Rd. (753-3777). About 5 mi. from town, accessible only by car. The Motel 6 basic: cheap and clean. Singles $25, doubles $31.

University Inn Bed and Breakfast, 340 A St. (756-8648). A few small steps across the street from the UCD campus, one giant step above budget quality and price. A charming B&B with elegant country decor. TVs and bikes. Elegant country decor. 4 rooms, from $42 each. Weekly $250.

Food

Murder Burger, 978 Olive Dr. (756-2142). "Burgers so good they're to die for"—and they're not kidding. Half-pound—*after* cooking—burgers ($4.50). Creamy strawberry shakes made with fresh strawberries $2.25. Gooey cheese fries covered in cheddar, tomato and onions are $1.15 for a small (which is plenty). Outdoor tables, black and white checkered floor, James Dean on the wall. Definitely not a restaurant to pass by; it makes an offer you can't refuse. Open Mon.-Thurs. and Sat. 10am-8pm, Fri. and Sun. 10am-9pm.

Caffé Helia, 1121 Richards Blvd. (758-7200). Down the street from Murder Burger. Very popular—hang with the hanging plants. Pasta, pizza and salads. Large portions. Entrees $7.50-12. If you're smooching TRW and BNG-style, half orders will fill you up—$3.50-5, including french bread. Open Mon.-Thurs. 6am-10pm, Fri.-Sat. 6am-11pm, Sun. 7-10pm.

Caffé Tutti, 231 F St. (758-0704). Chrome and black decor. A late-night hang-out and caffeine supplier in downtown Davis. Try their *panini*— a prosciutto ham, cambzola, basil, spinach and pear sandwich $4. The trendy sun-dried tomato sandwich is $2.50. Coffee 57¢. Open daily 8am-midnight.

The Graduate, 805 Russell Blvd. (758-GRAD) In the University Mall. Right next to campus, in a big barn. The Grad is a popular student hangout. Cavernous dining area has eight different large-screen TVs, tuned to eight different stations. Video games, pool table, outdoor tables. Music and dancing Fri.-Sat. nights. Regular comedy nights. Famous Gradburger w/fries $4.43. Well-stocked bar. Open daily 10:30am-1am.

Mei's Kitchen, 122 B St. (758-2823). Good food cheap. Lunch special—one entree, soup and rice—$3. Family dinner consists of soup, egg roll, chicken salad, rice and your choice of an entree, $4.25 per person. Open Mon.-Sat. 11:30am-8pm.

Sights

Davis is surrounded mainly by cow pastures and highways. The main excitement in town is supplied by the University of California at Davis, the largest campus in the UC network (and also one of the nation's finest agricultural universities). The Campus Events and Information Office presents a variety of tours (752-1011). The beautiful **Davis Botanical Park** (252-2222) is worth a stroll, and the **Quail Ridge Wilderness Conservancy** is proximate at 25344 Country Rd. 95, ½ mi. north of Country Rd. 31. Native California oaks, bunchgrasses, and a variety of wildlife thrive in this wilderness area, presenting a view of what California looked like before asphalt and steel gave her a facelift of dubious value. Tours by appointment (758-1387).

Davis holds a **Farmer's Market** on Wednesday evenings 5:30-8:30pm, June-August. Located on 2nd St. between C and E Sts., this gathering has just-picked produce, food vendors and music (756-8763).

Chico

The merchants and residents of Chico have their small-town America atmosphere down to a science. Don't go out of your way to come here, but if you happen to stumble upon Chico while in Northern California, you'll find the pervasive sense of tranquility a refreshing surprise. Borrow a dog or a little red wagon and savor the quiet shady streets. Consider how you'd love to raise kids and retire here. At least get a wholesome meal and a cheap, safe night's rest.

In contrast to downtown Chico's wide idyllic streets, the eastern side of town is dominated by the nation's formerly-foremost party school, Chico State. But being the collegiate party capital of America doesn't seem to have marred Chico's serenity—besides the popular late-night art-deco coffeehouse and a lively bar scene on weekends, you'd hardly know you were just a stone's throw from one of *Playboy's* favorite hot spots.

Practical Information

Visitors Information: Chamber of Commerce, 500 Main St. (891-5556). Wall-to-wall brochures cover Chico corner to corner. Check out the weekly *News and Review* for what's going on. Open Mon.-Fri. 9am-5pm.

State University Information Center: 895-6116.

Amtrak: 5th at Orange (800-872-7245). No ticket office, just the platform and station remnants. One train per day north to Seattle ($137) and south to Sacramento ($21).

Greyhound: 717 Wall (343-8266). Buses stop here 5 times per day on their north-south routes. To Sacramento ($12) and Red Bluff ($6.50). Express buses between Red Bluff and Sacramento bypass Chico on I-5. Pick up more frequent connections from either city. Open Mon.-Fri. 6:30am-6pm, Sat. 6-11:30am, 3-3:30pm, 5-5:30pm.

Buses: Butte County Transit, 893-4299 or 800-822-8145. Two routes link Chico with the nearby towns of Paradise and Oroville. Buses run Mon.-Fri. 6:30am-6:30pm, at the sluggish rate of 1 per hr. Fare 90¢, off-peak 70¢, in-town only 60¢. **Chico Area Transit System (CATS),** 893-5252. Five routes wend their way through Chico. Buses run Mon.-Fri. 6:30am-6:30pm, Sat. 8:30am-6:30pm. Fare 60¢, over 62 30¢, students 40¢. 20-ride pass $9.

Sacramento Airport Shuttle: 891-1219. Five buses per day to and from the Sacramento Airport (2 hr.). Buses leave from Jack's Restaurant at 6th and Main. One-way fare $25.

Car Rental: Ugly Duckling, 196 Humboldt Ave. (893-0838 or 800-843-3825). From $15 per day; 100 free miles. After that, 15¢ per mile. Open daily 8am-5:30pm.

AAA Emergency Road Service: 895-0344. **AAA Branch Office:** 1160 E. 1st St. (891-8601). Open Mon.-Fri. 8:30am-5pm.

Bicycle Rental: Sport Haus, 1433 Mangrove (343-2673). Mountain bikes $3 per hr. (2-hr. min.), $20 per day. Credit card or $200 deposit required. Also rents packs, tents, and sleeping bags. Open Mon.-Fri. 10am-6pm, Sat. 10am-5pm.

Laundromat: Wascomat, 254 E. 1st St., at Wall. Wash 50¢, dry 50¢, detergent 35¢. Restrooms and change machine. Open Sun.-Thurs. 6:30am-10pm, Fri.-Sat. 6:30am-8:30pm.

Gay Crisis: National Gay Task Force, 800-221-7044.

Women's Help Center: 2nd at Chestnut St. (891-1911), next to visitor parking. Open Mon.-Thurs. 7am-4:30pm.

Rape Crisis: 342-7273.

Chico Community Hospital: 560 Cohasset Rd. (345-2411).

Emergency: 911.

Police: 1460 Humboldt Rd. (895-4911).

Post Office: Downtown Office, W. 5th at Broadway (342-7765). Open Mon.-Fri. 8:30am-5pm. **Main Office,** 550 Vallombrosa (343-5531). Open Mon.-Fri. 7:30am-5pm. General Delivery ZIP Code: 95926.

Area Code: 916.

Accommodations and Camping

Though the nearest hostel is 35 mi. east in Oroville, who cares? Chico offers an ample collection of clean, safe, cheap motels catering mainly to state university visitors. For outdoor sleeping, pick up a copy of the useful camping brochure available at the Chamber of Commerce.

Chico Motor Lodge, 725 Broadway (895-1877). A fine specimen of the motor lodge species—right downtown, but quiet, with a small pool and spacious, spotless rooms. TV and A/C. Singles $30. Doubles $35.

Thunderbird Lodge, 715 Main St. (343-7911). Only the ornate sign distinguishes it from the other clean and quiet Chico motels. Rooms of magnitude. Pool. Coffee maker in room, TV, and A/C. Singles $30, weekends $35. Doubles $32, weekends $37.

Western Travel Inn, 740 Broadway (343-3286). The requisite A/C, TV, and swimming pool are in the care of an engaging and eccentric manager. Slightly more run-down, slightly more expensive than the other motels in town. Singles $34. Doubles $35. Winter rates: singles $32, doubles $33.

Motel 6, 665 Manzanita Ct. (345-5500), accessible only by car. From Rte. 99, take Cohasset Rd. exit. Pool, A/C, TV—hey, haven't I been here before? Singles $25, each additional adult $6.

Haven Motel, 2212 Park Ave. (342-5704). Despite the pink renovations this "haven" is still a little frayed. A hike from the center of town, but it's quiet, inexpensive and unsullied. Singles $30. Doubles $35. No reservations.

Mountain View Mobile Acres, 3156 Esplanade Rd. (342-2989). The usual trailer park. Full hookup $12.

Black Butte Lake Campgrounds: 865-4781. Just east of town, beyond I-5. Take Rte. 32 west and follow signs to Rd. 200. RV and tent sites, with showers and flush toilets. Sites $6.

Food

Chico's families and students enjoy a wide selection of cheap, filling, not too thrilling eating spots. There are several large supermarkets, including a 24-hr. **Safeway** at 860 East Ave. A **farmers' market** is held in the parking lot at 3rd and Broadway every Thursday in July and August from 5-8pm.

Café Sandino, 817 Main St. (894-6515). Tongue-zapping, south-of-the-border cuisine. Their famous tamales ($4-5) are shipped and sold throughout the state.

Pi-Zon's Pizza Parlor, 305 Nord Ave. (342-8389). This family-run restaurant offers a "smorgy" on Tues. and Wed. evenings: for $4.75, scarf down all-you-can-eat pizza, salad, pasta, sausage, and the best lasagna for miles. Thurs.-Sun. medium pizza and 2 salads $11. Open Tues.-Thurs. 5-11pm, Fri.-Sat. 5-11:30pm.

Rubino's, 133½ Broadway (891-5140). Small cheese fondues from $3, salads from $3.20. Open Tues.-Fri. 11am-2pm and 5-8:30pm.

Oy-Vey's, 146 W. 2nd. St. (891-6710). Very popular hang-out. A personal street sign guides the frazzled wait staff to your table. Terrace-dining for breakfast or lunch. Charbroiled chicken with excellent homefries $5. Open Mon.-Sat. 7am-5pm, Sun. 7am-3pm.

Café Sienna, 158 Broadway (345-7745). While absorbing this small-town art deco experience, check out the cappuccino ($1.15) and pastries. Chocolate Obsession cake $3. Open Mon.-Fri. 7am-midnight, Sat. 8am-midnight, Sun. 8am-11pm.

The Graduate, 344 W. 8th St. (343-2790). A great beer-burger-pool table experience. Burgers with the works $3.75, Mon. only $2. Open daily for meals 11am-10pm.

La Salles, 229 Broadway (893-0226). Regular jazz evenings in the bar. Kick back on the patio with a drink, but go elsewhere for dinner. Open Mon.-Wed. 11am-11pm, Thurs.-Sat. 11am-2am.

Sights

Chico is somewhat lean on sights, but parks, pedestrianization, and an active effort to avoid being mauled by malls all make Chico a charming place to browse. **Books,** 337 Broadway, offers excellent secondhand bargains, and is a fine place to start. Open Sun.-Wed. 10am-7:30pm, Thurs.-Sat. 10am-6pm. Books from 35¢. Outdoors, there are Friday concerts in the Plaza from May to September at 7pm. There is a **Chico Museum** at 141 Salem St. (891-4336; open Wed.-Sun. noon-4pm; free), but history buffs would do well to head instead for the **Bidwell Mansion,** 525 Esplanade (895-6144), a classic Victorian home that did time as a college dorm until preservationists came to its rescue. (Tours are given daily on the hour from 10am to 4pm; admission $1, ages 6-17 50¢). A ½ mi. from the mansion is **Bidwell Park.** The 2400-acre monstrosity is the nation's third-largest municipal park and extends 10 mi. from downtown. It has served as a setting for several movies including *Gone With the Wind* and *The Adventures of Robin Hood.* Both the park and mansion were bequeathed to Chico by General John Bidwell's estate. Highlights include two pools, a deer pen, and a selection of hiking, biking, and rock climbing trails. Alcohol is prohibited in the park.

For a historic picnic, go 5 mi. east on Humbug/Honey Run Rd. to the Honey Run Covered Bridge. Built in 1894, it is the only three level bridge in the United States. Ooh la la.

Although **Cal State Chico** isn't the most architecturally stimulating of campuses, it has distinguished itself as a perennial favorite in *Playboy's* list of the Top Ten Party Schools. Chico's raucous fêtes rage mostly during the term (Oct.-May), but a party school of this caliber doesn't shut down in the summer (the university **information center** offers tours daily at 11:30am). **Rancho Chico Days** (formerly Pioneer Days) are notoriously wild, and they kick off the summer on the first weekend in May.

For the more sedate-at-heart, the **University Art Gallery,** in Taylor Hall on campus, swings open its portals to budding connoisseurs. (Open Mon.-Fri. 10am-4pm, Sun. 1-5pm.) In summer, children's amusements compete with livestock for your silver dollars at the agricultural **Silver Dollar Fair** (admission $3).

Adventure Outings, a non-profit service organization sponsored by Chico State, runs self-described "low-buck adventures," which are in fact student-led hiking ($5-10) and rafting ($19-24) trips. Prices include transportation and permit fees. Equipment rental is under $10. During the school year, these trips are only for Chico State students, but in the summer, they're opened to adventurers of all ages and walks of life—what a country! Sign up at the Accounting Office in Bell Memorial Union, or call 895-4011. (Office open Mon.-Fri. 11am-1pm)

Red Bluff

Midway between Chico and Redding, Red Bluff perches on a steep, brick-colored bank of the Sacramento River (hence its name). If you're driving through the valley, stop here for a little lunchtime R 'n' R at the City Park. If you're taking the bus, this is a good place to catch a comfortable and cheap night's sleep. Red Bluff serves as the subdued seat of Tehama County, a farming region containing some of the world's most fertile acreage. The approach to town wends its way through groves of olive, peach, and walnut trees. Even the kiwi, a recent and trendy import, has taken root in Red Bluff's soil.

Red Bluff sits in the physical and financial shadow of the colossal Lassen volcanic range that rises to the east. Lassen-bound visitors file through the town to make a quick stop for groceries and to spread their largesse among local shop owners. But the relationship between town and volcano has not always been so placid. In

1915, after hundreds of years of inactivity, Mt. Lassen exploded suddenly and spectacularly, showering millions of tons of ashes and tephra over the Northwest and bringing darkness to Red Bluff at noon. Since that time the carefully monitored volcano has returned to its millennia-long slumber and wisps of steam are the only reminders that the giant is merely snoozing. You may rest up in Red Bluff before the 40-mi. drive to the park without fear of witnessing a command performance of *The Last Days of Pompeii.*

Practical Information and Orientation

Visitors Information: Chamber of Commerce, 100 N. Main St. (527-6220). Usual brochures and maps. Open Mon.-Thurs. 8:30am-5pm, Fri. 8:30am-4:30pm.

Forest Service Headquarters: 604 Antelope Blvd. (527-2213). Open Mon.-Fri. 8am-5pm.

Greyhound: 1023 Main St. (527-0434), 5 blocks north of Antelope Blvd. Frequent service to: Redding ($5.85), Chico ($7.35), and Sacramento ($21). Terminal open Mon.-Fri. 9am-5pm, Sat. 9am-noon.

Mt. Lassen Motor Transit: 529-2722. Limited county service. Fare $2, seniors and disabled $1. Mt. Lassen bus leaves weekdays at 8am and arrives in Mineral at 9:50am; you have to hitchhike to Lassen itself. Bus leaves Mineral at 3:30pm and arrives at Red Bluff after 5pm. One-way fare $6.45.

Taxi: Red Bluff Taxi Co., 529-2219.

Car Rental: Antelope Auto Rental, 790 Antelope Blvd. (527-5003). $22 per day and 10¢ per mile. Must be 25 with credit card.

Public Swimming Pool: 119 Sycamore St. (527-7211). Admission 50¢. Open daily 1-4pm.

Laundromat: Launderland, in the K-Mart shopping center on Marin St. Wash 50¢, dry 25¢. Open daily 7am-10pm.

Weather: 527-0279.

Helpline: 246-2711. Crisis intervention, suicide counseling. 24 hr.

Senior Information and Referral: Area Agency on Aging 800-822-0109.

Hospital: St. Elizabeth Community, Sister Mary Columbia Dr. (527-2112), at Main St.

Ambulance, 527-0250.

Road Conditions: 225-3028.

Highway Patrol: 2550 N. Main St. (527-2034).

Police: 555 Washington St. (527-3131).

Post Office: 447 Walnut St. (527-2012), at Jefferson. Open Mon.-Fri. 8:30am-5pm. General Delivery ZIP Code: 96080.

Area Code: 916.

Orientation

Red Bluff straddles the multiple lanes of I-5 at its junction with Rte. 99 (running from the Sacramento Valley south through the San Joaquin Valley) and Rte. 36 (running from Lassen Volcanic National Park to the east). Greyhound and local bus lines all provide complete service to the town.

Red Bluff can be covered in a half hour of leisurely walking. **Main Street,** which runs parallel to I-5, dominates the commercial center. **Walnut Street** branches off from Main to the west and supports a smaller business district about ¼ mi. from the central area. **Antelope Boulevard** intersects Main 2 blocks south of Walnut and crosses the river east of town, where motels, fast-food joints, and campgrounds abound.

Accommodations

An assortment of motels shelter the tentless. None of the places listed below should require reservations. Nearby camping is plentiful if you have a car. Check the Chamber of Commerce (see Practical Information) for information on availability.

Triangle Motel, 1175 Montgomery Rd. (527-4542). A brief stroll out of town. Serene and immaculate. Phones, TV, A/C, pool. Singles $19. Doubles $24.

Mt. Lassen Motel, 256 Main St. (527-2525), 7 blocks from Greyhound. Lava-free swimming pool, A/C, TV, and waterbeds on request. Singles $22. Doubles $24.

Flamingo Motel, 250 S. Main St. (527-3545). Clean, comfortable rooms with A/C, HBO and TV. A waterslide graces the pool. Singles $25. Doubles $30. Two rooms can be had for $20 each. Reservations recommended for summer weekends.

Sky Terrace Motel, 99 Main St. (527-4145), across from the Chamber of Commerce. Not exactly the great wide open; small-fry rooms, but spic-n-span. TV, A/C, petite pool. Singles $21. Doubles $25.

Crystal Motel, 333 S. Main (527-1021). A basic motel, minus the pool. Cute country decor. No incoming calls after 11pm. TV and A/C. Singles $22. Doubles $24.

The O'Nite RV Park, 130 Gilmore Rd. (527-5868), just over the river on Antelope Blvd. The closest camping in town. A 15-min. walk from Greyhound (turn right onto Main, left onto Antelope, right onto Gilmore). Rugged tent sites give a thrilling highway vista. Pool, lounge, restrooms, showers, and laundry bring you closer to the great outdoors. Sites $8, hookups $16. Each additional person $1.

Diversion Dam Recreation Area (824-5196), 4 mi. southeast of town. Cross the river on Antelope Blvd. and walk east to Sale Lane. Go south on Sale Lane to the Dam area. Campsites at the mosquito-infested river's edge. Operated by Forest Service. $6 fee for a maximum of 10 days.

Food

Red Bluff offers a fair selection of cheap food, most of it the greasy-spoon variety. Rte. 9 blossoms with orchards and roadside stands selling fresh produce: peaches, apricots, kiwi, cantelope, and plums in summer; pistachios, almonds, walnuts, and apples in fall. You can also pick up fresh produce at the **farmers' market** (527-6220; open June-Sept. Sat. 8am-whenever they run out of produce (usually around 10am), down the street from the Chamber of Commerce in the K-Mart parking lot on S. Main St.

The Feedbag, 200 S. Main St. (527-3777). Nothing superlative, but plenty to fill you up. Rope in the Ranch-hand: 2 eggs, large hash browns, 4 sausages, and 4 slices of toast for $4.25. Bottomless cup o' coffee 60¢. Open Mon.-Sat. 6:30am-9pm, Sun. 7:30am-3pm.

The Snack Box, 257 Main St. (529-0227). Soups, salads, and homemade pies ($3-6) all served daintily in a pink and blue pastel house. Open daily.

Blondie's Diner, 604 Main St. (529-1668). Pretends to be a diner, but the chef-prepared food, extensive wine list, and glossy interior blow its cover. If you crave something more refined than Red Bluff's standard freeway fare, feast on Blondie's near-gourmet pastas ($5-11) or salads ($6-10). Open Mon.-Sat. 11am-10pm.

Sights and Seasonal Events

Like life itself, Red Bluff is more a way station than a destination. If you find yourself needing a rest stop on the freeway of life, try the self-guided car tour of **Victorian houses,** which starts at the Chamber of Commerce on Main St. and rolls by Red Bluff's most distinguished buildings. Follow the rusty blue signs. The **Kelly-Griggs House Museum,** 311 Washington St., built in the 1880's, "invites you to walk into a vanishing America" by following their guides through the renovated rooms of this Victorian mansion. Tell a friend your whereabouts lest you vanish too. (Open daily 2-5pm; in winter Thurs.-Sun. 2-4pm.)

On Adobe Rd., a few miles north of Red Bluff off Rte. 99, the **William B. Ide Adobe State Historic Park** honors the man who led the 1846 Bear Flag Rebellion. In a drunken fit, he "seized" the then-important town of Sonoma from equally drunk Mexican officials and declared California's brief independence. The rebellion has since been immortalized with the phrase "Beware the march of Ide." The home of the first and only president of California has been restored with traditional adobe bricks. (Open daily 8am-5pm. Free.)

In April, Red Bluff makes it into the record books with the **Red Bluff Roundup,** "the world's largest two-day rodeo." The four-day **Sun County Fair** in mid-July includes carnival rides and games, live music, street dances, horseshoe tournaments, and a fiery chili cook-off. Almost all the entertainment is free. The same venue hosts a **Bull Sale** in late January (527-2045).

Redding

Woody Guthrie wrote "This Land is Your Land" while in Redding in the 1930s. Anyone who spends any time in the dry dusty town will understand why Guthrie was so anxious to share the land—or even give it away. Located at the northern end of the Sacramento Valley, and flanked on three sides by national forests, Redding has nonetheless remained uncannily dry, barren, ugly and, during the summer, unbearably hot. For those with cars, Whiskeytown Lake offers the closest relief.

Red Bluff is fast becoming a retirement haven, with the number of people over 65 predicted to quadruple by 2020. Redding's population is growing annually at 6%. We can only ponder the unanswerable question: why do so many people want to live here?

Practical Information and Orientation

Visitors Information: Redding Convention and Visitors Bureau, 777 Auditorium Dr. (255-4100), ½ mi. out of town. Take Park Marina Dr. east, turn north on Auditorium Dr. Open Mon.-Fri. 8am-6pm, Sat.-Sun. 9am-5pm. **Greater Redding Chamber of Commerce,** 747 Auditorium Dr. (243-2541). The maps are better here, the brochures similar. Open Mon.-Thurs. 8:30am-5pm, Fri. 8:30am-4:30pm. Both can be reached on foot by walking up Butte St. and over the freeway at the Convention Center interchange.

Shasta-Cascade Wonderland Association: 1250 Parkview Ave. (243-2643), 1 block south of the Safeway supermarket, at Pine St. Regional tourist information emphasizing forests, parks, and recreation. Plenty of news on all of northeastern California. Over 100 brochures, yours for the taking. Open Mon.-Fri. 8am-5pm.

Shasta Lake Ranger District: 6543 Holiday Dr. (275-1587). Call for local conditions or camping restrictions. Open Mon.-Fri. 9am-4:30pm.

Municipal Airport: Airport Rd. (224-4321), off Rte. 44 southeast of town. **Airport Bus,** 547-5678. Fare to downtown $8. Last bus leaves the airport at 6:40pm.

Amtrak: 1620 Yuba St. (241-1494 or 800-872-7245). Unstaffed station; buy your ticket on the train or through a travel agent. One train per day south to Sacramento ($29) and San Francisco ($45); 1 per day north to Portland ($94).

Greyhound: 1321 Pine at Butte St. (241-2531), downtown. Buses south to Sacramento (9 per day, $22.80) and San Francisco (3 per day, $21); north to Portland (2 per day, $50). Terminal open 24 hr.

Redwood Empire Lines: 1525 Pine St. (241-3944). One bus per day connects Redding with the Pacific Coast at Eureka via a serpentine mountain highway (4 hr.; $16.50, round-trip $28.50). Open Mon.-Fri. 9am-6pm, Sat.-Sun. 11am-4pm.

Municipal Bus: "The Ride," (241-2877). Eight routes in and around Redding. Pick up buses on Placer St. in front of the downtown mall. Fare 60-75¢. Also has a disabled service 50¢; call 241-8295 for reservations. Buses run Mon.-Fri. 6:30am-6:30pm, Sat. 9:30am-6:30pm.

Taxi: ABC Cab, 246-0577. **Yellow Cab,** 222-1234.

Car Rental: A Rent-A-Car, 875 Hartnell (221-7368). $16 per day with 100 free miles, 10¢ each additional mile. Must be 21, with a credit card or a $100 deposit.

Road Conditions: 244-1500.

AAA Emergency Road Service: 243-1874.

Equipment Rental: CAMPS, 3495 Market St. (241-4530). Four-day rentals of tents ($25), backpacks ($10), and sleeping bags ($10). Open Mon.-Sat. 9am-7pm, Sun. 9am-5pm.

Helpline: 225-5252. 24-hr. crisis intervention and counseling.

Rape Crisis: 244-0117. 24 hr.

Gay and Lesbian Task Force Crisis Line: 800-767-4297.

Crisis Line for Handicapped: 800-426-4263. 24 hr.

Redding Senior Center: 243-3209.

Hilltop Medical Clinic, 1374 Hilltop Dr. (221-1565), across from the Mt. Shasta Mall. Non-emergency, ambulatory care. Open daily 9am-9pm.

Hospital: Redding Medical Center, 1450 Liberty St. (243-2341), downtown. 24-hr. emergency service.

Police: 1313 California St. (225-4200).

Emergency: 911.

Post Office: Downtown office, 1647 Yuba St. (246-5502). Open Mon.-Fri. 7:30am-6pm. **Main office,** 2323 Churn Creek Rd. (223-7502). Open Mon.-Fri. 7:30am-5:30pm. General Delivery ZIP Code: 96049-9998.

Area Code: 916.

Redding lies at the crossroads of I-5 and Rte. 299 and 44. Roads radiate towards Sacramento in the south, Mt. Shasta in the north, Eureka in the west, and Lassen Volcanic National Park in the east and your best bet is to get on one of them as soon as possible. If you're traveling by bus, don't bother stopping here unless you must.

Accommodations and Camping

Market Street is the "strip" along which the cheapest motels cluster. Sleeping-baggers will find campsites a few miles north of town in the Whiskeytown-Shasta-Trinity National Recreation Area. Primitive campsites dotting the area require free wilderness permits. Most have pit toilets and no showers. Pick up permits at park headquarters (241-6584), west of Redding on Rte. 299, by the Whiskeytown Reservoir. (Open daily 9am-4:30pm.) There is no public transportation to the campsites.

Shasta Lodge, 1245 Pine St. (243-6133). Fresh, airy rooms. HBO, TV, A/C, pool, and coffee in office. Singles $28. Doubles $32.

Stardust Motel, 1200 Pine St. (241-6121), 3 blocks from Greyhound. Trim and cozy, with a budget motel feel. Mid-sized pool. HBO. Check-out 10am. Singles $27.90-32. Doubles $32-8.

Saratoga, 3025 S. Market St. (243-8586), about 2 mi. from Greyhound. Shabby rooms with TV; a few have A/C. Free HBO. No phones in rooms. Yet it fills fast—this is life in Redding. Check-out 10am. Singles from $25. Doubles $32.

El Rancho, 3295 S. Market St. (241-5275). All rooms with TV. A few rooms with A/C. Most guests leave their doors open in the vain hope of attracting a breath of cool air. Pool. HBO. Well-worn rooms. Singles $25. Doubles $32.

Oak Bottom Campground, on Rte. 299 (241-6584), 13 mi. west of Redding on Whiskeytown Lake. 105 sites. Cold showers, but a predominance of tents rather than RVs lend these sites an aura more engaging than most. $10 for tents, $8 for RVs. No hookups. Mid May-mid Sept. Reservations recommended; go through Ticketron (800-452-1111).

Bailey Cove Campground, on Rte. 6 (275-1587), ½ mi. southeast of O'Brien town (which is about 15 mi. north of Redding). 29 sites. Pit toilets. No showers, but plenty of nearby swimming. Sites $6.

Cooper Gulch Campground, on Rte. 299 (623-2131), in Lewiston about 30 mi. west of Redding. Take Rte. 299 west to the Lewiston turn-off; go north for 4¼ mi. on Rte. 105 to Lewiston Lake. 14 sites. Pit toilets, no showers, and no drinking water, but plenty of swimming. Free.

Solus Campground, just off I-5 (238-2451), 20 mi. north of Redding. The best of the commercial camprgound experience. Laundry, pool, showers, general store, and full hookups available. Sites $12.50.

Food

Redding, the culinary *and* fast-food capital of the Shasta and Trinity areas, attracts residents from as far as Red Bluff to dine in its handful of classier restaurants. The **Safeway Market,** 1191 W. Cypress (241-4545), at Pine St, is less a regional highlight than a pragmatist's place to pick up fruits and cold cuts for a trip to Lassen or Shasta-Trinity. (Open 24 hr.)

Buz's Seafood, 2159 East St. (243-2120), behind the Safeway. An exemplary seafood store and restaurant with the air of a market and the aroma of smoked fish. When local police officers eat here twice a day you know it's good. Fish and chips $2-5. Charbroiled snapper and swordfish $5.50-8. Dungeness crab in season. Open Sun.-Thurs. 11am-9pm, Fri.-Sat. 11am-9:30pm.

Jack's Grill, 1743 California St. (241-9705). The best steak for miles merits a little bit of financial imprudence. 16 oz. steak dinner $15. A bar where your best plaid shirt or a slinky cocktail dress would be equally appropriate. Open daily 5-11pm for dinner, 4pm-when they feel like it, at the bar.

Sakura Sushi, 2130 East St. (244-0201), across from Kathy's Pies. Tasty Japanese entrees and California's official fast food, *sushi* ($2.50-10), in a soothing bamboo-filled atmosphere. Open Mon.-Fri. 11am-2:30pm and 5-9pm, Sat. 5-9pm.

Kathy's Pies, 1040 Locust St. (246-0484). Bakery with yellow and green tables and a warm environment. Great pies $6 each. Serving Redding for 26 years with everything sweet under the sun. Open Mon.-Thurs. 7am-5pm, Fri. 7am-6pm, Sat. 8am-3pm.

Post Office Saloon, in the Redding Mall (246-2190), downtown in the alley between Placer and Tehama St. Locals await silent Trystero's empire beside the old-fashioned post office boxes in the walls. But where's Oedipa? Bud $1.20. Live entertainment Fri.-Sat. 9pm-1am.

The Shack, 1325 Eureka Way (241-5126), 3-4 blocks north from Greyhound. No-nonsense, breakfast-heavy place. Hefty portions of eggs, bacon, and pancakes $2-4. Chicken-fried steak $3. Burgers $4.25 w/fries and salad. Senior specials. Tabletop jukeboxes. Open daily 6am-midnight.

Sights

If you came to Redding to do a little sight-seeing, you're in luck. There are *very* few sights to see. The **Redding Museum and Art Center,** located in pleasant Caldwell Park at 56 Quartz Hill Rd. (225-4155), exhibits North and South American Native artifacts, including an extensive woven-basket collection. One gallery rotates work by California artists. (Open Tues.-Sun. 10am-5pm; in winter Tues.-Sun. noon-5pm. Free.) There's also a **town trail,** highlighting, among other things, a fine WPA **fire house** at 1445 Butte St. and the art deco **Cascade Theater.** You can pick up a map, along with three self-guided tours of the historic architecture, at the visitors bureau.

Redding also boasts the "best-equipped planetarium north of the Bay Area." **Schreder Planetarium,** 1644 Magnolia Ave. at Placer St. (225-0251), simulates the movement of the stars (since Redding's roaring nightlife obscures the real thing) in a 33-ft. dome-ceilinged theatre.

On summer Sundays, the **Riverfront Park Summer Concert Series,** 700 Auditorium Dr. (225-4095), presents free live concerts in varying genres at 6:30pm.

Waterworks Park, 151 N. Boulder Dr. (246-9550), the Burney/Alturas exit off I-5 north of Redding, might cool off the overheated traveler with its 3 giant water-slides and "Wild White Water Inner Tube River Ride." Admission for ages 12-65 $11, 4-11 $9, over 65 free. Open Memorial Day-Labor Day daily 10am-8pm.

Other than that, that's it. Now go. Get out of town. Now. Go on, you heard me. . .

Whiskeytown-Shasta-Trinity National Recreation Area

Set aside by President Kennedy in 1960 and designed by the idealistic outdoorsmen of the time, this National Recreation Area encompasses three separate areas, each focused on its very own artificial lake. While the dams keep California thirsts quenched, the lakes and surrounding hills satisfy the leisure needs of hikers, campers, fisherfolk, and boaters.

In the southern part of the region, small towns such as Shasta, O'Brien, Whiskeytown, and French Gulch cater directly to tourists with everything from visitor centers to supermarkets. On weekends, sailboats and powerboats battle it out on **Shasta** and **Whiskeytown Lakes. Trinity Lake** to the north takes its natural heritage more seriously. Bereft of RV parks and superettes, it's set in unspoiled wilderness and ringed with dozens of hike-in campsites.

Whiskeytown is run by the National Park Service while the Shasta and Trinity regions are run by the National Forest Service, so you'll have to go to the appropriate office for camping/hiking information in your region.

Practical Information

See Redding and Red Bluff for other nearby services.

Visitors Information: Shasta-Cascade Wonderland Association, 1250 Parkview Ave. (243-2643), in Redding. The best place to go for information on the area. Open Mon.-Fri. 8am-5pm.

U.S. Forest Service: (serves Shasta and Trinity) area headquarters in Redding, 2400 Washington St. (246-5222). Open Mon.-Fri. 7:30am-4:30pm. District stations also blanket the area and are responsible for issuing wilderness permits. These can be ferreted out at McCloud (964-2184), Mt. Shasta (926-4511), Redding (275-1587), Hayfork (628-5227), Platina (352-4211), Weaverville (623-2121), and Big Bar (623-6106).

National Park Service, (serves Whiskeytown) on Kennedy Memorial Drive off of Rte. 299 (241-6584). Visitors Center with lots of brochures and helpful staff. Further down the road is the park headquarters where you can get camping permits. Open June-Sept. daily 9am-5pm, Oct.-May Sat.-Sun. 9am-5pm.

Shasta Lake Ranger Station, 6543 Holiday Rd. (275-1589), off I-5 just north of Redding. Extensive brochures, helpful staff. Camping/fishing info and permits. Open daily 9am-6pm, in winter daily 8:30am-4:30pm.

24-Hour Information Line: 275-1587.

Emergency numbers: 911. **Sheriff,** 225-5651. **Medical Emergencies,** 246-1111. **Fire,** 246-5234. All 24 hr.

Area Code: 916.

Orientation

The Whiskeytown-Shasta-Trinity National Recreation Area is located north of Redding on I-5 and west of Rte. 299. You won't be able to get to the Recreation Area unless you have a car. Everyone seems to agree on the need for public transportation to the area, but so far no one has done anything about it and don't hold your breath in anticipation of that changing.

Activities and Sights

The **Whiskeytown Unit,** 8 mi. west of Redding on Rte. 299, is the recreation area's most popular sector. It circles Whiskeytown Lake, an extensive artificial lake with diamond-clear water, satiny beaches, and **sail and powerboat rentals** at **Oak Bottom Marina** (359-2269), on the lake (canoes $2 per hr., paddleboats $1.50 per hr., 13' fishing boats $31 for 4 hrs., ski boats $117 for 4 hrs., 17' canoes $8 for 4 hrs., 14' sailboats $37 for 4 hrs.; open daily 7am-8pm). The **Visitors Information Center,** on Rte. 299 at JFK Memorial Drive (246-1225), on the eastern side of the Whiskeytown Unit, offers regular walks and talks, and even goldpanning on Saturdays and Mondays at 1pm. (Open daily 9am-5pm.) To the west, there are fine old buildings in **Tower House Historical District.** Whiskeytown is all very pretty, but it also tends to be mobbed on weekends.

The discovery of gold at nearby Reading's Bar in 1848 marked the birth of Whiskeytown and the death of Wintu Indian culture. After a brief boom, when townspeople were shipping out $100,000 worth of gold monthly, the town went bust. Today all that is left of the original Whiskeytown is its general store and cemetery.

Brandy Creek Campground is a parking lot for self-contained RVs only (no fee). The only developed campground facilities on the lake are at **Oak Bottom Campground.** Oak Bottom has restrooms and tent sites, as well as RV spots, but no hookups. ($10 tents, $8 RVs.) Off Rte. 299 (241-6584).

Backcountry camping is allowed at a distance of at least 1 mi. from the lake shore with a permit from the Park Headquarters (see Practical Info). However, wilderness seekers are advised to head north to Trinity Lake—most of the sites are only a short walk to the road and all are used heavily in the summer. No potable water, 14-day max. Stay from May-Sept. Some sites have pit toilets.

Just to the east of the unit is **Old Shasta,** 5 mi. west of Redding on Rte. 299, which once shone as the gold-mining and commercial center of the North Valley. Shasta eased itself into picturesque inefficacy and was rescued with historic landmark status in 1950. Admire the economy of the gallows' positioning just a few feet from the courthouse door. The **Courthouse Museum** (243-8194) is open Mon. and Thurs.-Sun. 10am-5pm, Wed. 10am-2pm (admission $1). Appreciating the ruins of this old town requires some creative vision.

The town bestows its name upon the **Shasta Unit,** and several other attractions. About 15 mi. north on I-5, slightly to the west of Project City, is **Lake Shasta Dam,** a mammoth Depression-era WPA enterprise. The towering dam is the centerpiece of the Central Valley Project that provides irrigation to areas as far south as Modesto. (An interesting 30-minute film on the Central Valley Project is shown daily 8am-4pm; in winter at 10am, noon, and 2pm. Call 275-4463.) The dam, the second tallest in the world, stands 602 ft. high, 3,460 feet long, and holds back up to 4½ million acre-feet of water in Shasta Lake.

The Lake itself used to provide plentiful fishing opportunities for those hoping to hook salmon, steelhead, rainbow trout and bass—that is, until a massive pesticide spill contaminated the lake in 1991. The long-term effects remain to be seen, but for a while at least fishing at Shasta has lost its appeal, with all the little creatures floating belly-up. About 10 mi. north of the dam on I-5 are the **Lake Shasta Caverns** (238-2341), the largest—although by no means the most spectacular—caverns in California. Limestone formations drip from ceilings and grow from floors. (Tours $10, ages 4-12 $5. Expensive, but some say the breathtaking bus ride up the mountain and boat trip to the caverns merit the cost. Tours daily 9am-5pm; Nov.-March at 10am, noon, and 2pm.) The Shasta Unit's **Rangers Office,** 6543 Holiday Rd. (275-1589) at the I-5 Mountain Gate/Wonderland exit, offers information on camping, trails, and facilities for the disabled. (Open daily 8am-6pm; in winter 8:30am-4:30pm.) There are more than a dozen campgrounds in the Shasta Unit area, some with flush toilets, some with oven pits, others with boat launches. Among the finest of these are, **Lakeshore** ($7 car, $5 walk-in), **Antlers** ($8), and **McCloud Bridge** ($6), and **Hirz Bay** ($8). **Jones Inlet, Beehive Beach,** and **Gregory Beach** have water and primitive camping for free. Information is available at the ranger station. There are self-guided nature trails in the unit, including **Hirz Bay** (just by the campground), and Samuel Cave (1 mi. south of McCloud Bridge campground). More ambitious is the 4.7 mi. **Dry Fork Trail,** which starts from the west end of Shasta Dam, and affords excellent views of the area. During times of high water demand and low supply, old roads and new inlets are exposed by the "draindown."

There are many other outdoor wonders near Lake Shasta. About 40 mi. north of the lake on I-5 is **Castle Crags State Park,** where granite towers rise tall and stark. There's a **campground** (235-2684) here, just 6 mi. south of the town of **Dunsmuir** on I-5, with fishing, swimming and showers. (64 sites, $5; call MISTIX for reservations). Ten mi. farther north the distant, immense, and solitary Mount Shasta (14,126 ft.) looms out of the mist. Subterranean **Samuel Cave** features limestone tunnels (about 10 mi. east on Gilman Rd. off I-5). Obtain a key to the entrance of the cave as well as a free parking permit at the Shasta Ranger's Station ($10 deposit).

The third part of the National Recreation Area is the **Trinity Unit.** The town of **Weaverville** (Chamber of Commerce 623-6101), 5 mi. south of the area is a convenient starting point for exploring the area. The town thankfully does not feign an 1850s atmosphere, like so many of its neighbors. The biggest tourist draw, **Joss House** (the name is a Chinese corruption of the Spanish word for God, *Dios*), is a Chinese temple in continuous use since 1874 that contains excellent exhibits on the Chinese immigrants' contribution to the construction of the western railroads. (Tours every ½ hr. 10am-4pm; $1). Next door, the **J.J. Jackson Memorial Museum** houses an understated presentation of local history. Don't overlook the grafitti scrawled on the walls of the jail cells during the Gold Rush. (Open May-Oct. daily 10am-5pm; April and Nov. noon-4pm.)

Leaving the off-road vehicles and powerboats of Shasta Lake and Whiskeytown Reservoir far behind, head north on Rte. 3 from Weaverville to the **Trinity Lake region** itself. Exploration of this wilderness area and of the even less developed **Salmon-Trinity Alps Wild Area,** in the unit's far northwestern corner might begin at **Trinity Center,** a small town on the lake 27 mi. north of Weaverville.

Before planning even a daytrip into the wilderness area, check the local conditions. Swollen creeks and icy slopes frequently carry the inexperienced to an unhappy fate. Overnight campers need wilderness and camping permits, available at the **Coffee Creek Guard Center** (266-3211), on Rte. 3, or the **Big Bar Station** (623-6106). Both stations can leave a permit outside for campers arriving after 5pm. In the southwest corner of the lake, campgrounds without running water are free. Ranger Station 623-2121.

Lassen Volcanic National Park

Until Mount St. Helens blew its top in 1980, the volcanic activity at Lassen was the most extraordinary in recent Western history. In 1914, the enlightened earth radiated destruction as tremors, lava flows, black dust, and a series of enormous eruptions continued over several months, climaxing in 1915 when the earth sneezed up a 7-mi.-high cloud of ashes which were dumped as far distant as Reno, Nevada. Protected by Congress in 1916, Lassen's forests, lakes, peaks, and sulfurous springs forcefully demonstrate nature's processes—both destructive and recuperative. And the cycle could begin again—scientists consider Mt. Lassen the West Coast volcano most likely to blow its top in this century.

Practical Information and Orientation

Visitors Information: Lassen Volcanic National Park Headquarters, Mineral (595-4444). Open daily 8am-4:30pm. **Manzanita Lake Visitors Center** (335-7575), at the northwest entrances. Open daily 8am-5pm. Wilderness permits available in Mineral and from ranger stations scattered within the park. In the event of after-hour **emergencies,** call 911 or 335-7373.

Hat Creek Ranger Station (336-5521), off Hwy. 299 in Fall River Mills. Open Mon.-Fri. 7:30am-5pm.

Mount Lassen Motor Transit: 529-2722. Transportation from Red Bluff to Mineral on a mail truck (Mon.-Sat. at 8am). Return trip leaves at 10:25am and 3:50pm ($6.45 one way). Hitch into the park from Mineral. Red Bluff bus leaves from the Greyhound station.

Road Conditions: 225-3028.

Weather Conditions: 246-1311.

Emergency: 911.

Post Office: in Mineral and Shingletown. Both open Mon.-Fri. 8am-4:30pm. General Delivery ZIP Codes: 96063 and 96088, respectively.

Area Code: 916.

Lassen Volcanic National Park lies about 50 mi. east of Red Bluff and Redding, and is accessed by Rte. 36 and 44. Route 89, running north-south, intersects both roads just before they reach the park and carries travelers through the scenic area. It is the park's only thru-road. **Mineral,** along Rte. 36, and **Shingletown,** along Rte. 44, are the "gateway" towns furnishing supplies along the park's western entrances. From the southeast (Susanville and the Lake Almanor area), take Rte. 36 west to the intersection with Rte. 89. **Chester,** the nearest spot for gas and supplies on the north shore of Lake Almanor, provides access to the Warney Valley and Juniper Lake area in the park's southeastern corner. To the northeast, the remote Butte Lake region is reached by a dirt road farther east on Rte. 44. (Admission to Lassen $5 per car, $2 per hiker or biker.)

Weather in the park is vastly varied. In some years, 20-ft. snow drifts clog the main road until July 4; other years witness an early melt, with the road clear again by April. It's wise to call ahead, except during July and August when all is sure to be clear.

Camping and Food

Because of the chance of rockslides and lava flows, there are few permanent structures in the park, much less motels or cabins; the nearest indoor accommodations are 12 mi. north in **Old Station.** Less costly motels can be found in **Redding** and **Red Bluff,** to the west, and in **Chester,** to the east. Fortunately, camping in the park is beautiful and abundant. But expect near-freezing night temperatures, even in August. The maximum stay is 14 days, except at Summit Lake, which limits visitors to one week. All sites are doled out on a first-come, first-served basis.

South Summit Lake Campground, in the middle of the park, 12 mi. south of the Manzanita Lake entrance. 52 sites. Very popular. Summit Lake's deep blue glitters through sparse stands of pine trees. Be sure to bring a sleeping mat, as the soil is rocky. Water, pit toilets, no showers. Sites $6.

North Summit Lake Campground, just north of South Summit Lake Campground. 47 sites. Identical views, identical facilities (except flush toilets here), identical crowding on weekends. Be on the lookout for deer. Sites $7.

Manzanita Lake Campground, just inside the park border, near the northwest entrance. 179 sites. Not quite as scenic as the Summit Lake spots. Water, toilets, and showers. Sites $8.

Juniper Lake Campground, on the eastern shore of Juniper Lake, 12 mi. north up a dirt road from Chester. 18 sites. Pit toilets, fireplaces, lake water only (must be boiled or treated for parasites). Free.

Southwest, near the entrance. A walk-in campground for those weary of waking to the sweet strains of their neighbor's mufflerless car. 21 sites. Those near most of the volcanic hotspots are seldom crowded. Sites $6. RVs may park in the nearby chalet car park for $3.

Butte Lake, off Hwy. 44, in the northwest corner of the park. The best access to Cinder Cone trail. 98 sites on the lakeshore. Water and toilets, but no showers. Sites $8.

Crags Campground, 45 sites used for overflow from Manzanita Lake. Piped water and chemical toilets among the pine trees. Sites $6.

Rim Rock Ranch, Hwy. 44 (335-7114), in Old Station. Housekeeping cabins complete with linens, utensils, pots and pans from $25 per day. Group rates for 4-12 people are $32-36 per day. Open April-November.

Hat Creek Resort, Hwy. 44 (335-7121), in Old Station on Hat Creek. Popular with hunters and fishermen. Housekeeping cabins $64-100 for two days. Trailer park with full hookups $15 per day.

Backcountry camping is allowed at least one mile from developed areas and roads, with a free wilderness permit available from the park headquarters. Fires are prohibited, as is the use of all soaps (including biodegradable ones) in the lakes.

Lassen National Forest surrounds the park, encompassing scores of developed campgrounds. A half-dozen, all with water and toilets but no showers, line Rte. 89 to the north for the first 10 mi. out of the national park. **Big Pine** is the closest (19 sites at $5). Of the remaining five, **Bridge** and **Cave** campgrounds ($7) have only trailer sites (but tents may be used if you don't mind bumpy ground). **Rocky** has eight free sites with limited parking that are suited for tent camping. Scenically, they are all roughly comparable (read: not too exciting). Two campgrounds sit on Rte. 36, a few miles from the park entrance. To the west is **Battle Creek,** to the east **Gurnsey Creek;** sites at both are $4. These spots are prettier than the ones up north, but not as remote. Lassen is a major logging region; hundreds of dirt roads criss-cross the forest. Choose one, pull off the road, and camp in a beautiful, isolated, and free location (fire permits required). When camping, keep all food locked in your car or suspended above ground at least 10 ft. as a number of hungry bears populate the area.

The cheapest way to sustain yourself is to buy groceries in one of the outlying towns and cook for yourself. The **Lassen Chalet** (595-3376) is a relatively inexpensive cafeteria-style restaurant and grocery store near the Mineral entrance at the extreme southwest corner of the park. (Open daily 9am-5pm.) There is often a park volunteer stationed at the Chalet to answer questions. At the park's opposite end, the **Manzanita Camper Service Store,** at the Manzanita Lake Campground (335-2943), sells overpriced groceries, souvenirs, fishing licenses, guides and maps. (Open daily 8am-8pm.) The store's hot showers next door are open from 8am to 9pm (25¢ for 3 min.). A laundromat in the same building charges $1 to wash, and 25¢ per 10 minutes of drying (open daily 8am-9pm).

Sights and Activities

Most sights in Lassen are accessible from Rte. 89. Drivers can pick up the informative *Lassen Road Guide,* a booklet keyed to roadside markers, at any park entrance ranger station ($2.50). The best photographic scenery stretches along the 18-mi. length of road from the southwest entrance to Summit Lake—precisely the section of road that is closed for more than half the year. A comfortable drive through the park (including a few stops) should take about 1½-2 hours.

Among the most intriguing sights is the steaming, bubbling witch's pot of **Sulphur Works,** near the southwest entrance (roadside marker #5). The pungent fumes arising from natural vents are the continuing burps of a vent system that once created an ancient volcano. **Emerald Lake** (#15), a bit farther north, shimmers for a bright green, icy-cold hundred yards around a snow-covered center. When Mt. Lassen erupted, most of the lava flowed down the southwest side of mountain. On the northeast face, slower-moving lava melted the snow, creating an enormous mudflow. Three days later, a hot blast of gas took the same route, forming the vast **devastated area** (#41, 44 and 50). Fallen trees and scarred trunks still mark the destruction, which is slowly healing. Scientists conduct research here in the hope of aiding the recovery of the Mt. St. Helens area.

Beginning at marker #17, about ½ mi. past Emerald Lake, the 3-mi. trip to **Bumpass Hell** wanders through part of the park's largest hypothermal area. Pick up a guide (30¢) to this nature trail at the trailhead. A moderate path ambles up a mountainside, providing views of Lassen and the lower peaks. Bumpass Hell itself is a massive cauldron of boiling, steaming water in which its discoverer lost his leg; to avoid any danger to your own life and limb, you'd be wise to stay on the trail. Despite year-round snow, the water appears to ever-boil at **Cold Boiling Lake** (4 mi. farther, closer to the Kings Creek trailhead also known as marker #32). **Boiling Springs Lake,** 1½ mi. from Drakesbad Lodge, remains a toasty 125° year-round. The Boiling Springs nature trail is about 2½ mi. long and usually takes 1½-2 hours to complete. Pick up a guide (30¢) at the trailhead. Use caution when hiking in this area and do **not** leave the trail. **Devil's Kitchen,** 1½ mi. from the Warner Valley Campground parking lot, simmers away in violently bubbling pools like a pot of stew on Satan's stove.

Mt. Lassen itself is the world's largest plug-dome volcano. Despite its height (10,457 feet), there's a relatively easy trail to the summit. From marker #22, it's a steep 2½-mi. trek to the peak. Allow four to five hours to climb up and down the mountain. Even if it's sunny and 90° at the trailhead, take along extra clothes (especially a windbreaker), suntan lotion, and water. Hiking in shorts and a T-shirt is initially apropos, but you'll be glad you thought ahead when you reach the cool, windy crest. The view is incomparable from the summit: the sun shines on thousands of snow-covered acres and the volcanic craters sweep down toward Emerald Lake. From here you can see 4 varieties of volcano. **Brokeoff Mountain,** nearby, has similar views. (Trail begins at #2). The round-trip here meets less traffic but still takes up to five hours.

Given the heavy year-round snow cover, much of Lassen is not suitable terrain for backpackers. Of the 150 mi. of trails (including a stretch of the Pacific Crest Trail), only the **Manzanita Creek Trail,** near Manzanita Lake Campground, and the **Horseshoe Lake** area east of Summit Lake are usually free of snow by mid-June. Both make enjoyable overnight sojourns. Manzanita Creek Trail parallels a lovely creek which runs through rolling woodlands that bear scant resemblance to the boiling and sizzling cauldrons to the south. The Horseshoe Lake area is rich in ice-cold lakes and impressive pine forests, where deer forage among a marvelous variety of mountain flowers and shrubs. A number of challenging day hikes cut through the area, with parking available near most trailheads.

By mid-summer, the shallow waters of Lakes Manzanita and Summit usually warm to swimming temperatures. Several lakes in the park (including Summit) are stocked with rainbow trout. The usual state license is required, and some areas may have additional rules (Manzanita, for example, has a "catch and release" policy).

Near Lassen

The three nearby wilderness areas are even less spoiled than Lassen, if that's possible. **Thousand Lakes Wilderness,** a few miles northwest of the park, is full of alpine scenery and virgin pine forests. Access is possible from dirt roads west of Rte. 89; you must tote maps, information, and a wilderness permit (free from any ranger station; Chester's, Mineral's, and Red Bluff's are closest). Nearby **Subway Cave,** stalled off Rte. 89 about ¼ mi. north of its junction with Rte. 44, invites exploration of its 1/3-mi. lava tubes. Bring a lantern or a strong flashlight. Just south of the Rte. 44 junction, the gentle **Spattercone Trail** traverses lava domes, tubes, blowholes, and 16 spattercones formed by gas eruptions during lava flows.

Bordering the park on the east is the second of the wilderness areas—the forest plateau known as **Caribou Wilderness.** The area's many lakes are trout-stocked. There are no roads which cross the wilderness boundary, so you'll have to hike in from the Hay Meadow, Caribou Lake, or Cone Lake trailheads. Finally, **Ishi Wilderness** consists of a series of canyons and lava plateaus.

Just outside Hat Creek on Rte. 84 is a **radio telescope observatory** (335-2364; open Mon.-Fri. 8am-5pm).

Forty mi. north of Lassen on Rte. 89 lies the **McArthur-Burney Falls Memorial State Park** and its magnificent waterfall. The ranger station, located in Burney (335-2777), divulges information on a more demanding destination: the **Ahjumawi Lava**

Springs State Park, accessible only by boating across Big Lake from a launch near the town of McArthur.

Aside from hunting, camping, and hiking, the Lassen area's biggest draw is water sports. Two huge lakes, **Almanor** and **Eagle,** lie to the east. Almanor is closer, uglier, and less crowded. Several privately owned campgrounds, as well as one operated by the Forest Service, line its southern shore. Eagle Lake, about 15 mi. northwest of Susanville, is more remote but also more pleasant. The Forest Service maintains over 400 oft-used sites on the south shore. **Eagle** and **Merrill** campgrounds, both about 19 mi. from Susanville, carry water and toilets but no showers (sites $7). **Christie,** farther down, has the same facilities, but is cheaper and less crowded (sites $6).

Mt. Shasta

For centuries, residents of this part of the world have believed that Mt. Shasta (14,162 ft.) possesses mystifying powers. Some maintain that an ancient white-robed brotherhood called the Lemurians (the survivors of a nation which foundered beneath the Pacific 400,000 years ago) dwell within the massive volcano. By contrast, the Shasta Indians, whose name purportedly originates from the Russian word "tchastal" meaning "white and pure," worshipped a Great Spirit whom they believe created and resided in the snow-capped volcano.

Even today, in the late 20th century, Mt. Shasta still draws all kinds of mystical followers. Adherents to the IAM religion, a group founded in the 1930's by Guy Ballard after he supposedly encountered the notorious 18th-century occultist St. Germain while hiking on the mountain, have a monastery here. And in 1987, thousands of New Age believers converged here to witness the great celestial event of Harmonic Convergence, which climaxed when a resident turned on her TV set and saw an angelic vision displayed on the screen.

However, spiritual questers are not likely to find a guru here: common advice to would-be disciples and climbers alike is to "go where the mountain calls you." Just as most residents in this town have struck their own paths in life, most also refuse to lead others down an already-beaten one. And travelers skeptical of the mountain's communicative abilities should sit a spell on Shasta's isolated, colossal, majestic, and snow-capped slopes—she just might choose to speak to you.

Practical Information

Visitors Information: Shasta-Trinity National Forest Service, 204 W. Alma St. (926-3781), 1½ blocks across the railroad tracks from the intersection of Mt. Shasta Blvd. and Alma St. Maps, information, fire permits, and knowledgable help. Outside, there's a trail register that climbers and solitary hikers should sign. Open daily 8am-4:30pm; Labor Day-Memorial Day Mon.-Fri. 8am-4:30pm. **Chamber of Commerce,** 300 Pine St. (926-4865), 1 block west from Shasta Blvd. Brochures covering Siskiyou County services. Open Mon.-Fri. 8am-5pm, Sat.-Sun. 10am-4pm.

Greyhound: 305 S. Mt. Shasta Blvd. (926-2620), in Marconi's Market. Three departures south and four north per day. To: Redding ($10), Sacramento ($30.30), and Portland ($50). Open daily 7am-8pm.

Amtrak: The nearest connection is 5 mi. south in **Dunsmuir.** 1 train per day north and south.

The Stage: 842-3531. Siskiyou County minibus transit between Weed, Mt. Shasta, and Dunsmuir. Fare between each town 90¢. Operates daily 6:30am-6pm.

Car Rental: Mount Shasta Cabins, 500 S. Mt. Shasta Blvd. (926-5396). $29 per day, 19¢ per mile. Must have car insurance and either a credit card or $200 deposit.

Equipment Rental: 5th Season, 426 N. Mt. Shasta Blvd. 96067 (926-3606). Sleeping bags $12 for three days, $8 each additional day; 2 person tent $22 for three days. Cross-country ski rental in winter. Bike rentals $12 for ½ day, $18 full day. Includes helmet and pump. Additional days $12. Open Sun.-Fri. 9am-6pm, Sat. 8am-6pm.

Senior Info: Golden Umbrella. Information and referrals to senior citizen agencies, 241-6623.

Library: Mount Shasta Library, 515 E. Alma St.

Laundromat: Mt. Shasta Laundromat, 302 S. Mt. Shasta Blvd., across from the post office. $1 wash, 25¢ dry. Open 24 hr.

Sexual Assault Crisis Center: 842-3232.

Information: 926-5555. 24 hr. snow report.

Missing Climber Notification: County Sheriff's office, 842-4141.

Hospital: Mercy Medical Center, 914 Pine St. (926-6111).

Police: 926-2345.

Emergency: 911.

Post Office: 301 S. Mt. Shasta Blvd. (926-3801). Open Mon.-Fri. 8:30am-5pm. General Delivery ZIP Code: 96067.

Area Code: 916.

Orientation

Mt. Shasta is located 60 mi. north of Redding on I-5 and about 50 mi. west of Lassen Volcanic National Park. If you're traveling by car, it's a convenient base for exploring Lava Beds, Lassen, Burney Falls, and the Shasta Recreation Area. The city of Shasta is easy to find from any direction—just head towards the giant mountain with the snow on top.

Accommodations and Camping

Motels exist here so that mountaineers can reapply a thin veneer of civilization to their wilderness-worn hides. Weary walkers, too exhausted by sun or snow to drive home, shower, crash, and buy postcards, while hippies emerge from their spray-painted vans for a night or two.

Alpenrose Youth Hostel (AYH), 204 Hinckley St. (926-6724). This beautiful chalet sits regally at the base of the mountain and is much nicer than any of the motels in town. An herb garden, sundecks, and a beautiful flower garden surround the dazzling interior. Magnificent manager. 12 beds. Members $9, non-members $11.

Das Alpenhaus Motel, 504 S. Mt. Shasta Blvd. (926-4617), at High St. The closest lodging to downtown. Although the pseudo-Swiss-chalet exterior is somewhat incongruous (you keep expecting Julie Andrews and the Von Trapp brood to pour out the front door at any moment), the motel is nonetheless often full. Ski boots and poles decorate the pinewood walls, lending the rooms a rustic country feel. TV, no phones. Some rooms with kitchenettes. (Singles $25 in winter, in summer $30.)

Pine Needles, 1340 S. Mt. Shasta Blvd. (926-4811). A few blocks south, and slightly tired-looking, though the decor does its best to blend in with the rocks on its roof. TV, no phone. (Singles $25. Doubles $32.)

Alpine Lodge, 908 S. Mt. Shasta Blvd. (926-3145). They have an economical family suite available for $79 if you're traveling in a group.

Mountain View Motel, 305 Old McCloud Rd. (926-4704), about 1 mi. south of Greyhound on Mt. Shasta Blvd.; turn left on Old McCloud at the Shell station. Remote and rarely full. Cute country cottages with kitchenettes & TV, no phone. (Singles $28. Doubles $30.)

Following Old McCloud Rd. south after the Mountain View Motel for a mile up a moderate grade, you'll enter the national forest. You can camp anywhere from May to Sept., but prepare yourself for cold nights. Go to the Forest Service office for wilderness permits (free) and directions to water sources.

Regular campgrounds (reservations not accepted) are clustered several miles from the national forest boundary, and there's no trailhead parking. To find campgrounds or parking, take Alma St. east from the forest service office. After approximately 2 mi. (toward the mountain), Alma St. intersects Everett Memorial Highway. Three mi. up Mt. Shasta on the highway, you'll find **McBride Springs** campgrounds on the left, with water and toilets but no showers. (8 sites; $6.)

Closer to town, the **KOA Trailer Park,** 900 N. Mt. Shasta Blvd. (926-4029), has tent sites amid the RVs (tents $14 for 2, $2 each additional person). **Lake Siskiyou Campground,** 4½ mi. southwest of town (926-2618), gives access to a beach, swimming, boat rental (paddleboats, motorboats, and canoes), and a coin-operated laundry. (Sites $9.) Flee I-5 via the Central exit (second off-ramp), follow Hatchery Lane a ¼ mi., then go south on Old Stage Rd. and W.A. Barr Rd. Beautiful **Castle Lake,** ½ mi. southwest of town, is primitive (toilets but no water or showers) and free, but there are only 5 sites. Freestyle camping is permitted more than 200 ft. from the alpine lake ½ mi. beyond the campground. **Gumboat Lake,** 20 mi. west on South Fork Rd., is the most isolated and has only 4 sites. The drive is long, winding through corkscrew roads, and the sites are primitive, but the lake is utterly serene. Bug repellent is a prerequisite.

Food

Shasta has a variety of grocery stores, although the only full-fledged supermarket is **Sentry,** 160 Morgan Way, in the mall across from the Chamber of Commerce. (Open daily 7am-10pm.) In summer a produce stand across the street provides cheaper and fresher fruits and veggies. The **Mt. Shasta Supermarket,** at the corner of Chestnut and E. Alma Sts., is another source of produce and supplies for a picnic or hike. (Open Mon.-Fri. 8am-8pm, Sat. 8am-7pm, Sun. 8am-6pm.)

Mt. Eddy Bagel Bakery and Café, 105 E. Alma St. (926-2800). Locals fill this place for breakfast, but you can drop by anytime for hugs and espresso ($1). Just feel the positive vibes in the air. Friday evenings feature live "music." Soup and their thick bread can make a meal ($3.50). (Open Sun.-Thurs. 6:30am-8:30pm, Fri.-Sat. 6:30am-9.30pm.)

Bellissimo Café and Baker, 204A W. Lake St. (926-4461), next to the railroad tracks. Shastans recommend this place for those seeking a gourmet (though expensive) meal. Don't miss their award-winning desserts.

Willy's Bavarian Kitchen, 107 Chestnut St. (926-3686). Serves up *Gulasch mit nudeln* (goulash with noodles) for $7.40 (*mit* soup or salad) out of a wood shack on the corner. Enjoy the Old World atmosphere sipping one of their many imported beers. Offers numerous vegetarian options. (Open 11am-9pm daily.)

Sights

In town, the **Mt. Shasta State Fish Hatchery** on Old State Rd. (926-2215), ½ mi. west of I-5, monitors the production of more than 5 million baby trout every year in the state's oldest facility. You can pet the fish. (Open daily 7am-7pm.) One of the buildings here is the **town museum** (926-5508), which shows surprisingly well-done exhibits on the area's geology and Native American and white settlement history. Pick up trail maps here and check out the seismograph for the likelihood that Shasta will blow in the next hour. (Open Mon.-Sat. 10am-5pm; Sun. 1-5pm; in winter Mon.-Sat. noon-4pm, Sun. 1-4pm.)

Don't forget to stop at the public drinking fountain downtown and taste the water. Mountain spring water gurgles into a spring southeast of town, supplying the city with H2O so pure it can be used, without treatment, as distilled water. Locals like to say "once they taste the water, they always come back"—and some link the water supply's chaste qualities to the profound spiritual energy of the place. Either that, or somebody upstream is raising a colony of addicts.

The area's main attraction, of course, is **Mt. Shasta** itself. This beloved stratovolcano was declared a National Wilderness Area in 1984, and is the home of at least five active glaciers. With avalanches in winter, rockfalls in summer, and unpredictable and fast-changing weather year-round, a summit climb is not for beginners. *Relatively* easy ascents, sometimes not requiring ice equipment, are possible during August from trailheads at the Ski Bowl, or Horse Camp (where there's a Sierra

Club Lodge)—both off the Everitt Memorial Highway. Most climbers take two days, camping overnight and beginning their ascent around 3am. (The record, though, is 1 hour and 39 minutes set by Robert Webb on July 5, 1985 using only ski poles and light hiking boots.) If you dare to climb, chat first with the amiable folks at **5th Season** (see Practical Information), and pick up a copy of their *Mt. Shasta Climber's Review* ($3.20), and other useful literature. You should also sign in at the Forest Service register before departure (and sign out on your return).

Even hikers following some of the more modest trails—**Black Butte** or **Castle Lake** to **Bradley Lookout**—should be sure to take extra clothing, since the weather is always unpredictable, and bring lots of drinking water, as stream water along the trails is uniformly non-potable.

If you prefer a less confrontational experience with the mountain, start at the **Golden Bough Bookstore,** 219 N. Mt. Shasta Blvd. (926-3228). Information about the latest New Age activities in the area is posted on the bulletin board out front. Improve your azura by stepping inside to peruse the far-reaching spiritual book collection and chat with the store's friendly owner, who can fill you in on most every local going-on. (Open Mon.-Fri. 10am-5pm, Sat.-Sun. 11am-2pmish.)

The **Everitt Memorial Highway** provides excellent views of the mountain and the area as it winds its way 13 mi. from Mt. Shasta to the now-defunct Ski Bowl resort and trailhead.

Nearby **Black Butte** is a far easier climb, though still steep and rocky. Take the Truck Village exit off I-5, head east to the end of the block, then take a right and follow the road to the trail. The 2.6-mi. trail to an old fire lookout (only the foundation remains) should take 1-1½ hours each way, winding the tight curves up this volcanic dome.

The ranger station carries information on many other hiking trails in the area. The 9-mi. **Sisson-Callahan National Recreation Trail** offers great scenery and follows a route taken by 19th-century trappers and prospectors. Take the Gazelle exit off I-5 north of Weed and then turn right onto Hwy. 99. Follow this ½ mi. and turn left on Stewart Springs Rd. When you meet Forest Rd. turn right. Ten mi. later, you'll reach Parks Creek Summit, where you can join the **Pacific Crest Trail,** or go 2 mi. further to **Deadfall Lakes** to start your hike. Walking from Parks Creek Summit to Lake Siskiyou is at least a day-long trip for the average hiker. Bring water and beware unexpected weather. The trails to **Toad Lake** and **Porcupine Lake,** are also worth a walk. Contact **McCloud Ranger District** (964-2184) for more information.

Ten mi. east of Shasta, off Rte. 89 near McCloud, lies **Medicine Lake,** a volcanic cornucopia of lava flows, deposits, cones, faults, craters, and even an ice-cave.

In winter, cross-country skiing is popular throughout the region; ski season runs from mid-November to mid-April. A debate has raged in the area in recent years over proposals to develop a new ski area. Although increased tourism could help Shasta financially, many residents feel lift lines and lodges have no place on such a sacred and beautiful mountain. Whatever your opinion, development has been stalled indefinitely, so don't bother bringing snowbunny suit.

IAM Monastery stages a unique "life of Christ" pageant annually on the 2nd Sunday in August. Contact the IAM Reading Room (926-2525) for more info. Every February, Mt. Shasta sponsors the **Alpenfest,** a nordic Mardi Gras of snow sculptures, yodeling contests, and dogsled races. July 4 ushers in the biggest small-town foot race in California. And everyone do-si-does when the **Blackberry/Bluegrass festival** shuffle-steps into town on Labor Day.

Lava Beds National Monument

You probably won't be impressed by your first view of the Lava Beds National Monument. Driving in off a dusty access road (there is no public transportation here), acres of flat, dry, barren land, broken only by a few scrubby grasses, stretch out in front of you. But beneath this deceptively empty-looking land lies a complete network of lava-formed caves unlike anything else on earth: cool quiet and sometimes eerie, the lava beds range from intricate drag-yourself-through tube-size to awe-inspiring cathedrals. And since the beds are inconveniently located a significant distance from the interstate highway, the uncrowded trails, caves and campsites leave you plenty of time and space to explore at your own pace.

The human history here is almost as violent as the massive eruptions that formed the caves. The fertile regions around Lava Beds had been the home of the Modoc Indians for hundreds of years when white settlers arrived in the 1850s. In 1872-3, the beautiful area became the site of the Modoc War, the most costly conflict between U.S. troops and Native Americans. Earlier, the Modocs had been forcibly moved onto a reservation with the rival Klamath tribe, but they returned to reoccupy their homeland in 1872. The U.S. army arrived to drive them out again, but the Modoc chief, "Captain Jack," and 52 of his warriors held their ground against up to 2500 U.S. soldiers for over 5 months, making use of the natural fortifications of the lava beds.

Today, the neglected Lava Beds monument offers historical sights, wildlife, and an impressive natural environment of easily accessible caves and black lava beds. In spring and fall, nearby Tulelake is home to thousands of migratory birds, some of which have come from as far away as Siberia. The fall migration is particularly spectacular, with 1 million ducks and half a million geese literally darkening the sky. In winter, this area is also the best place in the lower 48 to sight a bald eagle.

Pick up free maps from the well-informed staff at **Lava Beds Visitors Center,** 30 mi. south of Tulelake on Rte. 139 (667-2282), and don't miss the exhibits (including videos) on geology and history. (Open daily 9am-6pm; Labor Day-June 15 8am-5pm. Admission $3 per vehicle.) The **area code** for the region is 916.

Orientation

The park has two entrances, both located off Rte. 139 south of the farming community of **Tulelake** (TOO-lee-lake). The southeast entrance (25 mi. south of town) is closest to the visitors center. The center has exhibits on Modoc culture and a short slide presentation on the war. The park staff also lends out heavy-duty **flashlights** (they are free and must be returned by 5:30pm) to cavers. The road to the northeast entrance leaves Rte. 139 about 4 mi. south of Tulelake. For 25 mi. it winds through the wilder northern areas of the monument before reaching the visitors center. You'll want to spend at least a half-day in the park (perhaps more, depending on your subterranean nerve), and you'll need a car or bike to see the northern areas. The cave areas are clustered around the visitors center and are accessible on foot. The nearest spot to catch a bus, rent a car, or find a hospital is all the way across the Oregon border in Klamath Falls, 30 mi. north of Tulelake. Alternatively, Chico, Redding, and Red Bluff are within a lava flow or two of the monument. There is no public transportation to this remote area and hitchhiking is difficult.

Accommodations and Food

The best place to spend the night in Lava Beds is at the **Indian Wells Campground** (667-2283), opposite the visitors center. Drinking water is available and there are slide shows Thurs.-Tues. at 9pm (40 sites, $6). **Modoc National Forest** hedges in the monument on three sides. The most accessible campground in the forest is at **Howard's Gulch,** 30 mi. south on Rte. 139. Here you'll find 11 quiet sites (for free). Off-road camping in the national forests is also free. Nearby are **Medicine Camp** and **Hemlock** ($5 each). More information on campsites is available at the **Modoc National Forest Doublehead Ranger Station,** 1 mi. south of Tulelake on Hwy. 39. (Open Mon.-Fri. 8:30am-4:30pm).

Tulelake's **Ellis Motel** (667-5242), 1 mi. north on Rte. 139, has clean rooms and is rarely full. Singles $24. Doubles $27. Just south of town, also on Rte. 139, is the **Park Motel** (667-2913). Singles $27. Doubles $29. **Jack's,** at Modoc Ave. and Main St. (667-2612), is the only thing in town resembling a supermarket. (Open Mon.-

Sat. 8am-8pm, Sun. 9am-6pm.) **Captain Jack's Stronghold Restaurant** (664-5566), 5 mi. south of Tulelake, at the turn off to the Lava Beds (664-5566), serves homemade soups and breads. (Open Mon. 7am-3pm, Tues.-Sat. 7am-9pm, Sun. 10am-7pm.)

Sights

Start your spelunking (to the uninitiated, this means crawling around in caves) at the **Mushpot Cave,** in the visitors car park. This clean, well-lit cave features exhibits on the area's geology. Next, stop at the visitors center for a giant flashlight (2 per party) and a copy of *Lava Beds Underground* ($1.25), which diagrams in detail the 19 caves open to the public. You can also pick up a plastic helmet ($2.50), an investment that your forehead will appreciate.

After that, you're on your own—it's just you and your flashlight. No matter how hot it is outside, underground it's always cool and slightly damp—take a sweatshirt or jacket. On the 3-mi. **Cave Loop,** starting and finishing at the visitors center, there are 13 caves with little more to guide you than an entrance stairway and sign. But lava caves are usually single rocky tubes, so confusing side passages are rare. Just remember to exercise some Daedalian foresight and be consistent—keep taking the left (or right) fork where one occurs, or tie one end of a spool of twine to a fixture at the entrance and unravel it as you go. The highlights of Cave Loop are **Golden Dome** and **Labyrinth.** Less popular but more interesting are **Skull Ice Cave** (35° a few miles north) and **Valentine's Cave** (a favorite of those who know the area, a few miles south). You're allowed to explore caves alone, but don't. Always take two flashlights and a friend. For those wanting a hand in the dark, ranger-led cave tours leave daily at 2pm, except Wednesday. Also when spelunking, don't pet the rodents as bubonic plague has been reported in this area. And try to avoid the rattlesnakes lurking in the darkness.

Two mi. north of the visitors center is **Schonchin Butte.** The 15-20 minute trail leads you to a working fire lookout that gives a broad view of the area. Farther towards the monument's northern entrance is **Captain Jack's Stronghold,** the natural lava fortress where Modoc warriors held back Colonel Wheaton's troops. There's an excellent self-guided trail through the area (maps 25¢). Just outside the northern entrace is **Petroglyph Point,** site of one of the largest collections of carvings in California, some of which date back to the first century AD. The images in the ancient rock are astoundingly vivid. **Fern Cave** contains underground carvings; on display by appointment only (contact the Lava Beds visitors center).

The monument encloses two undeveloped **wilderness areas,** one on each side of the main north-south road. A wilderness permit (free) is required for braving these desert places. Cooking is limited to stoves, and you must camp at least 100 ft. from trails. Don't worry about camping too near a stream—there aren't any. There is, however, plenty to explore, including over 200 lava caves whose locations have not been made known to the public in order to preserve them. **Klamatch Basin National Wildlife Refuge,** visible on the drive from Tulelake to Lava Beds, is a birdwatcher's Oz, teeming with waterfowl. For more information, contact the refuge manager in Tulelake (667-2231).

In Tulelake you can check out the **Japanese Internment Camps** where more than 18,000 Japanese-Americans were held by the U.S. government during World War II. In the nearby town of Newell the camps have been left undisturbed since their closing on March 20, 1946.

Since 1990, the 3rd weekend in July has been reserved at the Lava Beds for a Native American festival. More than 25 tribes gather in this area, which is thought to have been one of the largest and oldest centers of Native American civilization. The celebration climaxes with the smoking of a traditional peace pipe. The public is welcome to attend.

The Mother Lode

They came in search of gold, and they found it. Well, at least a few of them did. After John Sutter's assistant James Marshall stumbled across a nugget in 1848, word spread fast. Some 90,000 49ers from around the world left their families and headed for California and the 120 miles of gold-rich seams called the Mother Lode. In fact, few of the prospectors struck it rich. Living in a shantytown or tent city and working long hours, a miner might hope to squeeze an ounce a day from his fiercely guarded claim. The odds in Vegas are better than those facing 49ers hoping to strike it rich.

Before long a few women, mostly prostitutes and moral reformers, arrived to offer their respective services, but only slowly did families reunite and construct any semblance of household life in gold country. The few *nouveaux riches* built exuberant Victorian mansions, while many thousands more lived a hand-to-mouth existence through boom and bust.

Five years after the big discovery, the panning gold was gone, and miners could survive only by digging deeper and deeper into the rock. All but a few mines were abandoned by the 1870s, along with most of the towns that had sprouted parasitically around them. Some were repopulated when new industries arose, or when it became possible to commute from homes in the hills to nearby cities with stronger economic bases. A few of the old mines have since been reopened, using sophisticated chemical processing techniques to reclaim gold from the discarded ore of previous decades.

These days, the towns of the Mother Lode are once again delirious with gold fever—but most have a different object in their sights. These towns gussy themselves up as "Gold Rush towns" and now actively bait tourists traveling along the appropriately numbered Rte. 49, which runs through the foothills connecting dozens of small settlements. The area called the Mother Lode extends from Jamestown in the south to Nevada City in the north. On your way through the region, stop to spend some time seeing the odd reconstructed town, gold museum, and river bluff where so much gravel was panned for such little reward. The Mother Lode is perhaps better appreciated for the contemporary outdoor recreation opportunities it offers than for its exploitative recreation of history.

Sonora and Columbia

Sonora and Columbia together once ranked among the most prosperous and colorful of the old mining towns. The two cities were fierce rivals during the Gold Rush, each striving to top the other's gold production and become the richest city in the southern Mother Lode. Since that time, however, they have taken divergent paths. Sonora, named after Sonora, Mexico, is a modern town, and reminders of its mining past are increasingly scarce. By contrast, Columbia, just off Rte. 49 to the north of Sonora, is an historic park, a reconstructed Gold Rush town with a carnivalesque atmosphere. The saloons sell sasparilla, and the "working" blacksmith's shop rarely sees a real customer, meeting the rent by selling engraved horseshoes to tourists. In contrast to the cheez-wizardry of some other towns, Columbia's historic park has been done with some grace, and actually can be fun.

Practical Information

Visitors Information: Tuolumne County Visitors Bureau, 55 W. Stockton St. (533-4420 or 800-446-1333), in Sonora across from the Sonora Inn off Washington St. Lots of brochures and helpful stuff. Open Mon.-Fri. 9am-5pm, Sat.-Sun. 10am-3pm. **Chamber of Commerce** (532-4212), in the same building. **Yosemite Junction Visitors Bureau,** at the junction of Rte. 108 and 120 (948-4636). Open Memorial Day-Labor Day daily 10am-6pm.

Local Transportation: Tuolomne County Transit, 532-0404. Buses throughout the Mother Lode, except for Groveland. Call for schedules, routes and fares.

Taxi: Mother Lode Cab 533-1759, local and long distance. Jump start service.

Equipment Rental: Sonora Mountaineering, 173 S. Washington St. (532-5621), in Sonora. Head to the back for top-quality equipment (rented and sold). Standard sleeping bags—all you should need in the warm dry summers ($6 per day, 2 day minimum). External frame packs (same rate as bags); internal frame models ($18 for 2 days, $6 each additional day). Tents start at $17 per 2 days. Credit card deposit. Equipment reservations recommended. Open Mon.-Sat. 9:30am-6pm, Sun. noon-6pm.

Laundromat: F/C, 148 W. Stockton (532-8820), next to Sav-Mart on Rte. 49. A/C—a real boon in summer. Wash $1, dry 25¢. Open daily 6am-10pm.

AAA Emergency Road Service: 532-4117.

Mother Lode Women's Crisis Center, 101 Pine St. (532-4707), in Sonora. 24-hr. confidential crisis line. Occasional women's group meetings.

Senior Information: Area Agency on Aging 532-6272; **Senior Activities Line** 533-2622.

Tuolumne County Suicide Prevention Line 533-4357. 24 hr.

Crisis Intervention Line: (800) 444-9999.

Hospital: Tuolomne General Hospital, 101 Hospital Rd. (533-7100), in Sonora. 24-hr. emergency service.

Emergency: Dial 911. If no emergency, call: **Police** 532-8141, **Sheriff** 533-5815, **Forest Fire** 532-3671.

Post Office: 781 S. Washington (532-4304), in Sonora. General Delivery ZIP Code: 95370. Open Mon.-Fri. 8:30am-5pm, Sat. 10am-2pm. In Columbia, 11259 Jackson St. (532-7557). Open Mon.-Fri. 8am-4pm.

Area Code: 209.

Accommodations and Camping

Hotels and motels in town are expensive year-round. While the visitors bureau has a price list of motels throughout the county, it's best to head for the numerous campgrounds that ring Sonora. If you don't have a sleeping bag, you can rent one at Sonora Mountaineering (see Practical Information).

Columbia Gem Motel, 22131 Parrots Ferry Rd. (532-4508), 3 mi. north of Sonora on Rte. 49. Tiny, dark, but tastefully furnished cottages. Winter rates $35 for 1-2 people. Larger rooms $60. A/C, TV, bathtubs, coffeemaker in room. Make reservations one week in advance.

Columbia Inn Motel, 22646 Broadway just before the entrance to the park (533-0446). Clean, capacious rooms and a pool. Rooms for 1-2 people $46, $41 in winter. A/C, TV.

49ers Trailer Ranch, 23223 Italian Bar Rd. (532-9898), in Columbia. Convenient to the state park and quieter than most, but fairly expensive: $17 50 per site for 2 people and $2.50 per additional person. Amiable owners are full of factoids.

Marble Quarry RV Park, 11551 Yankee Hell Rd. (532-9539). Just past Columbia Park—follow the camping signs. Laundry, showers, and a heated pool. 85 sites, $17 a night.

No less than 10 campgrounds—some public, some commercial—are linked to Rte. 120, southeast of Sonora. They are all between 20 and 35 mi. from town on the road to Yosemite. The closest is **Moccasin Point** (989-2383), 6 mi. east of Chinese Camp off Rte. 120 in the Don Pedro Reservoir area. (Water, toilets, and showers. Tent sites $12, RV hook-up $15.) The other campgrounds, farther east on Rte. 120, are a hair-raising drive up the Old Priest's Grade between Moccasin and Groveland. **The Pines,** 2 mi. west of Buck Meadows, is administered year-round through the U.S. Forest Service. The 12 sites ($7) have water (May-Oct. only) and toilets, but no showers. The visitors bureau can give you a crude map of the area.

Food

Columbia, with its draft sasparilla, ice cream, and cotton candy, will spoil your appetite for the real food (i.e. sandwiches and groceries) to be had in Sonora. Check the *Union Democrat Weekend Guide* for church suppers and fund-raising pancake breakfasts—often the best and cheapest food around. To stock up for a nice picnic at Coffill Park on Sonora's Washington St., head for the 24-hr. **Safeway** in town, 659 Washington St., or the **Sav-Mart** on Rte. 49 just off Washington St.

Wilma's Café, 275 S. Washington St. (532-9957). Wilma is *not* the sweet stooped lady who makes the delicious pies ($2.15 a slice)—she's the wooden pig sitting on top of the pie case. Other pigs, especially the winged variety, can be found throughout the store. Early risers should take advantage of the Workers Weekday Special: 2 eggs, hash browns, bacon and toast for $2.49. Dinner entrees $8-10. Burgers $4.50-5.75. Wendy's (the real owner) specialty is the secret-ingredient tangy barbecue sauce that is slathered over tasty smoked meats. (Just hope it's not Wilma.) Open Sun.-Thurs. 6am-10pm, Fri.-Sat. 6am-midnight.

Mr. Hot Dog! 147 S. Washington St. Sonora (533-3008). The sign out front says Wee Kitchen—but inside 2-ft.-high letters spell out the correct name, complete with exclamation point, in case you're confused. A dozen varieties of dogs (cheese $2.15), and yummy milkshakes ($2.50). Open Mon.-Sat. 10am-6pm.

Hemingway's Café and Restaurant, 362 Stewart St. (532-4900). He walked in and sat down at a table. A past lover with whom he occasionally got tight had told him that the food was good. The Spanish waiter took his order, and he wired his office in New York to pay for it ($9-12). He ate, staring out the window and thinking of the Italian Alps, the African savannah, an Indian camp in Michigan. The jazz music reminded him of that rainy winter in Paris when he had written that lousy poetry. It seemed a very long time ago. He asked himself, "What the hell am I doing in Eastern California?" Perhaps he would return the next day for lunch ($8-10). Maybe he'd go fish instead. Open Tues.-Sat. 11:30am-2:30pm and 5pm-closing, Sun. 11am-2pm and 5pm-closing.

Hong Kong Restaurant, 267 S. Washington St. (532-1544). A dive, but at least it's cheap. Dinner for two with soup, fried wonton, egg roll, sweet and sour pork, cashew chicken and pork fried rice $6.50 per person. Special plates with three dishes are $4-5. Open Mon.-Thurs. 11:30am-9pm, Fri. 11:30am-9:30pm, Sat. 12:30-9:30pm.

Sights

Some of Sonora's buildings still appear much as they did when the town was the main supply post for thousands of miners in the area. The most distinguished houses cluster around Washington St. and on Novlin, which runs 1 block parallel. At the west end of Washington St. stands little red **St. James Episcopal Church** (1860), California's second-oldest Episcopal church of frame construction (by the way, this piece of information has officially been awarded the 1991 PWACH Most Ridiculous Attempt At A Superlative Award). Religion being a bedfellow of riches, across the street is a matching red building, the ornately domed **Street-Morgan Mansion** (1896), erected by local attorney Frank Street for his wife, Ada Bradford. At 42 S. Washington, the gaudily domed **Bradford Building,** lures visitors in through the fine copper doors. The Chamber of Commerce has a map showing locations of other historical homes. Near the chamber is the **Tuolumne County Museum,** 158 W. Bradford Ave., which served as a rather flimsy county jail until 1961 and now displays 19th-century memorabilia. (Open Mon., Wed., and Fri. 9am-4:30pm, Tues., Thurs., and Sat. 10am-3:30pm.) There are concerts in Courthouse Park July-August (532-2787).

Sierra Mac, based in Sonora, runs river trips down the Tuolumne and American Rivers with rapids up to Class V. One-day trips start at $85. Call 532-1327 or 800-457-2580 for information. **Sierra Adventures** (also in Sonora; 800-351-5041) leads rafting and backpacking trips through the region. Their shuttle will pick you up from the Bay Area, Stockton or Bakersfield ($40). Trips run the gamut from $15-675.

Sonora has one sonorously named **Wild West Film Fest** (533-4420) in Sept. and a sonorous 4-day **Bach Festival** (532-3120) in October.

North on Rte. 49 lies Columbia and the **Columbia State Historic Park** (532-4301), the most realistic reconstruction of a Gold Rush town in the Mother Lode. In the spirit of authenticity, automobiles are banned from the park and routed instead to large parking lots on the southern and western sides of town. (Park open daily 8am-5:30pm.) Several of the renovations are fascinating, despite your paranoid suspicion that a fudge shop lurks around every corner. Most reconstructed buildings are furnished à la Gold Rush era. The visitors center (532-4301) has useful free guides. Among the more interesting exhibits, a blacksmith's shop presents a smithy at work, and an old-time dentist's office plays a tape recording of an average 19th-century checkup—the patient was sent to the saloon for a post-op pain-killer. (Open daily 8am-5pm.)

The **Columbia Historical Museum,** at Main and State St., is a tastefully presented and instructive exhibition of Gold Rush history. The free slide show is interesting and brief. (Open daily 8am-5pm; showings hourly 11am-3pm.)

The main parking lot of the historic **City Hotel,** on Columbia's Main St. (532-1479), is sunk below ground as a result of hydraulic mining, a process in which desperate miners blasted away hundreds of square feet of soil with a water cannon in their furious quest for gold. For obvious reasons such techniques were soon outlawed.

In the park, the **Fallon House Theatre** has been entertaining locals and tourists for 140 years (at the southern end of the park, 532-4644). Tickets $6.50-11, but after 7:30pm they all go on sale for $5. Shows Thurs.-Fri. and 8pm, Sat. 2pm and 8pm, and Sun. at 2pm.

You can get robbed—and not lose much—by taking a 15-minute **Columbia Stage Line** trip, which includes a guaranteed hammy hold-up. (Open daily 10:30am-4:30pm, Labor Day-May Sat-Sun. 10:30am-4:30pm. Fare $3.50, seniors and children $3.) **Guided gold mine tours** leave daily at 10:30am from the Gold Mine Supply Store, where any findings can be sold upon return (532-9693).

Columbia has a number of its own annual celebrations including the humorous **Poison Oak Show** in Sept. (532-4301) and the **Fiddle and Banjo Contest** in Oct. (532-4301).

Walking around the dusty streets and picayune shops, you'll find it hard to believe that Columbia was once the 2nd largest city in California.

Stanislaus National Forest

Blanketing almost 900,000 acres, Stanislaus National Forest corners the market on national forest virtues—well-maintained roads, astonishing scenery, and acres of solitude. The dozens of cool aquamarine lakes in this area are surrounded by acres of Ponderosa pines, red and white fir trees, wildflower meadows and a number of well-planned campsites. Peregrine falcons, bald eagles, spotted owls, mountain lions and bears sometimes surprise the (un)lucky traveler. Although the excellent campgrounds and myriad activites (most coordinated by the Forest Service) make this region popular with tourists, space remains for solitary wandering. Stanislaus is divided into four ranger districts (Mi-Wok, Summit, Calaveras and Groveland) and three wilderness areas (Mokelumne, Emigrant, and Carson-Iceberg).

The **park headquarters** (532-3671, for 24-hour recorded information 532-9784), at 19777 Greenly Rd., in Sonora, sells fine maps for $2. (Open Mon.-Fri. 8am-5pm.) The **Mi-Wok Ranger Office,** on Rte. 108 in Mi-Wok Village (586-3234), administers the area closest to Sonora. (Open Mon.-Sat. 8am-5pm.) Not the prettiest area of the park, Mi-Wok's trails are mostly undeveloped. Hull Creek Campground, 12 mi. east of Long Barn on Road 3N01, has drinking water, tables, pit toilets, and 11 sites all in a secluded meadow—at no charge. Camping is available from May-Oct.

To the east along Rte. 120 lies **Summit Ranger District,** at Pinecrest Lake (965-3434), the forest's most popular spot. Several campgrounds surround the lake, and the trails in the area suit almost everyone's taste. Rangers lead many hikes and information sessions daily, several for children. Pick up a free copy of "The Summit

Passage" for details or consult the chalk board at the ranger station. (Open Mon.-Sat. 8am-6pm, Sun. 8am-4:30pm; in winter Mon.-Sat. 8am-4:30pm.) The nearby **Pinecrest Lake Loop Trail** circles the lake in an easy and scenic four miles. Off Herring Creek Rd., the 1½-mile **Trail of the Gargoyles** exposes the Sierra Nevada's fascinating geological history. The **Donnell Vista** trail, off Rte. 108 about 18 miles east of Pinecrest, leads ¼ mile through the trees to marvelous views. Swimming and boating are permitted in Pinecrest Lake. **Pinecrest Campground** and **Pioneer Trail Group Campground,** both in the Summit District, are the only sites in the forest which accept reservations through MISTIX.

In the **Calaveras Ranger District,** headquarters on Rte. 4 in Hathaway Pines (795-1381), herds of deer roam the forest and herds of skiers roam Bear Valley and Mt. Reba. Some of Stanislaus's best hiking trails begin near Lake Alpine. (Open Mon-Fri. 8am-4:30pm, Sat. 7am-3:30pm.) The **Osborne Trail** (11/3 miles) starts at Rte. 4, and presents lovely lake vistas. **Pacific Valley Campground,** ¼ mi. south of Highway 4 at Pacific Valley and midway between Lake Alpine and Ebbetts Pass, has stream water and pit toilets, with nearby fishing on Pacific Creek and Mokelumne River. Open June-Oct. Free. There are 22 other campsites in the Calaveras district—most are free, though **Stanislaus River** and **Sourgrass** cost $5 per night, and **Spicer Reservoir** about $10. **Marmot Campground** is a wheelchair-accessible site with water and toilets. (Take Rte. 49 north to Rte. 4, then head northeast to Lake Alpine; open June-Oct.; free.)

Finally, **Groveland Ranger District** (962-7825), reached by following Rte. 120 for seven miles east of Groveland, borders Yosemite's western edge. (Headquarters open Mon.-Fri. 8am-4:30pm, Sat. 7am-3:30pm.) The Rainbow Pool Picnic Area, off Rte. 120 from Yosemite, features a waterfall and the four-mile Preston Flat Trail, which climbs gently along the Tuolumne River. Ten campgrounds ring this area. **Carlon, Lumsden, Southfork, Middlefork** and **Moore Creek** are free. Moore Creek accepts reservations through the Groveland Ranger office.

Stanislaus's three designated wilderness areas offer the area's best backpacking. To camp overnight, you must obtain a wilderness permit, available (along with topographic maps) from any ranger station. **Mokelumne Wilderness,** whose 105,000 acres overlap into the Eldorado and Toiyabe National Forests, has some 32 miles of trails. There are trailheads off Rte. 4 at Lake Valley, Sandy Meadow, and Underwood Valley. **Emigrant Wilderness** drapes 185 miles of developed trails past volcanic domes, sub-alpine forest, lakes, and meadows. There are trailheads on Rte. 108 at Bell Meadow, Crabtree Camp, Gianelli Cabin, Coyote Meadow, and Kennedy Meadows, and on Rte. 120 at Cherry Lake. This region was the stomping ground of Jedediah Smith, the first European to cross the Sierras, Grizzly Adams, and the infamous hooligan Mac C. "Trapper" Ross. **Carson-Iceberg Wilderness** contains fewer lakes than the others, but, according to the Forest Service, more solitude as well—except for the overused Sword and Lost Lake area. There are trailheads off Rte. 108 at Clark Fork, Disaster Creek, Arnst Creek, County Line, and Wheats Meadow, and off Rte. 4 at Highland Lakes. Both the **Pacific Crest Trail** and the **Tahoe-Yosemite Trail** traverse the three wilderness areas.

Calaveras County

Unsuspecting Calaveras County turned out to be sitting on a literal goldmine—the richest part of the Mother Lode—when the big rush hit. Over 550,000 pounds of gold were pulled out of the county's earth. Among those who headed for these hills was a journalist from Virginia by the name of Samuel Clemens (a.k.a. Mark Twain). Hapless as a miner but gifted as a bullshitter, he allegedly based "The Celebrated Jumping Frog of Calaveras County," his first big hit, on a story he heard in the Hotel Angel's barroom one winter night. In the story, Jim Smiley proudly carries his champion leaper "Dan'l Webster" wherever he goes. When a stranger makes fun of him, Smiley offers to fetch the stranger a frog and bets on the success of Dan'l in a jumping contest. But he makes the mistake of leaving his champion in the stranger's hands. The out-of-towner fills ol' Dan'l with heavy buckshot, thereby weighing the poor frog down. The stranger wins the contest and rapidly rides away with his winnings. Life has since imitated (or in this case, capitalized on) art, and a frog-jumping contest has been an annual springtime event in Calaveras since 1928.

Frogs can be found in large quantities all over Calaveras County, though most are of the inanimate manufactured-for-tourists variety. Angels Camp even has goofy green frogs painted at sporadic intervals on its sidewalks. Ribbit.

Practical Information and Orientation

Visitors Information: Chamber of Commerce, 1301 S. Main St., Angels Camp (736-4444). Few brochures, but for 25¢ you can pick up a walking-tour map. Open Mon.-Fri. 9am-5pm.

Public Library: 1103 Main St., Angels Camp. Open Tues. 11am-2pm, Wed. and Fri. noon-5pm, Thurs. 10am-2pm.

Rape Hotline: Calaveras Women's Crisis Center, 736-4011.

Gay Crisis: National Gay Task Force (800) 221-7044.

Bike Rental: Bug's Bike and Lock Shop, 1087 Hwy. 4 (728-1315), in Douglas Flats. $15 per day.

Suicide Prevention Hotline: 754-3365. 24 hr.

Disabled Service: Calaveras Stagecoach Transportation, 754-1888.

Tuolumne/Calaveras Assoc. for the Handicapped: 533-0510.

Hospital: Mark Twain St. Joseph's Hospital, 768 Mountain Ranch Rd., San Andreas (754-3521). **Creekside Immediate Care,** 1300 Kurt Dr. in Stelte Park, Angels Camp (736-0813). For minor emergencies.

Emergency: 911.

Post Office: 1103 Main St., Angels Camp (736-2220). Open Mon.-Fri. 9am-5pm. General Delivery ZIP Code: 95222. 140 Big Trees Rd. at Main St., Murphys (728-2113). Open Mon.-Fri. 8:30am-4:30pm.

Area Code: 209.

Calaveras county is just hopping with small towns. The main population center is **Angels Camp,** on Rte. 49 between Sonora and Jackson, both in other counties. South of Angels Camp, Mark Twain's one-time home, **Tuttletown,** is now only a historic marker and a grocery store. To the east, **Murphys** is an interesting place if you happen to be passing through but is not worth a special trip. **Altaville** lies to the north of Angels Camp, and could easily be missed if it weren't on the map. **San Andreas, Valley Springs,** and **Mokelumne Hill** populate the northern part of the county. Mokelumne Hill is not a ghost town but rather a ghost *story* town. Once in the running to be state capital, this town's modern claim to fame is an affinity for spooky tales. Spirited storytellers haunt the **Leger Bar,** Main St. (286-1401).

Placerville

Historically, a lot of people have ended up hanging out in Placerville longer than they would have liked. And not just because the town is conveniently located at the juncture of Hwys. 50 and 49.

In 1848, William Daylor and Perry McCoon struck it rich when they discovered gold at a place called "Dry Diggin's." When the news broke, a flood of gold-crazed miners rushed into nearby Placerville and along with them, a small army of outlaws, calling themselves The Owls. Crime proliferated, but "justice" was swift. Street mobs sentenced men such as "Irish Dick" Crone and Bill Brown to death—stringing them up from the great oak (known as Hang Tree) in the middle of town. Placerville became known as Hangtown, a nickname that is absurdly celebrated by the modern Chamber of Commerce.

Today Placerville continues to provide food and lodging for weary travelers—as it did in the 1850s and 60s when it was the terminus of the Overland Trail and a way station for the Pony Express. But as for changes in its judicial system—well, you might want to think twice about littering or jaywalking.

Practical Information and Orientation

Visitors Information: Chamber of Commerce, 542 Main St. (621-5885). Open Mon.-Fri. 8am-5pm. Free maps of the county. **Parks and Recreation,** 549 Main St. (622-0832).

U.S. Forest Service: U.S. 50 West at Camino Heights Dr. All information is for the El Dorado National Forest 20 mi. east of Placerville. Open daily 7am-6pm.

Greyhound: 1750 Broadway (622-7200), 3 mi. from downtown. Open daily 8am-6pm. To Reno ($26) and Sacramento ($7.80).

Car Rental: Freedom Rent-A-Car 621-0868.

Bike Rental: Backcountry, 6110 Pony Express Trail, Pollock Pines (644-5271), about 10 mi. east of Placerville on U.S. 50. Mountain bikes $15 per day. Driver's license or other form of ID required as deposit. Open Mon.-Sat. 9am-5:30pm. Sun. only bike rental 9am-5:30pm.

Local Bus: El Dorado Transit, 3655C Chuckwagon Way (621-5617). Shuttle service from Point View Dr., west to Missouri Flat Rd., along a 2 mi. stretch north and south of U.S. 50. (Buses operate Mon.-Fri. 7am-6pm, Sat. 9am-5pm. Fare 75¢, seniors 35¢.) Shuttles to Coloma run on Tues. at 8am and 2:30pm ($1.60) from the Placerville Bell Tower.

Taxi: Yellow Cab 626-1010.

Suicide Prevention Center: 622-3345.

Senior Center: 937 Spring St. (621-6150).

Hospital: Marshall Hospital, Marshall Way at Cedar Ravine St. (622-1441, 24 hr. emergency 626-2678).

Emergency: 911.

Police: 730 Main St. (622-0111).

Post Office: 3045 Sacramento St. (622-6443), south of U.S. 50. Open Mon.-Fri. 8:30am-5pm. General Delivery ZIP Code: 95667.

Area Code: 916.

About one-third of the way from Sacramento to Lake Tahoe on U.S. 50, Placerville continues to act out its historic role as a pit stop, now strategically positioned to snare campers, boaters, and skiers. The town is clustered east-west along U.S. 50, extending northwards to encompass Hangtown Gold Bug Park. Most streets, including Main St., parallel U.S. 50. Route 49 also bisects the town, running north to Coloma (10 mi.) and Auburn, and south towards Calaveras County.

Accommodations and Camping

Budget motels in Placerville range from ugly but clean to just plain ugly. Prices vary depending on location and state of repair but are never outstandingly cheap. Placerville itself has no real campsites, but east on U.S. 50 you'll find all you need.

Hangtown Motel, 1676 Broadway (622-0637). Close to the bus station and cheap. HBO, A/C, kitchenettes. Call ahead to check availability, but reservations are not accepted—they don't want to be left hanging. Singles and doubles $32, weekends $34. Weekly rates from $210.

El Dorado Motel, 1500 Broadway (622-3884). Three long blocks from the bus station. Well-used furniture which creaks and groans almost by itself. Not bee-yoo-tiful, but rooms are secure and comfortable. Singles $35. Doubles $38. Reservations advised.

Mother Lode Motel, 1940 Broadway (622-0895). Neat, spacious rooms, HBO, A/C, pool, and a flower garden, too. Singles $33, doubles $41. In winter rates drop $5 a night. Not too far from the bus station. Enthusiastic manager

Sly Park (644-2545), 17 mi. east on U.S. 50 to County Rd. E16. Water, toilets, no showers. Swim in Lake Jenkinson. Popular with fishing folk. Lots of RVs. Sites $6.

Sunset (644-2348), on the banks of the Union Valley Reservoir, much farther from Placerville. Take U.S. 50 9 mi. past Pollock Pines, then 15 mi. north on County Rd. 17 N12. Water, toilets, no showers. Sites $6.

Food

There is much food to be had in Placerville: fast food joints, decrepit diners and cloying old-fashioned soda shops abound.

Poor Red's, Main St., El Dorado (622-2901), 5 mi south of Placerville on Rte. 49. Follow the tantalizing scent of barbecued ribs through the windowless metal door and past the ever-full circular bar. Portions big enough to sate Fred Flintstone. Dingy rooms host a "Who's Who" of Placerville society, from the mayor to the lumber magnate to the local Krishna holy man. Packed with locals from miles around; expect to wait up to 2 hours at peak eating times. To wash the ribs down—or better, to grieve their gradual departure—order a "gold Cadillac" ($2.50), a creamy, highly alcoholic drink whose exact ingredients are unknown. Barbecued ribs at dinner, $7.25. Lunch is cheaper and just as greasy: gigantic steak sandwich $5, barbecued pork lunch $2.75. Definitely *not* for vegetarians. French fries 75¢. Open Mon.-Fri. 11:30am-2pm and 5-11pm, Sat. 5-11pm, Sun. 2-11pm.

The Apple Café, 2740 U.S. 50 (626-8144), next to the exit for Point View Dr. An unassuming bulwark of natural goodness. Great turkey sandwiches with salad and fries $5. Three-egg omelettes with home fries and toast $4. Breakfast served at lunch, lunch at breakfast, dinner not at all. Terrific overlook of the valley from picnic tables under the apple trees. Open daily 6am-3pm.

Powell Brothers Steamer Company Saloon and Oyster Bar, 425 Main St. (626-1091). Sunday jazz is at the bar, fishnets are on the wall, oysters are in the half shell (½ doz. $6). Lunch specials $5-7. Delicious Lazyperson's (no shells) *Cioppino* (fish stews).

Sights and Seasonal Events

A walk along Placerville's well-preserved streets should satisfy anyone's appetite for 19th-century Victorian West nostalgia, but there's little here you can't find elsewhere on Rte. 49—except Placerville's relentless morbidity. Note the dummy being lynched from the second floor of the Hangman's Tree Bar on Main St.

Novice gold prospectors can pick up a how-to book at **Rivendell Books,** 352 Main St. (622-4540; open Mon.-Fri. 9:30am-5pm, Sat. 9:30am-4:30pm). **Hangtown Etc.** sells the pan to do it with at 400 Main St. (622-9488). Off Bedford St., in the **Gold Bug Park,** on Gold Bug Lane (622-0832), two gold mines exhibit the stampmill that miners used to extract gold from ore after the easy metal was gone. Extensive walking trails crisscross this large (6.1 acre) city park. Park open daily 8:30am-dusk; mine and museum open April-Oct. 10am-4pm.

The Chamber of Commerce's Placerville/Hangtown map (50¢) highlights several interesting buildings, including the **Druid Monument,** at Main St. and Cedar Ravine. The monument recalls the great Frederick Sieg, who brought the New Age to the West when he founded California's first Druids' Grove here in 1859. The **Placerville Historical Museum,** 524 Main St., just up from the Chamber provides an opportunity to get your bearings on local history. Exhibits are small and consist mainly of local family heirlooms, but they're nevertheless somewhat interesting. (Open Fri.-Sun. 10am-4pm.) The **County Fairgrounds Historical Museum,** at county fairgrounds on Placerville Dr., displays Victorian furnishings and decorations from an affluent local household.

Placerville is an apple town. Travelers with a bicycle or car can tour the apple orchards and wineries off U.S. 50 on Carson Rd., North Canyon Rd., and Carson Dr. in the area known as **Apple Hill.** Locals claim that **Denver Dan's,** 4344 Bumblebee Lane (644-2893), is the best orchard for consistently reasonable prices, while

Kid's, 3245 N. Canyon Rd. (622-0841), has the best apple pie in the area. The industry paper, the *Apple News,* available at the Chamber of Commerce, supplies information on area orchards. One consortium of 30 orchards, **Apple Hill Growers** (622-9595), publishes an exhaustive directory entitled *The Cider Press* (obtainable at the Chamber of Commerce).

You'll also get your chance to hunt for gold, of course. **Gold Country Prospecting,** 3119 Turner St. (622-2484), offers 1-hr. jaunts for $15 (children 7-12 $5), equipment provided—bring some old shoes and prepare to get wet.

For wine tasting, try local favorites **Lava Cap Winery,** at 2221 Fruitridge Rd. (621-0175; open daily 11am-5pm), or **Boeger Winery,** 1709 Carson Rd. (622-8094; open daily 10am-5pm). The **Harvest Festival** arrives in early autumn, when the masses flood local orchards in search of pears and chestnuts (the best buys) as well as every imaginable apple product. The vineyards get their turn in June with the region-wide **Fairplay Wine Festival.** This weekend of free wine-tasting and gourmet dinners is a fabulous gala put on by the local wineries, more in the spirit of fun than of profit.

Wagon Train Days in late June brings the Wild West back to life, albeit in a highly commercialized reincarnation. The **Hangtown Festival,** a morbid two days of food, crafts, and lynchings, takes place on the first weekend in July (expect entrance fees plus additional costs for everything inside the gates). A town-wide street dance on Saturday night is a Placerville tradition. The **El Dorado County Fair** livens up Placerville during the first week of August.

The **Dixieland Jazz Festival** blows through in April (223-0350). There's a certified **Farmer's Market** every Saturday June 1-Nov. 23 8am-noon at the El Dorado Fairgrounds, 100 Placerville Dr.

Coloma

See where it all began in Coloma, 8 mi. north of Placerville on Rte. 49. In the confusion of claims and counterclaims about the first, the richest, and the most important gold strike, remember just one thing: the 1848 Gold Rush began in Coloma at John Sutter's water-powered lumber mill, operated by James Marshall. Marshall's diary records events with this laconic entry: "This day some kind of mettle . . . found in the tailrace . . . looks like goald." Within five months, half of San Francisco was digging in the hills. Between 1848-52, California's population jumped from 14,000 to 223,000. 125 million ounces of gold were taken out of the hills in this area, but don't despair—scientists estimate sixty to ninety percent of the total Mother Lode remains in the ground (in case you're feeling lucky...). The **James Marshall Gold Discovery State Historic Park** (622-3470) is a masterpiece of intelligent understatement. Near the spot where Marshall discovered the precious metal, the water now flows quietly through the rushes, the tens of thousands of miners long since departed. A few hundred yards away is a replica of the original mill, constructed in 1968. Demonstrations of how it worked take place daily at 2pm. Picnic grounds across the street surround the **Gold Discovery Museum,** 310 Back St. (622-3470), which gives a rather simplified version of the events triggered by the discovery. Dioramas and a film give a feel for the time. For the record, neither Sutter nor Marshall made much from the discovery. (Open daily 10am-5pm. Winter hours may be shorter. Admission $3 per car, seniors $2.)

The entire town of Coloma is a historic park, with a day use fee of $5, seniors $4. The charge includes admission to the museum. Be sure to display your pass prominently in your car window or you will be ticketed.

Nearby **Consumnes** and **American Rivers** are full of places to swim; take Happy Valley Rd. to its intersection with the Consumnes. Another local swimming spot is the **Sky Park Reservoir** (Jenkinson Lake). Take Sky Park Rd. off U.S. 50. Timid folk might use the **city pool** (622-0832) on Benham Rd. (Admission 1:30-4:30pm $1, 7:30-9pm 75¢.)

Sadists should stake out a spot on the American River to see **whitewater rafting.** A popular spot from which to watch is near the famous "Troublemaker" rapid; ask locals for tips on where to perch. This part of the river has mostly Class III rapids, with intimidating names like "Satan's Cesspool," "Hospital Bar," "Bouncing Rock" and "Meatgrinder."

Should you want to test the waters yourself, **Whitewater Connection,** P.O. Box 270, Coloma 95613 (800-336-7238), is the largest carrier on the American River's South Fork. Two-day trips, including meals and overnight camping are $189 weekdays, $219 on weekends. One-day trips are $74 on weekdays, $89 on weekends, while a half-day on the river is $59 during the week, $69 weekends. Whitewater's offices are located right on Rte. 49 in Coloma and they recommend reservations in advance, but last minute spots are often available. Other raft-trip outfitters line the tranquil highway next to the river.

There are a number of campsites and "river resort" areas near town. **American River Resort,** 6019 New River Rd. (622-6700), a half mile from downtown Coloma, has campsites (from $18.50) and RV hookups on the river ($24). The resort also rents river cottages from $100 a night. Ask about raft trips. **Camp Lotus,** 2 mi. downstream from Coloma, at the end of Bassi Rd. off of Lotus Rd. (622-8672), has less expensive campsites. ($4 per person and $2 per vehicle per night. Sun.-Thurs. with weekend charges at $6 per person, $3 per vehicle. Reservations required on summer weekends.) The camp has showers, toilets, a volleyball court, a camp store, and plenty of swimming holes. They, too, run river-rafting trips. Reservations required on summer weekends.

The **Vineyard House,** off Rte. 49 at Cold Springs Rd. (622-2217), is worth a visit if only for a drink at the bar (the dinner prices are out of budget range). This old stagecoach stop has remained unchanged since the days when you ate with your horse. Excellent steak and chicken dinners cost $8.50. Apparently, Placerville does not have the only morbid fixation in the Mother Lode: a crazed man was once chained up by his even more crazed wife in the basement here—which, logically enough, is now a happening bar. His starved ghost supposedly haunts customers' appetites. Every Halloween the management throws him a party complete with a field trip to the cemetery across the street. (Open Tues.-Thurs. 5-9pm, Fri.-Sat. 5-10pm, Sun. 10am-2pm and 4-9pm; Oct.-May open Wed.-Sun.) Those who want something substantial in their stomachs should mosey over to the north side of the river and check out the **Coloma Deli, Coloma Club, Bar and Café,** and **Yossum's Pizza,** all within walking distance of one another.

From late July to early August, the county fair comes to the **El Dorado Fairgrounds,** next to the El Dorado Historical Museum, 1850 U.S. 50, with crafts, rides, and livestock. The anniversary of **Discovery Day** (622-3470) in January brings thousands to the Marshall Gold Discovery Park for crafts, food, and melodrama. Dedicated fans of histrionics can see a melodrama performed by the Coloma Crescent Players every Friday and Saturday at 8pm at the **Olde Coloma Theatre** (626-5282), near the Vineyard House. The Vineyard House hosts the brave folk who annually recreate a covered wagon journey across the old Emigrant Trail from Round Hill, Nevada to Cold Springs, all the while wearing coonskin caps, leather jerkins, and other period costumes. They stop in a different town every night on the way and party until they drop. Needless to say their arrival here at the end of June is the biggest party of all. Devotees of violent TV cop shows won't want to miss the **Police Demolition Derby** each summer at the fairgrounds. (Admission $5 for charity.)

San Joaquin Valley

While the rest of California speeds recklessly toward the millennium, the San Joaquin Valley quietly minds its own agribusiness. Known to most travelers as the "middle-of-nowhere" that separates Los Angeles and San Francisco, the area is nevertheless one of the most vital agricultural regions in the country. Throughout the triangle defined by 1009-ft. Altamont Pass to the northwest, Yosemite to the northeast, and 4144-ft. Tejon Pass to the south, the land is flat, the air is oven-hot, and the endless onion fields and rows of fruit trees are broken only by the razor-straight slashes of I-5 and Rte. 99. Lifestyles here are plain and conservative. Although the valley's livelihood is the bread and butter of California's economy, nowhere else in the state does one feel quite so removed from things typically Californian.

A word of caution: don't underestimate the heat. Temperatures reach three digits in early summer and sit there for weeks. It's a dry heat, so it's not uncomfortable, but the sun will blister and dehydrate the unwary. Stop frequently to pour in the liquids so you don't dry out. Winters can get very cold, especially at night, although snow on the valley floor is rare.

The valley is the only route to the national parks and forests of the Sierras, but the coast is practically inaccessible from here. Some of the larger towns such as Bakersfield and Visalia are peaceful places to live, but the tourist would do well to stock up on supplies, rest well for the night, and head on.

Fresno

Fresno has long been the butt of jokes by Californians: one of the few matters on which Angelenos and San Franciscans see eye-to-eye is their common contempt for this second-class citizen of the San Joaquin Valley. Fresno is hellishly hot, they chortle, and sprawls out forever in all directions. Fresno has no museums, no nightlife, and lacks panache. Fresno's idea of culture is what the doctor takes from your throat with a Q-tip.

What California's eighth-largest city lacks in ebullience it makes up for in efficiency; this is, after all, the banking center for the entire San Joaquin Valley. The trains run on time, the streets are freshly paved, and there are no lines at the post office. The new order has settled gracefully around the old, rather than barreling in and knocking it down. Fresno does in fact have art museums, a philharmonic orchestra, outstanding parks, and a rich history. This is also William Saroyan Country, and Ansel Adams survived here for many years. Fresno is not Partytown, U.S.A., and you certainly wouldn't want to spend an entire week here. But this centrally located city makes for a convenient stopover en route to or from the Sierras.

Practical Information and Orientation

Convention and Visitors Bureau: 808 M St. 93721 (233-0836). Professional staff divulges information on city and county businesses and attractions. Not used to budget travelers looking for a place to crash, but they'll try their best. They also publicize a variety of community events. Open Mon.-Fri. 8am-5pm. **Fresno County and City Chamber of Commerce:** P.O. Box 1469 (233-4651).

California State University at Fresno: Info on campus events: 278-2795. For info on fraternity room rentals: 278-7927.

Airport: Fresno Air Terminal, Clinton Way, northeast of downtown (buses #26, 39, 41). United, American, Delta and USAir offer connections to the rest of California and from there to other major cities nationwide.

Amtrak: Tulare at Santa Fe Ave. (486-7651, for ticket info call 800-872-7245). Three trains per day to San Francisco and Los Angeles (each destination $38; round-trip Mon.-Thurs. $45).

Greyhound: 1033 Broadway (268-9461). To San Francisco (10 per day, $22) and Los Angeles (13 per day, $28).

Fresno Area Express (FAX): 498-1122. Fifteen routes run north-south or crosstown, most originating at the courthouse (Fresno and Van Ness), or 2 blocks west at Fresno and Broadway. Fare 75¢, seniors and disabled persons 35¢, under 6 free. Transfers free. Service every

½ hr. on most routes Mon.-Fri. 6am-6:30pm, Sat. 9:30am-5:30pm. Route map is available at the main office (2223 G St.), in City Hall.

Car Rental: Action Rent-a-Car, 1811 De Visitell (266-3869). The cheapest wheels in town; $11 per day and 15¢ per mi., or $24.50 with 150 free mi. Must be 21 with a credit card.

Road Conditions (CalTrans): 227-7264 (tape) or 488-4020, Mon.-Fri. 8am-5pm.

Public Library: 2420 Mariposa (488-3209), at N St. Open Mon.-Tues. 9am-9pm, Wed.-Thurs. noon-9pm, Fri. 9am-6pm, Sat. 1-5pm.

Laundromat: Plaza, 3097 Tulare (266-1107), at U St. Wash 75¢, dry 25¢. Open 24 hr.

Camping Supplies: Army Surplus, 1715 E. Belmont Ave. (233-8309), at N. Blackstone. Mostly clothing, some equipment. Open Mon.-Sat. 8:30am-5:30pm. **Herb Bauer's Sporting Goods,** 6264 N. Blackstone (435-8600; open Mon.-Fri. 9am-9pm, Sat. 9am-6pm, Sun. 11am-5pm), and **Camp's City Surplus,** 6629 N. Blackstone (432-0168; open Mon.-Sat. 9am-6pm, Sun. 10am-4pm) have more. Fresno is a good place to stock up on camping supplies before heading into the Sierras.

Gay Community Center: 268-3541.

Rape Crisis: 227-1800. 24-hr. hotline for victims of rape, incest, or sexual molestation.

Medical Emergency: Fresno Community Hospital and Medical Center, Fresno at R St. (442-6000). Open 24 hr.

Police: 487-7700.

Post Office: 1900 E St. (487-7100). Clean, efficient, deserted. Open Mon.-Fri. 8:30am-5pm. General Delivery ZIP Code: 93706.

Area Code: 209.

Orientation

Fresno sits at the geographic center of the San Joaquin Valley, midway between the Coastal Ranges to the west and the Sierra Nevada to the east, as well as midway between Sacramento to the north and the low Tehachapi Range that marks the southern end of the valley. Greyhound and Amtrak both link Fresno with San Francisco 185 mi. to the northwest and Los Angeles 217 mi. to the southwest. If driving, it is far simpler to drive into Fresno along Rte. 99 which runs north-south through the Valley, than along any of the state or country routes that cross the Valley latitudinally.

Fresno is an ideal base for preparing a foray into the Sierra Nevada. The mountains are a cool alternative to the scorching summers of the Valley, and even the most dedicated Fresnophiles try to spend their leisure time at the higher elevations. Rte. 41 slices due north out of Fresno bound for Yosemite National Park, Rte. 168 winds its way northeast past Huntington Lake and Shaver Lake through among the peaks of the Sierra National Forest, and Rte. 180 traverses the eastern portion of the valley before climbing into Sequoia National Forest and Kings Canyon National Park.

Route 99 cuts northwest-to-southeast across metropolitan Fresno; **Route 180** runs due east-west, and **Route 41,** north-south. The confluence of these roads marks Fresno's **downtown.** Before entering downtown Fresno, arm yourself with a detailed map. The irregular road layout and one-way streets make navigation bewildering. Study the main roads before driving around; streets parallel to Rte. 99 are imaginatively named after famous letters of the alphabet. **Broadway,** where you'll find the bus stations, is where I St. ought to be; **Fulton St.** runs in J St.'s place; and **Van Ness Avenue** stands in for K St. Six blocks of Fulton Street are closed to traffic: this is **Fulton Mall,** a shopping area and convenient reference point. **Tulare Avenue** is the main thoroughfare crossing the alphabetized streets.

Accommodations and Camping

If you come by car, you'll find many variations on the Motel 6 motif along Rte. 99. North Motel Drive, north of Olive Ave., has some older motels that may be cheaper, but the neighborhood is none too wonderful. For those who aren't driving, the following are best downtown.

Motel 7, 888 Broadway (485-7550), near the bus stations. Don't wander alone in the neighborhood, but the hotel itself is secure and tastefully furnished. Singles $26. Doubles $28.

Motel 6, 933 N. Parkway Dr. (233-3913), off Rte. 99 at Olive St. exit; and 4245 N. Blackstone Ave. (221-0800), Rte. 99 at Rte. 41. A/C, pool, clean rooms. Singles $24. Doubles $30.

Travelers Inn, 2655 E. Shaw (294-0224). A cut above Motel 6; suitably decorated, copious rooms. Color TV, A/C, pool, spa. Reserve as far as a month in advance. Singles $30. Doubles $36.

Allstar Inns, 4080 N. Blackstone (222-2431), on the main drag north of downtown. This budget chain aims at the Motel 6 market. The accommodations are of the same variety; clean, but nothing to write home about. A/C, color TV, pool. Singles $24. Doubles $31.

Campgrounds in the area serve the purpose—but it's not much farther to Sierra National Park and national forest land.

Island Park Recreation Area, Army Corps of Engineers campground at Pine Flat Lake (787-2589), 17 mi. east of Fresno. Take Rte. 180 to Sanger, then northeast about 14 mi. to Trimmer Springs. Full-service campground with showers, but no hookups. 52 developed sites. 2-week max. stay. April-Sept. Sites $6, no charge in winter for limited facilities.

Millerton Lake State Recreation Area (822-2225), in Friant, 20 mi. northeast of Fresno on the western shore of Millerton Lake. Accessible by Friant Rd. from Rte. 41. Fishing, hot showers and flush toilets. Arrive early or reserve through MISTIX (800-444-7275). Sites $14.

Food and Entertainment

Thanks to the county's rich harvests and its Armenian, Mexican-American, and Japanese communities good food abounds in Fresno. The recent influx of Southeast Asian immigrants has added a few more Asian food stores to a thriving community on the west side of downtown.

The **Farmer's Market** (441-1009), at Divisadero and Tulare downtown, is an expansive indoor market. Half is fast-food; in the other half, local farmers and their families sell home-grown goods (open Mon.-Sat. 7am-9pm). You'll find the best selection Fridays and Saturdays. At the **outdoor produce market,** on the corner of Merced and N St. (Tues., Thurs., and Sat. 7am-3pm), vendors drive pickup trucks into a parking lot and, scales from their awnings, and sell, sell, sell.

Ethnic restaurants cluster north and west of downtown. The old Chinatown west of the railroad tracks at Kern St. and G, F, and E St. has many Asian (mostly Japanese) and Mexican restaurants and stores; be careful, though, the area may be dangerous after dark. American restaurants, clubs, and bars line N. Blackstone and Shaw, two main drags cruised by CSUF students in the more affluent part of Fresno.

The Tower District, bordered by Olive and Wishon, 1 mi. outside of downtown, is the Center of Fresno's nightlife, with movie theaters and clubs.

Old Fresno Hofbrau, 2820 Tulare (264-4014), at R St. has the feel of old Fresno, the kind of place where bankers and ranchers (yes, ranchers) eat lunch. Dark and cool, even in the heat of the day. Turkey, ham, roast beef, or pastrami sandwiches ($4.60, with salad). Top it all off with a slice of cheesecake or apple pie ($1.17). The bar serves cold drafts ($1). Open Mon.-Sat. 11am-10pm, bar open Mon.-Sat. 7pm-2am.

Santa Fe Hotel, 935 Sante Fe Ave. (266-2170), at Tulare. Family-style Basque lunches and dinners served at long tables. The decor might not be much, but they make up for it in quantity and quality of food. Enormous lunches $6, dinner $7-10, children under 12 $5. Open Mon.-Sat. 11:30am-1:30pm, Tues.-Sat. 5-8:30pm.

Central Fish Market, 1535 Kern (237-2049), at G St., a few blocks from Greyhound. Both a full grocery store and a Japanese restaurant. Owners pride themselves on clean, fresh fish and produce. The premises are fragrant, immaculate, and well stocked. The small, unadorned restaurant serves tasty Japanese meals for $3 and under. Filling combination plate $3. Market open Mon.-Sat. 8am-8pm, Sun. 8am-7pm; restaurant open daily 11am-6pm.

Fat Jack's, 3927 N. Blackstone (224-4141). Tasty burgers (double cheeseburger $3), real cherry, chocolate, lemon and vanilla cokes (large, $1.20) and excellent shakes ($2.40) in an authentic drive-in atmosphere. With limited seating, everyone eats in true drive-in style: in their cars. Open Mon.-Sat. 11am-10:30pm, 11:30am-10:30pm.

Rebecca's, 2405 Capitol Ave. (485-3399), in the Galleria, at N St. A modern café/deli, with lunch sandwiches and salads (½ sandwich with soup or salad, $4.50). Open Mon.-Fri. 6:30am-3pm, Sat. 8am-3pm.

George's, (264-9433), also in the Galleria, is an Armenian grill, with shish-kebab sandwiches ($6.25) and daily lunch specials ($6) as well as cheap breakfasts. Open Mon.-Sat. 6am-3pm.

Sights

Not only does Fresno possess a downtown, it's even got a historic skyline. Sort of. The tallest building in old Fresno is the 15-story **Pacific Southwest Building,** 1058 Fulton Mall, at Mariposa. Note the red-tile roof and white rooftop grillwork bestriding the "Security Bank" sign. Also note the building at 1015 Fulton Mall (built in 1917), and the art deco green of the now-abandoned Bank of America Building at 1255. The squat **Pacific Gas and Electric Building** anchors the Tuolumne St. end of the mall.

Fresno's major museum is the **Fresno Metropolitan Museum of Art, History and Science,** 1555 Van Ness (441-1444) at Calaveras. The museum shows both regional and traveling exhibits and strives to incorporate video and interactive displays. It features a permanent exhibit on the life of acclaimed writer (and Fresno native) William Saroyan. (Open Wed. 11am-7pm with free admission, Thurs.-Sun. 11am-5pm. Admission $2; seniors, students and children $1. Disabled access. Take bus #28.) The **Fresno Art Museum** houses changing contemporary exhibits on Mexican and American Art (2233 North First St.; 485-4810; adults $2, students and seniors $1; open Tues.-Sun. 10am-5pm).

The largest of Fresno's many neighborhood parks is **Roeding Park,** West Belmont Ave. at Rte. 99 (take any northbound bus and transfer at Belmont). Pick up a free map at the city parks office (488-1551) near the Belmont Ave. entrance. Roeding's 157 acres enclose the **Fresno Zoo** (266-9534), which contains the new South American Tropical Rainforest and the Australian Outback sections (open daily 10am-5pm, in winter 10am-6:30pm; admission $3, ages 4-14 $1), the Homer C. Wilson Camellia Garden (open upon request; free), and a surprisingly varied topography. Eat your lunch in the grove of your choice (pine, ash, eucalyptus). At Lake Washington, in the southwest corner of the park, you can rent a pedal boat. **Playland,** near the lake, offers the usual array of amusement park attractions, including 11 kid-sized thrill rides. (Open in warm-weather months Mon.-Fri. 10am-7:30pm, Sat.-Sun. and holidays 10am-dark.) **Storyland** (enter at north end of the lake) animates fairy tales and nursery rhymes with detailed, humorous sculptures in a garden of ivy and tall trees. (Open May-Sept. daily 10am-5pm; Oct.-Nov. and Feb.-April Sat.-Sun. and school holidays 10am-5pm. Admission $2.25, children $1.75, under 3 free.)

Fresno's other beautiful park is a scenic 5 mi. bicycle ride west of downtown, at the end of **Kearney Boulevard.** Martin Kearney laid out the boulevard early in this century to connect his home, now a museum, with the city. The road is long and mostly straight, lined with monster oleanders, palms, and eucalyptus trees, and paralleled by a bike route. (When the canopy of trees veers off to the left, bikers should too; the sign that says otherwise is directing you to a straighter, less inspiring route.) Kearney Park itself, near the end of the boulevard, is gracefully landscaped with an olive grove and other exotic plants. (Museum open Fri.-Sun. 1-4pm. Admission $2, children 75¢, under 2 free.)

Besides its parks, Fresno also takes pride in being the birthplace and longtime home of **William Saroyan,** the Pulitzer Prize-winning novelist and playwright. The convention center theater is named after him, and every May the city holds the Saroyan Festival, which includes writing contests and Armenian folk music.

California State University at Fresno, at Cedar and Shaw Ave. (278-2420), is the cultural heart of the city. Buses #28, 34, 38, and 39 all pass the university campus. The University supports the only serious theater in town, and the student union brings in guest lecturers and entertainers (278-2078). The city is extremely supportive of the "Red Wave" sports teams, especially football. If you're in town during the second weekend in March, don't miss the **Rodeo** on the campus grounds.

Nearby Clovis is home to **Wild Water Adventures,,** the San Joaquin Valley's only water park (open daily in summer; admission $7, seniors and under 48" $4; call 438-9453 for information).

Sierra Nevada

The Sierra Nevada is the highest, steepest, and most physically stunning mountain range in the contiguous United States. The heart-stopping sheerness of Yosemite's rock walls, the craggy alpine scenery of Kings Canyon and Sequoia National Parks, and the abrupt drop from the eastern slope into Owens Valley are unparalleled sights to take your breath away.

An enormous hunk of granite created by plate tectonics and shaped by erosion, glaciers, and volcanoes, the Sierra Nevada (Snowy Mountains) stretches 450 mi. north from the Mojave Desert to Lake Almanor. Before crustal plates thrust the rock skyward 400 million years ago, this entire area was just a giant puddle.

Appalled by the devastating logging that began threatening the giant sequoia during the mid- and late-1800s, preternatural naturalist John Muir convinced Congress to secure the region from the expanding sawmills and to establish Sequoia and Yosemite National Parks. Continuing environmental concern voiced by Californians resulted in the subsequent creation of other national parks in the Sierras, including Sequoia's fraternal twin, Kings Canyon, in 1940.

The High Sierra terrain is richly varied; the western slope rises gradually, from brush and chapparal of the San Joaquin Valley foothills to the pine trees of higher elevations. Meadows, glaciers, rivers, and lakes punctuate the rugged alpine landscape. The eastern slope is steeper and more barren. The entire region is home to hundreds of animal species, including bears, deer, mountain lions, and bobcats.

The popularity of the Sierras is reflected in the wide variety of books, maps, and brochures on the mountains. National park and forest visitor centers generally have comprehensive selections, as do some bookstores and libraries. Storer and Usinger's *Sierra Nevada Natural History* and Thomas Winnett's guide to the Pacific Crest Trail are both worth reading.

Cyclists should cross the mountains via Yosemite's Tioga Road (Rte. 120) to avoid the kamikaze logging trucks. Buses serve the valleys on the east and west of the Sierras, but cross the range only in the north on U.S. 50 and in the south from Bakersfield.

Muir called the Sierras the world's most hospitable mountain range, and they do indeed welcome the car-bound traveler as well as backpackers and climbers. Still, the high country can be treacherous (just ask the Donners); you should be prepared for any kind of weather. Snow comes early and leaves late.

Overnight lows can dip into the 20s year-round. Normally, only U.S. 50 and I-80 are kept open during the snow season. Exact dates vary from year to year, so check with a ranger station on local road and weather conditions from October through April. Come summer, your beachside tan will offer little protection against the high elevations' ultraviolet rays; always bring sunscreen. For additional hiking advice, see the Camping section in the General Introduction.

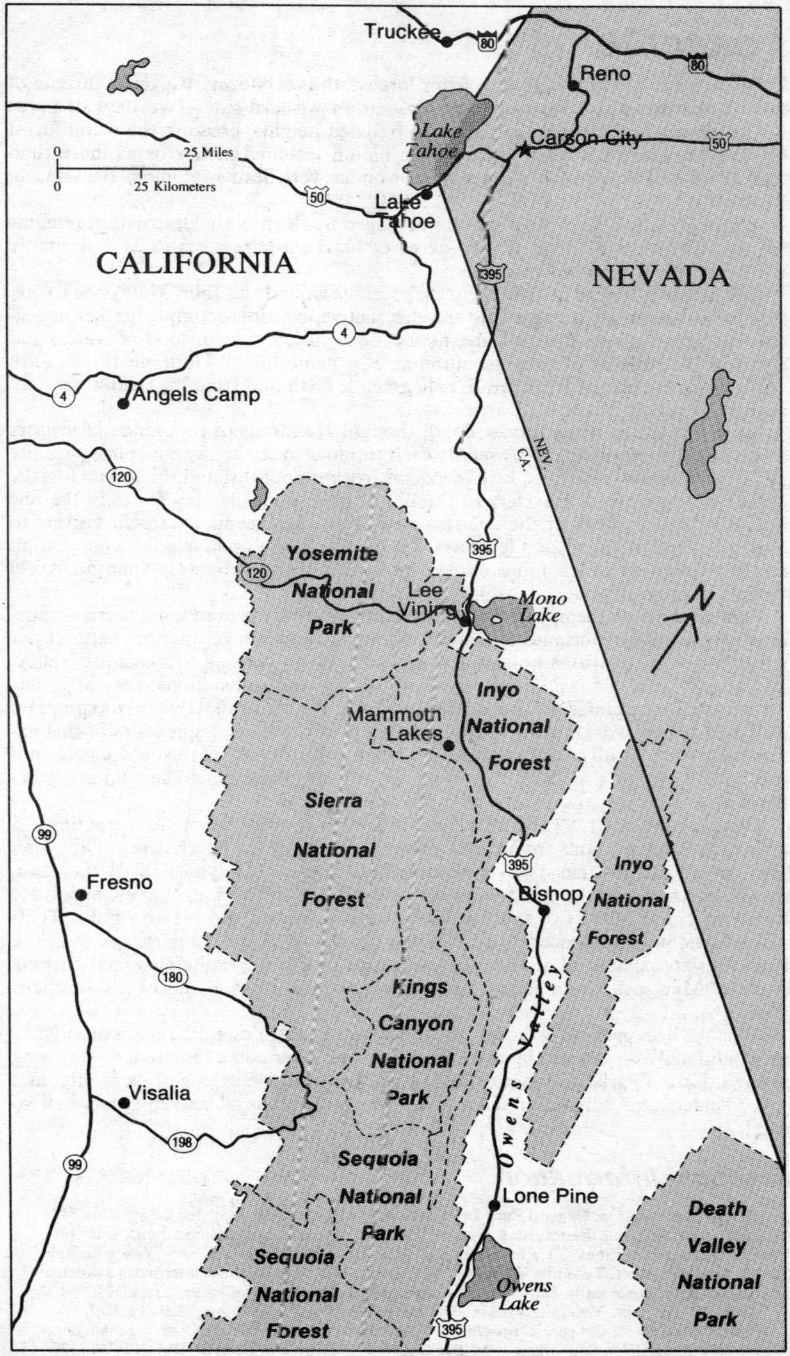
Truckee
80
Reno
80
Lake Tahoe
Carson City
50
0 25 Miles
0 25 Kilometers
50
Lake Tahoe
CALIFORNIA
395
NEVADA
4
4
Angels Camp
NEV.
CA.
120
395
Yosemite
120
National
Park
Lee Vining
Mono Lake
N
Inyo
Mammoth Lakes
National
Forest
Sierra
National
Forest
99
395
Inyo
Fresno
Bishop
National
Forest
180
Kings
Canyon
National
Park
Owens Valley
Visalia
198
99
Sequoia
National
Park
Lone Pine
Death
Valley
National
Park
Sequoia
National
Forest
Owens Lake
395

Yosemite

On August 7, 1990, lightning from intense thunderstorms triggered dozens of fires in the drought-dried forests of Yosemite's western side. Two days of fierce winds subsequently fueled the flames to frenzied heights, creating the worst forest fire in Yosemite's 100-year history. The nation watched in horror as more than 22,000 acres of the country's preeminent wonder were destroyed in one devastating week.

Although only 2% of the Park was damaged by the fire, the destruction remains highly visible along Tioga Road—acres of blackened trees stand as a dramatic marker to the 2-year-old tragedy.

Remarkably, time is healing the park's vicious wound. As John Muir once wrote, "By forces seemingly antagonistic and destructive, Nature accomplishes her beneficient designs—now a flood of fire, now a flood of ice, now a flood of water; and again in the fullness of time an outburst of organic life..." Underneath the dark tombstones of charred trees, fresh, pale green growth and stunning wildflowers are visible.

No fire could stop the tourist flood, though. Hundreds of thousands of visitors still make the pilgrimage to Yosemite each summer to see her awe-inspiring granite cliffs, thunderous waterfalls, lush meadows, rock monoliths, and thick pine forests. While the majority of travelers to the big ditch in Arizona stay for only the few hours it takes to gawk at the colorful view from each scenic overlook, visitors to Yosemite tend to linger for a few days. The resulting pile-up makes for a congestion in the wilderness which more closely resembles an L.A. freeway than an Ansel Adams photograph.

Though the park seems safe from condos and resorts, the number of tourists pouring into the valley continues to increase annually. Winnebago warriors battle it out with the rest of the three million annual visitors who journey to Yosemite Valley. With a plethora of snack shops, souvenir stands, and gas stations, the valley has descended into commercial chaos. Meanwhile, in the high country, purists complain of the park's crowds, but the ruling policy is that the unique splendors of this national park are for all to enjoy. Those who prefer the solitude of the outdoors should thus use the valley's facilities to commence a quiet journey into the wilderness beyond.

The park covers 1189 sq. mi. of mountainous terrain, the main attractions of which, **El Capitan, Half Dome,** and **Yosemite Falls,** lie in the Yosemite Valley, an area carved out by glaciers over thousands of years. Once you've seen this area, though, head out to the other parts of the park. Little Yosemite Valley, accessible by hiking trails, offers two spectacular waterfalls, Vernal and Nevada Falls. **Tuolumne Meadows** (pronouced twa-LUM-nay) in the northeastern corner of the park is an Elysian expanse of alpine meadows surrounded by granite cliffs and rushing streams. **Mariposa Grove** is a forest of giant sequoia trees at the park's southern end.

Whether backpackers or hotel guests, visitors to the Yosemite region are invariably delighted and uplifted by their stay. One can never come too often or stay long enough, for the park has infinite offerings. Experience the drama of its beauty, and you'll understand why Muir remarked, "No description of heaven seems half so fine."

Practical Information

Visitors Information: General Park Information, 372-0265; 24-hr. recorded information 372-0200. Informed and friendly staff gives telephone advice about accommodations, activities, and weather conditions. TTY users call 372-4726. Open Mon.-Fri. 8am-5pm. **Yosemite Valley Visitors Center,** Yosemite Village (372-4461, ext. 333). Sign language interpreter available daily 2-5pm. Open daily 8am-8pm. **Tuolumne Meadows Visitors Center,** Tioga Rd. (372-0263), 55 mi. from Yosemite Village. The headquarters of high-country activity, with trail information, maps, and special programs. Open in summer daily 8am-7:30pm. Sign language interpreter available Sun. 10am-1pm. **Big Oak Flat Information Station,** Rte. 120 W. (379-

2445), in the Crane Flat/Tuolumne Sequoia Grove Area. Open in summer daily 7:30am-6pm. **Wawona Ranger Station,** Rte. 141 (375-6391), at the southern entrance near the Mariposa Grove. Open Mon.-Fri. 8am-5pm, Sat.-Sun. 7am-5pm; in winter Mon.-Fri. 8am-5pm. **Backcountry Office,** P.O. Box 577, Yosemite National Park 95389 (372-0308; 24-hr. recorded information 372-0307), next to Yosemite Valley Visitors Center. Backcountry and trail information. Open daily 7:30am-7:30pm. With a map of the park and a copy of the informative *Yosemite Guide,* both available for free at visitors centers, you should be well-equipped to explore the park. Information folders and maps are available also in French, German, Spanish, and Japanese. Wilderness permits are available at all visitors centers. Campground information: 372-4845 (recorded).

Yosemite Park and Curry Co. Room Reservations, 5410 E. Home, Fresno 93727 (252-4848, TTY users 255-8345). Except for the campgrounds, Y. P. & C. has a monopoly on all the tourist facilities within the park. Contact them for information and reservations.

Tour Information: Yosemite Lodge Tour Desk (372-1240), in Yosemite Lodge lobby. Open daily 7:30am-7pm, or contact any other lodge in the park.

Gas: available at Chevron stations in Yosemite Valley (7am-8pm), Wawona, Crane Flat, and Tuolomne Meadows (all 8am-7pm). Fill up before you make the climb into the High Sierras—as the elevation rises, so do the gas prices.

Auto Service, Towing and Repair: Village Garage, 24 hr. towing (372-1221). Open 8am-5pm.

Equipment Rental: Yosemite Mountaineering School, Rte. 120 (372-1335, Sept.-May 372-1244), at Tuolumne Meadows. Sleeping bags $4 per day, backpacks $3.50-4 per day, snow shoes $6 per day. Climbing shoes rented to YMS students only. Driver's license or credit card required for deposit.

Bike Rentals: at **Yosemite Lodge** and **Curry Village** (372-1208 and 372-1200 respectively). Both open 8am-6pm daily. $4.25 per hr., $14.75 per day.

Camera Rental: Ansel Adams Gallery, in Yosemite Village next to the visitors center. Day rentals of tripods ($7) and both single-lens-reflex ($12) and compact 35mms ($7.50). Also offers a wonderful selection of prints and postcards for those who would rather not compete with Mr. Adams. A great place to browse. Open daily 9am-6pm.

Laundromat: Housekeeping Camp. $1 per wash, 25¢ to dry for 10 min. Open 7am-10pm in summer. In winter, laundry facilities available at Camp 6, across the street from the Village Store. 7am-10pm.

Showers: Housekeeping Camp $1.50 includes towel and soap, although at certain times of the day you'll have to wait in a long and dirty line. 7:30am-10pm. Showers also in **Curry Village** 6am-10pm.

Recycling: Village Store Recycling Center 10am-4:30pm. Collects paper, glass and plastic bottles and aluminum cans.

Money: Bank of America Versatel Machine, in Yosemite Village south of the Village Store (6am-midnight).

AAA Emergency Road Service: 372-1221.

Weather and Road Conditions: 372-4605 or 372-0200.

Lost and Found: P.O. Box 577L, Yosemite 95389 (372-4720). Open Mon.-Fri. 8am-4:30pm.

Medical Services: Yosemite Medical Clinic, in Yosemite Village near the Ahwanee Hotel (372-4637). 24-hour emergency service and regular appointments. Open Mon.-Fri. 9am-5:30pm, Sat. 9am-noon. **Dental Services** next to the clinic (372-4200) Mon.-Fri. 8am-4:30pm.

Stables: (372-1248); at Yosemite Valley (7am-7pm), Kennel (7:30am-5pm), Tuolumne Meadows (7:30am-5pm), Waroona (7:30am-5pm), and White Wolf (7:30am-5pm).

Emergency: 911; park rangers can be found thoughout the park.

Post Offices: Yosemite Village, next to the visitors center. Open Mon.-Fri. 8:30am-5pm; Sept.-May Mon.-Fri. 8:30am-12:30pm and 1:30-5pm. **Curry Village,** near Registration Office. Stamps available from machines year-round. Open June-Sept. Mon.-Fri. 9am-3pm. **Yosemite Lodge.** Open Mon.-Fri. 9am-4pm. General Delivery ZIP Code: 95389.

Area code: 209.

Orientation

Yosemite crowns the central Sierra Nevada, 180 mi. due east of San Francisco and 320 mi. northeast of Los Angeles. It can be reached by taking Rte. 140 from Merced, Rte. 41 north from Fresno, and Rte. 120 east from Sonoma or west from Lee Vining. Park admission is $2 if you're entering on foot, $5 for a 7-day vehicle pass. Overpriced gas stations litter the park's roadways.

Yosemite Via, 300 Grogan Ave., Merced 95340 (384-1315 or 722-0366), makes two round-trips per day from the Merced Greyhound station to Yosemite ($15, round-trip $28; discount for seniors). **Yosemite Gray Line (YGL),** P.O. Box 2472, Merced 95344 (383-1563), meets the morning train arriving in Merced from San Francisco and takes passengers to Yosemite. The bus returns to Merced in time to catch the return train to San Francisco. (One-way $15, round-trip $28.) YGL also runs to and from Fresno ($18). From July through Labor Day, the **Yosemite Transportation System (YTS)** connects the park with Greyhound in Lee Vining (372-1240; one way $32.50). Reservations are required.

For a "friendly" bus trip to Yosemite, take **Green Tortoise** from San Francisco for a two- or three-day journey. Buses leave San Francisco at 9pm—you sleep in a cushy, "sleep-aboard," violently green bus and arrive at popular sites before they get crowded. (Two-day trip $79, 3-day trip $99, food $8 per day; reservations required; see General Introduction for more information.) You can also take **Amtrak** (800-872-7245) from San Francisco to Merced (one-way $29) and connect with the waiting YGL bus. Amtrak also provides transport via shuttle bus and train from L.A. to Fresno and Merced (one-way to Fresno $37, one-way to Merced $44).

The best bargain in Yosemite is the free **shuttle bus system.** Comfortable but often crowded, the buses have knowledgeable drivers and broad viewing windows. They run through the valley daily at 10-minute intervals from 7:30am to 10pm. Hikers' buses run daily to Glacier Point spring-autumn and to Tuolumne Meadows/Lee Vining July 1-Labor Day. Call 372-1240 for tickets and information.

From any of the lodging facilities, you can purchase **tour tickets.** The basic Valley Floor Tour lasts two hours and points out sights such as Half Dome, El Capitan, Bridalveil Fall, and Happy Isles. The tour is conducted on open-air trams with an amiable guide, and costs $12.50 (children under 12 $6.25, under 5 free). The Glacier Point Tour lasts four hours and climbs to the point for a 3200 ft. view of the valley that'll take your breath away ($17.75, under 12 $9, under 5 free, June 1-Thanksgiving). The Mariposa Grove Tour spends half a day visiting the big trees ($27.75, children $13.75), and the Grand Tour ($34.50, children $17.25, June 1-Thanksgiving) is a comprehensive, full day's outing. Other tours include the Moonlight Tour; conducted on full moon nights and the three nights surrounding, it offers unique night-time views of the cliffs ($8). Call 372-1240 for reservations, departure times, and locations.

Although the inner valley is congested with traffic, the best way to see Yosemite is by car. Park at one of the lodging areas and ride the shuttle to see the valley sights, then hop back into your car to explore other places. Drivers intending to visit the highcountry in spring and fall should have snow tires; they are sometimes required in early and late summer. Of the five major approaches to the park, Rte. 120 to the Big Oak Flat entrance is particularly brutal. The easiest route from the west is Rte. 140 into Yosemite Valley. The eastern entrance, Tioga Pass, is closed during snow season; the road to Mirror Lake and Happy Isles is forbidden to private auto traffic, but is traversed by the free shuttle buses during the summer. In winter, snow closes the road to Glacier Point and sections of Tioga Road.

Bicycling is also an excellent way to see Yosemite Valley; bike paths burgeon, and most sights are within a 4 mi. diameter of the Valley. (See Practical Info. for rental information.)

You can also take guided horseback trips into Yosemite's backcountry. The park has four stables (see Practical Info.), and reservations are generally needed to secure a spot. A 2-hr. ride costs $26, and a full day will leave you $53 lighter and maybe more than a little saddle-sore. Call 372-1248 for reservations and information.

Accommodations

Lodgings in Yosemite Valley are monopolized by the park concessionaire, the Curry Company, and range from simple canvas tent cabins to the luxurious suites of the Ahwahnee Hotel (which start at $188.50 in season). Rates are in constant flux, varying between midweek and weekend, and in-season and off-season. All lodgings have access to dining and laundry facilities, showers, and supplies. Reservations are necessary for all park lodgings, some as far as a year in advance. Call 252-4848 for information. All rates are quoted for the high-season, and are as much as $15 more than midweek rates during the off-season.

Yosemite Lodge, in Yosemite Valley west of Yosemite Village. Small, spruce, sparsely furnished cabins under surveillance by deer. To catch cancellations, inquire before 4pm. Singles and doubles $40.50, with bath $53.75.

Curry Village, southeast of Yosemite Village. The flashing neon sign at the village entrance heralds the crowded camp area. Back-to-back cabins are noisy but clean. Ice cream and pizza only a minute away. $40.50, with bath $53.75. Less private canvas-sided tent cabins $28.50.

Housekeeping Camp, west of Curry Village. Canvas and concrete units accommodate up to 4 people, and include double beds, chairs, and stoves. Bring insect repellent. $32.25 for 1-4 people.

Wawona Hotel, off Rte. 41 in south end of park. Grand Southern-style mansion with gables and green shutters. Rooms $56, with bath $76.

Tuolumne Meadows Lodge, on Tioga Rd. in northeast corner of park. Canvas-sided tent cabins $32.35 for 2 people, $5 per additional adult ($2.50 for children).

White Wolf Lodge, west of Tuolumne Meadows on Tioga Rd. Cabins with bath $54.75. Canvas tent cabins $31.75 for 2, $6 for additional adults and $2.50 for children.

Camping

Yosemite provides many options for campers. Most of the Valley's campgrounds are crowded, many choked with trailers and RVs. In Yosemite Valley's drive-in campgrounds, reservations are required from April to November and can be made through Ticketron up to eight weeks ahead. If you've failed to make friends with Ticketron, try the people at the park; they may share their space with a spur-of-the-moment camper. Or show up at the **Curry Village Campground Reservations** office at 9am or 4pm to catch a cancellation. With the exception of major holidays, you should be able to camp in one of the first-come, first-served campgrounds (Wawona, Bridalveil Creek, Tamarack Flat, White Wolf, Yosemite Creek, and Porcupine Flat) if you arrive at a reasonable hour. In summer, there is a 14-day limit for campers outside Yosemite Valley and a seven-day limit for those in the valley. At **Backpacker's Camp** in the valley there is a 2-night limit, and a 1-day limit for the backpacker sites at Tuolumne. These camps are for backpackers with wilderness permits and without vehicles. "Walk-in" camps (Sunnyside and Tenaya Lake) do not require reservations. Sleeping in cars is strictly prohibited throughout the park.

Most campgrounds are close to supply stores (see Food). No campgrounds provide RV hookups, but showers are available at **Curry Housekeeping** from spring through fall (open 24 hr.; admission $1.50 including use of pool), and at **Tuolumne Meadows** and **White Wolf Lodges** in summer. At campgrounds served by natural stream water (Tamarack Flat, Yosemite Creek, Porcupine Flat), the *water must be boiled* to prevent giardia, a nasty instestinal disease akin to the scene in *Alien* where the thing comes out of the dude's stomach.

Backcountry camping is prohibited in the valley (you'll get slapped with a stiff fine if caught), but it's unrestricted along the high-country trails with a free wilderness permit (call 372-0307 for general information). Each trailhead limits the number of permits available. Reserve by mail between February and May (write Backcountry Office, P.O. Box 577, Yosemite National Park 95389), or take your chances with the 50% quota held on 24-hr. notice at the Yosemite Valley Visitors Center, the Wawona Ranger Station, or Big Oak Flat Station. Popular trails like **Little Yo-**

semite Valley and **Clouds Rest** fill the quotas regularly. To receive a permit, you must show a planned itinerary, although you needn't follow it exactly. Most hikers stay at the undeveloped mountain campgrounds in the high country for the company and for the **bear lockers,** used for storing food (not bears). Some of these campgrounds have chemical toilets.

Backpacker's Camp, 1½ mi. east of Yosemite Village across the river, behind North Pine Campground. Unadvertised. Low on facilities, high on camaraderie. Fishing is popular here. Running water, toilets, and showers nearby. Two-night max. stay. $2 per person. Open May-Oct.

Sunnyside, at the west end of Yosemite Valley past the Yosemite Lodge Chevron station. A walk to the climber's camp, called **Camp 4** by regulars, will immerse the innocent tourist in the spooky climbing subculture, where seasoned adventurers swap stories of exploits on vertical rock faces such as "Separate Reality," "Quicksilver," and "Outer Limits." Water, toilets, and tables. Sites $2. Open year-round.

Lower, Upper, and **North Pines,** in the eastern part of Yosemite Valley. Reserved sites, crowded with RVs. Water, toilets, and tables. Pets at Upper Pines only. Sites $12. Lower Pines open year-round; Upper Pines March-Nov.; North Pines April-Nov.

Lower and **Upper River,** 1 mi. east of Yosemite Village along the Merced River. Reserved sites, more secluded than the Pines campgrounds. No RVs at Upper River. No pets anywhere. Water, toilets, and tables. Sites $12. Lower River open April-Nov.; Upper River April-Oct.

Tamarack Flat, 23 mi. northeast of Yosemite Valley. Take Rte. 120 east. Drive-in sites, although the access road is not suitable for RVs. Fills up later than other campgrounds. Toilets and tables, but no drinking water. Stream water drinkable if boiled for 3 min. Pets allowed. Sites $4. Open June-Oct.

Tenaya Lake, a demanding 46-mi. drive from the valley east on Rte. 120, but worth it. Walk-in sites with gorgeous lake views. Swimming and fishing. Water, toilets, and tables. No pets. Sites $7. Open June-Oct.

Tuolumne Meadows, 55 mi. east on Rte. 120. Drive into the sprawling campground, or escape the RVs by ambling to the 25 walk-in sites. Great scenery and nearby trailheads. Pets allowed in the Western Section sites. Water, toilets, and tables. One-night max. stay. Drive-in sites $10, backpacker sites $2 per person. Open June-Oct.

Wawona, Rte. 41 in the southern end of the park. 100 sites beautified by tables, toilets, and water. Sites $7. Open year-round. Pets too.

Bridalveil Creek, on Glacier Point Rd. near Glacier Point. 110 sites consummated with water, tables, firepits, and toilets. Say "I do" to this place. Sites $7. Open June-Sept.

White Wolf, off Rte. 120 E. Water, toilets, tables, even firepits. Cabins here also. Pets. 87 sites. Sites $7. Open June-mid Sept.

Yosemite Creek, off Rte. 120 E. Access road fortunately not suitable for RVs or trailers. 75 Winnebago-free sites. Pit toilets, tables. Boil water from stream before drinking. Pets. Horse trails. Sites $4. Open June-Sept.

Porcupine Flat, off Rte. 120 E. RV access to front section only. Pit toilets, no tap water. 52 sites. Sites $4. Open June-Oct.

Food

Restaurants in Yosemite are expensive and dreary, dishing out bland American fare. Buy your own overpriced groceries for a campfire feast from the **Yosemite Lodge Store** or the **Village Store** (open daily 8am-10pm; Oct.-May 8am-9pm).

The Loft, in the Yosemite Village complex, above Degnan's Deli. Lunch sandwiches are $5.35-6.45, dinner entrees around $11, while burgers on French bread are $7.35. The atmosphere is casual—they call it "relaxed dining." Open May-Oct. daily 11:45am-2pm and 5:30-10pm.

Yosemite Lodge Cafeteria, in the Lodge complex. Provides schoolbox-type lunches for a picnic (2 sandwiches, a hard-boiled egg, fruit, and dessert $4.25). Order the day before you go. Open daily 6:30am-8pm; Oct.-May 8am-7pm.

Village Grill, in Yosemite Village. A snack bar with ultra-cheap prices: hamburgers $2.30, breakfast (2 eggs, sausage, biscuit, hash browns) $2. Open daily 7:30am-8pm.

Degnan's Delicatessan, in Yosemite Village. Sandwiches ($3.25), drinks, and an adjacent ice cream parlor. Part of a larger convenience market; there are tables outside for enjoying your meal. Prepare to share when the bugs come out in the evening. Open daily 7am-9pm.

Curry Village Cafeteria, in Curry Village. Pizza, standard cafeteria fare (complete meal around $6). Open daily 7-10am, 11:45am-1:30pm, 5:30-8pm. **Hamburger Stand** handles burgers, shakes, fries as well as late (11am) breakfast. Open daily 8am-8pm.

Sights

By Car or Bike

You can see a large part of Yosemite from the bucket seat. The drive along **Tioga Road** (Rte. 120 E.) presents one panorama after another and includes vistas of burned forest. The road through Tioga Pass is the highest highway strip in the country, exiting the eastern side of the park in the lunaresque landscape near Mono Lake. This miracle of highway engineering is buried under snow through May, in some years through June. Driving west from the Pass brings you to **Tuolumne Meadows** and its open, alpine spaces, shimmering **Tenaya Lake,** and innumerable scenic views of granite slopes and canyons.

Signs throughout the park indicate turnouts and points of interest. If you're not in a hurry, it's worthwhile to stop to gaze and perhaps take photographs. The *Yosemite Road Guide* ($3.25 at every visitors center) is keyed to these roadside markers, and provides a superb tour of the park—almost like as having a ranger tied to the hood.

The roads leading into Yosemite Valley, the center of the park, are not only among the world's most spectacular, but also among the most dangerous, simply because so many drivers are watching the scenery rather than the road. Do yourself a favor, and pull off to gawk. The approach from the south passes through **Wawona Tunnel.** The driver, upon exiting the tunnel, is greeted with an astonishing view of the valley. Dominating the spectacle are 7569 ft. **El Capitan** (the largest granite monolith in the world), misty **Bridalveil Falls,** and the **Three Brothers** (three adjacent granite peaks). A drive into the heart of the valley brings thunderous 2475-ft. **Yosemite Falls** (the highest in North America), **Sentinel Rock,** and **Half Dome** within view.

For a different perspective on the valley, drive up to **Glacier Point,** off Glacier Point Rd. Hovering 3214 ft. above the valley floor, this gripping overlook is guaranteed to impress the most jaded of travelers. Half Dome rests majestically across the valley, and the sight and sound of **Vernal Falls** and **Nevada Falls** punctuate the silence. Though it gets crowded at the point, most visitors gaze quietly, a testament to the power of Mother Nature.

You'll think you've stumbled into Brobdingnag as you walk among the giant sequoias at **Mariposa Grove,** off Rte. 41. The short hiking trail begins at the **Fallen Monarch,** a massive trunk lying on its side, and continues to the 209 ft., 2700 year old **Grizzly Giant,** and the fallen **Wawona Tunnel Tree.** Contemplate the fact that ancient Athens was in its glory when many of these trees were mere sproutlings.

In the northwestern region of the park lies **Hetch Hetchy,** a valley similar to Yosemite Valley, but dammed to an existence as an expansive reservoir. John Hunt tried unsuccessfully to establish this region as national park as well; instead, the artificial lake holds water for San Francisco's toilets.

Of course, when you drive through Yosemite you sacrifice intimacy with the land. One alternative is **cycling.** Roads are fairly flat near the villages, more arduous farther afield. Those near **Mirror Lake,** open only to hikers and bikers, guarantee a particularly good ride, and the valley roads, filled with traffic, are easily circumvented by the bike paths. For further information on bike routes, contact the bike rental stands at Yosemite Lodge or Curry Village (372-4461, ext. 298).

Day Hiking from the Valley

Many visitors to Yosemite find the Valley's motorized tourist culture a great distraction. The most splendid and peaceful experiences at Yosemite are had along the outer trails with just a backpack and canteen. There is a wealth of opportunities for anyone willing to lace up those hiking boots for a day-trip.

Day-use trails are usually fairly busy, sometimes positively crowded, and occasionally (July 4th weekend) there are human traffic jams. A colorful trail map, with difficulty ratings and average hiking times is available at the visitors center for 50¢. The easiest walks are to **Bridalveil Falls** and **Lower Yosemite Falls,** less than ¼ mi. from the shuttle bus stops. **The Mirror Lake Loop** is a level, 3-mi. walk to the glassy lake, which is slowly silting up to become a meadow. (All 3 trails are accessible to the handicapped with assistance.)

The steep 4-mi. trail to **Glacier Point** culminates in an extraordinary bird's-eye view of the valley 3214 ft. below. Ansel Adams took some of his most famous photographs from here. **Yosemite Falls Trail,** a similarly backbreaking trek to a windy summit, rewards the intrepid with an overview of the 2425-ft. drop. Leaving the marked trail is not a wise idea: every year someone wanders off and gets the ultimate tour of the Falls.

One of the most popular trails (and understandably so) begins at **Happy Isles.** From this point, one could reach Mt. Whitney via the John Muir Trail, but the 211-mi. trek is not for everyone. Most instead take the **Mist Trail** past Vernal Fall to the top of Nevada Fall, a steep and strenuous climb up hundreds of tiny stairs. The views of the falls from the trail are outstanding, and the proximity to the water shrouds the trail in a continuous drizzle that is welcome during the summer months. Take the free shuttle from the valley campgrounds to Happy Isles; there is no parking available.

The Mist Trail continues to the base of **Half Dome,** a monolithic testament to the power of glaciation. Expert climbers tackle its sheer front face; halfway up, a yard-wide ledge serves as a luxury resort on the otherwise smooth vertical wall. Look closely from below; the profile of an Ahwahnee Indian princess is supposedly stained into the rock. For novices who don't dare dangle from the dome's face, there is a route up the back side which is itself challenging and requires the aid of climbing cables. Skip the climb if it looks stormy; lightning has been known to strike the wet summit of Half Dome and run down along the metal cables. The cables are up only during the summer.

Activities

Park rangers lead a variety of high-quality hikes and other activities for younger visitors. **Junior Ranger** (ages 8-9) and **Senior Ranger** (ages 10-12) activities allow children to hike, raft, and investigate aquatic and terrestrial life. These three-hour summer programs, usually held mid-week, require reservations at least a day in advance through the **Valley Visitor Center** and cost $1 (open 8am-8pm). Rangers also guide visitors along a 90-minute walk, **A First Look at Yosemite,** which leaves daily at 9am from the Valley Visitor Center. An informative introduction to local history, legends, and scenery, the walk is accessible to disabled people. The three-hour, somewhat strenuous **Vernal Fall hike** explores the Merced River Canyon twice per week in summer (for reservations, call 372-0299). The park service sponsors unique adventures such as guided wading through Tenaya Creek, photographic hikes at sunrise, and star-gazing from Glacier Point. Check for other events and times in the free *Yosemite Guide* (available at all visitors centers).

John Muir gave Teddy Roosevelt a personal tour of the valley in 1903, and continues to guide visitors in more than just spirit. During warm weather months, dramatist Lee Stetson leads free, one-hour hikes in which he assumes the role of the man who fathered Yosemite Valley. (Meet at the visitors center. Check the *Yosemite Guide* for times.) Stetson also hosts *An Evening with John Muir,* a 90-minute one-man show and "Conversation with a Tramp" on alternate evenings Tues.-Fri., 8pm.

(Tickets $4, under 12 $3, infants not admitted. Buy tickets at the door or from the visitors center in advance to ensure seating. Check the *Yosemite Guide.*)

If you've got the courage (and the cash), join the stellar Yosemite rock climbers by taking a lesson with the Mountaineering School. The world's greatest climbers come here to test themselves at angles past vertical. Serious climbers train daily, with exercises such as one-armed, two-fingered pull-ups. The **basic rock climbing classes,** offered daily in summer (usually mid-April to Sept.), teach you the basics on the ground, then take you 80 ft. up a cliff and introduce you to bouldering and rappelling ($45 plus $6 for rock shoes rental). Advanced classes are also offered. Intermediate lessons on weekends and alternating weekdays are $50-55. You'll need to buy a lunch and beverage for the day of the climb. You must be at least 14 and "in reasonably good condition" to take the group lessons. Expert climbers wishing to tackle the ultimate challenge can hire Mountaineering School guides to lead them up the face of El Capitan—for a mere $3000. See if you can beat the world record time of just over 4 hours. (Good luck and don't look down.) Private lessons for younger children are also available. Reservations are useful and require a deposit of the day's fee, though drop-ins are accepted if space allows. Deposits are refundable if you cancel at least 48 hours in advance, or if the weather is inclement. All classes meet at the Tuolumne Meadows office at 8:30am. For information contact **Yosemite Mountaineering School,** Yosemite 95389 (372-1335, Sept.-May 372-1244; 8:30am-5pm).

Fish year-round in any of Yosemite's lakes, streams, or rivers, but don't expect to catch anything unless you're an expert. Each year a few of the lakes are selected to be stocked with trout, but the names of these lakes are not made public. Anglers over age 15 may obtain a fishing license from grocery stores in Yosemite Valley, Wawona, Tuolomne, and White Wolf. (Resident license $19.50, nonresident $46.50, 10-day nonresident $20.50.) Merced River **rafting** probably won't throw you through enough rapids to stimulate your adrenaline production, but you can drift peacefully along the river while dabbling feet in the water and gazing at the majestic Half-Dome. Rent rafts ($12.50 per adult, $10.50 per child) in **Curry Village,** between the Curry Village store and the ice-skating arena. (Open daily 11am-4pm, mid-May to mid-July.) A driver's license or a credit card serves as a deposit. Sharing the raft may be more economical. (Life preservers $2, paddles $2.) **Swimming** is permitted throughout the park except where posted. The public pools at Curry Village and Yosemite Lodge charge $1 for those who are not guests of the hotel. **Horseback tours** of Yosemite operate from stables in Wawona, White Wolf, and Tuolumne Meadows in the summer, and in the Valley from Easter to mid-October. (372-1248; tickets $26 for two hr., $35 for a half-day, $53 full-day.) Ponies, donkeys, and burros are also available for children.

Beyond Yosemite Valley

Purists believe that the asphalt surfaces and heavy traffic of Yosemite Valley aren't the Real Thing. For them, nothing short of a trek through the backcountry will do. Over 700 mi. of trails tempt these hikers; some connect to other national park or forest trails that continue as far as Washington state. The ridiculously overpriced mountain shop at Tuolumne rents and sells equipment (see Practical Information), but it's better to plan ahead and buy at a backpacking store in a major city (San Francisco or Fresno, for instance).

The two main trailhead areas, **Tuolumne Meadows** and **Happy Isles Nature Center,** are accessible from Yosemite Valley by bus after July 1 (372-1240); ask to be let off at the trailhead. You can also drive to the trailhead and park in the lots. Buy both a topographical and a trail route map from a visitors center. The best cheap map is the *Guide to Yosemite High Sierra Trails* ($2.50). A map of valley trails is also available (50¢). Be sure to acquire a wilderness permit from the Backcountry Office, the Tuolumne Permit Kiosk (both open daily 7:30am-7:30pm), Big Oak Flat Station (open daily 7am-6pm), or the Wawona Ranger Station (open daily 8am-5pm).

Wintertime in Yosemite

Yosemite is rapidly becoming a year-round park. Winter camping in Lower River, Sunnyside (Camp 4), Hodgen Meadows, and Wawona is possible, and most indoor accommodations offer reduced off-season rates. While some areas close down entirely when the snow falls, the main park facilities in the Valley (such as the visitors center) remain open. The Merced and Fresno buses continue to operate (see Orientation).

Cross-country skiing on your own is free. **Yosemite Park & Curry Co.** (372-1338) offers ski rentals starting from $12. Crane Flat and Badger Pass are considered the best skiing areas. Both areas have marked blazes on the trees so that the trails can be followed even when there's several feet of snow. Skiing season usually runs from late November to early April. Most summer hiking trails are transformed in winter into increasingly popular **snowshoe trails.** Rent snowshoes from the Tuolomne Mountaineering Shop (372-1244) for $5. Guided cross-country ski tours are also offered by the Curry Company (372-1244). A two-day trip costs $90, and the ultimate 6-day "Trans-Sierra Expedition" will run you $350.

The state's oldest ski resort, **Badger Pass Ski Area,** south of Yosemite Valley on Glacier Point Road, (372-1338) is the only downhill ski area in the Park. The Curry Co. has downhill lessons starting at $16 for 2 hrs., with private lessons starting at $35 (inexpensive if you form a small group). Rentals are $15.50 per day for a ski package, and lift tickets are $25 per day on Sat. and Sun., $21 on weekdays. Seniors (over 60) and anyone who skis on her 40th birthday gets in free. Discount ski packages (accommodation and rentals) are available through Yosemite Lodge for weekdays. Inquire at Curry Co.

Ice Skating at Curry Village costs $4.50 ($3.75 children) for a day's admission and $1.75 for skate rental. (Open mid-Nov. to early March Mon.-Fri. 2-10pm, Sat.-Sun. noon-11pm.)

Kings Canyon and Sequoia National Parks

Though they may not attract the throngs of visitors that the "Big Three" national parks of Yellowstone, Yosemite, and Grand Canyon do each summer, the twin parks of Kings Canyon and Sequoia can go sight-for-sight with any park in the United States. The added incentives of relatively uncrowded roadways and campsites even give these parks an advantage over the other contenders.

Glaciers sure did a number on King's Canyon. Spectacular rock cliffs and waterfalls line the deepest canyon walls in the United States. From the 8000-ft. depth of the canyon, it is possible to drive the 50 mi. (almost all uphill) to Giant Forest, at the heart (and near the top) of Sequoia National Park, and behold the towering sequoia trees and magnificent vistas of the southern Sierras.

For those seeking a more earthy experience, Kings Canyon and Sequoia have vast stretches of land accessible only by wilderness trails. The High Sierra Trail crosses Sequoia east-west, while the Pacific Crest Trail (which stretches from Mexico to Canada) skirts the parks' eastern border, passing Mt. Whitney (at 14,494 ft., the highest mountain in the continental U.S.).

Summer season in these parts goes from Memorial Day through Labor Day, snow season from November to March. When planning your sojourn, recall that the road into King's Canyon is closed from the first week of November until the last week of April due to winter storms and the threat of rockfall.

Practical Information

National Park Service Headquarters: Superintendent, Ash Mountain, Three Rivers 93271 (565-3456), 1 mi. beyond the Three Rivers entrance on Rte. 198 out of Visalia. Information on both parks provided. Books, maps, wilderness permits, and free brochures about the sequoia in German, French, Spanish, and Japanese. Open daily 8am-5pm; Nov.-April 8am-4:30pm. **Park Admission:** 7-day vehicle pass valid in both parks $5; 1-year pass valid in both parks $15.

Recorded Road, Weather, and Campground Information: 565-3351.

Backpacking Information: 565-3307.

Area Code: 209.

Kings Canyon

Grant Grove Visitors Center: Grant Grove Village (335-2315), 2 mi. east of the Big Stump Entrance by Rte. 180. Books, maps, and exhibits on the history of those big red trees. Open daily 8am-6pm, in winter 8am-5pm.

Cedar Grove Ranger Station: 565-3341, ext. 430. 30 mi. farther down Rte. 180 by the Kings River near the trailheads for hikes into the Kings Canyon high country. Books, maps, first aid, and the wilderness permits required for hikes and trips into a wilderness area. Open daily 9am-5pm. The **kiosk** at the end of Rte. 180 several miles east issues permits during summer months daily 7am-2:30pm, after which they are available until 4:30pm at the ranger station. Roads usually close during the snow season.

Food and Supplies: Grant Grove Market open daily 8am-9pm; in winter 8am-6pm; Cedar Grove Market open in summer daily 8am-9pm.

Gas: Chevron stations are located in Grant Grove and Cedar Grove. Open in summer daily 9am-5pm. Fill up before you enter the parks—prices are 30-40¢ per gallon less outside.

Showers: at Grant Grove Lodge (open 11am-2pm) and the Cedar Grove Chevron station (open in summer 8am-8pm). Both locations $2.

Laundromat: at Cedar Grove Chevron station (open in summer 8am-8pm).

AAA Emergency Road Service: 335-9071.

Post Office: in Grant Grove Village. Open June-Sept. Mon.-Fri. 8:30am-2pm and 3-4:30pm; Sat. 9am-2pm. In winter, contact the Grant Grove Visitors Center for more information. General Delivery ZIP Code: 93633

Sequoia

Ash Mountain Visitors Center: Three Rivers 93271 (565-3456), at the park headquarters 1 mi. beyond the Three Rivers entrance, on Rte. 198 out of Visalia. Information on both parks. Books, maps, and wilderness permits available. Open daily 8am-5pm; Nov.-April 8am-4:30pm.

Lodgepole Visitors Center: 565-3341, ext. 631, on Generals Hwy. 4 mi. east of the Giant Forest. In the heart of Sequoia National Park, near the big trees and gaping tourists. Open daily 8am-5pm; Oct.-April 9am-5pm. **Children's Nature Center** open daily 10am-5pm July-Labor Day. **Campground Reservations** daily 9am-7pm. **Wilderness Permits** daily 7am-4pm.

Giant Forest Village Information Booth: Information, park maps. Open daily 9:30am-3:45pm.

Mineral King Ranger Station: 561-3341, ext. 812, 1 mi. before the end of Mineral King Rd. The headquarters for the remote Mineral King region in southern Sequoia National Park (inaccessible in snow season). Maps, hiking information, general books, first aid, and wilderness permits. Open in summer daily 7am-5pm; early Sept.-snow season Sat.-Sun. 7am-5pm.

Cross-Country Ski Rental: Sequoia Ski Touring Center, Sequoia National Park 93262 (565-3435); **Grant Grove,** 335-2314. Open Mon.-Fri. 9am-5pm, Sat.-Sun. and holidays 8am-6pm.

Food and Supplies: Lodgepole Market, open daily 8am-9pm; **Giant Forest Market,** open daily 8am-9pm.

Gas: Chevron, Lodgepole Village, on Generals Hwy.; open daily 8am-8pm; in winter 8am-5pm.

AAA Emergency Road Service: 565-3381.

Showers and Laundromat: At the Lodgepole market, open in summer 7am-10pm.

Post Office: Lodgepole 93262. Open Mon.-Fri. 8am-1pm and 1:30-4pm.

Orientation

The two parks are accessible to vehicles from the west only. From the east, trails lead into the parks from the John Muir Wilderness and Inyo National Forest, both accessible from spur roads off U.S. 395. However, no roads traverse the Sierras here. From Fresno follow Rte. 180 through the foothills; it's about 60 mi. to the entrance of the detached **Grant Grove** section of Kings Canyon. Route 180 ends 30 mi. later in **Cedar Grove.** The road into this region is closed in winter. From **Visalia,** take Rte. 198 to Sequoia National Park. This road, which passes Lake Kaweah and runs alongside the Kaweah River, is punctuated with scenic views and turnouts. Both Rte. 180 and 198 are kept clear by snowplows in winter. **Generals Highway** (Rte. 198) connects the Ash Mountain entrance to Sequoia with the **Giant Forest,** and continues to Grant Grove in Kings Canyon. Snow more than 15 ft. deep covers the road in winter, and it is usually open only from mid-May to October. The road twists as it ascends 2000 ft.; allow two hours to drive from Ash Mountain to Grant Grove.

In summer, the treacherous road to **Mineral King** opens up the southern parts of Sequoia. From Visalia, take Rte. 198; the turnoff to Mineral King is 3 mi. past Three Rivers, and the **Lookout Point Ranger Station** lies 10 mi. along the Mineral King Rd. Take a break from driving here: Atwell Springs Campground and the nearby town of Silver City are 10 mi. (but 45 min.) farther. Cold Springs Campground, Mineral King Ranger Station, and several trailheads lie near the end of Mineral King Rd. in a valley formed by 12,000-ft. peaks on the north and east. The stunning route to Mineral King makes 698 turns between Rte. 198 and the Mineral King complex. Allow two hours for the trip from Three Rivers.

The northern two-thirds of Kings Canyon and the eastern two-thirds of Sequoia are untouched by roads; here the backpacker and packhorse have free rein. Check at a ranger station or visitors center for more detailed information.

Public transport to the parks is nonexistent. **Visalia KOA** (800-322-2336), however, offers one-day tours through both parks for groups of six people or more (round-trip fare $25).

Accommodations

Sequoia Guest Services, Inc., P.O. Box 789, Three Rivers 93271 (561-3314), monopolizes indoor accommodations and food in the parks. The four main lodging areas are Giant Forest, Grant Grove, Cedar Grove, and Stony Creek. At **Giant Forest,** rustic cabins are available for $28.50 without bath during the high season (May-Oct.). Low season (Nov.-April) motel rates are economical, ranging from $33-55. At **Grant Grove,** a cabin runs $28.50, $35 w/ electricity, $51.50 w/ bath; the low season rate is $23-41.50 (with bath only). These cabins have an outdoor feel and more character than the motel rooms. **Cedar Grove** and **Stony Creek** offer motel accommodations in the summer only for $72.

There are also a few cabins at the **Bearpaw Meadow Backcountry Camp,** 11 mi. along the High Sierra Trail from Giant Forest. Call Sequoia Guest Services for rates. If you don't have reservations, you might catch a cancellation at the lodge offices.

Camping

While campgrounds in these parks occasionally fill to the rim with trim, enthusiastic campers, you should be able to drive up late and snatch a spot somewhere. Memorial Day, the Fourth of July, and Labor Day are exceptions. Only Lodgepole in Sequoia brims regularly, owing partly to its proximity to the Giant Forest and partly to its position as the only campground in the parks that accepts summer reservations (through Ticketron, 800-452-1111). Most campgrounds are open from mid-May to October (2-week max. stay per year). For information about campgrounds, contact a ranger station or call 565-3351 for 24-hr. recorded information. The nearby sites in the Sequoia National Forest are convenient backups.

Kings Canyon

Sunset, Azalea, and **Crystal Springs,** are all within spitting distance of Grant Grove Village but still relatively quiet. Each is outfitted with restrooms and water. Azalea has a dump station and Sunset an amphitheater with daily programs. Sites $8, free in winter. Azalea is open year-round.

Sheep Creek, Sentinel, Canyon View, and **Moraine,** at the Kings River near Cedar Grove. Store, food service, laundry, and showers nearby. Within a few miles of Roads End and Kings Canyon trailheads. All have restrooms and water; Sheep Creek has a dump station, Sentinel is near the Cedar Grove Amphitheater. Remarkable vistas of Kings River Canyon and soaring peaks. Sites $8. Canyon View accepts reservations from organized groups only.

Sequoia

Lodgepole (900-370-5566), 4 mi. northeast of Giant Forest Village in the heart of Sequoia National Park by Kaweah River. Full of RVs. Phone, store. The center of the park's ranger-led activities year-round, including nature walks and snowshoeing in winter. No hookups. Sites $10 during peak summer season; free once snow accumulates, $8 otherwise. Sites can be reserved up to 8 weeks in advance through Ticketron mid-May to mid-Sept.

Atwell Mill and **Cold Springs,** about 20 mi. along the Mineral King Rd., in the Mineral King area. Primitive and secluded, but with piped water and picnic tables. Great trailheads and scenery. Store, restaurant, phone, and unleaded gas (from an antique pump) are 3 mi. away in Silver City. 60 sites $8.

Buckeye Flat, past park headquarters, a few miles into the park from the Ash Mountain entrance on Rte. 198. Buckeye prohibits trailers and RVs. Bring them instead to **Potishwa,** a full-service campground nearby with 44 sites. Both $8.

South Fork, on South Fork Rd., 12 mi. off Rte. 198. Near ranger station. Pit toilets; not recommended for trailers or RVs. Sites $8.

Food

Park food, like lodging, is monopolized by Sequoia Guest Services and offers as good an argument against government-granted monopolies as any Ec-10 formulas. Though service ranges from fast-food to sit-down restaurants, none of the offerings are very palatable. Bring a stove and fuel or rent a rustic cabin with kitchen accommodations and cook for yourself. A cabin with a woodburning stove (but no cooking utensils) in high season is $31.50 per night.

Lodgepole Deli, on General's Hwy. Passable deli sandwiches are $4, a 12" pizza $8.80. Breakfast (served 7-11am) runs $3-4. Neighboring ice cream store offers 2 scoops for $2. Open daily 7am-9pm.

Giant Forest Lodge Dining Room, in Giant Forest Village. The sit-down restaurant, overlooking Round Meadow, has dinner entrees from $10-12, breakfasts around $5. (Open Mon.-Sat. 7-11am and 4:30-9pm, Sun. 7am-2pm). There is also a **cafeteria,** located ¼ mi. down Generals Hwy. next to the Giant Forest Market. Dinner entrees here are $3-4.50, a full meal around $7. (Open daily 7-11am, 11:30am-4pm, and 4:30-9pm). Next door to the cafeteria is the **Fireside Room,** with cocktails daily from 5-11pm.

Grant Grove Restaurant, in Grant Grove Village. Sit-down service in a coffee-shop atmosphere. Breakfast $4-6, lunch $5-6, and dinner $8-11. Open daily 7am-9pm.

Cedar Grove Snack Bar, in Cedar Grove Village. Insipid fast-food. Cheeseburger with fries $4.20, fried chicken dinner $7.25, frozen yogurt $1.10. Open daily 7am-9pm.

Sights

The sights of this region, like lodging and food, are organized around four primary areas: Giant Forest and Mineral King in Sequoia National Park, and Grant Grove and Cedar Grove in Kings Canyon National Park. The two greatest attractions correspond to the names of the parks; most of the visitors are here to see the sequoia trees and breathtaking King's River Canyon.

Giant Forest is the center of activities in Sequoia and host to one of the greatest concentrations of giant sequoia trees in the world. The grove was named by John Muir, who explored the area and fought for its preservation. The contrast between the common pine and fir trees and the majestic sequoias is startling. The main marvel is **General Sherman,** believed to be the world's largest living thing. Discovered and named in 1879, it stands 275 ft. tall and 102 ft. around at its base. Its trunk is estimated to weigh 1385 tons. This 2700-year-old creature is at last mature, and, while still growing, gains only a millimeter in height each year. Don't gripe about the protective fence: the sequoia have shallow root systems that cannot survive compaction of the soil. Lying flat on your back affords the most dramatic view of the tree—ignore the tourists giving you funny looks. The **Congress Trail,** the park's most popular (and crowded) trail, boomerangs around General Sherman. A pamphlet (50¢) sold at the trailhead provides a quick lesson in sequoia forest ecology. Other trails wind through the Giant Forest, allowing you to see dozens of giants as well as younger trees. Tiny sprouts have begun the steady climb skyward in acres cleared by recent controlled fires. Pick up a trail guide to the Giant Forest region at the Lodgepole Visitors Center, and be sure to visit one of the rolling, alpine meadows such as **Crescent Meadow, Round Meadow,** and **Huckleberry Meadow,** all of which are filled with wildflowers in summer.

Perhaps the most spectacular sight in the Giant Forest area is the view from atop **Moro Rock,** 1½ mi. from the village. A rock staircase winds ¼ mi. up this granite monolith to the top, which offers a stunning 360° view of the southern Sierras. If the arduous climb up the stairs doesn't take your breath away, the view certainly will; the Great Western Divide lies to the east and the pine-covered foothills receding into the San Joaquin Valley are to the south and west. You might try coming at sunset, when the bare rock tops of the Western Divide become an otherworldly shade of orange. To behold the majesty of Moro Rock itself, stop 1/10 of a mile before it at **Hanging Rock. Sunnet Rock** is another exposed granite formation, accessible via an easy 1-mi. trail from the village. Lodgepole Campground is the trailhead for the **Tokopah Falls Trail,** a 2-mi. hike to a glaciated gorge and a series of cascades.

Nine mi. from Giant Forest Village on Rte. 198 is **Crystal Cave,** one of the few caves on the western side of Sequoia that is open to the public. Reached by a ½-mi. hike, the cave is lined with smooth stalagmites and stalactites moistened by a dark underground stream. The largest chamber is Marble Hall, 141 ft. long and over 40 ft. high. The temperature inside remains a constant 50°, so wear warm clothing. (Naturalists lead tours late June-Labor Day daily on the hour and ½-hour; May-June and Sept. Fri.-Mon. on the hour. Cave open 10am-3pm. Admission $3, ages 6-12 $1.50.)

The **Mineral King** area was acquired by the park system in 1978 after lawsuits prevented the Walt Disney Corporation from building a ski resort on the site. Although Disney probably would have built a better road, some of the best scenery in the park has been preserved for those willing to brave the winding drive to get here (don't take the Winnebago on this one). There is no lodge, but there are two campgrounds—**Atwell Mill** and **Cold Springs**—each with pit toilets and piped water. The valley is 7500 ft. deep, with steep trails leading up to mountain lakes and meadows. Some of the surrounding peaks stand over 12,000 ft. tall. A bonanza mining area in the 1800s, the region now offers magnificent day and backcountry hiking and climbing.

The most developed portion of King's Canyon National Park is **Grant Grove.** The General Grant Tree, the third-largest of the sequoias, gives the region its name. Only 267.4 ft., slightly smaller than General Sherman, it is perhaps the most aesthetically pleasing of the giants, displaying "classic" sequoia form. It has been designated the "Nation's Christmas Tree," and serves as a living shrine for the American war (especially Civil War) dead.

Off Rte. 180, 6 mi. north of Grant Grove Village, is the road to **Hume Lake,** in the Sequoia National Forest. The lake is rimmed by summer homes and group camps, and Hume Lake Rd. offers outstanding views of King's Canyon. **Panoramic Point,** located 2½ mi. from Rte. 180 off a steep, paved road starting at the village, overlooks yet another enthralling scene.

The most secluded region of the two parks is the Cedar Grove area, which rests inside King's Canyon, surrounded by its towering granite walls. The drive on Rte. 180 is a scenic and mountainous one. (Be sure to stop at roadside turnoffs to peer over the dizzying drop to the riverbed below.) The sheer rock walls dominate the view for much of the drive, and at the bottom of the canyon the brilliant blue-green of the King's River enlivens the roadside. The final approach to the grove passes **Boyden Cavern** (736-2708). Privately operated tours of the 5-mi. cavern are more expensive ($5, seniors $4.50, children $2.50) than at Crystal Cave in Sequoia. This cave crawls with massive stalagmites and stalactites, and sandcastle-like marble formations. If you want to avoid the $5 charge, you can explore similar caves on your own. Look for an opening just across the highway. Take a flashlight, and be careful in there. (Tours leave on the hour June-Sept. daily 10am-5pm; May and Oct. 11am-4pm.)

Once within the budding grove, you can explore the river's banks and marvel at the depth of the canyon. The floor is oh so flat, but the sides of the canyon rise 8000 ft. in some spots. **Zumwalt Meadows** is accessible via a 1½-mi. trail. The most secluded of the two Parks' meadows, and set inside Kings Canyon, Zumwalt Meadows is the most stunning, and the choice of white-tailed deer and afternoon sunshine. **Roaring River Falls** and **Mist Falls** are at their best in late spring and early summer, when the streams are swollen and swift. Roaring River Falls is easily reached by road, but Mist Falls requires a 3-hr. hike that may make you think twice about just how badly you want to see those falls. Exercise caution at all times near the water; it's cold and powerful. **Road's End** is exactly that, with parking for those entering the backcountry. The glacial valley is U-shaped, and the road turns back in a giant cul-de-sac.

There are also some more out-of-the-way sights in the parks. Garfield Grove is 5 mi. up the Kaweah River from South Fork campground, at the extreme southern boundary of Sequoia National Park. The Muir Grove, just west of the Dorst campground, is less pristine but more accessible. From Quail Flat, 4 mi. along Generals Hwy. from the turnoff to Grant Grove, you can hike down **Redwood Canyon.** True to its name, this small valley, a tributary of the North Fork of the Kaweah River, is filled with redwood trees. The trail forms two loops, allowing you to explore the whole grove.

Many visitors opt for longer forays into the wilderness. Mt. Whitney is on the **John Muir Trail,** which joins the **Pacific Crest Trail** inside King's Canyon Park. The John Muir leads north to Yosemite Valley, over 200 mi. away. Backpackers need to acquire a free wilderness permit by writing to the park or visiting any of the ranger stations.

During the summer especially, rangers organize a variety of activities including nature walks, campfire programs for children, day hikes, and films. They even arrange free **snowshoe walks** every weekend during snow season. Reservations are recommended (for Lodgepole area walks 565-3341, ext. 631; for Grant Grove 335-2315). Scheduling of other activities depends on demand, climate, and Smokey the Bear's mood. Contact a ranger station or look in the *Sequoia Bark,* the park newspaper handed out free at all park entrances, for a calendar of events.

For those with visions of riding the Western range, the parks also offer short or extended **horseback rides,** arranged at private stables in the Grant Grove, Cedar Grove, and Mineral King areas, and at Wolverton in Giant Forest. Horseback riding rates vary with the site (they're not government run), from $11 per hour to $30 for 2 hrs. Stop by the visitors centers or ranger stations for more information on the sundry park outfits, or call ahead to plan longer trips (565-3445).

Wolverton is the center of winter activities, with **downhill skiing** and snow play areas. **Cross-country ski** activities are organized in Giant Forest and Grant Grove Villages.

Sequoia National Forest

The Sierras continue their march southward for 60 mi. below Kings Canyon and Sequoia National Parks before petering out in the low ranges of the Mojave Desert. The Sequoia National Forest covers this southern tip of the Sierras, encompassing the region bounded on the north by the Kings River and on the west and east by two valleys—the San Joaquin and the Owens. The Kern River slices through the middle of the forest. Often overlooked and confused with the better-known Sequoia National Park, the region nevertheless has much to offer.

The Forest Service's mandate for the Sequoia National Forest dictates that it exist as a multi-use facility. Consequently, limited timber harvesting is permitted here, as is hunting and fishing, and several of the rivers are harnessed for hydroelectric power. The forest's main use, however, is for recreation, and much of the backcountry is left to serious campers and backpackers. In these parts, one can still explore untouched streams, alpine meadows, and rugged mountains.

The **forest headquarters** in Porterville, 900 W. Grand Ave. (209-784-1500), 15 mi. east of Rte. 99 midway between Fresno and Bakersfield, sells a detailed map of the forest for $2.10; you can also order it by mail from the Three Forest Interpretative Association (3FIA), 13098 E. Wire Grass Ln., Clovis 93612. The headquarters will burden you with as much free printed matter as you can carry. (Open Mon.-Fri. 8am-5pm; in winter 8am-4:30pm.) Whenever entering the forest, check with the appropriate ranger station on your way in to ascertain weather and fire conditions. A final caveat: Purify all water taken from rivers or streams by boiling or dissolving a purifying pill (available at most drugstores). There are all sorts of nasty microscopic parasites in unpurified water that could make your life very unpleasant (see Camping in the General Introduction).

Wilderness Areas

The Sequoia National Forest features five designated "wilderness areas," each administered by the district of the forest in which it lies. This is primitive land—no tourists, no developed campsites. If you enjoy being on your own, welcome; just be sure to pick up a free **wilderness permit** at a district ranger's office.

Dome Land Wilderness: the southeast portion of the forest, northeast of Lake Isabella. Glorious during the early spring and late fall, though scorching in the summertime. 94,000 acres; Cannell Meadow District.

Golden Trout Wilderness: immediately south of Sequoia National Park, east to the Kern River, west almost to the forest boundary. The California state fish, the golden trout, populates this part of the Kern River. 111,000 acres across 3 ranger districts.

Jennie Lakes Wilderness: off the Generals Hwy. between Sequoia and Kings Canyon parks. 10,000 acres; Hume Lake District.

Monarch Wilderness: north of Jennie Lakes, along the Kings River. 24,000 acres; Hume Lake District.

South Sierra Wilderness: along the eastern forest boundary, north of Dome Land. Cannell Meadow and Mt. Whitney Districts.

Hume Lake District

The northern section of Sequoia National Forest surrounds Kings Canyon Highway, the road which connects the Grant Grove and Cedar Grove areas of Kings Canyon National Park. The Hume Lake area, although only 10 mi. from Grant Grove Village, is uncrowded and beatific. The artificial lake once provided water for the world's longest lumber flume (a waterslide for transporting logs). The campground at the lake costs $10 per night for one of 75 sites with drinking water. (Open May-Sept.; trailer sites; fishing in season.) **Princess** campground, closer to Grant Grove, is similarly developed and costs $8. (Open May-Sept.; trailer sites.) The seven other forest service campgrounds in this area are free, and three are open year-round. Drive along Forest Service Rd. 13S01 from the south shore of Hume Lake to **Landslide** and **Tenmile** campgrounds. (Open May-Oct.) Neither has drinking water, but both are near the Tenmile and Bearskin **sequoia groves** and have water available at nearby streams. Six other virgin stands of the giant trees are within a few miles of Rte. 180 on forest service roads. The **Converse Basin Grove** on Rd. 13S014 is the most accessible. The grove's **Chicago Stump** is all that remains of a giant felled for display at the 1893 Columbian Exposition in Chicago. **Buck Rock** and **Big Meadow** (25 sites) campgrounds are free and can be reached from Generals Hwy. by Rd. 14S11.

The Hume Lake District contains most of the **Monarch Wilderness Area.** The area's remarkable **Grand Dike** rock outcropping and wildflowers are accessible to experienced hikers by the Deer Cove Creek Trail. Look for the trailhead a mile or so before Rte. 180 re-enters Kings Canyon National Park near Cedar Grove. This area is steep, rugged, and rarely used.

The **Hume Lake Ranger District Office** is located at 35860 E. Kings Canyon Rd. (Hwy. 180), Dunlap 93621 (209-338-2251), east of Fresno near the forest entrance. Be sure to stop there to check conditions before heading into the backcountry. (Open daily 8am-4:30pm; in winter Mon.-Fri. 8am-4pm.) After hours call 209-338-2251 for recorded information.

Southern Districts

By far the simplest way to explore this part of the forest is to drive along the **Western Divide Highway** (closed Nov.-March). The highway is a detour linking Rte. 99 on the western side of the Sierras with U.S. 395 hemming the eastern slope, and is for much of the year the only road route across the Sierras south of Yosemite. One of the precious few roads running perpendicular to the Sierra Crest, this highway provides wide-screen panoramas of rocky peaks and forested canyons.

Reach the Divide Highway from Rte. 190 out of Porterville. Rte. 190 winds gently through the foothills up to the mountains after passing Lake Success, an artificial lake and recreation area developed and maintained by the Army Corps of Engineers. From Lake Isabella and Bakersfield, you can also follow Rte. 178 east to Rte. 155, then take County Rd. 495 north to Kernville and Mountain 99, a road that connects to the Divide Highway. Keep in mind that all of these roads are quite tortuous and require slow and careful driving. When calculating traveling time, assume that your speed will average around 20 mph.

Among the sights along the Western Divide is **Dome Rock,** a massive granite monolith, about midway between Porterville and Kernville. A mile-long drive on unpaved road and a short walk up the side of the dome reward you with a 360° view of Kern River Canyon to the west, and of easterly peaks still snow-capped in June. In autumn, the **Quaking Aspen** area, 4 mi. north of Dome Rock, is vibrant with fall colors; there are several pretty trails, fishing holes, a campground with drinking water, and some large-group campsites. (Open May-Oct., sites $5.)

Numerous other established campgrounds also border the Divide Highway. The 19 free sites at **Peppermint,** between Quaking Aspen and Dome Rock, are shaded by birch and pine, with access to toilets, fire pits, and some picnic tables. (Open May-Oct. Water available at a nearby stream.) **Redwood Meadows,** 8 mi. south of Dome Rock, has drinking water and restrooms (open June-Oct., sites $5). This popular campground situates 15 tent sites in a forested nexus of old roads and hiking trails, across the road from the Long Meadow Grove of sequoia. View the grove from the **Trail of a Hundred Giants,** a ½-mi. loop trail accessible to the handicapped (maximum grade 6%).

This northern section of the lower Sequoia Forest is managed out of the **Tule River Ranger District Office,** 93256 Rte. 190, Springville 93256 (209-539-2607), between Lake Success and the forest boundary, and the **Hot Springs Ranger District Office,** 43474 Mt. Rd. 50, Rte. 4, P.O. Box 548, California Hot Springs 93207 (805-548-6503). Both offices are open mid-May to mid-September daily from 8am to 4:30pm; in winter Mon. through Fri. from 8am to 4:30pm. Both provide up-to-date information on the forest. Reach the town of California Hot Springs by taking Rte. 65 south from Porterville to Ducor.

Approaching the forest from the south, the road coils north along the Kern River from **Cannell Meadow Ranger District Office,** P.O. Box 6, Kernville 93238 (619-376-3781), at the northern tip of Lake Isabella. (Open daily 8am-4:30pm; in winter Mon.-Fri. 8am-4:30pm.) The office can supply information on campgrounds and on whitewater rafting along the swift Kern River above the lake.

Moving north from Lake Isabella, six campgrounds lie along Tulare County Rte. 99: **Camp #3, Fairview, Goldenledge, Headquarters, Hospital Flat, and Limestone.** All cost $5, except Limestone, which is free and overlooks the Kern River. An ideal campsite, Limestone has fantastic fishing but, alas, no piped water. (Open May-Nov.; 22 sites.) Only Headquarters is open year-round (water, pit toilets, 44 sites). Branching off to the east just north of Limestone, the **Sherman Pass Road** climbs to a lookout point at 9000 ft. and to several isolated campgrounds with piped water. After a 15-mi. stretch of unpaved road, the Sherman Pass connects with I-395 on the eastern slope. The tortuous switchbacks and steep inclines of Sherman's Pass may not be your cup of tea, but the road does offer a valuable and visually vivid alternative route through the Sierras. The road is closed in winter.

Several campgrounds line Rte. 155 west of Lake Isabella. The free **Cedar Creek** has drinking water, a stream, restrooms, and fine vistas (open year-round). Anglers and rafters can't get enough of this area, and most of the campgrounds along the Kern River fill up on busy summer days. The **Greenhorn Ranger District,** Federal Building #322, 800 Truxton Ave., Bakersfield 93301 (805-861-4212), has the scoop on this portion of the forest. After office hours call 861-4418 for recorded information on campgrounds and road conditions. (Open Mon.-Fri. 8am-4:30pm.)

Sierra National Forest

Covering 1.3 million acres south of the Merced River and north of the Kings River, the Sierra National Forest fills the gap between Yosemite National Park and Sequoia and Kings Canyon National Parks. The terrain is diverse: rolling, oak-covered foothills on the edge of the San Joaquin Valley to the alpine peaks of the Sierra Nevada crest. Though the park is a popular destination, you can go days without encountering another human being. Recreation centers around the region's rivers and lakes, including the always crowded Huntington Lake and Shaver Lake.

The forest is organized into four ranger districts. The excellent main **information office** for the forest is at the Sierra National Forest's Supervisor's Office, 1600 Tollhouse Rd., Clovis 93612 (209-487-5155; 24-hr. recorded information 487-5456). A big, bouncy, and beautiful map of the forest costs $2.10. Information on camping, hiking, pack and river outfitters, lodges, and boat rentals, as well as a number of publications on the Sierras and helpful advice from forest-lovers are all available here. (Open Mon.-Fri. 8am-4:30pm.)

Wildernesses

Designated wilderness areas comprise 46% of the forest and are popular with backpackers who want to explore the backcountry. A visitor's permit is required and can be acquired at any of the ranger stations (free). Trailhead quotas are in effect from July through Labor Day in the Ansel Adams, John Muir, Dinkey Lakes, and Kaiser Wildernesses; those who arrive without reservations are often disappointed, especially on weekends and holidays. If you're planning an extended trek, ask the rangers for information about pack stations that will cache your food.

Ansel Adams Wilderness: in the northeast section of the forest, near Yosemite and Devil's Postpile National Monument. Accessible from Rte. 120 or U.S. 395. 228,000 acres; Minarets and Pineridge districts.

Dinkey Lakes Wilderness: in the middle of the forest, between Huntington Lake and Courtright Reservoir. Not accessible in snow season. Mostly above 8000 ft. 30,000 acres; Pineridge and Kings River districts.

John Muir Wilderness: encompasses Kings Canyon National Park on west, north, and east (shared with Inyo National Forest). Access limited in snow season. 584,000 acres; Pineridge and Kings River districts.

Kaiser Wilderness: just north of Huntington Lake, divided by the east-west Kaiser Ridge. Southern half is densely forested. Northern half is more open and contains 18 small lakes. Winter access limited. 22,000 acres; Pineridge district.

Monarch Wilderness: along the Kings River. No wilderness permit required. 42,000 acres maintained jointly by the park services of both the Sequoia National Forest and the Kings River district.

Mariposa District

Information on this northwestern district, framed by Rte. 41 out of Fresno, can be obtained by calling or writing the **Mariposa Ranger District Office,** 41969 Rte. 41, Oakhurst 93644 (209-683-4665; open Mon.-Sat. 8am-4:30pm), or the **Mariposa Ranger Station,** 5158 Rte. 140, Mariposa 95338 (209-966-3638; open Mon.-Sat. 8am-4:30pm). **Bass Lake** is a pleasant enough body of water, thronged in summer by water-desperate San Joaquin Valley residents. The carnival atmosphere would make Bakhtin proud, but be sure to reserve a campsite ahead of time in July and August. Reservations can be made through MISTIX (800-283-2267) for the **Forks, Lupine, Spring Cove,** and **Wishon Point** campgrounds (sites $10). All five have toilets and drinking water. Maximum stay 10 days. When you reach the lake, stop first at the **Bass Lake Visitor Station,** 3990 Rd. 222 (209-683-3214; open daily 8am-4:30pm), at the western edge of the lake, for information about boating, swimming, fishing, waterskiing, and hiking. Nine more campgrounds lie near a mostly unpaved road east of Rte. 41 between Bass Lake and Sugar Pine. These are worth staying in for their own sake, especially **Nelder Grove,** which nestles among the redwoods and operates an interpretive center; ask the campground hosts for a tour of the big trees. (No regular hours.) All of these campgrounds have tables, outhouses, and some fire rings, but none have drinking water. Since only **Chilkoot** can be reached via paved road, you should call a ranger station for road conditions. The 30 sites in **Summerdale Campground,** at the border of Yosemite, are often used by spillover campers ($8 for pit toilets, piped water, a table, and a fire ring; usually full by Friday for the coming weekend).

Next to Nelder Grove Campground is the **Shadow of the Giants Trail,** a mile-long path extending through the grove's 106 sequoias. A separate trail leads to the largest tree in the grove, the 246-ft. **Bull Buck Tree.** You can also meander along the **Way of the Mono Trail,** a favorite among schoolchildren. Take Rte. 41 to the Bass Lake turn-off and follow Rd. 222 about 4 mi. to the parking lot at the trailhead. A brochure from the district ranger's office explains the "interpretive points" along the trail.

Food and fishing supplies are available at the **Old Corral Grocery & Tackle Shop** on Rte. 41 about 3 mi. south of the Bass Lake turn-off. (Open daily 8am-8pm.) For a better selection of fruits and vegetables, try the **Raley's** supermarket in Oakhurst on Rte. 41. (Open daily 7am-11pm.) In summer, buy produce straight from the growers at one of the **fruit stands** in the flats along Rte. 168 outside Clovis. **Gas** is readily available from several stations in Oakhurst. There's a Chevron on Rte. 41 (open 24 hr.).

Minarets District

Bordered on the south and east by the San Joaquin River, this region surrounds **Mammoth Pool Reservoir,** an aquatic body created by a dam that produces hydroelectric power for the Southern California Edison Company. The mountains around the pool soar 2000 ft. above the shore, forming a steep, narrow valley, dotted with oak and Ponderosa pine. Boating, fishing, hiking, and swimming are available when the road to Mammoth Pool is open (usually June-Oct.). There are seven campgrounds in the area; Mammoth Pool campground is the largest (47 sites) and closest to the lake, and drinking water is available. (Sites $5.) For more information, contact the **Minarets Ranger District Office,** North Fork 93643 (209-877-2218; open daily 8am-4:30pm), off Rte. 41 south of Bass Lake, or call 209-887-2218 for recreation information.

Kings River District

The far reaches of this district rise as high as 13,000 ft. at the Sierra Crest. Most of the region's activity centers around the **Dinkey Creek** area and the **Pine Flat Reservoir.** At the reservoir, **Kings River Ranger District Office,** 34849 Maxon Rd., 1 mi. off of Trimmer Rte., Sanger 93657 (209-855-8321; open Mon.-Fri. 8am-4:30pm), dispenses advice and permits. Named after an early settler's dog mauled by a bear, Dinkey Creek now offers three campgrounds (sites $8, filled on weekends) and a ranger station (841-3404; summer only). Bears are still a nuisance here, so lock your food and dogs in the car or sling them from a high limb. Dinkey Creek is reached from Shaver Lake on Rte. 168. Past Dinkey Creek, you approach the **McKinley Grove** of sequoia, where camping in **Gigantea's** seven sites is free. **Buck Meadows,** farther along, has 26 sites, and **Lily Pad,** on Wishon Reservoir, has 19. Lily Pad has water and costs $8. Buck Meadows is dry, but free. Wishon and nearby Courtright Reservoirs are the best trailheads for treks into the popular Woodchuck and Red Mountain Basin areas of the John Muir Wilderness. Taking a trip to Upper and Lower Indian Lakes is one of the surest ways to find real solitude.

Whitewater rafting on the Kings River is popular, especially in late spring. Operators include **Spirit Whitewater,** 1005 Rose Ave., in far-off Cotati 94706 (707-795-7305); **Kings River Expeditions,** 211 N. Van Ness Ave., Fresno (209-233-4881); and **Zephyr Expedition,** P.O. Box 510, Columbia 95370 (209-532-6249). All companies run trips 42 mi. east of Piedra on the Kings River in the heart of the dark forest. Trailbikes, ATVs, and four-wheel-drive vehicles raise dust on the five off-highway routes providing access to camping and fishing. Check at the district rangers office for more information.

One mile from Dinkey Creek Campgrounds is the **Dinkey Creek Inn** (209-841-3435; open Sun.-Thurs. 8am-7pm, Fri.-Sat. 8am-8pm). The inn offers several services, including a gas station, telephones, a grocery, rustic cabins ($23 for as many as 4 people) and showers ($1.50, open daily 9am-5pm). Reserve cabins two weeks in advance, earlier for holidays. 23 mi. away is **Wishon Village,** with a gas station, store, bar, and private campground.

Pineridge District

Easily accessible from Rte. 168, this is the most popular region of the national forest. Overseeing the activity here is the **Pineridge Ranger District Ofiice,** P.O. Box 300, Shaver Lake, 93664 (209-841-3311), one of the forest's busiest information centers (open daily 8am-4:30pm).

The road as far as Kaiser Pass is an easy drive, **Huntington Lake** and **Shaver Lake** (with fishing, swimming, and boating) are popular waterfronts. The Sierra Marina (209-841-3324) at the north end rents several kinds of boats, including 10-person pontoon boats ($105 per day, $65 per half-day) and fishing boats with motors ($35 per day, $25 per half-day, $8 per 2 hr.). The Shaver Lake Chamber of Commerce provides additional information (P.O. Box 58, Shaver Lake 93664; 209-841-3350). Huntington Lake lies farther east along Rte. 168, and its shimmering waters see a lot of use. Sailboat regattas, such as Fresno's monster race in July, occur throughout the summer. All of the lake's seven tent campgrounds cost $10, except the free **Badger Flat;** five of them require MISTIX reservations in July and August. **Deer Creek, Kinnikinnick,** and **Catavee** campgrounds lie beside Rte. 168, hugging Huntington Lake's north shore. All have toilets, water, fire pits, and tables. Popular Deer Creek offers views of the lake and lots of space for RVs. **Lakeview Cottages** (209-893-9228, in winter 213-697-6556), located on the lake's shore, rents cottages at $38-47 for two people, $60-68 for four. Reservations are necessary as far as six months in advance. There is the full complement of water recreation on and around the lake in summer, and in winter **cross-country skiing** is usually available. Cross-country and snowmobile routes, as well as frolicsome "snowplay" areas, are maintained along Rte. 168. Valley visitors or residents, sick of Fresno's sultry weather, zip up into the mountains to romp in clear air and pure snow.

Beyond Kaiser Pass, the road becomes narrow and slightly treacherous—honk your horn on the sharp blind turns. The terrain at the upper end of this road is definitively High Sierra—alpine lakes, flowers, and craggy summits. The **Mono Hot Springs Resort and Bathhouse,** P.O. Box 128, Oakhurst (209-227-2631), carries on up here with cabins, a restaurant, free mineral baths nearby, and natural hot springs. The road divides farther ahead, with routes going to **Edison** and **Florence Lakes.** The **Vermillion Valley Resort,** on Edison Lake, Mono Hot Springs 93642, has housekeeping cabins and a restaurant. Make reservations well in advance. The resort runs ferries along the lakes to trailheads right on the border of the lake-spangled country in the John Muir Wilderness.

All of the campgrounds above are $10 and close during the winter, when the entire High Sierra is entombed in snow. Opening dates are highly unpredictable, but sometimes arrive as early as May.

Eastern Slope

The magnificent eastern slope of the Sierra Crest is more of a wall than a "slope." While the Sierras descend slowly over a number of miles on their western side and melt into California's San Joaquin Valley, they drop off precipitously to the east, their jagged rock faces forming a startling silhouette. Although barely visible from Fresno and Merced in the San Joaquin Valley, the peaks of the High Sierra tower in a fearsome escarpment over the towns of the Owens Valley. To the south, decidedly uninviting to all but those with dirt bikes, the copper-brown sand dunes of the vast California desert strike a dramatic contrast with their snow-capped neighbors.

This contrast between east and west is a result of the lifting and faulting processes that shaped the Sierra ridge some 10 million years ago. Some areas have continued to rise relatively rapidly. The eastern slope traces the fault line where years ago the Owens Valley collapsed to expose 14,000-ft. slabs of rock to glaciation. The western slope, which *is* actually a slope, watered by cooling ocean air rising to its crest, is carpeted by dense forests at middle elevations. Once over the top, the clouds dissipate, leaving the eastern side remarkably arid.

Tioga Road in Yosemite traverses the Sierras and shows this pattern remarkably well. From the lush greenery of the flower-speckled Tuolumne meadows on the gently rising western slope, the road crosses 9941-ft. Fort Tioga Pass and plummets to desolate Mono Lake at 6400 ft. in just 6½ mi. (Bring a wide angle lens along for this ride.)

Tioga itself has risen 3 in. in the past 25 years from continued uplift. Hiking across the Sierras from east to west starts with a few hours' upward climb, followed by miles of gentle downhill slope. The shortest hike between paved roads is over **Kearsarge Pass** (about 16 mi.) from Onion Valley to Road's End near Cedar Grove in Kings Canyon National Park.

The tiny villages that stretch from Mt. Whitney to Yosemite National Park are linked by U.S. 395, the access route to the Sierras' eastern face. Small as they are, the towns eagerly support the crowds of campers, climbers, and camera-carriers who congregate in their valley each summer.

Lone Pine and Inyo National Forest

"Inyo" means "dwelling place of the great spirits" in the local Native American language, and the striking arid and forested landscapes in Inyo County lend credence to the name. The Inyo National Forest is comprised of a scattered collection of land parcels, many of which don't even have a single tree. The definition of "forest" was evidently stretched by politicians who wanted to preserve Los Angeles' water supply by maintaining public ownership of the Sierra watersheds.

The town nearest the forest is Lone Pine, named for the solitary pine tree which grew by its creek. Much has changed since Lone Pine was an active supply town for the mining industry during the 1870s: the tree is long gone, the mines closed, and the town totally rebuilt (following an earthquake which leveled all structures and created nearby Diaz Lake). The town, however, continues to provide supplies—except that now they're for the tourist gold mine.

Practical Information

Visitors Information: Interagency Visitors Center, U.S. 395 (876-4252), at Rte. 136 about 1 mi. south of town. Excellent selection of maps, brochures, guidebooks, nature books, and small exhibits. Knowledgeable staff. Open daily 8am-5:50pm; in winter 8am-4:50pm. **Chamber of Commerce:** 126 S. Main St. (876-4444), in Lone Pine. Same services and information as the visitors center, but at a more convenient location. Open Mon.-Fri. 9am-5pm.

Mt. Whitney/Inyo National Forest Ranger Station: 640 S. Main St. (876-5542), in Lone Pine. Pick up wilderness permits here. They also sell topographical and trail maps if you plan on camping overnight at a non-established campground. Open June 22-Oct. 15 daily 7am-4:30pm; call ahead during the winter. Write to P.O. Box 8, Lone Pine 93545. Between June and Sept. 15, quotas are enforced for some popular trails within the forest. Half the permits are reserved daily on a first-come, first-served basis, the other half can be obtained by mail between March 1 and May 31.

Greyhound: 107 N. Main St. (876-4244), in La Florista. One bus per day to Reno ($47) and to L.A. ($33.30). Open Mon.-Sat. 9am-5pm.

Car Rental: Lindsay Automotive, 316 S. Washington St. (876-4789). Rates from $38 per day. 150 free miles. Must be 21 with credit card. Open 8am-5pm.

AAA Emergency Road Service: 876-4600.

Bike Rental: Bent's Bikes, 132 N. Main (876-4547). Mountain bikes $5 per hr., $17 per day. Open Tues.-Sat. 10am-6pm.

Laundromat: Coin Op Laundromat, 105 Post St., at Main behind the High Sierra Inn. Wash 85¢, 12-min. dry 25¢. Open daily 8am-7pm.

Hospital: Southern Inyo, 501 E. Locust (876-5501).

Emergency Medical Service: 911.

Post Office: 121 Bush St. (876-5681), between Main and Jackson. Open Mon.-Fri. 9am-5pm. General Delivery ZIP Code: 93545.

Area Code: 619.

Lone Pine straddles U.S. 395. Fourteen miles to the north lies Independence, the county seat. Lone Pine is the first Sierra town you hit when traveling northeast on Rte. 136 from **Death Valley** and is a welcome center for the lush greens of the tallest mountain in the contiguous United States. Los Angeles is a 4-hr. drive (212 mi.) to the west.

Accommodations and Camping

Although motels abound in Lone Pine, cheap indoor lodging is scarce. Make reservations at least two weeks in advance for weekends and holidays, and call at least a day ahead for weekday reservations. Camping is cheap and within easy walking distance; again, be sure to arrive early on weekends and holidays.

Mt. Whitney Motel, 305 N. Main St. (876-4207). Amiable owners and relatively low prices make this the best deal in town. Cable TV, A/C, in-room coffee, pool. Rooms for 1-2 people Sun.-Thurs. $45, Fri.-Sat. $40.

Trails Motel, 400 S. Main St. (876-5555). TV, A/C, and in-room coffee. Pool, spa. Singles $36, on the weekend $39. Doubles $39, on the weekend $49.

Portagee Joe Campground, turn west on Whitney Portal Rd., ½ mi. to Tuttle Creek Rd.; turn south 1/10 mi. to campground. 15 sites. Pit toilets, tables, grills, piped water, and a stream. Sites $6.

Diaz Lake Campground, U.S. 395, 2 mi. south of Lone Pine. 200 sites. Overlooks an 86-acre lake with swimming, fishing, boating, and waterskiing. Flush toilets, tables, grills, well water, and concession stands. Sites $6.

There are 12 public campgrounds (all but Road's End have piped water) in the Lone Pine area of Inyo National Forest. Those at higher elevations, including the Whitney Trailhead, are ensconced in the cool evergreens with phenomenal views of the valley below. Contact the Mt. Whitney Ranger (876-5542) or call MISTIX (800-444-7275) for more information and reservations. (Sites $3-10. Road's End is free.) Hot showers ($2) for campers are available at **Kirk's Barber Shop,** 104 N. Main (876-5700).

Food

Lone Pine has its fair share of coffee shops and 24-hr. mini-marts, but not much else. If you're camping, grab groceries in town and do your own cooking under the western stars.

Joseph's Bi-Rite Market, 119 S. Main at Mountain View (876-4378). Slightly overpriced, but the only market in town. Open Mon.-Sat. 8:30am-9pm, Sun. 8:30am-8pm.

PJ's, 446 Main (876-5796). Down-to-earth local eatery with convincing prices. Their chicken-fried steak ($7) is mammoth and an excellent post-climb treat. (This is the only 24 hr. place in the area.)

Ernie's Tin Roof, U.S. 395 (876-4574), 2 mi. south of Lone Pine at Diaz Lake. Peaceful lakeside setting miraculously undisturbed by the minature golf course under the same management. Sun. brunch is substantial, including biscuits and coffee or tea with all entrees. Spanish omelette with crisp vegetables $4.75. Scrumptious seafood dishes; shrimp boat with fries $5. Open Tues.-Sat. 11am-10pm, Sun. 8am-10pm.

Sierra Cantina, N. Main St. (876-5740). All-you-can-eat Mexican lunch ($6) and dinner ($9). Buffet offers at least 4 hot entrees with fresh fruit. Open Thurs.-Mon. 11:30am-8pm (sometimes open later).

Sights and Activities

With the cragged edges of **Mount Whitney** as the star of the show, the parts of Inyo National Forest bordering Kings Canyon and Sequoia National Parks make up a suitable supporting cast. All of the Sierra's tallest peaks are here, generally within 10 to 15 mi. of U.S. 395. These regions can be explored by day hikes and overnight trips, using cheap national forest campgrounds as your base. All campsites have water and go for about $6 per site. Beware the high altitude and allow extra time and effort for hikes.

The **Whitney Trailhead** (876-5542) is 13 mi. west of Lone Pine. Turn west on Whitney Portal Rd. at the town's only traffic light. On the way, you'll pass through the geological anomalies known as the **Alabama Hills.** Recognize this landscape from the Western classics *How the West Was Won* or *The Lone Ranger?* One area made such a perfect natural amphitheater that it was used as a stage by the "Deepest Valley Theater Company" in the late 60s. The canyon entrance at **Whitney Portal** provides fantastic camping (sites $10). The 11-mi. trek to the top of the lower 48's highest peak usually takes two days. Most hikers start from the trailhead in the early afternoon. You can then camp midway up the trail your first night, leave your gear behind and continue upwards to the peak on the second day, and arrive back at the trailhead before dark. Stream water can be found as far up the trail as the mid-station, but it *must* be boiled and filtered: all water in the area carries the risk of the dreaded *giardiasis,* a parasitical infection of the intestine. Take your own supply of water from the mid-station to the summit. Do bring your camera—this is why you bought it.

If you intend to stop overnight on the trail to Mt. Whitney, plan ahead. On March 1, the Forest Service begins to accept reservations for wilderness permits, and quotas are filled rapidly (though the deadline is May 31). Unclaimed permits are released at 8am to those who show up on the doorstep; the line begins forming at 5am. Be warned: the trails are well-policed, and hikers without permits are likely to face high fines and an appearance before the local magistrate. Write or phone the Mt. Whitney Ranger District office (see Practical Information) for more information. The trail is generally free from snow between mid-July and early October, though ice patches exist year-round. While more a strenuous hike than a climb, you may nonetheless need an ice axe and crampons during the spring and early summer. For rock climbers, the East Face of Mt. Whitney is a year-round challenge. Contact the **Arête Climbing Center** (872-0294) for information and guides.

If your time is limited or if you simply want to choose the road less traveled, try one of the many day hikes that traverse the rest of the forest. The **Onion Valley Trailhead** (9200 ft.), 14 mi. west of Independence on Market St., is open May through November. A moderate hike along Kearsarge Pass will take you 2500 ft. above the trailhead. More difficult but also more rewarding are the **Robinson Trail** and the **Golden Lake Trail.** Expect snow early October through mid-July, and bring your own water on the trails whatever season you visit. You can camp at the trailhead or at **Grays Meadow,** 8 mi. east of Onion, for $6. Arrive very early (say, oh, 6am) on summer weekends and holidays.

You can **fish** at many of the lakes and streams within the forest, most of which are regularly stocked with golden mouth bass. Buy a fishing license for $7.50 per day at **Slater's Sporting Goods,** 130 S. Main St. (876-5020). Open daily 7am-9pm, in winter 7am-4pm.

Bishop and Owens Valley

In 1861, Samuel Bishop brought 600 cattle and his boots from Fort Tejon to settle among Native Americans at what is now Bishop Creek. Grazing herds still line Rte. 395 on the way into town. Bishop—easily the largest town in the eastern slope south of Mammoth—today dubs itself "Mule capital of the world," claiming the mule can do anything the horse can . . . and more. The town is the base for many mule-powered expeditions in the mountains and offers a lot more for vacationers besides.

Practical Information

Visitors Information: Visitors Center and Chamber of Commerce, 690 N. Main St. (873-8405), at the City Park. Maps, brochures, and information on the Owens Valley area. Get a free copy of the *Bishop Visitors Guide* for up-to-date listings of special events. Open Mon.-Fri. 9am-5pm, Sat.-Sun. 10am-4pm. Park open 24 hr. Community pool located directly behind the visitors center. Showers and changing rooms available. (Open Mon.-Sat. 1-5:15pm. Admission $1.50, 12-17 $1, under 12 50¢.)

White Mountain Ranger Station: 798 N. Main St. (873-4207). Excellent lists of campgrounds, roads, and nearby trails. Daily wilderness permits (free), up-to-date weather reports, and a message board. Topographical maps $2.65. Open Mon.-Fri. 8am-4:30pm.

Greyhound: 201 Warren St. (872-2721), behind the city parking lot. One bus per day to L.A. ($34) and to Reno ($39). Open Mon.-Fri. 1-5pm, Sat.-Sun. 1:30-2:30pm.

Dial-A-Ride: 872-1901. Serves Bishop and nearby trailheads. Fare 50¢ round-trip within city limits, 75¢ to areas just outside of the city; otherwise 60¢ per mile. Open Mon.-Fri. 9am-4pm.

Senior Information: Senior Center, 873-4248.

Car Rental: Ford Rent-A-Car, 1440 U.S. 6 North (873-4291). Their prices reflect their monopoly in Bishop: $38 per day with 150 free mi., 18¢ per mile after that. Driver's license and major credit card required. Open Mon.-Sat. 8am-5pm.

AAA Emergency Road Service: 873-8221.

Public Library: 210 Academy Ave. (872-8091). A large selection of books, with a special section on California and Inyo County. Open Mon.-Thurs. 10am-8pm, Fri. 10am-6pm, Sat. 10am-1pm.

Laundromat: Sierra Suds, Church at Warren (873-5524), behind Joseph's Bi-Rite. Wash $1.25, 10-min. dry 25¢. Open daily 7am-10pm.

Hospital: Northern Inyo, 150 Pioneer Lane (873-5811)

Emergency: 911.

Police: 873-5866.

Post Office: 595 W. Line St. (873-3526). Open Mon.-Fri. 9am-5pm. General Delivery ZIP Code: 93514.

Weather Information: 873-3213.

Area Code: 619.

Accommodations and Camping

You're best off camping in Bishop. Hotels aren't scarce; it's just that the cheap ones are hiding.

El Rancho Motel, 274 Lagoon St. (872-9251), 1 block west of Main St. near Greyhound. One of the nicest in town. Peppermint-fresh rooms, TV, A/C, in-room coffee. Singles and doubles $36. Kitchens $6 extra. Reservations recommended 2 wks. in advance. For Labor Day, 2 mos. in advance.

Town House Hotel, 625 N. Main St. (872-4541). Their welcome sign says "Once a guest, always a friend," and you get the feeling they mean it. TV, A/C, pool. Singles $37. Doubles $42.

Thunderbird Hotel, 190 W. Pine St. (873-4215 or 873-4214), west from the Union 76 station. Capacious rooms with bathtubs, TV, A/C, and in-room coffee. Singles Sun.-Thurs. $34, Fri.-Sat. $44. Doubles Sun.-Thurs. $44, Fri.-Sat. $50.

Brown's Town, 873-8522, 1 mi. south of town on U.S. 395. Turn west on Schrober Lane. Picnic area available for day use. Also on the premises: a daily video show and **Brown's Museum,** with antiques and original buildings of Bishop (both free). RV sites $12, tent sites $10, 7-min. showers 50¢. Open 24 hr.

Pleasant Valley Campground, 7 mi. northwest of Bishop on U.S. 395, along the Owens River. Turn north on Pleasant Valley Rd., 1 mi. to camp. 200 sites. Pit toilets, tables, grills, and well water. Sites $7.

Mill Pond Recreation Area (872-1301), 6½ mi. northwest of Bishop on U.S. 395, 1/5 mi. south on Ed Powers Rd., 4/5 mi. west on Sawmill Rd. Next to Mill Pond Riding Stables. Piped and stream water, pond for swimming and sailing, tennis courts, archery, horseshoe pits, and flush toilets. Sites $7.

There are over 20 **Inyo National Forest** campgrounds in the Bishop Ranger District. **First Falls** at Big Pine, **Grandview** in the Bristlecone Forest, and both **Sabrina** and **Willow** (closest to Bishop) at Bishop Creek are all free. Grandview has no water; the other three have only stream water, which must be boiled before drinking. Other sites are $7-8 and have piped water. Group units are $20-25; call MISTIX (800-444-7275) or the ranger (873-4207) for reservations.

If you're traveling in a group, the best option is the **Bishop Creek Lodge,** South Lake Rd. (873-4484). Take Rte. 168 north from Bishop. Rustic cabins for 4 with gas stoves, barbecue, linens, dishes, and shared bathroom facilities are $55 per night (2-day min. stay). With a general store, lodge, and cocktail bar, the Bishop Creek Lodge has been popular for over 60 years.

Food

Bar-B-Q Bill's, 187 S. Main St. (872-5535). A plastic heifer on the roof outside heralds wagon-wheel decor and cattle-train service within, but the food redeems all. You can select ribs, salads, or chili *a la carte* (each about $1), or order the satisfying BBQ combos starting at $5. Open Mon.-Thurs. 11am-9pm, Fri.-Sat. 11am-10pm.

Pyrenees Soup and Sandwiches, 150 N. Main St. (873-7275). Light lunches $3-4. Half a world away from its namesake, but well-frequented by locals for the delicious homemade soups and hearty sandwiches. Open Mon.-Sat. 10am-3pm.

Lee's Chinese Food, 285 Main St. (872-2189). The windowbox is filled with trinkets from every Chinese pawnshop in the valley, but the interior is fairly conventional. Dinner specials ($5-7) change weekly. Presentation—on paper plates—is unpretentious. The food's not unbeatable, but prices are (entrees from $3.25). Open Mon.-Fri. 11am-2pm and 4-8pm, Sat. 4pm-'til.

Schat's Bakery, 763 N. Main St. (873-7156). Enormous Dutch bakery that distributes throughout the valley. Wonderful fruit and nut breads ($4.20), sourdough ($1.80), and a cheese-bread big enough to serve ½ the Brady Bunch (excluding Alice; $4.80). Superb cream cakes, pastries, cookies, and chocolates. Open daily 6am-8pm.

Pizza Factory, 912 N. Main (872-8888); next to K-Mart. A standard red, white, and green pizza parlour with delectable pies. The calzone is filling; a large ($5) feeds two. Open Mon.-Sat. 11am-10pm and Sun. noon-10pm.

The Bishop Grill, 281 N. Main (873-3911). A downtown diner popular by knight. The way burgers and fries were intended to be: greasy. Complete dinners $5. Onion rings fit for a king ($1.65). Don't get rooked somewhere else. Pawn your watch if you must, but be sure to eat here. Open daily 6am-8pm.

Activities

The Owens Valley is a backpacker's Eden. East of Bishop, the **White Mountains** raise themselves to heights rivalling the Sierras. If you want to tackle the strenuous, 15-mi. climb to the top of White Mountain itself (14,246 ft.), park your car on White Mountain Rd., 22 mi. from Rte. 168. Camp for free at **Grandview Campground,** on White Mountain Rd., where you can use the pit toilets, tables, and grills. Carry your own water as none is available on this trail or at the campground.

Scattered across the face of the White Mountains like a five o'clock shadow are California's **bristlecone pines,** the oldest living things on the planet. Gnarled, twisted, and warped into fantastic shapes, the trees may grow only one inch every 100 years. The slow growth at extreme altitudes (up to 12,000 ft.) has allowed the "Methuselah" specimen to survive 4700 years to date (to preserve him, they don't tell you which one he is). Many of the pines are over 4000 years old. Take Rte. 168 off U.S. 395 at Big Pine. At the top of the pass turn left at the sign to the Bristlecone Pine Forest and the White Mountains Research station. The paved road takes you to Schulman Grove, where there are two short and interesting hikes. The 12-mi. drive on unpaved roads to Patriarch Grove is treacherous, though a tough family car should be able to make it. Along the way, there are several impressive viewpoints to inspire you to the top.

Continuing east on Rte. 168 from the Bristlecones takes you into **Deep Springs Valley,** home to **Deep Springs College,** the valley's only settlement. Deep Springs has a college program unique in the United States: twenty-four students, all men, attend the liberal arts institution for two years. Drugs, alcohol, and leaving the valley while classes are in session are not allowed. Students operate the school's cattle ranch and make decisions on matters such as faculty hiring and student admissions among themselves. The college doesn't encourage visitors, but a random backpacking student may be greeted with water and perhaps a meal. The valley itself is beautiful high desert (5900 ft.), surrounded by the stunning White Mountains and the shrub-covered Inyo Mountains.

Over the Inyos from Deep Springs lies the uninhabited **Eureka Valley.** The valley's magnificent and haunting **sand dunes** are the largest land-locked dunes in the world. Flip off your shoes, climb to the top of the dunes, and roll down. The friction between the sand you disturb and the nearly 700 ft. of grains beneath makes a bizarre, loud, unfathomably deep sound. These desolate and spooky dunes were once a favorite haunt of Charles Manson. You can try to cajole locals into telling some ghost stories.

Eureka Valley is also the home of madly reproducing **wild horses,** bane to ranchers and ecologists, but a delight to travelers. Seeing the horses is a matter of luck, but early morning is the best time to try. Getting to Eureka Valley and the dunes is tricky. Roads lead into the valley from the Owens Valley near Big Pine and from various points on the Nevada side, but none are reliable and not even the proverbial wild horses could drag you through when the road is washed out or snowed in. Check in with the Department of Transportation, next to the post office in Bishop, or with the rangers, for specifics. See The Desert for tips on desert travel.

Seven miles south of Big Pine on U.S. 395 is a wildlife viewpoint, where you can get a great view of the valley and, sometimes (particularly early morning or evening), elk herds. Elk also congregate on the mowed alfalfa fields, just south of Big Pine on 395.

The abundance of **day hikes** in and around Owens Valley will sate any nature lover. **Little Lakes Valley** and **Mono Lakes Trailhead** are favorites among area natives. From U.S. 395, turn at Tom's Place and continue up Rock Creek Canyon to the end of the road. Parking is available at Mosquito Flat. Little Lakes Valley is surrounded by 13,000-ft. peaks, and many of the lakes in its basin beckon fisherfolk seeking brook, rainbow, and brown trout. In 1864, William Brewer and his party of pioneers were the first white men lucky enough to cross **Mono Pass Trail** and set eyes on beautiful Ruby Lake and its staggering sheer granite walls. There are numerous campgrounds on the way to Mosquito Flat and plenty of day parking at each of the five trailheads. Campsites are $6-8 and include toilets—**Mosquito Flat Trailhead** is a free walk-in site with stream water only.

Sabrina Basin Trailhead offers more moderate hiking and fishing opportunities. From Bishop, turn west on Line St. (Rte. 168) and continue 18 mi. to the lake. Steeper switchbacks off the main trail lead to the less populated **George Lake.** Continue another 5 mi. along Rte. 168 to **South Lake Trailhead,** where leisurely trails lead to Green, Treasure, and Chocolate Lakes. Both trailheads have overnight parking and camping facilities. **High Sierra Limosine** (873-4453) and the **Eastern Sierra Shuttle** (934-3346) service most major trailheads, but are expensive.

To camp in the wilds, you *must* obtain a **wilderness permit** ($3) before your trip. These permits are limited, even if you reserve by mail. Write to the White Mountain Ranger District (see Practical Information) between March 1 and May 31 with their form complete. Some permits are saved for a day-to-day basis, but the competition for them is fierce. Arrive early.

Those who prefer traveling on four legs may be interested in **Pine Creek Saddle and Pack Trains** (387-2797), which provides guided tours of the area on gentle horses and mules. ($15 per 4 hr.; $35 per 5 hr.; $55 per day, including lunch.) Write P.O. Box 968, Bishop 93514, for more information. **Rock Creek Pack Station** (935-4493) offers 4-day wild mustang observation trips for the hardy (in May and June, $400). If you're into wheels, **The Outdoorsman,** 651 N. Main St. (873-3015), in Bishop rents mountain bikes for $5 per hour and $20 per day. **Alpine Adventures** (873-5838) offers a variety of exotic recreational packages from ballooning to river-tubing at reasonable rates; they also provide trailhead transport. Inquire at the Greyhound depot.

The **Paiute Shoshone Indian Cultural Center,** 2300 W. Line St., illustrates the history and culture of some of the seven local tribes (open Mon.-Sat. 9am-5pm, Sun. noon-5pm). For more Native American history, seek out the hidden **Red Rock Canyon Petroglyphs,** which are 4 mi. west of town on U.S. 6 (there are no signs). Take a left on Five Bridges Rd. and then a right on Fish Slough (they're around here somewhere—good luck).

Bishop hosts an eclectic group of annual events. The City Park (behind the visitors center) has been hosting **Monday evening concerts** for 40 consecutive summers (in the gazebo; 8-9pm; free). A massive **rodeo** is held in town every Labor Day

Weekend, and you can park your RV at the fairgrounds for $7 per night (873-8405). Each night, after the cowboys and girls finish taming the wild broncos, they settle down with some herbal tea and recite some of their favorite verse at the **Cowboy Poetry Festival.** Recently begun by the Inyo Council for the Arts, this is a truly remarkable event. Bishop's **Mule Days** are a Memorial Day Weekend tradition. An auction, parade, racing, and other celebrations launch the packing season. The **Ultra Marathon Mule Run,** also an annual event, entails a 30 mi. ascent to an elevation of 8,000 ft. and then a descent to the next valley. In order to compete, you must be as strong as a mule and somewhat stupider; call the Chamber of Commerce if you want to race.

In winter, the evergreen forests, the lake basins, and the peaceful "range of light" (as Muir described the Eastern Sierra) make for spectacular cross-country skiing. Bishop Creek and Rock Creek drainages are reportedly the best areas to explore. **Bishop Creek Lodge** offers 14 miles of groomed trails and a ski school (873-3015 or 873-4484). (Open Fri.-Sun.) The Forest Service occasionally grooms 3 km of trails through the **Four Jeffrey Campground** area. Call the ranger station for details (see Practical Information). Rock Creek Lodge (935-4464) offers access to other terrain considered excellent by locals.

Mammoth Lakes

Home to one of the most popular ski resorts in California, the town of Mammoth Lakes is a giant, year-round playground in the Sierras. In the summer, the ski resort is transformed into mountainbike terrain, and although the gondola carries you and your bike up the mountain, getting *down* is harder than it looks. Confronted with unpredictable weather (such as snow in June), locals and visitors, sharing a passion for the great outdoors, have threshed out a friendly and peaceful community.

Practical Information and Orientation

Visitors Information: Visitors Center and Chamber of Commerce, Main St. (934-2712 or 213-659-MMTH (659-6684)), inside Village Center Mall West, across from the post office. Better than the average visitors center: plenty of up-to-date information on the area as well as a congenial staff. Pick up a free copy of the *Mammoth Times.* Open Sat.-Thurs. 8am-5pm, Fri. 8am-8pm. Hours more restricted in winter.

Mammoth National Forest Visitors Center: east off U.S. 395 (934-2505), north of town. Rest rooms, pay phone. Updated information on which campgrounds, roads, and sights are open. Lists of nature walks and other organized activities. The *Mammoth Trails Hiking Guide* ($2) provides excellent descriptions of day and overnight hikes in the area. Nature exhibits. Open daily 6am-5pm; Oct.-June 8am-4:30pm.

Ski Conditions: 934-6166.

Mammoth Mountain Ski Area: 932-2571.

June Mountain Ski Area: 648-7733.

Mammoth/June Airport: 934-3825.

Greyhound: No phone number. No ticket office. No nothing. The bus stops in front of the McDonalds on Main St. One bus daily to Reno (at 1am) and to L.A. (at 12:30pm). Board here and buy your ticket at the next station. Information at Bishop (872-2721 or 800-531-5332).

Mammoth Area Shuttle (MAS): 934-2571. Runs only during the ski season. The red line services the main lodge and town (free). Other lines connect to various base chairlifts. Special daily service to Tamarack cross-country skiing, call 934-2442.

Taxi: Mammoth Cab (934-3346).

Car Rentals: Eastern Sierra (935-6445).

AAA Emergency Road Service: 934-3385.

Road Conditions: 934-6611 or CalTrans (873-6366).

Equipment Rental: Sandy's Ski Sport, Main St. (934-7518). Mountain bikes $7 per hr., $25 per day. Fishing poles $7 per day. Tents $9 for one day, $5 each additional day. Backpacks $7 for one day, $3 each additional day. Sleeping bags $10 one day, $3 each additional day. Rollerblades $7.50 per hr., $20 per day. Snowski rentals from $10 per day, ski packages $14 a day and up. Open Mon.-Sat. 8am-8pm, Sun. 8am-6pm. **Kittredge Sports,** Main St. (934-7566), is the best place to go for fishing information and equipment. Rod, reel and pole rentals from $5 per day. Also rents mountain bikes $7 per hr., $25 per day.

Snow Line: 934-6166. 24 hr.

Entertainment Hotline: Mammoth Direct Connection (934-7777).

Fire Department: 934-2200 for emergencies (or 911), 934-2300 for business information, on the corner of Main St. and Forest Trail.

Laundromat: on Laurel Mountain Rd., next to the 76 station. Wash $1.25, dry 25¢. Open daily 7:30am-9pm.

Hospital: Centinela Mammoth, 85 Sierra Park Rd. (934-3311). Open 24 hr. Adjacent to the **Medical Clinic** 934-3381.

Emergency: 911.

Post Office: Main St. (934-2205), across from the visitors center. Open Mon.-Fri. 8:30am-5pm. General Delivery ZIP Code: 93546.

Area Code: 619.

Mammoth Lakes is located on U.S. 395 about 160 mi. south of Reno and 40 mi. southeast of the eastern entrance to Yosemite National Park. Rte. 203 runs through the town as Main St., and then veers off to the right as Minaret Summit Rd. In the winter, the roads in from Southern California are jammed with weekend skiiers making the six-hour journey up to the slopes.

Accommodations and Camping

As with most ski resorts, indoor accommodations in Mammoth Lakes during the high season don't come cheap. If you're traveling with three or more people, look for condominium rentals. You enjoy all the comforts of home, including a kitchen and a garage, for as low as $60 per night in summer. Winter lodging is cheapest at the dormitory-style motels. Make reservations for these as far in advance as possible; they go fast. Hikers and bikers will find good deals here in the summer, when rates go down instead of up.

There are nearly 20 Inyo Forest public campgrounds in the area, at Mammoth Lakes, Mammoth Village, Convict Lake, and Reds Meadow. Call the Mammoth Ranger District (934-2505) for more information. Sites between $7-9, with discount rates for groups. Reservations taken only for Sherwin Creek and Pine Glen Group campgrounds ($7), through MISTIX (800-283-2267).

ULLR Lodge, Minaret Rd. just south of Main St. (934-2454). Ski-chalet style, with sauna, TVs in room. Kitchen shared by guests. The best deal in town is a night in their dorm-style rooms, with a shared bathroom at one end of the hall. Winter dorms $17-19. Singles $35, $41 on weekends, $42 on holidays. Doubles $38, $44 on weekends, $47 on holidays. Summer rates: dorm beds $12, private rooms $30-37. There are no dorm rooms for women (due to a lack of demand) but the helpful manager will rent lone women travelers a bed in a private room at the dorm rate, if available.

Innsbruck Lodge, 913 Forest Trail (934-3035). Motel rooms, housekeeping units, and dorm-style rooms all available in a cozy ski lodge with leftover 50s furniture. Sauna, fireplace, and TV. Reserve 4 weeks in advance in winter. "Dormettes" $21. Motel rooms for 1-2 people $50 in winter, $60 on weekends, $39 daily in summer. Housekeeping units for 2 people: $65 in winter, $75 on weekends, $50 for up to 4 people daily in summer.

Asgard Chalet, 19 Davison Rd. (716-962-6773). Excellent for groups. Dormitory and 7-18 person lodging units available. Small room sleeps 1 to 3 ($12-15 per person in summer, $18.50 per person in winter). Lower unit sleeps 7 ($115, weekends $125).

Kitzbuhel Lodge, Berner St. (934-2352), east of Minaret Rd. Dorm-style living ideal for lone travelers. Community kitchen, TV, spa, ski-storage, and piano. $10 per person, in winter $20. Make reservations well in advance.

Motel 6, 473372 Main St. (934-6660). Standard issue, and a bargain around here any day of the week. The 151 units move faster than polyester on the Love Boats, so book ahead up to a year in advance. Pool, TV, and A/C. Singles $32, each additional person $6; under 18 with parents free.

New Shady Rest Campground, on Rte. 203 across from McDonalds, a 2-min. walk from town. Piped-in water, flush toilets, no RV hookups. 97 sites. $8 per night. 14-day maximum stay. Open May 15-Oct. 31.

Mammoth Mountain RV Park (934-3822), across from the USFS Visitors Center. Free ski shuttle, hot showers, spa, and pool. Bike rentals $5 per hour. Hookups $24 in winter, $20 in summer. Tent sites $15. Open year-round.

Camp High Sierra, ¼ mi. west of New Shady Rest. Run by the L.A. Dept. of Recreation, this camp also has a helpful office stocked with information, a recreational lodge, sylvan sites with mountain vistas, and free hot showers. Tent sites $7, cabins $13. Open June-Sept. 15.

Lake Crowley, 12 mi. south of Mammoth Lakes on U.S. 395, cradles two beautiful hostels, by far the most enjoyable and economical accommodations around.

Long Valley Hostel (AYH), Lake Crowley Dr. (935-4377), off U.S. 395, 12 mi. south of Mammoth Lakes. Mailing address: Rte. 1, P.O. Box 189B, Long Valley, Mammoth Lakes 93546. Summer hostel with 10 beds in a beautiful self-contained chalet with kitchen; located on a ranch-style farm. Knowledgeable and amiable managers. Members $8.50, nonmembers $11.50. Open May-Oct. 15.

Hilton Creek International Hostel (AYH), 4 mi. along Lake Crowley Dr. (935-4989), off U.S. 395, 12 mi. south of Mammoth Lakes. Mailing address: Rte. 1, P.O. Box 1128, Crowley Lake 93546. New hostel in a converted park station, with 22 beds including a family room (by reservation). Young and engaging managers. Skiing, backpacking, inner-tubing, mountain biking, multilingual conversations, and local music. Beds $8, in winter $10. Seniors and under 18 with parents half-price.

Food

Mammoth Lakes is home to over 40 restaurants catering to a wide variety of tastes. Unfortunately, most of them are expensive. The usual fast-food franchises exert hegemonic control over cheap meals, but a few alternatives are listed below.

Brewhouse Grill, 170 Mountain Blvd. (934-8134). Cowboys and cowgirls ride in for the award-winning chili ($5.50) and 2 house brews: Bodie Bold and Dogtown Ale (16 oz. $2.25). Sun. night features live folk and bluegrass music, with live bands on other nights of the week, but no regular schedule. Open Tues.-Sat. 11:30am-whenever (later on weekends, Sun. 5-10:30pm.

Blondie's Kitchen, Sierra Center Mall, Old Mammoth Rd. (934-4048). Takes off on the cartoon fantasy of a Dagwood sandwich ($5.75). One skiier's breakfast special ($3.25) is enough for Mr. Snuffalufagus and a friend of his, too. Complimentary coffee and tea. Open daily 6:30am-1:30pm. (Afternoon hours fluctuate.)

Anything Goes, Old Mammoth Rd. at Chateau Rd. (934-2424), in Sherwin Plaza. Super gourmet food at not-so-super prices: dinner entrees $12-15. Breakfast and lunch are a little easier on the wallet—breakfast fritata $2.75, chicken sandwich $4. Outdoor patio. Open Thurs.-Tues. 7am-3pm, and Thurs.-Mon. 5:30-8pm.

Roberto's, 271 Old Mammoth Rd. (934-3667). Cute li'l shack with heavy Mexican food. Combos with rice, beans, and soup or salad from $5.75. "Loco Night" (Wed.) offers 50¢ drafts with dinner. Open Sun. and Tues.-Thurs. 11:30am-9pm; Fri. and Sat. 11:30am-10pm.

Matsu, Main St. (934-8277), 1 block past the post office. Multiple Asian cuisines at low prices. Known for their heaping platters, especially the vegetable stir-fry lunch ($5). Open Mon.-Fri. 11:30am-11:30pm, Sat. and Sun. 4:30-11:30pm.

Sights

There's plenty to see in Mammoth Lakes, but unfortunately most of it is accessible only by car. If you lack wheels, ask around for a ride at one of the campgrounds, hostels, or RV parks.

Devil's Postpile National Monument, an intriguing geological oddity, was formed when lava flows oozed through Mammoth Pass thousands of years ago and then cooled to form columns 40 to 60 ft. high. The column's cross-sections range from geometrically precise equilateral triangles to strange heptagons. Ancient glaciers exposed and polished the basalt posts to create the mammoth jewels that glitter today. A pleasant 3-mi. walk away from the center of the monument is **Rainbow Falls,** where the middle fork of the San Joaquin River drops 140 ft. past dark cliffs into a glistening green pool. From U.S. 395, the monument and its nearby bubbling hot springs can be reached by a 15-mi. drive past Minaret Summit on paved Rte. 203. It is operational only in summer, as is the campground near the ranger station (sites $7). To save the monument area from being completely trampled, the rangers have introduced a shuttle service between a parking area and the monument center, which all visitors—drivers and hikers alike—must use between 7:30am and 5:30pm. (Cars are let in for free between 5:30pm and 7:30am.) The shuttle takes about 30 min. from the car park to the Devil's Postpile trail, and the drivers give tours *en route* (round-trip $5, ages 5-12 $2.50).

Three mi. south of Mammoth Junction on U.S. 395 and 3 mi. east of the airport bubbles **Hot Creek,** open to bathers. Parking facilities, rest rooms, and changing areas are available here. (Open sunrise to sunset.) Ask locals about late-night skinny-dips.

Although there are over 100 lakes near town, not one actually goes by the name of "Mammoth Lake." The most mammoth lake in the basin, the mile-long **Lake Mary,** is popular for boating, fishing, and sailing. **Twin Lakes** is the closest lake to the village, only 3 mi. distant on Rte. 203. **Lake Mamie** has a picturesque picnic area, and many short hikes lead out to **Lake George.** Swimming is only allowed at **Horseshoe Lake,** which is also the trailhead for the impressive Mammoth Pass Trail. Twelve mi. south of town, **Lake Crowley** is popular with anglers. The lake yields over 80 tons of rainbow trout between May and October. Rowboats can be rented for $20 per day; parking is $3 per day, and campsites $4. Fishers converge on the area during **Flyfishing Days,** in mid-July, for some of the best trout in the contiguous U.S.

You can ride the **Mammoth Mountain Gondola** during the summer for a spectacular view of the area. Stop at the mid-station for lunch or coffee. (Open daily 11am-3pm. Round-trip $5, children $2.50.) **Obsidian Dome** lies 14 mi. north of Mammoth Junction and 1 mi. west of U.S. 395 on Glass Flow Rd. (follow the sign to "Lava Flow"). The dark, glassy volcanic rock is a wobbly climb, so take sturdy shoes.

Summers in Mammoth are packed with small festivals celebrating everything from chili cooking to motorcross racing. A new event, the **Mammoth Lakes Jazz Jubilee** in early July has already become a local favorite. Call 934-6243 for more information. A somewhat older tradition is the **Sierra Summer Festival,** held in August. Get a list of events from the visitors center (see Practical Information) or write to Sierra Summer Festival, P.O. Box 7710, Mammoth Lakes 93546 (934-2712), for tickets and information.

Mammoth ain't called mammoth for nothing. For the adventurer, Mammoth has it all: hot-air balloons, snowmobiles, mountain bike paths, and even dogsled trails. You can evaluate your options at the **Mammoth Adventure Connection,** in the Mammoth Mountain Inn (934-0606). One idea is the new **Mammoth Mountain Bike Park,** starting from 11,053 ft. up the side of the mountain and heading straight *down.* The park allows suicidal bikers to tackle the thawed winter-time ski trails, bared to expose many, many sharp rocks. As you ride up the gondola with your mountain bike secured in front of you, just remember that "what goes up must come down." Having come all the way up the mountain, only a wimp would miss the **Kamikaze** trail (2153 ft. down to the bike shop). $15 per day for gondola ticket,

$10 per day for trail use—and you have to *ride* up all the hills. $5 per day for helmet rentals (helmets required), bike rental $20 for 4 hrs., $30 per day. The Park has more than 50 miles of trails, as well as an obstacle arena and timed slalom race-course. Get tickets and information at the Mammoth Mountain Bike Center at the base of the mountain (934-0606). Park open daily 10am-5:30pm. Bike shop open 9:30am-6pm daily.

Skiing

With 132 downhill runs, over 26 lifts, and miles of nordic skiing trails, Mammoth is one of the country's premier winter resorts. Although "premier" can often mean "expensive," you can enjoy a skiing vacation without experiencing budgetary melt-down. Visit during off-season (at least 2 weeks before or after any major holiday and not on weekends), bring a handful of chums, and be prepared to cook your own meals. Economical multi-day lift tickets are available ($27 per day; $108 for 5 days). Rent skis either at home or in town, but not on the mountain; resort-run shops usually charge 10-20% more. Whatever happens, however, don't compromise on the quality of your equipment; stay in a run-down hotel if you have to, but make sure your boot bindings work. Be warned that there is a town ordinance against "stacking" more people in a condo than it was rented for. This law is enforced and can lead to fines or premature evacuation.

Mammoth Mountain lift tickets can be purchased at the **Main Lodge** at the base of the mountain on Minaret Rd. (934-2571 Mon.-Fri. 8am-3pm, Sat.-Sun. 7:30am-3pm), at **Stormriders** on the corner of Minaret Rd. and Canyon Blvd. (8am-9pm daily), or at **Warming Hut II** at the end of Canyon and Lakeview Blvds. (934-0771; open Mon.-Fri. 8am-5pm, Sat.-Sun. and holidays 7:30am-5pm). A free shuttle bus transports skiers between lifts, town and the Main Lodge. The ski area has 26 lifts and two gondolas that carry more than a million visitors annually.

June Mountain Ski Area, with lower-quality skiing than Mammoth, is located about 20 mi. north of Mammoth Lakes at Lake Hwy. 395 north and Rte. 158 west. Lift tickets are available in the Tram Haus next to the parking lot. For information call 648-7733.

Mono Lake

As fresh water from streams and springs drains into the "inland sea" of Mono Lake (pronounced MOE-no) it evaporates, leaving behind a mineral-rich, 13-mi. wide expanse that Mark Twain called "the Dead Sea of the West." The slippery, soap-like feel of the alkaline water prompted Twain to claim that he could clean his clothes simply by tying them to his boat and riding from one shore to the other. Although Mono supports no fishlife, brine flies, algae, and shrimp provide a buffet for migratory birds and the lake is full of wildlife activity. The lake's other attraction is its remarkable towers of calcium carbonate, known as "tufa," formed when calcium-rich fresh-water springs well up in the carbonate-filled salt water.

Tourists and ecologists love Mono for its unique rock formations and varied bird population, but thirsty Los Angeles loves it for its water. The steady diversion of water to the south has lowered the lake's level nearly 50 ft. since diversion began in 1941. Previously submerged areas have become dry land, exposing traditional bird nesting grounds to four-legged predators. Enough land has been uncovered to warrant the creation of a state park to protect the delicate tufa formations that were formerly submerged. The controversy over Mono Lake is bitter and ongoing: graffiti in a Bishop gas station restroom reads, "Flush twice—L.A. needs the water." The most recent court order prevents the Los Angeles Department of Water and Power from diverting water from all of the five tributaries leading into the lake.

Despite this environmentalist victory, the lake still rests at water levels much lower than its pre-diversion state. Increased salinity has devestated adjacent streams' trout stock, and newly exposed dust is seriously polluting local air. Locals and lake-lovers continue to fight for increased water flow to the lake, while Southern Californias's population continues to grow, sweat, bathe and thirst. At over 700,000 years, the extraordinary tub remains the Western Hemisphere's oldest enclosed body of water. For now.

The town of **Lee Vining** provides the best access to Mono Lake and the ghost town of Bodie. It is located 60 mi. north of Bishop on U.S. 395 and 10 mi. west of the Tioga Pass entrance to Yosemite.

Practical Information and Orientation

Visitors Information: Mono Lake Visitors Center and Lee Vining Chamber of Commerce, Main St. (647-6595), in the large blue building. Incredibly friendly staff, all of whom are part of the crusade to save Mono Lake from the L.A. Dept. of Water and Power. Examine the exhibits, articles, books, and free slide-show on the endangerment of the lake. They also have maps, brochures, and books covering all of Mono County. Call for information on road conditions. Open daily 9am-9pm. For information, write P.O. Box 29, Lee Vining, CA 93541.

Mono Lake/Tufa State Reserve Ranger Station: 4th St. (647-6525; recorded message 647-6331), behind the gift shop. Information on Mono County's wilderness areas and excellent interpretive tours. They also sell topographical maps and issue wilderness permits. Open sporadically between 9am-5pm daily.

U.S. Forest Service, Lee Vining Ranger Station: 2 mi. west of Hwy. 395 on Rte. 120 (647-6525). Large ranger station with camping information Obtain backcountry permits here (free). The **Rush Creek Trail** has a quota of 34 people per day from June-Sept. 15, so it's advisable to arrive early in the am. Permits given out daily on a first-come, first-served basis. Or obtain a reservation by contacting the ranger station March 1-May 31.

Greyhound, in the Lee Vining Grocery Store (647-6301; 800-237-8211 for fares and routes). One bus per day to L.A. (at 11am) and to Reno (at 1:50am). Buy your ticket at the next stop, because they don't sell them here. Open daily 8am-8pm.

AAA Emergency Road Service: 647-6444.

Laundromat: Main St. next to the grocery store. Open 24 hr. Wash $1, dry 25¢, soap 50¢.

Emergency Medical Service: 911.

Post Office: behind the car park in Lee Vining (647-6371). Open Mon.-Fri. 8:45am-2pm and 3-5:15pm. General Delivery ZIP Code: 93541.

Area Code: 619.

Because this bustling metropolis is only 2 blocks long, store owners don't bother with addresses or phone numbers. U.S. 395 runs through Lee Vining, making a cameo appearance as Main Street.

Accommodations and Food

Good news: Lee Vining does supply that rare human need, food. Bad news: it's pretty much the same heavy grub wherever you get it. Spend your nights camping, since the town's hotels are small and often expensive. Besides, the terrain is beautiful.

The King's Inn (647-6300), 2 blocks west of Main St. Cheapest in town. Munchkin-sized but comfortable rooms with TVs, showers, in-room coffee/tea, and magazines. Pets allowed. Cheapest in town. Rooms $27-40.

Blue Skies Motel, on Main St. (647-6440). TV and shower in clean, high-ceilinged and rather sparse rooms. Rooms for 1-2 people from $35.

Murphey's RV Park (647-6358), 1 block west of Main St., behind Murphey's Motel. Full hookups ($10) and tent sites ($6). Showers $2. Only a few overnight spaces available; on weekends and holidays arrive before 10am.

Mono Vista Trailer Park (647-6401), behind the Chevron station. 26 RV spots. Laundry $1, metered showers 25¢. Reservations are advisable in summer. Tent sites $10 for 1-4 people, $3 for each additional person.

Lee Vining's ideal location as a stopover on the way from Reno or Death Valley to Yosemite makes accommodations scarce on Friday afternoons and holidays. Go early, and reserve campsites in advance. There are also six campgrounds west of town on Rte. 120 within 15 mi. of Lee Vining and two north of town within 7 mi. All are based in Inyo National Forest and range from $3 to $10. **Sawmill Campground** and **Tioga Lake Campground** are 9000 ft. up, at the edge of Yosemite. Make reservations for these spectacular campgrounds at least 9000 days in advance. Obtain Inyo Forest campground information from the Lee Vining District Ranger (647-6525).

The **Lee Vining Market** is the town's closest thing to a grocery store (next to the laundromat on Main St. 647-6301). But the pickin's here are pretty slim. **Nicely's** restaurant seems to be a local favorite, but it can't because of the food. Maybe it's the crimson decor and the wait staff's matching crimson uniforms. Chili dog with cheese and onions $5. (647-6477, on Main St. north of the visitor center.)

Sights

In 1984, Congress set aside 57,000 acres of land surrounding the lake and called it the **Mono Basin National Forest Scenic Area** (647-6525), thereby preserving Mono Lake as one of the prime recreation spots in Mono County. Twain's "solemn, silent, sailless sea" is truly awe-inspiring. **South Tufa Grove,** 10 mi. from Lee Vining, harbors an impressive collection of calcium carbonate formations. Take U.S. 395 south to Rte. 120, then go 4 mi. east. Take the Mono Lake Tufa Reserve turnoff 1 mi. south of Tufa Grove. The tufa towers, which resemble giant drip sandcastles, poke through the smooth surface of the water. Four mi. north of Lee Vining, on U.S. 395, is **Mono Lake County Park,** a public playground with bathrooms, picnic tables, swings, wheelchair access to the lake, and a smaller tufa forest. The **Mono Lake Foundation** now offers guided **canoe tours** of the lake on weekends, an enlightening way to tour this enchanting body of water (8am, 9:30am, 11am; $10, ages 4-12 $4). ½ mi. from the South Tufa Grove is **Navy Beach,** one of the saltiest swimming holes in America. **Panum Crater** is a long-extinct volcano located 4 mi. east of town on Rte. 120. The Reserve Rangers at the crater offer excellent interpretive nature walks and evening presentations. Inquire at the Mono Lake Ranger Station for details. (Activities daily June 22-Sept. 2.)

June Lake, a glacially carved canyon filled with water, is 10 mi. south of Lee Vining on U.S. 395; take the scenic loop along Rte. 158 if you have the time. During the summer, the lake is an angler's heaven, with brook, golden, rainbow, and brown trout stocked weekly. Day hikes, wilderness backpacking, swimming, and boating are all within easy distance of the June Lake loop, and camping in the area is plentiful. (Sites $6-8, few have showers.) The **Oh! Ridge Campground** has water and flush toilets. (Sites $8. Open April-Sept.) In winter, sportsmen come in their snow pants for the area's alpine and cross-country **skiing.** Look for midweek specials at hotels and condominiums for discounts on lodging, equipment, and lift tickets. Traveling in large groups is the cheapest way to go; four people can rent fully equipped cabins for as little as $60. Call 800-648-JUNE (648-5863) for more information on accommodations. Make campground reservations through MISTIX: 1-800-283-CAMP.

Just when you thought you'd never find an authentic, unexploited old ghost town, there's **Bodie.** Tucked away in the high, forsaken desert, Bodie is the real McCoy, even if it does charge admission ($5, self-guide booklet $1). In 1880, the town was home to 10,000 people, 65 saloons, 22 tumbleweeds, and one homicide per day. Anne Cutler described it as "a sea of sin, lashed by the tempests of lust and passion." Not only has this once-booming, vice-ridden mining legend been well-preserved by the dry climate and by the state of California, Bodie was also spared the wartime pilfering of wood and metal that stripped many ghost towns of their original character. Though remote, it is accessible by a paved road which runs off of U.S. 395, 15 mi. north of Lee Vining (the last 3 mi. are a dusty delight), and by a dirt road all the way from Rte. 167 out of Mono Inn. Though ravaged by fire, many of the old buildings are still intact, and most are strewn with the original furnishings and objects of daily life. Old stagecoaches and fallen outhouses litter the town streets. Open 9am-4pm; Memorial Day weekend-Labor Day 9am-7pm. For information call Bodie State Historic Park at 647-6445 or write to P.O. Box 515, Bridgeport, CA 93517.

Lake Tahoe

The tectonic upheaval that brought the Sierras to their present height left a central basin which became the setting for North America's third deepest lake: Tahoe. Today, the cerulean waters, surrounded by evergreens and mountains, form an enormous Alpine oasis.

California mellowness meets Nevadan avarice in Tahoe, as the boundary of these two states splits the area's south-shore into two factions. To the west lies **South Lake Tahoe,** a nature lover's dream. Skiing, boating, and hiking draw lazy crowds to the scores of motels lining the water's edge. Just over the Nevada border, **Stateline** beckons more materialistic hedonists to the glittering world of casinos. Here, the perpetual clink of jackpots substitutes for the timeless lapping of waves upon the shore. For you, the intrepid traveler, the best bet is to eat cheap in Stateline, sleep cheap in South Lake Tahoe, and head to North Lake Tahoe to enjoy the splendor of the waves or woods.

Activity in **North Lake Tahoe** centers around **Tahoe City** where Western families come season after season, year after year, to enjoy the area's extraordinary recreational and natural resources. As such, the area has a warm, familiar atmosphere where everyone knows everyone and all are happy to escape the chaos and pollution of urban civilization. Tahoe City is not the most economical place to find a motel in Lake Tahoe, but it *is* rich with campsites and excellent trails. An active club and bar scene in the city offers an alternative to casino nightlife, with an energetic younger crowd and plenty of local entertainers.

Practical Information

Visitors Information: Visitors Bureau and Chamber of Commerce, 3066 U.S. 50 (541-5255), at San Francisco Ave. Tons of helpful brochures and maps. A local map, coupons, and a directory can be found in *101 Things to Do in Lake Tahoe* (free). Disabled visitors should pick up the complimentary *Handbook for the Handicapped,* an extensive directory of facilities and information. Open Mon.-Fri. 8:30am-5pm, Sat.-Sun. 9am-4pm. **Visitor's Bureau,** 950 North Lake Blvd. (583-3494, within North Tahoe 546-7100), in Tahoe City.

U.S. Forest Service, 870 Emerald Bay Rd., S. Lake Tahoe (541-6564). Supervises campgrounds and publishes the informative and free *Lake of the Sky Journal.* Open Mon.-Fri. 8am-4:30pm. The Visitor's Center, 3 mi further south on Rte. 89, is open 8am-4pm on most weekends.

Greyhound: 1099 Park Ave. (544-2241), on the state line. To San Francisco (10 per day, $28.50) and Sacramento (6 per day, $16.50). **Showboat Lines** (702-588-5300), Reno Airporter (8 per day, $12.50). Open daily 8:30am-5pm.

Tahoe Area Regional Transport (TART): 581-6365. Connects to the western and northern shores from Tahoma to Incline Village. Twelve buses daily 6:10am-6pm. Fare $1, unlimited travel day pass $2.50, children under 5 free.

Free Night Shuttle: Fri.-Sat. nights only, between Tahoma and Stateline. Stateline to Tahoe City: every ½ hr. on the hr. from 7pm-2am. From Tahoe City to Stateline: every hr. on the ½ hr. from 6:30pm-1:30am. From Tahoe City to Tahoma at 7:30pm, 8:30pm, 12:30am, and 1:30am. From Tahoma to Tahoe City: 8pm, 9pm, 1am, and 2am.

South Tahoe Area Ground Express (STAGE): 573-2080. 24-hr. bus service around town, 7-hr. daily service to the beach (1 per ½ hr.). Fare $1.25, under 8 free; 10-ride pass $10. Most of the Nevada-based casinos operate free shuttle service along U.S. 50 between ski resorts and motels in California. In particular **Harvey's** (702-588-2411) runs theirs daily from 8am-2am, but ask at any motel office for information on others.

South Lake Tahoe Dial-A-Ride: 577-7000. Door-to-door transportation for seniors and the disabled.

Taxi: Dial-A-Ride (577-7000) is best for solo travelers because it combines trips by picking up several passengers along the way. Open daily 7am-7pm. **Tahoe Ready Cab** (542-2424). Open 24 hr.

Car Rental: Budget (541-5777), at the airport. Rates from $34.80 per day. Check for leaflets offering discounts. Unlimited free mileage. Age 21-24 $10 extra per day, age 18-20 $20 extra per day.

Moped Rental: Country Moped, 800 Emerald Bay Rd. at Rte. 89 South and 10th St. (544-3500). $10 for the first hour; less for each additional hour. $38 per day. Scooters $50-100 per day. Helmets available. Open daily 10am-7pm.

Bike Rental: Anderson's Bicycle Rental, 645 Emerald Bay Rd. (541-0500), convenient to the well-maintained west shore bike trail. Parking. Mountain bikes $5 per hour, ½ day $15, full day $20. 3-speeds $4 per hour, half-day $12, full day $15. Leave driver's license as deposit. Open daily 8:30am-6:30pm. Bike rentals are generally the same price all over Lake Tahoe. Mountain bikes are most suited to the Tahoe terrain. A terrific bike path goes all the way along the west side of the Lake from Sugar Pine to Tahoe City.

Road Conditions: in California (577-3550), Trukee/Tahoe City (587-5005), in Nevada (702-793-1313).

Laundromat: Al Tahoe, 3111 U.S. 50 (541-9168) at Tallac. Wash $1.25, dry 25¢, soap 50¢. Open 24 hr. **Carnelian Bay Launderland,** 5083 N. Lake Blvd. (581-6830). Open daily 7am-10pm.

Public Pool and Recreation Center: 1180 Rufus Allen Blvd. (541-4611), across from El Dorado Beach. Open Mon.-Sat. 1:30pm-5pm, Sun. 1-4pm. Adults $2, children $1.25. Use of weight room same price as pool.

24-Hour Hotlines: Rape Crisis, 544-4444. **Mental Health,** 573-3251. **Gamblers Anonymous,** 800-322-8748. **Poison Control Center,** 800-342-9293; 24 hr. **Alcoholics Anonymous,** 546-2727 in North Tahoe, 541-1243 in South Tahoe.

Emergency: 911.

Hospital: Stateline Medical Center, 176 U.S. 50 at Kahle Dr. (588-3561). Open daily 8am-8pm.

Post Office: Stateline Station, 1085 Park Ave. (544-6162), next to Greyhound. Open Mon.-Fri. 8:30am-5pm. General Delivery ZIP Code: 95729. **Tahoe City,** 950 N. Lake Blvd., Suite 12 in the Lighthouse Shopping Center (583-3936). Open Mon.-Fri. 8:30am-5pm, Sat. noon-2pm. General Delivery ZIP Code: 96145.

Area Code: 916 in California, 702 in Nevada.

Orientation

Lake Tahoe is located 118 mi. northeast of Sacramento and 35 mi. southwest of Reno. U.S. 50, Rte. 89 and Rte. 28 overlap to form a ring of asphalt around the lake. U.S. 395 from Carson City and the Owens Valley area or I-80 from San Francisco or Reno are the most-traveled roads to the lake. In winter, tire-chains are required and 4-wheel drive is highly recommended. Consider staying in **Truckee,** California as a less expensive base for visits to North Lake Tahoe, especially Squaw Valley.

Accommodations

The strip off U.S. 50 on the California side of the state line supports the bulk of Tahoe's 200 motels. Others line Park Avenue, 1 block south, which is quieter. Be wary of shifty hotels; that $15 dump on Tuesday may become a regal $80 chamber on Friday. Book ahead and ask for written price confirmation. Lately, many of the smaller budget motels have been razed in order to erect luxury high-rise (and high-price) hotels in their place. The remaining inexpensive hotels are booked solid on weekends year-round. Look for discount coupons (as much as $10 off weekday rates) in newspapers. The cheapest deals are clustered near Stateline on U.S. 50 and may display their prices, although it is illegal to do so.

Motel 6, 2375 Lake Tahoe Blvd., 95731 (542-1400). One of the few places where the rate is constant. Standard issue but very popular, especially on weekends. Pool. TV. Singles $35.15, each additional adult $6. Make reservations in advance or hope someone cancels.

Midway Motel, 3876 U.S. 50 (544-4397). TV, A/C, phone. Try bargaining their prices down on weekdays. Clean and comfortable. One double bed (1-2 people) $22, weekends $59-95. 2 double beds (3-4 people) $30, weekends $75-95.

Jack Pot Inn, 3908 U.S. 50 (541-5587), about 1 mi. south of the casinos. Some rooms with kitchenettes. A bit worn but fine otherwise. Singles $20. Doubles $22. Fri.-Sat. rooms from $35. No reservations.

Edwards Lodge, in Tahoma along Rte. 89 (525-7207). A total of 17 cabins—11 for let during the summer, 7 during the winter—comprise this complex. Each is large, with two stories, several beds, a kitchen, and a TV, making them a perfect option for groups. Extremely convenient to many ski areas. Each cabin has a wood deck. Pool. Pay with cash; otherwise they'll hit you with a $10 surcharge. Check-in 2pm, check-out 11am. Cabins $55-85.

Camping

The Forest Service at the visitors bureau provides up-to-date information on camping near Lake Tahoe, surrounding which are over 30 sites. The prime camping locales are in West Lake Tahoe; Sugar Pine was rated #1 among all state parks by the *San Francisco Chronicle* in 1991. You can make reservations at state park campgrounds by calling MISTIX at 800-283-CAMP (283-2267) or 800-444-7275. Check with the Forest Service (see Practical Information) for more details. Free campgrounds include **Bayview** (544-6420, max. stay 1 night, open June-Sept.) and **Alpine Meadow** (639-2342, tents only; open May-Oct.).

El Dorado, in South Lake Tahoe (573-2059), to the west of downtown across from the lake. A few blocks from community pool, library, and golf course. Sites $16.50 for one vehicle with up to 4 adults, including showers; under 18 free. Open April-Oct.

Emerald Bay State Park, Rte. 89 (541-3030), 10 mi. west of town. Lovely scenery, with an oft-photographed tree-rimmed cove encircling a small island called Fannette. Peaceful. 15-day max. stay. Hot showers. Sites $14. Open June-Labor Day.

D.L. Bliss State Park, Rte. 89 (525-7277), a few miles west on Emerald Bay. Hot showers, wonderful beach. 14-day max. stay. 168 sites; $14, on-beach sites $19. The 8 mi. Rubicon trail leading to Emerald Bay and Vikingsholm, a stunning Scandinavian home noted for its impressive architecture. Open June-Labor Day. Make reservations at least 8 weeks in advance.

Sugar Pine Point: General Creek (525-7982), on the West Shore south of Tahoma. A modern campground ideal for groups. The picturesque views and the austere Ehrman Mansion which comprise the park's grounds was the perfect setting for filming David Mamet's *Things Change.* Tours of Ehrman Mansion are given on the hour from 11am-4pm. Located across Rte. 89 from the lake in a spacious evergreen forest. The campground accommodates groups of up to 40 (40 adults $60, 40 youths $30). Single sites $14, over 61 $13.

Nevada Beach, U.S. 50 and Country Rd. (573-2600), 1¾ mi. north of South Lake Tahoe. Quaint sandy beach. Sites $10 May-Sept, $12 Sept.-May.

Meeks Bay, Rte. 89 in West Lake Tahoe just south of Sugar Pine Point. Somewhat less crowded than the other campsites, with a good beach. 40 sites ($12 per night). Check-out 2pm. Two week max. stay.

Food

Over the Nevada border in Stateline, small casinos reign over the world of budget cuisine with their advertised specials—serving masses of reasonable quality food at coffee shop prices. In addition, Tahoe maintains a few traditional eating establishments for the locals and keen-eyed travelers. Check motel lobbies for sundry restaurant coupons. Groceries are cheaper on the California side of Tahoe. **Raley's,** 4018 U.S. 50 (544-3418), is particularly well-stocked.

Red Hut Waffles, 2723 U.S. 50 (541-9024). Breakfast beyond belief—try a plate-sized waffle with bananas and whipped cream ($3.50) or a massive omelette with toast and hash browns ($3.50-5). Open daily 6am-2pm.

The Siam Restaurant, 2210 U.S. 50 (544-0370). Family-run Thai restaurant with large portions at low prices. Entrees from $4. Order water; the spicy dishes are a fire hazard. Open Mon.-Tues. and Thurs.-Sun. 10am-9:45pm.

My Favorite Place, 3434 Lake Tahoe Blvd. (541-0225). Cute and cozy. Homemade buttermilk biscuits and portions suitable for pita-thief Miranda Spieler. The strawberry *crepes* ($5) are divine. Omelettes from $5.

Cantina Los Tres Hombres, Rte. 89 at 10th St. (544-1233), is the local margarita playland. Their fiesta from 4-6pm Mon.-Tues., Thurs.-Fri. is a lively place to munch on complimentary chips and salsa. Dinners from $6.50. Open 11:30am-10:30pm.

Firesign, 1785 West Lake Blvd. (583-0871). The stone hearth, wood tables, and amicable atmosphere contribute to the homey country-style feeling of this popular restaurant. A super place for out-of-the-ordinary cooking. Don't be put off by the long lines for Sunday brunch. Outdoor seating available. Dill and artichoke omelettes, with home fries, toast, and muffin $5.25. Sandwiches $3.50-4.25. Open daily 7am-3pm.

The Bridge Tender, 30 West Lake Blvd. (583-3342), in Tahoe City. Just look for the billows of smoke coming from the enormous outdoor grill. The specialty is burgers, and there is no lack of variety. Cajun bacon cheeseburger $5.25. Prices range from $3.85 to $5.25. Restaurant open daily 11am-10pm. At night, the tavern's pool table, the wide range of beers on tap, and late hours make this bar a popular spot for all ages (over 21, of course).

The Tahoe Yogurt Factory, 125 West Lake Blvd. (581-5253), in Tahoe City, has the best cappuccino in town ($1.65) and outdoor seating to enjoy it. Delicious smoothies $2.75. Open daily 6am-10pm.

Za's, 395 N. Lake Blvd. (583-1812), in Tahoe City behind **Pete and Peter's Bar.** Gourmet pizzas of large diameters that will melt in your mouth. Try something exotic like pesto with gorgonzola cheese ($6.25). Pizza by the slice ($1.50) available for take-out as well. Pasta $4.25 and up.

Wolfdales's, 640 North Lake Blvd. (583-5700), in Tahoe City, subtitled "Cuisine Unique". The gourmet food, prepared with ingredients from the restaurant's own garden, may be priced above the budget traveler's grasp, but the afternoon tea and cocktails (3-6pm) are a great way to taste the restaurant's perfection. English, Oriental, and medicinal teas ($2.50) are served in the exquisite garden tucked away behind the restaurant. The rock garden and Japanese fountain add to the feeling of isolation and charm. Have a scone with your tea, $2.50.

Tahoe Community Market, 505 West Lake Blvd. (583-3156). A small market catering to the health-conscious. Open Mon.-Sat. 9am-7pm, Sun. 10am-6pm.

Sights and Activities

There's not much to do in **Stateline** unless you're gambling. And in **South Lake Tahoe,** the only thing to do is sleep in the cheap motels. Call the Tahoe **Direct Connection** (800-272-3883 or 702-588-8861) for a listing of events and entertainment. The stylish way to see the lake itself is by glass-bottom boat. The *Tahoe Queen* (541-3364) departs from the Ski Run Blvd. for tours of Emerald Bay (3 per day, $12.50), and the *M.S. Dixie* (588-3508) departs from Zephyr Cove (5 per day, $9-30, April-Oct.). *Woodwinds* (588-3000), at Zephyr Cove, offers six 1½-hour sailing tours daily ($12, ages under 12 $6.

In the summer, **Windsurf Tahoe,** 5240 N. Lake Blvd. (546-5857), will rent you a sailboard for $12 per hour. You will want to rent a wet-suit, too, since the average temperature of the lake remains a chilling 39°F year-round. Most drowned bodies are never recovered, one tourist leaflet cheerfully reveals, because the cold prevents the decomposition that usually makes corpses float to the surface. In fact, the Indians who used to live around Lake Tahoe buried their dead by pushing them, fully garbed, off the side of their canoes into the Lake. The Lake's frigid temperatures kept the bodies perfectly preserved, suspended in the water. Surges of warm water or temperature changes and water movement have on occasion brought these perfectly preserved bodies to the surface. Several marinas rent out fishing boats, and you can rent paddle boats for under $10 per hour. It might be worth sharing the cost with several people and renting a motorboat and waterskis ($52 per hour) or a jet-ski ($45 per hour) at **Zephyr Cove** on U.S. 50 (702-588-3833), 4 mi. north of

Place
Stamp
Here

LET'S GO Travel

Harvard Student Agencies, Inc.
Harvard University
Thayer B
Cambridge, MA 02138 U.S.A.

Place
Stamp
Here

THE HOTEL
Atherton
SAN FRANCISCO

685 Ellis Street
San Francisco, CA 94109

the casino. Incidentally, you're far more likely to bump into the friendly green monster "Tahoe Tessie" in gift shops than in the water.

In the southwest corner of the lake, **Emerald Bay** is a magnificent inlet containing Tahoe's only island, Fannette. Off U.S. 50 away from the shore, are **Fallen Leaf Lake** and **Cascade Lake.** ¼-mi. from the road at Emerald Bay is **Vikingsholm,** a Scandinavian-style castle built in the 1920s (541-3030; open for tours daily mid-June-Labor Day 10am-4pm; admission $1, under 18 50¢, under 6 free). **Eagle Falls** waterfall is also a short hike away. The **North Tahoe Historical Museum** is housed in the Gatekeepers Cabin on Rte. 28 at 130 West Lake Blvd. (583-1762; open mid-May-Oct. daily 11am-5pm, Sept.-mid-May Mon.-Fri. 11am-5pm; free).

Incline Village, north of Tahoe just into Nevada, is named after an incline railway which supplied local mines in the late-19th century. The village is home to **Ponderosa Ranch,** of *Bonanza* fame (702-831-0691), on Tahoe Blvd. (Open April-Oct. daily 9am-6pm; admission $5.50, ages 5-11 $4.50, under 5 free.) Try the Waywagon Breakfast for a scenic buffet and hay ride (daily 8am). Both the **Forest Service Fire Lookout** and the **Mount Rose Scenic Overlook** (Rte. 431 from Incline to Reno) afford beautiful views of the lake. The **Heavenly Mountain** ski resort chairlift ride (541-1330) will take you 2000 ft. up the mountainside for a unique bird's-eye view (open Mon.-Sat. 10am-10pm, Sun. 9am-10pm).

For those who prefer to earn their views the old-fashioned way, the U.S. Forest Service (573-2674) publishes a series of leaflets and can advise on a variety of trails. On the western side of Tahoe, there is the **Tahoe State Recreation Area** (583-3074), **Sugar Pine Point Park** (525-7982), and the **D.L. Bliss** and **Emerald Bay State Parks** (both 525-7277). The ultimate hike is the grueling 150-mi. **Tahoe Rim Trail,** which loops around the entire lake and takes about 15 days (call 577-0676 for more information).

If the mere thought of a 150-mi. hike sounds like torture, take heart. Lake Tahoe is full of well-groomed bike trails and surrounded by several fine beaches. One of the most picturesque bike routes follows the Lake around from Tahoe City south to Sugar Pine Point, where several beaches lie. Though swimming in the chilly lake isn't particularly appetizing, lying on the beach is quite enjoyable in the summer. **Chambers Beach,** between Homewood and Tahoma, has volleyball nets on the public side and a pool, bathrooms, and bar on its private side. Although this beach is usually packed, it draws a sociable younger crowd and is very much a local hangout. **Meeks Bay,** 10 miles south of Tahoe City, is quieter and has a sandy beach. There is also the **El Dorado,** 1 mile north of Stateline on U.S 50 (open daily 7am-11pm). Fishing, horseback riding, mountain biking, and golfing are popular summer pass-times around the lake as well.

Skiing

Lake Tahoe in the winter is, surprisingly, no less crowded than in the summer. 16 ski resorts, nine cross-country areas, and snowmobile routes galore draw a myriad of visitors to this winter Valhalla.

Squaw Valley: (583-6985 or 800-545-4350) hosted the 1960 Winter Olympics and is one of the finest ski resorts in the world. There are 32 lifts and a wide variety of terrain. Lift tickets: full day $38, ½ day $26, children under 13 and seniors over 64 $10. First timers ski free.

Alpine Meadows: 6 miles northwest of Tahoe City on Rte. 89 (583-4232 or 800-TAHOE-4-U (824-6348)), is an excellent family vacation spot which is very accessible. Lift tickets: full day $38, 6-12 yr. $13; half-day $25, 6-12 yr. $9. Ski rentals $18 per day.

Homewood: 6 miles south of Tahoe City on Rte. 89 South (525-7256), is a smaller, uncrowded area beloved by locals. Lift tickets: full day $27, seniors and children under 13 $9; half-day $20, seniors and children $6.

Heavenly: in South Lake Tahoe (541-1330 or 800-2-HEAVEN) extends into both California and Nevada, but the Nevada side tends to be far less crowded. Another family ski resort. Lift tickets: full day $38.

North Star: on Rte. 267 and North Star Drive in Truckee (562-1010). Limits the number of lift tickets sold, to avoid mob scenes at the lift line. Thus, Mt. Jupiter is a great destination for families.

Mt. Rose: 11 miles from Incline Village on Rte. 431 (702-849-0704). One of the cheapest slopes in Lake Tahoe. Lift tickets: full day $23, children $8; half-day $17, children $5. Weekends: full day $28, children $10, seniors half-price.

Boreal Ridge: 10 miles west of Truckee on I-80 (426-3666). Has less challenging terrain than some of its neighbors, but offers night skiing for reduced rates. This is a popular group activity, especially for after-school trips, so don't expect a solitary midnight run.

Tahoe-Donner: in Truckee (587-9400), has slopes only for beginning to intermediate skiers. A confidence-building mountain for novices.

Cross Country Skiing

Royal Gorge: on Old Hwy. 40 (426-3871), offering 70 different trails totalling 300 km in length, is the nation's largest cross-country ski resort.

Incline: in North Tahoe (702-832-1150), is a more convenient location with 35 km of trails.

Spooner Lake, in Nevada where Rtes. 28 and 50 meet (702-749-5349) offers 25 scenic km of cross-country trails.

Entertainment

Casino's, of course, offer 24-hour entertainment, with concerts, flashy topless revues, and comedians. **Harrah's** in South Lake Tahoe, U.S. 50 at Stateline, has classic casino spectacles. Call 800-648-3773 for information or reservations. For down-to-earth entertainment, Tahoe City hosts local bands at two popular restaurants. **Emma Murphey's,** 425 North Lake Blvd. (583-6939), usually has bands Wed.-Sat. starting at 9pm. Just up the street, **Rosie's,** 571 North Lake Blvd. (583-8504), hosts *locals night* on Tuesdays from 9pm-2am with live music.

Sand Harbor at Incline Village provides a stunning Lakeside backdrop for the three *Shakespeare* plays staged in August. This popular event attracts an audience from all over the region, equipped with blankets, picnic lunches and champagne. Tickets $13, children 4-12 and seniors $11. Call 583-9048 for reservations and information. *Concerts* are held at Sand Harbor as well.

Truckee

Truckee got its name from a classic tale of miscommunication. When a Paiute Indian greeted the Stephen-Townsend-Murphy party in 1844 with the word "Tro-kay" ("peace"), they thought it was his name and gave it to a local river, and in turn, to the lumbering camp at the foot of the sierras.

Two years later, the ill-fated excursion led by George and Jacob Donner arrived from Illinois, and stubbornly ignored the tribe's advice not to attempt to cross the Sierras in winter. That year snowstorms hit a month early, dumping 20 feet by December 10. The 81 men, women, and children ended up eating each other.

Today, 20 ft. of snow in November would not be a boon for cannibalism, but for the skiing industry. Squaw Valley (which hosted the 1960 Winter Olympics) is the largest of the several area resorts and is home to the International Special Olympics. And when the skiers leave, hikers, river rafters, rock climbers, and mountain-bikers move in to take their places.

Practical Information

Visitor Information: Truckee-Donner Chamber of Commerce, 587-2757 or 800-548-8388, in the big yellow train station on Commercial Row. Excellent brochures, maps, and photocopied handouts. Open daily 9am-5pm, in winter 9am-4pm.

U.S. Forest Service Office: 587-3558, at the intersection of U.S. 89 and I-80. Open daily 8am-5pm.

Amtrak: 800-872-7245, in the Greyhound station. No lockers. One train per day east to Reno ($11) and Salt Lake City ($103), one per day west to Sacramento ($39) and San Francisco ($60).

Greyhound: 587-3822, in the Amtrak train station. To: Reno (gamblers special $5); San Francisco ($28); Sacramento ($15). Five eastbound buses per day, 9 westbound. Open Mon.-Sat. 9am-5:30pm.

Taxi: Truckee Yellow Cab, 587-6336. $1.50 per mi. with ski racks in winter, bike racks in summer.

Car Rental: Thrifty Rent-a-Car, 587-2588. Not so thrifty; rentals start at $34 per day with 150 free miles plus 16¢ per additional mile. Must be 21 with a major credit card. Open daily 8am-5pm. **AAA** in the train station, (582-8282). Same conditions and rates.

Bicycle Rental: Paco's Bicycles, 11400 Donner Pass Rd. (587-5561). All bikes $5 per hr., $22 per day. Open Mon.-Sat. 10am-6pm, Sun. 10am-4pm. The **Alpengloss,** on Bridge St. (587-2025), next to the post office, rents baby carriers for $5 per hr.

Equipment Rental: Basecamp, 505 West Lake Blvd., Tahoe City (583-5306), 15 mi. away on the Lake Tahoe shore. Rents backpacks, tents, and bicycles ($4 per hr., $18 per day).

Laundromat: Donner Center Launderland Rte. 89, in the mall with Pizza Junction. Wash $1, dry 25¢. Open daily 7am-10pm.

AAA Emergency Road Service: 583-6967.

Highway Patrol: 587-3518.

Road Conditions: 581-1400.

Rape Hotline: 544-4444. 24 hr.

Gay Crisis: National Gay Task Force: 800-221-7044.

Emergency: 911.

Hospital: Tahoe Forest, Pine Ave. and Donner Pass Rd. (587-6011).

Post Office: Rte. 267 (587-3442), 1 block north of Commercial Row. Open Mon.-Fri. 8:30am-5pm, Sat. noon-1:30pm. General Delivery ZIP Code: 95734.

Area Code: 916.

Truckee lies just off I-80 in the woody Sierra Nevadas. Sacramento sits 100 mi. southwest of Truckee, Reno 33 mi. east, and Lake Tahoe 15 mi. south. Tahoe City is the main city of the north shore. Officially known as Donner Pass Rd. (and also part of Rte. 89 *and* Old Hwy. 80), Commercial Row parallels the railroad tracks. Everything you'll need in Truckee lies within 2 blocks of this scenic avenue.

Accommodations and Camping

Twelve campgrounds lie within 10 mi. of town ($3-8). **U.S. Forest Service** sites (587-3558) are clustered northward along Rte. 89 at **Prosser Reservoir, Boca Reservoir,** and **Stampede Reservoir.** Of these, Prosser and Stampede charge $6, and Boca is free. South on Rte. 89 lie **Granite Flat** (3 mi., free), **Goose Meadows** (5 mi., $6), and **Silver Creek** (9 mi., $8). Three mi. west along I-80, **Donner Memorial** (587-3841) charges $10 for popular, fully equipped sites. Reservations at all of these campsites are always helpful, especially on weekends. Call MISTIX (800-444-7275) for reservations.

Star Hotel (AYH), 10015 W. River St. (587-3007), 1 block south of the railroad tracks on Bridge St. Excellent new management. Kitchen use and complimentary coffee and tea in a communal lounge. Always full during the ski season; make reservations early. Members only at the hostel ($11), but private rooms with shared bath are available at the hotel ($30-75). No smoking.

Alta Hotel, 10101 W. River St. (587-6668), across the railroad tracks from the yellow train station. Smoky rooms. Tanning room on the premises. Office open 8am-10pm. Singles $30. Doubles $33, in winter $37.

Cottage Hotel, Commercial Row (587-3108), near the west end of town, a 5-min. walk from the train station. Slightly more run-down than the other two. Singles $27. Doubles $33.

Donner Spitz Hütte ASI Lodge. At the end of Hwy. 40 (426-9108), in Norden. Only accessible by car. Swiss-style ski lodge on top of the historic Donner Pass offers sleeping bag bunks and breakfast for $17, $18 in the winter.

Food

Take your pick of touristy delis and greasy coffee shops, or else forage for yourself at the **Safeway** supermarket on Rte. 89, about 1 mi. west of downtown (open 24 hr.). The Forest Service has morbidly memorialized the starving pioneers by making their winter hellhole into a summer picnic site in the **Donner Memorial State Park.**

Squeeze-In, on Commercial Row, across from the Fire Station. 57 varieties of omelettes ($5-6) all squeezed into one little restaurant. Open daily 7am-2pm.

China Chef, on Commercial Row (587-1831). Expensive for dinner, but good bargains on lunch specials (soup, appetizer, entree, rice, tea, and fortune cookie for $4-5). Open Mon.-Sat. 11:30am-3pm and 4:30-10pm, Sun. noon-3pm and 4:30-10pm.

Bud's Fountain, 10108 Commercial Row. A clever entrepeneur, Bud merged an old-fashioned ice-cream parlor with a sporting goods store. Old-fashioned banana splits and other delights $1-2. Baseballs $3. Open Mon.-Sat. 9am-10pm.

The Cookery, on Commercial Row (587-6290.) The best of the touristy delis. An uneasy marriage of sophistication (cappucino $1.25) and small-town grub (Harry's Homemade Chili $3.25). Open daily 8am-6pm.

Basque Club Restaurant, Northstar's Golf Course Complex on Northstar Dr. (587-0260). Aprés-ski atmosphere with hearty, family-style, Basque dinners ($14.25, children $7). Dinner only.

Sights

Unlike its Mother Lode counterparts, Truckee did not have to rely on gold to survive. It developed instead as a logging center and railhead. Climb the **Rocking Stone Tower** on High St. to get a good view of the town at sunset (or sunrise). Legend has it that the 17-ton stone was used as a primitive Indian altar. In the late 19th century, the tower was attached to the house of Truckee's respected newspaper editor Charles McGlashen. His house has since been replaced with a hideously designed Veterans Memorial Building. Guaranteed a rockin' good time.

McGlashen came up with the profitable idea of an eye-catching 60-ft. "cultured" (i.e. artificial) icicle (no longer in existence). He was one of Truckee's "leading citizens" who backed a local group united under the slogan, "The Chinese must go." The "oriental ghetto" was forcibly moved to the south side of the Truckee river in 1879, and the population—perhaps the second-largest on the Pacific Coast—was driven out entirely in 1886 by boycotts and violence. The **Old Chinese Herb Shop,** on the corner of South River and Bridge St., though lacking as a tourist attraction, is one of the only vestiges of Chinatown today.

The local historical society has produced a brief town trail (maps obtainable from the Chamber of Commerce) and maintains part of the **Old Truckee Jail** on Jibboom St. as a small museum. (Open Fri.-Mon. 11am-4pm. Free.)

The Donner Party is remembered in the **Donner Memorial State Park** (587-3841), 1 mi. east of Truckee. Take I-80 to the Donner Lake exit, then go west on old U.S. 40 until you reach the park entrance. The park includes the excellent **Emigrant Trail Museum,** as well as a monument and trails to the cabin sites. (Museum open daily 10am-noon and 1-4pm. Admission 50¢.) There is another monument at the **Graves Cabin Site** on old U.S. 40, east of the I-80 interchange. Eighty-one mid-Westerners headed for the comfort of California in April 1846, taking a "shortcut" advocated by the dare-devil adventurer, Lansford Hastings. What Hastings didn't mention was that he'd never traveled the route, but just looked at a map and decided it would be fun to try. The party hacked through the wilderness, losing cattle and abandoning wagons as they went. The onset of an early winter at Truckee (later Donner) Lake in December forced them to eat mice, twigs, and bark, and finally, their friends and relatives. Only 45 survived.

Backpacking is easy and popular in summer. The well-traveled **Pacific Crest Trail** crosses I-80 near Donner Lake, a few miles west of town; this is an ideal place to pick up the trail going north. **Alpine Skills International** (426-9108) has all levels of classes ($75-400). For up-to-date information on hiking, backpacking, and climbing, talk to the folks at **Alpenglow Sports** (587-2025), next to the post office on Bridge St. (Open Mon.-Sat. 10am-6pm, Sun. 10am-5pm). They sometimes have spare packs and tents for rent. The Forest Service is, as always, particularly well-versed about federally owned lands. Rafting on the **Truckee River** is an excellent way to escape the summer heat (if there has been enough snowfall to let water out of Lake Tahoe; in 1990 all trips were cancelled). Call **Truckee River Raft Rentals** at 581-0123. (Open daily in summer 8:30am-3:30pm. Rentals $15, children under 12 $10.) Trips last 2-3 hours. Avoid disappointment by arriving before 10am.

For many, four legs are better than two, and horseback riding is both popular and plentiful. **Horsefeathers,** a horseback riding outfit, located at the Tahoe Donner Equestrian Center (587-9470), gives breakfast tours on horseback ($20) and 1 hr. trail rides ($15). **Mountain biking** has become the rage around here, and trails are rapidly being developed. Try the **Brockway Pass** trail at **NorthStar** or the **Flume Trail,** a 5-mi. uphill slope from the Spooner Lake campground.

Truckee sees the most activity in winter, though the area is licking its wounds from recent rejection as host of the 1992 Winter Olympics. **Squaw Valley** (583-6985) had the honor in 1960 and still proudly displays its Olympic symbol and flame. With 27 lifts, it is the largest of 11 ski resorts in the area. It lies 10 mi. south off Rte. 89. You can enjoy night skiing or cross-country here, as well as at several other resorts. In summer ride the Squaw Valley Tram to an elevation of 8200 ft. (open daily 10am-5pm; fare $8, ages 5-13 $5, under 5 free). Lesser known, **Sugar Bowl** (426-3651), which celebrates its 50th anniversary during the 1990/1991 season, is the closest to the Bay Area. Opportunities for excellent **nordic skiing** exist in the area as well. Prices run about $11-13 per day. Call **Tahoe-Donner Cross Country** (587-9484) for more information. March brings the **Snowfest** winter carnival (583-7625) and then celebrations in the sky with the **Truckee Air Show** (587-4119). And on Christmas Eve, a skilled professional dressed in Santa garb parachutes down from the sky. Ho ho ho.

The Desert

Mystics, misanthropes, and hallucinogenophiles have long been fascinated by the desert and its vast spaces, austere scenery, and often brutal heat. California's desert region has worked its spell on generations of passersby, from the Native Americans and pioneering fortune hunters of yesterday to the young Jim Morrison to modern city slickers disenchanted with smoggy L.A. The fascination stems from the desert's cyclical metamorphosis from a pleasantly warm refuge in winter to a technicolored floral landscape in spring, and then to a blistering wasteland in summer. The Western Desert is at once beautiful and desolate, and always awe-inspiring. Many come to California for the beaches, but you may weel find this sun-baked sandscape to be even more entrancing.

Orientation

Southern California's desert is at the fringe of the North American Desert, a 500,000-square-mile territory stretching east into Arizona and New Mexico, northeast into Nevada and Utah, and south into Mexico. Despite a climate that allows only 6 in. of rain to trickle onto the parched earth each year, the desert supports an astonishing array of plant and animal life as well as shabby towns around Death Valley, unlikely resorts such as Palm Springs, and dozens of bland highway settlements serving as pit stops for those speeding to points beyond.

California's desert divides roughly into two major regions with different climatic zones. The **Sonoran,** or **Low Desert,** occupies southeastern California from the Mexican border north to Needles and west to the Borrego Desert; the **Mojave,** or **High Desert** spans the southcentral part of the state, bounded by the Sonoran Desert to the south, San Bernardino and the San Joaquin Valley to the west, the Sierra Nevada to the north, and Death Valley to the east.

As their names imply, the Low and High Deserts lie at different elevations, resulting in their different climates. The Low Desert is flat, dry, and barren. The oases in this area are essential to the existence of human, animal, and plant life alike, with the largest of them supporting the super-resort of Palm Springs. Despite the arid climate, much of this region has become agriculturally important as water from the Colorado River irrigates the big city of Blythe, the Imperial Valley, and the Coachella Valley. Anza-Borrego Desert State Park and the Salton Sea are other points of interest here.

In contrast, the High Desert consists of foothills and plains nestled within mountain ranges approaching 5000 ft. Consequently, it is cooler (by about 10°F in summer) and wetter. Though few resorts are developed, Joshua Tree National Monument is a popular destination for campers. Barstow is the central city of the High Desert and an important rest station on the way from L.A. to Las Vegas or the Sierras.

Death Valley represents the eastern boundary of the Mojave but might best be considered a region unto itself, since it has both high and low desert areas. Major highways cross the desert east-west: I-8 hugs the California-Mexico border, I-10 goes through Blythe and Indio on its way to Los Angeles, and I-40 crosses Needles to Barstow, where it joins I-15, running from Las Vegas and other points west to L.A.

Desert Survival

Here, water, not bread, is the staff of life. The body loses at least a gallon of liquid per day in the desert, so keep drinking even when you're not thirsty. If you're using sweet beverages, dilute them with water to avoid over-reacting to high sugar content—even orange juice should be diluted at least 50%. Alcohol and coffee cause dehydration; if you indulge, compensate with lots more water. For long-term stays, a high-quality beverage with potassium compounds and glucose, such as ERG (an industrial-strength Gatorade), will help keep your strength up. Thirst is the first sign of dehydration, which comes on rapidly. Drinking enormous quantities of water after the fact is not effective—in fact, it's dangerous to do so in high temperatures.

If you arrive from a cooler climate, allow yourself a couple of days to adjust to the heat, especially if you're planning a hike or other strenuous activity. Make sure to carry sunglasses, a high-protection sunscreen, and a hat. A bandana or towel dipped in water and wrapped around the head Arabian-style will give added protection and relief. Keep clothing on, not off; a sweaty shirt, though uncomfortable, will prevent dehydration more effectively than removing it. Thick-soled shoes and two pairs of socks can help to keep feet comfortable on a hike during the summer as the sand can register a scorching 150-200°F. Whether you are driving or hiking, tote *two gallons of water per person per day;* a little less is adequate at higher altitudes and during winter months.

Heat is not the only concern for desert-goers. In fact, at high elevations, temperatures during winter nights can be well below freezing, even with afternoon temperatures in the 60s or 70s. Believe it or not, you should take along at least a sweater even in the summer. The desert is infamous for spring and fall flash floods. Avoid camping in dry gulches, which can turn into raging rivers with astonishing speed. Even if it's not raining where you are, water can come down from the higher elevations, where it is raining, and wreak Biblical devastation.

Hiking expeditions should be attempted only when the temperature is under 90°, and *never* alone. Almost all parks require hikers to register with the park office before setting out. If you're on private or unmanaged public land, *always* notify someone of your itinerary. The National Park Service recommends that a support vehicle follow all hikers.

Hitchhiking is risky year-round and suicidal in the summer. Between the searing desert floor, the isolation of most parts of the desert, and the uncertainty of getting a ride, this is the equivalent of spitting in the face of Fortuna.

Before **driving** in the desert, make sure that your car has been recently serviced and is in good running condition. Carry water for drinking and for the radiator, and make sure your car is equipped with a spare tire and necessary tools. Five gallons of water is recommended for each vehicle. For any trips off major roads, a board and shovel are useful in case your car gets stuck in sand; the board can be shoved under a tire to gain traction and the shovel can take care of minor quagmires. Although settlements are sometimes sparse, enough traffic usually passes on the roads to help you if you have car trouble. The isolated areas of the big parks pose more of a threat, especially in summer, when few tourists visit. *Stay with your vehicle if it breaks down;* it is easier to spot than a person. In the most nightmarish scenario—stranded, extreme heat, little or no water—find whatever shade you can, drench yourself with (but don't drink) cooled radiator water to ward off dehydration, burn motor oil in a hubcap to send smoke signals, and if you must move, do so only at night. If you see the temperature gauge climbing while driving, turn off the air conditioning. If an overheating warning light comes on, stop immediately and wait about a half hour before trying again. Never pour water over the engine to cool it; you can crack the engine block. Drivers should purchase a desert water bag for about $5 to $10 at a hardware or automotive store. This large canvas bag is strapped onto the front of the car and filled with water; the wind causes evaporation and prevents overheating. In an absolute emergency, turn the heater on full force to help cool the engine.

Palm Springs

With Mayor Sonny Bono providing mustachioed poolside politics, Palm Springs' beat goes on as a playground for the nouveau riche, and a low-cal slice of Southern California's pleasure pie. The medicinal waters given forth from the natural hot springs seem to ensure not only the health of the area's opulent residents but also Palm Spring's longevity as a resort town. Centuries ago, the Agua Caliente branch of the Cahuillian Indians settled here for a winter respite, and ever since then Palm Springs has continued to draw visitors pathetically hoping to snatch a piece of its glamorama lifestyle.

As Jaguars and Porsches prowl the strip, golden consumers compare prices at Gucci and Saks 5th Avenue. But have no fear, Budget Traveler! Cheap thrills are free; just have a seat and observe the parade of tacky affluence as it passes down Palm Canyon Drive.

Practical Information and Orientation

Visitors Information: Chamber of Commerce, 190 W. Amado (325-1577). Friendly advice and a map for $1. *The Desert Guide,* a free monthly magazine, scores high on most visitors' utility calculus. Open Mon.-Fri. 8am-5pm, Sat. 10am-2pm.

Palm Springs Recreation Department: 323-8272. Highlights of local arts and entertainment events.

Parks and Recreation Information: 401 S. Bavilon Way (323-8282). Information about activities at the leisure center (located at this address), the municipal golf course, and 8 city parks. Open daily 8am-5pm.

Airport: Palm Springs Regional Airport, 3400 S. Tahquitz-McCallum Way (323-8161). Easily connects to downtown via bus #2. Intrastate, as well as limited national service on American, United, and TWA Airlines.

Amtrak: Jackson St. at the railroad tracks (800-872-7245), in Indio, 25 mi. southeast of Palm Springs. Connect to Palm Springs via **Greyhound** (347-5888) in Indio. Three trains per week to and from L.A. ($29). Frequent stops make the trip much longer than the 2 hr. it takes to drive. This is getting to Palm Springs the hard way.

Greyhound: 311 N. Indian Ave. (325-2053), on one of the 2 main north-south streets. An easy walk from downtown. Five buses per day to and from L.A. ($18).

Desert Stage Lines: 367-3581. Bus service daily to Twentynine Palms, Joshua Tree National Monument (3 per day, $8.45, round-trip $16), and Yucca Valley. Fri. service to and from L.A. (from Twentynine Palms $20; from Palm Springs via Greyhound $20.75) and San Diego (from Palm Springs $23.45).

Sun Bus: 343-3451. The local bus system connects all Coachella Valley cities daily 6am-6pm. 50¢ to ride, plus 25¢ per zone and 25¢ per transfer. Bus #19 hits every mall in the valley on its way from Palm Springs to Indio (every ½-hr.). Bus #20 stays on a straight course along Palm Canyon Dr. and from there along Rte. 111 to Palm Desert, and eventually Indio (one bus per ½hr.). Bus #2 covers the downtown area, the airport, and Cathedral City. Schedules available at the Chamber of Commerce. Day pass $2. Seniors and disabled persons ride free on weekends; Mon.-Fri. 9am-2pm, 25¢.

Disabled and Senior Citizens' Transportation Information: 320-4906. *Tele-Ride* will take disabled people and those over 54 to their destinations. Fare $1.50. Runs Mon.-Fri. 8:00am-4pm. *Tele-Ride* to or from Palm Desert (341-7433) costs $1.25 each way and runs Mon.-Fri. 8am-noon and 1-4pm. 24-hr. notice required.

Taxi: Desert Cab, 325-2868. **Valley Cab,** 340-5845.

Car Rental: Rent-A-Wreck, 67501 Rte. 111 (324-1766). $19.95 per day. $119.95 per week with 700 free miles, plus 19¢ per additional mile. Must be 21 with major credit card.

Bicycle Rental: Burnett's Bicycles, 429 S. Sunrise Way (325-7844), at Ramon. Hidden in the bowels of the Alpha Beta shopping center. $16 per day, $45 per week. Ask for bike route maps. Take a pedal-powered tour of stars' homes in the Las Palmas suburb. Open Mon. and Thurs.-Sun. 8am-5pm, Tues. 8am-noon. Closed Wed.

Automobile Club of Southern California (AAA): 300 S. Farrell Dr. (320-1121). Emergency road service. In the Palm Springs to Palm Desert area 323-2721.

Road Conditions: 345-2767 (recording).

Road Emergency: California Highway Patrol (CHiPs). Dial 0, ask for Zenith 1-2000. Toll-free.

24-hr. Service Stations: Palm Springs Texaco, 610 N. Palm Canyon Dr. (320-9722); **Palms-to-Pines Shell,** Rte. 111 and 74, Palm Desert (346-3758).

Ticketron: 277 Avenida Caballeros (778-4100). Located in the lobby of the Convention Center.

Laundromat: Ramon Coin-Op, 222 E. Ramon Rd. (325-4949), at Indian Ave. Open daily 5am-9pm.

Weather: 398-7211. Coachella Valley forecast.

Clinic: Palm Springs Health Department, 3255 Tahquitz-McCallum Way (778-2210). Fees on a sliding scale. V.D. clinic, AIDS testing, family planning (no abortion counseling), pregnancy testing ($9). Open Mon.-Fri. 8am-5pm.

Desert Community Mental Health Center: 2150 Tahquitz-McCallum Way, #4 (320-0063). County-run out-patient mental health clinic. For emergency (including rape) counseling, call 800-472-4305. Open Mon. 8am-7pm, Tues.-Fri. 8am-5pm.

Desert Hospital: 1150 N. Indian Ave. (323-6511).

Emergency: 911.

Post Office: 333 E. Amado Rd. (325-9631). Open Mon.-Fri. 8:30am-5pm. General Delivery ZIP Code: 92262.

Area Code: 619.

Palm Springs basks off I-10, 120 mi. east of L.A., just beyond a low pass that marks the edge of the Colorado Desert. Palm Springs is one of several cities in the Coachella Valley, an agricultural oasis in the desert. The resort rests at the elbow of an arc, with Desert Hot Springs to the north, and Cathedral City, Rancho Mirage, Palm Desert, La Quinta, Indio, and Coachella to the east and southeast along Rte. 111.

The city's one-way, main drag is **Palm Canyon Drive** (Rte. 111), which runs south through the heart of town until it abruptly bends to become East Palm Canyon. Indian Avenue, the other major north-south street, 1 block east of Palm Canyon, runs north only. One of the two main east-west boulevards bears the unwieldy name of Tahquitz-McCallum (TAH-quits) and runs directly from downtown to the airport. Ramon Road, 4 blocks south, is the other east-west artery. **Palm Springs Regional Airport,** 3400 E. Tahquitz-McCallum Way (323-8161), is at the eastern edge of town. Take bus #2 to reach downtown.

Those coming to Palm Springs from within California are well advised to avoid high "domestic" airfares by taking the bus. You might check out some of the other airports in the region: Ontario is only an hour away and fares there are often cheaper than in Palm Springs.

Accommodations

Palm Springs caters mainly to those looking for a tax shelter, not a night's shelter. The prices are steep, but with Fortuna's guidance you'll escape with *some* cash still in hand.

State park and national forest **campgrounds** are only an hour away (see Idyllwild and Nearby Mountains or even Joshua Tree). The "campgrounds" closest to Palm Springs are RV parks. **Renting** a house, condominium, or apartment is not as outlandish as it sounds, especially if there are several of you to split the cost. Many homeowners use their porperty for only a small portion of the year and rent it out for the rest of the year. Look in the rental section of the classified ads in the *Desert Sun* (the daily paper), or call **Palm Springs Rental** (320-7451) or local brokers. Rentals range from one day to three months; summer is the best time but there is an available supply year-round. Luxury motels slash their prices by more than 50% in summer, smaller motels by 20-30%—don't be shy about bargaining.

Accommodations grow more expensive the closer you are to the action. If you have your own transportation, you may want to sojourn in the less swish Desert Hot Springs, a few miles northwest of Palm Springs. In the Springs itself, the cheaper motels are at the north end of town along Rte. 111. During peak winter months and especially during spring vacation, call ahead for reservations. Some motels have yet another tier of prices midway between the rock-bottom summer prices and inflated winter rates.

Motel 6, 2 locations: 660 S. Palm Canyon Dr. (327-4200), 149 units conveniently located south of city center (singles $29, doubles $35); 595 E. Palm Canyon Dr. (325-6129), 125 units (singles $25, doubles $31). Used to go by the name Hotel 6 as Palm Springs etiquette frowned upon the use of the word "Motel." Both locations boast pools and A/C, and are usually booked up—as much as 6 months in advance in the winter, 3 months in the summer. The best deal around. Reservations are accepted up to one year in advance. Some on-the-spot rooms are available around 9am, and no-shows are frequent.

Monte Vista Hotel, 414 N. Palm Canyon Dr. (325-5641). Convenient downtown location. Pleasant pool area with jacuzzi and shuffleboard 34 cheery chambers with color TV and A/C. Rooms $45-50; June-Aug. $35-37.50. Bungalows with kitchenette $60-65. Children allowed in summer only.

Mira Loma Hotel, 1420 N. Indian Ave. (320-1178). The 12 smartly decorated rooms in this one-story complex have refrigerators and color TVs; all open onto the poolside. Friendly management welcomes Europeans. Singles $35-58; $50-68 in winter. Children allowed in summer only. Reserve far in advance for spring weekends.

Allstar Inns, 69570 Higway 111, Rancho Mirage (324-8475). Located 5 mi. east of Palm Springs, just beyond Cathedral City. Incredible motel simulation. Large pool, A/C, color TV. Singles $27. Doubles $31.

Linda Vista Lodge, 67200 Hacienda Ave. (329-6401 or 800-334-7200), in Desert Hot Springs, 10 mi. north of Palm Springs. Large heated pool, 2 naturally hot mineral pools, sauna, and miniature golf. Sharp rooms, all with refrigerators and color TV. Lots of contented senior citizens lounging around the pool. Singles and doubles $29-40. Suite for 4 with kitchen $100. Rates $5-10 higher in winter. Stay 3 nights, get the 4th free.

Food

For those who prefer to stock up rather than eat out, there are plenty of chain supermarkets. **Ralph's,** 1555 S. Palm Canyon (323-8446), and **Vons,** in the Palm Springs Mall on Tahquitz-McCallum (322-2192), are reliably low-priced. The **Palm Springs Leisure Center,** on Sunrise at Ramon, and the **Ruth Hardy Park,** on Tamarisk, 4 blocks east of Indian Ave., are perfect places to picnic.

Enzo's Taco House, 494 N. Palm Canyon Dr. (325-6878). Honest Mexican chow executed with style. Ask for a business card and receive discounts on the pizza and platters. Open Mon.-Sat. 11:30am-9pm.

El Gallito Café, 68820 Grove St., Cathedral City (328-7794), within sight of Rte. 111, 2 blocks west of Date Palm Dr.; look for the Mag Gas station on Rte. 111. Take bus #20. The best *comida mexicana* in Palm Springs. The velvet paintings on the wall and the trinkets adorning the booths suggest a just-south-of-the-border ambiance. *Combinaciones* (2 entrees, beans, rice, and tortillas) fit for a glutton ($6.25). Try a burrito ($3.25) with complimentary chips and salsa and Mexican beers from their selection ($2). Always loud and busy. Open Sun.-Fri. 11am-9:30pm, Sat. 10am-9:30pm.

Carlo's Italian Delicatessen, 119 S. Indian Ave. (325-5571). Palm Springs' finest deli for the money. Overgrown sandwiches in the $4.50-5 range. Much a "New York" or "Chicago" sandwich ($4.75) while pondering the Palm Springs personalities portrayed on the wall. Open Sun 11am-5pm, Mon.-Thurs. 10am-6pm, Fri.-Sat 10am-7pm.

Las Casuelas Terazza, 222 S. Palm Canyon Dr. (325-2794). Cool Mexican mists pour out onto the sidewalk, inviting you to dine on this outdoor patio and indulge in margaritas as you watch the nightly entertainment. Two real macaws live in the mini-courtyard dining area. A hotspot, so make reservations. Entrees $7-12. Open Mon.-Sat. 11am-10pm, Sun. 10am-10pm.

Mama Chinn's, 260 N. Palm Canyon Dr. (320-5151), in downtown across from the Hyatt. Italian and Chinese cuisines fuse in a pizza parlor atmosphere. Grab a quick slice ($1.50), or maybe you'd rather sample the "Thai One Ahn" 6-incher ($5.95). Open 11am-midnight.

Hamburger Hamlet, 105 N. Palm Canyon Dr. (325-2321). Only in Southern California; a gourmet burger grill with a Shakespearean motif (the walls are adorned with playbills from various performances of *Hamlet*). These burgers are good—real, real, good. Holy guacamole! ½-lb. guacamole burger $7. Methinks the menu doth cholest too much. Entrees $5-9. Open Sun. 9am-11pm, Mon.-Thurs. 9am-10pm, Fri. 11am-11pm, Sat. 9am-11pm.

Paoli's Pizzeria and Pasta House, 68977 East Palm Canyon Dr. Cathedral City (324-3737). The tables in this Italian eatery are so close that you can't help but hear what your neighbors are saying. Chances are, however, they'll be talking about the pizza; it's the finest this side of the San Jacintos. (Family size pizza $11, $1 each additional topping.) The pasta dishes are generously proportioned ($7-14.) Open Tues.-Sun. 4pm-10pm.

The Wheel Inn, 849-7012. Cabazon exit on I-10, 15 mi. west of Palm Springs. You can't miss it. Two towering dinosaurs make this truck stop visible from a mile away. The gargantuan celebrities were granted oneiric immortality in *Pee Wee's Big Adventure.* One holds a small museum inside its shell. Alas, Large Marge is nowhere to be seen. Great homemade pies and fresh brewed coffee. Open 24 hr.

If you're not hungry for a meal, refresh yourself with a frozen yogurt from **Penguin's** or a scoop of award-winning ice-cream from the **Double Rainbow,** both on N. Palm Canyon Dr.

Sights

Towering above Palm Springs, only blocks from Palm Canyon Dr., stand the San Jacinto Mountains. Rising over 5000 ft., the **Palm Springs Aerial Tramway** climbs up the side of Mt. San Jacinto to an observation deck that affords excellent views of the far-off L.A. monster. The base station is located on Tramway Dr., which intersects Rte. 111 just north of Palm Spring. (Tram runs at least every ½ hr. Mon.-Fri. starting at 10am, Sat.-Sun. starting at 8am. Last car leaves at 9pm; Nov.-April at 7:30pm. Open year-round, except for maintenance work during the first week of August. Operation peaks in winter, especially on holidays. Round-trip tram fare $14, seniors $11.55, under 12 $9; with dinner on the mountain $18, under 12 $11.50.)

Eventually, the pathetic swankiness of Palm Springs' MTV hell will force you off of the main strip. A touch of true natural beauty has been carefully bought, cultivated, and marketed to please the rich at the remarkable **Desert Museum,** 101 Museum Dr. (325-7186), behind the Desert Fashion Plaza on Palm Canyon Dr. (325-7186). Underwritten, of course, by Palm Springs' philanthropists, the museum offers an impressive collection of Native American art, talking desert dioramas, and live animals. The museum also sponsors the performing arts in the 450-seat **Annenberg Theatre** as well as curator-led field trips into the canyons ($3). (Open late Sept.-early June, Tues.-Fri. 10am-4pm, Sat.-Sun. 10am-4pm. Adults $4, seniors $3, under 17 $2. Children free with adult. Free to all first Tues. of each month.

The **Indian Canyons** (327-2714), once home to the Agua Caliente Cahuilla Indians, are oases that contain both a wide variety of desert life and remnants of the communities they once supported. The site consists of 4 canyons just outside Palm Springs: Taquitz Canyon, Andres Canyon, Murray Canyon, and Palm Canyon. A permit is prerequisite to gain entrance to Taquitz ($10), and can be grabbed at the front gate. All four canyons can be accessed at the end of S. Palm Canyon Dr. (325-5673; open daily Sept.-July 7, 8am-5pm. Adults $3.50, seniors $2, children 6-12 $1, equestrians $3.50, students and military $2.50, pine-nuts free.)

The **Living Desert** located 1½ miles south of Highway 111 at 47900 Portola Ave. (346-5694), contains displays recreating various desert environments. Rare and exotic desert animals, such as Arabian oryces, St. Clair's iguani, desert unicorns, and Grery's zebras find a home here, alongside indigenous fauna in the **Botanical Gardens.** (Open daily Sept.-June 15 9am-5pm; adults $5.50, seniors $5, children $2.50. Disabled access.)

Less slick and more bizarre, **Moorten's Desertland Botanical Gardens,** 1701 S. Palm Canyon Dr. (327-6555), aims at extensive rather than precious landscaping. This is a botanist's heaven: ocotillo, yucca, prickly pear, and beavertail cacti to see, smell, and (sometimes) touch. The dinosaur footprints and petrified trees add an offbeat touch. The garden was started by Hollywood character actor "Cactus Slim" Moorten, and is now run by his wife and son, both of who are well-versed in desert lore. (Open Mon.-Sat. 9am-4pm, Sun. 10am-4pm. Admission $1.50, ages 5-16 50¢.)

The "Date Capital of the World" is *not* Zelda's disco (see Entertainment), but rather the **Coachella Valley,** although dates are not in fact native to this part of the world. Stop in at the **Oasis Date Garden** in Thermal (399-5665; open daily 8am-4:30pm) or the **Indian Wells Date Gardens,** on Rte. 111 in Palm Desert (346-2914; open daily 9:45am-5:15pm) for a date shake and a look around (should you decide to close your eyes it'll be a blind date). The **Shields Date Garden,** on Rte. 111 (347-0996; open daily 9am-6pm) toward Indio, features an epic slide presentation on the "Sex Life of The Date." Children must be accompanied by a parent.

For those travelers who saw more than enough desert simply getting to Palm Springs, a tour of **celebrity homes** offers an alternative view of mutant desert life forms. The budget method for this sight-seeing tour is to buy a map downtown and guide oneself. Alternately, Gray Line (325-0974) offers a 2½ hr. tour that includes a visit to the souvenir shop. (Adults $14.25, seniors $12.25, children $8.25; reservations required.) Be forewarned that these celebrities came to the desert for seclusion and your closest brush with greatness might be seeing Bob Hope's gardener working outside of his high adobe wall. To see celebrity Mayor Bono in action, take a seat in the audience of the **Palm Springs City Council,** which meets at City Hall, 3200 E. Tahquitz-McCallum Way, on the first and third Wednesday of every month. Bono's liberties with the English language can be painful to the ears and may make "I Got Youi Babe" seem eloquent in comparison. Ah, democracry in action. Mustaches, too. (Call 323-8299 for further information.)

For an introductory lesson in the area's history, visit the **Village Green Heritage Center,** 221 S. Palm Canyon Dr. (323-8297). The center consists of two homes built by the region's first non-native settlers, the McCallum Adobe and the Cornelia White Home, both of which have been moved from their original locations and converted into museums. (Open mid-Oct. to early June Sun. and Wed. noon-3pm, Thurs.-Sat. 10am-4pm.)

The most idiosyncratic sight in the region is **Cabot's Old Indian Pueblo,** 67616 E. Desert View Ave. (329-7610), 1 mi. east of Palm Dr. in **Desert Hot Springs.** Take bus #19 from downtown Palm Springs to Desert View Ave. The 35 rooms in the pueblo were built from materials found in the desert, Hopi pueblo style, over 23 years (1941-64) by Cabot Yerxa. Cabot, a black sheep of the upper-crust Boston Cabots, preferred the strenuous life of the desert to the Beantown Brahmin bull. When he built his four-story dream house (now surrounded by tract homes), there wasn't another soul for miles around: he had to walk 30 mi. to Garnet for water and concrete. (Open Wed.-Mon. 9:30am-4:30pm, last tour at 4pm. Hours vary in summer. Admission $2, seniors $1.50, ages 5-16 $1.)

Activities and Entertainment

In Robin Leach's lexicon, Palm Springs is synonymous with golf, tennis, and sunning by the pool—the rich and famous lifestyle. While this reputation is certainly justified (Palm Springs has more golf courses per capita than anywhere else in the world), there are other ways to take advantage of the area's near-perfect weather.

Those discontented with the swimming facilities at their lodgings may wish to take advantage of the **Olympic-sized pool** at the Palm Springs Leisure Center (323-8278), located on Ramon Rd. just east of Sunrise Way. (Open daily 11am-5pm, Tues. and Thurs. 7-9pm. Admission $3, ages 3-13 $2.) The Leisure Center also houses **Angeles Stadium** where the California Angels hold spring training. Thereafter, you'll have to settle for watching the lackluster class-A farm team, the Palm Springs Angels (admission $3, ages 4-14 $1.50; call the box office at 325-4487 for information).

Palm Springs has a number of public **tennis** and **golf** facilities. The eight courts at **Ruth Hardy Park,** 700 Tamarisk Dr., at Avenida Caballeros, come alive as early as 5am with people trying to beat the heat. **The Palm Springs Municipal Golf Course,** 1885 Golf Club Dr. (328-1005), claims to be one of the nation's top municipal golf courses ($18 for 9 holes, $9 in the summer). The visitors bureau has a list of other public golf courses, as does the *Desert Guide.* For complete information about facilities, call the city's Leisure Department at 323-8272. (How many cities do you know that have a Leisure Department?)

The Smoke Tree Stables, 2500 Toledo Ave. (327-1372), offers horseback riding at $18 per hour. Open Sept.-June 10am-8pm. Horsing around is undeniably costly, but the landscape easily justifies the expense. There are a number of companies that provide **balloon flights: Skysports Aviation,** P.O. Box 3164, Palm Desert (340-5545); **Sunrise Balloons,** 82550 Airport Blvd., Thermal (346-7591); and **Desert Balloon Charters,** P.O. Box 2713, Palm Desert (346-8575). Prices are lofty, generally over $100 per person, but many offer group rates. Shop around. Terrestrial transportation is provided by **Dune Enterprises,** 59511 Rte. 111 (325-0376), where you can rent 4-wheel, automatic All Terrain Vehicles for $25 per day.

A trip to Palm Springs would not be complete without a visit to the town's namesakes. The naturally hot mineral pools at the **Desert Hot Springs Spa,** 10805 Palm Dr. (329-6495), feature pools of different temperatures, saunas, professional masseurs and overflowing vanity. The spa epitomizes the town's "pool culture." On crowded days the deck unfortunately becomes littered with cups and cigarette butts, and the pools are awash in uninviting slicks of suntan oil. (Open daily 8am-10pm. Admission Mon.-Fri. $5, after 3pm $3; Sat.-Sun. $6, after 3pm $3; holidays $7. Refundable $3 lock deposit; $3 towel deposit, plus 50¢ rental.) **The Hacienda Riviera Spa,** 67375 Hacienda (329-7010), attracts a younger crowd of bathers. (Open Sept.-June daily 9am-5pm; July Wed.-Mon. 9am-5pm. Admission $4, children $1.)

To hear the rather incongruous roar of surf among the sagebrush, visit **Oasis Water Park,** (325-SURF (825-7873)) off Rte. 111 on Gene Autry Trail. In addition to a wave pool which generates 4½-ft. breakers, the park offers seven water slides of varying degrees of height and speed. Only a valiant few attempt the Scorpion, a stinging seven-story-tall near-free-fall plunge. (Admission $15, ages 4-11 $10, under 4 free.)

Back on the Main Strip, beautiful bodies promenade in poolside clothing. Shopping in Palm Springs is exclusively a sport for the well-heeled. Stores are outrageously expensive, but the *hoi polloi* find bargains in the numerous thrift shops in Cathedral City that take in the tired, poor, and huddled refuse of the rich. And for the shameless, there is the **Palm Desert Town Center,** an indoor shopping complex with an ice skating rink (340-4412) and 10 movie theaters.

Even if Mayor Bono were to leave politics and attempt a musical comeback, he would be hard-pressed to find a venue in Palm Springs. For live music of quality, residents in the know make the trek into L.A. The **Laff Stop,** 1000 E. Tahquite Way (327-8889), imports decent comedians from the City of Angels, but a two-drink minimum ($3-4 each) and a hefty cover ($7.50-10) may be reason enough to just stay home and play Pictionary. For a true taste of how Palm Springs steps out, cautiously approach **Zelda's,** 169 N. Indian Ave. (325-2375), off N. Palm Canyon Dr. No ripped jeans or ratty dreads are allowed.. Top 40 tunes pump from spinning speakers, while beautiful bodies sparkle for all to see. There is a $6 cover, but free passes are available for the lucky explorer. For a yuppier scene away from the 16-year-old crowd, try **Pernina's,** 340 N. Palm Canyon Dr. (325-6544).

Seasonal Events

If you happen upon the city during the second or third week in February, don't miss the **National Date Festival,** fashioned along the lines of a eupeptic Arabian fantasy complete with camel and ostrich races, harems, sheiks, and of course, mountains of dates. Call Date Festival Fairgrounds, Rte. 111 (342-8247), in Indio, for more information. Palm Springs is infamous for its professional golf and tennis tournaments named after aging celebrity has-beens: the **Bob Hope Desert Classic** in mid-January, the **Dinah Shore Ladies' Professional Golf Association Tournament (LPGA)** the first week in April, and the **James Franciscus Annual Celebrity Tennis Classic** the first week of May. In fulfilling his campaign promise to heighten Palm Springs' glamour quotient, Mayor Bono has instituted the **Palm Springs International Film Festival,** held each year during the second week of January. Films from around the world are screened in local theaters.

The last week of March and the first week of April elicit libidinous joy from the nation's college students and strike fear into the hearts of parents and resort-town officials everywhere. **Spring Break,** the rite of passage in which debauchery and a deep tan are the only orders of business, arrives with a vengeance in Palm Springs. Five years ago, riots forced the police to close Palm Canyon Drive; officers were attacked as they tried to make arrests and the chaos ended with the hijacking and looting of a catering truck (only in Palm Springs...). Since then, the city has cracked down with anti-revelry brochures distributed to most universities in the Southwest. Younger students yearning to kick up their heels should keep in mind the 10pm curfew for those under 18.

Near Palm Springs

At the **Morongo Reservation** near Banning, west of Palm Springs 1 mi. off I-10, the tiny **Malki Museum** (849-7289) exhibits Native American artifacts. Far from slick, the presentation is yet another collection of family heirlooms arranged with the ostensible purpose of preserving an era gone by. (Open Thurs.-Fri. 10am-4pm and Sat.-Sun. 11am-5pm.) The **Malki Spring Festival** takes place on Memorial Day weekend. Traditional music and dance are taken out of the closet and aired for a couple of days, and Hopi are brought in from Arizona to flesh out the *corps de ballet.*

Closer to Palm Springs is **Hadley's,** the Tiffany's of dried fruit. Walk around this warehouse-sized store munching on free samples. They also sell nuts, wine (there's a tasting room), and health foods, and will send gifts of California produce all over the world. Take the Apache Trail/Cabazon exit off I-10.

If time allows, take the scenic **Palms-to-Pines Highway** (Rte. 74) back to L.A., watching as the desert cactus and sagebrush give way to pine. You can pick up Rte. 74 at its junction with Rte. 111 in Palm Desert.

Joshua Tree National Monument

When the Mormons crossed this desert area in the 1800s, they named the enigmatic desert tree that grew in groves after the Biblical prophet Joshua. Its crooked limbs reminded them of the Hebrew leader, with his arms upraised, beckoning the weary traveler to the promised land. Indeed, after crossing the more arid Arizona desert, finding the slightly cooler and wetter Mojave must have been like arriving in God's country. As the meeting place between the Mojave and Sonoran Deserts, Joshua Tree National Monument hosts the spectrum of desert landscapes and life. Its 4000-ft. elevation offers a more hospitable climate for desert life, with temperatures 10-15° below those of the scorching Low Desert. Even so, during the summer the mercury regulary tops 100°.

The Joshua-dotted landscape is punctuated with great piles of quartz monzonite boulders, some over 100 ft. high. The campsites throughout the area center around these formations, as they provide shade and create rain-catching gullies, resulting in denser vegetation. The boulders were formed by subterranean lava flows seeping up through soft sandstone layers. Years of erosion have left the boulders exposed to the elements, and the two forces together have created fantastic textures and shapes, majestic to the viewer and irresistible to the climber. Beside the natural environment are vestiges of human existence: ancient rock pictographs, dams built in the 19th century to catch the meager rainfall for livestock, and the ruins of gold mines that operated as late as the 1940s.

In contrast to the rugged rock piles are the palm tree oases. Twentynine Palms, Fortynine Palms, Cottonwood Spring, and Lost Palms all grow out of springs of underground water rising through faults in the earth. Though perhaps not as large and luxurious as the oases of Arabian tales, they do support a remarkable diversity of plant and animal life, ranging from the California tree frog to bighorn sheep. They also sustained the earliest human residents of the region, some 10,000 years ago.

Cacti abound as well, and the short springtime is one of the park's loveliest (and most crowded) attractions. The *cholla* (CHOY-a) cactus is one to admire at a safe distance. The slightest brush against it will detach a spiny friend who will never leave your side. If you are one who relishes the thought of sleeping under the crystalline skies of the high desert, invest in a cot. Otherwise, rattlesnakes and scorpions may be uninvited bedfellows.

Most campgrounds do not have water; bring your own. And be sure to stop by the visitor center. The rangers are friendly and will help orient you to this fascinating wilderness.

Practical Information and Orientation

Visitors Information: Headquarters and Oasis Visitor Center, 74485 National Monument Dr., Twentynine Palms 92277 (367-7511), ¼ mi. off Rte. 62 Displays, lectures, maps. Brochures average about 20¢. Open daily 8am-4:30pm. **Cottonwood Visitor Center,** at the southern gateway, located approximately 7 mi. north of I-10; exit 4 mi. west of the town of Chiriaco Summit. Open daily 8am-4:30pm, but hours are sometimes interrupted due to staff problems. The south entrance has an honor system for entrance fees. **Indian Cove Ranger Station,** on the road to Indian Cove campground, but not located at a park entrance. Open Oct.-May daily 8am-5pm; summer hours vary. **West Entrance Information Kiosk,** Park Blvd., several miles southeast of the town of Joshua Tree. Those impatient to get into the monument may want to enter here rather than drive on to Twentynine Palms.

Buses: Desert Stage Lines, 367-3581, based in Palm Springs. Stops in Twentynine Palms before going on to the Twentynine Palms Marine Corps base.

Weather: summer highs 95-115°F; winter highs 60-70°F. Warmer in the eastern area. 4-5" of rain per year. The most comfortable places in summer are above 4000 ft.; in winter, stick to the lower elevations.

Emergency: call 914-383-5652 for a ranger.

Area Code: 619.

Joshua Tree National Monument covers 500,000 acres northeast of Palm Springs, about 160 mi. (3-3½ hr. by car) from L.A. It is ringed by three highways: I-10 to the south, Rte. 62 (Twentynine Palms Hwy.) to the west and north, and Rte. 177 to the east. From I-10, the best approaches are via Rte. 62 from the west, leading to the towns of Joshua Tree and **Twentynine Palms** on the northern side of the monument, and via an unnumbered road that exits the interstate about 25 mi. east of Indio, where the streets have no name. Joshua Tree is a popular destination for daytrips or weekend stays by residents of Palm Springs and coastal southern California who still haven't found what they're looking for.

Camping

Campgrounds in the monument accept no reservations, except for group sites at Cottonwood, Sheep Pass, and Indian Cove, where Ticketron (900-370-5566) handles reservations (mandatory at these 3 sites, except in summer). To secure a decent site for the weekend, arrive in the early afternoon hours on Friday, and earlier on holiday weekends. Campgrounds are often closed during the summer months; call in advance to check availability. Hidden Valley and Loop A of Cottonwood are almost always open. Many spring weekends find all campsites full *except* Black Rock Canyon, where the large size and relatively uninteresting site (at the monument's extreme northwest edge only 5 mi. from Rte. 62) almost guarantee availability. If even Black Rock is full, try the overflow campground outside the southern entrance off I-10, west of Chiriaco Summit.

All campsites have tables, fireplaces, and pit toilets, and are free unless otherwise noted. Water is available at Black Rock Canyon, Cottonwood, and the Indian Cove Ranger Station. There are no RV hookups or showers. BYOF (bring your own firewood). To secure a fee waiver for Cottonwood and Indian Cove group sites, write to the monument headquarters on your best official stationery and explain your bona fide educational/study group purposes (the activity is supposed to contribute to graduation requirements). There is unlimited backcountry camping, but tents must be more than 500 ft. from a trail and 1 mi. from a road. Your camping stay is limited to 14 days between October and May and to 30 days in the summer. An entrance fee to the monument ($2 per person or $5 per vehicle) is collected between October 1 and May 31. In the summer, only a few primitive sites are open; all are free. The central area of the park, where the Belle and Hidden Valley sites are located, is by far the prettiest during this time of year.

Hidden Valley (4200 ft.). Located in the center of the park off of Quail Springs Rd. With secluded alcoves in which to pitch a tent, and shade beneath enormous boulders, this is far and away the best and most wooded of the campsites. 62 sites in the Wonderland of Rocks. A haven for rock climbers. Near Barker Dam Trail. Loop C closed in summer.

Jumbo Rocks (4400 ft.). 130 well-spaced sites (65 in summer) surrounding (you guessed it) really big rocks. Located near Skull Rock Trail on the eastern edge of Queen Valley. Take Quail Springs Rd. 15 mi. south of visitors center.

Indian Cove (3200 ft.). 114 sites (45 in summer) on the northern edge of the Wonderland of Rocks (see Sights and Activities). Waterfalls after rain. Enter from north of park. 13 group sites, each $13.

Ryan (4300 ft.). 27 sites. With not as many rocks, as much privacy, or as much shade as nearby Hidden Valley. Three-mile, round-trip trail leads up 5470-ft. Ryan Mountain. Horses allowed. Closed in summer.

Cottonwood (3000 ft.). 62 sites (30 in summer) in the midst of arid, open desert. No shade. Located in the Colorado Desert portion of the park. Trail to Cottonwood Spring Oasis. Flush toilets, running water. Sites $6; 3 group sites $12.

White Tank (3800 ft.) Excellent for RVs. Closed in summer.

Belle (3800 ft.) 20 sites surrounding rock formations. Suitable for RVs and not much else. Little or no shade.

Black Rock Canyon (4000 ft.). 100 sites in a woodland environment. Take Joshua Lane off of Rte. 62, 2 mi. north of Yucca Valley. Horses permitted. Flush toilets, running water. Seldom full. Closed in summer. Sites $10. Reservations through Ticketron for families only.

Sheep Pass (4500 ft.). 6 group sites. No nightly fee, but a reservation fee of $13. Located in center of park near Ryan Mtn. trail. Call at least 3 months in advance for reservations.

Sights and Activities

Over 80% of the monument (mostly the southern and eastern areas) has been designated by Congress as a wilderness area—meaning trails but no roads, toilets, or campfire programs. For those seeking backcountry desert hiking and camping, Joshua Tree offers fantastic opportunities to explore truly remote territory. There is no water in the wilderness except when a flash flood comes roaring down a wash (beware your choice of campsite...), and even then, it doesn't stay long; carry at least a gallon of water per person per day. You *must* register at roadside boxes before setting out so that the monument staff knows where you are and so that your car is not towed from a roadside parking lot.

Less hardy desert rats should not be put off. Joshua Tree can be enjoyed for a day or a weekend in relative comfort. The most popular time, as with other desert parks, is **wildflower season** (mid-March to mid-May), when pilgrims by the thousands journey to see the floor of the desert exploding with yucca, verbena, cottonwood, mesquite, and dozens of other wildflowers. Bear in mind that no off-road driving or bicycling is permitted.

A drive through the center of the park along the winding road from Twentynine Palms to the town of Joshua Tree (34 mi.) passes by the **Wonderland of Rocks,** where piles of rocks approach a sort of surreal lapidarian art. The longer drive through the monument, between Twentynine Palms and I-10, traverses a sampling of both Low and High Desert landscapes. Along the way on both of these tours, explore as many of the side roads as time allows—some are paved, some are dirt, and some are suitable only for four-wheel-drive vehicles. Signs indicate for which vehicles each road is safe. One site that must not be missed is **Key's View,** (5185 ft.) 5 mi. off the park road just west of Ryan Campground. On a clear day, you can see forever—or at least to Palm Springs and the Salton Sea. The **Palm Oases** (Twentynine Palms, Forty-nine Palms, Cottonwood Spring, Lost Palms) also merit a visit, as does the **Cholla Cactus Garden,** off Pinto Basin Rd.

You may wish to explore the monument on foot, as many short trails provide access to some of Joshua Tree's most interesting sights. The **Lost Horse Mine** is reached by a 1½-mi. trail and evokes the region's gold prospecting days. Rusted machinery and ancient mine shafts eerily clutter the landscape. Information on many other hikes, ranging from 15-minute strolls to overnight treks, is available at the park center. Count on slow progress even on short walks; the heat is oppressive at times, and shade is a rare luxury.

Good food is as sparse as high desert vegetation. Stock up in Palm Springs or Desert Hot Springs. Nonetheless, **Everybody's Restaurant at C.B. Nutrition Center,** 71965 Twentynine Palm Hwy. (367-3164), offers several healthy sandwiches at even healthier prices ($1.25-2.75). Filipino dinner specialties average $6 a plate. Open Mon.-Sat. 11am-8pm.

Even if you view Joshua Tree merely as a break from the monotony of the interstate, do get out of your car once in a while to take a closer look at things. Note the adaptations that plants have made to the severe climate and admire the delicacy of their blooms. More animals can be seen at dusk than at high noon, but be alert to lizards and kangaroo rats. You may meet up with a enormous swarm of ladybugs near water. Golden eagles and bighorn sheep also inhabit the desert. If you come equipped with time, patience, and a sharp set of eyes, the beauty of the desert will gradually reveal itself.

Near Joshua Tree

The **Yucca Valley,** northwest of the monument, is graced with a couple of tourist sites and a genuinely helpful **Chamber of Commerce,** 56020 Santa Fe Trail, #B, 92284 (365-6323; open Mon.-Fri. 8am-5pm). The **Hi-Desert Nature Museum,** 57117 Twentynine Palms Hwy. (228-5452), has two rooms. Ignore the one on the left, which is stocked with arrowheads, cheap souvenirs from foreign countries, and bad paintings. The room on the right, however, has hundreds of gems, captive scorpions and snakes, and chunks of bristlecone pine, including a cone from the world's oldest living tree. In wildflower season, dozens of cut flowers from the properties of museum staff-members rest in vases along the tops of the display cases. This floral display allows armchair botanists to admire the hardy delicacy of desert wildflowers without tramping through cacti under the sun If you insist on seeing the wildflowers growing wild, take one of the two trails that start from the museum. The South Park Nature Trail (1 1/3 mi.) overlooks the Joshua Tree National Monument. The North Park Nature Trail (over 2 mi.) offers breathtaking views of the entire Morongo Basin area. (Museum open Wed.-Sun. 1-5pm. Free.)

Yucca Valley's other attraction is a series of bizarre hillside tableaux of 10- to 15-ft. concrete figures that tell biblical stories. **Desert Christ Park,** 57090 Twentynine Palms Hwy. (mail only), highlights Anton Martin's representations of Christ and the woman of Samaria, the Sermon on the Mount, and the Last Supper. The park is located at the end of Mohawk Trail; turn north off Twentynine Palms Hwy. The sentiment—that this be a world peace shrine bringing the Holy Land to Southern California—is admirable, but the Joshua trees down the road are more graceful and inspiring than these awkwardly pious icons. (Open dawn to dusk. Free.)

Mojave Desert

Scorching, silent, and barren, the Mojave is a picture of desolation. John Steinbeck called it a "terrestrial hell," and only the most sun-crazed desert rats would disagree with this description. Today, the empty spaces and scattered trailer towns serve as the bleak backdrop for a rootless subculture of military itinerants and Sam Shepherd impersonators. No one has heard of Häagen-Dazs ice cream at the imperative roadside EAT stands. Entrepreneurs fence off parcels of tumbleweeds and sell them as "Five Acre Tracts" with attractive and profitable "highway frontage." And travelers usually hurry through, too scared to explore, too anxious to reach gentler climes.

It's hard to argue with such instincts. Genuine attractions are rare indeed, and the summer heat would wither many mortals. Still, the Mojave leaves a mark on the undaunted adventurers patient enough to explore it. Winter temperatures are pleasant, even chilly. Hike or drive a four-wheel-drive vehicle across dizzying sand dunes; poke around the colorful gulches rife with fossils, obsidian, and Native American petroglyphs; inspect ghost towns. Do not, however, expect to revel in Barstow, the commercial hub of the Mojave, or Baker, a roadside settlement that comes in a distant second (which says a lot). Go into town only to sleep or to stock up on supplies.

Barstow

Barstow is the place to prepare for forays into the desert. Once a booming mining town, this desert oasis (pop. 20,000) now thrives on business from local military bases, tourists, and truckers. Stop in at the California Desert Information Center (see Practical Information), which has superb exhibits on the forest and a large topographical model of the Mojave, as well as free maps and information on hiking, camping, and exploring.

Practical Information and Orientation

Visitors Information: California Desert Information Center, 831 Barstow Rd., Barstow 92311 (256-8313), off I-15. Run by the **Bureau of Land Management** and staffed by the **Chamber of Commerce.** Best tourist information on the area, including local off-road vehicle areas. Open daily 9am-5pm.

Amtrak: N. 1st St. (800-872-7245), well past Main St., over the bridge that crosses the railroad tracks. An eerily silent and chilly shell of a station. You can get on or off a train here—that's all. Buy tickets on board or at a travel agency. To: L.A. (2 per day, $32), San Diego ($52), and Las Vegas ($43).

Greyhound: 120 S. 1st St. (256-8757), at W. Main. Cheerful personnel and lots of uniforms making their way to or from nearby bases. Cafeteria. To L.A. ($17.50) and Las Vegas (13 per day, $29). Open daily 8am-6pm.

Laundromat: 300 E. Main St.

Emergencies: Police, 256-2211. **Sheriff,** 256-1796. **Fire,** 256-2251. **Highway Patrol,** 256-1617.

Post Office: 425 S. 2nd St. (256-8494) Open Mon.-Fri. 9am-5pm. General Delivery ZIP Code: 92311.

Area Code: 619.

Barstow is midway between Los Angeles and Las Vegas on I-15; it is the western terminus of I-40. The Greyhound and Trailways stations are downtown. It is impossible to rent dune buggies or all terrain vehicles (ATVs) here.

Greyhound makes Mojave crossings east and west via Rte. 58 and I-15 (between Las Vegas and Los Angeles or Bakersfield) or via I-40 (between Flagstaff, AZ and Los Angeles or Bakersfield), serving the towns of Barstow, Baker, and Mojave. Buses also traverse the desert north and south between Los Angeles and Bishop via Rte. 14/U.S. 395 through Mojave, following the Los Angeles Aqueduct along the eastern foothills of the Sierra Nevada.

Accommodations, Food, and Entertainment

What Barstow lacks in charm (and boy, does it lack) is made up for by its abundant inexpensive motels and eateries. Every restaurant chain west of the Mississippi has a representative on Main St. You'll find a more inviting variety on E. Main St. than along W. Main St. For campgrounds outside of Barstow, see Near Barstow and Eastern Mojave Desert below.

El Rancho Motel, 112 E. Main St. (256-2401). Convenient to Greyhound and Amtrak stations, the building was constructed with railroad ties from the Tidewater and Tonopah Railway. Clean and newly decorated rooms complete with TV w/ cable, A/C. Pool. Kitchenettes available. Singles and doubles $26.45-33.

Economy Inns of America, 1590 Coolwater Lane (256-1737). Off of W. Main near I-40. Pool. Singles $22. Doubles $31.90. Quads $36.90. 10% discount for AAA members, military, and senior citizens.

Motel Calico, 35556 Yermo Rd. (254-2419), at I-15 and Ghost Town Rd. in Yermo, 8 miles east of Barstow. Seven attractive rooms decorated with desert photographs taken by the owner. Singles $22. Doubles $24.

Barstow/Calico KOA (254-2311), 7 mi. northeast of Barstow on north side of Outer Hwy. 15, between Ft. Irwin Rd. and Ghost Town Rd. exits. For corporate campers. Pool, showers, snack bar. Can get uncomfortably crowded. Tent sites for 2 $15, additional person $2.50. RVs $14. Electric and water hookup $4, sewer hookup $2.

The **Barstow Station McDonalds,** on E. Main St., made from old locomotive cars, is the busiest in the U.S., and is complete with a kid's playground, gift shop, and liquor store. If the idea of a Filet-O-Fish does not agree with you, you may wish to try **Vons** on E. Main St., where you may purchase a variety of supermarket specialties. Main St. also hosts ethnic restaurants of varying quality.**Carlo's and Toto's,** 901 W. Main. St. (256-7513) offers huge platters of Mexican specialties for south-of-the-border prices (entrees $4-$7.)

Barstow is studded with rough and rowdy bars, such as the **Katz,** 1st and Main (256-3275; open 6am-2am). The **Play-Mor,** 129 W. Main (256-5343), a video arcade, dispenses beer for $1. (Open Mon.-Fri. noon-midnight, Sat.-Sun. noon-2am.) A better entertainment alternative is the **Barstow Station Cinema 4,** 1503 E. Main St. (256-0065), where first-run movies are shown.

If you thought that Barstow fashion was an oxymoron, think again. Barstow is home to the **Factory Merchants Outlet Plaza,** 2837 Lenwood Rd. (253-7342), just south of town off of I-15. Over 50 shops sell the surplus of such designers as Ralph Lauren, Bass, and Anne Klein at prices 20-70% below retail in this fashion oasis. (Open daily 9am-8pm.)

Near Barstow

What happens when Walter Knott of Knott's Berry Farm gets his hands on a Yermo ghost town? **Calico Ghost Town,** Ghost Town Rd. (254-2122), 10 mi. northeast of Barstow via I-15, is the answer. Set high in multi-colored hills (hence the name), Calico flourished from 1881 to 1896 and died in 1907 after having produced $86 million in silver and $9 million in borax. At its height, the city supported about 4000 people and eight saloons along Main St. Circumvent the expensive admission package (tram, mine tour, train ride, "mystery shack" and vaudeville show $5.25, ages under 16 $3.25) by climbing the staircase at the tram/tour entrance and walk around for free. This sanitized Old West town is a restored and commercialized version of the mining town, and the number of visitors and shops sure puts the "ghost" label into question. There are discount rides for children in the amusement parks. For extended visits, there are 110 campsites in a shady canyon. Call 254-2122 for reservations. ("Town" open daily 7am-dusk, shops 9am-5pm. Parking $3.)

For a less tarted-up look at a much older period (Pleistocene, to be exact), visit the **Calico Early Man Site** (256-3591), farther east along I-15 to the Minneola Rd. off-ramp. This is the only New World site Louis Leakey ever bothered to excavate, and no wonder: the 20,000-year-old stone tools unearthed here make Calico the oldest find in the Western Hemisphere. On display are artifacts from the excavations and photographs of the dig. (Open Wed.-Sun. 8:30am-4:30pm. Free.)

Twelve mi. north of Barstow along Barstow Rd. are **Rainbow Basin** and **Owl Canyon,** colored with jasper, agate, and turquoise. Know, however, that rockhounding is illegal, and bears a steep penalty. The **BLM campground,** equipped with fireplaces, drinking water, and toilets, has 31 sites ($4).

Eastern Mojave Desert

The land between I-15 and I-40 east of Barstow is among the most isolated in California, hence the name Devils' Playground. Washes, dry lakes, and lava beds are some of the variations in this largely homogeneous landscape of sand and brush.

For most people, this region is only meant for passing through on the way to Las Vegas. Serene as the emptiness may be, it is still empty, and most press east to the glittering Strip, praying that their cars remain faithful.

Near **Kelso** is the most spectacular system of dunes in California. Four mi. long and reaching heights of 700 ft., the dunes are protected by the prohibition of off-road vehicles. Kelso is about 30 mi. southeast of Baker via Kelbaker Rd. from Barstow; either take I-40 to the Kelbaker Rd. exit 80 mi. to the east or I-15 to Baker. The routes are comparable in distance and difficulty.

Providence Mountains State Recreation Area, P.O. Box 1, Essex 92332 (389-2281), a popular, high-altitude (4000-5000 ft.) hiking, horseback riding, and spelunking region, is 10 mi. east of Kelso as the vulture flies. You can camp here in six primitive campsites for $6. But unless you have a Jeep, you'll have to backtrack from Kelso northward along Kelso Rd. toward Cima, then U-turn onto Black Canyon Rd. south to Essex Rd. and into the park. Or backtrack southward to I-40 via Kelbaker Rd. and find the northbound Essex Rd. exit, 20 mi. farther east along the freeway. (Open Sept. 17-June 14.) The BLM maintains 39 sites at the **Mid Hill** and the **Hole-in-Wall** campgrounds. **Mitchell Caverns Natural Preserve** offers 1½-mi. tours through its stalactite-cluttered limestone chambers. (1½-hr. tours Sept. 16-June 15 Mon.-Fri. at 1:30pm, Sat.-Sun. at 10am, 1:30pm, and 3pm; arrive ½ hr. early. Tours $3, ages 6-17 $1.) Gas and supplies are available in Essex and Goffs.

Dune buggies and Jeeps are still permitted free reign at the **DuMont Dunes,** about 25 mi. north of Baker, just off Rte. 127. Ask one of the locals to show you on a map exactly where they are—there is no sign. The **Bun Boy Restaurant** in Baker is a good place to stop for coffee and information.

Death Valley and Environs

Milton, Dante, and Blake could have found inspiration for further visions of Hell in Death Valley. No place in the Old World approaches the searing temperatures that are the summer norm here. Much of the landscape resembles photographs of the surface of Mars, with its reddish crags and canyons, stark and desolate. The highest temperature ever recorded in the Western Hemispere (134° in the shade) was measured at the Valley's Furnace Creek Ranch on July 10, 1913. Of that day, the ranch caretaker Oscar Denton said, "I thought the world was going to come to an end. Swallows in full flight fell to the ground dead, and when I went out to read the thermometer with a wet Turkish towel on my head, it was dry before I returned." The place names adhere to the infernal rhetoric: Devil's Golf Course, Coffin Peak, Funeral Mountains, Dante's View.

Fortunately, the fatal barrier of 130° is rarely crossed, and the region sustains a surprisingly intricate web of life. The otherworldliness of the landscape is strangely beautiful, as the earth-tones of the sands and rocks change hourly in the variable sunlight. The elevation ranges from Telescope Peak at 11,049 ft. down to Badwater, the lowest point in the hemisphere, at 282 ft. below sea level. There are pure white salt flats on the valley floor, impassable mountain slopes, and enormous, shifting sand dunes. Nature focuses all of its extremes and varieties here at a single location. And Milton and Dante thought Hell was interesting . . .

The history of Death Valley is a Wild West success story. In Pre-Columbian times, Native Americans eked a living from the land they called Tomesha. In 1849, a group of immigrants looking for a shortcut to California's gold country stumbled into the valley. After weeks of searching for a western pass through the Pantamint Range and suffering starvation and desertion, the group found a way out of the valley. Looking back at the scene of misery, one member exclaimed, "Good bye, death valley!" thus naming it for posterity. After this tragedy, few were anxious to return. Then in 1883 borax was discovered here. The mining of this salt, used as an antiseptic and water-softener, provided fortunes for a few and a livelihood for many in towns like Rhyolite and Skidoo. But these boom towns became ghost towns with alarming speed and have been preserved by the area's low humidity. With the borax mines depleted and no promise of new industry, most folks have forsaken the valley itself, leaving it a largely untouched desert wilderness.

When to Visit

Few venture to the valley floor during the summer, when Death Valley meets all hellish expectations; indeed, the *average* high temperature in July is 116°, with a nighttime low of 88°. Ground temperatures hover near an egg-frying 200°. The information given above under Desert Survival should be followed with extra care. In addition, check at the visitors center for the free pamphlet, *Hot Weather Hints.* Each of the towns and resorts within the monument provide water, but be sure to keep a supply for yourself and your car, as rest stops are often dozens of miles apart. Hiking is possible during the summer only at the high elevations and only for experts well-versed in desert trekking. Light sight-seeing is bearable if ucomfortable.

Late November through February are the coolest months (40-70° in the valley, freezing temperatures and snow in the mountains) and also the wettest, with infrequent but violent rainstorms that can flood canyons. Desert wildflowers bloom in March and April, accompanied by moderate temperatures and tempestuous winds that whip sand and dust into an obscuring curtain for hours or even days. Over 50,000 people crowd into Death Valley's facilities during the **49ers Encampment** festival, held the last week of October and the first two weeks of November. Traffic jams, congested trails and campsites, hour-long lines for gasoline, and four-hour waits at Scotty's Castle visit the area also on three-day winter weekends, Thanksgiving, Christmas through New Year's, and Easter.

Practical Information

Visitors Information: Furnace Creek Visitor Center (786-2331), on Rte. 190 in the east-central section of the valley. For information by mail, write the Superintendent, Death Valley National Monument, Death Valley 92328. A simple and informative **museum** dispels some myths (such as the claim that all the original settlers perished here). (Open daily 8am-5pm.) Slide show every ½-hour and nightly lecture. Purchase guides and topographic maps (the park service map/guide is free), get a schedule of activities and guided ranger hikes, check the latest weather forecast, and have a cool drink from the water fountain. Office open daily 8am-5pm. Center open Nov.-Easter daily 8am-8pm; in summer 8am-5pm.

Ranger Stations: Grapevine, junction of Rte. 190 and 267 near Scotty's Castle; **Stovepipe Wells,** on Rte. 190; **Wildrose,** Rte. 178, 20 mi. south of Emigrant via Emigrant Canyon Dr.; and **Shoshone,** outside the southeast border of the valley at the junction of Rte. 178 and 127. Weather report, weekly naturalist program, and park information posted at each station. Also provides emergency help. All are open year-round.

Gasoline: tank up outside Death Valley at Olancha, Shoshone, or Beatty, NV. Otherwise, you'll pay about 20¢ per gallon more at the stations across from the Furnace Creek Visitors Center, in Stove Pipe Wells Village, and at Scotty's Castle (all Chevron). Don't play chicken with the fuel gauge: Fortuna does not smile on the foolish and Death Valley takes no prisoners. **Propane gas** is available at the Furnace Creek Chevron, **white gas** at the Furnace Creek Ranch and Stove Pipe Wells Village stores, **diesel fuel** pumped in Las Vegas, Pahrump, and Beatty, NV, and in Lone Pine, Olancha, Ridgecrest, and Trona, CA.

Death Valley Hikers' Association: write for information c/o Darrell Tomer, P.O. Box 123, Arcata 95521. Ask for a copy of the *Dustdevil.*

Bike Rental: at the Furnace Creek Chevron station (786-2343). A maintained bike path leads from there to the Harmony Borax Works, 2 mi. north. Rugged, slightly rusty, single-seaters $2.50 first hr., $1 per additional hr., $6 per day. Tandems $3.50 first hr., $1 per additional hr., $7.50 per day. Open daily 8am-5pm.

Horseback Riding: Furnace Creek Ranch (786-2345). Two-hr. guided tours $12 per person. Trail rides offered Oct.-May, and Sept. if it's cool enough. Minimum age 8 years. Ages 8-11 must be accompanied by adult.

Groceries and Supplies: Furnace Creek Ranch Store, is well-stocked and expensive. Open daily 7am-9pm. **Stove Pipe Wells Village Store,** is in the same price range. Treat yourself to a can of real venison hotter-'n-hell chili for $3.50. Open daily 7am-8pm. Both stores are regulated by the National Park Service; both sell charcoal, firewood and ice.

Swimming Pools and Showers: swimming $2, shower $2 for non-guests at Stove Pipe Wells Village (9am-9pm); swimming $2, showers $1 for non-guests at Furnace Creek Ranch (9am-10pm; showers 9am-9pm). Towel and soap not included.

Police: 786-2330.

Post Office: Furnace Creek Ranch (786-2223). Open Mon.-Fri. 8:30am-5pm. General Delivery ZIP Code: 92328.

Area Code: 619.

Orientation

Death Valley spans over 2 million acres (1½ times the size of Delaware) and is extremely isolated. However, visitors from the south will find it only a small detour on the road to the Sierra Nevada's Eastern slope, and those from the north will find it convenient to Las Vegas. The monument lies about 300 mi. from Los Angeles, 500 mi. from San Francisco, and 140 mi. from Las Vegas.

There is no regularly scheduled public transportation into Death Valley. Bus tours are monopolized by **Fred Harvey's Death Valley Tours,** the same organization that runs Grand Canyon tours. They begin at Furnace Creek Ranch, which also handles reservations (786-2345, ext. 61), and are offered from early October to late May. A two-hour tour of the lower valley costs $15 (children $8) and leaves at 8:30am, stopping at Zabriskie Point, Mushroom Rock, Devil's Golf Course, Badwater, and Artists' Drive. For the same price and duration, a tour focusing on borax mining history leaves for the higher elevations of Dante's View at 11am. A five-hour tour to the north begins at 8am and explores Scotty's Castle, Ubehebe Crater, Sand Dunes, and Stovepipe Wells ($25, seniors $23, children $13).

The best way to get into and around Death Valley is by car. With two or more people to share gas expenses, renting a car will prove far cheaper and more flexible than any unreliable bus tour. The nearest agencies are in Las Vegas, Barstow, and Bishop; see listings in those sections. Be sure to rent a reliable car: this is *not* a place to tempt fate. Upon arrival each vehicle will be charged a $5 entrance fee, valid for 7 days.

Of the 13 monument entrances, most visitors choose Rte. 190 from the east. The road is well maintained, the pass is much less steep, and you arrive more quickly at the visitors center, located about mid-way along the 130-mi. north-south route through the valley. But since most of the major sights adjoin not Rte. 190 but the north/south road, the day-tripping visitor with a trusty vehicle will be able to see more of the monument by entering from the southeast (Rte. 178 west from Rte. 127 at Shoshone) or the north (direct to Scotty's Castle via NV Rte. 267 from U.S. 95). Unskilled mountain drivers should probably not attempt to enter via the smaller Titus Canyon or Emigrant Canyon Drive roads, since neither has guard rails to prevent your car from emigrating over the canyon's precipitous cliffs.

Eighteen-wheelers have replaced 18-mule teams, but driving in Death Valley still takes stubborn determination. Overheating is a common problem, especially on trips from the hot valley floor up into the mountains. Radiator water (*not* for drinking) is available at critical points on Rte. 178 and 190 and NV Rte. 374, but not on any unpaved roads. There are only three service stations in the park (see listings above), and the combination of extreme heat, rapid increases in altitude, and air conditioning will drain your tank more rapidly than expected; keep your tank as close to full as possible at all times.

Believe the signs that say "four-wheel-drive only." Those who do bound along the backcountry trails by four-wheel-drive should carry extra tires, gas, oil, water (both to drink and for the radiator), and spare parts. Know how to make minor repairs, bring along appropriate topographic maps, leave an itinerary with the visitors center, and bring a CB radio. Many of the most isolated four- and two-wheel-drive routes are spectacular. Get information and suggestions at the Visitors Center and see Sights below. Check ahead for road closings—especially in summer.

Hitchhike and die. It's that simple

Death Valley has **hiking** trails to challenge the mountain lover, the desert daredevil, the backcountry camper, and the fair-weather dayhiker. Ask a ranger for advice, and see Sights below. Backpackers and dayhikers alike should inform the visitors center of their trip, and take along the appropriate topographic maps. During the summer, the National Park Service recommends that valley floor hikers spend several days prior to the hike acclimating to the heat and low humidity, plan a route along roads where assistance is readily available, and outfit a hiking party of at least two people with another person following in a vehicle to monitor the hikers' progress. Carrying salve to treat feet parched by the nearly 200° earth is also wise.

Check the weather forecast before setting out—roads and trails can disappear during a winter rainstorm. The dryness of the area, plus the lack of any root and soil system to retain moisture, transforms canyon and valley floors into deadly torrents during heavy rains. For other important tips, read the Desert Survival section in the introduction to The Desert.

Accommodations and Food

To stay solvent, snooze and booze in one of the towns outside Death Valley (see Near Death Valley), or pack your food and camp out. For, you see, **Fred Harvey's Amfac Consortium** retains a vise-like grip on the trendy, resort-style concessions in Death Valley. The Consortium offers golf, tennis, and bingo (Wed. 8:30pm) at the **Furnace Creek Ranch** complex (786-2345, for reservations 800-528-6367), a former terminus that once housed and fed the people and mules working the Death Valley borax mines. With all the charm of a suburban shopping mall, this "true refuge" is deluged with video arcades and tour bus refugees. June through Oct. 7 is the only "budget" time to stay here; air-conditioned rooms with two double beds go for $65. The room price rises to $98 during the high season.

Furnace Creek's **cafeteria** is open daily from 5:30 to 9am and from 11am to 8:30pm, from November through April. A coffee shop is also open from 7 to 9pm. Breakfasts average $4, dinners $7, and you'll have to shell out $5.50 for the fruit plate. Last call at the adjacent bar, the Corkscrew Saloon, sounds at 12:45am. The ranch comes equipped with a general store, post office, and nearby Chevron station. Book sight-seeing tours and horseback rides (see Practical Information) at the front desk, but beware that Furnace Creek's sole concessions to the budget traveler remain the commodious free public toilets.

Stove Pipe Wells Village (786-2387) is Amfac's other Death Valley development. Less plastic than Furnace Creek, it comes complete with pseudo-ranch houses, a large heated mineral pool, and a beauty salon. When Helene and Bob Eichbaum owned the place in the 20s and 30s, you could stay in tents for $1.50-4; today's hotel charges $60 per night for one or two people, each extra person $9. The hotel office is open October to May; in other months inquire at the General Store. Across from the hotel are a general store and a service station, both open year-round daily 8am to 6pm. Stove Pipe Wells resort also operates a **restaurant** (open Nov.-May daily 7-10am, 11:30am-2pm, and 5:30-8:30pm) and a gift shop. During the off-months grilled food is served in the **saloon,** from 11am to 1am.

Camping

The National Park Service maintains nine campgrounds, none of which accepts reservations. The visitors center keeps tabs on how crowded the sites are. Call ahead to check availability and be prepared to do battle if you come during peak periods (see When to Visit). All campsites have toilets; all except Thorndike and Mahogany Flat have water; and all except Sunset and Stove Pipe Wells have tables. Open fires are prohibited at Stove Pipe Wells, Sunset, and Emigrant; bring a stove and fuel unless you like your meat *rare.* Collecting wood, be it alive or dead, is *verboten* everywhere in the monument. Be sure to stock up before setting off to camp. Dispersed (roadside) camping is not permitted, but **backcountry camping** is free and legal, provided you check in at the visitors center and pitch tents at least 1 mi. from main roads and 5 mi. from any established campsite. The campgrounds listed below are in geographic order from north to south. Fees, where charged, are technically collected all year, but exacted less vigorously in the summer. The farther one moves from the Visitors Center, the less commercialized and spoiled is the area.

Wildrose (4100 ft.), on the road to the Charcoal Kilns in Wildrose Canyon, 40 mi. north of Trona, 21 mi. south of Emigrant campground. The most secluded location that is still easily accessible for cars and RVs. 30 sites. Convenient base for trips to Skidoo ghost town, Aguereberry Point, Telescope Peak, and other Panamint Range sights. Pleasant in summer, chilly to frigid in winter (when there is no water available). Free. Open year-round.

Texas Springs (sea level), in the hills above the Furnace Creek Inn, 200 yd. beyond the Sunset campground on the same road. Best place for tenters near the Furnace Creek and Visitors Center activities. Some of 93 sites are umbrageous. For wind protection stick close to the walls of the hills. Generators prohibited. Sites $5. Open Nov.-April.

Mesquite Springs (1800 ft.), near Scotty's Castle, 2 mi. south of the Grapevine Ranger Station. 50 sites sans umbrage. Overlooks Death Valley Wash and alluvial fans. Listen for coyote and owls. Ideal for tenters. Sites $5. Open year-round.

Emigrant (2100 ft.), off Rte. 190, 8 mi. west of Stove Pipe Wells Village across from the ranger station, on the way down from Towne Pass through the Panamint Range. The 10 sites are comfortable in summer. No fires. Free. Open April-Oct.

Thorndike (7500 ft.) and **Mahogany** (8200 ft.), 10 mi. east of Wildrose and over ½ mi. higher, just beyond the Charcoal Kilns in Wildrose Canyon. Depending on conditions, a sturdy car with an able driver can make it to either site, although a 4-wheel-drive vehicle may be needed for the push up to Mahogany Flat. Gets cold and dark early as the sun sets quickly in the canyon. Can be snowy even in April and Oct. No water. Free. Open March-Nov.

Furnace Creek (196 ft. below sea level), north of the visitors center. Convenient to Furnace Creek Ranch facilities—pool, showers, laundry. A few of the 168 sites are shaded. Positively furnacious in summer. Packed with trailers, first to get crowded. Sites $8. (Don't confuse with $14 sites offered by the Furnace Creek Ranch.) Open year-round. Reservations through Ticketron (800-452-1111).

Stove Pipe Wells (sea level). Near an airstrip, Jeep trails, and sand dunes. Tenters will have to compete with clumps of RVs for one of 200 gravel sites. Try for a spot close to the trees for protection from spring sandstorms. Short walk to all the hotel and general store amenities. Sites $4. Open Nov.-April. (Don't confuse the park service campground with the Fred Harvey-operated trailer park, which costs $9 per day, including use of the Stove Pipe Wells Village hotel's pool and shower.)

Sunset (190 ft. below sea level), across from the visitors center. An RV city of 1000 sites. No fires. Sites $4. Pool at nearby Furnace Creek. Open Nov.-April.

Sights and Activities

It pays to figure out ahead of time the optimal approach to Death Valley. See the end of Orientation for a discussion of the various entrances. If you're doing the Valley in a day, you should adopt a north-south or south-north route, rather than heading directly to the Furnace Creek visitors center via Rte. 190, which connects east with west.

South of the Visitor Center

The **Visitor Center and Museum** (see Practical Information) is a pleasant stop. You can expand your knowledge of tours and hikes before venturing too deeply into the stony places. No programs are available in the summer, but some of the more popular programs (such as the car caravan tours and star-gazing talks) have been recently reinstated for the winter season. If you're interested in astronomy, speak to one of the rangers; some set up telescopes at Zabriskie Point and offer free-lance star-gazing shows. In **wildflower season** (Feb. to mid-April), there are tours to the choicest bloom-sites. **Hells Gate** and **Jubilee Pass** are beautiful, and **Hidden Valley** even more so, though it is accessible only by a difficult, 7-mi. four-wheel-drive route from Teakettle Junction (itself 25 mi. south of Ubehebe Crater).

Both the **Harmony Borax Works** and the **Borax Museum** are a short drive from the visitors center. The first successful borax operation in Death Valley, the Harmony plant is not terribly scenic, although the museum (originally the company's bunkhouse, kitchen, and office) merits investigation. Inside, there's a stunning mineral display as well as plenty of mining implements, Native American artifacts, and historical trinkets and trivia. Outside is parked an original 20-mule-team wagon, which hauled 18-ton loads and put in appearances at the 1904 St. Louis World's Fair and at President Wilson's inauguration. Old Dinah, the "Iron Mule" replacement for the real thing, languishes nearby.

Artist's Drive is a one-way loop off Rte. 178, beginning 10 mi. south of the visitors center. The road twists and winds its way through rock and dirt canyons on the way to **Artist's Palette,** a rainbow of green, yellow, and red mineral deposits in the hillside. The effect is most intense in the late afternoon as the colors change rapidly with the setting sun. Be aware that the dizzying 9 mi. drive turns back upon itself again and again, ending up on the main road only 4 mi. north of the drive's entrance. About 5 mi. south of this exit, you'll reach **Devil's Golf Course.** Don't bring your clubs; there's no green here. The true green is next to the golf course—witness the miracle of commercial irrigation. Palm trees, too. Nevertheless, the "Golf Course" is a expansive plane of spiny salt crust made up of the precipitate left from the evaporation of ancient Lake Manly, the 90-mi.-long pond that once filled much of the lower valley.

Three miles south of Devil's Golf Course lies **Badwater,** an aptly named briny pool saltier than the ocean. Magnitudinous in the winter, it contracts to a large puddle a few inches deep in the summertime. With nothing living nearby except several species of water beetles, insect larvae, and rare snails, you'll feel you've reached the bottom of the earth. And you nearly have—a 4-mi. trudge west across the salt flat takes you from 280 ft. below sea level to the lowest point in the Western Hemisphere—282 ft. down under. Unless your two feet will get a kick out of these two feet, you're better off not attempting this feat, especially since the marker has long since been removed by a brazen footpad.

The unpaved **West Side Road** (open Oct.-April) begins just beyond the Artist's Drive exit and parallels the route that follows the east side of the valley south. It provides four-wheel-drive access to frequently washed-out Trail Canyon, Hanaupah Canyon, Johnson Canyon, and Warm Springs Canyon. Roadrunners frequent Butte Valley, beyond the two-wheel-drive stretch of Warm Springs Canyon. The grave of Death Valley's most famous gold digger, 20 mi. down the West Side Road, bears the inscription: "Here lies Shorty Harris, a single blanket jackass prospector."

Immortalized by Antonioni's film of the same name, **Zabriskie Point** is a marvelous place (particularly at sunrise) from which to view Death Valley's corrugated badlands, formed when the prehistoric lake evaporated. Later on, scamper the 2 mi. (and 900 ft.) down Gower Gulch to colorful **Golden Canyon** (just 3 mi. south of Furnace Creek). Just before Zabriskie Point is the turn-off for four-wheel-drive Echo Canyon, and beyond is the turn-off for the two-wheel-drive **Twenty Mule Team Canyon Road,** a twisting 3-mi. one-way trek past abandoned borax prospects which exits onto Rte. 190.

Perhaps the most spectacular sight in the entire monument is the vista at **Dante's View,** reached by a 15 mi. paved road from Rte. 190. Just as the Italian poet stood with Virgil looking down on the damned, so the modern observer gazes upon a vast inferno. The desolation below is punctuated only by the virgin-white expanse of the salt flats. At 5475 ft. you can see Badwater, Furnace Creek Ranch, the Panamint Range, and, on a clear day, the Sierra Nevadas. In fact, on a really clear day, you can see both the highest point in the continental United States (Mt. Whitney, evel. 14,494 ft.) and the lowest point (Badwater, 282 ft. below sea level). It can be snowy up here in mid-winter and cold anytime but mid-summer.

North of the Visitor Center

For an entertaining one-day excursion, take **Beatty Road** (turn-off 12 mi. north of the visitors center) east toward the Nevada border. Five miles along you'll reach the turn-off to the **Keane Wonder Mine and Mill,** a site that died hard and fast, but not before yielding sacks of gold. You'll need the four-wheel-drive to reach the mine, and take care when poking around the mill's ramshackle wooden trams. Continuing along Beatty Rd., you'll cross Hell's Gate (a springtime beauty mark) before traversing Daylight Pass, the apex of which marks the California/Nevada border. Ten miles downhill bring you to **Rhyolite,** a ghost town, and then to Beatty, Nevada. The return trip to Death Valley via **Titus Canyon Road** (open Oct.-April) is the reason for all the fuss. Reminiscent of the Grand Canyon in its diversity and color, this gorge's jagged cliffs, hewn by ancient rivers, offer startling vistas. The journey down this rough, 30-mi., narrow way, full of dips and difficult switchbacks, justifies the toll it will take on any passenger car. Make sure you have gas, water, and a non-flooded canyon, and don't attempt the road in a camper. Along the route you will pass **Leadfield,** a mining boomtown that survived less than a year, and a grotesquely twisted stand of faulted rock monoliths.

About 10 mi. farther along is the turn-off to Death Valley's tallest **sand dunes.** (The dunes were favorites of Ansel Adams. If you decide to try and compete with the master, keep in mind that sand, like glass, is composed of reflective quartz that will fool your light meter; increase your exposure one F-stop to catch such details as footprints and ripples.) The largest of these constantly shifting behemoths is hundreds of feet high. Although barefoot galumphing on the dunes can be sensuous when the sands are cool, be wary of nasty tumbleweeds and mesquite spines. Winter wanderings in the moonlight are particularly transplendant.

Scotty's Castle has little to do with the desert, and therein lies its interest. Chicago insurance millionaire Albert Johnson became enamored of the infamous flim-flam man Walter Scott (a.k.a. "Scotty") during the latter's flamboyant days promoting the Los Angeles-to-Chicago railway. When Johnson fell ill, Scotty convinced him to come to the desert and build this palatial hacienda as a vacation retreat. Blueprints submitted by Frank Lloyd Wright were summarily rejected, but the end product, erected by an enormous crew of Shoshone people, is impressive nonetheless. Albert Johnson named it Death Valley Ranch and resided here until he expired in 1948. The original sign still hangs over the door to the inner courtyard. Scotty, who lived on the ranch for the remaining six years of his life, called it The Castle. Unfortunately, the waterfall in the living room has been switched off, but you can still see the remote-controlled piano and organ. Rumor has it that Scotty played the organ maniacally to cover up the machinery noise generated by his ill-fated attempt to mine for gold directly below the castle. This pseudo-Moorish folly is complete with minaret and Arabian-style colored tiles. Park service tours (1 hr.) depart frequently; you can purchase tickets until one hour before closing, but there are often massive lines to get in. (Open daily 9am-5pm. Tours $6, seniors and ages 6-11 $3.)

Ubehebe Crater, 5 mi. west of Grapevine Ranger Station, just south of Scotty's Castle, is nearly a ½ mi. wide and 462 ft. deep. This blackened volcanic blast site lies only a few miles from the brown sands. The view from the vantage point is spectacular, but steady yourself for the gale-force winds that assault the edges of this humongous hole. An unpaved road continues for 20 mi. south of the crater to the vast and muddy **Racetrack,** a dried-up lake basin providing access to four-wheel-drive routes into Hidden Valley and up White Top Mountain.

Mosaic Canyon is a ½-mi. long narrows of collaged, polished marble, which can be viewed by a 2½-mi. walk, horseback ride, or drive up an alluvial fan from a turn-off a mile west of Stove Pipe Wells. Winding **Emigrant Canyon Road** leads from the Emigrant Campground to Wildrose Canyon Drive. On the way, you'll pass the turn-off for the four-wheel-drive skedaddle to the ruins of **Skidoo,** yet another ghost town 5700 ft. up in the Panamint Range. A few miles farther is the turn-off for the unpaved road up to **Aguereberry Point** (named for Basque prospector Pete Aguereberry), known for its fine morning views.

A right turn at Wildrose Canyon Drive follwed by a 10 mi. drive will bring you to the 10 conical furnaces known as the **Charcoal Kilns,** which are 25 ft. high, 30 ft. in diameter, and which once held 45 cords of wood. Fire up the barbecue!

The infamous Death Valley **burros** no longer welcome the visitor. These pariahs, unwanted beasts of burden transported from their native Middle East in the 1850s and freed when the automobile made them obsolete, unwittingly but relentlessly decimated the monument's bighorn sheep population by wolfing down edible shrubs and by fouling all the water. Several years ago the park service authorized a three-year burro banishment plan to fly the asses out with helicopters (they were sold as pets). Over 6000 have been removed, and almost none remain.

Near Death Valley: West

Only such ghost towns as **Darwin** and a few slightly more populated community species are fit to survive on U.S. 395 near the Rte. 190 turn-off. In **Olancha,** the **Ranch Motel** (764-2387) on U.S. 395 provides spruce, attractive rooms in cottage-type buildings. (Singles $26. Doubles $30. $4 per additional person. Four-day "Getaway Special" Mon.-Thurs. for $80. Open year-round.) The truckers' rigs outside signal that the finest place to eat in town is the **Ranch House Café** (764-2363). The Ranch House's egg, bacon, toast, and coffee breakfast ($4.10) or chili with beans ($3.45) will stick with you far into Death Valley. (Open 24 hr.)

The **Rustic Motel** (764-2209) rests 3 mi. south of the Rte. 190 turn-off. A yappy dog protects the lodgings, which are in surprisingly good repair. (Singles $26. Doubles $32. Rooms have A/C and black and white TV.) A wee bit farther north than the Rustic, and a lot more hideous, is the **Wagon-Wheel Camper-Tel** (764-2222). There's no greenery in sight (except for the off-green sagebrush) so pitch tents on the gravel. Tents for two are $6 (each additional person 50¢). Hot shower and impromptu navy jet shows included. A dip in the pool is free to those with full trailer hookup ($12 per night). The wise travler tanks up here; at the Texaco station across from the Ranch Café reasonable prices abound.

Near Death Valley: Southeast

Amid the natural splendor of this region, you can meet a human wonder at **Death Valley Junction** (junction of Rte. 127 and 190, 29 mi. from Furnace Creek) in the person of mime and ballet dancer Marta Becket. With the exception of Wayne Newton concerts in Vegas, Becket's **Amargosa Opera House** (852-4316) is the sole outpost of desert high culture. Becket, the Californian Fitzcarraldo, fell in love with the tiny, decaying town when her car decayed here in 1968. While waiting for help, she and her husband revitalized the old movie theater that had entertained employees of the Pacific Coast Borax Company during the early 20s. Following a 16th-century Spanish style, Marta commissioned the painting of a continuous wall and ceiling mural depicting a fanciful audience of cupids, kings, angels, monks, and nuns. In her one-woman shows, Becket incorporates classical ballet, modern dance, and pantomime. (Performances given Nov.-April Mon. and Fri.-Sat.; May and Oct. Sat. Doors open at 7:45pm, shows begin at 8:15pm. Donation $5, ages under 12 $3.) Death Valley Tours (see Getting Around) will take you from Furnace Creek to the Opera House. (Tours $18, ages under 12 $10. Admission price included.)

The town of **Shosone** stands at the junction of Rte. 127 and 178, 56 mi. southeast of Furnace Creek. Tourists traveling on the Tonopah and Tidewater Railroad used the town as an entrance point to the monument back in the 20s. Today, it serves a similar purpose as an automotive gateway to the valley. The **Charles Brown General Store and Service Station** (852-4224) is open daily 8am-8pm (there's no Snoopy in sigh though). The friendly **Shoshone Inn** (852-4224) next door offers use of a natural spring swimming pool. (Singles $36. Doubles $44.) The **Red Buggy Café and Crowbar** (852-9988) serves generous meals at reasonable prices daily from 7am-9:30pm. The **Shoshone RV and Trailer Park** (852-3467) is ready for tired, gas-burning travelers.

Legend records that Paiute Chief Tecopa ceded the lands and springs now comprising **Tecopa** and **Tecopa Hot Springs** (towns 1 mi. east off Rte. 127, 5 mi. south of Shoshone) to the government for public use on the condition that they would not be privately developed. Either the legend is false or the chief was taken for a ride, because today the miserable, smelly baths and their accompanying resorts and RV parks are choked with visitors. The best of the lot is Dallas and Pat Schultz's **Tecopa Hot Springs Resort** (852-4373), where motel doubles cost $35, a room opening onto hot springs $38, RV sites $7.50. (Market and office open daily 7am-6pm; after hours go to the nearby trailer to register. A **laundromat** on the premises is open daily 7am-8pm; soap, wash, and dry $1.35.)

Near Death Valley: Northeast

When approaching Death Valley from the north, consider kicking back for a brief spell in the homey town of **Beatty.** Located about 90 miles northwest of Las Vegas on Rte. 95, Beatty offers the weary traveler relaxation and air conditioning, as well as ample gambling facilities, before the desolation of the valley.

Just outside of town, heading toward Death Valley on Rte. 374, lurks **Rhyolite,** a ghost town, complete with stone foundations and rusted cars. Further information can be collected at the **Beatty Visitor Information Center** (702-553-2424) on Main and 4th St. Open daily 8am-4pm. The Center will also gladly to help plan your trip into Death Valley.

Sleep in heavenly pee-eece at the **Stagecoach Hotel** (533-2333) ½ mile north of town through the silent night on Highway 95. Doubles start at $25 ($30 on weekends). With pool, jacuzzi, casino and bar, this place could prove your salvation. Eat your last supper before journeying across the desert at the **Burro Inn** (553-2445), at Highway 95 and 3rd St. Break bread with truck drivers over a meal fit for the king of kings ($2.50 cheeseburger). Don't pass over the gas and water at the service station before heading out of town. Should you break down in the sandy desert without a star to guide you, that's *your* cross to bear.

According to one resident, the favorite pastime in this town, which has the feel of a hick Las Vegas, is "drinkin' an' gamblin'." Compared to those in Reno and Las Vegas, Beatty's several casinos are homespun. Wager as little as $1 at blackjack and jaw with the dealers, regular folk in jeans and cowboy boots who play slow and seem genuinely sorry to take your money. (But take it they do; some things are universal.) All casinos are theoretically open 24 hr., but by 2am the dealers start eyeing the clock.

Prostitution is the other great vice of Beatty. In fact, Beatty is a scheduled stop on the Hell's Angels' annual "Whorehouse Run." Exercise caution, though; there are no physicians in this town of 1500. Residents must go to nearby Tonopah (92 mi. away) for medical care.

NEVADA

Nevada once walked the straight and narrow path. Explored by Spanish missionaries and settled by Mormons, the Nevada Territory's harsh and arid climate seemed a perfect place for ascetics to strive for moral uplift. But the discovery of gold in 1850 and silver in 1859 won the state over permanently to the worship of filthy lucre. Tales of the Comstock Lode spread, triggering a stampede of prospectors.

New mineral finds in the 20th century sent the state on a boom-bust roller coaster, which stalled at the bottom during the Great Depression. Nevadans responded by shaking off all vestiges of traditional virtue: unprecedented in America, they made gambling and marriage-licensing the state industries. Logically, Nevada has also become home of the drive-through divorce. In a final break with the rest of the country, Silver Staters legalized prostitution (though not in Las Vegas) and began paying Wayne Newton enormous amounts of cash for his concerts.

But there is a Nevada outside the gambling towns. The forested slopes of Lake Tahoe, shared with California, are speckled with little resorts of serenity and sanity in an otherwise expansive and arid state. It is in this "basin-and-range" countryside that the true West lingers in its barren glory.

Practical Information

Tourist Information: Nevada Commission on Tourism, #2C75 Valley Bank Building, U.S. 50, Carson City 89710 (885-4322). Pamphlets and maps. Open Mon.-Fri. 8am-5pm. **Nevada Division of State Parks,** Nye Building, 201 S. Fall, Carson City 89701 (885-4384). Brochures, maps, schedule of activities. Open Mon.-Fri. 8am-5pm.

Capital: Carson City.

Drinking and Gambling Age: 21.

Time Zone: Pacific (3 hr. behind Eastern).

Emergency: 911.

Postal Abbreviation: NV.

Area Code: 702.

Impractical Information

Nicknames: Silver State, Sagebrush State.

Motto: All for Our Country.

State Flower: Sagebrush.

Date of Statehood: October 31, 1864.

Las Vegas

Only in Vegas could there be a major museum devoted to Liberace. As close as the modern, civilized world is going to come to Sodom and Gomorrah, this arena of mild, middle-aged debauchery has exchanged pagan idols for worship of that twentieth century deity, *Kapital,* and sacrifices from all major credit cards are gleefully accepted. As an arena for mild, middle-aged debauchery, Vegas simply replaces Mickey and Minnie with blinding neon marquees, monolithic hotel/casinos, besequined Ziegfeldesque showgirls, and rococo wedding chapels. Divine punishment is unlikely considering the minor transgressions committed here, so only your sanity and not your mortal soul is at risk. The innumberable lights of Las Vegas are no doubt what keep General Electric in the black; their flashing cacophony is designed to confuse unwary visitors, making them forget that the money dropping into the shiny maw of that slot machine was hard-earned. Vegas, with its cigarette girls, Kwik-chapels, Elvis impersonators and Keno junkies, can be justified; just think of gambling as a tax on the stupid. As alien to the rest of the world as it is to the surrounding desert, the normal rules of conduct do not apply in this monument to the baser impulses of humanity. Neither feminism, nor energy conservation, nor anything the Surgeon General has to say seems to have affected anything in this gaudy fantasyland.

There is plenty in Las Vegas to keep you occupied. Like Jon Bon Jovi or Joan Collins, you can be married in a Kwik-chapel for less than $60. You can also gamble. You can get a home-delivered stripper quicker than a pizza, and a pizza probably quicker than a cop. You can gamble. You can go hiking in the hellishly hot desert. Or you can gamble. Las Vegas makes *its* money by taking *yours* away, so every minute you spend outside a casino in the 110° heat is a fraction of the casino's dinero down the tubes.

Like capitalism itself, the city began on a small, seemingly innocent scale. Until 1931, Las Vegas was a humble Mormon mining town. Then came the Great Depression and, faced with economic catastrophe, the Nevada legislature legalized gambling. While construction of the Hoover Dam brought electricity and water into the thirsty wasteland, it was not until the 1940's that Las Vegas took its first steps toward its present resort magnificence. Bugsy Seigel, L.A. gangster on the lam, opened the Flamingo Hotel and hit upon a magic formula that has kept the slot machines and roulette wheels well-lubricated ever since: by offering cheap lodging, cheap food and cheap drinks, the casinos keep guests' expenses small and encourage them to wager big at the gaming tables. The stakes have risen over the intervening half-century, but the formula remains the same.

Even if you wisely abandon the idea of winning enough for the down-payment on that yacht you've had your eye on, the inexpensive food and lodging alone can justify a visit to Vegas. Disciplined customers can take advantage of the inexpensive buffets and cheap drinks without throwing a single chip, and the visiting voyeur will find the best show in town is not an opulent "stage spectacular" but simply the bizarre (and free) spectacle of decadent Las Vegas itself.

Practical Information and Orientation

Visitors Information: Las Vegas Convention and Visitors Authority, 3150 Paradise Rd. (733-2471), at the Convention Center, 4 blocks from the Strip, next to the Las Vegas Hilton. Up-to-date literature on hotel bargains, floor shows, and buffet specials, as well as maps and general information on Las Vegas and Lake Mead. Open Mon.-Fri. 8am-5pm. Hostels are also excellent sources of information.

McCarran International Airport: 798-5410, at the southeast end of the Strip. The main terminal is on Paradise Rd. Within walking distance of the University of Nevada campus and the southern casinos. Buses and taxis to downtown.

Amtrak: 1 N. Main St. (386-6896, for fares and schedules 800-872-7245), in the Union Plaza Hotel. To: L.A. ($64, round-trip $75; reservations required); San Francisco ($115, round-trip $122; with bus connection); and Salt Lake City ($84, round-trip $126).

Greyhound: 200 Main St. (382-2640), at Carson Ave. downtown. Open 24 hr. To L.A. ($34), Reno ($37.60), Salt Lake City ($45), and Denver ($86). **Las Vegas-Tonopah-Reno Lines** provides service to Phoenix ($30).

Las Vegas Transit: 384-3540. Common transfer point at 200 Casino Center downtown. Trolley shuttle runs downtown along Fremont St. (50¢, over 65 and under 12 25¢). Most buses run 5:30am-9:05pm; strip buses (#6) every 15 min. 7am-12:45am. every ½-hr. 12:45am-2:45am, every hr. 2:45-6:30am. Buses $1.15, ages 6-17 40¢. Seniors and disabled persons can purchase 10 rides for $4.20 by showing ID to driver or at Downtown Transportation Center. Adults $7.30 for 10 rides. Transfers 15¢.

Tours: Gray Line Tours, 1550 S. Industrial Rd. (384-1234). Bus tours to: Hoover Dam/Lake Mead (5 hr., $19, departs Mon.-Sat. 9 and 11am, Sun. 9am); the Grand Canyon (2 days, $99 double occupancy, departs Mon. and Wed. 7am, Oct.-April also on Fri. for $129, reservations required); and Old Nevada (7 hr., $29, departs daily 10am). **City tours** (6 hr., $20). **Ray and Ross Tours:** 300 W. Owens St. (646-4661). Bus tours to Hoover Dam (6 hr., $17) and Hoover Dam/Lake Mead (7 hr., $24).

Taxi: Checker Cab, 873-2227. $2.20 for first 1/7 mi., 20¢ each additional 1/7 mi.

Car Rental: Avon, 387-6717. $24 per day with unlimited mileage in Nevada. $44 per day for those under 21. Must have credit card. Open daily 7am-11pm. **Fairway Rent-A-Car,** 5300 S. Paradise Rd. (736-1786 or 800-634-3476), near airport. $17 per day with 100 free mi. daily. 35¢ each additional mile. Local use, must be 21. Open daily 8am-9pm.

American Automobile Association: 3312 W. Charlestown Blvd. (870-9171), emergency road service 878-1822. Open Mon.-Fri. 8:30am-5pm.

Laundromat: 252 Convention Center Dr. (369-3696), in Sommerset Shopping Center. Drop-off service 80¢ per pound. Open Mon.-Fri. 8am-6pm, Sat. 8am-4pm.

Help Lines: As with most everything in Vegas, lines are open 24 hr. **Crisis Line,** 876-4357; **Rape Crisis,** 366-1640; **Alcoholics Anonymous,** 382-1888; **Gambler's Anonymous,** 385-7732; **Suicide Prevention,** 731-2990; **Mental Health Crisis,** 486-3540.

Women's Health Center/Pregnancy Counseling Services of Nevada: 2225 E. Flamingo Rd. #101 (733-7850). Open Mon.-Fri. 8am-3:45pm.

Post Office: 301 E. Stewart (385-8944), behind Lady Luck. Open Mon.-Fri. 9am-5pm. General Delivery open 10am-3pm. General Delivery ZIP Code: 89125.

Area Code: 702.

Las Vegas (population 232,370) lurks in the southeast corner of Nevada, about 290 driving miles northeast of Los Angeles and 589 mi. southeast of San Francisco. From L.A., the drive takes five to six hours, going east on I-10 and turning north at San Bernadino onto I-15, which passes through Las Vegas.

"Gambler's specials" are among the cheapest and most popular ways to reach Las Vegas. These bus tours leave early in the morning and return late at night or early the next day. Brochures advertising these deals can be found in tourist information centers in L.A., San Francisco, and San Diego. You can also call casinos for information. Prices include everything except food and gambling; the catch is that you are supposed to eat, drink, and gamble with the tour group once you reach the city. Sneaking off is seldom difficult, though.

There are two major casino areas. The **downtown** area, around Fremont and 2nd St., is much more amenable to walkers: casinos cluster close together, their big doors open and all-too-welcoming, and some of the sidewalks are even carpeted. It's easy to spend a night shuffling from one casino to its neighbor, and the methods doormen use to lure you from their competitors are always amusing. The other main area, known as the **Strip,** is a longer stretch that holds a collection of mammoth casinos on both sides of busy Vegas Blvd. S. Unless you have a car or an unnatural affinity for long, hot, umbrageless stretches of sidewalk, stay downtown during the day and sally forth along the Strip at night, when bourgeoisie from every nook and cranny of the globe gather to flash their peacock feathers.

Ironically, vice-ridden Vegas is generally a safe place for late-night strolling. Security guards and lights are plentiful, and there is almost always pedestrian traffic. However, the neighborhoods just north and west of downtown can be dangerous at night, so the Strip is safer for cruising after dark.

There are several free weekly magazines which include coupons, show listings, and other information. *What's On* is particularly helpful, but *Las Vegas Today, Vegas Visitor,* and *Fun & Gaming* are also quite valuable.

Accommodations and Camping

Las Vegas is one of the easiest cities in which to find cheap food and lodging, thanks to casino owners who make their money on gambling. The bargains change constantly, so watch the travel and entertainment sections of local newspapers across the Southwest for special deals. Even the largest casinos sometimes offer rooms for $10 a night. Prices go up on weekends and holidays, when the crowds move in. But with over 67,000 hotel rooms, Las Vegas should be able to accommodate you. Vegas' two hostels are located near each other on Las Vegas Blvd., about 1 mi. north of the closest major casino, the Sahara.

Las Vegas Independent Hostel, 1208 Las Vegas Blvd. S. (385-9955). Not AYH-affiliated, but offers discounts to AYH members. Spartan but airy rooms with foam mattresses. Free coffee, tea, and lemonade. Runs tours every Mon. to the North Rim of the Grand Canyon and has a ride board in kitchen. Offers a 3-day tour to Bryce and Zion ($95). Rooms open 24 hr. Office open daily 7-10am and 3-11pm, Nov.-Mar. 8am-10pm and 5-11pm. Check-out 10am. Students and AYH members $8, nonmembers $10. Key deposit $5.

Las Vegas International Hostel (AYH), 1236 Las Vegas Blvd. S. (382-8119). Small kitchen. Carpeted. Rooms are in separate cabins. More common area than in the Independent, including a grassy space. No curfew. You can work in exchange for lodging. Office open daily 7-10am and 5-11pm. Members $8.50. Non-members $11.50. Key deposit $5.

Nevada Hotel, 235 S. Main St. (385-7311, for reservations 800-637-5777), across from Greyhound station. Capacious, pleasant rooms with TV and phone. Singles and doubles $18, plus $3 per extra person.

Crest Motel, 207 N. 6th St. (382-5642 or 800-777-1817), at Ogden St. Friendly management. TV, phone, VCR, and refrigerators in room. Pool. Singles Sun.-Thurs. $25, Fri.-Sat. $35, kitchenettes $35. Breakfast at El Cortez included. Key deposit $5.

Downtowner Budget Motel, 129 N. 8th St. (384-1441 or 800-777-2566). A little out of the way, but still just a short walk from downtown. Pool, phone, TV. Singles Sun.-Thurs. $25, Fri.-Sat. $35. Doubles Sun.-Thurs. $29, Fri.-Sat. $50.

Motel 6, 195 E. Tropicana Ave. (798-0728), near the airport, 3 blocks from the Strip. Pool and jacuzzi. Large and reliable. But even with 577 rooms, you need reservations a day or two in advance to stay weekend nights. Maybe the only town in America where Motel 6 seems expensive. Singles and doubles $30.

El Cortez, 600 E. Fremont St. (385-5200, for reservations 800-634-6703). TV, phone, and A/C. Singles and doubles $23.

Budget Inn, 301 S. Main St. (385-5560), 1 block from Greyhound. TV, phone, and A/C. Diminutive, but trim rooms. Singles and doubles Sun.-Thurs. $21, Fri.-Sat. $25. Key deposit $5.

Aztec Inn, 2200 Las Vegas Blvd. S. (385-4566). Pool, phone and A/C. Singles and doubles $25, with the second night free.

Ambassador East, 916 E. Fremont (384-8281). Pool, phone, TV, and A/C. Stark but satisfactory. Singles and doubles $21.

For all the luxuries of a hotel except room service, park your RV next door to a casino. The **Hacienda,** 3950 Las Vegas Blvd. S. (739-8214 or 800-634-6942), charges $9.60 per night. **Circus Circus,** 500 Circus Circus Dr. (734-0410, for reservations 800-634-3450), charges $10.70 per night and runs a free shuttle service to the Strip. Tent campers have to settle for the **KOA Campground,** 4315 Boulder Hwy. (451-5527), east of the Desert Inn. Prices start at $16 for two people, plus $4 for each additional adult and $2.50 for each additional child. Pool, spa, recreation hall, and free shuttle to the Strip included.

You'll need a car to reach any of the noncommercial campsites around Vegas. Twenty mi. west of the city on Rte. 159 is **Red Rock Canyon** (363-1921), where you can see an earthquake fault-line and other geological marvels. Camp here for free, but only in the designated area of **Oak Creek Park.** Twenty-five mi. east, **Lake Mead National Park** (293-4041) has several campgrounds (see Lake Mead). Fifty-five mi. northeast via I-15 and Rte. 169, **Valley of Fire State Park** also has campsites. The red and white sandstone formations here are marvelous at dawn and dusk.

Food

Prime rib dinners, all-you-can-eat buffets, and champagne brunches at astonishingly cheap prices beckon high- and low-rollers alike into the casinos. Cruise the Strip or roam around downtown at any time of day and look for advertisements and specials; prices in Vegas change as quickly as fortunes. The Visitors Authority (see Practical Information) keeps an up-to-date list of buffets.

Breakfast specials are the cheapest, especially downtown, where it's actually difficult to find a full breakfast for more than $2. Lunch buffets are the best bargains around, costing about $1 less than dinner buffets and offering nearly the same fare. In most cafeterias, buffet food is served nonstop from 11am to 10pm. Don't expect too much; while the volume of food served ensures freshness, the fare is more institutional than restaurant-quality. Also, since they must appeal to the lowest common palate, dishes tend to be unimaginative.

The standard buffet consists of roast beef, ham, other entrees, salads, vegetables, dessert, and sometimes beverages. **Circus Circus's** is the largest. You pay $5, join a line, grab a 16-in. plate, and pile on food enough to sate Andre the Giant (4:30-11pm). The Circus cooks up an enormous variety of food (with comparable feasts at breakfast and lunch), but the atmosphere is more zoo-like than circusy. **El Rancho,** 2755 Las Vegas Blvd. S. (796-2222), serves a brunch buffet on weekends and is not as crowded as the bigger casinos ($3.25, Sat.-Sun. 8am-3pm). The **Hacienda,** 3950 Las Vegas Blvd. S. (739-8911), is a cut above comparably priced buffets, with champagne at breakfast and 12 entrees at lunch (Mon.-Fri. breakfast 7-11am, $4.75; lunch 11:30am-3pm, $6). **Caesar's Palace,** 3570 Las Vegas Blvd. S. (731-7110), is more expensive than most, but its comfortable chairs, friendly service, and especially appetizing displays of desserts, sliced meats, fresh salads, fruits, and cheeses make it *the* place for a gastro-orgy. Go for breakfast to get the most for your money (Mon.-Fri. breakfast 7:30-10:30am, $6.50; lunch 11am-2:30pm, $8). Downtown's **Golden Nugget,** 129 E. Fremont St. (385-7111), serves a similarly high-class morning meal ($5.75, Mon.-Fri. 7-10:30am). The **Aladdin,** 3667 Las Vegas Blvd. S. (736-0111), offers a partial escape from blandness with its "International Buffet." Although it does serve rice and several Asian dishes, the Kung Pao Chicken is the mildest you will ever taste, and you will find that even here you can't escape the omnipresent the roast beef and mashed potatoes are inescapable. (Open daily $4.75 7:30-10:30am, $5.75 11:30am-2pm, $8 4-10pm, $5 11pm-4am. Under 13 pay $1 less.)

Most of the casinos offer "Graveyard Specials" from midnight to morning. **The Barbary Coast,** 3595 Las Vegas Blvd. S. (737-7111) has a number of specials for under $2, as well as cocktail waitresses in the kind of embarrassing costumes that only Vegas can offer.

Drinks operate on the same principle as the food, since the casino operators have realized over the years that an empty wallet follows an inebriated mind. Drinks usually cost 75¢-$1.50, and are free to those who look like they're playing, so practice that feverish expression. Most players tip the improbably dressed cocktail waitresses with some of their gambling money, however, so even free drinks end up not being so cheap. Keep your wits about you and be on the prowl for 50¢ shrimp cocktail specials and offers of free champagne at entrances to some casinos.

"Lay" restaurants—those independent of casinos—cannot match the prices of the buffets (dinners average $9), but are a respite for those suffering the effects of too many helpings of chipped beef and fish croquettes. On the Strip, there are only expensive steakhouses and the usual fast-food joints, but downtown is home to a number of Thai, Chinese, and Italian restaurants; **Sahara Boulevard** and **Flamingo Road** both cut across the Strip and are studded with such places. One of the best is the **Silver Dragon Restaurant,** 1510 E. Flamingo Rd. (737-1234), 1 block east of Maryland Parkway, which serves Cantonese and Szechuan meals. Their "graveyard menu" offers nocturnal nourishment. (Open daily 11:30am-5am.) Those who desire more traditional Southwestern fare should visit **Mi Casa,** 2710 E. Desert Inn Rd. (369-5440) which offers enchiladas, strawberry *sopapillas,* and live Latin music nightly. (Open daily 11am-3am.) Those borne by wheels should beat a tire-track to **Komol Kitchen,** 2536 E. Fremont St. (388-0560), for the Thai-Chinese experience of a lifetime. The sedate, almost *normal* atmosphere makes it welcome shelter from the Vegas whirlwind.

Casino-Hopping and Nightlife

Casinos and their coffee shops, nightclubs, and even wedding chapels are all open 24 hr lending life in Las Vegas an eerie, timeless feel. Older folks and kids who under normal conditions are in bed by 9pm can be seen toddling off to hotel rooms at three or four in the morning. You'll almost never see clocks or windows in a casino; the owners are afraid of players who, realizing it's past midnight, will turn into pumpkins, and be unable to lose a nickel more. Casinos also fear card-counters; walking computers who usually fly in from some university's physics department to roll in big money at the card tables. If the casino thinks you're keeping track of the cards played, its rent-a-cops could make you feel *very* unwelcome.

To experience true Vegas you should at least gamble a little. You'll quickly discern which games are suited for novices and which require a degree of expertise. 5¢ video poker is probably the slowest way to lose your money, $5000 baccarat the fastest, but no matter how it is chewed, it all ends up in the same place—the casino's bank account. If you wish to learn how to play the table games (craps, blackjack, roulette, baccarat, and several varieties of poker) many casinos offer free classes, usually on weekday mornings and early afternoons, when the tables aren't very busy. Most casinos offer "fun-books," coupons meant to get you into their doors, and "slot clubs," which function like airline frequent-flyer clubs and are meant to create brand loyalty. But since casinos function on the assumption that tourists will exit considerably closer to the poverty line than when they entered, don't bring more dinero than you're prepared to lose cheerfully. Keep your wallet in your front pocket, and be wary of the thieves who prowl casinos to nab big winnings from unwary jubilants. You can get an escort from the casino security, or leave your winnings with the cashier, to be picked up later. Seniors are favorite targets and should be especially careful.

For best results, put on your plaid favorite suit, bust out the cigar and the pinky rings, and commence to go a' gamblin'. The atmosphere, decor, and clientele differ from casino to casino, so visit several if you can. For the ultimate Las Vegas experience hustle on over to **Caesar's Palace,** 3570 Las Vegas Blvd. (731-7110). Caesar's has taken the "theme" aspect of Vegas life to an extreme; where other casinos have miniature, mechanized horse racing, Caesar's has chariot racing. In addition to having actors who walk around in centurion's garb, there are replicas of classical and Renaissance statuary scattered about. Next door, the **Mirage,** 3400 Las Vegas Blvd. S. (791-7111), numbers among its attractions Siberian white tigers, an enormous tank filled with tropical fish, and a "volcano" that erupts with fountains and flame every quarter hour from 8pm-1am, (unless it is too windy). Take in the performing dolphins, but try not to get lost in the bewildering, mazelike casino as you make your way bakc to the street.

Circus Circus, 2880 Las Vegas Blvd. S. (734-0410), attempts to cultivate a family atmosphere, embodied by the gigantic clown on its marquee. While parents sit around the card tables and slot machines downstairs, their children can spend 50¢ tokens upstairs on the souped-up carnival midway. Tightrope walkers, fire-eaters, and rather impressive acrobats perform from 11am to midnight, two stories over the casino floor. The state-of-the-art video game arcade is enough to entertain even the most jaded video addict. The **Excalibur,** 3850 Las Vegas Blvd. S. (597-7777), is another family-oriented extravaganza that takes its theme from Merry Olde England, forcing its young workers to prance around in medieval clothing. Live jousts satisfy that nostalgic craving for the good old days, and the Magic Motion Machine ride on the bottom floor will keep the little ones occupied. The whole spectacle is enough to make one pine for the Black Plague.

Aside from gambling, every major casino has nightly shows. Many feature free performances by live bands. Caesar's Palace houses multi-storied **OMNIMAX theaters** (731-7900) with domed screens and daily shows every hour on the hour from 11am to midnight. Extra bucks will buy you a seat at a made-in-America phenomenon: the Vegas spectacular ($4, seniors and under 13 $3). Silly but stunning, the twice-nightly, staged productions feature technical marvels such as waterfalls, explosions, fireworks, and a cast of a thousand (men, women, and animals). The "Lido de Paris" at the **Stardust,** 3000 Las Vegas Blvd. S. (732-6325), costs $24.50 and includes two drinks (Wed.-Mon. 7 and 11pm). "Les Folies Bergère," a similarly francophile musical farce at the **Tropicana,** 3801 Las Vegas Blvd. S. (739-2411), offers an all-inclusive dinner for $27. (Fri.-Wed. 8pm $20, and 11pm $14.) Other casinos feature magicians, comedians, or Diana Ross impersonators. Some of the "production shows" are topless and most are tasteless. If you are traveling with children, consider seeking the "family" version of the show, which is usually the first performance of the evening. Be warned that show prices do not include sales tax, entertainment tax, or tip, which can add several bucks onto your tab.

You can also see Broadway plays and musicals, ice revues, and individual entertainers in concert. Musical stars in Las Vegas tend to be such libido-driven performers as Mel Tillis and Frank Sinatra, and their shows are invariably over-priced. The lowest charge for a cocktail show is $5. Dinner shows (steak is the norm) start at $10. To see someone such as Ann-Margret or Charo, people fork over $35 or more. More reasonably priced are the many "revues": impersonators of (generally deceased) cultural icons. You can't walk around Vegas for long without finding an aspiring would-be Elvis hankering to thrust his pelvis a' this way and a' that. The free weeklies often have complete listings of shows.

Nightlife in Vegas starts around midnight, and keeps going until everyone collapses. The Casino Lounge at the **Las Vegas Hilton,** 3000 Paradise Rd. (732-5111), has a disco every night (no cover charge, 1-drink minimum). **Gipsy,** 4605 Paradise Rd. (731-1919), southeast of the Strip, is a popular disco. At 11pm the place is deserted, but by 1am the medium-sized dance floor is packed. The crowd is mixed—gay and straight, women and men. **Carrow's**, 1290 E. Flamingo Rd. (796-1314), has three outdoor patios, plus plenty of people and plants. During the 4-7pm Happy Hour, filling hors d'oeuvres are free.

Public display of homosexuality is illegal in Nevada and strictly enforced with summonses and even arrests.

Sights and Activities

Shocking as it may sound, Las Vegas does offer more than just slot machines and scantily clad performers with feathered head-dresses. Classical music aficionados will be delighted by the **Liberace Museum,** 1775 E. Tropicana Ave. (798-5595), an establishment devoted to the preservation of "Mr. Showmanship"'s contribution to the world of art. As America's Most Beloved Entertainer explained, "When you have something beautiful, it's a shame not to share it." There's fur, velvet and rhinestones in combinations that boggle the rational mind. Though $6.50 might seem a bit much to pay for the privilege of "sharing" the "beauty," proceeds do go to The Liberace Foundation for the Performing and Creative Arts. (Open Mon.-Sat. 10am-5pm, Sun. 1-5pm. Seniors $4.50, ages 6-12 $2.)

The **Antique Auto Collection,** at the Imperial Palace, 3535 Las Vegas Blvd. S. (731-3311), is a privately owned collection of over 200 gleaming classic cars, from a 1908 Sears two-seater that was sold by catalog for $395 to a 1923 Model T Ford snowmobile. Also included are several bullet-proof vehicles used by heads of state, including Dwight Eisenhower and Adolf Hitler. The price might be justified for car lovers, but the adjacent casino often hands out free passes, making the museum a worthwhile diversion for even the moderately interested. (Open daily 9:30am-11:30pm. Admission $8, seniors and under 12 $4).

The most refreshing break from the casinos is the **Wet and Wild Water Park,** 2601 Las Vegas Blvd. S. (737-7873), between the Strip and Paradise Rd. A 26-acre water-ride extravaganza, the park is a cool attraction for people of all ages. The adventurous will free-fall down "Der Stuka," while the more sedate can sunbathe in lounge chairs and splash in the "Surf Lagoon," a simulated ocean with 4-ft. waves. Picnics are allowed, but alcoholic beverages are not. (Open daily June-Aug. 10am-8pm; May and Sept. 10m-5pm. Admission $14, under 12 $10. Discounts can be found in the weekly magazines.)

Sports fans can catch **Stars Baseball** (the AAA farm team for the San Diego Padres) at Cashman Field Center. Call 386-7200 or Ticketron (800-992-2128) for tickets and information. The **Rodeo National Finals** are held in Vegas early every December; call 739-3900 or Ticketron for tickets.

The **State Museum and Historical Society,** 700 Twin Lakes Dr. (486-5205), holds anthropology, biology, and history exhibits on Nevada's past and present. (Open Mon.-Tues. 11:30am-4:30pm, Wed.-Sun. 8:30am-4:30pm. Free.) **Ripley's Believe It or Not,** 202 E. Fremont St. (385-4011), in the Four Queens Casino, has displays more grotesque than Las Vegas proper; believe it or not. Exotica includes shrunken heads, bending rocks, and other bizarre stuff. (Open daily 9am-midnight. Admission $7, seniors $5, under 12 $3.50.) In a similar vein, the **Guiness World of Records** (792-0640), on the Strip just north of Circus Circus, uses mannequins, clippings, and videotapes to document such wonders as the world's fastest oyster-eater (open daily 9am-midnight; admission $5, seniors and students $4, under 13 $3).

Lake Mead NRA

Thirty mi. east of Las Vegas, the **Hoover Dam** plunges 726 ft. into a valley to slow the headlong rush of the Colorado River. Built in the 1930s as part of a New Deal program to provide jobs, water, flood control, and electricity for the Southwest, the monolithic concrete dam spawned two minor cities in the desert. As they labored on the dam, construction workers founded **Boulder City** along Boulder Hwy., which dried up the minute they outlawed gambling and liquor. A cruise ship, the *Echo* (293-6180), makes daily excursions to the dam from Lake Mead. Tours (75 min.) leave daily at 10:30am, noon, 1:30pm, and April to November at 3pm. (Boat tours $7.50, children $4.) Tours of the dam (30-40 min.) include an elevator ride to the powerhouse. (Open daily in summer 8am-6:45pm; in winter 9am-4:15pm; tours $1, under 15 free.)

Stretching from Grand Canyon National Park, 115 miles along the Colorado River, to a point 67 miles south of the Hoover Dam is the **Lake Mead National Recreation Area.** With its crystal blue waters lying beneath towering desert mesas, Lake Mead is a panorama of contrasts. The lake is artificial and was created by the building of the Hoover Dam and the subsequent flooding of previously arid desert. Home to bass, catfish, and trout, the lake draws fishing and boating enthusiasts year round.

The **Temple Bar Resort** ((602) 767-3211), about 80 miles northwest of Kingman, Arizona and 40 miles southeast of Las Vegas on Rte. 15, is a dramatic rest area. The resort is named for the monumental stone temples which overlook the nearby lake, which are especially beautiful when seen in twilight. The marina rents a variety of boats, from 16-foot fishing boats ($32 for 4 hr., $55 per day) to a 30-foot "Family Adventure Patio," complete with upholstered seats, gas barbeque, ice chest, and a souped-up cigarett boat engine for a *real* family adventure ($85 for 4 hr., $150 per day). Fishing gear and water skiing apparati are also available. Cash or credit deposits required.

Lodging is available at the motel at Temple Bar—but it *is* a resort. Doubles start at $39 for a cabin without bathroom facilities. The campsite at Temple Bar, relete with desert fauna, is more suited to the budget traveler ($6 per night). Also at the resort is a general store and diner (Hamburgers and fries $4. Open daily 8am-8pm.)

Over 1500 campsites in nine campgrounds are available on a first-come, first-served basis (293-4041; sites at National Park Service Campgrounds, $6). Boats and water equipment can be rented at **Boulder Beach** (293-3484); fishing boats are $15 per hour, $75 per day. The canyons around the lake are best suited for hiking in the spring and fall. From Las Vegas, take U.S. 95 south to Boulder City. The main **visitors center** (293-3484) is a few miles northeast of Boulder City.

Little-known **Mount Charleston** (388-6254) in Toiyabe National Forest, only 45 minutes northwest of town, is shawled in snow much of the year; skiing, horseback riding, hiking, and camping ($7 per night, 180 sites spread over 5 campgrounds) are popular diversions. From Las Vegas, take Rancho Dr. (U.S. 95) to the Kyle Canyon turn-off (Rte. 157) and drive 15 mi. or so to the first campground. Others are farther along the way.

The road to Hoover Dam leads past the **Ethel M Chocolate Factory and Cactus Garden,** 2 Cactus Garden Dr., Henderson (458-8864), 7 mi. from the Strip. This prickly sweet oasis grows 350 species of cactus and other desert flora in its 2½ acre garden. For no apparent reason, there is a chocolate factory next door. (Open daily 8:30am-5:30pm. Self-guided tours. Free.)

Carson City

Carson City may not be El Dorado, but it was nevertheless created out of gold. Named after explorer "Kit" Carson, this frontier town thrived during the Gold Rush, and six years after its founding in 1858, Abraham Lincoln designated it the capital of the newly created state of Nevada. It also was home to Nevada's first short line railroad, which is still operational today.

You may arrive in Carson City expecting raucous saloons and gunfights in the streets, but the golden years are over and this wild west town has grown considerably less wild since the end of the mining days.

Unlike its avaricious neighbours, government, not gambling, is Carson City's lifeblood. About 1/3 of the population works for the government (although the dynamic state legislature meets only once every two years).

With a single commercial street (which moonlights as U.S. 395), and a population of about 40,000, this is hardly a seething metropolis. It is, however, one of the most balanced industrial and residential communities in the state. Casinos exist, but they don't overwhelm. In fact, its compactness and the range of alternative attractions make Carson City well worth a stopover—at least for a few hours.

Practical Information and Orientation

Visitors Information: Chamber of Commerce, 1900 S. Carson St. (882-7474). Open Mon.-Fri. 8am-5pm, Sat.-Sun. 10am-3pm. A number of brochures, plus an excellent town trail map, and information on activities in the area beyond the city.

Carson Ranger Station: 1536 S. Carson St. (882-2766). Extremely knowledgeable staff and maps of local trails. Open in winter Mon.-Fri. 7:45am-4:30pm. Summer hours Tues.-Wed. 7:45am-4:30pm, Thurs.-Fri. and Mon. 7:45am-6pm, Sat. 7:45am-4pm.

Greyhound: 111 E. Telegraph (322-4511). Open Mon.-Fri 7am-5:40pm, Sat. 8am-noon. To: Reno (3 per day, $5.75); Vegas (2 per day, $50.75). **Showboat** (702-882-0786), service to South Lake Tahoe and the Reno airport.

Taxi: Capital Cab Company, 885-0300. Open 24 hr.

Car Rental: Enterprise, 2250 S. Carson St. (883-7788). From $30 per day, 150 free miles, 15¢ each additional mile. Must be 21, with a credit card.

Road Conditions: 793-1313.

Laundromat: Economy Wash and Dry, 207 Hot Springs Rd. (882-9964). A Renaissance laundromat, complete with TV, video poker and free hot beverages. Open daily 8am-8:30pm.

Public Library: 401 N. Carson St. (687-5160). Open Mon.-Fri. 8am-5pm.

Hospital: Carson-Tahoe, 775 Fleischmann Way (882-1361), between Division and Mountain St.

Poison Control: 789-3013 or 328-4129.

Post Office: 311 E. Washington St. at Stewart St. (887-7000). Open Mon.-Fri. 8:30am-5pm. General Delivery ZIP Code: 89701.

Area Code: 702.

Carson City is 30 mi. south of Reno on U.S. 395 and 14 mi. east of Lake Tahoe on U.S. 50. The bus station and the historic district are centered on Carson St. between 3rd and Washington St. King St. divides Carson St. into North and South and is a useful landmark.

Accommodations and Camping

Budget accommodations abound in Carson City. With its warm, small town flavor and proximity to both Reno and Lake Tahoe, Carson City is an ideal homebase for those traveling by car and an excellent stopover for bus travelers. The city's slow pace and historic charm offer relief from the bedlam of Reno.

City Center Motel, 800 N. Carson St. (800-338-7760 or 882-5535). If you are 21 or older (and they will ask for proof), the drive-up fun-pack coupon available at the visitors center offers the best deal in town. Two buffet dinners, $10 in gambling credits, $8 worth of cocktails, and a double room all cost a mere $33. The second night is $21.

Frontier Motel, 1718 N. Carson St.(882-1377). A little rough around the edges, but the Frontier has its own 24 hr. laundry and minimart on the premises (hot dog and draft beer 99¢). Private bath, TV w/ cable, phone, and A/C. Singles on weekdays $26.90. A three-day weekend is $149. Doubles are $20-30 more. As always, be sure to verify rooms and rates beforehand.

Motel 6, 2749 S. Carson St. (885-7710). The usual, this time with pool. Singles $30, each additional adult $6, children under 18 free when accompanied by their parents. Reserve 2 months in advance, but check for last-minute openings if you are stuck.

Motel Orleans, 2731 S. Carson St. (882-2007). Comfortable rooms that Mom would be happy with. Complimentary coffee, too. Pool and hot tub. Some waterbeds available as well. Singles $35, $30 with AAA card. Doubles $43. Each additional person $4. Reservatons should be made one month ahead.

Pioneer Motel, 907 S. Carson St. (882-3046). Simple accommodations with the usual facilities. TV hounds will eat up the free HBO. Singles with a queen-sized bed $36, weekends $44. Doubles $38, weekends $44.

Deer Run Ranch Bed & Breakfast, 5440 East Lake Blvd. (882-3643), in Washoe Valley. From Carson City take US 395 north to East Lake Blvd., the ranch is on the right. Owned by a friendly young couple and situated next to Washoe Lake and the Sierra Nevada, this alfalfa ranch is a perfect introduction to the area. Despite the seeming ruggedness of ranch life, this home actually comes complete with solar-heated pool, VCR, and spruce rooms kept at moderate temperatures despite the extreme changes from day to night. The sprawling farm claims to have "room to roam," and lives up to the statement. Hearty breakfasts, access to a telephone, and a separate entrance to the ranch with room for parking. This is a place to "splurge". Check-in after 3pm, check-out 11am. Single and double occupancy with one double bed: $75 weekdays, $85 weekends.

Oasis Trailer Haven, 4550 S. Carson St. (882-1375). $15.66 for two people. Rate goes up in proportion to number of people.

Nevada State Parks (687-4387) maintains campgrounds at **Washoe Lake,** 4855 East Lake Blvd. ($5, week maximum). There is also the **Comstock County Park,** 5400 S. Carson St. (882-2445), at U.S. 50 West. (Pool, spa, tennis courts. $18 per night up to 2 people, each additional person $2.)

Food

Catering mainly to the senior set, Carson City's casinos supply standard fare at ultra cheap prices.

Curry Street Buffet, 600 S. Carson St. (882-1890), at the Ormsby House. Chinese and other thematic buffets. Lunch $6. Dinner $7. Kids under 12 are half-price. Open Mon.-Fri. 11am-2pm and 5-8:30pm, Sat. 11am-2pm, 5-9pm. Sunday brunch 9am-3pm, $8.50.

Carson Nugget, 507 N. Carson (882-1626), has an extensive buffet. Lunch $5. Dinner $6. Champagne brunch $6. Open Mon.-Fri. 11am-2pm and 4:30-8pm; Sun. champagne brunch 9am-2pm.

Cactus Jack's, 420 N. Carson (882-8770). Why anyone would want to eat breakfast at 10pm is a mystery, but Jack does a healthy business selling 99¢ breakfasts around the clock. Customers must be at least 21 yr.

In addition to the 24-hr. breakfasts and buffets, Carson City also supports several conventional restaurants.

Cracker Box, 402 E. William (882-4556), has everything a diner could want: sassy waitresses, alcohol (wine and draft beer), and food of quality. French toast $2.75, linguine $5.50, and wedges of homemade pie $2. Open daily 6:30am-3pm.

Heidi's Dutch Mill, 1020 N. Carson St. (882-0486), is a standard pancake house serving gargantuan portions for about $5. Look for the bright yellow building. Open daily 6am-2pm.

Capital Chinese Restaurant, 1214 N. Carson (883-6668). Standard surroundings, but exceptional prices—lunch $3, dinner $5. Open Mon.-Thurs. 11:30am-9pm, Fri.-Sat. 11:30am-10pm.

The Happy Steak, 2300 U.S. 50 (883-7628), about 1 mile east of Carson St. A popular and inexpensive grill, with genial T-bone steak for $9, and teriyaki chicken $6.25. Open Mon.-Sat. 6am-9pm, Sun. 7am-8pm.

The Pickle Barrel Deli, 110 W. 10th St. (883-3358). Specialty sandwiches with garlic mayonnaise $3.90-4.50. Open Mon.-Fri. 8am-6pm, Sat. 9am-5pm

Sights and Activities

While casinos are an omnipresent diversion in the state of Nevada, Carson City's rich frontier history and sublime location in the Sierras offer many other options. It requires extra effort to get beyond the historic district museums, but nearby hot springs, off-road biking and four-wheeling are your waiting reward.

The **Nevada State Railroad Museum,** 2180 S. Carson St. at Fairview Dr. (687-6953), displays vintage railroad coaches and engines of the **Virginia and Truckee Railroad,** a railway which runs the Washoe Zephyr motor car ($1, ages 12 50¢) and the steam train ($2.50, age 5-12 $1, under 5 free) on short rides around the park. (Museum open in winter Wed.-Sun. 8:30am-4:30pm; in summer, daily 8:30am-4:30pm) About 2 mi. south on U.S. 395, **The Stewart Indian Museum,** 5366 Snyder Ave. (882-1808), is located next to a Nevada State Prison. Once a boarding school for Native American youths, one building houses a small three-room gallery of Native American crafts and artwork. The museum hosts the annual **Powwow Festival** on the second weekend in June. (Open daily 9am-4pm; free.)

The rest of Carson City's museums are concentrated in the center of town, between 3rd and Washington. The Chamber of Commerce provides self-guided walking tours of the **Historic District,** which bring out the finer points of Carson City's history.

To get a sense of early local history and the harsh life of a miner, visit the **Nevada State Museum,** 600 N. Carson at Robinson St. (687-4810). Exhibits include a ghost town and a well-reconstructed silver mine in the basement. The interactive **Children's Museum** is a superb and interesting recent addition. (Open Tues.-Fri. 9am-3pm, Sat. 10am-4pm, Sun. 2-4pm; same admission as museum.) **The Brewery Arts Center,** 449 W. King St. at Division (883-1976), hosts rotating exhibits of the work of Nevada artists in the Nevada Artists Association Gallery, in addition to theatrical productions and concerts. (Gallery open Mon.-Fri. 10am-4pm. Evening theater Fri. 7pm, Sat. 7pm and 9pm. Tickets $6, $5 for seniors and students.) **Kit Carson Days,** held in early June, provide the best chance to relive the frontier past of Carson City. With mountain men, a wagon ride, and a mock village, it's a fun way to play cowboys and cowgirls in the place where it all began.

Outdoor activities in Carson City are abundant and varied. For horseback riding, **Butterfield Country Stables,** 2595 Snyder Ave. (887-3605), offers rides ranging in price from $15 to $120. Open Thurs.-Tues. 8am-sunset. **Hoofbeats** (882-8147) in town runs wagon rides ($7, senior and under 12 $4). If you prefer the modern horse, there are seven mountain-bike trails in the area, although no bike rental outfits. Dog Valley Area and Genoa Peak Road are recommended hot spots, but call the Carson Ranger (882-2766) or Capital Bicycles, 900 N. Carson St. (883-3210), for more information. Those without horses of any kind, but with hooves of their own may hike **Mt. Rose** (10,776 ft.). It's a difficult 6-mi. climb, but the summit affords jaw-dropping views of Lake Tahoe. Less strenuous (suitable for children) is the **Hangman's Trail** at Washoe Lake State Park. Take U.S. 395 north to the East Lake Blvd. exit, and then turn right.

In addition to nearby Lake Tahoe, there are a few locales suitable for aquatic endeavors. The excellent fishing of Alpine County is outlined in a 35 site list at the Ranger Station. Local fishermen suggest **Horsethief Canyon,** a 1½ mi. walk off Hwy. 88, just below Hope Valley Resort, or **Forestdale Creek,** which runs beside Blue Lakes Rd. Permits are $12 for three days and are available at local sporting goods stores. Swimming is another option at the **Community Center,** 851 E. Williams St. (887-2290). (Open daily 1-5pm and Wed.-Fri. 6-8pm. Admission $2.25, ages 5-17 $1.25, under 5 75¢.) Slightly more refined, the **Carson Hot Springs Resort,** 1500 Hot Spring Rd. (882-9863), has a spring-fed mineral pool heated to a comfy 99°. (Open daily 8am-11pm. Admission $7, under 12 and over 55 $5; Tues. half-price for women, children and seniors.)

For a day trip to the locale of *The Misfits,* which starred Clark Gable and Marilyn Monroe, head over to Dayton, 12 mi. northeast on U.S. 50. One of the early gold and silver trading posts, Dayton is home to some beautiful historic buildings and a large flea market on summer weekends.

Three homegrown institutions offer quiet testimony to the simple and relaxed lifestyle of a town where it seems everybody knows everybody.

The Old Globe Saloon, 407 N. Curry (882-1816), has been in operation since 1881. The Carsonite after-work crowd will know you're a visitor, but don't worry, they're all friendly. A real wood bar, a shuffleboard, and billiard tables only enhance the natural style of this bar. "Here comes a regular..." Bottled beer $1.50. Open 9am-midnight, later on weekends.

Jack's Bar, 418 S. Carson St. (882-9865), at 5th St., has all the basics: pool table, slots, and a pinball machine. The decor is provided by the patrons. Draft beer 75¢, bottled $1, well drinks $1-$2.50. Open 24 hr.

El Charro, 4389 S. Carson St. (883-6261). This Mexican restaurant features dancing every Wed. with specials on margueritas ($6.50 for a large pitcher) starting at 7:30pm.

Reno

Reno, the so-called "biggest little city in the world," is not much more than a branch outlet of Las Vegas. With the same artificial, non-stop environment (the casinos are immune to the rhythm of the sun), Reno feeds on gambling and not much else. Unless you are motivated to escape downtown, you will be faced with two options: risk your travel budget on the tables, or extend it by eating at one of the many cheap buffets.

It may be difficult to believe when dazzled by the glare of innumerable flashing lights, but Nevada's second largest city has a long history apart from casinos. Originally a working town, Reno became famous when several renowned public figures, including America's Sweetheart, actress Mary Pickford, came to get divorced in the early 1920s. Reno's nouveau fame attracted wealthy people and one-armed bandits alike. With only 40% of its workforce linked to the gaming industry today, Reno is not yet one big casino; there are, in fact, several notable cultural attractions in the town, and some intriguing ones in the region, including a publicly owned, legalized brothel.

Practical Information and Orientation

Visitors Information: Reno Tahoe Visitors Center, 135 N. Sierra (348-7788), between 1st and 2nd. Engaging and expedient staff with the usual deluge of maps and brochures. Open Mon.-Fri. 9am-5pm, Sat. noon-5pm. **Ticket Station,** located in the center, sells tickets for shows on the Ticketron system at the Lawlor Coliseum in Reno and for other local events (348-7403). Open Mon.-Fri. 9am-5pm, Sat. 9am-2pm. **Reno-Sparks Convention and Visitors Center,** at the corner of Kitsky and Virginia (800-4-RENO). Open Mon.-Sat. 7am-9pm, Sun. 7am-6pm.

Cannon International Airport: 2001 E. Plumb Lane at Terminal Way (328-6400), on I-580 3 mi. southeast of downtown. Most major hotels have free shuttles for their guests; otherwise, take bus #24 from the visitors center. Taxi fare from hotel taxi stands runs around $8.

Amtrak: E. Commercial Row and Lake St. (329-8638 or 800-872-7245). Open 8:45am-noon, 2pm-4:45pm. To: San Francisco (1 per day, $58); Salt Lake City (1 per day, $106); Chicago (1 per day, $202).

Greyhound: 155 Stevenson St. (322-2970), ½ block from W. 2nd St. Open 24 hr. A modern depot. To: San Francisco (14 per day, $45); Salt Lake City (4 per day, $63); L.A. (10 per day, $55-60). **Arrow Trans** (786-2376) and **Reno-Tahoe Connection** (825-3900) both offer service to S. Lake Tahoe for $18 with a four person minimum (fewer, and the travelers split the $72 base fare). **Showboat:** Zephyr Cove at Lake Tahoe (323-3088 or 324-5333.

Gray Line Tours: 2570 Tacchino St. (329-1147; outside NV 800-822-6009). Open 8am-5pm. To Virginia City (5 hr., Mon.-Fri. $16) and Lake Tahoe/Virginia City (8½ hr., daily at 9am, $35).

Reno Citifare: Local bus system at 4th and Center St. (348-7433). Most routes operate 5am-7pm, though some operate 24 hr. Fare 75¢, senior citizens and disabled persons 35¢, ages 6-18 50¢.

Car Rental: Lloyd's International Rent-a-Car, 2515 Mill St. (800-654-7037 or 348-4777). Must be 21 with credit card. $25 per day, $145 per week; 150 free miles per day. **Apple Rent-a-Car,** 550 W. Fourth St. (800-537-9034 or 329-2438). $22.50 per day, $120 per week. Budget, at the Reno Cannon International Airport (785-2545), $33.80 per day with unlimited mileage. $10 added charge per day for 21-25 yr., $20 added on if you're 18-21. Open 6am-midnight.

AAA Emergency Road Service: 826-5322.

Road Conditions: Nevada (793-1313). California (916-577-3550).

Laundromat: Reliable Cleaners, 727 W. 5th St. (323-6001). Wash $1, 10 min. dry 25¢. Open Mon.-Fri. 7am-6pm, Sat. 8am-5pm.

Crisis Hotline: 323-6111 or 800-992-5757. 24 hr.

Gambling Hotline: 364-2625.

Northern Nevada Language Bank, 323-0500. 24 hr. help in most major languages.

Pharmacy: Cerveri Drug Store, 1901 E. 1st St., at First and Lake St. (322-6122). Open Mon.-Fri. 7:30am-6pm, Sat. 9am-5pm.

Hospital: St. Mary's, 235 W. 6th St. (323-2041), near Arlington. **Emergency Medical Care:** 789-3188. 24 hr.

Post Office: 50 S. Virginia St. at Mill (786-5523). Open Mon.-Fri. 7am-5pm. General Delivery ZIP Code: 89501. General Delivery office open Mon.-Fri. 10am-3pm.

Area Code: 702.

Only 14 mi. from the California border and 443 mi. north of Las Vegas, Reno glitters at the intersection of I-80 and U.S. 395, which runs along the eastern slope of the Sierra Mountains. Scan West Coast big-city newspapers for **gambler's specials** on bus and plane fare excursion tickets. Some include casino credits.

Although the city sprawls for miles, most of the major casinos are clustered downtown along Virginia and Sierra Streets, between 2nd and 4th St. The adjacent city of **Sparks** also has several casinos along I-80. Many of the buses stop at the major casinos, but the bus station and all the hotels listed are located downtown or within five to 15 minutes' walking distance. The *Reno/Tahoe Travel Planner,* available at the Chamber of Commerce contains a local map and is an excellent guide to the city. The weekly *Showtime* lists current events and performers and is a prime place to look for gambling coupons. Also check the local *Reno-Gazette Journal.*

Accommodations and Camping

Downtown Reno is compact, and its wide streets and well-lit 24-hr. activity are heavily patrolled in the summer. Be streetwise and avoid walking near the northeast corner alone after dark. Reno is blessed with a battery of inner-city hotels. Head towards the southwestern part of town for the cheapest accommodations.

Windsor Hotel, 214 West St. (323-6171), 1½ blocks from Greyhound Station toward Virginia St. The hall showers and rooms are wonderfully clean. Fans turn lazily overhead in compensation for the lack of A/C. Laundry facilities, amicable owner. Singles $17.44, with bath $21.80; Fri.-Sat. $26, with bath $28. Doubles $26.16; Fri.-Sat. $30.

Motel 6, 3 locations in Reno, each about 1½ mi. from the downtown casinos: 866 N. Wells Ave. (786-9852), north of I-80 off Wells Ave. exit; 1901 S. Virginia St. (827-0255), 1½ mi. down Virginia St. to Plumb Lane, near Virginia Lake; 1400 Stardust St. (747-7390), north of I-80 off Keystone Ave. exit, then west on Stardust St. Singles $30.47, each additional adult $7. The place to stay if you're traveling with children; under 18s are free when accompanied by parents. All 3 have pools.

El Cortez, 239 W. 2nd St. (322-9161), 1 block east of Greyhound station. Pleasant management and terrific bargains. TV. Ask for a private bath. The cheapest singles don't have A/C. Singles and doubles $27. Triples $37. Off-season: singles and doubles $24; triples $33. Add $3 on weekends and holidays. Make reservations for weekends at least 2 weeks in advance.

The Grand Hotel, 239 E. Plaza St. (322-2944), 1 block north of Amtrak station. Timeworn and a bit ragged, but clean. Shared bathrooms for most rooms. Singles and doubles $17-21; Fri.-Sat. $27, with bath $30.

Some of the best deals in town can be found in the major casinos, where all sorts of hidden discounts exist on rooms which ordinarily run $100 per night. Be nosy and ask enough questions and you may find yourself paying $35 for a room on the 20th floor of the Hilton. Usually there is a Welcome Center in the casino which can advise on discounts and specials.

You can park your RV overnight at **Bally's,** 2500 E. 2nd St. (789-2000), for $17. But the **Toiyabe National Forest** begins only a few miles southwest of Reno, and if you're equipped to camp, you might make the drive to the woodland sites of **Davis Creek Park** (849-0684), 17 mi. south on U.S. 395 then ½ mi. west (follow the signs), with full service, including showers, but no hookups. (Sites $9, each extra vehicle $3. Picnic area open 8am-9pm.) **Boca Basin,** a beautiful Forest Service campground is located on the **Boca Basin Lake,** just over the California line, 23 mi. west on I-80. No hookups. Two week maximum. Free.

Food

Eating in Reno is amazingly cheap. The casino buffets make even McDonalds seem expensive. To entice gamblers in, or to prevent them from wandering out in search of food, there is a range of all-you-can-eat casino cuisine.

Fitzgeralds, 255 N. Virginia St. (786-3663). The 3rd floor feels a bit like the bridge of the *U.S.S. Enterprise* with its domed roof, but the setting is pleasant, the buffet cheap, and the service superb. Breakfast (7:30-11am, $3), lunch (11am-4pm, $3.30), dinner (4-10pm, $4.80). Beverages included.

Cal Neva, 38 E. 2nd St. (323-1046). Features a 2-egg breakfast with sausage, toast and jelly (99¢) and an excellent prime rib dinner (5-11pm, $6), as well as all-you-can-eat spaghetti ($2.75).

Circus Circus, 500 N. Sierra (329-0711). With a 90 ft. blinking neon clown out front, you can't miss it. Offers enormous quantities on plastic plates. "Eat all you want, but eat all you take," they ask. Think twice before feeding here—this buffet is *not* frequented by locals. Breakfast (6-11:30am, $2.30), brunch (noon-4pm, $3), dinner (4:30-11pm, $4). Beverages included.

Sadly stereotypical bunny-girls hop around the casino floor serving cheap alcohol (beer nominally priced at 75¢, but usually free if you look like you are gambling). But beware: no matter how drunk you are, you'll still be held responsible for your gambling debts.

For a brief taste of culinary civilization, look past the casino "restaurants" and try one of Reno's many inexpensive restaurants. The large Basque population, which originally came from the Pyrenees to herd sheep in Nevada, brought with them a spicy and hearty cuisine which locals adore.

Santa Fe Motel, 235 Lake St. (323-1891), offers Basque dinners in a classic dining room with green and white checked tablecloths. Real wood bar, ancient slots, and juke box take you back to the 50s. Hefty portions, served family-style (everyone eats at one sitting). Dinner $12; discounts for children under 10. Open daily 12:30-1:30pm and 6:30-9pm.

Louis' Basque Corner, 301 E. 4th St. (323-7203), at Evans, 3 blocks east of Virginia, is a local institution. The friendly bar, family-style dining, and hearty full course dinner with wine, make the price ($14) happily bearable. Under 10 $6.50. Open Mon.-Sat. 11am-2:30pm, Sun. 4-11pm.

Landrum's, #3, 6770 S. Virginia St. (852-5464). With only eight seats, salmon-colored counters and turquoise walls, Landrums is the quintessential diner. Dinners with salad, vegetables, potato, and bread about $5. Thick shakes $2. Open Sun.-Thurs. 6am-3am, Fri.-Sat. 24 hr.

The Blue Heron, 1091 S. Virginia St. (786-4110), at Vassar St. A haven for vegetarians. Somewhat expensive natural foods in a large, sunny room. The carrot cake ($1.50) is excellent. Open Mon.-Fri. 11am-9:30pm, Sat. noon-9pm.

Bamboo Garden, 231 W. 2nd St. (323-6333), across from the Comstock. Largely undiscovered, this jungle-green spot concocts spicy Thai and Chinese lunches for $4-5 (served Mon.-Fri. 11:30am-2:30pm). Dinner entrees $6-10. Open daily 10:30am-10pm.

Sights

Gambling is what lures most tourists to Reno; there is even a bank of slot-machines in the local supermarket (**J.J.'s Food Co. Market,** Virginia and 5th St., 786-8870). Each casino claims fame and uniqueness for its "loosest slots" or accountant-certified "highest paybacks." The **Cal Neva,** 38 E. 2nd St. (323-1046), currently holds the world jackpot record ($6.8 million, won in Feb. 1988). The most famous piece of lighting architecture in a town which knows no night is the **Reno Arch,** on Virginia at Commercial, which originally proclaimed its "Biggest little city in the world" slogan in 1926 and was remodeled with 1600 bulbs a few years ago.

Before you "stack 'em or rack 'em" (your chips, that is), you might try the "Behind the Scenes" gaming tour, which takes you to the other side of the one-way mirrors, and teaches you the rudiments of the games, teaching you exactly how they take your money. (Daily tours ($5) leave from Ticket Station at 12:30pm; 135 N. Sierra, 348-7788.) The 2 hr. tours show the surveillance at Calvera, and the tourists get a chance to play a few practice games. Don't forget: gambling is illegal for persons under 21 years of age; if you win the jackpot at age 20, it'll be the casino's lucky day and not yours.

Most venues have live music in the evenings, while at **Bally's,** 2500 E. 2nd St (789-2285, open 10am-10pm), the enormous stage hosts aging has-beens like Frank Sinatra and Mel Torme. Check details in the weekly freebie *Showtime.* A free shuttle runs every 40 min. from El Dorado on Plaza St. to Bally's and every ½ hr. between Bally's and the airport (6:15am-11:45pm). **Circus Circus,** 500 N. Sierra (329-0711), has free 10-15 min. "big-top" performances running every ½ hr. from 11:15am-4:45pm, 6:10-11:35pm. **Harrah's,** at Virginia and Commercial (800-648-3773) presents musical groups geared to younger crowd.

Gay and lesbian travelers should know that public affection displayed by homosexual couples is illegal in Nevada and strictly enforced with summonses and even arrests. However, Reno has a fairly large homosexual community and 10 gay bars. The **Chute No. 1,** 1099 S. Virginia St. (323-7825), is a popular bar for dancing (open 24 hr.), or try the quieter **Ron's Piano Bar,** farther south on Virginia St., at 145 Hillcrest St. (829-7667). Open daily 11am-3am.

During the day, there are plenty of alternative attractions. The **Sierra Nevada Museum of Art,** 160 W. Liberty St. (329-3333), displays art of the Great Basin, as well as other 20th-century American works, in the E.L. Wiegand Gallery. The Educational Gallery offers hands-on experience for children that meshes with rotating art exhibits in the museum. (Open Tues.-Sat. 10am-4pm, Sun. noon-4pm. Admission $3, seniors and students $1.50.) Gambling rears its ubiquitous head at the **William F. Harrah Automobile Museum,** 10 S. Lake St. at Mill St. (333-9300). The displays demonstrate just how rich casino owners can get. Over 500 antique cars are on display, including models made of gold, papier mâche, and leather, and autos owned by JFK, Sinatra and Mary Pickford. (Open daily 9:30am-5:30pm. Admission $7.50, 62 and over $6.50, 6-18 $2.50, under 6 free. Discount coupons available at the Chamber of Commerce and most hotels.)

Not every millionaire in Reno made his money from casinos, or even *made* his money. The **Wilbur D. May Museum,** 1502 Washington St. (785-5961), in Rancho San Rafael Park, displays only some of the eclectic collection assembled by the son of the founder of the May Co. Department Store. Mr. May made over 40 trips around the world and brought back a South American shrunken head, an elephant's ear, rare T'ang Dynasty porcelain, as well as other artifacts. (Open Tues.-Sun. 10am-5pm; in winter Wed.-Sun. 10am-5pm. Admission $2, seniors and under 13 $1.) The grounds also house an arboretum (open year-round) and a Great Basin Adventure theme park (open May-Sept.; admission $2, seniors and under 13 $1). The state's oldest museum, the **Nevada Historical Society Museum,** 1650 N. Virginia St. (688-1190), houses Indian artifacts and mining antiques. (Open Mon.-Sat. 10am-5pm, admission free).

Next door, the **Fleischmann Planetarium,** at the University of Nevada, Virginia St. and N. McCarran Blvd. (784-4812), screens a new neck-straining, 360° ceiling show every 3 months. (Open Mon.-Fri. 8am-5pm and 7-9pm, Sat.-Sun. 10:30am-5pm and 7-9pm. Museum free. Shows daily at 11am, 1pm, 3pm, 5pm, 7:30pm, and 9:15pm. Movie admission $5, seniors and under 13 $3.50.)

The **Wild Island Adventure Park** (331-9453), located 3½ mi. east of Reno at the Sparks Blvd. exit, is yet another West Coast water world, with four slides, a pool with volleyball, and a tanning deck. (Open late May-Sept. 10am-midnight; admission $13.50, under 10 $10.) A 36-hole **Adventure Golf** course is next door (open May-Sept. Mon.-Thurs. 3-9pm, Fri. 3pm-midnight, Sat. 10am-midnight, Sun. 10am-9pm; admission $4 for 18 holes, $5 for 36). Those who brought their ice skates to the desert (just in case) are in luck; the **Sierra Nevada Ice Arena,** 1855 E. Lincoln Way (355-1033), has year-round recreational skating. (Open Mon.-Wed. and Fri. 10am-3:30pm, 7:30-9:30pm, Thurs. 9:30am-3:30pm, Sat. 12:45-4pm, 7:30-9:30pm, Sun. 12:45-4pm.; admission $5, seniors and under 13 $4; skate rentals $1.50.)

Tying and untying the knot has become a veritable industry in Reno. A six-week residency form for quickie divorces and marriages is *not* available from midnight to 8am; it is available only from 8am to midnight daily (including holidays) at the Courthouse, 117 S. Virginia St. (328-3274, $35). Ceremonies are, however, available 24 hr. a day ($20-100) at a wedding chapel near you, or dial 800-MARRY-US.

A rather less sanctimonious alternative is 10 mi. east on Rte. 80: the **New Mustang Ranch** (342-0176), which apparently receives 200,000 "clients" annually. This particular legal brothel came to fame in 1988 when it launched a share issue on Wall Street to avoid paying taxes on earnings.

The Basque influence is reflected in Reno's annual **Basque Festival** (323-3073), held in early August. This weekend of frenetic celebration features traditional contests, dancing, live music, and more food than the Circus Circus buffet. The annual **Reno Rodeo** (323-0924), one of the biggest in the West, spreads over eight days at the end of June. (Tickets $5.) Reno is also working to build itself a reputation in the arts. Freebie enthusiasts will enjoy the **summer band concerts** in Wingfield Park at 1st and Arlington, sponsored by the Chamber of Commerce (June-Aug. Mon.-Fri. noon-1pm; free). Call 334-2260 for information. The **Hot Air Balloon Race** (826-1181, in Rancho San Rafael) and the **National Air Races** (972-6663, at the Stead Airport) draw an international group of contestants and spectators. In September, nearby Virginia City hosts **Camel Races** (847-0311), where camels and ostriches race through town. Take U.S. 395 south, then Rte. 341 about 25 mi. Concerts are held in the Quad at the U. of Nevada-Reno July-Aug. at 6pm.

Grand Canyon

At 277 mi. long, 13 mi. wide, and over 1 mi. deep, the Grand Canyon is almost vast enough to hold the countless pilgrims that travel to this, the Mecca of American tourist attractions. Any trip through the Southwest requires you to stop here, if only to have that snapshot to show Aunt Sally, who will doubtless be impressed by the Canyon's general bigness.

Six million years ago, long before Bobby and Cindy Brady visited the region, the Colorado River decided to disobey the usual laws governing the flow of rivers, coursing over the mountains instead of around them. Ages later, Greg would point out to his younger siblings that the river was quick to cut through the canyon's soft limestone, sandstone, and shale, exposing countless years of strata. The result, Marcia quickly adds, is that the Canyon provides a glimpse into millions of years of geological change. Alice has nothing to add, her mind filled with thoughts of her butch meat-man, Sam.

Grand Canyon National Park consists of three areas: the South Rim (which includes Grand Canyon Village), the North Rim, and the canyon gorge itself. Because it is more accessible, the slightly lower South Rim draws 10 times more visitors than the more heavily forested North Rim. As long as you are within sight of the edge, the teeming masses don't seem to matter. The instant you step back, however, you enter a world of overpriced curio shops, expensive lodges, Winnebago-filled parking lots, and innumerable tour buses. You can avoid these nuisances on the North Rim, the side where locals go to elude the flocks of tourists. The 13-mi. distance that traverses the canyon floor is a two-day adventure for sturdy hikers; the 214 mi. of road is a scenic 5-hour drive for those who would rather do their exploring from above. Although park rangers do their best to make movement around the canyon as safe as possible, each year careless tourists decide to take what locals call "the 12-second tour" of the Canyon. Please remember to observe all safety precautions and the rules of common sense: drinking and climbing don't mix.

South Rim

In summer, anything on two legs or four wheels converges from miles around on this side of the Grand Canyon. If you plan to visit during the summer, make reservations for lodging, campsites, and mules, and be prepared for crowds. During the winter there are fewer tourists, but many of the canyon's hotels and facilities are closed.

Practical Information and Orientation

Park Headquarters: 638-7888. Open daily 8am-5pm. 24 hr. information on programs. (ext. 1,3,2,3)

Main Switchboard: 638-2631. This number puts you through to the Bright Angel Lodge travel info desk. 24 hr.

Nava-Hopi Bus Lines: 774-5003. Leaves Flagstaff Greyhound station for Grand Canyon daily 7am, 9am, and 4pm; departs from Bright Angel Lodge at Grand Canyon for Flagstaff daily 9:45am and 5:45pm. Round-trip $26, children $12; with Ameripass $13.20, $2 entrance fee not included.

Visitor Activities Line: 638-9304. 24-hr. recorded information.

Lodging Reservations: Reservations Dept., Grand Canyon National Park Lodges, Grand Canyon 86023 (638-2401). Reservations can also be made through Ticketron.

Camper Services: Coin-op showers and laundry next to **Mather** Campground. Open daily 6am-10pm.

Transportation Information Desk: in Bright Angel Lodge (638-2631). Reservations for mule rides, bus tours, Phantom Ranch, and taxi. Open daily 6am-6pm.

Equipment Rental and Sales: Babbit's General Store, in Mather Center Grand Canyon Village (638-2262 or 638-2234) near Yavapai Lodge. Rents comfortable hiking boots ($5 for the first day; children's sizes not available), sleeping bags ($5-6), tents ($10), and other camping gear. Also sells a wide variety of hats, water bottles, and other canyon necessities. Open daily 8am-8pm.

Valley National Bank: located across from Babbit's (638-2437). Does not accept out-of-state checks, but will cash traveler's checks. Cash can be drawn from 24-hr. ATM machines with ATM or credit cards. Open Mon.-Thurs. 10am-3pm, Fri. 10am-3pm and 4-6pm.

Backcountry Information Line: 638-2474. Current trail and weather conditions. 11am-5pm.

Weather and Road Conditions: 638-2245, 24-hr. recording.

Lost and Found: NPS Warehouse, (638-7798), across from the Albright Training Center. Open Mon.-Fri. 8am-noon and 1-4pm.

Emergency: 638-2477 or 911. 24 hrs.

Post Office: 638-2512, next to Babbit's. Open Mon.-Fri. 9am-4:30pm, Sat. 10am-2pm; lobby open 5am-10pm. ZIP Code: 86023.

Area Code: 602.

From Las Vegas, the fastest route to the canyon is on U.S. 93 south to I-40 east, and then Rte. 64 north. From Flagstaff, I-40 east to Rte. 89 north is the most scenic, passing by Navajo jewelry tourist traps and entering the park from the East at Desert View. The alternative and quicker route up Rte. 180 north is more commercial but also passes the yabbadabbadistic Bedrock City at the Rte. 64 junction. Pose for pictures with Bam Bam Rubble and Wilma Flintstone (children and adults, 4 clams). From Los Angeles and Southern California the quickest route is I-15 north to I-40 east at Barstow, then to Rte. 64 north. Admission to the Grand Canyon is $10 per car, $2 for travelers using other modes of transportation—even bus passengers must pay. Admission is valid for seven days; you can leave the park and re-enter without paying again. The entrance fee is sometimes waived at sunset.

Maps, schedules of free events, and information on accommodations are available at the **visitors center** in Grand Canyon Village (open 7:30am-8:30pm; in winter 8am-5pm). The park ranger staff is friendly and knowledgeable.

Upon arriving at the South Rim, grab a copy of *The Guide,* a small but comprehensive reference available at the entrance gate and the visitors center (free).

The National Park Service operates two **free shuttle buses.** The **West Rim Loop** runs between West Rim Junction and Hermit's Rest, with stops at all the scenic vistas along the way (Memorial Day-Labor Day every 15 min. 7:30am-sunset); the **Village Loop** covers Bright Angel Lodge, West Rim Junction, the visitors center, Grand Canyon Village, and Yavapai Point (year-round, every 15 min. 6:30am-9:30pm).

Thanks to the efforts of the National Park Service, the South Rim is accessible by wheelchair; pick up the free pamphlet *Access for Visitors* at the visitors center.

Accommodations and Camping

Compared with the six million years it took the Colorado River to cut the Grand Canyon, the six months it takes to get a room on the South Rim is pretty quick. With the closing of the hostel in 1990, it is now near impossible to sleep indoors anywhere near the South Rim without reservations—although you can check at the visitors center for last-minute vacancies.

Most accommodations on the South Rim other than those listed below are outrageously expensive. The campsites listed are usually full by 10am in summer. Campground overflow usually winds up in the **Kaibab National Forest,** adjacent to the park along the southern border, where you can pull off a dirt road and camp for free. Spending the night in cars is not permitted within the park, but is allowed in the Kaibab Forest. The Nava-Hopi bus stops at the Bright Angel Lodge, where you can check your luggage for 50¢ per day.

Bright Angel Lodge, Grand Canyon Village. Scout-style rustic cabins with plumbing but no heat. Very convenient to Bright Angel Trail and both shuttle buses. Singles $45-52, depending on how much plumbing you want. Each additional person $6.

Maswik Lodge, Grand Canyon Village. Small, clean cabins with shower $46 (single or double). Each additional person $8. Reservations required.

Trailer Village, next to Mather Campground. Campsites resemble driveways and offer little privacy. Sites with hookups $15 for two people, 50¢ each additional.

Reservations for Bright Angel Lodge, Maswik Lodge, Trailer Village, and more expensive rooms can be made through Grand Canyon National Park Lodges, P.O. Box 699, Grand Canyon 86023 (638-2401). Reservations can also be made through Ticketron. All rooms should be reserved six months in advance for summer, six weeks for winter.

Mather Campground, Grand Canyon Village, ½ mi. from the visitors center. Mather has shady, relatively isolated campsites without hookups. Sites $10. Reservations are a smart idea, but can only be made through Ticketron outlets 8 weeks in advance.

Desert View Campsite, 25 mi. east of Grand Canyon Village. Sites $8. Open May 15-Oct. 30. No hookups. No reservations, so arrive early in the day.

Ten-X Campground, in the Kaibab National Forest (638-2443), 10 mi. south of Grand Canyon Village on Rte. 64. Chemical toilets, water. 70 sites ($9 each). No reservations or hookups. Open April-Nov.

Phantom Ranch, on the canyon floor, a 4-hr. hike down the Kaibab Trail. The ranch has a snack bar and serves expensive meals; save money by bringing your own food. Reservations required 6 months in advance for the April-Oct. season, but check at the Bright Angel Transportation Desk (see above) for last-minute cancellations. Don't show up without reservations—they'll send you back up the trail, on foot. Dorm bed $27. Cabin for 1 or 2 people $53, each additional person $10.

If you plan on camping overnight on the canyon floor (free), you'll need reservations from the **Backcountry Reservations Office,** South Rim, Grand Canyon National Park, Grand Canyon 86023 (638-2474; open daily 7am-noon and 3-5pm). They start taking reservations for the following year on October 1; reserve a site as early as possible.

Food

It's a shame the fast chains have not sunk their razor sharp claws into the rim of the Canyon. Food in the canyon tends to leave your body in more ways than two. Luckily, none of it costs too much.

Babbit's General Store (638-2262), in Maswik Lodge, is more than just a restaurant—it's a superdupermarket. Stock up on trail mix, water and gear (open daily 8am-8pm; deli open 8am-7pm). The **Maswik Cafeteria,** also in Maswik Lodge, has a variety of inexpensive options, grill-made and served in a swish cafeteria atmosphere (open daily 6am-10pm). The **Yavapai Lodge Cafeteria** in Grand Canyon Village (638-7509) (open daily 6-11am and 11:30am-10pm) serves the same food but features a more varied clientele of blond international teens. **Bright Angel Restaurant,** in Bright Angel Lodge (638-6389), has hot sandwiches at prices slightly higher than the cafeteria's ($4-6); add the tip, and it's not such a bargain (open daily 6:30am-10pm). The **soda fountain** at Bright Angel Lodge offers sixteen flavors of ice cream (single scoop $1) to hikers emerging from the Bright Angel Trail, but alas . . . no milkshakes (open daily 11am-9pm).

Activities

After first glimpsing the canyon you will be struck by an overwhelming passion to hike down into it, an enterprise much harder than it appears. Much woe has come to the plaid-clad, would-be hiker armed with only a telephoto lens and an unopened can of Diet Coke—park rangers average over three rescues per day in the National Park that has the highest fatality rate in the country. Use your noggin: what seems like a light hike downhill becomes a nightmarish 100° journey on the return. Heat exhaustion, the second greatest threat after slipping, is marked by a monstrous headache and termination of sweating. Taking at least two quarts of water along on your hike is an absolute necessity. A list of hiking safety tips can be found in the *Grand Canyon Guide,* available at the entrance gate and the Visitor's Center, and should be read thoroughly before you hit the trail. Overestimating your limits is a common mistake when tackling the canyon, and parents should think strongly about bringing children more than a mile down the trails—kids have long memories and they might exact revenge when they get bigger.

The two trails down into the canyon are the **Bright Angel Trail,** which begins at Bright Angel Lodge, and **South Kaibab Trail,** originating at Yaki Point. Bright Angel is outfitted to accommodate the average tourist, with its rest houses stationed strategically 1½ mi. and 3 mi. from the rim. **Indian Gardens,** 4½ mi. down, presents the weary hiker with restrooms, picnic tables, and blessed umbrage. Kaibab is trickier, since it is steeper and has no shade or water, but it rewards the intrepid with a better view of the canyon's hypnotic contours (not unlike Hawaiian lava flowing into the night ocean). Consult *The Guide* for a more detailed description of these trails.

While a short hike down either of those two trails is enough to imbue one with an awe of the canyon's size, a real glutton for punishment wil want to go all the way to the canyon floor and back, an arduous nine-mile trek. It is important to remember that the difficult part of canyon hiking is the return trip, which typically takes twice as long as the trip down. Round trips to the canyon floor require a full two days; remember to prepare for chilly nights. Backcountry permits are required for any overnight stay. The best route descends the Kaibab Trail (3-4 h., depending on the condition of the trail) and ascends the rim via Bright Angel (7-8 hr.) the next day, as that trail's more shallow grade takes some of the punch out of the upward trek. You can catch the free **Hiker's Special Bus** to the head of South Kaibab from the Backcountry Reservation Office. It departs at 7:30am and 10:30am and returns from the same point back to the office at 8:30am and 11:30am. In addition to following the hiking tips in *The Guide,* make sure you bring along a hat, moleskin for blisters, and broken-in hiking boots.

If hiking requires too much sweat, or if you dislike the ubiquitous mules (who like to leave their mark on the trails, so watch your step), there are plenty of other options to explore. The trails along the rim lack fences or railings, you can still enjoy a hiker's sense of danger without the panting and exhaustion. The **Rim Trail** runs east, winding its way to the Grandeur Point lookout and the **Yavapai Geological Museum,** which fleshes out the history and importance of the canyon, while a westward route brings you to **Hermit's Rest.** Convenient shuttles run between these points, so you needn't hoof it.

In addition to the trails, which are open to all after the entrance fee to the park has been handed over, the National Park Service makes available a number of other free offerings, from informative slideshows and lectures to ranger-led hikes of varying lengths. The **Mather Amphitheater,** located behind the visitors center, shows a presentation on the Canyon every day at 8:30pm in the summer, and 7:30pm in the winter. The younger set will be kept busy with the *Grand Canyon's Young Adventurer,* a magazine full of stories of the canyon and a variety of puzzles for children ages 5-12. By finishing all the games inside, the kids can become Junior Rangers, an entry-level civil service position which could eventually lead to the White House.

For those willing to pay the improbably high prices demanded, a number of companies provide commercial tours of the South Rim. While generally out of the budget traveler's reach, tours of the canyon can be made by helicopter, airplane, mule, and inflatable raft. You can book plane and chopper tours in the town of **Tusayan,** 7 mi. south of Grand Canyon Village. Bus shuttle service provided from the Village.

($4, round-trip $7.) Air trips start at $50 per person per hour; raft trips start at around $70 per day. The Bright Angel Lodge runs mule trips for $70 per day, including lunch. Of the three bus tours offered, the Sunset and West Rim tours cover mostly places accessible by the free shuttle buses. If you have the time and the money, however, you might want to take the tour to **West Desert View** (2 per day in summer, 1 per day in winter; 3 hr. 45 min.; $17, children $8.50). Unless you have a car, this tour is the only way to reach Desert View, 26 mi. east of the village. The aptly named point commands a panoramic view of the canyon to the north and west, and gives a peek at the Painted Desert to the east. Contact the Bright Angel Transportation Desk for information on all commercial tours (638-2401). The 15-minute Kodak **slide show** presented at the visitors center offers photography tips for the snapshot enthusiast that will ensure the brightest sunrises and the most exquisite sunsets. The **Grand Canyon IMAX Theatre** (638-2203; take the Tusayan shuttle from the Yavapai lodge) in Tusayan allows rugged hikers and sedentary spectators alike the chance to "live" the canyon experience vicariously on their enormous screen. (Shows daily 8:30am-8:30pm in the summer, 10:30am-6:30pm in the winter; $6.50.) For the musically inclined, the annual **Chamber Music Festival** sounds off each September in the **Shrine of Ages.** For ticket information, call the festival office at 638-9215, or write the Grand Canyon Chamber Music Festival, P.O. Box 1332, Grand Canyon 86023.

No trip to America's biggest ditch would be complete without viewing one of the most spectacular sunsets imaginable, as the dying light works with the growing shadow to draw out shifting shades of red, orange and purple from the canyon walls. Show up about 45 minutes before the sun goes down, have a seat, and watch the show unfold. It's a natural spectacle that might capture even Blythe Grossberg's attention. The Eastern Rim trail is very popular and if you venture to the end of the trail you can have a sweeping view of the canyon on the observation deck of the Yavapai Museum (Open daily 8am-8pm. Free.) The **Watchtower** by Desert View, rebuilt from Indian ruins over 800 years old, may have a fabricated, plastic appearance, but it will be swarming at dusk with fellow sunset watchers. Along the Western Rim, a number of excellent panoramic vistas can be had, among them **Hopi Point** and the **Abyss,** where the canyon wall drops almost vertically to the Tonto plateau 3000 ft. below.

North Rim

If you are coming from Utah or Nevada, or if you simply want a more rugged, less crowded Grand Canyon experience, consider the North Rim. Only one-in-ten park visitors contemplates the canyon from this side—things are a bit wilder, a bit cooler, and a lot more serene. More important, the view from the North Rim is at least as remarkable, and decidedly less familiar, than the view from the South Rim.

Unfortunately, getting to the North Rim without a car is easier said than done: virtually no public transportation crosses the area. The only rim-to-rim transportation is available from **Transcanyon,** P.O. Box 348, Grand Canyon 86023 (638-2820), between late May and mid-October ($50, round-trip $85). Departs South Rim 1:30pm; arrives North Rim around 6pm. Call for reservations. Canyon drivers seem wary of those on foot, so hitching is not really an option. From the South Rim, the North Rim is a 200-mi. plus, stunningly scenic drive away. Take Rte. 64 east to U.S. 89 north, which runs into Alt. 89; off Alt. 89, take Rte. 67 south to the edge. Between the first snows at the end of October and May 15, Rte. 67 is closed to traffic; only a snowmobile will get you to the North Rim.

There is no visitors center on this side of the park, but you can direct questions to rangers at the entrance station and at the information desk in **Grand Canyon Lodge** (638-2611, open daily 8am-5pm). The lodge is at the very end of Rte. 67. (Front desk serviced 24 hrs.) The North Rim **emergency phone** (638-7805) is monitored 24 hrs.

Accommodations, Camping, and Food

Since camping within the confines of the Grand Canyon National Park is limited to designated campgrounds, only a lucky few among North Rim visitors get to spend the night "right there." If you can't find in-park lodgings, the fine Canyonlands Hostel is available in nearby Utah, and the Kaibab National Forest runs from north of Jacob Lake to the park entrance. Camp in an established site here, or pull off the main road onto any forest road and "at large" camp for free. Campsite reservation can be made through Ticketron (800) 452-1111.

Canyonlands International Hostel, 143 E. South, Kanab, UT 84741 (801-644-5554). 1½ hr. north of the Grand Canyon on U.S. 89, an equal distance south of Bryce Canyon. Free beverages, large kitchen, newly restored cabins; can accommodate 40. Office open daily 8-10am and 5-10pm. No curfew. Non-AYH, but all hostel cards honored. Members $8; nonmembers $10. Reservations advised, but not essential (can be made at Las Vegas Independent Hostel).

Grand Canyon Lodge, on the edge of the rim. Doubles from $50. Front desk is open 24 hrs. Write or call TW Recreational Services, P.O. Box 400, Cedar City, UT 84720 (801-586-7686).

Kaibab Lodge, Rte. 67 (638-2389), 5 mi. north of the Park Entrance Station. This secluded lodge is delightful, its restaurant delicious, and the private management delovely. Singles $43. Doubles $54. Call or write Kaibab Lodge, North Rim, Rural Route, Fredonia 85719 for reservations (526-0924 or 800-525-0924). Open May 28-Oct. 1.

Jacobs Lake Lodge (643-7232). 30 mi. north of the North Rim in Jacob Lake. Doubles $45-60.

North Rim Campground, Rte. 67, near the rim. You can't really see into the canyon from the pine-covered site, but it's close. Nearby grocery, recreation room, and showers. 82 sites. $8 per night. Reserve by writing to North Rim Campground, Grand Canyon National Park, Grand Canyon 86023. $10. Pay showers ($1 for 5 minutes) and coin-operated laundry machines are available across the street. (Open daily 8am-8pm.)

Kaibab National Forest Sites: (800) 283-CAMP. 18 mi. north of the North Rim Entrance Station. No sites; only free "at-large" camping on a first-come, first-served basis. **Jacob Lake Campground,** Jacob Lake, 32 mi. north of the North Rim, at Alt. 89 and Rte. 67 junction (643-7395). 48 sites, $6 per night. Reserve ahead.

There are two eating options on the North Rim, both strategically placed at the Grand Canyon Lodge. The restaurant slaps together dinners for $4.50-12 and breakfasts for around $3.50. A skimpy sandwich at the "buffeteria" costs about $2. North Rim hostelers are far better off eating in Kanab.

Activities

Starting at the Grand Canyon Lodge, **Bright Angel Point Trail** is an excellent introduction to the North Rim. The easy half-mile paved walk affords splended views of the canyon, including the San Francisco Peaks. **Point Imperial,** an 11 mile drive from the lodge, is the highest point on the rim of the canyon at 8,803 ft., and overlooks Marble Canyon and the Painted Desert. Beginning at **Cape Royal,** the one mile **Cliff Springs Trail** meanders into a forested ravine and past an Anasazi Ruin. **North Kaibab Trail** is the only trail into the canyon from the North Rim. The adventuresome and prepared hiker can tackle the 9.4 mile round trip to Pouring Springs, lying some 3401 feet below the rim.

A wide variety of nature walks and lectures are offered by the park throughout the day. For a complete list and schedules check the lodge information desk and bulletin boards. Those seeking alternative means of travel in and around the North Rim can investigate mule trips ($25 for a half-day journey) which leave from Grand Canyon Lodge (638-2292, open daily 7am-8pm) or rafting along the Colorado River (638-2389).

On warm evenings, the **Grand Canyon Lodge** overflows with an eclectic group of international travelers, Brady Bunches, and rugged adventurers. Some frequent the **Lodge Saloon** for drinks, jukebox disco, and a young crowd's enthusiasm. Others find the warm air rising from the canyon, a full moon, and the occasional shooting star a sufficient and most intoxicating mixture at day's end.

BAJA CALIFORNIA

US$1 = 3041 pesos	**1000 pesos = US$0.33**
CDN$1 = 2654 pesos	**1000 pesos = CDN$0.38**
UK£1 = 5069 pesos	**1000 pesos = UK£0.20**
AUS$1 = 2352 pesos	**1000 pesos = AUS$0.43**
NZ$1 = 1723 pesos	**1000 pesos = NZ$0.58**

Baja California is a 40,000-square-mile finger of desert, mountains, and jagged coastline that points southeast toward Central America, parallel to mainland Mexico. Earthquakes peeled this skinny peninsula away from the mainland, and now the Gulf of California and the Sea of Cortés separate the two. In the centuries after Mexico was subdued by the *conquistadores,* Baja's isolation served it well, as the area remained free of outside influence except for a few dozen Jesuit enclaves (now ruined missions hidden in the hills). Just a few decades ago, large tracts of Baja remained empty: recently, however, the government has sought to open up *La Frontera* through the construction of the Transpeninsular Highway (Rte. 1) and the introduction of regular ferry service to the mainland. Now Californians take full advantage not only of Northern Baja's under-age partying opportunities but also Southern Baja's beach-lined deserts.

Resorts have sprung up on scattered ribbons of sand, and tourist magnets, like Tijuana and Ensenada, pull *norteamericanos* across the border. As you travel southward, however, the raging torrent of Californians slackens. The Bahía de Concepcion in particular offers beautiful if not unspoiled beaches.

It will require more than a few slapped-together condo complexes to settle, let alone overpopulate, the Baja's mountain ranges, *saguaro* forests, and thousands of miles of perpetually sunny coastline, though secluded beaches are hard to come by unless you've got a car. With effort, though, Baja can be a freelance camper's paradise; simply stash some food, homestead a seaside acre, and vacation on some of the most gorgeous beaches in Western North America.

Getting Around

By Land

In the 1930s it took 10 days of rugged travel to get from La Paz to Tijuana. The completion of the **Transpeninsular Highway** has made a quicker journey possible, but driving through Baja is still far from easy. A sign at the onset warns that the road was not designed for high-speed driving—and once warned, don't expect to be reminded. Often you'll be safely cruising along at 60mph and suddenly careen into a hidden, poorly banked, rutted curve that can only be taken at 30mph. Still, a car allows you the invaluable freedom to break away from main arteries clogged by your fellow humans.

If you do run into trouble, stay by your car and wait for the *Angeles Verdes* (Green Angels), who pass along Rte. 1 twice per day. These English-speaking mechanics employed by the government provide gas, water, oil, and service and charge only the cost of the materials. Remember that extra gas (unleaded) may be in short supply along this highway, so don't pass a Pemex station without topping off your tank.

All major towns in Baja are served by bus. The gruelling 25-hour bus trip from Tijuana to La Paz costs 97,000 pesos, while you may zip directly to the mainland on ferry for as little as 30,000 pesos. If you plan to navigate the peninsula by bus, be forewarned that almost all *camiones* between Ensenada and La Paz are *de paso.* This means you have to leave at inconvenient times, fight to procure a ticket, and then probably stand the whole way. A much better idea is to buy a reserved seat

UNITED STATES OF AMERICA
Tijuana
Tecate
Mexicali
Ensenada
San Quintin
BAJA CALIFORNIA NORTE
Nogales
Nogales
El Paso
Ciudad Juarez
Casas Grandes
SONORA
Rio Grande
Punta Prieta
Hermosillo
Bahia Kino
CHIHUAHUA
SIERRA MADRE OCCIDENTAL
Piedras Negras
Chihuahua
GOLFO DE CALIFORNIA
Guerrero Negro
Guaymas
Creel
Santa Rosalia
Ciudad Obregon
COAHUILA
Mulege
Navojoa
Alamos
Hidalgo del Parral
Monclova
El Fuerte
Loreto
Los Mochis
Topolobampo
Torreon
BAJA CALIFORNIA SUR
DURANGO
Saltillo
SINALOA
Culiacan
La Paz
Durango
ZACATECAS
San Jose del Cabo
San Lucas
Cabo San Lucas
Mazatlan
Fresnillo
Zacatecas
Chicomoztoc
San Luis Potosi
5
NAYARIT
Aguascalientes
San Blas
Tepic
Lagos de Moreno
Guanajuato
Guadalajara
Irapuato
Puerto Vallarta
4
Chapala
PACIFIC OCEAN
JALISCO
Ciudad Guzman
Morelia
Barra de Navidad
Uruapan
Manzanillo
6
Colima
Tecoman
MICHOACAN
Playa Azul
Ixtapa/Zihuatanejo

in Tijuana, Ensenada, La Paz, or the Cabos, and traverse the peninsula in one shot while seated. Unfortunately you'll miss the fantastic Mulege-Loreto beaches. If you do cover the Baja in stages, always try to be the last to board. This way, you can place yourself in the front, where the air is freshest and where you can watch the scenery through the large driver's windows. Gambling this way means a higher risk of not getting a ticket, though you can usually sit on the floor or the steps.

Anyway you cut it, though, the Baja beaches and other points of interest off the main highway are often inaccessible on public transportation; buses don't stop at coastal spots between Tijuana and San Quintín. Near Muelegé, Loreto, La Paz, and the Cabos (capes) on Baja's southern tip, travelers tied to the bus system can make a short walk from the main road to some of the beaches.

By Sea

Ferry service was instituted in the mid-60s as a means of supplying Baja with food and supplies, not as a source of tourist transportation. Boats have come to serve *viajeros,* and passenger vehicles may take up any space left over after the first-priority commercial vehicles. For those who plan to take a car over to Baja from the mainland, the best advice is to make reservations one month in advance, either through a travel agent or with the ferry office directly. (See La Paz, Getting There for details.)

There are three different ferry routes: Santa Rosalía to Guaymas (7 hr.); La Paz to Topolobampo/Los Mochis (9 hr.); and La Paz to Mazatlán (16 hr.). If you wish to avoid the less interesting northern half of the peninsula, take the Guaymas-Santa Rosalía route. This allows you to wind your way southward to La Paz before taking a boat back to the mainland. The La Paz to Topolobampo/Los Mochis route provides direct access to the train from Los Mochis through the Barranca del Cobre (Copper Canyon).

Ferry tickets are generally expensive (prices listed below are for the La Paz to Topolobampo/Los Mochis route), even for *turista*-class berths—two to a cabin with a sink (bathrooms and showers down the hall, 60,000 pesos). It's extremely difficult to find tickets for *turista* class and *cabina* class (bathroom in the room, 90,000 pesos), and snagging an *especial*-class berth (a real hotel room, 120,000 pesos) is as likely as stumbling upon a snowball in the central Baja desert; there are only two such suites on each ferry. This leaves the bottom-of-the-line *salón*-class ticket (30,000 pesos), which entitles you to a bus-style seat. If, as is likely, you find yourself traveling *salón* at night, ditch the seats and stake out a spot on the floor early on—just spread out your sleeping bag and snooze. For exact prices, check the Getting There section of the towns, and for further ferry information call Mr. Martín Vargas at the State Tourist Department (tel. 81-94-92, 93, or 94).

Always bring food on ferry trips; boat restaurants are prohibitively expensive.

By Air

A 20-min. flight from La Paz to Los Mochis costs about 90,000 pesos; the flight between Tijuana and La Paz takes one and a half hours and will set you back 357,116 pesos. From Tijuana, **Aeroméxico,** 1236 Revolucion (tel. 85-44-01) flies to Mexico City and Guadalajara five times per day; **Mexicana,** 2800 Gobernador Baladezo, (tel. 81-75-72) flies to Mexico City twice per day (via La Paz or Zacatecas); **Aerocalifornia,** C-19 Paseo de los Heroes (tel. 84-20-06) has several planes per day to Guadalajara via Los Mochis, plus short flights from La Paz to the Cabos.

Baja California Norte

Tijuana

Tijuana's "Mexican culture" is about as authentic as the cheap tissue-paper flowers that adorn every vendor's cart, but there's a certain raunchy charm about this city that attracts tourists by the bushel. For only a few dollars, you can settle back in a side bar where the beer flows freely and enjoy the music as it drifts through the streets. In typical Mexican fashion, food is zesty, spicy, and salty and will satisfy the cravings of your stomach without testing the limits of your wallet.

If shopping for that which is small and purely ornamental is your passion, Tijuana is your long-lost homeland. There are enough black-velvet portraits of Jesus and Elvis for sale here to start your own gallery back home. The mounds of kitsch for sale astound—but be strong and make sure you're truly, deeply in love before you buy. That day-glo *serape* could haunt the back of your closet for generations.

Banners boldly proclaim Av. Revolución the "Most Visited Street in the World," and when you see the crowds, you'll find that boast easy to believe. Every weekend, swarms of people abandon themselves into the pulsating wave of music at the numerous flashy discos, drowning their sorrows in drink and dancing till dawn. If you can make it past the dirty streets (and mangy dogs), you'll find yourself in the eye of the Republic's free-est party.

Since World War II, Tijuana's population has swelled to nearly 2 million in the metropolitan area. First settled by the Cochimie, Tijuana made it onto the map in 1829, when Don Santiago Argüello received the title to the Rancho de Tía Juana (Aunt Jane's Ranch). After the 1848 Mexican-American War, the ranch became the new border, and its name was amalgamated.

Nowadays, thousands use this northernmost Mexican point as a springboard for undocumented emigration to the States. Thousands more await their turns in shantytown shacks along the border. Other Mexicans come here to study at the Ibero-American University, one of the finest in northern Mexico. Most, however, arrive to buy discounted non-Mexican goods: cameras, leather, alcohol, name-brand clothing, and perfume.

On Sundays, the city puts on immensely popular bullfights and horse races. Thick crowds of San Diegans descend upon Tijuana throughout the weekend; unless you're here for the fights or the races, try to visit on a weekday.

Orientation and Practical Information

Getting from San Diego to Tijuana is easy: take the **San Diego trolley** from downtown (US$1.50), or join it anywhere along the route. It lets you off right at the border-crossing. Returning is not so simple, thanks to long customs inspection lines. Motorists can drive across the border, but the hassles of obtaining Mexican insurance (U.S. policies are useless in Mexico) make this a bad idea for daytripping gringos. You must buy insurance—if you get into an accident without it, your car will probably be confiscated and you may be thrown into jail. A better idea is to leave your car in a parking lot on the U.S. side of the border and either walk or take a taxi into town. To go the opposite direction, catch a bus at Calle 3 and Niños Heroes.

Almost everything worth seeing in Tijuana is within walking distance. Buses (700 pesos) marked "Centro" run to *el centro;* look to the left as you exit the bus station. The ride from the terminal to Revolución takes a half hour because the bus stops every ten feet. If you're in a hurry, take a taxi from the terminal to town.

Tourist Office: De Comercio and Revolución (tel. 88-16-85). English-speaking staff with oodles of information. Ms. Cirramy Dupoux is especially helpful. Open daily 9am-7pm. **ASETUR** tourist office at the border (88-17-31).

State Attorney for the Protection of the Tourist: Same address as tourist office (tel. 81-94-92). Phone service Mon.-Sat. 9am-7pm. Open 24 hrs.

State Dept. of Tourism of Baja California: Tel. 84-21-27. **Baja California Information Center in San Diego:** Tel. (800) 522-1516.

Customs Office: At the border (tel. 83-13-88).

Consulates: U.S., Tapachula Sur 96 (tel. 81-74-00), at Colonia Hipódromo, adjacent to the Agua Caliente racetrack southeast of town. Open Mon.-Fri. 8am-4:30pm. **Canada,** German Gedovius 5-202 (tel. 84-04-61), Zona del Río.

Currency Exchange: Banks along Revolución change at the same rate. **Bánamex** and **Internacional** accept traveler's checks. Open daily 8:30am-1:30pm.

Post Office: Negrete at Calle 11. Lista de Correos. Open Mon.-Fri. 8am-7pm. Sat.-Sun. 9am-1pm. **Postal Code:** 22000.

Telephones: Farmacia Mayo, 1st and Mutualismo (tel. 855-600). No collect calls. Local calls 1000 pesos. Open daily 8am-midnight. Pay phones on the street are unreliable and operators are few and far between. Long-distance phone calls are much cheaper from the U.S. **Telephone Code:** 668.

Telegrams: At the post office (tel. 84-77-65). Open Mon.-Fri. 8am-8pm. Sat.-Sun. 8am-1pm.

Bus Station: (tel. 261-701). Huge station laid with spiffy marble floors. **Transportes Norte de Sonora** (tel. 86-90-26) to: Guadalajara (12 per day, express at 9am, 132,000 pesos); Mexico City (12 per day, 166,000 pesos); Mazatlán; Los Mochis; Hermosillo; Puerto Peñasco. **Autotransportes de la Baja California** to: Ensenada (every hr., 1½ hr., 6000 pesos); Guerrero Negro (3 per day, 47,000 pesos); Mulege (1 per day, 65,000 pesos); Loreto (74,000 pesos); La Paz. Other companies at the station include **Tres Estrellas de Oro** (tel. 86-91-86) and **Transportes de Pacífico** (tel. 85-49-81). **Greyhound** reaches northward to San Diego and beyond. Green-and-white **Autotransportes de la Baja California** buses leave for Rosarito (every hr., 1 hr., 2000 pesos) from the old bus station at Madero and Calle 1, 1 block from the tourist office on Revolución. *Taxis de ruta* to Rosarito leave from Madero between Calles 4 and 5. (See Rosarito for details.)

Car Insurance: If you'll be driving in Mexico, spend US$9.50 in San Ysidro to get insurance. There are several drive-through insurance vendors just before the border at Sycamore and Primero, who distribute a free booklet with maps and travel tips. Without insurance, you'll go to jail if you're involved in an accident.

Red Cross: Tel. 132. For non-emergencies, dial 85-81-91.

Pharmacy: Botica Sherr, Constitución at Calle 31 (tel. 85-39-38). Open 24 hr.

Hospital: Hospital General, Río Tijuana Ote. (tel. 84-09-22).

Police: Constitución at Calle 8. In case of emergency, dial 134. For other matters, dial 85-70-90. There is always a bilingual officer at the station.

Accommodations

Budget hotels in Tijuana are trapped in the vortex of the town, off Revolución and Calle 1. Prices are monstrous by Mexican standards. Reservations are a necessity on weekends. Most hotels accept dollars and pesos.

Hotel Texano, Calle 1 #1710 (tel. 38-43-15). Large, clean rooms with visually offensive furniture. If you get tired of the TV in your room, there's one in the lobby. Singles US$16, with bath US$21. Doubles all with bath US$35.

Motel Díaz, Revolución Nte. 375 (tel. 85-71-48), near Calle 1. Designed to the dictator's specifications: clean and comfortable. Singles and doubles US$25.

Hotel Poinsettia (Super 8), Constitución 1206 (tel. 85-19-12), between Calles 9 and 10. Brand new place proudly advertises its cable TV, phones, and chilly A/C. Perfect, except for the price. Singles US$30. Doubles US$35.

Hotel Plaza de Oro (Best Western), Revolución 277 (tel. 38-41-12), near Calle 1. Has TV, peach-toned phone, and still-lifes of lilies, just like the one in Moscow, Idaho. Singles US$35. Doubles US$40.

Hotel Nelson, Revolución 503 (tel. 85-43-02). Large well-kept rooms with wall-to-wall carpeting, clean bathroom, A/C, color TV, and phone. Great location and elevator. Singles and doubles 61,000 pesos. With TV 72,500 pesos.

Motel Alaska, Calle 1 #1950 (tel. 85-36-81), entrance at Revolución. Clean rooms are popular with families, probably because of the good rates for large rooms and private parking ample enough for station wagons. Singles 75,000 pesos. Doubles 85,000 pesos. Six people 95,000 pesos.

Hotel Perla del Occidente, Mutualismo 528 (tel. 85-13-58), between Calles 1 and 2. Sullen management. The green skylight lends a gloomy air to the hallways, but clean rooms and bathrooms are an anomalous surprise. Wall-to-wall carpeting and mammoth beds. Singles 45,000. Doubles 70,000 pesos.

Hotel Las Palmas, Calle 1 #1637 (tel. 85-13-48), near Mutualismo. Colorful courtyard decorated in the popular rosebush and dripping laundry motif. Tidy rooms with clean communal bathrooms. Singles 40,000 pesos. Doubles 60,000 pesos.

Food

The less expensive *típico* restaurants are on Madero and the streets leading from glitzy Revolución to Madero. On every corner, people sell fruit cocktails and melon cups (2500 pesos).

Deep-fried *churros,* a heart-stopping snack, cost 1500 pesos. As always, use your head when choosing what to eat; some vendors are not picky about how long they hold on to stock. If you'd rather not gamble with your health on the street, bar munchies are cheap, filling, and safe. Water is generally safe to drink in Tijuana, which shares its main water supply, the diminishing Colorado River, with San Diego.

Restaurant May, Callejon El Travieso #10, (tel. 85-06-74), on a small street that connects Calles 2 and 3 just off of Revolución. Scarf Mexican staples in yellow booths and off the overly-beaten track. *Enchiladas,* tacos, *flautas* all 9500 pesos. Open Mon.-Sat. 8am-6pm.

Restaurant Nelson, Revolución 503, under Hotel Nelson. Good, cheap, and undiscovered as yet by San Diegans. *Huevos revueltos* 3500 pesos. Hamburger 4200 pesos. *Antojitos* 7-9000 pesos. Open daily 7am-11pm.

Tilly's Fifth Avenue, at Revolución and Calle 5. Expect blaring music and lots of ravenous bourgeois in search of the perfect T-shirt. An *enchilada,* taco, and soup cost US$4. Open Mon.-Thurs. 9am-2am and Fri.-Sun. 9am-4am.

La Casa de Alicia, Madero 1246, off Calle 9. The enthusiasm of the management compensates for the insufficient size of the portions. *Comida corrida* 9000 pesos. Standard Mexican fare 11,000 pesos. Open daily 8am-6pm.

The original and vaguely legendary **Tía Juana Tilly's** is next door to the Jai Alai Palace at Revolución and Calle 7a. Since 1947, the bar, now with restaurant, dance floor, and outside patio, has been generating high-action, high-price atmosphere. Enjoy one of their rocket-fuel margaritas (4000 pesos) and people-watch from the patio. All-you-can-eat tacos (US$5) Fri.-Sun. 11am-3pm (terrace open daily 11am-11pm. Dancing Fri.-Sun. 9pm-2am).

Activities

For mild, inexpensive fun, try snacking and people-watching while strolling down **Revolución. Teniente Guerrero Park,** between 5 de Mayo and González Ortega, off Díaz Mirón, is one of the most pleasant parts of Tijuana, and only a few blocks from Revolución. Tijuana is also a great place to get your car re-upholstered—really.

The cultish game of **jai-alai** is played every night (except Thurs.) at 8pm in the Frontón Palacio, Revolución at Calle 7, a building decorated more like a palace than a sports center. Two two-player teams, identified by colored arm bands, compete inside the walled court. A Brazilian ball of rubber and yarn encased in goatskin is thrown at speeds reaching 180 mph and caught in arm-baskets after hitting the back wall of the court. The fast-paced game is played to 21, with lots of betting each round. All employees are bilingual, and the gambling is carried out in greenbacks. General admission US$3, reserved seats US$4. Gates open at 7pm. Call 85-16-12 for more information, (619) 260-0452 from the U.S.

Agua Caliente Racetrack (tel. 81-78-11), also called the Hipódromo, attracts enormous crowds year-round with greyhound races (Fri. and Mon. at 2pm and Wed.-Mon. at 7:45pm) and horse races (Sat.-Sun. at 12:45pm). The track's enclosed **Turf Club** (tel. 86-39-48) has comfortable seating and a restaurant; grandstand admission (nearly 11,000 seats) is free.

The bullfight is one of the great cultural signifiers of the 20th century; to Hemingway it was the last gasp of Romantic heroism, to Picasso it embodied the intense, inevitable cruelty of sexuality. Olé. Tijuana has two bullrings, **El Toreo de Tijuana,** downtown, and **Plaza Monumental,** 3km east on Agua Caliente, by the sea. The former presents *corridas* (bullfights) on Sundays at 4pm from early May to late September; the latter is more modern, features famous *matadores,* and hosts fights from early August to mid-September. Tickets are sold at Revolución 815 (tel. 85-22-10) from 10am to 7pm, or at the gate. Admission ranges from US$5-22, depending on the seat. San Diego (tel. (619) 231-3554).

The **Tijuana Centro Cultural,** Paseo de los Héroes and Mina (tel. 84-11-11), is worth visiting for its architecture alone. The center displays an elegant geographical and chronological survey of Mexico, as well as rotating exhibitions of modern art. (Admission 2500 pesos.) A performance center **(Sala de Espectáculos)** and open-air theater **(Caracol al Aire Libre)** host visiting cultural attractions, including the **Ballet Folklórico,** *mariachis,* and various drama performances.

Entertainment

Clubs is what we mean. A brief stroll down Revolución at dusk will get you bombarded by thumping music and abrasive club promoters all hawking basically the same thing (2-for-1 margaritas, starting from an inflated price). Although a few sleazy strip joints stud the strand, most clubs scream out for old-fashioned boozin' and *bailando,* and they get it. All Tijuana clubs check ID's (18+), with varying criteria for what is acceptable.

Peanuts and Beer, on a small walking street sandwiched between Calles 3 and 4. Glow in the dark psychedelic paint splashes spur on the young crowd. Drinks US$3.50. Cover US$2 on Sat. only. Open in summer Wed.-Sun. 8pm-3am. All other seasons Fri.-Sun. ID (and ID) necessary.

Tilly's 5th Avenue, on Revolución at 5a. Calle. Lights flash and the floor vibrates; the walls are laden with hats, photos, and sports and music equipment. A big-screen TV projects sporting events. Beer US$1, tequila US$2. No cover. Open Mon.-Thurs. 9am-2am and Fri.-Sun. 9am-4am. DMV only ID.

Margarita Village, Revolución 1020. No cover. Margaritas US$2.50. Open Sun.-Thurs. 10am-2am and Fri.-Sat. 10am-4am. Strict ID.

Escape,Revolución 938. A real thumper. Beer US$1. Margaritas US$2. No cover. Open daily noon-2am. ID necessary.

Tequila Sunrise, Revolución 918. They advertise a free tequila shot. Beer US$1.50. No cover. Open daily 5pm-2am. ID necessary.

Ensenada

The secret is out: beachless Ensenada is fast becoming a top weekend hotspot south of the border. The masses of Californians that arrive every Friday night have gringoized the town to an extreme degree; everything here is in English, down to the taco sales-pitches, and the store clerks whip out calculators if you try to buy something with pesos. Still, Ensenada is less brash than its insatiable cousin, Tijuana, to the north, and becomes quite pleasant Monday morning when the *gringos* head home and the cool sea breeze kicks in.

The drive from Tijuana to Ensenada is beautiful, if you take the Ensenada Cuota (toll road), which costs 6000 pesos. The *libre* (free) road is atrocious—poorly maintained, dangerous, and about as scenic as a municipal garbage dump. Along the toll road you'll enjoy sparkling ocean vistas, large sand dunes, stark cliffs, and broad mesas. Drive in the right lane only; the left is strictly for passing and the law is enforced. Also, drive only in daytime as the road is not lit.

Orientation and Practical Information

Ensenada is 108km south of Tijuana on Rte. 1. Buses from Tijuana arrive at the main terminal, at Calle 11 and Miramar, every half hour between 7am and 10pm and every hour between 11pm and 1am.

Ten blocks down Miramar from the bus station is Mateos (tel. 867-70), also called 1st, the main tourist drag, and 5 blocks south along Mateos you'll find the less expensive hotels. Prepare yourself for a nice jaunt or a 10,000-15,000-peso cab ride.

Tourist Office: Mateos 1350 (tel. 622-22), at Espinoza, office 13-B. Brochures from expensive hotels, some town maps, and other Baja travel material. Open Mon.-Fri. 9am-7pm. Sat. 9am-3pm and Sun. 10am-2pm. **Chamber of Commerce,** Mateos 693 (tel. 837-70), at Macheros. Closer to the center of town, with brochures, city maps and more helpful English-speaking staff. Open Mon.-Fri. 9am-6pm.

Customs: At Ruíz and Reyersow (tel. 408-997). Open Mon.-Fri. 8am-3pm.

Attorney for Protection of Tourists: Mateos 1360 (tel. 638-86), office 12-B. In the tourist office. Open Mon.-Fri. 9am-7pm, Sat. 9am-3pm, and Sun. 10am-2pm.

Currency Exchange: The banks clump along Juárez Ave., four blocks east of Mateos. They are generally open Mon.-Fri. 9am-12:30pm. **Banco Internacional** at Gastelum and Juárez stays open until 1:30pm. If it's after hours, there's an abundance of *casas de cambio.*

Post Office: Mateos at Floresta (tel. 637-18). Open Mon.-Fri. 8am-7pm, Sat.-Sun. 9am-noon. **Postal Code:** 22860.

Telephones: Casa de Larga Distancia. No collect calls. Open daily 8am-8pm. Collect calls can be made from any of the many public pay phones: dial 02 for the international operator. **Telephone Code:** 607.

Laundromat: Blanca, Cortés at Reforma (tel. 626-48), in the Limón shopping center. Large wash 5000 pesos, dry 750 pesos, detergent 800 pesos. Open Mon.-Sat. 7am-9:30pm, Sun. 7am-4pm.

Red Cross: Clark Flores at Colonia Ampliación Moderna (tel. 812-12 or 814-88). In medical emergencies, dial 132.

Pharmacies: Farmacia Regia, Mateos 628-B. (tel. 405-57) Open daily 8am-10pm. **Farmacia El Sol,** Centro Comercial Limón (tel. 637-75). Open 24 hrs

Hospital: Ruíz 1380 (tel. 403-08), at Calle 14. **Sanatorio St. Gabriel,** 4th and Espinoza (tel. 625-19). Open 24 hrs.

Police: Calle 9 at Floresta (tel. 624-21 or 626-96). Branch at Mateos and Espinoza (tel. 613-11 or 636-40), next to the tourist office. In emergencies, dial 134.

Supermarket: Calimax at Juárez and Espinoza. Open daily 7am-10pm.

Accommodations

Rooms in Ensenada might seem inexpensive if you're arriving from the U.S., but compared to the rest of Mexico, they're not. Cheaper hotels line Mateos between Espinoza and Granada, while the nicer lodging zone is along Mateos north of Castillo. It's simple to get a room in the middle of the week, but on weekends if you want a bed you should be lounging in a hotel lobby at check-out time. Although most prices are quoted in greenbacks, pesos are accepted by all.

Motel Bungalows Playa, Mateos 1487 (tel. 614-30), about a block from the tourist office. If only every bungalow on the beach were like this. Freshly remodeled, with cable TV and wall-to-wall carpeting. Spic-and-span. Singles and doubles US$35. Rooms in the old wing are US$20.

Motel America, Espinoza 1309 (tel. 613-33), at Mateos. If you went on vacation looking to cook and sleep under lavender felt, look no further. Large rooms have kitchenettes with stove, refrigerator, and purified water. Singles US$20. Doubles US$28.

Coronado Motel, Mateos 1275 (tel. 614-16). All rooms are doubles, but should you desire a single, no problem: they'll happily remove one of the beds. However, if you don't like the tacky wall-to-wall carpeting or fake-wood veneer, you'll have to tough it. Singles US$15. Doubles US$25. Quad US$25.

Motel Colón, ½ block from Bungalows Playa (tel. 619-10), on the right-hand side of Guadalupe. Full kitchenettes with stove, sink, cabinets, and table. Very friendly, English-speaking proprietor. Singles US$20. Doubles US$25. Owner will lend utensils.

Pancho Motel, Alvarado at Calle 2 (tel. 823-44), 1 block off Mateos. Super location. Chic it's not: orange plastic bus-station-type chairs and shredded nylon bedspreads. Check-out noon. Singles US$15. Doubles US$18.

Food

The cheapest restaurants are along Juárez near Ruíz and Gastelum; those on Mateos and near the water are more expensive.

Cafetería Anali, Calle 9 and Espinoza (tel. 640-41). Near the budget hotel district. Local crowd fills the tables around dinnertime. Cheap breakfasts, too. Open Mon.-Sat. 6am-11pm.

Antojitos de la Chispa, across from Bungalows Playa on Mateos. This tiny cafeteria serves the tastiest tacos (2500 pesos) in Baja California. Phenomenal *burritos* (with *tortillas* 1 ft. in diameter) 6500 pesos. Open daily 1-11pm.

Restaurant-Patio Las Brasas, Mateos 486 (tel. 811-95). An open grill with 12 fowl roasting, 11 cooks a-tortilla-patting, and 10 waiters scurrying. Dark palette and lots of wood set the tone. Large portions, but rather expensive. Half chicken with potatoes 16,000 pesos. No partridge in a pear tree, though. Open Wed.-Mon. 11am-10pm.

Restaurante Los Cabas, Gastelum 167. Green-and-white tiled floor. Vinyl booths and fake vines. *Enchiladas rojas* (8500 pesos) or ham and eggs 8000 pesos. Open daily 7am-9:30pm.

La Uva, 1433 4th at Floresta (tel 703-01). Red carnations match the trucks in the beer-ad-posters, "health" and vegetarian foods are the specialty. *Pollo con mole* or vegetarian *hamburguesas* 8000 pesos. Fruit salad 7000 pesos. *Licuados* 5500 pesos. Open daily 8am-8pm.

Sights and Activities

Seeing Ensenada requires more than a quick cruise down Mateos. Climb the **Chapultepec Hills** for a view of the entire city. The steep road leading to the top of the hill begins at the foot of Calle 2. Any number of dirt paths also wind over the nearby hills, which afford a pleasant ocean view. Watch out for broken glass and pack sunscreen and water.

The English-language *Baja Times* is full of bureaucratic propaganda and upcoming event announcements. Enormous quantities of low-quality curios are for sale along Mateos, but the **FONART** government store, Mateos 1306 (tel. 915-36), next to the tourist office at Espinoza, has high-quality authentic work. Most things you will see here are produced in southern Mexico, where they can be had for less is you're headed that way. Bargaining is verboten. (Open daily 9am-2pm and 3-6pm.) Baja's free-port status makes Ensenada a good place to purchase imported goods. Try the various shops along Juárez, including **La Joya,** at Ruíz.

The mild, dry climate of Northern Baja's Pacific coast has made it Mexico's prime grape-growing area, and **Bodegas de Santo Tomás,** Miramar 666 (tel. 678-25-09), produces 5000 cases of wine every year. The Bodegas have been in business since 1888. Tours (US$1.50) are conducted Monday through Saturday at 11am, 1pm, and 3pm and include winetasting with bread and cheese.

The **Vapor Catalina,** a tycoon's old cruise ship that has been converted into a floating mall, is tethered to the docks at the end of Av. Riviera. There are two restaurants on board (the informal San Valentín, on deck, serves Mexican/American cuisine; below, the semi-formal Restaurante Catalina specializes in nouvelle cuisine) as well as a disco, a snack bar, several curio shops, and a tourist office booth (tel. 832-22).

Entertainment

Most of the popular hangouts along Mateos are members of that common hybrid species, the restaurant/bar/disco. In most, food and drink are served only until 6pm or so; they turn into full-fledged discos after 8pm. The best of these is **Bananas,** at Mateos 477 (tel. 820-04). Cover charges here average US$3.50 and apply only on weekend nights. Get there before 8pm and you won't have to pay. Some other popular spots include: **Confetti's,** Alvarado at Paseo Costero (tel. 812-56); **El Osito,** Blancarte near Mateos (tel. 816-01), at the Travel Lodge, drinks 5000 pesos; **Valentino's,** #915 Paseo Costero, between Blancarte and Alvarado (tel. 400-22). Open noon-11pm; **Las Cazuelas,** #6 General Agustín Sanguines (tel. 610-44) at Las Dunas. Beer 5000 pesos. Open 10am-2am.

Better known than Ensenada itself is **Hussong's Cantina,** on Ruíz between Mateos and Calle 2. A vastly overrated, overcrowded, and overpriced hangout, its main claims to fame are the Hussong's bumper stickers and T-shirts which crop up all over the Baja. When you tire of the pencil drawings and continuous stream of *mariachi* musicians, cross the street to **Papas and Beer**. This upscale, glitzy restaurant/bar/disco fills with San Diegan weekend warriors, who swill huge margaritas (12,000 pesos) and spend corresponding amouts of cash. Beer 6000 pesos (Open daily noon-3am).

Near Ensenada

Since the town's beaches suffer from their proximity to a major fishing port, visitors to Ensenada concentrate on shopping, eating, and partying. About 11km north lies **Playa San Miguel.** About 8km to the south are **Playas Santa María** and **Estero.** All are sandy and clean, but the hyperactivity might drive you crazy. Farther south you'll find quieter beaches: try **San Quintín,** two hours south of town by car. Locals make their way to the Bahía San Quintín for three reasons: the cool climate, the lack of tourists, and the large clam population near the *Molino Viejo,* by El Presidente 6km south of the city of San Quintín.Rosario, another modest beach town, lies 58km south of San Quintín on the Transpeninsular Hwy.

La Bufadora, the largest geyser on the Pacific coast, is 30km south of Ensenada. On a good day, the "Blowhole" shoots water 40m into the air. Share the spectacle with the local sea lions. **Agua Caliente** hot springs (admission US$3) are 35km east on Rte. 3. **San Carlos** hot springs, accessed by a dirt road 16km south of town, are not especially clean (admission US$4) Both are hotspots.

HAWAII

No alien land in all the world has any deep, strong charm for me but that one, no other land could so longingly and beseechingly haunt me, sleeping and waking, through half a lifetime, as that one has done. Other things leave me, but it abides; other things change, but it remains the same....In my nostrils still lives the breath of flowers that perished twenty years ago.

—Mark Twain

Mark Twain's effusive recollections of his 1889 trip to what were then called the Sandwich Islands foreshadow the exotic image that Hawaii conjures today. Dribbled across the ocean blue of the Pacific, 2400 miles off mainland America, the state is both physically and psychologically set apart from the rest of the United States. Here, as nowhere else, you will find lush vegetation, expansive beaches, towering surf, and sultry breezes that keep the islands' weather uniformly wonderful. Acres of untainted tropical forest abut luxurious resort areas and bustling urban enclaves. Meanwhile, active volcanoes crag the horizon and release billows of grey into the air. It sounds Elysian. Indeed, it *is.*

The state's cultural geography is as varied as its land's. Hawaii is one of the most ethnically diverse regions in the world; as a community with no racial majority, the state serves as a bridge between East and West and as a melting pot for a multitude of cultures. This diverse cultural heritage expresses itself in the arts, literature, and cuisine of Hawaii's residents.

162 islands comprise the Hawaiian chain, though only seven are inhabited. The cosmopolitan capital of Honolulu makes its home on the island of Oahu, as do over 80% of the state's one million residents. Virtually all of the tourists stay in the hotel district of Oahu's Waikiki. The Big Island (officially called Hawaii) is famed for its Kona coffee, volcanoes, macadamia nuts, and black sand beaches. Maui, with the historic whaling village of Lahaina, fantastic surfing, and the extinct volcanic crater of Haleakala, is the "neighbor island" to which Oahuans most frequently escape. The green isle of Kauai at the northwestern end of the inhabited islands ranks first for sheer beauty. Molokai, once stigmatized by its leper colony, now crawls with imported African wildlife, while on tiny Lani the pineapple is ubiquitous. The seventh populated isle, Niihau, is taboo to most, supporting just a few hundred plantation families who still converse in the Hawaiian language. Together, the islands present an astonishing variety of geography and culture; they are, to continue with the words of Twain, "the loveliest fleet of islands that lies anchored in any ocean."

When in Hawaii, do as the Bradys do. First, you must enjoy the weather and the islands' natural environs. Witness lava ooze out of Kilauea and drift down to the sea, investigate off-shore aquatic life with a snorkel, amble along the beach and into caves, or enter a surfing competition as Mike, Carol, and the rest of your picture-perfect family look on in support. Tourist-tailored traps will draw you of course, and you might well beckon their call. Take in a family luau or sign up for hula lessons (just be careful not to throw your back out, as dear old Alice did). All the while, attune your sixth sense to the mysteries of the islands; join Bobby in learning about the taboos and gods which rule Hawaiian spiritual life.

Above all, explore the indigenous culture of the islands. Take in exhibits of the native handicrafts on display in markets and museums or delve into a book about the region. Not everyone will be treated to a ukulele lesson from Don Ho, as Cindy was, but with a little effort you can escape the islands' jejune commercialism and get a true taste of Hawaii's unique flavor. With this prescription to guide you, we

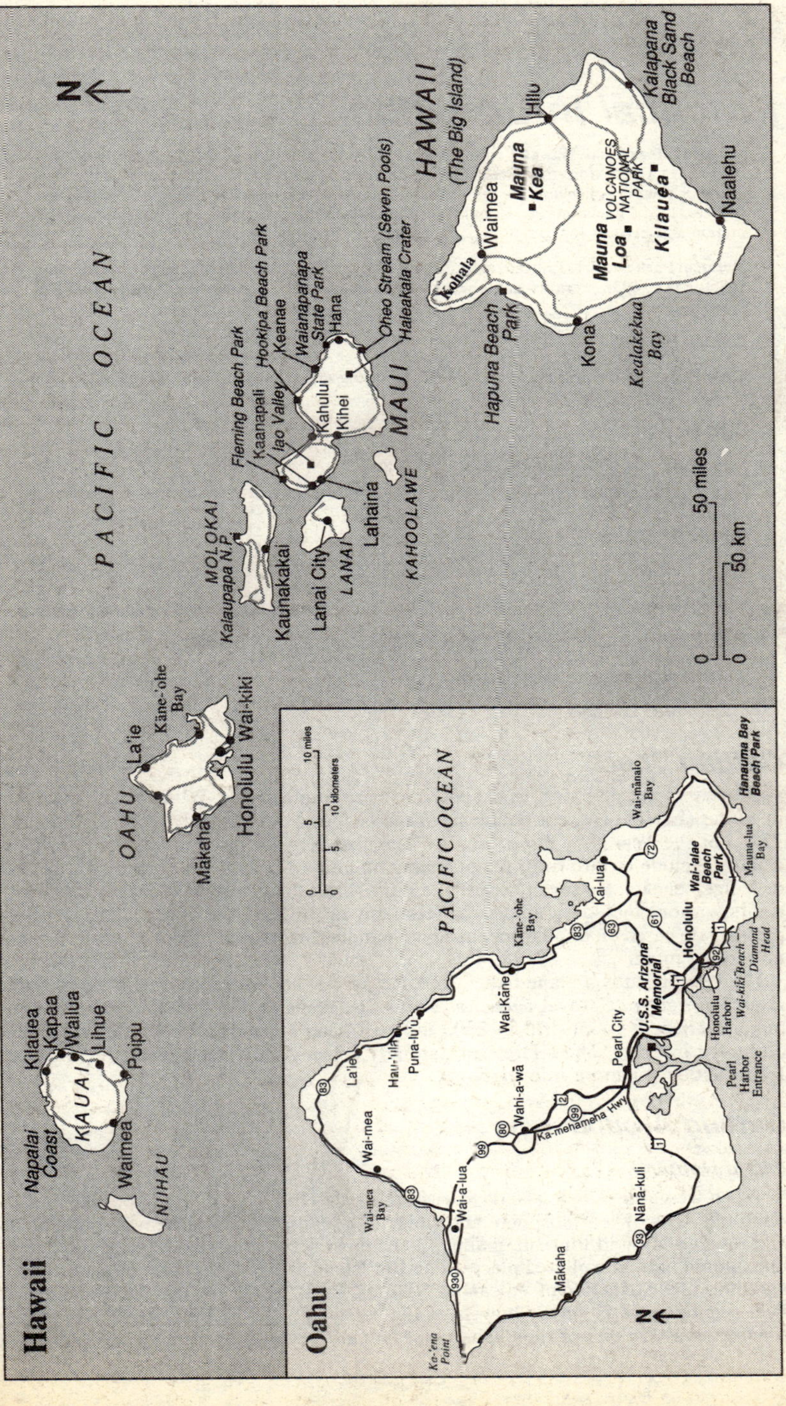
Hawaii
N
PACIFIC OCEAN
Napalai Coast
Kilauea
Kapaa
Wailua
Lihue
Poipu
Waimea
KAUAI
NIIHAU
OAHU
La'ie
Kāne-'ohe Bay
Honolulu
Wai-kiki
Mākaha
MOLOKAI
Kalaupapa N.P.
Kaunakakai
Lanai City
LANAI
Lahaina
KAHOOLAWE
Fleming Beach Park
Kaanapali
Iao Valley
Hookipa Beach Park
Keanae
Waianapanapa State Park
Hana
Kahului
Kihei
MAUI
Oheo Stream (Seven Pools)
Haleakala Crater
HAWAII
(The Big Island)
Hapuna Beach Park
Kohala
Waimea
Mauna Kea
Hilo
Mauna Loa
VOLCANOES NATIONAL PARK
Kilauea
Kalapana Black Sand Beach
Naalehu
Kona
Kealakekua Bay
0 50 miles
0 50 km
Oahu
N
PACIFIC OCEAN
0 5 10 miles
0 5 10 kilometers
Ka-'ena Point
Wai-mea Bay
Wai-mea
La'ie
Hau'ula
Puna-lu'u
Wai-Kāne
Kāne-'ohe Bay
Kai-lua
Wai-mānalo Bay
Hanauma Bay Beach Park
Mauna-lua Bay
Wai-'alae Beach Park
Diamond Head
Wai-kiki Beach
Honolulu
Honolulu Harbor
U.S.S. Arizona Memorial
Pearl City
Pearl Harbor Entrance
Wahi-a-wā
Wai-a-lua
Ka-mehameha Hwy
Mākaha
Nānā-kuli
83
99
80
930
93
1
2
61
63
72
92

at *Let's Go* know (it's much more than a hunch) that you'll enjoy your island stay a whole bunch.

Practical Information

Visitors Information: Hawaii Visitors Bureau, 2270 Kalakaua Ave., #1108, Honolulu 96815 (923-1811). Open Mon.-Fri. 8am-4:30pm. The ultimate source. The other islands staff offices at major towns, as listed in the appropriate sections. **Department of Land and Natural Resources,** 1151 Punchbowl St., Honolulu 96813 (548-7455). Open Mon.-Fri. 8am-4pm. Information and permits for camping in state parks, and trail maps.

National Park Service, Prince Kuhio Federal Bldg., #6305, 300 Ala Moana Blvd., Honolulu 96850 (541-2693). Permits are given at individual park headquarters. Open Mon.-Fri. 7:30am-4pm.

Capital: Honolulu.

Time Zone: Hawaii (3 hrs. behind Pacific in spring and summer; 2 hrs. otherwise). 11-13 hrs. of daylight year-round.

Drinking Age: 21.

Sales Tax: 4%; hotel rooms 9%.

Postal Abbreviation: HI.

Area Code: 808.

Major Newspapers: the *Advertiser* and the *Honolulu Star-Bulletin.* On Maui, *The Maui News.*

Motto: *Ua mau ke ea o ka aina i ka pono.* (The life of the land is perpetuated in righteousness.)

State Fish: Humuhumunukunuku-a-pua'au ("fish with pig-like snout").

State Bird: Nene, a rare clawed goose.

State Flower: Hibiscus.

Getting There

Reaching paradise isn't as expensive as you might think. While prices increase in winter (Feb.-April), reasonable fares can be found even then. Investigate the *L.A. Times* or the *New York Times* Sunday Travel section for discount packages, which usually include airfare from major mainland cities, accommodations, and a bevvy of fringe benefits. Be sure to learn the nitty gritty details: tour packages often list sights without including admission fees, and rates listed are almost always a per person rate based on double occupancy. An individual traveling alone usually winds up paying more.

If all you need is a plane ticket, look for special advance purchase fares or bulk rates from cut-rate travel agencies. From Los Angeles and San Francisco, many major carriers fly round-trip for $300 and up. **Cheap Tickets** (808-947-3717) in Honolulu, for instance, offers fares substantially below APEX rates. (See the General Introduction for more information.)

Getting Around

Island Hopping

When weighing which islands to visit, think carefully about what you like to do. Each offers its own atmosphere and range of activities. Oahu is heavily populated and revolves around tourism, making it the most accessible island, but leaving few unexplored and unexploited places. The Big Island (Hawaii) has lots of open space and the added attraction of Volcanoes National Park, where you can see the goddess Pele spit hot lava from the bowels of the earth into the boiling ocean. Kauai, at the northwestern end of the chain, comes a close second for pure visual splendor;

nicknamed the Garden Island, Kauai's lush green cliffs and dramatic waterfalls are surrounded by cherished surfing waters. Maui's strong winds have made it one of the premier windsurfing destinations of the world and with the windsurfers comes a hopping nightlife. Molokai is for the solitude-seeking traveler. With 6,000 inhabitants, the "Friendly Isle" still moves to the slow, quiet rhythms of the Pacific. Lanai, the most remote island of all, is for the off-road adventurer who enjoys hiking and diving—and pineapples. Regular ferry service exists only between Maui, Molokai, and Lanai. Cruise ships and private fishing boats will carry passengers to the other islands, but their prices are often exorbitant. Airlines are faster and more convenient, and often offer special deals on car rentals. The major inter-island carriers, **Hawaiian** and **Aloha Airlines,** can jet you quickly (about 40 min.) from Honolulu to any of the islands. Travel agents, such as **Pali Tour and Travel, Inc.,** 1304 Pali Hwy. (533-3608), in Honolulu, sell Hawaiian Air inter-island coupon books that are extremely convenient for island-hopping (6 flights for $250). Check the miscellaneous section of the classified ads in the *Star-Bulletin* or *Advertiser* for individuals selling these coupons at cut-rate prices. Most carriers offer the same fare to each island they serve. Inter-island flights are often extremely scenic, particularly in the early morning or late afternoon. For the best views, sit on the right side heading north and on the left flying south.

Hawaiian Airlines (537-5100), on Oahu. One way $65. 1st and last flights of the day to/from Honolulu $45. 24-hr. service.

Aloha Airlines (836-1111), on Oahu. One way $65. 1st and last flights of the day discounted to $45. Flies to every island except Lanai and Molokai. Open daily 6am-9pm.

Aloha Island Air (833-3219), on Oahu. Owned by Aloha Airlines. Smaller planes to major resorts and rural airports. Also fills in service to Molokai and Lanai for Aloha. About $69. Open daily 6am-10pm.

Surfboards cost an extra $20 each way as regular baggage, but if you ask to air freight the board you'll only pay about $12. Get to the ticket counter early, if you wish to fly through the air with the greatest of ease.

Package Tours

Aloha and Hawaiian often coordinate with resorts and/or car rental agencies to create economical packages. Ask a local travel or reservations agent about deals best suited to your needs, and keep an eye out for ads in pamphlets and newspapers.

Many companies offer one-day airplane and helicopter cruises of the islands (kind of like on Magnum, P.I.). Consult a travel agent about current deals and specials or look in the Sunday paper travel section.

On the Islands

While the **bus** system is fairly reliable and extensive on Oahu, it is patchy on the Big Island and local transit is nonexistent on the other islands (see individual island listings). You will probably want to rent your own set of wheels for a sojourn on any island other than Oahu.

Car rental agencies fill major island airports and tourist areas in towns. If you have not booked a rental through an airline or other package deal, check local weekly and monthly travel guides for specials and ask about weekly rates. Because car rental agencies are not state-regulated, a day's use of an automatic, air-conditioned compact car can range from $12 to $40. Hawaii is a no-fault insurance state, so insurance coverage is *optional,* but most companies will not honor your individual coverage, even if you already own a car. **Budget** is one of the few agencies that will rent to those ages 18 to 20, but only with a major credit card and a hefty surcharge atop the regular price. Waiting to start your car rental search until arrival at an airport is a sure way to be stuck with the most expensive rates. Whenever possible, do your research before you get there and make reservations at least 24 hrs. in advance.

Bicycle and **moped rentals,** available in most tourist centers, are an enjoyable way to see Hawaii in an easy-going, close-up manner. The congestion in Honolulu may be too much for two wheels; mopeds and bikes are more useful on the other side of Oahu, or on the neighbor islands.

If you bring your own bicycle, you may register it (for $3.50) at the **Pawaa Police Station,** 1455 S. Beretania St., Honolulu (943-3324; open Mon.-Fri. 7:45am-4:15pm). You can also pick up the free *Bicycle Regulations Pamphlet* here. More information is available at **The Bike Shop,** 1149 S. King St. (531-7071), in Honolulu (open Mon.-Thurs. and Sat. 9am-5:30pm, Fri. 9am-8pm, Sun. 10am-5pm), or from the **Hawaii Bicycling League,** P.O. Box 4403, Honolulu 96813 (732-5806). Inter-island airlines charge about $20 to bring your bike with you on the flight. Mainland airlines charge about $15.

Accommodations and Camping

Despite rumors to the contrary, reasonable room rates do exist on the islands. In general, the closer hotels are to the major tourist attractions and the better the view, the more they charge. Rates at larger resorts also vary frequently with seasons and special events. If you come to town for a canoe race, a golf tournament, or a marathon, expect prices to skyrocket. In general, high tourist season runs from mid-December to late April. Look for special deals that often include rental car and air transportation. **Hukilau, Sands, and Seaside Hotels,** (922-5737 or 922-1228 on Oahu, 800-451-6754 from the outer islands, 800-367-7000 from the mainland), manages some of the cheapest resort hotels ($35-55 per night) and is the only locally owned chain of hotels on the islands.

Hostels and the **YMCA** provide cheap shelter on most islands. Another alternative is the ever-growing number of bed and breakfast organizations which offer rooms in private homes. **B&B Hawaii,** P.O. Box 449, Kapaa 96746 (536-8421 on Oahu; 822-7771 on Kauai; 1-367-8047, ext. 339 on neighbor islands) and **B&B Honolulu,** 5242 Keehinani Dr., Honolulu 96817 (595-7533), operate statewide. Prices usually range from $30 to $55 for a double room with breakfast. B&B Hawaii tends to have the most extensive offerings and the lowest rates.

Camping can kill two birds with one sleeping bag—it'll save you money and bring you closer to the natural beauty you came to Hawaii to see. **State parks** are popular and rigidly regulated. Free **camping permits** are required, and applicants must be at least 18 years old to receive a permit for an individual or group. Camping is limited to five nights per 30 days. Sites are open Friday through Tuesday on Oahu, daily on the other islands. Two sorts of shelters are also available in state parks, but usually require reservations at least a month in advance. **A-Frames** are single rooms with wooden sleeping platforms, cooking facilities, bathroom, and shower facilities ($7 per night, 4-person max.); **housekeeping cabins** come with kitchen, living room, and one or two bedrooms, as well as utensils, linen, and heating or fireplace wood ($15 per night for 1 person, rate decreases as number in group increases, 6-person max.). For more information, reservations, and permits, write or visit one of the **State Parks Division** offices (also called the **Department of Land and Natural Resources**). (All open Mon.-Fri. 8am-4:15pm.) The **national** and **county parks** on each island also maintain campsites; refer to the appropriate sections for more information. Though illegal, free camping outside of designated parks is widely practiced throughout the state by locals, although visitors might be harassed by the police (or locals) if they are too obvious or too permanent (especially on Oahu and Maui). Nevertheless, with some discretion and enough sense to avoid four-wheel-drive tire tracks and empty beer cans, many consider picking their own quiet beach. Camping on Oahu is not a good idea.

Life in Hawaii

History

Between 25 and 40 million years ago, molten rock welled up from the depths of the earth and burst through the ocean floor at the bottom of the Pacific Ocean. Over millenia, giant shield volcanoes built up to puncture the ocean's surface. As the Pacific Plate shifted to the northwest, the underlying source of the eruptions remained stationary beneath it. As a result, the original island volcanoes moved beyond the active zone of volcanic intrusion while new eruptive fissures progressively surfaced farther southeast. In this conveyor belt fashion, the 1600 mi. archipelago known as the Hawaiian Islands formed. The oldest islands in the northwest have been worn away to tiny coral atolls by the erosion of the sea while at the other end of the chain fiery eruptions pull new land from the ocean's depths.

Long before plate tectonics were in vogue, the ancient Hawaiians grasped the volcanic mechanism at work. Their legends told of the Fire Goddess, Pele, who fled from island to island, moving southeast down the chain to escape the watery intrusions of her older sister, the ocean. These early Polynesian settlers arrived long after Pele's voyage had brought her to her current abode on the Big Island, but their own odyssey is no less remarkable. Traveling across thousands of miles of unbroken ocean as early as the 6th century AD, the first inhabitants carried with them roots, seeds, dogs, chickens, and a pig or two in their double-hulled canoes. They formed several constantly warring kingdoms, worshipped a host of gods, and considered themselves *keiki o ka aina* ("children of the land").

In 1778, Captain Cook sailed through Hawaii while searching for the Northwest Passage. He was received as a god but was accidentally killed in a skirmish when he returned eight months later. His inadvertent discovery propelled Hawaii into the modern world. King Kamehameha I of the Big Island exploited the introduction of Western arms and conquered all of the other islands except Kauai within 20 years of Cook's arrival. Today he is revered as the leader who united the islands and created modern Hawaii. In addition to the key weapons, the European trade ships brought more than Kamehameha had bargained for. Western influences slowly eroded Hawaiian culture. Western diseases decimated the Hawaiian population; in 1778 there were a quarter of a million native Hawaiians, one hundred years later, only 50,000. After Kamehameha II sat down to eat with women in 1819, the traditional taboo structures of Hawaiian society quickly collapsed.

Following the arrival of Calvinist missionaries from Boston in 1820, the *haole*—Caucasian, pronounced "HOW-lee"—presence in island life became entrenched. By 1853, 30% of Hawaiians belonged to Christian churches. An expanding sugar (and later pineapple) industry supplanted the original whaling and sandalwood trade. Chinese, Japanese, and Filipinos were brought in as indentured plantation laborers to replace the dying Hawaiians. American sugar magnates, leery of a strong monarchy and seeking to ensure a market for their product, overthrew King Kalakaua in 1893, and requested that the U.S. annex the islands. In 1898, having acquired Spain's interests in the Pacific and desiring Hawaii as a military base, the U.S. did just that.

Hawaiian commerce developed uneventfully until the Japanese attack on Pearl Harbor half a century later dramatically summoned the U.S. into World War II. In the heat of the Red Scare, the Hawaiian Nisei Japanese were at first denied the right to serve in the U.S. armed forces. The government's eventual relaxation of these unjust structures, and the Nisei Japanese's unusually valiant service in two Pacific combat divisions, was one factor in mitigating racial prejudice. In 1959, Hawaii became the 50th state.

Today, of the 162 volcanic islands which still stand above the highest tide, only seven are inhabited (one, Niihau, is privately owned). Although every ethnic group is a minority, there is little racial tension. Instead, Hawaii's residents have merged parts of each ethnic heritage into a "local" culture, which manifests itself everywhere from the menus of the island lunchwagons to the linguistic pot-pourri of Pidgin (the islands' English dialect).

Literature

Although the most widely famed are those who visited the area only briefly, many foreign and indigenous writers have chronicled the Hawaiian spirit in their novels, stories and poems. Most of the earliest verses are lost forever, as the "genealogical songs" of the Hawaiians, poems and stories handed down through generations, had an intimate family quality and were carefully guarded, and because a written language did not arrive on the islands until James Cook and his crew did. Mary K. Pukui and Alfons L. Korn's anthology presents selected Hawaiian verses spanning ancient through missionary times and their translations. The picaresque adventures in O.A. Bushnell's novels are an interesting cultural introduction to the Hawaii of one hundred years ago. Three renowned authors, Mark Twain, James Michener, and Jack London, have captured their impressions in stories or essays; Michener's mammoth text takes the reader all the way from the island's volcanic formation through to statehood. Novelists Earl Derr Biggers (whose Charlie Chan was modeled on a member of the Honolulu police force) and Marjorie Sinclair have infused intrigue and enchantment into 20th-century Hawaii. The best-known poet to hail from the region is Genevieve Taggard, whose reflective poems capture the Hawaii of her youth and are collected in one volume. For an overview of the Hawaiian *literati,* page through one of the anthologies listed below. Several of these books may not be found in the neighborhood bookstore; check your local library, or special order them at a bookstore.

Earl Derr Biggers, *The House Without a Key.*

O.A. Bushnell, *Ka'a'awa: A Novel About Hawaii in the 1850's.*

A. Grove Day and Carl Stroven eds., *A Hawaiian Reader.*

Gerrit P. Judd IV, *A Hawaiian Anthology.*

Jack London, *Stories from Hawaii.*

James A. Michener, *Hawaii.*

Mary Kawena Pukui and Alfons L. Korn, *The Echo of Our Song: Chants and Poems of the Hawaiians.*

Marjorie Sinclair, *Kona.*

Genevieve Taggard, *Origin: Hawaii.*

Mark Twain, *Letters from Hawaii.*

Art and Architecture

Visitors of an artistic bent will find in Hawaii a rich heritage of native crafts, and a smattering of famous works and Western imports. Perhaps the islanders' most celebrated handicraft is the production of *leis.* Although commercial vendors have bastardized the original craft with synthetic materials, you can still find the traditional garlands of leaves, flowers, nuts, and shells in local shops. Ornate **woodcarvings** and baskets, slippers, and table mats woven out of *lauhala* (the leaf of the pandanus tree) are still crafted by native artisans and are offered throughout the islands. **Scrimshaw** first came to Hawaii when mainland sailors idled away their free time on the island by carving images onto whales' bones and teeth; today the craft is refined and practiced by residents.

European fine arts landed on the islands with Captain Cook. Two members of his crew, John Webber and James Clevely, sketched the first Western impressions of Hawaii. In the 19th and early 20th century several artists grew to world-wide prominence. Most renowned of these is Madge Tennent, who came to the islands in 1823. Known as "Hawaii's Gauguin," Tennent painted dramatic oils of Hawaiian women, which are on exclusive display at the Tennent Art Foundation Gallery in Honolulu. Engravers Huc M. Luquiens and John M. Kelly are fêted for their arresting etchings of island landscapes and individuals, respectively. First celebrated for his Mexican murals, Jean Chalet came to Hawaii in 1949 and took the indigenous culture as his subject, becoming a leader in the Hawaiian artistic community until his death in 1979. Several **art marts** throughout the islands display the works of contemporary Hawaiian artists; the most notable show is held every weekend outside the entrance to the Honolulu Zoo (see Honolulu Sights).

The Bishop Museum in Honolulu houses the state's, and world's, best collection of Polynesiana and Hawaiiana, with extensive galleries, archives and demonstrations of Hawaiian crafts. The Honolulu Academy of Art has a wide collection of Western works, while the Contemporary Museum of Art hosts exhibitions on present-day artistic themes. Hawaii's most impressive collection of Asian art is housed at the East-West Center Learning Institute (at the Univ. of Hawaii), where arts and crafts both Eastern and Western are on display.

Hawaii's cities are an amalgamation of contrasting architectural styles. Oriental temples, Hawaiian huts and Western structures coexist with one another, but there has been no recognizable cohesion into an architectural style particular to the islands (although the State Capital, built in 1969, is a remarkable attempt). Landscape design, rather than architecture, is the forte of Hawaiian designers, as a stroll through the island's sculpted parks and gardens will attest.

Food

Hawaii offers the most unusual array of foods in the U.S. Many of the meat and dairy products are imported and island fish is in high demand in foreign markets, making everything but fruit relatively expensive. Still, a profusion of restaurants and take-out vendors make eating out affordable. All the islands except Molokai and Lanai support large, 24-hr. supermarkets, and each island offers its own specialties. The Big Island is the macadamia nut capital of the world and home to premium Royal Kona, the only coffee commercially grown in the U.S. Kauai has its cookies and sugar-cane ice cream; Maui, its potato chips; and Oahu, its international restaurants.

For a taste of Hawaii as pleasing to the wallet as the palate, go to one of the local take-out establishments. Plate lunches, a longstanding island tradition, are served at lunchwagons and take-out stands everywhere for about $3. A typical plate includes rice, macaroni salad, *kim chee* (pickled cabbage), and an entree such as chicken *katsu* (a breaded cutlet) or teriyaki beef. Wash it all down with passion-orange, passion-guava, or pineapple-orange juice. Many plate lunch specials feature such Hawaiian staples as *kalua* pig, *lau lau* (pork or chicken wrapped in *ti* and *taro* leaves), *lomi lomi* salmon (a mixture of tomatoes, onions, and salmon), *haupia* (coconut pudding), and two-finger *poi* (a taro root pudding thick enough to be eaten with two fingers, although most people usually use silverware). You can get all of these items at a full-blown commercial *luau* with Polynesian entertainment for about $40 per person at many restaurants, like **Germaine's,** 1451 S. King, Honolulu (941-3338).

You can constuct an interesting meal out of a potpourri of island *pupus,* or appetizers. *Sashimi,* fresh raw fish, is a favorite delicacy, usually served with *soyu* (soy sauce), fresh ginger and hot horseradish.

On the whole, the islands' Chinese restaurants offer some of the most economical meals, including varieties of *mein* (noodles), *manapua* (pork-filled dough), *won ton* and *dim sum* (various dumplings and small dishes). Be sure to go for *dim sum* early in the day (before 1:30 or 2pm). Japanese fare is usually a bit more expensive with delicate, delicious servings. Japanese fast foods, such as *saimin* (*ramen* noodles), served even in McDonalds, and *bento* (box lunches), are the least expensive varieties. Be sure to try sashimi and sushi. Other local favorites include Korean *kalbi* ribs and *kim chee,* Portuguese *pao duce* (sweet bread) or *malasadas* (doughnuts), and shaved ice.

Since it's in a sub-tropical zone, Hawaii is blessed with a variety of produce that does not grace mainland supermarkets. Fresh pineapple, sugar cane, and papaya are all cheap and plentiful in the islands. Try a tangy mango in summer. More exotic are lychee, guava, and the round bread fruit. Pomegranates and star fruit are also worth searching for as is the *lilikoi* (passion fruit). For a visually confounding taste sensation, try the yellow watermelon grown on the Big Island in summer. It's much sweeter than its pink cousin; unfortunately, it's yellow skin is so thin that it can't even be shipped to Oahu, so you'll have to go to the Big Island to indulge.

Recreation

The Hawaiian Islands are punctuated with hidden treasures: rare birds, tropical fish, botanical delights, and sandy beaches with glassy waves. Hiking, snorkeling, swimming, bird- and whale-watching, and fishing number among the outdoor activities visitors can enjoy with little or no expense. Despite the admonishments of 19th century missionaries, who objected to the religious, gambling and sexual connotations surfing then had (and still does?), the sport was invented in Hawaii during the islands' nativity and has since burgeoned into an world-wide activity. Diehard surfer dudes from California and beyond traverse the oceans to hang ten on the gnarly 20-footers breaking off Oahu's North Shore. The hybrid sport of windsurfing dominates the beaches of Maui, while between the islands the seafaring paddle traditional outrigger canoes or sail cata- and tri-marans.

Less aqautically inclined mammals should explore the islands singular geographical features. Oahu's mountains are perfect for climbers, and the beauty of the islands is consciously preserved in the twenty state and two national parks (Hawaii Volcanoes and Haleakala). The former of these boasts the world's only "drive-in" volcano and the enormous craters born of Mauna Loa and Kiluaea's eruptions. The Inland valleys of Maui, the Big Island, and Oahu—prime spots for illegal marijuana cultivation—can put hikers in danger of trespassing, so stay on defined trails. Robert Smith has authored some excellent guides to island hiking on sale at local bookstores. Brooks Brothers naturalists will find no dearth of fine golf courses.

The variety of island spectator sports is relatively limited. Polo tournaments and surfing competitions are the more exotic events, but college and pro-football players make an annual trek from the mainland for the Aloha, Hula and Pro Bowls during the winter months.

The Hawaii Visitors Bureau has planted "warrior" markers along the highway to point out historical landmarks. Consult the following organization for maps and campsite listings. Whatever you do, don't pick up any Tiki idols lying around construction sites.

Hawaiian Trail and Mountain Club, P.O. Box 2238, Honolulu 96804. Watch for listings of free hikes in the weekly "Pulse of Paradise" column of the *Honolulu Star-Bulletin.*

Sierra Club Hawaii Chapter, 1212 University Ave., Honolulu 96826 (946-8494), behind the Church of the Cross Roads. Phone for a recorded hiking update on Oahu. A major source of hiking information and organized weekend hikes. Open Mon.-Sat. 8-11am.

State Forestry Division, 1179 Punchbowl St., #325, Honolulu 96813 (548-8856). Provides free maps for its 24 trails. Open Mon.-Fri. 7:45am-4:30pm.

Weather

On Kauai, the wettest spot on the Earth (400-600 in. per year) is only 15 mi. from the year-round sun at Poipu. Sometimes it seems that the annual rainfall varies with the street address. Equatorial ocean currents and north-easterly trade winds converge to keep Hawaii's climate agreeable year-round. Seasons are virtually non-existent, although local weather around any given island fluctuates constantly. Coastal areas are usually drier; the leeward side of a mountain is usually calmer as well as hotter than the windward side. From April to October, temperatures range 73-88°; November to March, it's slightly cooler (65-83°) and wetter. The Big Island's Hilo is a tropical rain forest—precipitation is over a hundred inches per year—while the land to the south at Kau is a sun-scorched desert. Even some of the lower mountains catch a cool breeze, especially at night and early morning, so pack a sweater. On any island, be prepared for mountain showers and "liquid sunshine," a cool mixture of rain sprinkles, sunshine, and rainbows that is prevalent in the lower mountain areas.

Oahu

At the time of Captain Cook's landing, Oahu was something of a backwater among the settled Hawaiian islands. Its rulers preferred to spend their time on Molokai, the other island in their domain. King Kamehameha's victory on Oahu in 1795 consolidated his rule over the lower six islands and made the island the launching pad for his planned invasion of the kingdom of Kauai. Oahu's real importance, however, came with the creation of Honolulu harbor. The harbor established Oahu as a regular stopover for vessels plying the China trade, prompting many *haoles* (Caucasians) to settle in Honolulu. By the time the first missionaries arrived in 1820, the city had become the economic and cultural center of Hawaii, and the migrating royal court was obliged to spend more and more time there. Oahu's preeminence increased in ensuing decades as Honolulu's commercial traffic expanded and the U.S. Navy acquired exclusive rights to the neighboring inlet at Pearl Harbor. The dredging of Pearl Harbor's mouthway in 1900 allowed Oahu to develop almost overnight into the headquarters of the U.S. Pacific fleet. An uninvited visit by Japanese bombers on December 7, 1941 signaled the entrance of the U.S. into World War II and, twenty years later, the arrival of American jets took Hawaii's tourism industry to a higher plane.

Honolulu itself is a vibrant multi-ethnic city, inhabited by a diverse mixture of native Hawaiians, Caucasians, Japanese, Chinese, Samoans, Koreans, and Filipinos. Despite the severe discrimination many of these groups have faced in the past, relations among them are now remarkably friendly; nearly half of all island marriages are interracial.

Oahu can be roughly divided into four sections. **Honolulu** and its suburbs constitute the metropolitan heart of the state. The **North Shore,** from Kahuku to Kaena Point, is the home of the winter swells that surfers around the world dream of at night. The **Windward Coast,** especially around Hanauma Bay, is rife with tropical fish and coral reefs (not to mention reefer). The **Leeward Coast** is raw and rocky, strikingly beautiful, and a great escape for campers seeking solitude.

The slopes of two now-extinct volcanic mountain ridges, **Waianae** in the west and **Koolau** in the east, run parallel from northwest to southeast and make up the bulk of Oahu's 600 square miles. The narrow inlets of **Pearl Harbor** push in from the sea at the southern end of the valley between the two ridges. **Honolulu** spreads along 6 mi. of oceanfront southeast of Pearl Harbor, hemmed in by the Koolau Range in the northeast. Three mi. east of downtown, **Waikiki Beach** extends to the volcanic crater of Diamond Head, the island's southernmost extremity. The Honolulu district continues around Diamond Head to Koko Head in **Hawaii kai.** Skipping only the Leeward Coast and Kaena Point, well-maintained highways circle the island and navigate the central valley. White sand beaches drape Oahu's shores and hiking trails ramble through the inland mountains and vales.

Honolulu

As the cultural, commercial and political focal point of modern Hawaii, the city of Honolulu is a schizophrenic mix of high-rise buildings and white sand beachs, business suits and bikinis. The trade winds keep Honolulu free of stagnant pollution, and the pleasant climate brightens this prosperous urban environment. Despite

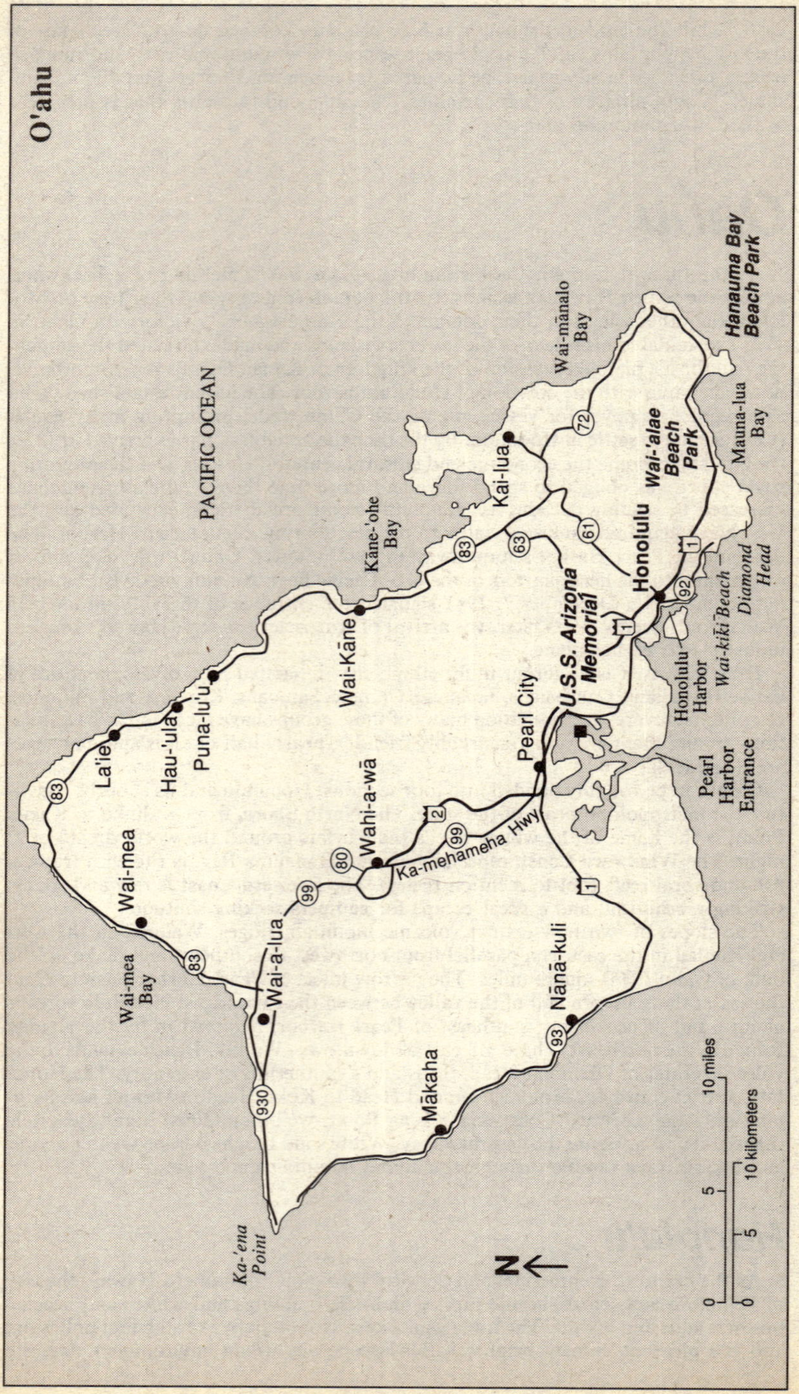
O'ahu
PACIFIC OCEAN
Hanauma Bay Beach Park
Wai-mānalo Bay
Kai-lua
Kāne-'ohe Bay
Wai-'alae Beach Park
Mauna-lua Bay
Honolulu
Diamond Head
Wai-kiki Beach
Honolulu Harbor
U.S.S. Arizona Memorial
Wai-Kāne
Pearl City
Pearl Harbor Entrance
Puna-lu'u
Hau-'ula
La'ie
Wahi-a-wā
Ka-mehameha Hwy
Wai-mea
Wai-mea Bay
Wai-a-lua
Nānā-kuli
Mākaha
Ka-'ena Point
72
61
63
83
1
92
2
99
80
93
930
N
0 5 10 miles
0 5 10 kilometers

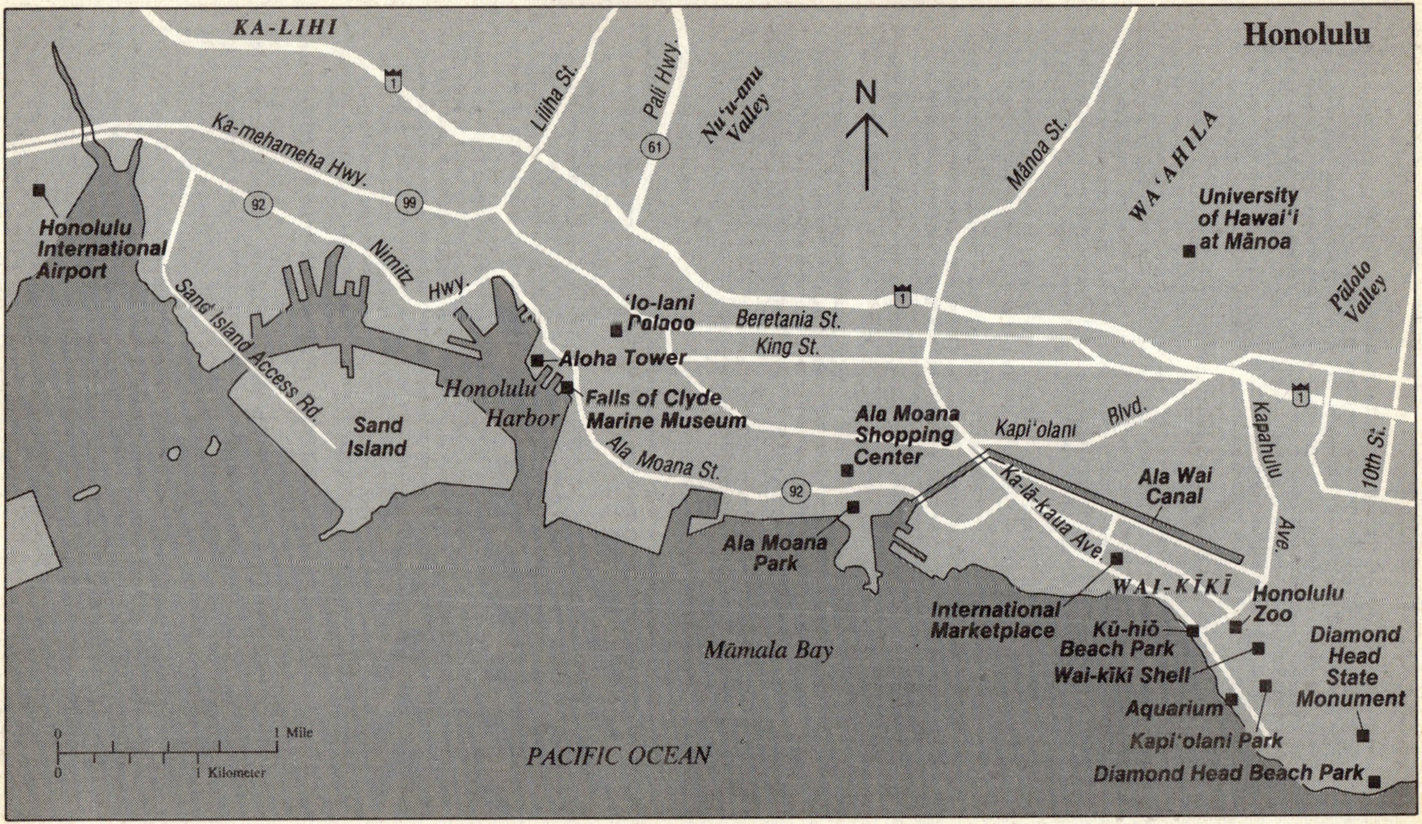
Honolulu
KA-LIHI
Ka-mehameha Hwy.
Liliha St.
Pali Hwy.
Nu'u-anu Valley
N
Mānoa St.
WA'AHILA
University of Hawai'i at Mānoa
Pālolo Valley
Honolulu International Airport
Nimitz Hwy.
Sand Island Access Rd.
Sand Island
'Io-lani Palace
Beretania St.
King St.
Aloha Tower
Honolulu Harbor
Falls of Clyde Marine Museum
Ala Moana St.
Ala Moana Shopping Center
Kapi'olani Blvd.
Kapahulu Ave.
10th St.
Ala Wai Canal
Ka-lā-kaua Ave.
Ala Moana Park
WAI-KĪKĪ
International Marketplace
Honolulu Zoo
Kū-hiō Beach Park
Wai-kīkī Shell
Aquarium
Kapi'olani Park
Diamond Head State Monument
Diamond Head Beach Park
Māmala Bay
PACIFIC OCEAN
0 1 Mile
0 1 Kilometer

ever-sprawling suburbs, the serenity of mountain and ocean remains close at hand. Waikiki, the world's quintessential vacation destination, is a great place to people-watch and enjoy the sun—if you can find space to spread your towel. Honolulu's temperate island setting even influences the lifestyle of its residents. Motorists in rush hour retain an amazingly friendly disposition toward their fellow roadwarriors. In the office, informal dress is the rule, especially on "Aloha Friday" and Food Fest days. And at night, the city vibrates with transient revelers, on whom residents capitalize by selling everything from party cruises to the odd sexual favor. Neither are likely to be a bargain, but hell, you're on vacation; book 'em Kemo.

Practical Information and Orientation

Visitor Information: Hawaii Visitors Bureau, 2270 Kalakaua Ave., 4th Floor, Honolulu 96815 (923-1811). Information on Oahu and the rest of the state. Pick up the *Accommodation Guide* and *Restaurant Guide,* a map of points of interest, and a walking tour of downtown Honolulu. Also has a travel guide for the disabled. All are free. Open Mon.-Fri. 8am-4:30pm. Information centers located in both the overseas and inter-island air terminals and at the Ala Moana Shopping Center. **Chinese Chamber of Commerce,** 42 N. King St. (533-3181 or 533-6967). Information on the Chinese community. Open Mon.-Fri. 8am-4pm, Sat. 8:30am-noon. Tour of Chinatown Tues. 9:30am-noon. Tour $4, with lunch (noon-1pm) $7.

Outdoor Information: Department of Parks and Recreation, 650 S. King, Honolulu 96817 (523-4525). Information and permits for county parks. Open Mon.-Fri. 7:45am-4pm. Permits available no earlier than 2 weeks in advance. **Department of State Parks,** 1151 Punchbowl St., Honolulu 96813 (548-7455). Information, trail maps, and permits for camping in state parks. Open Mon.-Fri. 8am-4pm.

Foreign Currency Exchange: Hyatt Regency at Hemmeter Center, 2nd Floor (922-3327). Open daily 8:15am-11pm. Many others in Waikiki.

American Express: 1778 Ala Moana Blvd. (946-7741). In the Beachcomber Hotel.

Bus: 848-5555. Covers the entire island, but different lines start and stop running at different times. Call to avoid getting stuck somewhere remote. Also, backpackers beware: they won't let you carry on big packs or luggage. Fare 60¢. $15 bus passes valid for 1 month are available at satellite city halls, or at Foodland grocery stores and Bank of Hawaii branches. Free senior citizens pass takes 1 week to process. Free Honolulu/Waikiki route maps available at tourist pamphlet stands throughout Waikiki. More extensive route maps and guides available in bookstores and at Foodland stores ($2.50).

Transit for Disabled: Handi-Van, 905 Ahuh St. (833-2222). Curb-to-curb service if reservations are made at least a day in advance. Service runs Mon.-Fri. 8am-4pm. Disabled travelers can obtain a bus pass from the City Department of Transportation Services. Write in advance to **Handicapped Bus Pass,** 650 S. King St., Honolulu 96813 (523-4083). **Handi-Cabs of the Pacific,** P.O. Box 22428 (524-3866), a private taxi company with van ramps for wheelchairs. $28 for airport-to-Waikiki service. Call for reservations.

Taxi: Sida, 439 Kalewa St. (836-0011). All cabs charge 20¢ per 1/6 mi. Flag rates are about $1.50. Airport to Waikiki $15-18. Also try **Charley's** (622-4177).

Car Rental: Hertz, Dollar, Avis and Budget all have outlets on the islands, but Budget is the only major one that will rent to drivers between 18 and 25, and they charge an extra $20 per day for this service. Alamo rents to those 21 and over with a major credit card and has weekly rates that are substantially cheaper than those available at Budget. Phone first, since each agency offers occasional special rates. For used cars, try **Honolulu Rent-a-Car,** 1856 Kalakaua Ave. #105 (941-9099 or 942-7187) or **Maxi Rentals,** 413 Seaside Ave. (923-7381). Both from $10 per day. Insurance mandatory if under 25 ($7). **Waikiki Rentals,** 224 McCully (946-2181). $20 per day including insurance. Three-day min. rental.

Moped and Bike Rentals: Mopeds, though less safe than a car, are a great way to "do" Honolulu, especially on Kalanianaole Hwy., the route to Hanauma Bay. They run about 40 mi. on $1 worth of gas. Most rental agencies require credit cards and a minimum age of 18. **Aloha Funway Rentals,** 1778 Ala Moana (942-9696) and 2976 Koapakapaka St. (834-1016), near the airport. Mopeds $16 per half day, $20 per day, $75 per week; bikes $13.50 per day. Open daily 8am-5pm. **Inter-Island Rentals,** 353 Royal Hawaiian Ave. (946-0013), features Honda, Suzuki, and PGO mopeds. Must be 18 with cash or credit card deposit and valid driver's license. Mopeds $25 per day, $125 per week, negotiable. Bikes $12 per day. Open daily 8am-6pm.

Water Equipment Rentals: All rental outfits are located on beaches and look like homemade lemonade stands, surrounded by surfboards and locals. Cash only. **Kuhio Beach Service,** to the right of the Kuhio Beach park pavilion, offers surfboard rentals with lessons ($15 per hr.), outrigger canoe rides ($5), and boogie boards ($5 per day). **Ohana Rentals,** near the breakers at Queen's Beach, also rents boogie boards ($8 per day) and fins ($8 per day). Open daily 8am-6pm. The best boards, along with helpful lessons, can be found at **Star Beachboys,** Kuhio Beach, to the left of the pavilion. Canoe rides $5, surfboard lessons $10 per hr., boogie boards $5 per hr. **Snorkel Bob's,** 819 Kapahulu Ave. (735-7944) is *the* place for snorkel equipment rentals. Decent equipment is $15 per week and $30 per week gets you higher quality equipment. Fish map and the a copy of the legend of Snorkel Bob included. For island hoppers, there is an inter-island return policy on Kauai and Maui.

Laundromats: The hostels have laundromats on the premises. For others wanting to air their dirty laundry, Waikiki Laundromats has 5 locations open daily 7am-10pm (923-2057), including one across from the International Market Place, and one in the Outrigger West Hotel, 2330 Kuhio Ave.

Weather Report: Sunny and 80°F. If in doubt, call 836-2102, 836-0121, or 836-0234 for confirmation.

Surf Report: 526-SURF (526-7873). 24 hrs.

Swimming Pools: Manoa Recreation Center, 2721 Kaaipu Ave. (988-6868). Take bus #5 from Ala Moana Center. Open Mon., Wed., and Fri. 3:30-5pm and 7:30-9pm, Tues. and Thurs. 2-5pm, Sat.-Sun. 12:30-5pm. **McCully Pool,** 831 Pumehana St. (947-6070). Take bus #1 or #4 from Ala Moana Center.

Crisis Lines: Sex Abuse Treatment Center, 524-7237. **Coast Guard Search/Rescue,** 536-4336. **Alcohol and Drug Abuse Hotline,** 548-4280. **Suicide and Crisis Center,** 521-4555. **AIDS Hotline,** 735-5303. **Multilingual Translation Help,** 521-4566. **The Ultimate Number,** 521-4566; for general help.

Gay Information Services: 2139 Kuhio Ave., #213 (926-2910). Lists gay-supported community programs and businesses.

TDD: 643-8TDD for hearing impaired users, 643-TALK for hearing users.

Health Centers: Queen's Medical Center, 1301 Punchbowl St. (538-9011). 24-hr. Emergency Room, 547-4311. Ask-a-Nurse Referrals, 533-5877. **Waikiki Health Center,** 277 Ohua St., Waikiki (922-4787).

Emergency: 911.

Post Office: Main Office, 3600 Aoleilei Ave. (423-3990). Near the airport. The only one that accepts General Delivery. Open daily 8am-4:30pm. General Delivery ZIP Code: 96813. **Waikiki Branch,** Royal Hawaiian Shopping Center, 2nd floor, Bldg. B. Open Mon.-Fri. 8:15-11:45am and 1-3:30pm. General Delivery ZIP Code: 96815.

Area Code: 808.

Honolulu International Airport is 20 minutes west of downtown, off the Lunalilo Freeway (H-1). If Waikiki is your destination, take the Honolulu exit, then move immediately into the left lane to get the interchange onto the freeway into town. Although 15 minutes longer, the **Nimitz Highway** (Rte. 92) will take you all the way into the concrete jungle. Bus #8, among others, goes the 9 mi. to Waikiki, but you won't be able to bring your luggage; you can, however, bring one pinenut per person (eeeh). Several companies will tote you and your luggage between the airport and Waikiki or downtown for $5. **Grayline** (834-1033) operates from 5am to 11:30pm. No reservations are required from the airport; look for the Grayline desk in the baggage claim area. **Waikiki Express** (942-2177) operates from 7am to 9pm, and requires reservations. **Airport Motor Coach** (926-4747) operates from 6:30am to 10pm and requires reservations.

The **H-1 Freeway** stretches the length of Honolulu. Downtown Honolulu is about 6 blocks long and 4 blocks wide, wedged between Honolulu Harbor and Punchbowl Street. In Waikiki, Ala Wai Boulevard, Kuhio Avenue, and Kalakaua Avenue run parallel to the ocean and are the main routes of transit.

Honolulu and the surrounding environs contain a plethora of places for biking and running. **Ala Moana Beach Park,** near Waikiki, has a scenic running path.

The Shower Tree (Airport) 836-3044

Write to the Hawaii Council for Safe Running, P.O. Box 23169, Honolulu 96822, for information on routes. For the latest running events, call 245-4144 or write the Department of Parks and Recreation. (See Practical Information.) Bike paths are found mostly in Manoa and near the University of Hawaii. **Hitchhiking** is illegal on Oahu, but it is done by some, particularly on the other side of the island.

Besides *mauka* (inland) and *makai* (seaward), you are also likely to hear such directions as *ewa* (west; pronounced EHVA) and *diamond head* (east).

Accommodations

Honolulu's reputation as a tourist town tends to drive prices for the transient sky high, but bargains are there for those willing to search and do without the grass-skirted frills. Because Hawaii is a stop on many round-the-world tickets, hostels are great places to meet travelers bound for the West Coast, Australia, or Europe. They do fill up, so reserve early by telephone with a credit card or by mail. Another option is to share a hotel room with other travelers, or to check for housing specials in the *Honolulu Advertiser,* available on most street corners for 35¢, for good deals. As Bed and Breakfast establishments proliferate, they too are becoming a convenient and inexpensive housing option.

Interclub Waikiki, 2413 Kuhio Ave. (924-2636). Close to Waikiki Beach and city nightlife. Clean, comfortable, friendly surroundings. Co-ed or single sex dorms. Laundry but no kitchen facilities. Lounge and pool table. No curfew or lights out, but Americans must be headed overseas to stay here.

Honolulu International (AYH), 2323A Seaview Ave., (946-0591), 1½ mi. north of Waikiki, near University of Hawaii at Manoa. By car, take University Ave. exit off H-1. By bus, take #6 from Ala Moana Shopping Center, to Metcalf and University Ave. (near Burger King). Kitchen, locker, and clean single sex facilities. Common area and recreation room with TV and free movies. Beds guaranteed for 3 nights; if you want to stay longer in Honolulu, the management can usually arrange to move you to the Hale Aloha hostel. Price includes 50¢ chore deposit. Lights out at 11pm; rooms are locked from 9:30am-5pm. Members $9, non-members $11. Sheet sack rental $1. Reservations recommended year round.

Hale Aloha (AYH), 2417 Prince Edward St. (926-8313), in Waikiki, 2 blocks from the beach. Members only. Beds guaranteed for 3 nights. Open daily 8am-noon and 5-9pm. Lights out at 11pm, but no curfew. Dorm bunks $12 per night. Studio doubles for $26. Reservations required.

Waikiki Prince, 2431 Prince Edward St. (922-1544). A/C and parking lot vistas. Much needed renovations were planned for October 1991. TV and laundry facilities. Small double occupancy studio without kitchen $28-36, with kitchen $38-45. Newly acquired building nearby offers bunks and hostel facilities, which were scheduled to open in July 1991, $15.Functional rooms $30, with kitchenette $35, with full kitchen $37.

Driftwood Hotel, 1696 Ala Moana Blvd. (949-0061), near Ala Moana Shopping Center and Ala Moana Beach Park. Funky pink headboards and turquoise counter tops. Laundry facilities and a small pool. Rooms with fridge and balcony are $55 single or double occupancy.

Royal Grove Hotel, 151 Uluniu Ave. (923-7691). Clean, simple, carpeted rooms close to Waikiki Beach. Economy rooms have a stirring view of Vivian's Bar-B-Q. Single or double room with bath, TV and fridge, $36. With kitchenette, $40.50.

Big Surf, 1690 Ala Moana Blvd. (946-6525), near Ala Moana Canal. Sparse and slightly gloomy, but safe, since the gate is always locked and only guests have keys. Suites for up to four people with twin beds and a sofabed, full kitchen and color TV are $45 from September 15-December 15 and February 15-June 15. $65 other times. Studios with patio for 1 or 2 people, $35 low season, $39 high and $42 with TV.

YMCA, 401 Atkinson Dr. (941-3344), across from Ala Moana Shopping Center downtown. Men over 18 only, lots of semi-permanent residents. Check in or out at noon. Singles $28, with bath $34.50. Doubles $40, with bath $48.50.

B&B Pacific Hawaii, 19 Kai Nani Place (262-6026). Bed and breakfast rooms all over the island from $45 per couple.

Outrigger Waikiki Surf Hotel ($40 single)
Others at back of book →

YWCA: Fernhurst Residence, 1566 Wilder Ave. (941-2231) near the University. Take bus #14 to Punahou School. For single women over 18. Two persons per room, 2 rooms per bath. Single occupancy $33, shared room $25.

Camping

Camping on Oahu is less convenient than on the other islands. Police strictly patrol parks and beaches across the island and won't balk at kicking off crashers. Campgrounds are located in rural areas, and native Hawaiians often consider the campgrounds their domain, especially on Oahu's western shore. Four state parks and 13 county parks allow camping. For free required **permits** contact the Department of Parks and Recreation (see Practical Information). In Honolulu, tent camping is allowed at two state parks, **Sand Island** and **Keaiwa Heiau State Recreation Area.** There is a five-day limit and an 11am check-out time. Apply at the Division of Land and Natural Resources (see Practical Information). Sand Island, outside of Honolulu Harbor, offers flat camping. Take Sand Island Access Rd. from Nimitz Hwy. (Rte. 92). Keaiwa Heiau State Recreation Area, at the end of Aiea Heights Dr. (488-6626), has forest sites—a short hike from the ruins of the *heiau hoosola* (temple of healing). For more information on camping, contact Division of State Parks, 1151 Punchbowl St. #310, Honolulu (548-7455) or County and Regional Parks, 650 South King St. (523-4525).

A complete selection of **camping equipment** is available at **The Bike Shop,** 1149 S. King St. (531-7071). From Waikiki, take Ala Wai Blvd. to McCully Ave., go left at Beretania St. onto Pensacola Ave., then turn left after 2 blocks to King St. The friendly staff offers suggestions on hiking trails and organized trips. (Open Mon.-Thurs. and Sat. 9am-5:30pm, Fri. 9am-8pm, Sun. 10am-5pm.)

Food

Eating in Honolulu can be an international dining experience. There's little reason for eating in Waikiki; if you're trapped there try the **Waikiki Shopping Plaza.** Look for breakfast specials at many hotel coffee shops and scan the "Dining Out" sections in the Sunday papers for the most recent plate lunch and other specials throughout Oahu. And don't miss Ala Moana's **Food Market** for a cornucopia of cuisines.

For truly local flavor, take a trip to the Farmers market across from Kewalo Basin, just west of Ala Moana Park. They have wonderfully fresh seafood and the delicate Hawaiian lau lau—a taro leaf stuffed with fresh fish. Go early in the morning and bargain for the day's catch.

The neighborhoods surrounding Waikiki support many inexpensive restaurants that avoid the corny tourist ambience. The Kapahulu, Kaimuki, Moiliili, and downtown districts are all within 10 minutes of Waikiki by bus, and with a good map, you can walk from one district to the next quite easily. Small Chinese and other Asian food counters serve excellent lunch snacks and *dim sum* all over Chinatown, especially on Hotel Street. A variety of ethnic restaurants, including Hawaiian, Japanese, Thai, and French, are located between the 500 and 1000 blocks of **Kapahulu Avenue** and in the surrounding area. Catch bus #2 going *mauka* up Kapahulu Ave. from the Diamond Head area of Waikiki.

Finally, travelers to Waikiki will be deluged with ads and flyers recommending *luaus.* These Brady Bunch-style feasts with Polynesian dancing rake in the tourist bucks and are often pretty cheesy, but some can be fun and belly-filling (and a few are even reasonably priced). The **Queen Kapiolani**, 150 Kapahulu Ave. (922-1941), offers a $11 unlimited *luau* luncheon buffet with entertainment, Mon.-Wed. and Fri.-Sat. 11am-2pm.

Ono Hawaiian Food, 726 Kapahulu Ave., Waikiki (737-2275), next to the Ala Wai golf course. Family-style restaurant that lives up to its name (*ono* means good). Try the *poi* or *opihi* (limpets) if you're adventurous. Go early—the lines often extend out the front door. *Kalua* plate $4.55. Combination plate $6. Open Mon.-Sat. 11am-7:30pm.

Perry's Smorgy, 2380 Kuhio Ave. (922-1904). Standard, filling fare. They offer an extensive all-you-can-eat buffet of chicken, spaghetti, rice, potatoes, roast beef, and breads. Gaily decorated, with a view of Waikiki Beach. Breakfast $4. Lunch $5.45. Dinner $8. Open daily 7-10:30am, 11am-2:30pm, and 5-9pm.

Rainbow Drive-In, 3308 Kanaina Ave. (737-0177). Probably the best plate lunches around. Heaps and heaps of tasty local food. Plate lunches come on a bed of rice and macaroni salad. Try the mixed plate of Hawaiian-style barbecued pig, boneless chicken and *mahi mahi* for $4.35.

Leonard's Bakery, 933 Kapahulu Ave. (737-5591). A fabulous bakery, this Hawaiian institution has served hot *malasadas* (a Portugese dessert) for years. Leonard's *malasadas* are, quite simply, the best on this planet (40¢); you'll forget that you were ever on a diet. Virtually a landmark. Open daily 6am-10pm.

KC Drive-In, 1029 Kapahulu Ave. (737-5581). Home to the decadent *ono-ono* shake made with peanut butter and your choice of flavoring ($2.35), and the puzzling waffle-wrapped hot dog ($1.50), apparently an original. They also serve plate lunches ($3-5), *sai min* noodles, and a variety of salads and croissant sandwiches ($4-5). Open Sun.-Thurs. 6am-8pm, Fri.-Sat. 6am-1am.

Wo Fat, 115 N. Hotel St. (533-6393). Very Cantonese, very old, and very popular. Lots of downtown Honolulu atmosphere. All-you-can-eat Peking Duck buffet lunch ($8.50), served Wed. 11am-1:30pm. A la carte dishes $4-6. Open daily 10:30am-9pm.

Auntie Pasto's, 1099 S. Beretania (523-8855). Cozy red-brick *ristorante* serving exceptional Italian meals. Stuffed calamari $6.50. Open Mon.-Fri. 11am-10:30pm, Sat.-Sun. 4-10:30pm.

Compadres, 1200 Ala Moana, Bldg. 3 (523-1307), at the Ward Centre. A festive Mexican bar and grill. Thurs. is especially lively as the young islanders gather to sip margaritas and munch on complimentary chips and salsa. Ask about half-portions. Dinners $6-8. Open Sun.-Thurs. 7am-11pm, Fri.-Sat. 7am-2am.

Patti's Kitchen, Ala Moana Shopping Center (946-5002), also in the Windward Mall in Kaneohe. Build your own buffet-style Chinese plate lunches ($3.85-5.50). Also has a counter selling *dim sum.* Rice cakes cost 40¢. An incredible bargain; apparently Elizabeth Taylor has eaten here, and when you see the portions you won't be surprised. Open Mon.-Sat. 10am-8pm, Sun. 10am-4:30pm.

Tsuruya Noodle Shop, Ala Moana Shopping Center (946-7214). Enormous cauldrons of *Soba* and *Udan* (noodles and soup) for $3.30-7. Open Mon.-Sat. 9:30am-9pm.

Island Manapua Factory, 2752 Woodlawn Dr., Manoa (988-5441). Pick up a box of freshly steamed *manapua,* an island favorite made from Chinese sweet dough filled with pork or chicken (60¢ each). Sticky rice cakes are a favorite *keiki* (kiddie) treat (30¢). Open Mon.-Sat. 8:30am-8pm, Sun. 8:30am-5pm.

Kengo's Restaurant, 1529 Kapiolani (941-2241). You can get entrees from $5-7 until 9:30pm, or wait until 10pm and eat double portions of pu-pu's for the price of one in the lounge ($5). Lunch served daily 11am-2pm, dinner daily 5-9:30pm.

Ruffage Natural Foods, 2443 Kuhio Ave. (922-2042). Serves up great vegetarian classics to go: tofu-burger with tomato and sprouts ($4.50), large container of vege-chili with brown rice ($2.85). They also serve fresh fruit smoothies ($2.50-3.50) and sell all-natural vitamins and skin care products. Open Mon.-Sun. 8:30am-7pm, Sun. 9am-7pm.

Sights and Activities

Gone are the early 80s, when Honolulu was littered with tokens of excessive commercialization tourism. Plastic grass skirts, Kon-Tiki idol replicas, and clamshell windchimes—not to mention billions of yards of plastic leis—have retreated in the face of the swish and cosmopolitan city that is the emerging Honolulu.

The one-hour loop on the #14 bus cuts across a sampling of Honolulu's diverse neighborhoods. Waikiki is, of course, centered around Waikiki Beach; Kaimuke and Kapahula are small, close-knit communities; Moliliili's lifeblood is the university; and downtown is the shipping and business district, along with Chinatown.

Waikiki

Originally a marshy swampland and hideaway for Hawaiian royalty, Waikiki's wetlands were drained into the Ala Canal to launch the island's tourist industry. In the 1950s, the image of a ¾-mi. crescent of white sand beach set against the profile of Diamond Head lured platoons of vacationers and honeymooners, eager to spend their post-war boom bucks, to wonderful Waikiki. Hotels sprouted everywhere, with each successive high-rise further obscuring the view of the ocean and mountain. Today, more savvy visitors spend time on the less crowded isles. Nevertheless, despite its glitzy facade, Waikiki remains fascinating.

When you want a break from the beach scene, hike the one mile into the **Diamond Head Crater.** To get there, take bus #58 from Waikiki. Bring a flashlight to guide you through a pitch-dark section of the tunnel. The view of Waikiki is spectacular, and if you go on a day full of liquid sunshine you might catch a rainbow arching over the U.S. military base in the center of the crater.The beautful estates on the slopes of Diamond Head belong to scions of Hawaii's original missionary families. It has been said that the missionaries came to do good, and did very well indeed.

If the gods do not favor your excursion to Diamond Head try visiting the **Damien Museum,** 330 Ohua St. (behind the St. Augustine Church), for a peek at the dark side of Hawaii's past. Through original documents and a one-hour video, the museum displays the history of Father Damien's Molokai leper colony. (Open Mon.-Fri. 9am-3pm, Sat. 9am-noon. Free.) For the animal inside you, the **Honolulu Zoo,** 151 Kapahulu Ave. (971-7171), across from Kapiolani Park, is located on the east end of Waikiki. This is the best zoo on the islands. Daily activities for children include shows and animal demonstrations. The Australian section is currently being expanded to make room for new arrivals. Call the above number for a recorded schedule of events. (Admission $4, ages under 13 free. Open daily 8:30am-4pm.) Outside the zoo local painters exhibit their work in the Art Mart (Wed. and Sat.-Sun. 10am-4pm). For a close encounter of the nautical kind, the **Kahala Hilton Hotel** has free dolphin feedings every day at 11am, 2pm and 4pm.

Across the street from the zoo is the **Waikiki Shell,** home to many concerts as well as the **Kodak Hula Show** (833-1661), which is Waikiki at its photogenic tackiest. This production packages *hula* dancing and palm tree climbing into bite-size tourist portions. You may have a Brady Bunch-esque flashback, but it is a laugh. (Shows Tues.-Thu. at 10am. $2.50 adults, under 12 free.) For more authentic dancing performances, contact the **Hawaii Visitor's Bureau** (923-1811) and ask about any upcoming performances or competitions among the **hula halau** (schools). Major competitions are usually held in the spring. The **Queen Kapiolani Rose Garden,** Monsarrat and Paki Ave., is always a welcoming and fragrant retreat. Look, but don't touch; the roses are protected by magic **kahuna stones** (open 24 hours; free). You can also ogle fish (and 2 dolphins) at the **Waikiki Aquarium,** 2777 Kalakaua Ave (923-9741). The aquarium has been undergoing expansion since 1988, and has recently added a wave machine and an exhibit on Mahimahi (dolphin fish). (Open daily 9am-5pm; $2.50 donation requested, ages under 16 free).

Waikiki Beach, actually comprised of several smaller beaches, is lined with shops and hotels of all varieties and is generally packed with tourists. Farthest to the east is the **Sans Souci Beach,** in front of the Kaimona Otani Hotel. Site of an old natatorium (an outdoor swimming pool by the sea with impressive stone bleachers) built as a war memorial, Sans Souci (carefree) has shower facilities but no public restrooms. The **Queen's Surf Beach,** closer to downtown, attracts swimmers and roller skaters. The area to the left of the snack bar is a popular tanning spot for gays. On Sunday evenings, bongo players gather under the banyan tree. Between the Hawaiian Regent and the Hyatt Regency, breakers shelter **Kuhio Beach Park** from the heavy surf. Enjoy the calm waters, and watch the adventurous stand on the rocks, while surfers venture beyond the breakers for the big waves. Next to the Waikiki Beach Center (across from the Hyatt Regency) are four more *kahuna stones,* which are supposed to possess healing powers. For a taste of an earlier age in Hawaiian tourism, wander through the lobbies of the newly renovated turn-of-the-century

Moana Hotel, which surrounds a phenomenal banyan tree on Waikiki Beach, or visit the historic Royal Hawaiian Hotel, whose pink grandeur was unveiled in 1927. At the far end of the beach, **Fort de Russy Beach Park** features the liveliest games of two-player beach volleyball this side of Orange County.

Downtown

Several cultural and historic attractions are found around the downtown area. If you are in Chinatown, stop and smell the beautiful strands of ginger *leis* ($3 each) at the *lei* shops on Maunakea St. Each lei holds a specific symbolic meaning, but they are best known as signs of welcome. Before the advent of jet planes, locals would celebrate "Boat Day" by purchasing leis at these stalls and walking a few blocks to garland arriving friends and relatives at the pier.

Get a seagull's-eye view of all Oahu from the **Aloha Tower** (536-6373) on the 10th floor of Pier 9. (Free, though unimpressive.) Or get a view of the sea at the **Maritime Museum,** on the 9th floor of the pier, with its collection of old ships from the Honolulu Harbor. (Open daily 9am-8pm. Admission $6, children $3.) The **Falls of Clyde,** a unique four-masted ship once used as an oil tanker, is dry docked in the harbor.

The **Iolani Palace,** at King and Richard St. (538-1471), was first the residence of King Kalakaua and Queen Liliuokalani and later served as the nerve center in the TV show *Hawaii Five-0.* The deposed Liliuukalani spent nine months here as a prisoner. The stunning breakfast room was once used to entertain heads of state from all over the world. Now it's a fabulous museum in the process of a multimillion dollar search for the original furniture. In the interim, the palace displays sumptuously carved *koa* furniture and elegant European decor. You can tour the grounds on your own, but the official tour inside the building gives interesting historical facts and lasts only 45 min. (Wed.-Sat. 9am-2:15pm., adults $4, ages 5-12 $1, under 5 not admitted). Call 522-0832 for reservations or go to the barracks or the palace grounds at least a half an hour beforehand to reserve tickets. The palace grounds include the Coronation Pavilion, where the Royal Hawaiian Band gives free concerts on Fridays at noon.

Across King St. stands the Kamehameha I statue, erected in 1883 in honor of the islands' early 19th-century ruler. In commemoration of the king's unification of the islands, his statue is draped with *leis* on June 11, when *palau* (horseback) riders parade through Waikiki. At the corner of Beretania and Richard St. stands Hawaii's modern **State Capitol,** an architectural melange reflecting all facets of the state's landscape. The pillars represent palm trees, while the inverted dome of the house chambers rises like a volcano, and reflecting pools call to mind the blue Pacific nearby. Outside stands a controversial sculpture of Father Damien. (Open Mon.-Fri. 9am-4pm. Free.) South of the State Capital at the intersection of Punchbowl and King St. is **Kawaiahao Church,** completed in 1942 and built from coral rocks. Services are at 10:30am on Sundays. The graves of early missionaries lie on the grounds between the church and the **Honolulu Mission House Museum,** 553 S. King St. (531-0481). Using Hawaii's oldest western buildings as their backdrop, museum actors transport visitors to the missionary age of the 1830s. The museum also offers walking tours for $7 at 9:30am (includes refreshments and admission to the homes). (Open Tues.-Fri. and Sun. noon-4pm. Admission $3.50, under 15 $1.) For a complete guide to this district, pick up the Capital District Walking Tour from the Hawaii Visitor's Bureau.

Nearby, the **Honolulu Academy of Arts,** 900 S. Beretania St. (538-1006), houses one of the finest collections of Asian art in the U.S. The 30 galleries and six garden courts also display 17th-century samurai armor, African art, and temporary exhibits. (Open Tues.-Sat. 10am-4:30pm, Sun. 1-5pm. Tours Tues.-Wed. and Fri.-Sat. at 11am, Thurs. at 2pm, and Sun. at 1pm. Free.) The **Bishop Museum,** 1525 Bernice St. (848-4129), in Kalihi, houses an eclectic and well-respected if somewhat disorganized collection of artifacts from the Indo-Pacific region. It is the best Hawaiiana museum in the world, and deserves a good portion of your day. Their planetarium features a show entitled "Journey by Starlight" (Mon.-Fri. at 11am and 3pm, Fri.-

Sat. at 8pm) which projects the history of Polynesian celestial navigation; the Atherton Halau is the scene of daily craft demonstrations ranging from *lei*-making to *Kapa* cloth-pounding and printing. (Open daily 9am-2:30pm; call 848-4106 for further information. Museum open Mon.-Sat. 9am-5pm. Admission $5, ages 6-16 $2.50.) Take bus #2 ("School St.") from Waikiki.

51 years ago this December 7th, a stunned nation listened to the reports of the Japanese obliteration of the U.S. Pacific Fleet in **Pearl Harbor.** Today, the **U.S.S. Arizona National Memorial** (422-2771) can be viewed with quiet respect. An austere, three-part structure was built over the sunken aircraft carrier hull in which over a thousand servicemen perished. The memorial's unique sagging center represents the demoralizing defeat of the *Arizona*: the higher ends of the structure symbolize the U.S.'s ultimate victory. The Navy offers free tours of the memorial from 7:45am to 3pm, including a 30-minute film, and sends launches out to the hull every 15 minutes. No children under six years of age or under 45 " are admitted on the launch. Dress is casual, but swimsuits and flip-flops are prohibited, in light of the somber and respectful mood. Veterans often throw leis into the viewing well over the hull. The **visitors center** is open Tuesday through Sunday 7:30am to 5pm. Take the #20 from Waikiki or the #50, 51, or 52 from Ala Moana or the $2 shuttle from major Waikiki hotels (926-4747). Tickets to the memorial are free, but 2-hour-plus waits are not unusual. If you are at Pearl Harbor on the first Saturday of the month, stop by from noon to 4pm for a free tour of the **Navy Visit Ship** at the Pearl Harbor Navy Base (471-0281).

Wake up early on Saturday and Sunday mornings and pop over to the **"swap meet"** held between 8:30am and noon in Aloha Stadium. It's a great chance to people-watch or buy a gift. Rows of vendors sell everything from T-shirts to fruits and vegetables. (Admission $1 per car, 8:30am-noon.)

Mauka (Inland)

Looking *mauka* from downtown you'll see the lush **Nuuanu Valley;** the next valley to the east is the **Manoa Valley.** At the mouth of the Manoa Valley lies the **University of Hawaii,** where lecture attendance drops as the surf rises. The campus bulletin boards are a great place to find out about apartments for rent, tickets for sale and upcoming film, theater and music events.

One of the best dayhikes on the island begins at the end of Manoa Rd. and trails through 1 mile of lush tropical greenery to Manoa Falls. Once there you can take a cold freshwater dip in the pool under the falls. Trail conditions are as unpredictable as the weather: visit after a dry spell and the falls are less impressive but more accessible. After a heavy rain you'll be mud-sliding and torrent-watching at the same time. Take bus #5 from Waikiki to the end of Manoa Rd.

The **Lyon Arboretum,** 3860 Manoa Rd. (988-3177), at the end of Manoa Valley 4 mi. from Waikiki, maintains a superb collection of tropical plants, shrubs, and trees. Free tours (1½ hr.) of the grounds are offered on the first Friday, third Wednesday (both at 1pm), and third Saturday (at 10am) of every month. (Open Mon.-Fri. 9am-3pm, Sat. 9am-noon. Donation $1.) Catch the bird shows in **Paradise Park,** 3737 Manoa Rd. (988-0200). This natural Hawaiian rain forest shelters hundreds of tropical birds, some of which perform their own musical compositions daily. (Open daily 9:30am-5pm. Shows three times a day. Admission $14, ages 8-13 $9, 3-7 $7.)

The ridge just *ewa* (west) of Manoa with its expansive views is the perfect place to watch the sunset. Go up Makiki St. to Round Top Dr. and follow this snake-like road to romantic **Puuualakaaa Park,** where you can gaze upon the twinkling city lights at night. After sunset, drive back down about 1 mi. to the parking area on the side of the road, watch Honolulu light up for the night, and feel the wind cascading down the valley. It's quite popular—ask the teenage couples in the parked cars.

The **National Memorial Cemetary of the Pacific,** 2177 Puowaina Dr. (546-3190), better known as the **"Punchbowl Cemetery",** commemorates servicemen who died

Royal Hawaiian Tavern 2 Merchant St (531 0422)

in both World Wars, Korea and Vietnam. It is located in the Puowaina Crater, where human sacrifice rituals were once performed. No irony intended.

Parallel to the Manoa Valley, the **Pali Highway** (Rte. 61) winds its way through **Nuuanu Valley** and over into Kailua, on the windward side of the island. On the way, stop at the **Queen Emma Summer Palace (Hanaiakamalama),** 2913 Pali Hwy. (595-3167), formerly the posh summer retreat for the Kamaaina elite. Queen Emma, a close friend of Queen Victoria as a result of her youthful travels to England, furnished her lavish estate in a manner that reflects the impact that Western civilization had upon the islands during her husband Kamehameha IV's reign. A non-profit organization offers tours. (Open daily 9am-4pm. Admission $4, seniors $3, ages 12-18 $1, under 12 50¢.) Take bus #4 "Waikiki" (1 hr.) or any bus that begins with "Kailua" or "Kaneohe" from Ala Moana Shopping Center. As you near the top of the Pali, pull into the **Pali Lookout.** Although this observation point is always packed with tourists, the view overlooking the windward side is undoubtedly one of the finest in all of the islands. From the lookout, you can look down onto an enormous valley studded with small mountains and then out to the sea beyond. But hang onto your hat—the wind blusters. Kamehameha the Great consolidated his kingdom by defeating Oahu's soldiers and driving them over this dramatic cliff.

Entertainment

Bars, restaurants, and theaters abound in Waikiki, making nightlife as wild as your feet and liver can take. Indoor cinemas allow the less rambunctious to escape the city's bright lights. The University of Hawaii's **Hemenway Theatre,** (948-8111), in the Physical Sciences Building, shows classic films for $2. The **Honolulu Academy of Arts,** 900 S. Beretania St. (528-1006), features foreign films. There is a full season of symphony and opera at the **Niel Blaisdell Center** (527-5400). Year-round theater (musical and dramatic) is staged at the **Honolulu Community Theater** (734-0274), near Diamond Head, and at the **Manoa Valley Theater** (988-6131). Don't miss the Honolulu Zoo's "wildest show in town" summer series of Wednesday night entertainment (923-7723). Admission is free, starting at 4:30pm, and performances begin at 6pm.

Seagull Bar and Restaurant, 2463 Kuhio Ave. (924-7911), in Waikiki. Drink up with a truly international crowd. A lot of young hostelers hang out here for the low drink prices; slam a beer for a mere $1.50. Open daily 4:30pm-2am.

Anna Bananas, 2440 S. Beretania (946-5190), near the university. Two floors of reggae, Afro-pop and blues. The crowd is generally local bikers and surfers with a liberal sprinkling of college students. Don't miss the exceedingly tastefully decorated bathrooms. Steinlager on draft $2.25. Open until 2am.

Hula's Bar and Leis, 2103 Kuhio Ave. (923-0669), at Kalaamoku. Popular gay bar. No cover. Open daily 2pm-4am.

Moose McGillycuddy's Pub & Café, 1035 University Ave. (944-5525), near the university (also 310 Lewers St., 923-0751, near the hostels). Student domain serving huge sandwiches for lunch and dinner. Pub happy hour offers half-price draft beer. Drinks and some margaritas and daquiries ($2). Must be 21 for the disco after 9pm. No cover. Happy Hour 4-8pm. Open Mon.-Sat. 11:30am-2am, Sun. 10am-2am.

The Wave, 1877 Kalakaua Ave. (941-0424), on the edge of Waikiki. A fine locale for loud music and dancing. Mixed crowd. Open daily 9pm-4am.

Pink Cadillac, 478 Ena (942-5282). One of the few dancing options for the 18-21 crowd, featuring cutting-edge progressive music. Open 'til 2am.

Cilly's, 1909 Ala Wai Blvd. (942-2952), corner of Ala Wai and McCully. 18 and over dancing, 9pm-4am.

The Other Side of the Island

Everything on Oahu outside Honolulu is considered "the other side." In general, the farther from the city you scoot, the fewer tourists you will encounter. Concrete and glass quickly fade into pineapple and sugarcane fields sprinkled with small outlying communities. Highway #2 going north traverses a fertile plateau before descending at the sugar-and-surfer town of Haleiwa on the North Shore. Well-maintained highways lead from there to the east, and the scenic windward coast. To the west of Haleiwa you can only travel as far as Kaena Point, where the paved road ends and a rough, rocky trail begins. You can see the Leeward coast by traveling west on H-1 from Honolulu until it becomes Fanington Highway.

A tour of the island can be done in five hours, but it's best to give yourself at least a day. Start on the Windward Coast and work your way around the perimeter. To reach the southern Windward Coast, take bus #58 from Waikiki. To see the North Shore, hop on bus #55 at Ala Moana. Both buses run every hour daily from 7am until 6pm.

Accommodations and Camping

There is a smaller pool of accommodations in these less densely populated areas, but if you find a place you like you might just have it to yourself. If you're flexible you can house yourself without spending a lot of money. Camping can be beautiful along the coast, but unfortunately, there have been reports of violence against tourists at some campgrounds in recent years. It's not always easy to pick a safe place by sight, but piles of empty beer cans and lots of trash are sure signs that someone considers the place their territory; it's best to steer clear and pick another spot. Remember that rangers patrol the beach to roust illegal campers. Don't risk it; get a permit and camp legally. Also seek out good deals at bed and breakfasts.

Backpacker's Vacation Inn and Plantation Villas, 59-788 Kamahameha Hwy. (638-7838), ¼ mi. north of Waimea Bay. Adjacent to Three Table Bay and neighboring Shark's Cove. International crowd of travelers and water sport enthusiasts. Plantation Village consists of cottages with bunks, bathroom, shared kitchen and laundry facilities, and color TV. The rowdy, youthful atmosphere may be a turn-off to some, but it's simple, comfortable, and so close to the ocean. Weekend B-B-Qs. Co-ed bunks rooms and free use of boogie boards and snorkeling equipment. Bunks $14-16, doubles $35-45.

Malaekahana State Recreation Area (293-1736), north of Laie. Ranger-patrolled for safety. At low tide, wade across the water to Mokuauia Island, a bird refuge and great picnic spot. Showers, toilets, picnic tables, barbecue pits. Permits obtainable at state offices (see Practical Information).

Bellows Field Beach Park (523-4525), just north of Warmanalo Bay. Facilities are a little rough and it can be crowded, but the beach is beautiful and good for swimming or windsurfing. Permits can be obtained at 650 South King St. in Honolulu from the County and Regional Parks people, in person only. Free.

Bed and Breakfast—Hawaii, P.O. Box 449, Kapau, HI 96746 (536-8421). Locations all over the island, including Kailua. Prices vary, starting at about $50 double occupancy.

Windward Oahu and Hanauma Bay

Miles of beaches and rural towns span the 40-mi. coast, running from Laie in the north to Mokapu Point in the south. This is one of the most scenic drives on the island, and good snorkeling abounds. Farther south, Kalanianaole Hwy. wraps around a rugged 4-mi. stretch to Koko Head, the eastern boundary of Honolulu.

Food

Starvation is not a danger here; fruit vendors and drive-in restaurants with plate lunches and shave ice are plentiful on the Windward Coast.

Kaaawa Country Kitchen and Grocery, 51-480 Kamehameha Hwy. (237-8485), Kaaawa. Across from Swanz Beach Park. This mom-and-pop country drive-in has kept the locals of

Kaaawa satisfied for more than 30 years. The teri-beef ($4.15) is tasty. Open Sun.-Thurs. 6:30am-6:30pm, Fri.-Sat. 6:30am-7pm.

Warmanolo BBQ, 41-857 Kalanianaole Hwy. (259-8700). Great place to stop after beaching all day. D-lishous ice cream ($1) and all flavors of shave ice. Plate lunches and island food $3.75-5.75. Open "from the time I get here 'til the time I go home," but 8:30am-4:30pm is safe.

Frankie's Drive-In, 41-1610 Kalanianale Hwy. (259-7819), Waimanolo. Frankie has been serving up 95¢ cheeseburgers since 1953. Hamburg D-lux for a wallet-pleasing $1.05. Plate lunches. Open Mon.-Sat. 9:30am-4:30pm.

Texas Paniolo Café, 53-146 Kam Hwy. (237-8521). Just south of Punaluu Beach Park. Restaurant and bar serves a yummy spicy veggie soup ($5.75) and 16 oz. Mason jars of Coors ($3). Open 'til midnight. Closed Tuesdays after 4pm.

Bueno Nalo, 41-865 Kalanianaole Hwy. (259-7186), in Waimanalo. The best restaurant for miles, Bueno serves flavorful Mexican meals ($6.25-7.75). Open Tues.-Fri. 5-9pm, Sat.-Sun. 3-9pm.Sights and Activities

From Waikiki, take **Kalanianaole Highway** (Rte. 72) east to **Koko Head Crater.** Some of the friendliest and most colorful fish in the Pacific reside in **Hanauma Bay,** formed where the ocean has washed away the crater's eastern wall. These federally protected waters are the spot supreme for snorkeling. For the clearest underwater trip, come early in the morning (before 10am), since the tourists flock here in droves. Park officials stop letting cars into the parking lot when it gets too crowded. A 10-minute walk to the left of the bay brings you to the less well-known **Toilet Bowl.** This bowl-shaped phenomenon is great fun to play around in. Climb in when it's full and get flushed up and down as waves fill and empty the chamber through natural lava plumbing. When the surf's high position yourself in the middle with plenty of human padding between you and the rocky sides—things can get rough in the Bowl.

A mile farther, a similar mechanism drives the **Halona Blow Hole** to release its spray. The dramatic effect is dependent upon tidal conditions and can vary from a weak squirt to a full-blown Moby Dick Spout. From here, the island of Molokai, 20 mi. away, can be viewed, and on a clear day, as many as four of the neighbor islands may be sighted. **Secret Beach,** to the right of Halona Blow Hole, was the site of Burt Lancaster and Deborah Kerr's famous "kiss in the sand" in *From Here to Eternity.* Readers of *Let's Go* may wish to re-enact this great moment in cinematic history when they see the tiny, romantic cove. The lone traveler may find consolation in watching the sea turtles that sometimes flip around the bay (although they probably won't be up for a passionate smooch).

Sandy Beach, just beyond Halona, is a prime spot for bodysurfing and boogie-boarding, the center of the summer surf circuit, and a year-round hangout for locals. The beach is expansive and pleasantly sandy, but the summer swells burst onto the shore with spine-crashing force, making swimming a bit awkward. The road continues toward Mokapu Point with views worthy of cinematic attention.Rabbit Island (so named because it resembles a swimming hare with flattened ears) and smaller Turtle Island (Kaohikaipu) are anchored offshore. **Makapuu Beach,** 41-095 Kalanianaole Hwy., is another prime place to bodysurf; but when the lifeguards put up red flags, stay out of the water. Across from Makapuu lies **Sea Life Park** (259-7933), a minor-league Sea World, with performing penguins and all. (Admission $8.50, seniors and children $6. Open Mon.-Wed. and Sat. 9:30am-5pm, Thurs.-Fri. and Sun. 9:30am-10pm.)

Past Makai Pier, but before you get to Kaiona Beach Park, you may experience déja vù. Not to worry. You've just been watching too many Magnum P.I. reruns (the show was often filmed in this area). **Waimanola Beach Park** has a shady tree area, clean facilities, and a cooling onshore breeze. For novices, the best bodysurfing can be found at **Sherwoods** and, on weekends, at **Bellows Air Force Base.** Both are on Kalanianaole on the road to Kailua. Be warned, however, that neither of these parks provides lifeguards.

Kalanianaole ends by intersecting **Kailua Road.** Follow this road toward **Kailua Town** and **Kailua Beach Park.** This is prime sailboarding territory. The sandy beach and strong, steady onshore winds are perfect for learning waterstarts. Beginners will thank the wind gods that they are being blown in rather than out to sea. If you feel an irresistable urge to "shred," but you left your rig at home, two companies rent from vans in the parking lot. **Windsurfing Hawaii** (261-6067) rents beginner boards for $30 per day (harness $5 extra) and shortboards for $40 per day. They also have boogie boards ($10 per day), water skis ($25 per day) and two-man kayaks ($35 per day). Sailboarding lessons run $35 per person for a 3 hour group clinic. **Kailua Sailboard Company** (262-2555), rents "standard" longboards for $27 per day, 8:30am-5pm (harness is $5 extra) and Bic Ace tech shortboards for $30 per day. They offer 3 hour beginner lessons for $35 at 10:30am and 2pm. When the winds are blowing, however, those left on shore may cringe as they are pelted with the powdery sand (particularly perilous to contact lens wearers). If you can bear the grit, this is a great place to swim. Nearby Lanikai's (Mokulva Dr.) white sand and deep green waters make it the best place on Oahu to savor the sunrise. Kailua Rd. in the other direction takes you to **Kaneohe** via Kamehameha Hwy. Visit the free **Haiku Gardens,** 46-316 Haiku Rd. (247-6671), where many weddings are held. Open daily sunrise to sunset.You might also check out the **Ulupo Heiau** (1200 Kailua Rd.), next to the YMCA. Supposedly built by the legendary *menehunes,* a mischievous little people, the temple still stands as a platform of black lava rock overlooking the Keanui swamp. Smooth stones lead across the jagged lava of the *heiau* and down the far side to the roots of a great banyan tree, where a natural spring wells up. Swimmers will love the smooth waters of **Kailua Beach Park** (450 Kawailoa Rd.) and **Lanikai Beach** (Mokulua Dr.)

Look for the **Valley of the Temples,** 47-200 Kahekili Hwy., a burial ground matching the Punchbowl for beauty. The serene **Byodo-In Temple** can be found on the grounds. A replica of a temple in Uji, Japan, it was built in 1968 to commemorate the 100th anniversary of Japanese immigrants' first arrival in Hawaii. Stroll through the tropical gardens and by the running stream, filled with brightly colored Japanese carp (but watch out for the resident peacock with attack-dog tendencies). Ring the three-ton brass bell to bring happiness and the blessings of the Buddha. (Open daily sunrise to sunset. Admission to the valley $2 per person.)

Approaching the North Shore on the Kamehameha Hwy., you will reach **Kualoa Regional Park** and **Chinaman's Hat,** an island named for its conical shape. Its Hawaiian name is *Mokolii,* which means little dragon. Much of *Karate Kid II* was filmed on the island. If you're a strong swimmer and careful about the tides, snorkel out to the island and climb to the top. The swim probably takes longer than the hike. North of here, **Swanzy Beach State Park, Kaaawa Beach Park,** and **Kahana Bay Park** are good places to picnic or swim. Right around the bend from **Punaluu** is the entrance to **Sacred Falls Park,** legendary birthplace of the pig god. The falls are a 2 mile walk from the parking lot. The trail crosses a stream twice and takes about an hour each way. The falls and the cool, refreshing pool underneath make the hike worthwhile.

Farther up the coast, the city of **Laie** is home to the **Polynesian Cultural Center,** 55-370 Kamehameha Hwy. (293-3333), a carefully re-created village representing the indigenous cultures of New Zealand, Samoa, Tonga, Fiji, Hawaii, Tahiti, and the Marquesas. Special performances include *hula* dancing on canoes and coconut-husking. Walk through the park at your own leisure. (Open Mon.-Sat. from noon-6:30pm for daytime activities Dinner served 4:30-7pm, followed by an evening spectacle from 7:30-9pm. Admission to the grounds is $25, with dinner and show $40.

Past Laie the land gives way to abandoned sugar plantations. **Amorient Aquafarms** (293-5311) runs a 175-acre shrimp and fish farm near Kahuku. Stop at their roadside stall to sample fresh catfish or Black Tiger Shrimp. Rounding the island's northern tip at Kahuku, you will also see strange two-armed windmills gyrating on the hillside—another experimental energy project.

North Shore and Central Oahu

Home to the sugar cane fields and surfers, the North Shore is a different world from Honolulu (and most other parts of the world). You'll find a plethora of people here who, Odysseus-like, have turned quick stops into six or eight year sojourns. The pace is slow and peaceful in the summer, with beautiful sunsets and plenty of empty beaches. Things heat up in the winter when the surfer crowd decends to shred the infamous waves along Sunset Beach and the Banzai Pipeline, and the North Shore hops with surfing competitions and bikini contests. The best things to see here are those you stumble across on your own—secluded bays free from tourists' footprints, coral reefs full of crabs and sea anemones or, if you're lucky, the perfect wave.

Food

Country Drive-In, 66-200 Kam Hwy. (637-9122), in Haleiwa. Twenty varieties of plate lunches and *shaka min.* Also sells yummy smoothies. Plate lunches $3-5. Open 7am-6pm, breakfast served 'til 11:30am.

China Inn, 66-250 Kam Hwy. (637-5876). For the broke and hungry, the super-mini-plate is anything but: a large serving of any meat or vegetable dish and rice or noodles for $2.50. Open Tues.-Sun. 9am-10pm. Closed Mondays.

Café Haleiwa, 66-460 Kam Hwy. (637-5516). Funky music, surfer and local crowd. Peace symbols on the menu. Daily specials $4.50-6.50, burgers with the works $5.35. Breakfast from 6am-7am.

Rosie's Cantina, Haleiwa Shopping Center (637-3538). Colorful interior and truly tasty food. $1 drafts on special nights. Sandwiches ($4.95-5.75) served until 5pm. Entrees ($9.50-12) until 10pm Sun.-Thu., 11pm Fri.-Sat.

Steamers Seafood Restaurant, Haleiwa Shopping Center (637-5071). At $9-18, the entrees are a bit pricey. Go for drinks and graze on salads ($2.50) and chowder ($2), baked potato or local steamed rice. Cover charge on weekends when local bands play, $3.

The Sugar Bar and Restaurant, 67-069 Kealohanui (637-6989). The ultimate in dive bar excitement. An interesting mix of bikers, surfers and locals. Area bands play sporadically to an enthusiastic crowd. No cover.

Sights

Even if you left your supply of Dr. Zog's Sex Wax (and your surfboard) at home, you still have ample opportunity to frolic in the untamed waters. The action on the North Shore centers around **Haleiwa,** the surfers' Lourdes. Haleiwa once was a plantation town, but now is enlivened by surf shops and art galleries. **Hawaii Surf and Sail,** 66-214 Kamehameha Hwy. (637-5373), rents all kinds of watersport equipment and gives surfing and sailboarding lessons ($30 for 2-hr. lesson). To the North of Haleiwa is **Waimea Beach Park,** where locals jump off a high rock formation into the sea. This is not to be confused with **Waimea Falls Park** (638-8511), a 1800-acre nature preserve with tropical gardens and a 45-ft. waterfall extravaganza. There, the divers are sent off the cliffs daily at 11am, 12:30pm, 2pm, 2:45pm and 3:30pm. Admission to the Falls Park is $14 for adults. Ask about free nighttime strolls offered around the time of the full moon. About ¼ mile north of Waimea Pupukea Rd. lies **Puuomahuka Heiqu,** the largest temple of its kind on the Island, which was used for human sacrifices until 1794. Today, visitors leave gifts of fruit or flowers on and between the rocks. Make a right off of Kamehameha onto Pupukea at the Foodland and follow the signs that say "State Monument."

Back on Kamehameha, another few minutes drive will get you to **Sunset Beach,** and the Banzai Pipeline, infamous winter waveland of the world. The beaches are big enough to stay sprinkled rather than packed with people. On Sundays, drop your board and head over to **Mokuleia** for a chukka or two of polo. (Along Rte. 930, $6 admission.) The field is right on the beach so if you get tired of the action you can go for a swim. Rte. 82 leads you through Wahiawa, another plantation town and home to the Sacred Healing Stones, which became so popular in the first part of this century that they had to be enclosed in a concrete, cubical "temple" for their protection. On the way, take a poke around the **Dole Pineapple Pavilion,** 64-1550 Kamehameha Hwy. (621-8468). Displays offer the visitor a crash course on the ins and outs of the pineapple breeding business. Inside you can buy classy pineapple memorabilia, from T-shirts to the puzzling Dole Whip. Honolulu is less than an hour away along Rte. 99 and H-2. As you drive back, you'll notice the suburban sprawl of Mililani extending Honolulu's tentacles further into the countryside, destroying the rural atmosphere.

Seasonal Events

A variety of events deify Hawaii's ethnic diversity and celebrate its outdoor spirit. The Hawaii Visitors Bureau publishes *He Kukiki Hawaii* (the Hawaiian Messenger), which gives a complete listing. Check also the "What's-On" listings in the Friday paper.

Narcissus Festival, late Jan., celebrates the Chinese New Year with fireworks and a raucous lion dance in Chinatown. Call 533-3181.

Punahou School Carnival, the 1st weekend in Feb. At the Punahou School, Punahou St. and Wilder Ave., near U. of H. The biggest of the many high school carnivals. Usually jam-packed, it features a variety of shows, rides, rummage sales, and famous mango chutney and *malasadas.*

Buffalo's Annual Big Board Surfing Classic, in late Feb. On Makaha Beach, Leeward Oahu. A surfing meet with entertainment and food. Call Bunky Bakutis (696-3878).

Cherry Blossom Festival, in late Feb.-March. The Japanese community puts on tea ceremonies, cooking demonstrations, fashion shows, and more all over the island, especially in downtown Honolulu. Also, look for *bon* dances most weekends in summer.

Annual Hawaiian Festival of Music, in mid-April. Waikiki Shell, Honolulu. Hawaiian and mainland groups compete for awards in a festival of symphonic strings, concert choirs, madrigal monks, swing groups, and marching bands. Call Robert Schriver (637-6566).

Lei Day, May 1. Kapiolani Park. Many flowers, *lei*-making contests, and pageants. Local schools celebrate by singing Hawaiian songs, dancing, and stringing *leis.* A great place to get *lei*ed.

Annual Bankoh Kayak Challenge, late May. 32 mile race from Moloaki to Koko Marina. Call Ocean Promotions in Kona at 326-1011.

Annual "Gotcha" Pro Surf Championships, in mid-June. Sandy Beach, Windward Oahu. Summer surfing event with prizes for the public.

King Kamehameha Day, June 11. A parade through downtown and Waikiki follows *lei* draping ceremony at the diminutive Kamehameha statue on King St.

King Kamehameha Annual Hula and Chant Competition, in late June. Neil Blaisdell Center, Honolulu. Modern and ancient *hula* and chant competition. Amateur and professional *halaus* compete amidst cheers from a boisterous crowd.

Hawaii State Farm Fair, late June-early July. McKinley High School Grounds. Agricultural exhibits, petting zoo, mud wrestling, rides, games, and food booths. Call Wendell Koga (848-2074).

Annual Prince Lot Hula Festival, late July. Authentic Hula performances, Moanalua Gardens. Call 839-5334 for additional information.

Aloha Week Festivities, in mid-Sept. The highlight of week-long events is the elaborate parade with *pau* riders on horseback. Call 944-8857.

Kanikapila (Let's Play Music), in mid.-Oct. at U. of H. campus. Singers, musicians, and dancers in the open-air Andrews Amphitheater.

Honolulu Marathon, Dec. 10. Also the Honolulu Wheelchair Marathon the day before. Call Honolulu Marathon Association (734-7200), or write 3435 Waialae Ave, #208, Honolulu 96816.

Triple Crown of Surfing, in Dec.-Jan., contingent upon weather and surfing conditions. The finals are always held at Banzai Pipeline and aired on national TV.

Hawaii (The Big Island)

Pele, Polynesian goddess of the volcanoes, is believed to reside on Hawaii, southeasternmost island in the Hawaiian chain. She prefers the hot, dry weather of the Kona (leeward) side while her lover, Kamapua'a, is responsible for the rain and wet of the Hilo (windward) side. Their frequent meetings mix things up a bit, creating the seventeen-odd climatic zones found on the Big Island, ranging from the desert-like North Kona coast to the snow-covered peaks of Mauna Kea to the rainforests, valleys, and waterfalls of the Hamakua Coast. Mark Twain captured the diversity when he said that here he "could see all the climes of the world at a single glance of the eye."

Visitors to the volcano region take heed: Pele is very much alive, and very powerful. She appears to some as a beautiful young woman, and to others as an old, drunken hag. Offerings left at sacred places or in the volcanoes themselves include leis, fruit or sweets, and rocks wrapped in Ti leaves. You will also see stacks of rocks a few feet high dotting the strange landscape of the lava flows. If you truly want to appease Pele and protect yourself from her wrath, take a bottle of gin with you and pour it into one of the lava lakes; Pele will appreciate it and smile on your adventure. Rumor has it that the cause of the Brady family's three-part misadventures in Hawaii nearly 20 years ago was a failure tp appease the vengeful goddess. Above all, never remove rocks from the island as souvenirs—thousands of tourists mail their stones back to the National Parks Service every year, begging forgiveness and an end to their otherwise inexplicable string of bad luck.

The Big Island emerged from the confluence of the five major volcanoes, the result of Hawaii's position on top of the hot spot in the Pacific Plate. The only two which are still active are Mauna Loa, the still-active Long Mountain (13,677 ft.) and Kilauea (4000ft.), home of the very active Halemaumau Crater. Kilauea is currently in its 49th phase of eruption without showing any signs of exhaustion, and crowds flock daily to the island to watch the molten rock pour into the boiling sea. Although the eruptions are tremendously powerful, the volcanoes do not emit dangerous ash clouds, and the lava flow is quick only near the summit and in underground lava tubes.

Coastal highways circle both mountains, cutting across barren lava fields. In Volcanoes National Park, both the old Saddle Road (Rte. 200), running between the mountains, and the Chain of Craters Road in Kilauea Crater permit closer views of the volcanoes.

The Big Island is twice the size of all the other islands combined, but is home to scarcely a tenth of the state's population. It's vast and varied agricultural production supports Hawaii's post-sugar economy. The towns of Hilo and Kailua-Kona, on opposite sides of the island, are the main arrival points for tourists.

The rest of the island is considered "country" by residents. The northwestern corner is the Kohala Peninsula, former sugar land and the northern border of the island's gigantic cattle range. The southern land mass is Kau, where the first Polynesian immigrants settled. You'll need a car to get out to the countryside, but keep a careful eye on the fuel gauge as distances between gas stations can be great. If you decide to rent a car in Kailua and drop it off in Hilo (or vice versa), ask about the drop-off charge—it can be steep (about $30). The Big Island does have a rudimentary bus system, and you should find most of the island's sights accessible.

Hilo

After Honolulu, Hilo is the largest city in the state, a sleepier and less tourist-ridden version of its big cousin. Moist tradewinds have imparted to it a lush climate. The center of the Hawaiian orchid and anthurium industry, the city is primarily residential; Hilo works best as a base from which to visit the island's other attractions—the rugged Hamakua (½ hr. north), green Waipio Valley north of Hamakua, *paniolo* (cowboy) country above that, and last but not least Volcanoes National Park (45 min. southwest).

Practical Information and Orientation

Visitor Information: Hawaii Visitors Bureau, 180 Kinoole St. (961-5797). Bus schedules, brochures, island guides, and maps (all free). Ask for the pamphlet describing a walking tour of historic Hilo. Open Mon.-Fri. 8am-noon and 1-4pm. **Wailoa Center,** P.O. Box 936, Hilo 96720 (961-7360), Kamehameha Ave. and Pauahi St., on the *makai* (seawards) side of the State Building. Helpful in planning itineraries. Maps, displays. Open Mon.-Fri. 8am-4:30pm. **State Visitor Information Center,** Hilo Airport (935-1018). **Big Island Center for Independent Living,** 1190 Wainuenue (935-3777), in Hilo. Assistance for disabled visitors. A good source of unofficial but useful information is the **Old Town Printers** shop, 201 Kinoole St. (935-8927), across from the HVB, where you can browse among informative booklets covering Hawaiiana from hiking to folklore.

Outdoors Information: For information on County Parks, contact the **Parks and Recreation Office,** 25 Aupuni St., #210, Hilo 96720 (961-8311). From the Kamehameha Hwy. turn left onto Pauahi St.; past Wailua Park, turn left onto Aupuni St. Open permits, allowing you to camp wherever you wish, are available for $1 per night per person. Open Mon.-Fri. 7:45am-4:30pm. Information on State Parks is available at the **Division of Land and Natural Resources,** 75 Aupuni St. #204, Hilo 96720 (933-4200). Free permits with a 5 day max. stay. Open Mon.-Fri. 7:45am-4pm. **Volcanoes National Park Visitor Center,** Volcano, Hawaii 96785 (967-7311), on Rte. 11, 13 mi. from Hilo. Offers trail maps, free ranger-guided hikes and important safety information. Open daily 8am-5pm. **Division of Forestry and Wildlife,** Dept. of Enforcement (next to the State Parks Office), P.O. Box 936, Hilo 96720 (961-7291). Information on hunting, fishing, hiking, and forest regulations. Open Mon.-Fri. 7:45am-4pm.

Buses: Hele-on-Bus, 25 Aupuni St. (935-8241). Information on bus schedules. Operates Mon.-Sat. 6:30am-6pm. Fare ranges from 50¢ to $6. Luggage and backpacks $1. Additional charge is 50¢ per piece. Runs between Kona and Hilo at least once per day, making a convenient circuit of the island ($5.25). Handicapped travelers can be accommodated on a day's advance notice with curb-to-curb service. (Call 961-3418 in Hilo or 323-2085 in Kona.)

Taxi: Ace Taxi, 935-8303. **ABC Taxi,** 935-0755. The trip from the airport into the city runs about $10.

Car Rentals: All national and state chains are located at Hilo airport. Make reservations several days in advance or take advantage of fly/drive deals for cheaper rates. **Dollar Rent-A-Car,** 961-6059. Must be 25 or over with a major credit card in your own name. $30 per day. **Budget,** 935-7293, rents to those 18-25 for a $20 surcharge per day. Basic economy car rate is $34 per day. They run frequent specials that can knock the price down to about $20 per day. Rental cars are not permitted on Saddle Rd.

Water Equipment Rentals: Nautilus Dive Center, 382 Kamehameha Ave. (935-6939). Mask/snorkel $3 per day, underwater camera $15 per day. $10 deposit. Also offers beginner and certified dive charters, $45. Open Mon.-Sat. 8:30am-5pm.

Laundromat: Hilo Quality Coin Laundrette, 2.0 Hoku St. (961-6490), between Kilauea Ave. and Kinoole St. Open daily 5am-9pm.

Western Union: 261 Kekuanaoa St. (969-1166), in the Computer Store. Open Mon.-Fri. 8am-5pm, Sat. 8am-4pm.

Coast Guard: 935-6370 or 800-331-6176.

Weather: 935-8555. (Hilo can be wet; Kona is generally sunny.)

Eruptions Bulletin: 967-7977. 24-hr. recording.

Sexual Assault Crisis Line: 935-0677.

Crisis/Help Line: 969-9111.

Senior Citizens Events: 935-1666 ext. 1801

Local Attractions and Cultural Events: 935-1666 ext. 1800.

Hospital: Hilo, 1190 Wainuenue St. (969-4111), by Rainbow Falls. 24-hr. emergency service.

Emergency: 961-6022 or 911.

Police: 961-2211, emergencies 935-3311.

Post Office: Waianuenue Ave. (935-6685), in the Federal Bldg. Open Mon.-Fri. 8:30am-4:30pm, Sat. 9am-noon. General Delivery ZIP Code: 96720.

Area Code: 808.

Hilo rests at the mouth of the Wailuku River. Its airport, **General Lyman Field,** is accessed by inter-island service and flights from the mainland. Travelers should stop and talk to the folks at the airport's visitor information booth; their maps and information are great for directions and orientation.

Accommodations and Camping

With the exception of Kona, tourism on the Big Island has never been as expensive or as popular as on other islands. Even the hotels clustered on Banyan Dr. by the bay are quiet and often empty. Rooms become scarce only during spectacular volcanic eruptions or events such as the total solar eclipse of July 1991. Booking rooms locally, rather than from the mainland, can save you $5-10 per day.

Arnott's Lodge, 98 Apapane Rd. (969-7097). By car, from Airport Rd, turn right at first traffic light. Turn right again at the next light (next to Dairy Queen) onto Kalanianaele St. Go 1½ miles and make a left onto Keokea. Apapane Rd. is on the right about 50 yds. down. Totally renovated and scrupulously clean. Michael, the manager, is a tour guide supreme and cooks a mean burrito to boot. Laundry, TV and cooking facilites, beach within walking distance. Hilo is a 10-15 minute bike ride away. Mountain bike rentals $7 per day. Bunks $15, private single $25, suite for 5 $80. Stay 6 nights and get the seventh free.

Hilo Hotel, P.O. Box 726, Hilo 96720 (961-3733), at 142 Kinoole St. downtown, across from Kalakaua Park. Old, but neat, clean, and charming in its on way. Most convenient hotel to Hilo activities. A/C, refrigerators, free coffee and sweet rolls in the morning. Cocktail lounge offers free *pupus* Tues.-Fri. 4-6pm. Singles and doubles $39-48.

Country Club Hotel, 121 Banyan Dr. (935-7171). Excellent rooms sandwiched between the bay and the banyan trees. A/C, TV, *lanai* (porch), kitchenette, and phones for low rates. Close to major Hilo activities. Restaurant offers an unlimited buffet for $6. Singles and doubles $45, with kitchenette $55.

Waiakea Villas Hotel, 400 Hualani St. (961-2841). A secluded resort with wooden Polynesian buildings. A/C, TV, tennis courts. Singles and doubles from $45. A bit remote without a car.

Dolphin Bay Hotel, 333 Iliahi St., Hilo 96720 (935-1466), in the Puueo section of town, across the river. 18 units, some plush. Cool, tropical gardens. Managers can help plan your excursions. Fans, TV, kitchens at no extra cost. Singles from $36. Doubles from $42. Pre-payment required; make deposit 10 days prior to stay to confirm reservations, although the management seems pretty flexible about everything except room rates.

Onekahakaha Beach Park and **Kealoha Beach Park** (both 961-8311) are within 3 mi. of Hilo, but visitors should be aware that these are known as local tough-guy hangouts. Tent camping, bathrooms, and shower facilities. $1 permit required (see Practical Information).

MacKenzie State Park (961-8311), off Rte. 137 in the Puna district, 32 mi. from Hilo. Tent or trailer camping near good shore fishing and an old Hawaiian coastal trail. Secluded; camping alone *not* recommended. No drinking water. Free permit required.

Food

You'll find macadamia nut bread, cookies, cakes and pies galore to accompany cups of steaming Kona coffee grown on the island. Free samples of the nuts are given out at the **Hawaiian Holiday Macadamia Nut Company** in Haina, off Rte. 19 near Honokaa. Downtown Hilo is loaded with cheap restaurants, sushi counters, and *okazu-ya.* Inspect a bit and choose one that's *ono* (good). You can always find a fast-food chain nearby and there are plenty of small Chinese restaurants with excellent lunch plates.

Reuben's Mexican Food, 336 Kamehameha Hwy. (961-2552). Authentic Mexican food served on colorful tablecloths. Choose from 34 entrees for $6-8. Wide selection of beers and margaritas. Open Mon.-Fri. 11am-9pm, Sat. noon-9pm.

Mun Cheong Lau, 172 Kilauea Ave. (935-3040). Cantonese in gigantic portions for under $6. Try the fried wanton with plum sauce. Take out available. Open Wed.-Mon. 11am-11pm.

Lani Truffels, 1477 Kalanianole (969-7871). Delectable lunch plates for $4 and mouth-watering confections for dessert. Open Tues.-Sat. noon-7pm.

Bear Coffee, 106 Keawe St. (935-0708), in old Hilo. Ignore the teddy bear motif and enjoy cappuccino, espresso and *café au lait* with delicious homebaked pastries. Behind the bears lurk local artists and café denizens. Also serves pizza, burritos and sandwiches for $3-4. Open Mon.-Fri. 7am-5pm, Sat. 8am-4pm.

Ken's Pancake House, 1730 Kamehameha Ave. (935-3711). Imagine a Hawaiian IHOP. Serves breakfast all day, as well as burgers, hot dogs, etc. ($2-5). Macadamia nut, coconut, or fresh banana pancakes $3-4. Choose from a variety of syrups (coconut, maple, fruits). But where are the chocolate chip pancakes and strawberry syrup? Open 24 hr.

Sights and Activities

Averaging nearly 125 in. of rain per year, Hilo is the soggiest side of the island. But this wet climate has also created a setting of true tropical splendor. Hilo is carpeted with lush mountain greenery and studded with plunging waterfalls, a testament to the Big Island's stunning beauty. And if things get too wet for you, just head for the sunny Kona-Kohala coast (about a 2-hr. drive away).

To get the most out of Hilo, start your sightseeing early in the day. Rte. 11 will take you directly from the Hilo airport to the national park, but it's more rewarding to explore the town first. Early risers with time on their hands will enjoy taking a morning stroll around **Liliuokalani Garden** (an elaborate Japanese-style garden named after one of the royal princesses), which is linked by a little footbridge to palm-covered **Coconut Island.** You'll get a great view of Mauna Kea before the clouds roll in. According to legend, Coconut Island is a bit of Maui that broke off when the demigod Blarthu tried to unite it with the islands of Maui and Hawaii. Early birds get the fish at **Suisan Fish Market's** fish auction (935-8051; Mon.-Sat., get there before 8am), where all the bidding and bartering is in Pidgin, a blend of Hawaiian and English. The market is at 85 Lihiwai St. off the harbor, at the mouth of the Wailoa River.

Another early bird possibility is the lovely **Rainbow Falls,** up Waianuenue Ave. As the sun begins to peek over the trees, a rainbow is formed in the mist of the plunging falls, the legendary home of goddess Hina.

Hilo is the orchid capital of the world; enough botanical gardens and nurseries have sprung up around the city to supply every senior prom in the country. **Orchids of Hawaii,** 2801 Kilauea Ave., immediately past the first one-lane bridge (959-3581) features beautiful *leis* and an exotic variety of orchids and anthuriums. (Open Mon.-Fri. 7:30am-4:30pm). The **Hilo Tropical Gardens,** 1477 Kalanianaole Ave. (935-4957 or 935-1146) are a lush botanical experience, perfect for an afternoon stroll (open Mon.-Fri. 9am-4:30pm). Many of the nurseries charge a tour fee or request donations. Your cheapest option is to simply explore the spectacular front-yard flora along any residential street, and take the 4 mile scenic drive off Rte. 19 north of Hilo. The **Panaewa Zoo Rainforest,** tucked away in the Panaewa forest reserve (halfway between Hilo and Volcanoes National Park on Rte. 11), is an entertaining diversion, especially for kids. The baby hippo named Kamakanaokalewalani (Gift of the Sky) has been the show-stealer of late; also performing are tigers, goats, monkeys, and colorful tropical birds. (Open daily 9am-4pm. Feeding at 9:15am and 8pm. Free.)

To see historic Hilo, pick up a walking tour pamphlet at the visitors bureau. Follow early Hawaiian missionaries into the **Lyman House Museum,** 276 Haili St. (Seven 25-min. tours daily. Open Mon.-Sat. 9am-5pm. Admission $4, ages 13-18 $3, 6-12 $2.) The research library contains over 26,000 volumes and is a center for Hawaiiana scholarship.

Near Hilo

Recent lava flows have covered the once-glistening shores of **Kaimu Black Sand Beach** and various parts of the highway as well, making Rte. 11 the only way to round South Point from Hilo. **Lava Tree State Park,** which blooms year round with lava casts of trees formed during the 1790 eruption, is still accessible. From Hilo, take Rte. 11 south to Keaau, turn onto Rte. 130 to Pahoa, and then take Pahoa-Pohoiki Rd. (Rte. 132). Continue around the loop on Rte. 132 past the **Kapoho Lighthouse** and the gardens nearby. Here a 1960 lava flow covered Kapoho Village; only trees and the lighthouse remain.

The Volcano Area

The volcanoes of the Big Island are unique in their size, frequency of eruption, and accessibility. Resting above the geological hot spot that fashioned each of the Hawaiian islands in turn, the two mountains in **Volcanoes National Park** continue to heave and grow, adding acres of new land each year. **Kilauea Caldera,** with its steaming vents, sulfur fumes, and periodic "drive-in" eruptions, is the star of the park although the less active **Mauna Loa** and its dormant northern neighbor, **Mauna Kea,** are in some respects more amazing. Each towers nearly 14,000 ft. above sea level and drops some 16,000 ft. to the ocean floor. Mauna Loa is the largest volcano in the world, while Mauna Kea, if measured from its base on the ocean floor, would be the tallest mountain on earth. Entrance to the park is $5, and is good for seven days.

At the visitors center in **Kilauea,** Crater Rim Rd. (967-7311), visitors can see 10-minute films shown hourly from 9am to 4pm and receive the bulletins on the latest volcanic activity. One of the films depicts the fiery destruction of the Wahaula ranger station. Trails of varying difficulty lead around Kilauea and to the summit of Mauna Loa; speak to a ranger before setting out.

Accommodations and Camping

Staying in the volcano area is expensive because of the limited number of hotels. The area is only 40 minutes from Hilo and a bit over an hour from Kona, so it's cheaper (and far more exciting at night) to stay in the larger cities and commute.

Morse Volcano B&B, P.O. Box 100, Volcano, 96785 (967-7216), in Volcano Village just outside the park. A historic missionary-style home with roomy common areas. Singles $26, with bath $31. Doubles $42, with bath $46.

Volcano House, P.O. Box 53, Hawaii Volcanoes National Park 96718 (967-7321). A bit expensive, but affords the opportunity to eat and sleep on the rim of an active volcano. The 1220-ft. vantage point is certainly a unique perspective. Rooms start at $59. The hotel also runs the **Namakanipaio** cabins, located 3 mi. behind the Volcano House in an *ohia* forest. Check-in after 3pm. 4-person cabins $25. Linen and some blankets provided.

Volcanoes National Park, 967-7311. Free campsites at **Kipukanene, Namakanipaio** (near Kilauea Crater), and **Kamoamoa** (on the coast)—each with shelters and fireplaces, but no wood. Seven-day maximum. No reservations.

Mauna Kea State Park, 935-7237, on the slopes of Mauna Kea off Saddle Rd. (Rte. 200). Largest state park. Good views of both Mauna Kea and Mauna Loa. 7 cabins available. Camping is officially prohibited. Nights at the 6500 ft. elevation can be chilly, so bring a sweater. One of the few places where you might see rare *nene* geese in the wild. Keep in mind that Saddle Rd. is off-limits to most rental cars. Permit required.

State Recreation Areas: Kalopa, end of Kalopa Rd. (775-7114), 3 mi. *mauka* (inland) from Mamalahoa Hwy. 19. Camping, group lodging, picnicking, nature trails. Sites surrounded by a wonderful *ohia* forest.

Two patrol cabins on the Mauna Loa summit trail may be used for free by hikers en route to the summit. One is at **Red Hill,** bordering Puuulaula caldera, 7½ mi. from the end of Mauna Loa Strip Rd. (10,000 ft.). The other is 9½ mi. farther, at **Mauna Loa Summit,** next to Mokuaweaweo caldera (13,250 ft.). Bunks, mattresses, and blankets are sometimes provided; bring your own sleeping bag, stove, and fuel. The ascent usually takes three days. No reservations are necessary, but register at the Kilauea visitors center. **Pepeia Cabin** is 5 mi. from the end of Hilina Pali Rd. There are several shelters along the coast.

Sights

Watching fresh earth being borne into the ocean may be the most spectacular scene you'll witness on these islands. The site at the end of **Crater Rim Drive** is expected to flow through the summer of 1992. To get there take Crater Rim Drive, turn on Chain of Craters Road and follow it 25 miles.

You'll have to hike from the point where the hardened lava has smothered the road. The flows are extremely rough, uneven and disorienting, so be sure to wear sturdy shoes and socks, take plenty of water (there is none available on the volcano), and wear sunscreen or a hat. Keep in mind where the ocean lies and if you get disoriented head toward it. Although extraordinary anytime, **Pele's Playground** becomes phenomenal at night, the red of the molten lava coloring the great clouds of steam that are formed as it hits the cold water. Even as the ongoing lava flows displace the ocean the restless waters off the Puna Coast smash methodically against the cliffs—a reminder that one day Pele's fires will cool and the ocean will reclaim this land. The lava is so hypnotizing that you won't be able to move.

The 11-mi. scenic drive around the Kilauea Caldera on **Crater Rim Drive** is a good way to see the volcano by car. The road is accessible via Rte. 11 from the east and west or via the Chain of Craters Rd. from the south. Well-marked trails and lookouts dot the way, so stop frequently to explore. You might also take the easy hike along the vista-filled **Crater Rim Trail,** which traverses *ohia* and giant fern forests, *aa* (rough) and *pahoehoe* (smooth) lava flows, and smoldering steam and sulfur vents. *Pilau!* ("Stinks!") Walk through the **Thurston Lava Tube,** formed by lava that cooled around a hot core which continued to move, leaving the inside of the flow hollow. **Devastation Trail** is a mile-long psychedelic trip though landscape out of Dali's imagination. The cinder cones and dead ohia trees were blasted by Kilauea Iki ("little Kilauea", west of "big" Kilauea Crater) in 1959. Halemaumau Crater, the goddess Pele's official residence, consumes daily offerings of gin, fruit and red ohia blossoms.

The **Hawaiian Volcano Observatory** is closed to the public, but the free **Jaggar Museum** next door explains the geological background with a pictorial history of the volcano. Other displays focus on Hawaiian legends. (Open daily 8:30am-5pm.)

Four-mi. **Kilauea Iki Trail** starts at the Kilauea Iki overlook on Crater Rim Rd. It leads around the north rim of Kilauea Iki, through a forest of tree ferns, down the wall of the little crater, past the vent of the '59 eruption, over steaming lava, and back to Crater Rim Rd. (Whew!) On the way you'll pass *ohelo* bushes laden with red berries. Legend has it that you must offer some berries to Pele before eating any or you'll incur her wrath. The 3½-mi. **Mauna Iki Trail** begins 9 mi. southwest of park headquarters on Rte. 11. It leads to ashen footprints left in 1790. From here you can hike down into the coastal area.

Kipuka Puaulu (Bird Park), north off Mauna Loa Rd., is a patch of green land that eons of lava flows have miraculously missed. An easy mile-long loop trail leads through Kipuka Pauulu from the parking lot, 1 mi. up Mauna Loa Rd. from Rte. 11. Keep an eye out for native Hawaiian birds such as the bright-red, black-winged *apapane.* The drops and strands of lava along the way bear names such as Pele's Tears and Pele's Hair. Heed the rangers' advice, however, and leave these excretions with Pele lest she bring you bad luck. Many tourists spirit them away, only to regret the thievery and mail the rocks back. The park keeps an amusing collection of the lava fragments tourists have sent back along with the apologetic letters accompanying them on display at the Kilauea Visitors Center.

Moving from the terrestrial to the celestial, **Mauna Kea,** to the north, has long served as an international center for visual astronomy. An unpaved road, navigable by four-wheel drive only, leads to the summit from Rte. 200 (Saddle Rd.). Resembling Maui's Haleakala, the terrain is stark and the views unearthly. The notion of altitude sickness at 13,796 ft., however, can be deterring.

Kona

Occupying the western side of Hawaii, Kona claims a disproportionate share of the Big Island's white sand beaches, resorts, and realtors. It is also home to the town of Kailua (officially hyphenated as Kailua-Kona), a booming resort center with shops, nightlife, and perfect weather. Hot and gorgeous, the white sand beaches at Hapuna and Kawaihae, and the coves of the major hotels (all hotels must have public access paths to the beach) are perfect for tanning (or burning). The calm deep waters along this coast of the Big Island offer splendid snorkeling, scuba diving, and big game fishing. Upland, the fertile slopes of Mauna Kea and Haulalai yield the nation's best and only domestic coffee harvest.

Kailua-Kona itself is small enough to see in a short walk, and a number of historic sites are right in the heart of the city. Take time to visit King Kalaukaua's summer home or the national historic park at Puuhonua O Honaunau. Many resorts feature petroglyphs or *heiaus* on their grounds. Kealakekua Bay holds a different historical interest: Captain Cook, the islands' first recorded Western visitor, dropped anchor and later met his death in this idyllic cove.

Practical Information and Orientation

Visitor Information: Hawaii Visitors Bureau, 75-5719 Alii Dr. (329-7787), across from the Kona Inn Shopping Center. Very helpful. Bus schedules, brochures, maps, and accommodations information. Open Mon.-Fri. 8am-noon and 1-4pm. See also Hilo Practical Information.

Outdoors Information: Department of Parks and Recreation, Yano Stall, Captain Cook (323-3046 or 323-3060), by the police station. Information on county parks, camping, and permits. Open Mon.-Fri. 7:45am-4:30pm. See also Hilo Practical Information.

Bus: Hele-on-Bus, 935-8241. Traverses the west coast out of Kona 6:15am-4:30pm, 3 times per day via Alii Dr., once via Hulualoa. To Hilo $5 at 6:15am. Because of infrequent runs, the bus is not a practical way to get around Kona.

Car Rental: at Kona airport. **Dollar Rent-A-Car,** 329-3161. $30 per day. Must be 21 with credit card. Open Mon.-Tues. 6am-11pm, Wed.-Thurs. 6am-9pm, Fri.-Sat. 6am-10pm. **Avis Rent-A-Car,** 329-1745. $26 per day. Must be 21 with credit card. Open daily 6:30am-8pm. **Budget,** 329-8511. $22 per day. Must be 18 with credit card, and if you're under 25 they add a $20 per day surcharge. Drop-off charges can be as steep as $28. In town, **Honolulu Rent-A-Car,** 74-5588 Pawaii Pl. (329-7328), rents used cars with a three-day minimum for as little as $15 per day.

Bikes and Mopeds: Ciao, 75-5663A Palani Rd. (326-4177), across from the King Kamehameha Hotel. Scooters $20 per day. Cruiser bikes $10 per day. Cash or credit card deposit. Open daily 8am-8pm. **B&L Bike & Sports,** 74-5576B Pawai Pl. (329-3309), at Kaiwi St., offers 12-speeds for $12 per day, $60 per week; 15-speed mountain bikes $15 per day, $75 per week. Open Mon.-Fri. 9am-5:30pm, Sat. 9am-3pm.

Water Equipment Rentals: Big Island Divers, Kona Market Place (329-6068), all the way in the back. Masks, fins, and snorkels $6 per day, prescription masks $8. Boogie boards $6 and $8 per day. Charters, introductory dives, and scuba rentals are also available at affordable rates. Open daily 8am-8pm.

Coast Guard: 935-6370 or 800-331-6176.

Library: 75-138 Hualalai Rd. Open Mon., Wed.-Fri. 10am-6pm, Tues. 11am-8pm, Sat. 10am-1pm.

Laundromat: Kona Laundry, 75-5705 Kuakini Hwy. Open daily 8:30am-10pm.

Crisis/Help Line: 329-9111.

Sexual Assault Crisis Line: 935-0677.

Kailua-Kona Medical Clinic: 75-5595 Palani Rd. (329-1346), in the Lanihau Shopping Center. Open 24 hr. **Ambulance:** 961-6022.

Hospital: Kona, in Honalo off Rte. 11 (322-9311). Follow well-marked signs on road.

Emergency: 323-2645 or 911.

Police: 329-3838 or 911.

Post Office: Palani Rd. (329-1927). Open Mon.-Fri. 9am-4pm, Sat. 9am-noon. General Delivery ZIP Code: 96740.

Area Code: 808.

Kailua-Kona is served by **Keahole Airport,** 9 mi. (15 min.) north of town. Taxi rides into town are about $16, plus 30¢ per bag. Kailua-Kona is a small settlement and can be toured in one day without a car. The three or four car-rental agencies located in town are for those who wish to rent without returning to the airport. The city is split by two streets running parallel to the ocean: Alii Drive, nearest the ocean, and Kuakini Highway, 1 block *mauka.* Kealakekua Bay and the town of Captain Cook are another 9 mi. south on Rte. 11.

Accommodations

Staying overnight in Kailua-Kona can be expensive, since its hotels cater to the affluent traveler. It's cheaper and more adventurous to stay away from the resort area, and daytrip into Kailua to use the hotel's beaches. (All hotels must have public access paths to the beach. If you behave yourself, and dress appropriately, you can use their pools and lounges—if they figure out you're not a guest they'll ask you to leave, but it's not likely). For the nearest **camping,** see Kohala.

Kona Hotel, Holualoa (324-1155), on Rte. 18 southeast of Kona, near the arts center. Clean, comfortable surroundings and friendly management. Make sure to reserve well in advance as this small, fabulous find fills up frighteningly fast. Singles $15, doubles $23.

Manago Hotel, P.O. Box 145, Captain Cook, 96704 (323-2642). The dark, shadowy exterior is forbidding, but the interior is comfy and clean. Generally older clientele. Inexpensive restaurant is a lunchtime favorite for guests and townies alike (open daily 7-9am and 11am-2pm; dinner Mon.-Thu. 5-7:30pm, Fri.-Sun. 5-7pm). Austere singles $20, doubles $23. More spacious and elegant rooms with bath and view in newer wing from $35, doubles $38.

Kona Seaside, 75-5646 Palani Rd., Kailua-Kona 96740, (922-5333; from the outer islands 800-451-6754; from the mainland 800-367-7000). What this place lacks in character, it makes up for in comfort and price. Pool, A/C, TV. Right in the resort area for $49 single or double.

Food

Kailua-Kona has a wide range of tourist-oriented restaurants. You can search for atypical homestyle establishments or dive right into the early-bird specials (5-6pm) at most hotels.

Ocean View Inn, 75-5683 Alii Dr. (329-9998), across from the boat dock. Popular establishment serving seafood, American, Chinese, and Hawaiian fare in a diner setting and price range. Furniture and menus give this place an authentic 50s aura. Breakfast $4, lunch $4-7, dinner $7-10. Try some *laulau* and *poi* for $3. Special vegetarian dishes average $3. Open Tues.-Sun. 6:30am-2:45pm and 5:15-9pm.

Sibu, 75-569 E. Alii Dr., in Banyon Court Mall across from the Kailua Seawall. Indoor/outdoor café serving naturally prepared Indonesian food. Plenty of vegetarian options. Dinner entrees $8-10. Open 7 days, 11:30am-9pm.

Stan's, 75-5646 Palani Rd. (329-2455), in the Kona Hukilau. Breakfast specials include coconut hotcakes ($3.35). Complete dinners ($7). Enjoy the harbor view while you try the fresh *ahi* in season ($8.75). Open daily 7-9:30am and 5:30-8:30pm.

Betty's Chinese Kitchen, Palani Rd., in the KTA Shopping Center. More local Chinese food. Large portions and a daily buffet. Daily plate for $3-4. Open Mon.-Sat. 10am-8:30pm.

Aloha Café Theatre, (322-9924), off Rte. 11 in Kealakekua. Sip an espresso ($1) at frequent film revivals and live productions—plays, concerts, dance performances. During the day enjoy the quiet *lanai* overlooking a park and the ocean. Healthy meals ($7) and fresh baked muffins daily ($1). Open Mon.-Sat. 8am-8pm. Theater schedule changes constantly, and nothing seems definite until a day or so before.

Quinn's, 75-5655A Palani Rd. (329-3822). A local institution, Quinn's offers excellent food for medium money. Bar and terrace. Steamed clams with bread $7.50. The stuffed artichokes will make you scream for more. Open Mon.-Sat. 11am-1am, Sun. 11am-11pm.

Entertainment

Kona's weekday nightlife centers around resort activities. **Kimo's Restaurant,** in the Kona Bay Hotel, 75-5739 Alii Dr. (329-1393), presents two dinner hula shows nightly at 6:30pm and 7:30pm. (No cover. Dinner served 5:30-9pm.) On the weekends, the nightclubs and discos fill with locals and visitors.

Jolly Roger Restaurant, 75-5776 Alii Dr. (329-1344). Full bar and live music 5-6 nights a week. No cover.

Kona Surf, 78-128 Ehukai St. (322-3411). The place to catch real headliner acts. Jerry Garcia has played here, among illustrious others. Call for information on current acts.

Eclipse, 75-5711 Kuakini Hwy. (329-4686). A small restaurant/disco with a young crowd dancing to top 40 music every evening starting at 10pm. No cover; drink prices are steep.

Bombadil's Food and Drink, across from the Hilton tennis courts (329-2173). Sports bar with a fun crowd, though it's a bit pricey.

Sights and Activities

About the only things that break up the sparkling sands are fast-food restaurants, hyperkinetic nightclubs, and history. **Magic Sands** (also called "Disappearing Sands" because the sand gets washed away for a couple of weeks every winter and then mysteriously returns) at the Kona Magic Sands Hotel, 77-6452 Alii Dr. (329-9177), is a good place to park your towel and wade, but make sure you park it when the sand isn't about to go on vacation. It's also a perfect place for snorkeling, bodysurfing, and boogie boarding. **Hulihee Palace** (built in 1838), 75-5718 Alii Dr. (329-1877), King Kalakaua's former pad, has been beautifully restored—much more completely than Queen Emma's summer cottage on Oahu. (Open daily 9am-4pm. Admission $4, ages 12-18 $1, under 12 50¢.) Across from the palace is **Mokuaikaua,** the first church in Hawaii (1836). Also called the "church of the chimes," the building has been lovingly cared for and is still used for sermons and as a museum. The chimes sound daily at 4pm. (Open daily sunrise-sunset.) The church maintains an extensive collection of information on the first missionaries to arrive in "Owyhee", including copies of original documents and newspaper articles.

The expensive hotels in Kailua are an attraction in themselves. **The Sheraton has beautiful gardens full of native plants, and the head gardener gives knowledgeable lectures and answers questions. The Hilton** was built by an architect inspired by depictions of King Kamehameha's waterslide.

Up Hualalai Rd. on Rte. 180, **Holualoa** enjoys a different lifestyle from the resort-swamped coast. This tiny coffee town features a number of arts and craft vendors as well as a fresh perspective of the bay below. At the end of the day, stop by the harbor pier to see the sport fishing charter boats weigh in their largest catches. Giant billfish and 800-lb. marlin are not uncommon.

Despite other attractions, the beaches remain the main drawing card in Kona. White, sandy stretches line the coast through Kailua and up Rte. 19 to prime **Hapuna Beach** and **Spencer Beach Parks,** 35 mi. north. Both parks have wheelchair-accessible facilities. Check out the hotel-owned coves where you can rent sailboards at make-shift stands (see Practical Information).

Farther south on Rte. 11 is **Kealakekua Bay.** From Rte. 11 turn right onto Napoopoo Dr.; this winding road leads down to the historic bay (about 15 min.) where, in 1778, Captain Cook tried to restock his ship during the *Makahiki,* a holy season honoring the god Lono. The Hawaiians thought Cook's white sails and masts heralded the return of Lono, and they proclaimed Cook a god at the **Hikiau Heiau** on the bay. A year later Cook was killed on the far side of the bay when he tried to break up a fight between his men and the islanders. A white monument marks the site.

Southeast of Kona: Kau

Driving south from Kaiwa toward Ka Lae (South Point), you come to **Puuhonua O Honaunau,** often referred to as the City of Refuge (take Rte. 160 off Rte. 11, admission $1). This was a last ditch sanctuary for Hawaiians fleeing from battle or escaping punishment for breaking the *kapu* (the sacred laws that ruled Hawaiian life). Having reached the *puuhonua* and received absolution at the hands of the *kahuna pule* (priest), the ritually purified offender could safely resume life at home. King Kamehameha II destroyed all other such sanctuaries when he abolished the *kapu* in 1819, but saved this one because it contained the bones of his ancestors. Stop by the **visitors center** (328-2288) for a map. (Open daily 7:30am-5:30pm. Admission $1.) Picnicking and sunbathing are forbidden, and swimming in Keoneele Cove is highly inappropriate. Instead, play a round of **konane;** instructions for this ancient Hawaiian checkerboard game are available at the visitors center.

Two detours on the road to Puuhonua O Honaunau, are worth investigating. Though officially called **St. Benedict's Catholic Church,** this Gothic church has been dubbed **Painted Church,** because of the many murals and frescoes painted on its side panels and ceiling. The church was built in the 1900s by a Belgian priest and painted to look like the Cathedral of Burgos in Spain. (Free. Open daily sunrise-sunset.) The other noteworthy stop is **Wakefield Botanical Gardens and Restaurant,** 1 Rodeo Rd. (328-9930), a relatively unknown tropical garden along the yellow coconut trail. The restaurant's Mexican entrees aren't as exciting as their desserts: try the blueberry cheesecake or the macadamia nut pie ($2). (Open daily 11am-8pm.) The café offers free tours of the garden, a fine opportunity to work off your desert.

Farther south, you can camp at the county park in **Milolii,** a fishing village. Villagers live in the traditional manner without electricity, far from the currents of modern life. In the friendly town of **Waiohinu,** you can also stay at the southernmost hotel in the U.S. **Shirikawa's Hotel and Motel,** P.O. Box 467, Naalehu 96722 (929-7462), lies 58 mi. southeast of Kailua-Kona on Rte. 11. It's near a monkeypod tree planted by Mark Twain in 1866. There are only 13 of these comfortable, clean units, so reserve a month in advance (singles $25, with kitchen $32; doubles $30, with kitchen $35).

From the town of Waiohinu, you can drive 12 miles down a rough, one lane road to South Point, the southernmost point in the U.S. Get out where the cars are parked and hike the 2½ mile trails to **Green Sands,** where a high copper content has turned the beach—you guessed it—pure natural green.

Around Haalehu and heading north back toward Volcanoes National Park and Hilo, camp at **Punalu'u Black Sand Beach.** A county park, Punalu'u has wheelchair-accessible bathrooms, pavilions, outdoor showers, fire pits, public phones, and an unsurpassed view of the rising sun.

Kohala

The drive along the northwestern coast takes you into rural Hawaii. (Kohala without a car means hitchhiking—it is inaccessible by bus. Many are able to catch rides in Waimea.) Once home to several sugar mills, much of the area has deteriorated into ghost towns with the death of the sugar economy. The Kona side of Kohala offers camping near beaches, and the flat, wide-shouldered roads are ideal for cycling; the center is *paniolo* (cowboy) country; and the Hilo side guards the emerald Waipio Valley. Kohala is remarkably empty of tourists, despite its physical beauty.

Camping

The permit required at Hapuna Beach State Park is a free permit, but all the other parks require a $1 camping permit, available at the county parks office (see Hilo Practical Information). Mahukona and Kapaa Beach Parks have restroom facilities and allow camping, but neither is on a beach. Instead, they are perched on rocky coastlines, unsuitable for sunbathing.

Hapuna Beach State Park, off Rte. 19 (882-7995), 3 mi. south of Kawaihae. Great beach for swimming, volleyball, sunning, and relaxing. The wide, white, sandy beach is good for people-watching. Let it suffice to say that swimming is not the first thing on everyone's mind. Lots of shaded picnic tables. A-frame shelters only; no tent camping. A-frame $7 (4 people max.). Reserve in advance, as this spot is popular.

Spencer Beach Park, off Rte. 27 near Kawaihae. Crowded. Wheelchair-accessible facilities. Not quite as exciting a beach as Hapuna, but good for tent camping.

Keokea Beach Park, off Rte. 27, 6 mi. past Hawi. Beautiful spot, rarely crowded. Good fishing, showers, restrooms, electricity.

Sights

Driving up the coast north of Kona, turn left at the road to Waikoloa to see the ancient Hawaiian markings along the petroglyph trail. Farther north, just off the intersection of Rte. 19 and 270, stop at the **Puukohola Heiau visitors center** (882-7218), for a brief introduction and a guide (open 7:30am-4pm). The **Puukohoa Heiau** is the last major religious structure of the old culture. Kamehameha the Great built this *heiau* 200 years ago in honor of his family war god, Ku Kailimoku, before his conquest of the Big Island. In 1791, a prophet told him that constructing the temple would enable him to conquer the entire chain of Hawaiian islands. About four years later, the prophecy was realized. Hungry travelers can invade the nearby **Harbor Hut Restaurant** (882-7783), on Kawaihae Rd. (Rte. 270). Besides its $4 all-you-can-eat breakfast special, the hut stands out for its 99-bottle beer-bedecked wall. Try the *beer du jour* for 99¢, or work through them all to compare flavors. (Open daily 7:30am-2:30pm; dinner Sun.-Thurs. 5:30-9pm, Fri.-Sat. 5-9:30pm.) Sorry, no Hawaiian beers.

Rte. 270 will lead you out of the desert and around the Kohala Mountains to the tropical plantation town of **Hawi.** The birthplace of King Kamehameha is marked by the original cast of a statue that stands in Honolulu (thr original fell off a ship and was lost, then later recovered, but not before an identical copy was cast). Accommodations can be found at the **Kohala Club Hotel** off Rte. 270, in a clean, plantation-style home just past the 550 ft. elevation marker. Rte. 270 ends at the **Pololu Valley Lookout.** A ½-hour hike leads down from here to a broad, black sand beach.

From the Kona Coast beyond Hapuna Beach, head up the mountain on Rte. 19 toward **Kamuela,** which is the Hawaiian equivalent of "Samuel." The area was originally called Waimea but was renamed Kamuela after Samuel Parker of Parker Ranch. Founded in 1847 by a Boston missionary, the ranch spans 225,000 acres and is home to 40-50,000 head of Hereford cattle; the ranch annually produces enough beef for 40 million Quarter-Pounders. Stop in at the **Parker Ranch Visitors**

Center and Museum (885-7655), for audio-visual presentations on the fascinating history, operations, and lifestyles of Parker Ranch and its *paniolos,* Hawaiian cowboys. (Open daily 9:30am-4:30pm. Admission $4, ages 4-11 $2). Mr. Richard Smart, present owner of the Parker Ranch, has recently opened his private home, **Puuopelu** (855-5666), to the masses. Also open is **Mana House,** the original residence built by John Palmer Parker in 1847. From the visitors center, turn left onto Rte. 19. The gates appear shortly after a green Quonset hut on your right. (Open daily 9:30am-4:30pm.) Comprehensive tours of the ranch, including admission to the private homes, cost $15 (ages 4-11 $7.50) and leave daily from the visitors center (every 20 min. 9am-3:30pm).

The **Kamuela Museum** (885-4724) houses the largest collection of artifacts of the Hawaiian monarchy, as well as WWII relics. The museum's exhibits explain the monarchs' relationship with the Parkers of Parker Ranch. (Museum open daily 8am-4pm. Admission $2.50, under 12 $1.)

A 30-minute drive on Rte. 19 from Kamuela to **Honokaa** will take you through cattle country strewn with foggy, rolling hills. Looking at the cattle, horses, and landscape, it's hard to believe that the desert-like Kohala coast is just 45 minutes away. If it's mid-May, you might happen on the **Honokaa Rodeo.** Otherwise, hop along down Rte. 24 to the edge of the lush **Waipio Valley,** 8 mi. away, for one of the most striking panoramas anywhere in the islands. This 2000-ft. gorge is the crowning point of a series of breathtaking canyons between Waipio and Pololu. Bountiful flora and fauna made Waipio (the islands' largest gorge) the center of ancient Hawaiian civilization. In 1780, King Kamehameha was singled out here by reigning chiefs to be the future ruler. Consider walking down into the valley only if you don't have vindictive knees. The jaunt takes a ½ hour down, then one hour back up along a paved road. Many trails lead back into the valley and along the beach.

Paradise Safari's four-wheel-drive wagons will take you into the valley or up Mauna Kea (329-9282). A day-long trip with lunch costs $60. The **Waipio Valley Shuttle** (775-7121) takes visitors on a 1½-hour drive to 1200-ft. waterfalls, lotus ponds, and other exotic and historic sights. Catch the Jeep shuttle at the top of the valley. Purchase tickets and check in at the **Waipio Woodworks Art Gallery** (775-0958), ½ mi. from the Waipio Valley lookout. Reservations are highly recommended. (Tour $20, under 12 $10. Mon.-Sat. 8am-5pm. Write P.O. Box 5128, Kukuihaele 96727 for more information.) The adventurous should consider the 9-mi. hike between the Waipio Valley Lookout and Waimanu Bay. Waimanu Valley holds ancient Hawaiian ruins, and the scenery can't be beat. Expect a five-hour hike each way.

Seasonal Events

Great Waikoloa Rodeo Horse Races, in mid-Feb. at the Waikoloa Stables. Call Warren Miura (883-9335).

Kona Stampede, 2nd weekend in March at Honaunau Arena. Call Dr. William Bergin (885-7941).

Merry Monarch Festival, in late March-early April. Hula contests, local music, and festivities.

Annual Keauhou Kona Triathlon, in late April at Keauhou Bay, western Hawaii. Half the distance of the Ironman (see below). Call Toni Fortin (326-9575).

Annual Naalehu Carnival and Rodeo, July 4-6 in Naalehu. Rodeo events, farm fairs, games, contestants, beer garden, and Hawaiian entertainment.

Annual Big Island Invitational Marlin Tournament, July in Kailua-Kona. Call Jody Wright (329-4112).

Jamie Rosen Invitational East-Meets-West Face-Off, in late February. One 350-lb. *sumo* wrestler climbs into the ring with 3 118-lb. collegiate wrestlers, and they have it out. First of its kind.

Macadamia Nut Harvest Festival, mid-July in Honakaa. Races, jamborees, and a parade. Call Clarence Garcia (775-7792). (A delightful Macadamia Nut Pie recipe is available from Bart St. Clair, Winthrop House, Harvard College, Cambridge, MA 02138.

Bud Light Ironman World Triathlon Championship, mid-Oct. in Kailua-Kona. The original and ultimate test of endurance: a 2.4-mi. swim, 112-mi. cycle, and 26.2-mi. marathon. If you don't feel up to the challenge, at least pick up a t-shirt and tell your friends back home about how Dave Scott beat you by a yard at the end.

Maui

Long before college athletes proclaimed "We're Number One," Maui's warlike chieftains proudly announced their island's supremacy over the aricpelago with the words *Maui No Ka Oi.* After the Big Island's Kamehameha Dynasty united the islands in 1810, it chose Lahaina, on Maui, as its capital city. Honolulu's commercial preeminence forced a royal relocation to Oahu in 1845, as Waikiki took the lead in tourism development. Despite the slight of being dethroned as capital, Maui retains its high profile.

The island was named for the demi-god Maui, who, according to legend, pulled the islands up from the sea-bottom with fish hooks. "The Valley Island," as it is known, features everything from clapboard cane towns to concrete condos, sunny beaches to a (sometimes) snowcapped volcano, Hana's lush rain forest to arid Lahaina (which means "merciless sun"). Maui's popularity will seem justified once you've toured its contrasting corners: sleepy West Maui, with its rugged mountains; the windy central isthmus that holds Wailuku, Kahului, and acre upon acre of sugar cane; the mystifying Haleakala volcano, which dominates East Maui; and the remote splendor of the spearfisher, snorkeler, and windsurfer inhabited Hana coast.

Practical Information and Orientation

Visitors Information: Visitor Information Kiosk (877-6431), at the Kahului Airport terminal. Helpful orientation with free map. Open daily 6am-9pm. **Hawaii Visitors Bureau,** 380 Dairy Rd., Kahului (871-8691). Friendly assistance with itinerary planning, activities, and accommodations, but they won't make reservations. Information on Molokai and Lanai. Open Mon.-Fri. 8am-4:30pm.

Outdoors Information: Haleakala National Park, P.O. Box 369, Makawao 96768 (572-7749), provides recorded information on weather conditions, daily ranger-guided hikes and special activities. For information on camping and cabins call 572-9177. Park Headquarters (572-9306) is open daily 7:30am-4pm. **Visitor Center,** 65 Hana Hwy., Paia (579-8000). Details on Paia's windsurfing tournaments available. Open Mon.-Sat. 9am-noon and 5-6pm. **Department of Parks and Recreation,** War Memorial Gym, 1580 Kaahumanu Ave. (244-9018), between Kahului and Wailuku. Information and permits ($4) for county parks. Open Mon.-Fri. 8-11am and noon-4:15pm. You may have to knock on the window. **Division of State Parks,** 54 High St. (244-4354), in Wailuku. Maui and Molokai state parks information. Helpful, but tough to find; go downstairs by the parking area at 54 High St. (corner of High and Main St.). Open Mon.-Fri. 8-11am and noon-4:15pm.

American Express: The Wharf, 658 Front St. #174 (667-4381, for refunds 800-221-4950), in Lahaina. Open daily 9am-5pm. **Activities desk,** street level (667-2112). Offers prestige, tickets, reservations, cruises, and traveler's check information and services, all for only $55 a year. Open daily 8am-9:30pm.

Bus: There is no public transportation on Maui. **Gray Line Shuttle** (on Maui 877-5507, from Oahu 833-8000, from mainland 800-367-2420) runs between Kahului Airport and the Lahaina-Kaanapali area. Fare $10, reservations required. Tours to Iao Valley and Lahaina ($15-25), to Hana ($35-48). Operates daily 7am-9pm.

Boats: Ferries are an ideal mode of transport to Molokai and Lanai. Going by boat is more exciting and cheaper than flying. The **Maui Princess** (661-8397) runs daily from Lahaina, Maui to Molokai at 6:30am and 4:30pm, and from Molokai to Maui at 5:30am and 3:30pm. The crossing takes about 1½ hours and costs $21 one way. **Expeditions** (661-3756) sails to Lanai twice per day for $25.

Tours: Those to Hana provide an alternative to driving your moped down tortuous roads. **Akamai Tours,** 50 Hana Hwy., and 532 Keolani Pl. (871-9551), offers frequent tours in air-conditioned mini-buses. To Haleakala/Iao Valley ($35), and Hana ($60).

Taxi: Kaanapali Taxi (661-5285). $6 ride into town from the airport.

Car Rental: A capital ideer on this island. Make reservations in advance and save money. 21-and-underlings will find renting anything with four wheels exceedingly problematic. Try hooking up with older travelers at hostels. **Word of Mouth,** Dairy Rd. (877-2436), near Kahului Airport. $15 per day for a used car, $17 with A/C; $85 per week, $95 with A/C. Must be 25. **Avis,** Kahului Airport (871-7575). $22 per day with frequent specials. Must be 25. **Thrifty,** Kahului Airport (871-7596). $30 per day. 21 and over with a major credit card.

Bicycle: Bicycle touring on West Maui, with its flat roads, is highly rewarding. The twisting and crowded Hana Hwy., on the other hand, is deadly. **The Island Biker,** Kahului Shopping Center (877-7744), rents 21-speed mountain bikes for $18 per day. 5% discount with student ID. Open Mon.-Fri. 9am-5pm, Sat. 9am-3pm. **A&B Rentals,** 3481 Lower Honoapilani Rd. (669-0027), near Kaanapali. $10 per day for Beachcruiser bikes, or $50 per week. Open daily 9am-5pm.

Moped and Scooter Rentals: A&B Moped and Scooter Rentals, 3481 Lower Honoapilani Rd. (669-0027). Scooters $20 for 8 hours, $25 for 24 hours. Ask about weekly rates. Must be 18 with a major credit card. Open daily 9am-5pm.

Hitchhiking: Illegal, but that doesn't stop some. The usual method is to stand roadside without the thumb signal. Drivers know what's up, but cops may not jump on you quite so quickly. Remember that you are taking your life into your own hands.

Water Equipment Rentals: If you are on the island for an extended stay, consider buying your equipment. Several places offer used boogie boards at sale prices. **The Dive Shop,** 1975 S. Kihei Rd. (879-5172), Kihei. Snorkel set or boogie board $5 per day, $15 per week. **Maui Dive Shop,** Azeka Pl. (879-3388), Kihei, and Wakea Ave. (661-5388), Kahalui. Complimentary scuba lessons with equipment rental, and free 1-hr. introductory snorkeling lessons. Mask $3, snorkel $2, boogie board $8, wetsuit $6, underwater camera $20 per day. Open Mon.-Fri. 8am-9pm, Sat.-Sun. 8am-6pm. **Hunt Hawaii,** 120 Hana Hwy., (579-8129), Paia. Surf, boogie, and sailboards for rent or sale. Biggest surfboard rental fleet on Maui. Surfboards $15 per 2 hr., $25 per day. Windsurfers $30 per day, $150 per week. Surf or sailboard lessons $35 per 2 hr. Open daily 9am-6pm. **Hawaiian Reef Divers,** 129 Lahainalua Rd. (667-7647 or 667-6002), Lahaina. Good deals, friendly advice, and an excellent beach map. Snorkel set $2.50, boogie boards $5 per day. Boat trips with snorkeling or scuba offered. Open daily 8am-5pm. **The Maui Windsurf Company,** 520 Keolani Pl. (877-4816 or 800-872-0999), near the Kahului Airport. Fanatic and Angulo sailboards $45 per day, $200 per week. Roof rack and harness included. 2½-hr. beginner lessons (equipment included) $50. Inquire here about short-term accommodations as well. Open daily 8am-6pm.

Weather: Land, 877-5111. Marine, 877-3477.

Whale Report Center: 661-8527. Information on humpback whale sightings.

Laundromat: Happy Valley Wash 'n' Wear, 340 N. Market St., Wailuku. Wash 75¢, wear 25¢. Detergent vending machine. Open 24 hr.

Library: 254 High St., Wailuku. Open Mon.-Fri. 8:30am-4:30pm, Sat. 9-11am.

Help Lines: Sexual Assault Crisis Center, 242-4357. 24 hr. **Suicide Crisis Center,** 244-7407. **Gay and Bisexual Information,** 572-1884 (serves Maui, Molokai, Lanai). 24 hr. **Coast Guard Rescue,** 800-331-6176. **Family Shelter,** 579-9581.

Handicapped Information: the *Maui Traveler's Guide* is available from the Commission on the Handicapped, c/o State Department of Health, 54 High St., Wailuku, Maui 96793 (244-4441).

Hospital: Maui Memorial, 221 Mahalani St. (244-9056), Wailuku. 24-hr. **Emergency Room,** 242-2343.

Post Office: Lahaina, Baldwin Ave. Open Mon.-Fri. 8:15am-4:15pm. General delivery ZIP Code: 96761. **Paia,** Baldwin Ave. Open Mon.-Fri. 8am-4:30pm, Sat. 10:30am-12:30pm. Mail collection Mon.-Sat. 1:15-3:45pm. General delivery ZIP Code: 96799. Wailuku, next to State Office Building, on High St. Open Mon.-Fri. 8:30am-4:30pm, Sat. 9-11am. General Delivery ZIP Code: 96793. **Kihei,** 1254 S. Kihei Rd., in Azeka Market Place. Open Mon.-Fri. 9am-4:30pm, Sat. 9-11am. General Delivery ZIP Code: 96753.

Kahului is the major **airport,** landing regular flights from the mainland and other islands. Planes also fly into **Kaanapali** and **Hana.** Hawaiian flys from Honolulu 18 or more times daily, 2 times daily from Hilo, 3 times from Kona, several times from Kauai, and 2 times from Molokai. The visitors information booth in front of the Kahului terminal's entrance provides free maps, information, and directions. A taxi to hotels costs $8-10, but the wise traveler will rent a car upon arrival; it's the only way to travel around the island efficiently. Numerous national, state, and local firms have handy booths at Kahului Airport. Rates at local firms fluctuate; always make advance reservations.

Maui consists of two mountains joined at an isthmus. The highways follow the shape of the island in a broken figure eight pattern. The **Kahului Airport** sits on the northern coast of the isthmus. To the west lie **Kahului** and **Wailuku,** business and residential communities offering less expensive food and supplies than the resort towns. From Kahului, Rte. 30 will lead you clockwise around the smaller western loop of the figure eight to hot and dry **Lahaina,** the former whaling village, and **Kaanapali,** the major resort area. Rte. 34 leads counterclockwise around the same loop from the isthmus to where the paved road ends at **Kapuna.**

Circling the slopes of Haleakala along the eastern loop, Rte. 31 passes white sand beaches as it runs south past **Kihei** and **Wailea.** Kihei is a major resort on the south side of the isthmus, but is not particularly picturesque. Past Wailea, however, the condos cease and the snowy beaches are more sparsely populated.

On the north side of this eastern loop, Rte. 36 winds through rainy terrain, over 57 one-lane bridges, to **Hana.** Rte. 40 or 37 will lead you to Rte. 377, and then 378, which head up 10,023-ft. **Haleakala.** Most roads are well marked but poorly lit. Heed the warnings "road recommended for four-wheel-drive vehicles only"; a passing rainstorm can quickly drain your funds, since most rental car contracts stipulate that dirt road driving is at the driver's risk.

Accommodations

One of the fringe benefits of increasing tourism on Maui is the rise in the number of vacation rentals and bed and breakfasts, many catering to windsurfers and offering space to store equipment. Some go for as little as $20 per night. Check the classified section of the *Maui News.* The classifieds also list house-swap opportunities.

Hostels are another way to sidestep tourist traps. They get jammed during windsurfing events, so make it your maxim to book a month in advance.

In East Maui camping is the watchword. The few hotels near Hana, Kula, or Wailea are expensive (minimum $50); besides, the outdoor facilites are great.

Northshore Inn, 2080 Vineyard St. (242-8999), Wailuku, above Hazel's. Among the amenities: super-clean shared bathrooms, comfy common room with TV, perked coffee on tap and lots of high-wind adventure stores. Space to store windsurfing equipment. Microwave, refrigerator, and laundry facilites. Periodic barbecues in the garden. Bunks $12. Singles $32. Doubles $43.

Banana Bungalow Hotel and International Hostel, 310 North Market St., Wailuku (244-5090 or 800-846-7835). Reasonably priced hostelesque accommodations. Lots of international travelers and windsurfers. Laundry room and information board with key facts on hikes, dives and deals. Bunks $13. Singles with a double bed $29. Doubles $35.

The Bungalow, 2044 Vineyard St. (244-3294), Wailuku. Primitive quarters with shared baths. Some rooms with picnic coolers. A bit daunting. Singles $10. Doubles $15. Check also for openings at **Cabebe Apartments** (244-9077) at the same address.

Maui Palms Resort, 170 Kaahumanu Ave. (877-0071), Kahului. Unpretentious hotel by the sea. TV. Singles $48. Doubles $51.

Nani Kai Hale, 73 N. Kihei Rd. (879-9120, 800-367-6032 from the mainland), Kihei. Condominium on a sandy beach. Doubles with bath $32.50, three-day minimum; Dec. 16-April 15 $42.50, seven-day min. stay. Reserve ahead by phone.

Wailana Sands, 25 Wailana (879-2026 or 879-3661), off the 500 block of S. Kihei Rd. in Kihei. In a quiet cul-de-sac. One of the few places surviving the tourist onslaught. Full kitchen, small pool. Four-day min. stay. Two-person studio $40. Reserve a month in advance.

Pioneer Inn, 658 Wharf St. (836-1411), Lahaina. One of Hawaii's 2 oldest hotels, this popular meeting spot is directly in front of the boat harbor, next to the famous giant banyan tree. Two buildings make up the hotel, the "original" and the "Mauka." The lively Old Whaler's Saloon spouts liquor long into the night. Pool. Ask for a room with a view of the harbor. Singles and doubles $25, with bath $30; in Mauka building $60. All rooms on the 2nd floor are inaccessible to the disabled. Call months in advance for reservations, especially for Dec.-March.

Camping

Renting a car and camping on the island may be the best and cheapest way to ebulliate in Maui's natural magnificence. Sadly, the increasing number of tourists has made Maui, like Oahu, less tolerant of campers. East Maui, with its safe and well-organized campgrounds, is perhaps the surest option, although the opening of Camp Pecosa gives West Maui its first organized campsite. If you choose to camp, be selective, avoid areas that may be local hangouts, and stay away from the road. Police ask campers to leave when they come across them, but rarely get sand in their shoes by actively searching for them. Some campers park their cars at a public park, and then walk down the road or beach for some distance. Early morning rain showers, especially along the Hana Coast, and mosquitoes, make a light tent a sound investment. Long pants, sweaters, and blankets are a must, as the nights get cold.

The county maintains **H.A. Baldwin Park** in Paia about 5 miles east of the Kahului Airport. The maximum stay is three nights. A tent and permit are prerequisite. $3 per person, ages under 18 50¢. For more information contact the Department of Parks and Recreation (see Practical Information).

On West Maui, the only recognized camping is at **Camp Pecosa,** 800 Olowalu Village (661-4303), ¼ mi. north of the 14-mi. marker on Hwy. 30. The facilites are not really glamorous and the site provides little umbrage. Shower, washbasin, pit toilets, and tables are provided for $3 per person on a walk-in basis.

The state maintains three parks for camping with a five-night maximum stay. Required permits can be obtained free at the Department of Parks and Recreation. (See Practical Information.) **Waianapanapa State Wayside** in Hana, about 52 mi. east of Kahului Airport, has the best state camping facilities on the island. Cabins $5 per person. All sites include restrooms, picnic tables, barbecue grills, and outdoor showers, and are convenient to a black sand beach, blow holes, a *heiau* (temple), and Waianapanapa Cave. You can take advantage of the hiking trail to reach Hana. If Waianapanapa happens to be full, continue down 360 toward Hana. This is not tourist territory, but if you're careful, respectful, and quiet there are some great beaches that the locals will suffer you to curl up on. Hamoa, about 3 miles south of Hana, is tinted red due to oxidized iron deposits in the sand. **Polipoli State Park,** off Rte. 377 on the west slope of Haleakala Crater, sits in a wooded area 6200 ft. up the mountain. Winter nights are below freezing; you'll need a four-wheel-drive vehicle or strong legs to reach it any time of year. Although there are no showers or electricity, there is one 10-person cabin with gas lanterns ($10 for one person, $14 for two). The site also offers plenty of hiking. **Kaumahina State Park,** 28 mi. east of Kahului Airport on Rte. 36 (halfway to Hana), occupies a rain forest area, which may be an asset since there are no showers. To camp, head up the hill to find the only flat spot in the park, or, two valleys closer to Hana, turn off at the short gravel road that heads down to the ocean. The beach is a popular, though unofficial, campsite. There is a stream and plenty of rain, but no facilities.

Maui's two federal parks require no permit. **Hosmer Grove,** 7000 ft. up Haleakala's slope, is a small campground with drinking water, toilet, grills, and firewood. On a weekend night, however, you'll have to squeeze your tent in with a crowbar. Groups are limited to 15 people and a three nights' stay. **Oheo** is at sea level, about 67 mi. from Kahului Airport, ¼ mi. south of **Oheo Stream** near the Seven Pools. There's a paucity of drinking water and firewood. Three nights per month is the maximum stay.

Camping at the **national campsites** within the Haleakala Crater requires a permit and a hike to the site. Be sure to read the permit conditions before signing. Cabins (equipped with pit toilets, wood-burning cooking stove, basic utensils, 12 bunks without pillows or bedding, and a limited supply of water and firewood) are available at the **Kapalaoa, Paliku,** and **Holua** sites through a lottery. You must send in your request at least 60 days before the month when you wish to camp, and the odds of success are low. Campers are limited to two consecutive nights in each campground with a maximum of three nights per month inside the crater. Include an alternate request as each site accommodates a maximum of 25 people. Permits are available from the **Haleakala National Park Headquarters,** P.O. Box 369, Makawao, Maui 96768 (572-9306).

For unequipped campers, **Maui Sporting Goods,** 92 Market St. (244-0011), in Wailuku, rents and sells tents, backpacks, sleeping bags, ground pads, beef jerky, and more. (Open Mon.-Fri. 8am-6pm, Sat. 8am-5pm, Sun. 10am-3pm.)

Food

Gilligan would like Maui. The waters around the coast teem with fish so numerous even he could spear them, and the trees drip breadfruit, mango, coconut, pine nuts, papaya, and guava. The ground bears it's share of delicacies as well, including pineapple and the sweet Kula onion, world famous and sold for up to $6 per pound at the local market. But since this is a *charted* desert isle, Maui also has supermarkets which stock thick, crispy, kettle-cooked Maui chips (not "Maui style" potato chips, which are different and not as tasty), with or without chocolate coating. *Guri Guri,* a locally made pineapple or strawberry sherbet, has lured generations of islanders to its main supply source **Tasaka Guri Guri,** in Kahului's Maui Mall (871-4512; open daily Hawaiian time (i.e. whenever).

The cheapest places to eat are away from the resorts. Wailuku supports the largest concentration of inexpensive restaurants. To dine in style, however, visit the hotels' attractive restaurants. Try the **Gazebo Bar** in the Naplili Shores Hotel in Kaanapali for breakfast (open daily 7:30am-noon; $3.50 and up).

Hazel's Café, 2080 Vineyard St. (244-7278), Wailuku. Uncorrupted by tourist dollars, Hazel's remains a simple, unadorned café offering inexpensive local food. Copious lunch entrees, with salad, bread and tea $5-7. A wide selection of daily homestyle specials. If you can't get enough at home, Hazel serves pigs' feet soup every Fri. Open Mon.-Fri. 6am-9pm, Sat. 6am-8pm.

The Maui Boy, 2102 Vineyard St. (244-7243), at Church St. in Wailuku. The visual amenities of curtains and potted plants give this "local American" diner an edge over competitors. Large New York-style deli menu with many American sandwiches and Asian dishes for about $5. Open Tues.-Fri. 10am-2pm and 5-9pm, Sat.-Sun. 7am-2pm and 5-9pm.

Tasty Crust, Mill St., Wailuku. A bare-bones backpacker diner serving beverages in paper cups and hearty food at unbeatable prices. Fill up on giant hot cakes (85¢, served all day). Open Mon.-Sat. 6am-8pm.

Ichiban the Restaurant, Kahului Shopping Center (871-6977). Japanese cuisine with a Hawaiian atmosphere. Lunches $5.25, dinner entrees $6-8. Open Mon.-Sat. 7am-2pm and 5-9pm.

The Bakery, 991 Limahana Place (667-9062), near the railroad depot in Lahaina. It's hard to find, but have faith, for breads and pastries await your arrival. Good pizza, too. Made-to-order sandwiches $4. Open Mon.-Sat. 6am-4pm, Sun. 6am-noon.

Longhi's, 888 Front St. (667-2288), Lahaina. Elegant but informal. Excellent gourmet Italian food, and yet this is not Italy. Dinners are costly, but you can admire the ocean view and fill up on the marvelous complimentary pizza bread. Open daily 7:30am-10pm.

Azeka's, S. Kinei Rd. (879-0078), in Azeka Marketplace, Kihei. In the same building as Azeka's Market, this window-service snack shop sells inexpensive box lunches ($3-4). Hamburgers and sandwiches start at $1.25. Open Mon.-Fri. 9:30am-4pm, Sat.-Sun. 9:30am-5pm.

Paia Drive-In, Hana Hwy., next to the General Store in Paia. Cheap local "grinds." Savor the *ono* ("good") fish sandwich ($2). Open Mon.-Fri. 6am-6pm, Sat.-Sun. 7am-3pm.

Charlie P. Woofers Saloon and Restaurant, 142 Hana Hwy. (579-9453), Paia. Known simply as "Charlies" Packed with surfers. Giant breakfasts. The pancakes come ¼-in. thick ($3.25). Fresh flowers adorn wooden tables. Dinner menu of Italian and Mexican selections, burgers and pizza ($6-11). Hearty portions assembled by friendly cooks. Open daily 7am-2pm and 4-11pm.

PicNics, 30 Baldwin Ave., (579-8021), Paia. Delicious sandwiches around $4.25, and a wide variety of take-out pasta salads. Clean formica tables provided, but everyone takes the food out for PicNics. Accepts phone-in orders. Open daily 7:30am-3:30pm.

Mana Foods, 49 Baldwin Ave. (579-8078), in Paia. Full service health food grocery store and deli. Try the Maui Ginger Blast drink to wash down your tofu on wheat (all natural, no preservatives). Open daily 8am-8pm.

Paia Fish Market, 2A Baldwin Ave. (579-8030), in Paia. Elegant but casual, with woody, net-filled interior. Freshest fish around. Dinner specials around $10. Open daily 11am-9:30pm.

Komada's Market, Mukawoa (572-7261). Neighboring islanders make special trips here to buy their cream puffs (80¢). *Please* don't leave without trying them. Open Mon.-Sat. 6:30am-5pm.

Kitada's KauKau Korner, Makawao (572-7241). a truly Mom-and-Pop establishment, established in the 1940s. Mrs. Kitada serves sandwiches for $1.50, plate lunches $3-6. Open Mon.-Sat. 6:30am-1:30pm.

Casanova's Italian Restaurant and Deli, 1188 Makawao Ave. (572-0220), in Makawao. In addition to serving moderately priced Italian cuisine, Casanova's is one of Makawao's central night spots, with a front lanai convenient for drinking and chatting. Local bands some nights. Deli open daily 8:30am-7:30pm. Restaurant 5:30-8:30pm, closed sundays.

Paradise Fruit, 1935 Kihei Rd. (879-1723). A great last or first resort. Paradisical fruit at the 24-hr. stand.

Sights and Activities

The "Valley Island" can be divided into four areas—the Upcountry, the Hana Coast, West Maui, and the isthmus. You could spend weeks hiking the myriad trails on Mt. Haleakala in the upcountry, exploring the tropical wilderness around Hana, enjoying the beaches of West Maui, or wandering through the old neighborhoods of the towns on the isthmus. Resorts in Kaanapali, Kihei, and Kapalua pander to tourists and virtually monopolize water activities. Maui's real treasures, however, are not controlled by developers: silky beaches, rainforests on the Hana Hwy., the barren beauty of Haleakala, the endless rows of crops in the central valleys, and the seasonal humpback whale population near Lahaina.

The free *Maui Beach Press* provides listings of both local and tourist resort happenings.

Upcountry

Haleakala Crater, the "House of the Sun," dominates the eastern end of the island from its perch 10,000 ft. above the sea. According to Polynesian legend, the demigod Maui ascended Haleakala to slow the sun's trip across the sky so that his mother would have more time to dry her *tapa* cloth in the sun's rays. When the sun arose from his house at the end of the sky, Maui lassoed him by his genitals, and the sun quickly agreed to cruise across the sky more slowly. Today you can glory in the sun during Maui's long days, and the House of the Sun is still a wondrous place for watching the sun rise. **Haleakala National Park** is open 24 hr., but daily admission is $3 per car per day. Bring coffee and blankets and watch the sky gradually brighten through infinite shadings as the sunrise approaches. Be sure to stop at the **park headquarters** (572-9306) about a mile from the Rte. 378 entrance.

The famous volcano, the largest dormant volcano in the world, presents a moonscape of volcanic cinder cones. As you hike to lower elevations within the crater, you'll find the rare silversword plant and Hawaiian *nene* geese. If you drive the 36 mi. from Kahului Airport up the mountain for the sunrise, the views, the chilly weather, and the number of people who had the same bright idea will astound you. Early morning temperatures are generally in the low 40s (call 572-7749 for the Haleakala Park weather report). Clouds usually roll in about 10am. Before hiking into the crater, register at the trailhead ($3 per car, $1 per person). Be sure to call the weather information—it's a long trip up the mountain and you'd be surprised how fast you can get fogged in.

Haleakala Visitors Center (572-9172), near the summit, has exhibits on the geology, archaeology, and ecology of the region. Free ranger talks are given at 9:30, 10:30, and 11:30am. During summer months, the park sponsors a variety of free events. (Open daily 6:30am-4pm.) The **Puuulaula Center,** at Haleakala's summit, is where you'll probably have to stay if you forget a sweater or jacket (open 24 hr.). An 11-mi. descent into the crater via **Sliding Sands Trail** and out again via **Halemauu Trail** could be the most impressive seven hours of your trip to Hawaii. Heed the park's advice about sturdy walking shoes, water, and sun screen. **Kaluuokaoo Pit,** also called bottomless, is one of several exposed lava tubes in the crater. Early Hawaiians threw the umbilical cords of their newborns into the pit to safeguard the sacred coils from the valley's evil rodents. (See Camping, above, for information on campgrounds in Haleakala National Park.) If only to satisfy your curiosity, drive farther south on Rte. 37 to **Tedeschi Winery** (878-6058). You can stop and taste their "Maui Blanc" pineapple wine (free). Yum. (Open Mon.-Fri. 9am-5pm, Sat.-Sun. 10am-5pm.) Makawao is a small agricultural town. Try dancing at **Partners,** 1188 Makawao Ave. (572-6611).

Hana Coast

You could spend a full day driving to Hana. The northern route (Hana Hwy. 360) through **Paia** and **Keanae** is incredibly tortuous, but the scenery is equally rewarding. Make sure you start out from Paia with a full tank of gas, and don't go if the road is wet—it's a long way down.

Windsurfers enjoying nearby **Hookipa Beach Park** have brought their colorful sensibilities to Paia. The city hosts an active nightlife, and several stores sell creative clothing. Fill your PicNic basket at **PicNics** (see Food above).

On the way to Hana, you'll pass through bamboo forests and several tiny towns. Take a look around **Puohokamoa Falls, Puaakaa State Park** (home of two waterfalls, several natural pools, and clean restrooms), and **Waianapanapa State Park.** Choose from the many hikes on the Hana Coast, from balmy oceanside walks near rocky cliffs to trails through the dense jungle. The **Hana-Waianapanapa Coastal Trail,** the ancient Hawaiian "King's Highway," from the campground on Pailoa Bay to Kainalimu Bay, is a real jewel; a few of the stepping stones placed on the jagged lava can still be found, though most have eroded. Between Kuaiwa Point and Paina Point, the trail passes an ancient Hawaiian *heiau,* about ½ mi. from the Waianapanapa campground. North of the campground, about ½ mi. past Hana Airport, are the **Waianapanapa** and **Waiomao Caves.** Bring a flashlight and swim in the underground lava tubes, now filled with fresh water. According to legend, an Hawaiian princess once hid from her cruel husband in these caves. Her feather *kahili* was reflected by the water, however, and the prince found and murdered her. Every spring, red shrimp turn the cave waters crimson, a living reminder of the slain princess.

The city of **Hana** on the eastern slope of Haleakala is a picturesque one-horse town, immortalized in song for its **Hasegawa General Store** (248-8231; open Mon.-

Sat. 7:30am-6pm, Sun. 9am-3:30pm). The original store burned down in 1990, but they have relocated in a nearby warehouse. **Hale Waiwai o Hana,** the Hana Cultural Museum, 1 block *makai* (inland) off Rte. 31 on Keanini St., recounts the city's past as an agricultural oasis. Look through the town's family album of class photos, old bottles, and Hawaiian quilts. 1½ mi. past Hana, turn seaward on Haneoo Rd. to get to sandy **Haneoo Beach,** the only bodysurfing beach for miles. Farther south from Hana along Rte. 31, is the **Kipahulu District,** part of Haleakala National Park. Over 20 pools exist in the mile of the **Oheo** stream immediately above the ocean. Known to tourists as the Seven Sacred Pools, *Oheo,* which means "the gathering of pools," is the historically accurate name. From the Pools there is a lovely path (400 ft.) up Oheo Gulch to Waimoku Falls. The trail, in the Haleakala National Park, is rough, but the beauty of the undisturbed waterfalls, pools, and bamboo groves compensate for the effort. **Charles Lindbergh's Grave** lies in the Kipahulu Hawaiian Church's idyllic graveyard, about 2 mi. down the road from the Pools. The supreme aviator spent his last years here and helped to restore the church.

Central Maui

While near the saddle of the island, be sure to step into the unspoiled **Iao Valley,** on the southern slope of Puu Kukui. The valley is especially beautiful in the moonlight. West on Rte. 32, toward the valley, lies calm **Kepaniwai Park.** In 1790, Kamehameha I slaughtered the Maui army here, filling the brook with the dead (*kepaniwai* (meaning "the damming of the waters"). Their blood reputedly ran all the way down to the Wailuku ("bloody") River. Today, the park is home to a host of pavilions dedicated to the peoples who have populated Maui—Japanese, Filipino, Chinese, Hawaiian, early American, and Portuguese. The **Iao Valley State Park,** at the end of Rte. 32, includes the **Iao Needle,** a 1200-ft. basalt spire (open daily 7am-7pm). Tour buses arrive by 10am, and clouds by 2pm; both leave by 6pm. The name is onomatopoetic—the cry of an unfortunate god who sat on this pointed peak. Wailuku itself is a tranquil plantation town, worth an afternoon stroll. The government buildings on High St. and vintage shops on Market St. remain oblivious to the depredations of resort development in the south.

In the 19th century, the Baileys, a New England missionary family, sailed around Cape Horn to reach Maui's pagan paradise. Now cared for by the cordial Mrs. Bosworth and still decked in period decor, the Bailey's home serves as the **Maui Historical Society Museum,** on Rte. 32 between Wailuku and Iao Valley. (Open daily 10am-4:30pm.)

On a nearby hill, you can visit a relic of the ancient religion that the Baileys came to stifle. The **Hale Kii** (House of Images) served as a place of worship throughout the 18th century until it was destroyed by natural erosion in 1819. Reconstructed in 1958, the *heiau* is now a temple of love. High school sweethearts make the pilgrimage uphill on Thursday evenings for the island's most idyllic views. Follow Main St. (Rte. 32) to the traffic light at Rte. 330. Make a left, pass the macadamia nut grove, and turn right on Rte. 340. Continue to Kuhio Place, and follow the nerve-wracking route to the right.

Wailuku is populated by a curious mix of international travelers and hard-core windsurfers. The **Vineyard Tavern,** 2171 Vineyard (242-9938), is close to the hostels and a good nighttime hangout. It's a dim, dusty bar and grill with a shuttleboard table and a hefty dose of charm. Budweisers $2. Last call 1:30am.

The **Maui Community Theatre,** 68 Market St. (242-6969), Wailuku, presents a variety of productions performed by community actors. The theater is a creaky remnant of the past, with hard wooden chairs and dust. (Admission $7, juniors $6, children $3.)

West Maui

Between the Kaanapali Airport and Lahaina stretches the 4-mi. **Kaanapali Beach,** a resort area from which you can often see the neighboring islands of Molokai, Lanai, and Oahu. **Launiupoko State Wayside Park** is a swimming beach with picnic tables, restrooms, outdoor showers, and barbecue grills. At the **14 mile**

marker, near Olowalu, you can enjoy some of the calmest and most spectacular snorkeling in Hawaii, although it is unsuitable for sunbathing. Near Lahaina, **Fleming Beach Park** is a favorite for both snorkeling and bodysurfing.

Lahaina, an old whaling port, was the capital of the islands during the time of Kamehameha the Great. The Cannery in Lahaina and Whaler's Village in Kaanapali are two made-for-tourists shopping malls. Whaler's Village displays rusting relics of the whaling days. In the middle of the mall on the second floor, a one-room museum exhibits an extensive collection of scrimshaw (the art of detailed etching on whale bones). (Open daily 9:20am-1pm and 1:30-10pm.) Whale-watching is a popular activity along the coast in spring and fall. Lahaina itself is a sunny, dry town that infects visitors with drowsy calm. When Mark Twain visited, he planned to stay one week and work; he stayed a month and never lifted a pen. The enormous tree in Lahaina's town square is a 114-year-old East Indian **banyan tree,** rivaling Kaui's for the title of the islands' largest. Pick up a free copy of the *Lahaina Historical Guide* from one of the many tourist centers that crowd the town. The sugar mill at the end of Lahainaluna Rd. still operates, and the island's only remaining steam locomotive still carries tourists, if not sugar, between Lahaina and Kaanapali. (One way $5; round-trip $8; under 12 half-price.) A new OMNI theater, 824 Front St. (661-8314), Lahaina, presents Hawaii's history on the big, big screen with *Hawaii: Island of the Gods!* shown daily on the hour from 10am-10pm. (Admission $6, children under 12 $4. $1 discount coupons available at nearby tourist centers.)

Club Lanai, Inc., 355 Hukilike Suite 211 (871-1144), sends shuttles from Lahaina harbor to the club facilities on Lanai every other hour from 8am to 4pm. The shuttle costs $20 round trip. Once there you can eat, drink ($2-10) and play merrily with the club's water equipment for $5-20. Call for reservations.

West Maui hosts the island's hottest dance scene. **Spats,** in the Hyatt Regency Maui (667-7474), has two bars and two dance floors, a cover charge ($5-10), and a dress code, rocking until 4am. **Banana Moon,** in the Maui Marriott (667-1200), offers the same scene but just 'til 2am.

Seasonal Events

Maui Marathon, early March. Kahului to Kaanapali.

O'Neil Invitational, 1st week in April at Hookipa Beach Park, Paia. International windsurfing tournament. Call Paul Ehman (579-9765).

Wenkai Story-Telling Festival, June 16 on Pali Beach by the volleyball courts.

Makawao State Rodeo, July 4 in the Oskie Rice Arena.

Na Mele O Maui Music Festival, early August.

Hawaiian Pro Am, early September at Hookipa Beach Park, Paia. International windsurfing tournament. Speed competition at the Molokai Channel Crossing. Call Paul Ehman (579-9765).

Maui Grand Prix, mid-October at Hookipa Beach Park, Paia. No, not a car race, but a major wave surfing event. Surfers from twelve countries compete.

Aloha Citizen's Classic, late October at Hookipa Beach, Paia. One of the biggest windsurfing events at Hookipa.

Maui County Fair, October in Kahului.

Halloween, October 31. This is a big event Lahaina. Party, trick, and treat. Neighboring islanders come specially for the night.

Kauai

Kauai is the oldest, the wettest, and perhaps the most magnificent of all the inhabited islands. Father Time, Mother Nature, and Fortuna herself have woven a web of streams and waterfalls running from Mt. Waialeale (the wettest spot on earth, with 400-600 in. of rainfall annually) down through the lush Waimea Canyon, creating 459 square miles of visual paradise. Filmakers have used Kauai as a shooting location for *South Pacific, Blue Hawaii,* and the television series *Fantasy Island.* If you're coming to Kauai seeking nightlife and decadence, seek elsewhere. Above all, Kauai abounds in peaceful, natural splendor.

Practical Information and Orientation

Visitors Information: Hawaii Visitors Bureau, Lihue Plaza Bldg., 3016 Umi St. #207, Lihue (245-3971), at Rice St. Write for their vacation planner, a directory of services, events, and coupons: P.O. Box 507, Lihue 96766. Open Mon.-Fri. 8am-4:30pm. **Kauai County Parks Office,** 4193 Hardy St., Lihue (245-8821). The office is located behind the convention center in a long building by the parking lot. Information and permits for camping in county parks. Open Mon.-Fri. 8am-4:30pm. **Division of State Parks,** 3060 Eiwa St., Lihue 96766 (241-3444), at Hardy St., in the State Office Bldg. Information on camping in state parks, permits issued Mon.-Fri. 8am-4pm. **Kauai Chamber of Commerce,** P.O. Box 1969, Lihue 96766 (245-7363).

Local Attractions and Cultural Events: 246-4441 ext. 1800.

Taxis: An expensive last resort. **Hanamaulu Taxi** (245-3727). 24-hr. service. **ABC Taxi** (822-7641), island-wide. **North Shore Cab** (826-6189) offers end-of-the-road specials for hikers.

Car Rental: The best deals come as part of hotel-car or air-car packages. Make reservations. **Alamo Rent-a-Car,** Lihue Airport (800-327-9633 or 245-8953). $29 per day with unlimited mileage. Must be 25 with credit card or $50 per day deposit. Open daily 6:30am-9:30pm. **Budget Rent-a-Car,** Lihue Airport (800-527-0700 or 245-9031). $25 per day. $20 surcharge for those 18-21, $7 under 25. Open daily 6am-9pm. **Thrifty,** Lihue Airport (245-7388). $24 per day, $10 surcharge for unlimited mileage. Must be 21 with a major credit card.

Bicycle and Moped Rentals: Kauai's main roads leave little room for slow 2-wheelers, so think twice before renting. **Peddle 'n' Paddle,** P.O. Box 1413, Ching Young Village, Hanalei 96714 (826-9069). Bikes $20 and mopeds $50 per day. Credit card required. Also rents boats, canoes, surfboards, and windsurfers. Open daily 9am-5pm.

Camping Equipment: Hanalei Camping and Backpacking, Ching Young Village, P.O. Box 1245, Hanalei 96714 (826-6664), on the northern side of Kauai. Stocks tents, backpacks, camp stoves, and child carriers. Open Mon.-Sat. 8am-7pm, Sun. 9am-6pm.

Water Equipment Rentals: Progressive Expressions, Old Koloa Town (742-6041), near Poipu. Also in Kapaa (822-9211). Boogie boards for sale and rent, $10 per day. Open daily 9am-9pm. **Aquatics Kauai,** 733 Rte. 56 (822-9213), in Kapaa across from the Sheraton. A dive shop offering lessons and charters. Masks (prescription lenses available), fins, and snorkel $8 per day. Boogie boards $7.50 per day. Bodysurfing fins $5 per day. Open daily 7am-7pm. **Kayak Kauai,** P.O. Box 503, Hanalei 95314 (826-9844). Instruction, extended tours, and rentals. Two-person inflatable kayaks $45 per day. Hard-shell ocean kayaks start at $35 per day. Soft racks and life preservers included.

Laundromat: Kapaa Laundry Center, Kapaa Shopping Center, Kuhio Hwy. (822-3113). Drop off and self-service. 7am-7:30pm daily.

Weather: 245-6001.

Water Conditions: 245-3564.

Surf Report: 335-3611.

Coast Guard: 245-4521 or 245-8111.

Help Lines: Crisis, 245-7838. 24 hr. **Kauai Women's Center,** 3094 Elua St. (245-5959), in Lihue. **Sexual Assault Center,** 245-4144. 24 hr. **SCUBA Recompression Chamber,** 338-1422. **Kauai Helpline,** 822-3411.

Hospitals: Wilcox, O.N. Memorial Hospital and Health Center, 3420 Rte. 56, Lihue (245-1010). **Kauai Veterans** (338-9431), in Waimea.

Police: 3060 Umi St., Lihue (245-9722 or 911).

Post Office: 4441 Rice St., Lihue (245-4994). Open Mon.-Fri. 8:30am-4pm, Sat. 10am-2pm. General Delivery ZIP Code: 96766.

Area Code: 808.

Kauai is the farthest north and west of the large islands in the Hawaii chain. Roughly circular, the island falls away from Waialeale at its center to a coastline ringed by one highway. The road connects Lihue and the Lihue Airport with the major towns: **Wailua** is 7 mi., **Kapaa** 10 mi., Hanalei 35 mi., and Haena 41 mi. counterclockwise on Rte. 56. Clockwise on Rte. 50, **Poipu** lies 14 mi. and **Waimea** 25 mi. from Lihue. The Rte. 50/56 circuit leaves a wide, roadless gap on the remote northwestern **Napali Coast** of Kauai. Thirty miles from Lihue, Rte. 55 branches off Rte. 50 and heads up **Waimea Canyon.**

Lihue Airport, a 26-minute flight from Honolulu, is Kauai's major airfield. **Grayline Airport Service** (800-367-2420) can take you to the resort towns of Wailua ($6) and Poipu ($10); call for reservations. **Princeville Airport** serves mainly the Princeville resort area and is serviced only by **Aloha Island Air** (800-652-6541; flights to all islands from $60).

Accommodations

Kauai lacks a hostel, but does feature several affordable hotels as well as a number of B&Bs and camping sites with cabins. In general, you'll find better accommodations for less money on Kauai than on Oahu or Maui.

Garden Island Inn, 3445 Wilcox Rd., Nawiliwili 96766 (245-7227), about 3 mi. ($9 taxi) from Lihue airport. Across from Kalapaki Beach, this newly renovated inn offers comfortable, airy rooms in a garden setting, complete with goldfish-stocked pools, TV, fridge, phone, coffee machines, and some rooms with wet bar. Near the Westin Kauai Lagoons Hotel. Singles and doubles $45-65.

Kauai Sands Hotel, 420 Papaloa Rd., Coconut Plantation, Wailua 96746 (822-4951). "Resort-scaped" grounds along a white sand beach. Affordable restaurant. All-you-can-eat pancakes (Boy!) ($3.65). Comfortable rooms with A/C, ceiling fans, and refrigerators. Two pools. Singles and doubles $64. Double room with car $79.

Kay Barker's B&B, P.O. Box 740, Kapaa 96746 (822-3073), in the lush Wailua homesteads off Rte. 580 past the Opaekaa falls. A gracious country home offers spacious rooms with private bath. Generous breakfasts. Singles $30. Doubles $40-60. Call early for reservations, but last-minute openings are not unheard of. Knowledgeable caretaker will give you any information you still need after reading *Let's Go.* Hike up the short trail starting at the back of the house for a remarkable view from the top of **Sleeping Giant** (so named for its shape).

Tip Top Motel, P.O. Box 1231, Lihue 96766 (245-2333). From the airport, take Akuhini Rd. past Umi and Elua, turn left onto Akahi St.; the motel is on the right. Restaurant and bakery downstairs. Not in the Most Aesthetically Pleasing Top Ten, but serviceable and cheap. Cement façade and bare rooms. Singles $30. Doubles $39. Key deposit $5.

Hotel Coral Reef, 1516 Rte. 56, Kapaa 96746 (800-843-4659 or 822-4481), 10-mi. drive on Rte. 56 from the airport. Beachfront hotel with spacious rooms and amiable management. Fans, no phones. Singles or doubles in older section $40; in newer wing $45.

Camping and Cabins

Camping is an economical way to enjoy Kauai's beauty. State and county parks are plentiful (permits required), and free camping spots along the beaches are hard to avoid. Obtain permits from the County Parks Office or from the police station on weekends (see Practical Information). County permits cost $3 per person per day for a maximum of 7 days per park and/or 60 days total. Be prepared with specific dates and campgrounds. Check also for available cabins. Permits for the three state parks are available at the Division of State Parks (see Practical Information). These permits are free and are for a maximum five nights in one park. For more information on camping and hiking on Kauai, contact **Kauai Sports,** Lihue (245-8052; open Mon.-Thurs. 9am-6pm, Fri. 9am-9pm, Sun. 10am-4pm); or the **Sierra Club** (822-7654 or 822-7141; open Mon.-Thurs. 7:30am-4:30pm; also offers $2 guided hikes).

While camping, keep in mind that the water on Kauai may contain harmful bacteria. *Always* treat any water from mountain streams with tablets (or boil the water for at least five minutes) before drinking.

Polihale State Park, Rte. 50, about 37 mi. northwest of Lihue at the end of 5 mi. of dirt road. A beautiful beach park for swimming, bodysurfing, and shore fishing beneath the cliffs of the Napali Coast. Waters may be treacherous, especially in fall and spring. Picnicking, tent, and trailer camping facilities. Five-day max. stay. Permit required.

Napali Coast State Park. Primitive camping facilities along the scenic Kalalau Trail (11 tough mi. each way) in **Haena Beach Park.** Haena, at the end of Rte. 56, is 40 mi. from Lihue. Kalalau Valley is also accessible by boat May-Sept. Three-night max. stay at Milolii (accessible only by boat) and at Kalalau Beach, one-night max. at Hanakapiai and Hanakoa Valleys. Permit required.

YMCA, Camp Naue (246-9090), on the northshore beach near Kalalau trail, in Haena. Close to some very good snorkeling spots and Haena Beach Park. Space for 40 people in 4 rooms. Individual shower stalls. Tent sites available. Members $9. Nonmembers $10. Linen $3. Sites with tents $8, plus $5 per each additional person.

Kokee State Park, P.O. Box 819, Waimea 96796 (335-6061). On Kokee Rd., 16 mi. north of Kekaha. Tent and trailer camping near trails, picnic facilities, scenic forests, and canyon. Plum picking, pig hunting, and trout fishing in season. More information at the visitors center. Permit required.

Cabins: Kokee Lodge, P.O. Box 819, Waimea 96796 (335-6061), offers cabins which sleep three to seven people, with refrigerators, stoves, showers, utensils, and linens. Kind of rough, but what do you expect? Five-day max. stay. Check-in 2pm. Check-out 11am. Office open Sun.-Thurs. 8:30am-5:30pm, Fri.-Sat. 8:30am-9pm. Cabins $35-45 per night. First night deposit required, refundable on 2-week cancellation notice. Book early for summer.

YWCA, Camp Sloggett (335-6060), ½ mi. down the dirt road from Kokee Lodge in Kokee. Think rustic; bring your own food and bedding. Hot showers. Cabin and bunks $12 per person.

Kahili Mountain Park (742-9921), off Rte. 50, 10 mi. west of Lihue. 200 acres with a small lake and a few hiking trails. December and January are especially busy; reserve well in advance. Two-day min. stay. Cabins for two with private bath, shower, and kitchen $39; cabinettes for two with kitchen, communal shower, and bath $22. Each additional person $4. Linen, dishes, and detergent included. Tent sites $6.

Food

Travelers enjoying Kauai's visual delights need not fear that their tastebuds will be left in the dark. Consider satisfying the two senses simultaneously: pack a picnic and take to the road, find a superlative vista, and feast your eyes while you feed your face.

For groceries, check out the **Big Saves** in Lihue at Hardy St. and Rte. 56 and in Waimea at 9861 Rte. 56 (both open daily 7am-11pm), and **Old Koloa** at 5510 Rte. 530 (open daily 6am-11pm). **Papaya's Natural Foods,** Kauai Village in Kapaa (823-0190), has organic produce and bulk-bin oat bran as well as healthy, prepared take out meals to fill your picnic basket.

Hamura's Saimin Stand, 2956 Kress St. (245-3271), in Lihue. Doesn't look like much, but locals line up for *saimin* (noodles $2-2.90, add-ins 65-70¢). *Malasadas* 35¢, *manapua* 75¢, banana bread $1.20. Patrons are kindly requested not to leave their gum under the corrugated counter. **Holo Holo Shave Ice Shack,** in the same building. Open Mon. 10am-1am, Tues.-Thurs. 10am-2am., Fri. and Sat. 10am-4am, Sun. 10am-11pm.

Ma's Family Restaurant, on Halenani St. one block off of Rice St. (245-3143), in Lihue. Ma opens her doors by 5am daily, making her place *Let's Go's* number one pick for early morning Kalua pig omelettes. Free coffee to wash it down. Open Mon.-Fri. 5am-1:30pm, Sat.-Sun. 5am-10am.

Barbecue Inn, 2982 Kress St. (245-2921), in Lihue. The only restaurant on Kress St. that isn't a diner. Bar starts serving drinks around noon to give you an early start on the nightlife. Breakfast $3-5; lunch $5-8; complete Japanese dinner from $6. Open Mon.-Sat. 7:30am-1:30pm and 4:30-8:30pm.

Island Pleasures Tropical Food and Drink, Anchor Cove, 3416 Rice St. (245-9000), in Nawiliwili. Abundant Life, Boogie Burgers, or Sun Dried Tomato Sandwiches on your mind? This café on the bay will service you. Sandwiches $3-6. Also offers vegetarian specials. Baked Potato Mexicali with veggie chili and cheese is cheap and filling at $3.75. Eat at the counter or sit at outside tables. Open daily 7am-9pm.

Perry's Smorgy, Kapaa (822-3111), off Rte. 56 at the Kauai Beachboy Hotel in the Market Place. A surprisingly palatable array of island offerings served in unlimited portions. Breakfast $4, lunch $5.45, dinner $8. Open daily 7-10am, 1-2:30pm and 5-9pm.

Duane's Ono Charburgers, on Rte. 56 in Kealia. Little red shack just past Whale's General Store, on the right side of the road going north on Rte. 56. Multitudinous fries ($1.40) and juicy burgers ($3-5). There's a place to tie up your horse, and Walter Cronkite has eaten here! Though "ono" is a kind of fish, it is also Hawaiian for "good," and the ono-burgers are 100% beef, not fish. Open Mon.-Sat. 10am-6pm, Sun. 11am-6pm.

Village Snack and Bakery Shop, Ching Young Village (826-6841), off Rte. 56 in Hanalei. A breakfast bonanza. Banana pancakes with bacon and coffee $3. Overstuffed sandwiches $2.50-3. Open daily 6am-3pm.

Hanalei Shave Ice, 5-5183 Rte. 56 (826-7408), behind Bali Hai Charters in Hanalei across from Ching Young Village. Miss not their *lilikoi* (passion fruit, $1-1.20). Open Mon.-Sat. 10am-6pm, Sun. noon-6pm.

Taquería Norteños, 2827A Poipu Rd. (742-7222), in the Poipu Plaza. Giant quasi-health-food burritos from $2. All entrees under $5. Open Mon.-Tues. and Thurs.-Sun. 11am-11pm, Wed. 11am-5:30pm.

Sights and Activities

Explore Kauai from the two coastal highways (Rte. 50 going south and Rte. 56 going north) that embrace the island from Lihue Airport.

Kauai has some of the best surf spots on the islands, and the classic Hawaiian Reef diving beckons to the nautically inclined. For beach potatoes, white sand and calm waters abound.

Lihue

The **Kauai Museum,** 4428 Rice St. (245-6931), has a remarkable collection of Hawaiiana as well as presentations on the geological and cultural history of Kauai. While there, don't miss the 40-minute video of the island as seen from a helicopter and by underwater scuba divers. Large exhibits feature crafts made from koa wood and native Hawaiian quiltmaking. (Open Mon.-Fri. 9am-4:30pm, Sat. 9am-1pm. Admission $3, under 18 free.) South of Lihue sit the ancient **Menehune Gardens** (245-2660), off Nawiliwili Rd., Rte. 58. Named after the mysterious little people said to have inhabited the island before the Polynesians, the gardens are home to the Weeping Banyan, Hawaii's oldest and largest tree. (Admission $2.50, under 12 50¢. Open daily 10am-4pm.) Legend has it that Kauai was the Menehunes' island of choice. Just southeast of Lihue, at Niumalu, is the Alakoko fish pond, purportedly built in one night by the resourceful little magic sprites, who then caught a red-eye to Dublin and started hanging out under the shamrocks. The fish pond is still in use. **Kilohana Plantation,** 3-2087 Rte. 50 (245-5608), 1.7 mi. south of Lihue, was the plantation estate of Gaylord Park Wilcox. The nostalgic can take a 20-minute carriage ride through the 35 acres of lush tropical gardens ($7, children $4.50). There is no charge for roaming around the plantation house itself, although most of the rooms are now occupied by shops. The original furnishings in the dining and living rooms, however, provide a singular glimpse of Old Hawaii. **Gaylords** serves pleasant but expensive meals on the veranda. (Plantation opens daily at 9am.) Fulfill your fantasies at **Wailua Falls,** where the diminutive Hervé Villechaise would carry out his weekly spotting of "da plane" on the late *Fantasy Island* television series.

Heading north on Rte. 56, turn *mauka* (inland) on Rte. 583 to get to **Wailua Falls.** The falls cascade 400 ft. into a blue-green pool. Steep and unimproved trails lead down to the top of the falls from the end of the road. Turn right after the Wailua Golf Course on Rte. 56 North to get to **Lydgate State Park.** Look for the *heiau* (temple of refuge) just past the white sand beach and sheltered wading pool.

At **Wailua Marina State Park,** 7 mi. from Lihue before the Wailua River Bridge, you can take a boat up the Wailua River to the **Fern Grotto** ($9, ages under 12 $4.50). **Smith's Tropical Paradise** (822-4654 or 822-9599) and **Waialeale Boats** (822-4908) run boats that leave every half hour from 9am to 4pm. The complete trip takes one hour. In addition, Smith's Tropical Paradise, Kapua, is a striking 30 acres of colorful flora and peaceful lagoons. Maroon yourself here for at least ½ a day. Admission $5.

At Rte. 580, turn *mauka* again and you'll find the **Holoholoku Heiau,** once used for human sacrifices. Farther along the road lie the **Pohakuhoohanau,** sacred stones where Hawaiian royalty came to give birth. Beyond, at the top of the hill, is a *heiau* where the king of Kauai once lived. Check out the view of **Opaekaa Falls** from this road. Opaekaa means "rolling shrimp," referring to the days when shrimp filled the turbulent waters at the base of the falls. Across from Opaekaa Falls at 6060 Kuamoo Rd., on the banks of the Wailua River, is the **Kamokila Hawaiian Village** (822-1193). This reconstructed Hawaiian village features demonstrations of traditional local activities: poi-pounding, hula, and lei-making (open Mon.-Sat. 9am-4pm. Admission $5, ages under 12 $1.50).

North and East From Lihue: Princeville, Hanalei, and Haena

The best sights in eastern Kauai lie farther along Rte. 56. On the drive, stop at **Kilauea Lighthouse National Park** (828-1413), 709 ft. above sea level on a bluff near Kilauea Bay, off Kuhio Ave. To get here, follow the signs from the highway. Share the beautiful vista with nearly three million sea birds and an occasional dolphin or seal. (Open Mon.-Fri. 10am-4pm.) The **Hanalei Valley Lookout,** off the left side of the road, spans a valley of *taro* patches and rice paddies. Stop at **Pooku Stable,** P.O. Box 888 (826-6777, 826-7473, evenings 826-6484), to ride horseback through Hanalei Valley ($25), on the bluffs above the beach ($46), or to the waterfalls for a picnic ($70).

The town of Princeville sparkles with the glitz of tourism. The **Princeville Hotel-Sheraton** is a super-charged multi-million dollar resort establishment that merits inspection. But be careful—breathe too hard and your wallet will shrink. This lair of the rich and famous overlooks Hanalei Bay.

If watersports are your passion, the area around Hanalei Bay can keep you amused for a day or more. The bay is perfect for snorkeling and spearfishing on calm days. The Kalihiwai area, a few miles east of Princeville, offers a bit more shelter in rough weather, but watch out—the murky waters can be shark-infested, and the currents are too strong for beginners.

Surfers and those who just like to watch should head for the spot known as **Cannons,** opposite Princeville off **Lumahai Beach.** This shallow reef locale breaks close to shore, making it dangerous for the guys on the boards and exciting for the spectators on shore. The nurses in *South Pacific* happy-talked right here. Lazy folks can get a clear view of the action from above without making the hike down.

Drive on toward **Haena** past the enormous **Maninholo Cave,** named after the head fisherman of the Menehunes. One mile farther you can walk directly from the road into **Waikapalae Cave,** which contains a small pool. To experience the cooler side of paradise, dip into the lagoon at the **Waikanaloa Cave.** The Cave has two sections. Before you reach the section that is adjacent to the road you will see a parking area on your right. Walk up the road a few yards and directly across from the King Kahmehameha-shaped sign you will see an old road with cracked pavement. The entrance to a much more secluded section of the cave, called the **Blue Room,** lies a short walk up this road. The water is usually a deeper blue here because it is hidden from the onslaught of silt-churning tourists. Lore-mongers claim that Pele dug these caves when she was first trying to find a home on the islands, but hit water instead of lava.

All along this route you'll find dead-end roads and turn-offs leading to beautiful beaches. Try to ignore the buzz of helicopter sight-seeing flights whirring overhead. At the end of Rte. 56 are **Haena Point, Kee Beach,** and the trailhead for the **Kalalau Valley Trail,** which follows an ancient Hawaiian trail 11½ mi. down spectacular Napali Coast. Be sure to allow at least two hours for a hike to **Hanakapiai Beach.** Hikes into the valley or to **Kalalau Beach** can range from several hours to many days in length (see Camping). The wilderness coastal areas beyond Haena are accessible only by hiking or by boat. Rip currents from September through April make swimming perilous.

South and West From Lihue: Poipu, Waimea, and Kokee

On Rte. 50 west from Lihue, detour onto Rte. 520. You'll pass through a tunnel of eucalyptus trees to the restored **Old Koloa Town,** Hawaii's first sugar mill town, now gentrified by boutiques. A right off 520 at Kapili Rd. leads to **Kiahuna Plantation** (742-6411), Hector Moir's lavish gardens filled with 3000 varieties of plants. (Open daily 9am-6pm. Free.) At the end of Rte. 520 is a fork in the road at the "Welcome to Poipu Beach" sign. A right turn takes you past **Prince Kuhio's birthplace** and the **Spouting Horn,** where waves force water to spout through lava tubes, as at the Blow Hole on Oahu. Beyond the Spouting Horn, the daring will find secluded beaches among steep cliffs. Going left at the fork, wide-open beaches line the coast from the resort area on Poipu Rd. Continue through the dirt road end of **Poipu Beach Rd.** to more secluded locales. Two such beaches, **Brenneckies** (known for bodysurfing) and **Acid Drops** (for boardsurfing), are some of Kauai's more accessible wave spots.

Thirty mi. west of Lihue, Rte. 50 meets Rte. 550 at tiny **Waimea.** 1 mile east of Waimea is **Infinities,** the best "left" (a beach where the waves break left instead of right) in all off Hawaii. Park alongside the road (there will be cars there if the surf is pumping) and hike through the bull pasture to reach the shore. Try not to intrude upon the locals or the regular surfers; they can be hostile to outsiders. Off the highway, 1½ mi. down Menehune Rd., a marker points to the interlocking stones of **Peekauai Ditch** (also known as Menehune Ditch). It is the famed creation of the Menehunes, those legendary little guys known for their masonry and mischievousness.

Turning inland, Rte. 550 begins an ascent past the dramatic **Waimea Canyon Lookout.** With its stunning colors, this is serious Kodak Perfect Moment material. Farther up Rte. 550, **Kokee Lodge** offers a place to eat, pitch a tent, or just visit the small but free museum (open daily 10am-4pm). Kokee Lodge is part of Kokee State Park, and a permit is required for camping. (See Camping for information on permits and the lodge.) The park has an abundance of hiking trails, including some that venture into **Alakai Swamp**—ask at park headquarters for directions to the trailhead. Near the end of Rte. 550 is the exquisitely lush **Kalalau Valley Lookout.** Still farther up the road, where tractors aborted an attempt to build a road to Haena, rests the entrance to the muddy Pihea Trail. Take some time to hike along the ridge overlooking Kalalau Valley before turning inland down into the Alakai swamp. On the way back down the mountain to the coast, thrill-seeking drivers will enjoy the twisted majesty of **Waimea Canyon Drive,** to the left of Rte. 550.

In days gone by, many visitors took Rte. 50 west to hear the sands speak at **Barking Sands Beach,** but, as local residents say, "The dog stay old already," and these days the sand seldom barks, yips, or even woofs. If peaceful beaches are your thing, drive out to the end of Rte. 50 and continue along 5 mi. of dirt road to **Polihale Beach Park.** This secluded park and surf spot, equipped with showers, shelters, tables, grills, and the ever popular toilet, is bordered by the **Napali Cliffs** and a swimming beach. It is also your best bet for guaranteed sunshine on Kauai. Camping is free, but a state permit is required from the Division of State Parks (see Camping).

Entertainment

Visitors to Kauai will discover that nightclubs aren't the only places to go for an exciting evening. It's a good thing too, considering that there aren't very many on the island. If you happen to be on the Garden Isle at the right time, however, you might catch some celebrating, local-style. Take a sunset cruise along the northern coast with **Bali Hai Charters,** 5-5183 Rte. 56, Hanalei 96714 (826-9787; from $25), or indulge in a festive *luau* ($45, under 13 $27.25) at the Sheraton Coconut Beach Hotel, P.O. Box 830, Coconut Plantation, Kapaa (822-3455, ext. 651 for reservations). Better yet, take in Sheraton-sponsored native music, daily at 7:45pm with no cover. **Club Jetty,** on the Nawiliwili pier (245-4970) near Lihue, offers dancing to live music Wednesday through Saturday for $2. No cover Wednesday. Free *pupus* and a musicians' jam Sunday. **Riptide Bar,** 4-1378 Kuhio Hwy. (822-2441), Kapaa, has live dance music and pu-pus.

Seasonal Events

Captain Cook Festival, late Feb. in Waimea. Canoe race in honor of Captain Cook's first landing in the Hawaiian Islands. Call Sylvia Dobry (338-1226).

LPGA Women's Kemper Open, late Feb. at the Princeville Makai Golf Course. Call Mac Hunter (826-3580).

Prince Kuhio Festival, March 26 in Lihue. Pageantry, song, and dance from the era of Prince Kuhio. Canoe races and a royal ball. Call the visitors bureau (245-3971) for more information.

King Kamehameha Day, June 11 in Lihue. Parade, *hoolaulea* (festive gathering), arts and crafts.

Hanalei Stampede, in late July, at Pooku Stables, Hanalei. A foot-stompin' rodeo that drifted 2000 mi. west. Call 826-6777 for more information.

Kauai County Fair, in early Sept. at the Kauai Memorial Convention Hall, Lihue. Exhibits, entertainment, games, and food booths.

Molokai

The fifth largest island in the chain, Molokai has always been set apart as a refuge for Hawaiians escaping misfortune and seeking peace. Deer cavort alongside wild goats and pigs on the mountainous eastern end. On the island's western side, pineapples grow under the shadow of Puu Nana (Viewing Hill), where the *hula* was conceived. When Hansen's disease (leprosy) swept through Hawaii in the mid-1800s, those afflicted were exiled to Makanalua ("the Living Grave"), a completely isolated peninsula on Molokai's north coast. Those banished to the colony, which relocated to the western side at Kalaupapa during the 1870s, were cut off from family and friends for the remainder of their abject lives. Under the stigma of leprosy, many Hawaiians shunned Molokai as the "Lonely Isle."

In 1873, the famous Belgian priest Joseph De Veuster, more popularly known as Father Damien, arrived at the settlement with nothing but his Bible. The rest of his life was devoted to offering spiritual and physical comfort to the community. Damien became known as the "Martyr of Molokai" after he died of the disease 16 years later. His efforts led to increased awareness of the plight of the lepers, and today leprosy can be controlled with drugs. The Kalaupapa settlement, on the site of the original colony, is Molokai's most notable tourist sight. In an effort to shed its rather grisly image, Molokai has been re-nicknamed the "Friendly Isle," after its 6000 genuinely amiable inhabitants.

Although most of the sights are either on private land or are inaccessible to the main road, this is designed only to deter a full-scale tourist onslaught. Those who do come to Molokai will discover that the locals are in fact quite welcoming to low-key outsiders and that none of Molokai's sights are "guarded." Be respectful, however, of all of the signs associated with the Molokai Ranch Wildlife Park on the western end of the island, to which endangered African animals have been transported within the last 30 years.

Practical Information and Orientation

Visitors Information: Molokai Chamber of Commerce, P.O. Box 515, Kaunakakai 96748. They sponsor an information booth at the airport. Free maps and cheerful advice. Open Mon.-Fri. 8am-4pm. Obtain a brochure map from the Hawaii Visitors Bureau on Oahu or Maui. Call **Destinations Molokai** (553-3876), a non-profit organization dedicated to introducing visitors to the island, for accommodations and car rental information.

Parks: Molokai Division of Parks, P.O. Box 526, Kaunakakai 96748 (553-5141), at the east end of Kaunakakai, behind the baseball field and fire station in the Mitchell Pauole Center. Information on camping and county parks on Molokai. Open Mon.-Fri. 8am-4pm. Issues camping permits ($3). Free permits for Palau State Park issued at the **Division of Water and Land,** near the post office in Hoolehua, 1 mi. from the airport. Open Mon.-Fri. 8am-4pm. Write or visit the **Department of Parks and Recreation,** Maui County, Wailuku, Maui 96793 (243-7230) for maps of Molokai and information on camping in county parks on Molokai, Lanai, and Maui. Open Mon.-Fri. 7:45am-4:30pm. The **Division of State Parks,** P.O. Box 1049, Wailuku, Maui 96793 (243-5354), also has information on state parks on Molokai, Lanai, and Maui. Open Mon.-Fri. 7:45am-4:30pm.

Airlines: Hawaiian Air (567-6510) and **Aloha Island Air** (836-1111) run frequent flights to Molokai. Fare is about $65 one way. If you're traveling between Molokai and Maui it's cheaper to take the Maui Princess. ($21 one way, see Maui section for more info.)

Tour Services: Gray Line Tours, P.O. Box 253, Hoolehua 96729 (567-6177). Island tours $23-42 per person. Children under 12 are half-price. **Robert's Hawaii** (552-2751) offers also a variety of tours ($18-28).

Car Rentals: Avis (567-6814 on Molokai or 800-331-1212 from the mainland). $29 per day with unlimited mileage. Must be 21 with credit card. Insurance $11 per day. **Tropical** (567-6118). $25 per day. Must be 21 with credit card. **Budget** (567-6877 on Molokai or 800-527-0700). $25 per day. Insurance $10 per day. **Dollar** (567-6156 or 800-367-7006). $25 per day. $5 per day surcharge if under 25. Credit card required. All agencies are at the airport and are open daily 6:30am-6:30pm.

Public Transportation: None. Plan ahead, as it is difficult to obtain transportation of any sort after 5pm. You will probably have to rent a car, but call the organized bus tours, and you may be able to strike a deal that works for you (see Tour Services above).

Water Equipment Rentals: Molokai Fish and Dive Shop, Ala Malama St., Kaunakakai 96748 (553-5926). The only place to rent masks, snorkels, fins, and diving gear. Masks $3, snorkels $1.50, fins $4, complete set $8, boogie boards $7, ice chest and ice $4, friendly info free. The staff has the inside scoop on the best snorkeling and fishing spots. Open Mon.-Sat. 9am-6pm, Sun. 8am-2pm.

Laundromats: Kaunakakai Launderette, Makaena Pl. behind the outpost's store. Cold wash 75¢, hot wash $1. Open daily 7am-9pm.

Western Union, Ala Malama St., Kaunakakai, in the Friendly Market Center. Open Mon.-Fri. 9:30am-6pm, Sat. 9:30am-5pm.

Crisis Lines: Hale Laiku Women's Shelter, Grace Episcopal Church, Farrington Ave. (Rte. 480), Hoolehua (567-6420). Open 24 hr. **Senior Outreach,** 553-5242. **Molokai Family Support Services,** 553-3301. **Sexual Assault Crisis Center,** call collect to Maui, 242-4357.

Hospitals: Molokai General (553-5331), in Kaunakakai. **Molokai Family Health Center,** in Kaunakakai. Follow signs up the hill from Ala Malama St. Emergency room open 24 hr.

Post Office: Ala Malama at Kamoi St. (553-5845), in Kaunakakai. Open Mon.-Fri. 8am-4:30pm. General Delivery ZIP Code: 96748.

Police: 553-5355. Located in the Mitchell Pauole Center at the eastern end of Ala Malama St., Kaunakakai.

Area Code: 808.

Molokai, situated between Maui and Oahu in the middle of the Hawaiian chain, is shaped roughly like a trapezoid, and is 10 mi. wide and 40 mi. long. **Kamehameha V Highway** (Rte. 450) snakes along the southeastern coast and between the island's two dormant volcanoes, low Puu Nana and forested Kamakou. The highway forks into two roads: **Mauna Loa Highway** (Rte. 460), which travels to Mauna Loa on the western side of the island, and **Kalae Highway** (Rte. 470), which goes north toward Kalaupapa. **Hoolehua Airport,** a 55-mi. (22-min.) flight from Honolulu, lies between the mountains in the island's center, and is accessed by all major roads. **Kaunakakai,** Molokai's principal town, sits 8 mi. south on the southern shore.

Accommodations and Camping

Molokai is not known as a tourist island. Accommodations tend to be simple and reasonably priced, outside of the token swish resort, **Colony's Kaluakoi Hotel and Golf Club** (552-2555), in Mauna Loa near Papohaku Beach. To get there, turn right off Mauna Loa Hwy. onto Kaluakoi Rd. and continue to the end. The **Ke Nani Kai** condominiums, also on Kaluakoi Rd., may have vacant units.

Campsites on Molokai are easily accessible, uncrowded, and tremendously beautiful. Free camping is possible along the far end of Kamehameha V Hwy. and in **Halawa Valley.** Because of the dearth of people on Molokai, you're likely to have the parks to yourself. Contact the Department of Parks and Recreation (see Practical Information) before you set off to hike or camp and be careful where you pitch camp—much of the island wilderness is private land. Don't forget to stock up on insect repellent to ward off the island's unofficial bird, the mosquito.

Bed and Breakfast Hawaii, P.O. Box 449 Kapaa, Kauai (800-773-1632, 822-7771). Singles and doubles, cottages, homes, and hotel units $27.50-45.

Pau Hana Inn, P.O. Box 860, Kaunakakai 96748 (553-5342, 536-7545 from Oahu, 800-423-MOLO (423-6656) from the mainland), turn inland off Rte. 450 at the modern, white church across from the school. "Pau Hana" means "after work" or leisure time. Easily the most reasonable inn on the island. Popular with locals. Rooms are diminutive and spare, but antiseptic. Swimming pool and oceanfront garden complete with banyan trees. Inexpensive restaurant features entertainment Fri. and Sat. nights. Ceiling fans, no room phone. Singles and doubles from $45.

Hotel Molokai, P.O. Box 546, Kaunakakai 96748 (553-5347, 531-4004 in Honolulu, 800-423-MOLO (423-6656) from the mainland), about 1½ mi. east of Kaunakakai. On Kamehameha V Hwy. (Rte. 450). Two units equipped for the disabled. Family rooms available. Clean pool and authentic Polynesian architecture. On the beach. Fabulous restaurant. Rooms with bath, living room, ceiling fans, and *lanai* (porch) TVs $10 extra per day. Singles and doubles from $59.

Palaau State Park, about 9 mi. northwest of the airport off Rte. 470. An isolated state campground with restrooms, picnic tables, barbecue grills, and a view of the Kalaupapa Settlement nearby. For the camper who prefers woods to beaches. But be careful: wandering off the well-groomed hiking trails might send you over the 1500 ft. sea cliffs, where you will quickly have an up-close-and-personal meeting with the picturesque rocky coastline below. Purify the water here before drinking. Five-day max. stay. Free. Contact the Division of State Parks (see Practical Information).

Papohaku County Beach, near Kaluakoi resort on the west end. A beautifully maintained secluded spot with restrooms and Molokai's most breathtaking beach (with strong winter surf). Tent "officially" required (lots of ants). Permit available from the Molokai Division of Parks ($3; see Practical Information).

Onealii County Beach Park, on the south shore just east of Kaunakakai on Rte. 450. The most complete camping park on the island and the best place to camp with children, but not in a particularly attractive setting. The park is flanked by the highway and an average beach. The town's proximity is convenient, but the Papohaku County Beach is just as well-equipped and much more secluded and picturesque. Three-day max. stay. Sites $3 per person, ages under 18 50¢. Permits required from the Molokai Division of Parks (see Practical Information).

Food

Restaurants cluster in Kaunakakai, but you might want to stock up on groceries at **Friendly Market Center** (open Mon.-Fri. 8:30am-8:30pm, Sat. 8:30am-6:30pm; credit cards accepted) or **Misakis Inc.** (open Mon.-Sat. 8:30am-8:30pm, Sun. 9am-noon), both on Ala Malama St.

Kanemitsu Bakery, Ala Malama (553-5855), in Kaunakakai. Kanemitsu's fresh bread is famous throughout the islands—french onion, wheat, raisin, and a number of fruity flavors, including peach, coconut, and pineapple ($1.50-2.50). Restaurant serves coffee, sausage, 2 eggs, and toast ($2.75), and lunch plates ($3-3.85). Open Wed.-Mon. 5:30am-8pm.

Hop Inn, Ala Malama St. (553-5465), in Kaunakakai. A wonderful Cantonese restaurant, which also serves some American food. Meals $4-7. Hop in for the sweet 'n' sour spare ribs dinner plate ($5.35). Be sure to try the almond pudding, a strange, sweet, melt-in-your-mouth dessert ($1). Open daily 11am-9pm.

Molokai Drive-Inn, Kamoi Ave. at Kamehameha V Hwy., in Kaunakakai, near the Pau Hana Inn. American and island take-outs include 2 scoops of rice and macaroni salad ($3-4.50). A legion of fries $1.10. Located in the yellow building with no sign, just the number "101" on the awning. Open daily 7am-10:30pm, sometimes as late as 11:30pm on weekends.

Oviedo's Lunch Counter, at the *mauka* end of Ala Malama St. (553-5014), in Kaunakakai. More energy is put into the cooking than the interior decorating. The result is fine Filipino food at reasonable prices. Select two entrees with steamed white rice for $6.75. Ice cream $1.15 per scoop. Open daily 9:30am-6:30pm.

Mid-Nite Inn, Ala Malama St. (533-5302), in Kaunakakai. This restaurant got its name from dock workers waiting for the midnight ship to moor. "No Fool Aroun'." A classic hang-out—a favorite with locals and visitors alike. Breakfast special ($2.75) is their forte. Steak is not. Open Mon.-Sat. 6am-1:30pm and 5:30-9pm. Set to reopen in January, 1992.

Outposts Natural Foods (553-3377), Makaena Pl. off Ala Malama St. Fresh fruits and local vegetables. Cereals, rice cakes, homemade sandwiches and salads, as well as tropical fruit smoothies made with papayas, mangoes, bananas, and pineapples ($2.75). Open Sun.-Thurs. 9am-6pm, Fri. 9am-3:30pm. Juice bar lunch counter open Mon.-Fri. 10am-3pm ($4-5).

Holo Holo Kai, in the Hotel Molokai (553-5347), 2 mi. east of Kaunakakai. Grilled *mahi mahi* (fish) and *huli huli* (chicken teriyaki) for $11. Box lunches of size $6. Sandwiches served poolside 1:30-6pm. Open daily 7-10:30am, 11:30am-1:30pm, and 6-9pm. The hotel features local entertainers Thurs.-Sat. nights.

Sights and Activities

Central Molokai and Kalaupapa

To reach **Palaau State Park** from Hoolehua Airport take Mauna Loa Hwy. (Rte. 460) west and take a left onto Rte. 470. A short trail leads to the **Kalaupapa Overlook,** where you can view the site where lepers were forced to settle and the spectacular Makanalua Peninsula, 1500 ft. below. The overlook displays photographs of the settlement. For a closer look, hike 3 mi. of switchbacks down the steep cliff trail. On the way down, remind your legs that they are obliged to carry you back up as well. Call **Damien Tours** (567-6171) for a $17.50 half-day tour of the site (bring your own lunch).

Only people of age 16 or above are allowed by state law to enter Kalaupapa Settlement, and you may not enter the settlement unescorted. In other words, if you don't buy a town ticket you'll have to settle for the view from the lookout.

The development of sulfone drugs in the 1940s has ensured that Hansen's disease is no longer a dreaded malady. Although the number of residents at Kalaupapa has steadily decreased over the years, many have chosen to remain. Now, they may come and go as they please. Several churches guard **Kalawao,** the original settlement area. Residents of the colony appreciate any sincere interest in their history and in Father Damien, the "Martyr of Molokai." But unless you explore aggressively, you will come in contact only with sales personnel and state employees. Bring comfortable walking shoes. Just outside Palaau Park a sign will point you down a road toward the original **Kalaupapa Overlook.** The road is closed to traffic, but you can walk down. The view here is even better than from the new overlook.

Another short trail, well-marked and well-trodden, leads to **petroglyphs** carved on the bottom face of a suspended stone and to Kauleo Nanahoa, lovingly nicknamed the **Phallic Rock.** According to legend, when a childless woman spends the night under its moonlit shadows (presumably alone), she becomes pregnant.

Kaunakakai and East from Kaunakakai

Take Kamehameha V Hwy. (Rte. 450) east from Kalae Hwy. (Rte. 470) to tiny Kaunakakai. Before you reach town, glance at Father Damien's century-old **Kapuaina Grove** of coconut trees. Before the canoe shack on Ala Malama, you will come across a stone foundation—all that remains of Kamehameha V's summer home.

Continuing east on Kamehameha V Hwy. (Rte. 450) past Kaunakahai, you'll run into the first in a series of **Hawaiian fishponds.** These coral and basalt pools, essential to the livelihood of ancient Hawaiian warriors, were used to raise salt-water fish. Some fishponds were up to 2000 ft. long, and although overgrown, their outlines are still visible. A little past the 10-mi. marker is **St. Joseph Church,** built by Father Damien in 1876, a tiny and picturesque church with a small graveyard. Go right in, even though the door is shut. Farther down the road, you'll see the red steeple of **Our Lady of Sorrows Church,** built by Damien in 1874. Of the four churches he built, only these two remain.

Continuing along the Kamehameha Hwy., about 1 mi. off the road from Pukoo, you'll come across the 13th-century **Iliiliopai Heiau,** one of the most magnificent temples on the islands. Once used for human sacrifices, the *heiau* is on land owned by late 70s pop diva Olivia Newton-John, and admission is by her permission only. **Molokai Wagon & Horse Ride** (558-8380) offers daily tours of the *heiau* and a giant mango grove, as well as a chance to see Hawaiian crafts in a refreshingly noncommercial atmosphere ($25 includes a small *luau,* daily at noon). Farther down the road toward Halawa Valley, you'll find the ruins of the **Moanui Sugar Mill,** which operated from 1870 to 1900.

The water near mile marker 20 on Kamehameha V Hwy. is known as having the best snorkeling on Molokai. The shallow reefs and calm waters are ideal for beginners.

The road ends a bit farther along with a spectacular descent into **Halawa Valley** and a striking black sand beach. If you survive the nerve-shattering drive down into the valley, hike to **Moaula Falls** for a swim in fresh water. Watch out, however, for the falls' fabled sea-monster: an enormous *moo* (lizard). A 2-mi. trail leads to the falls' lower pool (take the left branch where it forks). The slippery stepping-stones make the wide stream difficult to cross—impossible if it has rained recently. Think twice about bringing along your camera, unless it could stand an accidental swim. From the lower pool, clamber over to Hipuapua Falls by following Halawa Stream. The valley's lone snack bar offers parking and directions for the hike up to the falls (open daily 6am-5pm).

The **Halawa Valley** was devastated by a *tsunami* in 1946, and the salt water left the area unfit for agriculture. Only a handful of inhabitants returned to the ruins. Although there are no established parks, it is possible to camp here.

West from Kaunakakai: Papohaku and Mauna Loa

Traveling west on Mauna Loa Hwy (Rte. 460), you'll pass over **Puu Nana** (Viewing Hill), past the Kaluakoi turn-off for Papohaku and Kepuhi beaches, and smack into the excruciatingly quiet plantation town of **Mauna Loa.** Once a thriving pineapple-plantation community, rows of brown company cottages now stand barren among overgrown roads. Dole shut down its operations in 1976, but recently residents have been attempting to turn Mauna Loa into a cultural cornucopia. Refresh yourself at **Jo Jo's Café,** with a bowl of Portuguese bean soup ($2.50) or freshly caught island fish ($4-8). (Open Mon., Tues., Thurs.-Sat. 11:45am-2:45pm and 5-7:45pm.)

To reach Molokai's most fabulous beaches, take a right off Rte. 460 back at the Kaluakoi turn-off. **Kepuhi** is a long white sand cove, where the **Kaluakoi Resort** now stands. The resort consumes much of the island's limited water supply, causing resentment among Molokai's farmers. Beyond the hotel's golf course and to the right, dirt tracks lead to several secluded white sand coves with protected waters and spectacular snorkeling. The deep water and offshore currents, however, make this area suitable only for the more experienced snorkeler.

A left off Rte. 460 leads to **Papohaku,** a 2-mi. long beach with excellent camping facilities (see Accommodations and Camping). Come here to watch the sun set over the choppy waves of the Pacific. At the end of the road is the entrance to the **Molokai Ranch Wildlife Park,** a 1000-acre refuge for African endangered species. Barbary sheep, Rhea axis deer, antelopes, and technicolor pheasants roam incongruously in the tropical shade of a Pacific island. Miles of dry land surround the green acres, protecting the transplanted beasts in a re-creation of the Serengeti desert. Tour departures 8am, 10am, 1pm, 3pm. Adults $25, under 13 $15.

Seasonal Events

The **Great Molokai Mule Drag Race,** held on September 19, enlivens Molokai's main street with an old Hawaiian festival which is part luau, part rodeo. On September 26, canoes powered by women race from Molokai to Oahu (22 mi.) in the **Na Wahine O Ke Kai.** The finish line is at Fort Derussy Beach in Waikiki. October brings **Aloha Week,** with street dances, luaus, athletic events, and parades. Later in the month, there's the **Molokai-to-Oahu Outrigger Canoe Race,** the male rebuttal to the *Na Wahine O Ke Kai.*

Lanai

More than 1000 years after the Polynesians had inhabited the other Hawaiian islands, Lanai (pronounced La-NYE or La-NAH-ee) remained empty. Empty of people, that is—it was believed that evil spirits dwelled on the island. Legend has it that Kaululaau, the exiled nephew of a Maui king, was banished to Lanai, where he eradicated the spirits and opened the island for settlement. The uneven land was thought unfit for agricultural enterprises, but an American entrepreneur named James Dole changed all that in 1922. Pineapples proved to be the perfect crop for Lanai's reddish, volcanic soil, and the island soon received the sobriquet "Pineapple Isle."

Castle and Cooke Company, of which Dole is a subsidiary, still owns 98% of the island. A hefty portion of the rest belongs to Club Lanai, a resort used mainly as a day escape by Maui tourists arriving via motorboat from Lahaina. Two new hotels are being built on the island, flooding quiet Lanai City with construction workers and prefiguring a deluge of pina coladas and suntan oil by century's end. In the meantime, horns still sound before dawn and at dusk, rousing plantation employees.

Lanai is a paradise for those who bask in back-road solitude, but be prepared to rough it. Only 20 mi. of paved roads touch the island; the rest must be explored via jarring Jeep rides or by foot. Stores close daily for lunch (noon-1:30pm) and often close before scheduled hours, at the whim of the owner. Lanai scatters one hotel, one campground, two gas stations, and 12 of the state's 15 best scuba diving locations along its craggy coast. There are two expensive resorts on the island, both run by Rockresorts at Manele Beach, near Lanai City. They are worth visiting just to wander around their landscaped settings or to browse among the beautiful furnishings. An overnight sojourn, however, will set you back about $275 per night.

Practical Information

Visitors Information: None. The closest you'll get is speaking with the people at **Oshiro's** (see Car Rentals) or at the **Koele Company,** Lanai Ave. (565-6561), across from the post office (open Mon.-Fri. 7:30am-5pm). Most locals are also generous with advice and assistance.

Fish and Game Division Office: 8th St. next to Pine Isle Market (565-6688).

Taxi: Oshiro's, 850 Fraser Ave. (565-6952). Airport to Lanai City $7. Open Mon.-Sat. 8am-noon and 1:30-5:30pm.

Car Rentals: Lanai City Services, 1036 Lanai Ave. (565-7227, from Maui 244-9538, from Oahu 533-3666). Cars $50 per day; Jeeps $100. Open Mon.-Fri. 7am-6pm, Sat.-Sun. 8am-6pm. **Oshiro's,** 850 Fraser Ave. (565-6952). Cars $50; Jeeps from $75 per day. Must be 21 with a major credit card. Make reservations, especially for weekends. Also runs a shuttle between airport and town ($5 round-trip). Open Mon.-Sat. 8am-noon and 1:30-5:30pm. Jeeps are crucial because most of the best sights are on unpaved roads, where "non-Jeeps" are forbidden.

Library: Fraser and 6th. Open Mon. noon-8pm, Tues-Fri. 9am-5pm.

Laundromat: Laundrette Lanai, 7th St., near Dahang's Bakery.

Hospital: Lanai, 628 7th. (565-6411). 24-hr. emergency room. Day clinic, 565-6423.

Police: 565-6525.

Emergency: 911.

Post Office: Lanai Ave. (565-6517), in Lanai City, on the other side of Dole Park from Hotel Lanai. Open Mon.-Fri. 8am-4:30pm, Sat. 9:30-10am. General Delivery ZIP Code: 96763.

Area Code: 808.

Aloha Island Air, Air Molokai, and Hawaiian Airlines will take you to **Lanai Airport,** near the southern end of the island. (See Getting Around in the Hawaii introduction.) **Expeditions** (661-3756) runs twice daily to Manele harbor for $25. You can also cruise to Lanai on a day-long boat trip from Maui. Most cruises include breakfast or lunch and island tours. **Tom Barefoot's Cashback Tours,** 626 Front St. (661-8889), in Lahaina, Maui, will sail tourists to Lanai for $67. Round-trip travel time is four hours, and the tour spends the day at Club Lanai. **Seabird Cruises** (661-3643), on Maui, offers a daytrip aboard a luxurious catamaran to Hulopoe Beach Park for a bounteous barbecue, with snorkeling, underwater photography, volleyball, nature hikes, and land tours. (Tours leave Mon.-Fri. at 8am. $80, children $40, under 4 free.) Contact the Maui branch of the Hawaii Visitors Bureau for information on other one-day tours to the island.

Accommodations, Camping, Food, and Entertainment

If arriving by sea, don't wait until you disembark to phone for hotels. Telephones are not available at the beach or harbor, and construction workers have taken most of the rooms anyway. Make reservations early if you plan to stay on a weekend, especially between January and May (hunting season for quail, deer, and turkey). Lanai residents often camp on secluded beaches, but this is not a good idea for visitors.

Provisions can be procured at **Richard's Shopping Center,** 434 8th St., or at **Pine Isle Market,** 356 8th St. (565-6488), next to the Fish and Game Department.

Hotel Lanai, 828 Lanai Ave. (565-7211 or 800-624-8849), Lanai City. Built in the 1927 as a home for Dole supervisors and guests, the island's only moderately priced hotel is now owned by Rockresorts and run by locals. There are only 10 rooms, so book at least two months in advance. Singles $56. Doubles $63. Triples $71. The hotel's restaurant serves inexpensive meals all day long in a comfortably furnished, wood-paneled dining room. Open Mon.-Sat. 7:30-9am, 11:30am-1:30pm, and 6:30-8:30pm; Sun. 7:30am-noon and 6:30-8:30pm.

Camping: the only sites available are at **Hulopoe Beach,** one of the island's best swimming and fishing beaches, 20 min. from the city. Restroom facilities and outdoor showers. $5 per person per day. 7-day max. stay. Reservations should be made at least a week in advance; contact the Koele Company (see Practical Information).

Dahang's Bakery on 7th St. (565-6363), walking distance from the Hotel Lanai. Doughnuts and coffee. Sandwiches and hamburgers ($2-4). Open daily 5:30am-1:30pm.

S.T. Property, Inc., 419 7th St. (565-6537), next to Dahang's. Cheap snack food served Thurs.-Tues. 6:30am-12:30pm. Chips, candy, and drugstore items sold until 5pm.

Entertainment is generally of the create-your-own variety on this quiet isle, but check local bulletin boards for community events and organized boat excursions to the Lahaina cinema.

Sights

Some common sense and a dose of adventure will help you conquer Lanai. It's not easy driving on pockmarked dirt tracks through 12,000 acres of pineapple fields. Obtain a map from the Koele Company or the Hawaii Visitors Bureau on Oahu, Maui, or the Big Island, and always notify someone when and where you'll be exploring. Be wary of year-round hunting in progress; wear clothing that will distinguish you from the average pheasant, turkey, quail, deer, or antelope.

Lanai's most celebrated sights lie along the **Munro Trail,** a loop through the rainforest where naturalist George C. Munro planted specimens of plantlife from his native New Zealand about 80 years ago. Start north on Rte. 440 out of Lanai City, and turn right onto the well-beaten dirt road at Koele cemetery. You'll pass **Hookio Ridge,** where Lanai warriors unsuccessfully tried to defend their home against invaders from the Big Island in 1778.

The four-wheel-drive trail becomes exceedingly treacherous after climbing the **Lanaihale Overlook,** as Alewi Rd. snakes back down toward Rte. 441, 4 mi. south of Lanai City. If you go all the way up to the 3370-ft.-high overlook on a clear day, you'll see as many as five other islands: Oahu far to the northwest, Molokai and Maui close by to the north and northeast, Hawaii looming on the southeastern horizon, and little Kahoolawe (which has been appropriated by the navy as a bombing range) between Lanai and Hawaii. Don't fret about losing your way on Lanai. The island's routes are either short and circular or dead ends; you'll eventually end up where you started, or you won't be able to continue farther.

If you strike out to the northwest on Polihua Rd. (a dirt road), you'll come to the **Garden of the Gods** after 7 miles. This landscape of eerie rock formations is best viewed at sunset and at night. The road becomes more difficult as it winds toward the northern tip of Lanai, **Kaena Point.** The paved Keomuku Highway (Rte. 44) from Koele runs northeast about 6 mi. to **Shipwreck Beach,** an aptly named graveyard for two scuttled ships. This is a narrow, windswept beach, unsuitable for sunbathing. Skin divers might enjoy poking around the ship carcasses and the reef they rest on. It's about a 250 yard swim to the wreck in 30-40 foot water. The reef itself is—ahem—captivating. The beach is also home to some well-preserved **petroglyphs.** From the beach, the highway turns to dirt as it hugs the shoreline south to **Keomuku,** a ghost town that was once a bustling sugar-producing community.

The best beach on Lanai, if not the entire Hawaiian chain, is **Hulopoe Beach Park,** more commonly called White Manele Beach, at the southern end of Manele Rd. (Rte. 441), 9 mi. from Lanai City. This is the perfect spot for all sports, with a fully developed park, superb surf, and a partially protected beach for swimming (showers and restrooms available, but no lifeguards). Skin diving here is rewarding, but leave your spearfishing gun at home—it's a protected park. Next to Hulopoe Bay is **Manele Bay,** a black sand beach with a small boat harbor. If you detour left off Rte. 441 halfway to the beach, and climb onto a bunch of boulders, you might be able to find the **Luahiwa Petroglyphs,** one of the state's best collections of rock carvings. Evidently drawn after *haoles* had come to the island, some of these glyphs depict men on horseback. Summer is pineapple harvesting time; try calling the Koele Company to arrange a tour of a pineapple plantation (see Practical Information).

At the southernmost tip of the island, take the rugged ride or hike down to **Kaunolu,** an ancient Hawaiian village housing the **Halulu Heiau,** one of the island's best-preserved temples. Kamehameha the Great had a home on the nearby bluffs. Look for **Kahekili's Jump,** the tallest cliff on Lanai, from which the king's warriors cliff-dived into the sea to prove their bravery. Don't even think about it—you're better off being wimpy and alive.

One of the more recent additions to the tiny island is the privately owned resort, bar, and restaurant **Club Lanai,** an active oasis amid limp rows of vegetation. Like a country club and national park rolled into one, it sponsors diving trips, swimming, volleyball, snorkeling, horseshoes, glass bottom boat rides, and nature walks. Go north from Lanai City on Keomuku Rd. (Rte. 44) to the northern coastline, turn right to travel southeast on a rough dirt road to **Halepalaoa Landing.** The eight-acre resort is frequented primarily by daytrippers from Maui (see Practical Information). The one-hour drive from Lanai City requires jeeps and a sturdy stomach.

Mahalo.

INDEX

Hotels Honolulu

Hawaiian King 417 Nohonani St, Waikiki
(Tel 922-3894)

Outrigger East 150 Kaiulani Av, Waikiki
(Tel 922-5353)

||| Waikiki Circle 2464 Kalakaua Av, Waikiki
(Tel 923-1571)

LA

Figueroa Hotel 939 S. Figueroa St. (627-8971)

Oasis Motel 2200 W. Olympic Boul.
(385 4191)

Holiday Lodge 1631 W. 3rd St, (482-4920)

Alexandria Corner of Spring & 5th Sts
(626-7484)